# Contemporary Authors®

## NEW REVISION SERIES

# Explore your options!

## Gale databases are offered in a variety of formats

**GALE**

The information in this Gale publication is also available in some or all of the formats described here. Your Gale Representative will be happy to fill you in. Call toll-free 1-800-877-GALE.

*GaleNet* SM
your information community

### GaleNet

A number of Gale databases are now available on GaleNet, our new online information resource accessible through the Internet. GaleNet features an easy-to-use end-user interface, the powerful search capabilities of BRS/SEARCH retrieval software and ease of access through the World Wide Web.

### Diskette/Magnetic Tape

Many Gale databases are available on diskette or magnetic tape, allowing systemwide access to your most-used information sources through existing computer systems. Data can be delivered on a variety of mediums (DOS-formatted diskettes, 9-track tape, 8mm data tape) and in industry-standard formats (comma-delimited, tagged, fixed-field).

### CD-ROM

A variety of Gale titles are available on CD-ROM, offering maximum flexibility and powerful search software.

### Online

For your convenience, many Gale databases are available through popular online services, including DIALOG, NEXIS, DataStar, ORBIT, OCLC, Thomson Financial Network's I/Plus Direct, HRIN, Prodigy, Sandpoint's HOOVER, the Library Corporation's NLightN and Telebase Systems.

# Contemporary Authors®

A Bio-Bibliographical Guide to
Current Writers in Fiction, General Nonfiction,
Poetry, Journalism, Drama, Motion Pictures,
Television, and Other Fields

**JEFF CHAPMAN**
**JOHN D. JORGENSON**
Editors

NEW REVISION SERIES
*volume* 54

GALE

DETROIT • NEW YORK • TORONTO • LONDON

# STAFF

Jeff Chapman and John D. Jorgenson, *Editors, New Revision Series*

Daniel Jones, *Pre-Manuscript Coordinator*
Thomas Wiloch, *Sketchwriting Coordinator*

Brigham Narins, Deborah A. Stanley, Aarti Dhawan Stephens,
Kathleen Wilson, and Janet Witalec, *Contributing Editors*

George H. Blair and Polly A. Vedder, *Associate Editors*

Bruce Boston, Frank DeSanto, Lane A. Glenn, Joan Goldsworthy, Anne Janette Johnson,
Jane Kosek, Robert Miltner, Julie Monahan, Trudy Ring, Jean W. Ross,
Bryan Ryan, Pamela L. Shelton, Kenneth R. Shepherd, Denise Wiloch,
Michaela Swart Wilson, and Tim Winter-Damon, *Sketchwriters*

Tracy Arnold-Chapman, Jane Kosek,
Emily J. McMurray, and Trudy Ring, *Copyeditors*

James P. Draper, *Managing Editor*

Victoria B. Cariappa, *Research Manager*

Barbara McNeil, *Research Specialist*

Laura C. Bissey, Julia C. Daniel, Tracie A. Richardson
Norma Sawaya, and Cheryl L. Warnock, *Research Associates*

Alfred A. Gardner and Sean R. Smith, *Research Assistants*

⊚™ This book is printed on acid-free paper that meets the minimum requirements
of American National Standard for Information Sciences-
Permanence Paper for Printed Library Materials, ANSI Z39.48-1984.

Library of Congress Catalog Card Number 81-640179

ISBN 0-7876-0125-X
ISSN 0275-7176

359913

Printed in the United States of America.

Gale Research, an International Thomson Publishing Company.

10  9  8  7  6  5  4  3  2  1

# Contents

Preface . . . . . . . . . . . . . . . . . . . . . . . . . . . . . . . . . . . . . . . . . . . . . . . . . . . . . . . . vii

*CA* Numbering System and
Volume Update Charts . . . . . . . . . . . . . . . . . . . . . . . . . . . . . . . . . . . . . . . . . . . xi

Authors and Media People
Featured in This Volume . . . . . . . . . . . . . . . . . . . . . . . . . . . . . . . . . . . . . . . . . xiii

Author Listings . . . . . . . . . . . . . . . . . . . . . . . . . . . . . . . . . . . . . . . . . . . . . . . . . . 1

**Indexing note:** All *Contemporary Authors New Revision Series* entries are indexed in the *Contemporary Authors* cumulative index, which is published separately and distributed with even-numbered *Contemporary Authors* original volumes and odd-numbered *Contemporary Authors New Revision Series* volumes.

**As always, the most recent *Contemporary Authors* cumulative index continues to be the user's guide to the location of an individual author's listing.**

Contemporary Authors
*was named an*
*"Outstanding*
*Reference Source,"*
*by the*
*American Library*
*Association Reference*
*and Adult Services*
*Division after its*
*1962 inception.*
*In 1985 it was listed by*
*the same organization*
*as one of the*
*twenty-five most*
*distinguished reference*
*titles published in the*
*past twenty-five years.*

# Preface

The *Contemporary Authors New Revision Series* (*CANR*) provides completely updated information on authors listed in earlier volumes of *Contemporary Authors* (*CA*). Entries for individual authors from *any* volume of *CA* may be included in a volume of the *New Revision Series*. *CANR* updates only those sketches requiring significant change.

Authors are included on the basis of specific criteria that indicate the need for significant revision. These criteria include bibliographical additions, changes in addresses or career, major awards, and personal information such as name changes or death dates. All listings in this volume have been revised or augmented in various ways. Some sketches have been extensively rewritten, and many include informative new sidelights. As always, a *CANR* listing entails no charge or obligation.

## How to Get the Most out of *CA*: Use the Index

The key to locating an author's most recent entry is the *CA* cumulative index, which is published separately and distributed with even-numbered original volumes and odd-numbered revision volumes. It provides access to *all* entries in *CA* and *CANR*. Always consult the latest index to find an author's most recent entry.

For the convenience of users, the *CA* cumulative index also includes references to all entries in these Gale literary series: *Authors and Artists for Young Adults, Authors in the News, Bestsellers, Black Literature Criticism, Black Writers, Children's Literature Review, Concise Dictionary of American Literary Biography, Concise Dictionary of British Literary Biography, Contemporary Authors Autobiography Series, Contemporary Authors Bibliographical Series, Contemporary Literary Criticism, Dictionary of Literary Biography, Dictionary of Literary Biography Documentary Series, Dictionary of Literary Biography Yearbook, DISCovering Authors, DISCovering Authors: British, DISCovering Authors: Canadian, DISCovering Authors: Modules, Drama Criticism, Hispanic Literature Criticism, Hispanic Writers, Junior DISCovering Authors, Major Authors and Illustrators for Children and Young Adults, Major 20th-Century Writers, Native North American Literature, Poetry Criticism, Short Story Criticism, Something about the Author, Something about the Author Autobiography Series, Twentieth-Century Literary Criticism, World Literature Criticism,* and *Yesterday's Authors of Books for Children.*

## A Sample Index Entry:

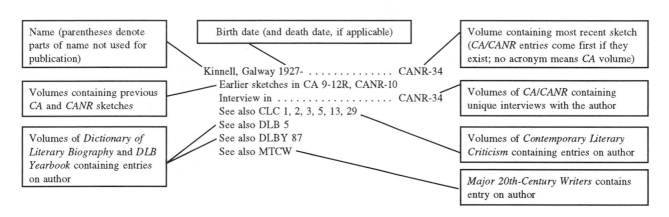

For the most recent *CA* information on Kinnell, users should refer to Volume 34 of the *New Revision Series,* as designated by "CANR-34"; if that volume is unavailable, refer to CANR-10. And if CANR-10 is unavailable, refer to CA 9-12R, published in 1974, for Kinnell's First Revision entry.

# How Are Entries Compiled?

The editors make every effort to secure new information directly from the authors. Copies of all sketches in selected *CA* and *CANR* volumes previously published are routinely sent to listees at their last-known addresses, and returns from these authors are then assessed. For deceased writers, or those who fail to reply to requests for data, we consult other reliable biographical sources, such as those indexed in Gale's *Biography and Genealogy Master Index,* and bibliographical sources, such as *National Union Catalog, LC MARC,* and *British National Bibliography.* Further details come from published interviews, feature stories, and book reviews, and often the authors' publishers supply material.

*\* Indicates that a listing has been compiled from secondary sources believed to be reliable but has not been personally verified for this edition by the author sketched.*

# What Kinds of Information Does an Entry Provide?

Sketches in *CANR* contain the following biographical and bibliographical information:

- **Entry heading:** the most complete form of author's name, plus any pseudonyms or name variations used for writing

- **Personal information:** author's date and place of birth, family data, educational background, political and religious affiliations, and hobbies and leisure interests

- **Addresses:** author's home, office, email, or agent's addresses, as available

- **Career summary:** name of employer, position, and dates held for each career post; resume of other vocational achievements; military service

- **Membership information:** professional, civic, and other association memberships and any official posts held

- **Awards and honors:** military and civic citations, major prizes and nominations, fellowships, grants, and honorary degrees

- **Writings:** a comprehensive, chronological list of titles, publishers, dates of original publication and revised editions, and production information for plays, television scripts, and screenplays

- **Adaptations:** a list of films, plays, and other media which have been adapted from the author's work

- **Work in progress:** current or planned projects, with dates of completion and/or publication, and expected publisher, when known

- **Sidelights:** a biographical portrait of the author's development; information about the critical reception of the author's works; revealing comments, often by the author, on personal interests, aspirations, motivations, and thoughts on writing

- **Biographical and critical sources:** a list of books and periodicals in which additional information on an author's life and/or writings appears

## Related Titles in the *CA* Series

*Contemporary Authors Autobiography Series* complements *CA* original and revised volumes with specially commissioned autobiographical essays by important current authors, illustrated with personal photographs they provide. Common topics include their motivations for writing, the people and experiences that shaped their careers, the rewards they derive from their work, and their impressions of the current literary scene.

*Contemporary Authors Bibliographical Series* surveys writings by and about important American authors since World War II. Each volume concentrates on a specific genre and features approximately ten writers; entries list works written by and about the author and contain a bibliographical essay discussing the merits and deficiencies of major critical and scholarly studies in detail.

## Available in Electronic Formats

**CD-ROM.** Full-text bio-bibliographic entries from the entire *CA* series, covering approximately 100,000 writers, are available on CD-ROM through lease and purchase plans. The disc combines entries from the *CA, CANR,* and *Contemporary Authors Permanent Series* (*CAP*) print series to provide the most recent author listing. It can be searched by name, title, subject/genre, and personal data, and by using boolean logic. The disc will be updated every six months. For more information, call 1-800-877-GALE.

**Magnetic Tape.** *CA* is available for licensing on magnetic tape in a fielded format. Either the complete database or a custom selection of entries may be ordered. The database is available for internal data processing and nonpublishing purposes only. For more information, call 1-800-877-GALE.

**Online.** The *Contemporary Authors* database is made available online to libraries and their patrons through online public access catalog (OPAC) vendors. Currently, *CA* is offered through Ameritech Library Services' Vista Online (formerly Dynix), and is expected to become available through CARL Systems. More OPAC vendor offerings will follow soon.

**GaleNet.** *CA* is available on a subscription basis through GaleNet, a new online information resource that features an easy-to-use end-user interface, the powerful search capabilities of the BRS/Search retrieval software, and ease of access through the World-Wide Web. For more information, call Melissa Kolehmainen at 1-800-877-GALE, ext. 1598.

## Suggestions Are Welcome

The editors welcome comments and suggestions from users on any aspects of the *CA* series. If readers would like to recommend authors whose entries should appear in future volumes of the series, they are cordially invited to write: The Editors, *Contemporary Authors,* 835 Penobscot Bldg., Detroit, MI 48226-4094; call toll-free at 1-800-347-GALE; fax to 1-313-961-6599; or e-mail at conauth@gale.com.

# *CA* Numbering System and Volume Update Chart

Occasionally questions arise about the *CA* numbering system and which volumes, if any, can be discarded. Despite numbers like "29-32R," "97-100" and "150," the entire *CA* series consists of only 134 physical volumes with the publication of *CA New Revision Series* Volume 54. The following charts note changes in the numbering system and cover design, and indicate which volumes are essential for the most complete, up-to-date coverage.

*CA* **First Revision**
- 1-4R through 41-44R (11 books)
  *Cover:* Brown with black and gold trim.
  There will be no further First Revision volumes because revised entries are now being handled exclusively through the more efficient *New Revision Series* mentioned below.

*CA* **Original Volumes**
- 45-48 through 97-100 (14 books)
  *Cover:* Brown with black and gold trim.
- 101 through 153 (53 books)
  *Cover:* Blue and black with orange bands.
  The same as previous *CA* original volumes but with a new, simplified numbering system and new cover design.

*CA* **Permanent Series**
- *CAP*-1 and *CAP*-2 (2 books)
  *Cover:* Brown with red and gold trim.
  There will be no further *Permanent Series* volumes because revised entries are now being handled exclusively through the more efficient *New Revision Series* mentioned below.

*CA* **New Revision Series**
- *CANR*-1 through *CANR*-54 (54 books)
  *Cover:* Blue and black with green bands.
  Includes only sketches requiring extensive changes; **sketches are taken from any previously published *CA*, *CAP*, or *CANR* volume.**

## If You Have:

## You May Discard:

| If You Have: | You May Discard: |
|---|---|
| *CA* First Revision Volumes 1-4R through 41-44R **and** *CA Permanent Series* Volumes 1 and 2 | *CA* Original Volumes 1, 2, 3, 4 and Volumes 5-6 through 41-44 |
| *CA* Original Volumes 45-48 through 97-100 **and** 101 through 153 | **NONE:** These volumes will not be superseded by corresponding revised volumes. Individual entries from these and all other volumes appearing in the left column of this chart may be revised and included in the various volumes of the *New Revision Series*. |
| *CA New Revision Series* Volumes *CANR*-1 through *CANR*-54 | **NONE:** The *New Revision Series* does not replace any single volume of *CA*. Instead, volumes of *CANR* include entries from many previous *CA* series volumes. All *New Revision Series* volumes must be retained for full coverage. |

# A Sampling of Authors and Media People
# Featured in This Volume

## Edward Albee

A highly acclaimed American playwright, Albee gained international fame with his 1962 play *Who's Afraid of Virginia Woolf?* He has earned many of drama's most prestigious awards, including three Pulitzer Prizes, his most recent for his autobiographical drama *Three Tall Women.* He was inducted into the Theater Hall of Fame in 1985.

## Kingsley Amis

Known primarily for his satire, including his acclaimed first novel *Lucky Jim,* Amis also wrote poetry, criticism, short stories, science fiction, and espionage thrillers. His works include *Ending Up, Jake's Thing,* and the Booker Prize-winning *The Old Devils.*

## Martin Amis

Highly acclaimed English novelist Amis, son of the late Kingsley Amis, is occasionally compared by critics to Nabokov, Bellow, Flaubert, and Joyce. Cited for his command of language, Amis received the Somerset Maugham Award in 1974 for his first novel, *The Rachel Papers.*

## Nina Bawden

Writer of both children's novels and fiction for adults, Bawden's works frequently satirize upper-middle-class familial relationships. Her works include *The Peppermint Pig, Afternoon of a Good Woman,* and the Booker Prize-nominated *Circles of Deceit.*

## Madison Smartt Bell

Recognized largely for *All Souls' Rising,* his popular novel detailing Haiti's fight for independence in the late 1700s, Bell has been described by one critic as "a prose poet of aloneness, and the best writer of his generation." His other works include *Waiting for the End of the World, Ten Indians,* and *Save Me, Joe Louis.*

## Edmund Blunden

A diverse writer, Blunden's works include poetry, criticism, memoirs, and novels. Considered an authority on the Romantic movement of the late 1700s and early 1800s, Blunden's biographies include the highly respected *Leigh Hunt: A Biography* and *Shelley: A Life Story.*

## J. M. Coetzee

Considered one of South Africa's most accomplished novelists, Coetzee is known for works which explore the lives of characters as they struggle in oppressive societies. His works include *In the Heart of the Country, The Master of Petersburg,* and the James Tait Black Memorial Prize-winning *Waiting for the Barbarians.*

## Michael Crichton

One of America's most popular contemporary authors, Crichton is known for pioneering "techno-thriller" novels such as *Congo, Jurassic Park,* and *The Lost World.* Crichton is also a director and screenwriter, and is the creator of the television series *ER.*

## Thomas M. Disch

A versatile and prolific author, Disch's works include science fiction, poetry, historical novels, and computer-interactive fiction. Cited by a critic as "the most formidably gifted unfamous American writer," Disch received an American Book Award nomination for *On Wings of Song,* and Hugo Award and Nebula Award nominations for *The Brave Little Toaster.*

## Erica Ducornet

Known primarily for her acclaimed surrealist novels, Ducornet is also an illustrator and poet. Her works include *The Stain, The Fountains of Neptune, The Jade Cabinet,* and *Phosphor in Dreamland.* She was a finalist for the National Book Critics Circle award in 1994.

## Howard Fast

Fast is an American novelist, playwright, screenwriter, and biographer. Known initially as an historical novelist, one of Fast's most famous works is his 1951 novel *Spartacus.* He received the National Jewish Book Award in 1949 for *My Glorious Brothers.*

## Athol Fugard

South African Fugard is a highly respected playwright, actor, and director. His works include the Obie Award-winning *Boesman and Lena,* and the Drama Desk Award- and New York Drama Critics Circle Award-winning *"Master Harold" ... and the Boys.*

## William Golding

English novelist Golding's reputation rests largely on his first novel *Lord of the Flies*, considered by some critics to be one of the most important novels published in the 1950s. Golding's other works include the Booker Prize-winning *Rites of Passage*. He received the Nobel Prize for Literature in 1983.

## Neil Jordan

Jordan is an Irish film director, screenwriter, novelist, and short story writer. After gaining critical acclaim for fiction with *Night in Tunisia and Other Stories,* Jordan earned international recognition in film with *Mona Lisa* and *The Company of Wolves.* He received an Academy Award for Best Original Screenplay in 1993 for his highly successful film, *The Crying Game.*

## Donald Justice

Considered one of America's most distinguished and significant poets, Justice is known for the elegance and technical mastery of his verse. He received a nomination for the National Book Award in 1973 for *Departures* and was awarded the Pulitzer Prize in 1979 for *Selected Poems.*

## Jack Kerouac

Kerouac, along with others like William S. Burroughs and Allen Ginsberg, was one of the defining voices of the Beat Generation. Kerouac's novel *On the Road* has come to be known as the quintessential statement of the Beats and their philosophy, its publication considered by some critics to be a defining and revolutionary moment in contemporary American literature.

## Doris Lessing

Lessing is widely considered among the world's most powerful contemporary novelists. Her works also include short stories, essays, poetry, and travel literature. She received a Booker Prize nomination for her novel *The Sirian Experiments: The Report of Ambien II, of the Five,* and her autobiography *Under My Skin* won both the *Los Angeles Times* Book Prize and the James Tait Black Memorial Prize.

## Julian May

May is an American novelist whose works include science fiction and juvenile nonfiction. A prolific writer, her more than 250 nonfiction works focus mainly on science, sports, and biography. Her science fiction novel *The Many-Colored Land* garnered Hugo and Nebula Award nominations and won the *Locus* Award in 1982.

## Arthur Miller

One of America's most celebrated playwrights, Miller is known primarily for his first four plays, *All My Sons, Death of a Salesman, The Crucible,* and *A View from the Bridge.* He has received numerous prestigious drama awards, including two Drama Critics Circle Awards, three Tony Awards, and the Pulitzer Prize for Drama.

## Neil Simon

Simon is one of contemporary theater's most popular playwrights. His comedies, including *The Odd Couple, Brighton Beach Memoirs, Biloxi Blues,* and *Broadway Bound,* have dominated Broadway and many of his works have been adapted as motion pictures. He received the Pulitzer Prize for Drama in 1991 for *Lost in Yonkers.*

## Stephen Spender

One of the generation of English writers known as the "Oxford Poets," Spender is known for works which examine the turbulent social and political issues of the 1930s. In addition to verse, Spender also wrote criticism, plays, and essays. He received the Queen's Gold Medal for Poetry in 1971 and a *Los Angeles Times* Book Award nomination in 1986 for *Collected Poems: 1928-1985.*

## Amy Tan

Tan is a Chinese-American novelist whose first work *The Joy Luck Club* was both a critical and popular success, garnering nominations for the National Book Critics Circle Award and the *Los Angeles Times* Book Award. Focusing on the lives of Chinese-American women, Tan's works are praised for their poignant, engaging drama.

## John Wain

Wain was an acclaimed English novelist, critic, poet, short story writer, and biographer. Grouped with authors such as Kingsley Amis, John Braine, and John Osborne, and dubbed the "Angry Young Men," Wain was known for works which expressed disenchantment with the class-based hierarchy of English society. His works include the Whitbread Award-winning *The Free Zone Starts Here.*

## Tobias Wolff

Praised by critics for his lyrical prose, Wolff is an American novelist, short story writer, and memoirist often compared to Raymond Carver and Ann Beattie. His works include the PEN/Faulkner Award-winning *The Barracks Thief* and the National Book Award-nominated *In Pharaoh's Army: Memories of the Lost War.*

# *Contemporary Authors®*

## NEW REVISION SERIES

*\*Indicates that a listing has been compiled from secondary sources believed to be reliable but has not been personally verified for this edition by the author sketched.*

---

## ACKERMAN, Diane 1948-

*PERSONAL:* Born October 7, 1948, in Waukegan, IL; daughter of Sam (a restaurant owner) and Marcia (Tischler) Fink. *Education:* Attended Boston University, 1966-67; Pennsylvania State University, B.A., 1970; Cornell University, M.F.A., 1973, M.A., 1976, Ph.D., 1978. *Avocational interests:* Gardening, bicycling.

*ADDRESSES: Agent*—Janklow and Nesbitt, 598 Madison Ave., New York, NY 10022.

*CAREER:* Writer. Social worker in New York City, 1967; government researcher at Pennsylvania State University, 1968; Cornell University, Ithaca, NY, teaching assistant, 1971-78, lecturer, 1978-79; University of Pittsburgh, Pittsburgh, PA, assistant professor of English, 1980-83; Washington University, St. Louis, MO, director of writers' program and writer in residence, 1984-86; *New Yorker,* New York City, staff writer, 1988-94. Host, *Mystery of the Senses,* Public Broadcasting System (PBS), 1995. Writer in residence, William and Mary College, 1983, Ohio University, 1983; visiting writer, Columbia University, 1986, New York University, 1986, Cornell University, 1987. Member of literature panels, including New York State Council on the Arts, 1980-83; member of advisory board, Planetary Society, 1980—. Has participated in readings, residencies, and workshops.

*AWARDS, HONORS:* Academy of American Poets Poetry prize, Cornell University, 1972; Corson Bishop French Prize, Cornell University, 1972; Abbie Copps Prize, Olivet College, 1974; Rockefeller graduate fellowship, 1974-76; Heermans-McCalmon Playwriting Prize, Cornell University, 1976; creative writing fellowships, National Endowment for the Arts, 1976 and 1986, and Creative Artists Public Service Program, 1980; Corson Bishop Poetry Prize, Cornell University, 1977; poetry prize, *Black Warrior Review,* 1981; Pushcart Prize VIII, 1984; Peter I. B. Lavan Younger Poet Award, Academy of American Poets, 1985; Lowell Thomas Award, Society of American Travel Writers, 1990; National Book Critics Circle Award nomination, 1991; Wordsworth Award, 1992; Golden Nose Award, Olfactory Research Fund, 1994; named "Literary Lion," New York Public Library, 1994; semifinalist, Journalist-in-Space Project.

*WRITINGS:*

*POETRY*

(With Jody Bolz and Nancy Steele) *Poems: Ackerman, Bolz, and Steele* (chapbook), Stone Marrow Press (Cincinnati), 1973.
*The Planets: A Cosmic Pastoral,* Morrow (New York City), 1976.
*Wife of Light,* Morrow, 1978.
*Lady Faustus,* Morrow, 1983.
*Jaguar of Sweet Laughter: New and Selected Poems,* Random House (New York City), 1991.

*NONFICTION*

*Twilight of the Tenderfoot: A Western Memoir,* Morrow, 1980.
*On Extended Wings* (memoir), Atheneum (New York City), 1985, published as *On Extended Wings: An Adventure in Flight,* Scribner (New York City), 1987.

*A Natural History of the Senses,* Random House, 1990.

*The Moon by Whale Light, and Other Adventures among Bats, Penguins, Crocodilians, and Whales,* Random House, 1991.

*A Natural History of Love,* Random House, 1994.

    *The Rarest of the Rare: Vanishing Animals, Timeless Worlds,* Random House, 1995.

*Monk Seal Hideaway* (juvenile), Crown (New York City), 1995.

*Bats: Shadows in the Night* (juvenile), Crown, 1997.

*A Slender Thread,* Random House, 1997.

OTHER

*Reverse Thunder* (play), Lumen, 1988.

*Mystery of the Senses,* Public Broadcasting System, 1995.

Contributor to anthologies, including *The Morrow Anthology of Younger Poets,* edited by Dave Smith and David Bottoms, Morrow, 1985; *Norton Introduction to Literature,* edited by Jerome Beaty and J. Paul Hunter, 4th edition, Norton, 1986; *Norton Introduction to Poetry,* edited by Hunter, 3rd edition, Norton, 1986; *The Paris Review Anthology,* edited by George Plimpton, Norton, 1989; and numerous other poetry and prose anthologies. Contributor of poems and nonfiction to literary journals, periodicals, and newspapers, including *New Yorker, Poetry, Life, Omni, Kenyon Review, American Poetry Review, Parnassus: Poetry in Review, Michigan Quarterly Review, Paris Review,* and *New York Times;* contributor of reviews to *New York Times Book Review.*

*ADAPTATIONS: On Extended Wings: An Adventure in Flight* was adapted for the stage in 1987 by Norma Jean Griffin.

*SIDELIGHTS:* Diane Ackerman has been hailed by several critics for her poetry and for her prose explorations into the world of science and natural history. Although the two genres are seemingly very different from each other, Ackerman's sensibility blends the two, bringing a poetic touch to her nonfiction work and incorporating the subjects of chemistry and biology into her verse. She once said in *Contemporary Poets:* "People sometimes ask me about all of the Science in my poetry, thinking it odd that I should wish to combine Science and Art, and assuming that I must have some inner pledge or outer maxim I follow. But the hardest job for me is trying to keep Science out of my poetry. We live in a world where amino acids, viruses, airfoils, and such are common

ingredients in our daily sense of Nature. Not to write about Nature in its widest sense, because quasars or corpuscles are not 'the proper realm of poetry,' as a critic once said to me, is not only irresponsible and philistine, it bankrupts the experience of living, it ignores much of life's fascination and variety."

Ackerman's voracious appetite for knowledge and her eager appreciation of the natural world are evident in *Jaguar of Sweet Laughter: New and Selected Poems,* according to *New York Times Book Review* contributor David Kirby. He asserted: "Diane Ackerman's poems not only operate in the present but press toward the future. . . . Just about everything Ms. Ackerman writes, prose or poetry, is exploratory. . . . [Her] speakers push ahead; they probe, open, take off lids, peel back covers, inspect, taste, sniff." Her constant sense of wonder is the key to the appeal of her work, concluded Kirby: "Ms. Ackerman trains her telescope on the bend in the river, all but pitching over the rail as she strains toward the next surprise."

Ackerman explored the world of animals in *The Moon by Whale Light, and Other Adventures among Bats, Penguins, Crocodilians, and Whales,* a collection of four essays expanded from articles previously published in the *New Yorker.* Allying herself with experts on each species, Ackerman went into the field to gain first-hand experience with the animals. She recorded her observations in detail, along with thoughts on the folklore of each animal. Fraser Harrison noted in *New Statesman and Society,* "Ackerman is at her best when describing the animals in her own eloquent words. She is a hands-on journalist in a very literal sense, for, as befits the author of *A Natural History of the Senses,* she always insists on touching her subjects, even the whales. Especially vivid is her account of sitting astride an alligator, its mouth bound with tape, and feeling her way round its 'beautiful, undulating skin.'" Harrison found Ackerman's portrayal of penguins "shamelessly anthropomorphic" yet justifiable; her depiction of their habitat, he added, has a poetic quality. "And it is this quality," he concluded, "that makes her a considerable nature writer as well as an intrepid, sharp-eyed journalist, for she has the imaginative gift to identify with the character of her animals and the intelligence to keep them in their ecological place."

Michiko Kakutani of the *New York Times* offered similar praise, writing that Ackerman "has a gift for sparkling, resonant language, and her descriptions of various animals and their habitats are alive with verbal energy and delight. She describes bats as delicately assembled packages of 'fur and appetite' and characterizes their high-pitched cries as 'vocal Braille.'" Kakutani further praised the author for providing a great deal of "fascinating" information about the lives of each species. Franklin Burroughs, writing in *Southern Review,* enthusiastically endorsed Ackerman's "fine eye for detail, her adventurousness, and her humor" and noted: "When these essays first appeared in the familiar milieu of *The New Yorker,* they seemed to fall within its civilized, flexible conception of an American middle voice: informative, engaging, modest, witty, and thoroughly *professional,* not subject to the enthusiasms, large claims, and idiosyncrasies of the writer for whom writing itself remains the central, animating adventure."

Ackerman shifted her focus from the animal world to the human province of romantic love with her 1994 collection of essays, *A Natural History of Love.* *Washington Post Book World* contributor Barbara Raskin characterized this volume as "an audaciously brilliant romp. . . . Using an evolutionary history as her launchpad, Ackerman takes off on a space flight in which she describes, defines, theorizes, analyzes, analogizes, apologizes, generalizes, explains, philosophizes, embellishes, codifies, classifies, confesses, compares, contrasts, speculates, hypothesizes and generally carries on like a hooligan about amatory love. It's a blast." Beginning with a quick survey of 2,000 years of love, Ackerman proceeds with an analysis of famous literary passages on romance, the chemistry of love, the effects of lovelessness on children and cultures, and many more subjects. Some critics believed too many topics were included and too many different writing styles used. Chris Goodrich, writing in the *Los Angeles Times,* praised *A Natural History of Love* as an enjoyable read, but found it "surprisingly shapeless," with contents "that vary between the arresting and the superficial, the illuminating and the irksome. Reading the book, you spend half your time wishing it were better, and the other half captivated by those passages in which Ackerman . . . has found a particularly good lens through which to view her subject." Still, he allowed that the book was "a pleasure," and described Ackerman as "a beguiling, even seductive writer." Raskin also emphasized the author's power with words, stating: "Of all the loves Ackerman describes, none is greater than her own love of language. . . . She produces hard-hitting metaphors and sweet constellations of similes that are like confectionery recipes for fresh insights."

*BIOGRAPHICAL/CRITICAL SOURCES:*

BOOKS

*Contemporary Authors Autobiography Series,* Gale (Detroit), 1995.
*Contemporary Poets,* St. James (Chicago and London), 1985.
*Dictionary of Literary Biography,* Volume 120: *American Poets since World War II, Third Series,* Gale, 1992.

PERIODICALS

*Boston Globe,* July 3, 1994, p. A16; June 12, 1995, p. 26.
*Chicago Tribune,* September 6, 1994, section 5, p. 2.
*Los Angeles Times,* October 20, 1985; July 8, 1994, p. E8; February 18, 1995, p. F14.
*Los Angeles Times Book Review,* November 29, 1992, p. 10; October 29, 1995.
*Mirabella,* September, 1991, pp. 76-78.
*New Republic,* November 20, 1976.
*New Statesman and Society,* May 21, 1993, pp. 35-36.
*Newsweek,* September 22, 1986.
*New York Times,* November 29, 1991, p. C27.
*New York Times Book Review,* June 29, 1980; December 22, 1985; November 3, 1991, p. 14; December 29, 1991, p. 7; June 26, 1994, p. 12; February 18, 1996, p. 11.
*Philadelphia Inquirer,* October 22, 1995, pp. K1-2.
*Publishers Weekly,* September 11, 1995, p. 71.
*San Francisco Examiner & Guide,* October 29, 1995.
*Southern Review,* October, 1992, pp. 928-36.
*Vogue,* September, 1991, pp. 384-88.
*Wall Street Journal,* November 26, 1991, p. A12.
*Washington Post,* June 10, 1980; November 28, 1991, p. C3.
*Washington Post Book World,* June 19, 1994, p. 2.

\*   \*   \*

**ALBEE, Edward (Franklin III)   1928-**

*PERSONAL:* Surname pronounced *All*-bee; born March 12, 1928, probably in Virginia; adopted son of Reed A. (part-owner of Keith-Albee theatre circuit) and Frances (Cotter) Albee. *Education:* Attended Trinity College, Hartford, CT, 1946-47. *Re-*

*ligion:* None. *Avocational interests:* Travel, playing the harpsichord.

*ADDRESSES: Home*—Montauk, NY. *Office*—14 Harrison St., New York, NY 10013.

*CAREER:* Writer, producer, and director of plays. Worked as continuity writer for WNYC-radio, office boy for Warwick & Legler (advertising agency), record salesman for G. Schirmer, Inc. (music publishers), and counterman in luncheonette of Manhattan Towers Hotel; messenger for Western Union, 1955-58. Producer, with Richard Barr and Clinton Wilder, New Playwrights Unit Workshop, 1963—; director of touring retrospective of his one-act plays including, *The Zoo Story, The American Dream, Fam and Yam, The Sandbox, Box, Quotations from Chairman Mao Tse-Tung, Counting the Ways,* and *Listening,* produced as *Albee Directs Albee,* 1978-79; co-director of Vivian Beaumont Theatre at Lincoln Center for the Performing Arts, New York, NY, 1979-81. Founder of William Flanagan Center for Creative Persons in Montauk, NY, 1971. Member of National Endowment grant-giving council; member of Dramatists Guild Council; member of governing commission of New York State Council for the Arts. Lecturer at colleges, including Brandeis University, Johns Hopkins University, and Webster University. Cultural exchange visitor to U.S.S.R. and Latin American countries for U.S. State Department. President of Edward F. Albee Foundation. Instructor/Artist-in-Residence at University of Houston.

*MEMBER:* PEN American Center, National Academy of Arts and Letters, Dramatists Guild.

*AWARDS, HONORS:* Berlin Festival Award, 1959, for *The Zoo Story,* and 1961, for *The Death of Bessie Smith;* Vernon Rice Memorial Award, and Obie Award, 1960, and Argentine Critics Circle Award, 1961, all for *The Zoo Story; The Death of Bessie Smith* and *The American Dream* were chosen as best plays of the 1960-61 season by Foreign Press Association, 1961; Lola D'Annunzio Award, 1961, for *The American Dream;* selected as most promising playwright of 1962-63 season by New York Drama Critics, 1963; New York Drama Critics Circle Award, Foreign Press Association Award, Antoinette Perry ("Tony") Award, Outer Circle Award, *Saturday Review* Drama Critics Award, and *Variety* Drama Critics' Poll Award, 1963, and *Evening Standard* Award, 1964, all for *Who's Afraid of Virginia*

*Woolf?;* with Richard Barr and Clinton Wilder, recipient of Margo Jones Award, 1965, for encouraging new playwrights; Pulitzer Prize, 1967, for *A Delicate Balance,* and 1975, for *Seascape;* D.Litt., Emerson College, 1967, and Trinity College, 1974; American Academy and Institute of Arts and Letters Gold Medal, 1980; inducted into Theater Hall of Fame, 1985; Pulitzer Prize and New York Drama Critics Circle Award, 1994, for *Three Tall Women.*

*WRITINGS:*

*PLAYS, EXCEPT AS INDICATED*

*The Zoo Story, The Death of Bessie Smith, The Sandbox: Three Plays* (*The Zoo Story,* first produced [in German] in Berlin at Schiller Theater Werkstatt, September 28, 1959, produced Off-Broadway at Provincetown Playhouse, January 14, 1960; *The Death of Bessie Smith,* first produced in Berlin at Schlosspark Theater, April 21, 1960, produced Off-Broadway at York Playhouse, February 28, 1961; *The Sandbox,* first produced in New York, NY at Jazz Gallery, May 15, 1960, produced Off-Broadway at Cherry Lane Theatre, February, 1962, directed by author), Coward, 1960, published with *The American Dream* (also see below) as *The Zoo Story and Other Plays,* J. Cape, 1962.

(Author of libretto with James Hinton, Jr.) *Bartleby* (opera; adaptation of story by Herman Melville; music by William Flanagan), produced Off-Broadway at York Playhouse, January 24, 1961.

*The American Dream,* with introduction by the author (produced Off-Broadway at York Playhouse, January 24, 1961), Coward, 1961.

*Fam and Yam* (produced in Westport, CT at White Barn Theatre, August 27, 1960), Dramatists Play Service (New York City), 1961.

*Who's Afraid of Virginia Woolf?* (produced on Broadway at Billy Rose Theatre, October 13, 1962), Atheneum (New York City), 1962.

*The Ballad of the Sad Cafe* (adaptation of novella of same title by Carson McCullers; produced on Broadway at Martin Beck Theatre, October 30, 1963), Houghton (Boston), 1963.

*Tiny Alice* (produced on Broadway at Billy Rose Theatre, December 29, 1964), Atheneum, 1965.

*Malcolm* (adaptation of novel of same title by James Purdy; produced on Broadway at Sam S. Shubert Theatre, January 11, 1966), Atheneum, 1966.

*A Delicate Balance* (produced on Broadway at Martin Beck Theatre, September 22, 1966), Atheneum, 1966.

*Breakfast at Tiffany's* (musical; adaptation of story of same title by Truman Capote; music by Bob Merrill), produced in Philadelphia, 1966, produced on Broadway at Majestic Theatre, December, 1966.

*Everything in the Garden* (based on play by Giles Cooper; produced on Broadway at Plymouth Theatre, November 29, 1967), Atheneum, 1968.

*Box* [and] *Quotations from Chairman Mao Tse-Tung* (two interrelated plays; first produced at Studio Arena Theatre, Buffalo, NY; produced on Broadway at Billy Rose Theatre, September 30, 1968), Atheneum, 1969.

*All Over* (produced on Broadway at Martin Beck Theatre, January 26, 1971; produced in London by Royal Shakespeare Co. at Aldwych Theatre, January 31, 1972), Atheneum, 1971.

*Seascape* (produced on Broadway at Sam S. Shubert Theatre, January 26, 1975, directed by author), Atheneum, 1975.

*Counting the Ways* [and] *Listening: Two Plays* (*Counting the Ways*, first produced in London by National Theatre Co., 1976, produced by Hartford Stage Co., Hartford, CT, January 28, 1977; *Listening: A Chamber Play* [produced as radio play by British Broadcasting Corp. (BBC), 1976], first produced on stage by Hartford Stage Co., Hartford, January 28, 1977), Atheneum, 1977.

*The Lady from Dubuque* (produced on Broadway at Morosco Theatre, January 31, 1980), Atheneum, 1980.

*Lolita* (adaptation of novel of same title by Vladimir Nabokov), first produced in Boston at Wilbur Theatre, January 15, 1981, produced on Broadway at Brooks Atkinson Theatre, March 19, 1981, published as *Lolita: A Play*, Dramatists Play Service, 1984.

*The Man Who Had Three Arms*, first produced in Miami, FL, at New World Festival, June 10, 1982, directed by the author; produced in Chicago, IL at Goodman Theater, October 4, 1982, directed by the author.

*Finding the Sun*, (first produced in 1983, New York premiere at the Signature Theatre Company, February, 1994), Dramatists Play Service, 1994.

*Marriage Play*, first produced at the English Theatre in Vienna, 1987, American premiere at the McCarter Theater in Princeton, N.J., February 22, 1992.

*Three Tall Women*, (two-act play; first produced at the English Theatre in Vienna, June, 1991, New York City premiere at the Vineyard Theatre, February 13, 1994), Dutton (New York City), 1995.

*Fragments: A Sit Around,* (premiered at Ensemble Theater of Cincinnati, Cincinnati, OH, November, 1993, New York opening at Signature Theatre Company, 1994), published as *Edward Albee's Fragments: A Sit-Around,* Dramatists Play Service, 1995.

*A Delicate Balance: A Play,* Plume (New York City), 1997.

*AUTHOR OF INTRODUCTION*

Noel Coward, *Three Plays by Noel Coward: Blithe Spirit, Hay Fever,* [and] *Private Lives,* Delta (New York City), 1965.

Phyllis Johnson Kaye, editor, *National Playwrights Directory,* 2nd edition, Eugene O'Neill Theater Center (Waterford, CT), 1981.

(With Sabina Lietzmann) *New York,* Vendome Press (New York City), 1981.

*Louise Nevelson: Atmospheres and Environments,* Clarkson N. Potter (New York City), 1981.

Also author of screenplays, including an adaptation of *Le Locataire* (title means "The Tenant"), a novel by Roland Topor, an adaptation of his *The Death of Bessie Smith,* one about the life of Nijinsky, and one about Stanford White and Evelyn Nesbitt. Also contributor of articles to magazines.

*ADAPTATIONS: Who's Afraid of Virginia Woolf?* was adapted and filmed by Warner Bros. in 1966.

*SIDELIGHTS:* Reviewing the numerous commentaries written about Edward Albee's plays, C. W. E. Bigsby notes in *Edward Albee: A Collection of Critical Essays* that in comparison to Albee "few playwrights . . . have been so frequently and mischievously misunderstood, misrepresented, overpraised, denigrated, and precipitately dismissed." Capsulizing the changing tone of Albee criticism since the early 1960s (when his first play appeared), Bigsby offers this overview: "Canonized after . . . *The Zoo Story,* [Albee] found himself in swift succession billed as America's most promising playwright, leading dramatist, and then, with astonishing suddenness, a 'one-hit' writer. . . . The progression was essentially that suggested by George in [Albee's] *Who's Afraid of Virginia Woolf?,* 'better, best, bested.'"

To symbolize the curve of Albee's reputation as a dramatist, Bigsby chooses a phrase from a play designated by many critics as a dividing line in the playwright's career. T. E. Kalem, for example, in *Time* remarks: "Albee almost seems to have lived through two careers, one very exciting, the other increasingly depressing. From *The Zoo Story* through *The American Dream* to *Who's Afraid of Virginia Woolf?,* he displayed great gusto, waspish humor and feral power. In the succeeding . . . years, he has foundered in murky metaphysics, . . . dabbled in adaptations, . . . and gone down experimental blind alleys."

However, many critics have praised these same plays. Albee continues to win awards; he has received three Pulitzer Prizes since *Virginia Woolf,* one in 1967 for *A Delicate Balance,* one in 1975, for *Seascape,* and, in 1994, a third for his autobiographical drama *Three Tall Women.* His three Pulitzer Prizes place him in the ranks of such notable dramatists as Tennessee Williams, holder of two Pulitzers, Robert E. Sherwood, a three-time winner, and four-time honoree Eugene O'Neill.

Walter Wagner in *The Playwrights Speak* notes, "[Albee] is a successful dramatist because of his intelligence, perceptions, talent and willingness to treat questions that few American playwrights examined before him." Brian Way, in *American Theatre,* while conceding what he judges to be limitations in the scope of Albee's writing, also praises the dramatist: "It is only fair that one should return to an assertion of the importance of Albee's good qualities in the American theatre. If it is true that he inhabits a finite world, he does so with brilliance, inventiveness, intelligence, and moral courage." And, according to Ruby Cohn in *Dialogue in American Drama,* Albee is "the most skillful composer of dialogue that America has produced."

Bigsby offers an explanation of the ongoing critical attacks on Albee's ability as a playwright: "There is no doubt that the Broadway production of . . . *Virginia Woolf* provided the basis for Albee's amazing popular reputation; . . . equally certainly, it was also the primary reason for the suspicion with which some reviewers and critics approached his work. . . . The success of . . . *Virginia Woolf* established Albee's reputation around the world. . . . And now, public and reviewers alike expected him to repeat his earlier success. [But] the truth was that Albee has remained at heart a product of Off-Broadway, claiming the same freedom to experiment and, indeed, fail, which is the special strength of that theatre."

The playwright, in spite of negative criticism, has not been "bested" by the critics. He continues in his

role as dramatist, and teacher, with a post as an instructor and artist-in-residence at the University of Houston. In a *Washington Post* interview with David Richards, Albee explained his own reaction to the critics: "I have been both overpraised and underpraised. I assume by the time I finish writing—and I plan to go on writing until I'm ninety or gaga—it will all equal itself out. . . . You can't involve yourself with the vicissitudes of fashion or critical response. I'm fairly confident that my work is going to be around for a while."

Although stylistically varied, Albee's plays are thematically connected. Gerald Weales in *The Jumping Off Place: American Drama in the 1960's* notes: "Each new Albee play seems to be an experiment in form, in style, . . . and yet there is unity to his work as a whole. This is apparent in the devices and the characters that recur, modified according to context, but it is most obvious in the repetition of theme, in the basic assumptions about the human condition that underlie all his work."

Reviewing Albee's touring retrospective of eight of his one-act plays, "Albee Directs Albee," Sylvie Drake of the *Los Angeles Times* observes: "This condensation of work reveals Albee's consistent and enduring concern with loss. . . . 'Pain is understanding,' says someone in [Albee's play] 'Counting the Ways.' 'It's really loss.' Yes. These plays are *all* about loss." In her analysis of Albee's plays Drake also discovers the following themes: "the chasm between people, [and] their inability to connect except through pain."

John MacNicholas, writing in *Dictionary of Literary Biography,* says the development of these themes in Albee's plays started with his first play, *The Zoo Story.* According to Way, this play, a tale of a fairly prosperous married man and his confrontation on a Central Park bench with a totally alienated young drifter, "is an exploration of the farce and agony of human isolation." George Wellwarth, in *The Theater of Protest and Paradox: Development in the Avant-Garde Drama,* explains the play's thematic content in more detail: "[Albee] is exemplifying or demonstrating a theme. That theme is the enormous and usually insuperable difficulty that human beings find in communicating with each other. More precisely, it is about the maddening effect that the enforced loneliness of the human condition has on the person who is cursed (for in our society it undoubtedly is a curse) with an infinite capacity for love."

Albee's thematic preoccupation with loss of contact between individuals is tied to the playwright's desire to make a statement about American values, as Weales points out. "In much of his work," according to the critic, "there is a suggestion . . . that the emptiness and loneliness of the characters are somehow the result of a collapse of values in the Western world, in general, in the United States, in particular." Albee finds the feelings of loss and emptiness prevalent in the society that surrounds him.

Howard Schneider elaborates on this idea in a *Pittsburgh Press* article: "[Albee] hammers incessantly [at this theme] when he talks at college campuses. The 'disengagement' of the population. The passivity of Americans drawn to a television set six hours a day. The religious, political and social structures that men have created to 'illusion' themselves from the world and each other." Schneider quotes Albee's own explanation of the themes present in his work: "People who are passive and who are careless contribute to the decline of the system, especially in a democracy. . . . People still refuse to think and act honorably with each other. They are still mean and vicious and these are the subjects of my plays."

Following *The Zoo Story,* three Albee plays opened in New York during 1960-61. All of these—*The Sandbox, The American Dream,* and *The Death of Bessie Smith*—"attack certain features in American society," according to MacNicholas. *The Death of Bessie Smith,* for example, deals with the death of the black singer who bled to death after an automobile accident, apparently because she was denied care at a nearby all-white hospital. *The American Dream* and *The Sandbox* share the same characters— Mommy, Daddy, and Grandma. MacNicholas feels that these two plays "form a continuum in subject matter and technique; both attack indifference to love, pity, and compassion. In both, . . . the characters . . . live in a kind of moral narcosis."

Allen Lewis, in *American Plays and Playwrights of the Contemporary Theatre,* comments: "*The American Dream* is a wildly imaginative caricature of the American family. . . . [In this play] Albee is the angry young man, tearing apart the antiseptic mirage of American middle-class happiness." The American family of the play is comprised of characters known only as "Mommy" (a domineering shrew), "Daddy" (a weak, hen-pecked husband), and "Grandma" (an older version of "Mommy"). Set in the family's stuffy apartment, the play includes the story of the couple's adoption of a "bumble of joy" whom they

destroy after discovering his various defects. (For example, they cut out his tongue when he says a dirty word.) As he grows up, Mommy and Daddy complain that the baby has no head on his shoulders, is spineless, and has feet of clay. They complain again when he dies after having already been paid for. Near the end of the play, the baby's twin appears. He is a handsome young man who describes himself as a "clean-cut midwest farm boy type, almost insultingly good-looking in a typically American way." "The young man," as Frederick Lumley notes in *New Trends in Twentieth Century Drama,* "feels that he is incomplete, he doesn't know what has happened to something within him, but he has no touch, he is unable to make love, to see anything with pity; in fact he has no feeling." Continuing his interpretation of the play, Lewis states: "The American Dream [of the title] is the young man who is all appearance and no feelings. . . . He says: 'I cannot touch another person and feel love. . . . I have no emotions. . . . I have now only my person . . . my body, my face. . . . I let people love me. . . . I feel nothing.'"

In his preface to *The American Dream,* Albee explains the play's content: "The play is an examination of the American Scene, an attack on the substitution of artificial for real values in our society, a condemnation of complacency, cruelty, emasculation and vacuity; it is a stand against the fiction that everything in this slipping land of ours is peachy-keen." According to MacNicholas, Albee continues his critique of American society in his first three-act play, *Who's Afraid of Virginia Woolf?.* Many critics note a relationship between this play and *The American Dream.* Martin Esslin, writing in *The Theatre of the Absurd,* comments: "A closer inspection reveals elements which clearly . . . relate [*Virginia Woolf*] to Albee's earlier work. . . . George and Martha [a couple in the play] (there are echoes here of George and Martha Washington) have an imaginary child which they treat as real, until in the cold dawn of that wild night [in which the action of the play takes place] they decide to 'kill' it by abandoning their joint fantasy. Here the connection to *The American Dream* with its horrid dream-child of the ideal all-American boy becomes clear. . . . Is the dream-child which cannot become real among people torn by ambition and lust something like the American ideal itself?"

Drake finds George and Martha of *Virginia Woolf* directly related to Mommy and Daddy of *The American Dream.* Lumley describes this evolution: "The

Mommy and Daddy of . . . *Virginia Woolf* are this time given names, Martha and George, thus becoming individuals instead of abstract characters. . . . They have been unable to have children; so that their love is mixed-up sexual humiliation, a strong love-hate relationship which makes them want to hurt and claw and wound each other because they know each other and cannot do without one another." In the *Arizona Quarterly,* James P. Quinn describes the combination of social criticism and the theme of human isolation in *Virginia Woolf:* "In [the play] the author parodies the ideals of western civilization. . . . Thus, romantic love, marriage, sex, the family, status, competition, power all the 'illusions' man has erected to eliminate the differences between self and others and to escape the . . . burden of his freedom and loneliness come under attack."

Critics note the continuation of theme and social awareness throughout Albee's work. For example, Harold Clurman, in his *Nation* review of *All Over,* writes: "Albee is saying [in this play] that despite all the hasty bickering, the fierce hostility and the mutual misunderstandings which separate us, we need one another. We cry out in agony when we are cut off." Bigsby, commenting on the same play, concludes: "Albee's concern in *All Over* is essentially that of his earlier work. He remains intent on penetrating the bland urbanities of social life in an attempt to identify the crucial failure of nerve which has brought individual men and whole societies to the point of not merely soulless anomie but even of apocalypse."

Bigsby also finds similar characteristics in Albee's play *Box,* calling it "a protest against the dangerously declining quality of life—a decline marked . . . by the growth of an amoral technology with a momentum and direction of its own." MacNicholas notes Albee's preoccupation with loss in *A Delicate Balance:* "[The play] concerns itself with loss: not loss which occurs in one swift traumatic stroke, but that which evolves slowly in increments of gentle and lethal acquiescence."

A handful of interested readers and viewers, however, was not enough to sustain critical and popular success for the playwright in the United States from the late 1970s through the 1980s. In this period, his only play to receive a generally favorable response, the 1975 Pulitzer-winning *Seascape,* closed after only sixty-five performances. Though he continued to write and produce, on average, a play every two years, his work often found more enthusiastic audiences abroad. At home his plays generated mainly academic interest. Commenting on some of Albee's efforts from this era, critic Stefan Kanfer writes in the *New Leader:* "His reward for all this industry has been a latter-day neglect. Too many of Albee's major works have failed on the main stem, and lesser plays have not prospered Off-Broadway. Who remembers *The Lady from Dubuque, The Man Who Had Three Arms, Finding the Sun?*"

Then, in what several critics have referred to as phoenix-like fashion, Albee was seemingly reborn as a popular and critically successful artist during the 1993-94 New York theatre season in Off- and Off-Off-Broadway houses similar in spirit to the fringe theaters Albee and his contemporaries helped nourish in the 1960s, during the early days of avant-garde American playwriting. One such artistic enclave, the Signature Theatre, a non-profit company in lower Manhattan, brought Albee aboard as its playwright-in-residence and dedicated an entire season to his works, proving that at least some producers remembered his allegedly forgotten plays. The lineup included a variety of full-length dramas and one-acts, old and new. Among them were *Finding the Sun,* a long 1983 one-act in twenty-two vignettes, involving the interaction of eight characters on a New England beach; *Marriage Play,* Albee's 1987 sparring match between a long-wed husband and wife that elicited several comparisons to *Virginia Woolf;* and *Fragments: A Sit Around.*

Rounding off the list were two one-act collections. The first, *Listening: A Chamber Play,* and *Counting the Ways* were originally presented in London at the National Theatre in 1976, then in America at the Hartford Stage Company in Connecticut. These plays represent Albee's experimental writing in the middle part of his career. In a *New York Times* review, Ben Brantley suggests that both "are essentially linguistic chamber works. . . . Though they are radically different in tone, their preoccupation with the slipperiness of language and perception and with the opacity of what truly lies behind it is much the same. The questions posed reverberate without answers and are often as unapologetically naked as 'Who am I?' 'Who are you?' and 'Do you love me?'"

The next short play bill, collectively entitled *Sand,* was directed by Albee himself and included three representative pieces, *Box* (1968), *The Sandbox* (1960) and *Finding the Sun.* While the Signature season provided him a rare opportunity to revisit several old works and try out new ideas, it was the

New York premiere of his 1991 play *Three Tall Women* a few blocks north at the Vineyard Theater that earned Albee his greatest accolades since *Virginia Woolf,* including a third Pulitzer Prize and the New York Drama Critics Circle Award.

Autobiographical in content, *Three Tall Women* is an examination of the life of a wealthy, boisterous, strong-minded woman nearly a century old. The first act consists of a conversation between this often cantankerous dowager, known only as A; her sympathetic, middle-aged caretaker, B; and C, her 26-year-old lawyer. These are Albee's "three tall women" in their first incarnation. A's physical condition is deteriorating rapidly—she is frequently incontinent and has recently broken an arm that will not heal—and her mental state is precarious. As she attempts to put her affairs in order with C and reminisces about her experiences, she alternates between an amazing perceptiveness and scandalous wit, and amnesic episodes accompanied by childlike tantrums. She can't remember if she is ninety-one or ninety-two, or whether close friends are alive or dead, but can relate tales from her courtship and early years of marriage in great detail.

The fifty-two-year-old B has become inured to the abuse A frequently heaps upon her, and to the personal tasks she must help the older woman perform. In her own climbing years B waxes philosophically about the natural aging process. C is both attracted to and repulsed by the behavior of her elders. She giggles at A's anecdotes of her early sexual escapades (though A claims to have been the "wild one" her behavior was prudish by C's youthful standards), then she is shocked at A's casual, overt racism, bigotry, and insensitivity. The first act ends with A lying in bed lamenting the breakdown in her relationships with her own mother, whom she cared for in her old age, and her homosexual son, who couldn't stand her intolerance and left her when he was still a teenager. Her rambling diatribe ends suddenly, and upon examining her, B announces A has suffered a stroke.

A transformation occurs between acts, and when the curtain rises on the second half of *Three Tall Women,* a mannequin representation of A occupies the bed while the actresses playing A, B, and C are revealed as the same woman at three different stages of life, all attending what will soon be her own deathbed. This partition of the elderly A's life allows the playwright the opportunity to examine his character from three distinct, yet similar points of view.

C remembers her glory days, when she and her sister worked as department store models and cavorted innocently, and not so innocently, with boys, all the while waiting for "the man of my dreams." Hers is the voice of youth and naivete, silly yet romantically appealing. B, the realist, has fresher adult memories of the man of her dreams, including both her and her husband's extramarital affairs. She also recalls, quite vividly, opening her son's mail and finding admiring notes from older men, then arguing with him, and watching him exit her life for the next twenty years. A remembers the six agonizing years it took for her husband to die of cancer, and how she sold her jewelry a little at a time to meet expenses, replacing it with replicas to maintain appearances. In the final moments of the play, the three tall women, multiple facets of the same spirit, share what they feel has been their happiest moment. For the youthful C it is uncertain. It may have been her confirmation or, better yet, perhaps they are still to come. B's happiest moment is the here and now, "half of being adult done," she says, "the rest ahead of me. Old enough to be a *little* wise, past being *really* dumb." As they all join hands A reveals her happiest moment will be "coming to the end of it; yes. . . . That's the happiest moment. When it's all done. When we stop. When we can stop."

Following the success of *Three Tall Women* in New York, Albee admitted in interviews that the play's main character was directly inspired by his own adoptive mother, Frances Cotter Albee, who expelled the eighteen-year-old Edward from his family's home for his homosexuality, and later removed him from her will. As Albee told David Richards of the *New York Times,* "The play is a kind of exorcism. . . . I didn't end up any more fond of the woman after I finished it than when I started. But it allowed me to come to terms with the long unpleasant life she led and develop a little respect for her independence. She was destructive, but she had lots of reasons to be. It's there on the stage, all the good stuff and the bad stuff." Though elements of his own life and family had crept into his plays before, notably in *The American Dream* and *Finding the Sun,* Albee did not feel free enough to write particularly about his mother until after her death at the age of ninety-two in 1990. In the *New Yorker,* John Lahr suggests that the "last great gift a parent gives to a child is his or her own death, and the energy underneath *Three Tall Women* is the exhilaration of a writer calling it quits with the past." Robert Brustein asserts in the *New Republic* that "*Three Tall Women* is a mature piece of writing . . . in which Albee seems to be coming to terms not only with a socialite foster parent, . . . but with his own advancing age."

Not all reviews were glowing, however. In a *New York Times* review, Ben Brantley complains, "*Three Tall Women* . . . is by no means an entirely successful play. . . . It makes its points so blatantly and repeats them so often that one perversely longs for a bit more of the cryptic obliquity that is Mr. Albee's signature." Vincent Canby, another *New York Times* critic, opines, "*Three Tall Women* initially seems to be about the process of dying and death itself, though that's not the full story. It's more about the inevitable changes effected by time and circumstances, about the accumulation of events that can shape a character and that are so many they eventually become meaningless. It doesn't help that at no one of her three ages is A a very interesting woman. She's bossy and gauche as young C, bitter and tired as B and self-absorbed as old A."

While *Three Tall Women* stands apart in the Albee oeuvre as a popular and critical success, the dramatist himself insists it does not mark a fundamental departure from his preferred method of writing, nor should it be read as an indicator of plays to come. In a *Los Angeles Times* interview Albee declared: "I want to reach as wide an audience as possible but, alas, on my own terms. I don't want to compromise or oversimplify just to give myself the illusion of accomplishment. You start lying, telling half-truths, well, what's the point? Ascribe it to my arrogance—an arrogance that any artist in the United States has got to have to survive—but I can't really approach my work in any other way."

*BIOGRAPHICAL/CRITICAL SOURCES:*

BOOKS

Amacher, Richard E., *Edward Albee,* Twayne (New York City), 1969.
*Authors in the News,* Volume I, Gale (Detroit), 1976.
Bigsby, C. W. E., *Albee,* Oliver & Boyd, 1969.
Bigsby, editor, *Edward Albee: A Collection of Critical Essays,* Prentice-Hall, 1975.
Bloom, Harold, editor, *Edward Albee,* Chelsea House, 1987.
Brown, John Russell, and Bernard Harris, editors, *American Theatre,* Edward Arnold, 1967.
Cohn, Ruby, *Edward Albee,* University of Minnesota Press (Minneapolis, MN), 1969.

Cohn, *Dialogue in American Drama,* Indiana University Press (Bloomington, IN), 1971.
*Contemporary Literary Criticism,* Gale, Volume 1, 1973, Volume 2, 1974, Volume 3, 1975, Volume 5, 1976, Volume 9, 1978, Volume 11, 1979, Volume 13, 1980, Volume 25, 1983, Volume 53, 1989, Volume 86, 1995.
Debusscher, Gilbert, *Edward Albee: Tradition and Renewal,* American Studies Center (Brussels), 1967.
*Dictionary of Literary Biography,* Volume 7: *Twentieth-Century American Dramatists,* Part I, Gale, 1981.
Downer, Alan S., editor, *American Drama and Its Critics,* University of Chicago Press (Chicago, IL), 1965.
Esslin, Martin, *The Theatre of the Absurd,* Doubleday (New York City), 1969.
Giantvalley, Scott, *Edward Albee: A Reference Guide,* G. K. Hall, 1987.
Hughes, Catharine, *American Playwrights, 1945-75,* Pitman, 1976.
Kolin, Philip C., editor, *Conversations with Edward Albee,* University Press of Mississippi, 1988.
Kostelanetz, Richard, *On Contemporary Literature,* Avon (New York City), 1964.
Lewis, Allan, *American Plays and Playwrights of the Contemporary Theatre,* Crown (New York City), 1965.
Lumley, Frederick, *New Trends in Twentieth Century Drama,* 4th edition, Oxford University Press, 1972.
Mayberry, Bob, *Theatre of Discord: Dissonance in Beckett, Albee, and Pinter,* Fairleigh Dickinson University Press, 1989.
Paolucci, Anne, *From Tension to Tonic: The Plays of Edward Albee,* Southern Illinois University Press (Carbondale, IL), 1972.
Roudanae, Matthew Charles, *Who's Afraid of Virginia Woolf?: Necessary Fictions, Terrifying Realities,* Twayne Publishers, 1990.
Rutenberg, Michael E., *Edward Albee: Playwright in Protest,* Avon, 1969.
Tyce, Richard, *Edward Albee: A Bibliography,* Scarecrow Press, 1986.
Wagner, Walter, editor, *The Playwrights Speak,* Delacorte (New York City), 1967.
Weales, Gerald, *The Jumping Off Place: American Drama in the 1960's,* Macmillan (New York City), 1969.
Wellwarth, George, *The Theater of Protest and Paradox: Development in the Avant-Garde Drama,* New York University Press (New York City), 1964.

*PERIODICALS*

*America,* April 2, 1994, p. 18.
*Arizona Quarterly,* autumn, 1974.
*Atlantic,* April, 1965.
*Books,* July, 1966.
*Chicago Tribune,* March 26, 1979; September 26, 1982; April 9, 1995, sec. 13, p. 2.
*Chicago Tribune Book World,* September 26, 1982.
*Christian Science Monitor,* November 10, 1993, p. 12.
*Commonweal,* January 22, 1965; April 10, 1992, p. 18; December 3, 1993, p. 17.
*Contemporary Literature,* spring, 1968.
*Current Biography,* April, 1996, p. 3.
*Detroit News,* June 27, 1982.
*Hudson Review,* spring, 1965; winter, 1966-67.
*Life,* October 28, 1966; May 26, 1967; February 2, 1968.
*London Magazine,* March, 1969.
*Los Angeles Times,* October 18, 1978; April 21, 1994, pp. F1, F6.
*Nation,* December 18, 1967; March 25, 1968; April 12, 1971; February 23, 1980; April 18, 1981; March 14, 1994, p. 355.
*National Observer,* December 4, 1967.
*New Leader,* December 18, 1967; April 19, 1971.
*New Republic,* January 23, 1965; April 17, 1971; February 2, 1975; April 11, 1981; April 4, 1994, pp. 26, 28.
*Newsday,* March 26, 1971.
*New Statesman,* January 23, 1970.
*Newsweek,* January 4, 1965; March 18, 1968; April 5, 1971; February 10, 1975; March 30, 1981.
*New York,* May 6, 1996, p. 86.
*New Yorker,* January 22, 1966; April 3, 1971; March 3, 1980; May 30, 1981; May 16, 1994, pp. 102-105; May 27, 1996, p. 138.
*New York Times,* December 27, 1964; January 21, 1965; January 13, 1966; August 16, 1966; September 18, 1966; September 24, 1966; October 2, 1966; August 20, 1967; November 26, 1967; April 4, 1971; April 18, 1971; January 27, 1975; February 4, 1977; May 23, 1978; January 27, 1980; March 1, 1981; March 20, 1981; March 29, 1981; February 23, 1992; November 20, 1993, p. A11; December 1, 1993, p. C17; February 14, 1994, pp. C13, C16; February 20, 1994, sec. 2, p. 5; April 13, 1994, p. C15; August 28, 1994, p. WC1; May 5, 1996, p. H4; June 16, 1996, p. H33.
*New York Times Magazine,* February 25, 1962.
*New York World Journal Tribune,* September 22, 1966; October 2, 1966.
*Observer Review,* January 19, 1969.
*Paris Review,* fall, 1966.
*People,* February 25, 1980; April 6, 1981.
*Pittsburgh Press,* February 3, 1974.
*Prairie Schooner,* fall, 1965.
*Reporter,* December 28, 1967.
*Saturday Review,* June 4, 1966; April 17, 1971; March 8, 1975; May, 1981.
*Theatre Arts,* March, 1961.
*Time,* April 5, 1971; February 10, 1975; May 20, 1996, p. 77.
*Transatlantic Review,* summer, 1963.
*Tulane Drama Review,* spring, 1963; summer, 1965.
*Variety,* March 4, 1991, p. 66; January 20, 1992, p. 147; November 8, 1993, p. 30; February 14, 1994, p. 61; November 6, 1995, p. 80.
*Village Voice,* December 7, 1967; March 21, 1968; October 31, 1968.
*Washington Post,* February 18, 1979; August 14, 1994.
*World Literature Today,* autumn, 1995, pp. 799-800.
*Writer's Digest,* October, 1980.*

—*Sketch by Lane Glenn*

\* \* \*

## ALLEN, Charlotte Vale 1941-
### (Katherine Marlowe; Claire Vincent)

*PERSONAL:* Born January 19, 1941, in Toronto, Ontario, Canada; came to the United States in 1966; Canadian citizen; married Walter Bateman Allen, Jr. (an insurance broker), July 21, 1970 (divorced, 1976); married Barrie Baldaro (an actor and writer), January 23, 1980 (divorced, 1982); children: (first marriage) Kimberly Jordan Allen (daughter). *Education:* Attended drama school in Toronto, Ontario. *Politics:* No affiliation. *Religion:* No affiliation.

*ADDRESSES: Home*—144 Rowayton Woods Dr., Norwalk, CT 06854. *Agent*—Harold Ober Associates, 40 E. 49th St., New York, NY 10017; David Higham Associates Ltd., 5-8 Lower John St., London W1R 4HA, England.

*CAREER:* Actress and singer, 1959-63; revue performer and singer, 1963-71; insurance broker, 1971-74; writer, 1975—. Lecturer on the sexual abuse of children, 1980—.

*WRITINGS:*

NOVELS

*Love Life,* Delacorte (New York City), 1976.
*Hidden Meanings,* Warner Books (New York City), 1976.
*Sweeter Music,* Warner Books, 1976.
*Gentle Stranger,* Warner Books, 1977.
*Another Kind of Magic,* Warner Books, 1977.
*Mixed Emotions,* Warner Books, 1977.
*Running Away,* New American Library (New York City), 1977.
*Becoming,* Warner Books, 1977.
*Julia's Sister,* Warner Books, 1978.
(Under pseudonym Claire Vincent) *Believing in Giants,* New American Library, 1978.
*Acts of Kindness,* New American Library, 1979.
*Moments of Meaning,* New American Library, 1979.
*Promises,* Dutton (New York City), 1979.
*Times of Triumph,* New American Library, 1980.
*Gifts of Love,* Dutton, 1980.
*The Marmalade Man,* Dutton, 1981.
*Perfect Fools,* New English Library, 1981.
*Intimate Friends,* Dutton, 1982.
*Meet Me in Time,* Berkley Publishing (New York City), 1983.
*Pieces of Dreams,* Berkley Publishing, 1985.
*Matters of the Heart,* Berkley Publishing, 1986.
*Time/Steps,* Atheneum (New York City), 1986.
*Illusions* (also see below), Atheneum, 1987.
*Dream Train* (also see below), Atheneum, 1988.
*Night Magic* (also see below), Atheneum, 1989.
*Painted Lives,* Atheneum, 1990.
(Under pseudonym Katherine Marlowe) *Heart's Desires,* Fine (New York City), 1991.
(Under pseudonym Katherine Marlowe) *Secrets,* Fine, 1992.
*Leftover Dreams,* Doubleday (New York City), 1992.
*Charlotte Vale Allen: Three Complete Novels* (contains *Illusions, Dream Train,* and *Night Magic*), Wings Books (New York City), 1993.
(Under pseudonym Katherine Marlowe) *Nightfall,* Tor (New York City), 1993.
*Dreaming in Color,* Doubleday, 1993.
*Somebody's Baby,* Mira, 1995.

NONFICTION

*Daddy's Girl* (memoir), Wyndham Books, 1980.

*SIDELIGHTS:* Charlotte Vale Allen once told *CA* that although her books are about women, they are not just *for* women but "for everyone. I like to include issues of both social and emotional significance." After having written a number of successful novels, she published *Daddy's Girl,* an autobiographical work in which she comes to grips with a childhood made almost intolerable by her sexually abusive father. It is, writes Marilyn Murray Willison in the *Los Angeles Times Book Review,* "the harrowing tale of a childhood spent amidst a bitter, exploited mother and a manipulative and selfish father. Charlotte and her two older brothers were victims trapped by circumstance, but Charlotte bore the added indignity of being forced to suffer through her father's incestuous demands." *Library Journal* reviewer Janet Husband says *Daddy's Girl* is "altogether a powerful story, told with the considerable skill and restraint necessary to keep the facts from seeming sensational or maudlin." And Eleanor Wachtel, in a *Books in Canada* article, states that Allen "writes effectively. . . . She has written a genuinely troubling book, annoying, uncomfortable, and compelling."

Intertwined with the childhood recollections in *Daddy's Girl* are what Willison calls "verbal snapshots" of the author's struggle to free herself from her past. She had been conditioned to think of herself as ugly and unlovable, and thus "learning to love herself (much less a man) became a full-time assignment" during her adulthood. Writes Willison: "One finishes the book thinking that if it weren't for the kind and understanding attention of a high-school teacher (as well as the earlier ministrations of an aunt and uncle) the author would surely not be with us today." In addition to these early positive influences, Allen was aided by two friends, Norman and Lola, who helped her to face her distasteful childhood and rebuild her life. As a result, she is able to write about her past with complete candor. As she says in *Daddy's Girl:* "It's impossible to forget what happened. I can't use Liquid Paper on 10 years of my life [from the ages of seven to seventeen] and put a nice, thick white coat over it the way I do typing errors."

At one time in her life, Allen did try to forget by changing her name when she began to pursue a new life away from her family. Since then, she has turned her painful past into positive social action. She travels throughout North America "lecturing to professionals about how to deal with sexually abused children," reports Sybil Steinberg in *Publishers Weekly.* Mary Lassance Parthun remarks in the Toronto *Globe and Mail,* "A significant aspect of public education is the dissemination of information about social, psychological and medical problems through popular novels favored by women. Charlotte Vale Allen is a notable practitioner of this important social function. Her work is approved by human service professionals because she takes on the tough problems (incest, for example) and handles them in a tasteful and nonexploitative manner." In *Pieces of Dreams,* for example, a woman who was once abandoned by her mother later meets the challenge of facial disfigurement prolonged by an inept surgeon. The victim of a sexual kidnapping ordeal gives her perspective on the experience in the novel *Illusions.* "I think I'm uniquely qualified to write about certain areas of female experience," Allen told Steinberg. "When you get into abusive situations, you have to find a way to explain what happened. So I've narrated this whole entrapment scenario, and then I tell what happens afterwards. And believe me, when you read the ending of this book the hair all over your body will stand on end. In fact, it's the only time I couldn't wait to finish writing a book, it upset me so much."

Not all of Allen's novels are as "upsetting." Reviewers call *Dream Train* a romance because the major challenge to heroine Joanna James is to choose between two suitors who are equally sincere and attractive. Particularly well-written, says *Times Literary Supplement* reviewer Roz Kaveney, is the scene in which Joanna "is given good advice by an older woman, one of her companions on the train to Venice," a scene which stresses "the theme of female friendships: as important to women's lives as any relationships, sexual or other, with men."

The capacity of women to survive and overcome adversity has continued to inspire Allen. In *Painted Lives,* an aging widow named Mattie Sylvester uncovers her past as the partner of an ambitious and unscrupulous artist. Surrounded by a staff with troubles of their own, Mattie reveals the sacrifices she made in 1920s New York after giving in to her passion for painter Gideon Sylvester. "Allen's energy and enthusiasm are much in evidence in the animated Mattie and she is at her most compelling with simple, quiet narratives," writes *Quill & Quire* reviewer Jean Sheppard.

Equally dynamic, but in a much more destructive vein, is Maggie Parker, one of the heroines of *Leftover Dreams.* Deserted by her husband, Maggie vents her bitterness and rage on her two young daughters, Faye and Louise, who are forced to seek help from a gentle grandmother and, eventually, each other. When Faye dies after a rape and a bungled abortion, Louise tries to outrun her past, only to find that she must face it in order to achieve happiness. In a *Chicago Tribune Books* review of *Leftover Dreams,* Joyce Slater commends Allen for her "smooth prose style" and "intuitive understanding of family dynamics," adding that with its "vibrant characters," the novel is "not nearly as grim as it might sound."

Allen has never shied from topical issues in her fiction. Her characters may be victims of child or spouse abuse, but they are survivors as well, using their wits and strength to defy their tormentors. Such is the theme of *Dreaming in Color,* the tale of one battered woman's recovery with the help of a well-to-do Connecticut family. Bobby escapes the brutal treatment of her husband Joe by taking a job as a caretaker for a stroke victim. As she and her daughter Penny find healing and solace in the home of Alma Ogilvie, they confront not only their own demons but those of the household as well. A *Kirkus Reviews* contributor notes that the story is "a cautionary tale, but with a cheerful domestic overcast as a victim is given back her life." In addition, Allen's book includes a list of real organizations dedicated to helping victims of domestic violence—testament once again to her conviction that women can find help from one another and empowerment in themselves.

*BIOGRAPHICAL/CRITICAL SOURCES:*

*BOOKS*

Allen, Charlotte Vale, *Daddy's Girl,* Wyndham Books, 1980.

*PERIODICALS*

*Booklist,* January 1, 1992, p. 794; July 1995, p. 1858.
*Books in Canada,* January 1981.
*Globe and Mail* (Toronto), May 26, 1984; April 30, 1988.
*Kirkus Reviews,* June 15, 1993, p. 735.
*Library Journal,* December 1, 1980.
*Los Angeles Times Book Review,* September 18, 1980.
*Maclean's,* October 15, 1990, p. 13.
*Publishers Weekly,* July 4, 1986; February 2, 1990, p. 77; January 6, 1992, p. 48; July 5, 1993, p. 62.
*Quill and Quire,* March 1990, p. 61.
*Times Literary Supplement,* June 3, 1988.
*Tribune Books* (Chicago), April 26, 1992, p. 6.
*Washington Post,* July 28, 1986.*

**ALLPORT, Susan    1950-**

*PERSONAL:* Born July 5, 1950, in New Haven, CT; daughter of Alexander Wise (an administrator) and Jane (Raible) Allport; married David C. Howell (a designer), September 10, 1978; children: Liberty, Cecil. *Education:* Pitzer College, B.A., 1972; Tulane University of Louisiana, M.S., 1977. *Politics:* Independent. *Religion:* None.

*ADDRESSES: Home and office*—333 Hook Rd., Katonah, NY 10536. *Agent*—Virginia Barber, 101 Fifth Ave., New York, NY 10003.

*CAREER:* Writer.

*MEMBER:* American Medical Writers Association, National Association of Science Writers.

*WRITINGS:*

*Explorers of the Black Box: The Search for the Cellular Basis of Memory,* Norton (New York City), 1986.
*Sermons in Stone: The Stone Walls of New England and New York,* Norton, 1990.
*A Natural History of Parenting,* Harmony (New York City), 1997.

*BIOGRAPHICAL/CRITICAL SOURCES:*

PERIODICALS

*Atlantic Monthly,* March, 1991.
*Boston Magazine,* November 30, 1990.
*Los Angeles Times,* October 28, 1986.
*Nature,* January, 1987.
*New York Times,* March 10, 1991.
*New Yorker,* January 28, 1991.
*Washington Post Book World,* February 22, 1987.

\*   \*   \*

**AMIS, Kingsley (William)    1922-1995**
    **(Robert Markham, William Tanner)**

*PERSONAL:* Born April 16, 1922, in London, England; died after suffering severe injuries in a fall, October 22, 1995, in London, England; son of William Robert (an office clerk) and Rosa Annie (Lucas) Amis; married Hilary Ann Bardwell, 1948 (divorced, 1965); married Elizabeth Jane Howard (a novelist), 1965 (divorced, 1983); children: (first marriage) Philip Nicol William, Martin Louis, Sally Myfanwy. *Education:* St. John's College, Oxford, B.A. (first class honors in English), 1947, M.A., 1948. *Avocational interests:* Music (jazz, Mozart), thrillers, television, science fiction.

*CAREER:* University College of Swansea, Swansea, Glamorganshire, Wales, lecturer in English, 1949-61; Cambridge University, Peterhouse, Cambridge, England, fellow, 1961-63; full-time writer, 1963-95. Princeton University, visiting fellow in creative writing, 1958-59; Vanderbilt University, visiting professor of English, 1967-68. *Military service:* British Army, Royal Signal Corps, 1942-45; became lieutenant.

*MEMBER:* Authors' Club (London), Bristol Channel Yacht Club, Garrick Club.

*AWARDS, HONORS:* Somerset Maugham Award, 1955, for *Lucky Jim;* Booker-McConnell Prize nomination, Great Britain's Book Trust, and *Yorkshire Post* Book of the Year Award, both 1974, for *Ending Up;* fellowship, St. John's College, Oxford, 1976; Commander of the Order of the British Empire, 1981; fellowship, University College of Swansea, 1985; Booker-McConnell Prize for Fiction, Great Britain's Book Trust, 1986, for *The Old Devils;* Cholmondeley Award, 1990; knighted, 1990.

*WRITINGS:*

NOVELS

*Lucky Jim,* Doubleday (New York City), 1954 (though title page of first printing reads 1953), edited and abridged edition by D. K. Swan, illustrations by William Burnard, Longmans (London), 1963, abridged edition with glossary and notes by R. M. Oldnall, Macmillan (New York City), 1967.
*That Uncertain Feeling,* Gollancz (London), 1955, Harcourt (New York City), 1956.
*I Like It Here,* Harcourt, 1958.
*Take a Girl Like You,* Gollancz, 1960, Harcourt, 1961.
*One Fat Englishman,* Gollancz, 1963, Harcourt, 1964.
(With Robert Conquest) *The Egyptologists,* J. Cape (London), 1965, Random House (New York City), 1966.
*The Anti-Death League,* Harcourt, 1966, Gollancz, 1978.

(Under pseudonym Robert Markham) *Colonel Sun: A James Bond Adventure,* Harper (New York City), 1968.

*I Want It Now,* J. Cape, 1968, collected edition, 1976, Harcourt, 1969.

*The Green Man,* J. Cape, 1969, Harcourt, 1970.

*Girl, 20,* J. Cape, 1971, Harcourt, 1972.

*The Riverside Villas Murder,* Harcourt, 1973.

*Ending Up,* Harcourt, 1974.

*The Alteration,* J. Cape, 1976, Viking (New York City), 1977.

*Jake's Thing* (also see below), Hutchinson (London), 1978, Viking, 1979.

*Russian Hide-and-Seek: A Melodrama,* Hutchinson, 1980, Penguin (New York City), 1981.

*Stanley and the Women* (also see below), Hutchinson, 1984, Summit Books (New York City), 1985.

*The Old Devils* (also see below), Hutchinson, 1986, Summit Books, 1987.

*The Crime of the Century,* Dent (New York City), 1987.

*A Kingsley Amis Omnibus* (includes *Jake's Thing, Stanley and the Women,* and *The Old Devils*), Hutchinson, 1987.

*Difficulties with Girls,* Summit Books, 1988.

*The Folks That Live on the Hill,* Hutchinson, 1990.

*The Russian Girl,* Viking, 1994.

*You Can't Do Both,* limited edition, Hutchinson, 1994.

*POETRY*

*Bright November,* Fortune Press (London), 1947.

*A Frame of Mind: Eighteen Poems,* School of Art, Reading University, 1953.

*Poems,* Oxford University Poetry Society (Oxford), 1954.

*Kingsley Amis,* Fantasy Press (Oxford), 1954.

*A Case of Samples: Poems, 1946-1956,* Gollancz, 1956, Harcourt, 1957.

(With Dom Moraes and Peter Porter) *Penguin Modern Poets 2,* Penguin, 1962.

*The Evans Country,* Fantasy Press, 1962.

*A Look Round the Estate: Poems 1957-1967,* J. Cape, 1967, Harcourt, 1968.

*Collected Poems: 1944-1979,* Hutchinson, 1979, Viking, 1980.

*OTHER*

*Socialism and the Intellectuals,* Fabian Society (London), 1957.

*New Maps of Hell: A Survey of Science Fiction,* Harcourt, 1960.

*My Enemy's Enemy* (short stories; also see below), Gollancz, 1962, Harcourt, 1963.

*Reading His Own Poems* (recording), Listen, 1962.

(With Thomas Blackburn) *Poems* (recording), Jupiter (London), 1962.

(Under pseudonym William Tanner) *The Book of Bond; or, Every Man His Own 007,* Viking, 1965.

*The James Bond Dossier,* New American Library (New York City), 1965.

*Lucky Jim's Politics,* Conservative Political Centre (London), 1968.

*What Became of Jane Austen? and Other Questions* (essays), J. Cape, 1970, Harcourt, 1971, published as *What Became of Jane Austen and Other Essays,* Penguin, 1981.

*Dear Illusion* (short stories; also see below), Covent Garden Press (London), 1972.

*On Drink* (also see below), illustrations by Nicolas Bentley, J. Cape, 1972, Harcourt, 1973.

*First Aid for ABA Conventioneers* (excerpt from *On Drink*), Harcourt, 1973.

*Rudyard Kipling and His World,* Scribner (New York City), 1975.

*Interesting Things,* edited by Michael Swan, Cambridge University Press, 1977.

*Harold's Years: Impressions of the Harold Wilson Era,* Charles River Books (Boston, MA), 1977.

*The Darkwater Hall Mystery* (also see below), illustrations by Elspeth Sojka, Tragara Press (Edinburgh), 1978.

(Editor) *The New Oxford Book of English Light Verse,* Oxford University Press, 1978.

*An Arts Policy?,* Centre for Policy Studies, 1979.

(Editor) *The Faber Popular Reciter,* Faber & Faber (London), 1979.

*Collected Short Stories* (includes "My Enemy's Enemy," "Dear Illusion," and "The Darkwater Hall Mystery"), Hutchinson, 1980, Penguin, 1983, revised edition, 1987.

*Every Day Drinking,* illustrations by Merrily Harper, Hutchinson, 1983.

*How's Your Glass? A Quizzical Look at Drinks and Drinking,* Weidenfeld & Nicolson (London), 1984, with cartoons by Michael Heath, Arrow, 1986.

*The Amis Anthology,* Century Hutchinson (London), 1988.

*The Amis Collection: Selected Non-Fiction, 1954-1990,* Hutchinson, 1990.

*The Pleasure of Poetry,* Cassell (London), 1990.

*Kingsley Amis, in Life and Letters,* edited by Dale Salwak, Macmillan (Basingstoke, Hants), 1990, St. Martin's (New York City), 1991.

*Memoirs,* Summit Books, 1991.

*We Are All Guilty* (for children), Viking Children's Books, 1992.

*Mr. Barrett's Secret and Other Stories,* Hutchinson, 1993.

*The Biographer's Mustache,* HarperCollins (New York City), 1995.

Also author of a science fiction radio play, *Something Strange,* and of television plays *A Question about Hell,* 1964, *The Importance of Being Harry,* 1971, *Dr. Watson and the Darkwater Hall Mystery,* 1974, and *See What You've Done,* 1974. Also editor of *Spectrum: A Science Fiction Anthology,* Amereon. Author of column on beverages in *Penthouse.* Editor of and contributor to literary anthologies. Contributor to periodicals, including *Spectator, Encounter, New Statesman, Listener, Observer,* and *London Magazine.*

*ADAPTATIONS: Lucky Jim* was adapted as a motion picture, written by Jeffrey Dell and Patrick Campbell, directed by John Boulting, starring Sharon Acker and Ian Carmichael, British Lion, 1957; *That Uncertain Feeling* was adapted as a motion picture as *Only Two Can Play,* written by Bryan Forbes, directed by Sidney Gilliat, starring Peter Sellers, Mai Zetterling, Virginia Maskell, and Richard Attenborough, Columbia, 1962; *Take a Girl Like You* was adapted as a motion picture, written by George Melly, directed by Jonathan Miller, starring Hayley Mills and Oliver Reed, Columbia, 1970; *Jake's Thing* was recorded on audiocassette, Books on Tape, 1988; *The Old Devils* was adapted as a play, 1989; *The Green Man* was adapted for television, 1990.

*SIDELIGHTS:* "I think of myself like a sort of mid- or late-Victorian person," said Kingsley Amis in *Contemporary Literature,* "not in outlook but in the position of writing a bit of poetry (we forget that George Eliot also wrote verse), writing novels, being interested in questions of the day and occasionally writing about them, and being interested in the work of other writers and occasionally writing about that. I'm not exactly an entertainer pure and simple, not exactly an artist pure and simple, certainly not an incisive critic of society, and certainly not a political figure though I'm interested in politics. I think I'm just a combination of some of those things."

Though an eclectic man of letters, Amis was best known as a prolific novelist who, in the words of Blake Morrison in the *Times Literary Supplement,* had the "ability to go on surprising us." He won critical acclaim in 1954 with the publication of his first novel, *Lucky Jim.* After producing three other comic works, Amis was quickly characterized as a comic novelist writing in the tradition of P. G. Wodehouse and Evelyn Waugh. Critics ranked him among the foremost "Angry Young Men," a school of British writers who disdained post-World War II British society throughout the 1950s. "Amis," stated *Los Angeles Times* writer William D. Montalbano, "rejected the label as 'a very boring journalistic phrase.'" After his early works, however, Amis produced a spate of novels that differed radically in genre and seriousness of theme. He kept "experimenting with ways of confounding the reader who hopes for a single focus," claimed William Hutchings in *Critical Quarterly,* though Clancy Sigal suggested in *National Review* that Amis simply had "the virtue, rare in England, of refusing to accept an imposed definition of what a Serious Writer ought to write about." His place in British literature was recognized in 1986, when his seventeenth novel *The Old Devils* won the Booker Prize, Britain's highest literary award. In 1990, he was knighted by Queen Elizabeth II.

Amis, who admitted in *Contemporary Literature* that he considered poetry a "higher art" than prose writing, was publishing poems before he began publishing novels. "I would have been a poet entirely if I had had my way," Amis told *CA* interviewer Jean W. Ross. A respected poet influenced by Philip Larkin, Amis not only eschewed the grandiose subject matter and lofty tones of romanticism; as editor of several collections of British verse, he encouraged his peers to do the same. Because his poems focus on the realities of contemporary life, which he renders with "innovative technique," Amis has a place in British poetry as an important minor poet, Neil Brennan noted in a *Dictionary of Literary Biography* essay.

Clive James, writing in the *New Statesman,* suggested, "Only the fact that he is so marvelously readable can now stop Kingsley Amis from being placed in the front rank of contemporary poets." Yet it was through his early novels that Amis became widely known and respected as a writer. When *Lucky Jim* first appeared, it attracted unusually wide review attention and led to a Somerset Maugham Award, a successful film, and a paperback sale of over a million copies in America. Edmund Fuller praised it in the *New York Times* as "written with the cool, detached, sardonic style which is the trademark of the British satirical novelist. *Lucky Jim* is funny in something approaching the Wodehouse vein, but it cuts a bit deeper." Other critics also likened it to P. G. Wodehouse's works, and Walter Allen in *The Modern Novel* called it "the funniest first novel since [Evelyn Waugh's] *Decline and Fall.*" William Van O'Connor summed up the book's virtues this way in *The New University Wits and the End of Modernism,* "The characterizations are extremely good, the dialogue is natural, the narrative pacing is excellent, and Jim himself is not only a wonderfully funny character, he is almost archetypical."

Jim Dixon, the protagonist, is, according to Anthony Burgess in *The Novel Now,* "the most popular anti-hero of our time." Though a junior lecturer at a provincial university, Jim has no desire to be an intellectual—or a "gentleman"—because of his profound, almost physical, hatred of the social and cultural affectations of university life. This characteristic of Jim's has led several critics to conclude that he is a philistine, and, moreover, that beneath the comic effects, Amis was really attacking culture and was himself a philistine. Brigid Brophy, for example, wrote in *Don't Never Forget: Collected Views and Reviews* that the "apex of philistinism" is reached "when Jim hears a tune by the composer whom either he or Mr. Amis . . . thinks of as 'filthy Mozart.'"

Ralph Caplan, however, claimed in Charles Shapiro's *Contemporary British Novelists* that *Lucky Jim* "never [promises] anything more than unmitigated pleasure and insight, and these it keeps on delivering. The book [is] not promise but fulfillment, a commodity we confront too seldom to know how to behave when it is achieved. This seems to be true particularly when the achievement is comic. Have we forgotten how to take humor straight? Unable to exit laughing, the contemporary reader looks over his shoulder for Something More. The trouble is that by now he knows how to find it."

Amis himself stated in a *Publishers Weekly* interview that to see *Lucky Jim* as a polemic on culture was to misinterpret it: "This is the great misunderstanding of it. People said I was part of an emergent group of angry young men writing novels of protest. But the idea that Jim was an 'outsider' just won't do. He was an *insider.* This still eludes people, especially Americans." As to the charges of philistinism, Amis said to Dale Salwak in *Contemporary Literature:* "Jim and I have taken a lot of bad mouthing for being philistine, aggressively philistine, and saying, 'Well, as long as I've got me blonde and me pint of beer and me

packet of fags and me seat at the cinema, I'm all right.' I don't think either of us would say that. It's nice to have a pretty girl with large breasts rather than some fearful woman who's going to talk to you about Ezra Pound and hasn't got large breasts and probably doesn't wash much. And better to have a pint of beer than to have to talk to your host about the burgundy you're drinking. And better to go to see nonsensical art exhibitions that nobody's really going to enjoy. So it's appealing to common sense if you like, and it's a way of trying to denounce affectation."

Critics generally see the three novels that followed *Lucky Jim* as variations on this theme of appealing to common sense and denouncing affectation. Discussing *Lucky Jim, That Uncertain Feeling, I Like It Here,* and *Take a Girl Like You* in the *Hudson Review,* James P. Degnan stated: "In the comically outraged voice of his angry young heroes—e.g., Jim Dixon of *Lucky Jim* and John Lewis of *That Uncertain Feeling*—Amis [lampoons] what C. P. Snow . . . labeled the 'traditional culture,' the 'culture of the literary intellectuals,' of the 'gentleman's world.'" James Gindin noted in *Postwar British Fiction* that the similarity of purpose is reflected in a corresponding similarity of technique: "Each of the [four] novels is distinguished by a thick verbal texture that is essential comic. The novels are full of word play and verbal jokes. . . . All Amis's heroes are mimics: Jim Dixon parodies the accent of Professor Welch, his phony and genteel professor, in *Lucky Jim;* Patrick Standish, in *Take a Girl Like You,* deliberately echoes the Hollywood version of the Southern Negro's accent. John Lewis, the hero of *That Uncertain Feeling,* also mimics accents and satirically characterizes other people by the words and phrases they use."

The heroes in these four novels are in fact so much alike that Brigid Brophy charged Amis with "rewriting much the same novel under different titles and with different names for the characters," although Walter Allen insisted that the "young man recognizably akin to Lucky Jim, the Amis man as he might be called, . . . has been increasingly explored in depth." Consistent with her assessment of Jim Dixon in *Lucky Jim,* Brophy saw the other three Amis heroes also as "militant philistines," a view that was not shared by Caplan, Burgess, or Degnan. Caplan explained that though the Amis hero in these novels is seemingly anti-intellectual, he is nonetheless "always cerebral," and Burgess pointed out that the hero "always earns his living by purveying culture as teacher, librarian, journalist, or publisher." Representing a commonsensical approach to life, the Amis protagonist, according to Degnan, is an inversion of a major convention of the hero "as 'sensitive soul,' the convention of the 'alienated' young man of artistic or philosophical pretensions struggling pitifully and hopelessly against an insensitive, middle-class, materialistic world. . . . In place of the sensitive soul as hero, Amis creates in his early novels a hero radically new to serious contemporary fiction: a middle-class hero who is also an intellectual, an intellectual who is unabashedly middle-brow. He is a hero . . . whose chief virtues, as he expresses them, are: 'politeness, friendly interest, ordinary concern and a good natured willingness to be imposed upon. . . .' Suspicious of all pretentiousness, of all heroic posturing, the Amis hero . . . voices all that is best of the 'lower middle class, of the non-gentlemanly' conscience."

Degnan, however, did believe that Patrick Standish in *Take a Girl Like You* came dangerously close to "the kind of anti-hero—e.g., blase, irresponsible, hedonistic—that Amis's first three novels attack," and that this weakened the satirical aspect of the novel. Echoing this observation in *The Reaction against Experiment in the English Novel, 1950-1960,* Rubin Rabinovitz detected an uncertainty as to what "vice and folly" really are and who possesses them: "In *Take a Girl Like You* Amis satirizes both Patrick's lechery and Jenny's persistence in preserving her virginity. . . . The satire in *Lucky Jim* is not divided this way: Jim Dixon mocks the hypocrisy of his colleagues in the university and refuses to be subverted by it. [In *Lucky Jim*] the satire is more powerful because the things being satirized are more boldly defined."

After *Take a Girl Like You,* Amis produced several other "straight" novels, as *Time*'s Christopher Porterfield described them, as well as a James Bond spy thriller, written under the pseudonym of Robert Markham, called *Colonel Sun: A James Bond Adventure;* a work of science fiction, *The Anti-Death League;* and a ghost story, *The Green Man.* When Gildrose Productions, the firm to which the James Bond copyright was sold after Ian Fleming's death, awarded the first non-Fleming sequel to Amis, the literary world received the news with a mixture of apprehension and interest. Earlier, Amis had done an analysis of the nature of Fleming's hero, *The James Bond Dossier,* and he appeared to be a logical successor to Bond's creator. But the reactions to *Colonel Sun* were mixed. Though Clara Siggins stated in *Best Sellers* that Amis "produced an exciting narrative

with the expertise and verve of Fleming himself," S. K. Oberbeck claimed in the *Washington Post Book World* that the changes Amis made "on Bond's essential character throw the formula askew. . . . In humanizing Bond, in netting him back into the channel of real contemporary events, Amis somehow deprives him of the very ingredients that made his barely believable adventures so rewarding." Similarly, David Lodge, discussing the book in *The Novelist at the Crossroads and Other Essays on Fiction and Criticism,* considered *Colonel Sun* "more realistic" yet "duller" than most of the Fleming novels, because "the whole enterprise, undertaken, apparently, in a spirit of pious imitation, required Amis to keep in check his natural talent for parody and deflating comic realism."

Amis's comic spirit, so prominent in his first four novels and muted in *Colonel Sun,* is noticeably absent from *The Anti-Death League,* which was published two years before the Bond adventure. Bernard Bergonzi commented in *The Situation of the Novel* that in *The Anti-Death League* Amis "has written a more generalised kind of fiction, with more clearly symbolic implications, than in any of his earlier novels. There is still a trace of sardonic humor, and his ear remains alert to the placing details of individual speech; but Amis has here abandoned the incisive social mimicry, the memorable responses to the specificity of a person's appearance or the look of a room that have previously characterized his fiction."

The story concerns a British army officer who becomes convinced that a nonhuman force of unlimited malignancy, called God, is responsible for a pattern of seemingly undeserving deaths. Bergonzi viewed the work as a provocative, anti-theological novel of ideas and maintained that it "represents Amis's immersion in the nightmare that flickers at the edges of his earlier fiction." He did, however, find one shortcoming in the novel: "*The Anti-Death League* . . . is intensely concerned with the questions that lead to tragedy—death, cruelty, loss of every kind—while lacking the ontological supports—whether religious or humanistic—that can sustain the tragic view of life." A *Times Literary Supplement* reviewer admitted that the rebellion against the facts of pain and death "seems rather juvenile, like kicking God's ankle for doing such things to people," but asserted: "[Amis] takes the argument to more audacious and hopeful lengths. . . . We do care about his creatures; the agents intrigue us and the victims concern us.

The handling is vastly less pompous than the theme: oracular, yes, but eloquent and earthly and even moving."

Amis followed *The Anti-Death League* with *The Green Man* and *Girl, 20,* a comic novel with serious overtones. Paul Schleuter in *Saturday Review* viewed *Girl, 20* as a harmonious addition to Amis's body of work. He wrote: "[Amis's] talent for creating humorous situations, characters, and dialogue is as fresh as ever. . . . Amis also has a distinct undercurrent of pathos, darkness, and trauma. The result is not really a 'new' Amis so much as a more mature examination of human foibles and excesses than was the case in his earlier novels." But Amis's next novel, *The Riverside Villas Murder,* "offers no comfort to those who look for consistency in [his] work," according to a *Times Literary Supplement* reviewer.

A departure from Amis's previous works, *The Riverside Villas Murder* is a detective story, though there was some debate among critics whether it is to be read "straight" or as a parody of the genre. Patrick Cosgrave, for example, claimed in *Saturday Review/World* that the book was "a straight detective story, with a murder, several puzzles, clues, a great detective, and an eminently satisfying and unexpected villain. So bald a statement is a necessary introduction in order to ensure that nobody will be tempted to pore over *The Riverside Villas Murder* in search of portentiousness, significance, ambiguity, or any of the more tiresome characteristics too often found in the work of a straight novelist who has turned aside from the main road of his work into the byways of such subgenres as crime and adventure. More, the book is straight detection because Amis intended it to be such: It is written out of a great love of the detective form and deliberately set in a period—the Thirties—when that form was . . . most popular." The *Times Literary Supplement* reviewer, however, considered the book "something more and less than a period detective story. Mr. Amis is not one to take any convention too seriously, and on one plane he is simply having fun." Patricia Coyne, writing in the *National Review,* and *Time*'s T. E. Kalem expressed similar opinions. Coyne described the story as "a boy discovers sex against a murder-mystery backdrop," and Kalem concluded that by making a fourteen-year-old boy the hero of the novel, "Amis cleverly combines, in mild parody, two ultra-British literary forms—the mystery thriller with the boyhood adventure yarn."

Some critics considered the plot of *The Riverside Villas Murder* weak, but the characterization and style particularly strong. Angus Wilson wrote in the *New York Times Book Review* that the "mechanism of the murder, who did it and how, is at once creaky, obvious, and entirely improbable," yet he believed that the book contains "an almost perfect creation of the character of a young adolescent boy." Moreover, Wilson lauded Amis's prose as "probably the most pleasant to read of any good writers of English today. I know no other writer who can forgo all ornament without either aridity or pseudo-simplicity. . . . Each sentence, each paragraph, each chapter is organized to do its job, and the whole is therefore always satisfactory within its limits." Coyne, who also maintained that the mystery was not engaging enough, found the characterization and the style of the highest quality: "[Amis's] may be the best secondary characters—most notably, his old men—since Dickens. And equally satisfying is his style, the often complex sentences falling clear and true with that deceptive ease that marks the master craftsman."

Almost as if to befuddle readers searching for consistency in his work, Amis followed his detective story *The Riverside Villas Murder* with a straight novel, *Ending Up,* before producing *The Alteration,* which *Time*'s Paul Gray said "flits quirkily between satire, science fiction, boy's adventure, and travelogue. The result is what *Nineteen Eighty-Four* might have been like if Lewis Carroll had written it: not a classic, certainly, but an oddity well worth an evening's attention." According to Bruce Cook in *Saturday Review, The Alteration* belongs to a rare subgenre of science fiction: "the so-called counterfeit- or alternative-world novel." Though set in the twentieth century (1976), the book has as its premise that the Protestant Reformation never occurred and, as a result, that the world is essentially Catholic. The plot centers on the discovery of a brilliant boy soprano, the Church's plans to preserve his gift by "altering" his anatomy through castration, and the debate on the justice of this decision.

Thomas R. Edwards noted in the *New York Review of Books* that though "Amis isn't famous for his compassion," in *The Alteration* he "affectingly catches and respects a child's puzzlement about the threatened loss of something he knows about only from descriptions." John Carey insisted in the *New Statesman* that the book "has almost nothing expectable about it, except that it is a study of tyranny." What Carey referred to was the destructive power of the pontifical hierarchy to emasculate life and art, which he saw as the theme of the novel. Bruce Cook shared this interpretation. Calling *The Alteration* "the most overtly and specifically theological of all [Amis's] books," Cook argued: "Fundamentally, *The Alteration* is another of Kingsley Amis's angry screeds against the Catholic faith and the Catholic idea of God. And it is not just what Amis sees as the life-hating, sex-hating aspect of High Christianity—something that made possible such monstrous phenomena as the castrati—that concerns him here [but] . . . Christianity itself. At the end of *The Anti-Death League,* his oddest and most extreme book and in some ways his best, Amis allows some talk of reconciliation, of forgiving God the wrongs He has done humanity. But there is none of that in *The Alteration.* It is an almost bitter book by a man grown angry in middle age."

William Hutchings, however, did not regard the novel as an attack on Catholicism. Despite sharing Cook's conviction that Amis's concern in his works after *The Anti-Death League* was increasingly metaphysical, even theological, Hutchings maintained that the novel presented Amis with a way of making sense of a world "both absurd and threatening." "Death, which dominates much of his fiction (for example, *The Anti-Death League, The Green Man,* and *Ending Up*), may be meaningless, but it cannot be viewed dispassionately. If death is horrible and God, should he exist, is either cruel or teasing, life has all the more to be lived for its present values. If we don't want it now, we'll never get it. . . . It is here that *The Alteration* represents a fascinating new step in Amis's career. If art is to have any value in such a world, then it must be part of the reason for wanting it now. The structure of the novel and its use of a musically talented main character bring a consciousness of the importance of art directly into its presentation of some problems of life."

From *The Alteration* to *Jake's Thing,* Amis again made the transition from science fiction to "comic diatribe," according to V. S. Pritchett in the *New York Review of Books.* Pritchett considered *Jake's Thing* "a very funny book, less for its action or its talk than its prose. . . . Mr. Amis is a master of laconic mimicry and of the vernacular drift." A reviewer wrote in *Choice* that this is "the Amis of *Lucky Jim,* an older and wiser comic writer who is making a serious statement about the human condition."

The story focuses on Jake Richardson, a sixty-year-old reader in early Mediterranean history at Oxford who in the past has been to bed with well over a hundred women but now suffers from a loss of libido. Referred to sex therapist Dr. Proinsias (Celtic, pronounced "Francis") Rosenberg, Jake, said *Nation*'s Amy Wilentz, "is caught up in the supermarket of contemporary life. The novel is filled with encounter groups, free love, women's liberation, and such electronic contrivances as the 'nocturnal mensurator,' which measures the level of a man's arousal as he sleeps." Christopher Lehmann-Haupt of the *New York Times* noted that Amis "makes the most of all the comic possibilities here. Just imagine sensible, civilized Jake coming home from Dr. Rosenberg's office with . . . assignments to study 'pictorial pornographic material' and to 'write out a sexual fantasy in not less than six hundred words.' Consider Jake struggling to find seventy-three more words, or contemplating the nudes in *Mezzanine* magazine, which 'had an exotic appearance, like the inside of a giraffe's ear or a tropical fruit not much prized by the locals.'"

But for all the hilarity, there is an undercurrent of seriousness running through the novel. "It comes bubbling up," wrote Lehmann-Haupt, "when Jake finally grows fed up with Dr. Rosenberg and his experiments." Wilentz argued that the novel expresses "outrage at, and defeat at the hands of, modernity, whose graceless intrusion on one's privacy is embodied in Dr. Rosenberg's constantly repeated question, 'I take it you've no objection to exposing your genitals in public?'" Malcolm Bradbury shared this interpretation, writing in the *New Statesman:* "Amis, watching [history's] collectivising, behaviourist, depersonalizing progress, would like nice things to win and certain sense to prevail. Indeed, a humanist common sense—along with attention to farts—is to his world view roughly what post-Heideggerian existentialism is to Jean-Paul Sartre's."

John Updike, however, offered another interpretation. Reviewing the book in the *New Yorker,* he called the satire "more horrifying than biting, more pathetic than amusing." Updike claimed that the book does not demonstrate that Dr. Rosenberg, in peddling the ideas and techniques of sex therapy, is a charlatan, "though Jake comes to believe so, and the English reader might be disposed to expect so. To an American, conditioned to tolerance of all sorts of craziness on behalf of the soul, the exercises of group therapy seem at least a gallant attack upon virtually intractable forms of human loneliness and mental misery." Updike viewed *Jake's Thing* as a portrait of a man infuriated by the times in which he lives. As such, he concludes it is "satisfyingly ambiguous, relentless, and full. Jake has more complaints than the similarly indisposed Alexander Portnoy [in *Portnoy's Complaint* by Philip Roth]. . . . He suffers from moments of seeing 'the world in its true light, as a place where nothing had ever been any good and nothing of significance done.' He is in a rage. Yet he is also dutiful, loyal in his fashion, and beset; we accept him as a good fellow, an honest godless citizen of the late twentieth century, trying hard to cope with the heretical possibility that sex isn't everything."

After the problems of libido in *Jake's Thing,* wrote Blake Morrison in the *Times Literary Supplement, Russian Hide-and-Seek* "signals the return of the young, uncomplicated, highly sexed Amis male; . . . the more important connection, however, is with Amis's earlier novel, *The Alteration.*" Another example of the "alternative world" novel, *Russian Hide-and-Seek* depicts an England, fifty years hence, that has been overrun by the Soviet Union; oddly enough, though, the Soviets have abandoned Marxism and returned to the style of Russia under the czars. Paul Binding described the book in the *New Statesman* as "at once a pastiche of certain aspects of nineteenth-century Russian fiction and an exercise in cloak-and-dagger adventure. The two genres unite to form a work far more ambitious than those earlier *jeux*—a fictional expression of the author's obsessive conviction that, whatever its avatar, Russian culture is beastly, thriving on conscious exploitation, enamoured of brutality."

Binding considered the indictment of Russian culture only moderately successful, citing as a weakness Amis's characterizations: "For the most part he has accorded his twenty-first-century Russians only the outward rituals and attitudes—and indeed attitudinisings—of their ancestors. . . . If Amis believes that [the ideologies and social structure of the Soviet Union] now contain the germinating seeds of reversion, then—even in a fictional parable—evidence should be given." Morrison admitted *Russian Hide-and-Seek* "is not all it might be" but maintained it is a novel "of interest and subtlety." He believed that along with *The Alteration, Russian Hide-and-Seek* confirms in Amis's body of work "a development away from the provincial, lower-middle class comic novels of the 1950s and the metropolitan, upper-middle, satirical ones of the 1960s and early 1970s towards an interest in serious politico-histori-

cal fiction (*The Anti-Death League* was an early forerunner)."

Amis placed himself at the center of political controversy with his next novel, *Stanley and the Women.* Well received upon publication in England, the book was rejected by publishing houses in the United States twice because of objections to its main character's misogyny, said some sources. "When rumors that one of Britain's most prominent and popular postwar novelists was being censored Stateside by a feminist cabal hit print [in early 1985], the literary flap echoed on both sides of the Atlantic for weeks," reported *Time*'s Paul Gray. After the book found an American publisher a critical debate ensued, with some reviewers condemning its uniformly negative depiction of women, and others defending the book's value nonetheless.

In a *Washington Post Book World* review, Jonathan Yardley charged, "Amis has stacked the deck against women, reducing them to caricatures who reinforce the damning judgments made by Stanley and his chums." Though Yardley felt that "much else in the novel is exceedingly well done," he also felt that its "cranky misogynism" is too prominent to be ignored. Indeed, Stanley casts himself as the victim of a gang of female villains: a self-centered ex-wife; a current wife who stabs herself and accuses Stanley's emotionally unstable son; and a psychiatrist who deliberately mishandles the son's case and blames Stanley for the son's schizophrenia. On the other hand, "the men in the novel hardly fare any better," remarked Michiko Kakutani of the *New York Times*. In her view, shared by Susan Fromberg Schaeffer in the *New York Times Book Review, Stanley and the Women* proves Amis to be "not just a misogynist, but a misanthrope as well. Practically every character in the novel is either an idiot or a scheming hypocrite." Amis, who observed that British women take less offense from the book, claims it is not anti-female; *Time* presented his statement that "all comedy, . . . all humor is unfair. . . . There is a beady-eyed view of women in the book, certainly . . . . But a novel is not a report or a biographical statement or a confession. If it is a good novel, it dramatizes thoughts that some people, somewhere, have had."

Viewing the book from this perspective, some critics find it laudable. *Spectator* contributor Harriet Waugh argued, "It does have to be admitted . . . that Mr. Amis's portrayal of Stanley's wives as female monsters is funny and convincing. Most readers will recognise aspects of them in women they know. . . . [Amis] has written a true account of the intolerableness of women in relation to men." Such a tract, she felt, is comparable in many respects to novels by women that show women "downtrodden" by men. Wrote Gray, "Amis has excelled at rattling preconceptions ever since the appearance of his classically comic first novel, *Lucky Jim* . . . . Is this novel unfair to women? Probably. Is the question worth asking? No. . . . The females in the world of this book all commit 'offences' . . . at least in the eyes of Stanley, who is . . . nobody's idea of a deep thinker." In the *Times Literary Supplement*, J. K. L. Walker concluded, "*Stanley and the Women* reveals Kingsley Amis in the full flood of his talent and should survive its ritual burning in William IV Street unscathed."

The author's next novel, *The Old Devils*, "manifests little of the female bashing that made the satiric *Stanley and the Women* (1985) so scandalous. In fact, dissatisfied wives are given some tart remarks to make about their variously unsatisfactory husbands. . . . Even so, these concessions never denature Amis's characteristic bite," wrote Gray. In a London *Times* review, Victoria Glendinning concurred: "This is vintage Kingsley Amis, 50 percent alcohol, with splashes of savagery about getting old, and about the state of the sex-war in marriages of thirty or more years' standing." Reviewers admired most the book's major female character; Amis gives her a relationship with her daughter "so close, candid and trusting that the most ardent feminist must applaud," noted Champlin in the *Los Angeles Times Book Review*. Her husband, Alun, an aggressive womanizer, drew the most disfavor. In what Gray felt was the author's "wisest and most humane work," both sexes enjoy their best and worst moments. "This is one of Amis's strengths as a novelist, not noticeably to the fore in recent work but making a welcome return here: 'bad' characters are allowed their victories and 'good' characters their defeats. Yet Amis comes down against Alun in a firmly 'moral' conclusion," commented Morrison in the *Times Literary Supplement*.

Alun's funeral near the close of the book is balanced with "the reconciliation of two of the feuding older generation, and the marriage of two of the younger," such that the ending has "an almost Shakespearean symmetry," stated Morrison. But the mood, he warned, is not exactly one of celebration. He explained that the character Amis seems to most approve of "belongs in that tradition of the Amis hero

who would like to believe but can't," whose "disappointed scepticism" keeps him from seeing a romantic encouragement behind a pleasant scene. "Finally," reflected Bryan Appleyard in the London *Times*, "it is this sense of an empty, somewhat vacuous age which seems to come close to the heart of all [Amis's] work. His novels are no-nonsense, well-made, good-humored products. They are about the struggle to get by in the gutter and their heroes seldom roll over to gaze at the stars. Like Larkin he is awestruck by the *idea* of religion but he cannot subscribe. Instead, his novels are happily committed to the obliteration of cant without thought of what to put in its place."

For *The Old Devils*, Amis received the Booker-McConnell Prize for Fiction, the most prestigious book award in England. Among critics who felt the prize was well deserved was Champlin, who referred to "its sheer storytelling expertise, and its qualities of wit, humanity, and observation." In the *New York Times Book Review*, William H. Pritchard recognized *The Old Devils* as Amis's "most ambitious and one of his longest books, . . . neither a sendup nor an exercise in some established genre. It sets forth, with full realistic detail, a large cast of characters at least six of whom are rendered in depth . . . . *The Old Devils* is also Mr. Amis's most inclusive novel, encompassing kinds of feeling and tone that move from sardonic gloom to lyric tenderness." Also to the author's credit, said Pritchard, "one is constantly surprised by something extra, a twist or seeming afterthought signifying an originality of mind that is inseparable from the novelist's originality of language." Added Champlin, "For long-term admirers of the Amis of *Lucky Jim* and after, *The Old Devils* is welcome evidence that the master remains masterful, able now to conjoin the mischievous with the mellow. As always, he is an insightful guide through the terrain where what is said is not meant and what is felt is not said, but where much of life is lived."

Critics celebrated Amis's return to the satiric comic-novel again in *Difficulties with Girls*, a sort of sequel to his 1960 work *Take a Girl Like You*. "In returning to the characters of . . . *Take a Girl Like You*," wrote *New York* magazine contributor Rhoda Koenig, "Amis has also . . . reverted to his style of that period, the sprightly, needling tone he had only six years after *Lucky Jim*." Patrick Standish has not changed much from the "dedicated sexual predator" who married the girl he raped after getting her drunk at a party, declared Judith Grossman in the *New York Times Book Review*. He has left his job as a high school teacher and entered the world of publishing, which provides him with just as many opportunities for sexual conquests. When his wife Jenny discovers the latest of these, she leaves him; then, discovering she is pregnant, she returns. "Amis is one of the best chroniclers we have of the lost world [of 1950s-era male chauvinism]," stated Michael Wood in the *Times Literary Supplement,* "in large part because he knows it's not lost at all, but lies around us everywhere. . . . Amis is not a praiser of the old world, but he is very suspicious of the new one. Maybe it's not even there; maybe it's just a phantom bred of our lame trendiness, our cult of tolerance."

Reviewers found in *Difficulties with Girls* some of the same controversies that characterized his novels of the 1980s and 1990s. "In recent years," wrote *New Yorker* contributor Charles McGrath, "Amis has perversely made a point of finding humor in subjects that are difficult or unpleasant; three of his four novels before this one dealt corrosively with impotence, madness and misogyny, and the debilities of old age." In *Difficulties with Girls,* the author confronts adultery, homosexuality, and anti-Semitism, usually from the point of view of the protagonist. "Amis writes here, as he has written before, about the distance between men and women; he shows that it is not all roses for the rational hedonist who deceives the woman he lives with and loves," explained Karl Miller in the *London Review of Books.* "It isn't every comic genius who would undertake to send his talent into such painful places; it isn't easy to be light, and right, about the marriage of Count Almaviva." "It will be difficult," he concluded, "for him to be baleful about the Millennium."

*The Folks That Live on the Hill* again looks at problems in modern life—alcoholism, prostate surgery, divorce—in a serio-comic vein. "Formally," stated *New Statesman and Society* contributor Anthony Quinn, "it's another funny-sad comedy of social and sexual manners, cast in the old-farts-ensemble mould of *Ending Up* and *The Old Devils.*" It tells of the struggles of retired librarian Harry Caldecote to resolve the problems of different members of his extended family—his son's financial irresponsibility, his brother's suffering marriage, and the various problems of relatives of his ex-wives. "Mr. Amis is, however, less interested in exploring Harry's burden of obligation toward others than in focusing on the novel's different characters as they undergo their troubles," declared William H. Pritchard in the *New York Times Book Review.* Although critics recognized that *The Folks That Live on the Hill* covers ground

that Amis had covered before, they agreed with Quinn that "Amis is still *funny.* The knack of capturing the false starts and dead ends of everyday chatter, the gift for mimicry, the elaborate expressions of outrage—time has withered none of these. You wince as he drives a coach and horses over the liberal consensus, but you find yourself cackling like a maniac."

Amis reviewed his own career in *Memoirs,* published four years before his death. "Television interviewers and others who expected him to be uniformly reactionary on every issue," wrote Merle Rubin in the *Christian Science Monitor,* "were often surprised to discover that he was not an advocate of capital punishment, a racist, or an America-basher, after all." However, many critics deplored the work, declaring that it lacked focus and personal insight. "The faint hope might have been that, in writing directly about himself, the irascible old shag would come over as . . . cuddlier than his usual public image makes him seem," said *London Review of Books* critic Ian Hamilton. "To any such tender expectations, though, Amis offers here a close-to-gleeful 'In a pig's arse, friend'—i.e. you bastards will get nothing out of me, or not much and what you do get you won't like." "Amis," Craig Brown stated in the *Times Literary Supplement,* "has created his autobiographical persona along the lines of one of his most comically pitiless characters."

Amis "earned his fame in the 1950s as a debunker of pomposity, privilege, pretension and hypocritical opportunism," Michael Horovitz declared in *New Statesman and Society.* "Now he publishes an apotheosis of all four, in paralysed prologation of the pratfall so many ageing bigots wallow in—a supposed superiority to the imaginative, rebellious youth they've put behind them." "The book's essays—nasty, British and short—typically err on the side not of commending his friends but of settling old scores," stated *New York Times Book Review* contributor Joel Conarroe, "or, more often, of humbling those he is unwilling to suffer gladly." Dylan Thomas, Lord Snowdon, Roald Dahl, and Leo Rosten all suffer at Amis's hands. "These sketches of fleeting encounters with the famous are well matched to their saloon-bar tone," Brown wrote, "for their mercilessness is not encumbered with friendship, and the targets fit well into the savagery of the anecdotal form. Any anthologist of twentieth-century gossip would find perfect examples of the genre in these sections of *Memoirs.*"

In his twenty-first novel, *The Russian Girl,* Amis returned to skewer one of his prime targets: the halls of Academe. Richard Vaisey is an academic at a British university who specializes in Russian literature. Like other Amis protagonists, he is also over-sexed and unhappily married—to Cordelia, whose good points are that she is good in bed and independently wealthy. Vaisey is approached by an expatriate Russian poet named Anna Danilova, who is circulating a petition to have her brother released from prison in Russia. "Anna Danilova is a terrible poet but sweet, gentle and deferential," explained Diane Roberts in the *Atlanta Journal-Constitution.* "Richard must choose between Cordelia (and money) and Anna (and true love)." "Amis, the old master, somehow orchestrates all these themes, and several more, into a wonderful new concert of plot and language," Gary Abrams declared in the *Los Angeles Times Book Review,* "that provokes both belly laughs and twinges of discomfort over the silly messes we humans make while blundering through life." "*The Russian Girl,*" stated *New York Times Book Review* contributor Christopher Buckley, "is . . . vintage Amis: smooth, dry and not overpriced."

Amis's unexpected death late in 1995—he was being treated in St. Pancras hospital, London, after having crushed several vertebrae in his back in a severe fall—prompted many retrospectives and assessments of his career. His first novel, *Lucky Jim,* is widely regarded as his masterpiece. "It established him as a master of invective and a man well able to raise a guffaw from his readers, especially the male ones," stated a London *Times* obituary writer. "For the next 40 years Amis produced a regular flow of books which established him as the leading British comic novelist of his generation. The tone varied considerably, but Amis picked his targets carefully and his aim was deadly accurate. He wrote about what he knew well and made sure that he did not too much like what he saw around him."

Amis continued to elude categorization throughout his life partly because he actively fought it. "He loves to bait his readers," observed Frederick Busch in a *Chicago Tribune Book World* review of *Stanley and the Women.* More importantly, Amis loved to explore his own capabilities as a novelist. "I agree with Kipling," he explained in a *Publishers Weekly* interview, that "as soon as you find you can do something, try something you can't. As a professional writer one should range as widely as possible." Reflecting on efforts to categorize him and on his excursions into new areas of fiction, Amis mused

in *Contemporary Literature:* "So I'm a funny writer, am I? [*Ending Up*], you'll have to admit, is quite serious. Oh, so I'm primarily a comic writer with some serious overtones and undertones? Try that with *The Anti-Death League* and see how that fits. So I'm a writer about society, twentieth-century man and our problems? Try that one on *The Green Man.* Except for one satirical portrait, that of the clergyman, it is about something quite different. So there is a lot of sex? Try that on [*Ending Up*], in which sexual things [are] referred to, but they've all taken place in the past because of the five central characters the youngest is seventy-one. So you dislike the youth of today, Mr. Amis, as in *Girl, 20?* Try that on [*Ending Up*] where all the young people are sympathetic and all the old people are unsympathetic. This can be silly, but I think it helps to prevent one from repeating oneself, and [Robert] Graves [said] the most dreadful thing in the world is that you're writing a book you've written before. Awful. I haven't quite done that yet, but it's certainly something to guard against."

*BIOGRAPHICAL/CRITICAL SOURCES:*

*BOOKS*

Allen, Walter, *The Modern Novel,* Dutton (New York City), 1984.

Allsop, Kenneth, *The Angry Decade,* P. Owen (London), 1958.

*Authors in the News,* Volume 2, Gale (Detroit), 1976.

Bergonzi, Bernard, *The Situation of the Novel,* University of Pittsburgh Press, 1970.

Brophy, Brigid, *Don't Never Forget: Collected Views and Reviews,* Holt (New York City), 1967.

Burgess, Anthony, *The Novel Now: A Guide to Contemporary Fiction,* Norton (New York City), 1967.

*Contemporary Literary Criticism,* Gale, Volume 1, 1973, Volume 2, 1974, Volume 3, 1975, Volume 5, 1976, Volume 8, 1978, Volume 13, 1980, Volume 40, 1987, Volume 44, 1988.

*Dictionary of Literary Biography,* Gale, Volume 15: *British Novelists, 1930-1959,* 1983, Volume 27: *Poets of Great Britain and Ireland, 1945-1960,* 1984, Volume 100: *Modern British Essayists, Second Series,* 1990, Volume 139: *British Short-Fiction Writers, 1945-1980,* 1994.

Feldman, Gene, and Max Gartenberg, editors, *The Beat Generation and the Angry Young Men,* Citadel (Kent, England), 1958.

Fussell, Paul, *The Anti-Egotist: Kingsley Amis, Man of Letters,* Oxford University Press (Oxford, England and New York City), 1994.

Gardner, Philip, *Kingsley Amis,* Twayne (Boston), 1981.

Gindin, James, *Postwar British Fiction,* University of California Press (Berkeley), 1962.

Gooden, Philip, *Makers of Modern Culture,* Facts on File (New York City), 1981.

Johnson, William, compiler, *Focus on the Science Fiction Film,* Prentice-Hall (Englewood Cliffs, NJ), 1972.

Karl, Frederick R., *The Contemporary English Novel,* Farrar, Straus (New York City), 1962.

Lodge, David, *Language of Fiction,* Columbia University Press (New York City), 1966.

Lodge, *The Novelist at the Crossroads and Other Essays on Fiction and Criticism,* Cornell University Press (Ithaca, NY), 1971.

Moseley, Marritt, *Understanding Kingsley Amis,* University of South Carolina Press (Columbia, SC), 1993.

Nemerov, Howard, *Poetry and Fiction: Essays,* Rutgers University Press (New Brunswick, NJ), 1963.

Rabinovitz, Rubin, *The Reaction against Experiment in the English Novel, 1950-1960,* Columbia University Press, 1967.

Salwak, Dale, *Kingsley Amis, Modern Novelist,* Barnes & Noble (Lanham, MA), 1992.

Shapiro, Charles, editor, *Contemporary British Novelists,* Southern Illinois University Press (Carbondale), 1963.

Wilson, Edmund, *The Bit between My Teeth: A Literary Chronicle of 1950-1965,* Farrar, Straus, 1965.

*PERIODICALS*

*America,* May 7, 1977.
*Atlanta Journal-Constitution,* July 24, 1994, p. N10.
*Atlantic,* April, 1956; April, 1958; July, 1965; June, 1968; June, 1970; February, 1977; November, 1985.
*Best Sellers,* May 15, 1968; April 4, 1969.
*Bloomsbury Review,* March, 1992, p. 2.
*Books and Bookmen,* December, 1965; July, 1968; January, 1969; September, 1969; October, 1978.
*Bookseller,* November 11, 1970.
*Boston Globe,* May 22, 1994, p. B18; September 7, 1994, p. 74.
*British Book News,* June, 1981.

*Chicago Tribune,* August 1, 1989.
*Chicago Tribune Book World,* October 13, 1985.
*Choice,* November, 1979.
*Christian Science Monitor,* January 16, 1958; September 24, 1970; September 11, 1985; March 10, 1987; October 7, 1991, p. 13.
*Commonweal,* March 21, 1958.
*Contemporary Literature,* winter, 1975.
*Critical Quarterly,* summer, 1977.
*Critique,* spring-summer, 1966; Volume 9, number 1, 1968; summer, 1977.
*Economist,* March 9, 1991, p. 89.
*Encounter,* November, 1974; January, 1979; September/October, 1984.
*Essays in Criticism,* January, 1980.
*Harper's Bazaar,* May 1989, p. 76.
*Hudson Review,* summer, 1972; winter, 1973-74; winter, 1974-75; winter, 1980-81.
*Library Journal,* July, 1970.
*Life,* May 3, 1968; March 14, 1969; August 28, 1970.
*Listener,* November 9, 1967; January 11, 1968; November 26, 1970; May 30, 1974; October 7, 1976; May 22, 1980; October 23, 1980; May 24, 1984; October 16, 1986.
*London Magazine,* January, 1968; August, 1968; October, 1968; January, 1970; January, 1981; October, 1986.
*London Review of Books,* June 7-20, 1984; September 18, 1986; December 4, 1986; April 2, 1987; September 29, 1988, pp. 14, 16; March 22, 1990, p. 20; March 21, 1991, p. 3; November 16, 1995, p. 8.
*Los Angeles Times,* September 25, 1985; July 6, 1989.
*Los Angeles Times Book Review,* May 4, 1980; April 26, 1987; June 12, 1994, p. 3.
*Manchester Guardian,* February 2, 1954; August 23, 1955; November 30, 1956.
*Nation,* January 30, 1954; August 20, 1955; April 28, 1969; May 5, 1969; October 5, 1970; April 7, 1979.
*National Observer,* September 15, 1969; June 29, 1977.
*National Review,* June 18, 1968; June 3, 1969; August 25, 1970; October 27, 1973; February 1, 1974; March 14, 1975; October 27, 1983; February 22, 1985; May 8, 1987; August 1, 1994, p. 62.
*New Leader,* September 21, 1970; December 6, 1976.
*New Republic,* March 24, 1958; September 19, 1970; October 12, 1974; May 28, 1977; November 26, 1977; February 25, 1985; May 30, 1987.

*New Statesman,* January 30, 1954; August 20, 1955; January 18, 1958; September 24, 1960; November 28, 1963; July 7, 1967; December 1, 1967; October 11, 1968; November 21, 1975; October 8, 1976; September 15, 1978; April 13, 1979; May 23, 1980; December 5, 1980; September 19, 1986.

*New Statesman & Society,* March 30, 1990, p. 38; October 5, 1990, p. 44; March 29, 1991, p. 38.

*Newsweek,* March 2, 1964; May 8, 1967; May 6, 1968; September 14, 1970; September 30, 1974; January 17, 1977; February 4, 1985.

*New York,* April 17, 1989, p. 73.

*New Yorker,* March 6, 1954; March 24, 1958; April 26, 1969; September 13, 1969; October 21, 1974; March 14, 1977; August 20, 1979; April 27, 1987; June 12, 1989, pp. 121-24.

*New York Review of Books,* October 6, 1966; August 1, 1968; March 9, 1972; March 20, 1975; April 15, 1976; March 3, 1977; May 17, 1979; March 26, 1987; June 9, 1994, p. 29.

*New York Times,* January 31, 1954; February 26, 1956; February 23, 1958; April 25, 1967; April 25, 1968; March 12, 1969; August 17, 1970; January 6, 1972; May 11, 1979; September 14, 1985; October 8, 1985; November 8, 1986; February 25, 1987; March 28, 1989.

*New York Times Book Review,* April 28, 1963; July 25, 1965; April 28, 1968; May 19, 1968; March 23, 1969; August 23, 1970; November 11, 1973; October 20, 1974; April 18, 1976; January 30, 1977; May 13, 1979; January 13, 1985; June 13, 1985; September 22, 1985; March 22, 1987; April 2, 1989, p. 11; July 1, 1990, p. 5; September 8, 1991, p. 7; May 15, 1994, p. 11.

*Observer* (London), October 10, 1976; December 12, 1976; February 12, 1978; July 23, 1978.

*Observer Review,* November 12, 1967; October 6, 1968.

*Paris Review,* winter, 1975.

*Poetry,* spring, 1968; July, 1969.

*Publishers Weekly,* October 28, 1974.

*Punch,* April 24, 1968; August 28, 1968; October 12, 1968; October 22, 1969; November 18, 1970; October 4, 1978.

*Saturday Review,* February 20, 1954; May 7, 1955; February 25, 1956; July 27, 1957; March 8, 1958; April 6, 1963; April 5, 1969; February 5, 1977; May/June, 1985.

*Saturday Review/World,* May 8, 1973.

*Spectator,* January 29, 1954; September 2, 1955; January 17, 1958; September 23, 1960; October 11, 1969; October 9, 1976; June 2, 1984; Sep-

tember 13, 1986; November 29, 1986; December 6, 1986; December 14, 1991, pp. 40-42.

*Sunday Times* (London), September 28, 1986.

*Time,* May 27, 1957; August 31, 1970; September 10, 1973; September 30, 1974; January 3, 1977; June 12, 1978; September 20, 1985; September 30, 1985; March 9, 1987; September 16, 1991, p. 74.

*Times* (London), May 15, 1980; December 31, 1980; May 17, 1984; May 24, 1984; December 15, 1984; September 4, 1986; September 11, 1986; October 23, 1986; December 12, 1987; March 26, 1988; March 31, 1990.

*Times Literary Supplement,* February 12, 1954; September 16, 1955; January 17, 1958; September 21, 1962; November 23, 1967; March 28, 1968; September 24, 1971; April 6, 1973; October 8, 1976; September 22, 1978; May 16, 1980; October 24, 1980; November 27, 1981; May 25, 1984; September 12, 1986; December 26, 1986; September 23-29, 1988, p. 1039; March 30-April 5, 1990, p. 339; October 5-11, 1990, pp. 1061-62; March 8, 1991, p. 9; November 22, 1991, p. 24.

*Tribune Books* (Chicago), March 8, 1987.

*Vanity Fair,* May, 1987.

*Village Voice,* October 25, 1973.

*Washington Post,* September 10, 1973; May 30, 1994, p. C2.

*Washington Post Book World,* May 5, 1968; August 8, 1968; October 20, 1968; September 1, 1985; March 1, 1987; March 26, 1989.

*Wilson Library Bulletin,* May, 1958; May, 1965.

*World,* May 8, 1973.

*World Literature Today,* summer, 1977; winter, 1977.

*Yale Review,* autumn, 1969; summer, 1975.

*OBITUARIES:*

*PERIODICALS*

*Los Angeles Times,* October 23, 1995, p. A16.

*Times* (London), October 23, 1995, p. 21.*

\*    \*    \*

## AMIS, Martin (Louis) 1949-

*PERSONAL:* Born August 25, 1949, in Oxford, England; son of Kingsley William (a writer) and Hilary (Bardwell) Amis; married Antonia Phillips, 1984 (divorced); children: two sons. *Education:* Oxford University, B.A. (with honors), 1971.

*ADDRESSES: Home*—14 Kensington Gardens Sq., London W2, England. *Agent*—A. D. Peters, The Chambers, Chelsea Harbour, Lots Road, London SW10 0XF, England.

*CAREER: Times Literary Supplement,* London, editorial assistant, 1972-75; *New Statesman,* London, assistant literary editor, 1975-77, literary editor, 1977-79; writer, 1980—. Actor in the film *A High Wind in Jamaica,* 1965.

*AWARDS, HONORS:* Somerset Maugham Award, National Book League, 1974, for *The Rachel Papers.*

*WRITINGS:*

*The Rachel Papers* (novel), J. Cape (London), 1973, Knopf (New York City), 1974, reprinted, Vintage Books (New York City), 1992.

*Dead Babies* (novel), J. Cape, 1975, Knopf, 1976, reprinted, Vintage, 1991, published as *Dark Secrets,* Panther, 1977.

(With others) *My Oxford,* edited and introduced by Ann Thwaite, Robson Books (London), 1977, revised edition, 1986.

*Success* (novel), J. Cape, 1978, Crown (New York City), 1987, reprinted, Vintage, 1991.

(Contributor) Caroline Hobhouse, editor, *Winter's Tales 25,* Macmillan (London), 1979, St. Martin's (New York City), 1980.

*Other People: A Mystery Story* (novel), Viking (New York City), 1981, reprinted, Vintage, 1994.

*Invasion of the Space Invaders* (autobiographical), with an introduction by Stephen Spielberg, Hutchinson (London), 1982.

*Money: A Suicide Note* (novel), J. Cape, 1984, Viking, 1985.

*The Moronic Inferno and Other Visits to America* (articles, reviews and interviews), Harcourt (New York City), 1986.

*Einstein's Monsters* (essay and short stories), J. Cape, 1987, Harmony (New York City), 1987.

*London Fields* (novel), J. Cape, 1989, Vintage, 1991.

*Time's Arrow; or, the Nature of the Offense,* Harmony, 1991.

*Visiting Mrs. Nabokov and Other Excursions* (essays), J. Cape, 1993, Harmony, 1994.

*The Information* (novel), Harmony, 1995.

Also author of a screenplay, *Saturn 3,* 1980. Contributor of short stories to *Encounter, Penthouse, Granta 13, London Review of Books,* and *Literary Review.* Contributor of articles and reviews to numerous periodicals, including *Times Literary Supplement, Observer, New Statesman, New York Times,* and *Sunday Telegraph.*

*SIDELIGHTS:* Since his publication of *The Rachel Papers* at age twenty-four, Martin Amis has established himself as one of the leading British writers of the late-twentieth century. Regularly compared to writers like Vladimir Nabokov and Saul Bellow, Amis's books are usually filled with various wordplays and often appear to be very conscious of themselves as works of fiction. In fact, John Greenya reports in the *Detroit News* that Amis has been "called by one critic 'the nearest thing to a Nabokov that the punk generation has to show.'" The reason, notes Charles Champlin in the *Los Angeles Times,* is that Amis is "a writer with what can only be called a furious command of words, a social commentator of lethal invention and savage wit." Bellow himself compared Amis's stylistic skills to Gustave Flaubert and James Joyce in a *New York Times Magazine* profile. Amis's biting, yet moralistic satire has also drawn comparisons to the work of Jonathan Swift and Angus Wilson. Margaret Drabble suggests in the *New York Times Book Review* "that Amis is so horrified by the world he sees in the process of formation that he feels compelled to warn us all about it."

Inevitably, Amis has also been compared to his father, Kingsley Amis, the late writer of the post-World War II generation of British comic novelists. "Both father and son write of intellectual phonies and pretenders, assorted degenerates and a rotted-out youth in an England of depraved popular culture and not the slightest social or moral structure," writes Richard Eder in the *Los Angeles Times Book Review.* Eder continues that like his father, "Martin Amis is dark, satirical and gifted with irascibility. But what we get under the satire is not a sense of protest but of contempt." Blake Morrison notes in the *Times Literary Supplement* that Martin Amis takes his satire to another level of nastiness, making it "the comedy of the grotesque." In many ways, Amis's works occupy a place well beyond the imposing shadow of his father's works.

For Amis becoming a writer was not, as some have supposed, a matter of "taking over the family business," he told Amanda Smith in a *Publishers Weekly* interview. In some ways, exposure to other cultures, including Spain and the United States, did more to shape his perceptions and writings than did his family background. "Some of the anthropologist's detachment when commenting on human behavior is evident in Amis's novels and essays," notes Sven Birkerts in the *New Republic*. In fact, the elder Amis "didn't really take much notice of my efforts to write until I plonked the proof of my first novel on his desk," Martin told Smith.

In 1973, Amis entered the British literary scene with *The Rachel Papers,* a novel that "caused a stir in Britain—and, it may be, a dreadful thrill of excitement at what may by some be regarded as the spectacle of a crusadingly nasty adolescent unburdening himself in print," writes Karl Miller in the *New York Review of Books*. In the *New Leader,* Pearl K. Bell elaborates: "*The Rachel Papers* offers a candid, groin-level view of teen-age sex, circa 1970, in Swinging Britain. Amis' hero, Charles Highway, is no slouch at telling us exactly what-he-did-and-then-she-did. But since he is also a precocious and totally self-absorbed intellectual, this indefatigable swordsman is more interested in what he thought, pretended, felt, and above all what he *wrote* in his journal about his sexual happenings, than he is in the act itself." Assessments of room for improvement in the novel take up limited space in reviews that recognize Amis's uncannily mature comic talent. Clive Jordan, for instance, remarks in *Encounter,* "Martin Amis directs a determined, dead-pan stare at his chosen patch of the lush teenage jungle, teeming with characters who are about as appealing as bacilli on a face flannel, described with the detached, excessively detailed physicality common to satirists down the ages. What holds the attention are not these limited characters, but the author's verbally inventive scrutiny of them." Reviews of *The Rachel Papers* helped Amis to become known in England as a young writer of substantial promise.

Many American readers first became aware of Amis as the British author who charged that his novel *The Rachel Papers* had been plagiarized by Jacob Epstein, an American. Amis alleged in an October 19, 1980, article in the London *Observer* that some fifty sizable chunks of Epstein's first novel, *Wild Oats,* were virtual duplications of wording from *The Rachel Papers,* which had been published seven years earlier in 1973. Susan Heller Anderson of the *New York Times* writes that when Amis first made the discovery, he "pondered what action to take. 'My own resentment was largely one of embarrassment,' he said. 'I am no real admirer of my first novel or

indeed my second, regarding them as a mixture of clumsy apprenticeship and unwarranted showing off. It shamed me to see sentences exhumed for reinspection ten years on.'" Anderson reports that the London *Observer* article was Amis's only revenge and quotes him as saying: "'I'm not terrifically indignant, but just feel it ought to be made public. . . . The saddest thing about the case is that *Wild Oats* is the work of a genuinely talented writer.'"

Two days after Amis's article appeared, Jacob Epstein verbally admitted that he had indeed copied passages and images from Amis, as well as from other writers. Epstein then explained in the October 26, 1980, issue of the *Observer* that out of admiration and a desire to learn his craft, he had copied passages from *The Rachel Papers* and from books by Nabokov, Turgenev, and Goethe into several notebooks. "After several rewrites and homogenizations," writes Anderson, "Mr. Epstein . . . assumed he was working with virtually original wording." When Epstein discovered in June of 1979 that several phrases and images in his novel had come verbatim from *The Rachel Papers,* he asked his editor at Little, Brown about making revisions. Though this was impossible for the first printing, Epstein did make thirteen deletions for the second American edition and asked that the British publisher work from the revision. The letter to the British publisher, however, went astray.

Embarrassed by the British edition, Amis was infuriated by the revised American edition, because Epstein, who had recognized and regretted his error, only made thirteen deletions. According to an interview quoted by Anderson, Amis replied: "'There aren't thirteen bits, there are fifty odd bits from my book. Looking at his revisions, he had lost track of what he'd taken from me. How do you rewrite a novel and leave word-for-word passages?'"

*Dead Babies,* though not as popular as *The Rachel Papers,* "shows Amis's usual humor and satire but with an especially decadent setting and bizarre violence," notes Levy. Short on suspense but long on the sadness and horror well known to the "post-permissive" generation, the novel castigates "our contemporary practice with drugs and sex, or some features of it," Michael Mason maintains in the *Times Literary Supplement*. Amis's youth of the future, "the heirs of liberation," says Mason, "only respect glamour and violence. That process of degeneration which led from Bob Dylan and Ken Kesey to David

Bowie and Charles Manson is complete. The novel's only spokesman for other values . . . turns out to be by far the most evil and brutal member of the group." Hailed as a comic success by some, the novel, says Drabble, is "too extreme" and "not at all funny." Publishers granted its paperback edition a new title, *Dark Secrets,* to make it more appealing. It was generally received in the United States "like a smirk at a funeral," according to *Esquire* critic James Wolcott; however, argues Mason, its formal structure and black humor confirm its author's affinities with the great satirists Menippe and Jonathan Swift.

Amis's next offering, *Success,* is the "first of three fictions, a series of turmoils, in which orphan and double meet," observes Karl Miller in *Doubles: Studies in Literary History.* Terry Service, bereft of his father (a man who murdered his own wife and baby daughter), sets himself against his upper-class foster brother Gregory Riding. As they begin with opposite fortunes, so they end, Gregory having fallen from what seemed to be a charmed position of wealth and sexual opportunity, Terry rising to a higher level of success. "At the crossing-point of their two lives lies the smashed body of Ursula, Gregory's sister, successful at the second attempt in a suicide nurtured in an incestuous childhood with Gregory, and triggered by a more recent relationship with Terry," Neil Hepburn notes in the *Listener.*

Both brothers relate this turn of events "in alternating and remarkably distinct voices," Jay Parini writes in the *New York Times Book Review.* Terry's voice is marked by extensive vulgarity, a feature that perhaps contributed to the nine-year delay between the book's publication in England and its first American edition, Amis believes. Reviewers generally express disappointment with the book's style, but *Encounter* contributor Tom Paulin sees a method behind the author's "madness": "Amis heaps up verbal triplets and refuses to write well. But in a valueless world style may be a value that he is deliberately rejecting."

To Wolcott, *Success* is "a doomsday reverie, in which Terry represents the brutal, heartless spirit of Urban Apocalypse," while Miller calls it a "comedy of orphan malice and adolescent trauma." "The malice these brothers level at women is nearly equal to their hatred of themselves," says Parini. Jonathan Yardley, writing in the *Washington Post,* guesses that Amis means to express his contempt for both young men; Paulin feels that Amis targets the entire

contemporary world. Paulin contends, "Central to Amis's vision is a sense of deprivation which annihilates the past and makes the present moment seem an exhausted bundle of vicious, fetid and desperate energies. . . . The only constants in the dead secular world are 'self-pity, self-disgust, and self-love.'"

Reviewers offer differing views about the book's success as a satire. "It may be that Amis is attempting to take the negative way through the hell he depicts, but there is a helpless uncertainty in his treatment of it. Far from subverting or qualifying his demonic competence he tends to recommend it," notes Paulin, who, like Parini and Yardley, feels the book is less successful than other novels by Amis. *Village Voice* contributor Graham Fuller, on the other hand, sees in *Success* an enjoyable "parody of England's class war, with Gregory and Terry symbolizing the spiritual decay of the landed gentry and the greedy self-betterment of the 'yobs,' each appraising the other's position with eloquent disgust or shameless envy." In exposing "his characters' self-absorption and the past transgressions that will maim their futures," Fuller finds Amis without peer among British contemporary satirists.

A profusion of doubles complicates Amis's second orphan delirium, or madman's diary, *Other People: A Mystery Story.* Mary Lamb, an amnesiac, faintly recalls her past as bad girl Amy Hide, who nearly died after being attacked by a sadistic psychopath. Two voices tell her story; its ending suggests a return to the beginning for a second take. Her social worker may be sincere, or may be her abductor, setting her up for more abuse. Numerous ambiguities throughout the book make the mystery hard to solve, say some reviewers, while others, like Miller, feel that "its obscurities may be considered a necessary element." Amis provides the answer to this long riddle in literary allusions too subtle for some readers to decipher, but *Encounter* contributor Alan Brownjohn and others recognize the voice of Amis throughout, musing on his own godlike power to manipulate his characters. When read this way, *Other People* appears to be an analysis of the process of making fiction. Extending the analogy, Charles Nichol declares in the *Saturday Review,* "Not all readers will agree with Martin Amis that writing a novel is necessarily a sado-masochistic process, but the force and brilliance of his speculation are undeniable."

In *Other People,* Brownjohn sees "a familiar Martin Amis world made more hideously surprising through the eyes of this lamb on the way back to the slaughter," a vision of uncertainty and violence that makes it "a most original and memorable fable for the Eighties." Evan Hunter muses in the *New York Times Book Review* that Amis "would seem far too young to have acquired such a dismal view of the world." Others, like Brownjohn, indicate that the novel is "more sorry than cynical" about Mary's fate. For this reason, several critics call the book a notable accomplishment. "To confront the fact that one's trusted 'savior' might be full of diabolical intent takes remarkable courage," suggests Geoffrey Stokes in a *Village Voice* review. Stokes, who sees *Other People* as a slight departure from the stance Amis established in prior books, claims, "The great virtue of *Other People* is that Amis has harnessed his cleverness, turned it into a vehicle for the compassionate exploration of the world—and of the received ideas that shape it. . . . Instead of giving the finger to life, he is trying to embrace it."

Amis elicits sympathy for another unlikely character in *Money: A Suicide Note.* Narrator John Self lost his mother when he was seven and later received a bill from his father to cover the cost of his upbringing. Obsessed with money and overcome by his appetites, Self, says John Gross in the *New York Times,* "embodies . . . just about everything your mother told you not to play with." Yardley elaborates in the *Washington Post,* "[Money] is one long drinking bout, interrupted only briefly by a period of relative sobriety; it contains incessant sexual activity, much of it onanistic; it has a generous supply of sordid language. . . and it has an unkind word for just about every race, creed or nationality known to exist." According to *Time* reviewer R. Z. Sheppard, Self demonstrates that "a culture geared to profit from the immediate gratification of egos and nerve endings is not a culture at all, but an addiction. As an addict, he discovers that bad habits and ignorance are the bars of self-imprisonment." *Listener* contributor Angela Huth deems *Money* "a grim book; a black study of the humiliations and degradations of an alcoholic, a warning of the corruptibility of money and the emptiness of a life with no culture to fall back on." In any other novel, Self's indecencies might cause offense, says Yardley, but in this case, Amis "has created a central character of consummate vulgarity and irresistible charm."

In Self's defense, Amis told Smith, "I'm very, very fond of all my characters. . . . The central character, repulsive though he is in many ways, is a sort of

very dedicated sufferer. Nothing ever goes too well for him. And all his attempts to drain as much pleasure out of life as he has entails such suffering on his part. This is a book in a way about the cost of pleasure." In the end, when Self's avarice culminates in his ruin, he is penniless, but better off, Amis told Stephanie Mansfield of the *Washington Post.* The book's popularity with readers confirms his belief that everyone finds stories of misfortune more interesting than stories of success.

"It is a measure of Amis's narrative and stylistic gifts that he makes of his deeply unpromising material an exhilaratingly readable long novel," Nigel Andrew states in the London *Times.* However, many reviewers find fault with the drunken Self's repetitive account of his demise, wrought behind the scenes in the American film industry. Labeled tedious by some, "that ack-ack prose" is the novel's strength, claims Melvyn Bragg in *Punch.* Self's language, he feels, "has impact and often a breathless force," and captures the real world of the eighties in a way "which can lift the roof of your brain." In a more balanced view, Yardley concedes that *Money* "is amply endowed with flaws," but they are less in number than its achievements. "It takes great risks, it boils with energy, . . . it even manages . . . to shock. And for all of that it is so unremittingly, savagely hilarious that reading it is quite literally an exhausting experience from which one emerges simultaneously gasping for air and pleading for more." Yardley concludes, "If there is excess here, then there is also excess in John Self and excess in the 20th century he so pornographically and flamboyantly mirrors."

"*Money* really needs to be read twice (at least): the first time for the sheer pleasure of encountering the grotesque and lovable John Self, for the laughs, the plot, the extraordinary urban atmospherics. The second time round . . . you can begin to relish the book's marvelously intricate design," Ian Hamilton observes in the *London Review of Books.* Doubling, for instance, takes many forms in the novel. In addition to literary allusions which Self repeats but doesn't fully comprehend, parodies and double-talk, double takes and alter egos abound. At one point, Self approaches a London-based writer named Martin Amis to rewrite a movie script. "From that point on the writer—the fictional writer—threatens to usurp the novel—the real novel. It is like the Escher drawing of a hand drawing itself," muses Gross. Disciplined and cultured, the character Martin Amis has a female counterpart in New York, a Martina Twain, who befriends Self, introduces him to opera, and encourages him to sample great books. Miller indicates that, on another level, the auto-eroticism and self-examination so frequent in the book require the narrator to see himself objectively with an awareness equal to doubling on a psychological plane. Other notable semblances Miller sees in *Money* are its affinities with the works of Norman Mailer, Mickey Spillane, Saul Bellow, and Nabokov's novel of doubling, *Despair*. Commenting on these complexities, Amis told Michael Billingsworth for the *New York Times Book Review,* "What I've tried to do is create a high style to describe low things," which he described to Smith as "a very solid thread in English literature." In addition, "*Money* owes much of its drive to contemporary American fiction," observes Sheppard, who compares it to Joseph Heller's *Catch-22* and Philip Roth's *Portnoy's Complaint*. Hamilton expects that "*Money* will be thought of for years to come as one of the key books of the decade."

*The Moronic Inferno and Other Visits to America* shows the same fascinated disdain for American culture through essays, reviews, and interviews about and with American writers. Reviewers on both sides of the Atlantic mention the negative slant of these pieces, most of which first appeared in the *Observer*. London *Times* reviewer Fiona MacCarthy suggests, "Amis . . . is answering some devastating inner urge to search out and describe in minute detail the worst side of America, the false, silly, double-thinking land of violence, vulgarity, of grid-lock and decay. He ignores have-a-nice-day America completely. Almost all his cast of characters have absolutely dreadful days. At best, Truman Capote in the grip of a grand hangover. At worst, Sunny von Bulow, so well cared for in her coma." Perhaps anticipating charges of anti-Americanism, Amis claims in the introduction that the cultural ailment diagnosed in *The Moronic Inferno* is not "a peculiarly American condition. It is global and perhaps eternal." His America is "primarily a metaphor . . . for mass, gross, ever-distracting human infamy."

In *Einstein's Monsters,* a collection of short stories centered on the danger of a nuclear holocaust, Amis continues his "attack on the apocalyptic folly of the age," as Hepburn once called it. "In addition to high verbal energy and flashes of satiric genius, the stories hum with resentment and loathing of a man who fears for his natural patrimony, the earth, the sky and time itself," Sheppard writes in a *Time* review.

Bruce Cook, writing in the *Washington Post Book World,* comments on the author's emotional intensity: "Usually a writer with a cool, commanding manner (utterly unflappable in . . . *The Moronic Inferno*) he comes unglued before us here, attributing his high excitement over the nuclear issue to his impending fatherhood and to a relatively late reading of Jonathan Schell's *The Fate of the Earth.*" Speaking to John Blades in the *Chicago Tribune,* Amis said Schell's book helped him identify the previously felt but unnamed concern that distinguishes his generation from all others: "We are at the evolutionary crisis point, it seems to me. We're in a new moral universe. We can unmake the world. Extinction is a possibility." He feels that rabid consumerism and many other "present-day peculiarities have to do with this damaged set of time we have. We don't think into the future. People behave as if there were no future." Meanwhile, Amis maintains in the opening essay, the generation that invented and proliferated the A-bomb (or "Z-bomb," in his view) does not give the matter much thought. "The argument is really with our fathers," Amis told Ruth Pollack Coughlin of the *Detroit News*. "But it's also about our children. And all the unborn children."

In the *Times Literary Supplement,* Adam Mars-Jones observes that the stories in *Einstein's Monsters* attempt to make the threat of apocalypse an emotional reality for its readers. The collection lives up to its ambitions, says Norman Snider in the Toronto *Globe and Mail:* "Like that of the Nazi death camps, the subject of nuclear annihilation is one of such appalling magnitude that it takes the strongest of minds to see it whole, without flinching, and at the same time manage a response that avoids the bathetic. Amis succeeds for the most part, although his tone at times sounds the characteristically strident note of the newly converted." Even so, Snider adds, "most of these stories are of the laughing-out-loud variety, the blackest humor of the eighties. . . . It's not every writer who can peer over the brink of human extinction and make you laugh at the same time."

This comparatively thin Amis book has the taut energy of an athlete's body, says Francis King in a *Spectator* review; yet it also rewards connoisseurs of Amis's characteristic style, which so fills *Einstein's Monsters* that Mars-Jones compares it to "a painting composed entirely of signatures." No Amis book has failed to receive accolades for distinctive style. Phrases such as "the commodious cellarage of her eyes" in *The Rachel Papers* moved Grace Glueck of the *New York Times Book Review* to say "Shakespeare lives"; Christopher Lehmann-Haupt's negative assessment of *Dead Babies* deems its verbal wittiness "elegant"; and Fuller qualifies his few complaints about *Success* with his comment that its "Nabokovian wordplay is beautifully wrought." At the same time, Amis has consistently exposed and scorned civilization's decay through unappealing characters that he somehow makes interesting. Says Sheppard, "Amis is quite the scold. His Rabelaisian comic gift cuts savagely at the patchwork of relativism and materialism that passes for modern social fabric." Offers Mansfield, "In fact, were it not for his undisputed command of language, his comedic genius and keen ear for dialogue, Amis might be dismissed as just another clever and, yes, snotty young Brit armed with an arsenal of Chelsea one-liners such as 'Style is sort of everything and nothing, but it's mostly everything.'" Summing up, Coughlin remarks, "It is no wonder that [Amis] has been called 'diabolically talented.'"

Amis's *London Fields* is "a mordant allegory of *fin de millenaire* entropy in the post-Thatcherite toilet that Britain has become by 1999," according to Fuller in the *Village Voice*. The London of this novel, as well as the world it is in, is heading toward some undefined but seemingly inevitable apocalypse. Amis's characters are all headed toward a more personal apocalypse. Nicola Six is a beautiful, self-destructive, thirty-four-year-old woman who, having foreseen that she will be murdered on her thirty-fifth birthday, sets out to be killed on her own terms. She lures two married men, Keith and Guy, into a bizarre sex triangle. Keith is a course pub regular with no morals, but with the ambition to be a champion at darts. Guy is a handsome, wealthy British gentleman. One of these two men will kill Nicola, the other will be taken along for a ride. A third man, Sam, a Jewish-American writer who is dying of an incurable disease, is attracted to the triangle for its story value.

As a novel, *London Fields* has received a wide variety of critical attention. For some, Amis is to be commended for capturing a decaying world on the edge of destruction and raising it up as a mirror to our own times. "*London Fields* is a virtuoso depiction of a wild and lustful society," comments Bette Pesetsky in the *New York Times Book Review*. "In an age of attenuated fiction, this is a large book of comic and satirical invention." According to Jonathan Yardley in another *Washington Post Book World* review, "Amis plunges like Dickens reincarnate into the life of the city, wallowing in its messi-

ness and nastiness and desperation." Yet, as Martyn Harris suggests in *New Statesman and Society,* in his preoccupation with creating a setting and scenes of decay and decadence, the author slights some of the other elements of his novel: "Amis isn't interested in character, plot, motivation. . . . In denying motive Amis denies his characters the capacity for change, which in turn rules out the manipulation of reader sympathy—the strongest lever in fiction." Harris continues, "Instead of character the book offers chronocentrism—the conceit that your own age is more special, more scary, more apocalyptic than any other."

Still other reviewers find Amis's vision of decay with allusions to a nuclear or environmental catastrophe now in the making too one-sided and sermonizing. Luc Sante, writing in the *New Republic,* calls the novel "a panoramic cartoon that takes in a whole world of culture and custom and speech. . . . What keeps *London Fields* from being anything more than a cartoon, however, is the complete absence of a heart. The deadly accurate pinpointing of human weaknesses has no counterweight in acknowledgment of human value." Pesetsky finds the novel's merit elsewhere. She writes, "As a tale of nuclear warning, *London Fields* is unconvincing. It succeeds, however, as a picaresque novel rich in its effects." For Jonathan Yardley, "*London Fields* is in sum a mad and maddening book, irate and deranged, and the reader can expect no compromises or comforts from it. In my judgment it borders on but never quite achieves brilliance, largely because of Amis's insistence on mounting the pulpit, but its shortcomings are more than outweighed by its heartbreaking ambition and the huge risks it takes in trying to do nothing less than tell the story of our times."

As with Amis's other novels, *London Fields* has drawn critical notice not only for its story, but also for its style. In fact, in the view of *Spectator* contributor Francis King, "What makes this book so much worth reading is the brilliance of its style. . . . There is no English novelist whose writing can match Amis's in this combination of fastidiousness and power." Harris offers a similar view. He observes, "Amis was always great with the words, of course: the only English writer of his generation to kick his way out of the reticent, genteel language of the contemporary novel into a modern idiom which manages to be both coarse and eloquent, demotic and cerebral." To Bragg, Amis's stylistic fireworks at times threaten to overwhelm the book. He notes in the *Listener,* "Sometimes it is too pummelling, occasionally straining. Alliterations and repetitions threaten to become cluttered and self-imitative, hammering at the prose like hail until you want to stop." Even so, concludes Bragg, "Taken all in all, *London Fields* is a rare achievement. . . . The jokes work, the character/caricatures convince, the ambition is laudable, and the energy ferociously impressive."

By the time the "bad boy" of British letters reached middle age, his writing, particularly *The Information,* reflected a change in his perspective. It is a novel about two middle-aged friends and how their careers, each headed in a different direction, affect them and their friendship. The two men, Richard Tull and Gwyn Barry, are writers. In addition to looking at middle age, the book is also about how writers react to success and failure. As Gail Caldwell describes in a *Boston Globe* review, "*The Information* is a novel about literary envy, the kind that most writers swear isn't their own affliction, though they all seem to know someone else who's succumbed. It is a frighteningly funny, erudite and mostly compelling novel, dragging you along through London's rough side and Tull's sewers and staircases of consciousness until you beg for mercy. Tull will go to any length, almost, to torment his rival." This literary battle, believes *Vanity Fair* contributor Michael Shnayerson, is at the novel's core. He writes: "*The Information* lampoons a publishing world driven by vacuous best-sellers and foolish prizes; for all the grim fun it makes of male midlife confusion, the literary crisis is real, Amis is saying, and must be met."

Tull is the failing author. He has written a couple of experimental novels that have received only an inkling of critical attention. However, his four more recent works have gone unpublished. His most recent work places such demands on its readers that the few who have attempted it have been rendered physically ill. Barry, on the other hand, has of late achieved fame, wealth, and critical acclaim with a bestselling novel. Tull does not take his friend's good fortune well. In fact, he begins to plot Barry's downfall. Through a variety of farfetched schemes, Tull attempts to destroy Barry's career, his marriage, and his life. Some readers may wonder, as Christopher Buckley does in the *New York Times Book Review,* "Is an envious writer enough to sustain a whole novel? Surprisingly, yes. Mr. Amis is quite dazzling here." Caldwell offers a similar view. She writes that Amis's main character is "an intelligence of enough dimension and humanity, however soiled, to make us

stay for the whole performance. Richard Tull is smart, he is demented, sometimes he is even deeper than his depression. . . . His sullied passion is what fuels him, and the wicked mind that spawned him is what fuels the novel."

Amis's characteristic style and humor are once again on display in this novel. "*The Information* drags a bit around the middle," comments Buckley, "but you're never out of reach of a sparkly phrase, stiletto metaphor or drop-dead insight into the human condition. And there is the humor; Mr. Amis goes where other humorists fear to tread." *Washington Post Book World* contributor David Nicholson feels that Amis missed an opportunity to capitalize on the novel's humor. "*The Information* is quite good. There is, however, a wonderful sidesplitting smaller book trapped inside it. *The Information* would have been far better had Amis allowed it to come out." *New York Times* reviewer Michiko Kakutani finds in *The Information* "Amis's own idiosyncratic vision and his ability to articulate that vision in wonderfully edgy, street-smart prose." He suggests that Amis "has written just the sort of novel his bumbling hero dreams in vain of writing: an uncompromising and highly ambitious novel that should also be a big popular hit."

For some reviewers, the strength of *The Information* goes beyond its style and humor. Kakutani also contends that "*The Information* marks a giant leap forward in Mr. Amis's career. Here, in a tale of middle-aged angst and literary desperation, all the themes and stylistic experiments of Mr. Amis's earlier fiction come together in a symphonic whole." Amis's "Nabokovian devices are not only employed to frame the story of a failed novelist, Richard Tull," adds Kakutani, "but are also cunningly used to open out his hilarious tale of envy and revenge into a glittering meditation on the nervous interface between the real world and the world of art." Chris Heath also sees the book in a larger context. In a profile of Amis for *Details,* he writes, "Only in the smallest way is *The Information* about what happens when Richard Tull and Gwyn Barry start scheming around each other. It's about messier, more troubling matters: competitiveness and jealousy and vanity, the vacuum of middle age, the need to be remembered, the ways we corrupt innocence. It is also, in all its side alleys, simply about describing the modern world in all its vain, grotesque minutiae." Yardley calls Amis "a force unto himself among those of his generation now writing fiction in English; there is, quite simply, no one else like him."

*BIOGRAPHICAL/CRITICAL SOURCES:*

BOOKS

*Contemporary Literary Criticism,* Gale (Detroit), Volume 4, 1975, Volume 9, 1978, Volume 38, 1987, Volume 62, 1992.
*Dictionary of Literary Biography,* Volume 14: *British Novelists since 1960,* Gale, 1983.
Diedrick, James, *Understanding Martin Amis,* University of South Carolina Press (Columbia, SC), 1995.
Miller, Karl, *Doubles: Studies in Literary History,* Oxford University Press, 1985.

PERIODICALS

*American Spectator,* May, 1987.
*Atlanta Journal-Constitution,* March 4, 1990, p. N8.
*Booklist,* January 15, 1994, p. 894.
*Boston Globe,* February 18, 1990, p. B41; March 25, 1990, p. B37; April 30, 1995, p. B15; May 31, 1995, p. 59.
*Chicago Tribune,* April 21, 1985; February 23, 1986; June 11, 1987; September 1, 1987; May 14, 1995.
*Christian Science Monitor,* September 4, 1987, p. B4; April 11, 1990, p. 12; May 17, 1995, p. 14.
*Cosmopolitan,* August, 1978.
*Details,* June, 1995, p. 92.
*Detroit News,* June 16, 1985; June 14, 1987.
*Encounter,* February, 1974; February, 1976; September, 1978; May, 1981.
*Esquire,* November, 1980; November, 1986; January, 1987; October, 1987.
*Globe and Mail* (Toronto), January 26, 1985; September 6, 1986; June 6, 1987.
*Interview,* June, 1985; May, 1995, p. 122.
*Listener,* August 15, 1974; October 30, 1975; April 13, 1978; March 5, 1981; September 27, 1984; April 30, 1987, p. 28; September 21, 1989, p. 30.
*London Magazine,* February/March, 1974.
*London Review of Books,* May 7-20, 1981; September 20-October 3, 1984; July 24, 1986, p. 5; May 7, 1987, p. 11; September 28, 1989, p. 7; September 12, 1991, p. 11.
*Los Angeles Times,* June 28, 1987; September 27, 1987; March 29, 1990, p. E1.
*Los Angeles Times Book Review,* March 31, 1985, p. 3; June 28, 1987, p. 13; March 4, 1990, p. 3; November 10, 1991, p 3; April 30, 1995, p. 3.
*Nation,* April 23, 1990, p. 565; December 30, 1991, p. 852.

*National Review,* August 14, 1987, p. 44; November 20, 1987, p. 60; May 28, 1990, p. 46; May 29, 1995, p. 61.
*New Criterion,* February, 1987; May, 1990.
*New Leader,* May 13, 1974.
*New Republic,* May 6, 1985, p. 34; January 26, 1987, p. 36; April 30, 1990, p. 45.
*New Statesman,* November 16, 1973; October 17, 1975; March 13, 1981; May 29, 1987, p. 24; September 22, 1989, p. 34; September 27, 1991, p. 55; October 1, 1993, p. 39; March 24, 1995, p. 24.
*Newsweek,* May 6, 1974; March 25, 1985, p. 80; March 5, 1990, p. 62; May 8, 1995, p. 66.
*New Yorker,* June 24, 1974; August 10, 1981; June 10, 1985; April 15, 1991, p. 25; May 25, 1992, p. 85; March 6, 1995, p. 96.
*New York Magazine,* April 29, 1974; October 21, 1991, p. 117; May 29, 1995, p. 38.
*New York Review of Books,* July 18, 1974.
*New York Times,* March 15, 1985, p. 36; February 13, 1990, p. C17; July 5, 1990, p. C11; October 22, 1991, p. C17; January 31, 1995, p. C13; May 2, 1995, p. C17.
*New York Times Book Review,* May 26, 1974; February 8, 1976; July 26, 1981; March 24, 1985, p. 36; May 17, 1987, p. 28; September 6, 1987, p. 8; March 4, 1990, p. 1; December 2, 1990, p. 1; November 17, 1991, p. 15; February 27, 1994, p. 17; April 23, 1995, p. 1.
*New York Times Magazine,* February 4, 1990, p. 32.
*Observer* (London), December 2, 1984, p. 19; April 7, 1985, p. 21; September 24, 1989, p. 47; September 22, 1991, p. 59; November 24, 1991, p. 2; October 17, 1993, p. 16; March 26, 1995, p. 17.
*Publishers Weekly,* February 8, 1985.
*Punch,* October 10, 1984, p. 82; May 27, 1987, p. 66.
*Quill and Quire,* September, 1987, p. 86.
*Rolling Stone,* May 17, 1990, p. 95.
*San Francisco Review of Books,* April, 1991, p. 32.
*Saturday Review,* June, 1981.
*Spectator,* November 24, 1973; April 15, 1978; March 21, 1981; October 20, 1984; July 12, 1986, p. 29; December 6, 1986, p. 33; May 2, 1987, p. 31; September 23, 1989, p. 36; July 20, 1991, p. 25; September 28, 1991, p. 37; October 16, 1993, p. 38.
*Sunday Times* (London), March 8, 1981; September 26, 1982.
*Time,* March 11, 1985, p. 70; June 22, 1987, p. 74; February 26, 1990, p. 71; May 1, 1995, p. 90.
*Time Out,* March 27, 1981.

*Times* (London), September 27, 1984; August 14, 1986; April 30, 1987; July 25, 1987.

*Times Educational Supplement,* November 5, 1993, p. 12.

*Times Literary Supplement,* October 17, 1975; March 6, 1981; November 26, 1982; October 5, 1984; July 18, 1986, p. 785; May 1, 1987, p. 457; September 29, 1989, p. 1051; September 20, 1991, p. 21; October 15, 1993, p. 21.

*Tribune Books* (Chicago), May 29, 1988, p. 6; March 4, 1990, p. 1; May 6, 1990, p. 8; November 24, 1991, p. 3; May 14, 1995, p. 5.

*Vanity Fair,* March, 1990, p. 62; May, 1995, p. 132.

*Village Voice,* January 26, 1976; June 10-June 16, 1981; February 24, 1987, p. 43; December 1, 1987, p. 66; April 24, 1990, p. 75.

*Voice Literary Supplement,* October, 1991, p. 31.

*Wall Street Journal,* April 24, 1985; March 13, 1990, p. A14; December 23, 1991, p. A7; February 14, 1994, p. A16; April 25, 1995, p. A18; May 1, 1995, p. A12.

*Washington Post,* April 28, 1985; January 7, 1987; September 16, 1987; November 26, 1991, p. B1; February 9, 1994, p. B2; February 6, 1995, p. C2.

*Washington Post Book World,* March 24, 1985 p. 3; July 5, 1987, p. 4; June 5, 1988; February 18, 1990, p. 3; October 27, 1991, p 1; May 7, 1995, p 3.

*World Literature Today,* spring, 1982.*

\*    \*    \*

**APPLE, Max (Isaac)  1941-**

*PERSONAL:* Born October 22, 1941, in Grand Rapids, MI; son of Samuel (a baker) and Betty (Goodstein) Apple; divorced; children: Jessica, Sam. *Education:* University of Michigan, A.B., 1963, Ph.D., 1970; graduate study at Stanford University, 1964.

*ADDRESSES: Office*—Department of English, Rice University, Houston, TX 77001. *Agent*—Amanda Urban, International Creative Management, 40 West 57th St., New York, NY 10019.

*CAREER:* Reed College, Portland, OR, assistant professor of literature and humanities, 1970-71; Rice University, Houston, TX, assistant professor, 1972-76, associate professor, 1976-80, professor of English, 1980—.

*MEMBER:* Modern Language Association of America, PEN Club, Texas Institute of Letters.

*AWARDS, HONORS:* National Endowment for the Humanities younger humanists fellowship, 1971; Jesse Jones awards from Texas Institute of Letters, 1976, for *The Oranging of America, and Other Stories,* and 1985, for *Free Agents;* Hadassah magazine-Ribalous Award, for best Jewish fiction of 1985.

*WRITINGS:*

(Contributor) David Madden, editor, *Nathanael West: The Cheaters and the Cheated,* Everett/Edwards (DeLand, FL), 1972.

(With others) *Studies in English,* Rice University (Houston, TX), 1975.

*The Oranging of America, and Other Stories,* Grossman (New York City), 1976.

*Zip: A Novel of the Left and the Right,* Viking (New York City), 1978.

(Editor) *Southwest Fiction,* Bantam (New York City), 1980.

*Three Stories,* Pressworks (Dallas, TX), 1983.

*Free Agents,* Harper (New York City), 1984.

*The Propheteers: A Novel,* Perennial Library (New York City), 1987.

*Roommates: My Grandfather's Story* (memoir), Warner Books (New York City), 1994.

Contributor of stories to *Esquire, Mademoiselle, American Review, Georgia Review, Ohio Review,* and numerous other periodicals.

*SIDELIGHTS:* With the 1976 publication of his popular collection *The Oranging of America, and Other Stories,* Max Apple established a reputation for comic intelligence that has persisted through his subsequent works. According to Celia Betaky in *Saturday Review,* Apple's fictions "take American obsessions and fads, myths and habits, and explode them into ingenious symbols with a life all their own. . . . Life is not only a game, Apple's stories seem to say, but a game show. . . . They mimic peculiarly American aspirations in matters as grave as economics, politics, and literature." Calling Apple a "friendly critic of American culture," *New York Times* reviewer Anatole Broyard adds: "What distinguishes him from other critics is the affection in his voice, as if he were remonstrating with someone he loved—like parents, children or friends. There's something saintly about him; he's patient and amused, rather than angry. His wit is tender, soft-edged, insidious."

"It was my fascination with the English language itself that made me a writer," Apple declared in an essay for the *New York Times Book Review.* "Its endless suggestiveness has carried me through many a plot, entertained me when nothing else could." Born and raised in Grand Rapids, Michigan, Apple spoke Yiddish in his home as a child. "I remember in kindergarten being surprised that everything happened in English," he wrote. "To [my family] English was the official language, useful perhaps for legal documents and high school graduation speeches but not for everyday life." Apple recalled elsewhere in the *New York Times Book Review* that he did not feel unusual growing up in a kosher Jewish household in a small midwestern city. "It's a Calvinist town," he said of Grand Rapids. "There were no movies, no dances. So being Jewish was just a different kind of craziness."

A professor of English who has taught at Rice University since 1972, Apple has for some time considered himself "a Texan but not an academic," according to Martin Levine in the *New York Times Book Review.* Indeed, Apple wrote in his essay: "I'll conjure lives far richer than mine, which is so pedestrian that it would make you seem heroic were you here."

This rather self-effacing assessment provides an accurate description of one aspect of Apple's work. As Nicholas Delbanco notes in the *New Republic,* the cast in a typical Apple offering "teeters . . . between the imagined and the actual." Famous historical figures and national pop cultural heroes often interact with Apple's fictional characters. In *The Oranging of America,* for instance, Apple includes short stories about Howard Johnson, Norman Mailer, Gerald Ford, and Fidel Castro, among others. "Apple's parables are about pioneers," writes Betaky, "because in America that is what our deluded dreamers, mad visionaries, and inspired madmen turn out to be." Joe David Bellamy, writing in the *New York Times Book Review,* praises the "charming nostalgia that Apple generates for these characters and their times, even as they are butts of ridicule. It is a quality that makes [*The Oranging of America*] far more than just another cute barrage of pot shots at the ravaged American dream."

Critics have also cited *The Oranging of America* for its imaginative humor. *Newsweek* reviewer Peter S. Prescott notes: "Apple's principal asset is his star-

tling imagination. Original, witty, writing deftly and economically, he translates the most battered of our cultural cliches into glistening artifacts. . . . He means to make us feel a little better about ourselves, about American life, by polishing the rubble and hinting that man's spirit is frisky yet." Bellamy takes a similar view of the work: "In addition to an eye for cultural cliches, an ear attuned to the self-satirizing vagaries of American business jargon and a lot of heart, is the scrupulous and generally unpretentious elegance and balance of the Apple prose style, and the throaty gratification the reader feels at his sense of a patient intelligence at work along the way." According to Eliot Fremont-Smith in the *Village Voice,* Apple's stories "are positive and cheerful (in the face of insanity) and at root optimistic; they stimulate the aesthetic imagination and gracefully bypass the social concerns and fashionable guilts they obviously acknowledge and to a degree employ." Fremont-Smith also concludes of *The Oranging of America:* "I *am* sure that it is quite the most lovely piece of imaginative writing I have encountered in some years. You go from it happy. That happiness may be viewed as an insult to pressing moral issues that indeed do matter, but I find it reenergizing. . . . That's the feel I get from Apple's book, and I'm grateful for it."

In 1978, Apple published his *Zip: A Novel of the Left and the Right.* In a *New York Times* article, John Leonard comments that the full-length work "seems to me to be less a novel than a box of toys, epigrams, firecrackers, political pot shots, Talmudic maunderings, whistles and screams. What distinguishes it from other, similar exercises in Pop Modernism is its affection." The story revolves around a Jewish Detroiter who manages a Puerto Rican middleweight named Jesus Goldstein. Consistent with previous Apple fiction, historical figures such as Fidel Castro, J. Edgar Hoover, and Jane Fonda make cameo appearances. Terence Winch, reviewing the work in the *Washington Post Book World,* notes that it belongs to the fictional tradition of the American Jewish novel. Apple's prose, writes Winch, "has the humor and poise of [Saul] Bellow's or [Henry] Roth's. . . . The spiritual exchange between Jew and Gentile was a parable of modern salvation that [Edward Lewis] Wallant and [Bernard] Malamud took very seriously. In *Zip,* however, Apple parodies the salvation parable. But rather than transforming the myth through humor, he simply discredits it."

Though generally well-received, *Zip* has also drawn some less than favorable critical responses. Leonard writes: "A fine comic intelligence, a superb ear, and a brilliant way with slapstick do not automatically add up to a coherent, satisfying book." Winch comments that though Apple is "a good writer," he seems in *Zip* "to be taking on too much in too brief a novel." Likewise, Philip Stevick notes in the *Nation:* "Apple, no doubt, has a range of human responsiveness that is greater than most men's." Stevick concludes, nevertheless, that the final impression of *Zip* is "of a novel with wonderful moments, a splendid sense of verbal play, and a keen eye for the styles of the '60s but without the imaginative power of Apple's best shorter work." Despite their reservations, these reviewers and others have found praiseworthy aspects of the author's novel. "Mr. Apple uses a feather, not a blowtorch, on his characters," claims Leonard. "He would tickle politics out of business." Stevick calls the work "Apple's most telling comment on the '60s, that depressing tendency to derive energy from other energetic people, irrespective of what those other people *do.*" In a *New York Times Book Review* piece about *Zip,* Jerome Charyn concludes: "Max Apple doesn't seem to have a wicked bone in his body. He can laugh at our heroes and villains of the left and the right, without needing to savage them. *Zip* is good for you. It's a novel that can tickle us all."

*Free Agents,* Apple's 1984 publication, contains short stories and essays "on such recondite subjects as ice fishing, Aristotle as a model for post-modern writing, and a basketball-sized Japanese American who lobbies in Washington for Taiwan," in the words of Ralph B. Sipper for the *Los Angeles Times Book Review.* Sipper continues: "The unifying principle in all these sendups is an author who expresses himself in some of the niftiest satirical prose this side of Jonathan Swift. . . . The most enduring pieces are those grounded in what seems autobiography crossed with wild invention—the literary equivalent of a Magritte painting where surrealism emerges less from subject than from juxtaposition." In a *New Republic* review, Tom LeClair also notes the autobiographical bent of some of the stories in *Free Agents:* "Self is the shortcut . . . the quick starter for a story, but Apple doesn't push far enough into that self or send it wide enough to matter in most of these twenty pieces." LeClair nevertheless admits about the author: "For all his Apple absorption, he's a likable fellow, a little nostalgic and guilty, well intentioned and concerned with continuity—his family's past and kids' future." *New Leader* contributor Simon Wincelberg finds *Free Agents* "a cheerful mixture of Apple's deceptively bland sense of fantasy and airy humor—a humor free of malice, aggression, or shy nudges to share a laugh at another's expense."

Apple's 1986 novel, *The Propheteers,* brings three eccentric and well-known Americans together for a showdown over a piece of Florida real estate. Howard Johnson the motel magnate returns here to Apple's fiction, along with his trusted companions Mildred and Otis. They are joined in the novel by the wealthy heiress Margery Post and by creative genius Walt Disney and his bullying brother. These principals collide over the future use of some land in Orlando: Disney wants to develop a theme park on it, Johnson wants to set it aside as a haven for weary travelers, and Post wants the property to be left alone. According to Roz Kaveney in the *Times Literary Supplement,* "Much of Max Apple's *The Propheteers* is concerned with demystifying the very rich by showing them as compulsive neurotics; much partakes of myth or comic book."

*London Review of Books* correspondent Peter McDonald notes that in *The Propheteers,* "post-war American society is caricatured with remorseless precision, its values inflated into religious terms that seem ludicrous only at first. The book projects the visionary nature of the marketplace, the apotheosis of the entrepreneur, the patriarchal grandeur of the major corporations, and takes this religion seriously enough to understand the raptures of its more mystical reaches, its dream of pure consumerism, pure wealth, pure leisure and, of course, the life eternal." The critic concludes that the novel is "an original, amusing, shockingly far-fetched parable of the sad successes of a profit-society in which everyone, even among the winners, ends up losing." *New York Times Book Review* contributor Cyra McFadden writes of Apple: "No one has a kinder, more avuncular voice . . . no one's funnier, in his own singular fashion."

Most critics have been particularly praiseworthy of Apple's memoir, *Roommates: My Grandfather's Story.* In this work Apple recounts his close and quirky relationship with his grandfather, who shared a room with the author in the family home and later in an apartment in Ann Arbor, Michigan. "This family memoir bursts onto the American literary scene incongruously," declares Tova Reich in the *New Leader.* "It is so out of joint with our television-celebrated, Hollywood-promoted, magazine-vaunted culture of generational conflict, teenage independence, single-mother liberation, and geriatric horror that in a perverse but triumphant way it seems destined to provide a rigorously encouraging vision of how generative and salvational families can be. . . . It is nothing less than a blessing." *New York Times Book Review* correspondent Andrew Bergman likewise calls the work "an enthralling and novelistic tale of family, guilt and the rules of survival as they apply during illness, job-and school-related migrations, and the arrival and growth of children. Relying on the steady accretion of detail and the simplest of prose, Mr. Apple . . . has written a moving and satisfying book." Bergman concludes: "Max Apple's tribute to [his grandfather] is free of treacle but full of sentiment. *Roommates* is a terrific book."

Apple wrote in the *New York Times Book Review*: "Fiction seems sometimes like my [ventriloquist's] dummy, like that part of myself that should get all the best lines. I want to be the 'straight man' so that the very difference between us will be a part of the tension that I crave in each sentence, in every utterance of those wooden lips redeemed from silence because I practiced." Apple, whose stories Charyn feels "give us a feel for our own loony culture that is so recognizable, we blink with shame and delight," has admitted that he was in his late twenties before he got all the sentences right in a single story. His careful craftsmanship and evocation of comic absurdity have led *Newsweek*'s Walter Clemons to dub him "a satirist without scorn, an affectionate ironist," who "masters the lingoes of postmodernism, incorporation and Washington lobbying and comes up grinning, as if he's found diamonds, not dreck."

*BIOGRAPHICAL/CRITICAL SOURCES:*

BOOKS

*Contemporary Literary Criticism,* Gale (Detroit, MI), Volume 9, 1978, Volume 33, 1985.
*Dictionary of Literary Biography,* Volume 130: *American Short-Story Writers since World War II,* Gale, 1993.

PERIODICALS

*Atlantic Monthly,* February 1977.
*Chicago Tribune Book World,* September 10, 1978.
*Coda,* September/October 1978.
*London Review of Books,* October 1, 1987, p. 12.
*Los Angeles Times Book Review,* August 26, 1984; March 8, 1987, p. 3.
*Michigan Quarterly Review,* winter 1988, p. 77.

*Nation,* January 15, 1977; August 19-26, 1978.
*New Leader,* July 9-23, 1984; June 6-20, 1994, p. 36-37.
*New Republic,* June 24, 1978; October 22, 1984.
*Newsweek,* December 6, 1976; July 10, 1978; June 25, 1984.
*New York Times,* November 20, 1976; July 17, 1978; June 8, 1984.
*New York Times Book Review,* February 13, 1977; July 16, 1978; March 22, 1981; June 17, 1984; March 15, 1987, p. 13; June 19, 1994, pp. 9-10.
*Observer* (London), July 26, 1987, p. 22.
*Partisan Review,* Volume XLVII, number 2, 1980.
*Saturday Review,* January 22, 1977; July 22, 1978.
*Southwest Review,* summer 1979, p. 230-37.
*Time,* July 9, 1984.
*Times Literary Supplement,* October 9, 1987, p. 1106.
*Village Voice,* February 14, 1977; August 7, 1978.
*Washington Post Book World,* August 6, 1978.*

—*Sketch by Anne Janette Johnson*

\* \* \*

**AXTELL, James Lewis 1941-**

*PERSONAL:* Born December 20, 1941, in Endicott, NY; son of Arthur J. (an accountant) and Laura (England) Axtell; married Susan Hallas (a preschool teacher), August 31, 1963; children: Nathaniel, Jeremy. *Education:* Yale University, B.A., 1963; Cambridge University, Ph.D., 1967.

*ADDRESSES: Home*—109 Walnut Hills Dr., Williamsburg, VA 23185. *Office*—Department of History, College of William and Mary, Williamsburg, VA 23187.

*CAREER:* Yale University, New Haven, CT, assistant professor of history, 1966-72, Morse fellow, 1969-70; Sarah Lawrence College, Bronxville, NY, associate professor of history, 1972-75; Northwestern University, Evanston, IL, visiting professor of history, 1977-78; College of William and Mary, Williamsburg, VA, professor of history, beginning 1978, William R. Kenan, Jr., Professor of Humanities, 1986—.

*MEMBER:* American Historical Association, Organization of American Historians, American Society for

Ethnohistory, Society of American Historians, Champlain Society, Hakluyt Society, Colonial Society of Massachusetts, Pilgrim Society, French Colonial Historical Society.

*AWARDS, HONORS:* Social Science Research Council fellow, 1965-66; National Endowment for the Humanities fellow, 1976-77, 1986, 1992; Guggenheim fellow, 1981-82; Gilbert Chinard Prize, 1985; Erminie Wheeler-Voegelin Prize, 1986; Albert B. Corey Prize, 1986, for *The Invasion Within: The Contest of Cultures in Colonial North America;* American Council of Learned Societies fellow, 1987.

*WRITINGS:*

*The School upon a Hill: Education and Society in Colonial New England,* Yale University Press (New Haven, CT), 1974.
(With James P. Ronda) *Indian Missions: A Critical Bibliography,* Indiana University Press (Bloomington), 1978.
*The European and the Indian: Essays in the Ethnohistory of Colonial North America,* Oxford University Press (New York City), 1981.
*The Invasion Within: The Contest of Cultures in Colonial North America,* Oxford University Press, 1985.
*After Columbus: Essays in the Ethnohistory of Colonial North America,* Oxford University Press, 1988.
*Beyond 1492: Encounters in Colonial North America,* Oxford University Press, 1992.
*The Rise and Fall of the Powhatan Empire: Indians in Seventeenth-Century Virginia,* Colonial Williamsburg Foundation (Williamsburg, VA), 1995.

*EDITOR*

*The Educational Writings of John Locke: A Critical Edition with Introduction and Notes,* Cambridge University Press (New York City), 1968.
*The American People in the Colonial South,* Pendulum Press (West Haven, CT), 1973.
*The American People in Colonial New England,* Pendulum Press, 1973.
*The Native American People of the East,* Pendulum Press, 1973.
*American Perceived: A View from Abroad in the Seventeenth Century,* Pendulum Press, 1974.
*American Perceived: A View from Abroad in the Eighteenth Century,* Pendulum Press, 1974.

*The Indian Peoples of Eastern America: A Documentary History of the Sexes,* Oxford University Press, 1981.

Contributor to history journals and *American Heritage.*

*WORK IN PROGRESS:* The Cultural Origins of North America, Volume II: *American Encounter: The Confluence of Cultures in Colonial North America,* for Oxford University Press; *The Pleasures of Academe* (familiar essays).

*SIDELIGHTS: The Invasion Within: The Contest of Cultures in Colonial North America,* by historian James Axtell, explores the impact of early French and English missionaries on Indian culture. "As James Axtell claims in his trenchant, sometimes belligerent study of early America, the English teachers and preachers were guilty of cultural annihilation," writes Mark Abley in the *Times Literary Supplement.* According to *New York Times Book Review* contributor William Cronon, "Few historians have focused more closely on this cultural warfare than James Axtell. . . . Unlike more materialist historians, Mr. Axtell pursues a frontier that is mental rather than geographical. 'For many natives and Europeans,' he writes, frontier conflict 'remained primarily a contest between two concepts of spiritual power.'"

Axtell admires the French Jesuits, who adapted themselves to the Indian way of life, far more than the English missionaries, who attempted to make the Indians both Christian and European. However, in covering Axtell's descriptions of the Protestant missionaries, Abley remarks that Axtell's "zeal to discredit the English goes some way beyond the frontiers of historical objectivity." Despite its shortcomings, Abley recommends *The Invasion Within.* "Lucid, packed with detail and written with a sad passion, . . . the book stands as a provocative study of the psychology and consequences of missionary work, and of the resistance to it." Cronon also praises the book: "*The Invasion Within* is the best introduction now available to the problem of cultural conversion in the New World. For anyone wishing to learn the significance of soap and education in the tool kit of European empire, it is essential reading."

Axtell once commented to *CA:* "I always try to write for both college sophomores and professional colleagues. If I can engage and hold the former and convince the latter, I am satisfied."

*BIOGRAPHICAL/CRITICAL SOURCES:*

*PERIODICALS*

*American Historical Review,* April, 1976; February, 1994, p. 292.
*Historian,* February, 1990, p. 333.
*Journal of American History,* December, 1989, p. 906; March, 1994, p. 1427.
*New York Times Book Review,* December 9, 1979; November 3, 1985.
*Times Literary Supplement,* December 21, 1979; June 13, 1986.
*World Literature Today,* autumn, 1979.*

# B

## BACKHOUSE, Janet    1938-

*PERSONAL:* Born February 8, 1938, in Corsham, England; daughter of Joseph Helme and Jessie (Chivers) Backhouse. *Education:* Attended Stonar School, Melksham, 1946-56, Bedford College, London, 1956-59, and Institute of Historical Research, London, 1959-62.

*ADDRESSES: Office*—Department of Manuscripts, British Library, Great Russell St., London WC1B 3DG, England.

*CAREER:* British Museum/Library, London, England, assistant keeper of manuscripts/curator of illuminated manuscripts, 1962—. Member of Comite International de Paleographie Latine, 1993; member of Advisory Council of the National Art Collections Fund, 1995; council member of the Henry Bradshaw Society; member of steering committee of the Harlaxton Medieval Symposium.

*MEMBER:* British Archaeological Association, Bibliographical Society, Society of Antiquaries of London (fellow, 1983), Friends of the National Libraries, National Art Collections Fund, Society of Art Historians, Wiltshire Archaeological and Natural History Society.

*WRITINGS:*

*John Scottowe's Alphabet Books,* Roxburghe Club, 1974.
*The Madresfield Hours,* Roxburghe Club, 1975.
*The Illuminated Manuscript,* Phaidon (Oxford, England), 1979.
*The Lindisfarne Gospels,* Phaidon, 1981.

*Books of Hours,* British Library Publications (London), 1985.
(With Christopher de Hamil) *The Becket Leaves,* British Library Publications, 1988.
*The Luttrell Psalter,* British Library Publications, 1989.
*The Bedford Hours,* British Library Publications, 1990.
*The Isabella Breviary,* British Library Publications, 1993.
(With Yves Giraud) *Pierre Sala's Petit Livre d'Amour,* Faksimile Verlag Luzern, 1994.
(With James H. Marrow and Gerhard Schmidt) *Biblia Pauperum,* Faksimile Verlag Luzern, 1994.
*The Lindisfarne Gospels: A Masterpiece of Book Painting,* British Library Publications, 1995.

Author, editor, or contributor to many exhibition catalogs. Also contributor of articles and reviews to scholarly journals, conference proceedings and newspapers.

\*    \*    \*

## BALLSTADT, Carl A.    1931-

*PERSONAL:* Born December 28, 1931, in Sault Ste. Marie, Ontario, Canada; son of Paul A. (a paper maker) and Hilda (Liedtke) Ballstadt; married Dorothy Copeland (a nurse), July 8, 1967; children: Kurt, Marnin (daughter). *Education:* University of Western Ontario, B.A., 1957, M.A., 1959; University of London, Ph.D., 1965. *Religion:* Lutheran.

*ADDRESSES: Office*—Department of English, McMaster University, 1280 Main St. W., Hamilton, Ontario, Canada L8S 4L9.

*CAREER:* Teacher at schools in Sault Ste. Marie, Ontario, 1953-60; University of Saskatchewan, Saskatoon, instructor, 1962-64, assistant professor of English, 1964-66; University of Guelph, Guelph, Ontario, assistant professor of English, 1966-76; McMaster University, Hamilton, Ontario, assistant professor, 1967-72, associate professor, 1972-85, professor of English, 1986—.

*MEMBER:* Bibliographical Society of Canada, Association for Canadian Studies.

*WRITINGS:*

*Major John Richardson: A Selection of Reviews and Criticism,* Lawrence M. Lande Foundation at McGill University (Montreal, Quebec, Canada), 1972.

*The Search for English-Canadian Literature,* University of Toronto Press (Buffalo, NY), 1975.

(Coauthor) *Catharine Parr Traill and Her Works,* ECW Press (Toronto, Ontario, Canada), 1983.

(Editor with Elizabeth Hopkins and Michael Peterman) *Susanna Moodie: Letters of a Lifetime,* University of Toronto Press, 1986.

(Editor) Susanna Moodie, *Roughing It in the Bush,* Carleton University Press, 1988.

*Letters of Love and Duty: The Correspondence of Susanna and John Moodie,* University of Toronto Press, 1993.

(Editor with Michael Peterman) *Forest and Other Gleanings: The Fugitive Writings of Catharine Parr Traill,* University of Ottawa Press (Ottawa, Ontario, Canada), 1994.

(Coauthor and editor with Hopkins and Peterman) *I Bless You in My Heart: Selected Correspondence of Catherine Parr Traill,* University of Toronto Press, 1996.

*SIDELIGHTS:* Carl A. Ballstadt told *CA:* "Canadian literature has 'come into its own' in the past two decades with the emergence of writers such as Margaret Atwood, Margaret Laurence, Alice Munro, and Timothy Findlay—writers whose work has commanded a good deal of attention in other parts of the world. But the work of these people often reflects their sense of a particular and fascinating Canadian past with which they can identify. Works by both Atwood and Laurence, for example, include a recognition of kindred spirits in Susanna Moodie and Catharine Parr Traill, two of our prominent nineteenth-century writers. And yet, there is still much that we do not know about Moodie and Traill. As is the case with so many early Canadian authors, their literature has been much considered while their letters have been ignored, at least until recently.

"My own scholarship has been devoted to establishing a better basis for knowing ourselves by understanding how our colonial ancestors felt about emerging nationhood and about the status of literature and other modes of cultural expression in a colony or a new nation. My work began with a broad study of early critical materials concerning the desire for and the nature of literature in the British American colonies and the Canadian Confederation. The main discovery of that survey was the high degree to which nineteenth-century observations of Canadian literature anticipated and were consistent with those made by our twentieth-century writers and critics with respect to such matters as moderation in nationalism, an eclectic outlook, our experience of 'northernness,' and our cultural relationships to Britain and the United States.

"One other concern of those early critics was the process of transition from Old World to New World culture. Moodie and Traill offer a rich basis for the examination of that transition—hence, my interest in their lives and writings along with those of other nineteenth-century figures. The process of transition continues to be a major theme in Canadian literature."

*BIOGRAPHICAL/CRITICAL SOURCES:*

*PERIODICALS*

*Globe and Mail* (Toronto), February 8, 1986.

\*     \*     \*

### BARBOUR, Douglas (Fleming) 1940-

*PERSONAL:* Born March 21, 1940, in Winnipeg, Manitoba, Canada; son of Harold Douglas (a fundraising executive) and Phyllis (Wilson) Barbour; married M. Sharon Nicoll, May 21, 1966. *Education:* Acadia University, B.A., 1962; Dalhousie University, M.A., 1964; Queen's University, Kingston, Ontario, Ph.D., 1976. *Politics:* "Anarchist (at heart)."

*ADDRESSES: Home*—11655 72nd Avenue, Edmonton, Alberta, Canada T6G 0B9. *Office*—Department of English, University of Alberta, Edmonton, Alberta, Canada T6G 2E5.

*CAREER:* Alderwood Collegiate Institute, Toronto, Ontario, teacher of English, 1968-69; University of Alberta, Edmonton, assistant professor, 1969-77, associate professor, 1977-82, professor of English, 1982—. Member of editorial board of NeWest Press and Longspoon Press, 1980-87.

*MEMBER:* Association of Canadian College and University Teachers of English, League of Canadian Poets (co-chair, 1972-74).

*WRITINGS:*

POETRY

*Land Fall,* Delta Books (Montreal), 1971.
*A Poem as Long as the Highway,* Quarry Press (Kingston), 1971.
*White,* Fiddlehead Books (Fredericton), 1972.
*Song Book,* Talonbooks (Vancouver), 1973.
*He. &. She. &.,* Golden Dog Press (Ottawa), 1974.
*Visions of My Grandfather,* Golden Dog Press, 1977.
*Shore Lines,* Turnstone Press (Winnipeg), 1979.
*Vision/Sounding,* League of Canadian Poets (Toronto), 1980.
(With Stephen Scobie) *The Pirates of Pen's Chance: Homolinguistic Translations,* Coach House Press (Toronto), 1981.
*The Harbingers,* Quarry Press, 1984.
*Visible Visions: The Selected Poems of Douglas Barbour,* NeWest Press (Edmonton), 1984.
*Story for a Saskatchewan Night,* RDC Press (Red Deer, Alberta), 1990.

EDITOR

*The Story So Far Five* (short stories), Coach House Press, 1978.
(And author of introduction) Robert Kroetsch, *The 'Crow' Journals,* NeWest Press, 1980.
(With Stephen Scobie) *The League of Canadian Poets,* League of Canadian Poets, 1980.
(With Scobie) *The Maple Laugh Forever: An Anthology of Canadian Comic Poetry,* Hurtig Press (Edmonton), 1981.
(With Marni Stanley) *Writing Right: New Poetry by Canadian Women,* Longspoon Press (Edmonton), 1982.

(And author of preface) *Three Times Five: Short Stories by Beverly Harris, Gloria Sawai, Fred Stenson,* NeWest Press, 1983.
(And author of introduction) Richard Sommer, *Selected and New Poems,* Vehicule Press (Montreal), 1983.
(With Phyllis Gotlieb) *Tesseracts 2: Canadian Science Fiction,* Porcepic Press (Victoria), 1987.
*Beyond Tish: New Writing, Interviews, Critical Essays,* NeWest Press, 1991.

CRITICISM

*Worlds Out of Words: The SF Novels of Samuel R. Delany,* Bran's Head Books (Frome, UK), 1978.
*Canadian Poetry Chronicle (1984),* Quarry Press, 1985.
*John Newlove and His Works,* ECW (Toronto), 1992.
*Daphne Marlatt and Her Works,* ECW, 1992.
*bpNichol and His Works,* ECW, 1992.
*Michael Ondaatje,* Twayne (New York City), 1993.

Author of "Canadian Poetry Chronicle," in *Dalhousie Review,* 1969-77, *West Coast Review,* 1977-82, and *Quarry,* 1983. Member of editorial board of *Quarry,* 1965-68, *White Pelican,* 1972-76, *Canadian Forum,* 1978-80, and *On-Spec,* 1990—.

*WORK IN PROGRESS:* Poetry.

*SIDELIGHTS:* Douglas Barbour told *CA:* "I share with those writers I most admire a sense of language as alive, as something which speaks out its own life rather than simply as a tool to be 'used'; the language shaped *by* desire gives shape *to* desire."

\*        \*        \*

**BARKER, Sebastian 1945-**

*PERSONAL:* Born April 16, 1945, in Gloucestershire, England; son of George Granville (an author) and Elizabeth (an author; maiden name, Smart) Barker; married Julie Rosalind Ellis, August 29, 1969 (divorced May 12, 1980); married Sally Louise Rouse (a teacher), March 29, 1986 (divorced, November 3, 1992); children: (first marriage) Chloe Therese Katherine, Miranda Rose Korinne Faith; (second marriage) Daniel Stathis, Xanthi Rafaella. *Education:* Corpus Christi College, Oxford, M.A.

(natural science), 1968; University of East Anglia, M.A. (English literature), 1970.

*ADDRESSES: Home and office*—22a Lawford Rd., London NW5 2LN, England.

*CAREER:* Writer. Writer-in-residence at South Hill Park Arts Centre, Stamford Arts Centre, Stamford College for Further Education, Grantham City Library, Spalding City Library, and Berkshire County Council, 1980-85; director or co-director of Bracknell Literature Festivals, Surrey Literature Festival, and Royal Berkshire Poetry Festival, 1980-85.

*MEMBER:* Poetry Society (general council, chair, 1988-92), Oxford Union (life member), English PEN (executive committee, 1990-93), Nietzsche Society of Great Britain (executive committee, 1990-95), English College Foundation in Prague (founder and director, 1990).

*AWARDS, HONORS:* Arts Council award, 1976; Ingram Merrill Foundation award, 1988; Royal Literary Fund award, 1993.

*WRITINGS:*

POETRY EXCEPT AS NOTED

*Poems,* Cygnet Press (Oxford, England), 1974.
*The Dragon,* Quill Books (Harlington, TX), 1976.
*On the Rocks,* Martin Brian & O'Keeffe (London), 1977.
*Who Is Eddie Linden?* (documentary novel), Jay Landesman (London), 1979.
*Epistles,* Martin Brian & O'Keeffe, 1980.
*A Fire in the Rain,* Martin Brian & O'Keeffe, 1982.
*A Nuclear Epiphany,* Friday Night Fish Publications, 1984.
*Boom,* Free Man's Press Editions, 1985.
(Editor) Christopher Barker, *Portraits of Poets* (poetry and photography), Carcanet Press (Manchester), 1986.
*The Dream of Intelligence,* Littlewood Arc, 1992.
*Guarding the Border: Selected Poems,* Enitharmon Press (London), 1992.
*The Hand in the Well,* Enitharmon Press, 1996.

*WORK IN PROGRESS: The Animated Dynamo* (poetry); *Between the Establishment and Vision* (prose on poetry and philosophy).

*SIDELIGHTS:* Sebastian Barker told *CA:* "When I first wrote to *CA,* I was in the middle of what turned out to be a seven year project to write a poem which used the life and works of Friedrich Nietzsche as its starting material. As a 'work in progress,' the poem was called *The Autobiography of a Philosopher.* Its published title was *The Dream of Intelligence.* I was published at the Brighton Festival in 1992. Readings from it have taken place at philosophy faculties in universities, international philosophy conferences, schools, arts centres, public reading venues, and the like. It was voted a Book of the Year in *The Spectator* and *The Independent* and was a key factor in the founding of the Long Poem group in Great Britain. Essentially dramatic in conception, it reaches back to the roots of tragedy in 6th century B.C. Greece. But it may also be described as a Christian tragedy, a notion which George Steiner has thought of as a contradiction in terms. Such a notion undersells Christianity. I believe Christian theology by no means bars its gates to tragedy. In short, like Greek dramatic tradition, which is Dionysian, and the Western Christian dramatic tradition, which reaches from the 9th century A.D. and is liturgical, meet in the Enlightenment age especially, most noticeable in Shakespeare. Such a dual inheritance, rightly understood, does possess, I maintain, the possibility of Christian tragedy. The implications of this are to say the least far-reaching. It is the aim of my future writings to explore some of them."

\*    \*    \*

**BARNARD, Robert    1936-**
**(Bernard Bastable)**

*PERSONAL:* Born November 23, 1936, in Burnham-on-Crouch, Essex, England; son of Leslie (a writer) and Vera (Nethercoat) Barnard; married Mary Louise Tabor (a librarian), February 7, 1963. *Education:* Balliol College, Oxford, B.A. (with honors), 1959; University of Bergen, Ph.D., 1972. *Politics:* "Vaguely left-wing."

*ADDRESSES: Home and office*—Hazeldene, Houghley Lane, Leeds LS13 2DT, England.

*CAREER:* University of New England, New South Wales, Australia, lecturer in English, 1961-66; University of Bergen, Bergen, Norway, lecturer, later senior lecturer in English, 1966-76; University of Tromsoe, Tromsoe, Norway, professor of English literature, 1976-83; full-time writer, 1983—.

*MEMBER:* Dickens Fellowship, Bronte Society (chair, 1996—), Society of Authors, Crime Writers Association (committee member, 1988-91).

*AWARDS, HONORS:* Edgar Award nomination for best novel, 1981, for *Death of a Literary Widow,* for best critical study, 1981, for *A Talent to Deceive: An Appreciation of Agatha Christie,* and five others, all from Mystery Writers of America.

*WRITINGS:*

MYSTERY NOVELS

*Death of an Old Goat,* Collins (London), 1974, Walker & Co. (New York City), 1977.
*A Little Local Murder,* Collins, 1976, Scribner (New York City), 1983.
*Blood Brotherhood,* Collins, 1977, Walker & Co., 1978.
*Death on the High C's,* Collins, 1977, Walker & Co., 1978.
*Unruly Son,* Collins, 1978, also published as *Death of a Mystery Writer* (also see below), Scribner, 1979.
*Posthumous Papers,* Collins, 1979, also published as *Death of a Literary Widow,* Scribner, 1980.
*Death in a Cold Climate* (also see below), Collins, 1980, Scribner, 1981.
*Death of a Perfect Mother* (also see below), Scribner, 1981, published in England as *Mother's Boys,* Collins, 1981.
*Sheer Torture,* Collins, 1981, also published as *Death by Sheer Torture* (also see below), Scribner, 1982.
*Death and the Princess,* Collins, 1982, Scribner, 1982.
*The Case of the Missing Bronte,* Scribner, 1983, published in England as *The Missing Bronte,* Collins, 1983.
*Little Victims,* Collins, 1983, also published as *School for Murder,* Scribner, 1984.
*Corpse in a Gilded Cage,* Scribner, 1984, published in England as *A Corpse in a Gilded Cage,* Collins, 1984.
*Out of the Blackout,* Collins, 1985, Scribner, 1985.
*Faete Fatale,* Scribner, 1985, published in England as *Disposal of the Living,* Collins, 1985.
*Political Suicide,* Collins, 1986, Scribner, 1986.
*Bodies,* Collins, 1986, Scribner, 1986.
*The Cherry Blossom Corpse,* Scribner, 1987, published in England as *Death in Purple Prose,* Collins, 1987.

*The Skeleton in the Grass,* Collins, 1987, Scribner, 1988.
*At Death's Door,* Collins, 1988, Scribner, 1988.
*Death and the Chaste Apprentice,* Collins, 1989, Scribner, 1989.
*A City of Strangers,* Bantam (London), 1990, Scribner, 1990.
*A Scandal in Belgravia,* Bantam, 1991, Scribner, 1991.
*A Fatal Attachment,* Bantam, 1992, Scribner, 1992.
*Four Complete Mysteries* (contains *Death by Sheer Torture, Death of a Perfect Mother, Death in a Cold Climate,* and *Death of a Mystery Writer*), Wings Books (New York City), 1993.
*A Hovering of Vultures,* Bantam, 1993, Scribner, 1993.
*The Masters of the House,* HarperCollins (Scranton, PA), 1994, Scribner, 1994.
*The Bad Samaritan: A Novel of Suspense Featuring Charlie Peace,* HarperCollins, 1995, Scribner, 1995.

MYSTERY NOVELS; UNDER NAME BERNARD BASTABLE

*To Die Like a Gentleman,* Macmillan (London), 1993, St. Martin's Press (New York City), 1993.
*Dead, Mr. Mozart,* Little, Brown (Boston), 1995, St. Martin's Press, 1995.
*Too Many Notes, Mr. Mozart,* Little, Brown, 1995, Carroll and Graf (New York City), 1996.

OTHER

*Imagery and Theme in the Novels of Dickens,* Universitetsforlag (Oslo, Norway), 1974.
*A Talent to Deceive: An Appreciation of Agatha Christie,* Collins, 1980, Dodd (New York City), 1980.
(Author of introduction) Agatha Christie, *The Best of Poirot,* Collins, 1980.
(Contributor) H. R. F. Keating, editor, *Whodunit,* Windward, 1982.
*A Short History of English Literature,* Basil Blackwell (London and Cambridge, MA), 1984.
(Contributor) Dilys Winn, editor, *Murder Ink,* revised edition, Workman Publishing (New York City), 1984.
*Death of a Salesperson, and Other Untimely Exits* (short stories), Scribner, 1989.
*The Habit of Widowhood, and Other Murderous Proclivities,* HarperCollins, 1996, Scribner, 1996.

Contributor of short stories to *Alfred Hitchcock's Mystery Magazine* and *Ellery Queen's Mystery Maga-*

*zine;* contributor of articles to *Books and Bookmen, London Magazine, Armchair Detective,* and *Times Literary Supplement.*

*SIDELIGHTS:* Drawing from his knowledge of English society and his teaching experience in Australia's "down under" and Norway's "land of the midnight sun," Robert Barnard has been able to establish himself as an innovative figure among British mystery writers. Newgate Callendar of *New York Times Book Review* calls him "one of the deftest stylists in the field (and out)." "[His] books are maliciously funny, closely plotted, acutely observed, and genuinely puzzling," writes Robin Winks in *New Republic.* But *Newsweek*'s Peter S. Prescott suggests that "if the puzzle were what mattered in Robert Barnard's mysteries, few would read them. Barnard's success lies in his wit, his social satire and his deftly drawn characters."

Well-drawn though they may be, Barnard's characters are not known for their pleasantness. As Maude McDaniel notes in *Washington Post,* his "gift for satire is so biting that, except for protagonists, he has trouble turning out really likable characters." For instance, *A City of Strangers* introduces what *New York Times Book Review* contributor Josh Rubins calls "Mr. Barnard's most exuberantly nasty corpse-to-be thus far." The author explains in a *Contemporary Authors* interview with Jean W. Ross: "All my characters are pretty awful in one way or another, partly because they are suspects in a murder investigation and I don't really believe that nice people are potential committers of murder."

Barnard uses the act of murder as the focal incident in his novels, but as Jean M. White writes in the *Washington Post Book World,* he "has never allowed murder—however well-planned and executed—to interfere with his fun as a playfully irreverent observer of the human scene." He has investigated the nature of Australian academia in *Death of an Old Goat,* the opera in *Death on the High C's,* and various facets of the literary world in a number of other books. *A Little Local Murder,* Callendar notes, is "a comedy of manners that looks back to Jane Austen and Trollope." "[In] *Blood Brotherhood,* [the author] accomplished two things: he wrote a good mystery and also exposed, gently but surely, the hypocrisies and the human frailties of modern churchmen," observes White in another *Washington Post Book World* article. Barnard also casts a cold eye on English society, one equally critical of the working class, middle classes, aristocracy, and royalty.

Though keeping to the same genre, Barnard manages to vary the setting and focus of each of his novels to investigate a new slice of life, and he adds new twists to his murder cases. *The Bad Samaritan* is set in a traditional English parish but the featured detective is a black man, Charlie Peace. The setting of *Death and the Chaste Apprentice* is a modern London suburb, but the plot centers on the performance of an Elizabethan drama (devised by Barnard for the novel). *Death in Purple Prose* (published in the United States as *The Cherry Blossom Corpse*) is set at a romance novelists' convention in Bergen, Norway. *The Skeleton in the Grass* takes place during the Spanish Civil War and looks at the question of Socialism. "Barnard has produced a most beautifully crafted novel composed in a yearning elegiac style," writes Gerald Kaufman in *Listener* about *The Skeleton in the Grass,* "which at the same time is sharply acute on the subjects of arrogance and snobbery." "He plots a mystery as well as any other writer alive," observes a *Time* reviewer, "and he never takes the easy path of repeating a winning formula."

Barnard's versatility is one aspect of his writing on which many reviewers have commented. David Walton writes about *The Bad Samaritan* in *New York Times Book Review* article, expounding on Barnard's "keen social satire and ear for dialogue." *Christian Science Monitor* contributor Michele Ross assesses *A City of Strangers,* suggesting that "Its strength and appeal lie in Barnard's depiction of human nature at its best, worst, and most indifferent. He takes what would normally be stock characters and turns them into people we recognize." She concludes by calling the book "a thought-provoking morality tale." "It is . . . a sign of Barnard's skill," declares *Listener* critic Gerald Kaufman in a review of *Death in Purple Prose,* "that his wry comments on the diuretic effect of costly Norwegian liquor are an important clue in a whodunnit which, if only the motive for murder were more convincing, would be one of this excellent author's best-crafted plots." "In one sense," states John Gross in *New York Times,* "Mr. Barnard is thoroughly contemporary—in his settings, his topical references, his whole tone. But he is also a traditionalist, constructing puzzles in the spirit of Agatha Christie . . . and, in a number of stories, playing with literary themes in the spirit of a Michael Innes or an Edmund Crispin."

In *Out of the Blackout,* Barnard weaves a different, more serious kind of mystery. The novel begins in 1941 in war-torn England. A train full of children fleeing the London blitz arrives in a small rural town. With them is one child who is able to give few details about his home and family. He is adopted and embarks on a new life, but memories haunt him as he grows. As an adult, he becomes obsessed by the mystery that is his past, and he sets out to recover his life in wartime London. "For *Out of the Blackout,* I did a quite a bit of reading in '30s history in Britain," Barnard tells Ross, "the history of the fashions, the history of people who were interned during the Second World War as possible enemies. But it was on a subject that already interested me and that I already felt I knew something about. The reading was just to back up the book on specific points."

Although the author may have ventured into new territory in choosing his historical setting, John Gross of the *New York Times* feels that "he shows himself as adept at capturing the flavor of a period (without recourse to obvious props) as he is at evoking the feel of a neighborhood or pinning down a social type." Carolyn See recommends the book in her *Los Angeles Times* review. She writes that she "learned a lot about the political climate of the prewar British under-class [and] gained the satisfaction of learning once again that right (often) triumphs over wrong, and intelligence is better than ignorance and stupid cruelty." Derrick Murdock of Toronto's *Globe and Mail* came away from *Out of the Blackout* with the conviction that "Barnard is an inventive, witty writer and skillful satirist, but without question this is the most original novel he has yet written, with an ending as totally satisfying as it is unexpected."

In addition to his mysteries, Barnard has written *A Talent to Deceive: An Appreciation of Agatha Christie,* "a long critical essay, in which Professor Barnard discusses the weaknesses and then the strengths of Agatha Christie's detective fiction," notes Janet Morgan in the *Times Literary Supplement.* "Mr Barnard's main thesis is that paradoxically, Agatha Christie's defects as a writer contributed to her success as a popular entertainer. . . . Even the stereotyped characterization, so far from detracting from the books, contributes to their universality," P. D. James explains in the London *Times.* In this study, adds James, "Christie's supreme skill, the talent to deceive, or rather, the tricks by which with gentle cunning, she seduces us into deceiving ourselves, are analysed by Mr Barnard with a crime-writer's perception." "It's the wonderful professionalism of her that I admire very much," Barnard tells Ross. "When it came to the moment when Crime Club was celebrating its fiftieth anniver-

sary, they were going to reprint a terrible old book about Christie. Finally, after various hints that I would like to write one, which were not taken up, I said, 'For God's sake, I'll write you one in three months or something.' They agreed immediately, and I did it."

Barnard's other nonfictional works include a study of Charles Dickens, who was a personal inspiration, and a history of English literature. "To me, Dickens is the Shakespeare of the novel," the author tells Ross, "and I'm always pinching things from him. I like his sharp, near-caricature style of characterization. To me Dickens is the writer in English who is closest to me, whom I love most, so inevitably he comes in into the books in one way or another. Every word lives in Dickens, even the terrible sentimental bits. He never writes dully, so that I think he makes one weigh up one's words and see that they have a vitality of their own." And the *Short History of English Literature?* "It's actually earning me money," Barnard confesses to Ross, "which is a rather delightful thing to happen. Usually with academic books you don't expect to earn money from them, just academic prestige and what you call tenure and all the rest of it. But this one has earned quite a decent amount of money so far, so I assume students are finding it useful or some colleges are plugging it."

*BIOGRAPHICAL/CRITICAL SOURCES:*

*PERIODICALS*

*Christian Science Monitor,* November 30, 1990, p. 14.
*Globe and Mail* (Toronto), April 6, 1985.
*Listener,* April 2, 1987, pp. 24-25; January 21, 1988, p. 24.
*Los Angeles Times,* July 25, 1985.
*New Republic,* February 7, 1981.
*Newsweek,* December 31, 1984; February 24, 1986.
*New York Times,* July 12, 1985; October 31, 1986; October 14, 1988, p. C29.
*New York Times Book Review,* November 22, 1981; February 6, 1983; May 8, 1983; March 25, 1984; December 22, 1985, p. 30; June 8, 1986; September 27, 1987, p. 27; October 15, 1989, p. 47; January 7, 1990, p. 29; October 14, 1990, pp. 38, 40; August 25, 1991, p. 23; October 22, 1995, p. 27.
*Publishers Weekly,* October 25, 1985; June 12, 1987, p. 75; November 17, 1989, p. 44.
*Time,* July 29, 1985.

*Times* (London), April 29, 1980.

*Times Literary Supplement,* February 27, 1981; October 9-15, 1987, p. 1124; July 22-28, 1988, p. 818; December 29, 1989, p. 1448; September 6, 1991, p. 22.

*Tribune Books* (Chicago), August 9, 1992, pp. 4-5.

*Washington Post,* August 5, 1983.

*Washington Post Book World,* November 19, 1978; October 19, 1980; April 19, 1981; January 19, 1986.

\*    \*    \*

### BARNES, Julian (Patrick) 1946-
### (Dan Kavanagh; Edward Pygge)

*PERSONAL:* Born January 19, 1946, in Leicester, England; son of Albert Leonard (a French teacher) and Kaye (a French teacher) Barnes; married Pat Kavanagh (a literary agent), 1979. *Education:* Magdalen College, Oxford, B.A. (with honors), 1968.

*ADDRESSES: Agent*—Peters, Fraser and Dunlop, The Chambers, Chelsea Harbour Rd., London SW10 0XF, England.

*CAREER:* Freelance writer, 1972—. Lexicographer for *Oxford English Dictionary Supplement,* Oxford, England, 1969-72; *New Statesman,* London, England, assistant literary editor, 1977-78, television critic, 1977-81; *Sunday Times,* London, deputy literary editor, 1979-81; *Observer,* London, television critic, 1982-86; London correspondent for *New Yorker* magazine, 1990-94.

*AWARDS, HONORS:* Somerset Maugham Prize, 1980, for *Metroland;* Booker Prize nomination, 1984, Geoffrey Faber Memorial Prize and Prix Medicis, all for *Flaubert's Parrot;* American Academy and Institute of Arts and Letters award, 1986, for work of distinction; Prix Gutembourg, 1987; Premio Grinzane Carour, 1988; Prix Femina for *Talking It Over,* 1992; Shakespeare Prize (Hamburg), 1993; Officier de l'Ordre des Arts et des Lettres.

*WRITINGS:*

NOVELS

*Metroland,* J. Cape (London), 1980, St. Martin's (New York City), 1981.

*Before She Met Me,* J. Cape, 1982, McGraw (New York City), 1986.

*Flaubert's Parrot,* J. Cape, 1984, Knopf (New York City), 1985.

*Question and Answer,* J. Cape, 1986.

*Staring at the Sun,* J. Cape, 1986, Knopf, 1987.

*A History of the World in 10 1/2 Chapters,* Knopf, 1989.

*Talking It Over,* Knopf, 1991.

*The Porcupine,* Knopf, 1992.

*Letters from London,* Vintage (New York City), 1995.

*Cross Channel,* Knopf, 1996.

UNDER PSEUDONYM DAN KAVANAGH; CRIME NOVELS

*Duffy,* J. Cape, 1980, Pantheon (New York City), 1986.

*Fiddle City,* J. Cape, 1981, Pantheon, 1986.

*Putting the Boot In,* J. Cape, 1985.

*Going to the Dogs,* Pantheon, 1987.

OTHER

Contributing editor, under pseudonym Edward Pygge, to *New Review* in the 1970s. Regular contributor to the *Times Literary Supplement* and the *New York Review of Books.*

*SIDELIGHTS:* "Julian Barnes," writes *Dictionary of Literary Biography* contributor Merritt Moseley, "is one of the most celebrated, and one of the most variously rewarding, of Britain's younger novelists." His work, the critic continues, "has been acclaimed by readers as different as Carlos Fuentes and Philip Larkin; reviewers and interviewers sum him up with praise such as Mark Lawson's claim that he 'writes like the teacher of your dreams: jokey, metaphorical across both popular and unpopular culture, epigrammatic.'" In addition to novels such as *Flaubert's Parrot* (nominated for the prestigious Booker Prize, Britain's highest literary award), *A History of the World in 10 1/2 Chapters* and *The Porcupine,* Barnes has also won a reputation as a writer of innovative detective fiction and an essayist. "Since 1990," Moseley concludes, "he has been the London correspondent of the *New Yorker* magazine, contributing 'Letters from London' every few months on subjects such as the royal family and the quirkier side of British politics."

Barnes published four novels, *Metroland, Before She Met Me,* and the detective novels *Duffy* and *Fiddle City* (both written under the pseudonym Dan

Kavanagh) before he completed *Flaubert's Parrot,* his first great success. Critics acclaim these early books for their comic sensibility and witty language. *Metroland* tells the story of two young men who "adopt the motto *epater la bourgeoisie,*" explains *New Statesman* contributor Nicholas Shrimpton. "But this grandiose ambition is promptly reduced to the level of 'epats,' a thoroughly English field-sport in which the competitors attempt to shock respectable citizens for bets of sixpence a time." "After this vision of the Decadence in short trousers," the reviewer concludes, "it is hard to take the idea of outrage too solemnly." *Before She Met Me* is the tale of an older man who falls into an obsession about his actress wife's former screen lovers. The book, states Anthony Thwaite in the *Observer,* presents an "elegantly hardboiled treatment of the nastier levels of obsession, full of controlled jokes when almost everything else has got out of control."

Barnes's detective fiction also looks at times and characters for whom life has gotten out of control. The title character of *Duffy* is a bisexual former policeman who was blackmailed out of his job. "The thrillers are active, louche, violent, thoroughly plotted," states Moseley. "*Duffy* shows the result of serious research into the seamy world of London's sex industry; in *Duffy,* as in its successors, the crime tends to be theft or fraud rather than murder, though Barnes successfully imbues the book with a feeling of menace." *Fiddle City,* for instance, takes place at London's Heathrow airport and looks at the smuggling of drugs and other illegal items.

It was with the publication of *Flaubert's Parrot,* though, that Barnes scored his greatest success to date. The novel tells of Geoffrey Braithwaite, a retired English doctor, and his obsession with the great French novelist Gustave Flaubert. After his wife's somewhat mysterious death, Braithwaite travels to France in search of trivia concerning Flaubert; his chief aim is to find the stuffed parrot that the writer kept on his desk for inspiration while writing *Un Coeur Simple,* the story of a peasant woman's devotion to her pet. Barnes "uses Braithwaite's investigations to reflect on the ambiguous truths of biography, the relationship of art and life, the impact of death, the consolations of literature," explains Michael Dirda in the *Washington Post Book World.*

Far from a straightforward narrative, *Flaubert's Parrot* blends fiction, literary criticism, and biography in a manner strongly reminiscent of Vladimir Nabokov's *Pale Fire,* according to many critics.

*Newsweek* reviewer Gene Lyons calls it "too involuted by half for readers accustomed to grazing contentedly in the best-seller list," but recommends it to readers "of immoderate literary passions." Other reviewers stress that, while a complex and intellectual work, *Flaubert's Parrot* is also "endlessly fascinating and very funny," in the words of London *Times* contributor Annabel Edwards. Dirda concludes that this "delicious potpourri of quotations, legends, facts, fantasies, and interpretations of Flaubert and his work . . . might seem dry, but Barnes' style and Braithwaite's autumnal wisdom make the novel into a kind of Stoic comedy. . . . Anyone who reads *Flaubert's Parrot* will learn a good deal about Flaubert, the making of fiction, and the complex tangle of art and life. And—not least important—have a lot of rather peculiar fun too."

Of Barnes's later works, *A History of the World in 10 1/2 Chapters* and *The Porcupine* are probably best known to American readers. "*A History of the World in 10 1/2 Chapters* builds on Barnes's reputation as one of Britain's premier postmodernists," states *Village Voice Literary Supplement* contributor Rob Nixon. "The anti-novel that emerges attempts to double as a novel of ideas—never Brit lit's forte. . . . The principal concern of the novel, which begins with corruption on the Ark and ends in the tedium of heaven (pretty much like life with lots of shopping), is to debunk religion and that most seductive of theologies, History." Barnes conceives of history in the book as a series of different, mostly unrelated events, and the connections we ourselves invent to link them together. "One of Barnes's characters rather improbably describes her supposed mental condition—imagining that she has survived a nuclear disaster, which, as it turns out, she has—as 'Fabulation. You keep a few true facts and spin a new story about them,'" declares Frank Kermode in the *London Review of Books.* "This is what Barnes himself, in this book, attempts. He fabulates this and that, stitches the fabulations together, and then he and we quite properly call the product a novel." "As a 'historian,'" states Anthony Quinn in the *New Statesman and Society,* "he is unlikely to dislodge Gibbon or Macaulay; but as satirist and story-teller he has few equals at present."

*The Porcupine* is a short novel set in a fictional Eastern European country in the post-Communist era. "Stoyo Petkanov, the former president, a cross between [former Rumanian premier] Nicolae Ceaucescu and Bulgaria's Georgi Dimitrov," explains *New York Times Book Review* contributor

Robert Stone, "is on trial in the courts of the shakily democratic successor government." His prosecutor is Peter Solinsky, born into a family prominent under the Communists. Solinsky is shaken by Petkanov's sincere belief in the principles of Communism. Contrasting them with the poverty and lack of respect that the reforms have brought, Solinsky begins to turn away from his new democratic ideals. "In the end," Mary Warner Marien declares in the *Christian Science Monitor,* "nothing is resolved except a clearer vision of the stupendous obstacles facing the former communist country." "Admirers of the earlier, Francophile Julian Barnes may regret that in his latest work . . . the author of *Flaubert's Parrot* and *Talking It Over* has shed his brilliance and dandyism to become a rather sombre recorder of his times," states *London Review of Books* contributor Patrick Parrinder. "The greyness seems inherent in his subject-matter, but it has not infected his acute and spiny prose."

*BIOGRAPHICAL/CRITICAL SOURCES:*

BOOKS

*Contemporary Literary Criticism,* Volume 42, Gale (Detroit), 1987.
*Dictionary of Literary Biography Yearbook: 1993,* Gale, 1994.
Moseley, Merritt, *Understanding Julian Barnes,* University of South Carolina Press (Columbia), 1996.

PERIODICALS

*Booklist,* July, 1995, p. 1856.
*Chicago Tribune,* January 3, 1993, p. 3.
*Christian Science Monitor,* January 20, 1993, p. 13.
*Commonweal,* May 8, 1992, pp. 22-24.
*Independent,* July 13, 1991, pp. 34-36.
*Journal of Literature and Theology,* June, 1991, pp. 220-232.
*Library Journal,* March 15, 1996, p. 98.
*London Review of Books,* June 22, 1989, p. 20; February 11, 1993, pp. 18-19.
*Los Angeles Time Book Review,* March 17, 1985; November 8, 1992, p. 3.
*New Statesman,* March 28, 1980, p. 483.
*New Statesman & Society,* June 23, 1989, p. 38; November 13, 1992, pp. 34-35; January 16, 1996, pp. 39-40.
*Newsweek,* April 29, 1985.
*New York Times,* February 28, 1985; March 30, 1987, p. C16; July 5, 1990, pp. C11, C15; April 16, 1996, p. B2.

*New York Times Book Review,* March 10, 1985; December 13, 1992, p. 3.
*New York Times Magazine,* November 22, 1992, pp. 29, 68-72, 80.
*Observer* (London), April 18, 1982, p. 31; July 7, 1991, pp.25-26.
*Publishers Weekly,* November 3, 1989, pp. 73-74; February 19, 1996, p. 204.
*Salon* (Internet magazine), Issue 15, May 13-17, 1996.
*Sunday Times* (London), June 18, 1989, p. G9.
*Time,* April 8, 1985.
*Times* (London), March 21, 1980; October 4, 1984; November 7, 1985.
*Times Literary Supplement,* March 28, 1980; April 23, 1982; January 6, 1984, pp. 4214-4215; October 5, 1984, p. 1117.
*Village Voice Literary Supplement,* November, 1989, p. 5.
*Wall Street Journal,* December 11, 1992, p. A10.
*Washington Post Book World,* March 3, 1985; November 15, 1992.
*Yale Review,* summer, 1988, pp. 478-491.

\* \* \*

**BARON, Dennis E(mery)    1944-**

*PERSONAL:* Born May 9, 1944, in New York, NY; son of R. C. Roy (a historian) and Sylvia (a teacher; maiden name, Mayer) Baron; married Iryce White (a teacher), October, 1979; children: Cordelia, Rachel, Jonathan. *Education:* Brandeis University, B.A., 1965; Columbia University, M.A., 1968; University of Michigan, Ph.D., 1971.

*ADDRESSES: Home*—Urbana, IL. *Office*—Department of English, University of Illinois, 608 South Wright St., Urbana, IL 61801.

*CAREER:* Eastern Illinois University, Charleston, IL, assistant professor of English, 1971-73; City College of the City University of New York, New York City, assistant professor of English, 1973-74; University of Illinois, Urbana, assistant professor, 1975-81, associate professor, 1981-84, professor of English and linguistics, 1984—, director of rhetoric, 1985—. Fulbright lecturer at Universite de Poitiers, France, 1978-79; member of Conference on College Composition and Communication.

*MEMBER:* American Dialect Society, Modern Language Association of America, National Council of Teachers of English, Linguistic Society of America.

*AWARDS, HONORS:* National Endowment for the Humanities fellow, 1989.

*WRITINGS:*

*Case Grammar and Diachronic English Syntax,* Mouton (Hawthorne, NY), 1974.

*Going Native: The Regeneration of Saxon English* (monograph), University of Alabama Press (University), 1982.

*Grammar and Good Taste: Reforming the American Language,* Yale University Press (New Haven, CT), 1982.

*Grammar and Gender,* Yale University Press, 1986.

*Declining Grammar and Other Essays on the English Vocabulary,* National Council of Teachers of English (Urbana, IL), 1989.

*The English-Only Question: An Official Language for Americans?,* Yale University Press, 1990.

*Guide to Home Language Repair,* National Council of Teachers of English, 1994.

Contributor of articles to language and linguistics journals, including *American Speech, English Today, College English, Journal of Literary Semantics, Language Problems and Language Planning, Journal of Popular Culture, Verbatim, Righting Words,* and *Language and Style.* Associate editor of *Publications of the American Dialect Society,* 1982-85, editor, 1985-93.

*WORK IN PROGRESS: The First Draft: A Book for College Writers;* and *The Literacy Complex.*

*SIDELIGHTS:* Dennis E. Baron, professor of English and Linguistics at the University of Illinois, Urbana, writes not only history and guidebooks for the college student of English, but also of contemporary issues that deal with the present and future of the English language. As Baron told *CA:* "I'm interested in how people's attitudes toward language affect their linguistic production. I also write about language reform movements and their interesting and unpredictable effects on the course of language."

Stuart B. Flexner writes in the *New York Times Book Review* that Baron's *Grammar and Good Taste: Reforming the American Language* is a "well-researched, . . . excellent and useful dissertation" on the history of American English. According to Ed-

ward B. White in the *Los Angeles Times Book Review,* Baron has written a "sensible and careful book . . . a wonderfully amusing collection of oddities, testimony to the vanity, pedantry and earnestness of those who seek to hold back or make more rational the tides of language." Both reviewers further express that the crucial chapters of *Grammar and Good Taste* are those devoted to the movements for a federal English and other reform efforts present in the United States since the eighteenth century.

Baron further told *CA:* "I am interested in a variety of topics dealing with the history of the English language, literacy, the question of sexism and language, attitudes toward language use, the movement to make English the official language of the United States, and attempts to change language. My audience is the general educated reader, as well as the language specialist, and I talk about the English language frequently on WILL-Radio, the central Illinois National Public Radio affiliate. My graduate training is in medieval English language and literature, and I have developed a subsidiary interest in detective fiction, trying my hand at writing a novel and children's books. My cartoons have appeared in a number of journals and newsletters."

*BIOGRAPHICAL/CRITICAL SOURCES:*

*PERIODICALS*

*American Library Book Review,* October, 1994, p. 12.

*American Political Science Review,* June, 1991, p. 636.

*Bookwatch,* February, 1991, p. 6.

*Choice,* March, 1991, p. 1126.

*Journal of English and Germanic Philology,* April, 1989, p. 211.

*Los Angeles Times Book Review,* March 6, 1983.

*Modern Language Journal,* winter, 1993, p. 556.

*New York Times Book Review,* November 28, 1982.

*Psychology Today,* August, 1986.

*Signs: Journal of Women in Culture and Society,* spring, 1988, p. 600.

*Times Literary Supplement,* July 4, 1986; May 31, 1991, p. 8.

\*     \*     \*

**BASTABLE, Bernard**
**See BARNARD, Robert**

## BAWDEN, Nina (Mary Mabey) 1925-
### (Nina Mary (Mabey) Kark)

*PERSONAL:* Born January 19, 1925, in London, England; daughter of Charles and Ellalaine Ursula May (Cushing) Mabey; married H. W. Bawden (divorced); married Austen Steven Kark (an executive for British Broadcasting Corporation), 1954; children: (first marriage) Nicholas Bawden (deceased), Robert Humphrey Felix Bawden; (second marriage) Perdita Emily Helena Kark. *Education:* Somerville College, Oxford, B.A., 1946, M.A., 1951; additional graduate study at Salzburg Seminar in American Studies, 1960. *Avocational interests:* Traveling, reading.

*ADDRESSES: Home*—22 Noel Rd., London N1 8HA, England. *Agent*—Curtis Brown Ltd., 575 Madison Ave., New York, NY 10022; fax 1071-359-7103.

*CAREER:* Writer. Assistant, Town and Country Planning Associates, 1946-47; Justice of the Peace, Surrey, England, 1968-76.

*MEMBER:* PEN, Royal Society of Literature (fellow), Society of Women Writers and Journalists (president), Authors Lending and Copyright Society, Lansdowne, Ski Club of Great Britain.

*AWARDS, HONORS: Guardian* Award for Children's Fiction, 1975, for *The Peppermint Pig; Yorkshire Post* Novel of the Year Award, 1977, for *Afternoon of a Good Woman;* Booker Prize nomination, 1987, for *Circles of Deceit;* Phoenix Award from Children's Literature Association of North America, 1993, for *Carrie's War;* United Kingdom nominee for International Board of Books for Young Children Hans Andersen Award, 1996; *Granny the Pag* part of British nominee shortlist for Carnegie Medal, 1996.

*WRITINGS:*

*Eyes of Green,* Morrow (New York City), 1953, published in England as *Who Calls the Tune,* Collins (London), 1953.
*The Odd Flamingo,* Collins, 1954.
*Change Here for Babylon,* Collins, 1955.
*The Solitary Child,* Collins, 1956.
*Devil by the Sea,* Collins, 1957, abridged edition for children, Lippincott (Philadelphia, PA), 1976.
*Glass Slippers Always Pinch,* Lippincott, 1960, published in England as *Just Like a Lady,* Longmans, Green (London), 1960.

*In Honour Bound,* Longmans, Green, 1961.
*Tortoise by Candlelight,* Harper (New York City), 1963.
*Under the Skin,* Harper, 1964.
*A Little Love, a Little Learning,* Longmans, Green, 1965.
*A Woman of My Age,* Harper, 1967.
*The Grain of Truth,* Harper, 1968.
*The Birds on the Trees,* Longmans, Green, 1970.
*Anna Apparent,* Harper, 1972.
*George beneath a Paper Moon,* Harper, 1974.
*Afternoon of a Good Woman,* Harper, 1976.
*Familiar Passions,* Morrow (New York City), 1979.
*Walking Naked,* St. Martin's (New York City), 1981.
*The Ice House,* St. Martin's, 1983.
*Circles of Deceit,* St. Martin's, 1987.
*Family Money,* St. Martin's, 1991.
*In My Own Time: Almost an Autobiography,* Clarion (New York City), 1994.

*JUVENILE*

*The Secret Passage,* Gollancz (London), 1963, also published as *The House of Secrets,* Lippincott, 1964.
*On the Run,* Gollancz, 1964, also published as *Three on the Run,* Lippincott, 1965.
*The White Horse Gang,* Lippincott, 1966.
*The Witch's Daughter,* Lippincott, 1966.
*A Handful of Thieves,* Lippincott, 1967.
*The Runaway Summer,* Lippincott, 1969.
*Squib,* Lippincott, 1971.
*Carrie's War,* Lippincott, 1973.
*The Peppermint Pig,* Lippincott, 1975.
*Rebel on a Rock,* Lippincott, 1978.
*The Robbers,* Lothrop (New York City), 1979.
(Adapter) *William Tell,* illustrated by Pascale Allamand, Lothrop, 1981.
*Kept in the Dark,* Lothrop, 1982.
*St. Francis of Assisi* (nonfiction), Lothrop, 1983.
*The Finding,* Lothrop, 1985.
*Princess Alice,* Deutsch (London), 1985.
*Henry,* Lothrop, 1988, published in England as *Keeping Henry,* Gollancz, 1988.
*The Outside Child,* Gollancz, 1989.
*Humbug,* Houghton, 1992.
*The Real Plato Jones,* Houghton, 1993.
*Granny the Pag,* Clarion, 1996.

*OTHER*

Contributor to newspapers, including *Evening Standard* and *Daily Telegraph.*

*ADAPTATIONS:* Many of Bawden's children's stories have been adapted for television, including *Carrie's War,* broadcast in the United States on PBS-TV; *Circles of Deceit* was made into a BBC film; *Family Money* is in production as a four-part television serial, to be broadcast in 1997.

*WORK IN PROGRESS:* Novel, *A Nice Change.*

*SIDELIGHTS:* Author of numerous novels for both children and adults, "Nina Bawden is perhaps best known for her incisive satirical inquiry into the family relationships of the educated middle class," notes Gerda Seaman in a *Dictionary of Literary Biography* essay. Since beginning her career with less well-known mystery, gothic, and horror stories, Bawden "has moved toward the psychological investigation of modern middle-class existence," continues Seaman. "With an urbane irony and often surprising violence, she exposes the uneasy alliances which keep chaos at bay and provides a circumstantial account of the domesticated brutality at the heart of modern life."

In *The Ice House,* for example, Bawden introduces Daisy Brown and Ruth Perkins, two women who have been close friends since childhood. When Daisy's husband is killed in an accident, Ruth comes to realize that her friend's marriage was not as happy as it appeared. Indeed, Ruth finds her own marriage in jeopardy upon discovering her husband's longtime affair. *Washington Post* contributor Elizabeth Ward finds Bawden's use of this situation ironic: "What [the death] catalyzes is not, as one might expect, the unraveling of Ruth's and Daisy's secure family lives. It is the gradual realization of both families that their lives were pretty unraveled already, shredded by false expectations, misplaced trust and betrayal." In addition, the author's portrayal of Ruth's increasingly perplexing search to discover and oust her husband's mistress leads Ward to comment that "it is impossible not to admire the ease with which Bawden manipulates the intricate elements of her plot."

Bawden creates a similarly tangled group of misleading relationships in *Circles of Deceit,* a novel which was nominated for the prestigious Booker Prize. The story is narrated by an artist who, appropriately, paints fine copies of the Old Masters; his first wife betrayed him by having an affair, while his second wife is hiding the abuse of her own son. "Ms. Bawden makes comic use of these characters' foibles, but there is considerable sadness beneath her evocative scenes and lively dialogue," observes Laurel Graeber in *New York Times Book Review.* In

showing the characters's lies and deceptions, the author also reveals the distress they cause themselves. As Jennifer McKay states in the *Listener,* "emotional pain is something Bawden portrays well, perhaps because she knows it is as likely to show itself in banal words and actions as in heroics." Although the pace of the book is slow, Graeber remarks that Bawden "makes the reader care about these people's trials. However much her characters deceive," concludes Graeber, "it's refreshing to see that Nina Bawden's own talent is nothing less than genuine."

Bawden has also written many novels for young adults, and in them "we see a real world," asserts Nicholas Tucker in *Children's Literature in Education;* a world "stretching from junk yards to prim, over-immaculate front parlours. Yet it would be facile to place this author in any simple 'social realist' category, since at the same time she is also taken up with the theme of fantasy, both in her characters' lives and in the stories themselves as she writes them." Tucker explains: "The result, then, is neither fantasy nor realism, but the tension between them."

*Carrie's War* is perhaps Bawden's best known children's novel, relating the evacuation of a young girl and her brother to a bleak Welsh mining town during World War II. A *Times Literary Supplement* reviewer observes that while Bawden's work has been "immensely readable and accessible yet often thought-provoking," *Carrie's War* is "altogether more moving, richer and stranger than anything she has achieved before. If it is not partly autobiographical, it certainly feels as if it is." "Miss Bawden has written outstanding books," maintains Catherine Storr in her *New Statesman* review. "It's because she writes with compassion and with insight and above all with honesty." Similarly, Bawden's *Henry,* a story again set on a Welsh farm during the War, recalls autobiography. Deborah Singmaster writes in the *Times Literary Supplement* that the story is "so artfully remembered and retold that it will charm both children and adults alike."

"All Nina Bawden's books have a definite quality," says Tucker; "the humour is abundant and never forced, and there are always moments of great pace and excitement." Seaman concludes, "to read [Bawden's] work is to encounter a writer of great integrity. . . . Her clear-eyed satiric studies of men, women, and children have always probed the hypocritical motive and the mechanical response. Most recently they have also offered us honest alternatives."

*BIOGRAPHICAL/CRITICAL SOURCES:*

*BOOKS*

*Children's Literature Review,* Volume 2, Gale (Detroit), 1976.
*Dictionary of Literary Biography,* Volume 14: *British Novelists since 1960,* Gale, 1982.
*Something about the Author Autobiography Series,* Volume 16, Gale, 1993.

*PERIODICALS*

*Booklist,* October 1, 1992, p. 328.
*Children's Literature in Education,* number 13, 1974.
*Horn Book Magazine,* May, 1988, p. 349; January, 1990, p. 61; March, 1990, p. 231; March, 1993, pp. 206, 231; March, 1994, p. 197.
*Kirkus Reviews,* July 15, 1992, p. 918.
*Listener,* September 10, 1987.
*New Statesman,* May 25, 1973.
*Newsweek,* August 29, 1983.
*New Yorker,* February 24, 1992, p. 102.
*New York Times Book Review,* June 3, 1973; November 29, 1987.
*Times* (London), July 14, 1983.
*Times Educational Supplement,* May 15, 1992, p. 11.
*Times Literary Supplement,* April 6, 1973; April 17, 1981; July 22, 1983; July 17, 1987; June 24, 1988; April 19, 1991, p. 21.
*Washington Post,* August 29, 1983.

\*    \*    \*

**BELL, Madison Smartt   1957-**

*PERSONAL:* Born August 1, 1957, in Nashville, TN; son of Henry Denmark (an attorney) and Allen (a farmer; maiden name, Wigginton) Bell; married Elizabeth Spires (a poet), June 15, 1985. *Education:* Princeton University, B.A. (summa cum laude), 1979; Hollins College, M.A., 1981.

*ADDRESSES: Office*—Department of English, Goucher College, Towson, MD 21204.

*CAREER:* Security guard at Unique Clothing Warehouse (boutique), 1979; production assistant for Gomes-Lowe Associates (commercial production house), 1979; sound man for Radiotelevisione Italiana (Italian national network), 1979; Franklin Library (publishing firm), New York City, picture research assistant, 1980, writer of reader's guides, 1980-83; Berkley Publishing Corp., New York City, manuscript reader and copy writer, 1981-83; Goucher College, assistant professor of English, 1984-86, writer-in-residence, 1988—. Visiting writer, Poetry Center, 92nd Street Y, New York City, 1984-86, Iowa Writers Workshop, 1987-88, and Johns Hopkins Writing Seminars, 1989-93. Director of 185 Corporation (media arts organization), 1979-84.

*MEMBER:* PEN American Center, Authors Guild, Authors League of America, Poets and Writers, Phi Beta Kappa.

*AWARDS, HONORS:* Ward Mathis Prize, 1977, for short story "Triptych," Class of 1870 Junior Prize, 1978, Francis LeMoyne Page Award, 1978, for fiction writing, and Class of 1859 Prize, 1979, all from Princeton University; Lillian Smith Award, 1989; Guggenheim fellowship, 1991; George A. and Eliza Gardner Howard Foundation Award, 1991-92; National Endowment for the Arts fellowship, 1992; National Book Award finalist, 1995, PEN/Faulkner Award finalist, Maryland Library Association Award, and Annisfield-Wolf Award, all 1996, all for *All Souls' Rising;* selected as one of the "Best American Novelists under Forty," *Granta,* 1996; Andrew James Purdy Fiction Award from Hollins College.

*WRITINGS:*

*NOVELS*

*The Washington Square Ensemble,* Viking (New York City), 1983.
*Waiting for the End of the World,* Ticknor & Fields (New York City), 1985.
*Straight Cut,* Ticknor & Fields, 1986.
*The Year of Silence,* Ticknor & Fields, 1987.
*Soldier's Joy,* Ticknor & Fields, 1989.
*Doctor Sleep,* Harcourt (San Diego, CA), 1991.
*Save Me, Joe Louis,* Harcourt (New York City), 1993.
*All Souls' Rising,* Pantheon (New York City), 1995.
*Ten Indians,* Pantheon, 1996.

*OTHER*

*History of the Owen Graduate School of Management* (nonfiction), Vanderbilt University, 1985.
*Zero db* (short fiction), Ticknor & Fields, 1987.

*Barking Man and Other Stories* (short stories; contains "Holding Together," "Black and Tan," "Customs of the Country," "Finding Natasha," "Dragon's Seed," "Barking Man," "Petit Cachou," "Witness," "Move on up," and "Mr. Potatohead in Love,"), Ticknor & Fields, 1990.

Contributor of short fiction to periodicals and anthologies, including *Best American Short Stories, The New Writers of the South, New Stories from the South, Atlantic, Harper's, Hudson Review,* and *North American Review.* Contributor of reviews and essays to *Harper's, New York Times Book Review, Village Voice,* and *Los Angeles Times Book Review.*

*WORK IN PROGRESS:* Two sequels to *All Souls' Rising,* continuing the history of the Haitian revolution: *The War of Knives* and *The Stone That the Builders Refused.*

*SIDELIGHTS:* "Madison Smartt Bell has been called a postmodernist, a minimalist, a prose poet of aloneness, and the best writer of his generation," states Donna Seaman in *Booklist.* "His distinctively riling fiction sizzles with tension and menace." Bell, who had published six novels and two short-story collections by the time he was 35 years old, usually writes about society's misfits. Most of his main characters are petty criminals, drifters, and lost souls whose lives Seaman describes as "fateful and apocalyptic."

*Save Me, Joe Louis* exemplifies the themes and situations found in much of Bell's fiction. In this novel, Macrae, an AWOL Southerner, and Charlie, an unstable ex-con, forge a dangerous partnership soon after meeting in New York City. Together they embark on a small-time crime spree that eventually leads them to flee for Macrae's backcountry homeland. There, the relationship sours and violence erupts.

Macrae and Charlie are typical of Bell's protagonists in that there is little to like about them; many commentators find that one of the great strengths of Bell's writing is his ability to generate characters for such people. Andy Solomon writes in the *Chicago Tribune* that Bell "moves among modern thieves and lepers with charity. His is a Robert Browning empathy that creates no character so defiled that Bell cannot ask, 'What is at the heart of this man that is in me as well?' In Macrae, Bell once again takes a character you'd be disturbed to find living anywhere near your neighborhood, then moves relentlessly

against the grain of popular thought to find the embers of Macrae's humanity beneath the ashes of his pain." Reviewing the novel for *Booklist,* Seaman calls *Save Me, Joe Louis* "a work of ferocious intensity and poetic nihilism" in which Bell examines the "soul's disturbing capacity for both good and evil and the pointlessness of unexamined lives lived wholly by instinct and rage."

Rage is at the center of *All Souls' Rising,* an epic history of Haiti's war for independence, which broke out shortly after the French revolution in the late 1700s. The strange alliances, hatred, and tensions between Haiti's rich white ruling class, the poor whites, the free mulattoes, and the island's mistreated slave population culminated in a 15-year bloodbath. In just the first few months of the revolution, 12,000 people perished and nearly 200 plantations were burned. Writing in the *New York Times Book Review,* John Vernon describes Bell's historical novel as a "carefully drawn roadmap through hell." "*All Souls' Rising,*" he continues, "is historical fiction in the monumental manner, heavily prefaced, prologued, glossaried and chronologized. It admirably diagrams the complex muddle of 18th-century Haiti, a slave society constructed along clearly racist lines but with surprising alliances. Haitian whites, split into royalists and revolutionaries, alternately compete for and spurn the loyalties of free mulattoes, for whom gradations of color are of central importance. . . . This bizarre and rich stew is the perfect stuff of fiction, whose subject is never reality but competing realities."

Countless atrocities were committed on all sides in the Haitian revolution, and Bell's book details many examples. For some reviewers, the gore was too much. Brian Morton expresses little enthusiasm for the novel, stating in *New Statesman & Society* that *All Souls' Rising* "is an ugly book about ugly times. The author can claim historical veracity. . . . But there are undercurrents that recall the violent pornography of another triple-barrelled American novelist, Bret Easton Ellis." Vernon concurs that the scenes of mutilation, rape, and violence are relentless and warns that such repeated gore may numb the novel "into a handbook of splatter-punk. To his credit," Vernon continues, "Mr. Bell knows that violence may be the writer's hedge against mawkishness, but it also threatens to become mere slush, the sentimentality of gore." Still, Vernon finds much to praise, especially Bell's ability to humanize all types of characters and concludes that while there are flaws in the novel, they are overshadowed by its power and intelligence. "Mr. Bell can manage epic slabs of action remarkably well, has a feel for the panoramic and iconic, and, above all, seeks to understand and probe the mysterious intersection of history and flesh by which historical forces become incarnate. *All Souls' Rising,* refreshingly ambitious and maximalist in its approach, takes enormous chances, and consequently will haunt readers long after plenty of flawless books have found their little slots on their narrow shelves."

A *Publishers Weekly* reviewer expresses unreserved enthusiasm for *All Souls' Rising,* deeming it an "astonishing novel of epic scope." The reviewer argues that "Bell avoids the sense of victory that mars so many novels about revolution." After the many scenes of massacre, rape, and violence, the critic continues, "there can be no question of a winner of the battle for Haitian liberation. Surviving it was feat enough. In Bell's hands, the chaos . . . that surrounds these characters somehow elucidates the nobility of even the most craven among them."

Discussing *All Souls' Rising* with Ken Ringle of the *Washington Post,* Bell compares Haiti's race conflict with conditions in the contemporary United States. "Haiti's was a full-blown race war," he explains, "over issues we've never really come to terms with in this country. Now we're having our own race war. But it's a slow-motion race war, disguised as crime in the streets. And nobody, black or white, wants to admit what's happening."

*BIOGRAPHICAL/CRITICAL SOURCES:*

*PERIODICALS*

*Atlanta Journal-Constitution,* April 22, 1990, p. N8; January 13, 1991, p. N10; June 13, 1993, p. N8; November 26, 1995, p. C1.
*Booklist,* April 15, 1993, pp. 1468-1469; September 1, 1995, p. 4.
*Boston Globe,* May 23, 1993, p. B40; October 22, 1995, p. B38.
*Chicago Tribune,* January 13, 1991, section 14, p. 1; May 30, 1993, section 14, p. 6; October 22, 1995, section 14, p. 1.
*Entertainment Weekly,* November 10, 1995, p. 55.
*Harper's,* August, 1986.
*Library Journal,* October 1, 1995, p. 118.
*Los Angeles Times,* September 16, 1985; September 15, 1986; February 20, 1987; November 3, 1987.

*Los Angeles Times Book Review,* February 27, 1983; September 30, 1990, p. 12; January 20, 1991, p. 8; July 11, 1993, p. 7.
*New Statesman & Society,* February 9, 1996, pp. 37-38.
*New York Times Book Review,* February 20, 1983; August 18, 1985; October 12, 1986; February 15, 1987; November 15, 1987; December 27, 1987; April 8, 1990, p. 11; January 6, 1991, p. 11; June 20, 1993, p. 9; October 29, 1995, p. 12.
*Publishers Weekly,* August 28, 1995, p. 102; November 6, 1995, p. 58.
*Times* (London), November 14, 1985; November 19, 1987.
*Times Literary Supplement,* August 26, 1983; November 22, 1985; November 6, 1987.
*Tribune Books* (Chicago), November 22, 1987.
*Washington Post,* October 25, 1986; January 24, 1991, p. B3; November 28, 1995, pp. C1-C2.
*Washington Post Book World,* February 16, 1983; September 1, 1985; October 26, 1986; February 1, 1987; November 22, 1987; April 15, 1990, p. 7; June 24, 1993, p. C2; November 5, 1995, p. 4.*

—*Sketch by Joan Goldsworthy*

\*   \*   \*

**BELLINGHAM, Brenda 1931-**

*PERSONAL:* Born August 14, 1931, in Liverpool, England; daughter of Thomas (a foreman at a feed mill) and Beatrice (Morris) Brown; married Ramsay Stephen Bellingham, February 20, 1959; children: Sheena, Kevin. *Education:* Received Certificate in Social Science and Diploma in Industrial Sociology from University of Liverpool; University of Alberta, Teacher's Diploma, 1970.

*ADDRESSES: Home*—266-52249 Range Rd. 233, Sherwood Park, Alberta, Canada T8B 1C7.

*CAREER:* Provincial Government of Alberta, Calgary, social worker, 1958-62; schoolteacher in Strathcona County, Alberta, 1971-77; writer.

*MEMBER:* Canadian Authors Association (president of Edmonton branch, 1974-75); Canadian Society of Children's Authors, Illustrators, and Performers; Writers Union of Canada; Society of Children's

Book Writers and Illustrators; Writers Guild of Alberta.

*WRITINGS:*

*Joanie's Magic Boots* (juvenile), Tree Frog Press (Edmonton), 1979.
*Two Parents Too Many* (juvenile), Scholastic Canada (Toronto), 1985.
*Storm Child* (juvenile), Lorimer (Toronto), 1985.
*The Curse of the Silver Box,* Scholastic Canada, 1989.
*Like a TV Hero,* General, 1991.
*Princesses Don't Wear Jeans,* Scholastic Canada, 1991.
*Dragons Don't Read Books,* Scholastic Canada, 1992.

*WORK IN PROGRESS:* An historical novel for teenagers.

*SIDELIGHTS:* Brenda Bellingham told *CA:* "As a child I was an enthusiastic reader and I also enjoyed writing stories. I used to bore my family with my efforts while we sat in the candlelight in our Anderson shelter in the backyard of our home during World War II. Later, my writing energies were used up by school and university demands for essays, reports, and projects. Imagination was not a requirement.

"It was not until I had my own two children and a classroom full of children that I re-entered the rich world of children's fiction. The experience of reading aloud to children inspired me to try writing for them. I was lucky enough to get my first book published and consequently decided 'to be a children's writer.' Since then I've learned that this is not as easy as it looks. I've had a few minor successes and my share of failures. What keeps me writing? The challenge! I'm sure writing is an activity I'll never totally master. There's always a new problem to work out, some skill I haven't properly developed. Besides, there's nothing else I know that allows me to live in my imagination for hours on end and call it work."

Bellingham's 1985 novel *Storm Child* is a work of historical fiction set in the rugged wilderness of Canada's western frontier. It explores the relationships and tensions between several characters of mixed heritage. The main character, Storm Child, is part Scottish and part Indian. She leaves her mother and the security of Fort Edmonton to live with her Indian grandparents. There the young girl experiences the fullness and the hardship of tribal life, and, ultimately, discovers some of the universal truths that apply to all people, red and white alike.*

\*          \*          \*

**BIANCHI, Robert Steven     1943-**

*PERSONAL:* Born November 30, 1943, in New York, NY; son of Robert Vincent and Bessie (Litrakis) Bianchi; divorced; children: Kyria Marcella Osborne. *Education:* Rutgers University, B.A., 1965; New York University, M.A., 1969, Ph.D., 1976. *Avocational interests:* Travel, visiting archaeological sites and museums.

*ADDRESSES: Home and office*—1056 Fifth Ave., Suite 18D, New York, NY 10028-0112.

*CAREER:* Rutgers Preparatory School, Somerset, NJ, teacher, 1965-74; Metropolitan Museum of Art, New York City, assistant in Egyptian Department, 1974-75; Brooklyn Museum, Brooklyn, NY, curatorial assistant, 1976, associate curator, 1976-90, curator of Egyptian art, 1990; Metropolitan Museum of Art, J. Clawson Mills fellow, 1992-93. Upsala College, instructor, 1971-73; New York University, adjunct professor, 1979, 1986-89; Columbia University, adjunct professor, 1981. 1059 Corp., member of cooperative board, 1992—. International Congress of Egyptologists, North American representative, 1979; International Congress of Papyrology, member, 1980; American Research Center in Egypt, member of board of governors, 1979-81; American School of Classical Studies in Athens, class coordinator for development, 1980-83; Royal Academy of Arts, London, consulting curator of ancient Egyptian art. Author, director, and host of the television series *Ancient Egyptian Art,* WCBS-TV, 1979; guest on television programs, including *Nickelodeon's Total Panic.*

*MEMBER:* International Association of Egyptologists (American representative), American Association of Museums, Archaeological Institute of America (member of executive committee of New York society, 1982-89; traveling lecturer), Corpus Antiquitatum Aegyptiacarum (member of executive board, 1979), Association of Hellenes From Egypt in America (member of board of directors, 1992—),

Egyptological Seminar of New York (member of board of governors, 1987-84; president, 1984—), Explorers Club (fellow resident, 1979), Oriental Club of New York.

*AWARDS, HONORS:* Fulbright-Hayes fellow, Aegyptisches Musem, Berlin, Germany, 1977; Andrew W. Mellon Humanist, Howard University, 1980; Bourse Jacques Vandier grant from the Louvre, Paris, France, 1981; Honorary Friend of Egyptian Art, Boston Museum of Fine Arts, 1989; J. Clawson Mills Fellow, Egyptian Department, Metropolitan Museum of Art, New York City, 1992-93.

*WRITINGS:*

*Ancient Egyptian Sculpture From the Brooklyn Museum,* Abrams (New York City), 1978, Museo de la Fondacion Archeologica (San Juan), 1979.
*Egyptian Treasures,* Abrams, 1979.
*Treasures of the Nile: Art of the Temples and Tombs of Egypt,* Newsweek (New York City), 1980.
*Museums of Egypt,* Newsweek, 1980.
*Ann Chernow: The Candace Series; Recent Paintings and Drawings,* [New York City], 1982.
*Egyptian Treasures From the Cairo Museum at the World's Fair in Knoxville, Tennessee, at the Egyptian Pavilion in 1982,* [Cairo], 1982.
*Cleopatra's Egypt: Age of the Ptolemies,* Brooklyn Museum (Brooklyn, NY), 1988.
*In the Tomb of Nefertari: Conservation of the Wall Paintings,* [Malibu], 1992.
*The Nubians: People of the Ancient Nile,* Millbrook Press (Brookfield, CT), 1994.
(Editor) *Who's Who in Egyptian Mythology,* 2nd edition, Scarecrow Press (Metuchen, NJ), 1995.

Work represented in anthologies, including *Marks of Civilization: Artistic Transformations of the Human Body,* edited by Arnold Rubin, [Los Angeles], 1988; and *Mummies and Magic: The Funerary Arts of Ancient Egypt,* [Boston], 1988. Contributor of over three hundred articles and reviews to professional journals, books, and art catalogs. Book review editor, *Journal of the American Research Center in Egypt,* 1984-89; member of editorial board, *Archaeology,* 1987-89, and *Selene,* 1989; editorial adviser, *Archaeology.*

*WORK IN PROGRESS: The Temple of Dendur,* for Metropolitan Museum of Art, New York City; research for a catalog of the masterpieces of Greek and Roman art in the Graeco-Roman Museum, Alexandria, Egypt.

*SIDELIGHTS:* Robert Steven Bianchi told *CA:* "I write extensively and lecture on archaeology and art history. I do so, I suppose, because of my family traditions. My father's Italian family includes several gifted uncles, a jeweler whose firm created breathtaking jewels based on the designs of Salvatore Dali, a textile designer who studied with the futurist Robert Delauney in Paris, and a recognized American painter and sculptor. My mother's family comes from the Ionian Greek island of Samos and from Alexandria in Egypt. As a child, I spoke Greek before I spoke English, and was raised on Homer's epics, the fables of Aesop, the ageless myths from Greece and Rome and, of course, on Egypt's glorious civilization.

"After my maternal grandfather's failed attempt to place me in a Greek Orthodox seminary, I went on to college, majoring first in Greek and Latin, and eventually earning advanced degrees in classical art, Egyptology, and aesthetics. I consider myself fortunate to have been awarded fellowships which enabled me to study for extended periods of time in Europe and the Middle East where, quite frankly, I feel very much at home because I reside there for as long as six months every year. I, therefore, derive a great deal of personal satisfaction and pleasure from being able to write for both the general public and academics on subjects relating to ancient Greek, Roman, and Egyptian art and culture.

"During the course of the last two years, I have had the unexpected opportunity to write magazine articles and catalogs about modern artists, thereby using my training in aesthetic appreciation and criticism gained during my postgraduate work in Europe, particularly in Paris. The chronological gap between antiquity and the twentieth century is not that great, because art criticism and aesthetics, as disciplines, were first developed by the ancient Greeks.

"As I attempt to formulate future goals, I entertain the idea of working with film, either in the form of television programs or video cassettes. I harbor these aspirations because I am convinced that the book, as we presently know it, will still exist as hard copy, but will be supplemented by film in various forms. Authors must acknowledge the approaching century's media orientation and do all they can to integrate their works into these new and exciting technologies."*

## BLUM, Lawrence A. 1943-

*PERSONAL:* Born April 16, 1943, in Baltimore, MD; son of Irving and Lois (Hoffberger) Blum; married Judith Smith (a college professor), June 22, 1975; children: Benjamin, Sarah, Laura. *Education:* Princeton University, A.B., 1964; Harvard University, M.A., 1965, Ph.D., 1974; attended Linacre College, Oxford, 1968-69. *Religion:* Jewish.

*ADDRESSES: Home*—149 Prospect St., Cambridge, MA 02139. *Office*—Department of Philosophy, University of Massachusetts, 100 Morrissey Blvd., Boston, MA 02125.

*CAREER:* University of Massachusetts, Boston, assistant professor, 1973-80, associate professor of philosophy, 1980—. Visiting associate professor at University of California, Los Angeles, spring, 1984.

*MEMBER:* American Philsophical Association.

*AWARDS, HONORS:* Fellow of National Endowment for the Humanities, 1986-87.

*WRITINGS:*

*Friendship, Altruism, and Morality,* Routledge & Kegan Paul (London), 1980.
(With V.J. Seidler) *A Truer Liberty: Simone Weil and Marxism,* Routledge & Kegan Paul, 1989.
*Moral Perception and Particularity,* Cambridge University Press (Cambridge, England), 1994.

Contributor to books, including *The Virtues: Contemporary Essays in Moral Character,* edited by R. Kruschwitz and R. Roberts, Wadsworth, 1987; *The Emergence of Morality in Young Children,* edited by J. Kagan and S. Lamb, University of Chicago, 1988; and *Public Education in a Multicultural Society,* Cambridge University Press, 1996. Also contributor to philosophy journals.

*SIDELIGHTS:* In his book *Friendship, Altruism, and Morality,* Lawrence A. Blum argues that morality is as much a matter of emotion as rationality. This places him opposite great moral philosophers such as Immanuel Kant and more in line with classical thinkers like Aristotle. Blum asserts in particular that compassion, sympathy, and friendship are central moral phenomena neglected in Kantian-influenced traditions of morality.

*BIOGRAPHICAL/CRITICAL SOURCES:*

*PERIODICALS*

*Boston Magazine,* October, 1982.
*New Republic,* June 18, 1990, p. 40.
*Signs: Journal of Women in Culture and Society,* spring, 1990, p. 663.
*Times Literary Supplement,* February 20, 1981.

\*     \*     \*

## BLUNDEN, Edmund (Charles) 1896-1974

*PERSONAL:* Born November 1, 1896; died January 20, 1974; son of Charles and Georgina (Tyler) Blunden (joint-headmasters of a London school); married Mary Davies (divorced); married Sylva Norman, 1933 (divorced); married Claire Margaret Poynting, 1945; children: four daughters. *Education:* Queen's College, Oxford, M.A. and C.Lit.

*CAREER:* Joined the staff of *The Athenaeum,* 1920, as assistant to Middleton Murry and continued (until 1924) as a regular contributor when *The Athenaeum* was amalgamated with *The Nation,* returned, 1928; Tokyo University, Tokyo, Japan, professor of English, 1924-27; Oxford University, Oxford, England, fellow and tutor in English literature at Merton College, 1931-43, staff member of Senior Training Corps, 1940-44; worked with United Kingdom liaison mission in Tokyo, 1948-50; University of Hong Kong, professor of English, 1953-64; Oxford University Chair of Poetry, 1966-68. *Military service:* Royal Sussex Regiment, 1916-19; served in France and Belgium; Military Cross, 1917.

*AWARDS, HONORS:* Hawthornden Prize, 1922, for *The Shepherd, and Other Poems of Peace and War;* Commander, Order of the British Empire, 1951; Queen's Gold Medal for Poetry, 1956; Benson Medal, Royal Society of Literature; Order of the Rising Sun, third class, Japan, 1963; Litt.D., University of Leeds.

*WRITINGS:*

*POETRY*

*Poems 1913 and 1914,* [Horsham], 1914.
*Poems Translated from the French,* [Horsham], 1914.

*Three Poems,* J. Brooker, 1916.

*The Barn* (also see below), [Uckfield], 1916.

*The Silver Bird of Herndyke Mill; Stane Street; The Gods of the World Beneath,* [Uckfield], 1916.

*The Harbingers,* [Uckfield], 1916.

*Pastorals: A Book of Verses,* E. Macdonald (London), 1916.

*The Barn with Certain Other Poems,* Sidgwick & Jackson (London), 1920, Knopf (New York City), 1921.

*The Waggoner and Other Poems,* Knopf, 1920.

*The Shepherd, and Other Poems of Peace and War,* Knopf, 1922.

*Old Homes, A Poem,* Ward (Clare), 1922.

*To Nature: New Poems,* Beaumont Press (London), 1923.

*Dead Letters,* Pelican (London), 1923.

*To Nature,* Beaumont Press, 1923.

*Edmund Blunden,* Benn (London), 1925.

*Masks of Time: A New Collection of Poems Principally Meditative,* Beaumont Press, 1925.

(Contributor) Edward Thompson, editor, *The Augustan Books of Modern Poetry,* Benn, 1925, reissued as one part of *Modern Poetry,* L. B. Hill, 1925.

*English Poems,* Knopf, 1926, revised edition, Duckworth (London), 1929.

*Japanese Garland,* Beaumont Press, 1928.

*Retreat,* Doubleday, Doran (Garden City, NY), 1928.

*Winter Nights: A Reminiscence,* Faber & Gwyer (London), 1928.

*Near and Far: New Poems,* Cobden-Sanderson (London), 1929, Harper (New York City), 1930.

*The Poems of Edmund Blunden, 1914-1930,* Cobden-Sanderson, 1930, Harper, 1932.

*A Summer's Fancy,* Beaumont Press, 1930.

*To Themis: Poems on Famous Trials, with Other Pieces,* Beaumont Press, 1931.

*Constantia and Francis: An Autumn Evening,* [Edinburgh], 1931.

*Halfway House: A Miscellany of New Poems,* Cobden-Sanderson, 1932, Macmillan, 1933.

*Choice or Chance: New Poems,* Cobden-Sanderson, 1934.

*Verses: To H. R. H. The Duke of Windsor,* Alden Press, 1936.

*An Elegy and Other Poems,* Cobden-Sanderson, 1937.

*On Several Occasions, by a Fellow of Merton College,* Corvinus Press (London), 1938.

*Poems, 1930-1940,* Macmillan, 1940.

*Shells by a Stream: New Poems,* Macmillan (London), 1944, Macmillan (New York City), 1945.

*After the Bombing, and Other Short Poems,* Macmillan, 1949, reprinted, Books for Libraries Press, 1971.

*Eastward: A Selection of Verses Original and Translated,* Benrido (Kyoto), 1950.

*Edmund Blunden: A Selection of Poetry and Prose,* Hart-Davis (London), 1950, Horizon (New York City), 1962, reprinted, Books for Libraries Press, 1970.

*Records of Friendship: Occasional and Epistolary Poems Written during Visits to Kyushu,* Kyushu University Press (Kyushu), 1950.

*Poems of Many Years,* Collins (London), 1957.

*A Hong Kong House,* Poetry Book Society, 1959, published in England as *A Hong Kong House: Poems 1951-1961,* Collins, 1962.

*Eleven Poems,* Golden Head Press (Cambridge), 1965.

*A Selection of the Shorter Poems,* White (Long Melford), 1966.

*Poems on Japan, Hitherto Uncollected and Mostly Unprinted,* Kenkyusha (Tokyo), 1967.

*The Midnight Skaters: Poems for Young Children* (chosen and introduced by C. Day Lewis), Bodley Head (London), 1968.

*A Selection from the Poems,* Restoration Fund Committee of the Great Church of the Holy Trinity (Long Melford), 1969.

*Selected Poems* (edited by Robyn Marsack), Carcanet Press (Manchester), 1982.

PROSE

*The Appreciation of Literary Prose: Being One of the Special Courses of the Art of Life,* [London], 1921.

*The Bonadventure: A Random Journal of an Atlantic Holiday,* Cobden-Sanderson, 1922, Putnam (New York City), 1923.

*Christ's Hospital: A Retrospect,* Christophers (London), 1923.

*More Footnotes to Literary History,* Kenkyusha, 1926.

*On the Poems of Henry Vaughn: Characteristics and Intimations, with His Principal Latin Poems Carefully Translated into English Verse,* Cobden-Sanderson, 1927, reprinted, Russell (New York City), 1969.

*On Receiving from the Clarendon Press,* Clarendon Press (Oxford), 1927.

*Lectures in English Literature,* Kodowkan (Tokyo), 1927.

*Leigh Hunt's "Examiner" Examined,* Cobden-Sanderson, 1928, Harper, 1931, reprinted, Archon Books (Hamden), 1967.

*Undertones of War* (narrative), Cobden-Sanderson, 1928, Doubleday, Doran, 1929, with new preface by the author, Oxford University Press, 1956, revised edition, Collins, 1965, Harcourt (New York City), 1966.

*Shakespeare's Significances: A Paper Read before the Shakespeare Association,* Oxford University Press, 1929, reprinted, Folcroft (Folcroft, PA), 1974.

*Nature in English Literature,* Harcourt, 1929, reprinted, Kennikat (Port Washington, NY), 1970.

(Contributor) Takeshi Saito, *Keats' View of Poetry: To Which is Prefixed an Essay on English Literature in Japan, by Edmund Blunden,* Cobden-Sanderson, 1929, reprinted, Norwood (Norwood, PA), 1975.

*De Bello Germanico: A Fragment of Trench History,* G. A. Blunden (Hawstead), 1930.

*Leigh Hunt and His Circle,* Harper, 1930, published in England as *Leigh Hunt: A Biography,* Cobden-Sanderson, 1930, reprinted as *Leigh Hunt: A Biography,* Archon Books, 1970.

*The Somme Battle: Selected Chapters from Undertones of War,* Velhagen & Klasing, c. 1930.

*In Summer: The Rotunda of the Bishop of Derry,* privately printed for Fytton Armstrong, 1931.

*Votive Tablets: Studies Chiefly Appreciative of English Authors and Books,* Cobden-Sanderson, 1931, Harper, 1932, reprinted, Books for Libraries Press, 1967.

*The Face of England in a Series of Occasional Sketches,* Longmans, Green (New York City), 1932.

*Fall in, Ghosts: An Essay on a Battalion Reunion,* White Owl Press (London), 1932.

*Charles Lamb and His Contemporaries, Being the Clark Lectures Delivered at Trinity College, Cambridge, 1932,* Cambridge University Press (Cambridge), 1933, also published as *Charles Lamb and His Contemporaries,* 1937, reprinted, Archon Books, 1967, also published as *Charles Lamb: His Life Recorded by His Contemporaries,* Norwood, 1976.

(With Sylva Norman) *We'll Shift Our Ground: or, Two on a Tour,* Cobden-Sanderson, 1933.

*The Epilogue for King John: Presented by the O.U.D.S. February 25, 1933 on the Occasion of the Closing of the New Theatre Oxford,* Holywell Press (Oxford), 1933.

*The Mind's Eye: Essays,* J. Cape (London), 1934, reprinted, Books for Libraries Press, 1967.

*Edward Gibbon and His Age,* University of Bristol Press (Bristol), 1935, reprinted, Folcroft, 1975.

*Keats's Publisher: A Memoir of John Taylor (1781-1864),* J. Cape, 1936, Kelley (Clifton, NJ), 1975.

*On Shelley,* Oxford University Press, 1938, reprinted, Norwood, 1975.

*English Villages,* Hastings House (New York City), 1941.

*Thomas Hardy,* Macmillan, 1941, Macmillan (New York City), 1942, reprinted, St. Martin's (New York City), 1967.

*Cricket Country,* Collins, 1944.

*Shelley: A Life Story,* Collins, 1946, Viking, 1947, 2nd edition, Oxford University Press, 1965.

*Shakespeare to Hardy: Short Studies of Characteristic English Authors Given in a Series of Lectures at Tokyo University,* Kenkyusha, 1948, reprinted with corrections, 1949, reprint of 1948 edition, Folcroft, 1969.

*Two Lectures on English Literature,* Kyoiku Tosho (Osaka), 1948.

*Shelley's Defence of Poetry and Blunden's Lectures on "Defence",* Hokuseido (Tokyo), 1948, reprinted, Folcroft, 1969.

*Sons of Light: A Series of Lectures of English Writers,* Hosei University Press (Hosei), 1949, Folcroft, 1969.

*Addresses on General Subjects Connected with English Literature Given at Tokyo University and Elsewhere in 1948,* Kenkyusha, 1949, 2nd edition, 1958.

*Poetry and Science and Other Lectures,* Osaka Kyoiku Tosho, 1949.

*Hamlet, and Other Studies,* Yuhodo (Tokyo), 1950.

*Favorite Studies in English Literature: Lecture Given at Keio University in 1948 and 1949,* Hokuseido, 1950.

*Influential Books: Lectures Given at Wasdea University in 1948 and 1949,* Hokuseido, 1950.

*Reprinted Papers: Partly Concerning Some English Romantic Poets with a Few Postscripts,* Kenkyusha, 1950, Folcroft, 1971.

*Chaucer to "B. V.", with an Additional Paper on Herman Melville,* Kenkyusha, 1950, reprinted, Folcroft, 1971.

*A Wanderer in Japan,* Asahi-shimbun-sha (Tokyo), 1950.

*John Keats,* Longmans, Green, 1950, 2nd revised edition, 1966.

*Sketches and Reflections,* Eibunsha (Tokyo), 1951.

*Lectures in English Literature,* 2nd edition, Kodokwan (Tokyo), 1952.

*Essayists of the Romantic Period,* Kodokwan, 1952.

*The Dede of Pittie: Dramatic Scenes Reflecting the History of Christ's Hospital and Offered in Cel-*

ebration of the Quatercenary 1953 at the Fortune Theatre (poems and prose), Christ's Hospital (London), 1953.

*Charles Lamb,* Longmans, Green, 1954, revised edition, 1964.

*War Poets, 1914-1918,* Longmans, Green, 1958, revised edition, 1964.

*Three Young Poets: Critical Sketches of Byron, Shelley and Keats,* Kenkyusha, 1959, Folcroft, 1970.

*A Wessex Worthy: Thomas Russell,* Toucan Press (Beaminster), 1960.

*English Scientists as Men of Letters,* Hong Kong University Press (Hong Kong), 1961.

*William Crowe (1745-1829),* Toucan Press, 1963.

*A Corscambe Inhabitant,* Toucan Press, 1963.

*Guest of Thomas Hardy,* Toucan Press, 1964.

*A Brief Guide to the Great Church of the Holy Trinity, Long Melford,* East Anglican Magazine (Ipswich), 1965.

*A Few Not Quite Forgotten Writers?,* English Association (London), 1967.

*John Clare: Beginner's Luck,* Bridge Books (Wateringbury), 1971.

### EDITOR

(With Alan Porter) John Clare, *Poems Chiefly from Manuscript,* Cobden-Sanderson, 1920, Putnam, 1921.

Christopher Smart, *A Song to David, with Other Poems,* Cobden-Sanderson, 1924.

John Clare, *Madrigals and Chronicles,* Beaumont Press, 1924.

*Shelley and Keats as They Struck Their Contemporaries,* C. W. Beaumont, 1925, Folcroft, 1970, reprint of 1925 edition, Haskell, 1971.

Benjamin Robert Hayden, *Autobiography,* Oxford University Press, 1927.

(Compiler) *A Hundred English Poems from the XIVth Century to the XIXth,* Kenkyusha, 1927, 2nd revised edition, 1968.

(Author of introduction and compiler with Cyril Falls, H. M. Tomlinson, and R. Wright) *The War, 1914-1918: A Booklist,* The Reader, 1929.

William Collins, *The Poems,* Haslewood Books, 1929.

*Great Short Stories of the War: England, France, Germany, America,* Eyre & Spottiswoode (London), 1930.

John Clare, *Sketches in the Life of John Clare,* Cobden-Sanderson, 1931.

Wilfred Owen, *Poems,* Viking, 1931, new edition, 1947, New Directions, 1949, author of introduction to amended edition entitled *Collected Poems,* New Directions, 1964.

(Compiler) *Charles Lamb: His Life Recorded by His Contemporaries,* Hogarth Press (London), 1934.

(With Earl Leslie Griggs) *Coleridge: Studies by Several Hands on the Hundredth Anniversary of His Death,* Constable (London), 1934, reprinted, Russell, 1970.

*Return to Husbandry,* J. M. Dent, 1943.

Francis Carey Slater, *Selected Poems,* Oxford University Press, 1947.

Christopher Smart, *Hymns for the Amusement of Children,* Blackwell (Oxford), 1948.

(With others) *The Christ's Hospital Book,* Hamish Hamilton (London), 1953.

Ivor Gurney, *Poems Principally Selected from Unpublished Manuscripts,* Hutchinson (London), 1954.

John Keats, *Selected Poems,* Norton (New York City), 1955.

Percy Bysshe Shelley, *Poems,* Collins, 1955.

Alfred, Lord Tennyson, *Selected Poems,* Heinemann (London), 1960.

Thomas Bewick, *A Memoir of Thomas Bewick, Written by Himself, 1822-1828,* Centaur Press, 1961, Southern Illinois University Press (Carbondale), 1962.

(With Bernard Mellor) *Wayside Poems of the Seventeenth Century: An Anthology,* Hong Kong University Press, 1963.

(With Mellor) *Wayside Poems of the Early Eighteenth Century: An Anthology,* Oxford University Press, 1963.

(With Mellor) *Wayside Sonnets, 1750-1850: An Anthology,* Hong Kong University Press, 1971.

### OTHER

Contributor to anthologies. Also author of numerous pamphlets and booklets on literary subjects. Translator of the poetry of Mezzetin and Loret, and of Henry Vaughan's Latin verse. Author of libretto for Gerald Finzi's *An Ode for St. Cecilia's Day,* Boosey & Hawks (Oceanside, NY), 1947. Contributor to *Times Literary Supplement.*

*SIDELIGHTS:* Margaret Willy said of Edmund Blunden: "[He is] in direct line of descent from Crabbe and Clare—his roots firmly planted in the sturdy pastoral tradition of English poetry." Another critic, Charles Morgan, noted: "Blunden has within his range both the poetry of observation penetrated and the poetry of the unperceived. In the first respect, he has an affinity with Wordsworth; in the second, with Coleridge." This was not to say, however, that he merely continued a tradition. According to Hugh l'Anson Fausset, Blunden "seldom treads ground which his imagination has not intimately worked, circumscribed as that ground may be. Consequently the tradition which he maintains, he also renews." He "followed no school or fashion," wrote Alec M. Hardie. "The post-war disillusion hit hard at the literary world, old gods apparently had feet of clay, and newness, originality and revolt were the catchwords. To believe [as Blunden did] in the immediate past was [according to many of his contemporaries] to believe in sterility and decadence. Edmund Blunden was [erroneously] labelled a 'Georgian' by many of the rebels." G. S. Fraser added: "With Sassoon, Read and Graves, Blunden is a last important survivor of that generation of first world war poets who passed through and surmounted an ordeal of initiation. . . . [He] is the last surviving poet of the school of Hardy, the last writer of a natively English poetry."

Fausset allowed that the dismissal of Blunden by certain contemporaries was possibly somewhat justified: "The charge brought against him that he has failed to come to grips with contemporary reality and is for that reason inevitably only a minor poet has some truth in it. His very virtues are here his defects. His rootedness in the past and the soil make him impervious to the distractions, the mechanized tensions, the life-and-death struggle of the modern world. He does not stand between two worlds, one dead, one struggling to be born, but in a world of his own, secure and at peace, though tempests rage without or its tranquil air quivers now and then at the thud of distant explosions."

Yet within the limits he had set for himself, Blunden was a notable poet. His subjects include English rural life (for which he is probably best known, though he is no "bucolic escapist," wrote Richard Church) and trench warfare during World War I. He also wrote occasional verse and "personal" poems which Hardie saw as representing "the pilgrimage of a poet often bewildered and in doubt, but rarely in despair, and it is hardly to be wondered at that his imagination and thought have explored more widely the metaphysical realms in ever-increasing persistence. . . . A similar atmosphere pervades his purely imaginative poems; he opens his wings in the clouds of mystery, the kingdom of 'The Ancient Mariner' and 'Christabel.' The riddle of man's power and mind

are challenged." Hardie continued: "'Blunden's country' cannot be confined. He has found a common link between England and France, England and Japan. Imaginative and poetic reasoning is his country. He seems the legitimate inheritor of the legacy of English literature, and has increased the value of his inheritance, not least by his modesty, tolerance and artistic sincerity."

Writing in the *University of Toronto Quarterly,* Philip Gardner expressed the opinion that although Blunden wrote on many subjects over the course of his career, he "in fact, never ceased to be a war poet, and this 'war element' in his poetry is all-important. This is not simply because his direct experience of war is expressed with a moving eloquence and immediacy for which he has received little critical credit. These harsh realities also deepened and enlarged his compassion and his awareness of the human virtues of kindness, friendship, loyalty, and sacrifice." He concluded: "Even when Blunden's poetry bears no marks whatever of war, when it is gentle, ruminative, 'literary' in subject, working at low pressure in an old-fashioned idiom—when it is, in short, 'verse'—it is made acceptable not just by its well-turned accomplishment but by the reader's knowledge that it proceeds from a mind which contains, and has expressed, far more unpleasant themes."

Blunden's prose memoirs of World War I struck numerous reviewers as moving and powerful. Reviewing *Undertones of War,* Catherine Peters remarked in *Spectator:* "Blunden's book has a peculiar intimacy, which adds to the horror and yet makes one rejoice in the beauty of spirit of the man who is writing it. . . . There is no attempt to gloss over the mass carnage, the smells, sights and sounds . . . of total, senseless destruction, or the lunatic incompetence and insistence on 'correct' details of procedure. But Blunden also includes, as other memorialists of the war do not, the incongruous saving detail, field-mice playing round the trenches . . ., the snatched hour in the tall grass of an orchard with a book."

Blunden was respected as a scholar as well. He was considered to be a leading authority on the English Romantic poets, and was responsible for rediscovering John Clare. Hardie wrote, "English literature owes much to him for his biographical discoveries, critical originality and perspicuity; literary periods are now the fuller for his researches." According to *Dictionary of Literary Biography* contributor John Henry Raleigh, *Thomas Hardy* is Blunden's most significant and "best-sustained piece of literary criticism. First, it is discriminatory and judicious, pointing out flaws, which he does not usually do, as well as virtues; second, the literary criticism is often very specific, pointing out, for example, the specific words Hardy used for obtaining his effects. . . . Blunden's evaluation of Hardy's prose and verse is discriminating and subtle."

"Edmund Blunden remains one of the neglected—an irony if we consider how much of his effort he devoted to resuscitating the neglected figures of the past," declared Paul Fussell in *Sewanee Review.* "But to revisit Blunden is to realize how much life there is in even the neglected."

*BIOGRAPHICAL/CRITICAL SOURCES:*

*BOOKS*

Bridges, Robert, *The Dialectical Words in Blunden's Poems,* [Oxford], 1921.
Church, Richard, *Eight for Immortality,* Dent, 1941.
*Contemporary Literary Criticism,* Gale (Detroit), Volume 2, 1974, Volume 56, 1989.
*Dictionary of Literary Biography,* Gale, Volume 20: *British Poets, 1914-1915,* 1983, Volume 100: *Modern British Essayists, Second Series,* 1990, Volume 155: *Twentieth-Century British Literary Biographers,* 1995.
Edwards, Oliver, *Talking of Books,* Heinemann, 1957.
Fausset, Hugh I'Anson, *Poets and Pundits,* Yale University Press (New Haven, CT), 1947.
Fung, Sydney S. K., *Edmund Blunden, a Bibliography of Criticism,* Kelly & Walsh (Hong Kong), 1983.
Giese, Rolf, *Die Versdichtung Edmund Blundens: Traditionalistischer Ansatz und Moderne Wirklichkeitserfahrung,* Studienverlag Brockmeyer (Bochum), 1982.
Graham, Desmond, *The Truth of War: Owen, Blunden, Rosenberg,* Carcanet Press, 1984.
Hardie, Alec M., *Edmund Blunden,* Longmans, Green, for the British Council, 1958.
Hart-Davis, Rupert, *Edmund Blunden, 1896-1974: An Address,* [privately printed], 1974.
Hirai, Masao, and Peter Milward, editors, *Edmund Blunden: A Tribute from Japan,* Kenkyusha, 1974.
Kirkpatrick, B. J., *A Bibliography of Edmund Blunden,* Clarendon, 1979.
Mallon, Thomas, *Edmund Blunden,* Twayne (Boston), 1983.

Midzunoe, Yuichi, *Edmund Blunden in Japan: Bibliographical Documents and Two Unpublished Poems,* Hokuseido, 1981.
Morgan, Charles, *Reflections in a Mirror,* second series, Macmillan, 1947.
Okada, Sumie, *Edmund Blunden and Japan: The History of a Relationship,* Macmillan, 1988.
Squire, J. C., *Essays on Poetry,* Hodder & Stoughton, 1923, pp. 171-81.
Swinnerton, Frank, *The Georgian Scene,* Farrar & Rinehart, 1934.
Thorpe, Michael, *The Poetry of Edmund Blunden,* Bridge Books, 1971.
Webb, Barry, *Edmund Blunden: A Biography,* Yale University Press, 1990.
Williams, Charles, *Poetry at Present,* Clarendon, 1930.

*PERIODICALS*

*English,* fall, 1957, pp. 213-18.
*Nation,* May 25, 1921, p. 747.
*Observer* (London), August 4, 1968, p. 22.
*Poetry,* May, 1941.
*Sewanee Review,* fall, 1986, pp. 583-601.
*Spectator,* May 8, 1982, p. 18.
*Times Literary Supplement,* May 11, 1922, p. 305; December 6, 1928, p. 949; November 16, 1962, p. 874; March 31, 1966, p. 264; October 3, 1968, p. 1109; July 9, 1982, p. 733.
*University of Toronto Quarterly,* spring, 1973, pp. 218-40.

*OBITUARIES:*

*PERIODICALS*

*Newsweek,* February 4, 1974.
*New York Times,* January 22, 1974.
*Publishers Weekly,* February 18, 1974.
*Washington Post,* January 2, 1974.*

\*    \*    \*

**BOND, William Henry    1915-**

*PERSONAL:* Born August 14, 1915, in York, PA; son of Walter Loucks and Ethel (Bossert) Bond; married Helen Elizabeth Lynch, December 6, 1943; children: Nancy Barbara, Sally Lynch. *Education:* Haverford College, A.B. (with honors), 1937; Harvard University, M.A., 1938, Ph.D., 1941.

*ADDRESSES: Home*—109 The Valley Rd., Concord, MA 01742-4923. *Office*—The Houghton Library, Harvard University, Cambridge, MA 02138.

*CAREER:* Research fellow with Folger Shakespeare Library, 1941-42; Harvard University, Cambridge, MA, assistant to librarian at Houghton Library, 1946-48, curator of manuscripts, 1948-64, lecturer at university, 1964-67, librarian, 1965-82, professor of bibliography, 1967-86, librarian and professor emeritus, 1986—. Assistant keeper of manuscripts at British Museum, 1952-53; Sandars Reader in Bibliography at Cambridge University, 1981-82. Member of board of trustees of Emerson Memorial Association, 1964-89, Historic Deerfield, Inc., 1965-89, honorary trustee, 1991—, and Concord Free Library, 1966-71. *Military service:* U.S. Naval Reserve, active duty, 1943-46; became first lieutenant.

*MEMBER:* Bibliographical Society of America (president, 1974-76), American Antiquarian Society (member of council, 1975-89, honorary councillor, 1991—), Bibliographical Society (England), Massachusetts Historical Society, Colonial Society of Massachusetts (president, 1982-93, honorary member, 1994—), Johnsonians, Grolier Club, Club of Odd Volumes, Phi Beta Kappa.

*AWARDS, HONORS:* Senior Fulbright fellow, 1952-53; Guggenheim fellow, 1982-83.

*WRITINGS:*

EDITOR UNLESS OTHERWISE NOTED

Christopher Smart, *Jubilate Agno,* Harvard University Press (Cambridge, MA), 1954.
*Supplement to the Census of Medieval and Renaissance Manuscripts in the United States* (originated by C. U. Faye) Bibliographical Society of America (New York City), 1962.
*The Houghton Library, 1942-1967,* Harvard College Library, Harvard University (Cambridge, MA), 1967.
(And compiler) William Alexander Jackson, *Records of a Bibliographer: Selected Papers,* Harvard University Press, 1967.
(And compiler) *Eighteenth Century Studies in Honor of Donald F. Hyde,* Grolier Club (Danbury, CT), 1970.
(Author) *Thomas Hollis of Lincoln's Inn: A Whig and His Books,* Cambridge University Press (New York City), 1990.

Also editor (with Reuben A. Brower) of Alexander Pope's translation of Homer's *Iliad,* 1965. Contributor of numerous articles and reviews to scholarly journals.

\*    \*    \*

## BOUCHER, Alan (Estcourt)  1918-1996

*PERSONAL:* Born January 3, 1918, in Frowlesworth, Leicestershire, England; died January 10, 1996; son of Robin Estcourt (a civil servant) and Kathrine Veronica (Burns) Boucher; married Aslaug Thorarinsdottir, February 28, 1942; children: Alice Kristin, Robin Gunnar, Antony Leifur. *Education:* Attended Winchester College, England; Trinity College, Cambridge, B.A., 1939, M.A., 1942, Ph.D., 1951; University of Iceland, postgraduate study, 1948-50. *Religion:* Roman Catholic.

*CAREER:* Ampleforth School, York, England, assistant master in English, 1946-48; British Broadcasting Corp., London, England, producer and program organizer in the schools broadcasting department, with special responsibilities in field of English literature and travel, 1951-96; former supervisor in old Icelandic studies, Cambridge University, Cambridge, England; professor of English, University of Iceland, Reykjavik, 1972-1988. *Military service:* British Army, Royal Artillery and Intelligence Corps, 1939-46; became captain.

*AWARDS, HONORS:* Dame Bertha Phillpots Award for northern research, 1950, 1951; M.B.E., 1980; Knight's Cross, Icelandic Order of the Falcon, 1983.

*WRITINGS:*

*Iceland, Some Impressions,* [Reykjavik], 1949.
*The Runaways,* Nelson (Surrey, England), 1959.
*The Path of the Raven,* Constable (London), 1960.
*Venturers North,* Nelson, 1962.
*The Greenland Farers,* Constable, 1962.
*The King's Men,* Doubleday (London and New York City), 1962.
*The Empty Land,* Nelson, 1963.
*The Wineland Venture,* Constable, 1963.
*The Cottage in the Woods,* Nelson, 1963.
*The Wild Ones,* Nelson, 1964.
*Sea-Kings and Dragon Ships,* Walker (London), 1964.

*The Land-Seekers,* Deutsch (London), 1964, Farrar, Straus (New York City), 1968.

*The Raven's Flight,* Constable, 1964.

*The Hornstranders,* Constable, 1966, Meredith (New York City), 1969.

(Compiler and translator) *Mead Moondaughter, and Other Icelandic Folktales,* Hart-Davis (London), 1967, Chilton Book (Philadelphia), 1967.

*Stories of the Norsemen,* Burke, 1967.

*The Sword of the Raven,* Scribner (New York City), 1969.

*Modern Nordic Plays,* Universitets Forlag Oslo, 1973.

(Selector and Translator) *Northern Voices: Five Contemprary Icelandic Poets,* Wilfion Books (Paisley, Scotland), 1984.

(Editor) *A Student's Anthology of English Poetry,* Boksala Studenta, 1984.

*The Lily and Lay of the Sun,* Boksala Studenta, 1985.

*The Stars of Constantinople,* Louisiana State University Press (Baton Rouge), 1992.

*TRANSLATOR FROM THE ICELANDIC; PUBLISHED BY ICELAND REVIEW LIBRARY (REYKJAVIK)*

*Poems of Today from Twenty-Five Modern Icelandic Poets,* 1972.

*Short Stories of Today,* 1973.

*A Quire of Seven,* 1974.

*Icelandic Folktales,* Volume 1: *Ghosts, Witchcraft and the Other World,* Volume 2: *Elves, Trolls and Elemental Beings,* Volume 3: *Adventures, Outlaws and Past Events,* 1977.

O. J. Sigurdsson, *The Changing Earth and Selected Poems,* 1979.

*A Tale of Icelanders,* 1980.

*The Saga of Hallfred,* 1981.

*Tales from the Eastfirth,* 1981.

*The Saga of Gunnlaug, together with the Tale of Scald-Helgi,* 1983.

*The Saga of Hord and the Holm-Dwellers,* 1983.

*The Saga of Havard the Halt, together with the Saga of Hen-Thorir,* 1986.

*The Saga of Viga-Glum,* 1986.

(Compiler and author of introduction and notes) *The Iceland Traveller: A Hundred Years of Adventure,* 1989.

*IN ICELANDIC*

*Enskur Ordafordi Fyris Islandinga,* Prentfell, 1951.

*Litil Synisbok Enskra Bokmennta,* Isafold, 1952.

*Vid Sagnabrunninn,* Mal og Menning, 1971.

*Vid Timans Fljot,* Mal og Menning, 1985.

*OTHER*

Also translator of plays, *Delerium Bubonis, Dufnaveislan,* and of radio plays. Contributor to publications in Iceland.

*WORK IN PROGRESS:* Poems, personal and biographical. Also translating a sonnet sequence (in Danish) by Gunnar Gunnarsson.

*SIDELIGHTS:* Boucher told *CA:* "Since retiring at the legal maximum age for government employees in January 1989, I continued to undertake some advanced supervision work for the University until the latter ran out of money to pay me. Since then I have divided my time between Iceland and England, using the library of my old university in Cambridge for research in the field of stylistics and poetics. I prefer to spend the summers in England and the winters in Iceland, where the art of living in a cold climate (with the help of geo-thermal heating) is at a more advanced stage. I also travel on the continent of Europe during the summers, though I have also managed a visit to the U.S. where I spent some time working on my anthology of English poetry for Icelandic students in consultation with American teachers, chiefly in the area around Boston. My main occupations during the dark days of the Icelandic winter are bathing in open-air thermally heated swimming pools, drinking countless cups of coffee with friends and relations of my Icelandic wife, and wrestling with the English language in the composition of poetry."

*BIOGRAPHICAL/CRITICAL SOURCES:*

*PERIODICALS*

*Books,* February, 1970.

*Washington Post Book World,* February 9, 1969.

*Young Readers Review,* December, 1968.

*[Verified by daughter, Alice K. Boucher]*

\*      \*      \*

**BRAMSON, Robert M(ark)   1925-**

*PERSONAL:* Original name, Robert M. Abramson; name legally changed in 1949; born November 12, 1925, in Los Angeles, CA; son of Max J. (a physician) and Sylvia L. (a dress designer; maiden name, Barsha) Abramson; married Susan J. Batkin (a management consultant), July 18, 1970; children: Wendy Bramson Waits, Marni Bramson Welch, Robert, Sean, Patrick, Jeremy. *Education:* University of California, Los Angeles, A.B., 1949; San Francisco State College (now University), M.A., 1965; University of California, Berkeley, Ph.D., 1969.

*ADDRESSES: Home*—Greeley Hill, CA. *Office*—10513 Converse Rd., Greeley Hill, CA 95311. *Agent*—Carol Mann Literary Agency, 55 Fifth Ave., New York, NY 10003-4301.

*CAREER:* Consolidated Hotels of California, Los Angeles, electrician, 1948-51; State of California, parole officer, 1951-54, educational administrator, 1954-57, training specialist, 1957-63, chief of health training, 1963-70; Bramson-Parlette Associates (management consultants), Berkeley, CA, senior partner, 1973-89; senior partner, Bremson-Gill Associates, 1989—; writer. Property manager/owner for Les-Rob/Paxton, 1966-69. Lecturer at University of Southern California, 1963-73, San Francisco State College (now University), 1966-73, and Stanford University, 1978-86. Director of Control Resources Development Corp. *Military service:* U.S. Army, 1943-46; served in Europe; received Bronze Star and Combat Infantry Badge with three battle stars.

*MEMBER:* American Psychological Association, Authors Guild, Oakland Museum Association, Psi Chi.

*WRITINGS:*

*Coping with Difficult People,* Doubleday (New York City), 1981.
(With Allen Harrison) *Styles of Thinking,* Doubleday, 1982.
(With Susan Bramson) *The Stressless Home,* Doubleday, 1985.
*Coping with the Fast Track Blues,* Doubleday, 1989.
*Coping with Difficult Bosses,* Carol Publishing (New York City), 1992.
*When Your Boss Doesn't Tell You Until It's Too Late,* Simon & Schuster (New York City), 1996.

Contributor to academic journals.

*WORK IN PROGRESS: First Hired, Last Fired: Becoming an Indispensable Person.*

*SIDELIGHTS:* Robert M. Bramson once told *CA:* "As a writer I try to bridge the gap between behavioral scientists who don't fully realize how the knowledge which they have uncovered might be used, and those who could and would be eager to use it if they knew just what was available.

"My qualifications for undertaking this role are these: a bifurcated set of thinking styles which, to quote my wife, 'has my head in the clouds and my feet on the ground'; nineteen years of varied work experience prior to getting my Ph.D.; twenty-five years as a consultant, listening to bosses, their subordinates, and their spouses talking about themselves and each other.

"Susan and I have worked together as spouses, parents, and management consultants since 1970, and recently as authors. We have made these crossed-over relationships work in a way that helps us find that fine balance between intimacy and separateness that is at the heart of any well-working family."

Bramson indicated to *CA* that he has finally found the right balance as an author, speaker and consultant with just the right number of clients to keep fully involved with life in the fast track.

*BIOGRAPHICAL/CRITICAL SOURCES:*

*PERIODICALS*

*Booklist,* January 15, 1994, p. 955.
*Library Journal,* June 15, 1990, p. 120.

\*   \*   \*

**BROOKS, James L. 1940-**

*PERSONAL:* Born May 9, 1940, in Brooklyn, NY; son of Edward M. and Dorothy Helen (Sheinheit) Brooks; married Marianne Catherine Morrissey, July 7, 1964 (divorced, 1971); married Holly Beth Holmberg, July 23, 1978; children: (first marriage) Amy Lorraine; (second marriage) Chloe, Cooper, Joseph. *Education:* Attended New York University, 1958-60.

*ADDRESSES: Office*—Gracie Films, Columbia Pictures, Poitier Building, 10202 W. Washington Blvd., Culver City, CA 90232. *Agent*—International Creative Management, 8899 Beverly Blvd., Los Angeles, CA 90048.

*CAREER:* Writer, producer, and director. Columbia Broadcasting System (CBS) News, New York, NY, reporter and writer, 1964-66; Wolper Productions, Los Angeles, CA, writer and producer of documentaries, 1966-67; American Broadcasting Co. (ABC), Los Angeles, executive story editor and creator of television series *Room 222,* 1968-69; CBS, Studio City, CA, executive producer and creator of television series *The Mary Tyler Moore Show,* 1970-77; founder of Gracie Films, 1984. Producer, co-creator, and writer for numerous television series and films, 1968—, including *Thursday's Game, Cindy* (musical), *Rhoda, The New Lorenzo Music Show, Friends and Lovers, Lou Grant, Taxi, The Associates, Broadcast News, The Tracey Ullman Show, Sibs, The Simpsons, I'll Do Anything,* and *The Critic;* also producer of films *Big,* 1988, *War of the Roses,* 1989, and executive producer of *Say Anything,* 1989. Appeared as an actor in the film *Modern Romance,* 1981. Guest lecturer, Stanford Graduate School of Communications.

*MEMBER:* Television Academy of Arts and Sciences, Writers Guild of America, Directors Guild of America, Screen Actors Guild, Academy of Motion Picture Arts and Sciences.

*AWARDS, HONORS:* National Academy of Television Arts and Sciences, Emmy Award for best new series, 1969, for *Room 222,* for outstanding comedy writing, 1971, and 1974-77, and for outstanding comedy series, 1975-77; Peabody Award, Writers Guild of America Award nomination, best teleplay, TV Critics Achievement in Comedy Award, TV Critics Achievement in Series Award, and Humanitas Prize, all 1977, all for *The Mary Tyler Moore Show;* Humanitas Prize, 1977 and 1982, both for *Rhoda;* Peabody Award, 1977 and 1978, Emmy Award for outstanding writing in a drama, 1978-82, and Emmy Award nomination for outstanding drama series, 1978, all for *Lou Grant;* TV Film Critics Circle Award for achievement in comedy and in a series, 1977, Golden Globe Award for best comedy, 1978-80, Humanitas Prize, 1979, and Emmy Award for outstanding comedy series, 1979-81, all for *Taxi;* Academy Award for best film and best adapted screenplay from American Academy of Motion Picture Arts and Sciences, Golden Globe Award, and New York Film Critics Circle Award, all 1984, all for *Terms of Endearment;* Academy Award nomination for best picture and winner of best original screenplay from American Academy of Motion Picture Arts and Sciences, and best picture and best original screenplay from New York Film Critics Circle, both 1987, for *Broadcast News;* Emmy

Award for outstanding animated special and outstanding animated program, 1990, for *The Simpsons.*

*WRITINGS:*

*SCREENPLAYS*

(Co-writer and co-producer) *Thursday Game* (television film), 1971.
(And co-producer) *Starting Over,* Paramount, 1979.
(And co-producer and director) *Terms of Endearment* (based on the novel by Larry McMurtry), Paramount, 1983.
(And producer and director) *Perfect,* 1985.
(And producer and director) *Broadcast News,* Twentieth Century-Fox, 1987.
(And co-producer and director) *I'll Do Anything,* Columbia Pictures, 1994.

*TELEVISION SERIES*

(And creator) *Room 222,* ABC, 1968-69.
(And co-creator and executive producer) *The Mary Tyler Moore Show,* CBS, 1970-77.

*SIDELIGHTS:* With everything from tear-jerking dramas to irreverent comedies to his credit, screenwriter/producer/director James L. Brooks has established himself as a Hollywood mainstay. *New York Times* correspondent Aljean Harmetz notes that with his "long jaw, black mustache and heavy beard," Brooks "might be Mephistopheles as a stand-up comic. The comedy that gushes out like water from a lawn sprinkler has no edge of nastiness. It is sweet and cheerful and aimed at no one but himself." Brooks made a name for himself in the 1970s as a television writer, and in the ensuing years has performed a myriad of tasks for both television series and feature films. He is variously described as a mercurial man who can bubble effusively one minute and turn apprehensive the next, and an engaging eccentric who has made a career of mining his own inner turmoil for laughs.

A self-described "early latchkey" kid who grew up in the New Jersey suburbs of New York City, Brooks dropped out of college in the late 1950s to take a job as a copy boy for CBS News. After four years of toil in the newsroom (later the source for his television news-based *The Mary Tyler Moore Show* and *Broadcast News*), he managed to work his way up to newswriter and reporter. He left New York City in 1966 to work as a television writer in Los Angeles.

In Hollywood, Brooks began writing and selling scripts for various situation comedies, including *The Andy Griffith Show* and *That Girl*. He landed a full-time job with ABC in 1968 as executive story editor and went on to create the award-winning television series *Room 222*. He returned to CBS in 1970 and scored an immediate hit as creator, writer, and producer of *The Mary Tyler Moore Show*. The series was the first in a string of television hits which eventually included the comedies *Rhoda* and *Taxi* and the drama *Lou Grant*. As the 1970s drew to a close, Brooks had three series running simultaneously (*Taxi, Rhoda,* and *Lou Grant*), all of which reflected the troubled spirit of the decade. Having received numerous Emmy Awards and other citations from the television industry, Brooks decided to move into feature films.

As a would-be movie producer and director, Brooks found himself, in the early 1980s, with an adaptation of a Larry McMurtry novel, an idea for directing it, and no encouragement from the studio brass. "Not commercial," "too downbeat," and "Who would be interested in the problems of this mother and daughter?" were, according to Harmetz's article, just some of the rejection remarks Brooks got when he was trying to pitch *Terms of Endearment*. Finally Brooks got a deal from Paramount, and *Terms of Endearment*, starring Shirley MacLaine, Jack Nicholson, and Debra Winger, was released in 1983. The reaction seemed instantaneous, with critics and public alike responding to the bittersweet comedy of family loyalty and romantic infidelity. Among the many gifted artists involved in the movie, Brooks was singled out for particular praise—even in his handling of the touchy subject of death in what ostensibly appears to be a comedy.

"In adapting [McMurtry's] entertaining and affecting but dramatically diffuse novel, Brooks has contrived to finesse most of the structural defects built into its rambling, episodic nature," notes *Washington Post* critic Gary Arnold. "His touch is so pleasant and the cast so skillful and enjoyable that it may seem immaterial to ask yourself if this narrative is really getting someplace, rather than passing the time agreeably." Arnold continues: "When a decisive crisis [in the film] occurs, Brooks takes even more impressive advantage of the novel's belated, arguably underhanded resort to incurable illness as a cure-all for plot drift. Spectators who feel resentful about the way the movie activates and exploits its concluding, heartbreaking twist of fate will probably be in a clear

minority, but it will be difficult for the rest of us to deny that they have a legitimate esthetic complaint."

In a *New York Times* review of *Terms of Endearment*, Vincent Canby admits that the film "is not a perfect movie," with its scenes of fatal illness and family breakdown. The critic went on to conclude, however, that the work "must be one of the most engaging films of the year, to be cherished as much for the low-pressure way in which it operates . . . as for the fact that it contains what are possibly the best performances ever given by Shirley MacLaine and Jack Nicholson." *Terms of Endearment* went on to capture three major Academy Awards, including best picture and best adapted screenplay for Brooks.

After what is commonly acknowledged as a false start, the 1985 aerobics-love story *Perfect*, Brooks came back with an original screenplay culled from his own past as a writer in a television newsroom. *Broadcast News*, released in 1987, presents the traditional love triangle—between Jane, a savvy network-news producer, Aaron, a brilliant but uncharismatic reporter, and Tom, an attractive if less-than-gifted news anchorman—that evolves into a love quadrangle, as careerism becomes a consuming part of each character. "The story unfolds as a series of 'days in the life of' a network news bureau, and a cautionary tale it is," remarks Sheila Benson in the *Los Angeles Times*. "Brooks is understandably distressed at the state of the news we're getting, in bright, flashy, easily digested 'bites,' a *USA Today*, 'Entertainment Tonight' version of the news."

*Broadcast News* is "funny, it's intelligent, and it's aimed at the upscale, but what will sell it . . . is that it's all about Washington Media Folk, the people America loves to hate and who, it might be speculated, love to hate themselves," according to *Washington Post* reviewer Tom Shales. *Chicago Tribune* correspondent Dave Kehr observes: "Though Brooks begins with a slightly sitcom-like sense of narrowly defined, single-trait characters—there's the dumb one, the smart one and the compulsive one—he builds on the archetypes to create remarkably full, complex figures, in whom strengths and weaknesses, generous impulses and selfish interests exist side by side." Benson feels that Brooks's "talent for observation and for truthful, careful writing borders on the eerie. He's captured these young people and their pressure-cooker jobs exactly—their banter, their rationalizations, the balance of their lives between work and whatever comes a close second. . . . [Brooks] has seen that a playful sort of ego-speak guards their vulnerability, and he understands that there is a distinct pragmatism to his whiz kids. But he likes them. And there's no way in the world that we won't either."

In *Washington Post* critic Hal Hinson's opinion, *Broadcast News* "never comes close to being a great, penetrating work about television news. It's not a scathing satire like 'Network,' nor is it to broadcast journalism what 'All the President's Men' was to print. But Brooks' ambitions for [this movie] appear to have been far less exalted. [He instead has crafted] a teasing, affectionately critical satire of his former profession. In the process, he's created a spunky romantic comedy with some of the snappiest lines heard onscreen in a long while." Members of the Motion Picture Academy agreed with these assessments, awarding Brooks a best original screenplay Oscar, along with a nomination for best picture.

*Broadcast News* was the first motion picture released by Brooks's own production company, Gracie Films, named after the famous comedienne Gracie Allen. Brooks created Gracie Films as a refuge for the writer, as he explains in an *American Film* profile. "The justification for Gracie was to try this idea out," he states, "that we'd consider it a personal failure if more than the original writer's name appeared on the [film] credits. . . . We wanted authorship of movies, not the latest draft from the latest person hired." In addition to its screenwriting and film producing mission, Gracie Films has provided a launching point for several television series, including the highly irreverent animated comedy *The Simpsons*. In a *Rolling Stone* piece on *The Simpsons*, Bill Zehme states: "Without Brooks, of course, it is doubtful Simpsonia would have gripped the land. He sponsored the Simpsons' rise by hiring [creator Matt] Groening." Zehme concludes that *The Simpsons* has become "the soul of Fox Broadcasting, dependably notching Top Twenty Nielsen ratings."

The renewed television success brought to Brooks by *The Simpsons* has not interfered with his movie projects. In 1994 he released *I'll Do Anything*, a satire of Hollywood that was originally conceived as a musical but ended up being reshaped into a comedy-romance with one song. Featuring a score largely written by Prince and choreography by the eminent modern dancer Twyla Tharp, *I'll Do Anything* exhibited "the kind of crackling comedic dialogue that is a hallmark of all of Jim Brooks's work," to quote Nancy Griffin in *Premiere*. Griffin adds that even after the musical numbers had been

excised, "what remains is, incredibly enough, a dazzling, urbane comedy of which Brooks can be justly proud, rich in its navigation through the ethical flytraps and seductions of the entertainment industry." The film failed to draw at the box office, however, a consequence—so Brooks thought—of its inherent complexity. "There is something about me that's at war with simplicity," he tells *Premiere*. "And if it is true that the form requires some simplicity, maybe that is it."

Throughout his career Brooks has remained a writer with an ear for snappy dialogue that lashes out at the listener, that has the ring of authenticity but at the same time tells the viewer: here is something you have never heard before. And he has remained, too, an iconoclastic, almost capricious teller of darker truths. "I'm telling you," Brooks explains in *Premiere*, "I'm a guy trying to get the people right." In *Interview* magazine he concludes: "The truth about making movies is—is God help us if it's all that important."

## BIOGRAPHICAL/CRITICAL SOURCES:

*PERIODICALS*

*American Film*, May, 1989, p. 44.
*Chicago Tribune*, April 8, 1984; December 16, 1987; January 3, 1988.
*Commonweal*, January 29, 1988, p. 49.
*Cosmopolitan*, February, 1988, p. 40.
*Forbes*, November 12, 1990, p. 188.
*Interview*, April, 1988, p. 92.
*Los Angeles Times*, November 23, 1983; December 16, 1987; December 20, 1987; January 11, 1988.
*Movieline*, April, 1994, p. 36.
*Ms.*, March, 1988, p. 26.
*Nation*, January 23, 1988, p. 94.
*National Review*, February 5, 1988, p. 56.
*New Republic*, February 1, 1988, p. 26.
*Newsweek*, April 17, 1989, p. 72.
*New York*, February 1, 1988, p. 54.
*New Yorker*, January 11, 1988, p. 76.
*New York Times*, November 20, 1983; November 23, 1983; December 4, 1983; December 20, 1987; January 7, 1988.
*New York Times Magazine*, April 8, 1984.
*People*, December 21, 1987, p. 10.
*Premiere*, September, 1989, p. 105; March, 1994, p. 49.
*Rolling Stone*, June 28, 1990, p. 41.
*Vogue*, February, 1988, p. 86; April, 1988, p. 198.

*Washington Post,* October 5, 1979; November 23, 1983; December 13, 1987; December 25, 1987.*

\* \* \*

## BROWN, Laurene Krasny 1945-
### (Laurene Krasny Meringoff)

*PERSONAL:* Born December 16, 1945, in New York, NY; daughter of Morris (an accountant) and Helen (a teacher; maiden name, Meyer) Krasny; married Stephen Meringoff, August 27, 1967 (divorced September, 1974); married Marc Brown (an author and illustrator), September 11, 1983; children: Eliza Morgan; (stepchildren) Tucker Eliot, Tolon Adam. *Education:* Cornell University, B.S., 1966; Columbia University, M.A., 1967; Harvard University, Ed.D., 1978. *Religion:* Jewish. *Avocational interests:* Reading, writing letters and adding little pictures, cooking and baking, piano, walking, jogging, bicycling, gardening, canoeing, and collecting buttons, ribbons, and interesting scraps of paper and cloth.

*ADDRESSES: Home and office*—562 Main St., Hingham, MA 02043; Pilot Hill Farm, Tisbury, MA 02568 (summer). *Agent*—Phyllis Wender, 3 East 48th St., New York, NY 10017.

*CAREER:* Federal Headstart Program, Boston, MA, evaluator, 1967-68; Child Guidance Center, Cape Cod, MA, staff psychologist, 1968-71; Gene Reilly Group (consumer research), Darien, CT, senior research associate, 1972-74; Harvard University, Cambridge, MA, researcher at Center for Research in Children's Television, 1975-76, research associate and co-director of Project Zero (researching cognitive development in the arts), 1978-83; writer, 1983—. Consultant and expert witness for the Federal Trade Commission, 1978-79; consultant to better business bureaus and children's film producers.

*MEMBER:* Derby Academy (board of trustees).

*AWARDS, HONORS:* Grants from National Association of Broadcasters, 1976-77, and John and Mary R. Markle Foundation, 1977-83; *The Bionic Bunny Show* was selected a Notable Children's Book by the Association for Library Service to Children of the American Library Association, runner-up for *Redbook*'s Best Children's Book of the Year and one of *School Library Journal*'s Best Books of the Year, all 1984; silver honor for picturebooks, *Parent's Choice,* 1995.

*WRITINGS:*

(Contributor under name Laurene Krasny Meringoff) R. Adler, editor, *Effects of TV Advertising on Children,* Lexington Books (Lexington, MA), 1980.

(Editor under name Laurene Krasny Meringoff) *Children and Television: Annotated Bibliography,* Council of Better Business Bureaus, 1980.

(Contributor under name Laurene Krasny Meringoff) J. Bryant and D. R. Anderson, editors, *Children's Understanding of TV,* Academic Press (New York City), 1983.

*Taking Advantage of Media: A Manual for Parents and Teachers,* Routledge & Kegan Paul (Boston and London), 1986.

*Baby Time: A Grownup's Handbook to Use with Baby,* illustrated by husband, Marc Brown, Knopf (New York City), 1989.

*Yellow Fish, Blue Fish,* illustrated by M. Brown, Heath (Lexington, MA), 1989.

*Toddler Time: A Book to Share with Your Toddler,* illustrated by M. Brown, Joy Street Books (Boston), 1990.

*Rex and Lilly Family Time,* illustrated by M. Brown, Little, Brown (Boston), 1995.

*The Vegetable Show,* Little, Brown, 1995.

*Rex and Lilly Playtime,* illustrated by M. Brown, Little, Brown, 1995.

*Rex and Lilly Schooltime,* illustrated by M. Brown, Little, Brown, 1997.

Contributor to periodicals, including *School Library Journal, Journal of Aesthetic Education, Language Arts,* and *Journal of Educational Psychology.*

*JUVENILE; WITH HUSBAND, MARC BROWN*

*The Bionic Bunny Show* (children's picture book), Atlantic/Little, Brown (Boston), 1984.

*Visiting the Art Museum,* Dutton (New York City), 1986.

*Dinosaurs Divorce: A Guide for Changing Families,* Atlantic/Little, Brown, 1986.

*Dinosaurs Travel: A Guide for Families on the Go,* Joy Street Books, 1988.

*Dinosaurs Alive and Well: A Guide to Good Health,* Little, Brown, 1990.

*Dinosaurs to the Rescue! A Guide to Protecting Our Planet,* Joy Street Books, 1992.

*When Dinosaurs Die: A Guide to Understanding Death,* Little, Brown, 1996.

*WORK IN PROGRESS: What's the Big Secret?: A Guide to Sex for Girls and Boys,* for Little, Brown, 1997.

*SIDELIGHTS:* In *The Bionic Bunny Show* Laurene Krasny Brown and Marc Brown give young readers a behind-the-scenes look at the making of one episode of a superhero cartoon series called *The Bionic Bunny Show.* Portraying the Bionic Bunny as an actor-rabbit who is clumsy, nearsighted, and doesn't know his lines, the book "debunks the myth of the effortless superhero by showing us how much help the Bionic Bunny needs to pull off his heroism" and capture the dirty rat bank robbers, noted Carrie Carmichael in the *New York Times Book Review.* The critic deemed *The Bionic Bunny Show* "a very funny book" whose "humor and sarcasm" leaves children with the valuable perception "that television's superheroes are not what they seem"; Carmichael also commended the work's informative glossary of television terms.

Laurene Krasny Brown told *CA:* "Having spent many years as an educational psychologist and researcher of children, stories, and media, I find myself yearning to create fiction for young audiences instead of evaluating it. I suffer from Renaissance-woman fantasies of narrating stories for radio, producing films for children, illustrating their picture books, designing their computer software. Wishes come easily, however; seeing an idea through to a finished product is something else again. We shall see."

*BIOGRAPHICAL/CRITICAL SOURCES:*

PERIODICALS

*New York Times Book Review,* July 22, 1984.
*Publishers Weekly,* April 10, 1995; April 1, 1996.
*School Library Journal,* March, 1992.

\*    \*    \*

**BROWNE, William P(aul)   1945-**

*PERSONAL:* Born May 15, 1945, in Cherokee, IA; son of William D. (an automobile salesman) and Irene Etta (a hair stylist; maiden name, Lopau) Browne; married Linda S. Thomas (an elementary school principal), June 1, 1968. *Education:* Iowa State University, B.S., 1967, M.S., 1969; Washington University, St. Louis, Mo., Ph.D., 1971.

*ADDRESSES: Home*—5332 South Nottawa Road, Mt. Pleasant, MI 48858. *Office*—Department of Political Science, Central Michigan University, Mount Pleasant, MI 48859.

*CAREER:* Florissant Valley Junior College, St. Louis, MO, instructor in state and local politics, 1970; Central Michigan University, Mount Pleasant, assistant professor, 1971-74, associate professor, 1974-77, professor of political science, 1977—. Program manager, Institute for Personal and Career Development, 1973-75. Consultant to government agencies and private businesses.

*MEMBER:* American Agricultural Economics Association, American Political Science Association, American Society of Public Administration, Policy Studies Organization, Midwest Political Science Association, Michigan Conference of Political Scientists (member of board of directors, 1981-86; president, 1984-85), Weidman Lions Club (president, 1982).

*AWARDS, HONORS:* Creative Endeavors Award, Central Michigan University, 1973, 1975, 1977-82, 1984-85, 1990; University Achievement Award, 1974, for research in bureaucratic operations; grants from Ford Foundation, Dirksen Congressional Research Center, Farm Foundation, Resources for the Future, Economics Research Service, 1976, 1979-80, 1983-88; *Choice* Outstanding Academic Book award, 1987, 1989; Quality of Communiations award, American Agricultural Economics Association, 1993.

*WRITINGS:*

(Editor with Don Hadwiger) *The New Politics of Food,* Lexington Books (San Diego, CA), 1978.
(Editor with Hadwiger and Richard Fraenkel) *The Role of U.S. Agriculture in Foreign Policy,* Praeger (New York City), 1979.
*Politics, Programs and Bureaucrats,* Kennikat (Port Washington, NY), 1980.
(Editor with Hadwiger) *Rural Policy Problems: Changing Dimensions,* Lexington Books, 1982.
(Editor with Laura Katz Olson) *Public Policy and the Elderly: The Politics of Growing Old in America,* Greenwood Press (Westport, CT), 1983.
(Editor with Hadwiger) *World Food Policies: Toward Agricultural Interdependence,* Rienner Publishers (Swengel, PA), 1986.

(Editor with Hadwiger) *Public Policy and Agricultural Technology,* St. Martin's (New York City), 1987.

*Private Interests, Public Policy, and American Agriculture,* University Press of Kansas (Lawrence), 1988.

(With Allan Cigler) *U.S. Agricultural Groups: Institutional Profiles,* Greenwood, 1990.

(With Jerry Shees, Lou Swanson, Paul Thompson and Laurian Unnevehr) *Sacred Cows and Hot Potatoes: Agrarian Myths in Agriculture Policy,* Westview (Boulder, CO), 1992.

(With Kenneth Verburg) *Michigan Politics and Government: Facing Change in a Complex State,* University of Nebraska Press (Lincoln), 1995.

*Cultivating Congress: Constituents, Issues, and Interests in Agricultural Policymaking,* University Press of Kansas, 1995.

Contributor of about eighty articles to scholarly journals, including *Policy Studies Journal, Public Administration Review, State and Local Government Review,* and *Polity.* Member of editorial board of Policy Studies Organization, 1979-81.

*WORK IN PROGRESS:* Books on interest groups and their public policy effects.

*SIDELIGHTS:* William P. Browne told *CA:* "I've always been struck by the observation that professors, in particular, are little involved in the areas of their individual interest. As a result, they too often seem shallow and aloof from real world problems. Life should be advancement of knowledge, the identification of problems, and the search for solutions.

"Because I feel so strongly, I've operated under the personal rule that research and writing are the most critical parts of my professional life. To do neither, seems to me, an affront to those who hope to learn something under my direction. As a political scientist, my greatest contribution seems to be possible in the areas of public policy analysis, for the bottom line for government is how well it meets its goals in meeting social needs.

"I guess that food policy will always be my favorite area of policy studies. I was born in farm country, raised among those who produce food, and appreciate the prominent part food plays in both national and international politics. We all gravitate to those things that are most familiar to us. I've been extremely fortunate to spend so much time with members of Congress, lobbyists, food and farm activists, and administrators who share that familiarity and interest."

# C

## CAMPBELL, Maria 1940-

*PERSONAL:* Born June Stifle in April, 1940, in Park Valley, Saskatchewan, Canada; married (marriage dissolved); children: four.

*ADDRESSES: Home*—Gabriel's Crossing, Batoche, Saskatchewan, Canada. *Office*—Coach House Press, 401 Huron St., Toronto, Ontario, Canada, M5S 2G5.

*CAREER:* Writer. Cofounder of Edmonton Women's Halfway House and Women's Emergency Shelter. Writer-in-residence at University of Alberta, 1980, and University of Regina, 1982. Editor of *New Breed* (a newspaper).

*WRITINGS:*

*Halfbreed* (autobiography; also see below), Saturday Review Press (New York City), 1973.
*People of the Buffalo: How the Plains Indians Lived* (juvenile), illustrated by Douglas Tait and Shannon Twofeathers, Douglas & McIntyre, 1976.
*Little Badger and the Fire Spirit* (juvenile), illustrated by David Maclagan, McClelland & Stewart, 1977.
*The Red Dress* (screenplay), National Film Board, 1977.
*Riel's People* (juvenile), Douglas & McIntyre, 1978.
(With Linda Griffiths and Paul Thompson) *Jessica* (drama, based on *Halfbreed*), produced in Saskatoon, Saskatchewan, by 25th Street Theatre, 1982.
(Editor and author of introduction) *Achimoona* (short fiction), Fifth House (Saskatoon, Canada), 1985.

(With Linda Griffiths) *The Book of Jessica: A Theatrical Transformation* (nonfiction), Coach House Press (Toronto), 1989.
*Stories of the Road Allowance People,* Orca, 1995.

Author of radio plays, and *Edmonton's UnWanted Women,* a collective documentary for Canadian Broadcasting Corporation (CBC-TV); author of screenplay, *The Road Allowance People.* Contributor to magazines, including *Maclean's,* and newspapers.

*SIDELIGHTS:* Maria Campbell is a Canadian Metis writer and political activist whose first and best-known work is her autobiography, *Halfbreed.* "I write this for all of you," Campbell states in the introduction to *Halfbreed,* "to tell you what it is like to be a Halfbreed woman in our country. I want to tell you about the joys and sorrows, the oppressing poverty, the frustrations and the dreams." *Halfbreed* has been described as a passionate, moving fulfillment of this promise, and at the time of its publication in 1973, it was considered a unique literary endeavor. *The Bloomsbury Guide to Women's Literature* called Campbell's autobiography "the first book to articulate the oppressions and frustrations of Canadian Metis women." Campbell has also written several works for young people based on Native folklore and on Canadian Native history. Her coauthored publications, *Jessica* and *The Book of Jessica: A Theatrical Transformation,* both with Linda Griffiths, document the transformation of *Halfbreed* into a play, and the relationship that evolved between Campbell and Griffiths as they worked together over the course of more than five years.

Campbell's literary reputation rests on *Halfbreed,* in which she recounts her first thirty-three years: the poor but happy times of her early childhood, the struggle to keep her family together after the death of her mother, marriage at age fifteen, her husband's abandonment, and her subsequent recourse to prostitution, drugs, and alcohol. Throughout the narrative, critics have argued, Campbell attempts to place her own experience in the context of the Metis, people of mixed ancestry who are not officially recognized as Natives by the government. Campbell depicts the official treatment of her people as manipulative and abusive, when they are noticed at all, and the unofficial treatment as prejudiced, discriminatory, and scornful. The final sections of the book concern Campbell's work in the Native Rights movement and with young women writers.

In an interview with Hartmut Lutz and Konrad Gross in *Contemporary Challenges: Conversations with Canadian Native Authors,* Campbell stated that *Halfbreed* began as a letter to herself, "because I had to have somebody to talk to, and there was nobody to talk to." The resulting book, however, pared down from the original two thousand-page manuscript, has been viewed as a work with strong literary qualities. In an early review in *Best Sellers,* Cornelia Holbert remarked that *Halfbreed* contains "at least a dozen perfect short stories which could stand independently. Among the other credits accruing to [Campbell] are a Greek-drama simplicity, honesty neither shamed nor exhibitionist, and sensitivity." Writing in *Canadian Literature,* Agnes Grant commented that "though remarkable for its understatement, *Halfbreed* is a book choking with emotion. The author's sense of place and her dependence on that sense show up again and again in the first part of the book." Similarly, Penny Petrone remarked in *Native Literature in Canada: From the Oral Tradition to the Present* that *Halfbreed* is "rich with a sense of place and time, . . . a disturbing testimony to the ugliness of racism that is part of Canada's social history."

In *Jessica,* Campbell collaborated with actor/writer Linda Griffiths to create a play that follows the autobiographical outline of *Halfbreed* while also dramatizing the role of dreams and the spirit world in the heroine's life. The actors therefore have dual roles, as human characters and animal spirits. Wearing masks, they interact on an upper level of the set as spirits, influencing events; without their masks, they move to the middle level of the stage and take part in Jessica's Metis world; or they enter the lower level, which represents the white world. "The play's achievement lies in its vivid theatrical integration of

fabular elements and contemporary realities," wrote Diane Bessai in an essay collected in *Writing Saskatchewan: 20 Critical Essays.* In *The Book of Jessica* Campbell's voice is again joined with that of Linda Griffiths, as the two explain the difficulties of literary collaboration when the subject is the life of one of the collaborators.

Campbell is also the author of several children's books based on Native legends. *Little Badger and the Fire Spirit,* for instance, "was written because my grandson wanted to know where we got fire," the author told Lutz and Gross. "I don't think of myself as a writer," Campbell remarked in the same interview. "My work is in the community. Writing is just one of the tools that I use in my work as an organizer." Like *Halfbreed* and *Jessica,* Campbell's teleplay, *The Road Allowance People,* has been viewed by commentators as the author's attempt to use writing as a means toward a political end. The story, based on an actual event, takes place in 1948, in Saskatchewan, when a community of Metis is convinced by the Canadian government and the Catholic Church to leave their homes for land the government will give them some distance away. Transported in unheated cattle cars and left to freeze in the open when the homes they were promised do not materialize, many of them die; others attempt to return to their homes, only to find them destroyed. The story demonstrates the power of the church and the government over the Metis and explains why many mixed-blood Natives came to live along the side of the roads, earning the name "Road Allowance People."

Maria Campbell is considered an important voice in Native and feminist literary circles, primarily due to the historic, sociological, and literary import of her autobiography, *Halfbreed.* Commenting on *Halfbreed* in their book *American Indian Women: Telling Their Lives,* Gretchen M. Bataille and Kathleen Mullen Sands remarked: "This confessional and personal account by Maria Campbell marks a dramatic change in the autobiographies of American Indian women. Her life story is more like those of other contemporary women writers than those of previous Indian writers." Campbell's work with Native communities across Canada, documented in the last part of her autobiography, has inspired several of her other works, including *Achimoona,* an edited anthology of fiction written by young Natives; her rendering of Native lore in *Little Badger and the Fire Spirit;* and her writings on Native history—*People of the Buffalo: How the Plains Indians Lived* and *Riel's*

*People.* Campbell has also brought her message to works written for the stage and for television.

*BIOGRAPHICAL/CRITICAL SOURCES:*

*BOOKS*

Bataille, Gretchen M., and Kathleen Mullen Sands, *American Indian Women: Telling Their Lives,* University of Nebraska Press (Lincoln), 1984, pp. 113-26.

Blain, Virginia, Patricia Clements, and Isobel Grundy, *Feminist Companion to Literature in English: Women Writers from the Middle Ages to the Present,* Yale University Press, 1990.

Buck, Claire, editor, *The Bloomsbury Guide to Women's Literature,* Prentice Hall General Reference, 1992.

Campbell, Maria, *Halfbreed,* Saturday Review Press, 1973.

*Contemporary Literary Criticism,* Volume 85, Gale, 1995.

Hamilton, K. A., *Canada Writes! The Members' Book of the Writers' Union of Canada,* Writers' Union of Canada (Toronto), 1977.

King, Thomas, Cheryl Calver, and Helen Hoy, editors, *The Native in Literature,* ECW Press, 1987, pp. 188-205.

Lutz, Hartmut, editor, *Contemporary Challenges: Conversations with Canadian Native Authors,* Fifth House Publishers, 1991, pp. 41-65.

*Native North American Literature,* Gale, 1994.

Petrone, Penny, *Native Literature in Canada: From the Oral Tradition to the Present,* Oxford University Press Canada, 1990, pp. 113-37.

Probert, Kenneth G., editor, *Writing Saskatchewan: 20 Critical Essays,* University of Regina, 1989, pp. 100-10.

Schwartz, Narda Lacey, *Articles on Women Writers,* Vol. 2, *1976-1984: A Bibliography,* ABC-Clio (Santa Barbara, CA), 1986.

Vrana, Stan A., *Interviews and Conversations with 20th-Century Authors Writing in English: An Index,* series II, Scarecrow Press (Metuchen, NJ), 1986.

*PERIODICALS*

*American Indian Culture and Research Journal,* Volume 12, number 1, 1988, pp. 1-37.

*Best Sellers,* November 1, 1973, p. 344.

*Booklist,* December 15, 1973, pp. 418, 440.

*Books in Canada,* December, 1985, p. 12.

*Canadian Children's Literature,* number 31, 1983, p. 98, 105.

*Canadian Dimension,* September-October, 1993, p. 37.

*Canadian Journal of Native Studies,* Volume 12, number 2, pp. 321-23.

*Canadian Literature,* spring, 1990, p. 124; spring-summer, 1990, pp. 124-32; summer, 1992, p. 197; spring, 1993, pp. 24-39.

*Choice,* January, 1972, p. 1450.

*Emergency Librarian,* January, 1984, p. 39.

*Instructor,* summer, 1986, p. 50.

*Journal of Reading,* December, 1982, p. 220.

*Kirkus Reviews,* July 1, 1973, p. 722.

*Kliatt,* winter, 1983, p. 36.

*Library Journal,* November 1, 1971, p. 3594; July, 1973, p. 2079.

*Maclean's Magazine,* November 15, 1982, p. 78.

*Performing Arts in Canada,* spring, 1990, p. 36.

*Publishers Weekly,* July 2, 1973, p. 76.

*Quill and Quire,* December, 1985, p. 24.

*Saturday Night,* August, 1973, pp. 31-32; November, 1976, p. 72.

*School Library Journal,* November, 1978, p. 41.

*Washington Post Book World,* September 23, 1973, p. 15.*

      \*    \*    \*

**CAMPBELL, Tom D.**    **1938-**

*PERSONAL:* Born March 3, 1938, in Glasgow, Scotland; son of Sidney Thomson (a lawyer) and Bessie (Barrow) Campbell; children: Flora M., A. Magnus. *Education:* University of Glasgow, M.A., 1962, Ph.D., 1969; Oxford University, B.A., 1964.

*ADDRESSES: Home*—50 Brereton St., Garran, ACT 2605, Australia. *Office*— Faculty of Law, Australian National University, ACT 0200, Australia; fax 06-249-0097.

*CAREER:* University of Glasgow, Glasgow, Scotland, lecturer in politics, 1964-69, and moral philosophy, 1970-73; University of Stirling, Stirling, Scotland, professor of philosophy, 1973-79; University of Glasgow, professor of jurisprudence, 1979-90; Australian National University, professor of Law, 1990—. *Military service:* British Army, 1956-58; became lieutenant.

*MEMBER:* Academy of Social Sciences of Australia (fellow), United Kingdom Association of Legal and Social Philosophy (president, 1986), Royal Society of Edinburgh (fellow).

*WRITINGS:*

*Adam Smith's Science of Morals,* Allen & Unwin (London), 1971.
*Seven Theories of Human Society,* Oxford University Press (Oxford, England), 1981.
*The Left and Rights: Conceptual Analysis of the Idea of Socialist Rights,* Routledge & Kegan Paul (London), 1983.
(Editor with David Goldberg, Sheila McLean, and Tom Mullen) *Human Rights: From Rhetoric to Reality,* Basil Blackwell (Oxford, England), 1986.
*Justice,* Macmillan (London, England), 1988.
*Mental Illness: Prejudice, Discrimination and the Law,* Gower (Aldershot, Hants, England), 1989.
*The Legal Theory of Ethical Positivism,* Dartmouth (Brookfield, VT), 1996.

*BIOGRAPHICAL/CRITICAL SOURCES:*

*PERIODICALS*

*Times Literary Supplement,* August 22, 1986.

\*　　\*　　\*

**CARBALLIDO, Emilio 1925-**

*PERSONAL:* Born May 22, 1925, in Cordoba, Veracruz, Mexico; son of Francisco Carballido and Blanca Rosa Fentanes; children: Juan de Dios. *Education:* Universidad Nacional Autonoma de Mexico, 1945-49. *Politics:* Third positionist. *Religion:* Catholic.

*ADDRESSES: Office*—Instituto Nacional de Bellas Artes, Bosque de Chapultapec, 11580 Miquel Hidalgo, Mexico D.F., Mexico.

*CAREER:* Universidad Veracruzana, Xalapa, Mexico, sub-director of Escuela de Teatro, 1954, member of Editorial Council, 1959—, Faculty of Philosophy and Letters, professor, 1960-61; Instituto Nacional de Bellas Artes, Escuela de Arte Teatral, Mexico City, Mexico, professor, 1955—; Ballet

Nacional A.C., Mexico, literary advisor, 1957—, public relations representative on European and Asian tours, 1957-58; Instituto Politecnico Nacional, Mexico City, Mexico, Departamento de Difusion Cultural, staff member, 1960-74, Taller de Composicion Dramatica, director, 1969-74; Universidad Nacional Autonoma de Mexico, Mexico City, professor of dramatic theory and composition and head of Seminario de Teatro Mexicano, 1965-68. Visiting professor at Rutgers University, 1965-66, and University of Pittsburgh, 1970-71.

*MEMBER:* Sindicato de Trabajadores de la Produccion Cinematografica (secretary, Seccion de Autores y Adaptadores).

*AWARDS, HONORS:* Second prize in Concurso Nacional de Teatro, 1950, for *La zona intermedia: Auto sacramental;* Rockefeller fellowship, 1950; Centro Mexicano de Escritores fellowship, 1951-52, and 1955-56; second prize in libretto contest, Opera Nacional, 1953, for *El pozo;* first prize in Universidad Nacional Autonoma de Mexico contest, 1954, for *La hebra de oro; El Nacional* prize, 1954, for *La danza que suena la tortuga;* first prize in theatre, Festival Regional, Instituto Nacional de Bellas Artes, 1955, and Ruiz de Alarcon Critics' Prize for the best work of 1957, both for *Felicidad; El Nacional* prize, 1958, for *El dia que se soltaron los leones;* Premio de los Criticos No-asociados for the best work of 1960, for *El relojero de Cordoba;* Menorah de Oro prize for best film continuity of 1961, for *Macario;* Instituto Internacional de Teatro prize, Mexican branch, 1962, and honorable mention, Paris, 1963, both for *Medusa; Casa de las Americas* prize, 1962, for *Un pequeno dia de ira;* Ruiz de Alarcon Prize for best play of the year, 1966, for *Yo tambien hablo de la rosa,* and 1968, for *Medusa; El Heraldo* prize, 1967, for *Te juro, Juana, que tengo ganas,* and 1975, for *Las cartas de Mozart;* Asociacion de Criticos y Cronistas prize, 1976, for *Un pequeno dia de ira.*

*WRITINGS:*

*PLAYS*

*La triple porfia* (title means "The Triple Cross"; one-act farce), first produced in Mexico City, Mexico, at the theatre of Escuela de Arte Teatral, Instituto Nacional de Bellas Artes, 1949.
*El triangulo sutil* (title means "The Subtle Triangle"; one-act farce), privately produced in Mexico City, 1949.

*La zona intermedia: Auto sacramental* (also see below; first produced in Mexico City at Teatro Latino, 1950), published in English translation by Margaret Sayers Peden as *The Intermediate Zone* in *The Golden Thread and Other Plays* (also see below).

*Escribir, por ejemplo* (title means "To Write, For Example"; monologue; also see below) first produced in Mexico City at Teatro del Caracol, 1950.

*Rosalba y los llaveros* (title means "Rosalba and the Turnkeys"; three-act comedy; also see below), first produced in Mexico City at Palacio de Bellas Artes, 1950.

*La sinfonia domestica* (title means "The Domestic Symphony"; three-act comedy), first produced in Mexico City, at Teatro Ideal, 1953.

(With Sergio Magana) *El viaje de Nocresida* (three-act juvenile comedy), first produced in Mexico City at Palacio de Bellas Artes, 1953.

*Felicidad* (title means "Happiness"; three-act), first produced in Mexico City, at Teatro Reforma, 1955, published in *Concurso Mexicano de Teatro: Obras premiadas,* Instituto Nacional de Bellas Artes, 1956.

*La danza que suena la tortuga* (title means "The Dance the Turtle Dreams About"; three-act comedy), first produced as *Palabras cruzadas* in Mexico City at Teatro de la Comedia, 1955, Fonda de Cultura Economica, 1957.

(With Luisa Bauer and Fernando Wagner) *Cinco pasos al cielo* (title means "Five Steps to Heaven"; three-act juvenile comedy), first produced in Mexico City at Palacio de Bellas Artes, 1959.

*La hebra de oro* (three act, first produced in Mexico City at Teatro Reforma, 1959), translation by Peden published as *The Golden Thread* in *The Golden Thread and Other Plays* (also see below).

*Selaginela* (monologue; also see below), first produced in Mexico City at Teatro de la Feria del Libro, 1959.

*El censo* (comedy; also see below), first produced in Mexico City at Teatro de la Feria del Libro, 1959; produced in New York City by Repertorio Espanol, 1977.

*Las estatuas de marfil* (title means "The Ivory Statues"; three-act), first produced in Mexico City at Teatro Ofelia, 1960, Universidad Veracruzana, 1960.

*El relojero de Cordoba* (two-act comedy), first produced in Mexico City at Teatro del Bosque, 1960, translation by Peden published as *The Clockmaker from Cordoba* in *The Golden Thread and Other Plays* (also see below).

*La lente maravillosa* (juvenile), first produced in Mexico City at Teatro Orientacion, 1960.

*El jardinero y los pajaros* (title means "The Gardener and the Birds"; juvenile), first produced in Mexico City at Teatro Orientacion, 1960.

*Guillermo y el nahual* (juvenile), first produced in Mexico City at Teatro Orientacion, 1960.

*Homenaje a Hidalgo* (pageant with actors, dance company, chorus, soloists, and symphony orchestra), with music by Rafael Elizondo, first produced in Mexico City at Palacio de Bellas Artes, 1960, expanded version produced in Mexico City at Plaza de la Alhondiga, 1965.

*Teseo* (tragicomedy), first produced in Mexico City at Teatro Xola, 1962, published in *La Palabra y El Hombre,* Number 24, 1962; translation by Peden published as *Theseus* in *The Golden Thread and Other Plays* (also see below).

*Parasitas* (monologue; also see below), first produced in German as *Die Parasiten* in Kiel, West Germany, at Theatre of the State Capital, 1963.

*La perfecta casada* (title means "The Perfect Wife"; one-act; also see below), first produced in Xalapa, Mexico, at Teatro del Estado, 1963.

*El dia que se soltaron los leones* (three-act farce; also see below), first produced in Havana at Teatro del Sotano, 1963, translation by William Oliver published as *The Day They Let the Lions Loose* in *New Voices in Latin American Theatre,* University of Texas Press (Austin), 1971.

*Silencio, pollos pelones, ya les van a echar su maiz . . . !* (farce), first produced in Ciudad Juarez, Mexico, at Teatro de Seguro Social, 1963; produced in Mexico City at Teatro Urueta, 1964; translation by Ruth S. Lamb produced as *Shut Up, You Plucked Chickens, You're Going to Be Fed!* in Claremont, CA, at Scripps College, 1969, Aguilar, 1963.

*Los hijos del capitan Grant* (three-act melodrama for children, based on a novel by Jules Verne), first produced in Mexico City by Compania Estudiantil de la Preparatoria Numero 5 at their theatre, 1964; produced in Mexico City at Palacio de Bellas Artes, 1966.

*Medusa* (five-act tragicomedy; also see below), first produced in English translation by Mary Madiraca under same title in Ithaca, NY, at Cornell University, 1966.

*Yo tambien hablo de la rosa,* first produced in Mexico City at Teatro Jimenez Rueda, 1966; translation by Myrna Winer produced as *I Also Speak about the Rose* in Northridge, CA, at San Fernando Valley State College, 1972, Departamento de Teatro, Instituto Nacional de

Bellas Artes, 1966, 2nd edition, 1970, translation by Oliver published as *I Too Speak to the Rose* in *Drama and Theatre,* Number 1, 1970.

*Te juro, Juana, que tengo ganas* (title means "I Swear to You, Joan, I Want To"; farce), first produced in Mexico City at Teatro del Granero, 1967; produced in New York City by the Repertorio Espanol, 1977, published in *La Palabra y El Hombre,* Number 35, 1965.

*Almanque de Juarez* (dramatic collage-spectacle), first produced in Mexico City at Teatro del Bosque, 1968.

*Tianguis!* (spectacle), first produced in Mexico City at Auditorio Nacional, 1968.

*Las noticias del dia* (title means "The News of the Day"; dialogue), Coleccion Teatro de Bolsillo, 1968.

*Un pequeno dia de ira,* first produced in Havana on Cuban television, 1969; produced in Mexico City, 1976; translation by Peden produced as *A Short Day's Anger* in Pittsburgh, PA, at University of Pittsburgh, 1970, Casa de las Americas (Havana), 1962.

*Un vals sin fin por el planeta* (title means "An Endless Waltz around the Planet"; comedy), directed by Carballido, first produced in Mexico City at Teatro Orientacion, 1970.

*Acapulco, los lunes* (title means "Acapulco, On Mondays"; farce), first produced in Mexico City at Teatro Antonio Caso, 1970, Ediciones Sierra Madre, 1969.

*La fonda de las siete cabrillas* (farce; based on *Don Bonifacio* by Manuel Eduardo de Gorostiza), first produced in Mexico City by Compania Popular de la Ciudad de Mexico, 1970.

*Conversacion entre las ruinas,* first produced in English translation by Myra Gann as *Conversation among the Ruins* in Kalamazoo, MI, at Kalamazoo College, 1971; produced in New York City at Puerto Rican Traveling Theater, June, 1989.

*Las cartas de Mozart,* first produced in Mexico City at Teatro Jimenez Rueda, 1975.

*Nahui Ollin* (commissioned by Consejo Nacional de Cultura, Venezuela), first produced in Caracas, Venezuela, 1977.

*13 veces el D.F.,* Editores Mexicanos Unidos, 1985.

*Rose of Two Aromas,* translation by Peden, produced in New York City at Puerto Rican Traveling Theater, March, 1987.

*Flor de abismo,* Grupo Editorial Planeta, 1994.

*Querataro imperial,* H. Ayuntamiento de Querataro Coordinacion de Publicaciones, 1994.

Also author, with Luisa Josefina Hernandez, of *Pastores de la ciudad* (also see below), first produced at Teatro Universitario de Puebla.

*PLAY COLLECTIONS*

*La zona intermedia: Auto sacramental* [and] *Escribir, por ejemplo,* Coleccion Teatro Mexicano, 1951.

*La hebra de oro* (contains *La hebra de oro* and *El lugar y el boro* [translation by Peden published as *The Time and the Place: Dead Love* in *The Golden Thread and Other Plays* (also see below)]), Imprenta Universitaria, Universidad Nacional Autonoma de Mexico, 1957.

*D.F.,* (title means "Federal District"; contains nine one-act plays: *Misa primera, Selaginela, El censo, Escribir, por ejemplo, El espejo* [English translation by Margaret Sayers Peden published as *The Mirror* in *The Golden Thread and Other Plays* (also see below)], *Hipolito, Tangentes, Parasitas,* and *La medalla*), Coleccion Teatro Mexicano, 1957, 2nd edition published with preamble and five additional plays (also contains: *La perfecta casada, Paso de madrugada, El solitario en octubre, Un cuento de Navidad,* and *Pastores de la ciudad*), Universidad Veracruzana, 1962, revised and enlarged edition published as *D.F.: 26 obras en un acto* (title means "Federal District: 26 One-Act Works"), Editorial Grijalbo, 1978.

*Teatro* (contains *El relojero de Cordoba, Medusa, Rosalba y los llaveros,* and *El dia que se soltaron los leones*), Fondo de Cultura Economica, 1960, French & European Publications, 1969.

*The Golden Thread and Other Plays* (contains *The Mirror, The Time and the Place: Dead Love, The Glacier, The Wine Cellar, The Golden Thread, The Intermediate Zone, The Clockmaker from Cordoba,* and *Theseus*), translation and introduction by Peden, Unversity of Texas Press, 1970.

*Tres comedias* (contains *Un vals sin fin por el planeta, La danza que suena la tortuga,* and *Felicidad*), Extemporaneos, 1981.

*Silencio pollos pelones, ya les van a echar su maaiz; Un pequeno dia de ira; Acapulco, los lunes,* Editores Mexicanos Unidos, 1985.

*Orinoco; Las cartas de Mozart; Felicidad,* Editores Mexicanos Unidos, 1985.

*Teatro 2,* Fondo de Cultura Economica, 1988.

*Teatre de Emilio Carballido,* Gobierno del Estado de Veracruz, 1992.

*Orinoco, Rosa de dos aromas y otra piezas dramaticas,* Fondo de Cultura Economica, 1994.

*Fotographia en la playa; Sonar la noche; Las cartas de Mozart,* Grupo Editorial Gaceta, 1994.

OTHER

*La veleta oxidada* (title means "The Rusty Weathervane"; novel), Los Presentes (Mexico), 1956.
*El norte* (novel), Universidad Veracruzana, 1958, translation by Peden published as *The Norther,* with introduction by Peden, University of Texas Press, 1968.
*La caja vacia* (title means "The Empty Box"; short stories), Fondo de Cultura Economica, 1962.
*Macario* (filmscript), Azteca, 1968.
*Las visitaciones del diablo: Folletin romantico en XV partes* (novel; also see below), J. Mortiz (Mexico), 1965, 2nd edition, 1969.
*El sol* (novel), J. Mortiz, 1970.
(Compiler) *Teatro joven de Mexico* (anthology), Editorial Novaro, 1973.
(Compiler and contributor) *El arca de Noe* (anthology), Secretaria de Educacion Publica, 1974.
*Los zapatos de fierro* (novel), J. Mortiz, 1977.
*Tiempo de ladrones: La historia de Chucho el Roto,* Grijalbo, 1983.
*El tren que corria,* Fondo de Cultura Economica, 1984.
(Compiler) *Nueve obras jovenes,* Editores Mexicanos Unidos, 1985.
(Editor) *Avanzada: Mas teatro joven,* Editores Mexicanos Unidos, 1985.
(Compiler) *Le teatro Mexicano, 1999: Un anthologie,* Editora del Gobierno del Estado de Veracruz-Llave, 1993.

Also author of play, *Auto del juicio final* (title means "Auto of the Judgment Day"); and of filmscripts, including *Felicidad* (adapted from his play of the same title), *Los novios, Las visitaciones del diablo* (adapted from his novel of the same title), *Rosa Blanca, El aguila descalza,* and *La torre de marfil.* Also author of two ballets, *El invisible* and *Ermesinda,* both first produced in Mexico City at Palacio de Bellas Artes, 1952, and of operas, *Misa de seis,* first produced at Palacio de Bellas Artes, 1962, and *El pozo.* Contributor to anthologies. Contributor of plays to *Revista de Bellas Artes, Revista de la Universidad de Mexico, Novedades, El Nacional,* and *America: Revista Antologica;* contributor of stories to *Texas Quarterly* and *Izvestia* (Moscow). Founder and director of *Tramoya,* theatre quarterly published by Universidad Veracruzana, 1975—.

ADAPTATIONS: *El censo* was produced on Spanish television in 1970, and *Yo tambien hablo de la rosa* was produced on French television, 1973; several of Carabillido's other plays have also been adapted for production on Spanish television, including *Felicidad, La danza que suena la tortuga,* and *El relojero de Cordoba.*\*

\*　\*　\*

CARO, Francis G(eorge)　1936-

PERSONAL: Born September 28, 1936, in Milwaukee, WI; son of Walter (an engineer) and Elizabeth (Voss) Caro; married Carol Bauer (a librarian), December 28, 1965; children: Paul, David. *Education:* Marquette University, B.S., 1958; University of Minnesota, Ph.D., 1962. *Politics:* Democrat.

ADDRESSES: *Home*—27 Elba St., Brookline, MA 02146. *Office*—Gerontology Institute, University of Massachusetts—Boston, Boston, MA 02125.

CAREER: Community Studies, Inc., Kansas City, MO, research associate, 1962-64; Community Progress, Inc., New Haven, CT, research associate, 1964-65; Marquette University, Milwaukee, WI, assistant professor of sociology, 1965-67; University of Colorado, Boulder, associate professor of sociology, 1967-70; Brandeis University, Waltham, MA, associate professor of social welfare, 1970-74; Community Service Society, New York City, director of Institute for Social Welfare Research, 1974-88; University of Massachusetts—Boston, Gerontology Institute, director of Manning Research Division, 1988—.

MEMBER: Gerontological Society.

WRITINGS:

(Editor) *Readings in Evaluation Research,* Russell Sage (New York City), 1970, 2nd edition, 1977.
(With Dwight L. Frankfather and Michael J. Smith) *Family Care of the Elderly,* Lexington Books (Lexington, MA), 1981.
(With Arthur E. Blank) *Quality Impact of Home Care for the Elderly,* Haworth Press (New York City), 1988.
(Co-editor with Scott A. Bass and Yung-Ping Chen) *Achieving a Productive Aging Society,* Auburn House (Westport, CT), 1993.

Contributor to gerontology and evaluation research journals.

*WORK IN PROGRESS:* Book on Future of long-term care with Robert Morris.

\* \* \*

**CAVERHILL, Nicholas**
**See KIRK-GREENE, Anthony (Hamilton Millard)**

\* \* \*

**CHANDLER, David Porter 1933-**

*PERSONAL:* Born February 7, 1933, in New York, NY; son of Porter R. (a lawyer) and Gabrielle (Chanler; an artist) Chandler; married Susan Saunders (a consultant), June 3, 1967; children: Elizabeth Margaret, Thomas. *Ethnicity:* "Caucasian." *Education:* Harvard University, B.A., 1954; Yale University, M.A., 1968; University of Michigan, Ph.D., 1973. *Politics:* Democrat.

*ADDRESSES: Home*—6 Orford Rd., Ashburton, Victoria 3147, Australia; fax 613-9905-2210. *Office*—Centre of Southeast Asian Studies, Monash University, Clayton, Victoria 3168, Australia. *E-mail*—dchandle@arts.monash.edu.au.

*CAREER:* Department of State, Washington, DC, foreign service officer, 1958-66; Monash University, Clayton, Australia, lecturer in history, 1972-81, associate professor, 1981-92, professor, 1993-96. Centre of Southeast Asian Studies, research director, 1978-96. *Military service:* U.S. Army, 1955-57.

*MEMBER:* Asian Studies Association of Australia, Association of Asian Studies, Australian Academy of the Humanities, Phi Beta Kappa.

*WRITINGS:*

*The Land and People of Cambodia,* Lippincott (Philadelphia, PA), 1972, completely revised edition, HarperCollins (New York City), 1987.
(Translator) *The Friends Who Tried to Empty the Sea: Eleven Cambodian Folk Stories,* Monash University (Clayton, Australia), 1976.

(With Ben Kiernan and Muy Hong Lim) *The Early Phases of Liberation in Northwestern Cambodia* (booklet), Centre of Southeast Asian Studies, Monash University, 1977.
(Translator) *Favourite Stories from Cambodia,* Heinemann in Asia Educational Books (London, England), 1978.
*A History of Cambodia,* Westview (Boulder, CO), 1983, revised edition, 1996.
(Editor with Kiernan) *Revolution and Its Aftermath in Kampuchea: Eight Essays,* Yale University Southeast Asia Monograph Series (New Haven, CT), 1983.
(Editor and translator with Kiernan and Chanthou Boua) *Pol Pot Plans the Future: Confidential Leadership Documents from Democratic Kampuchea, 1976-1977,* Yale University Southeast Asia Monograph Series, 1988.
*The Tragedy of Cambodian History: Politics, War and Revolution since 1945,* Yale University Press, 1991.
*Brother Number One: A Political Biography of Pol Pot,* Westview Press, 1992.
(With Ian Mabbett) *The Khmers,* Blackwell (Oxford, England), 1995.
*Facing the Cambodian Past: Selected Essays, 1971-1995,* Allen & Unwin (London), 1996.

Contributor to *World Book Encyclopedia* and *Encyclopaedia Britannica.* Also contributor to periodicals, including *Commonweal, Current History, Journal of the Siam Society,* and *Pacific Affairs.*

Chandler's *Brother Number One: A Political Biography of Pol Pot* has been translated into French, Japanese and Thai.

*WORK IN PROGRESS:* A book-length study on the pathology of terror in Pol Pot's Cambodia, based on the archive of the regime's secret prison; an historical dictionary of Cambodia; a translation of a 19th century Cambodian verse chronicle dealing with warfare with Vietnam in 1830s.

*SIDELIGHTS: History* contributor Ian Brown notes that David P. Chandler's *A History of Cambodia* "is the first scholarly history of Cambodia to appear in English, and the first in any European language for some seventy years." In a *Times Literary Supplement* review, Anthony Barnett recommends the book's second section which deals with Cambodian history from the late eighteenth century through the end of French control of the area. In this part of the book, according to Barnett, Chandler "writes as someone whose own primary researches . . . have made him a foremost authority."

David P. Chandler told *CA*: "With hindsight, my most important decision as a writer was to volunteer for Cambodian language training when I was a fledgling Foreign Service Officer in Washington in 1959. The choice led to my spending two extraordinary years in Cambodia (1960-1962); these, in turn, led me to specialize in Cambodian history as a graduate student when I resigned from the Foreign Service in 1966.

"The Khmer Rouge era with its fierce totalism, thoughtless cruelty and horrific effects took me by surprise but as an historian I felt obliged to study this daunting period in depth so as to understand how it connects with human nature, with earlier times in Cambodia and with terrorist regimes in other countries.

"Research on the Khmer Rouge took me to France, Canada, Thailand and the United States as well as Cambodia, which I began to visit again after a twenty-year absence in 1990. Since then, I have visited the country seven times, on three occasions on missions for Amnesty International. These trips have sharpened my insights and softened some of my more dogmatic notions about Cambodia and its past."

*BIOGRAPHICAL/CRITICAL SOURCES:*

PERIODICALS

*History,* June, 1985.
*Pacific Affairs,* winter, 1994, p. 625; spring, 1995, p. 140.
*Times Literary Supplement,* September 14, 1984.

\*     \*     \*

## COETZEE, J(ohn) M(ichael)    1940-

*PERSONAL:* Born February 9, 1940, in Cape Town, South Africa; son of an attorney (father) and a schoolteacher (mother); married, 1963 (divorced, 1980); children: Nicholas, Gisela. *Education:* University of Cape Town, B.A. 1960, M.A., 1963; University of Texas, Austin, Ph.D., 1969.

*ADDRESSES: Home*—P.O. Box 92, Rondebosch, Cape Province 7700, South Africa. *Agent*—Peter Lampack, 551 Fifth Ave., New York, NY 10017.

*CAREER:* International Business Machines (IBM), London, England, applications programmer, 1962-63; International Computers, Bracknell, Berkshire, England, systems programmer, 1964-65; State University of New York at Buffalo, assistant professor, 1968-71, Butler Professor of English, 1984, 1986; University of Cape Town, Cape Town, South Africa, lecturer in English, 1972-82, professor of general literature, 1983—; Johns Hopkins University, Hinkley Professor of English, 1986, 1989; Harvard University, visiting professor of English, 1991.

*MEMBER:* International Comparative Literature Association, Modern Language Association of America.

*AWARDS, HONORS:* CNA Literary Award, 1977, for *In the Heart of the Country;* CNA Literary Award, James Tait Black Memorial Prize, and Geoffrey Faber Award, all 1980, all for *Waiting for the Barbarians;* CNA Literary Award, Booker-McConnell Prize, and Prix Femina Etranger, all 1984, all for *The Life and Times of Michael K;* D. Litt., University of Strathclyde, Glasgow, 1985; Jerusalem Prize for the Freedom of the Individual in Society, 1987; *Irish Times* International Fiction Prize, 1995, for *The Master of Petersburg;* Life Fellow, University of Cape Town.

*WRITINGS:*

NOVELS

*Dusklands* (contains two novellas, *The Vietnam Project* and *The Narrative of Jacobus Coetzee*), Ravan Press (Johannesburg), 1974, Penguin Books (New York City), 1985.
*From the Heart of the Country,* Harper (New York City), 1977, published in England as *In the Heart of the Country,* Secker & Warburg, 1977, reprinted as *In the Heart of the Country,* Penguin Books, 1982.
*Waiting for the Barbarians,* Secker & Warburg, 1980, Penguin Books, 1982.
*The Life and Times of Michael K.,* Secker & Warburg, 1983, Viking (New York City), 1984.
*Foe,* Viking, 1987.
*Age of Iron,* Random House (New York City), 1990.
*The Master of Petersburg,* Viking, 1994.

OTHER

(Translator) Marcellus Emants, *A Posthumous Confession,* Twayne (Boston), 1976.

(Translator) Wilma Stockenstroem, *The Expedition to the Baobab Tree,* Faber, 1983.

(Editor with Andre Brink) *A Land Apart: A Contemporary South African Reader,* Viking, 1987.

*White Writing: On the Culture of Letters in South Africa* (essays), Yale University Press (New Haven, CT), 1988.

*Doubling the Point: Essays and Interviews,* edited by David Attwell, Harvard University Press (Cambridge, MA), 1992.

*Giving Offense: Essays on Censorship,* University of Chicago Press (Chicago), 1996.

ADAPTATIONS: An adaptation of *In the Heart of the Country* was filmed as *Dust,* by ICA (Great Britain), 1986.

SIDELIGHTS: Often using his native South Africa as a backdrop, J. M. Coetzee explores the implications of oppressive societies on the lives of their inhabitants. As a South African, however, Coetzee is "too intelligent a novelist to cater for moralistic voyeurs," Peter Lewis declared in *Times Literary Supplement.* "This does not mean that he avoids the social and political crises edging his country towards catastrophe. But he chooses not to handle such themes in the direct, realistic way that writers of older generations, such as Alan Paton, preferred to employ. Instead, Coetzee has developed a symbolic and even allegorical mode of fiction—not to escape the living nightmare of South Africa but to define the psychopathological underlying the sociological, and in doing so to locate the archetypal in the particular."

Though many of his stories are set in South Africa, Coetzee's lessons are relevant to all countries, as *Books Abroad*'s Ursula A. Barnett wrote of *Dusklands,* which contains the novellas *The Vietnam Project* and *The Narrative of Jacobus Coetzee.* "By publishing the two stories side by side," Barnett remarked, "Coetzee has deliberately given a wider horizon to his South African subject. Left on its own, *The Narrative of Jacobus Coetzee* would immediately have suggested yet another tale of African black-white confrontation to the reader." Although each is a complete story, "their nature and design are such that the book can and should be read as a single work," Roger Owen commented in *Times Literary Supplement. Dusklands* "is a kind of diptych, carefully hinged and aligned, and of a texture so glassy and mirror-like that each story throws light on the other." Together the tales present two very different outcomes in confrontations between the individual and society.

*The Vietnam Project* introduces Eugene Dawn, employed to help the Americans win the Vietnam War through psychological warfare. The assignment eventually costs Dawn his sanity. The title character of *The Narrative of Jacobus Coetzee,* a fictionalized ancestor of the author, is an explorer and conqueror in the 1760s who destroys an entire South African tribe over his perception that the people have humiliated him through their indifference and lack of fear. H. M. Tiffin, writing in *Contemporary Novelists,* found that the novellas in *Dusklands* are "juxtaposed to offer a scarifying account of the fear and paranoia of imperialists and aggressors and the horrifying ways in which dominant regimes, 'empires,' commit violence against 'the other' through repression, torture, and genocide."

Coetzee's second novel, *In the Heart of the Country,* also explores racial conflict and mental deterioration. A spinster daughter, Magda, tells the story in diary form, recalling the consequences of her father's seduction of his African workman's wife. Both jealous of and repulsed by the relationship, Magda murders her father, then begins her own affair with the workman. The integrity of Magda's story eventually proves questionable. "The reader soon realizes that these are the untrustworthy ravings of a hysterical, demented individual consumed by loneliness and her love/hate relationship with her patriarchal father," Barend J. Toerien reported in *World Literature Today.* Magda's "thoughts range widely, merging reality with fantasy, composing and recomposing domestic dramas for herself to act in and, eventually introducing voices . . . to speak to her from the skies," Sheila Roberts noted in *World Literature Written in English.* "She imagines that the voices accuse her, among other things, of transforming her uneventful life into a fiction." *World Literature Today*'s Charles R. Larson found *In the Heart of the Country* "a perplexing novel, to be sure, but also a fascinating novelistic exercise in the use of cinematic techniques in prose fiction," describing the book as reminiscent of an overlapping "series of stills extracted from a motion picture."

Coetzee followed *In the Heart of the Country* with *Waiting for the Barbarians,* in which the author, "with laconic brilliance, articulates one of the basic problems of our time—how to *understand* . . . mentality behind the brutality and injustice," Anthony Burgess wrote in *New York.* In the novel, a magistrate attempting to protect the peaceful nomadic people of his district is imprisoned and tortured by the army that arrives at the frontier town to destroy the "barbarians" on behalf of the Empire. The horror of what he has seen and experienced affects the magistrate in inalterable ways, bringing changes in his personality that he cannot understand. Doris Grumbach, writing in the *Los Angeles Times Book Review,* found *Waiting for the Barbarians* a book with "universal reference," an allegory which can be applied to innumerable historical and contemporary situations. "Very soon it is apparent that the story, terrifying and unforgettable, is about injustice and barbarism inflicted everywhere by 'civilized' people upon those it invades, occupies, governs." "The intelligence Coetzee brings us in *Waiting for the Barbarians* comes straight from Scripture and Dostoevsky," Webster Schott asserted in the *Washington Post Book World.* "We possess the devil. We are all barbarians."

In *Waiting for the Barbarians* Coetzee "succeeded in creating a tragic fable of colonialism that surpassed the boundaries of his native South Africa and made universal the agony of its conscience-stricken European protagonist," Christopher Lehmann-Haupt remarked in the *New York Times.* "In . . . *The Life and Times of Michael K.,* Mr. Coetzee goes even further in the same direction." The story follows the title character as he helps his dying mother on a journey to her childhood home. She dies along the way, leaving Michael, a disfigured and supposedly slow-witted young man, to fend for himself in a country at war. "Mr. Coetzee's landscapes of suffering are defined by the little by little art of moral disclosure—his stories might be about anyone and anyplace," Cynthia Ozick commented in the *New York Times Book Review.* "At the same time they defy the vice of abstraction; they are engrossed in the minute and the concrete. It would be possible, following Mr. Coetzee's dazzlingly precise illuminations, to learn how to sow, or use a pump, or make a house of earth." In a review for *Maclean's,* Mark Abley found that the book "begins as a study of an apparently ordinary man; it develops into a portrait of an exceptional human being, written with unusual power and beauty."

Coetzee's work is often compared to that of Franz Kafka, a reference that appears in many reviews of *The Life and Times of Michael K.* In the *Chicago Tribune Book World,* Charles R. Larson described the author as "writing from a tradition that might be identified as Kafkaesque," noting that Michael K. "shares the same initial as Kafka's heroes. Moreover, the world in which he tries to operate is unknowable in many of the same ways as Kafka's in-

explicable reality. South Africa, one concludes, has become the reality of Kafka's nightmares."

*Foe,* a retelling of Daniel Defoe's *Robinson Crusoe,* marked a transitional stage for Coetzee, according to Maureen Nicholson in *West Coast Review.* Nicholson found many areas in which *Foe* differs from Coetzee's previous work. "Coetzee initially appeared to me to have all but abandoned his usual concerns and literary techniques" in *Foe,* Nicholson commented. "I was mistaken. More importantly, though, I was worried about why he has chosen *now* to write this kind of book; I found his shift of focus and technique ominous. Could he no longer sustain the courage he had demonstrated [in *Waiting for the Barbarians* and *The Life and Times of Michael K.*], turning instead to a radically interiorized narrative?" Nicholson concluded, "Perhaps *Foe* is best viewed as a pause for recapitulation and evaluation, transitional in Coetzee's development as a writer." Ashton Nichols, however, writing in *Southern Humanities Review,* found that Coetzee had not strayed far from his usual topics. "Like all of Coetzee's earlier works, *Foe* retains a strong sense of its specifically South African origins, a sociopolitical subtext that runs along just below the surface of the narrative," Nichols remarked. The reviewer emphasized Coetzee's role as "an archeologist of the imagination, an excavator of language who testifies to the powers and weaknesses of the words he discovers," a role Coetzee has performed in each of his novels, including *Foe.* Central to this idea are the mute Friday, whose tongue was cut out by slavers, and Susan Barton, the castaway who struggles to communicate with him. Daniel Foe, the author who endeavors to tell Barton's story, is also affected by Friday's speechlessness. Both recognize their duty to provide a means by which Friday can relate the story of his escape from the fate of his fellow slaves who drowned, still shackled, when their ship sank, but also question their right to speak for him. "The author, whether Foe or Coetzee, . . . wonders if he has any right to speak for the one person whose story most needs to be told," Nichols noted. "Friday is . . . the tongueless voice of millions."

While he found *Foe* somewhat lighthearted in places, *Tribune Books*'s John Blades also recognized the serious element embedded in the story. Noting that readers familiar with *Robinson Crusoe* will enjoy Coetzee's "mischievous little touches," such as replacing the goats on the island with apes, thereby forcing Cruso (Coetzee's spelling) to wear "apeskin" clothing, Blades remarked that the author "is not simply an exalted mischief maker," and concluded that in *Foe* "what is now considered a preadolescent classic is transformed into an infinitely intriguing adult conundrum, a vessel that overflows with mystery and allusion, a novel that is both a funhouse and a madhouse." In a *New York Times* review, Michiko Kakutani asserted that in *Foe* "the operative forces are not so much history or politics as art and imagination—how can one individual's story be apprehended and translated through language by another?" Kakutani concluded that *Foe* "which remains somewhat solipsistically concerned with literature and its consequences—lacks the fierceness and moral resonance of *Barbarians* and *Michael K.,* and yet it stands, nonetheless, as a finely honed testament to its author's intelligence, imagination, and skill."

In *Age of Iron* Coetzee addresses the crisis of South Africa in direct rather than allegorical form. The story of Mrs. Curren, a retired professor dying of cancer and attempting to deal with the realities of apartheid in Cape Town, *Age of Iron* is "an unrelenting yet gorgeously written parable of modern South Africa, . . . a story filled with foreboding and violence about a land where even the ability of children to love is too great a luxury," Michael Dorris wrote in *Tribune Books.* As her disease and the chaos of her homeland progress, Mrs. Curren feels the effects her society has had on its black members; her realization that "now my eyes are open and I can never close them again" forms the basis for her growing rage against the system. After her housekeeper's son and his friend are murdered in her home, Mrs. Curren runs away and hides beneath an overpass, leaving her vulnerable to attack by a gang. She is rescued by Vercueil, a street person she has gradually allowed into her house and her life, who returns her to her home and tends to her needs as the cancer continues its destruction. The book takes the form of a letter from Mrs. Curren to her daughter, living in the United States because she cannot tolerate apartheid. "Dying is traditionally a process of withdrawal from the world," Sean French commented in *New Statesman and Society.* "Coetzee tellingly reverses this and it is in her last weeks that [Mrs. Curren] first truly goes out in the baffling society she has lived in." As her life ends, Mrs. Curren's urgency to correct the wrongs she never before questioned intensifies. "In this chronicle of an aged white woman coming to understand, and of the unavoidable claims of her country's black youth, Mr. Coetzee has created a superbly realized novel whose truths cut to the bone," Lawrence Thornton declared in the *New York Times Book Review.* In a *Washington Post Book*

*World* review, Michael Heyward found that *Age of Iron,* "like Coetzee's other novels, leaves an indelible image of the South Africa it is set in—but it is not simply a novel about politics or nationality. The detail with which Coetzee inscribes Mrs. Curren's inner life makes this an absorbing book, a powerful account of an old woman's descent into death."

Reviewers voiced mixed opinions of Coetzee's next novel, *The Master of Petersburg.* The central character in the book is the Russian novelist Fyodor Dostoevsky, but the plot is only loosely based on his real life. In Coetzee's story, the novelist goes to St. Petersburg upon the death of his stepson, Pavel. He is devastated by grief for the young man, and begins an inquiry into his death. He discovers that Pavel was involved with a group of nihilists and was probably murdered either by their leader or by the police. During the course of his anguished investigation, Dostoevsky's creative processes are exposed; Coetzee shows him beginning work on his novel *The Possessed.*

In real life, Dostoevsky did have a stepson named Pavel; but he was a foppish idler, a constant source of annoyance and embarrassment to the writer. The younger man outlived his stepfather by some twenty years, and as Dostoevsky died, he would not allow Pavel near his deathbed. Some reviewers were untroubled by Coetzee's manipulation of the facts. "This is not, after all, a book about the real Dostoevsky; his name, and some facts connected to it, form a mask behind which Coetzee enacts a drama of parenthood, politics and authorship," Harriett Gilbert explained in *New Statesman and Society.* She went on to praise Coetzee's depiction of "the barbed-wire coils of grief and anger, of guilt, of sexual rivalry and envy, that Fyodor Mikhailovich negotiates as he enters Pavel's hidden life. From the moment he presses his face to the lad's white suit to inhale his smell, to when he sits down, picks up his pen and commits a paternal novelist's betrayal, his pain is depicted with such harsh clarity that pity is burnt away. If the novel begins uncertainly, it ends with scorching self-confidence."

*New York Times Book Review* contributor Patrick McGrath also rated *The Master of Petersburg* a powerful novel. Noting that "a ferociously bleak sense of human isolation has characterized the work of [Coetzee]," he went on to say that this is his "grimmest book yet, and suggests a new degree of darkness in an outlook that has yet to find much to celebrate in the human condition." McGrath found *The*

*Master of Petersburg* inferior to some of Coetzee's earlier work, and he described it as "dense and difficult, a novel that frustrates at every turn." Still, he also found much to admire, particularly Coetzee's portrait of "the figure who emerges from these pages, the master himself [Dostoevsky], in his tortured unhappiness, his terror of the next epileptic seizure, his restless sexuality and his desperate gambling with God." McGrath affirms that Coetzee's Dostoevsky "will seize any imagination still susceptible to the complicated passions of the Slav soul. He will reveal himself as a profound man in the throes of a furious struggle to wring meaning and redemption from the death of a son."

Less enthusiastic was Michiko Kakutani, who in the *New York Times* deplored Coetzee's pastiche of fact and fiction. Kakutani declared: "The effect is similar to that of mixing the pieces from two separate if thematically related jigsaw puzzles. Although fascinating but distorted portraits can be assembled from the mess, other pieces refuse to fit, leaving the reader with a confusing jumble of enigmas and loose ends. . . . Mr. Coetzee's manipulation of these facts and fictions is perfectly nimble, [but] it also feels completely arbitrary. For the reader, at least, there seems to be no larger purpose to his clever sleight of hand. . . . Indeed, one finishes *The Master of Petersburg* marveling at the waste of Mr. Coetzee's copious talents on such an odd and unsatisfying enterprise."

John Skow was more enthusiastic, writing in his *Time* review that *The Master of Petersburg* was "a brilliant, brooding novel, a literary work of the first class"; yet like Kakutani, Skow was deeply disturbed by the discrepancies between the reality of Dostoevsky's life and the story presented in Coetzee's fiction. The author's manipulation of the truth spoiled the novel for Skow, who concluded that the "confounding falsification by the author . . . reduces the entire book to the level of a clever and nearly meaningless stunt." Still other reviewers, such as Edward Hower of *Wall Street Journal,* found Coetzee's use of real-life characters and events fascinating but, in the end, unimportant. Hower emphasized that "Mr. Coetzee's book can stand on its own as a powerful study of grief, of relationships between fathers and sons, and of the great Russian themes of love and death. His picture of 19th-century Petersburg is convincingly drawn in spare and eloquent prose. His characters, especially Fyodor, are fascinating creations. And the ambitious issues Mr. Coetzee explores—the nature of tyranny and rebellion—are as important in this century as they were in the last." Coetzee's controversial book won the *Irish Times* International Fiction Prize in 1995.

Coetzee's nonfiction works include *White Writing: On the Culture of Letters in South Africa, Doubling the Point: Essays and Interviews,* and *Giving Offense: Essays on Censorship.* In *White Writing,* the author "collects his critical reflections on the mixed fortunes of 'white writing' in South Africa, 'a body of writing [not] different in nature from black writing,' but 'generated by the concerns of people no longer European, yet not African,'" Shaun Irlam observed in *MLN.* The seven essays included in the book discuss writings from the late seventeenth century to the present, through which Coetzee examines the foundations of modern South African writers' attitudes. Irlam described the strength of *White Writing* as its ability "to interrogate succinctly and lucidly the presuppositions inhabiting the language with which 'white writers' have addressed and presumed to ventriloquize Africa." In the *Rocky Mountain Review of Language and Literature,* Barbara Temple-Thurston noted, "Coetzee's book reiterates impressively how cultural ideas and language bind and limit the way in which we interpret our world." In *Doubling the Point: Essays and Interviews,* a collection of critical essays on Samuel Beckett, Franz Kafka, D. H. Lawrence, Nadine Gordimer, and others, Coetzee presents a "literary autobiography," according to Ann Irvine in a *Library Journal* review. Discussions of issues including censorship and popular culture and interviews with the author preceding each section round out the collection.

In addition to his writing, Coetzee produces translations of works in Dutch, German, French, and Afrikaans, serves as editor for others' work, and teaches at the University of Cape Town. "He's a rare phenomenon, a writer-scholar," Ian Glenn, a colleague of Coetzee's, told the *Washington Post*'s Allister Sparks. "Even if he hadn't had a career as a novelist he would have had a very considerable one as an academic." Coetzee told Sparks that he finds writing burdensome. "I don't like writing so I have to push myself," he said. "It's bad if I write but it's worse if I don't." Coetzee hesitates to discuss his works in progress, and views his opinion of his published works as no more important than that of anyone else. "The writer is simply another reader when it is a matter of discussing the books he has already written," he told Sparks. "They don't belong to him anymore and he has nothing privileged to say about them—while the book he is engaged in writing is far too private and important a matter to be talked about."

BIOGRAPHICAL/CRITICAL SOURCES:

*BOOKS*

Atwell, David, *J. M. Coetzee: South Africa and the Politics of Writing,* University of California Press (Berkeley), 1993.
*Contemporary Literary Criticism,* Gale (Detroit), Volume 23, 1983, Volume 33, 1985, Volume 66, 1991.
*Contemporary Novelists,* fourth edition, St. James Press (Detroit), 1986, pp. 190-91.
Huggan, Graham, and Stephen Watson, editors, *Critical Perspectives on J. M. Coetzee,* St. Martin's (New York City), 1994.
Jolly, Rosemary Jane,*Colonization, Violence, and Narration in White South African Writing: Andre Brink, Breyten Breytenbach, and J. M. Coetzee,* Ohio University Press (Athens), 1996.
Renders, Luc, in *Literary Gastronomy,* edited by David Bevan, Rodopi (Amsterdam), 1988, pp. 95-102.

*PERIODICALS*

*Africa Today,* third quarter, 1980.
*America,* September 25, 1982.
*Ariel: A Review of International English Literature,* April, 1985, pp. 47-56; July, 1986, pp. 3-21; October, 1988, pp. 55-72.
*Books Abroad,* spring, 1976.
*Books in Canada,* August/September, 1982.
*Boston Globe,* November 20, 1994, p. B16.
*British Book News,* April, 1981.
*Chicago Tribune Book World,* April 25, 1982; January 22, 1984, section 14, p. 27; November 27, 1994, p. 3.
*Christian Science Monitor,* December 12, 1983; May 18, 1988, pp. 503-05.
*Contemporary Literature,* summer, 1988, pp. 277-85; fall, 1992, pp. 419-431.
*Critique: Studies in Modern Fiction,* winter, 1986, pp. 67-77; spring, 1989, pp. 143-54.
*Encounter,* October, 1977; January, 1984.
*English Journal,* March, 1994, p. 97.
*Globe and Mail* (Toronto), August 30, 1986.
*Library Journal,* June 1, 1992, p. 124.
*Listener,* August 18, 1977.
*London Review of Books,* September 13, 1990, pp. 17-18.

*Los Angeles Times Book Review,* May 23, 1982, p. 4; January 15, 1984; February 22, 1987; November 20, 1994, p. 3.
*Maclean's,* January 30, 1984, p. 49.
*MLN,* December, 1988, pp. 1147-50; December 17, 1990, pp. 777-80.
*Nation,* March 28, 1987, pp. 402-05.
*New Republic,* December 19, 1983; February 6, 1995, pp. 170-72.
*New Statesman and Society,* September 21, 1990, p. 40; February 25, 1994, p. 41.
*Newsweek,* May 31, 1982; January 2, 1984; February 23, 1987.*New York,* April 26, 1982, pp. 88, 90.
*New Yorker,* July 12, 1982.
*New York Review of Books,* December 2, 1982; February 2, 1984; November 8, 1990, pp. 8-10.
*New York Times,* December 6, 1983, p. C22; February 11, 1987; April 11, 1987; November 18, 1994, p. C35.
*New York Times Book Review,* April 18, 1982; December 11, 1983, pp. 1, 26; February 22, 1987; September 23, 1990, p. 7; November 20, 1994, p. 9.
*Publishers Weekly,* January 22, 1996, p. 52.
*Research in African Literatures,* fall, 1986, pp. 370-92.
*Rocky Mountain Review of Language and Literature,* Volume 53, Nos. 1-2, 1989, pp. 85-87.
*Sewanee Review,* winter, 1990, pp. 152-59; April, 1995, p. R48.
*South Atlantic Quarterly,* winter, 1994, pp. 1-9, 33-58, 83-110.
*Southern Humanities Review,* fall, 1987, pp. 384-86.
*Spectator,* December 13, 1980; September 20, 1986.
*Time,* March 23, 1987; November 28, 1994, pp. 89-90.
*Times* (London), September 29, 1983; September 11, 1986; May 28, 1988.
*Times Literary Supplement,* July 22, 1977; November 7, 1980, p. 1270; January 14, 1983; September 30, 1983; September 23, 1988, p. 1043; September 28, 1990, p. 1037; March 4, 1994, p. 19.
*Tribune Books* (Chicago), February 15, 1987, pp. 3, 11; September 16, 1990, p. 3.
*Tri-Quarterly,* spring-summer, 1987, pp. 454-64.
*Village Voice,* March 20, 1984.
*Voice Literary Supplement,* April, 1982.
*Wall Street Journal,* November 3, 1994, p. A16.
*Washington Post,* October 29, 1983.
*Washington Post Book World,* May 2, 1982, pp. 1-2, 12; December 11, 1983; March 8, 1987; September 23, 1990, pp. 1, 10; November 27, 1994, p. 6.

*West Coast Review,* spring, 1987, pp. 52-58.

*World Literature Today,* spring, 1978, pp. 245-47; summer, 1978, p. 510; autumn, 1981; autumn, 1988, pp. 718-19; winter, 1990, pp. 54-57; winter, 1995, p. 207.

*World Literature Written in English,* spring, 1980, pp. 19-36; spring, 1986, pp. 34-45; autumn, 1987, pp. 153-61, 174-84, 207-15.

\*   \*   \*

## COLBERT, James   1951-

*PERSONAL:* Born November 2, 1951, in New Orleans, LA; son of Charles R. (an architect) and Rosemary (Schrafft) Colbert; married Veronica C. Trau (an architect), August 17, 1985. *Education:* Louisiana State University, B.A., 1977.

*ADDRESSES: Home*—8 South University Avenue, Fayetteville, AR 72701.

*CAREER:* Writer; affiliated with Jefferson Parish Sheriff's Office, Jefferson, LA, 1976-78. *Military service:* U.S. Marine Corps, 1970-72; served in Vietnam.

*MEMBER:* The Authors Guild.

*WRITINGS:*

FICTION

*Profit and Sheen* (novel), Houghton Mifflin (Boston), 1986.
*No Special Hurry,* Houghton Mifflin, 1988.
*Skinny Man,* Atheneum (New York City), 1991.
*All I Have Is Blue,* Atheneum, 1992.

OTHER

*God Bless the Child* (nonfiction), Atheneum, 1993.

Contributor to books and anthologies, including *A Catalogue of Crime,* edited by Jacques Barzun and Wendell Hertig Taylor, Harper (New York City), 1987; *Hardboiled: The Best of American Crime Writing,* edited by Stuart Coupe and Julie Ogden, Allen & Unwin (Winchester, MA), 1992; and *Above Ground,* edited by Thomas Bonner, Jr., and Robert E. Skinner, Xavier Review Press, 1993. Also contributor of reviews and articles to publications, in-

cluding *Washington Post, Times-Picayune* (New Orleans), *Southern, Rave Reviews, Baton Rouge Morning Advocate, Writer, Writer's Handbook, Los Angeles Times, Chicago Tribune,* and *Nexus.* Contributor with Andrew Vachss to *Hard Looks* and *Underground.*

*ADAPTATIONS:* The film *Replay* was based on the stage play by Andrew Vachss and the Dark Horse Comics Adaptation by Colbert and was released by Independent Media Arts Production, 1995.

*SIDELIGHTS:* James Colbert's first mystery novel pits a drug dealer named Profit against a bodyguard named Sheen Vice-domini. Sheen works in New Orleans, and, like the author, is a Vietnam veteran and a former policeman. In the *Washington Post Book World,* critic Charles Willeford described *Profit and Sheen* as "a stunning first novel," with "excellent characterizations, down to and including every minor character." The reviewer commented that Colbert writes with great sensitivity and authority, "a unique blend rarely seen in today's mystery fiction."

*BIOGRAPHICAL/CRITICAL SOURCES:*

PERIODICALS

*Chicago Tribune,* July 31, 1988; August 11, 1992.
*Los Angeles Times,* July 12, 1992; February 21, 1993.
*New Yorker,* October 13, 1986.
*New York Times,* October 26, 1986; October 16, 1988; July 19, 1992.
*Times* (London), February, 1990.
*Washington Post Book World,* September 7, 1986; September 8, 1988; September 7, 1990; July 26, 1992.*

\*   \*   \*

## COLSON, Charles W(endell)   1931-

*PERSONAL:* Born October 16, 1931, in Boston, MA; son of Wendell Ball (a lawyer) and Inez (Ducrow) Colson; married Nancy Billings, June 3, 1953 (divorced); married Patricia Ann Hughes, April 4, 1964; children: (first marriage) Wendell Ball II, Christian Billings, Emily Ann. *Education:* Brown University, A.B. (with distinction), 1953; George Washington University, J.D., 1959. *Religion:* Christian.

*ADDRESSES: Office*—Prison Fellowship, P. O. Box 17500, Washington, DC, 20041-0500.

*CAREER:* Admitted to the Bar of Virginia, 1959, the Bar of Washington, DC, 1961, and the Bar of Massachusetts, 1964; assistant to assistant secretary of Navy, 1955-56; administrative assistant to Senator Leverett Saltonstall, 1956-61 Gadsby & Hannah, Boston, MA, senior partner, 1961-69; special counsel to president of the United States, White House, Washington, DC, 1969-73; Colson & Shapiro, Washington, DC, partner, 1973-74; Fellowship House, Washington, DC, associate, 1975-76; Prison Fellowship Ministries, Washington, DC, founder and president, 1976-84, chair of the board, 1984—; chair of the board for Prison Fellowship International, 1979—; Justice Fellowship, chair of the board, 1983-84, vice chair of the board, 1984—. Speaker on syndicated radio program, *BreakPoint.* Associate member, Fellowship House, Washington, DC, 1975; member of board of directors, Voice of Calvary and Ligonier Valley Study Center, both 1980—. *Military service:* U.S. Marine Corps, 1953-55; became captain; served during Korean conflict.

*MEMBER:* Order of Coif, Beta Theta Pi.

*AWARDS, HONORS: Born Again* was named outstanding evangelical book of 1976 by *Eternity* magazine; Religious Heritage of America Award, Freedom Foundation, 1977; L.L.D., Wheaton College, 1982, Houghton College, 1983, Eastern College, 1983, Anderson College, 1984, Taylor University, 1985, Geneva College, 1987, John Brown University, 1988, Asbury College, 1989, and LeTourneau University, 1990; Layman of the Year Award, National Association of Evangelicals, 1983; Abe Lincoln Award, Southern Baptist Radio and TV Commission, 1984; fellow, Christianity Today Institute, 1985; Poverello Award, University of Steubenville, 1986; Salvation Army distinguished service award, 1990; Humanitarian Award, Southern Baptist Convention, 1991; Templeton Prize for Progress in Religion, 1993; also received Domino's Pizza Award.

*WRITINGS:*

*Born Again* (autobiography), Chosen Books (Lincoln, VA), 1976.
*Life Sentence* (autobiography), Chosen Books, 1979.
*Loving God,* Zondervan (Grand Rapids, MI), 1983.
*Who Speaks for God?: Confronting the World with Real Christianity,* Crossway (Westchester, IL), 1985.

*Kingdoms in Conflict: An Insider's Challenging View of Politics, Power, and the Pulpit,* Morrow & Zondervan, 1987.
*Against the Night: Living in the New Dark Ages,* Servant Books (Ann Arbor, MI), 1989.
(With Daniel W. Van Ness) *Convicted: New Hope for Ending America's Crime Crisis,* Crossway, 1989.
*The God of Stones and Spiders: Letters to a Church in Exile,* Crossway, 1990.
(With others) *Christ in Easter: A Family Celebration of Holy Week,* NavPress, 1990.
*Why America Doesn't Work,* Word Publishing (Waco, TX), 1991.
*The Body: Being Light in Darkness,* Word Publishing, 1992.
*Inspirational Writings of Charles Colson,* Arrowood Press, 1992.
(With Nancy R. Pearcey) *A Dance with Deception— Revealing the Truth behind the Headlines,* Word Publishing, 1993.
*Faith on the Line,* edited by Barbara Williams, Victor Books, 1994.
*A Dangerous Grace* (daily readings), Word Publishing, 1994.
(With Ellen Vaughn) *Gideon's Torch* (novel), Word Publishing, 1995.
(Editor with Richard John Neuhaus) *Evangelicals and Catholics Together: Toward a Common Mission,* Word Publishing, 1995.

Contributor of articles on prison reform to *Policy Review* and other periodicals. Contributing editor, *Christianity Today,* 1983—.

*SIDELIGHTS:* Charles Colson has had a high profile career in both politics and the ministry. As a special counsel to President Richard Nixon, Colson was a prominent figure in the Watergate scandal of the early 1970s. For his role in acquiring confidential FBI files on political opponents, among other charges, Colson served a brief prison sentence. Upon his release from prison, Colson turned from politics to religion, founding the Prison Fellowship Ministries to bring Christian teachings and assistance to those incarcerated in America's prisons. In the years since its founding in 1976, the Prison Fellowship Ministries has become one of the largest organizations of its kind and has spun off several related groups helping the victims of crime and the children of prisoners. It also works to bring about reforms in the American justice system.

Colson's political career began with his appointment as a special counsel to President Nixon in 1969. His loyalty to the president was strong. "I would walk over my grandmother if necessary to get Nixon re-elected," he was quoted explaining. This loyalty led Colson to involve himself in several activities meant to protect the president from hostile opponents, including a burglary of Daniel Ellsberg's psychiatrist's office to find damaging information about the man who had released the "Pentagon Papers." Another of these actions was to help cover-up the involvement of campaign workers in a break-in at Democratic Party headquarters at the Watergate office building in Washington, DC. In the ensuing Watergate scandal, Colson was among those charged with wrongdoing and sentenced to seven months in prison.

While awaiting trial, Colson met an old friend who had become a born again Christian. He also read C. S. Lewis' book *Mere Christianity.* These influences inspired him to accept Christ as well, and to plead guilty to an obstruction of justice charge rather than delay his court proceedings with further legal maneuvers. Convicted and sentenced in 1974, Colson spent seven months in prison.

After his time in prison, Colson began working with the Christian ministry organization known as Fellowship House. He also published his first book, *Born Again,* which details his spiritual conversion. Many people were skeptical about Colson's convenient change of heart in 1974. Molly Ivins of the *New York Times Book Review* concedes that when "his conversion was made public in mid-Watergate, it produced a spell of coast-to-coast sniggering." But Ivins judges that Colson in *Born Again* "is not only serious, but also . . . manages to make his conversion entirely credible." She adds, "There is no doubting his sincerity."

One sign of Colson's sincerity is his fervent devotion to Christian ministry in the more than twenty years since Watergate. He has become a leading spokesman for criminal justice reforms, encouraging Christians in particular to become actively involved with this and other social issues. Prison Fellowship Ministries, which he founded in 1976, "is today the largest evangelical outreach into prisons in America. It has spread to England, Australia, New Zealand, and Canada," Colson once told *CA.* The organization includes several subsidiaries: Prison Fellowship, U.S.A. (with a network of more than thirty-thousand volunteers and affiliated with Prison Fellowship International, a larger network connecting prison ministries in more than thirty countries); Justice Fellowship (formed in 1983, to assist government officials

and private sector groups working for change in the nation's criminal justice system); Fellowship Communications (developed in 1984 to produce publications to mobilize the Christian church for social action); Neighbors Who Care (founded in 1993 to assist the victims of crime); and Angel Tree (a ministry to the children of prisoners).

Colson's second book, *Life Sentence,* describes his experiences after he left prison and began to organize Prison Fellowship. Later books, such as *Kingdoms in Conflict: An Insider's Challenging View of Politics, Power and the Pulpit,* warn American Christians to re-evaluate the proper relationship of faith and politics. A believer who has never identified "with any one camp," Colson, reports Kathleen Hendrix in the *Los Angeles Times,* is equally concerned about "those who see religion as a completely private affair that should have no influence in public life, and those who would use political power to play God, dominating society through legislation and court decisions, taking it upon themselves to fulfill Biblical prophecies." Reading current events as elements of Armageddon, for instance, could lead us prematurely into conflict with other nations, he argues in the book. Hendrix cites Colson's statement in *Kingdoms in Conflict* that sums up the challenge: "The real issue for Christians is not whether they should be involved in politics or contend for laws that affect moral behavior. The question is how."

## BIOGRAPHICAL/CRITICAL SOURCES:

### BOOKS

Colson, Charles W., *Born Again* (autobiography), Chosen Books, 1976.
Colson, *Life Sentence* (autobiography), Chosen Books, 1979.
Colson, *Kingdoms in Conflict,* Morrow, 1987.

### PERIODICALS

*Booklist,* November 15, 1987, p. 514; May 15, 1989, p. 1582; September 1, 1995, p. 5.
*Chicago Tribune,* November 3, 1987; January 26, 1988.
*Christianity Today,* June 15, 1984, p. 42; January 15, 1990, p. 58; April 5, 1993, p. 86; September 11, 1995, p. 40.
*Commonweal,* July 1, 1976.
*Human Events,* January 6, 1990, p. 13.
*Journal of Christian Studies,* winter, 1993, p. 179.

*Library Journal,* February 15, 1984, p. 380; June 1, 1989, p. 112; September 1, 1995, p. 156.
*Los Angeles Times,* October 28, 1987.
*Nation,* February 19, 1996, p. 25.
*National Review,* August 6, 1976; February 5, 1988, p. 49; September 15, 1989, p. 52; December 25, 1995, p. 58.
*Newsweek,* June 17, 1974; July 1, 1974; September 9, 1974; February 17, 1975; October 25, 1976; October 8, 1984.
*New York Times,* March 29, 1973; March 2, 1974; March 28, 1976.
*New York Times Book Review,* March 28, 1976.
*Publishers Weekly,* May 12, 1989, p. 258; September 11, 1995, p. 41.
*Time,* June 17, 1974; July 8, 1974; February 2, 1976; November 13, 1995, p. 105.
*USA Today,* October 27, 1982.
*Washington Post,* July 24, 1983; December 25, 1987.
*West Coast Review of Books,* September, 1986, p. 47; Volume 15, number 1, 1989, p. 76; Volume 15, number 6, 1990, p. 40.

\* \* \*

## CONFORD, Ellen 1942-

*PERSONAL:* Born March 20, 1942, in New York, NY; daughter of Harry and Lillian (Pfeffer) Schaffer; married David Conford (a professor of English), November 23, 1960; children: Michael. *Education:* Attended Hofstra College (now Hofstra University), 1959-62.

*ADDRESSES: Home*—26 Strathmore Rd., Great Neck, NY 11023; fax: 516-466-6547.

*CAREER:* Writer of books for children and young adults.

*AWARDS, HONORS: The Alfred G. Graebner Memorial High School Handbook of Rules and Regulations* was chosen Notable Young Adult Book of 1976 by the American Library Association; Pacific Northwest Young Reader's Choice Award, 1981, and California Young Reader's Medal, 1982, both for *Hail, Hail, Camp Timberwood; Lenny Kandell, Smart Aleck* was named one of *School Library Journal*'s Best Books of the Year, 1983; South Carolina Young Adult Book Award, 1987, for *If This Is Love, I'll Take Spaghetti;* South Dakota Prairie Pasque Award, 1989; Garden State Children's Book Award, 1996, for *Nibble, Nibble, Jenny Archer.*

*WRITINGS:*

*Impossible, Possum* (Junior Literary Guild selection), Little, Brown (Boston), 1971.
*Why Can't I Be William?,* Little, Brown, 1972.
*Dreams of Victory* (Junior Literary Guild selection), Little, Brown, 1973.
*Felicia, the Critic* (Junior Literary Guild selection), Little, Brown 1973.
*Just the Thing for Geraldine,* Little, Brown, 1974.
*Me and the Terrible Two,* Little, Brown, 1974.
*The Luck of Pokey Bloom,* Little, Brown, 1975.
*Dear Lovey Hart: I Am Desperate,* Little, Brown, 1975.
*The Alfred G. Graebner Memorial High School Handbook of Rules and Regulations,* Little, Brown, 1976.
*And This Is Laura,* Little, Brown, 1977.
*Eugene the Brave,* Little, Brown, 1978.
*Hail, Hail, Camp Timberwood* (Junior Literary Guild selection), Little, Brown, 1978.
*Anything for a Friend,* Little, Brown, 1979.
*We Interrupt This Semester for an Important Bulletin,* Little, Brown, 1979.
*The Revenge of the Incredible Dr. Rancid and His Youthful Assistant, Jeffrey,* Little, Brown, 1980.
*Seven Days to a Brand New Me,* Little, Brown, 1982.
*To All My Fans, with Love, from Sylvie,* Little, Brown, 1982.
*Lenny Kandell, Smart Aleck,* Little, Brown, 1983.
*If This Is Love, I'll Take Spaghetti* (story collection), Scholastic Book Services (New York City), 1983.
*You Never Can Tell* (Junior Literary Guild selection), Little, Brown, 1984.
*Why Me?,* Little, Brown, 1985.
*Strictly for Laughs,* Putnam (New York City), 1985.
*A Royal Pain,* Scholastic Book Services, 1986.
*The Things I Did for Love,* Bantam (New York City), 1987.
*A Job for Jenny Archer,* Little, Brown, 1988.
*A Case for Jenny Archer,* Little, Brown, 1988.
*Genie with the Light Blue Hair,* Bantam, 1989.
*Jenny Archer, Author,* Little, Brown, 1989.
*What's Cooking, Jenny Archer?,* Little, Brown, 1989.
*Jenny Archer to the Rescue,* Little, Brown, 1990.
*Can Do, Jenny Archer,* Little, Brown, 1991.

*Dear Mom, Get Me Out of Here,* Little, Brown, 1992.

*Nibble, Nibble, Jenny Archer,* Little Brown, 1993.

*Get the Picture, Jenny Archer?,* Little, Brown, 1994.

*I Love You, I Hate You, Get Lost,* Scholastic, 1994.

*Norman Newman: My Sister, the Witch,* Troll, 1995.

*Norman Newman and the Werewolf of Walnut Street,* Troll, 1995.

*The Frog Princess of Pelham,* Little, Brown, 1997.

*Lovelinks: A Collection of Stories for Valentine's Day,* HarperCollins (New York City), 1997.

Contributor of short stories to books, including *Short Circuits,* Delacorte, 1992, and *A Night to Remember,* Avon. Contributor of stories and poems to *Teen, Reader's Digest, Modern Bride,* and other periodicals, and of reviews to *New York Times* and *American Record Guide.*

ADAPTATIONS: *Dear Lovey Hart, I Am Desperate, And This Is Laura,* and *The Alfred G. Graebner Memorial High School Handbook of Rules and Regulations* have been filmed for television; *The Revenge of the Incredible Dr. Rancid and His Youthful Assistant, Jeffrey* was adapted as the American Broadcasting Companies (ABC) after-school special *Getting Even: A Wimp's Revenge.*

SIDELIGHTS: Ellen Conford is "a very clever, very intelligent young writer of children's books whose reputation as a writer children like to read and who teachers, librarians and parents like to have children like to read, is growing at a steady rate," states John G. Keller, her editor at Little, Brown in *Elementary English.* Critics appreciate Conford's ability to understand young adults and the problems they face. Her books for children and young adults, which are hallmarked by a sprightly style and much witty dialogue, are characterized by Conford's "ability to make everyday events interesting and amusing," writes Harriet McClain in *School Library Journal.* Noting that Conford writes quickly once the idea for a story is formulated, Keller suggests that there is a thematic unity of optimism in her work: "Believe in yourself. You are worthwhile and have something to contribute. You may have a problem, but we all have problems and, basically, life is good and people care what happens to you."

Conford told *CA:* "The reason I write for children is probably because I was a kid who loved to read. I turned into an adult who loves to read. I am disturbed by the number of children *and* adults who have never experienced the joys of reading a book just for pleasure. Therefore, I write the kinds of books for children and teenagers that *I* liked to read at their age, books meant purely to entertain, to amuse, to divert. I feel that I am competing with the television set for a child's mind and attention, and if I receive a letter that says, 'I never used to like to read until I read one of your books, and now I really enjoy reading,' I feel I've won a great victory. A child who discovers that reading can be pleasurable may become an educated, literate, well-informed adult. I like to think I'm doing what I can to help the cause."

BIOGRAPHICAL/CRITICAL SOURCES:

BOOKS

*Children's Literature Review,* Volume 10, Gale (Detroit), 1986.

PERIODICALS

*Elementary English,* September, 1974.

*New York Times Book Review,* June 24, 1973; November 4, 1973; April 17, 1983.

*School Library Journal,* March, 1981.

\*　　\*　　\*

## CONNER, K. Patrick 1952-

PERSONAL: Born November 27, 1952, in San Rafael, CA; son of John (a salesperson) and Gaylo (a teacher) Conner. *Education:* Chico State University, B.A., 1976, M.A., 1977.

ADDRESSES: *Office—San Francisco Chronicle,* 901 Mission, San Francisco, CA 94103.

CAREER: *San Francisco Chronicle,* San Francisco, CA, journalist, 1989—.

WRITINGS:

*Blood Moon* (novel), Doubleday (New York City), 1987.

*Kingdom Road* (novel), Donald I. Fine (New York City), 1991.

(With Debra Heimerdinger) *Horace Bristol: An American View* (nonfiction), Chronicle Books (San Francisco, CA), 1996.

## COOPER, Artemis 1953-

*PERSONAL:* Given name accented on first syllable; born April 22, 1953, in London, England; daughter of John-Julius (a writer) and Anne (a painter; maiden name, Clifford) Norwich; married Antony Beevor (a writer). *Education:* Attended St. Hugh's College, Oxford.

*ADDRESSES: Home—*54 St. Maur Rd., London SW6 4DP, England. *Agent—*Felicity Bryan, 2A North Parade, Oxford OX2 6PE, England.

*CAREER:* Writer.

*WRITINGS:*

(Editor) *A Durable Fire* (letters), Collins (London), 1983.
*The Diana Cooper Scrapbook,* Hamish Hamilton (London), 1987.
*Cairo in the War, 1939-1945,* Hamish Hamilton, 1989.
(Editor) *Mr. Wu and Mrs. Stitch* (letters), Hodder & Stoughton (London), 1991.
*Watching in the Dark,* John Murray (London), 1992.
(With husband, Antony Beevor) *Paris after the Liberation, 1945-1949,* Hamish Hamilton, 1994.

*BIOGRAPHICAL/CRITICAL SOURCES:*

*PERIODICALS*

*Times* (London), September 26, 1987.

*       *       *

## COOPER, J(ean) C. 1905-

*PERSONAL:* Born November 27, 1905, in Chefoo, China; daughter of Tom Gear (in holy orders) and Florence (Campbell) Willett; married Vincent Morse Cooper (a naval commander), June 21, 1945 (deceased). *Ethnicity:* "English-Scottish." *Education:* University of St. Andrews, LL.A. (with honors), 1930. *Politics:* Conservative. *Religion:* Taoist.

*ADDRESSES: Home—*Bobbin Mill, Ulpha, Broughton-in-Furness, Cumbria LA20 6DU, England.

*CAREER:* Lecturer to philosophical and literary societies, 1930-39; lecturer to the armed forces, 1939-45; lecturer in adult education on comparative religion, philosophy, and symbolism, 1945—. Justice of the peace; past member of local prison board and review committee; chair of the board of governors of two schools.

*MEMBER:* International PEN, Royal Commonwealth Society.

*WRITINGS:*

*Taoism: The Way of the Mystic,* Aquarian Press (Wellingborough, Northants, England), 1972.
*An Illustrated Encyclopaedia of Traditional Symbols,* Thames & Hudson (London), 1978, revised edition, 1987.
*Yin and Yang,* Aquarian Press, 1981.
*Symbolism,* Aquarian Press, 1982.
*Fairy Tales: Allegories of the Inner Life,* Aquarian Press, 1983.
*Chinese Alchemy,* Aquarian Press, 1984.
*The Aquarian Dictionary of Festivals,* Aquarian, 1990.
*Symbolic and Mythological Animals,* Aquarian, 1992.
(Editor) *Brewer's Dictionary of Myth and Fable,* Cassell (London), 1992.
(Editor) *Cassell's Christian Dictionary,* Cassell, 1996.

Contributor of articles and reviews to *Studies in Comparative Religion.*

*WORK IN PROGRESS:* Research on festivals.

*SIDELIGHTS:* J. C. Cooper told *CA:* "I was born in China and spent my early formative years there, my father having been in the consular service and later a director of one of the missions then operating in the country, so I was brought up by Christian parents and Taoist-Buddhist amahs, seeing more of the latter than the former. Thus, if one follows the Jesuit adage 'give me a child for the first seven years,' it is easy to see why those years were more influenced by Eastern than Western thought and attitudes. I also grew up with the vivid contrasts between the imported Western opulence and the squalor of the city back-streets, and, against these, the breath-taking and magical beauty of the mountain country where I was sent to boarding school at an early age. Overall, too, I learned the charm of the Chinese character, with its balance between Confucian social decorum and Taoist gamin individuality as well as the beauty of the arts and crafts with which one was surrounded.

"I see very few 'motivating factors' in my life or career. Things happen and I let them develop and watch with interest—often the smallest incidents initiate events of major importance. I now find myself, via my marriage, living in an ideal state of rural seclusion and beauty. The Taoists say that one should have a simple dwelling, facing south, with running water by it and woods behind it. I have just that.

"I read philosophy at the university and studied comparative religion and lectured in these subjects in adult education. My writing career started when I was asked to write on Taoism and most of my books have been commissioned or have developed from courses of lectures. They are now in eighteen languages including Greek, Serbo-Croat, Finnish, Japanese, and practically all European languages.

"My interest in writing on mysticism is to join with those who feel that the West has largely grown to ignore its heritage in this respect and is now turning to the East so that a strong East-West exchange of thought and belief has developed; those who have a foot in both camps can contribute to this dialogue. The monumental work of Joseph Needham in his *Science and Civilization in China* is an outstanding example of this inter-communication. And in America the equally impressive work of Joseph Campbell in his books on mythology is another invaluable contribution to world understanding. The practical work in the various branches of Taoist art taught and demonstrated by Chungliang Al Huang in his Living Tao Foundation brings the ancient wisdom of the East to the West and now exports it back to China."

\*     \*     \*

## COREN, Alan   1938-

*PERSONAL:* Born June 27, 1938, in London, England; son of Samuel (a builder) and Martha (Phelps-Cholmondeley) Coren; married Anne Kasriel (a doctor), October 14, 1963; children Giles, Victoria. *Education:* Wadham College, Oxford University, B.A., 1960, M.A., 1980; attended University of Minnesota, 1961, Yale University, 1962, and University of California, Berkeley, 1962-63.

*ADDRESSES: Home*—26 Ranulf Rd., London, England.

*CAREER: Punch* magazine, London, England, assistant editor, 1963-67, literary editor, 1967-69, deputy editor, 1969-77, editor, 1977-87; *Listener* magazine, London, editor, 1987-89. Television critic for the *Times* (London), beginning 1971. Author of columns for *Daily Mail,* 1972-77, *Evening Standard,* beginning 1977, *Times,* 1987—, and *Sunday Express,* 1990-95. Rector of St. Andrew's University, 1973-76.

*AWARDS, HONORS:* Editor of the Year, British Society of Magazine Editors, 1986; D. Litt., Nottingham University, 1994.

*WRITINGS:*

*FICTION*

*The Dog It Was That Died,* Hutchinson (London), 1965.
*All Except the Bastard,* Gollancz (London), 1969.
*The Sanity Inspector,* Robson (London), 1974, St. Martin's (New York City), 1975.
*The Collected Bulletins of Idi Amin,* Robson, 1974.
*The Further Bulletins of Idi Amin,* Robson, 1975.
*Golfing for Cats,* Robson, 1975, St. Martin's, 1976.
(Editor) *The Punch Book of Crime,* Robson, 1976.
*The Lady from Stalingrad Mansions,* St. Martin's, 1977.
*The Peanut Papers: In Which Miz Lillian Writes,* St. Martin's, 1977.
(Editor) *Pick of Punch,* Hutchinson, 1978, Beaufort Books, 1985.
*A Rhinestone as Big as the Ritz,* Robson, 1979.
*Tissues for Men,* Robson, 1980.
(Editor) *Punch Book of Short Stories,* Robson, 1980, St. Martin's 1982.
(Editor) *Punch Book of Short Stories II,* St. Martin's, 1981, published as *The Second Punch Book of Short Stories,* Penguin (London), 1982.
*The Best of Alan Coren,* St. Martin's, 1981.
*The Cricklewood Diet,* Robson, 1982, Parkwest, 1984.
(Editor) *Present Laughter: A Personal Anthology of Modern Humour,* Robson, 1982.
(Editor) *Penguin Book of Modern Humour,* Penguin, 1984.
*Bumf,* Robson, 1984, Parkwest, 1985.
*Something for the Weekend,* Robson, 1986.
*Bin Ends,* Robson, 1987.
*Seems like Old Times,* Robson, 1989.
*More like Old Times,* Robson, 1990.

*A Year in Cricklewood,* Robson, 1993.
*Toujours Cricklewood?,* Robson, 1993.
*Sunday Best,* Robson, 1993.
*Animal Passions,* Robson, 1994.
*A Bit on the Side,* Robson, 1995.
*The Alan Coren Omnibus,* Robson, 1996.

*FICTION; FOR CHILDREN*

*Buffalo Arthur,* Robson, 1976, Little, Brown, 1978.
*Arthur the Kid,* Robson, 1976, Little, Brown, 1978.
*The Lone Arthur,* Robson, 1976, Little, Brown, 1978.
*Railroad Arthur,* Robson, 1977, Little, Brown, 1978.
*Klondike Arthur,* Robson, 1977, Little, Brown, 1978.
*Arthur's Last Stand,* Robson, 1977, Little, Brown, 1979.
*Arthur and the Great Detective,* Little, Brown, 1979.
*Arthur and the Bellybutton Diamond,* Robson, 1979.
*Arthur and the Purple Panic,* Robson, 1981, Parkwest, 1984.
*Arthur Versus the Rest,* Robson, 1981, Parkwest, 1985.

*TELEVISION SCRIPTS*

*That Was the Week That Was,* British Broadcasting Corp. (BBC-TV), 1963-64.
*Not So Much a Programme,* BBC-TV, 1965-66.
*At the Eleventh Hour,* BBC-TV, 1967.
*The Punch Review,* BBC-TV, 1976-77.
*Every Day in Every Way* (play), BBC-TV, 1977.
*Nuts* (situation comedy), Yorkshire TV, 1977.
*The Losers,* 1978.

*RADIO PLAYS*

*The Shelter,* BBC-Radio, 1965.
*End As a Man,* BBC-Radio, 1965.
*Black and White and Red All Over,* BBC-Radio, 1966.

*ADAPTATIONS:* Some of Coren's *Arthur* books have been adapted into children's television films.

*SIDELIGHTS:* Alan Coren became the venerable *Punch* magazine's twelfth editor in 1977, a post he inherited after serving as assistant, literary, and deputy editors. Despite his success at the helm of the magazine, however, Coren announced his retirement from full-time work at *Punch* in 1987. Libby Purves, a contributor to the periodical under Coren's leadership, recalls in a London *Times* article that the humorist's qualifications "lay not in management . . .,

but strictly on the printed page. Here was a joker, a parodist, a savage but romantic clown, the sort of man who shut himself in his office, banging his typewriter, frowning and laughing maniacally to himself."

Coren stated at the time that he was leaving *Punch* to pursue his writing career. In the same *Times* article, he adds that his stint as editor contributed to the decision: "I came to *Punch* because I loved comedy. I wanted to be in a place surrounded by comic writers. Being an editor has changed me: it took a long while, but it has." Purves adds that Coren "can be crusty, short and woundingly decisive (he once rejected an idea of mine with the syllable 'Naah!'), but he is generous and perceptive, and worth rewriting anything to please. And in conversation, it is still blessedly easy to make him laugh immoderately. Not bad after 25 years laughing for a living."

*BIOGRAPHICAL/CRITICAL SOURCES:*

*BOOKS*

James, Clive, *The Metropolitan Critic,* Faber, 1974.

*PERIODICALS*

*New Yorker,* December 19, 1977.
*New York Times Book Review,* March 21, 1976.
*Times* (London), June 10, 1987.

\*    \*    \*

**CRICHTON, (John) Michael   1942-**
    **(Jeffrey Hudson, John Lange; Michael Douglas, a joint pseudonym)**

*PERSONAL:* Surname is pronounced "*cry*-ton"; born October 23, 1942, in Chicago, IL; son of John Henderson (a corporate president) and Zula (Miller) Crichton; married Joan Radam, January 1, 1965 (divorced, 1970); married Kathleen St. Johns, 1978 (divorced, 1980); married Suzanne Childs (marriage ended); married Anne-Marie Martin, 1987; children: (fourth marriage) Taylor (a daughter). *Education:* Harvard University, A.B. (summa cum laude), 1964, M.D., 1969.

*ADDRESSES:* c/o Alfred A. Knopf, Inc., 201 E. 50th St., New York, NY 10022.

*CAREER:* Salk Institute for Biological Studies, La Jolla, CA, post-doctoral fellow, 1969-70; full-time writer of books and films; director of films and teleplays, including *Pursuit* (based on his novel *Binary,*), American Broadcasting Companies, Inc. (ABC-TV), 1972, *Westworld,* Metro-Goldwyn-Mayer (MGM), 1973, *Coma,* United Artists (UA), 1978, *The Great Train Robbery,* UA, 1979, *Looker,* Warner Bros., 1981, and *Runaway,* Tri-Star Pictures, 1984. Creator of National Broadcasting Company (NBC-TV) series *ER.*

*MEMBER:* Mystery Writers Guild of America (West), Authors Guild, Authors League of America, Academy of Motion Picture Arts and Sciences, Directors Guild of America, PEN, Aesculaepian Society, Phi Beta Kappa.

*AWARDS, HONORS:* Edgar Award, Mystery Writers of America, 1968, for *A Case of Need,* and 1979, for *The Great Train Robbery;* writer of the year award, Association of American Medical Writers, 1970, for *Five Patients: The Hospital Explained.*

*WRITINGS:*

NOVELS

*The Andromeda Strain,* Knopf (New York City), 1969.
(With brother Douglas Crichton, under joint pseudonym Michael Douglas) *Dealing: Or, The Berkeley-to-Boston Forty-Brick Lost-Bag Blues,* Knopf, 1971.
*The Terminal Man,* Knopf, 1972.
*Westworld* (also see below), Bantam (New York City), 1974.
*The Great Train Robbery* (also see below), Knopf, 1975.
*Eaters of the Dead: The Manuscript of Ibn Fadlan, Relating His Experiences with the Northmen in A.D. 922,* Knopf, 1976.
*Congo,* Knopf, 1980.
*Sphere,* Knopf, 1987.
*Jurassic Park,* Knopf, 1990.
*Rising Sun,* Knopf, 1992.
*Disclosure,* Knopf, 1994.
*The Lost World,* Knopf, 1995.
*Airframe,* Knopf, 1996.

NONFICTION

*Five Patients: The Hospital Explained,* Knopf, 1970.
*Jasper Johns,* Abrams (New York City), 1977; revised and expanded, 1994.

*Electronic Life: How to Think about Computers,* Knopf, 1983.
*Travels* (autobiography), Knopf, 1988.

SCREENPLAYS

*Extreme Close-up,* National General, 1973.
*Westworld* (based on novel of same title), Metro-Goldwyn-Mayer, 1973.
*Coma* (based on novel of same title by Robin Cook), United Artists, 1977.
*The Great Train Robbery* (based on novel of same title), United Artists, 1978.
*Looker,* Warner Bros., 1981.
*Runaway,* Tri-Star Pictures, 1984.
*Twister,* Warner Bros., 1996, screenplay published by Ballantine (New York City), 1996.

UNDER PSEUDONYM JOHN LANGE

*Odds On,* New American Library (New York City), 1966.
*Scratch One,* New American Library, 1967.
*Easy Go,* New American Library, 1968, published as *The Last Tomb,* Bantam, 1974.
*Zero Cool,* New American Library, 1969.
*The Venom Business,* New American Library, 1969.
*Drug of Choice,* New American Library, 1970.
*Grave Descend,* New American Library, 1970.
*Binary,* Knopf, 1971.

UNDER PSEUDONYM JEFFREY HUDSON

*A Case of Need,* New American Library, 1968.

*ADAPTATIONS: The Andromeda Strain* was filmed by Universal, 1971; *A Case of Need* was filmed by Metro-Goldwyn-Mayer, 1972; *Binary* was filmed as *Pursuit,* ABC-TV, 1972; *The Terminal Man* was filmed by Warner Bros., 1974; *Jurassic Park* was filmed by Steven Spielberg and released in 1994; *Congo* was filmed by Frank Marshall and released by Paramount, 1995; *Disclosure* was filmed and released in 1995.

*SIDELIGHTS:* Michael Crichton has had a number of successful careers—physician, teacher, film director, screenwriter—but he is perhaps best known for pioneering the "techno-thriller" with novels such as *The Andromeda Strain, Sphere,* and *Jurassic Park.* Whether writing about a deadly microorganism, brain surgery gone awry, or adventures in the Congo, Crichton's ability to blend the tight plot and suspense of the thriller with the technical emphasis of science fiction has made him a favorite with readers of all ages. Crichton's fame is not limited to literary endeavors; he has also directed a number of popular films with subjects ranging from body organ piracy (*Coma*) to advertising manipulation and murder (*Looker*) and he is the creator of the award-winning television drama *ER*. Summing up Crichton's appeal in the *Dictionary of Literary Biography Yearbook,* Robert L. Sims wrote: "His importance lies in his capacity to tell stories related to that frontier where science and fiction meet. . . . Crichton's best novels demonstrate that, for the immediate future at least, technological innovations offer the same possibilities and limitations as their human creators."

Crichton's first brush with literary success occurred after he entered medical school. To help pay for tuition and living expenses, he began writing paperback thrillers on the weekends and during vacations. One of these books, *A Case of Need,* became an unexpected hit. Written under a pseudonym, the novel revolves around a Chinese-American obstetrician who is unjustly accused of performing an illegal abortion on the daughter of a prominent Boston surgeon. Critical reaction to the book was very positive. "Read *A Case of Need* now," urged Fred Rotondaro in *Best Sellers,* "it will entertain you; get you angry—it will make you think." Allen J. Hubin, writing in the *New York Times Book Review,* similarly noted that the "breezy, fast-paced, up-to-date first novel . . . demonstrates again the ability of detective fiction to treat contemporary social problems in a meaningful fashion."

Also published while the author was still in medical school, *The Andromeda Strain* made Crichton a minor celebrity on campus (especially when the film rights were sold to Universal Studios). Part historical journal, the novel uses data such as computer printouts, bibliographic references, and fictional government documents to lend credence to the story of a deadly microorganism that arrives on Earth aboard a NASA space probe. The virus quickly kills most of the residents of Piedmont, Arizona. Two survivors—an old man and a baby—are taken to a secret government compound for study by Project Wildfire. The Wildfire team—Stone, a bacteriologist, Leavitt, a clinical microbiologist, Burton, a pathologist, and Hall, a practicing surgeon—must race against the clock to isolate the organism and find a cure before it can spread into the general population.

The mix of science and suspense in *The Andromeda Strain* brought varied reactions from reviewers.

While admitting that he stayed up all night to finish the book, Christopher Lehmann-Haupt of the *New York Times* observed that he felt cheated by the conclusion. "I figured it was all building to something special—a lovely irony, a chilling insight, a stunning twisteroo. . . . The whole business had to be resolved before I could sleep," the critic wrote. ". . . It wasn't worth it, because . . . Mr. Crichton resolves his story with a series of phony climaxes precipitated by extraneous plot developments." Richard Schickel, writing in *Harper's,* was more concerned with a shortage of character development. "The lack of interest in this matter is . . . amazing. Perhaps so much creative energy went into his basic situation that none was left for people," he wrote. Not all critics were as harsh in their evaluation of the novel, however. "The pace is fast and absorbing," claimed Alexander Cook in *Commonweal,* "the writing is spare and its quality is generally high; and the characters, if not memorable, are at any rate sufficiently sketched in and have been given little personal touches of their own."

Crichton also used the world of science and medicine as a backdrop for *The Terminal Man.* The title refers to computer scientist Harry Benson who, as the result of an automobile accident, suffers severe epileptic seizures. As the seizures grow in intensity, Benson has blackouts during which he commits violent acts. At the urging of his doctors, Benson decides to undergo a radical procedure in which an electrode is inserted into his brain. Hooked up to a packet in the patient's shoulder, the electrode is wired to locate the source of the seizures and deliver a shock to the brain every time an episode is about to occur. Unfortunately, something goes wrong, and Benson's brain is overloaded; as the shocks increase, Benson becomes more irrational, dangerous, and eventually, murderous.

John R. Coyne in the *National Review* found *The Terminal Man* "one of the season's best." He added: "Crichton proves himself capable of making the most esoteric material completely comprehensible to the layman. . . . Even more important, he can create and sustain that sort of suspense that forces us to suspend disbelief." And, in an *Atlantic Monthly* review of the novel, Edward Weeks opined that Crichton has "now written a novel quite terrifying in its suspense and implication."

In *The Great Train Robbery,* Crichton moved out of the realm of science and into the world of Victorian England. Loosely based on an actual event, the book explores master criminal Edward Pierce's attempt to steal a trainload of army payroll on its way to the Crimea. "*The Great Train Robbery* combines the pleasures, guilt, and delight of a novel of gripping entertainment with healthy slices of instruction and information interlarded," declared Doris Grumbach in the *New Republic.* Lehmann-Haupt enthused that he found himself "not only captivated because it is Mr. Crichton's best thriller to date . . . but also charmed most of all by the story's Victorian style and content." And Weeks, writing in the *Atlantic Monthly,* called the novel "an exciting and very clever piece of fiction."

*Congo* marked Crichton's return to the field of science and technology. In the novel, three adventurers travel through the dense rain forests of the Congo in search of a cache of diamonds with the power to revolutionize computer technology. The trio is accompanied by an intelligent, linguistically-trained gorilla named Amy, the designated intermediary between the scientists and a band of killer apes who guard the gems. The small band's search is hampered by cannibals, volcanos, and mutant primates; it is also marked by a sense of desperation, as the team fights to beat a Euro-Japanese rival company to the prize. In a review of *Congo* for *Best Sellers,* Justin Blewitt termed the novel "an exciting, fast-paced adventure. It rang very true and at the same time was a terrific page-turner. That's a rare combination. . . . [*Congo* is] really a lot of fun."

A scientific—and monetary—search is also the emphasis in *Sphere.* An American ship laying cable in the Pacific hits a snag; the snag turns out to be a huge spaceship, estimated to be at least three centuries old. An undersea research team is ordered to investigate the strange craft from the relative safety of an underwater habitat. Among the civilian and military crew is psychologist Norman Johnson, whose apprehension about the entire project is validated by a number of increasingly bizarre and deadly events: a bad storm cuts the habitat off from the surface, strange messages begin appearing on computer screens, and an unseen—but apparently huge—squid attacks the crew's quarters.

"Michael Crichton's new novel . . . kept me happy for two hours sitting in a grounded plane," wrote Robin McKinley in the *New York Times Book Review,* adding that "no one can ask for more of a thriller. . . . Take this one along with you on your next plane ride." While noting that he had some problems with *Sphere*—including stilted dialogue and

broad characterizations—James M. Kahn mused that Crichton "keeps us guessing at every turn. . . . [He is] a storyteller and a damned good one." And Michael Collins of the *Washington Post Book World* noted that "the pages turn quickly." He urged readers to "suspend your disbelief and put yourself 1,000 feet down."

Huge creatures—in this case, dinosaurs—are also integral to the plot of Crichton's thriller *Jurassic Park. Jurassic Park* chronicles the attempts of self-made billionaire John Hammond to build an amusement park on a remote island off the coast of Costa Rica. Instead of roller coasters and sideshows, the park features actual life-sized dinosaurs bred through the wonders of biotechnology and recombinant DNA. There are some problems before the park opens, however: workmen begin to die in mysterious accidents and local children are attacked by strange lizards. Fearful that the project's opening is in jeopardy, Hammond calls together a team of scientists and technicians to look things over. Led by a paleontologist named Grant, the group is initially amazed by Hammond's creation. Their amazement quickly turns to horror when the park's electronic security system is put out of commission and the dinosaurs are freed to roam at will. What ensues is a deadly battle between the vastly under-armed human contingent and a group of smarter-than-anticipated tyrannosaurs, pterodactyls, stegosaurs, and velociraptors.

*Time* correspondent John Skow considered *Jurassic Park* the author's "best [techno-thriller] by far since *The Andromeda Strain.*" Skow added that Crichton's "sci-fi is convincingly detailed." In a piece for the *Los Angeles Times Book Review,* Andrew Ferguson remarked that, "having read Crichton's fat new novel . . . I have a word of advice for anyone owning real estate within 10 miles of the La Brea tar pits: Sell." Ferguson ultimately stated that *Jurassic Park*'s "only real virtue" lies in "its genuinely interesting discussion of dinosaurs, DNA research, paleontology, and chaos theory." Gary Jennings of the *New York Times Book Review* was more appreciative, arguing that the book has "some good bits. . . . All in all, *Jurassic Park* is a great place to visit."

Crichton left the world of science in *Rising Sun,* a political thriller revolving around the murder of a young American woman during a party for a huge Japanese corporation. The case is given to detective Peter J. Smith, who finds himself up against an Oriental syndicate with great political and economic power. As Smith gets closer to the truth, the Japanese corporation uses all its influence to thwart his investigation—influence that includes corruption and violence. John Schwartz in *Newsweek* recognized that Crichton had "done his homework," but the critic still felt that *Rising Sun* is too full of "randy propaganda instead of a more balanced view" to be effective.

If *Rising Sun* was criticized as having a xenophobic view of the Far East, *Disclosure,* Crichton's 1994 best-seller, opened a whole new vista for debate and discussion. A techno-thriller with a twist, *Disclosure* opens as a computer company executive named Tom Sanders discovers that he has been passed over for a promotion in favor of a woman executive with whom he had once been romantically involved. When he arrives at his new boss's office, she makes a pass at him. Now happily married, Sanders dodges the boss's advances, only to find within days that he has been named as the aggressor in a sexual harassment suit. How Sanders digs his way from beneath the spurious charges—while simultaneously unearthing wider corruption in the computer company—forms the core of the novel.

Crichton told *People* magazine that he was inspired to write *Disclosure* by a true story told to him in 1988. He was well aware, he said, that the story went against the common assumption that men are more apt to harass women. He noted that while the general perception of college-educated white women has changed for the better, "the perception of males has contracted into an emotionally closed and physically violent stereotype." In the afterword for *Disclosure,* he explained his rationale further, saying "a role-reversal story . . . may enable us to examine aspects concealed by traditional responses and conventional rhetoric."

While critics duly observed the theme of sexual harassment in *Disclosure,* they tended to dwell more upon the thriller aspect of the novel. In *New Statesman and Society,* Douglas Kennedy commended *Disclosure* as an "acidic glimpse into the nasty gamesmanship of U.S. corporate life," adding: "Sexual harassment becomes a minor consideration in a narrative more preoccupied by the wonders of virtual reality and the vicious corporate battlefield." *People* magazine reviewer Susan Toepfer found that by casting the woman as the wrongdoer, "Crichton offers a fresh and provocative story," but contended he did not sufficiently explore the situation's possibilities. *National Review* contributor Michael Coren likewise noted of the novel: "This is provocative stuff, for to

question the racial or gender exclusivity of self-awarded victim status is to kick at the very foundations of modern liberalism." While he deemed the characters too black-and-white and criticized the lack of a woman's viewpoint, Coren concluded, "On one level *Disclosure* is a literary pebble tossed into a political pond, and the ripples just might dampen some of the strident howls and emotional spasms that currently dominate discussion of the issue. On another it is a refreshingly uncluttered and sinewy entertainment, free of pretension and eminently readable."

Both *Disclosure* and *Jurassic Park* were produced as feature films, the latter proving to be one of the top-grossing movies of all time. Perhaps the vast success of *Jurassic Park* as a book and a film inspired Crichton to re-visit his scheming raptors and vicious tyrannosaurs in *The Lost World.* Also set on an island off the coast of Costa Rica, *The Lost World* follows the adventures of another team of scientists—with a return appearance by mathematical theorist Ian Malcolm—as they try to escape the clutches of the dinosaurs *and* thwart the ambitions of some egg-stealing opportunists. "One doesn't read Crichton's books for intimate peeks at inner worlds, but for heaping helpings of plot, suspense and cosmological maunderings from popular literature's most noted polymath," observed Neal Karlen in the *Los Angeles Times Book Review.* ". . . But in *The Lost World* . . . the author has done the sequel step just right, keeping the tropes of the earlier novel familiar for the fans while changing the ideas and story line enough to keep even his severest and most envious critics turning the pages to find out what happens next." Noted Susan Toepfer in *People,* "Characteristically clever, fast-paced and engaging, Michael Crichton's . . . work accomplishes what he set out to do: offer the still-harrowing thrills of a by-now-familiar ride."

Although Crichton is best known for his works of fiction, he has also written a number of nonfiction books that reflect his varied interests. *Five Patients: The Hospital Explained* uses five case studies to explore how a modern hospital functions. The topics Crichton discusses in *Five Patients* include the rising cost of health care, advancing technology, and the relationships between doctors and their patients. According to Sims, "*Five Patients* is written by a doctor who prefers writing about medicine to practicing it." Some of the issues raised in *Five Patients* are also touched on in Crichton's autobiographical *Travels.* In *Travels,* the author talks with candor about both his personal and professional life, a life that includes journeys to mysterious lands. "I was ultimately swept away, not just by [Crichton's] richly informed mind, but his driving curiosity," remarked Patricia Bosworth in the *New York Times Book Review.*

Crichton's ability to mesh science, technology, and suspense is not limited to novels. Many of the films that the author has directed, such as *Westworld* and *Runaway,* feature a struggle between humans and technology. Despite the often grim outlook of both his films and novels, Crichton revealed in an interview with Ned Smith of *American Way* that his primary intention in making movies and writing books is to "entertain people." He noted that one of the rewards he gets from filmmaking and writing comes from telling stories. "It's fun to manipulate people's feelings and to be manipulated. To take a movie, or get a book and get very involved in it—don't look at my watch, forget about other things," he said. As for critical reaction to his work, Crichton told Smith: "Every critic assumes he's a code-breaker; the writer makes a code and the critic breaks it. And it doesn't work that way at all. As a mode of working, you need to become very uncritical."

What the critics say hardly matters anyway. As Douglas Kennedy observed, Crichton is "the most bankable commercial novelist of the moment," an author who has achieved success by becoming "a *serious* popular writer." In *Newsweek,* David Gates concluded that despite Crichton's use of contemporary subjects, the author is "a throwback: a hard-working pop novelist who spots the trend, does the research, retools familiar characters, works out the plot, plants the clues, ties up the loose ends and keeps you turning the pages."

## BIOGRAPHICAL/CRITICAL SOURCES:

### BOOKS

*Authors and Artists for Young Adults,* Volume 10, Gale (Detroit), 1993, pp. 63-70.
*Contemporary Literary Criticism,* Gale, Volume 2, 1974, Volume 6, 1976, Volume 54, 1989, pp. 62-77.
*Dictionary of Literary Biography Yearbook: 1981,* Gale, 1982.
Trembley, Elizabeth A., *Michael Crichton: A Critical Companion,* Greenwood Press (Westport, CT), 1996.

### PERIODICALS

*American Spectator,* May, 1992, p. 71.
*American Way,* September, 1975, pp. 66-69.
*Atlantic Monthly,* May, 1972, pp. 108-110.
*Best Sellers,* August 15, 1968, pp. 207-208; February, 1981, p. 388.
*Commonweal,* August 9, 1969, pp. 493-94.
*Entertainment Weekly,* December 3, 1990, p. 80; December 16, 1994, p. 16; December 30, 1994, p. 30; January 13, 1995, pp. 52-53; September 22, 1995, pp. 72-73.
*Forbes,* June 21, 1993, p. 24; September 13, 1993, p. 26; February 14, 1994, p. 26; February 21, 1994, p. 108.
*Harper's,* August, 1969, p. 97.
*JAMA: Journal of the American Medical Association,* September 8, 1993, p. 1252.
*Los Angeles Times Book Review,* July 12, 1987, pp. 1, 13; November 11, 1990, p. 4; October 29, 1995, p. 2.
*Nation,* May 11, 1992, p. 637.
*National Review,* June 23, 1972, pp. 700-701; August 17, 1992, p. 40; February 21, 1994, p. 63.
*New Republic,* June 7, 1975, pp. 30-31.
*New Statesman and Society,* March 1, 1991, p. 34; February 4, 1994, p. 49.
*Newsweek,* November 19, 1990, p. 69; February 17, 1992, p. 64; January 17, 1994, p. 52.
*New Yorker,* February 7, 1994, p. 99; June 27, 1994, p. 81.
*New York Review of Books,* April 23, 1992, p. 3; February 29, 1996, pp. 20-22; August 12, 1993, p. 51.
*New York Times,* May 30, 1969, p. 25; June 10, 1975.
*New York Times Book Review,* August 18, 1968, p. 20; July 12, 1987, p. 18; June 26, 1988, p. 30; November 1, 1990, pp. 14-15; November 11, 1990, p. 14; February 9, 1992, p. 1; January 23, 1994, p. 7; October 1, 1995, pp. 9-10.
*People,* January 17, 1994, p. 24; September 18, 1995, p. 37.
*Publishers Weekly,* September 28, 1990, p. 84; January 27, 1992, p. 91.
*Time,* November 12, 1990, p. 97; February 24, 1992, p. 63; January 10, 1994, p. 52; September 25, 1995, pp. 60-67.
*U.S. News and World Report,* March 9, 1992, p. 50.
*Vanity Fair,* January, 1994, p. 32.
*Washington Monthly,* April, 1994, p. 54.
*Washington Post Book World,* June 14, 1987, pp. 1, 14.

**CUNNINGHAM, Bob**
  See MAY, Julian

\*  \*  \*

**CUNNINGHAM, E. V.**
  See FAST, Howard (Melvin)

\*  \*  \*

**CUSHMAN, Doug  1953-**

*PERSONAL:* Born May 4, 1953, in Springfield, OH; son of Donald E. (a business manager) and Juney (maiden name, Fasick) Cushman; married Kim F. Mulkey (an illustrator), June 16, 1979. *Education:* Attended Paier School of Art, 1971-75.

*ADDRESSES: Home*—31 West Prospect St., New Haven, CT 06515.

*CAREER:* Apprentice to book illustrator Mercer Mayer, 1975-77; writer and illustrator, 1977—. Instructor at Paier College of Art, 1980, and Southern Connecticut State University, 1981—.

*MEMBER:* Society of Children's Book Writers, National Cartoonists Society.

*AWARDS, HONORS:* Child Book of the Year Award, 1979, for *Haunted Houses on Halloween.*

*WRITINGS:*

*JUVENILE; SELF-ILLUSTRATED*

(And editor and contributor) *Giants* (stories and poems), Grosset (New York City), 1980.
(And editor) *Trolls* (stories), Grosset, 1981.
*Once Upon a Pig,* Grosset, 1982.
*The Pudgy Fingers Counting Book,* Grosset, 1983.
*Nasty Kyle the Crocodile,* Grosset, 1983.
*Aunt Eater Loves a Mystery,* Harper (New York City), 1987.
*Secret of the Nile: Missing Mystery,* Macmillan (New York City), 1987.
*Uncle Foster's Hat Tree,* Dutton (New York City), 1988.
*Possum Stew,* Dutton, 1990.
*Camp Big Paw,* Harper, 1990.

*Possum Stew,* Dutton, 1990.
*Aunt Eater's Mystery Vacation,* HarperCollins (New York City), 1992.
*The ABC Mystery,* HarperCollins, 1993.
*Mouse and Mole and the Year-'Round Garden,* Scientific American Books for Young Readers (New York City), 1994.
*Mouse and Mole and the Christmas Walk,* Scientific American Books for Young Readers, 1994.
*Aunt Eater's Mystery Christmas,* HarperCollins, 1995.
*Mouse and Mole and the All-Weather Train Ride,* Scientific American Books for Young Readers, 1995.
*The Mystery of King Karfu,* HarperCollins, 1996.

*ILLUSTRATOR*

Lillie Patterson, *Haunted Houses on Halloween,* Garrard (Easton, MD), 1979.
Elizabeth Norine Upham, *Little Brown Bear,* Platt & Munk (New York City), 1979.
F. Kaff, *Monster for a Day; or, The Monster in Gregory's Pajamas,* Gingerbread House (New York City), 1979.
Leonard Kessler, *The Silly Mother Hubbard,* Garrard, 1980.
Kessler, *Hickory Dickory Dock,* Garrard, 1980.
Michaela Muntean, *Bicycle Bear,* Parents Magazine Press (New York City), 1983.
Ida Lutrell, *Tillie and Mert,* Harper, 1985.
Suzanne Gruber, *Chatty Chipmunk's Nutty Day,* Troll Associates (Mahwah, NJ), 1985.
Michael J. Pellowski, *Benny's Bad Day,* Troll Associates, 1986.
Rose Greydanus, *Bedtime Story,* Troll Associates, 1987.
Sharon Gordon, *The Jolly Monsters,* Troll Associates, 1987.
Jack Long, *Sunken Treasure Mystery,* Macmillan, 1987.
Long, *The Vanishing Professor,* Macmillan, 1987.
Pellowski, *Mixed-Up Magic,* Troll Associates, 1988.
Terry Webb Harshman, *Porcupine's Pajama Party,* Harper, 1988.
Melanie Martin, *Itsy-Bitsy Giant,* Troll Associates, 1988.
C. S. White, *The Monsters' Counting Book,* Platt & Munk, 1988.
Dorothy Corey, *A Shot for Baby Bear,* Albert Whitman (Niles, IL), 1989.
Michaela Muntean, *Bicycle Bear Rides Again,* Parents Magazine Press, 1989.

Marcia Leonard, *The Three Little Pigs,* Silver Press (Englewood Cliffs, NJ), 1990.

Joan Davenport Carris, *Aunt Morbelia and the Screaming Skulls,* Little, Brown (Boston), 1990.

Leonard, *The Elves and the Shoemaker,* Silver Press, 1990.

Teresa Noel Celsi, *The Fourth Little Pig,* Raintree Publishers (Milwaukee, WI), 1990.

Lois G. Grambling, *An Alligator Named Alligator,* Barron's (New York City), 1991.

Michael Berenstain, *1 + 1 Take Away Two,* Western Publishing (Racine, WI), 1991.

William H. Hooks, Joanne Oppenheim, and Barbara Brenner, *How Do You Make a Bubble?,* Bantam (New York City), 1992.

Hooks, *Feed Me!: An Aesop Fable,* Bantam, 1992.

Gary Richmond, *The Early Bird,* Word (Dallas, TX), 1992.

Muntean, *Bicycle Bear,* Parents Magazine Press, 1993.

Naomi Baltuck, *Crazy Gibberish: And Other Story Hour Stretches from a Storyteller's Bag of Tricks,* Linnet (Hamden, CT), 1993.

Bethany Roberts, *Halloween Mice!,* Clarion (New York City), 1995.

Pat Lakin, *Get Ready to Read!,* Raintree Steck-Vaughn (Austin, TX), 1995.

Lakin, *The Mystery Illness,* Raintree Steck-Vaughn, 1995.

Lakin, *Trash and Treasure,* Raintree Steck-Vaughn, 1995.

Lakin, *A Good Sport,* Raintree Steck-Vaughn, 1995.

Lakin, *Up a Tree,* Raintree Steck-Vaughn, 1995.

Lakin, *A True Partnership,* Raintree Steck-Vaughn, 1995.

Lakin, *Where There's Smoke,* Raintree Steck-Vaughn, 1995.

Lakin, *Signs of Protest,* Raintree Steck-Vaughn, 1995.

Lakin, *Aware and Alert,* Raintree Steck-Vaughn, 1995.

Lakin, *A Summer Job,* Raintree Steck-Vaughn, 1995.

Lakin, *Information, Please,* Raintree Steck-Vaughn, 1995.

Lakin, *Red Letter Day,* Raintree Steck-Vaughn, 1995.

Gail Herman, *Teddy Bear for Sale,* Scholastic Inc. (New York City), 1995.

Alice Cary, *Nat the Crab,* Open Court (Chicago, IL), 1995.

Robin Dexter, *Frogs,* Troll Associates, 1996.

*SIDELIGHTS:* Doug Cushman once told *CA:* "My earliest memories of books are of the bookmobile that arrived on our street every other week or so. I pored over every book my mother would let me check out, absorbing every detail, sometimes even copying the pictures on a pad of notebook paper. I've never stopped making my own books. Even today I like making stories and pictures out of everything I see. Character is the most important aspect of a book, I think. Once I got Nasty Kyle down as a solid character the stories went very quickly. A good character will almost write a book by himself with a little nudge or two from the author.

"My trip to Kenya provided a wealth of material that still has yet to be organized. I've done many paintings of the land and the Masai. But one of the most enjoyable moments was sitting one evening with our guide, a Kamba tribesman, and sharing folktales from our respective countries. His always began, 'Once upon a time when the lion lay down with the lamb. . . .' That's beautiful. I'd like to do something with that."*

\* \* \*

**CUTHBERT, Diana Daphne Holman-Hunt 1913- (Diana Holman-Hunt)**

*PERSONAL:* Born October 25, 1913, in London, England; daughter of Hilary Lushington and Gwendolyn (Freeman) Holman-Hunt; married Villiers Bergne, 1933 (divorced); married David Cuthbert, 1946 (deceased); children: (first marriage) Paul Bergne.

*ADDRESSES: Home*—50 Onslow Gardens, London SW7 3QA, England. *Agent*—Curtis Brown Ltd., 1 Craven Hill, London, W2.

*WRITINGS:*

UNDER NAME DIANA HOLMAN-HUNT

*My Grandmothers and I,* Hamish Hamilton (London), 1960, Norton (New York City), 1961.
*My Grandfather, His Wives and Loves,* Hamish Hamilton, 1969, Norton, 1969.
*Latin among Lions: Alvaro Guevara,* M. Joseph (London), 1974.

Contributor of articles and reviews to *Connoisseur, Harpers & Queen,* and *Spectator.*\*

# D

**DAICHES, David    1912-**

*PERSONAL:* Born September 2, 1912, in Sunderland, England; son of Salis and Flora (Levin) Daiches; married Isobel Janet Mackay, July 28, 1937 (died, 1977); married Hazel Neville, 1978 (died, 1986); children: (first marriage) Alan H., Jennifer R., Elizabeth M. *Education:* University of Edinburgh, M.A. (with first class honors), 1934; Balliol College, Oxford, M.A., 1937, D.Phil., 1939; Cambridge University, Ph.D., 1939.

*ADDRESSES: Home*—22 Belgrave Crescent, Edinburgh EH4 3AL, Scotland.

*CAREER:* Oxford University, Balliol College, Oxford, England, fellow, 1936-37; University of Chicago, Chicago, IL, assistant professor of English, 1939-43; British Embassy, Washington, DC, second secretary, 1944-46; Cornell University Ithaca, NY, professor of English, 1946-51, chairman of Division of Literature, 1948-51; Cambridge University, Cambridge, England, university lecturer, 1951-61, fellow of Jesus College, 1957-62; University of Sussex, Brighton, England, professor of English, 1961-77, dean of School of English and American Studies, 1961-67. Visiting professor, University of Indiana, 1956-57; Hill Foundation visiting professor, University of Minnesota, spring, 1966. Fellow, Center for Humanities, Wesleyan University, 1970, and National Humanities Center, North Carolina, 1987. Elliston Lecturer, University of Cincinnati, spring, 1960; Whidden Lecturer, McMaster University, 1964; Ewing Lecturer, University of California at Los Angeles, 1967; Carpenter Memorial Lecturer, Ohio Wesleyan University, 1970; Alexander Lec-

turer, University of Toronto, 1980; Gifford Lecturer, University of Edinburgh, 1983; lecturer at the Sorbonne. Lecturer on tours in America, Germany, India, Finland, Norway, Italy, Holland, and Denmark.

*MEMBER:* Royal Society of Literature (fellow), Royal Society of Edinburgh (fellow), Scottish Arts Club.

*AWARDS, HONORS:* Brotherhood Award, 1957, for *Two Worlds: An Edinburgh Jewish Childhood;* Litt.D., Brown University, 1964; Abe Prize, Tokyo, 1965, for best educational television programme; doctor honoris causa, Sorbonne, Paris, 1973; D.Litt., University of Edinburgh, 1976, University of Sussex, 1978, University of Stirling, 1980, University of Glasgow, 1987; Saltire Book Award, 1987, for *God and the Poets;* honorary doctorate, Bologna University, 1988.

*WRITINGS:*

CRITICISM

*The Place of Meaning in Poetry,* Oliver & Boyd (Edinburgh), 1935.
*New Literary Values: Studies in Modern Literature,* Oliver & Boyd, 1936.
*Literature and Society,* Gollancz (London), 1938.
*The Novel and the Modern World,* University of Chicago Press (Chicago), 1939, revised edition, 1960.
*Poetry and the Modern World,* University of Chicago Press, 1940, reprinted, Octagon Books (New York City), 1978.

*Virginia Woolf,* New Directions (San Francisco), 1942, revised edition, 1963.

*Robert Louis Stevenson,* New Directions, 1947.

*A Study of Literature for Readers and Critics,* Cornell University Press (Ithaca, NY), 1948, reprinted, Norton (New York City), 1964.

*Robert Burns,* Rinehart (New York City), 1950, revised edition, Macmillan (New York City), 1966.

*Willa Cather: A Critical Introduction,* Cornell University Press, 1951, reprinted, Greenwood Press (Westport, CT), 1971.

*Stevenson and the Art of Fiction,* privately printed, 1951, reprinted, Darby (Darby, PA), 1980.

*Walt Whitman: Man, Poet, Philosopher,* Library of Congress (Washington, DC), 1955.

*Critical Approaches to Literature,* Prentice-Hall (Englewood Cliffs, NJ), 1956.

*Literary Essays,* Oliver & Boyd, 1956, Philosophical Library (New York City), 1957.

*Milton,* Hutchinson (London), 1957, revised edition, Norton, 1966.

*The Present Age in British Literature,* Indiana University Press (Bloomington, IN), 1958 (published in England as *The Present Age: After 1920,* Cresset Press, 1958).

*A Critical History of English Literature,* two volumes, Ronald Press (New York City), 1960, 2nd edition, 1970.

*George Eliot: Middlemarch,* Edward Arnold (London), 1962, Barron's (New York City), 1963.

*Carlyle and the Victorian Dilemma,* Carlyle Society, 1963.

*English Literature,* Prentice-Hall, 1964.

*Time and the Poet,* University of Swansea College, 1965.

*More Literary Essays,* Oliver & Boyd, 1967, University of Chicago Press, 1968.

*The Teaching of Literature in American Universities,* Leicester University Press (Leicester), 1968.

*Some Late Victorian Attitudes,* Norton, 1969.

*Shakespeare: Julius Caesar,* Edward Arnold, 1976.

(With Tamas McDonald) *Introducing Robert Burns, his Life and Poetry,* Macdonald Publishers (Edinburgh, Scotland), 1982.

*Milton, Paradise Lost,* E. Arnold (London, England), 1983.

*Robert Burns, the Poet,* Saltire Society (Ediburgh), 1994.

### EDITOR

(With William Charvat) *Poems in English, 1530-1940,* Ronald Press, 1950.

*A Century of the Essay, British and American,* Harcourt (San Diego), 1951.

(With others) *The Norton Anthology of English Literature,* two volumes, Norton, 1962, revised edition, 1974.

Joseph Conrad and Robert Louis Stevenson, *White Man in the Tropics: Two Moral Tales,* Harcourt, 1962.

*The Idea of a New University: An Experiment in Sussex,* Deutsch, 1964, 2nd edition, 1970, MIT Press (Cambridge, MA), 1970.

Emily Bronte, *Wuthering Heights,* Penguin (New York City), 1965.

Sir Walter Scott, *Kenilworth,* Limited Editions Club, 1966.

*The Penguin Companion to Literature,* Volume 1: *Britain and the Commonwealth,* Allen Lane (London), 1971.

(With others) *Literature and Western Civilization,* six volumes, Aldus Books, 1972-75.

*Andrew Fletcher of Saltoun: Selected Political Writings and Speeches,* Scottish Academic Press (Edinburgh), 1979.

*A Companion to Scottish Culture,* Edward Arnold, 1981, revised edition published as *The New Companion to Scottish Culture,* Polygon (Edinburgh), 1993.

(With Peter Jones and Jean Jones) *A Hotbed of Genius: The Scottish Enlightenment, 1730-1790,* University Press (Edinburgh), 1986.

*A Wee Dram: Drinking Scenes from Scottish Literature,* Deutsch, 1990.

### OTHER

*The King James Version of the English Bible: A Study of Its Sources and Development,* University of Chicago Press, 1941, reprinted, Archon Books (Hamden, CT), 1968.

*Two Worlds: An Edinburgh Jewish Childhood* (autobiography), Harcourt, 1956, 3rd edition, Canongate Classics, 1987.

*The Paradox of Scottish Culture: The Eighteenth Century Experience,* Oxford University Press (New York City), 1964.

(Author of introduction) Robert Burns, *Commonplace Book, 1783-1785,* Centaur Press (Eastergate, England), 1965.

*Scotch Whisky: Its Past and Present,* Deutsch, 1969, 3rd edition, 1978.

*A Third World* (autobiography), Sussex University Press (Sussex), 1971.

*Robert Burns and His World,* Thames & Hudson (London), 1971, Viking (New York City), 1972.

*Sir Walter Scott and His World,* Viking, 1971.

*Robert Louis Stevenson and His World,* Thames & Hudson, 1973.

*The Last Stuart: The Life and Times of Bonnie Prince Charlie,* Putnam (New York City), 1973 (published in England as *Charles Edward Stuart: The Life and Times of Bonnie Prince Charlie,* Thames & Hudson, 1973).

*Was: A Pastime from Time Past,* Thames & Hudson, 1975.

*James Boswell and His World,* Thames & Hudson, 1975, Braziller (New York City), 1976.

*Moses: The Man and His Vision,* Praeger (New York City), 1976 (published in England as *Moses: Man in the Wilderness,* Weidenfeld & Nicolson [London], 1976).

*Scotland and the Union,* J. Murray (London), 1977.

*The Quest for the Historical Moses* (booklet), The Council of Christians and Jews, 1977.

*Glasgow,* Deutsch, 1977.

*Edinburgh,* Hamish Hamilton (London), 1978.

(With John Flower) *Literary Landscapes of the British Isles: A Narrative Atlas,* Paddington Press (London), 1979.

*Literature and Gentility in Scotland,* Edinburgh University Press (Edinburgh), 1982.

*Robert Fergusson,* Scottish Academic Press, 1982.

*God and the Poets,* Oxford University Press, 1984.

*Edinburgh: A Traveller's Companion,* Constable (London), 1986.

*A Weekly Scotsman and Other Poems,* Black Ace Books, 1994.

*SIDELIGHTS:* Robert Alter, a reviewer for *Commentary,* offers this summation of David Daiches as a literary critic: "He commands a very impressive range of English and American literature, with a minutely-informed sense of its classical and Continental backgrounds, and he uses all this knowledge gracefully, relevantly, without a trace of pedantry. . . . Virtually everything he writes is sane, lucid, and tactful, and in an age when the language of most literary people is tainted with learned barbarism or stylistic exhibitionism, he writes an eminently civilized prose that seems effortless in its clarity and directness." Daiches is known for several studies of leading English literary figures.

Published in 1942, Daiches's *Virginia Woolf* has long been considered an excellent introduction to that author's work. Howar Doughty, writing in *Books,* calls it a "competent and intelligent guide" that is "informed with insight into the relation of technical problems to currents of thought and feeling in the writer's time." In a *Canadian Forum* article, Robert Finch commends Daiches for his "brilliance that illuminates more often than it dazzles."

Daiches's 1950 study of Robert Burns has been recognized as one of the best modern books on the subject. A critic for the *Economist* considers *Robert Burns* one of "the most perceptive books about Scottish literature." Writing in *Commonweal,* Virginia Mercier voices a similar opinion: "[Daiches] deserves a nobler title than scholar—that of humanist. . . . No critical study has done fuller justice to Burns' work as a song-writer or supplied more information about it." The *New York Herald Tribune Book Review*'s G. F. Whicher believes that the book "is notable for its vigorous grasp of crucial issues and for its success in clearing the air of misapprehensions that have often blurred the understanding of Robert Burns' position and achievement."

*Book World* writer Joel Sayre notes that while Daiches's "vocation is English . . . his avocation [is] Pot-Still Highland Malt Scotch Whisky." In *Scotch Whisky: Its Past and Present,* Daiches contends: "The proper drinking of Scotch whisky is more than an indulgence. It is a toast to civilization, a tribute to the continuity of culture, a manifesto of man's determination to use the resources of nature to refresh mind and body and enjoy to the full the senses with which he has been endowed."

Daiches points out that the United States leads the world in Scotch consumption and that approximately ninety-nine percent of all Scotch consumed there is a blended rather than a single malt whisky. He laments that too many Scotch drinkers are unaware that the single malts can be obtained. Sayre relates the following anecdote: "When he was a member of the Cornell faculty, Daiches once casually mentioned in a lecture . . . that Mortlach [a single malt] was to be had at Macy's in New York. On his next trip to Manhattan he dropped in at Macy's to stock up his Mortlach supply. 'Sorry, but some damn fool prof up at Ithaca recommended it to his students, and we're all out.'"

*BIOGRAPHICAL/CRITICAL SOURCES:*

*BOOKS*

Daiches, David, *Two Worlds: An Edinburgh Jewish Childhood,* Harcourt, 1956, 3rd edition, Canongate Classics, 1987.

Daiches, David, *A Third World,* Sussex University Press, 1971.

*PERIODICALS*

*Books,* September 27, 1942.
*Book World,* March 8, 1970.
*Canadian Forum,* November, 1942.
*Commentary,* May, 1969.
*Commonweal,* February 23, 1951.
*Economist,* May 28, 1977.
*Newsweek,* March 26, 1956.
*New York Herald Tribune Book Review,* August 26, 1951.
*New York Times Book Review,* April 12, 1970.
*Washington Post,* March 30, 1979.
*Yale Review,* winter, 1970.

\*    \*    \*

## DALEY, Brian 1947-1996
### (Jack McKinney, a joint pseudonym)

*PERSONAL:* Born December 22, 1947, in Englewood, NJ; died of cancer, February 11, 1996, in Arnold, MD; son of Charles J. and Myra A. (de la Cruz) Daley. *Education:* Jersey City State College, B.A., 1974.

*ADDRESSES:* c/o Ballantine/Del Ray Books, 201 East 50th St., New York, NY 10022.

*CAREER:* Novelist. Worked as house painter, waiter, and county welfare case worker. *Military service:* U.S. Army, 1965-69; served in Vietnam and West Germany.

*WRITINGS:*

*SCIENCE FICTION NOVELS; PUBLISHED BY BALLANTINE/ DEL REY (NEW YORK CITY)*

*The Doomfarers of Coramonde,* 1977.
*The Starfollowers of Coramonde,* 1979.
*Han Solo at Stars' End* (see also below), 1979.
*Han Solo's Revenge* (see also below), 1979.
*Han Solo and the Lost Legacy* (see also below), 1980.
*The Exploits of Han Solo* (contains *Han Solo at Stars' End, Han Solo's Revenge,* and *Han Solo and the Lost Legacy*), 1982, published as *Star Wars: The Han Solo Adventures,* 1994.

*Tron,* 1982.
*A Tapestry of Magics,* 1983.
*Requiem for a Ruler of Worlds,* 1985.
*Jinx on a Terran Inheritance,* 1985.
*Fall of the White Ship Avatar: A Hobart Floyt-Alacrity Fitzhugh Adventure,* 1986.
*Gamma L.A.W.,* four volumes, 1996.

*WITH JAMES LUCENO; UNDER PSEUDONYM JACK McKINNEY; "ROBOTECH" SERIES; PUBLISHED BY BALLANTINE/DEL REY*

*Genesis,* 1987.
*Battle Cry,* 1987.
*Homecoming,* 1987.
*Battlehymn,* 1987.
*Force of Arms,* 1987.
*Doomsday,* 1987.
*Southern Cross,* 1987.
*Metal Fire,* 1987.
*The Final Nightmare,* 1987.
*Invid Invasion,* 1987.
*Metamorphosis,* 1987.
*Symphony of Light,* 1987.
*The End of the Circle,* 1990.
*The Zentraedi Rebellion,* 1994.
*The Masters Gambit,* 1995.
*Before the Invid Storm,* 1996.

*WITH JAMES LUCENO; UNDER PSEUDONYM JACK McKINNEY; "SENTINELS" SERIES; PUBLISHED BY BALLANTINE/DEL REY*

*The Devil's Hand,* 1988.
*Dark Powers,* 1988.
*Death Dance,* 1988.
*World Killers,* 1988.
*Rubicon,* 1988.

*WITH JAMES LUCENO; UNDER PSEUDONYM JACK McKINNEY; "BLACK HOLE TRAVEL AGENCY" SERIES; PUBLISHED BY BALLANTINE/DEL REY*

*Event Horizon,* 1991.
*Artifact of the System,* 1991.
*Free Radicals,* 1992.
*Hostile Takeover,* 1994.

*RADIO PLAYS; PUBLISHED BY BALLANTINE/DEL REY*

*Star Wars: The National Public Radio Dramatization,* 1994.
*The Empire Strikes Back: The National Public Radio Dramatization,* 1995.

*Return of the Jedi: The National Public Radio Dramatization,* 1996.

OTHER

Scriptwriter for television series *Adventures of the Galaxy Rangers,* 1986. Author of scripts for record albums *Wargames* and *Rebel Mission to Ord Mankell,* both released by Disneyland/Buena Vista Records. Contributor to science fiction and fantasy periodicals.

*SIDELIGHTS:* Brian Daley once told *CA:* "The most horrible thing that can possibly happen to a novelist is to have Del Rey Books senior editor and veteran science fiction/fantasy writer Lester Del Rey point to a plot device and sneer, 'How convenient for the author!' I recommend it, however, the earlier the better, for the breaking of certain bad habits. The phrase makes a great cautionary mantra."

*[Sketch verified by James Luceno]*

\*   \*   \*

## DARY, David A.  1934-

*PERSONAL:* Born August 21, 1934, in Manhattan, KS; son of Milton Russell and Ruth (Long) Dary; married Carolyn Sue Russum, June 2, 1956; children: Cathy, Carol, Cindy, Cris. *Education:* Kansas State University, B.S., 1956; University of Kansas, M.S., 1970. *Religion:* Episcopalian.

*ADDRESSES: Home*—Norman, OK. *Office*—H. H. Herbert School of Journalism and Mass Communication, University of Oklahoma, Norman, OK 73019. *Agent*—Eleanor Wood, Spectrum Literary Agency, 111 Eighth Ave., Ste. 1501, New York, NY 10011.

*CAREER:* WIBW Radio-TV, morning news editor, 1956-57; KWFT Radio, Wichita Falls, TX, news editor, 1957-60; KTSA Radio, San Antonio, TX, managing news editor, 1960; Columbia Broadcasting System, Inc., Washington, DC, reporter and editor, 1960-63; National Broadcasting Company, Inc., Washington, DC, manager of local news, 1963-67; Studio Broadcasting System, Topeka, KS, director of news, 1967. Kansas Republican State Committee, Topeka, KS, director of public affairs, 1968. University of Kansas, William Allen White School of Journalism, Lawrence, assistant professor, 1969-75, associate professor, 1975-81, professor of journalism,

1981-89; University of Oklahoma, School of Journalism and Mass Communication, Norman, director and professor, 1989—.

*MEMBER:* Westerners International (president, 1986-88; chair, 1990-92; executive committee member, 1992—), Association for Education in Journalism and Mass Communications, Society of Professional Journalists, Western History Association, Western Writers of America (president, 1988-90), Kappa Tau Alpha.

*AWARDS, HONORS:* Golden Spur Award from Western Writers of America, 1982, for *Cowboy Culture,* and 1995, for *Seeking Pleasure in the Old West;* Wrangler Award from National Cowboy Hall of Fame, 1982.

*WRITINGS:*

*Radio News Handbook,* TAB Books (Thurmont, MD), 1967, 2nd edition, 1970.
*Television News Handbook,* TAB Books, 1971.
*How to Write News for Print and Broadcast,* TAB Books, 1973.
*The Buffalo Book* (Book-of-the-Month Club selection), Swallow Press (Athens, OH), 1974, new edition, 1989.
*Comanche,* Museum of Natural History, University of Kansas (Lawrence), 1976.
*True Tales of the Old-Time Plains,* Crown (New York City), 1979.
*Cowboy Culture—A Saga of Five Centuries,* Knopf (New York City), 1981.
*Lawrence Douglas County, Kansas: An Informal History,* Allen Books (Lawrence, KS), 1982.
*True Tales of Old-Time Kansas,* University Press of Kansas (Lawrence), 1984.
*Kanzana, A Selected Bibliography, 1854-1900,* Allen Press, 1986.
*Entrepreneurs of the Old-West: The Silent Army,* Knopf, 1986.
*More True Tales of Old-Time Kansas,* University Press of Kansas, 1987.
*Pictorial History of Lawrence, Douglas County, Kansas,* Allen Books, 1992.
*Seeking Pleasure in the Old West,* Knopf, 1995.

Author of introduction to books, including Charles C. Howes, *This Place Called Kansas,* University of Oklahoma Press (Norman, OK), 1984; Don Coldsmith, *Follow the Wind: The Spanish Bit Saga. . .,* Bantam Books (New York City), 1987; William Francis Hooker, *The Bullwhacker: Adven-*

*tures of a Frontier Freighter,* University of Nebraska Press (Lincoln, NE), 1988; Alexander Majors, *Seventy Years on the Frontier,* University of Nebraska Press, 1989; John R. Cook, *The Border and the Buffalo,* State House Books (Austin, TX), 1989; and Francis Haines, *The Buffalo,* University of Oklahoma Press, 1995. Also contributor of book chapters, book reviews, encyclopedia entries, and newspaper and magazine articles dealing with the Old West.

*SIDELIGHTS:* Among David Dary's many books on the Old West, his *Cowboy Culture, Entrepreneurs of the Old West: The Silent Army,* and *Seeking Pleasure in the Old West* have attracted attention from critics for their combination of scholarly history and popular folklore. "*Cowboy Culture* takes us all the way," notes a *Detroit News* contributor, "from the early, stringy longhorn bulls right down to the Wild West shows, dime novels, rodeos, and movies. It untangles the myths. It exposes the Spanish and European roots of the cowboys, cattle, and horses. It connects the raw and reckless frontier to history." Dary asserts that the cowboy's secure place in the American consciousness is as much a product of legend as of historical fact. According to J. D. Reed's *Time* review, Dary "deflates the mythic machismo of the bunkhouse and the open range. His real cowpoke is hardly an existential drifter on the Plains. Rather, he is a common laborer beset by the pressures of a hard life and slim wages."

Similarly, in *Entrepreneurs of the Old West: The Silent Army,* Dary unmasks the myth surrounding the early settlers of the West. Wray Herbert observes in the *Washington Post* that in the book Dary asserts that despite fanciful portrayals in popular films and novels "it was the search for personal wealth rather than any romantic urge or sense of adventure . . . that was the driving force behind the move west" by the early pioneers.

David Drury told *CA:* "My interest in the history of the American West started in Kansas during the depression '30s, when I grew up hearing countless stories about the pioneer days from my grandmother and many great aunts and uncles. As a young man I sought to understand my heritage and the reasons why two grandfathers came west to settle, one in 1864, another in 1873. My research that followed naturally gave way to writing about the American West.

"Because I write about history, I am often described as a historian, but I am more a writer who has chosen to write about history than a pure historian. As a writer I seek to chronicle the past, especially those vanished years of the American West from 1800 into the 20th century. I believe it is my responsibility as a writer to seek the truth, but facts alone are not sufficient. Too many pure historians get bogged down reporting fact after fact. Many of them may be fine historians, but most of them are not good writers. They avoid the process of rewriting, editing and more rewriting. Too many fail to find the best combinations of words to relate the story they are trying to tell. They believe their writing is done once they have organized the facts on paper. Their books reflect this. They are dull. Their writing does not reflect facts *and* emotion, essential ingredients for good writing and wide readership."

*BIOGRAPHICAL/CRITICAL SOURCES:*

*PERIODICALS*

*Detroit News,* September 13, 1981.
*Kansas City Star,* January 21, 1996.
*Los Angeles Times,* July 2, 1981; January 31, 1996.
*New York Times,* August 28, 1986.
*Time,* September 7, 1981.
*Washington Post,* August 10, 1986.

\*    \*    \*

**DAUGHERTY, Tracy 1955-**

*PERSONAL:* Born June 5, 1955, in Midland, TX; son of Don Eugene (a geologist) and Joanne (Stephenson) Daugherty; married Martha Grace Low (a teacher), December 31, 1985. *Ethnicity:* "White." *Education:* Southern Methodist University, B.A., 1976, M.A., 1983; University of Houston, Ph.D., 1986.

*ADDRESSES: Office*—Department of English, Oregon State University, Corvallis, OR 97331. *E-mail*—daughert@cla.orst.edu. *Agent*—Heather Shroder, International Creative Management, 40 West 57th St., New York, NY 10019.

*CAREER:* High School for Performing and Visual Arts, Houston, TX, writing consultant, 1984-86; Oregon State University, Corvallis, OR, associate professor of English, 1986—.

*MEMBER:* Associated Writing Programs, Modern Language Association, Pacific Northwest American Studies Association, Sigma Tau Delta, English Honor Society.

*AWARDS, HONORS:* Awards from Southwestern Booksellers Association and Texas Literary Festival, both 1986, both for *Desire Provoked;* A. B. Guthrie Jr. Short Fiction Award, for "The Women in the Oil Field," 1996; Associated Writing Programs award for *What Falls Away,* 1996.

*WRITINGS:*

*Desire Provoked* (novel), Random House (New York City), 1987.
*What Falls Away* (novel), Norton (New York City), 1996.
*The Women in the Oil Field* (short story collection), Southern Methodist University Press (Dallas, TX), 1996.

*WORK IN PROGRESS: The Boy Orator,* a novel about the Socialist movement in Oklahoma in 1917.

*SIDELIGHTS:* Described by Ron Loewinsohn in the *New York Times Book Review* as "an uneven but still impressive first novel," *Desire Provoked,* Tracy Daugherty's first novel, is the story of Sam Adams, a cartographer whose ordered world becomes suddenly confused by his wife's desertion, pressure from his boss to be dishonest on the job, and visits from a dark, mysterious stranger. Only after a near-fatal map-making trip to the Arctic, taken to escape the turmoil of his life, is Adams able to resolve his difficulties. Although Loewinsohn noted that the author tends to preach, he also wrote that Daugherty "is a serious, ambitious, highly gifted artist whose narration shifts between a straightforward, terse, no-nonsense prose and interludes of expressionistic or surreal free association."

Daugherty told *CA:* "I am interested in the connections between public and private lives—a territory Grace Paley has explored so well—and in various definitions of 'culture.' I'm intrigued by what happens when cultures clash. I've been heavily influenced by Donald Barthelme's experiments with language; I want to test the extremes of narrative and characterization, in light of the aforementioned cultural definitions. How does 'culture' shape our notions of 'story'?

"In the years since the publication of my first novel, I have attempted, in my work, to marry my earlier impulses toward innovation in form with more traditional structures and characterizations. This doesn't mean my aesthetics have become more conservative; rather, I hope it indicates a growing ease with the art of narrative, a maturing outlook. New forms will always be necessary to accurately describe a changing universe; but the best fiction, I believe, will always be strongly grounded in character. Novels and stories do their work through detail and human emotions. I am still intrigued by the new patterns of speech innovative writers such as Grace Paley and Donald Barthelme have given us, but my own vision now leans toward inclusiveness and expansion, rooted in historical knowledge, along the lines of William Kennedy's magnificent Albany series of novels. If I could write *Billy Phelan's Greatest Game* as seen through the eyes of the Dead Father, I could die happy."

*BIOGRAPHICAL/CRITICAL SOURCES:*

*PERIODICALS*

*Chicago Tribune,* February 15, 1987.
*Los Angeles Times Book Review,* March 8, 1987; February 11, 1996, p. 10.
*New York Times Book Review,* February 1, 1987.

\* \* \*

**DAVIES, R(obert) W(illiam) 1925-**

*PERSONAL:* Born April 23, 1925, in London, England; son of William and Gladys Hilda (Hall) Davies; married Frances Rebecca Moscow (a researcher and teacher), December 29, 1953; children: Maurice William, Catherine Gladys Anne. *Education:* University of London, B.A., 1950; University of Birmingham, Ph.D., 1954.

*ADDRESSES: Office*—Center for Russian and East European Studies (CREES), University of Birmingham, Birmingham B15 2TT, England; fax 0121-414-3423. *E-mail*—Y.K.M.Hall@bham.ac.uk.

*CAREER:* University of Glasgow, Glasgow, Scotland, senior research scholar and assistant in department of Soviet institutions, 1954-56; University of Birmingham, Birmingham, England, research fellow, 1956-59, lecturer, 1959-62, senior lecturer in department of economics and institutions of the U.S.S.R., 1962-63, director of Center for Russian and East European Studies, 1963-79, professor of Soviet economic studies, 1965—. Chair of British academic committee for cooperation with Russian archives. *Military service:* Royal Air Force, 1943-46; served as aircraftsman.

*MEMBER:* British Association of Slavonic and East European Studies (member of National Committee, 1965-76; elected honorary life member, 1996).

*WRITINGS:*

*The Development of the Soviet Budgetary System,* Cambridge University Press (Cambridge, England), 1958.
(With E. Zaleski and others) *Science Policy in the U.S.S.R.,* Organisation for Economic Cooperation and Development, 1969.
(With E. H. Carr) *Foundations of a Planned Economy, 1926-1929,* Volume 1, two parts, Macmillan (London and New York City), 1969.
*The Socialist Offensive: The Collectivization of Soviet Agriculture, 1929-1930,* Macmillan, 1980.
*The Soviet Collective Farm, 1929-1930,* Macmillan, 1980.
*The Soviet Economy in Turmoil, 1929-1930,* Macmillan, 1989.
*Soviet History in the Gorbachev Revolution,* Macmillan/Indiana University Press (Bloomington), 1989.
*Crisis and Progress in the Soviet Economy, 1931-1933,* Macmillan, 1996.
*Soviet History in the Yeltsin Era,* Macmillan, 1996.

Contributor of articles on Soviet science and technology, and history of Soviet economic institutions, to periodicals.

*EDITOR*

(With R. Amann and J. Cooper) *The Technological Level of Soviet Industry,* Yale University Press (New Haven, CT), 1977.
*The Soviet Union,* Allen & Unwin (London), 1977, 2nd edition, 1989.
*Soviet Investment for Planned Industrialization, 1929-1937: Policy and Practice,* Berkeley Slavic, 1983.
(Coeditor) *Materials for a Balance of the Soviet National Economy, 1928-1930,* Cambridge University Press, 1985.

E. H. Carr, *What is History?,* 2nd edition, Macmillan, 1986.
*From Tsarism to the New Economic Policy: Continuity and Change in the Economy of the USSR,* Macmillan/Cornell, 1988.
(With M. Harrison and S. G. Wheatcroft) *The Economic Transformation of the Soviet Union, 1913-1945,* Cambridge University Press, 1994.

Joint general editor, series on Russian and East European History and Society, Macmillan/CREES. Member of editorial board, *Economics of Planning.*

*WORK IN PROGRESS:* A multivolume history of Soviet industrialization, 1929-1937; research on Soviet economic statistics.

\*　　\*　　\*

**DAVIS, Peter (Frank) 1937-**

*PERSONAL:* Born January 2, 1937, in Santa Monica, CA; son of Frank (a screenwriter) and Tess (a writer; maiden name, Slesinger) Davis; married Johanna Mankiewicz, September 13, 1959 (died, 1974); married Karen Zehring (in publishing), June 10, 1979; children: Timothy, Nicholas, Jesse, Antonia. *Education:* Harvard University, A.B. (magna cum laude), 1957. *Politics:* Independent Democrat.

*ADDRESSES: Home and office*—P. O. Box 357, Castine, ME 04421. *Agent*—Amanda Urban, International Creative Management, 40 West 57th St., New York, NY 10019.

*CAREER: New York Times,* New York City, copyboy, 1958-59; Columbia Broadcasting System, Inc. (CBS-TV), New York City, producer and writer of documentary films, 1968-72; screenwriter and director of documentary films, 1972—. Associated with Yale University, 1972. *Military service:* U.S. Army, 1959-60.

*MEMBER:* Writers Guild of America.

*AWARDS, HONORS:* Award from Writers Guild of America, 1968, for *Hunger in America;* award from *Saturday Review,* 1970, for *The Battle of East St. Louis;* Emmy Award, National Academy of Television Arts and Sciences, Peabody Award, George Polk Award, and awards from Writers Guild of

America and *Saturday Review,* all 1971, all for *The Selling of the Pentagon;* Academy Award for best documentary film, Academy of Motion Picture Arts and Sciences, 1975, for *Hearts and Minds.*

*WRITINGS:*

*Hometown* (nonfiction), Simon & Schuster (New York City), 1982.
*Where Is Nicaragua?* (nonfiction), Simon & Schuster, 1987.
*If You Came This Way,* John Wiley (New York City), 1995.

DOCUMENTARIES; WRITER AND DIRECTOR

*The Heritage of Slavery,* Columbia Broadcasting System (CBS-TV), 1968.
(With Martin Carr) *Hunger in America,* CBS-TV, 1968.
*Once upon a Wall,* CBS-TV, 1969.
*The Battle of East St. Louis,* CBS-TV, 1969.
*The Selling of the Pentagon,* CBS-TV, 1971.
*Hearts and Minds,* Warner Brothers, 1975.
*Middletown,* Public Broadcasting Service (PBS-TV), 1982.
*The Best Hotel on Skid Row,* Home Box Office (HBO), 1990.
*Jack,* CBS-TV, 1993.

OTHER

Also co-author of screenplay for made-for-television film *Haywire,* adapted from the book by Brooke Hayward. Contributor to periodicals, including *Esquire, Nation, New York Times,* and *New York Woman.*

*SIDELIGHTS:* Outspoken documentary filmmaker and nonfiction writer Peter Davis has explored such topics as inner city poverty, the Vietnam War, the American military and the leftist government of Sandinista Nicaragua. In such works as *Hearts and Minds,* a study of the North Vietnamese view of the Vietnam War, *Hometown,* a semi-fictional look at Midwestern America, and *Where Is Nicaragua?,* a sympathetic view of the Sandinistas of that Central American nation, Davis gains attention even when he is sometimes offending his audience. *Hearts and Minds* won Davis an Academy Award in 1975.

Davis received a great deal of attention in the mid-1970s as the director of the controversial *Hearts and Minds,* a look at the Vietnam War. Davis created

*Hearts and Minds* using film footage featuring President Johnson and General Westmoreland making, respectively, pro-war and racist statements; the documentary also uses interviews and sequences of actual encounters between American troops and the Viet Cong and North Vietnamese Army. The film is an examination, according to Paul D. Zimmerman for *Newsweek,* of "loss, both personal and national, of ideals and illusion, sons and brothers, lives, limbs, liberties, and, finally, of a collective ability to connect with human suffering" during the Vietnam War.

Supporters of *Hearts and Minds* praise its impassioned plea for peace and its expose of war as folly. Zimmerman calls it a "thoroughly committed, brilliantly executed and profoundly moving document." The film's detractors, however, contend that it is too disorganized and too eager to elicit an emotional response. *Time*'s Stefan Kanfer writes: "Throughout, *Hearts and Minds* displays more than enough heart. It is mind that is missing. Perhaps the deepest flaw lies in the method: the Viet Nam War is too convoluted, too devious to be examined in a style of compilation without comment. And righteous indignation may tend to blind the documentary film maker to his prime task: the representation of life in all its fullness, not only those incidents that conform to the thesis." But Kanfer quotes Davis's conviction that the film "is not a chronology of war so much as a study of people's feelings."

In *Hometown,* an account of six years of observations and experiences in Hamilton, Ohio, Davis turns his attention to the "average America" of the Midwest. He was led to the town after asking the Census Bureau for a location where he could "understand America by going into one community and penetrating its society as deeply and widely as possible," records Susan Allen Toth in the *New York Times Book Review.* Davis uncovered some lively characters in his chosen town, whom he presents under such fictional names as "Mayor Witt" and "Congressman Kindness," and finds some exciting events, such as a basketball game between rival high schools, a murder between brothers-in-law, and a sex scandal that causes the entire town to reexamine its morals.

*Hometown* has received enthusiastic praise from several critics. The *Los Angeles Times*'s Elaine Kendall calls it "social science with heart and soul," and adds that "such attempts to straddle fact and fiction can easily fall between them in a no-man's land: 'Hometown' strikes a precarious balance." While Toth concedes that "no single 'hometown' could reveal it all," she feels that "Davis has made an honorable effort, and the stories he tells so effectively in 'Hometown' will doubtless resonate in other American hometowns as well." Christopher Lehmann-Haupt similarly remarks in the *New York Times* that "one doesn't absolutely have to make anything symbolic" of the characters in *Hometown.* "That they stand intensely and dramatically for themselves," Lehmann-Haupt concludes, "is really satisfying enough."

In *Where Is Nicaragua?,* Davis turned from examining small-town America to a friendly look at the Central American nation of Nicaragua. Run at the time by the leftist Sandinista government which had recently taken power, Nicaragua provided Davis with the opportunity to show how such a regime operated. He speaks with individuals from all classes, religions, and political affiliations—including sympathetic Americans living in the country—and presents their ideas and viewpoints in what Lehmann-Haupt calls "a camera's-eye view of Nicaragua." In a *New York Times Book Review* commentary on *Where Is Nicaragua?,* Jefferson Morely notes that "Davis suggests . . . that we take Nicaragua seriously and at face value." Although *Washington Post Book World* critic Lloyd Grove wishes Davis had spent more time interviewing, he finds Davis's work "seldom tendentious, and often refreshingly clear-headed. . . . He has the sharp eye of a film maker and a sharp pen as well."

*BIOGRAPHICAL/CRITICAL SOURCES:*

PERIODICALS

*Boston Globe,* May 2, 1982.
*Los Angeles Times,* March 8, 1982; March 20, 1982.
*Newsweek,* March 3, 1975; March 29, 1982.
*New York Times,* March 14, 1982; March 18, 1982; April 6, 1987.
*New York Times Book Review,* April 4, 1982; April 12, 1987.
*People,* March 29, 1982.
*Time,* March 17, 1975.
*USA Today,* March 27, 1987.
*Washington Post Book World,* April 4, 1982; April 19, 1987.

\*    \*    \*

**DEMIJOHN, Thom**
  **See DISCH, Thomas M(ichael)**

**DIKTY, Julian May**
  **See MAY, Julian**

\*    \*    \*

**DISCH, Thomas M(ichael)   1940-**
  **(Tom Disch; Leonie Hargrave; Thom Demijohn and Cassandra Knye, joint pseudonyms)**

*PERSONAL:* Born February 2, 1940, in Des Moines, IA; son of Felix Henry and Helen (Gilbertson) Disch. *Education:* Attended Cooper Union and New York University, 1959-62.

*ADDRESSES: Office*—31 Union Square West, No. 11E, New York, NY 10003. *Agent*—Karpfinger Agency, 500 Fifth Ave., Suite 2800, New York, NY 10110.

*CAREER:* Freelance writer, 1964—. Majestic Theatre, New York City, part-time checkroom attendant, 1957-62; Doyle Dane Bernbach, New York City, copywriter, 1963-64; theater critic for *Nation,* 1987-91; theater critic for the *New York Daily News,* 1993—. Artist-in-residence, College of William and Mary, 1996—. Lecturer at universities.

*MEMBER:* PEN, National Book Critics Circle (board member, 1988-91), Writers Guild East.

*AWARDS, HONORS:* O. Henry Prize, 1975, for story "Getting into Death," and 1979, for story "Xmas"; John W. Campbell Memorial Award, and American Book Award nomination, both 1980, both for *On Wings of Song;* Hugo Award and Nebula Award nominations, 1980, and British Science Fiction Award, 1981, all for novella *The Brave Little Toaster.*

*WRITINGS:*

NOVELS

*The Genocides,* Berkley Publishing (New York City), 1965.
*Mankind under the Leash* (expanded version of his short story, "White Fang Goes Dingo" [also see below]), Ace Books (New York City), 1966, published in England as *The Puppies of Terra,* Panther Books, 1978.

(With John Sladek under joint pseudonym Cassandra Knye) *The House That Fear Built*, Paperback Library, 1966.

*Echo Round His Bones*, Berkley Publishing, 1967.

(With Sladek under joint pseudonym Thom Demijohn) *Black Alice*, Doubleday (New York City), 1968.

*Camp Concentration*, Hart-Davis, 1968, Doubleday, 1969.

*The Prisoner*, Ace Books, 1969.

*334*, MacGibbon & Kee, Avon (New York City), 1974.

(Under pseudonym Leonie Hargrave) *Clara Reeve*, Knopf (New York City), 1975.

*On Wings of Song*, St. Martin's (New York City), 1979.

*Triplicity* (omnibus volume), Doubleday, 1980.

(With Charles Naylor) *Neighboring Lives*, Scribner, 1981.

*The Businessman: A Tale of Terror*, Harper, 1984.

*Amnesia* (computer-interactive novel), Electronic Arts, 1985.

*The Silver Pillow: A Tale of Witchcraft*, M. V. Ziesing (Willimantic, CT), 1987.

*The M.D.: A Horror Story*, Knopf, 1991.

*The Priest: A Gothic Romance*, Knopf, 1995.

STORY COLLECTIONS

*One Hundred and Two H-Bombs and Other Science Fiction Stories* (also see below), Compact Books (Hollywood, FL), 1966, revised edition published as *One Hundred and Two H-Bombs*, Berkeley Publishing, 1969, published in England as *White Fang Goes Dingo and Other Funny S.F. Stories*, Arrow Books, 1971.

*Under Compulsion*, Hart-Davis, 1968, also published as *Fun with Your New Head*, Doubleday, 1969.

*Getting into Death: The Best Short Stories of Thomas M. Disch*, Hart-Davis, 1973, revised edition, Knopf, 1976.

*The Early Science Fiction Stories of Thomas M. Disch* (includes *Mankind under the Leash* and *One Hundred and Two H-bombs)*, Gregg (Boston, MA), 1977.

*Fundamental Disch*, Bantam, 1980.

*The Man Who Had No Idea*, Bantam, 1982.

POETRY

(With Marilyn Hacker and Charles Platt) *Highway Sandwiches*, privately printed, 1970.

*The Right Way to Figure Plumbing*, Basilisk Press, 1972.

*ABCDEFG HIJKLM NPOQRST UVWXYZ*, Anvil Press Poetry (Millville, MN), 1981.

*Orders of the Retina*, Toothpaste Press (West Branch, IA), 1982.

*Burn This*, Hutchinson, 1982.

*Here I Am, There You Are, Where Were We?*, Hutchinson, 1984.

*Yes, Let's: New and Selected Poetry*, Johns Hopkins University Press (Baltimore, MD), 1989.

*Dark Verses and Light*, Johns Hopkins University Press, 1991.

JUVENILE

*The Tale of Dan de Lion: A Fable*, Coffee House Press, 1986.

*The Brave Little Toaster: A Bedtime Story for Small Appliances*, Doubleday, 1986.

*The Brave Little Toaster Goes to Mars*, Doubleday, 1988.

EDITOR

*The Ruins of the Earth: An Anthology of Stories of the Immediate Future*, Putnam, 1971.

*Bad Moon Rising: An Anthology of Political Foreboding*, Harper, 1975.

*The New Improved Sun: An Anthology of Utopian Science Fiction*, 1975.

(With Naylor) *New Constellations: An Anthology of Tomorrow's Mythologies*, Harper, 1976.

(With Naylor) *Strangeness: A Collection of Curious Tales*, Scribner, 1977.

OTHER

(Ghost editor with Robert Arthur) *Alfred Hitchcock Presents: Stories that Scared Even Me*, Random House, 1967.

(Librettist) *The Fall of the House of Usher* (opera), produced in New York City, 1979.

(Librettist) *Frankenstein* (opera), produced in Greenvale, NY, 1982.

*Ringtime* (short story), Toothpaste Press, 1983.

(Author of introduction) Michael Bishop, *One Winter in Eden*, Arkham House (Sauk City, WI), 1984.

*Torturing Mr. Amberwell* (short story), Cheap Street (New Castle, VA), 1985.

(Author of preface) Pamela Zoline, *The Heat Death of the Universe and Other Stories*, McPherson & Company (New Paltz, NY), 1988.

(Author of introduction) Philip K. Dick, *The Penultimate Truth*, Carroll & Graf, 1989.

*Ben Hur* (play), first produced in New York City, 1989.

*The Cardinal Detoxes* (verse play), first produced in New York City by RAPP Theater Company, 1990.

*The Castle of Indolence: On Poetry, Poets, and Poetasters,* Picador (New York City), 1995.

Contributor to *Science Fiction at Large,* edited by Peter Nicholls, Harper, 1976.

Contributor to numerous anthologies. Also contributor to periodicals, including *Playboy, Poetry,* and *Harper's.* Regular reviewer for *Times Literary Supplement* and *Washington Post Book World.*

*ADAPTATIONS: The Brave Little Toaster* was produced as an animated film by Hyperion-Kushner-Lockec, 1987.

*WORK IN PROGRESS: The Teddy Bear's Tragedy; The Pressure of Time; A Child's Garden of Grammar,* for Story Line Press.

*SIDELIGHTS:* An author of science fiction, poetry, historical novels, opera librettos, and computer-interactive fiction, Thomas M. Disch has been cited as "one of the most remarkably talented writers around" by a reviewer for the *Washington Post Book World.* Disch began his career writing science fiction stories that featured dark themes and disturbing plots. Many of Disch's early themes reappear in his short stories and poetry; the result, according to Blake Morrison in the *Times Literary Supplement,* is "never less than enjoyable and accomplished." While many of his best-known works are aimed at an adult audience, Disch is also the author of well-received children's fiction, including two fantasies, *The Brave Little Toaster* and *The Brave Little Toaster Goes to Mars.* Describing the diversity of Disch's work in *Dream Makers: The Uncommon People Who Write Science Fiction,* Charles Platt notes that the author "has traveled widely, through almost every genre and technique. . . . And in each field [Disch] has made himself at home, never ill-at-ease or out-of-place, writing with the same implacable control and elegant manners."

Hard to pigeon-hole, Disch's versatility has made both marketing his work and developing a loyal following of readers difficult. In refusing to let critics stamp his work with labels, Disch has been granted a relative anonymity, a phenomenon that led *Newsweek* critic Walter Clemons to call the author "the most formidably gifted unfamous American writer."

Disch grew up in Minnesota and graduated from high school in St. Paul. As a youngster he devoured horror comic books and science fiction magazines, including the influential *Astounding Science Fiction.* He learned his craft by reading and re-reading the work of authors such as Robert A. Heinlein and Isaac Asimov—found in the pages of *Astounding Science Fiction.* Although Disch did not publish his first short story until 1952, he had been writing science fiction for a decade or more under the inspiration of his favorite childhood authors.

After a series of low-paying jobs in Minnesota (which included employment as night watchman in a funeral parlor), Disch moved to New York City. While living in New York, he worked as a checkroom attendant and advertising copywriter. His first fiction appeared in a magazine called *Fantastic Stories* in 1962. Between that periodical and another one called *Amazing Stories* he would publish nine more stories that year and the next. Although Disch has admitted to not thinking that highly of his first publishing success, he found his second effort at writing a full-length story more satisfactory. This story, entitled "White Fang Goes Dingo," was first published in its short form, then in an expanded version as the author's second novel, *Mankind under the Leash* (later published under the title Disch prefers, *The Puppies of Terra).*

In 1964, having secured an advance from Berkley Books, Disch left advertising to become a full-time writer. He published his first novel the following year, a science fiction tale entitled *The Genocides.* In large part the story of an alien invasion of Earth, *The Genocides* describes the last grim days of human existence, an existence where people are reduced to little more than insects in the aliens' global garden. Critics found the book frightening. "The novel . . . is powerful in the way that it forces the reader to alter his perspective, to reexamine what it means to be human," writes Erich S. Rupprecht in the *Dictionary of Literary Biography.* Disch followed *The Genocides* with a series of thought-provoking science fiction tales, such as *Camp Concentration* and *334,* as well as horror novels such as *The Businessman* and *The M.D.*

Confident of his continued success as a writer, Disch would soon find himself near the center of an upheaval in the world of science fiction. Having published stories in the influential British magazine *New Worlds,* he became a force in what has since been labeled the New Wave of science fiction. Brian Aldiss, in his *Trillion Year Spree: The History of Science Fiction,* noted: "At the heart of *New Worlds's* New Wave—never mind the froth at the edges—was a hard and unpalatable core of message, an attitude to life, a skepticism about the benefits of society or any future society." More specifically, the New Wave was interested in new forms of expression and new themes never dreamed of by the older generation of science fiction writers. "In a broad sense," write Robert Scholes and Eric S. Rabkin in *Science Fiction: History, Science, Vision,* "the New Wave represents an attempt to find a language and a social perspective for science fiction that is as adventurous and progressive as its technological vision." The skepticism of its writers made their works on a whole pessimistic, and Disch was no exception. Although the New Wave has been followed by succeeding generations of writers, its impact on Disch's work—and the reverse—is undeniable.

*Camp Concentration, 334,* and *On Wings of Song* are widely considered Disch's best works. All three appeared in a mid-1980s survey by David Pringle entitled *Science Fiction: The 100 Best Novels.* Scholes and Rabkin describe *Camp Concentration* as Disch's "first major breakthrough" under the influence of the New Wave. It is set at a secret prison camp run by the U.S. Army where selected prisoners are being treated with a new drug that increases their intelligence. Unfortunately, this drug also causes the prisoners' early deaths. The novel is in the form of a diary kept by one of the prisoners. The diary's style grows more complex as the narrative develops, reflecting the prisoner's increasing intelligence. According to Scholes and Rabkin, the novel "combines considerable technical resources in the management of the narrative . . . with a probing inquiry into human values." Rupprecht draws a parallel between *Camp Concentration* and *The Genocides.* In both novels, he argues, the characters must survive inescapable situations. Disch's continuing theme, Rupprecht summarizes, is "charting his characters' attempts to keep themselves intact in a world which grows increasingly hostile, irrational, inhuman."

This theme is also found in *334,* a novel set in a New York City housing project of the future. Divided into six loosely-related sections, the novel presents the daily lives of residents of the building, which is located at 334 East Eleventh Street. The characters live in boredom and poverty; their city is rundown and dirty. The world of the novel, Scholes and Rabkin believe, "is not radically different from ours in many respects but is deeply troubling for reasons that apply to the present New York as well. Above all, the aimlessness and purposelessness of the lives chronicled is affecting." In his analysis of the book Rupprecht also notes the similarity between the novel's setting and the world of the present. He finds *334* to be "a slightly distorted mirror image of contemporary life." Although the *Washington Post Book World* reviewer judges the setting to be "an interesting, plausible and unpleasant near-future world where urban life is even more constricted than now," he nonetheless believes that "survival and aspiration remain possible." Rupprecht praises *334* as Disch's "most brilliant and disturbing work. . . . One can think of few writers—of science fiction or other genres—who could convey a similar sense of emptiness, of yearning, of ruin with this power and grace. . . . Like all great writers, Disch forces his readers to see the reality of their lives in a way that is fresh, startling, disturbing, and moving." Speaking of *Camp Concentration* and *334,* David Lehman of the *Times Literary Supplement* states that these two novels "seem to transcend their genre without betraying it; they manage to break down the barriers separating science fiction from 'literature,' and they do so by shrewdly manipulating the conventions of the former."

Like *334, On Wings of Song* deals with a future time that resembles our own. Describing the general atmosphere of the novel in the *New York Times Book Review,* Gerald Jonas notes: "Politically and economically, things seem to be going downhill, but in between crises, people can still assure themselves that they are living in 'normal' times." In the *Village Voice,* John Calvin Batchelor calls *On Wings of Song* Disch's "grandest work." The critic maintains that the novel links Disch with other great social critics of the past, including H. G. Wells and George Orwell. "Disch," he writes, "is an unapologetic political writer, a high-minded liberal democrat, who sees doom in Western Civilization and says so, often with bizarre, bleak scenarios."

Along with his novels, Disch has also contributed numerous short stories to periodicals. These have been gathered in several well-received short story collections and appeared in anthologies, including several volumes of *The Best from Fantasy & Science Fiction.* Reviewers of his short stories have also been reluctant to classify Disch as "merely" a science fiction writer. *Time* reviewer Paul Gray, for instance, observes that in Disch's collection *Getting into Death and Other Stories* there is only one story that is traditional, space-oriented science fiction, while the others are deemed comparable to the work of *Alice's Adventures in Wonderland* creator Lewis Carroll. Finding yet another notable author with whom to compare Disch, *Voice of Youth Advocates* reviewer Wain Saeger refers to the stories in *Fundamental Disch* as "somber, even eerie, more like Edgar Allan Poe than today's space opera."

Continuing to explore many literary avenues, in the 1980s and 1990s Disch published novels, stories, poetry, a libretto and an interactive computer novel. Three novels published during this period further the social criticism seen in earlier works. In *The Businessman: A Tale of Terror, The M.D.: A Horror Story,* and *The Priest: A Gothic Romance,* Disch combines classic thriller techniques with a critical look at the corruption he sees in the three professions mentioned in the titles. The plots are replete with the type of strange occurrences Disch's readers have grown to expect, and the works show Disch's usual blend of styles. Writing about *The M.D.* in *Kliatt,* Larry W. Prater notes: "The novel combines elements of the macabre, of fantasy and of SF." Evidently, in life as well as literature, categories aren't important to Disch. In a *Publishers Weekly* interview with David Finkle, Disch refuses to see *The M.D.* as just a horror novel and with equal fervor defends his right to remain unburdened by a convenient label. "Every book has its own slightly different ground rules from the others," he maintains. ". . . As long as the book plays by its own rules and those are clear, I don't think genre borderlines are especially helpful. I don't spend my life trying to determine what category I'm in." Disch tells Platt: "Part of my notion of a proper ambition is that one should excel at a wide range of tasks."

The variety found in Disch's novels and stories also extends to his poetry and work for children. Lehman praises Disch's poetry by noting that "the distinctive qualities of Disch's prose fiction—wit, invention, and the gift of gab—are the virtues of his verse as well. . . . Disch has . . . an excellent ear and clever tongue." Disch has also had success as a children's author with titles such as *The Brave Little Toaster* and *The Tale of Dan de Lion.* In these works, Disch fully embraces the fantastic. *The Brave Little Toaster* tells the story of a group of small appliances (including the toaster, a clock radio, and an electric blanket) who come to life in order to search for their missing master. *The Tale of Dan de Lion,* presented in a series of couplets, concerns the adventures of a dandelion, his weedy family, and the rose breeder who wants to destroy them. Critics praised Disch's children's works both for the author's use of language and sense of whimsy. *The Brave Little Toaster* gained further recognition when it was produced as a popular animated film in 1987.

In most evaluations of his work, Disch is lauded for his great imagination, the diversity of his narrative style, and the ease with which he works in a number of different genres. Because Disch is able to move so effortlessly through these different thematic and stylistic concerns, Rupprecht concludes that Disch is "one of the finest writers of fiction today," a writer who "seems to delight . . . in blurring easy distinctions."

## BIOGRAPHICAL/CRITICAL SOURCES:

### BOOKS

Aldiss, Brian W., *Trillion Year Spree: The History of Science Fiction,* Atheneum, 1986.

Bleiler, E. F., editor, *Science Fiction Writers: Critical Studies of the Major Authors from the Early Nineteenth Century to the Present Day,* Scribner, 1982, pp. 351-56.

*Children's Literature Review,* Volume 18, Gale (Detroit), 1989.

*Contemporary Literary Criticism,* Gale, Volume 7, 1977, pp. 86-87; Volume 36, 1986, pp. 123-28.

*Contemporary Poets,* St. James Press (Chicago), 5th edition, 1991.

Delany, Samuel R., *The American Shore: Meditations on a Tale of Science Fiction by Thomas M. Disch,* Dragon (Elizabethtown, NY), 1978.

*Dictionary of Literary Biography,* Volume 8: *Twentieth-Century Science Fiction Writers,* Gale, 1981, pp. 148-154.

Disch, Thomas M., *334,* Gregg, 1976, pp. v-xiii.

Nee, David, *Thomas M. Disch: A Preliminary Bibliography,* Other Change of Hobit (Berkeley, CA), 1982.

Nicholls, Peter, editor, *Science Fiction at Large,* Harper, 1976, pp. 141-55.

Platt, Charles, *Dream Makers: Uncommon People Who Write Science Fiction,* Berkley Publishing, 1980.

Pringle, David, *Science Fiction: The One Hundred Best Novels* [London], 1985.

Scholes, Robert and Eric S. Rabkin, *Science Fiction: History, Science, Vision,* Oxford University Press, 1977, pp. 88, 96.

*Something about the Author Autobiography Series,*
  Volume 15, Gale, 1993, pp. 107-23.
Stephens, Christopher P., *A Checklist of Thomas M.
  Disch,* Ultramarine (Hastings-on-Hudson, NY),
  1991.

PERIODICALS

*Chicago Tribune Book World,* March 22, 1982.
*Kliatt,* September, 1992, p. 20.
*Los Angeles Times,* February 3, 1981; November 21,
  1982, p. 13; August 13, 1989, p. 3.
*New Statesman,* July 13, 1984, p. 28.
*Newsweek,* March 9, 1981; July 2, 1984; July 11,
  1988, pp. 66-67.
*New York Times Book Review,* March 21, 1976, p. 6;
  October 28, 1979, p. 15, 18; August 26, 1984,
  p. 31; April 20, 1986, p. 29.
*Publishers Weekly,* January 7, 1974, p. 56; January
  5, 1976, p. 59; August 29, 1980, p. 363; April
  19, 1991, pp. 48-49.
*Science Fiction Chronicle,* February, 1993, p. 35.
*Spectator,* May 1, 1982, p. 23.
*Time,* July 28, 1975; February 9, 1976, pp. 83-84;
  July 9, 1984, pp. 85-86.
*Times Literary Supplement,* February 15, 1974, p.
  163; June 12, 1981, p. 659; August 27, 1982, p.
  919; May 25, 1984, p. 573; November 28,
  1986, p. 343; September 15-21, 1989, p. 1000;
  November 11, 1994, p. 19.
*Village Voice,* August 27-September 2, 1980, pp. 35-
  36.
*Voice of Youth Advocates,* April, 1981, p. 39.
*Washington Post,* September 23, 1979, p. 7.
*Washington Post Book World,* July 26, 1981, pp. 6-
  7; August 6, 1989, p. 5.

\*     \*     \*

**DISCH, Tom**
  **See DISCH, Thomas M(ichael)**

\*     \*     \*

**DIXON, Stephen    1936-**

*PERSONAL:* Original name, Stephen Ditchik; name
changed at age six; born June 6, 1936, in New York,
NY; son of Abraham Mayer (a dentist) and Florence
(an interior decorator; maiden name, Leder) Ditchik;

married Anne Frydman (a translator and lecturer),
January 17, 1983; children: Sophia Cara, Antonia.
*Education:* City College of New York (now City
College of the City University of New York), B.A.,
1958. *Avocational interests:* Reading, writing, listening to serious music, "reading the *New York Times*
over several cups of black coffee."

*ADDRESSES: Home*—1315 Boyce Ave., Towson,
MD 21204. *Office*—The Writing Seminars, Johns
Hopkins University, Baltimore, MD 21218.

*CAREER:* Writer. Worked as fiction consultant, junior high school teacher, tour leader, school bus
driver, department store sales clerk, artist's model,
waiter, bartender, reporter for a radio news service,
magazine editor, and assistant producer of a television show, *In Person,* for the Columbia Broadcasting
System (CBS); New York University, School of
Continuing Education, New York City, instructor,
1979; Johns Hopkins University, Baltimore, MD,
assistant professor, 1980-85, associate professor,
1985-89, professor of fiction, 1989—.

*AWARDS, HONORS:* Stegner fellow, Stanford Uni-
versity, 1964-65; National Endowment for the Arts
grant for fiction, 1974-75, 1990-91; O. Henry
Award, 1977, for "Mac in Love," and 1982, for
"Layaways"; Pushcart Prize, 1977, for "Milk Is
Very Good for You"; American Academy-Institute
of Arts and Letters prize for literature, 1983;
Guggenheim Fellowship for fiction, 1984-85; John
Train Humor Prize, *Paris Review,* 1986; National
Book Awards finalist in fiction, 1991, and PEN/
Faulkner finalist in fiction, 1992, both for *Frog;*
National Book Awards finalist in fiction, 1995, for
*Interstate.*

*WRITINGS:*

SHORT STORY COLLECTIONS

*No Relief,* Street Fiction Press (Newport, RI), 1976.
*Quite Contrary: The Mary and Newt Story,* Harper
  (New York City), 1979.
*14 Stories,* Johns Hopkins University Press (Balti-
  more), 1980.
*Movies,* North Point Press (Berkeley, CA), 1983.
*Time to Go,* Johns Hopkins University Press, 1984.
*The Play and Other Stories,* Coffee House (Minne-
  apolis), 1989.
*Love and Will,* British American Publishing, 1989.
*All Gone,* Johns Hopkins University Press, 1990.

*Friends: More Will & Magna Stories,* Asylum Arts, 1990.

*Moon,* British American Publishing, 1993.

*Long Made Short,* Johns Hopkins University Press, 1994.

*The Stories of Stephen Dixon,* Holt (New York City), 1994.

*Man on Stage: Playstories,* Hi Jinx (Davis, CA), 1996.

Contributor to *Making a Break,* Latitudes Press (New York City), 1975.

*NOVELS*

*Work,* Street Fiction Press, 1977.

*Too Late,* Harper, 1978.

*Fall & Rise,* North Point Press, 1985.

*Garbage,* Cane Hill Press (New York City), 1988.

*Frog,* British American Publishing, 1991.

*Interstate,* Holt, 1995.

*Gould: A Novel in Two Novels,* Henry Holt (New York City), 1997.

*OTHER*

Contributor to anthologies. Contributor of more than 350 short stories to periodicals, including *Harpers, Glimmer Train, Western Humanities Review, Viva, Playboy, Paris Review, American Review, Atlantic, Pequod, Esquire, Yale Review, South Carolina Review, Triquarterly,* and *Chicago Review.*

*SIDELIGHTS:* Stephen Dixon has published more than 400 pieces of short fiction and several novels. His work has appeared in a wide variety of magazines, from the venerable *Paris Review* to such popular glossies as *Playboy* and *Esquire,* to little magazines with a few hundred subscribers. Some critics have seen the success of his published short story collections as an indication of a "boomlet" of interest in that genre. Dixon, who worked odd jobs for years while trying to sell his fiction, admitted in a *Baltimore Sun* article that he didn't really start publishing books until he was forty. "By being published late, I learned I could endure and survive and still write," he said. "If I lost my job [as professor of creative writing at Johns Hopkins University], . . . I would get a job as a waiter or a bartender and go on writing."

Pervasive themes in Dixon's work include "relationships of couples, complexities of even the simplest

jobs, and ways in which information so easily becomes misinformation or even disinformation," to quote Jerome Klinkowitz in the *Dictionary of Literary Biography.* A native New Yorker, Dixon often sets his fiction's action in that city. Paul Skenazy notes in the *San Francisco Chronicle* that Dixon "writes about people who live in rundown apartments, . . . he gives a reader the irritating, wearing feel of city life. He captures that rubbing of noise and excitement against the grain of one's inertia, that constant intrusion of human traffic. But at its best the tone is less tough than worn-at-the-cuffs, frayed and slightly frantic from observing people who let their pride escape while they were watching TV or doing the laundry." "Dixon's imagination sticks close to home," writes John Domini in the *New York Times Book Review.* "His principal subject is the clash of the mundane and aberrant, those unsettling run-ins with wackos or former lovers all too familiar to anyone who's ever lived in a city." Skenazy feels that Dixon's urban stories "frequently have a powerful impact that, while distasteful, is bracing; and there is something of the feel of that part of life too often ignored by fiction."

Much of Dixon's work also chronicles the pitfalls and problems of male-female relationships, painting "a harrowing portrait of therapeutic man and therapeutic woman trying to experience love," according to Anatole Broyard in the *New York Times.* A *Kirkus Reviews* critic writes that the author's theme becomes clear: "love affairs are like fiction—stories that are added to, rubbed out, obsessively changed, matters of chosen order and nuance and correction." His male protagonists "are generally so yearning and irritably hungry for sex and/or intimacy that they either don't look before they leap, or if they do look, leap anyway no matter what they see ahead," claims David Aitken in the *Baltimore Sun.* "As a result, their lives are almost always in uncontrollable comic disarray."

This theme is apparent in Dixon's novel *Fall & Rise,* in which the leading character tries, through a long New York night, to woo a woman he met at a party earlier in the evening. It is also the controlling idea behind Dixon's O. Henry Award-winning short story "Mac in Love," in which a repulsed suitor yells wistful nonsense at his date's balcony until the beleaguered woman calls the police. The final effect in many of Dixon's male-female imbroglios is, in Aitken's opinion, "vaguely Woody Allenish. Dixon's comedy is stronger than Allen's though, in being less stylized and drawn with a fresher eye for the particulars of life."

Some critics have found fault with aspects of Dixon's work. In his review of *Time to Go,* Aitken comments: "One wishes Dixon didn't republish so many of his weaker stories. It dilutes the impression his best work makes." Domini similarly finds that in *Time to Go,* "all Mr. Dixon's encounters lack any but the most general physicality. . . . The repression of rhetoric and an emphasis on the trivial are hallmarks of many contemporary short stories. But Mr. Dixon is so unrelenting in both regards that he ends up compounding a lack of imagination with a near absence of passion." James Lasdun writes in the *Times Literary Supplement:* "One has the feeling that Dixon begins most of his stories with little more in mind than a vague idea, a couple of characters, or a briefly observed scene, relying on his ready wit to transform it into a convincing piece of fiction. This is fine when it works, but occasionally the initial impulse is too flimsy and the story fails to take off."

In general, however, Dixon's literary output has elicited considerable critical approval. Lasdun notes: "The best of these stories have a certain manic quality about them, caused largely by Dixon's delight in speeding life up and compressing it, to the point where it begins to verge on the surreal." In the *Chicago Tribune Book World,* George Cohen concludes: "Dixon's best is superb, tragic, funny, cynical. He's telling us all the bizarre things we already know about ourselves, and he's right on the mark." "Every overworked adjective of praise in the literary criticism business applies to Dixon's writing, beginning with versatile," comments a reviewer in the *Baltimore Sun.* Richard Burgin, in an article for the *St. Petersburg Times,* calls Dixon "a prolific and versatile writer whose strong vision balances anxiety and darkness with humor and compassion. . . . It is high time that the larger American literary community recognized that he is one of our finest writers of short fiction."

*The Stories of Stephen Dixon,* a collection of many of the author's favorite and most representative work, was published in 1994 and shows the writer playing "intelligent variations on a few great themes," observes William Ferguson in the *New York Times Book Review.* Ferguson also notes Dixon's penchant for characters who "reinvent themselves, time and again, in a retractile language that always seems to be more substantial than they are."

Praising Dixon's stories generally for their depth of feeling and their technical merit, Klinkowitz notes: "Although their humor is often based on the inanity of human needs caught up in and mangled by the infernal machinery of systematics, his narratives can also use this same facility to convey great sensitivity and emotion." Concludes Klinkowitz: "Like a jazz soloist improvising exuberantly, yet within the contours of melody and progressions of chords, Dixon uses the structures of language and circumstance to produce effective prose."

The same distinctive style Dixon employs in his short stories can also be found in his novels. A reviewer for the *Virginia Quarterly Review* explains that Dixon "writes rapid-fire fiction; the action is fast and unceasing." Once again mostly employing urban settings, the author often moves the action along via run-on sentences that imitate real-life speech and thought patterns, complete with pauses, self-contradictions, and digressions. "One doesn't exactly read a story by Stephen Dixon, one submits to it," claims Alan H. Friedman in the *New York Times Book Review.* "An unstoppable prose expands the arteries while an edgy, casual nervousness overpowers the will."

In one of Dixon's longer works, a novel titled *Garbage,* this quick-paced delivery intensifies the action of the plot, helping to create a dark and hopeless mood. An average bar owner, Shaney Fleet, has two choices when a garbage collection service tries to extort money—pay or fight. Fleet decides to fight, and in the process his apartment is burned down and he goes to jail where he is so badly beaten that he ends up in the hospital, at which point his neighbors help themselves to whatever he has left. The police are remote and unable to help. In the end, Fleet loses his bar, but retains his fighting spirit. "In *Garbage,* the good guys don't triumph over the bad guys. What triumphs is simply the human spirit," declares Margo Hammond in the *Baltimore Sun. Library Journal* contributor Albert E. Wilhelm calls *Garbage* "a well-wrought parable of modern urban life," and Cleveland *Plain Dealer* correspondent Michael Heaton concludes: "More than an entertainment, Dixon's novel is an achievement. He is a writer's writer whose mastery of the mundane elevates the common life experience to high art. Put simply, *Garbage* is glorious."

In *Frog,* a National Book Award finalist, Dixon brings together a collection of short stories, novellas, letters, essays, poems and two novels surrounding the life of one protagonist—Howard Tetch, a teacher and family man. The stories, or chapters, are arranged without regard to chronology, so Tetch's marriage, childhood, anecdotes of his children's lives, and aging and death intermix, creating a conglomeration of his fantasies and memories. Episodes overlap, variations on the same story are presented, and the reader is often left to decipher the "truth." Within the space of two chapters, for example, Tetch's daughter Olivia is lost forever at the beach, only to show up as a member of the family at his funeral, without the separation indicated. "Events rotate in a kaleidoscope, the bright fragments fall, and the author's eye focuses on his protagonist's self-absorption, through chains of immense paragraphs, each a story in itself," describes Friedman. Sybil Steinberg in *Publishers Weekly* advises: "Readers attuned to the author's run-on style may warm to a cunning, sexy, audacious performance; others will find this an arty bore." Jim Dwyer in the *Library Journal* praises *Frog* for its "labyrinthine structure, rapid-fire wordplay, vivid descriptions, and raw emotional power." *Washington Post Book World* contributor Steven Moore concludes: "For readers who can see through such bad writing and relish the immediacy it offers, its vitality, its feel of catching life on the wing as Dixon's characters endlessly try to explain themselves to others or to themselves, *Frog* will be a memorable experience."

The same permutations of repetitious event and imagery form the basis of Dixon's 1995 novel *Interstate*. Through eight divergent versions of the story, a father named Nathan Frey grapples with the horror of losing a daughter in a freak murder on the highway. Over and over again the events of the shooting are re-visited, each time from an entirely different perspective. "Italo Calvino and Alain Robbe-Grillet have also written novels that begin again and again, revising themselves, but the subjects of these novels are only themselves," observes George Stade in the *New York Times Book Review.* "Neither of them has brought off anything like the broken eloquence of Nathan's voice, which is as distinct and original and American as Mark Twain's, if otherwise very different." In the *Los Angeles Times Book Review,* Allen Barra commends Dixon for his experimental style, noting: "In this, his 17th book, Stephen Dixon has honed his radical techniques to their finest sheen." Barra concludes: "There is the intriguing possibility that the narrator, in recounting the story, can't recall all the details himself and keeps changing its landscape slightly. There is also the even more intriguing possibility that each narrative is simply a blueprint of

the father's subconscious fears for his children and his own helplessness to protect them in the outside world."

"My writing comes first in my work," Dixon once told *CA.* "But to get to my writing, I first must finish all my school work. And I have lots of school work to do, but I never feel free to write, and I have to feel free and unburdened of looming work of other kinds, so I do all my school work before I do my writing. That sometimes means I'll stay up to 3:00 a.m. finishing student papers; I'll go to bed tired but I wake up liberated, and ready to write. I must teach in order to pay the bills. I like teaching, but I'd prefer just to read and write. I've a lot to write and I write every single day. New ideas always come when I'm writing, so the process of writing is very important for me. . . . I write only for myself, my writing has to excite me or it's worthless, boring, and I then have to try something else; and I must always do something new. If I ever find myself going over familiar ground in a familiar way, meaning my familiar or other writers, I'd give up writing—that wouldn't be so hard; I've written plenty, more than anyone would ever want to read—and try something else, or just read, walk, think, and keep my manual typewriter polished and clean for possible future writing days."

## BIOGRAPHICAL/CRITICAL SOURCES:

### BOOKS

*Contemporary Literary Criticism,* Volume 52, Gale, 1989.
*Dictionary of Literary Biography,* Volume 130, Gale, 1993, pp. 124-32.
Klinkowitz, Jerome, *The Self-Apparent Word: Fiction as Language/Language as Fiction,* Southern Illinois University Press (Carbondale), 1988, pp. 95-108, 122-124, 136-37.
Klinkowitz, Jerome, *Structuring the Void: The Struggle for Subject in Contemporary American Fiction,* Duke University Press (Durham, NC), 1992, pp. 8-14, 165-67, 171-73.
*Short Story Criticism,* Volume 16, Gale, 1994, pp. 202-19.

### PERIODICALS

*Baltimore Sun,* January 22, 1984; July 22, 1984, pp. F1, F8-9; October 19, 1988; April 31, 1989, pp. F8, F11, F13-15.
*Chicago Sun-Times,* June 4, 1978.

*Chicago Tribune Book World,* July 15, 1979; January 4, 1981.

*Kansas City Star,* August 12, 1984.

*Kirkus Reviews,* May 1, 1979.

*Library Journal,* August, 1988, p. 173; December, 1989, p. 166; January, 1992, p. 172.

*Los Angeles Times Book Review,* December 3, 1989, p, 2; May 28, 1995, pp. 1, 11.

*New York Times,* June 9, 1979.

*New York Times Book Review,* July 31, 1977; May 7, 1978; October 14, 1984; July 7, 1985, p. 16; June 4, 1989, p. 19; December 17, 1989, p. 23; November 17, 1991, p. 14; February 20, 1994, p. 22; September 4, 1994, p. 12; May 21, 1995, p. 46.

*North American Review,* March, 1981, pp. 54-56.

*Plain Dealer* (Cleveland), January 22, 1988.

*Publishers Weekly,* September, 29, 1989, p. 58; November 8, 1991, p. 48; June 19, 1995, pp. 40-41.

*St. Petersburg Times,* August 26, 1984.

*San Francisco Chronicle,* January 29, 1984.

*Small Press,* May/June 1985.

*Soho Weekly News,* December 2, 1976.

*South Carolina Review,* November, 1978.

*Time,* August 13, 1984.

*Times Literary Supplement,* May 29, 1981.

*Tribune Books* (Chicago), June 11, 1995, p. 6.

*Virginia Quarterly Review,* autumn, 1988.

*Washington Post Book World,* February 22, 1981, p. 10; August 5, 1984, pp. 8-9; July 20, 1985; January 19, 1992, pp. 6-7.*

\*   \*   \*

## DONALD, David Herbert   1920-

*PERSONAL:* Born October 1, 1920, in Goodman, MS; son of Ira Unger and Sue Ella (Belford) Donald; married Aida DiPace, 1955; children: Bruce Randall. *Education:* Attended Holmes Junior College, 1937-39; Millsaps College, A.B., 1941; University of Illinois, A.M., 1942, Ph.D., 1946. *Religion:* Episcopalian.

*ADDRESSES: Home*—41 Lincoln Rd., P.O. Box 6158, Lincoln, MA 01773. *Office*—Harvard University, Cambridge, MA 02138.

*CAREER:* University of North Carolina at Chapel Hill, teaching fellow, 1942; University of Illinois at Urbana-Champaign, research assistant, 1943-46; research associate, 1946-47; Columbia University, New York City, instructor, 1947-49, assistant professor, 1951-52, associate professor, 1952-57, professor of history, 1957-59; Smith College, Northampton, MA, associate professor of history, 1949-51; Princeton University, Princeton, NJ, professor of history, 1959-62; Johns Hopkins University, Baltimore, MD, professor of history, 1962-73, Harry C. Black Professor of American History, 1963-73, director of the Institute of Southern History, 1966-72; Harvard University, Cambridge, MA, Charles Warren Professor of American History, 1973-91, chair of graduate program in American civilization, 1979-85, professor emeritus, 1991—. Visiting associate professor of history, Amherst College, 1950; Fulbright lecturer in American history, University College of North Wales, 1953-54; member, Institute for Advanced Study, Princeton, NJ, 1957-58; Harmsworth Professor of American History, Oxford University, 1959-60; John P. Young lecturer, Memphis State University, 1963; Walter Lynwood Fleming lecturer, Louisiana State University, 1965; visiting professor, Center for Advanced Study in the Behavioral Sciences, 1969-70; Benjamin Rush Lecturer, American Psychiatric Association, 1972; Commonwealth Lecturer, University College, University of London, 1975; Samuel Paley lecturer, Hebrew University, Jerusalem, Israel, 1991.

*MEMBER:* American Historical Association, Society of American Historians, Organization of American Historians, Southern Historical Association (president, 1969-70), Phi Beta Kappa, Phi Kappa Phi, Pi Kappa Delta, Pi Kappa Alpha, Omicron Delta Kappa.

*AWARDS, HONORS:* Social Science Research Council fellowship, 1945-46; George A. and Eliza G. Howard fellowship, 1957-58; Pulitzer Prize in biography, 1961, for *Charles Sumner and the Coming of the Civil War,* and 1988, for *Look Homeward: A Life of Thomas Wolfe;* Guggenheim fellowship, 1964-65, and 1985-86; American Council of Learned Societies fellowship, 1969-70; National Endowment for the Humanities senior fellow, 1971-72; C. Hugh Holman prize, Modern Language Association, 1988; Benjamin L. C. Wailes award, Mississippi Historical Society, 1994; Lincoln Prize, Gettysburg College, Jefferson Davis Award, Museum of the Confederacy, and Christopher Award, all 1996, all for *Lincoln.*

*WRITINGS:*

*Lincoln's Herndon,* introduction by Carl Sandburg, Knopf (New York City), 1948, reprinted with a new introduction by Donald, Da Capo Press (New York City), 1988.

(Author of text) *Divided We Fought: A Pictorial History of the War, 1861-1865,* Macmillan (New York City), 1952.

(Editor) *Inside Lincoln's Cabinet: The Civil War Diaries of Salmon P. Chase,* Longmans, Green (New York City), 1954.

*Lincoln Reconsidered: Essays on the Civil War,* Knopf, 1956, 2nd enlarged edition, Random House (New York City), 1961, reprinted, Vintage Books (New York City), 1989.

(Author of introduction) George Cary Eggleston, *A Rebel's Recollections,* Indiana University Press (Bloomington, IN), 1959.

(Editor) *Why the North Won the Civil War,* Louisiana State University Press (Baton Rouge, LA), 1960; revised and expanded edition, Simon & Schuster (New York City), 1996.

*An Excess of Democracy: The American Civil War and the Social Process,* Clarendon Press (Oxford, England), 1960.

*Charles Sumner and the Coming of the Civil War* (also see below), Knopf, 1960, collector's edition, Easton Press (Norwalk, CT), 1987.

(With James G. Randall) *The Divided Union,* Little, Brown (Boston), 1961.

(With Randall) *The Civil War and Reconstruction,* 2nd edition, Heath (Boston), 1961, revised and enlarged edition, 1969.

(Editor with wife, Aida Donald) *Diary of Charles Francis Adams,* two volumes, Harvard University Press (Cambridge, MA), 1964.

(With others) *Grant, Lee, Lincoln and the Radicals,* Northwestern University Press (Evanston, IL), 1964.

*The Politics of Reconstruction, 1863-1867,* Louisiana State University Press, 1965, reprinted, Harvard University Press, 1984.

*The Nation in Crisis, 1861-1877,* Appleton, 1969.

*Charles Sumner and the Rights of Man,* Knopf, 1970, unabridged edition, published with *Charles Sumner and the Coming of the Civil War,* with new introduction by Donald published as *Charles Sumner,* Da Capo (New York City), 1996.

*Gone for a Soldier,* Little, Brown, 1975.

(With others) *The Great Republic: A History of the American People,* Heath, 1977, 4th edition, 1992.

*Liberty and Union,* Little, Brown, 1978.

*Look Homeward: A Life of Thomas Wolfe,* Little, Brown, 1987.

*Lincoln,* Simon & Schuster, 1995, revised edition, Touchstone, 1996.

Contributor to historical journals. General editor, "The Making of America" series and "Documentary History of American Life" series.

*SIDELIGHTS:* Historian and Pulitzer Prize-winning biographer David Herbert Donald has made a career of exploring and interpreting the American Civil War and its central figure, Abraham Lincoln. Donald's first biography eliminated some of the shadows surrounding Lincoln's life by shedding new light on Lincoln's law partner and early biographer, William Henry Herndon. *Lincoln's Herndon* was published in 1948 and used strong scholarship to question some of Herndon's claims about Lincoln's early life, loves, and work. Donald earned his first Pulitzer Prize for biography in 1961 for *Charles Sumner and the Coming of the Civil War,* an examination of the life of a radical New England abolitionist. "Subtly interweaving social and psychological insights with a crisply written narrative," in the opinion of John McCardell in the *Dictionary of Literary Biography,* "Donald graphically depicted a man of many facets who achieved national political prominence despite, rather than because of, his personal traits."

In *Liberty and Union,* Donald has made "admirable contributions" to the scholarly literature on the Civil War, according to C. Vann Woodward of the *New York Times Book Review.* Woodward places the book, an account of American history from 1830 to 1890, as "traditional history, main-line history in brief, the march of events in double time, the big events of national concern." He qualifies his praise of the book with a criticism of Donald's organization. Woodward feels that Donald's attempt, in the interest of completeness, to include advances in all fields of enterprise and social development is thwarted by space limitations. Because Donald lacks time to fully develop theories and interpretations, says Woodward, his attempt to provide a broad perspective of the period from 1830 to 1890 is not entirely successful. According to *New York Times* critic Herbert Mitgang, Donald does successfully provide that sort of overview in *The Great Republic: A History of the American People.* Mitgang contends that the book, coauthored by Donald and five other prominent historians, is "not a flag-waving tract but a surprisingly hard-hitting view of why, somehow, the nation worked," and that it serves to "provide a wide-angle view of the government and the people."

After having written about the Civil War, several figures of the period, and parts of Lincoln's career for almost five decades, Donald published a biography of President Lincoln in 1995. In the book, titled simply *Lincoln,* Donald "has steered clear of legends and delivered a one-volume study of Lincoln's life that will augment and replace the previous modern standards by Benjamin Thomas (1953) and Stephen Oates (1977)," comments David W. Blight in the *Los Angeles Times Book Review.* Blight continues, "Donald's biography is foremost the product of painstaking research and a lifetime of reading in the Lincoln archives and literature. It is a definitive version of Lincoln's personal story." One of the most noteworthy features of this biography, according to Blight, is that "Donald has effectively used Lincoln's own language—the famous speeches and state papers, public letters and the inexhaustible trove of the President's own jokes and tales—to develop the story." As a result, finds Blight, "Donald's Lincoln is a humanized, demystified figure: cautious, brilliant and lucky, the pilot who kept trying to steer the ship to the middle of the river while imagining the gradual, if inevitable, abolition of slavery."

James M. McPherson suggests in the *Atlantic Monthly* that Donald's long and respected career as a Civil War historian had prepared him well for writing this biography. McPherson points out that "Donald weighs the evidence, navigates skillfully among the shoals of apocrypha, myth, and self-serving recollections, avoids reductionism, and advances interpretations that mostly rely on common sense as well as on informed insight." The primary weakness of the book, McPherson finds, has to do with the war itself. Donald "includes a good analysis of Lincoln's concept of military strategy, but these pages do not sparkle as brightly as those on politics, personalities, and the emancipation issue." He adds, "Donald's grasp of military matters is sometimes a bit shaky."

Some other reviewers also offer reservations. Thomas Fleming comments in the *Spectator,* "This latest book on the 16th American president may be as honest a biography as we are likely to see, but it stops short of holding Lincoln accountable for his personal and political failings." *New York Times* book reviewer Michiko Kakutani finds that Donald's approach—focusing narrowly on Lincoln and utilizing the president's own words so much—has its shortcomings. "In drawing this portrait, Donald helps give the reader an understanding of the everyday difficulties besetting the Lincoln administration," observes the reviewer, "but in doing so he often loses sight of the huge moral and historical issues faced by the country in the years before, during and

after the Civil War." Kakutani adds, "His determination to write 'from Lincoln's point of view,' 'to explain rather than to judge' also has practical consequences for the reader: it results in an almost purely chronological account of Lincoln's life, devoid of the sort of retrospective analysis that might have situated his decisions and beliefs in some broader context." Still, in the analysis of a *New York Times Book Review* contributor, *Lincoln* "is so lucid, richly researched, scrupulous and gritty that one cannot imagine a more satisfying [biography]."

Donald won his second Pulitzer Prize for biography not for a book about the Civil War, nor even for a study of a political or military figure. Instead, it was awarded for his biography of a twentieth-century literary figure, Thomas Wolfe. For *Look Homeward: A Life of Thomas Wolfe,* notes Kakutani in the *New York Times,* Donald "was granted full access to Wolfe's diaries, letters and manuscripts, and he has used this information to write a comprehensive and absorbing book that both underlines the correspondences between Wolfe's fiction and his life and illuminates the psychological underpinnings of his art." As Hugh Kenner observes in the *Times Literary Supplement,* Donald "would seem to be Wolfe's ideal biographer. He writes cleanly; he can select. Moreover, he can testify to the spell. Now in his late sixties, he speaks candidly for his own American generation." And, continues Kenner, "Normally he is mesmerized by his dishevelled subject; that is indeed one merit of his book, which spares us any subliminal intimation that academic caution would be a creator's best guide."

"Yet," as Kakutani points out, "for all his sympathy for his subject, Mr. Donald is unable to make Wolfe very sympathetic." As a person, Wolfe had many faults, including drinking, treating women poorly, and making his anti-Semitic views clear. Even as a writer, Wolfe offered much to criticize. His major works were deemed overwritten by his publishers and had to be severely cut and reworked by his editors—Maxwell Perkins at Scribner's and Edward Aswell at Harper and Brothers—before they could be published. "Donald's thorough, fastidious research—as well as the inherent appeal of the freakish and the famous—enables us to share his fascination with this often unsavory man and his unfashionable work," writes David Gates in *Newsweek.* The outcome of his balanced approach to Wolfe is an account of the writer that neither raises him up to a literary pinnacle nor dismisses him.

---

Harold Bloom notes in the *New York Times Book Review*, "Though he thinks that Wolfe was a great novelist, Mr. Donald is actually persuasive in showing us Wolfe rather as a cultural and social journalist, a passionate beholder of America in trouble." And, while Bloom questions Donald's literary criticism, he concludes, "Mr. Donald's book deserves to be called a critical biography, is very well informed, and clearly surpasses its predecessors."

*BIOGRAPHICAL/CRITICAL SOURCES:*

BOOKS

*Dictionary of Literary Biography,* Volume 17: *Twentieth-Century American Historians,* Gale (Detroit), 1983.
*A Master's Due: Essays in Honor of David Herbert Donald,* edited by William J. Cooper, Jr., Michael F. Holt, and John McCardell, Louisiana State University Press, 1985.

PERIODICALS

*American Spectator,* March, 1987, p. 40.
*Atlantic Monthly,* November, 1995.
*Boston Globe,* January 25, 1987, p. A25; November 28, 1995, p. 43.
*Chicago Tribune,* November 5, 1978.
*Christian Science Monitor,* February 6, 1987, p. 24.
*Commonweal,* December 4, 1987, p. 715.
*London Review of Books,* January 7, 1988, p. 20.
*Los Angeles Times Book Review,* February 22, 1987, p. 4; October 22, 1995, p. 3.
*Macleans,* March 2, 1987, p. 49.
*National Review,* February 13, 1987, p. 49.
*New Republic,* March 23, 1987, p. 30.
*New Republican,* January 9, 1971.
*Newsweek,* February 2, 1987, p. 69.
*New York Review of Books,* September 24, 1987, p. 34.
*New York Times,* January 30, 1971; May 4, 1977; February 18, 1987, p. C21; April 1, 1988, p. B4; October 3, 1995.
*New York Times Book Review,* March 12, 1961; November 19, 1978; February 8, 1987, p. 13; December 3, 1995, p. 27.
*Observer,* April 12, 1987, p. 23.
*Publishers Weekly,* January 20, 1987, p. 366.
*Saturday Review,* February 20, 1971.
*Spectator,* April 25, 1987, p. 26; January 20, 1996, p. 27.
*Time,* March 16, 1987, p. 80.
*Times Literary Supplement,* April 17, 1987, p. 403.

*Tribune Books* (Chicago), January 25, 1987, p. 1.
*USA Today,* February 6, 1987, p. D2.

\*   \*   \*

**DOUGLAS, Michael**
   **See CRICHTON, (John) Michael**

\*   \*   \*

**D'SOUZA, Dinesh    1961-**

*PERSONAL:* Born April 25, 1961, in Bombay, India; immigrated to United States, 1978; son of Allan L. (an executive) and Margaret (a homemaker; maiden name, Fernandes) D'Souza. *Education:* Dartmouth College, A.B., 1983.

*ADDRESSES: Office*—American Enterprise Institute, 1150 17th Street NW, Washington, DC 20036.

*CAREER: Dartmouth Review,* Hanover, NH, editor, 1982-83; *Prospect,* Princeton, NJ, editor, 1983-85; *Policy Review,* Washington, DC, managing editor, beginning in 1985; worked as an assistant domestic policy adviser in the Ronald Reagan administration, Washington, DC, 1987-88.

*MEMBER:* Phi Beta Kappa.

*AWARDS, HONORS:* Award from Society for Professional Journalists, 1982, for outstanding reporting.

*WRITINGS:*

*Falwell: Before the Millennium,* Regnery Gateway (Washington, DC), 1985.
*The Catholic Classics,* introduction by John J. O'Connor and William F. Buckley Jr., Our Sunday Visitor (Huntington, IN), 1986.
*My Dear Alex: Letters from the KGB,* Regnery Gateway, 1987.
*Illiberal Education: The Politics of Race and Sex on Campus,* Free Press (New York City), 1991.
*The End of Racism: Principles for a Multi-Cultural Society,* Free Press, 1995.

An abridged version of *Illiberal Education: The Politics of Race and Sex on Campus* was recorded on audio cassette and released by Dove, Audio, 1991.

Contributor to periodicals, including *New York Times, Washington Post, Boston Globe, Los Angeles Times,* and *Wall Street Journal.*

*SIDELIGHTS:* Dinesh D'Souza is among conservatives who during the 1980s and 1990s pushed to continue the Reagan revolution by challenging the nation's social, economic, and political thought. D'Souza's experience in the public policy arena has given him strongly conservative credentials.

D'Souza is an immigrant from India. His family was Catholic, so his father, a pharmaceutical company executive, sent him to Jesuit schools. In his final year of high school, D'Souza came to the United States as an exchange student. After graduation, he went to Dartmouth, where he began to pursue his interest in public policy. In addition to his studies and other campus activities, D'Souza went to work at the *Dartmouth Review,* a conservative magazine not affiliated with the college. He later became editor. After graduating from Dartmouth, he took the position of editor with *Prospect,* a magazine published by Princeton alumni. He also began contributing to conservative magazines like the *National Review* and *Policy Review.* In 1987, he joined the Reagan administration as an assistant in the domestic policy office.

While pursuing his interests and his career as a journalist, D'Souza began writing longer works on conservative issues. His biography of Jerry Falwell, *Falwell: Before the Millennium,* examines the life and career of the American fundamentalist preacher and leader of a conservative political lobby. Investigating numerous charges leveled against the minister by the liberal Left, the author argues that many are exaggerations or propaganda; he contends, for example, that accusations of segregations and anti-Semitism belie Falwell's vigorous support of civil rights issues and the perpetuation of Israel. D'Souza also sees the preacher's secular activities as twentieth-century methods to disseminate traditional fundamentalist teachings, disavowing the perceived threat of Falwell's political activism to the Bill of Rights' separation of Church and State. "Falwell did what Martin Luther King, William Sloane Coffin, Jesse Jackson, the Berrigans, and thousands of other leftist clergymen had been doing for generations, with liberal benedictions," asserted Joseph Sobran in a *National Review* summary of D'Souza's position. Falwell, Sobran concluded, "is a 'menace' only to liberalism."

Reproaching the publisher of *Falwell* for presenting it as a "critical biography," *New York Times Book Review* contributor Marty Zupan found D'Souza's treatment far from "an objective assessment" of Falwell. "Mr. D'Souza might object that he is careful to note Mr. Falwell's failings," wrote the reviewer. "Indeed, he does, and then he generally excuses them. . . . Meanwhile, Falwell's controversial positions are not discussed." Zupan dismissed the biography as a book "written for the faithful." Sobran, too, noted the volume's "friendly" approach but emphasized instead its factual and informative nature, commenting that the book "is written with unfailing color and energy. . . . Its main virtue is simply that it brings new information in every paragraph. The details add up to a warm but accurate portrait of the man." In the *American Spectator,* Malcolm T. Gladwell viewed *Falwell* as "a case of the right dealing with its own." Yet the critic discounted the publisher's mislabeling, remarking that the book "never pretends to be anything but a defense of Falwell." He added: "To his credit D'Souza treats his subject with grace and thoroughness, and turns what could easily be shrill justification into a genuinely good read. But in the process he steers clear of the implications of Falwell's move into the political arena. . . . D'Souza doesn't want to believe that Falwell's secular activities have tainted him and pushed him in any way from the traditional fundamentalist pattern."

In *Illiberal Education: The Politics of Race and Sex on Campus,* D'Souza examines the contemporary American university. The cultural revolution of the 1960s, he observes, has not disappeared from campuses, but rather has become institutionalized as the revolutionary students have become the faculty and administrators of today's academia. Ideas such as affirmative action, a multicultural curriculum, preferential treatment for some groups, and restrictions of speech to protect these groups have come to shape the university. These changes, D'Souza believes, have caused a decline in American higher education. He maintains that the study of classic literature is out, as is Western culture itself. Merit is out, with respect to disciplines, texts, faculty, and students. Instead, all choices are made with an eye to welcoming groups traditionally left out, groups defined by race, gender, and sexual orientation.

D'Souza's conclusions sparked debate among reviewers over the state of the American university. Charles J. Sykes, writing in *National Review,* found that "*Illiberal Education* is both a primer on the breadth of the crisis and a penetrating critique of the fundamental issues that underlie the assault on academic values, free speech, and intellectual integrity in American higher education." Sykes added, "The triumph of *Illiberal Education* is D'Souza's success in exposing the dishonesty and hypocrisy of what James Coleman has called policies of 'conspicuous benevolence.'" Catherine R. Stimpson, on the other hand, labeled the book "a document in a political campaign. Like most campaigns, it polarizes reality. The target is higher education." She concluded in her review in the *Nation,* "*Illiberal Education* saturates educational debate with slippery rhetoric, inconsistency and falsehood. *Illiberal Education* debases thought for a heap of bony power."

In *Illiberal Education* D'Souza explores the current state of the university through six case studies, including the University of California at Berkeley, the University of Michigan, Duke, and Harvard. He constructs the case studies from interviews of students, faculty, and administrators, as well as information gathered from other sources. According to Jacob Weisberg in the *Washington Monthly,* D'Souza "describes with clarity and fair-mindedness the recent disputes at six elite universities." Sykes called the book "exhaustively researched, cogently argued, and sweeping in its range." Yet a number of reviewers questioned D'Souza's reliance on secondary sources. Louis Menand conceded that the interviews provide new material to debate, but he observed in the *New Yorker* that "much of D'Souza's book is drawn from information that has already appeared in newspapers, news magazines, and journals of opinion." Still others faulted D'Souza's interviews. "For a quasi-scholarly study," wrote James Bowman in the *Times Literary Supplement,* "his interviewing technique is annoying." *Time*'s Walter Shapiro said, "His interviewing style is that of a patronizing pedant." *New York Times Book Review* contributor Nancy S. Dye had difficulty with D'Souza's entire approach. She wrote, "What we read in *Illiberal Education* is seriously misleading. Mr. D'Souza has constructed his argument by cobbling together anecdotal accounts of campus incidents, clippings from *The Chronicle of Higher Education* and highly selective statements from students, admissions officers, deans and faculty members. There is a place for good muckraking, but this book does not fill it."

Among the remedies that D'Souza suggests to turn universities around are to tie affirmative action not to race but to economic need and to create a curriculum rooted in the classics that still addresses modern issues. Sykes found some of the author's solutions "somewhat disappointing and even misguided." However, he concluded, "Even so, this hardly detracts from the immense value of D'Souza's book, which seems certain to become a touchstone for the debate over liberal learning in America's colleges and universities." Dye believed that books such as *Illiberal Education* distract the public. She maintained, "The tragedy of these endless battles over the canon is that they divert attention from understanding and finding creative solutions."

*The End of Racism: Principles for a Multi-Cultural Society* gives an outsider's view of racism in America. "Not since Gunnar Myrdal's classic, *An American Dilemma,* just over half a century ago," wrote Hoover Institution economist Thomas Sowell in *Forbes,* "has any book looked so searchingly at the role of race in American society as Dinesh D'Souza's new book, *The End of Racism.*" As Peter Brimelow explained in *National Review,* "By skillfully marshalling facts that are publicly available but rarely brought together in a systematic way, D'Souza argues that the plight of black Americans must be largely attributed to their own dysfunctional culture." To reach this conclusion, D'Souza reexamines the long history of blacks in America, through slavery, segregation, and discrimination. He reevaluates recent events, including the civil rights movement and policy and social trends since. What he finds is both a failure of liberal policies and the dependence on the part of some blacks on these failed policies. Overall, in the opinion of Sean Wilentz in the *New Yorker,* "D'Souza tells only half the story of our racial travails, and that obliquely. The part that he does describe is the tragedy of modern liberalism, especially that of the Democratic Party. . . . The other half of the story, the half that D'Souza does not tell, is the tragedy of modern conservatism—especially that of the Republican Party."

As with his previous books, *The End of Racism* stirred a great deal of discussion. Harvard historian Stephan Thernstrom disputed D'Souza's reassessment of the historical record. He contended in the *Times Literary Supplement,* "D'Souza has had no professional training in history, but that does not stop him from writing a good many pages on the history of slavery and the intellectual origins of racism. He is simply beyond his depth here and never should have made the attempt." Specifically, Thernstrom found that "D'Souza . . . is naively generous in his assessment of the motivation of the 'southern ruling elite,' which he believes favoured segregation because of its commitment to the benevolent 'code of the Christian and the gentleman.'" He offered stronger words to describe D'Souza's view of recent events. "His analysis is so muddled that it is difficult to criticize," maintained Thernstrom. "He tells us that the notion that 'the civil rights movement represented a triumph of justice and enlightenment over the forces of Southern racism and hate' is a mere 'myth.'"

In the eyes of some reviewers, *The End of Racism* provides justification for racism. A reviewer for the *Economist* commented, "This book is a defence of bigotry and prejudice. Its message, crudely put, is that discrimination against blacks in America is not racial but rational—meaning wise in circumstances—and that the disadvantages they suffer are largely their fault." It also overgeneralizes, according to this reviewer: "His whole book is written in the language of blame and in the language of stereotypes. It treats black America as 'the Other,' as an undifferentiated statistical mass, as a social 'dysfunction,' as a problem." Yet, for Sowell, *The End of Racism* does not justify racism; rather, it deflates it. As he puts it, the book "argues that the explanatory power of racism is very weak when put to the test, and it now serves largely as a distraction from the hard work of dealing with other factors behind very real problems." In the estimation of Peter Brimelow, "In *The End of Racism*, D'Souza takes many courageous stands; his book has a powerful major argument and endlessly fascinating detail." He concluded, however, that "it remains ultimately incomplete, in terms both of fact and of theory." Sowell summed up the book in the following terms: "*The End of Racism* is . . . a thorough reappraisal of race and racism in American today."

## BIOGRAPHICAL/CRITICAL SOURCES:

### PERIODICALS

*American Spectator,* January, 1985; November, 1987, p. 46.
*Chicago Tribune,* February 4, 1985, sec. 1, p. 11.
*Christian Science Monitor,* November 30, 1987, p. 20.
*Economist,* October 14, 1995, p. 101.
*Forbes,* October 9, 1995, p. 74.
*Los Angeles Times Book Review,* June 28, 1987, p. 3.
*Modern Language Journal,* spring, 1993, p. 113.
*Mother Jones,* January, 1991, p. 74.
*Nation,* September 30, 1991, p. 378.
*National Review,* February 22, 1985; November 21, 1986, p. 67; April 15, 1991, p. 49; September 30, 1991, p. 378; November 27, 1995, p. 60.
*Nature,* September 30, 1991, p. 384.
*New Republic,* April 15, 1991, p. 30.
*New Yorker,* May 20, 1991, p. 101; October 2, 1995, p. 91.
*New York Review of Books,* July 18, 1991, p. 32.
*New York Times Book Review,* December 30, 1984; March 31, 1991, p. 12.
*Time,* May 6, 1991, p. 71.
*Times Literary Supplement,* May 31, 1991, p. 7; December 8, 1995, p. 4.
*Village Voice,* May 21, 1991, p. 71.
*Wall Street Journal,* March 28, 1991.
*Washington Monthly,* April, 1991, p. 56.
*Washington Post,* April 16, 1991, p. B1.*

\*          \*          \*

## DUCORNET, Erica          1943-
### (Rikki; Rikki Ducornet)

*PERSONAL:* Born April 19, 1943, in Canton, NY; daughter of Gerard and Muriel De Gre; married Guy Ducornet (a painter and potter; divorced); children: Jean-Yves. *Education:* Bard College, B.A., 1962.

*ADDRESSES: Office*—English Department, University of Denver, Denver, CO 80208.

*CAREER:* Writer and illustrator. Drawings have been exhibited widely, notably in Czechoslovakia, 1966, Museum of West Berlin, 1969 and 1972, Museum of Lille (France), 1973, Museum of Fine Arts (Belgium), 1974, International Surrealist Exhibition, Chicago, 1977, Museo de Bellas Artes (Mexico), 1979, Centre Culturel Francaise (Sweden), 1982, and Centre Culturel Mexican (Paris), 1984. Writer in residence, University of Denver, Denver, CO.

*MEMBER:* PEN International, Amnesty International.

*AWARDS, HONORS:* Bunting Fellow, Mary Ingraham Bunting Institute, 1986-87; Merrill Ingram Foundation award, 1988; Eben Demarest Trust, 1990; Copeland Colloquium fellowship, 1992; Lannan Literary Fellowship, 1993; National Book Critics Circle Award finalist, 1994; Critic's Choice Award, 1995.

## WRITINGS:

### FICTION

(Adapter and illustrator) D'Aulnoy, *The Blue Bird* (juvenile), Knopf (New York City), 1970.

*Shazira Shazam and the Devil* (juvenile; Junior Literary Guild Selection), illustrations by husband, Guy Ducornet, Prentice-Hall (Englewood Cliffs, NJ), 1970.

(Under name Rikki) *The Butcher's Tales* (short stories), Aya Press, 1978, expanded and revised edition published as *The Complete Butcher's Tales,* Dalkey Archive (Normal, IL), 1994.

(Coeditor and contributor) *Shoes and Shit* (short stories), Aya Press, 1984.

(And illustrator) *Haddock's Eyes* (short stories), Editions du Fourneau, 1987.

Work represented in anthologies, including *The Stonewall Anthology,* University of Iowa Press (Iowa City), 1974, *The Myth of the World,* Dedalus, 1994, *After Yesterday's Crash,* Penguin, 1995, and *Two, or; The Book of Twins and Doubles,* Virago, 1996. Contributor of short stories and poetry to *Iowa Review, Parnassus, Witness, The City Lights Review, Conjunctions,* and other periodicals.

### NOVELS; UNDER NAME RIKKI DUCORNET

*The Stain,* Grove (New York City), 1984, Dalkey Archive (Normal, IL), 1995.

*Entering Fire,* Chatto and Windus, 1984, City Lights (San Francisco), 1986.

*The Fountains of Neptune,* McClelland and Stewart (Toronto), 1989, Dalkey Archive, 1992.

*The Jade Cabinet,* Dalkey Archive, 1993.

*Phosphor in Dreamland,* Dalkey Archive, 1995.

### POETRY; SELF-ILLUSTRATED; UNDER NAME RIKKI

*From the Star Chamber* (for adults; includes short stories), Fiddlehead (Canada), 1974.

*Wild Geraniums,* Actual Size Press (London), 1975.

*Weird Sisters,* Intermedia (Canada), 1976.

*Knife Notebook,* Fiddlehead, 1977.

*The Illustrated Universe,* Aya Press (Toronto), 1978.

*The Cult of Seizure,* Porcupine's Quill (Erin, Ontario, Canada), 1989.

### ILLUSTRATOR

Paris Leary and Muriel De Gre, *The Jack Spratt Cookbook,* Doubleday (New York City), 1965.

G. Ducornet, *Silex de lavenir* (poems), Pierre Jean Oswald, 1966.

Mme. Leprince de Beaumont, *Beauty and the Beast* (translated from the French by P. H. Muir), Knopf, 1968.

G. Ducornet, *Trophes en selle* (poems), Traces, 1970.

(Under name Rikki) Susan Musgrave, *Gullband Thought Measles Was a Happy Ending,* J. J. Douglas, 1974.

(Under name Rikki, with G. Ducornet) *Bouche a bouche* (erotic game book), Soror, 1975.

(Under name Rikki) Matt Cohen, *The Leaves of Louise,* McClelland and Stewart, 1978.

Robert Coover, *Spanking the Maid,* Bruccoli Clark (Columbia, SC), 1981.

Jose Luis Borges, *Tloen, Uqbar, Orbis Tertius,* Porcupine's Quill, 1983.

Also illustrator of *Canada: Gullband,* by Susan Musgrave, 1974.

*ADAPTATIONS: Shazira Shazam and the Devil* was put to music by Benjamin McPeek and performed by the Canadian Brass.

*SIDELIGHTS:* Reviewing Erica Ducornet's *The Stain* in the *Guardian,* Robert Nye remarks: "This is the most brilliant first novel that I have read in years." Nye asserts that *The Stain* is "accomplished, and memorable . . . by any standards. Imagine *Cold Comfort Farm* revamped by Ronald Firbank, or *Clochemerle* sent up rotten by Angela Carter after a night on the sloe gin, and you may have some small notion of its outrageous flavour." Calling *The Stain* a "highly disciplined extravaganza" in the *Times Literary Supplement,* Jayne Pilling focuses on the novel as a new facet of the author's work: "Illustration and short story writing have in common a technique of concentration within spatial constraints; but Ducornet's first novel is a promising demonstration of her talent for the longer form. And the writing itself is highly impressive; the grim humour has the verbal spontaneity of a natural idiom, and the prose, however polished, never seems strained."

*The Stain* is the first work in a series based on the elements of earth, fire, water, and air. While *The Stain* was based on earth imagery, *Entering Fire* dwells on fire metaphors and deals thematically with bigotry. The novel begins in turn of the century France, with a boy, Septimus, whose father has had an affair and a son with a Chinese woman, and later flees to South America. Septimus grows up full of hatred—he sympathizes with Nazi ideology, despises his father for giving him a half-Chinese brother, and eventually ends up in the Hudson Valley trying to put the FBI onto his father. "This headlong roller-coaster ride through the black tunnels of the twentieth-century nightmare lights up occasionally with a little wit and some rococo invention," writes Hanif Kureishi in the *Times Literary Supplement.* He concludes, however, that generally *Entering Fire* "is a schematic, strained and exaggerated pursuit of unreality in a period of history when surely reality itself was sufficiently charged to be interesting." Oliver Conant, in the *New York Times Book Review* comments: "*Entering Fire* displays a cheerfully gruesome audacity and an imagination both lively and bizarre."

Water forms the imagery in *The Fountains of Neptune.* The novel revolves around a French boy, Nicolas, who spends nearly sixty years in a trauma-induced coma. He is awakened by psychoanalyst Venus Kaiserstiege and spends the remainder of his life dreaming and gardening in the sanitarium. Toronto *Globe and Mail* contributor Beverley Daurio finds the story "an excellent metaphor for the writer who needs to bypass modernism and the horrific imagery of trenches and holocaust to get back in touch with the roots of human myth-making." Daurio continues, "Ducornet builds and layers meaning into an almost dizzyingly brilliant tower. Her writing is relentless, breathless and energetic, and if one were to complain it might be because the lights are occasionally too bright, shining on too many things too quickly." Still, she concludes, *The Fountains of Neptune* "is a complex work that takes the basic tenet of magic realism, the supremacy of imagination over all, and bends it back into the greater stream of literary tradition." Philip Marchand states in the *Toronto Star* that *The Fountains of Neptune* "is a meditative work, too poetic for some tastes, perhaps, but with a very engaging story to tell."

The fourth and final entry in Ducornet's elemental series is *The Jade Cabinet,* the title meant to symbolize air. Set in nineteenth-century England, *The Jade Cabinet* is narrated by a character named Memory Sphery. The story revolves around Memory's mute, yet lovely and captivating, older sister, Etheria. The sisters' unconventional upbringing includes sessions of nude modeling for a Mr. Dodgson (the real-life name of Lewis Carroll, who did indeed enjoy sketching young girls, and whose writing is often cited as an influence on Ducornet's). Etheria is married young, to a distasteful industrialist whom Memory loathes; Etheria flees him after he brutalizes her, and

he then spends the rest of his life trying to recapture her. "As usual, Ducornet manages to deliver striking physical imagery while challenging the intellect," *Belles Lettres* reviewer Patty O'Connell remarks. She goes on, "Feminists who narrowly define their 'isms' may find fault with Ducornet's novels, which are often bawdy and flirtatious, evocative of Lewis Carroll and Rabelais; however, those readers taking offense will be cheating themselves out of some of the most magical and merciful writing available today." Adds *American Book Review* contributor Corinne Robins, "*The Jade Cabinet* . . . intrigues and delights."

Sinda Gregory voices high praise for Ducornet's "alchemy" quartet, and its completion led her to pose this question in an *American Book Review* essay: "Would the exhaustion of natural elements to employ lead to any sort of creative exhaustion?" She reassures readers: "Not to worry. Ducornet's first 'post-elemental' novel, *Phosphor in Dreamland,* makes it clear that Ducornet is perfectly comfortable working outside the framework she employed in her earlier novels. Indeed, *Phosphor in Dreamland* is arguably Ducornet's richest and most ambitious work to date." Like much of the author's earlier work, *Phosphor* mixes reality and unreality, and takes on a variety of weighty subjects: sex, language, parents and children, good and evil, and the productive and destructive ways in which people deal with their fear of the unknown. Ducornet's skill, however, keeps her work from growing stale, asserts Gregory: "In *Phosphor* she again invents storylines and characters which introduce these core concerns within contexts whose peculiar textures and unexpected juxtapositions produce the sorts of epiphanies the surrealists hoped to achieve."

Set on an imaginary Caribbean island called Birdland, *Phosphor in Dreamland* describes the coming of the first Europeans there in the seventeenth century, and the life of a young orphan, called Phosphor, who grows into a brilliant inventor and poet, only to be destroyed because his sexually explicit verse shocks the inquisitional authorities. Phosphor's story is interwoven with a modern romance and told through a series of letters. Gregory finds the book both an effective satire of Western culture and a paean to physical passion, calling it "a celebration of the human capacity to revel in our flesh." Identifying Ducornet as "one of America's most incandescent satiric writers," Michelle Latiolais points out in the *Los Angeles Times Book Review* that in addition to all its other fine qualities, *Phosphor* is a very funny book. It is, in her words, "like finding superbly enchanting aboriginal reliquiae in the sifting screens on an archeological dig, the finer points being that you're far less dusty and your body aches not from the tedium of recovery but from laughing. . . . Rikki Ducornet is a writer whose work deserves our joyous attention." Not all reviewers are captivated by *Phosphor,* however; for instance, in the *Chicago Tribune* Michael Harrington pronounces it "a nice but ultimately shapeless trifle." Although Ducornet's style is usually charming, he says, here it fails to create a compelling story. He asserts that one significant problem is that the characters "remain distant and not fully formed."

Ducornet's body of work has won substantial praise. "It's startling and refreshing to encounter a writer whose work insists so relentlessly upon the magic of making tales," enthuses Robert Chatain in a Chicago *Tribune Books* review of *The Complete Butcher's Tales* and *The Jade Cabinet.* "Rikki Ducornet's work has been called surrealism; this may be true, but not in the sense that 'surreal' is usually applied to describe (or dismiss) fiction that stretches beyond the everyday. Surreal means more than unreal; it means a heightened look at reality in unexpected wavelengths of light generated by the unconscious. Ducornet achieves this intensity again and again; her rare achievement illustrates how difficult it is to make surreal insights seem inevitable, not just arbitrary." The Lannan Foundation, from which Ducornet received a fellowship in 1993, cited her for works which are "eccentric, sensuous, elegant, perverse, and entirely unforgettable."

*BIOGRAPHICAL/CRITICAL SOURCES:*

*PERIODICALS*

*American Book Review,* December, 1993, pp. 17, 28; February-March, 1996, pp. 9, 30.
*Belles Lettres,* summer, 1993, pp. 2, 11.
*Booklist,* October 1, 1995.
*Chicago Tribune,* December 5, 1995, section 5, p. 3.
*Globe and Mail* (Toronto), June 10, 1989.
*Guardian,* February 2, 1984.
*Los Angeles Times Book Review,* May 29, 1994, p. 8; December 17, 1995, pp. 2, 12.
*Nation,* June 6, 1994, pp. 809-812.
*New York Times Book Review,* June 7, 1987, p. 30; June 14, 1987; January 10, 1988, p. 34; October 29, 1995, p. 30.
*Publishers Weekly,* January 4, 1993, p. 58; February 7, 1994, p. 70; August 14, 1995, p. 76; October 9, 1995, pp. 66-67.
*Times Literary Supplement,* March 2, 1984; February 21, 1986, p. 198; May 14, 1993, p. 25.
*Toronto Star,* December 2, 1989.
*Tribune Books* (Chicago), July 17, 1994, p. 5.
*Washington Post Book World,* August 7, 1994, p. 6.

\* \* \*

**DUCORNET, Rikki**
  **See DUCORNET, Erica**

# E

## EDBERG, Rolf 1912-

*PERSONAL:* Born March 14, 1912, in Lysvik, Sweden; married Astrid Persson, 1937; children: Joergen, Ranveig Jacobsson, Birgitta.

*ADDRESSES: Home*—Hybelejens gata 4,65340 Karlstad, Sweden.

*CAREER: Oskarshamns Nyheter,* Oskarshamm, Sweden, chief editor, 1934-37; *Oestgoeten,* Linkoeping, Sweden, chief editor, 1938-44; *Ny Tid,* Gothenburg, Sweden, chief editor, 1945-56; Swedish ambassador to Norway, 1956-67; governor of Swedish province of Vaermland, 1967-77. Member of Swedish Parliament, 1940-44 and 1948-56. Delegate to Council of Europe, 1949-52, United Nations, 1952-55, 1957, 1960-61, Northern Council, 1953-56, and Disarmament Conference, 1961-65.

*MEMBER:* Swedish Press Club (president, 1951-53), Swedish Association of Writers, Pen Club, Swedish Association of Biologists, Swedish Royal Academy of Sciences, Swedish Society for Anthropology and Geography.

*AWARDS, HONORS:* Socrates Prize, 1972, from School of Adult Education; gold medal, 1974, from Royal Swedish Academy of Science; Doctor Honoris Causa, 1974, from University of Gothenburg; gold medal, 1976, from Geographical-Anthropological Society; Selma Lagerloef Prize, 1976 and 1996; Dag Hammarskjoeld Medal, 1978; King's Medal, 1981; gold medal from government of Sweden, 1984; Nordic Environmental Prize, 1984; Let Live! Award, 1985; Premio Mondiale delle Cultura, 1985; Natur och Kultur's Cultural Prize, 1987; Maarbacka Prize, 1994; Sclmalagerloef Prize, 1996.

*WRITINGS:*

*Nansen, europein: En studie i vilja och god-vilja* (title means "Nansen, the European: A Study in Will and Good Will"), Tiden, 1961.

*Spillran av ett moln,* Norstedt, 1966, translation by Sven Aahman published as *On the Shred of a Cloud: Notes in a Travel Book,* University of Alabama Press, 1969, same translation published as *On the Shred of a Cloud: Reflections on Man and His Environment,* Harper (New York City), 1971.

*Vid traedets fot,* Norstedt, 1971, translation by David Mel Paul and Margareta Paul published as *At the Foot of the Tree: A Wanderer's Musings before the Fall,* University of Alabama Press, 1974.

*Brev till Columbus* (title means "Letters to Columbus"), Norstedt, 1973.

*Ett hus i kosmos* (title means "A House in the Cosmos"), Esselte Studium, 1974.

*Dalens Ande,* Norstedt, 1976, translation by Keith Bradfield published as *The Dream of Kilimanjaro,* Pantheon (New York City), 1979.

*Skuggor oever Savannen* (title means "Shadows across the Savannah"), Bra Boecker & Trevi, 1977.

*De glittrande vattnens land* (title means "The Land of Glittering Waters"), Bra Boecker & Norstedts, 1980.

(Editor) *Haer aer vi hemma* (title means "This Is Our Home"), Bra Boecker & Norstedts, 1982.

(Editor) *Vaart hotade hem* (title means "Our Threatened Home"), Bra Boecker & Norstedts, 1983.

*Droppar av vatten, droppar av H aar* (title means "Drops of Water, Drops of Years"), Bra Boecker & Norstedts, 1984.

*. . . och de seglade staendigt* (title means ". . . And They Always Sailed"), Norstedts, 1986.

*Aarsbarn med Plejaderna* (title means "Born with the Pleiades"), Bra Boekerts & Norstedts, 1987.

(With Alexey Yablokov) *Soendag aer foer sent* (title means "Sunday Is Too Late"), Norstedts, 1988, translation by Sergei Chulaki published as *Tomorrow Will Be Too Late: East Meets West on Global Ecology,* University of Arizona Press, 1991.

*Jordens oega* (title means "The Eye of the Earth"), Nystroms, 1989.

*Att leva med ord* (title means "To Live with Words"), Vaermlamdslitteratur, 1990.

*Raststaellen* (title means "Resting Places"), Streifferts, 1992.

*Vilopunkter* (title means "Points of Peace", Wiken, 1993.

*And the Sea Never Rests,* originally published as *Ock havet vilar aldrig,* Journal, 1995.

Also author of *Ge dem en chans* (title means "Give Them a Chance"), 1939; *I morgon Norden* (title means "Tomorrow Nordic"), 1944; *Demokratisk linje* (title means "Democratic Line"), 1948; *Femte etappen* (title means "The Fifth Stage"), 1949; *Oeppna grindarna* (title means "Open the Gates"), 1952; and *Paa jordens villkor* (title means "On Earth's Terms"), 1974.

*ADAPTATIONS: Dalens Ande* was adapted as a symphony by the Finnish composer Henrik Otto Donner.

*SIDELIGHTS:* Rolf Edberg once told *CA:* "I grew up in a fresh and beautiful countryside and very early I got in contact with the science of evolution, which started a lifelong interest in natural sciences. [My] first book about man's condition was created in order to disentangle my own meditating threads and to put man's moment on earth [into] a bigger continuity. We have in our constantly greedy searching acquired an ever increasing richness in knowledge of details and have been forced into an even harder specialization. However, nature is interaction, not separation. What we have to do today is to place our varying knowledge under a unifying comprehensive view giving us a vision of our destiny. My ambition as a layman has been to arrive at such a comprehensive view.

"The scientific literature—especially in the environmental field—published in the United States has

given me great inspiration in my work. Europe has a lot to learn from the American research which is the most advanced in the world. But I believe that America, highly urbanized, has some to learn from the Scandinavian people with their natural love of nature. And that is the way it ought to be: that we learn from each other's research, thinking, and experience."

The Edberg Foundation, named in honor of Rolf Edberg, was founded in 1990 to organize annual seminars on environmental issues. The foundation also awards a prize worth $50,000 to persons who have initiated and carried through a project of environmental improvement in a country with severe environmental problems. The award is intended to be used to promote further studies that will increase the effectiveness of the recipient's work.

*BIOGRAPHICAL/CRITICAL SOURCES:*

*PERIODICALS*

*Chicago Tribune Book World,* May 20, 1979.

\*    \*    \*

**EDDENDEN, A(rthur) E(dward) 1928-**

*PERSONAL:* Born September 21, 1928, in Hamilton, Ontario, Canada; son of Frederick Arthur (a policeman) and Marjorie (a homemaker; maiden name, Beckwith) Eddenden; married Elizabeth Bettine Weir (a secretary), December 1, 1951; children: Michael, Peter, Leslie, Sarah. *Ethnicity:* "English." *Education:* Attended high school in Hamilton, Ontario, Canada.

*ADDRESSES: Home*—3458 Spruce Ave., Burlington, Ontario, Canada L7N 1K3.

*CAREER:* Writer. D-L (printers), Hamilton, Ontario, apprentice artist, 1947-50; T.D.F. (art studio), Toronto, Ontario, artist, 1950-51; Graphic Associates (art studio), Hamilton, partner, 1951-53; Standard Engravers, Hamilton, art director, 1953-75; H.I.P. (advertising agency), Hamilton, art director, 1975-80; F.M.B.J. (advertising agency), Toronto, senior art director, 1980-85; Bozell Jacobs Kenyon Eckhardt (agency), Toronto, senior art director, 1985-87; Carter Advertising, Etobicoke, Ontario, senior art director, 1987; retired. *Military service:* Canadian Army Reserve, 1942-45.

*MEMBER:* Burlington Golf and Country Club.

*WRITINGS:*

*"INSPECTOR TRETHEWAY" SERIES; MYSTERY NOVELS*

*A Good Year for Murder,* Academy Chicago (Chicago, IL), 1988.
*Murder on the Thirteenth,* Academy Chicago, 1992.
*Murder at the Movies,* Academy Chicago, 1996.

Contributor of short stories to *Alfred Hitchcock's Mystery Magazine.*

*WORK IN PROGRESS: The Ugly Murders,* completed manuscript submitted to Academy Chicago (not a "Tretheway" novel); *The Radio Serial Killer* (fourth in the "Inspector Tretheway" series).

*SIDELIGHTS:* A. E. Eddenden told *CA:* "I like my job (graphic design, art directing, rendering) but I would love to write full time if it were financially possible (interrupted by golf games). I feel the mystery genre is underrated. I thoroughly enjoy reading (or watching) the masters—Arthur Conan Doyle, Rex Stout, and so on."

Eddenden updated *CA:* "Much the same, except for retiring. Still not financially possible. Now have three beautiful grandchildren: Michael Arthur, David Arthur and Alexander. Fourth on [the] way.

"I write for money and satisfaction. There's more of the latter. It's hard work, but does produce a sense of accomplishment. Especially being published. 'No man but a blockhead ever wrote except for money: S. Johnson.' Keeps you from vegetating.

"Work still influenced by masters. Cosies. I'd like readers to feel as comfortable in Tretheway's boarding house as I have felt in Nero Wolfe's brownstone or on Baker Street.

"[My writing] process: the Lots of research, four to five drafts on electric typewriter. Edging toward word processor.

"Like to write about late 30s, early 40s. Comfortable. I was there. More vivid memories of that time than of the 60s or later. Nostalgia influence I guess.

Simpler times but lots going on. Depression, prohibition, WWII. Great era."

\*    \*    \*

**EDWARDS, David L(awrence)  1929-**

*PERSONAL:* Born January 20, 1929, in Cairo, Egypt; son of Lawrence Wright (a civil servant) and Phyllis Edwards; married Hilary Phillips; children: Helen, Katharine, Clare, Martin. *Education:* Magdalen College, Oxford, B.A., 1952, M.A., 1959, D.D. (Lambeth), 1990.

*ADDRESSES: Home and office*—19 Cripstead Lane, Winchester SO23 9SF, England.

*CAREER:* Ordained a priest of the Church of England. All Souls College, Oxford, England, fellow, 1954-61; St. Martin-in-the-Fields, London, curate, 1958-66; SCM. Press, London, England, managing director and editor, 1959-66; Cambridge University, Cambridge, England, fellow and dean of King's College, 1966-70; canon of Westminster and rector of St. Margaret's, London, 1970-78; Norwich Cathedral, Norwich, England, dean, 1978-83; Southwark Cathedral, London, provost, 1983-94.

*AWARDS, HONORS:* Named member of Order of the British Empire (OBE), 1995.

*WRITINGS:*

*Not Angels but Anglicans,* SCM. Press (London), 1958.
*This Church of England,* Church Information Office (London), 1962.
*God's Cross in Our World,* Westminster (London), 1963.
*F. J. Shirley: An Extraordinary Headmaster,* Society for Promoting Christian Knowledge (London), 1969.
*The Last Things Now,* SCM. Press, 1969.
*Religion and Change,* Harper (London), 1969, revised edition, Hodder & Stoughton (London), 1974.
*Leaders of the Church of England, 1828-1944,* Oxford University Press (Oxford, England), 1971, revised edition published as *Leaders of the Church of England, 1828-1978,* Hodder & Stoughton, 1978.

*St. Margaret's, Westminster,* Pitkin (London), 1972.

*What Is Real in Christianity?,* Westminster, 1972.

*The British Churches Turn to the Future: One Man's View of the Church Leaders' Conference, Birmingham, 1972,* SCM. Press, 1973.

*Ian Ramsey, Bishop of Durham: A Memoir,* Oxford University Press, 1973.

*What Anglicans Believe,* Mowbray (Oxford, England), 1974, published as *What Anglicans (Episcopalians) Believe,* Forward Movement Publications, 1975.

*Jesus for Modern Man: An Introduction to the Gospels in Today's English Version,* Fontana for the Bible Reading Fellowship, 1975.

*A Key to the Old Testament,* Collins (London), 1976.

*Your Faith,* Mowbray, 1978.

*A Reason to Hope,* Collins & World, 1978.

*Christian England,* Volume 1: *Its Story to the Reformation,* Oxford University Press, 1981, Volume 2: *From the Reformation to the Eighteenth Century,* Eerdmans (London), 1983, Volume 3: *From the Eighteenth Century to the First World War,* Eerdmans, 1984.

*The Futures of Christianity,* Morehouse, 1988.

(With John R. W. Stott) *Evangelical Essentials: A Liberal-Evangelical Dialogue,* Inter-Varsity Press (Leicester, England), 1988.

*The Cathedrals of Britain,* Pitkin, 1989.

*Christians in a New Europe,* HarperCollins (London), 1990.

*Tradition and Faith,* Hodder and Stoughton, 1990.

*What is Catholicism?: An Anglican Responds to the Official Teaching of the Roman Catholic Church,* Mowbray, 1994.

*Glimpses of God: Seeing the Divine in the Ordinary,* Chalice Press (St. Louis, MO), 1995.

*The First Two Thousand Years: A History of Christianity,* Cassell (London), 1997.

Also author of *A History of King's School, Canterbury,* Faber, and *Movements into Tomorrow,* SCM. Press.

### EDITOR

*The Honest to God Debate: Some Reactions to the Book "Honest to God,"* Westminster, 1963.

*Preparing for the Ministry of the 1970s: Essays on the British Churches by H. G. G. Herklots, James Whyte and Robin Sharp,* SCM. Press, 1964.

*Christians in a New World,* SCM. Press, 1966.

*Unity: The Next Step?,* S.P.C.K., 1972.

### OTHER

Compiler of abridgements from *Good News Bible in Today's English* version, for Collins: *Good New in Acts,* 1974; *Today's Story of Jesus,* 1976; *The Catholic Children's Bible,* 1979; *The Children's Bible,* 1979; *Robert Runcie: A Portrait by His Friends,* 1990; and *Christianity and Conservatism,* 1990.

*SIDELIGHTS:* In his 1969 work *Religion and Change,* David L. Edwards considers the challenges to religion which have arisen during the twentieth century. As John H. Wright observes in his *Commonweal* review, Edwards "has attempted to survey and evaluate the social and intellectual forces operating in twentieth-century Christianity and to project both a new shape for the Christian church and a new statement of Christian belief." While Edwards himself has described the book's purpose as "absurdly audacious," many reviewers find the study a success. "Here," remarks a *Times Literary Supplement* contributor, "is a quite superb account of the present scene combining a scholarly depth with a breadth of vision." "While it is a masterly survey, brilliant in its detail," continues the critic, "there are excellent summaries and many constructive insights. It should be prescribed reading for all concerned with the Christian faith and its institutions as well as with the well-being of humanity."

In addition, Edwards has written a continuing series on the history of Christianity in Britain, *Christian England,* and it has received similar praise. In Volume 2, for example, *From the Reformation to the Eighteenth Century,* Edwards "has brought to his task a remarkable acquaintance with recent historical writing on a two-hundred-year period," comments Eamon Duffy in the *Times Literary Supplement.* "His narrative never flags, and for all its compression is never clotted with mere brute fact. . . . Difficult theological issues are sketched out with remarkably little distortion, and all this with an admirable breadth of comprehension." Although Duffy faults the author for neglecting the popular aspect of religious development, he notes that "within its own terms of reference, it is difficult to see how this [volume] could have been better done." Duffy presents a similar assessment of Volume 3, *From the Eighteenth Century to the First World War,* which he calls "a wide-ranging and lively book." While the critic notes in the London *Times* that "the book is not so much an analysis of a period as a gallery of significant characters," he admits that "this is a perfectly legitimate approach, [and] indeed it is difficult to see how [Edwards] could in any other way have produced so comprehensive and so entertaining a book."

*BIOGRAPHICAL/CRITICAL SOURCES:*

PERIODICALS

*Christian Century,* April 6, 1988, p. 348.
*Commentary,* January, 1970.
*Commonweal,* December 26, 1969.
*Contemporary Review,* August, 1991, p. 109.
*Ecumenical Review,* July, 1988, p. 546.
*Times* (London), August 16, 1984.
*Times Literary Supplement,* August 21, 1969, February 5, 1982, February 24, 1984, September 21, 1984, January 8, 1988, p. 32.

\*   \*   \*

**ELLERBEE, Linda (Jane)   1944-**

*PERSONAL:* Born August 15, 1944, in Bryan, TX; daughter of Lonnie Ray and Hallie Smith; married four times; children: Vanessa, Joshua. *Education:* Attended Vanderbilt University. *Avocational interests:* Music.

*ADDRESSES: Office*—Lucky Duck Productions, 96 Morton St., New York, NY 10014.

*CAREER:* WVON-Radio, Chicago, IL, newscaster and disc jockey, 1964-67; KSJO-Radio, San Francisco, CA, program director, 1967-68; KJNO-Radio, Juneau, Alaska, and Associated Press (AP), Dallas, TX, reporter, 1969-72; KHOU-TV, Houston, TX, reporter, 1972-73; WCBS-TV, New York City, reporter, 1973-76; National Broadcasting Co. (NBC-TV), New York City, *NBC Nightly News* correspondent in Washington, DC, 1975-78, co-anchor of weekly television program *NBC News Weekend,* 1978-80, co-anchor and general editor of nightly television program *NBC News Overnight,* 1982-83, co-anchor of weekly television program *Summer Sunday U.S.A.,* 1984; correspondent and reporter for *Today Show,* NBC-TV, 1984-85; American Broadcasting Company (ABC-TV), writer and anchor of *Our World,* 1986; president of Lucky Duck Productions, 1987—; Cable News Network (CNN), commentator, 1989; producer, writer, and host of *Nick News W/5* (news magazine program); producer of "A Conversation with Magic: It's Only Television" (TV

special), 1992; executive producer and host of "Strange Danger" (TV special), Nick News, 1994.

*AWARDS, HONORS:* Peabody Award, 1992, for "A Conversation with Magic: It's Only Television."

*WRITINGS:*

*"And So It Goes": Adventures in Television,* Putnam (New York City), 1986.
*Move On: Adventures in the Real World,* Putnam, 1991.

Author of foreword to John Callahan, *I Think I Was an Alcoholic—,* Morrow (New York City), 1993; Rex Stout, *Three Men Out,* Bantam (New York City), 1994; and Bob Wade, *Daddy-O: Iguana Heads and Texas Tales,* St. Martin's Press (New York City), 1995.

*SIDELIGHTS:* Linda Ellerbee gained prominence in the field of broadcast journalism as co-anchor of *NBC News Overnight,* the late-night television news program that aired five times weekly from July of 1982 to December of 1983. Described by *People Weekly*'s Kristin McMurran as "a bright light in the murky realm of night-owl newscasting," Ellerbee brought to the critically acclaimed show what McMurran called a "refreshing blend of stylish prose and wry delivery."

Ellerbee first joined the National Broadcasting Company (NBC) in 1975 as a news correspondent in Washington, D.C. Assigned to cover the U.S. House of Representatives, she soon developed a dislike for Washington politicians. She explained in an interview with McMurran: "I don't like the idea that the way to get a story is to cozy up to them. . . . It's a very bad practice to be socializing with those people." "Besides," Ellerbee chided, "they probably have diseases." After three years in the nation's capital, she moved to New York City, where she and Lloyd Dobyns anchored *NBC News Weekend,* a weekly program with a magazine format.

In 1982, the network launched *NBC News Overnight,* naming Ellerbee and Dobyns (who was later replaced by Bill Schechner) as the show's anchors. Critics attributed the success of *Overnight* to its mixture of a straight-forward, no-nonsense approach with what Christopher Connelly defined in *Rolling Stone* as "bracing wit and a dash of hard-won cynicism." Reviewing *Overnight* when it was first broadcast, Martin Kitman noted in *New Leader* that "After the most important stories, which take up only the first 10 minutes of the show, the last 50 minutes of Dobyns and Ellerbee gives you a feeling of what is actually going on in the country." Connelly praised the program for "news that emphasized the reporting and interpreting skills of its anchors and correspondents instead of flashy graphics or stagy, oncamera confrontations." Despite the show's popularity, NBC announced the cancellation of *Overnight* in the fall of 1983. The announcement prompted more than fifteen hundred letters from viewers protesting the show's demise, and many sympathetic *Overnight* fans sent money in hopes that their contributions would offset NBC's reported loss of $6 million in advertising revenues. "The loss of *Overnight* is a tough one," Connelly lamented, "for it deprives the airwaves of the only news show that embodied two of mankind's most appealing qualities: intelligence and a sense of humor."

"It's easy to be smug, doing what I do," writes Ellerbee in *"And So It Goes": Adventures in Television,* the first of two books she has written about her life. "Television news is the candy store. They pay me to read. They pay me to travel around the world. They pay me to watch things happen, to go to parades, fires, conventions, wars, circuses, coronations and police stations—all in the name of journalism— and they pay me well." *Library Journal* reviewer Rebecca Wondriska describes the memoir as the "breezy story of [Ellerbee's] days as a television reporter and anchor."

In 1991, Ellerbee published *Move On: Adventures in the Real World,* focusing on aspects of her life aside from her television career. Ellerbee writes: "This is not the story of my life, but some of these are stories from my life. . . . This is about Bugs Bunny and Texas, revolutions, rock 'n' roll, finding a style, finding a job, five networks, four marriages and two children." A *Publishers Weekly* reviewer calls the book an "entertaining, often moving collection of essays." Chet Hagan, reviewing the book in *Library Journal,* writes that Ellerbee's language is "unpretentious and entertaining."

*BIOGRAPHICAL/CRITICAL SOURCES:*

PERIODICALS

*Booklist,* March 1, 1991, p. 1281.
*Detroit Free Press,* May 17, 1994, p. 5D.
*Film Comment,* February, 1984.
*Kirkus Reviews,* March 1, 1991, p. 296.

*Library Journal,* May 1, 1986, p. 118; April 1, 1991, p. 133.
*Los Angeles Times,* November 11, 1983; November 23, 1983; December 5, 1983; June 14, 1984.
*Los Angeles Times Book Review,* May 18, 1986, p. 6.
*New Leader,* September 6, 1982.
*Newsweek,* July 2, 1984.
*New York,* May 30, 1983.
*New York Times,* November 26, 1983.
*New York Times Book Review,* June 14, 1987, p. 38; May 12, 1991, p. 22; May 10, 1992, p. 28.
*People Weekly,* June 27, 1983; May 13, 1991, pp. 117-29.
*Publishers Weekly,* April 11, 1986, p. 78; March 22, 1991, p. 66.
*Rolling Stone,* January 19, 1984.
*Washington Journalism Review,* May, 1991, p. 52.
*Washington Post,* October 18, 1983.
*Washington Post Book World,* May 26, 1991, p. 12.*

\*    \*    \*

## EMERSON, Kathy Lynn 1947-
### (Kaitlyn Gorton)

*PERSONAL:* Born October 25, 1947, in Liberty, NY; daughter of William Russell and Theresa Marie (Coburg) Gorton; married Sanford Merritt Emerson (in law enforcement), May 10, 1969. *Education:* Bates College, A.B., 1969; Old Dominion University, M.A., 1972.

*ADDRESSES: Home*—P.O. Box 156, Wilton, ME 04294.

*CAREER:* Tidewater Community College, Virginia Beach, VA, instructor in English, 1972-73; tutor and counselor in Franklin County Community Action Program, 1974-75; language arts teacher at Wilton Academy, 1975-76; University of Maine at Farmington, Farmington, library assistant, 1979-85, lecturer, 1985-87; free-lance writer, 1976—.

*MEMBER:* Mystery Writers of America, Novelists, Inc., Romance Writers of America, Sisters in Crime.

*WRITINGS:*

ROMANTIC SUSPENSE NOVELS

*Winter Tapestry* (historical), Harper (New York City), 1991.

*Echoes and Illusions* (contemporary), Harper, 1993.
*Firebrand* (historical), Harper, 1993.
*The Green Rose* (historical), Harper, 1994.
*Unquiet Hearts* (historical), Harper, 1994.

ROMANCE NOVELS; UNDER PSEUDONYM KAITLYN GORTON

*Cloud Castles,* Silhouette Books (New York City), 1989.
*Hearth, Home, and Hope,* Silhouette Books, 1995.
*Separated Sisters,* Silhouette Books, 1997.

NOVELS FOR CHILDREN

*The Mystery of Hilliard's Castle,* Down East (Camden, ME), 1985.
*Julia's Mending,* Orchard Books (London and New York City), 1987, Avon Camelot, 1990.
*The Mystery of the Missing Bagpipes,* Avon Camelot, 1991.

NONFICTION

*Wives and Daughters: The Women of Sixteenth-Century England,* Whitston (Troy, NY), 1984, trade paperback edition, 1993.
*Making Headlines: A Biography of Nellie Bly* (childrens), Dillon Press (Minneapolis, MN), 1989.
*The Writer's Guide to Everyday Life in Renaissance England,* Writer's Digest Books (Cincinnati, OH), 1996.

OTHER

*Face Down in the Marrow-Bone Pie* ("Chronicle of Lady Appleton" mystery series), St. Martin's Press (New York City), 1997.

Columnist, "Kathy's Corner" (a question-and-answer column appearing in each issue), for *Mainely Romance* (newsletter of Maine chapter of Romance Writers of America), 1995—. Contributor of articles and stories to periodicals, including *D.A.R. Magazine, First Person Female American, Highlights for Children, Medieval Chronicle, Mystery News, Notes on Teaching English, Primary Treasure,* and *Renaissance Papers.*

*WORK IN PROGRESS:* "The second chronicle of Lady Appleton is under contract with St. Martin's Press for 1998 publication; *Sleepwalking Beauty* and *E-Mail Bride* are under contract with Bantam Books for the Bantam Loveswept romance series."

*SIDELIGHTS:* Kathy Lynn Emerson told *CA:* "I alternate between writing contemporary and historical fiction with an occasional nonfiction project for variety.

"My favorite historical period is the sixteenth century, in which I have set several adult novels. The 1880s have provided background for *Julia's Mending* and a biography of Nellie Bly, both for young readers. I frequently use family stories as the basis for plot development. *Julia's Mending* incorporates many of the adventures my grandfather had as a young boy. If there is any single theme running through my work, it concerns the dangers of jumping to conclusions about people. My protagonists frequently must learn to be more open-minded and fight unintentional prejudices they discover within themselves."

\*   \*   \*

**ENDO, Shusaku    1923-**

*PERSONAL:* Born March 27, 1923, in Tokyo, Japan; son of Tsunehisa and Iku (Takei) Endo; married Junko Okado, September 3, 1955; children: Ryunosuke (son). *Education:* Keio University, Tokyo, B.A., 1949; Lyon University, Lyon, France, student in French literature, 1950-53. *Religion:* Roman Catholic.

*ADDRESSES: Home*—3-35 Tamagawagakiren, 2 chome, Machida Tokyo 194, Japan. *Office*—c/o Japanese PEN Club, 9-1-7 Akasaka Room 265, Minatu-ku Tokyo, Japan.

*MEMBER:* International PEN (president of Japanese Centre, 1969), Association of Japanese Writers (member of executive committee, 1966).

*AWARDS, HONORS:* Akutagawa prize (Japan), 1955, for *Shiroihito;* Tanizaki prize (Japan), 1967, and Gru de Oficial da Ordem do Infante dom Henrique (Portugal), 1968, both for *Chinmoku;* Sanct Silvestri, awarded by Pope Paul VI, 1970.

*WRITINGS:*

IN ENGLISH TRANSLATION

*Umi to Dokuyaku* (novel), Bungeishunju, 1958, translation by M. Gallagher published as *The Sea and Poison,* P. Owen (London), 1971, Taplinger (New York City), 1980.

*Kazan* (novel), [Japan], 1959, translation by Richard A. Schuchert published as *Volcano,* P. Owen, 1978, Taplinger, 1980.

*Obaka-san,* [Japan], 1959, translation by Francis Mathy published as *Wonderful Fool,* Tuttle (Tokyo), 1974.

*Ryugaku,* [Japan], 1965, translation by Mark Williams published as *Foreign Studies,* P. Owen, 1989, Linden Press/Simon & Schuster (New York City), 1990.

*Chinmoku* (novel), Shinchosha, 1966, translation by William Johnston published as *Silence,* P. Owen, 1969, Taplinger, 1979.

*Ougon no Ku* (play), Shinchosha, 1969, translation by Mathy published as *The Golden Country,* Tuttle, 1970.

*Iseu no shogai,* [Japan], 1973, translation by Schuchert published as *A Life of Jesus,* Paulist Press (New York City), 1978.

*Kuchibue o fuku toki* (novel), [Japan], 1974, translation by Van C. Gessel published as *When I Whistle,* Taplinger, 1979.

*Juichi no iro-garasu* (short stories), [Japan], 1979, translation published as *Stained Glass Elegies,* Dodd (New York City), 1985.

*Samurai* (novel), [Japan], 1980, translation by Gessel published as *The Samurai,* Harper (New York City), 1982.

*Sukyandaru,* [Japan], translation by Gessel published as *Scandal,* Dodd, Mead, 1988.

*Umi to dokuyaku* [Japan], translation by Michael Gallagher published as *The Sea and Poison,* New Directions, 1992.

*The Final Martyrs* (short stories), translation by Gessel, New Directions (New York City), 1994.

*Dipu riba,* [Japan], translation by Gessel published as *Deep River,* New Directions, 1995.

*The Girl I Left Behind,* translation by Williams, New Directions, 1995.

*IN JAPANESE*

*Shiroihito* (novel; title means "White Man"), Kodansha, 1955.

*Seisho no Naka no Joseitachi* (essays; title means "Women in the Bible"), Shinchosha, 1968.

*Bara no Yakat* (play), Shinchosha, 1969.

*Yumoa shosetsu shu* (short stories), Kodansha, 1974.

*France no daigakusei* (essays on travel in France), Kadokawashoten, 1974.

*Kitsunegata tanukigata* (short stories), Kodansha, 1976.

*Watashi ga suteta onna,* Kodansha, 1976.

*Yukiaru kotoba* (essays), Shinchosha, 1976.

*Nihonjin wa Kirisuto kyo o shinjirareru ka,* Shogakukan, 1977.

*Kare no ikikata,* Shinchosha, 1978.

*Kirisuto no tanjo,* Shinchosha, 1978.

*Ningen no naka no X* (essays), Chuokoronsha, 1978.

*Rakuten taisho,* Kodansha, 1978.

*Ju to jujika* (biography of Pedro Cassini), Shuokoronsha, 1979.

*Marie Antoinette* (fiction), Asahi shinbunsha, 1979.

*Chichioya,* Shinchosha, 1980.

*Kekkonron,* Shufunotomosha, 1980.

*Sakka no nikki* (diary excerpts), Toju-sha, 1980.

*Endo Shusaku ni yoru Endo Shusaku,* Seidosha, 1980.

*Meiga Iesu junrei,* Bungei Shunju, 1981.

*Onna no issho* (fiction), Asahi Shinbunsha, 1982.

*Endo Shusaku to Knagaeru,* PHP Kekyujo (Kyoto), 1982.

*Fuyu no yasashisa,* Bunka Shuppakyoku, 1982.

*Shin ryaugaku jijao,* Kawade Shobao Shinsa (Tokyo), 1982.

*Shiina Rinzao,* Kadokawa Shoten (Tokyo), 1983.

Also author of *Kuroihito,* 1955, *Hechima kun,* 1963, *Nanji mo mata,* 1965, *Watakusi no Iesu,* 1976, *Usaba kagero nikki,* 1978, *Shinran,* 1979, *Tenshi,* 1980, *Ai to jinsei o meguru danso,* 1981, and *Okuku e no michi,* 1981.

*ADAPTATIONS: Silence* has been optioned for a film to be directed by Martin Scorsese.

*SIDELIGHTS:* Of all leading modern Japanese novelists, Shusaku Endo is considered by many critics to be the one whose novels are easiest for Western readers to grasp. His Roman Catholic upbringing is often cited as the key to his accessibility, for it has given him a philosophical background shaped by Western traditions rather than those of the East. Christianity is a rarity in Japan, where two sects of Buddhism predominate. As Garry Wills explains in the *New York Review of Books,* "Christ is not only challenging but embarrassing [to the Japanese] because he has absolutely no 'face'. . . . He will let anyone spit on him. How can the Japanese ever honor such a disreputable figure?" While strongly committed to his adopted religion, Endo has often described the sense of alienation felt by a Christian in Japan. Many of his novels translated into English address the clash of Eastern and Western morals and philosophy, as well as illustrate the difficulty and unlikelihood of Christianity's establishment in Japan. John Updike writes in the *New Yorker* that Endo's first novel in English translation, *Silence,* is "a remarkable work, a somber, delicate, and startlingly empathetic study of a young Portuguese missionary during the relentless persecution of the Japanese Christians in the early seventeenth century." The young missionary, Rodrigues, travels to Japan to investigate rumors that his former teacher, Ferreira, has not only converted to Buddhism, but is even participating in the persecution of Christians. Updike notes, "One can only marvel at the unobtrusive, persuasive effort of imagination that enables a modern Japanese to take up a viewpoint from which Japan is at the outer limit of the world."

Endo seeks to illustrate Japan's hostility toward the Christ figure in another of his translated novels, *Wonderful Fool.* Set in modern times, this story centers on Gaston Bonaparte, a French former priest who is seen as a fool by the Japanese. At their hands he is "scorned, deceived, threatened, beaten and finally drowned in a swamp," reports *Books Abroad* contributor Kinya Tsuruta. "In the end, however, his total faith transforms all the Japanese, not excluding even a hardened criminal. Thus, the simple Frenchman has successfully sowed a seed of good will in the corrupting mud swamp, Endo's favorite metaphor for non-Christian Japan." *Wonderful Fool* is seen by some reviewers as Endo's condemnation of his country's values. "What shocks him," notes a *Times Literary Supplement* contributor, "is the spiritual emptiness of what he calls 'mud-swamp Japan,' an emptiness heightened by the absence of any appropriate sense of sin." In a *New Republic* review, Mary Jo Salter believes that "ultimately it is the novelist's humor—slapstick, corny, irreverent—that permits him to moralize so openly."

Louis Allen concurs in the *Listener* that Endo "is one of Japan's major comic writers." Praising the author's versatility, he continues, "In *When I Whistle,* he explores yet another vein, a plain realism behind which lingers a discreet but clear symbolism." *When I Whistle* tells two parallel stories, Ozu's and his son, Eiichi's. The parallel stories merge when Eiichi, in the hopes of furthering his career, decides to use experimental drugs on a terminal cancer patient— Ozu's former sweetheart, Aiko. Like *Wonderful Fool, When I Whistle* presents "an unflattering version of postwar Japan," notes Allen. But while *Wonderful Fool* is marked by its humor, "Sadness is the keynote [of *When I Whistle*], and its symbol the

changed Aiko: a delicate beauty, unhoused and brought to penury by war, and ultimately devoured by a disease which is merely a pretext for experiment by the new, predatory generation of young Japan." *When I Whistle* differs from many of Endo's novels in its lack of an overtly Christian theme, but here as in all his fiction, believes *New York Times Book Review* contributor Anthony Thwaite, "what interests Mr. Endo—to the point of obsession—are the concerns of both the sacred and secular realms: moral choice, moral responsibility."

Endo returns to the seventeenth century setting of *Silence* in *The Samurai.* This work has proved to be his most popular in Japan, and like *Silence,* it is based on historical fact. Whereas *Silence* gave readers a Portuguese missionary traveling to Japan, *The Samurai* tells of a Japanese warrior journeying to Mexico, Spain, and finally the Vatican. The samurai, Hasekura, is an unwitting pawn in his shogun's complex scheme to open trade routes to the West. Hasekura feigns conversion to Christianity in obedience to the shogun but against his own convictions. By the time he returns to Japan political policy has been reversed, and he is treated as a criminal for his "conversion." Through his own suffering, Hasekura comes to identify with Jesus and becomes a true Christian. In his *Village Voice* review, Geoffry O'Brien judges *The Samurai* to be Endo's most successful novel, giving particular praise to its engrossing storyline and to Endo's "tremendously lyrical sensory imagination." *Washington Post Book World* reviewer Noel Perrin agrees that *The Samurai* functions well as an adventure story but maintains that "Endo has done far more than write a historical novel about an early and odd encounter between East and West. Taking the history of Hasekuru's embassy as a mere base, he has written a really quite profound religious novel."

Endo followed *The Samurai* with *Scandal,* a novel with a modern setting. In it, the author once again confronts questions of morality and sin in modern Japan in what *Washington Post Book World* contributor J. Thomas Rimer calls "one of his most absorbing views to date of human spiritual darkness." *Scandal* tells the story of a respected Christian Japanese novelist named Suguro. The elderly writer is attending a reception when he is approached by drunken woman who claims to have met him in Tokyo's Shinjuku district in a house of prostitution. She even claims to have seen a portrait of him hanging there. Stung by these accusations, Suguro—who has built his reputation on the practice of Christian charity—begins an investigation of the quarter. He in turn is stalked by a reporter named Kobari, who is determined to expose what he believes to be Suguro's hypocrisy.

Critics note that *Scandal* displays the complex name of sin and morality in modern life. "Suguro," writes *New York Times Book Review* contributor Charles Newman, "is left with a knowledge more complex than that of a moral hypocrite and more human than that of a writer who had commonly confused the esthetic with the spiritual. For his acceptance of the neat dualism of sin and salvation has blinded Suguro to the possibility of multiple selves and allowed him to avoid the irreducible evil at the core of his own character." "The sure grip Suguro thought he had on his world is gradually prised loose," *Times Literary Supplement* critic Louis Allen states. "His relationship to his wife is falsified and his art is seen to be based on self-deception. He realises that 'sin' and the salvation that can arise from it are somehow shallow and superficial things. The reality is the magma that erupts and alters everyone's personal landscape for ever." "Endo has written greater novels than 'Scandal,'" declares Thomas Cahill in the *Los Angeles Times Book Review,* "but never has he combined profundity with entertainment to such a degree."

Endo originally published the three stories that make up *Foreign Studies* in 1965, but they were translated into English for the first time in 1989. John B. Breslin writes in the *Washington Post Book World* that there are "strong parallels" between *Foreign Studies* and his longer works. The stories look at the dissimilarities between Eastern and Western culture through the experiences of Christian Japanese. The first story tells of a young Japanese student studying, as Endo did himself, in France during the 1950s. The second tells of a theological student who studied in Rome and returned to Japan after Christianity was banned in 1614. The third is the story of Tanaka, an academic who specializes in French literature, who is in France researching the career of the Marquis de Sade. "Tanaka's shadow-figure here is Sade," declares Breslin, "just as, in . . . *Scandal,* it is a perverse doppelganger who haunts a popular contemporary Japanese novelist."

The theme that unites the stories of *Foreign Studies* is the conflict between Eastern and Western ways of life. "In an introduction, Endo notes that these stories . . . present a starker picture of the divide between Japanese and Western culture than the one he has come to hold," declares *Los Angeles Times Book Review* contributor Richard Eder. "Now he sees hopes of transcending it, he writes, perhaps by studying the subconscious." "By releasing [the book] to the West some 25 years after its Japanese debut," Scott Baldauf states in the *Christian Science Monitor,* "he clearly felt the novel could help us understand those who are torn between their own and a Western identity. And he's right. The points it makes are valid and harrowing, and beautifully developed." "Paradoxically," says a *Publishers Weekly* reviewer, "Endo transcends all cultural barriers; far from foreign, his work has the intimacy and the vastness of the universally true."

*The Final Martyrs,* like *Foreign Studies,* is a collection of stories; and, like the other collection, it contains eleven stories that range in time from the beginning of Endo's career to 1985. "They remind us," states Joseph R. Garber in the *San Francisco Review of Books,* "how central Endo's anguish at the gap between Christian and Shinto senses of good and evil is to all his work." Endo's dedication to his theme comes through very clearly in the collection. *Los Angeles Times Book Review* contributor Karl Schoenberger calls the stories "character sketches and rambling essays in the confessional *zuihitsu* style," and adds, "Copiously detailed footnotes grace one of these stories, apparently part of the original text. It should be noted that Endo made his mark as a man of letters in the genre of historical fiction. It pays to be patient with his dull, gray sincerity." "With their satire relieving their thin-skinned tenderness," writes Ruth Pavey in the *Observer,* "these stories, presented together and in English for the first time, deserve to bring Endo many more devoted readers."

*Deep River* takes its title from the well-known American spiritual hymn, and it mixes elements of the philosophies of the Hindu, Buddhist, and Roman Catholic Christian religions. It opens with the trip of a group of Japanese tourists to Varanasi, an Indian town and a place of Hindu pilgrimage. Each of the tourists has unresolved spiritual problems. The ex-soldier Kiguchi is haunted by memories of cannibalism during the 1944 invasion of India. Isobe is looking for the Indian child in which he believes his late wife has been reborn. Numada is a writer who is spiritually dedicated to animals: "Dogs and birds provide him with the companionship that others find in God," Michael Harris of the *Los Angeles Times* explains. Mitsuko is a cynic, who once seduced her

Christian classmate Otsu in an effort to undermine his faith. And Otsu himself lives in poverty on the banks of the Ganges, ministering to the Hindus who come to the holy river to die. He collects their bodies and brings them to funeral pyres so that they can find the salvation in which they believed.

"In *Deep River,*" declares Andrew Greeley in the *Washington Post Book World,* "Endo discovers grace in this convergence of three world religions—Hindu, Buddhist, and Catholic Christian—on the banks of the Ganges. He does not seek to combine the three religions into one." The image of the Ganges, the sacred river of the Hindus, represents one type of spirituality that many modern people have rejected. It is "a way station toward new kinds of life to be assumed rather than a spot that marks the end of things," explains *New York Times Book Review* contributor Robert Coles, "but for modern Japanese as well as Americans, reared on antisepsis and biotechnology, a place of absurdity if not danger—funeral pyres everywhere, and bodies of human beings and household pets floating downstream." "But Endo absorbs the wisdom of all three faiths into his vision," Greeley concludes, "and makes salvation available to all his pilgrims."

## BIOGRAPHICAL/CRITICAL SOURCES:

### BOOKS

*Contemporary Literary Criticism,* Gale (Detroit), Volume 7, 1977, Volume 14, 1980, Volume 19, 1981, Volume 54, 1989.

Rimer, J. Thomas, *Modern Japanese Fiction and Its Traditions: An Introduction,* Princeton University Press (Princeton, NJ), 1978.

### PERIODICALS

*America,* June 21, 1980; February 2, 1985; October 13, 1990; August 1, 1992; November 19, 1994, pp. 18, 28.

*Antioch Review,* winter, 1983.

*Best Sellers,* November, 1980.

*Books Abroad,* spring, 1975.

*Chicago Tribune Book World,* October 7, 1979.

*Christian Century,* September 21, 1966.

*Christianity Today,* March 17, 1989.

*Christian Science Monitor,* July 27, 1990, p. 13.

*Commonweal,* November 4, 1966; September 22, 1989.

*Contemporary Review,* April, 1978.

*Critic,* July 15, 1979.

*Listener,* May 20, 1976; April 12, 1979.

*London Magazine,* April/May, 1974.

*London Review of Books,* May 19, 1988, p. 24.

*Los Angeles Times,* November 13, 1980; December 1, 1983; May 22, 1995, p. E4.

*Los Angeles Times Book Review,* December 5, 1982; November 13, 1988; May 13, 1990; September 18, 1994.

*New Republic,* December 26, 1983.

*New Statesman,* May 7, 1976; April 13, 1979.

*New Statesman and Society,* April 30, 1993, p. 44.

*Newsweek,* December 19, 1983.

*New Yorker,* January 14, 1980; March 6, 1989, pp. 107-11.

*New York Review of Books,* February 19, 1981; November 4, 1982.

*New York Times,* August 5, 1988.

*New York Times Book Review,* January 13, 1980; June 1, 1980; December 26, 1982; November 13, 1983; July 21, 1985; August 28, 1988, pp. 15-16; May 6, 1990, p. 34; May 28, 1995, pp. 1, 21.

*Observer,* April 24, 1988; May 21, 1989; August 29, 1993.

*Publishers Weekly,* March 30, 1990, p. 50; July 4, 1994, p. 25; September 11, 1995, p. 72.

*San Francisco Review of Books,* October/November, 1994, p. 40.

*Saturday Review,* July 21, 1979.

*Spectator,* May 1, 1976; April 14, 1979; May 15, 1982.

*Times* (London), April 18, 1985.

*Times Literary Supplement,* July 14, 1972; January 25, 1974; May 5, 1978; May 21, 1982; October 26, 1984; April 29, 1988, p. 471; April 28, 1989, pp. 466-67; October 28, 1994, p. 22.

*Vanity Fair,* February, 1991.

*Village Voice,* November 16, 1982.

*Washington Post Book World,* September 2, 1979; October 12, 1980; October 24, 1982; June 23, 1985; August 14, 1988, pp. 3, 13; May 6, 1990; June 25, 1995.

*World Literature Today,* summer, 1979; winter, 1984.*

\*          \*          \*

**ERICSON, Walter**
**See FAST, Howard (Melvin)**

# F

## FAIRCLOUGH, Adam   1952-

*PERSONAL:* Born November 14, 1952, in London, England; son of Alan (a journalist) and Marian (Skea, now Wills) Fairclough; married Patricia Benard (an artist), 1976; married Mary Ellen Curtin (a historian); children: (first marriage) Jennifer Lee. *Ethnicity:* "English." *Education:* Balliol College, Oxford, B.A. (with first class honors), 1975; graduate study at University of Georgia, 1975-76; University of Keele, Ph.D., 1978; postdoctoral study at Institute of Education, London, 1982-83. *Politics:* Labour Party.

*ADDRESSES: Office*—School of History, University of Leeds, Leeds LS2 9JT, England; fax: 0113-234-2759. *E-mail*—a.fairclough@leeds._ac.uk.

*CAREER:* New University of Ulster (now University of Ulster), Coleraine, Northern Ireland, member of department of history, 1978-79; University of Liverpool, Liverpool, England, member of department of modern history, 1980-81; University of Wales, St. David's University College, Lampeter, member of department of history, 1983-94; University of Leeds, Leeds, England, professor of modern American history, 1994—. Visiting scholar at Tulane University, 1987; fellow at Carter C. Woodson Center, University of Virginia, 1990-91; fellow at National Humanities Center, 1994-95.

*MEMBER:* Association of University Teachers, British Association for American Studies, Southern Historical Association, Organization of American Historians, American Historical Association.

*AWARDS, HONORS:* Fellow of American Council of Learned Societies, 1987; Lillian Smith Award, 1995, Louisiana Literary Award, 1996, and General L. Kemper Williams Prize, 1996, all for *Race and Democracy: The Civil Rights Struggle in Louisiana, 1915-1972.*

*WRITINGS:*

*To Redeem the Soul of America: The Southern Christian Leadership Conference and Martin Luther King, Jr.,* University of Georgia Press (Athens), 1987.
*Martin Luther King, Jr.,* University of Georgia Press, 1990.
*Race and Democracy: The Civil Rights Struggle in Louisiana, 1915-1972,* Univeristy of Georgia Press, 1995.
*Forty Acres and a Mule: Horace Mann Bond and the Lynching of Jerome Wilson,* University of Georgia Press, 1997.

Contributor to history journals.

*WORK IN PROGRESS: Constant Struggle: Blacks and Equality, 1895-1995.*

*SIDELIGHTS:* Adam Fairclough told *CA:* "My work is sustained by the creative tension between political engagement and the ideal of objectivity implicit in the historian's craft. I absorbed a concern for social justice and an interest in Labour politics from my father, chief leader-writer for the London *Daily Mirror* until his death in 1973. It took exposure to the poverty of Liverpool, however, to transmute vague sympathies into concrete political activity. Whether political commitment helps or hinders my work as a historian of the American civil rights movement is not for me to say; but it has, I believe, deepened my understanding of the mechanics of power and of the political wisdom of Martin Luther King's leadership.

"My work on the civil rights movement in Louisiana, and my current research into the history of black education, have taken me much more deeply into the complexities of the civil rights movement, compelling me to question many of the assumptions that characterize recent interpretations—including my own."

*BIOGRAPHICAL/CRITICAL SOURCES:*

*PERIODICALS*

*Los Angeles Times,* July 30, 1987.
*Times Literary Supplement,* July 17, 1987.

\* \* \*

**FALCONER, Lee N.**
  **See MAY, Julian**

\* \* \*

**FARMER, David Hugh    1923-**

*PERSONAL:* Born January 30, 1923, in Ealing, London, England; son of Charles (a publisher) and Madeleine (maiden name, Beard) Farmer; married Ann Widgery (a teacher); children: Paul, John. *Education:* Studied at Quarr Abbey, 1941-58; attended St. Benet's Hall, Oxford, 1959-60; Linacre College, Oxford, B.Litt., 1967. *Avocational interests:* Travel (France, Italy, and Scandinavia), walking, swimming, music, exploring old buildings and art galleries, wine and its history.

*ADDRESSES: Office*—26 Swanston Field, Whitchurch-on-Thames, Reading, Berks RG8 7HP, England.

*CAREER:* Entered Prinknash Abbey (Benedictine), 1939; Benedictine monk at Quarr Abbey, Isle of Wight, 1941-58; University of Reading, Reading, England, lecturer, 1967-77, reader in history, 1977-88; Southampton University, external examiner, 1987-91; Oxford University, lecturer, 1988-95.

Broadcaster for British Broadcasting Corp., Radio Telefis Eirann, and local radio stations.

*MEMBER:* Royal Historical Society (fellow), Society of Antiquaries (fellow).

*AWARDS, HONORS:* Grant from British Academy, 1987; Emeritus Research Fellowship, 1988.

*WRITINGS:*

*The Magna Vita of St. Hugh of Lincoln,* Oxford University Press (Oxford, England and New York City), Volume I, 1961, Volume II, 1962, second edition, revised, 1985.
*The Monk of Farne,* Darton, Longman & Todd (London), 1962, second edition published as *Christ Crucified and Other Meditations,* Gracewing, 1994.
*The Rule of St. Benedict,* Rosenkild & Bagger, 1968.
*The Oxford Dictionary of Saints,* Oxford University Press, 1978, third edition, 1993.
(Editor and contributor) *Benedict's Disciples,* Fowler Wright Books (Herefordshire, England), 1980, revised and expanded edition, Gracewing, 1995.
(With J. F. Webb) *The Age of Bede,* Penguin (West Drayton, Middlesex and New York City), 1983, revised, 1988.
*St. Hugh of Lincoln* (biography), Darton, Longman & Todd, 1985, Cistercian Publications (Kalamazoo, MI), 1986.
(With L. Shirley Price) *Bede's Ecclesiastical History,* Penguin, 1990.

Work represented in anthologies, including *The Amesbury Millennium Lectures,* and *East Anglian and Other Studies.* Contributor to encyclopedias, including *Dictionnaire d'Hisotoire et geographie Ecclesiastique, New Catholic Encyclopedia, Bibliotheca, Sanctorum, Lexikon der Christlichen,* and *New Dictionary of National Biography.* Contributor to periodicals, including *Tenth-Century Studies, Millenium,* and *St. Wilfrid at Hexham.*

*The Oxford Dictionary of Saints* has been translated into Italian and Slovakian.

*WORK IN PROGRESS: The Gesta Pontificum of William of Malmesbury,* for Oxford University Press; a new edition of *Butler's Lives of the Saints.*

*SIDELIGHTS:* David Hugh Farmer described himself as "a medieval historian, with a special interest in the church." He has concentrated his research on the

Anglo-Saxons, Vikings, and Normans, particularly in the fields of monasticism, hagiography, and historiography. He likes to speak to, and write for, a wider audience than academics alone.

*BIOGRAPHICAL/CRITICAL SOURCES:*

PERIODICALS

*Times Literary Supplement,* January 9, 1981.

\* \* \*

**FASICK, Adele M(ongan)**    **1930-**

*PERSONAL:* Born March 18, 1930, in New York, NY; daughter of Stephen (an optometrist) and Florence (a teacher; maiden name, Geary) Mongan; divorced; children: Pamela, Laura, Julia. *Education:* Cornell University, B.A., 1951; Columbia University, M.A., 1954, M.L.S., 1956; Case Western Reserve University, Ph.D., 1970.

*ADDRESSES: Home*—51 Broadfield Drive #40, Etobicoke, Ontario, Canada M9C 5P2. *Office*—Faculty of Information Studies, University of Toronto, Toronto, Ontario, Canada M5S 1A1.

*CAREER:* New York Public Library, New York City, librarian, 1955-56; Long Island University, Brooklyn, NY, librarian, 1956-58; homemaker, 1958-67; Rosary College, River Forest, IL, assistant professor of library science, 1970-71; University of Toronto, Toronto, Ontario, professor of library science, 1971—; dean of faculty of Information Studies, 1990-95.

*MEMBER:* International Federation of Library Associations, Canadian Library Association, American Library Association, Association of Library Service to Children, Association of Library and Information Science Education, Ontario Library Association.

*WRITINGS:*

(With Claire England) *Childview: Evaluating and Reviewing Materials for Children,* Libraries Unlimited (Littleton, CO), 1987.
*The Beauty Who Would Not Spin* (childrens picture book), Scholastic-Tab (Toronto), 1988.

(Editor with R. Osler and M. Johnston) *Lands of Pleasure: Essays on Lillian H. Smith and the Development of Children's Libraries,* Scarecrow Press (Metuchen, NJ), 1990.
*Managing Children's Services in Public Libraries,* Libraries Unlimited, 1991.
(Editor) *International Guidelines for Library Services to Children,* International Federation of Library Associations (The Hague), 1991.
(Editor) *Young People and Reading: International Perspectives; Papers Presented and the Children's Section/Reading Research Round Table Joint Workshop, August 22, 1991,* International Federation of Library Associations, 1994.

Contributor to professional journals.

*WORK IN PROGRESS:* New edition of *Managing Children's Services in Pubic Libraries,* for Libraries Unlimited, in 1997; compiling and editing a database in electronic and print format of *International Research Abstracts: Youth Library Services,* second edition, scheduled for 1996; a new children's book.

*SIDELIGHTS:* Adele M. Fasick told *CA:* "As CD-ROMs and the Internet bring children more contact with electronic media, I am interested in exploring the ways in which these media are used and how they interact with children's reading. Public libraries are becoming hives of activity with books competing for space between the terminals and media racks. But the children have not changed as much as the media would suggest. The stories that hold their interest deal with the perennial topics of finding a place in the world, discovering courage to confront evil, and reaching out to other people. Much of the current media treats the world as if it were newly hatched and without a history. I hope in my writing for children to show that the world is complex and fascinating; that people in the past struggled with the same feelings and worries that we have now and that sometimes they succeeded in overcoming problems just as difficult as the ones we have today.

"Now that I have stepped down from my administrative position I expect to devote more time to writing for children. There are some needs that can only be met by books. Although videos and computer games can offer exciting stories, they are not internalized in the same way that books can be. Only books, I think, can tell us a story from inside a person's head. Instead of watching the action on a screen, we create the action inside our minds when we read and live for a little while the life of the character in the book.

In reading books boys and girls can discover that there are others who think and feel the way they do and that they are not alone. My goal as a writer is to open new and different worlds for children and to let them see that the possibilities are wide and deep and far more compelling than the vista of a shopping mall."

\*    \*    \*

**FAST, Howard (Melvin)    1914-**
    **(E. V. Cunningham, Walter Ericson)**

*PERSONAL:* Born November 11, 1914, in New York, NY; son of Barney (an ironworker, cable car gripper, tin factory worker, and dress factory cutter) and Ida (a homemaker; maiden name, Miller) Fast; married Bette Cohen (a painter andsculptor), June 6, 1937; children: Rachel, Jonathan. *Education:* Attended National Academy of Design. *Religion:* Jewish. *Avocational interests:* "My home, my family, the theater, the film, and the proper study of ancient history. And the follies of mankind."

*ADDRESSES: Home*—Greenwich, CT. *Agent*—Sterling Lord Agency, 65 Bleeker St., New York, NY 10012.

*CAREER:* Worked at several odd jobs and as a page in the New York Public Library prior to 1932; writer, 1932—. Foreign correspondent for *Esquire* and *Coronet,* 1945. Member of World Peace Council, 1950-55; American Labor Party candidate for U.S. Congress, 23rd New York District, 1952. Has given numerous lectures and made numerous appearances on radio and television programs. *Military service:* Affiliated with U.S. Office of War Information, 1942-44; correspondent with special Signal Corps unit and war correspondent in China-India-Burma theater, 1945.

*MEMBER:* Century Club.

*AWARDS, HONORS:* Bread Loaf Literary Award, 1937; Schomburg Award for Race Relations, 1944, for *Freedom Road;* Newspaper Guild award, 1947; National Jewish Book Award, Jewish Book Council, 1949, for *My Glorious Brothers;* International Peace Prize from the Soviet Union, 1954; Screenwriters annual award, 1960; Secondary Education Board annual book award, 1962; American Library Association "notable book" citation, 1972, for *The Hes-*

*sian;* Emmy Award for outstanding writing in a drama series, American Academy of Television Arts and Sciences, 1975, for episode of *Benjamin Franklin;* Literary Lions Award, New York Public Library, 1985; Prix de la Policia Award (France), for books under name E. V. Cunningham.

*WRITINGS:*

*Two Valleys,* Dial (New York City), 1933.
*Strange Yesterday,* Dodd (New York City), 1934.
*Place in the City,* Harcourt (New York City), 1937.
*Conceived in Liberty: A Novel of Valley Forge* (also see below), Simon & Schuster (New York City), 1939.
*The Last Frontier,* Duell, Sloan & Pearce (New York City), 1941.
*The Romance of a People,* Hebrew Publishing (New York City), 1941.
*Lord Baden-Powell of the Boy Scouts,* Messner (New York City), 1941.
*Haym Salomon, Son of Liberty,* Messner, 1941.
*The Unvanquished* (also see below), Duell, Sloan & Pearce, 1942.
*The Tall Hunter,* Harper (New York City), 1942.
(With wife, Bette Fast) *The Picture-Book History of the Jews,* Hebrew Publishing, 1942.
*Goethals and the Panama Canal,* Messner, 1942.
*Citizen Tom Paine* (also see below), Duell, Sloan & Pearce, 1943.
*The Incredible Tito,* Magazine House (New York City), 1944.
*Freedom Road,* Duell, Sloan & Pearce, 1944, new edition with foreword by W. E. B. DuBois, introduction by Eric Foner, M. E. Sharpe (Armonk, NY), 1995.
*Patrick Henry and the Frigate's Keel and Other Stories of a Young Nation,* Duell, Sloan & Pearce, 1945.
*The American: A Middle Western Legend,* Duell, Sloan & Pearce, 1946.
(With William Gropper) *Never Forget: The Story of the Warsaw Ghetto,* Book League of the Jewish Fraternal Order, 1946.
(Editor) Thomas Paine, *The Selected Works of Tom Paine,* Modern Library (New York City), 1946.
*The Children,* Duell, Sloan & Pearce, 1947.
(Editor) Theodore Dreiser, *Best Short Stories of TheodoreDreiser,* World Publishing, 1947.
*Clarkton,* Duell, Sloan & Pearce, 1947.
*Tito and His People,* Contemporary Publishers (Winnipeg, Canada), 1948.
*My Glorious Brothers,* Little, Brown (Boston), 1948, new edition, Hebrew Publications, 1977.

*Departure and Other Stories,* Little, Brown, 1949.

*Intellectuals in the Fight for Peace,* Masses & Mainstream (New York City), 1949.

*The Proud and the Free* (also see below), Little, Brown, 1950.

*Literature and Reality,* International Publishers (New York City), 1950.

*Spartacus* (also see below), Blue Heron (New York City), 1951, Citadel (Secaucus, NJ), 1952, reprinted with new introduction, North Castle Books (Armonk, NY), 1996.

*Peekskill, U.S.A.: A Personal Experience,* Civil Rights Congress (New York City), 1951.

*Tony and the Wonderful Door,* Blue Heron, 1952.

*The Passion of Sacco and Vanzetti: A New England Legend,* Blue Heron, 1953.

*Silas Timberman,* Blue Heron, 1954.

*The Last Supper, and Other Stories,* Blue Heron, 1955.

*The Story of Lola Gregg,* Blue Heron, 1956.

*The Naked God: The Writer and the Communist Party* (memoir), Praeger (New York City), 1957.

*Moses, Prince of Egypt,* Crown (New York City), 1958.

*The Winston Affair,* Crown, 1959.

*The Howard Fast Reader,* Crown, 1960.

*April Morning,* Crown, 1961.

*The Edge of Tomorrow* (stories), Bantam (New York City), 1961.

*Power,* Doubleday (New York City), 1962.

*Agrippa's Daughter,* Doubleday, 1964.

*Torquemada,* Doubleday, 1966.

*The Hunter and the Trap,* Dial, 1967.

*The Jews: Story of a People,* Dial, 1968.

*The General Zapped an Angel,* Morrow (New York City), 1970.

*The Crossing* (based on his play of the same title; also see below), Morrow, 1971, New Jersey Historical Society, 1985.

*The Hessian* (based on his screenplay of the same title; also see below), Morrow, 1972, reprinted with new foreword, North Castle Books (Armonk, NY), 1996.

*A Touch of Infinity: Thirteen Stories of Fantasy and Science Fiction,* Morrow, 1973.

*The Immigrants,* Houghton (Boston), 1977.

*The Art of Zen Meditation,* Peace Press (Culver City, CA), 1977.

*The Second Generation,* Houghton, 1978.

*The Establishment,* Houghton, 1979.

*The Legacy,* Houghton, 1980.

*The Magic Door* (juvenile), Avon (New York City), 1980.

*Time & the Riddle: Thirty-One Zen Stories,* Houghton, 1981.

*Max,* Houghton, 1982.

*The Outsider,* Houghton, 1984.

*The Immigrant's Daughter,* Houghton, 1985.

*The Dinner Party,* Houghton, 1987.

*The Call of Fife and Drum: Three Novels of the Revolution* (contains *The Unvanquished, Conceived in Liberty,* and *The Proud and the Free*), Citadel, 1987.

*The Pledge,* Houghton, 1988.

*The Confession of Joe Cullen,* Houghton, 1989.

*Being Red: A Memoir* (memoir), Houghton, 1990.

*The Trial of Abigail Goodman: A Novel,* Crown, 1993.

*War and Peace: Observations on Our Times,* M. E. Sharpe, 1993.

*Seven Days in June: A Novel of the American Revolution,* Carol (Secaucus, NJ), 1994.

*The Bridge Builder's Story,* M. E. Sharpe, 1995.

Author of weekly column, *New York Observer,* 1989-92; also columnist for *Greenwich Time* and *Stamford Advocate.*

*PLAYS*

*The Hammer,* produced in New York, 1950.

*Thirty Pieces of Silver* (produced in Melbourne, 1951), Blue Heron, 1954.

*George Washington and the Water Witch,* Bodley Head (London), 1956.

*The Crossing,* produced in Dallas, TX, 1962.

*The Hill* (screenplay), Doubleday, 1964.

*David and Paula,* produced in New York City at American Jewish Theater, November 20, 1982.

*Citizen Tom Paine: A Play in Two Acts* (produced in Washington, DC, at the John F. Kennedy Center for the Performing Arts, 1987), Houghton, 1986.

*The Novelist* (produced in Mamaroneck, NY, 1991), published as *The Novelist: A Romantic Portrait of Jane Austen,* Samuel French (New York City), 1992.

Also author of *The Hessian,* 1971, and teleplay, *What's a Nice Girl Like You. . .!,* based on his novel *Shirley.* Also wrote television episode for series *Benjamin Franklin,* 1975.

*UNDER PSEUDONYM E. V. CUNNINGHAM; NOVELS*

*Sylvia,* Doubleday, 1960, published under name Howard Fast, Carol, 1992.

*Phyllis,* Doubleday, 1962.

*Alice,* Doubleday, 1963.

*Shirley,* Doubleday, 1963.

*Lydia,* Doubleday, 1964.

*Penelope,* Doubleday, 1965.

*Helen,* Doubleday, 1966.

*Margie,* Morrow, 1966.

*Sally,* Morrow, 1967, published under name Howard Fast, Chivers, 1994.

*Samantha,* Morrow, 1967.

*Cynthia,* Morrow, 1968.

*The Assassin Who Gave Up His Gun,* Morrow, 1969.

*Millie,* Morrow, 1973.

*The Case of the One-Penny Orange,* Holt (New York City), 1977.

*The Case of the Russian Diplomat,* Holt, 1978.

*The Case of the Poisoned Eclairs,* Holt, 1979.

*The Case of the Sliding Pool,* Delacorte (New York City), 1981.

*The Case of the Kidnapped Angel,* Delacorte, 1982.

*The Case of the Angry Actress,* Delacorte, 1984.

*The Case of the Murdered Mackenzie,* Delacorte, 1984.

*The Wabash Factor,* Doubleday, 1986.

*UNDER PSEUDONYM WALTER ERICSON*

*Fallen Angel,* Little, Brown, 1951.

*ADAPTATIONS: Spartacus* was filmed in 1960 by Universal Pictures, directed by Stanley Kubrick (uncredited) and Anthony Mann, starring Kirk Douglas, Laurence Olivier, Tony Curtis, Jean Simmons, Charles Laughton, and Peter Ustinov; many of Fast's other works have been adapted to the screen, including *Man in the Middle,* based on his novel *The Winston Affair,* 1964, *Mirage,* based on a story he wrote under the pseudonym Walter Ericson, 1965, *Penelope,* based on his novel of the same title, 1966, *Jigsaw,* based on his novel *Fallen Angel,* 1968, and *Freedom Road,* based on his novel of the same title, 1980; *The Immigrants* was broadcast as a television miniseries in 1979; *April Morning* was adapted as a television program, 1988; *The Crossing* was recorded on cassette, narrated by Norman Dietz, Recorded Books, 1988; *The Immigrant's Daughter* was recorded on cassette, narrated by Sandra Burr, Brilliance Corporation, 1991.

*WORK IN PROGRESS:* An untitled novel, to be published by Harcourt Brace.

*SIDELIGHTS:* Howard Fast has published novels, plays, screenplays, stories, historical fiction, and biographies in a career that dates from the early days of the Great Depression. Fast's works have been translated into some eighty-two languages and have sold millions of copies worldwide; some observers feel that he may be the most widely read writer of the twentieth century. *Los Angeles Times* contributor Elaine Kendall writes: "For half a century, Fast's novels, histories and biographies have appeared at frequent intervals, a moveable feast with a distinct political flavor." *Washington Post* correspondent Joseph McLellan finds Fast's work "easy to read and relatively nourishing," adding that the author "demands little of the reader, beyond a willingness to keep turning the pages, and he supplies enough activity and suspense to make this exercise worthwhile."

In the *Dictionary of Literary Biography,* Anthony Manousos suggests that Fast's long and prolific career may be divided into three periods, reflecting crucial shifts in his political alignment. During his first decade as a novelist, Fast explored America's heritage of freedom, primarily from a liberal viewpoint. Toward the end of the Second World War, Fast became a member of the Communist Party, and his fiction through the mid-1950s dramatized mankind's struggle for a classless society. Eventually Fast renounced communism and began to create works with a more ambivalent political and religious view. Each period in Fast's career has yielded bestsellers—historical novels such as *Freedom Road* and *Citizen Tom Paine* are still in print, as is his historical novel *Spartacus.* "I've had a good long run," Fast tells *Publishers Weekly.* "I've survived, and there were times I never thought I would. And now, when I'm a bestseller again [with the 'Immigrants' series], my kids tell me, 'Dad, you've been recycled.'"

The grandson of Ukrainian immigrants and son of a British mother, Fast grew up in New York City. His family struggled to make ends meet, so Fast went to work as a teen and found time to indulge his passion—writing—in his spare moments. His first novel, *Two Valleys,* was published in 1933 when he was only eighteen. Thereafter Fast began writing full time, and within a decade he had earned a considerable reputation as a historical novelist with his realistic tales of American frontier life.

Fast found himself drawn to the downtrodden peoples in America's history—the Cheyenne Indians and their tragic attempt to regain their homeland (*The Last Frontier*), the starving soldiers at Valley Forge (*Conceived in Liberty: A Novel of Valley Forge*), and black Americans trying to survive the Reconstruction era in the South (*Freedom Road*). In *Publishers Weekly*, John F. Baker calls these works "books on which a whole generation of radicals was brought up." A *Christian Science Monitor* contributor likewise notes: "Human nature rather than history is Howard's Fast's field. In presenting these harassed human beings without any heroics he makes us all the more respectful of the price paid for American liberty." *Freedom Road* in particular was praised by the nation's black leaders for its depiction of one race's struggle for liberation; the book became a bestseller and won the Schomberg Award for Race Relations in 1944.

During the Second World War Fast worked as acorrespondent for several periodicals and for the Office of War Information. After the conflict ended he found himself at odds with the Cold War mentality developing in the United States. At the time Fast was a member of the Communist Party and a contributor of time and money to a number of antifascist causes. His writing during the period addressed such issues as the abuse of power, the suppression of labor unions, and communism as the basis for a utopian future. Works such as *Clarkton, My Glorious Brothers,* and *The Proud and the Free* were widely translated behind the Iron Curtain and earned Fast the International Peace Prize in 1954.

Baker notes that Fast's political views "made him for a time in the 1950s a pariah of the publishing world." The author was jailed for three months on a contempt of Congress charge for refusing to testify about his political activities. Worse, he found himself blacklisted to such an extent that no publishing house would accept his manuscripts. Fast's persecution seemed ironic to some observers, because in the historical and biographical novels he had already published—like *Conceived in Liberty: A Novel of Valley Forge* and *The Unvanquished*—as well as in his work for the Office of War Information, Fast emphasized the importance of freedom and illuminated the heroic acts that had built American society. He made the relatively unknown or forgotten history of the United States accessible to millions of Americans in books like *The Last Frontier,* and as a correspondent for the radio program that would become the Voice of America, he was entrusted with the job of assuring millions of foreigners of the country's greatness and benevolence during World War II. Yet even after Fast learned of Stalin's atrocities, which convinced him that he had been betrayed by the Communist Party and caused him to break his ties with it, he did not regret the decision he had made in 1944. His

experience as the target of political persecution evoked some of his best and most popular works. It also led Fast to establish his own publishing house, the Blue Heron Press.

Fast published *Spartacus* under the Blue Heron imprint in 1951. A fictional account of a slave revolt in ancient Rome, *Spartacus* became a bestseller after it was made into a feature film in 1960, starring Kirk Douglas, Sir Laurence Olivier, and Tony Curtis. By that time Fast had grown disenchanted with the Communist Party and had formally renounced his ties to it. In a discussion of Fast's fiction from 1944 through 1960, *Nation* correspondent Stanley Meisler contends that the "older writings must not be ignored. They document a unique political record, a depressing American waste. They describe a man who distorted his vision of America to fit a vision of communism, and then lost both."

Fast published five books chronicling the fictional Lavette family, beginning with *The Immigrants* in 1977. The saga ends in 1985's *The Immigrant's Daughter,* the story of Barbara Lavette, Dan Lavette's daughter, and her political aspirations. Denise Gess in the *New York Times Book Review* calls *The Immigrant's Daughter* "satisfying, old-fashioned story-telling" despite finding the novel occasionally "soap-operatic and uneven." Barbara Conaty, reviewing the novel in *Library Journal,* calls Fast a "smooth and assured writer." A reviewer for *Publishers Weekly* concurs, commenting that "[s]moothly written, fast-paced, alive with plots and subplots, the story reads easily."

"An old-fashioned Ibsenesque moral drama is what Howard Fast has undertaken in . . . *The Dinner Party,* about a wealthy liberal United States senator who is forced to confront his own limitations," comments the *New York Times*'s Christopher Lehmann-Haupt. *The Dinner Party* follows fictional senator Richard Cromwell on the day that he has planned a dinner party at his house in the country. During this time, Cromwell "reconnects with his wife, learns a tragic fact about his son and alters the direction of his career by standing up for his own needs and beliefs," summarizes a *Publishers Weekly* reviewer. James Idema, in Chicago *Tribune Books,* argues that in *The Dinner Party,* Fast is "more eloquent than ever in the cause of human rights and social justice." Although the critic finds that Fast's "soapbox has become too obvious," and that the dialogue is "less affecting" because of this, Idema concludes that "the predicaments [Fast's] characters must contend with nevertheless hold our attention." Lehmann-Haupt claims that Fast "succeeds . . . in dramatizing many of the major moral dilemmas of our age," and calls the novel "a powerful and absorbing drama."

The prolific Fast published another politically charged novel in 1989, with *The Confession of Joe Cullen.* Focussing on U.S. military involvement in Central America, *The Confession of Joe Cullen* is the story of a C.I.A. pilot who confesses to New York City police that, among other things, he murdered a priest in Honduras, and has been smuggling cocaine into the United States. Arguing that the conspiracy theory that implicates the federal government in drug trafficking and gun running has never been proved, Morton Kondracke in the *New York Times Book Review* has reservations about the "political propaganda" involved in *The Confession of Joe Cullen.* Robert H. Donahugh, however, highly recommends the novel in *Library Journal,* calling it "unexpected and welcome," and lauding both the "fast-moving" storyline and the philosophical probing into Catholicism. Denise Perry Donavin, in *Booklist,* concurs, finding the politics suiting the characters "without lessening the pace of a powerful tale."

Fast focuses on another controversial subject, the issue of abortion, in his 1993 novel *The Trial of Abigail Goodman.* As a *Publishers Weekly* critic notes, Fast views America's attitude toward abortion as "parochial" and is sympathetic to his protagonist, a college professor who has an abortion during the third trimester in a southern state with a retroactive law forbidding such acts. Critical reaction to the novel was mixed. Ray Olson in *Booklist* argues that "every anti-abortion character" is stereotyped, and that Fast "undermines . . . any pretensions to even-handedness," calling the novel "an execrable work." The *Publishers Weekly* critic, on the other hand, finds *The Trial of Abigail Goodman* "electrifying" and calls Fast "a master of courtroom pyrotechnics." Many critics, including Susan Dooley in the *Washington Post,* view the novel as too polemical, failing to flesh out the characters and the story. Dooley argues that Fast "has not really written a novel; his book is a tract for a cause, and like other similar endeavors, it concentrates more on making converts than creating characters." A reviewer for *Armchair Detective* concurs, concluding that the novel would have been much stronger if "there were some real sincerity and some well-expressed arguments from the antagonists." A *Rapport* reviewer agrees, and comments: "Fast is more than capable of compelling character studies. There's a kernel of a powerful trial

novel here, but this prestigious writer chooses not to flesh it out."

Fast returned to the topic of the American Revolution in his 1994 novel *Seven Days in June: A Novel of the American Revolution.* A *Publishers Weekly* critic summarizes: "Fictionalizing the experiences of British commanders, loyalists to the crown and a motley collection of American revolutionaries, Fast . . . fashions this dramatic look at a week of profound tension that will erupt [into] the battle of Bunker Hill." Some critics see *Seven Days in June* as inferior to Fast's *April Morning,* considered by some to be a minor masterpiece. Charles Michaud in *Library Journal* finds that *Seven Days* "is very readable pop history, but as a novel it is not as involving as . . . *April Morning.*" A *Kirkus Reviews* critic faults the novel for repetitiveness and a disproportionate amount of focus on the sexual exploits of the British commanders, concluding that *Seven Days* "has a slipshod, slapdash feel, cluttered with hurried, lazy characterizations." The critic for *Publishers Weekly,* however, argues that the novel "ekes genuine suspense" and lauds Fast's "accomplished storytelling."

Fast's time as a Communist in Cold War America provided him with an extraordinary story to share in his autobiographical works, including *Being Red: A Memoir.* Charles C. Nash of *Library Journal* calls *Being Red* "indispensable to the . . . literature on America's terrifying postwar Red Scare." Fast explains to Jean W. Ross in a *Contemporary Authors* interview: "There is no way to imagine war or to imagine jail or to imagine being a father or a mother. These things can only be understood if you live through them. Maybe that's a price that a writer should pay." Fast tells Ken Gross in *People Weekly* that he wrote the book with the inspiration of his son, Jonathan, who wanted to show it to his own children. Rhoda Koenig of *New York* magazine remarks that Fast's story is "a lively and gripping one," and that he "brings alive the days of parochial-school children carrying signs that read KILL A COMMIE FOR CHRIST."

With a critical eye, Ronald Radosh asserts in *Commentary* that *Being Red* contains information and perspectives that contradict portions of Fast's 1957 memoir, *The Naked God: The Writer and the Communist Party.* In Radosh's opinion, *Being Red* was the author's attempt to "rehabilitate" the Communist Party he had admonished in *The Naked God.* "Now, nearly thirty-five years later, it almost sounds as though Fast wants to end his days winning back the admiration of those unreconstructed Communists," Radosh claims, even calling them "some of the noblest human beings I have ever known." Clancy Sigal in the *Chicago Tribune* describes *Being Red* as "by turns, warm, cozy, angry and informative (if not always informed)," but faults Fast for not having "a sense of humor about anything having to do with himself." Christopher Hitchens in the *Washington Post Book World* argues that *Being Red* reveals Fast as different from the ex-Communist stereotype: "[Fast] left the Communist Party for the same reason that he joined it—which is to say he left it because he was interested in social justice and historical truth." Hitchens describes the narrative as "rambling first-person stream of consciousness," and claims that whether you "[l]ove [Fast] or hate him, it's very difficult to read him."

Quoted by Alvin Klein in the *New York Times,* Fast describes his passion for playwriting: "The novel is like my wife, and that has paid for my existence on this earth. . . . And the theater is my mistress." Fast's 1991 play *The Novelist,* the fictional love story of Jane Austen and Captain Thomas Crighton, a member of the Royal Navy, ran Off-Broadway at the Theatre Row Theatre. John Beaufort in the *Christian Science Monitor* argues that the "casual playgoer may well find *The Novelist* a slight but charming piece of romantic hypothesis." Stephen Holden in the *New York Times* calls *The Novelist* "a well-written if sentimental portrait of Austen by a playwright who is unabashedly enamored of his subject."

Fast has also published a number of detective novels under the pseudonym E. V. Cunningham, for which he received a Prix de la Policia Award. Many of these feature a fictional Japanese-American detective named Masao Masuto who works with the Beverly Hills Police Department. Fast tells *Publishers Weekly:* "Critics can't stand my mainline books, maybe because they sell so well, [but] they love Cunningham. Even the *New Yorker* has reviewed him, and they've never reviewed me." In the *New York Times Book Review,* Newgate Callendar calls detective Masuto "a well-conceived character whose further exploits should gain him a wide audience." Toronto *Globe and Mail* contributor Derrick Murdoch also finds Masuto "a welcome addition to the lighter side of crime fiction." "Functional and efficient, Fast's prose is a machine in which plot and ideals mesh, turn and clash," Kendall concludes. "The reader is constantly being instructed, but the manner is so disarming and the hectic activity so absorbing that the didacticism seldom intrudes upon the entertainment."

Fast's voice has interpreted America's past and present and helped shape its reputation at home and abroad. One of his own favorites among his novels, *April Morning,* has been standard reading about the American Revolution in public schools for generations, the film *Spartacus* has become a popular classic, and *Being Red* offers an account of American history that Americans may never want to forget, whether or not they agree with Fast's perspectives. As Victor Howes comments in *Christian Science Monitor,* if Howard Fast "is a chronicler of some of mankind's most glorious moments, he is also a register of some of our more senseless deeds."

*BIOGRAPHICAL/CRITICAL SOURCES:*

*BOOKS*

*Contemporary Authors Autobiography Series,* Volume 18, Gale (Detroit), 1994.
*Contemporary Literary Criticism,* Volume 23, Gale, 1983.
*Dictionary of Literary Biography,* Volume 9: *American Novelists, 1910-1945,* Gale, 1981.
Macdonald, Andrew, *Howard Fast: A Critical Companion,* Greenwood Press (Westport, CT), 1996.
Meyer, Hershel D., *History and Conscience: The Case of Howard Fast,* Anvil-Atlas, 1958.
Newquist, Roy, *Counterpoint,* Rand McNally (Chicago), 1964.
Rideout, Walter B., *The Radical Novel in the United States: Some Interrelations of Literature and Society,* Harvard University Press (Cambridge, MA), 1956.

*PERIODICALS*

*Armchair Detective,* spring, 1994, p. 218.
*Atlantic,* September, 1944; June, 1970.
*Best Sellers,* February 1, 1971; September 1, 1973; January, 1979; November, 1979.
*Booklist,* June 15, 1989, p. 1739; July, 1993, p. 1916.
*Books,* September 23, 1934; June 25, 1939.
*Book Week,* May 9, 1943.
*Catholic World,* September, 1953.
*Chicago Tribune,* February 8, 1987, pp. 6-7; April 21, 1987; January 20, 1991, section 14, p. 7.
*Christian Science Monitor,* July 8, 1939; August 23, 1972, p. 11; November 7, 1977, p. 18; November 1, 1991, p. 12.

*Commentary,* March, 1991, pp. 62-64.

*Detroit News,* October 31, 1982.

*Globe and Mail* (Toronto), September 15, 1984; March 1, 1986.

*Kirkus Reviews,* June 15, 1994, p. 793.

*Library Journal,* November 15, 1978; September 15, 1985, p. 92; May 15, 1989, p. 88; October 1, 1990, p. 96; August, 1991, p. 162; July, 1994, p. 126.

*Los Angeles Times,* November 11, 1982; November 11, 1985; November 21, 1988.

*Los Angeles Times Book Review,* December 9, 1990.

*Masses & Mainstream,* December, 1950.

*Nation,* April 5, 1952; May 30, 1959.

*New Republic,* August 17, 1942, p. 203; August 14, 1944; November 4, 1978.

*New Statesman,* August 8, 1959.

*New York,* November 5, 1990, pp. 124-25.

*New Yorker,* July 1, 1939; May 1, 1943.

*New York Herald Tribune Book Review,* July 21, 1963.

*New York Herald Tribune Books,* July 27, 1941, p. 3.

*New York Times,* October 15, 1933; June 25, 1939; April 25, 1943; February 3, 1952; September 24, 1984; February 9, 1987, p. C16; March 10, 1987; April 21, 1991, pp. 20-21; October 23, 1991, p. C19; November 19, 1993, p. A2.

*New York Times Book Review,* October 13, 1933; April 25, 1943; February 3, 1952; March 4, 1962; July 14, 1963; February 6, 1966; October 2, 1977, p. 24; October 30, 1977; May 14,1978; June 10, 1979; September 15, 1985, p. 24; March 29, 1987, p. 22; August 20, 1989, p. 23.

*People,* January 28, 1991, pp. 75-79.

*Publishers Weekly,* August 6, 1979; April 1, 1983; July 19, 1985, p. 48; November 28, 1986, p. 66; July 22, 1988, p. 41; June 30, 1989, p. 84; June 21, 1993, p. 83; July 11, 1994, p. 66.

*Rapport,* Volume 18, number 1, 1994, p. 38.

*Saturday Review,* March 8, 1952; January 22, 1966; September 17, 1977.

*Saturday Review of Literature,* July 1, 1939; July 26, 1941, p. 5; May 1, 1943; December 24, 1949.

*Spectator,* August 15, 1958; April 3, 1959; May 30, 1959.

*Springfield Republican,* November 5, 1933.

*Time,* November 6, 1977.

*Times Literary Supplement,* November 11, 1939.

*Tribune Books* (Chicago), February 8, 1987, p. 6.

*Washington Post,* October 4, 1979; September 26, 1981; September 25, 1982; September 3, 1985; February 9, 1987; March 3, 1987; September 6, 1993, p. C2.

*Washington Post Book World,* October 23, 1988; November 25, 1990.

*Weekly Book Review,* April 25, 1943.

*Yale Review,* September, 1941.


\*   \*   \*


**FEILEN, John**
   **See MAY, Julian**


\*   \*   \*


**FERLITA, Ernest (Charles)   1927-**

*PERSONAL:* Born December 1, 1927, in Tampa, FL; son of Giuseppe R. (a macaroni manufacturer) and Vincenta (Ficarrotta) Ferlita. *Education:* Spring Hill College, B.S., 1950; St. Louis University, S.T.L., 1964; Yale University, D.F.A., 1969.

*ADDRESSES: Home and office*—Department of Drama and Speech, Loyola University, New Orleans, LA 70118.

*CAREER:* Entered Order of Society of Jesus (Jesuits), 1950, ordained Roman Catholic priest, 1962; high school teacher in New Orleans, LA, 1956-59; Spring Hill College, Mobile, AL, instructor in English and speech, 1964-65; Loyola University, New Orleans, LA, professor of drama, 1969—, chair of department of drama and speech, 1970-88. Fulbright traveling scholar to Brazil, 1980. Member of board of directors, Loyola University, 1970-75, 1984-88, chair of board, 1972-75. *Military service:* U.S. Army, Medical Corps, 1946-47.

*AWARDS, HONORS:* American Radio Theatre Award, 1985, for *The City of Seven Rivers;* Miller Drama Award, 1986, for *The Truth of the Matter.*

*WRITINGS:*

*The Ballad of John Ogilvie* (three-act play), first produced Off-Broadway at Blackfriars' Theatre, October 9, 1968.

*The Theatre of Pilgrimage,* Sheed & Ward (Kansas City, MO), 1971.

(With John R. May) *Film Odyssey,* Paulist/Newman, 1976.

(With May) *The Parables of Lina Wertmuller,* Paulist/Newman, 1977.

*The Way of the River,* Paulist/Newman, 1977.

*Black Medea,* first produced in New York City at New Federal Theatre, 1978.

*The Obelisk,* first produced in New York City at Fordham College at Lincoln Center, 1982.

(With May and others) *Religion in Film,* University of Tennessee (Knoxville), 1983.

*Gospel Journey,* Winston Press (Minneapolis, MN), 1983.

*The City of the Seven Rivers* (play), American Radio Theatre, 1986.

*The Uttermost Mark,* University Press of America (Lanham, MD), 1989.

*The Paths of Life,* Alba House (Staten Island, NY), *Cycle A,* 1992, *Cycle B,* 1993, *Cycle C,* 1994.

Also author of *The Mask of Hiroshima.* Contributor to *Best Short Plays of 1989,* Applause Theatre Books (New York City), 1989.

*SIDELIGHTS:* Ernest Ferlita told *CA,* "Every scribe trained for the truth 'brings out of his treasure what is new and what is old' (Matthew 13:51). I like to think that I'm such a scribe when I tell an old story in another time and place, always with the hope that the truth will appear and be seen afresh."

\*     \*     \*

**FILOSA, Gary Fairmont Randolph de Marco II
1931-**

*PERSONAL:* Born February 22, 1931, in Wilder, VT; son of Gary F. R. de Viana (a publisher) and Roseline (a columnist; maiden name, Falzarano) Filosa; married Catherine Moray Stewart, December 21, 1963; children: Marc Christian Bazire de Villodon III, Gary Fairmont Randolph de Viana III. *Education:* University of Chicago, Ph.B., 1954; University of the Americas, B.A., 1967; California Western University, M.A., 1968; U.S. International University, Ph.D., 1970. *Politics:* Republican. *Religion:* Episcopal.

*ADDRESSES: Home*—Box 1207, Iowa City, IA 52244-1207. *Office*—Box 299, Beverly Hills, CA 90213-0299. *Agent*—Shirley Burke, 370 East 76th St., New York, NY 10021.

*CAREER:* Sports reporter for *Claremont Daily Eagle,* Claremont, NH, *Rutland Herald,* Rutland, VT, and *Vermont Informer,* White River Junction, VT, all 1946-50; *Clay Pipe News,* Chicago, IL, editor, 1953-54; Fuller, Smith & Ross, New York City, copywriter, 1954-55; *Esquire,* New York City, associate editor, 1955-56; *Teenage,* New York City, editor, 1957-61; *Science Digest,* New York City, associate editor, 1961-62; American Association of Social Directories, Los Angeles, CA, editor and publisher, 1969-75. Associate editor of *Apparel Arts,* 1955-56; editor of *Teen Life, Teenage,* and *Rock and Roll Roundup,* 1957-61. President of U.S. Surfing Foundation. *Military service:* U.S. Army, 1954-55.

*MEMBER:* International Surfing Committee (president), United States Surfing Committee (president), Authors Guild, Authors League of America, Sierra Club, Chapultapec Club (Mexico City), Embajadores (Puebla, Mexico), Los Angeles Athletic Club, Town Hall Club, Commonwealth Club, Kona Kai Club.

*WRITINGS:*

*Technology Enters the Twenty-First Century,* Columbia University Press (New York City), 1966.

*No Public Funds for Nonpublic Schools,* privately printed, 1968.

*Creative Function of the College President,* University of Michigan Press (Ann Arbor), 1969.

*Feather Light* (musical drama; music composed by Peter Duchin), first produced in London at Devonshire Theatre, January, 1969.

*The Surfers Almanac,* Dutton (New York City), 1977.

Author of *Let Me Call Ethel* (stage play), 1955; *Creative Function of the College President,* 1969; *Surfing U.S.A.* (television series), 1977; *The Olympic Almanac* (a quadrennial publication), 1978; *Bibliotherapy,* 1980; *Duke Paoa Kahanamoku* (screenplay), 1982; *Payne of Florida,* 1985; *Honolulu,* 1991; *The Gym,* 1992; *Sales Pitch,* 1992; *810 Ocean Avenue,* 1992; *One Father,* 1992; and *Holy Hawaii* (first part of trilogy on the history of Polynesian peoples), 1996. Also author of newsletters, *The Filosa Newsletter,* 1986-92, *Conversations with America,* 1989—, and *All American Beach Party,* 1989—. Contributor of numerous articles to professional journals and encyclopedias.

*WORK IN PROGRESS: God's Own Prince* and *A Plague on Paradise,* the second and third parts of a trilogy on the history of Polynesian peoples.

*SIDELIGHTS:* Gary Fairmont Randolph de Marco Filosa II's ancestors came to Mexico with Cortes and to Californiawith De Anza in 1776. He speaks Spanish, Italian, and French. Filosa told *CA:* "I devoted all my extracurricular time to the worldwide effort to make our oldest American sport, surfing, an Olympic event, which took place 5 June 1995. Now we are working to 're-amateurize' the Olympic Games."

\* \* \*

## FLANAGAN, Mary    1943-

*PERSONAL:* Born May 20, 1943, in Rochester, NH; immigrated to England, 1969; daughter of Martin James (a housing director) and Mary (a secretary; maiden name, Nesbitt) Flanagan. *Education:* Brandeis University, B.A., 1965. *Politics:* Socialist. *Religion:* Roman Catholic. *Avocational interests:* Gardening, playing the piano, environmental activism.

*ADDRESSES: Home*—London, England. *Office*—c/o Bloomsbury Publishing, 2 Soho Sq., London W1, England.

*CAREER:* Writer.

*MEMBER:* PEN, Authors Guild, Society of Authors (UK).

*WRITINGS:*

*Bad Girls* (stories), edited by Liz Calder, J. Cape (London), 1984, Atheneum (New York City), 1985.
*Trust* (novel), Bloomsbury Publishing (London), 1987, Atheneum, 1988.
*Rose Reason* (novel), Bloomsbury Publishing, 1991, Harcourt (New York City), 1992.
*The Blue Woman* (stories), Bloomsbury Publishing, 1994, Norton (New York City), 1995.

Author of introductions to books, including Kate O'Brien, *The Land of Spices,* Virago (London), 1988, and Edith Wharton, *Ethan Frome,* Virago, 1991. Work represented in several short story anthologies. Contributor to literary magazines, newspapers and radio.

*WORK IN PROGRESS:* A novel, *Adele,* publication by Bloomsbury Publishing expected in 1996.

*SIDELIGHTS:* Mary Flanagan, who was born in the United States to Irish parents, settled in England after spending a year in Morocco between 1968 and 1969. Her first book, *Bad Girls,* is a collection of short stories chronicling the morally"bad" behavior of a number of young and old women victimized by their own illusions. Assessing the work as an "impressive debut," Roz Kaveney in the *Times Literary Supplement* commented that "Flanagan writes well of the delicate balances by which friendship is constructed and maintained."

In her first novel, *Trust,* Flanagan examines both the elusive nature of and the quest for trust. Reviewing the book for the London *Times,* Chris Peachment compared this "excellent" debut to the works of novelists Henry James and sisters Charlotte, Emily, and Anne Bronte. In Kaveney's opinion, *Trust* brings to mind the fiction of Iris Murdoch, featuring "a world of high sensibility, profitable artistic taste, private incomes and . . . interlockings of familial and sexual intrigue." It is a "moral tale," wrote the reviewer, "in which solidarity between the more or less virtuous makes it possible for them to capture . . . some moments of pleasure in a world in which the selfish and unreliable usually make the running."

Flanagan told *CA:* "I write about people in extremes who are forced to satisfy the demands of both instinct and conscience. What interests me is the resultant play of conflicting elements in a character's nature, such as desire opposing ethics, the child and the beast straining against their social conditioning."

*BIOGRAPHICAL/CRITICAL SOURCES:*

*PERIODICALS*

*Booklist,* September 1, 1992, p. 31.
*Independent,* April 2, 1987.
*Irish Times,* April 8, 1987.
*Kirkus Reviews,* July 1, 1992, p. 799.
*Library Journal,* August, 1992, p. 148.
*Observer* (London), June 26, 1994, p. 19; July 10, 1994, p. 15.
*Publishers Weekly,* July 6, 1992, p. 37.
*Punch,* April 15, 1987.
*Times* (London), April 2, 1987.
*Times Literary Supplement,* November 9, 1984; April 3, 1987; July 1, 1994, p. 21.

**FOLLETT, Ken(neth Martin) 1949-**
  (Martin Martinsen, Symon Myles, Bernard L.
  Ross, Zachary Stone, pseudonyms)

*PERSONAL:* Born June 5, 1949, in Cardiff, Wales;
son of Martin D. (a tax inspector) and Lavinia C.
(Evans) Follett; married Mary Emma Ruth Elson,
January 5, 1968 (divorced September 20, 1985);
married Barbara Broer, November 8, 1985; children
(first marriage): Emanuele, Marie-Claire. *Education:*
University College, London, B A., 1970. *Religion:*
Atheist. *Avocational interests:* Music.

*ADDRESSES: Home*—P.O. Box 708, London SW10
ODH, England. *Agent*—Writers House, Inc., 21
West 26th St., New York, NY 10010.

*CAREER:* Trainee journalist and rock music columnist at *South Wales Echo,* 1970-73; *Evening News,*
London, England, reporter, 1973-74; Everest Books
Ltd., London, editorial director, 1974-76, deputy
managing director, 1976-77; full-time writer, 1977—.

*AWARDS, HONORS:* Edgar Award, Mystery Writers
of America, 1978, for *Eye of the Needle.*

*WRITINGS:*

NOVELS

*The Shakeout,* Harwood-Smart, 1975.
*The Bear Raid,* Harwood-Smart, 1976.
*The Secret of Kellerman's Studio* (juvenile), Abelard,
  1976.
*Eye of the Needle* (Literary Guild selection), Arbor
  House (New York City), 1978 (published in
  England as *Storm Island,* Macdonald & Jane's,
  1978).
*Triple,* Arbor House, 1979.
*The Key to Rebecca,* Morrow (New York City),
  1980.
*The Man from St. Petersburg,* Morrow, 1982.
*Lie Down with Lions,* Hamilton (London), 1985,
  Morrow, 1986.
*The Pillars of the Earth* (also see below), Morrow,
  1989.
*Mystery Hideout* (juvenile; illustrated by Stephen
  Marchesi), Morrow, 1990.
*Night over Water,* Morrow, 1991.
*A Dangerous Fortune,* Delacorte (New York City),
  1993.
*Pillars of the Almighty* (selections of text from *Pil-
  lars of the Earth*), Morrow, 1994.

*A Place Called Freedom,* Crown (New York City),
  1995.
*The Third Twin,* Crown, 1996.

NONFICTION

(With Rene Louis Maurice) *The Heist of the Century,*
  Fontana Books (London), 1978, published as *The
  Gentlemen of 16 July,* Arbor House, 1980, re-
  vised edition published as *Under the Streets of
  Nice: The Bank Heist of the Century,* National
  Press Books, 1986.
*On Wings of Eagles,* Morrow, 1983.

UNDER PSEUDONYM MARTIN MARTINSEN

*The Power Twins and the Worm Puzzle: A Science
  Fantasy for Young People,* Abelard, 1976, pub-
  lished under name Ken Follett as *Power Twins,*
  Scholastic, 1991.

UNDER PSEUDONYM SYMON MYLES

*The Big Needle,* Everest Books (London), 1974,
  published as *The Big Apple,* Kensington (San
  Diego, CA), 1975, published under name Ken
  Follett, Zebra, 1986.
*The Big Black,* Everest Books, 1974.
*The Big Hit,* Everest Books, 1975.

UNDER PSEUDONYM BERNARD L. ROSS

*Amok: King of Legend,* Futura (London), 1976.
*Capricorn One,* Futura, 1978.

UNDER PSEUDONYM ZACHARY STONE

*The Modigliani Scandal,* Collins (London), 1976,
  published under name Ken Follett, Morrow,
  1985.
*Paper Money,* Collins, 1977, published under name
  Ken Follett, Morrow, 1987.

SOUND RECORDINGS

(With Rene L. Maurice) *Under the Streets of Nice,*
  Dove Audio (Beverly Hills, CA), 1991.

OTHER

Also author of film scripts *Fringe Banking,* for British Broadcasting Corp., 1978, *A Football Star,* with
John Sealey, 1979, and *Lie Down with Lions,* for

Scott Reeve Enterprises, 1988. Contributor to *New Statesman* and *Writer*.

*ADAPTATIONS: Eye of the Needle* was adapted for the screen by Stanley Mann. The 1981 United Artists film was directed by Richard Marquand and starred Donald Sutherland and Kate Nelligan. *The Key to Rebecca* was filmed as an Operation Prime Time television miniseries in April, 1985; *On Wings of Eagles* was filmed by Edgar Schenick Productions and broadcast as a television miniseries in 1985.

*SIDELIGHTS:* Ken Follett has blended historical event and action-adventure fiction in a series of best-selling novels, including *Eye of the Needle, Triple, Lie Down with Lions,* and *The Pillars of the Earth.* Follett's work has proven immensely successful in the United States, making the native of Wales one of the world's youngest millionaire authors. Follett penned his first bestseller before he turned thirty, and each of his subsequent novels has made a debut with a massive first printing and vast publicity. *Washington Post* correspondent Paul Hendrickson claims that Follett has earned a reputation as an "international thriller writer with a genius for threading the eye of the literary needle."

"I was a great liver in fantasy worlds from an early age," Follett told the *Washington Post.* The son of an internal revenue clerk, Follett grew up in Cardiff, Wales and attended the University of London. After graduating with a degree in philosophy in 1970, he worked as a newspaper reporter, first in Cardiff and then in London. He began writing fiction on the side when he needed extra money for car repairs. "It was a hobby for me," he told the *Chicago Tribune.* "You know, some men go home and grow vegetables. I used to go home and write novels. A lucrative hobby. I sold them for far more than you could sell vegetables for."

Follett's early works were published under various pseudonyms. Most of these novels are murder mysteries or crime fiction, based loosely on cases he covered as a reporter for the London *Evening News.* The author admitted in the *Los Angeles Times* that he learned how to write good books "by writing mediocre ones and wondering what was wrong with them." In order to further his knowledge of the book business, Follett joined the staff of Everest Books in 1974. Remembering his decision to move to the publishing house, Follett told the *Chicago Tribune:* "A good deal of it was curiosity to know what made books sell. Some books sell and others don't. All the

books I had written up to that point fell into the category of those that did not."

Follett began to use his own name on his work in 1975, when he turned to spy fiction. Within three years his dream of writing a bestseller had been fulfilled with the publication of *Eye of the Needle,* a World War II thriller about a ruthless Nazi spy and a crippled pilot's wife. In the *Washington Post Book World,* Roderick MacLeish calls *Eye of the Needle* "quite simply the best spy novel to come out of England in years," and *Newsweek* correspondent Peter Prescott describes the work as "rubbish of the very best sort . . . a triumph of invention over convention." *Eye of the Needle,* which won the Edgar Allan Poe Award from the Mystery Writers of America, has since sold more than ten million copies worldwide.

With *Eye of the Needle* Follett established himself as a new sort of thriller writer—one who found a compromise between the serious and the popular. Follett's works have been cited for their special sensitivity to female characters as well as for an overall psychological complexity not often found in adventure stories. As Andrew F. Macdonald and Gina Macdonald note in the *Dictionary of Literary Biography,* a positive feature of Follett's novels "is his humanizing of his villains. All are well rounded and complete, with credible motives and understandable passions—if anything, they are sometimes so sympathetic that they jeopardize the reader's relationship with the hero." In another *Dictionary of Literary Biography* entry, Michael Adams contends that the author's heroines "are realistically portrayed women who have led fairly ordinary lives but who are capable of heroics when needed." By creating such sympathetic heroines, Follett has been able to lure female readers to novels that traditionally appeal primarily to men.

Follett's forte—in fiction and nonfiction—is the variation upon history. Every human relationship is somehow blighted or molded by the complexities of world politics, and all the emotional and sexual entanglements are played out against a backdrop of historical events. Andrew and Gina Macdonald write: "Each of [Follett's] best works grows out of news stories and historical events. Cinematic in conception, they follow a hunter-hunted pattern that leads to exciting chase scenes and games of wit and brinkmanship." Several of Follett's books confront the complex issues of Middle Eastern politics, and his novel *Lie Down with Lions* offers an ambiguous portrait of the factional strife in Afghanistan. *Time* contributor Michael Demarest claims that the author's strength remains "an acute sense of geographical place, and the age-old knowledge that character is action. . . . He brilliantly reproduces a distant terrain, complete with sounds and smells and tribal rites."

Adams relates some of the reasons for Follett's extraordinary success as a novelist, explaining that in his "exciting, intelligent, generally well-written . . . thrillers, not only are the major characters well developed, but the minor characters are given attention as well. The reader is always able to understand all the characters' political, social, economic, and sexual motives. Follett makes certain that even his villains have sympathetic sides. . . . He also reveals a thorough understanding not only of the history and techniques of espionage but of the intertwining complexities of twentieth-century world politics. Equally important is the skill of his plotting. While spy fiction is frequently complex and bewildering to the reader, Follett's work is consistently clear and easy to follow."

In 1989 Follett made a break with thriller fiction. Since then he has written three massive historical novels, *The Pillars of the Earth, A Dangerous Fortune,* and *A Place Called Freedom. The Pillars of the Earth,* set in twelfth-century England, recounts the four-decades-long construction of a cathedral and the efforts of Prior Philip and his master mason Tom Builder to complete the building and keep it from falling into the hands of a rival bishop. Critical reaction to that novel was mixed, perhaps because it was such an unexpected departure for Follett. Gary Jennings in the *Washington Post Book World,* for example, finds that "the legions of fanciers of Ken Follett's spy novels will likely be dismayed by his having turned now to historical fiction." On the other hand, Margaret Flanagan of *Booklist* calls *The Pillars of the Earth* "a towering triumph of romance, rivalry, and spectacle from a major talent." And Margaret Cannon of the Toronto *Globe and Mail,* while acknowledging the book's tendency toward overwriting, admits that "the period is so good and the cathedrals so marvelous that one keeps reading anyway."

The historical novel genre has proved compatible with Follett's skills. His subsequent works *A Dangerous Fortune* and *A Place Called Freedom* both weave complicated stories of intrigue in England and the Americas. In *A Dangerous Fortune,* an English

schoolboy's drowning sets off a chain of events that lead to national crisis as rival bankers seek to undermine each others' positions. "*A Dangerous Fortune* leaves us feeling as though we've visited an age very different from our own, and understand it far better than we did," writes a *Rapport* correspondent. "Follett's . . . tour through privileged Victorian society . . . won't be easily forgotten." In the *Los Angeles Times Book Review,* Thomas Hines cites *A Dangerous Fortune* for its "eye for the telling historical detail and a fair sense that people from the past weren't like us—and that's precisely what makes them so interesting." *A Place Called Freedom* tells the story of Malachi McAsh, a Scottish miner who rebels against his lifetime of servitude to the brutal local laird. McAsh's quest for freedom leads him to trouble in London and indentured servitude in America at a time when the very ideals of human liberty are being debated therein. *Publishers Weekly* reviewer Sybil S. Steinberg notes that in the novel, Follett "adroitly escalates the suspense by mixing intrigue and danger, tinged with ironic complications." The critic concludes that *A Place Called Freedom* is redeemed "by Follett's vigorous narrative drive and keen eye for character."

Between these various historical sagas, Follett completed yet another thriller, *Night over Water.* Set in the last dark days of 1939, the novel recounts the last transatlantic voyage of the opulent Pan American Clipper, its passengers all bent upon various deadly intrigues. According to *Spectator* reviewer Christopher Hawtree, *Night over Water* "marks a return to World War Two and top form" for Follett. Hawtree adds that the novel provides "a smoothly-controlled bumpy landing. There is no reverse-thrust to this narrative which sedulously leads one into the dark and all that is revealed therein."

Unlike many of his contemporaries, Follett positively relishes the label "popular writer." He told the *Dictionary of Literary Biography:* "I'm not under the illusion that the world is waiting for my thoughts to appear in print. People want to be told a story, and that's what I'm up to. I think of myself as a craftsman more than an artist." Although he likes to read such noted English writers as Thomas Hardy, Jane Austen, and George Eliot, Follett remains satisfied with his own aims and accomplishments. "What I enjoy," he told the *Chicago Tribune,* "is writing a book and then having *millions* of people read it and love it. I wouldn't want to write something that ten people loved; so I'm constrained by what I think are the preferences of my readers. If I'm careful, I'll take them along with me."

*BIOGRAPHICAL/CRITICAL SOURCES:*

*BOOKS*

*Authors and Artists for Young Adults,* Volume 6, Gale (Detroit, MI), 1991.
*Bestsellers 89,* Issue 4, Gale, 1990.
*Contemporary Literary Criticism,* Volume 18, Gale, 1981.
*Dictionary of Literary Biography,* Volume 87: *British Mystery and Thriller Writers since 1940,* first series, Gale, 1989.
*Dictionary of Literary Biography Yearbook: 1981,* Gale, 1982.
Turner, Richard Charles, *Ken Follett: A Critical Companion,* Greenwood Press, 1996.
*Twentieth-Century Crime and Mystery Writers,* third edition, St. James Press (Detroit, MI), 1991.

*PERIODICALS*

*Booklist,* June 15, 1989.
*Chicago Tribune,* October 14, 1983; October 25, 1987; September 10, 1989.
*Chicago Tribune Books,* August 30, 1992, p. 8.
*Chicago Tribune Book World,* October 5, 1980.
*Detroit Free Press,* September 10, 1989.
*Globe and Mail* (Toronto), September 2, 1989.
*Library Journal,* July 1989.
*London Review of Books,* August 19, 1982, p. 18.
*Los Angeles Times,* October 1, 1980; June 3, 1990.
*Los Angeles Times Book Review,* October 7, 1979; September 28, 1980; May 30, 1982; September 11, 1983; February 16, 1986; October 4, 1987, p. 6; December 12, 1993, p. 8.
*Nation,* April 26, 1980, p. 504-505.
*New Statesman,* April 10, 1987.
*Newsweek,* August 7, 1978; September 29, 1980.
*New Yorker,* August 21, 1978; August 16, 1982.
*New York Times,* May 12, 1978; October 3, 1979.
*New York Times Book Review,* July 16, 1978; September 21, 1980; May 9, 1982; October 23, 1983, pp. 20, 22; January 26, 1986; September 10, 1989; September 29, 1991, p. 22; January 9, 1994, p. 19.
*People,* September 25, 1978.
*Publishers Weekly,* January 17, 1986; June 30, 1989; July 21, 1989; April 13, 1990, p. 66; July 19, 1991, p. 44-45; June 5, 1995, p. 48-49.
*Rapport,* January 1994, p. 21.
*Saturday Review,* August 1978.
*Spectator,* November 16, 1991, p. 46.
*Time,* October 30, 1978; November 5, 1979; September 29, 1980; May 3, 1982.
*Times Literary Supplement,* December 26, 1980; June 4, 1982.
*Tribune Books,* September 10, 1989, p. 7.
*Washington Post,* October 11, 1979; September 15, 1980; September 7, 1983; September 21, 1983; June 1, 1985.
*Washington Post Book World,* April 25, 1982; February 2, 1986, p. 9; August 20, 1989; November 21, 1993, p. 4.
*Writer,* June 1979.*

—*Sketch by Anne Janette Johnson*

\* \* \*

**FOX, Connie**
**See FOX, Hugh (Bernard, Jr.)**

\* \* \*

**FOX, Hugh (Bernard, Jr.)    1932-**
**(Connie Fox)**

*PERSONAL:* Born February 12, 1932, in Chicago, IL; son of Hugh Bernard (a physician) and Helen M. (Mangan) Fox; married Lucia Alicia Ungaro (a Peruvian poet and critic), June 9, 1957 (divorced, 1969); married Nona W. Werner (a professor and writer), June, 1970; children: (first marriage) Hugh Bernard III, Cecilia, Marcella; (second marriage) Margaret, Alexandra, Christopher. *Education:* Loyola University, Chicago, B.A., 1954, M.A., 1955; University of Illinois, Ph.D., 1958. *Politics:* None. *Religion:* Jewish.

*ADDRESSES: Office*—Department of American Thought and Language, Michigan State University, East Lansing, MI 48823.

*CAREER:* Loyola University of Los Angeles (now Loyola Marymount University), Los Angeles, CA, professor of American literature, 1958-68; Michigan State University, East Lansing, professor of American thought and language, 1968—. U.S. Information Service lecturer throughout Latin America, 1958—. Fulbright Professor in Mexico, 1961, in Caracas, Venezuela, 1964-66, and in Brazil at Federal University of Santa Catarina, 1978-80.

*MEMBER:* Committee of Small Magazine Editors and Publishers (member of board of directors, 1968-76).

*AWARDS, HONORS:* John Carter Brown Library magazines grant, 1968; Organization of American States research grant, 1969-70, for study in Buenos Aires, Argentina, 1987, for archaeological fieldwork in the Atacama Desert, Chile.

*WRITINGS:*

*A Night with Hugh Fox* (three one-act plays), [Caracas], 1966.

*Countdown on an Empty Streetcar* (novel), Abyss Publications, 1969.

*Gnosis Knows Best: A Radiography of the North American Subconsciousness* (novella), [East Lansing, MI], 1969, reprinted, Semiotext, 1988.

*The Omega Scriptures,* Ghost Dance (East Lansing, MI), 1971.

*Peeple* (short stories), Dustbooks (Paradise, CA), 1972.

*The Invisibles* (novel), The Smith (New York City), 1976, *The Face of Guy Lombardo* (short stories), Fault (Union City, CA), 1976.

*Honeymoon* (semi-autobiographical novel), December Press (Highland Park, IL), 1978.

*Mom* (semi-autobiographical novel), December Press, 1978.

*Leviathan* (novel), Carpenter Press (Pomeroy, OH), 1981.

*Song of Christopher,* Clock Radio Press, 1988.

(Under pseudonym Connie Fox) *The Dream of the Black Topaze Chamber: The Portfolio* (contains selections from Fox's unpublished novel *The Dream of the Black Topaze Chamber*), Trout Creek Press, 1988.

*Shaman,* Permeable Press, 1993.

*The Last Summer,* Xenos Books (Gardena, CA), 1995.

*The Point of Points* (collected short fiction), French Bread Press, 1996.

NONFICTION

*America Today* (lectures), [Caracas, Venezuela], 1965.

*Problems of Our Time* (essays), [Caracas], 1966.

*Henry James: A Critical Introduction,* J. Westburg (Conesville, IA) 1968.

*Charles Bukowski: A Critical and Bibliographical Study,* Abyss Publications (Somerville, MA), 1969.

*The Living Underground: A Critical Overview,* Whitston (Troy, NY), 1970.

*The Gods of the Cataclysm: A Revolutionary Investigation of Man and His Gods before and after the Great Cataclysm* (anthropology), Harper's Magazine Press, 1976.

*The Poetry of Charles Potts* (criticism), Dustbooks, 1979.

*The Guernica Cycle: The Year Franco Died* (diary), Cherry Valley (Wheaton, MD), 1983.

*Lyn Lifshin: A Critical Study,* Whitston, 1985.

*The Mythological Foundations of the Epic Genre: The Solar Voyage as the Hero's Journey* (anthropology/mythology), Edwin Mellen (Lewiston, NY), 1988.

*The Stairway to the Sun* (anthropology/mythology), Permeable Press, 1996.

POETRY

*Soul-Catcher Songs,* Ediciones de la Frontera, 1967, second edition, 1968.

*Eye into Now,* Ediciones de la Frontera, 1967.

*Apotheosis of Olde Towne,* Fat Frog Press, 1968.

*Glyphs,* Fat Frog Press, 1969.

*The Permeable Man,* Black Sun Press, 1969.

*Son of Camelot Meets the Wolf Man,* Quixote Press (Houston, TX), 1969.

*Waca,* Ghost Dance, 1975.

*Almazora 42,* Laughing Bear Press, 1982.

*Papa Funk* (chapbook), Brian C. Clark, 1986.

*Jamais Vu,* Dusty Dog, 1991.

*F. Richard Thomas' 50th Birthday,* Zerx Press, 1992.

*The Sacred Cave,* Omega Cat Press, 1992.

*Now,* Permeable Press, 1995.

*Alexandra Saturday Night,* Mayapple Press (Kent, OH), 1996.

*Dragon Island,* Minotaur Press, in press.

UNDER PSEUDONYM CONNIE FOX; POETRY

*Blood Cocoon,* Zahir, 1980.

*The Dream of the Black Topaze Chamber: The Poem Cycle,* Ghost Pony (Madison, WI), 1983.

*Oma,* Implosion Press, 1985.

*Nachthymnen,* Mudborn (Santa Barbara, CA), 1986.

*Ten to the One Hundred Seventieth Power,* Trout Creek Press, 1986.

*Babicka,* Kangaroo Court Press, 1986.

*Skull Worship,* Applezaba, 1988.

*Our Lady of Laussel,* Spectacular Diseases Press (London), 1988.

*Noria,* Plain View (Austin, TX), 1988.

*EDITOR*

(With Sam Cornish) *The Living Underground: An Anthology of Contemporary American Poetry,* Ghost Dance, 1969, revised edition, Whitston, 1973.

*First Fire* (anthology of Amerindian poetry), Doubleday-Anchor (New York City), 1978.

*Other Kinds of Scores: The Ghost Dance Anthology,* Ghost Dance Pilot Editions, 1991, 1992, 1993, Whitston Press, 1994.

*The Living Underground: The Prose Anthology,* Whitston Press, 1996.

*OTHER*

Also author of several screenplays, including *The Laundromat.*

Unpublished works include: the novels *Shaman, Mandala, Sketches toward the Definition of a False Brazilian Messiah,* and, under pseudonym Connie Fox, *The Dream of the Black Topaze Chamber;* the prose piece "Dialogue"; and the play *Voices.*

Contributor of poetry, criticism, fiction, and articles on cultural history to periodicals, including *Abraxas, Arizona Quarterly, Asylum, Big Cigars, Black Bear Review, Bogg, Caliban, Choice, Exquisite Corpse, Kansas Quarterly, Long Story, Massachusetts Review, Michigan Quarterly, New Orleans Review, New York Quarterly, North American Review, Pacific Coast Review, Pan American Review, Portland Review, Prairie Schooner, Southern Humanities Review, Southwest Review, Transatlantic Review, Tri-Quarterly, West Coast Review, Western Humanities Review, Wisconsin Review,* and *Wormwood.*

Founder and editor, *Ghost Dance: The International Quarterly of Experimental Poetry.*

Editor, "Ghost Dance Portfolio" series, 1968—.

*ADAPTATIONS:* Poetry volume *Babicka* is available on cassette, Suburban Wilderness Aural Library, 1988; *Song of Christopher* is available on cassette, Suburban Wilderness Aural Library.

*SIDELIGHTS:* Hugh Fox once told *CA:* "The most 'releasing' experiences I've had were trips to Spain (1975-76) and Brazil (1978-80). While in Spain I fell under the influence of contemporary Spanish authors like Juan Bennett and Camilo Jose Cela. While in Spain I wrote a nonstop diary *The Guernica Cycle:*

*The Year Franco Died.* I also did some poetry in Spain . . . [published] as *Almazora 42* (my address in Valencia). When I came back to the United States in 1976, I went into a fit of depression and wrote a whole book of death meditations that John Bennett excerpted from to produce *Happy Deathday.* I also did three essays that came out as a special issue of *Camels Coming.*

"The Brazil trip activated everything. I fell in love with Brazilian *Modernismo,* especially the work of Oswald de Andrade, his 'mural novels,' which triggered my own [as yet unpublished] novel *Sketches toward the Definition of a False Brazilian Messiah. . .* and my first [a yet unpublished] novel as Connie Fox, *The Dream of the Black Topaze Chamber. . . .* I found Brazil itself a huge experiment, romantic, surrealistic, magical, a complicated syncretic blend of the African, the Portuguese, the Indian. Never stopped writing."

Fox later told *CA* that "all during the 1980s I worked on prehistory, both European and American, wrote a number of articles for *Pulpsmith,* and in 1987 got a grant from the Organization of American States as an archaeologist to spendthe winter in San Pedro de Atacama in the Chilean desert right *on* the Tropic of Capricorn, following up the work of Belgian Jesuit Gustavo le Page. . . . The conclusion I came to was that Atacama was a sun-worship point for ancient world peoples going back as far as 60,000 B.C. or earlier, which more or less agrees with le Page's theories.

"One by-product of these anthropological-archaeological books was *Our Lady of Laussel,* a poem-cycle (accompanied by prose meditations) attempting to use prehistoric (mainly European) ideas linked up with modern life to show that under the facade of The Modern, we are essentially the same as prehistoric man."

Fox more recently provided an update on his research and writing projects: "Three years ago in the Louvre and the Musee de l'Homme in Paris I noticed an iconographic similarity between a Greek-Sicilian pot portraying Herakles strangling Typhon and exactly the same theme portrayed on a Mochica Indian pot from Peru. When I got back to the U.S., in the Mochica collection at the Field Museum in Chicago, I found a Phoenician word written on one of the Mochica pots and a variant of the same word on another Mochican pot in the Chicago Art Institute, and within a few months I had written a book

(*Herakles Americanus: The Phoenician Presence in Ancient Peru*) demonstrating that the so-called 'Fanged-God' on Mochica pots is really Herakles (Hercules in Latin, Herakles in Greek) and that, in fact, *most* Mochica pottery portrays scenes from Herakles' myths.

"Then I kept studying early Greek and Anatolian pots and started to find totally unexpected stylistic and iconographic links between pots from ancient Hacilar (Turkey) and the Dimini Culture in Neolithic Greece and pots in Colombia, which in turn were close cousins to Anasazi and pre-Anasazi pottery in Northern Mexico and the American Southwest. I also found links between the Prodromo Culture in Greece and ancient Trinidad, Troy IV (Turkey) and the Atacama desert in Chile.

"All these new links I was discovering between the Neolithic Mediterranean, Middle East and Asia Minor really didn't come as much of a surprise to me, however, because for years I had known that the New World (very specifically Tiawanaku in Bolivia) was the mythical Land of the Sun King/Home of the Gods/World Center/Tin Lands in ancient world myth not only in Europe and the Middle East, but also in India, China and Japan.

"The ancient Sumerian epic *Gilgamesh* (3,000 B.C.) is about a voyage to ANAKU, the tin-lands across the ocean, and when you go to the tin-lands across the ocean, you find a place called TIAWANAKU. My book *The Mythological Foundations of the Epic Genre: The Solar Voyage as the Hero's Journey* (The Edwin Mellen Press, 1989) is a study of ancient myths about the solar hero's voyage across the ocean to the Land of the Sun King as an astrological-astronomical metaphor in which the mythological episodes are all derived from zodiac signs. Herakles killing the Nemean Lion, for example, is really a portrayal of the sun-god (Herakles) passing through the constellation of Leo the Lion. I see the zodiac itself as a star-chart for ancient mariners to navigate by on their way to South America (Tiawanaku).

"My first comprehensive book on all these matters, *The Stairway to the Sun,* was published by Permeable Press in San Francisco in September of 1996.

"Currently I am working on a book that attempts to transform all this mythological-archaeological material into a novel—*Immortal Jaguar*. Most of my insights came to me in libraries and museums, but in *Immortal Jaguar* I clothe all the research in terms of transformations occasioned by the taking of sacred psychedelic drugs. Among the Desana Indians in Colombia, the taking of the sacred drug supposedly transforms the individual into a jaguar shaman and I take all the data I have accumulated over the last forty [years] and turn it into jaguar shaman 'revelations' in a psychedelic context.

"I have also been trying to write a 'popular' novel, reading Danielle Steele, Judith Krantz, *The Bridges of Madison County,* etc., and trying to write, not literary clones, but second or third cousins.

"So far I have written two such novels, *The Coils of Eternity* and *Fate,* only I am finding out that I am not writing close enough to the formula-structure of my models. The message from New York agents is very clear—all novels must begin in the middle of things, in the midst of 'significant action,' things must be demonstrated cinematographically, never 'told,' the language must be aimed at a 14 year old level. For forty years I've been doing non-formula writing, exactly what I've wanted to do and now *Matta* in Prague is bringing out my novel *Shaman* in Czech. So my non-formula work is starting to reach a European market. It's almost as if there were two totally separate worlds, the slick, formula-bound commercial world and the free-form, inner-impulse-dominated small literary presses. In the commercial world you make money, in the literary world you write what you 'need' to write. My problem is that at age 65, on the edge of retirement, I would like to float off into the sunset, but I need money for a balloon.

"It's funny, even writing a novel like *Immortal Jaguar,* with the work of Carlos Castaneda and *The Celestine Prophecy* somewhat in the back of my mind as 'models,' I am creating a work that is 90 percent non-formula. It really is true that once you plug into the creative center inside you that Maritain talks about in *Creative Intuition in Art and Poetry,* it is difficult to ever become a literary hack again. I'll tell you who is standing in the wings offstage as I write, not Mickey Spillane and Erskine Caldwell, Edna Ferber and Danielle Steele, but Bela Bartok and Stravinsky, Jorge Luis Borges, Marguerite Duras and Jackson Pollock. Harry Smith used to tell me, 'Great writers write great works because of a certain inevitability in the nature of their performance; hacks turn out hack work because that is the essential *them.*' Maybe he was right.

"What I intend to do next is write sequels to my recent novels *Fate* and *The Coils of Eternity. The*

*Coils of Eternity* is about an old professor finally getting together with an ex-student of his in California after 40 years of separation. I was going to set the sequel in Paris (where *Coils* itself ends), but I intend to take off a sabbatical semester in the fall of 1997 and go to Prague instead and set the novel there. I've started studying Czech (my grandmother's language) and instead of shying away from all the horrible things done to Jews in Prague, I thought I would weave it in with the love story. I was raised as an Irish Catholic in Chicago—but had a secret, hidden Jewish grandmother who, more than anyone else, *raised* me. After 20 years of having no religion at all, under the influence of the great Kabbalist, Menke Katz, I converted to Judaism and that is giving a whole new slant to my world-view. I recently finished a spiritual autobiography that is still circulating with agents. I think perhaps it is time to go back over my 30 unpublished novels and rework them, perhaps try them out in England and elsewhere if the U.S. market seems too dogmatically mediocre. I am quite at home in German, Spanish, Italian, French and Portuguese and think of myself more as a kind of misplaced time-traveller from the 19th century Hapsburg Empire than anyone born in Chicago in 1932."

\* \* \*

## FRAZIER, Ian    1951-

*PERSONAL:* Born in 1951 in Cleveland, OH; son of David (a chemist) and Peggy (a teacher) Frazier; married Jacqueline Carey (a writer); two children. *Education:* Harvard University, B.A., 1973.

*ADDRESSES: Home*—Brooklyn, NY. *Office*—New Yorker, 20 West 43rd St., New York, NY 10036.

*CAREER:* Essayist and journalist. Staff writer for *New Yorker.*

*WRITINGS:*

*Dating Your Mom,* Farrar, Straus (New York City), 1986.
*Nobody Better, Better Than Nobody,* Farrar, Straus, 1987.
*Great Plains,* Farrar, Straus, 1989.
(Contributor) *They Went: The Art and Craft of Travel Writing,* Houghton (Boston, MA), 1991.
*Family,* Farrar, Straus, 1994.

*SIDELIGHTS:* Journalist and essayist Ian Frazier is known for his comic, ironic essays and for his affectionate explorations of rural America. A native of Ohio now living and working in New York City, Frazier has kept alive his ties to the Midwest by writing about it in the pages of the *New Yorker* magazine and in books. His humorous reflections upon home and country, city life, and modern society are collected in aseries of nonfiction books, including *Dating Your Mom, Great Plains,* and *Family. New York Times* reviewer Christopher Lehmann-Haupt cites Frazier for his "original point of view" and the "antic sense of fun he brings to whatever he writes."

Collections of essays Frazier originally wrote for the *New Yorker* form the basis of his first two books, *Dating Your Mom* and *Nobody Better, Better Than Nobody.* The twenty-five pieces that make up *Dating Your Mom* showcase Frazier's deadpan humor and wit. In the title story, for instance, Frazier counsels single men to give up the arduous process of dating strangers and instead date their mothers, since these men are already familiar with and loved by their moms. In "LGA-ORD," another piece from the book, Frazier offers a witty parody of playwright Samuel Beckett as a commercial pilot making his way from New York to Chicago. Critics have praised Frazier's bizarre fantasies and his ability to see humor in small details. As Mordecai Richler notes in the *New York Times Book Review:* "Frazier is an elegant miniaturist, a much-needed mockingbird with a fine eye for the absurd." *Los Angeles Times Book Review* contributor Shelly Lowenkopf comments that the essays in the book "sing with Frazier's understated irreverence, reminding us that there is nothing so sacred it cannot or should not be laughed at."

In his second collection of humorous essays, *Nobody Better, Better Than Nobody,* Frazier again turns to a wide range of seemingly average people and events. He writes of a fishing-store owner in New York City, of the woman who produces the *Hints From Heloise* newspaper column, and of bears in Montana. As in his first collection, his humor is often couched in the guise of serious storytelling, such as his description of an angry dog he encountered while fishing, as quoted by Paul Gray in *Time:* "The woman told me to hold still and the dog wouldn't bite me. I held still, and the dog bit me in the right shoulder. I told the woman that the dog was biting me." Reviewers have noted that Frazier tempered the wicked sarcasm of his first collection with sympathy for his subjects, while maintaining his astute eye for ironic detail. *New York Times* critic Lehmann-Haupt comments: "It's the rare combination of humor and empathy that gives these casual pieces their special appeal." Other reviewers laud Frazier's ability to heighten his comedic effects with stylistic devices, particularly with his tendency toward extremely long sentences and equally long series of oddly juxtaposed images. Gray praises the "loopy laziness" of Frazier's prose and noted that "the reader winds up laughing and knowing a great deal about subjects . . . that most people can live without."

For his third book, *Great Plains,* Frazier spent several years exploring the interior of the United States. Among many other sites, he visited gigantic ranches in Wyoming, Indian monuments in South Dakota, and obscure museums in Kansas. His observations of the area, while often funny and ironic, express a sadness that the rural lifestyle that characterizes the vast plains of inner America will inevitably disappear as people abandon farms for cities. Frazier describes the uniqueness of the plains landscape—flat and barren under an enormous sky—and the diversity of figures, both past and present, who inhabit that landscape. As quoted by Sue Hubbell in the *New York Times Book Review,* the author writes that "the Great Plains have plenty of room for the past. Often, as I drove around, I felt as if I were in an enormous time park." Critics praise the mix of humor, wit, nostalgia, and sadness with which Frazier infuses his observations. Writing in the *Washington Post Book World,* Ron Hansen states: "There is no mistaking Ian Frazier's respect for the integrity and majesty of the neglected worlds of the plains, nor of his tone of tender elegy for the lore and ways of living that soon may disappear. *Great Plains* is a great book."

Frazier continued his exploration of the American heartland in his well-received 1994 book *Family.* The work is a profile of Frazier's own white, Anglo-Saxon Protestant, Midwestern, middle-class forebears and their quite ordinary—if illuminating—lives. "*Family* . . . is more than an extended family photo album minus the photos," writes David Klinghoffer in the *National Review.* "There is an unmistakable tide in the history of these families, which Frazier notices early on and conveys in a powerful, because personal, way. It's the slow evaporation of noble sentiment, reflected in a wider way in American culture." *Los Angeles Times Book Review* contributor Hugh Nissenson contends that "Frazier's *Family* is hard to put down. He structures his narrative in both a lineal and thematic way. He occasionally jumps

around in time, while developing individual stories, but they all compel the reader's attention. . . . Ian Frazier's *Family* is a deeply moving book in a great American literary tradition." In the *New York Times Book Review,* David Willis McCullough characterizes *Family* as "a book of a lifetime, . . . that rarest of events, a family reunion worth inviting strangers to attend."

*BIOGRAPHICAL/CRITICAL SOURCES:*

BOOKS

*Contemporary Literary Criticism,* Volume 46, Gale (Detroit), 1988.

PERIODICALS

*Boston Globe,* January 10, 1995, p. 25.
*Los Angeles Times Book Review,* August 31, 1986; November 27, 1994, p. 3, 12.
*National Review,* December 19, 1994, p. 57-59.
*Newsweek,* February 3, 1986.
*New York Times,* December 23, 1985; April 16, 1987; June 5, 1989; November 21, 1994, p. C13.
*New York Times Book Review,* January 5, 1986; May 3, 1987; June 18, 1989; November 6, 1994, p. 9.
*Time,* March 3, 1986; May 25, 1987.
*Tribune Books* (Chicago), July 5, 1987; May 28, 1989; November 13, 1994, p. 5.
*Village Voice Literary Supplement,* October, 1994, p. 23.
*Washington Post Book World,* May 28, 1989, p. 3.

\*    \*    \*

**FUGARD, (Harold) Athol    1932-**

*PERSONAL:* Born June 11, 1932, in Middelburg, Cape Province, South Africa; son of Harold David (an owner of a general store) and Elizabeth Magdalena (a cafe manager) Fugard; married Sheila Meiring (a novelist, poet, and former actress), 1956; children: Lisa. *Education:* Attended Port Elizabeth Technical College, 1946-50, and University of Cape Town, 1950-53. *Avocational interests:* Jogging, music, poetry.

*ADDRESSES: Home*—P.O. Box 5090, Port Elizabeth, South Africa. *Agent*—Esther Sherman, William

Morris Agency, 1350 Avenue of the Americas, New York, NY 10019.

*CAREER:* Actor, director, and playwright. Crew member of a tramp steamer bound from Port Sudan, Sudan, to the Far East, 1953-55; *Port Elizabeth Evening Post,* Port Elizabeth, journalist, 1954; South African Broadcasting Corporation, Port Elizabeth and Cape Town, reporter, 1955-57; Fordsburg Native Commissioner's Court, Johannesburg, South Africa, clerk, 1958; African Theatre Workshop, Sophiatown, cofounder, 1958-59; New Africa Group, Brussels, cofounder, 1960; Serpent Players, Port Elizabeth, cofounder, director, and actor, 1963—; Ijinle Company, London, cofounder, 1966; The Space Experimental Theatre, Cape Town, cofounder, 1972. Has worked as actor and director in various theatre productions in New York City, London, and South Africa. Actor in television film *The Blood Knot* for British Broadcasting Corp. (BBC-TV), 1968; actor in motion pictures, including *Boesman and Lena,* 1973, *Meetings with Remarkable Men,* 1979, *Marigolds in August,* 1980, *Gandhi,* 1982, and *The Killing Fields,* 1984.

*MEMBER:* Royal Society of Literature (fellow), American Academy of Arts and Letters, Dramatists Guild, Mark Twain Society.

*AWARDS, HONORS:* Obie Award for distinguished foreign play from *Village Voice,* 1971, for *Boesman and Lena; Plays & Players* Award for best new play, 1973, for *Sizwe Banzi Is Dead;* London Theatre Critics Award, 1974; Ernest Artaria Award from Locarno Film Festival, 1977; Golden Bear, Berlin Film Festival, 1980; Yale University fellow, 1980; New York Drama Critics Circle Award for best play, 1982, for *A Lesson from Aloes;* Drama Desk Award and New York Drama Critics Circle Award for best play, 1983, and *Evening Standard* Award, London, 1984, for *"Master Harold" . . . and the Boys;* Commonwealth Award, 1984, for contribution to the American theatre; Drama League Award, 1986; New York Drama Critics Circle Award, 1988; Helen Hayes Award, 1990, for direction; honorary degrees from Yale University, Georgetown University, Natal University, Rhodes University, Cape Town University, Emory University, and the University of Port-Elizabeth, South Africa.

*WRITINGS:*

*Tsotsi* (novel), Collings, 1980, Random House (New York City), 1981.

*Notebooks, 1960-1977,* edited by Mary Benson, Faber (London), 1983, Knopf (New York City), 1984.
*Writer and Region: Athol Fugard* (essay), Anson Phelps Stokes Institute, 1987.

*PLAYS*

*No-Good Friday* (also see below), first produced in Cape Town, South Africa, 1956.
*Nongogo* (also see below), first produced in Cape Town, 1957; produced in New York City, 1978.
*The Blood Knot* (first produced in Johannesburg, South Africa, and London, 1961; produced Off-Broadway, 1964; also see below), Simondium, 1963, Odyssey, 1964; published with other plays as *Blood Knot and Other Plays,* Theatre Communications Group (New York City), 1991.
*Hello and Goodbye* (first produced in Johannesburg, 1965; produced Off-Broadway at Sheridan Square Playhouse, September 18, 1969; also see below), A. A. Balkema, 1966, Samuel French (New York City), 1971.
*The Occupation: A Script for Camera,* published in *Ten One-Act Plays,* edited by Cosmos Pieterse, Heinemann (New York City), 1968.
*Boesman and Lena* (first produced in Grahamstown, South Africa, 1969; produced Off-Broadway at Circle in the Square, June 22, 1970; produced on the West End at Royal Court Theatre Upstairs, July 19, 1971; also see below), Buren, 1969, revised and rewritten edition, Samuel French, 1971 (published with *The Blood Knot, People Are Living There* [also see below], and *Hello and Goodbye* as *Boesman and Lena, and Other Plays,* Oxford University Press [Oxford, England], 1978).
*People Are Living There* (first produced in Cape Town at Hofmeyr Theatre, June 14, 1969; produced on Broadway at Forum Theatre, Lincoln Center, November 18, 1971), Oxford University Press, 1970, Samuel French, 1976.
(With Don MacLennan) *The Coat* [and] *Third Degree* (the former by Fugard, the latter by MacLennan), A. A. Balkema, 1971.
*Orestes* (produced in Cape Town, 1971), published in *Theatre One: New South African Drama,* edited by Stephen Gray, Donker, 1978.
*Statements* (contains three one-act plays: [with John Kani and Winston Ntshona] *Sizwe Banzi Is Dead,* first produced in Cape Town, 1972, produced in New York City, 1974; [with Kani and Ntshona] *The Island,* first produced in South Africa, 1972,

produced on the West End at Royal Court Theatre, December, 1973, produced in New York at Edison Theatre, November, 1974; and *Statements after an Arrest under the Immorality Act*, first produced in Cape Town, 1972, produced in London, 1974), Oxford University Press, 1974.

*Three Port Elizabeth Plays: The Blood Knot, Hello and Goodbye, Boesman and Lena*, Viking (New York City), 1974.

*Dimetos*, first produced in Edinburgh, 1975, produced in London and New York City, 1976 (published with *No-Good Friday* and *Nongogo* as *Dimetos and Two Early Plays*, Oxford University Press, 1977).

(With Ross Devenish) *The Guest: An Episode in the Life of Eugene Marais* (screenplay), Donker (Johannesburg), 1977.

*A Lesson from Aloes* (first produced in Johannesburg, December, 1978, produced in New York, 1980), Oxford University Press, 1981.

*The Drummer*, produced in Louisville, 1980.

(With Devenish) *Marigolds in August* (screenplay), Donker, 1982; published with *The Guest* as *Marigolds in August and The Guest: Two Screenplays*, Theatre Communications Group, 1992.

*"Master Harold" . . . and the Boys* (first produced in New Haven, Connecticut, March, 1982, produced on Broadway at Lyceum Theatre, May 5, 1982), Oxford University Press, 1983 (published with *The Blood Knot, Hello and Goodbye*, and *Boesman and Lena* as *Selected Plays*, Oxford University Press, 1987).

*The Road to Mecca* (first produced in New Haven, 1984, produced in London at Lyttelton Theatre, March 1, 1985, produced in New York at Promenade Theatre, April, 1988), Faber, 1985.

*A Place with the Pigs* (produced in New Haven, 1987), Faber, 1988.

*My Children! My Africa!* (produced in Johannesburg and New York City, 1989), Theatre Communications Group, 1990.

*Playland* (first produced in Cape Town, 1992), published with *A Place with the Pigs* as *Playland and A Place with the Pigs*, Theatre Communications Group, 1993.

*Valley Song*, produced in market Theater, Johannesburg, and McCarter Theater, Princeton, NJ, 1995.

### OTHER

Author of teleplays *Mille Miglia* and *The Guest at Steenkampskraal*. Produced screenplays include *Boesman and Lena* (based on his play), 1972, *The Guest*, 1976, *Meetings with Remarkable Men*, 1979, *Marigolds in August*, 1980, *Gandhi*, 1982, and *The Killing Fields*, 1984. Plays reprinted in various anthologies, including *Text & Teaching: The Search for Excellence*, edited by Michael Collins, Georgetown University Press, 1991.

*SIDELIGHTS:* As a white child growing up in segregated South Africa, Athol Fugard resisted the racist upbringing society offered him. Nevertheless, the boy who would become, in the words of Gillian MacKay of *Maclean's*, "perhaps South Africa's most renowned literary figure, and its most eloquent anti-apartheid crusader abroad" did not completely escape apartheid's influence—he insisted that the family's black servants call him Master Harold, and he even spat at one of them. Fugard told MacKay that the servant, an "extraordinary" man who had always treated him as a close friend, "grieved for the state" of Fugard's soul and forgave him instead of beating him "to a pulp."

Fugard will never forget this incident, which he transformed into a powerful scene in the play, *"Master Harold" . . . and the Boys*. As he comments to Lloyd Richards in *Paris Review*, it is like a deep stain which has "soaked into the fabric" of his life. In Fugard's career as a playwright, director, and actor, he has forced himself and his audiences to consider their own "stains." As Frank Rich remarks in a 1985 *New York Times* review of *The Blood Knot*, "Mr. Fugard doesn't allow anyone, least of all himself, to escape without examining the ugliest capabilities of the soul."

Despite Fugard's insistence that he is not a political writer and that he speaks for no one but himself, his controversial works featuring black and white characters have found favor with critics of apartheid. According to Brendan Gill of the *New Yorker, The Blood Knot*, the play that made Fugard famous, "altered the history of twentieth-century theatre throughout the world" as well as the world's "political history." Not all critics of apartheid, however, have appreciated Fugard's works. Some "see a white man being a spokesman for what has happened to black people and they are naturally intolerant," Fugard explains to Paul Allen in *New Statesman and Society*.

Whether Fugard's theatrical explorations of passion, violence, and guilt played a role in undermining apartheid or not, it is clear that he was involved in breaking physical and symbolic barriers to integration. He defied the apartheid system by founding the first enduring black theater company in South Africa, by collaborating with black writers, and by presenting black and white actors on stage together for integrated audiences. He insisted upon performing plays for local audiences in South Africa as well as for those in New York City and London; his plays carried messages that people around the world needed to hear. Even after the government took Fugard's passport and banned his plays, he refused to consider himself an exile or to renounce his country. Love, and not hate for South Africa, Fugard maintained, would help it break the chains of apartheid. "Wouldn't it be ironic if South Africa could teach the world something about harmony?," he asks MacKay.

Fugard is highly regarded by literary and theater critics. Stephen Gray, writing in *New Theatre Quarterly,* notes that the author has been called "the greatest active playwright in English." His plays are noted for their multifaceted, marginalized characters, realistic yet lyrical dialogue, and carefully crafted, symbolic plots. Critics have also appreciated Fugard's ability to write scenes which elicit emotion without declining into melodrama. Fugard has forged new paths in theater by directing and acting in many of his own plays, and by writing and composing plays with the actors who perform in them.

Fugard credits his parents with shaping his insights about South African society. As a child, he developed close relationships with both his English-speaking South African father, Harold, and his mother, Elizabeth, the daughter of Dutch-speaking Afrikaners. Harold, a jazz musician and amputee who spent a great deal of time in bed, amused the boy with fantastic stories and confused him with his unabashed bigotry. Fugard's mother Elizabeth supported the family by efficiently managing their tea room. In an interview with Jamaica Kincaid for *Interview,* Fugard describes his mother as "an extraordinary woman" who could "barely read and write." In Fugard's words, she was "a *monument* of decency and principle and just anger" who encouraged Fugard to view South African society with a thoughtful and critical eye.

If Fugard learned the power of words from his father, and if he discovered how to question society from his mother, he gained an understanding of the complexity of human nature from both parents. Like Fugard's characters, his parents were neither entirely good or evil. Nevertheless, as Fugard explains to Kincaid, "I think at a fairly early age I became suspi-

cious of what the system was trying to do to me. . . . I became conscious of what attitudes it was trying to implant in me and what *prejudices* it was trying to pass on to me." Fugard fed his intellectual appetite with conversations with his mother and daily trips to the local library. By the time he began college, he knew he wanted to be a writer. He accepted a scholarship at the University of Cape Town and studied philosophy, but he left school before graduating to journey around the Far East on a steamer ship.

At this time in his life, Fugard entertained notions of writing a great South African novel. Yet his first attempt at writing a novel, as he saw it, was a failure, and he destroyed it. After Fugard met and married Sheila Meiring, an out-of-work South African actress, he developed an interest in writing plays. *The Cell* and *Klaas and the Devil* were the first results of this ambition.

Not until after Fugard began to keep company with a community of black writers and actors near Johannesburg did he experience a revelation in his work. During this time, he witnessed the frustration of the black writers and learned the intricacies of a system which shrewdly and cruelly thwarted their efforts to live and work freely. The plays he penned at this time, *No-Good Friday* and *Nongogo,* were performed by Fugard and his black actor friends for private audiences.

In 1959 Fugard moved to England to write. His work received little attention there, and Fugard began to realize that he needed to be in South Africa to follow his muse. Upon his return home in 1961, Fugard wrote a second novel. Although he tried to destroy this work, a pair of graduate students later found the only surviving copy, and it was published in 1981. Critics have noticed the presence of many of the elements which would re-emerge in Fugard's more famous plays in this novel, *Tsotsi.*

*Tsotsi* portrays the life of David, a young black man whose nickname, "Tsotsi," means "hoodlum." Tsotsi spends his time with his gang of thieving, murderous friends. He has no family and cannot remember his childhood. It is not until a woman he is about to attack gives him a box with a baby in it, and David gives the baby his name, that he begins to experience sympathy and compassion, and to recall his childhood. When David is about to kill a crippled old man he has been pursuing, he suddenly remembers how his mother was arrested and never came home, and how he began to rove with a pack of abandoned children. It is not long before he recalls the trauma that led to his violent life on the streets. Fugard does not allow David's character to revel in his newly discovered emotions or to continue his search for God: at the novel's end, David is crushed under a bulldozer in an attempt to save David, the baby.

Critics appreciate *Tsotsi* for the insight it provides into the lives of even minor characters. Fugard did not allow his readers to categorize characters as "good" or "bad"; instead, he forced them to understand their complexity. In a 1981 review of the book in the *New York Times Book Review,* Ivan Gold finds *Tsotsi* to be "a moving and untendentious book" which demonstrates Fugard's ability to "uncannily insinuate himself into the skins of the oppressed majority and articulate itsrage and misery and hope." Although Barbara A. Bannon in *Publishers Weekly* comments that *Tsotsi* is "altogether different in tone" from some of his plays, she observed that the "milieu is much the same as the one that has made Fugard . . . the literary conscience of South Africa."

While Fugard generally works on one project at a time (typically writing with pens instead of word processors), he wrote *Tsotsi* and *The Blood Knot* at the same time. Fugard explains the inspiration for *The Blood Knot* to Richards in *Paris Review.* Fugard walked in a room and saw his brother was asleep in bed one night; Fugard's brother had lived a difficult life, and his pain was apparent in his face and body. Fugard realized that there was nothing he could do to save his brother from suffering so, and he experienced guilt. By writing *The Blood Knot,* Fugard recalls, he "was trying to examine a guilt more profound than racial guilt—the existential guilt that I feel when another person suffers, is victimized, and I can do nothing about it. South Africa afforded me the most perfect device for examining this guilt."

*The Blood Knot* is the story of two brothers born to the same mother. Morris, who has light-skin, can "pass" for white; he confronts the truth about his identity when he returns home to live with his dark-skinned brother, Zachariah. Although the opening scene of the play finds Morris preparing a bath for hard-working Zachariah's feet, it soon becomes clear that the brothers' relationship is a tenuous one. The tension between the brothers is heightened when Zach's white pen pal (a woman who thinks Zach is white) wants to meet him, and Morris must pretend to be the white man with whom she has been corresponding.

Morris's attempts to look and sound white are painful for both brothers: to convincingly portray a white man, Morris must treat his black brother with the cruelty of a racist. In his role as a white man, Morris sits in the park and calls insults at his brother, who chases black children from the presence of his "white" brother. By the last scene, the "game" is out of control, and Zach tries to kill Morris. According to Robert M. Post in *Ariel: A Review of International English Literature,* the brothers in *The Blood Knot* "are typical victims of the system of apartheid and bigotry" and "personify the racial conflict of South Africa."

Fugard had little support in producing the play; it was not until actor Zakes Mokae joined the project that the production emerged. As a result of this collaboration, the first production of *The Blood Knot* in Johannesburg, in 1961, was controversial not only for its content, but because it featured a black actor and a white actor on stage together. Fugard played the light-skinned brother who "passes" for a white man, while Mokae played the darker-skinned brother. *The Blood Knot* opened in front of a mixed-race, invitation-only audience in a run-down theatre. As Derek Cohen writes in *Canadian Drama,* this first production of *The Blood Knot* "sent shock waves" through South Africa. "Those who saw the initial performance knew instinctively that something of a revolution had taken place in the stodgily Angloid cultural world of South Africa. . . . Whites, faced boldly with some inescapable truths about what their repressive culture and history had wrought, were compelled to take notice."

Responses to *The Blood Knot* varied. As Cohen notes, some Afrikaners believed that the play's message was that blacks and whites could not live together in peace, and some black critics called the work racist. Many critics now accept the interpretation of the play as a sad commentary on the way racism has twisted and tangled our understanding of brotherhood and humanity. More specifically, Cohen insists, *The Blood Knot* is "about the hatred which South African life feeds on."

According to Dennis Walder in his book *Athol Fugard,* Fugard's plays "approximate . . . the same basic model established by *The Blood Knot:* a small cast of 'marginal' characters is presented in a passionately close relationship embodying the tensions current in their society, the whole first performed by actors directly involved in its creation, in a makeshift, 'fringe' or 'unofficial' venue." Since the first production of *The Blood Knot,* the substance of Fugard's plays as well as the means of their production reflect the historical circumstances in which they evolved. Fugard insists that the actual performance, or rather each performance, of his plays is the legitimate play; he selects the actors to perform in his plays and continues to direct and act in them.

*Boesman and Lena,* produced in 1969, was Fugard's next great success; in the words of Cohen, it is "possibly the finest of Fugard's plays." This work develops around the image of an old, homeless woman Fugard once saw, presenting a homeless couple (both "colored") who wander without respite. According to Cohen, it is a "drama of unrelieved and immitigable suffering" which becomes "more intense as the characters, impotent against the civilization of which they are outcasts, turn their fury against each other."

Fugard suffered from writer's block after he wrote *Boesman and Lena,* but went on to work in collaboration with actors to create *Orestes* in 1971. *Orestes* developed as a collection of images which, writes Walder, "defies translation into a script" and explores "the effect of violence upon those who carry it out."

Fugard's next project began after two amateur actors, John Kani and Winston Ntshona, asked Fugard to help them become professional actors. As Fugard explains to Richards in his *Paris Review* interview, "At that point in South Africa's theater history . . . the notion that a black man could earn a living being an actor in South Africa was just the height of conceit." Nevertheless, the trio decided to create their own play. Three plays eventually emerged from this plan in 1972, known as *The Statements Trilogy* or *The Political Trilogy,* and include *The Island, Sizwe Banzi Is Dead,* and *Statements after an Arrest under the Immorality Act.*

In these plays, personal experiences, along with the direction of Fugard, combine to provoke audiences. Post comments that *The Island* and *Statements* share "the basic conflict of the individual versus the government." In *The Island,* prisoners (portrayed by John and Winston) in a South African jail stage Sophocles's *Antigone;* the play within the play suggests that, according to Post, the "conflict between individual conscience and individual rights . . . and governmental decrees . . . corresponds to the conflict between the individual conscience and the rights of black prisoners and white government." *Statements*

follows the relationship between a white librarian and a black teacher who become lovers despite their fear of being caught and castigated; eventually, their "illegal" love is uncovered by the police.

The development of *Sizwe Banzi Is Dead* began with an image of a black man in a new suit, seated and smiling, that Fugard saw in a photographer's store. Speculation about why the man was smiling led to a story about the passbook that blacks had to carry around with them under the apartheid system. Before Sizwe Banzi can get his passbook in order, he must trade his identity for another and, symbolically, die. This play was performed "underground" until, as Fugard tells Richards, it "had played in London and New York" and earned a reputation that "protected" its writers and cast. In 1974, Kani won a Tony Award for his New York performance in *Sizwe Banzi Is Dead.*

Fugard unveiled *A Lesson from Aloes* in 1978. Like his other works, this play demonstrates the extent to which apartheid effects everyone in South African society. Piet, a Dutch Afrikaner living in Port Elizabeth in 1963, tends his collection of hardy, bitter aloe plants and joins a group of political activists. When the group's bus boycott is disrupted by the police and Piet's only friend Steve is found to have mixed blood and sent away, Piet is blamed. Even Piet's wife, whose diaries have been read by the police, believes he betrayed Steve.

Instead of defending himself, Piet isolates himself in his quiet aloe garden, and even the audience is unsure of his innocence. At the same time, Gladys, his wife, laments the violation of her diaries and goes insane. Fugard explains that he wanted to demonstrate the "complexity" of the Afrikaner in *A Lesson from Aloes.* He tells Richards in his *Paris Review* interview that we will "never understand how we landed in the present situation or what's going to come out of it" if we "simply dispose of the Afrikaner as the villain in the South African situation."

*"Master Harold"* . . . *and the Boys* communicates similar notions. Hallie, whose childhood parallels Fugard's, is troubled by his father's thoughtless and unthinking attitude. Although he has a close relationship with his family's black servants, Sam and Willie, even he is not immune to the evil of apartheid; at one point in the play, the boy spits in Willie's face. Fugard tells Richards how the relationship shared by Hallie, Sam, and Willie is autobiographical, and how he really did spit in Willie's face.

He felt that it was "necessary" to deal with what he'd done by writing *"Master Harold" . . . and the Boys.*

*"Master Harold" . . . and the Boys* was the second of Fugard's plays to open in the United States, where it earned critical acclaim. Despite this American success, the play provoked criticism from individuals and groups who, as Jeanne Colleran notes in *Modern Drama,* either asserted that characters like Sam exhibit "Uncle Tom-ism," or demanded that Fugard present his plays in South Africa instead of abroad, in "languages of the black majority." Colleran suggests that because of this criticism, "Fugard cannot write of Johannesburg or of township suffering without incurring the wrath of Black South Africans who regard him as a self-appointed and presumptuous spokesman; nor can he claim value for the position previously held by white liberals without being assailed by the more powerful and vociferous radical left. . . . Ironically . . . Fugard has been forced to practice a kind of self-censorship by those whose cause he shared."

*"Master Harold" . . . and the Boys* also received negative attention from the South African government, which claimed that it was subversive. The government proclaimed it illegal to import or distribute copies of the play. Fugard later managed to present *"Master Harold" . . . and the Boys* in Johannesburg, because the government did not forbid the play's performance.

The publication of *Notebooks, 1960-1977* reinforced Fugard's growing popularity in the United States. This book provides what Pico Iyer of *Time* calls "the random scraps out of which Fugard fashioned his plays" and "a trail of haunting questions." Richard Eder of the *Los Angeles Times Book Review* asserts that, in addition to providing "the most vivid possible picture of an artist striving to shape his material even as it was detonating all around him," the *Notebooks* are "an illuminating, painful and beguiling record of a life lived in one of those tortured societies where everything refers back, sooner or later, to the situation that torments it."

When *The Road to Mecca* opened in 1984 at the Yale Repertory Theatre, American audiences were captivated by Fugard's mastery once again. Nevertheless, this play reinforced Fugard's reputation as a regional writer by reconstructing the character and life of a woman who lived in Karoo, where Fugard kept his South African home. Unable to take comfort from the Karoo community, Helen Martins isolates herself

at home; there, she produces sculpture after sculpture from cement and wire. Benedict Nightingale notes in *New Statesman* that while Helen Martins actually committed suicide by "burning out her stomach with caustic soda," Fugard recreates her as "a docile old widow" with a beautiful life; "that paranoia, that suicide are ignored" by the playwright. The central problem in the play consists of the local pastor's attempts to get Helen to enter a home for the elderly to hide his secret love for her. As Jack Kroll observes in *Newsweek,* although *The Road to Mecca* "doesn't seem to be a political play at all," it "concerns love and freedom, and for Fugard that is the germ cell of the South African problem."

With some exceptions, *The Road to Mecca* was lauded by critics. While Nightingale appreciates the presentation of the Afrikaner pastor "in the round, from his own point of view as much as that from the liberal outsider," he also finds the play to be "exasperatingly uneven, as unreal and real a play as Fugard has ever yet penned." According to Colleran, *The Road to Mecca* was "extraordinarily well received," playing at Britain's National Theatre and on Broadway. Graham Leach asserts in *Listener* that *The Road to Mecca* is "universal" and "a major piece of theatre. . . . Many people here believe it may well end up being judged Fugard's finest work."

*A Place with the Pigs,* as Colleran recounts in *Modern Drama,* is a personal parable "concerning the forty years spent in a pigsty" by a "Red Army deserter." It premiered at the Yale Repertory Theatre in 1987 with Fugard in the leading role. Unlike *The Road to Mecca, A Place with the Pigs* did not receive critical acclaim. Colleran suggests that the play may have failed to gain positive attention because it "simply does not conform to the audience's expectations of what a work by Athol Fugard should be like." In her opinion, the "dismissal" of *A Place with the Pigs* is unfortunate, in part because this "parable of one segment of South African society—the white South African who is committed both to dismantling apartheid and to remaining in his homeland—it adds a new voice, an authentic one, to those clamoring to decide the future of South Africa."

*My Children! My Africa!* was the first of Fugard's plays to premiere in South Africa in years. According to Gray in *New Theatre Quarterly,* Fugard believes that "South African audiences should have this play first." Fugard ensured that many audiences were exposed to this work: after a long run at the Market Theatre in Johannesburg, *My Children! My Africa!*

was performed for six weeks in a tour of black townships in South Africa in 1989 with Lisa Fugard, Fugard's daughter, and John Kani in starring roles.

Like *"Master Harold"* . . . *and the Boys, My Children! My Africa!* portrays the struggles of youths to live with or confront the division between races in South Africa. Yet, as Allen of *New Statesman and Society* observes, the play marks "the first time Fugard . . . put the struggle itself on stage." Fugard was inspired by the story of a black teacher who refused to participate in a school boycott and was later murdered in Port Elizabeth by a group that believed he was a police informer.

*Playland* was the first of Fugard's plays to appear after the fall of apartheid. It is set on New Year's Eve in a traveling amusement park in Karoo. Here, a black night watchman painting a bumper car and a white South African whose car has broken down meet, discuss their lives, and reveal their darkest secrets: the white man tells how he killed blacks in a border war, and the black man confesses that he killed a white man who tried to force his fiancee (who was working as the white man's servant) to have sexual intercourse with him. John Simon of *New York* criticizes the play: "There is hardly a situation, a snatch of dialogue, an object that isn't, or doesn't become, a symbol." But, according to Edith Oliver in a *New Yorker* review of the play, the spell cast by the actors' performances "is rooted in Mr. Fugard's moral passion." She concludes: "I have rarely seen an audience so mesmerized, or been so mesmerized myself."

Set after Nelson Mandela's election as South Africa's new president, *Valley Song* portrays four "colored" characters as they prepare to face the challenges of the future. Fugard was happy to premiere *Valley Song* at the Market Theatre in Johannesburg. As Donald G. McNeil, Jr., of the *New York Times* reports, Fugard was also optimistic about the future of South Africa: "We're pulling off a political miracle here."

If Fugard's plays have actually influenced history by undermining apartheid, the author may credit his native land and the power of art. "I come from a country which is so highly politicized that there is no act, even the most private you can think of, which does not resonate politically," Fugard tells Richards. "Art is at work in South Africa. . . . Art goes underground into people's dreams and surfaces months later in strange, unexpected actions."

*BIOGRAPHICAL/CRITICAL SOURCES:*

*BOOKS*

*Contemporary Literary Criticism,* Gale (Detroit), Volume 5, 1976, Volume 9, 1978, Volume 14, 1980, Volume 25, 1983, Volume 40, 1986, Volume 80, 1994.
*Drama Criticism,* Volume 3, Gale, 1993.
Fugard, Athol, *Notebooks, 1960-1977,* Faber (London), 1983, Knopf (New York City), 1984.
Gray, Stephen, *Athol Fugard,* McGraw Hill (New York City), 1982.
Hauptfleisch, Temple, *Athol Fugard: A Source Guide,* Donker, 1982.
Vandenbroucke, Russell, *Athol Fugard: A Bibliography, Biography, Playography,* TQ Publications, 1977.
Vandenbroucke, *Truths the Hand Can Touch: The Theatre of Athol Fugard,* Theatre Communications Group (New York City), 1985.
Walder, Dennis, *Athol Fugard,* Macmillan (New York City), 1984.

*PERIODICALS*

*America,* March 21, 1992, pp. 250-51.
*Ariel: A Review of International English Literature,* July, 1985, pp. 3-17.
*Booklist,* December 1, 1982, p. 478.
*Canadian Drama/L'Art dramatique canadien,* spring, 1980, pp. 151-61.
*Chicago,* March, 1989, p. 34.
*Commonweal,* June 3, 1988, pp. 342-43.
*Interview,* August, 1990, pp. 64-69.
*Kirkus Reviews,* December 1, 1980, p. 1530.
*Listener,* December 13, 1984, p. 20.
*Los Angeles Times,* March 13, 1982; July 17, 1983; July 29, 1983.
*Los Angeles Times Book Review,* April 8, 1984, pp. 3, 5.
*Maclean's,* June 18, 1990, pp. 58-59.
*Modern Drama,* March, 1990, pp. 82-92.
*New Republic,* July 25, 1970; December 21, 1974.
*New Statesman,* March 8, 1985, pp. 30-31.
*New Statesman and Society,* September 7, 1990, p. 38.
*Newsweek,* May 28, 1984, pp. 85-86; May 2, 1988, p. 73.
*New Theatre Quarterly,* February, 1990, pp. 25-30.
*New York,* June 6, 1970; December 2, 1974; February 20, 1978; May 17, 1982; January 6, 1986; June 21, 1993, pp. 71-72.

*New Yorker,* December 11, 1978; December 23, 1985, pp. 78, 80; June 28, 1993, p. 95.

*New York Review of Books,* February 19, 1981.

*New York Times,* September 19, 1969; May 17, 1970; June 4, 1970; July 6, 1970; December 17, 1974; February 2, 1977; April 1, 1980; April 5, 1980; November 16, 1980; February 1, 1981; June 6, 1981; March 21, 1982; May 5, 1982; November 12, 1982; December 5, 1982; May 15, 1984; December 11, 1985, p. C23; April 3, 1987; May 28, 1987; April 10, 1988; April 13, 1988; April 24, 1988; January 13, 1995, p. C2.

*New York Times Book Review,* February 1, 1981, pp. 8, 27.

*Paris Review,* summer, 1989, pp. 128-51.

*Publishers Weekly,* December 19, 1980, p. 38.

*Theater,* fall-winter, 1984, pp. 40-42.

*Time,* April 30, 1984, pp. 76-77.

*Times Literary Supplement,* May 2, 1980; March 1, 1985.

*Travel and Leisure,* December, 1992, pp. 118-22.

*Variety,* March 15, 1993, p. 70.

*Village Voice,* February 20, 1978.

*Washington Post,* April 13, 1985; September 29, 1987.

*World Literature Today,* summer, 1983, pp. 369-71.

# G

## GALLANT, Roy A(rthur)   1924-

*PERSONAL:* Born April 17, 1924, Portland, ME; children: Jonathan Roy, James Christopher. *Education:* Bowdoin College, B.A., 1948; Columbia University, M.S., 1949, and additional study. *Avocational interests:* Photography, oil painting, flying, horseback riding.

*ADDRESSES: Home*—Beaver Mountain Lake, Rangely, ME 04970. *Office*—Office of the Director, Southworth Planetarium, University of Southern Maine, 96 Falmouth St., Portland, ME 04103. *E-mail*—rgallant@Portland.maine.edu.

*CAREER:* Freelance writer. *Retailing Daily,* reporter, and *Boys' Life,* New York City, staff writer, 1949-51; *Scholastic Teacher,* New York City, managing editor, 1954-57; Doubleday & Co., Inc., New York City, author in residence, 1957-59; Aldus Books Ltd., London, England, executive editor, 1959-62; Natural History Press, New York City, editor in chief, 1962-65; member of faculty, Hayden Planetarium, American Museum, 1972-79; owner, publisher, and editor of *The Rangeley Highlander* (a weekly newspaper), 1977-78; University of Southern Maine, Portland, director of Southworth Planetarium, 1980—, adjunct professor, 1980-81, professor of English, 1981—. Instructor, Teachers College, Columbia University, 1958, and University of Maine, Farmington, 1975-76; guest lecturer, University of Illinois, 1964, 1965, and 1966. Science commentator, WCSH-TV, Portland, ME, 1985-86. Lecturer to professional, special interest and school groups on social problems associated with science and technology. Member of advisory board, Center for the Study of the First Americans. Consultant (temporary appointment) to President's Committee for Scientists and Engineers, The Edison Project, 1993, and Israel Academy of Arts and Science environmental sciences project, 1994. *Military service:* U.S. Army Air Forces, navigator, 1943-46; Military Intelligence, member of faculty and staff, Psychological Warfare School, Fort Riley, KS, and psychological warfare officer, Tokyo, Japan, during Korean War.

*MEMBER:* Authors Guild, Authors League of America, American Association for the Advancement of Science, Aircraft Owners and Pilots Association, Royal Astronomical Society (fellow), New York Academy of Sciences.

*AWARDS, HONORS:* Co-recipient of Thomas Alva Edison Foundation Award for best children's science book of the year, 1959, for *Exploring the Universe;* Boys' Clubs of America junior book award certificate, 1959, for *Exploring Chemistry;* National Science Teachers Association outstanding science book for children awards, 1980, for *Memory: How It Works and How to Improve It,* 1982, for *The Planets,* 1983, for *Once around the Galaxy,* 1984, for *101 Questions and Answers about the Universe,* 1986, for *The Macmillan Book of Astronomy,* and 1987, for *Rainbows, Mirages, and Sundogs;* Publication Award, Geographic Society of Chicago, 1980, for *Our Universe;* Distinguished Achievement Award, University of Southern Maine, 1981; Outstanding Science Trade Book for Children award, Children's Book Council, 1987, for *Rainbows, Mirages, and Sundogs;* John Burroughs Award, 1996, for *The Day the Sky Split Apart.*

*WRITINGS:*

*Exploring the Moon,* Doubleday (New York City), 1955, revised edition, 1966.

*Exploring the Universe,* Doubleday, 1956, revised edition published as *The Nature of the Universe,* Doubleday, 1968.

*Exploring Mars,* Doubleday, 1956, revised edition, 1968.

*Exploring the Weather,* Doubleday, 1957, second revised edition published as *The Nature of the Weather,* 1969.

*Exploring the Planets,* Doubleday, 1958, revised edition, 1967.

*Exploring Chemistry,* Doubleday, 1958.

*Exploring the Sun,* Doubleday, 1958.

*Man's Reach into Space,* Doubleday, 1959, revised edition, 1964.

*Exploring under the Earth,* Doubleday, 1960.

(Editor with F. Debenham) *Discovery and Exploration,* Doubleday, 1960.

*The ABC's of Astronomy: An Illustrated Dictionary,* Doubleday, 1962.

*Antarctica,* Doubleday, 1962.

*The ABC's of Chemistry: An Illustrated Dictionary,* Doubleday, 1963.

(Editor with G. E. R. Deacon) *Seas, Maps and Men,* Doubleday, 1963.

*Universe,* Doubleday, 1964.

(Editor with T. F. Gaskill) *World Beneath the Oceans,* Natural History Press (Garden City, NY), 1964.

(Editor with C. A. Ronan) *Man Probes the Universe,* Natural History Press, 1964.

*Weather,* Doubleday, 1966.

(With C. J. Schuberth) *Discovering Rocks and Minerals: A Nature and Science Guide to Their Collection and Identification,* Natural History Press, 1967.

(With Clifford Swartz) *Measure and Find Out: A Quantitative Approach to Science* (textbook series for grades 4-6), Scott, Foresman (Glenview, IL), 1969.

*Man Must Speak: The Story of Language and How We Use It,* Random House (New York City), 1969.

(Editor with McElroy) *Foundations of Biology,* Prentice-Hall (Englewood Cliffs, NJ), 1969.

(Editor) *The Universe in Motion,* Harper (New York City), 1969.

(Coauthor and editor) *Gravitation,* Harper, 1969.

(Coauthor and editor) *The Message of Starlight,* Harper, 1969.

*Man's Reach for the Stars,* Doubleday, 1971.

*Me and My Bones,* Doubleday, 1971.

*Man the Measurer: Our Units of Measure and How They Grew,* Doubleday, 1972.

*Charles Darwin: The Making of a Scientist,* Doubleday, 1972.

(With Roderick A. Suthers) *Biology: The Behavioral View,* Xerox Publishing (Middletown, CT), 1973.

*Explorers of the Atom,* Doubleday, 1973.

*Astrology: Sense or Nonsense?,* Doubleday, 1974.

*How Life Began: Creation versus Evolution,* Four Winds Press (Bristol, FL), 1975.

*Beyond Earth: The Search for Extraterrestrial Life,* Four Winds Press, 1977.

*Fires in the Sky: The Birth and Death of Stars,* Four Winds Press, 1978.

*Earth's Changing Climate,* Four Winds Press, 1978.

*Our Universe,* National Geographic Society (Washington, DC), 1980, revised edition, 1994.

*Memory: How It Works and How to Improve It,* Macmillan (New York City), 1980.

*The Constellations: How They Came to Be,* Four Winds Press, 1980.

*The Planets: Exploring the Solar System,* Four Winds Press, 1982.

*The Jungmann Concept and Technique of Anti-Gravity Leverage,* Institute for Gravitational Strain Pathology, 1982.

*Once around the Galaxy,* Watts (New York City), 1983.

(Contributor) Ashley Montague, editor, *Science and Creationism,* Oxford University Press (New York City), 1983.

*101 Questions and Answers about the Universe,* Macmillan, 1985.

*Fossils,* Watts, 1985.

*The Ice Ages,* Watts, 1985.

*Lost Cities,* Watts, 1985.

*The Macmillan Book of Astronomy,* Macmillan, 1986.

*Private Lives of the Stars,* Macmillan, 1986.

*The Solar System,* Macmillan, 1986.

*From Living Cells to Dinosaurs,* Watts, 1986.

*Our Restless Earth,* Watts, 1986.

*The Rise of Mammals,* Watts, 1986.

*Rainbows, Mirages, and Sundogs* (Junior Literary Guild selection), Macmillan, 1987.

*Ancient Indians: The First Americans,* Enslow (Hillside, NJ), 1989.

*Before the Sun Dies: The Story of Evolution,* Macmillan, 1989.

*The Peopling of Planet Earth: From Neanderthal to the Present,* Macmillan, 1990.

*Earth's Vanishing Forests,* Macmillan, 1991.

*A Young Person's Guide to Science,* Macmillan, 1993.

*The Day the Sky Split Apart,* Atheneum (New York City), 1995.

*Geysers: When Earth Roars,* Watts, 1997.

Also coauthor with Isaac Asimov and Jeanne Bendick of volumes in "The Ginn Science Program" series, Ginn, 1973-80. Author of study guides and instructors' manuals for science textbooks. Contributor to *Book of Knowledge, The Public Trust and the First Americans,* and to *Science-86, Omni, Reporter, American Biology Teacher, Science and Children,* and other magazines. Editorial advisor, Doubleday's "Pictorial Library" series and Prentice-Hall's high school biology textbook program. Member of editorial board, *Natural History,* 1962-64; consulting editor, *Nature and Science,* 1965-68; consultant in earth and space science to *Science and Children,* National Science Teacher's Association, 1980—.

*SIDELIGHTS:* In the realm of physical science, Roy A. Gallant's special interest is astronomy. As a science writer and editor, he believes that few subjects are too complex to present to children. "If a writer has command of the scientific concept he is dealing with," Gallant comments, "he can operate on the level of abstraction he chooses; and if he knows the capabilities of his audience, he can communicate with them."

*BIOGRAPHICAL/CRITICAL SOURCES:*

BOOKS

*Contemporary Literary Criticism,* Volume 17, Gale (Detroit), 1981.

*Something about the Author,* Gale, Volume 4, 1973, Volume 68, 1992.

PERIODICALS

*American Scientist,* November, 1993, p. 588.

*Appraisal: Science Books for Young People,* winter, 1994, p. 14.

*Booklist,* March 1, 1990, p. 1270.

*Book Report,* March, 1990, p. 52; January, 1994, p. 60.

*New York Times Book Review,* August 1, 1982.

*School Library Journal,* September, 1994, p. 145.

*Voice of Youth Advocates,* April, 1990, p. 48.

*Washington Post Book World,* May 12, 1985; May 13, 1990, p. 17.

## GARDAM, Jane 1928-

*PERSONAL:* Born July 11, 1928, in Coatham, Yorkshire, England; daughter of William (a schoolmaster) and Kathleen Mary (Helm) Pearson; married David Hill Gardam (a Queens counsel), April 20, 1952; children: Timothy, Mary, Thomas. *Education:* Bedford College, London, B.A. (with honors), 1949, graduate study, 1949-52. *Politics:* "Ecology." *Religion:* Anglo-Catholic. *Avocational interests:* Growing roses.

*ADDRESSES: Home*—Haven House, Sandwich, Kent, England. *Office*—c/o Hamish Hamilton, 27 Wrights Lane, London W8 5TZ, England. *Agent*—Bruce Hunter, David Higham Associates, 5-8 Lower John Street, London W1R 4HA, England.

*CAREER:* Writer. *Weldons Ladies Journal,* London, England, sub-editor, 1952-53; *Time and Tide,* London, assistant literary editor, 1953-55. Organizer of hospital libraries for Red Cross, 1950.

*MEMBER:* PEN, Royal Society of Literature (fellow), Arts Club, University Womens Club.

*AWARDS, HONORS: Book World's* Spring Book Festival award, 1972, for *A Long Way from Verona; Boston Globe-Horn Book* honor book for text, 1974, for *The Summer after the Funeral;* David Higham Prize for fiction and Winifred Holtby Award, both 1977, both for *Black Faces, White Faces;* runner-up citation, Booker Prize, 1978, for *God on the Rocks;* Whitbread Award, 1983, for *The Hollow Land,* and 1991, for *The Queen of the Tambourine;* Carnegie Medal "highly recommended" award, for *The Hollow Land* and "commended" award, for *Bridget and William,* both 1983; Katherine Mansfield Award, 1984, for *The Pangs of Love;* Phoenix Award, 1991, for *A Long Way from Verona.*

*WRITINGS:*

JUVENILE FICTION

*A Few Fair Days* (short stories), illustrated by Peggy Fortnum, Macmillan (New York City), 1971.

*A Long Way from Verona* (novel), Macmillan, 1971.

*The Summer after the Funeral* (novel), Macmillan, 1973.

*Bilgewater* (novel), Hamish Hamilton (London), 1976.

*God on the Rocks* (novel), Morrow (New York City), 1978.

*Bridget and William,* illustrated by Janet Rawlings, Julia MacRae (New York City), 1981.

*The Hollow Land* (stories), illustrated by Rawlings, Julia MacRae, 1981.

*Horse,* illustrated by Rawlings, Julia MacRae, 1982.

*Kit,* illustrated by William Geldart, Julia MacRae, 1984.

*Kit in Boots,* Julia MacRae, 1986.

*Swan,* Julia MacRae, 1986.

*Through the Dolls' House Door* (novel), Julia Mac-Rae, 1987.

*ADULT FICTION*

*Black Faces, White Faces* (stories), Hamish Hamilton, 1975, published as *The Pineapple Bay Hotel,* Morrow, 1976.

*The Sidmouth Letters* (stories), Morrow, 1980.

*The Pangs of Love* (stories; also see below), Hamish Hamilton, 1983.

*Crusoe's Daughter* (novel), Atheneum (New York City), 1986.

*Showing the Flag* (stories), Penguin (New York City), 1989.

*The Queen of the Tambourine* (novel), Sinclair-Stevenson, 1991, St. Martin's (New York City), 1995.

*Going into a Dark House* (stories), Sinclair-Stevenson, 1994.

*OTHER*

Also author of scripts for television films, including *The Easter Lilies,* based on the author's book *The Pangs of Love.* Contributor of short stories to magazines.

*SIDELIGHTS:* Hailed in Great Britain as a writer of talent and originality, Jane Gardam has enjoyed success with children's fiction as well as with short stories and novels written expressly for adults. In the *Dictionary of Literary Biography,* Patricia Craig argues that categorizing Gardam's fiction strictly as "juvenile" or "adult" does the writer's work a disservice. The appeal of Gardam's fiction, writes Craig, "should not be restricted by any factor of age in the reader. . . . All of Gardam's work is marked by certain admirable characteristics: economy of style, exuberance and humor, a special relish for the startling and the unexpected."

Proof of Gardam's ability to touch readers of various ages can be found in the awards she has won: the David Higham Prize for *Black Faces, White Faces,* a collection of short stories for adults; the prestigious Whitbread Award for *The Hollow Land,* a work ostensibly for juveniles; and for *The Queen of the Tambourine,* a novel for adults. Jane Miller outlines Gardam's strengths in a *Times Literary Supplement* review: "[She] has a spectacular gift for detail, of the local and period kind, and for details which make characters so subtly unpredictable that they ring true, and her humor is tough as well as delicate."

Young teens on the brink of adulthood are often the central characters in Gardam's juvenile fiction. Craig believes that Gardam's works "recreate directly the sensations and impressions of childhood." Craig also notes a slightly autobiographical cast in a number of the juvenile novels: "Although to an extent transformed in the course of writing, certain elements of Gardam's early life seem to have made a fairly consistent pattern in her books: the girl with a much younger brother; the schoolmaster or clergyman father; the Yorkshire or Cumbria locations. Each book, however, has a distinctive feeling, a mood and atmosphere all its own. Gardam repeats her motifs but not her effects. . . . [She] makes high comedy of the fidgets and fancies of adolescence, with her heroine constantly on the brink of some contretemps or social disaster; but the narrative is charged as well with a kind of muted fairy-tale glamour."

Gardam received critical acclaim for her first three children's books, but she was still virtually unknown as an author when she published *Black Faces, White Faces.* The short story collection, which appeared in the United States as *The Pineapple Bay Hotel,* won Britain's David Higham Prize, even though it was not a novel at all. Craig explains that the stories in Gardam's story collections are interrelated within each volume, but "what is important is not the classification [as novel or collection] but the degree of acuity brought to bear on a theme." Indeed, publication of *Black Faces, White Faces* expanded Gardam's critical audience considerably and accorded her highly favorable reviews that have continued with subsequent story collections and novels.

Among her critically acclaimed works is the Whitbread Award-winning novel *The Queen of the Tambourine,* which tells the story of Eliza Peabody, a middle-aged woman whose marriage is dull and unsatisfying. The novel consists of Eliza's letters to her friend Joan, who has left her husband to live in the Far East. As Jonathan Yardley states in the *Washington Post,* the letters "describe a woman slipping slowly into lunacy." These letters, Michael Harris reports in the *Los Angeles Times Book Review,* "are full of delusions, often not sent and never answered." Commenting on the novel's structure, Frances Spalding writes in the *Times Educational Supplement* that the narrative strays from the "demands of a traditional plot" and "has an improvisatory air." Eliza's experiences, Spalding continues "form a series of vignettes which ornament the thread of her mental journeying." Several critics also remark on Gardam's ability to create a character who, although unreliable as a narrator because of her delusions, is nonetheless likeable. Calling *The Queen of the Tambourine* "funny and moving," Nina Sonenberg of the *New York Times Book Review* praises Gardam's "devilish wit" and describes Eliza as another heroine driven insane by "splendid suburban isolation." Barbara Hardy, however, writing for the *Times Literary Supplement,* questions the efficacy of Gardam's portrayal of Eliza's insanity. "Everything is explained by Eliza's madness," Hardy states, "but there are too many ways in which she is sane to the point of banality, and the mad bits are hardly ever thoroughly mad." Yardley recommends the novel to "readers with a taste for psychological portraiture and subtle wit."

Several critics discuss Gardam's ability to write with wit and sharpness about the English upper class without resorting to polemics. In a review for *Room of One's Own,* Carroll Klein explains that Gardam's approach in her stories is subtle, and that "the subtlety of her writing salvages and often enhances her reticence in making direct statements. She sets up a situation, creates brilliantly realistic dialogue, and lets the reader conclude what she will." Victoria Glendinning describes Gardam in the *Times Literary Supplement* as "a very English writer, in that her observation is at its sharpest on matters of class and status, and her most poisonous darts reserved for the upper middle classes, or rather for the female residue who no longer have servants to exploit and are ending their days in seedy stinginess." "Her manifold traps are hidden away under glass and satin," notes Raymond Sokolov in the *Washington Post Book World.* "The voice you hear is an odd combination of girl and grande dame, a voice that trills out the most sinister truths as if they were part of the court circular." In a London *Times* review of *The Pangs of Love,* Elaine Feinstein suggests that Gardam "is a spare and elegant master of her art, which is neither genteel nor gentle, and she spares the well-bred less than the vulgar, and the predictably English abroad least of all."

Gardam's penchant for writing about the English middle class is clearly evident in her story collection, *Going into a Dark House.* Writing in the *Spectator,* Anita Brookner describes the world Gardam creates as "cautious, middle-class, respectable, and capable of extreme wildness." The majority of the characters are middle-aged or elderly and theme of death and chance are prominent in many of the stories. "Death is everywhere," states Alex Clark of the *Times Literary Supplement,* "and it provides the dominant motif through which character, motivation and story are revealed." Brookner considers the collection a tribute to Gardam's talent as a writer and states that though "robustly English and eschewing post-modern tricks, [Gardam's writing] conquers by stealth, as all good fiction should, and surprises one with a convincing account of eccentricities triumphing over the most mundane of circumstances."

Throughout Gardam's fiction, juvenile and adult alike, the author explores eccentric behavior. Klein notes that "Gardam peoples her stories with ineffectual, occasionally absurd, characters, with the walking wounded, the intellectually incompetent, and with those hovering on the edge of social approbation." A *Times Literary Supplement* reviewer also notes that Gardam's characters, "young and old, are observed with unwavering directness, their emotional hang-ups and outlets quietly understated so that the adolescent reader can take or leave the undertones." In Craig's view, Gardam "is interested in the discrepancy between the face one presents to the world and one's actual feelings, and the comedy which results from lack of face." Gardam's eccentric characters are matched by her eye for finding the strange hidden among the everyday. "She can pick on the small incident and find that behind it lies the bizarre, or the chilling, uncomfortable edge," writes Simon Blow in the *New Statesman.* According to Craig, however, "the fanciful and highly colored in Gardam's work are always disciplined by a northern toughness and plainness of expression."

An incisive comment on Gardam's talent comes from a *Times Literary Supplement* review of *A Long Way from Verona:* "Jane Gardam is a writer of such humorous intensity—glorious dialogue, hilarious set-pieces—that when one reads her for the first time one laughs aloud and when rereading her, the acid test for funny books, one's admiration increases a hundredfold." In the years since Gardam began publishing fiction, Craig concludes, she "has shown herself to be a novelist of rare inventiveness and power."

*BIOGRAPHICAL/CRITICAL SOURCES:*

BOOKS

Blishen, Edward, editor, *The Thorny Paradise: Writers on Writing for Children,* Kestrel, 1975.
*Children's Literature Review,* Volume 12, Gale (Detroit), 1987.
*Contemporary Literary Criticism,* Volume 43, Gale, 1987.
*Dictionary of Literary Biography,* Volume 14: *British Novelists since 1960,* Gale, 1983.
*Something about the Author Autobiography Series,* Volume 9, Gale, 1990.

PERIODICALS

*Booklist,* October 1, 1987.
*Horn Book,* October, 1978; December, 1978.
*Los Angeles Times Book Review,* December 21, 1980; October 22, 1995.
*New Statesman,* November 12, 1971; October 13, 1978; April 11, 1980, p. 558.
*New Statesman & Society,* April 12, 1996, p. 39.
*New York Times,* December 19, 1980.
*New York Times Book Review,* May 7, 1972; February 17, 1974; August 11, 1974; May 2, 1976; April 27, 1986; August 27, 1995, p. 18.
*Observer* (London), February 13, 1983; October 9, 1994.
*Publishers Weekly,* September 25, 1987, p. 111; July 8, 1988, p. 57.
*Room of One's Own,* Volume 8, number 3, 1983.
*School Librarian,* May, 1987, pp. 131-32.
*Spectator,* November 13, 1971; December 22, 1973; November 29, 1975; December 11, 1976; November 25, 1978; May 3, 1980; February 19, 1983; September 3, 1994, p. 36.
*Times* (London), February 10, 1983; February 9, 1985.
*Times Educational Supplement,* November 20, 1981; November 21, 1986, p. 31; September 18, 1987, p. 34; November 27, 1987, p. 45; January 6, 1989, p. 26; May 3, 1991, p. 23.
*Times Literary Supplement,* November 22, 1971; December 3, 1971; November 23, 1973; September 19, 1975; December 10, 1976; October 13, 1978; April 18, 1980; March 27, 1981; September 18, 1981; February 10, 1984; May 31, 1985; July 10, 1987, p. 751; July 7, 1989; April 12, 1991, p. 18; August 26, 1994, p. 20.
*Washington Post,* April 21, 1986; August 23, 1995, p. C3.
*Washington Post Book World,* May 2, 1976; January 8, 1978.

## GAREAU, Etienne 1915-1988

*PERSONAL:* Born October 21, 1915, in Saint-Jacques, Montcalm, Quebec, Canada; died November 27, 1988; son of Hector (a farmer) and Camilla (Martineau) Gareau. *Education:* Gregorian University, B.Ph., 1938; University of Ottawa, B.A., 1940, L.Th., 1946; Laval University, Licence es Lettres classiques, 1949; Sorbonne, University of Paris, Docteur de l'Universite de Paris en latin, 1952.

*CAREER:* Roman Catholic priest of Oblate Fathers of Mary Immaculate. Juniorat du Sacre-Coeur, Ottawa, Ontario, professor of classical studies, 1943-47; University of Ottawa, Ottawa, Ontario, professor of Greek and Latin, 1952-67, professor of classical studies, 1967-88, chair of department, 1957-67. President of pre-doctoral awards committee, Canadian Council, 1966-67, member, 1968-69.

*MEMBER:* Societe canadienne des Etudes classiques (vice president, 1960-62, president, 1964-66), Classical Association of Canada (president, 1964-66), Societe des Etudes latines (Paris), Societe des Etudes grecques et latines du Quebec (vice president, 1967-75), Humanities Association of Canada, Association Guillaume Bude.

*AWARDS, HONORS:* French Government fellow, 1949-50; Canadian Council fellow, 1967-68; Canadian Council award in the arts, 1967-68.

*WRITINGS:*

*L'Universite d'Ottawa,* University of Ottawa (Ontario, Canada), 1957.
(Editor) *L'enseignement des civilisations grecque et romaine,* University of Montreal, 1970.
(Editor) *Methodes nouvelles d'enseignement des disciplines anciennes,* Laval University, 1970.
(Editor) *Valeurs antiques et temps modernes/Classical Values and the Modern World,* Les Editions de l'Universite d'Ottawa (Ontario, Canada), 1972.
*Etudes classiques: Liste de ressources pedagogiques, cycles intermediaire et superieur,* Ministry of Education (Toronto), 1979.
*Melanges offerts en hommage au Reverend pere Etienne Gareau,* Editions de l'Universite d'Ottawa, 1982.

Contributor to books, including *Les Humanites classiques au Quebec,* edited by Maurice Lebel, Editions de l'Acropole et du Forum, 1967; and *Les*

*Editions de textes et de commentaires d'auteurs anciens en France de 1585 a 1615,* Editions du Sphinx, 1979. Also contributor to professional journals.*

[*Date of death provided by Eugene King, Rector, Saint Paul University Seminary.*]


\* \* \*


## GASCOYNE, David (Emery) 1916-

*PERSONAL:* Born October 10, 1916, in Harrow, England; son of Leslie Noel (a bank official) and Winfred Isabel (Emery) Gascoyne; married Judy Tyler Lewis, May 17, 1975; children: 2 stepsons, 2 stepdaughters. *Education:* Attended Salisbury Cathedral Choir School ("this had a lasting influence on my life") and Regent Street Polytechnic.

*ADDRESSES: Home*—48 Oxford St., Northwood, Cowes, Isle of Wight PO31 8PT, England.

*CAREER:* Poet and writer. Has given poetry reading tours in the United States, 1951-52, and 1981, and in Ireland, 1984. Representative on international committee, *Nuova Revista Europa,* Milan; president, Third European Festival of Poetry, Belgium, 1981. Attended poetry festivals in Rome, Paris, Amsterdam, Florence, Belgrade, and other cities.

*MEMBER:* Royal Society of Literature (fellow), World Organization for Poets (member of cultural committee), Committee of Belgian Biennales Internationales de Poesi (honorary member).

*AWARDS, HONORS:* Rockefeller-Atlantic Award, 1949; the British Council and the Centre Georges Pompidou presented an "Homage to David Gascoyne" in 1981; Biella European Poetry Prize, 1982, for *La Mano de Poeta;* Chevalier Sans l'Ordre National des Arts et Lettres, 1995.

*WRITINGS:*

*Opening Day* (novel), Cobden-Sanderson, 1933.
*A Short Survey of Surrealism,* Cobden-Sanderson, 1935, City Lights (San Francisco, CA), 1982.
(Editor and author of introduction) Kenneth Patchen, *Outlaw of the Lowest Planet,* Grey Walls Press, 1946.

*The Hole in the Fourth Wall; or, Talk, Talk, Talk* (play), first produced in London at the Watergate Theatre, 1950.
*Thomas Carlyle,* Longmans, Green, 1952.
*Paris Journal, 1937-1939,* preface by Lawrence Durrell, Enitharmon Press, 1978.
*Journal, 1936-1937,* Enitharmon Press, 1980.
*Rencontres avec Benjamin Fondane,* Editions Arcane, 1984.
*Collected Journals 1937-1942,* introduction by Kathleen Raine, Skoob Book Publishing (London), 1991.
*Lawrence Durrell,* privately printed, 1993.

*POETRY*

*Roman Balcony, and Other Poems,* Lincoln Williams, 1932.
*Man's Life Is This Meat,* Parton Press, 1936.
*Hoelderlin's Madness,* Dent (London), 1938.
*Poems, 1937-1942,* Editions Poetry (London), 1943.
*A Vagrant, and Other Poems,* Lehmann (Gateshead, England), 1950.
*Night Thoughts* (verse play; first broadcast on radio by the British Broadcasting Corp., December 7, 1955), Grove (New York City), 1956, with an introduction by Simon Callow, Alyscamps Press, 1995.
*Collected Poems,* edited and with an introduction by Robin Skelton, Oxford University Press (Oxford, England), 1965, enlarged editions published as *Collected Poems, 1988,* 1988, and *Selected Poems,* Enitharmon Press (London), 1994.
*The Sun at Midnight: Aphorisms, with Two Poems,* Enitharmon Press, 1970.
*Three Poems,* Enitharmon Press, 1976.
*Early Poems,* Greville Press (Warwick, England), 1980.
*La Mano de Poeta,* Edizioni S. Marco dei Giustiniani, 1982.
*Tankens Doft,* Ellerstroms, 1988.
*Miserere, Poemes 1937-1942,* Granit, 1989.
*Three Remanences,* privately published, 1994.

*TRANSLATOR*

Salvador Dali, *Conquest of the Irrational,* J. Levy, 1935.
(With Humphrey Jennings) Benjamin Peret, *A Bunch of Carrots: Twenty Poems,* Roger Roughton, 1936, revised edition published as *Remove Your Hat,* 1936.
(With others) Paul Eluard, *Thorns of Thunder,* Europa/Nott, 1936.

Andre Breton, *What Is Surrealism?*, Faber (London), 1936.

*Collected Verse Translations,* edited by Skelton and Alan Clodd, Oxford University Press, 1970, enlarged edition, Enitharmon Press, 1996.

(With others) Paul Auster, editor, *The Random House Book of 20th Century French Poetry,* Random House (New York City), 1982.

Breton and Philippe Soupault, *The Magnetic Fields,* Atlas Press (London), 1985.

O. V. de-L. Milosz, *Poems of Milosz,* Enitharmon Press, 1993.

*OTHER*

Contributor to numerous anthologies, including books published in France, Germany, Italy, Yugoslavia, Argentina, and Hong Kong.

Also contributor to *Ambit, Botteghe Oscure, Cahiers du Sud, Literary Review, London Review of Books, Malahat Review, New English Weekly, Partisan Review, PN Review, Poetry Review, Temenos, Times Literary Supplement, Two Rivers,* and other publications in England, France, Belgium and Italy.

*SIDELIGHTS:* The poetry of David Gascoyne has undergone several major changes during his long career. At first an imagist, then a dedicated surrealist, Gascoyne's early poems were visionary, fantastic works filled with hallucinatory images and symbolic language. By the 1940s, he was writing mystical poems in which Christian imagery played a large part and the ecstatic pain of the religious seeker was paramount. Since publishing a few more poems in the late 1940s, Gascoyne has published little new work. Since the 1950s, his writing has been curtailed due to a mental breakdown and continuing bouts of severe depression. But Gascoyne's place in modern British poetry is secure; writing in *Twentieth Century,* Elizabeth Jennings describes Gascoyne as the "only living English poet in the true tradition of visionary or mystical poetry." In an article for the *Dictionary of Literary Biography,* Philip Gardner calls Gascoyne's *Poems, 1937-1942* "among the most distinguished and powerful collections of the last fifty years."

According to Gardner, in an article for the *Times Literary Supplement,* Gascoyne "was the literary prodigy of the 1930s." *Roman Balcony, and Other Poems,* Gascoyne's first book of poetry, appeared when the author was sixteen, and was followed by a novel, a nonfiction study entitled *A Short Survey of*

*Surrealism,* several volumes of work translated from the French, and, before Gascoyne was twenty, a second volume of poems. This initial burst of activity was never to be repeated.

*Roman Balcony, and Other Poems* was published in 1936 while Gascoyne was still attending school. He had received a small legacy and used the money to finance the book's publication. Strongly influenced by the imagist poets and the fin-de-siecle writings of the 1890s, these early poems are "highly impressionistic, introspective, and word-conscious," Gardner explains in the *Dictionary of Literary Biography.* Robin Skelton, in his introduction to Gascoyne's *Collected Poems,* calls *Roman Balcony* "an astonishing performance for an adolescent. . . . Already in this book there is that interest in hallucinatory obsessive symbolism which gave so many of [Gascoyne's] poems of the later thirties their individual and disturbing quality."

Gascoyne's early interest in symbolism and the hallucinatory led him to study the surrealist writers of the 1930s, a school little known in England at that time. He was one of the first British poets to take note of the surrealists, and is generally credited with introducing their work to the English-speaking world. In 1935 and 1936, Gascoyne translated collections by the surrealists Salvador Dali, Benjamin Peret, and Andre Breton. His nonfiction introduction to the group's beliefs, *A Short Survey of Surrealism,* is described by Stephen Spender in the *Times Literary Supplement* as "a delightful book conveying, almost for the first time in English, the fascination of this movement."

This interest in surrealism is evident in the second collection of Gascoyne's poems, *Man's Life Is This Meat,* a book which contains works dedicated to such surrealists as Max Ernst, Rene Magritte, and Salvador Dali. The poems utilize the juxtapositions, intense imagery, and dream logic found in many surrealist works. Skelton says of the poems in this collection that "Gascoyne employed surrealist techniques to good effect. . . . Some poems look like products of a free-association game, [but] a second glance shows them to be full of profound implications."

With *Poems, 1937-1942,* published during the Second World War, Gascoyne first won widespread critical acclaim. "It was with publication of *Poems, 1937-1942* . . . that Gascoyne's stature became fully apparent," Skelton believes. The book, Derek Stanford maintains in *Poetry Review,* represents "the high-water-mark of Gascoyne's career." Containing poems that are more mystical than those he wrote during his brief association with the surrealists, the book is the first expression, according to Jennings, of Gascoyne's mature poetic voice. "I do not think, . . . that he really found his own voice or his own individual means of expression until he started writing the poems which appeared in the volume entitled *Poems, 1937-42,*" Jennings writes.

In these mystical poems Gascoyne writes as an agonized Christian seeker desperate for a transcendent realm beyond the mortal world. "The theme which emerges most clearly . . .," Skelton states, "is that of man's despair at his mortality, and his confusion; but often it seems that some illumination of the darkness is imminent." Speaking of the poem series entitled "Miserere" which forms part of the book, Kathleen Raine of the *Sewanee Review* explains that these works "are in praise of the 'Eternal Christ'; the poet speaks from those depths into which the divine Presence has descended in order to redeem our fallen world, in a voice of sustained eloquence, as if at last the angel spoke." Commenting on this same group of poems, Spender explains that Gascoyne was inspired to write these works by the outbreak of the Second World War. Gascoyne, Spender states, "employs the Christian theme of the Miserere to express and transform the agony of war. . . . The poems which Gascoyne wrote early in the war have the immediacy of terrifying events which, acting upon the poet's sensibility like a hand upon an instrument, produce music and images that become part of the larger religious history of mankind."

Gascoyne's ability to combine his visionary poetry with an awareness of the real world around him is remarked upon by Skelton, who states that in *Poems, 1937-1942,* Gascoyne "achieved a religious poetry which combines powerful symbolism with contemporary relevance." Writing in *The Freedom of Poetry: Studies in Contemporary Verse,* Stanford believes that "the poetry of Gascoyne creates a world that is no escape from or substitute for the world we already know. All the problems reality makes us face, we face again in this poetry; and meeting them here for a second time we find them no longer modified by the small distractions of daily life, or the comic relief which existence offers. In this verse we are made to experience the total impact of wickedness—evil itself assumes an image. So, without mercy or mitigation, we are forced to look on this picture of our guilt and

inhabit a sphere that seems to be sealed against the possible entry of hope."

Gascoyne's affiliation with the surrealists of the 1930s left its mark on these later poems, although the works are not strictly in the surrealist style. As Michael Schmidt writes in *A Reader's Guide to Fifty Modern British Poets,* "Gascoyne, in his mature work, adapted elements of surrealist technique to an English tradition." Raine comments that "from the surrealists Mr. Gascoyne learned to find, everywhere mirrored in objective reality, subjective states." Writing in *The Ironic Harvest: English Poetry in the Twentieth Century,* Geoffrey Thurley finds that Gascoyne's "capacity for feeling in the presence of rare affinities . . . springs from the same sensibility as created the Surrealist poems, tutored by the Surrealist discipline." Schmidt sees two major influences from the surrealists: "In [Gascoyne's] later poems the surreal elements serve to intensify a mental drama which is powerful for being rooted in the real. . . . The tension is between what he can say and what a language, wrenched and disrupted, can only hope to imply. . . . The main lesson he learned from surrealism was rhythmical. Throughout his work, his sense of line and rhythm units is subtle. In the surreal poems, it is rhythm alone that renders the distorted imagery effective, that fuses disparate elements into an apparent whole."

Beginning with *Poems, 1937-1942,* Gascoyne began to write in a distinctive narrative voice. As a writer for the *Times Literary Supplement* observes, "What makes Gascoyne's poetry so remarkable is its oracular quality." Raine believes that Hoelderlin's work inspired Gascoyne. She cites the metaphysical poems in the *Poems, 1937-1942* volume as bearing "the evident mark of Hoelderlin's influence; whose imaginative flights David Gascoyne from this time dared, finding in his own wings an eagle-strength upon which he outsoared, in sublimity, all his contemporaries."

*A Vagrant, and Other Poems* appeared in 1950 and contains works written between 1943 and 1950. "Though it contains nothing finer than [the poems found in *Poems, 1937-1942*], the high level of pure poetry, the perfect command of language, never falters," Raine states. "The tone," Skelton notes, "is generally more quiet. The same beliefs are expressed, but with greater delicacy, and often with humor." Gardner, too, sees a quieter mood in *A Vagrant, and Other Poems.* Many of the poems in this collection, he states in the *Dictionary of Literary*

_Biography,_ "transmit a quiet inner beauty one would call mellow, if that word did not carry overtones of a temperament too easily satisfied. Perhaps one may suggest their spiritual quality by saying that they convey a new acceptance of human limitations, a reconciliation."

Several critics believe that _Night Thoughts,_ Gascoyne's lone attempt at a dramatic verse play, is among his finest works. Skelton, for example, calls it "his single greatest achievement." The play, written for and first broadcast on radio, is meant to "break through to those other islands of humanity, to reach the drifting rafts of those who, being alone, are also ready to make contact," as Thurley explains. This attempted union with members of the listening audience has a mystical connotation. Stanford believes that the most successful section of _Night Thoughts_ is called "Encounter with Silence." This section of the play "is one of the most subtle expositions of man as a spiritually communicative animal to be found in contemporary literature," Stanford writes. "The voice we hear speaking is that of the Solitary, who slowly realises that silence is the music not of the Void but of the Spirit."

During the 1960s and 1970s, Gascoyne published little new work. His _Collected Poems_ appeared in 1965 to general critical appreciation, and two volumes of his journals appeared in the late 1970s and early 1980s. But problems in his personal life prevented Gascoyne from writing new work.

Bouts of severe depression and paranoia, along with a brief drug addiction, hindered his efforts. He suffered, too, Gardner notes in the _Dictionary of Literary Biography,_ "three serious breakdowns in the course of his life." During one such episode in 1973, Gascoyne met Judy Tyler Lewis, a part-time hospital worker. They married in 1975. Gascoyne has said that since that time, his life has vastly improved.

Gascoyne's _Paris Journal, 1937-1939_ and _Journal, 1936-37_ were written just after his initial burst of creative activity. They record his move to Paris in the mid-1930s, his break with the surrealists and brief affiliation with communism, and provide a fascinating insight into his thoughts and observations of the time. As Spender notes about _Paris Journal,_ "On several levels, Gascoyne's journal is a classic example of this genre." "Taken together," Gardner writes in the _Times Literary Supplement,_ "the two journals offer admirers of Gascoyne's work an en-

grossing record of his self-realization and artistic growth."

Especially noted by critics was Gascoyne's success at rendering the tone and flavor of the time, as well as his revealing expression of his own moods and thoughts. "Few at 20, which was Gascoyne's age when he began [_Paris Journal, 1937-1939_], could have known themselves so fully or have had the literary maturity for such a self-portrait . . .," Ronald Blythe comments in the _Listener._ "The _Journal_ certainly charms, but with something more than talent—perhaps by its ability to describe, with neither conceit nor tedium, all the initial _longeur_ of a writer's existence." Spender finds in _Paris Journal_ "some beautiful passages of prose poetry evoking Paris street scenes and the French countryside—and also some very somber ones. The young Gascoyne is a marvelously truthful and exact recorder of impressions made on him at concerts and art exhibitions." Alan Ross, writing in _London Magazine,_ sees the appearance of Gascoyne's journals as a hopeful sign that the poet may soon begin writing new work. "What is encouraging about the journals," he states, "is that they suggest a shrewd and amusing observer of contemporary foibles, to the extent that one could envisage a late period in the poetry that might be more anecdotal and idiomatic as well as lighter in mood. Gascoyne's literary career, after so long and distressing an interruption, deserves a happy ending. There are few writers from whom one would more welcome poems out of the blue."

In a letter to _CA,_ Gascoyne comments on the possibility of his writing new poetry: "After about 15 years of complete non-production, and hospitalizations following three severe mental breakdowns, I have at the age of 72 recovered sufficient self-confidence to make me feel I may be entering a new, closing period of creativity."

_BIOGRAPHICAL/CRITICAL SOURCES:_

BOOKS

Beford, Colin, _David Gascoyne: A Bibliography of His Works (1929-1985),_ Heritage Books, 1986.
_Contemporary Literary Criticism,_ Volume 45, Gale, 1987.
_Dictionary of Literary Biography,_ Volume 20: _British Poets, 1914-1945,_ Gale, 1983.
Gascoyne, David, _Collected Poems,_ Oxford University Press, 1965.

Gascoyne, *Paris Journal, 1937-1939,* Enitharmon Press, 1978.

Gascoyne, *Journal, 1936-1937,* Enitharmon Press, 1980.

Raine, Kathleen, *Defending Ancient Springs,* Oxford University Press, 1967.

Remy, Michel, *David Gascoyne, ou l'urgence de l'inexprime,* Presses Universitaires de Nancy, 1984.

Scarfe, Francis, *Auden and After: The Liberation of Poetry, 1930-1941,* Routledge, 1942.

Schmidt, Michael, *A Reader's Guide to Fifty Modern British Poets,* Heinemann Educational, 1979.

Stanford, Derek, *The Freedom of Poetry: Studies in Contemporary Verse,* Falcon Press, 1947.

Stanford, *Inside the Forties: Literary Memoirs, 1937-1957,* Sidgwick & Jackson, 1977.

Thurley, Geoffrey, *The Ironic Harvest: English Poetry in the Twentieth Century,* Edward Arnold, 1974.

*PERIODICALS*

*Book Forum,* fall, 1978.

*Listener,* September 7, 1978.

*London Magazine,* July, 1957; November, 1965; June, 1981.

*New Statesman,* September 22, 1978.

*Observer,* December, 1950.

*Poetry,* September, 1966.

*Poetry Review,* Volume LVI, 1965.

*Sewanee Review,* spring, 1967.

*Temenos,* Number 7.

*Times Literary Supplement,* August 12, 1965; October 1, 1971; October 27, 1978; February 6, 1981; August 26, 1988.

*Twentieth Century,* June, 1959.

—*Sketch by Thomas Wiloch*

*       *       *

**GETZ, Gene A(rnold) 1932-**

*PERSONAL:* Born March 15, 1932, in Francesville, IN; son of John A. (a farmer) and Matilda (Honegger) Getz; married Elaine Holmquist, June 11, 1956; children: Renee Elaine, Robyn Lynn, Kenton Gene. *Education:* Moody Bible Institute, diploma, 1952; attended Easter Montana College of Education (now Eastern Montana College), 1952-53; Rocky Mountain College, B.A., 1954; Wheaton College, Wheaton IL, M.A., 1958; New York University, Ph.D., 1969.

*ADDRESSES: Home*—2822 Woods Lane, Garland, TX 75042; fax 214-783-8841. *Office*—1700 Gateway Blvd., Richardson, TX 75080. *E-mail*—gene_getz @fbcn.com.

*CAREER:* Engaged in radio ministry with Montana Gospel Crusade and youth director of Church of the Air, Billings, 1952-54; assistant pastor of community church in Hinsdale, IL, 1954; director of Christian education at Bible church in Lisle, IL, 1956-58; Moody Bible Institute, Chicago, IL, instructor in Christian education, 1956-68, director of evening school, 1963-68; Dallas Theological Seminary, Dallas, TX, associate professor of Christian education, beginning 1968; Fellowship Bible Church, Dallas, pastor, 1972-81; Center for Church Renewal, Plano, TX, director, 1978—. Visiting professor, Word of Life Summer Institute of Camping, Schroon Lake, NY, 1964-68. President, Space Age Communications, Dallas.

*MEMBER:* National Association of Professors of Christian Education, National Sunday School Association (former president of research commission).

*WRITINGS:*

*Audio-Visuals in the Church,* Moody (Chicago, IL), 1959, revised edition published as *Audiovisual Media in Christian Education,* 1972.

*The Vacation Bible School in the Local Church,* Moody, 1962.

*The Christian Home,* Moody, 1967.

(With Roy B. Zuck) *Christian Youth: An In-Depth Study,* Moody, 1968.

*The History of the Moody Bible Institute,* Moody, 1969.

*The Story of the Moody Bible Institute,* Moody, 1969.

(Editor with Zuck) *Adult Education in the Church,* Moody, 1970.

(With Zuck) *Ventures in Family Living,* Moody 1971.

*Sharpening the Focus of the Church,* Moody, 1974, revised edition, Victor Books (Wheaton, IL), 1984.

*The Measure of a Man,* Regal Books (Ventura, CA), 1974.

*The Measure of a Church*, Regal Books, 1975.
*The Measure of a Family*, Regal Books, 1976.
*Building Up One Another*, Victor Books (Wheaton, IL), 1976.
*When You're Confused and Uncertain*, Regal Books, 1976.
*When You Feel Like You Haven't Got It*, Regal Books, 1976.
*The Measure of a Woman*, Regal Books, 1977.
*Loving One Another*, Victor Books, 1979.
*When You Feel Like a Failure*, Regal Books, 1979.
*When the Job Seems Too Big*, Regal Books, 1979.
*Encouraging One Another*, Victor Books, 1981.
*When Your Goals Seem Out of Reach*, Regal Books, 1981.
*Joseph: From Prison to Palace*, Regal Books, 1983.
*Pressing On When You'd Rather Turn Back*, Regal Books, 1983.
*Saying No When You'd Rather Say Yes*, Regal Books, 1983.
*Serving One Another*, Victor Books, 1984.
*When the Pressure's On*, Regal Books, 1984.
*Believing God When You're Tempted to Doubt*, Regal Books, 1984.
*Doing Your Part When You'd Rather Let God Do It All*, Regal Books 1984.
*Looking Up When You Feel Down*, Regal Books 1985.
*Living for Others When You'd Rather Live for Yourself*, Regal Books, 1985.
*Standing Firm When You'd Rather Retreat*, Regal Books, 1986.
*God's Plan for Building a Good Reputation*, Victor Books, 1987.
*Partners for Life*, Regal Books, 1988.
*Biblical Theology of Material Possessions*, Moody Press, 1990.
*Real Prosperity*, Moody Press, 1990.
*Filling the Holes in Our Souls*, Moody Press, 1992.
*The Walk: The Measure of Spiritual Maturity*, Broadman and Holman, (Nashville, TN), 1994.
*David: Seeking God Faithfully*, Broadman and Holman, 1995.
*Elijah: Remaining Steadfast through Uncertainty*, Broadman and Holman, 1995.
*Joshua: Living as a Constant Role Model*, Broadman and Holman, 1995.
*Nehemiah: Becoming a Disciplined Leader*, Broadman & Holman, 1995.
*Abraham: Holding Fast to the Will of God*, Broadman and Holman, 1996.
*Jacob: Following God without Looking Back*, Broadman and Holman, 1996.
*Joseph: Overcoming Obstacles through Faithfulness*, Broadman and Holman, 1996.

*WORK IN PROGRESS:* An exposition on Romans; books on leadership in the local church and on biblical renewal.

*SIDELIGHTS:* Gene A. Getz wrote *CA:* "One of the unique surprises for me is the way in which a number of my books have been translated into foreign languages. To date, over fifty titles have been translated into at least twelve different languages. Several of my titles are scheduled for translation and release in all of the Eastern European languages. This is encouraging in that I have attempted to write with a supracultural perspective."

*        *        *

## GILBERT, Michael (Francis) 1912-

*PERSONAL:* Born July 17, 1912, in Billinghay, Lincolnshire, England; son of Bernard Samuel (a writer) and Berwyn Minna (Cuthbert) Gilbert; married Roberta Mary Marsden, July 26, 1947; children: Harriett Sarah, Victoria Mary, Olivia Margaret, Kate Alexandra, Richard Adam St. John, Laura Frances, Gerard Valentine Hugo. *Education:* University of London, LL.B., 1937. *Politics:* "Me-ist." *Religion:* Church of England. *Avocational interests:* Cricket, contract bridge, walking.

*ADDRESSES: Home*—Luddesdown Old Rectory, Cobham, Kent, DA13 0XE, England. *Agent*—Curtis Brown Ltd., Haymarket House, 28129 Haymarket, London SW1 Y, England.

*CAREER:* Schoolmaster in Salisbury, 1931-38; Ellis, Bickersteth, Aglionby & Hazel, London, England, articled clerk, 1938-39; Trower, Still & Keeling, London, solicitor, 1947-51, partner, 1952-73. Legal advisor, government of Bahrain, 1960. British Army, Royal Horse Artillery, 1939-45; served in North Africa and Italy; held for a time in an Italian prisoner of war camp; escaped; became major; mentioned in dispatches.

*MEMBER:* Law Society, Society of Authors, Crime Writers Association (founder; member of committee, 1985-87), Mystery Writers of America, British Film Association, Garrick Club, Band of Brothers.

*AWARDS, HONORS:* Commander, Order of the British Empire, 1980; Grand Master Award, Mystery Writers of America, 1987, for lifetime achievement; Diamond Dagger, Crime Writers Association, 1996.

*WRITINGS:*

NOVELS

*Close Quarters,* Hodder & Stoughton (London), 1947, Walker & Co. (New York City), 1963, reprinted, Hamlyn (London), 1981.

*He Didn't Mind Danger,* Harper (New York City), 1948 (published in England as *They Never Looked Inside,* Hodder & Stoughton, 1948).

*The Doors Open,* Hodder & Stoughton, 1949, Walker & Co., 1962.

*Smallbone Deceased,* Harper, 1950, reprinted, Garland Publishing (New York City), 1976.

*Death Has Deep Roots,* Hodder & Stoughton, 1951, reprinted, 1975, Harper, 1952.

*The Danger Within,* Harper, 1952, reprinted, 1978 (published in England as *Death in Captivity,* Hodder & Stoughton, 1952).

*Fear to Tread,* Harper, 1953, reprinted, 1978.

*The Country-House Burglar,* Harper, 1955 (published in England as *Sky High,* Hodder & Stoughton, 1955).

*Be Shot for Sixpence,* Harper, 1956.

*Blood and Judgement,* Hodder & Stoughton, 1959, Harper, 1978.

*After the Fine Weather,* Harper, 1963.

*The Crack in the Teacup,* Harper, 1966.

*The Dust and the Heat,* Hodder & Stoughton, 1967, published as *Overdrive,* Harper, 1968.

*The Family Tomb,* Harper, 1969 (published in England as *The Etruscan Net,* Hodder & Stoughton, 1969).

*The Body of a Girl* (also see below), Harper, 1972.

*The Ninety-Second Tiger,* Harper, 1973.

*Flash Point* (also see below), Harper, 1974.

*The Night of the Twelfth,* Harper, 1976.

*The Empty House,* Harper, 1979.

*The Killing of Katie Steelstock,* Harper, 1980 (published in England as *Death of a Favourite Girl,* Hodder & Stoughton, 1980).

*End Game,* Harper, 1982 (published in England as *The Final Throw,* Hodder & Stoughton, 1982).

*The Black Seraphim,* Harper, 1984.

*The Long Journey Home,* Harper, 1985.

*Trouble,* Harper, 1987.

*Paint, Gold, and Blood,* Harper, 1989.

*The Queen against Karl Mullem,* Hodder & Stoughton, 1992.

*Roller Coaster,* Hodder & Stoughton, 1993.

*Ring of Terror,* Hodder & Stoughton, 1995.

STORY COLLECTIONS

*Game without Rules* (also see below), Harper, 1967.

*Stay of Execution and Other Stories of Legal Practice,* Hodder & Stoughton, 1971.

*Amateur in Violence,* Davis Publications (Worcester, MA), 1973.

*Petrella at Q,* Harper, 1977.

*Mr. Calder and Mr. Behrens,* Harper, 1982.

*The Young Petrella: Stories,* Harper, 1988.

*Anything for a Quiet Life,* Carroll and Graf (New York City), 1990.

PLAYS

*A Clean Kill* (also see below; first produced in London on the West End, 1959), Constable (London), 1961.

*The Bargain* (first produced in London on the West End, 1961), Constable, 1961.

*The Shot in Question* (first produced in London on the West End, 1963), Constable, 1963.

*Windfall* (first produced in London on the West End, 1963), Constable, 1963.

EDITOR

*Crime in Good Company: Essays on Criminals and Crime-Writing,* Constable, 1959.

*Best Detective Stories of Cyril Hare,* Faber (London), 1959, Walker & Co., 1961.

*The Oxford Book of Legal Anecdotes,* Oxford University Press, 1986.

Editor, "Classics of Detection and Adventure" series, Hodder & Stoughton.

OTHER

*Dr. Crippen,* Odhams Press, 1953.

*The Claimant,* Constable, 1957.

*The Law,* David & Charles (Devonshire, England), 1977.

Also author of radio scripts: "Death in Captivity," 1953, "The Man Who Could Not Sleep," 1955, "Crime Report" (also see below), 1956, "Doctor at

Law," 1956, "The Waterloo Table," 1957, "You Must Take Things Easy," 1958, "Stay of Execution," 1965, "Game without Rules" (based on his story of the same title), 1968, "The Last Chapter," 1970, "Black Light," 1972, "Flash Point" (based on his novel of the same title), 1974, "Petrella," 1976, "In the Nick of Time," 1979, "The Last Tenant," 1979, and "The Oyster Catcher," 1983.

Also author of television scripts: "The Crime of the Century," 1956, "Wideawake," 1957, "The Body of a Girl" (based on his novel of the same title), 1958, "Fair Game," 1958, "Crime Report" (based on his radio script of the same title), 1958, "Blackmail Is So Difficult," 1959, "Dangerous Ice," 1959, "A Clean Kill" (based on his play of the same title), 1961, "The Men from Room 13" (adapted from a story by Stanley Firmin), 1961, "Scene of the Accident," 1961, "The Betrayers" (adapted from a story by Stanley Ellin), 1962, "Trial Run," 1963, "The Blackmailing of Mr. S.," 1964, "The Mind of the Enemy," 1965, "The Man in Room 17," 1966, "Misleading Cases" (adapted from a story by A. P. Herbert), 1971, "Hadleigh," 1971, "Money to Burn" (adapted from the novel by Margery Allingham), 1974, and "Where There's a Will," 1975.

Contributor of short stories to *Ellery Queen's Mystery Magazine.* Also contributor to *The Mystery Writers' Handbook,* edited by Herbert Brean, Harper, 1956; *Winter's Crimes I,* edited by George Hardinge, St. Martin's, 1969; *The Mystery Story,* edited by John Ball, University of California Extension, 1976; *The World of Raymond Chandler,* edited by Miriam Gross, Weidenfeld & Nicolson, 1977; *Agatha Christie: First Lady of Crime,* edited by H. R. F. Keating, Weidenfeld & Nicolson, 1977; *Murder Ink: The Mystery Reader's Companion,* edited by Dilys Winn, Workman Publishing, 1977; *The Great Detectives,* edited by Otto Penzler, Little, Brown, 1978; *Verdict of Thirteen,* edited by Julian Symons, Harper, 1979; *Winter's Crimes 12,* edited by Hilary Watson, St. Martin's, 1980; *Who Done It?,* edited by Alice Laurance and Isaac Asimov, Houghton, 1980; *After Midnight Ghost Book,* Hutchinson, 1980; and *Crime Wave,* Collins, 1980.

*SIDELIGHTS:* Michael Gilbert has written over thirty novels of mystery and adventure, a similar number of works for radio and television, and four successful plays for the West End, all while working full time as a solicitor. Gilbert wrote most of his books during the train ride to and from his office in London. He tells Rosemary Herbert of *Publishers Weekly:* "The journey lasted 45 or 50 minutes, and I know it doesn't *sound* like a great deal of time, but it's true. . . . The train started; I started writing. The train pulled into Victoria station and I stopped." This method allowed Gilbert, writing some two-and-a-half pages a day, to finish a novel in about five or six months' time. In 1987 his efforts earned him a Grand Master Award from the Mystery Writers of America, the mystery genre's highest honor.

Before writing mysteries, Gilbert served in the British Army during the Second World War and was stationed in Canada and North Africa. He was captured by the Germans and held for a time in a prisoner of war camp in Italy. This experience was later re-created in the novel *The Danger Within,* the story of British prisoners who must uncover the traitor among them while they plot their escape. Following the war, Gilbert followed the advice of his uncle, who was the Lord Chief Justice of India, and joined a law firm in London, where he became a partner in 1952. At one time he served as mystery writer Raymond Chandler's legal advisor, and drew up the late author's will. Gilbert retired from the legal profession in 1983.

Gilbert's first novel, *Close Quarters,* is a tràditional mystery story set in a small English cathedral town, a setting Gilbert has used in many of his stories. His early novels follow the conventional pattern of classic English mystery fiction, presenting Agatha Christie-type puzzles that must be solved by the reader. They are noted, too, for their realistic depiction of police procedures and the workings of the legal system, subjects well known to Gilbert from his own law career.

As he became more comfortable with the writing of mysteries, Gilbert began to move away from the courtroom and police station, exploring other settings and characters and developing plots that are more than just puzzles. In *Fear to Tread,* Gilbert writes of a school headmaster who turns detective, while in *The Doors Open,* he writes of illegal activities in the insurance business. In other novels he has written of counterintelligence agents, the French resistance, and British diplomatic missions on the Continent. His work began to include more humor as well. His *Smallbone Deceased,* for example, concerns a corpse that is discovered in a bank's safe deposit box. M. H. Oakes of the *New York Times* calls the novel an "agreeably understated satire," while L. G. Offord of the *San Francisco Chronicle* praises the "excellent plot and characters, high literacy and that inimitable English trick of submerged humor."

Among the many strengths of Gilbert's stories, Anthony Boucher writes in the *New York Times Book Review,* are "the smooth ingenuity of plotting [and] the manner of telling, which disconcertingly combines elegance and harshness." "From Gilbert one expects supercivilized writing," Newgate Callendar explains in the *New York Times Book Review,* "and he does not disappoint." Reviewing the 1987 book *Trouble,* John Gross of the *New York Times* notes that "Gilbert published his first novel some 40 years ago, but you would never guess it from *Trouble.* The writing is as crisp as ever; there is the same professionalism, the same firm balance between atmosphere and plot."

Several critics have praised Gilbert for his ability to take his readers behind the scenes of a respected profession and show how it operates. T. J. Binyon of the *Times Literary Supplement,* for example, remarks on "how expert he is at creating the atmosphere of a profession." Speaking of the novel *Trouble,* Jon L. Breen of the *Armchair Detective* notes that it "demonstrates [Gilbert's] ability to impart specialized information and to deploy a large cast of characters effectively." The realism of Gilbert's stories has also been remarked upon by several reviewers. Boucher, for one, claims that the espionage stories found in the collection *Game without Rules* are "short works of art in social realism."

Gilbert has created several memorable detective characters who reappear from time to time in his novels. Perhaps his most popular has been Patrick Petrella, a detective chief inspector with the South London Division of the Metropolitan Police. Petrella's father was a police lieutenant in Franco's Spain, while his mother is a proper Englishwoman. He is fond of quoting from the classics of literature as well as from the police manual of English law. His only full-length adventure was recounted in 1959's *Blood and Judgement,* a novel in which then-sergeant Petrella investigated the murder of a convict's wife on the bank of a London reservoir. The novel earned high accolades as one of the best police novels of the year.

Writing in his contribution to *The Great Detectives,* Gilbert recalls how he invented his character. "Petrella," he writes, "was conceived in church. The moment of his conception is as clearly fixed in my mind as though it had happened yesterday. . . . It was a drowsy summer evening and the preacher had reached what appeared to be only the midpoint of his sermon. It was not an inspired address, and I turned, as I sometimes do in such circumstances, to the hymn book for relief." There, Gilbert found the words of a poem by Christina Rosetti and an idea for a story came to him. More importantly, the picture of the police officer who played the central role in the story came to him. "In that short sequence, which cannot have lasted for more than a few seconds," Gilbert comments, "a complete character was encapsulated." Since his initial case in the late 1950s, Petrella has gone on to solve a number of baffling mysteries and has appeared in many short stories.

Over the more than three decades that Gilbert had been writing mystery stories, he has earned the praise of many critics in the field. Gross calls Gilbert "one of the acknowledged masters of the contemporary crime story," while Anatole Broyard of the *New York Times* describes him as "a master of the classic English murder mystery." In an article for the *Times Literary Supplement,* Julian Symons maintains that Gilbert "has been writing intelligent, well-crafted detective stories and thrillers" for more than thirty years. "When at the top of his form," Symons concludes, "nobody excels Mr. Gilbert in posing and developing a mystery."

## BIOGRAPHICAL/CRITICAL SOURCES:

### BOOKS

Penzler, Otto, editor, *The Great Detectives,* Little, Brown, 1978.
*Twelve Englishmen of Mystery,* Popular Press, 1984.

### PERIODICALS

*Armchair Detective,* summer, 1988.
*Best Sellers,* February 15, 1966.
*New Republic,* October 16, 1976.
*New Yorker,* July 1, 1967.
*New York Times,* November 5, 1950; December 10, 1983; May 17, 1985; June 19, 1987.
*New York Times Book Review,* February 6, 1966; July 2, 1967; August 20, 1976.
*Publishers Weekly,* October 25, 1985.
*San Francisco Chronicle,* October 22, 1950.
*Times* (London), May 16, 1985.
*Times Literary Supplement,* May 23, 1980; August 21, 1987.

## GINSBURG, Mirra

*PERSONAL:* Born in Bobruisk (formerly Russia; now Belarus); daughter of Joseph and Bronia (Geier) Ginsburg. *Education:* Attended schools in Russia, Latvia, Canada, and the United States. *Avocational interests:* Poetry, cats (big and little), birds, ballet, baroque, folk and early music, early and primitive art.

*ADDRESSES: Home and office*—150 West 96th St., Apt. 9-G, New York, NY 10025.

*CAREER:* Freelance writer, editor, and translator from Russian and Yiddish. Served on translation juries, NBA, 1974, ABA, 1982, PEN, 1984.

*MEMBER:* American Literary Translators Association, Authors Guild, PEN.

*AWARDS, HONORS:* National Translation Center grant, 1967; Lewis Carroll Shelf Award, 1972, for *The Diary of Nina Kosterina;* Mildred L. Batchelder nomination, 1973, for *The Kaha Bird: Folk Tales from Central Asia,* and 1974, for *The White Ship;* Children's Book Showcase Title, 1973, for *The Chick and the Duckling;* Guggenheim fellow, 1975-76.

*WRITINGS:*

*TRANSLATOR*

Roman Goul, *Azef,* Doubleday (New York City), 1962.
Vera Alexandrova, *A History of Soviet Literature,* Doubleday, 1963.
Bulgakov, *Heart of a Dog,* Grove (New York City), 1968, third edition, 1987.
Fyodor Dostoyevsky, *Notes from Underground,* introduction by Donald Fanger, Bantam (New York City), 1974.
Lydia Obukhova, *Daughter of Night: A Tale of Three Worlds* (science fiction), Macmillan (New York City), 1974, Avon (New York City), 1982.

*TRANSLATOR AND AUTHOR OF INTRODUCTION*

Mikhail Bulgakov, *Master and Margarita,* Grove, 1967, reprinted, 1987.
*The Diary of Nina Kosterina,* Crown (New York City), 1968.

Bulgakov, *Flight* (play; also see below), Grove, 1969.
Bulgakov, *The Life of Monsieur de Moliere,* Funk and Wagnalls, 1970, New Directions, 1986, Oxford University Press, 1988.
Chingiz Aitmatov, *The White Ship,* Crown, 1972.
Yevgeny Zamyatin, *We,* Viking, 1972, Avon, 1983.
Andrey Platonov, *The Foundation Pit,* Dutton, 1975, Northwestern University Press (Evanston, IL), 1994.
Bulgakov, *Flight and Bliss* (two plays), New Directions (New York City), 1985.
Yuri Tynyanov, *Lieutenant Kije/Young Vitushishnikov,* Eridanos/Marsilio (New York City), 1991.

*EDITOR AND TRANSLATOR*

(And author of introduction) *The Fatal Eggs and Other Soviet Satire,* Macmillan, 1965, Grove, 1987.
(And author of introduction) *The Dragon: Fifteen Stories by Yevgeny Zamyatin,* Random House (New York City), 1966, second edition, University of Chicago Press (Chicago, IL), 1976.
(And author of introduction) *The Last Door to Aiya: Anthology of Soviet Science Fiction,* S. G. Phillips, 1968.
*A Soviet Heretic: Essays by Yevgeny Zamyatin,* introduction by Alex Shane, University of Chicago Press, 1970, Northwestern University Press, 1992.
(And author of introduction) *The Ultimate Threshold: Anthology of Soviet Science Fiction,* Holt, 1970, Penguin, 1978.
*The Air of Mars* (Soviet science fiction anthology), Macmillan, 1976.
Kirill Bulychev, *Alice* (science fiction), illustrated by Igor Galanin, Macmillan, 1977.

*FOLK TALE COLLECTIONS; EDITOR, ADAPTOR, TRANSLATOR*

*Three Rolls and One Doughnut: Fables from Russia,* illustrations by Anita Lobel, Dial (New York City), 1970.
*The Master of the Winds: Folk Tales from Siberia,* illustrations by Enrico Arno, Crown, 1970.
*The Kaha Bird: Folk Tales from Central Asia,* illustrations by Richard Cuffari, Crown, 1971.
*One Trick Too Many: Tales about Foxes,* illustrations by Helen Siegl, Dial, 1973.
*The Lazies: Folk Tales from Russia,* illustrations by Marian Parry, Macmillan, 1973.

*How Wilka Went to Sea: Folk Tales from West of the Urals,* illustrated by Charles Mikolaycak, Crown, 1975.

*The Twelve Clever Brothers and Other Fools: Folk Tales from Russia,* illustrations by C. Mikolaycak, Lippincott, 1979.

*PICTURE BOOKS; AUTHOR, ADAPTOR, TRANSLATOR*

*The Fox and the Hare* (Russian folk tale), Crown, 1969.

Vladimir Grigor'evich Suteyev, *The Chick and the Duckling,* illustrations by Jose Aruego and Ariane Dewey, Macmillan, 1972, reprinted, 1988.

*What Kind of Bird Is That?* (Weekly Reader Book Club selection), illustrations by Guilio Maestro, Crown, 1973, in *Merry-Go-Round,* Greenwillow, 1992.

Suteyev, *The Three Kittens* (Junior Literary Guild selection), illustrations by Maestro, Crown, 1973, second edition, 1987.

*Mushroom in the Rain: Adapted from the Russian of V. Suteyev,* illustrations by Aruego and Dewey, Macmillan, 1974.

*The Proud Maiden, Tungak, and the Sun* (Russian Eskimo tale), illustrations by Igor Galanin, Macmillan, 1974.

*How the Sun Was Brought Back to the Sky* (adapted from a Slovenian Folk Tale; Weekly Reader Book Club and Children's Choice Book Club selections), illustrations by Aruego and Dewey, Macmillan, 1975.

*The Two Greedy Bears: Adapted from a Hungarian Folk Tale* (Hungarian tale), illustrations by Aruego and Dewey, Macmillan, 1976.

*Pampalche of the Silver Teeth* (based on a Mari tale), illustrations by Rocco Negri, Crown, 1976.

Pyotr Dudochkin, *Which Is the Best Place?,* illustrations by Roger Duvoisin, Macmillan, 1976.

*The Strongest One of All* (based on a Kumyk tale), illustrations by Aruego and Dewey, Greenwillow, 1977.

*Little Rystu* (an Altay tale), illustrations by Tony Chen, Greenwillow, 1978.

*Striding Slippers* (based on an Udmurt folktale), illustrations by Sal Murdocca, Macmillan, 1978.

*The Fisherman's Son* (adapted from a Georgian tale; Caucasus), illustrations by Chen, Greenwillow, 1979.

*The Night It Rained Pancakes* (based on a Russian folktale), illustrations by Douglas Florian, Greenwillow, 1979.

*Ookie-Spooky* (based on a verse of Korney Chukovsky), illustrations by Emily McCully, Crown, 1979.

*Good Morning, Chick* (based on a verse of Korney Chukovsky; Young Parents Book Club, Book-of-the-Month Club, and Scholastic Magazine Book Club selections), illustrations by Byron Barton, Greenwillow, 1980.

*Kitten from One to Ten,* illustrations by Maestro, Crown, 1980.

*Where Does the Sun Go at Night?* (based on an Armenian song), illustrations by Aruego and Dewey, Greenwillow, 1980.

*The Sun's Asleep behind the Hill* (based on an Armenian poem), illustrations by Paul O. Zelinsky, Greenwillow, 1982.

*Across the Stream* (based on a verse of Daniel Kharms), illustrations by Nancy Tafuri, Greenwillow, 1982.

*The Little Magic Stove* (Russian tale), illustrations by Linda Heller, Putnam, 1983.

*Four Brave Sailors* (based on a verse of Daniil Kharms), illustrations by Tafuri, Greenwillow, 1987.

*The Chinese Mirror* (adapted from a Korean fairy tale), illustrations by Margot Zemach, Harcourt, 1988, Voyager Books, 1994.

*Asleep, Asleep* (based on a verse by A. Vvedensky), illustrations by Tafuri, Greenwillow, 1992.

*Merry-Go-Round, Four Stories,* illustrations by Aruego and Dewey, Voyager Books, Greenwillow, 1992.

*The King Who Tried to Fry an Egg on His Head* (based on a Russian tale), illustrations by Will Hillenbrand, Macmillan, 1994.

*The Old Man and His Birds* (based on a riddle by Vladimir Dal), illustrations by Donna Huff, Greenwillow, 1994.

*Clay Boy and the Little White Goat with the Golden Horns* (adapted from a Russian folk tale), illustrations by Joseph Smith, Greenwillow, 1996.

*OTHER*

Also translator of stories by Isaac Bashevis Singer, Alexey Remizov, Isaac Babel, and Zoshchenko, for various anthologies, collections by periodicals; co-translator of Isaac Babel's play, "Sunset," produced in 1966 and 1972.

*SIDELIGHTS:* Mirra Ginsburg told *CA:* "I was born and spent my early childhood in Bobruik, a small town in Byelorussia (now Belarus), which seems centuries away from my present home in New York.

"It was a town of small one-storey wooden houses, with only three brick buildings two storeys high. It was surrounded by woods and fields, and we lived simply. We had no running water and no plumbing. Most streets were not paved. When it rained, barrels were put out to collect the water, for washing and cleaning. Drinking water was brought from a neighbor's well. After rains there were huge puddles in the street, where pigs, big and little, came to wallow and luxuriate. Neighboring women often rinsed their wash in rivulets that ran along board sidewalks.

"After we left Russia, we lived for a time in Latvia, then Canada, finally coming to settle in this country [the United States].

"I have been fortunate in my work. I have translated into English a number of books by some of the greatest Russian writers of the 20th Century. I have also edited, translated and adapted many folk tales, mostly of the non-Russian peoples of the late Soviet Union (both in collections and picture books)—also a labor of love and joy—since folk literature, to me, is among the purest and most profound creations humans have been capable of. Another area, and this requiring a very different approach, has been in books for young children. Here, although I usually begin with a Russian original, it is necessary to work freely—change, delete and invent, *letting the story sing out* as something fresh and new and strange, so that it speaks directly to the child—here and now. I never try to teach or draw a moral. I love poetry and wit and play, and I hope that what delights me will in turn delight the reader and the listener. And if there is a lesson in the story, let it speak for itself. And if there isn't, let the story play and sing as it will.

"I have loved folktales since childhood, and have gone on collecting them and delighting in them ever since. I place folktales among the greatest works of literature. To me they are a distillation of man's deepest experience into poetry, wisdom, truth, sadness, and laughter."

Many of Ginsburg's books have also been published in England, and translated into various languages, including Afrikaans, Chinese, Danish, French, German, Japanese, Portuguese, Swedish, and Zulu.

## GOLDING, William (Gerald)    1911-1993

*PERSONAL:* Born September 19, 1911, in St. Columb Minor, Cornwall, England; died of a heart attack, June 19, 1993, in Perranarworthal, near Falmouth, England; son of Alex A. (a schoolmaster) and Mildred A. Golding; married Ann Brookfield, 1939; children: David, Judith. *Education:* Brasenose College, Oxford, B.A., 1935, M.A., 1960. *Avocational interests:* Sailing, archaeology, and playing the piano, violin, viola, cello, and oboe.

*CAREER:* Writer. Was a settlement house worker after graduating from Oxford University; taught English and philosophy at Bishop Wordsworth's School, Salisbury, Wiltshire, England, 1939-40, 1945-61; wrote, produced, and acted for London equivalent of "very, very far-off-Broadway theatre," 1934-40, 1945-54. Writer in residence, Hollins College, 1961-62; honorary fellow, Brasenose College, Oxford University, 1966. *Military service:* Royal Navy, 1940-45; became rocket ship commander.

*MEMBER:* Royal Society of Literature (fellow), Savile Club.

*AWARDS, HONORS:* Commander, Order of the British Empire, 1965; D.Litt., University of Sussex, 1970, University of Kent, 1974, University of Warwick, 1981, Oxford University, 1983, and University of Sorbonne, 1983; James Tait Black Memorial Prize, 1980, for *Darkness Visible;* Booker Mc-Connell Prize, 1981, for *Rites of Passage;* Nobel Prize for Literature, 1983, for body of work; LL.D., University of Bristol, 1984; knighted, 1988.

*WRITINGS:*

FICTION

*Lord of the Flies,* Faber (London), 1954, published with an introduction by E. M. Forster, Coward, 1955, casebook edition with notes and criticism, edited by James R. Baker and Arthur P. Ziegler Jr., Putnam, 1964.
*The Inheritors,* Faber, 1955, Harcourt (New York City), 1962.
*Pincher Martin,* Faber, 1955, new edition, 1972, published as *The Two Deaths of Christopher Martin,* Harcourt, 1957.
(With John Wyndham and Mervyn Peake) *Sometime, Never: Three Tales of Imagination,* Eyre & Spottiswoode (London), 1956, Ballantine (New York City), 1957.

*Free Fall,* Faber, 1959, Harcourt, 1960.

*The Spire,* Harcourt, 1964.

*The Pyramid* (novellas), Harcourt, 1967.

*The Scorpion God: Three Short Novels* (includes "Clonk Clonk," "Envoy Extraordinary" [also see below], and "The Scorpion God"), Harcourt, 1971.

*Darkness Visible,* Farrar, Straus (New York City), 1979.

*Rites of Passage* (first novel in trilogy), Farrar, Straus, 1980.

*The Paper Men,* Farrar, Straus, 1984.

*Close Quarters* (second novel in trilogy), Farrar, Straus, 1987.

*Fire Down Below* (third novel in trilogy), Farrar, Straus, 1989.

*The Double Tongue: A Draft of a Novel,* Farrar, Straus, 1995.

OTHER

*Poems,* Macmillan, 1934.

*The Brass Butterfly: A Play in Three Acts* (based on "Envoy Extraordinary"; first produced in Oxford, England, at New Theatre, 1958; produced in London, England, at Strand Theatre, April, 1958; produced in New York at Lincoln Square Theatre, 1965), Faber, 1958, new edition with introduction by Golding, 1963.

*Break My Heart* (play), produced for BBC Radio, 1962.

*The Hot Gates, and Other Occasional Pieces* (nonfiction), Harcourt, 1965.

*A Moving Target* (essays and lectures), Farrar, Straus, 1982.

*Nobel Lecture, 7 December 1983,* Sixth Chamber (Leamington Spa, UK), 1984.

*An Egyptian Journal* (travel), Faber, 1985.

Also author of radio plays and contributor to periodicals, including *Encounter, Holiday, Listener, New Left Review,* and *Spectator.*

ADAPTATIONS: *Pincher Martin* was produced as a radio play for the British Broadcasting Corp. in 1958; *Lord of the Flies* was filmed by British Lion Films in 1963 (from Golding's screenplay) and by Castle Rock Entertainment in 1990.

SIDELIGHTS: William Golding has been described as pessimistic, mythical, spiritual—an allegorist who used his novels as a canvas to paint portraits of man's constant struggle between his civilized self and his hidden, darker nature. With the appearance of

*Lord of the Flies,* Golding's first published novel, the author began his career as both a campus cult favorite and one of the late twentieth century's distinctive—and much debated—literary talents. Golding's appeal was summarized by the Nobel Prize committee, which issued this statement when awarding the author its literature prize in 1983: "[His] books are very entertaining and exciting. They can be read with pleasure and profit without the need to make much effort with learning or acumen. But they have also aroused an unusually great interest in professional literary critics [who find] deep strata of ambiguity and complication in Golding's work, . . . in which odd people are tempted to reach beyond their limits, thereby being bared to the very marrow."

Golding was born in England's west country in 1911. His father, Alex, was a follower in the family tradition of schoolmasters; his mother, Mildred, was a suffragette. The fourteenth-century family home in Marlborough was characterized by Stephen Medcalf in *William Golding* as "darkness and terror made objective in the flint-walled cellars . . . and in the graveyard by which it stood." By the time Golding was seven years old, Medcalf continued, "he had begun to connect the darkness . . . with the ancient Egyptians. From them he learnt, or on them he projected, mystery and symbolism, a habit of mingling life and death, and an attitude of mind sceptical of the scientific method that descends from the Greeks."

When he was twelve, Golding "tried his hand at writing a novel," reported Bernard Oldsey in the *Dictionary of Literary Biography.* "It was to be in twelve volumes and, unlike the kinds of works he had been reading [adventure stories of the Edgar Rice Burroughs and Jules Verne ilk], was to incorporate a history of the trade-union movement. He never forgot the opening sentence of this magnificent opus: 'I was born in the Duchy of Cornwall on the eleventh of October, 1792, of rich but honest parents.' That sentence set a standard he could not maintain, he playfully admitted, and nothing much came of the cycle."

Despite this setback the young man remained an enthusiastic writer and, on entering Brasenose College of Oxford University, abandoned his plans to study science, preferring to read English literature. At twenty-two, a year before taking his B.A. in English, Golding saw his first literary work published—a poetry collection simply titled *Poems.* In hindsight, the author called the pieces "poor, thin things," according to Medcalf. But, in fact, Medcalf remarked, "They are not bad. They deal with emotions—as they come out in the poems, rather easy emotions—of loss and grief, reflected in nature and the seasons."

After graduating from Oxford, Golding perpetuated family tradition by becoming a schoolmaster in Salisbury, Wiltshire. His teaching career was interrupted in 1940, however, when World War II found "Schoolie," as he was called, serving five years in the Royal Navy. Lieutenant Golding saw active duty in the North Atlantic, commanding a rocket launching craft. "What did I do?," he responded in Oldsey's article about his wartime experiences. "I survived." Having been present at the sinking of the *Bismarck* and the D-Day invasion, Golding later told Joseph Wersba of the *New York Post:* "World War Two was the turning point for me. I began to see what people were capable of doing."

On returning to his post at Bishop Wordsworth's School in 1945, Golding, who had enhanced his knowledge of Greek history and mythology by reading while at sea, attempted to further his writing career. He produced three novel manuscripts that remained unpublished. "All that [the author] has divulged about these [works] is that they were attempts to please publishers and that eventually they convinced him that he should write something to please himself," noted Oldsey. That ambition was realized in 1954 with *Lord of the Flies.*

The novel that established Golding's reputation, *Lord of the Flies* was rejected by twenty-one publishers before Faber & Faber accepted the forty-three-year-old schoolmaster's book. While the story has been compared to such works as Daniel Defoe's *Robinson Crusoe* and Richard Hughes's *A High Wind in Jamaica,* Golding's novel is actually the author's "answer" to nineteenth-century writer R. M. Ballantyne's children's classic *The Coral Island: A Tale of the Pacific Ocean.* These two books share the same basic plot line and even some of the same character names (two of the lead characters are named Ralph and Jack in both books). The similarity, however, ends there. Ballantyne's story, about a trio of boys stranded on an otherwise uninhabited island shows how, by pluck and resourcefulness, the young castaways survive with their morals strengthened and their wits sharpened. *Lord of the Flies,* on the other hand, is "an allegory on human society today, the novel's primary implication being that what we have come to call civilization is, at best, not more than

skin-deep," James Stern explained in the *New York Times Book Review.*

Initially, the tale of a group of schoolboys stranded on an island during their escape from atomic war received mixed reviews and sold only modestly in its hardcover edition. But when the paperback edition was published in 1959, thus making the book more accessible to students, the novel began to sell briskly. Teachers, aware of the student interest and impressed by the strong theme and stark symbolism of the work, assigned *Lord of the Flies* to their literature classes. As the novel's reputation grew, critics reacted by drawing scholarly theses out of what was previously dismissed as just another adventure story.

Golding provided in *Time* a simple explanation of his book. "The theme," he said, "is an attempt to trace the defects of society back to the defects of human nature." Indeed, the book begins with a company of highly-bred young men ("We've got to have rules and obey them. After all, we're not savages. We're English, and the English are best at everything," one of them states) and in just a few weeks strips them of nearly every aspect of "civilization," revealing what Golding described as man's "true" nature underneath. In *Lord of the Flies,* religion becomes pagan ritual—the boys worship an unknowable, pervading power that they call The Beast; even a group of choirboys becomes a chanting warrior troop. Democratic society crumbles under barbarism. "Like any orthodox moralist Golding insists that Man is a fallen creature, but he refuses to hypostatize Evil or to locate it in a dimension of its own. On the contrary Beelzebub, Lord of the Flies, is Roger and Jack and you and I, ready to declare himself as soon as we permit him to," John Peter pointed out in *Kenyon Review.* "One sees what Golding is doing," said Walter Allen in his book *The Modern Novel.* "He is showing us stripped man, man naked of all the sanctions of custom and civilization, man as he is alone and in his essence, or at any rate, as he can be conceived to be in such a condition."

In his study *The Tragic Past,* David Anderson saw Biblical implications in Golding's novel. "*Lord of the Flies,*" wrote Anderson, "is a complex version of the story of Cain—the man whose smoke-signal failed and who murdered his brother. Above all, it is a refutation of optimistic theologies which believed that God had created a world in which man's moral development had advanced *pari passu* with his biological evolution and would continue so to advance until the all-justifying End was reached." *Lord of the*

*Flies* presents moral regression rather than achievement, Anderson argued. "And there is no all-justifying End," the critic continued, "the rescue-party which takes the boys off their island comes from a world in which regression has occurred on a gigantic scale—the scale of atomic war. The human plight is presented in terms which are unqualified and unrelieved. Cain is not merely our remote ancestor: he is contemporary man, and his murderous impulses are equipped with unlimited destructive power."

The work has also been called Golding's response to the popular artistic notion of the 1950s that youth was a basically innocent collective, victims of adult society. In 1960, C. B. Cox deemed *Lord of the Flies* "probably the most important novel to be published . . . in the 1950s." Cox, writing in *Critical Quarterly,* continued: "[To] succeed, a good story needs more than sudden deaths, a terrifying chase and an unexpected conclusion. *Lord of the Flies* includes all these ingredients, but their exceptional force derives from Golding's faith that every detail of human life has a religious significance. This is one reason why he is unique among new writers in the '50s. . . . Golding's intense conviction [is] that every particular of human life has a profound importance. His children are not juvenile delinquents, but human beings realising for themselves the beauty and horror of life."

Not every critic responded with admiration to *Lord of the Flies,* however. One of Golding's more vocal detractors was Kenneth Rexroth, writing in the *Atlantic:* "Golding's novels are rigged. All thesis novels are rigged. In the great ones the drama escapes from the cage of the rigging or is acted out on it as on a skeleton stage set. Golding's thesis requires more rigging than most and it must by definition be escape-proof and collapsing." Rexroth added: "[The novel] functions in a minimal ecology, but even so, and indefinite as it is, it is wrong. It's the wrong rock for such an island and the wrong vegetation. The boys never come alive as real boys. They are simply the projected annoyances of a disgruntled English schoolmaster."

Jean E. Kennard voiced a different view in her study *Number and Nightmare: Forms of Fantasy in Contemporary Fiction:* "Golding's ability to create characters which function both realistically and allegorically is illustrated particularly well in *Lord of the Flies.* It is necessary for Golding to establish the boys as 'real' children early in the novel—something he achieves through such small touches as Piggy's

attitude to his asthma and the boys' joy in discovering Piggy's nickname—because his major thesis is, after all, about human psychology and the whole force of the fable would be lost if the characters were not first credible to us as human beings."

Golding took his theme of tracing the defects of society back to the defects of human nature a step further with his second novel, *The Inheritors.* This tale is set at the beginning of human existence itself, during the prehistoric age. A tribe of Neanderthals, as seen through the characters of Lok and Fa, live a peaceful, primitive life. Their happy world, however, is doomed: evolution brings in its wake the new race, *Homo sapiens,* who demonstrate their acquired skills with weapons by killing the Neanderthals. The book, which Golding has called his favorite, is also a favorite with several critics. And, inevitably, comparisons were made between *The Inheritors* and *Lord of the Flies.*

To Peter Green, in *A Review of English Literature,* for example, "it is clear that there is a close thematic connection between [the two novels]: Mr. Golding has simply set up a different working model to illustrate the eternal human verities from a new angle. Again it is humanity, and humanity alone, that generates evil; and when the new men triumph, Lok, the Neanderthaler, weeps as Ralph wept for the corruption and end of innocence [in *Lord of the Flies*]." Oldsey saw the comparison in religious terms: "[The *Homo sapiens*] represent the Descent of Man, not simply in the Darwinian sense, but in the Biblical sense of the Fall. Peculiarly enough, the boys [in *Lord of the Flies*] slide backward, through their own bedevilment, toward perdition; and Lok's Neanderthal tribe hunches forward, given a push by their *Homo sapiens* antagonists, toward the same perdition. In Golding's view, there is precious little room for evolutionary slippage: progression in *The Inheritors* and retrogression in *Lord of the Flies* have the same results."

Just as *Lord of the Flies* is Golding's rewriting, in his own terms, of *The Coral Island,* Golding claimed that he wrote *The Inheritors* to refute H. G. Wells's controversial sociological study *Outline of History.* "[One] can see that between the two writers there is a certain filial relation, though strained," commented a *Times Literary Supplement* critic. "They share the same fascination with past and future, the extraordinary capacity to move imaginatively to remote points in time, the fabulizing impulse, the need to moralize. There are even similarities in style. And surely now, when Wells's reputation as a great writer is beginning to take form, it will be understood as high praise of Golding if one says that he is our Wells, as good in his own individual way as Wells was in his." Taken together, the author's first two novels are, according to Lawrence R. Ries in *Wolf Masks: Violence in Contemporary Fiction,* "studies in human nature, exposing the kinds of violence that man uses against his fellow man. It is understandable why these first novels have been said to comprise [Golding's] 'primitive period.'"

Golding's "primitive period" ended with the publication of his third novel, *Pincher Martin* (published in America as *The Two Deaths of Christopher Martin,* out of the publishers' concern for American readers who would not know that "pincher" is British slang for "petty thief"). Stylistically similar to Ambrose Bierce's famous short story "An Occurrence at Owl Creek Bridge," *Pincher Martin* is about a naval officer who, after his ship is torpedoed in the Atlantic, drifts aimlessly before latching on to a barren rock. Here he clings for days, eating sea anemones and trying his best to retain consciousness. Delirium overtakes him, though, and through his rambling thoughts he relives his past. The discovery of the sailor's corpse at the end of the story in part constitutes what has been called a "gimmick" ending, and gives the book a metaphysical turn—the reader learns that Pincher Martin has been dead from the beginning of the narrative.

The author's use of flashbacks throughout the narrative of *Pincher Martin* was discussed by Avril Henry in *Southern Review:* "On the merely narrative level [the device] is the natural result of Martin's isolation and illness, and is the process by which he is gradually brought to his ghastly self-knowledge." In fact, said Henry, the flashbacks "function in several ways. First the flashbacks relate to each other and to the varied forms in which they themselves are repeated throughout the book; second, they relate also to the details of Martin's 'survival' on [the rock]. . . . Third, they relate to the six-day structure of the whole experience: the structure which is superficially a temporal check for us and Martin in the otherwise timeless and distorted events on the rock and in the mind, and at a deeper level is a horrible parody of the six days of Creation. What we watch is an unmaking process, in which man attempts to create himself his own God, and the process accelerates daily."

While acknowledging the influences present in the themes of *Pincher Martin*—from Homer's *Odysseus*

to *Robinson Crusoe* again—Medcalf suggests that the novel is Golding's most autobiographical work to date. The author, said Medcalf, "gave [to] Martin more of the external conditions of his own life than to any other of his characters, from [his education at] Oxford . . . through a period of acting and theatre life to a commission in the wartime Navy." Golding, too, has added another dimension from his own past, noted Medcalf: "His childhood fear of the darkness of the cellar and the coffin ends crushed in the walls from the graveyard outside [his childhood home]. The darkness universalizes him. It becomes increasingly but always properly laden with symbolism: the darkness of the thing that cannot examine itself, the observing ego: the darkness of the unconscious, the darkness of sleep, of death and, beyond death, heaven."

Each of Golding's first three novels, according to James Gindin in his *Postwar British Fiction: New Accents and Attitudes,* "demonstrates the use of unusual and striking literary devices. Each is governed by a massive metaphorical structure—a man clinging for survival to a rock in the Atlantic ocean or an excursion into the mind of man's evolutionary antecedent—designed to assert something permanent and significant about human nature. The metaphors are intensive, far-reaching; they permeate all the details and events of the novels. Yet at the end of each novel the metaphors, unique and striking as they are, turn into 'gimmicks' [Golding's own term for the device], into clever tricks that shift the focus or the emphasis of the novel as a whole." Gindin further stated that such endings fail "to define or to articulate fully just how [the author's] metaphors are to be qualified, directed, shaped in contemporary and meaningful terms."

Gimmick endings notwithstanding, V. S. Pritchett summed up Golding's early books as romantic "in the austere sense of the term. They take the leap from the probable to the possible." Pritchett elaborated in a *New Statesman* review: "All romance breaks with the realistic novelist's certainties and exposes the characters to transcendent and testing dangers. But Golding does more than break; he bashes, by the power of his overwhelming sense of the detail of the physical world. He is the most original of our contemporaries."

To follow *Pincher Martin,* Golding "said that he next wanted to show the patternlessness of life before we impose our patterns on it," according to Green. However, the resulting book, *Free Fall,* Green noted, "avoids the amoebic paradox suggested by his own prophecy, and falls into a more normal pattern of development: normal, that is, for Golding." Not unlike *Pincher Martin, Free Fall* depicts through flashbacks the life of its protagonist, artist Sammy Mountjoy. Imprisoned in a darkened cell in a Nazi prisoner-of-war camp, Mountjoy, who has been told that his execution is imminent, has only time to reflect on his past.

Despite the similarity in circumstance to *Pincher Martin,* Oldsey found one important difference between that novel and *Free Fall.* In *Free Fall,* a scene showing Sammy Mountjoy's tortured reaction on (symbolically) reliving his own downfall indicates a move toward atonement. "It is at this point in Golding's tangled tale that the reader begins to understand the difference between Sammy Mountjoy and Pincher Martin," Oldsey said. "Sammy escapes the machinations of the camp psychiatrist, Dr. Halde, by making use of man's last resource, prayer. It is all concentrated in his cry of 'Help me! Help me!'— a cry which Pincher Martin refuses to utter. In this moment of desperate prayer, Sammy spiritually bursts open the door of his own selfishness."

Medcalf saw the story as Dantesque in nature (Mountjoy's romantic interest is even named Beatrice) and remarked: "Dante, like Sammy, came to himself in the middle of his life, in a dark wood [the cell, in Sammy's case], unable to remember how he came there. . . . His only way out is to see the whole world, and himself in its light. Hell, purgatory and heaven are revealed to him directly, himself and this world of sense in glimpses from the standpoint of divine justice and eternity." In *Free Fall* Gold-ing's intent "is to show this world directly, in other hints and guesses. He is involved therefore in showing directly the moment of fall at which Dante only hints. He has a hero without reference points, who lives in the vertigo of free fall, therefore, reproachful of an age in which those who have a morality or a system softly refuse to insist on them: a hero for whom no system he has will do, but who is looking for his own unity in the world—and that, the real world, is 'like nothing, because it is everything.' Golding, however, has the advantage of being able to bring Dante's world in by allusion: and he does so with a Paradise hill on which Beatrice is met."

Several critics took special notice of Golding's use of names in *Free Fall*—and his selection of the novel's title itself. Peter M. Axthelm, in his book *The Modern Confessional Novel,* found that "almost every proper name . . . implies something about the character it identifies." The name Sammy Mountjoy, with its hedonistic ring, for example, contrasts sharply with that of his childhood guardian, Father Watts-Watt. The most crucial name in the book, though, stated Axthelm, is that of the woman whom Sammy loves and abuses, Beatrice Ifor. Sammy reads her surname as "I-for," an extension of his own sexual passion. But her name can also be read as "If-or," indicating a spiritual choice—"in other words, she is the potential bridge between Sammy's two worlds," as Axthelm noted. Unable to reconcile the two sides of her character, Sammy "ignores the spiritual side of the girl and grasps only the 'I-for,' the self-centered, exploitative lust. He upsets the balance and destroys the bridge," explained Axthelm.

"Many critics have commented that the title [*Free Fall*] has both a theological and a scientific significance," declared Kennard, "but Golding himself has, as usual, expressed it best: 'Everybody has translated this in terms of theology; well, okay, you can do it that way, which is why it's not a bad title, but it is in fact a scientific term. It is where your gravity has *gone*; it is a man in a space ship who has no gravity; things don't fall or lift, they float about; he is completely divorced from the other idea of a thing up *there* and centered on *there* in which he lives.' Sammy Mountjoy, narrator of *Free Fall,* has more insight and perhaps more conscience than Pincher Martin, but basically his is Pincher's problem. He is islanded, trapped in himself, 'completely divorced from the other idea of a thing up there.'" "Sammy is the character through whom Mr. Golding, one suspects, is beginning to be reconciled to the loss of his primal Eden," offered Green.

In Golding's fifth novel, *The Spire,* "the interest is all in the opacity of the man and in a further exploration of man's all-sacrificing will," wrote Medcalf. Fourteenth-century clergyman Dean Jocelin "is obsessed with the belief that it is his divine mission to raise a 400-foot tower and spire above his church," Oldsey related. "His colleagues protest vainly that the project is too expensive and the edifice unsuited for such a shaft. His master builder (obviously named Roger Mason) calculates that the foundation and pillars of the church are inadequate to support the added weight, and fruitlessly suggests compromises to limit the shaft to a lesser height. The townspeople—amoral, skeptical, and often literally pagan—are derisive about 'Jocelin's Folly.'" Dean Jocelin, nonetheless, strives on. The churchman, in fact, "neglects all his spiritual duties to be up in the tower overseeing the workmen himself, all the while choosing not to see within and without himself what might interrupt the spire's dizzying climb," Oldsey continued. The weight of the tower causes the church's foundations to shudder; the townspeople increasingly come to see Jocelin as a man dangerously driven.

Finally, despite setbacks caused by both the workers (they "drink, fornicate, murder, and brawl away their leisure hours," according to Oldsey) and by the elements of nature (storms ravage the tower in its building stage), the spire nears completion. Dean Jocelin himself drives the final nail into the top of the edifice—and as he does, succumbs to a disease and falls from the tower to his death. "Whether he has been urged by Satan, God, or his own pride (much like that of Pincher Martin) is a moot question," stressed Oldsey, who also noted that "again Golding returns to the most obsessive subject in his fiction—The Fall."

*The Spire* "is a book about vision and its cost," observed *New York Review of Books* critic Frank Kermode. "It has to do with the motives of art and prayer, the phallus turned spire; with the deceit, as painful to man as to God, involved in structures which are human but have to be divine, such as churches and spires. But because the whole work is a dance of figurative language such an account of it can only be misleading." Characteristic of all Golding's work, *The Spire* can be read on two levels, that of an engrossing story and of a biting analysis of human nature. As Nigel Dennis found in the *New York Times Book Review,* Golding "has always written on these two levels. But *The Spire* will be of particular interest to his admirers because it can also be read as an exact description of his own artistic method. This consists basically of trying to rise to the heights while keeping himself glued to the ground. Mr. Golding's aspirations climb by clinging to solid objects and working up them like a vine. This is particularly pronounced in [*The Spire*], where every piece of building stone, every stage of scaffolding, every joint and ledge, are used by the author to draw himself up into the blue."

With *The Spire* Golding completed his first decade in the literary eye. The author's prolific output—five novels in ten years—and the high quality of his work established him as one of the late twentieth century's distinguished writers, and in 1965 he was named a Commander of the British Empire.

Thus, by 1965, Golding was evidently on his way to continuing acclaim and popular acceptance—but "then matters changed abruptly," as Oldsey related. The writer's output dropped dramatically: for the next fifteen years he produced no novels and only a handful of novellas, short stories, and occasional pieces. Of this period—what Boyd refers to as the "hiatus in the Golding oeuvre"—*The Pyramid,* a collection of three related novellas (and considered a novel proper by some critics), is generally regarded as one of the writer's weaker efforts. The episodic story of a man's existence in the suspiciously named English town of Stilbourne, *The Pyramid* proved a shock to "even Golding's most faithful adherents [who] wondered if the book was indeed a novel or if it contributed anything to the author's reputation. To some it seemed merely three weak stories jammed together to produce a salable book," said Oldsey. *The Pyramid,* however, did have its admirers, among them John Wakeman of the *New York Times Book Review,* who felt the work was Golding's "first sociological novel. It is certainly more humane, exploratory, and life-size than its predecessors, less Old Testament, more New Testament." And to a *Times Literary Supplement* critic the book "will astonish by what it is not. It is not a fable, it does not contain evident allegory, it is not set in a simplified or remote world. It belongs to another, more commonplace tradition of English fiction; it is a low-keyed, realistic novel of growing up in a small town—the sort of book H. G. Wells might have written if he had been more attentive to his style."

*The Scorpion God: Three Short Novels,* another collection of novellas, was somewhat better received. One *Times Literary Supplement* reviewer, while calling the work "not major Golding," nevertheless found the book "a pure example of Golding's gift. . . . The title story is from Golding's Egyptological side and is set in ancient Egypt. . . . By treating the unfamiliar with familiarity, explaining nothing, he teases the reader into the strange world of the story. It is as brilliant a *tour de force* as *The Inheritors,* if on a smaller scale."

Golding's reintroduction to the literary world was acknowledged in 1979 with the publication of *Darkness Visible.* Despite some fifteen years' absence from novel writing, the author "returns unchanged," Samuel Hynes observed in a *Washington Post Book World* article. "[He is] still a moralist, still a maker of parables. To be a moralist you must believe in good and evil, and Golding does; indeed, you might say that the nature of good and evil is his only theme. To be a parable-maker you must believe that moral meaning can be expressed in the very fabric of the story itself, and perhaps that some meanings can only be expressed in this way; and this, too, has always been Golding's way."

The title *Darkness Visible* derives from Milton's description of Hell in *Paradise Lost,* and from the first scenes of the book Golding confronts the reader with images of fire, mutilation, and pain—which he presents in Biblical terms. For instance, noted *Commonweal* reviewer Bernard McCabe, the novel's opening describes a small child, "horribly burned, horribly disfigured, [who walks] out of the flames at the height of the London blitz. . . . The shattered building he emerges from . . . is called 'a burning bush,' the firemen stare into 'two pillars of lighted smoke,' the child walks with a 'ritual gait,' and he appears to have been 'born from the sheer agony of a burning city.'" The rescued youth, dubbed Matty, the left side of whose face has been left permanently mutilated, grows up to be a religious visionary.

"If Matty is a force for light, he is opposed by a pair of beautiful twins, Toni and Sophy Stanhope," continued Susan Fromberg Schaeffer in her *Chicago Tribune Book World* review. "These girls, once symbols of innocence in their town, discover the seductive attractions of darkness. Once, say the spirits who visit Matty, the girls were called before them, but they refused to come. Instead, obsessed by the darkness loose in the world, they abandon morality, choosing instead a demonic hedonism that allows them to justify anything, even mass murder." "Inevitably, the two girls will . . . [embark on a] spectacular crime, and just as inevitably, Matty, driven by his spirit guides, must oppose them," summarized *Time*'s Peter S. Prescott. "The confrontation, as you may imagine, ends happily for no one."

*Darkness Visible* received mixed reviews overall, with much of the negative reaction focusing on the author's "embarrassing fictional stereotypes . . . and his heavy-handedly ironic attempt to create a visionary-moron in [Matty]," as Joyce Carol Oates related in the *New Republic*. McCabe found that although the novel "has its undeniable fascinations . . . [nevertheless] what I end up with is an impression of a very earnest writer, blessed with remarkable skills and up to all sorts of ingenuities, struggling with a dark vision of man, trying to express it through a complex art, making another attempt at another *tour de force,* and getting nowhere."

On the other hand, Hynes, who conceded that *Darkness Visible* is a "difficult novel," added that "unlike many other contemporary novels, it is difficult because its meaning is difficult: it is not a complicated word game, or a labyrinth with a vacuum at the center. Golding, the religious man, has once more set himself the task of finding the signs and revelations, the parable, that will express his sense of the human situation. Difficult, yes—isn't morality difficult?—but worth the effort."

While *Darkness Visible* "could not by itself restore Golding to prominence," as Robert Towers pointed out in the *New York Review of Books,* the wave of renewed interest the book generated in its author paved the way for Golding's following novel, *Rites of Passage.* A tale of high-seas adventure, *Rites of Passage,* according to Towers, is "a first-rate historical novel that is also a novel of ideas—a taut, beautifully controlled short book with none of the windiness or costumed pageantry so often associated with fictional attempts to reanimate the past."

Some of the ideas explored in this book trace back to *Lord of the Flies* "and to the view [the author] held then of man as a fallen being capable of a 'vileness beyond words,'" stated *New Statesman* reviewer Blake Morrison. Set in the early nineteenth century, *Rites of Passage* tells of a voyage from England to Australia as recounted through the shipboard diary of young aristocrat Edmund Talbot. "He sets down a vivid record of the ship and its characters," explained Morrison. They include "the irascible Captain Anderson. . ., the 'wind-machine Mr Brockleband,' the whorish 'painted Magdalene' called Zenobia, and the meek and ridiculous 'parson,' Mr. Colley, who is satirised as mercilessly as the clerics in [Henry] Fielding's *Joseph Andrews.*" This latter character is the one through which much of the dramatic action in *Rites of Passage* takes place. For Colley, this "country curate . . . this hedge priest," as Golding's Talbot describes him, "is the perfect victim—self-deluding, unworldly, sentimentally devout, priggish, and terrified. Above all he is ignorant of the powerful homosexual streak in his nature that impels him toward the crew and especially toward one stalwart sailor, Billy Rogers," said Towers. Driven by his passion yet torn by doubt, ridiculed and shunned by the other passengers on the ship, Colley literally dies of shame during the voyage.

The ship, Towers argued, is a kind of microcosm that encapsulates a society. "It may even have occurred to some that the concealed name of this obsolete old ship of the line, with its female figurehead obscenely nicknamed by the crew, might well be *Britannia*. . . . Though there is indeed a schoolmasterish streak in Golding, inclining him toward the didactic, tempting him to embellish his work with literary references. . ., he has in *Rites of Passage* constructed a narrative vessel sturdy enough to support his ideas. And because his ideas—about the role of class, about the nature of authority and its abuses, about cruelty (both casual and deliberate) and its consequences—because these themes and others are adequately dramatized, adequately incorporated, they become agents within the novel, actively and interestingly, at work within the fictional setting."

The author faced his harshest criticism to date with the publication of his 1984 novel *The Paper Men*. A farce-drama about an aging, successful novelist's conflicts with his pushy, overbearing biographer, *The Paper Men* "tells us that biography is the trade of the con man, a fatuous accomplishment, and the height of impertinence in both meanings of the word," according to London *Times* critic Michael Ratcliff. Unfortunately for Golding, many critics found *The Paper Men* to be sorely lacking in the qualities that distinguish the author's best work. Typical of their commentary is this observation from Michiko Kakutani of the *New York Times:* "Judging from the tired, petulant tone of [the novel], Mr. Golding would seem to have more in common with his creation than mere appearance—a 'scraggy yellow-white beard, yellow-white thatch and broken-toothed grin.' He, too, seems to have allowed his pessimistic vision of man to curdle his view of the world and to sour his enjoyment of craft."

Some reviewers call *The Paper Men* a work unworthy of a Nobel Prize winner (Golding had received the award just months prior to the book's publication); reacting to the outpouring of negative criticism, Blake Morrison said in the *Times Literary Supplement* that "all that can be said with confidence is that Golding's previous novels, even those that were coolly received on publication, have stood up well to subsequent re-readings, and that *The Paper Men* is certain to get a more patient treatment from future explicators than it has had from its reviewers. As for the author, he will have to console himself with [his lead character's] rather specious piece of reasoning on the poor reception of [his own novel]: 'You have to write the bad books if you're going to write the good ones.'"

Departing briefly from fiction, Golding produced two books of "occasional pieces," works containing essays, reviews, and lectures. *The Hot Gates, and Other Occasional Pieces* was published in 1965; *A Moving Target* appeared in 1982, one year prior to the author's receipt of the Nobel Prize. Literary observations pervade *A Moving Target*. Golding speaks not only of the works of such authors as Samuel Richardson, Alexander Pope, and Jane Austen, but also offers "advice" to aspiring writers and, "with pristine clarity, he answers critics, academics and 'dangerous' postgraduate students who have subjected his *Lord of the Flies* to 'Freudian analysis, neo-Freudian analysis, Jungian analysis, Roman Catholic approval, . . . Protestant appraisal, nonconformist surmise, and Scientific Humanist misinterpretation," as *Los Angeles Times Book Review* contributor John Rechy observed.

But the most moving writing in the book, according to Gabriel Josipovici in the *Times Literary Supplement,* is a pair of mood pieces that find Golding reliving his youthful infatuation with Egyptology, and a travel essay that finds the boy, a lifetime later, finally exploring Egypt in person. "This volume," stated Josipovici, "is fascinating . . . because it gives us a glimpse of two Goldings. The pieces about place, about Homer, about fairy-tales, convey the power of his imagination, his extraordinary ability to enter into and convey to us the strangeness and incomprehensibility of the world we live in. The lectures, on the other hand, give us a glimpse of the writer turning into a monument, not graciously but uneasily."

Golding saw the publication of two more novels before his death in 1993. *Close Quarters,* published in 1987, and *Fire Down Below,* published in 1989, completed a trilogy begun with *Rites of Passage*. This first volume, according to Bernard F. Dick in *World Literature Today,* "portrayed a voyage to Australia on a ship that symbolized class-conscious Britain (circa 1810) facing the rise of the middle class. . . . *Close Quarters* continues the voyage, but this time the ship, which is again a symbol of Britain, is near collapse." The story is told through the journal entries of Edmund FitzHenry Talbot, "a well-meaning, somewhat uncertain, slightly pompous officer and gentleman enroute to Sydney and a career in His Majesty's service," a *Publishers Weekly* reviewer observed. When an inexperienced sailor's error destroys the ship's masts, the crew and passengers are left to ponder their mortality. "As with most of Golding's fiction," David Nokes asserted in the

*Times Literary Supplement,* "it is impossible to escape a brooding, restless intensity which turns even the most trivial incident or observation into a metaphysical conceit." As the ship founders and its captives become increasingly agitated, it seems to become a living thing itself, with twigs sprouting from its timbers and discernable creeping movements in its deck planks underfoot. "As a story-teller [Golding's] touch never falters," Nokes concluded. "His attention to details of idiom and setting show a reverence for his craft that would do credit to a master-shipwright. It is in the dark undertow of his metaphors and in the literary ostentation of his allusions that a feeling of strain and contrivance appears. As he steers us through the calms and storms, we are never quite sure whether we are in the safe hands of a master-mariner or under the dangerous spell of an Old Man of the Sea."

*New York Times Book Review* contributor Robert M. Adams had high hopes for the final book of the trilogy based on his reading of *Close Quarters*. He asserted that the second volume "will not stand up by itself as an independent fiction the way *Rites of Passage* did. . . . But this is the wrong time to pass final judgment on a project, the full dimensions of which can at this point only be guessed. In one sense, the very absence from this novel of strong scenes and sharply defined ironies confirms one's sense of a novelist who is still outward bound, firmly in control of his story, and preparing his strongest effects for the resolutions and revolutions to come." The *Los Angeles Times Book Review*'s Richard Hough also found *Close Quarters* unable to stand alone: "This reviewer confesses to being totally mystified by Golding's sequel to *Rites of Passage*. It is neither an allegory, nor a fantasy, nor an adventure, nor even a complete novel, as it has a beginning, a middle (of sorts) but an ending only at some unspecified future date when Golding chooses to complete it, if he does."

The final volume of the trilogy, *Fire Down Below,* appeared in 1989. The title refers to the plan for repairing the ship's masts which entails creating iron bands to pull together the split wood preventing the masts from bearing the weight of the sails, but which also carries the danger of fire in the hold: *Quill and Quire* reviewer Paul Stuewe described *Fire Down Below* as an "ambitious and satisfying novel" and "a rousing finale to an entertaining exercise in historical pastiche." While asserting that neither *Fire Down Below* nor *Close Quarters* "works as powerfully and coherently as *Rites of Passage* with its strongly struc-

tured story of a parson who literally died of shame," *New Statesman & Society*'s W. L. Webb observed that "what keeps one attending still, as to the other ancient mariner's tales of ice mast-high, are [Golding's] magic sea pictures: faces on the quarter-deck masked in moonlight, the eerie 'shadow' that falls behind solid bodies in mist and spray, storm-light and a droning wind, and the sailors swarming out like bees as the wounded ship yaws close to the ice cliffs. There's nothing quite like it in our literature."

"As a novelist, William Golding had the gift of terror," Joseph J. Feeney wrote in an obituary for *America*. "It is not the terror of a quick scare—a ghost, a scream, a slash that catches the breath—but a primal, fearsome sense of human evil and human mystery. . . . William Golding was, with Graham Greene, the finest British novelist of our half-century. His fellow novelist Malcolm Bradbury memorialized him as 'a writer who was both impishly difficult, and wonderfully monumental,' and a teller of 'primal stories—about the birth of speech, the dawn of evil, the strange sources of art.'"

Golding once provided a description of himself in Jack I. Biles's *Talk: Conversations with William Golding:* "I'm against the picture of the artist as the starry-eyed visionary not really in control or knowing what he does. I think I'd almost prefer the word 'craftsman.' He's like one of the old-fashioned shipbuilders, who conceived the boat in their mind and then, after that, touched every single piece that went into the boat. They were in complete control; they knew it inch by inch, and I think the novelist is very much like that."

## BIOGRAPHICAL/CRITICAL SOURCES:

### BOOKS

Allen, Walter, *The Modern Novel,* Dutton, 1964.

Anderson, David, *The Tragic Past,* John Knox Press, 1969.

Axthelm, Peter M., *The Modern Confessional Novel,* Yale University Press, 1967.

Babb, Howard S., *The Novels of William Golding,* Ohio State University Press, 1970.

Baker, James R., *William Golding: A Critical Study,* St. Martin's, 1965.

Biles, Jack I., *Talk: Conversations with William Golding,* Harcourt, 1971.

Biles, J. I., and Robert O. Evans, editors, *William Golding: Some Critical Considerations,* University Press of Kentucky, 1979.

Bloom, Harold, *William Golding's Lord of the Flies,* Chelsea House (New York City), 1996.

Burgess, Anthony, *The Novel Now: A Guide to Contemporary Fiction,* Norton, 1967.

*Contemporary Literary Criticism,* Gale, Volume 1, 1973, Volume 2, 1974, Volume 3, 1975, Volume 8, 1978, Volume 10, 1979, Volume 18, 1981, Volume 27, 1984, Volume 58, 1990, Volume 81, 1994.

Dick, Bernard F., *William Golding,* Twayne (New York City), 1967.

*Dictionary of Literary Biography,* Volume 15: *British Novelists, 1930-1959,* Gale, 1983.

*Dictionary of Literary Biography Yearbook: 1983,* Gale, 1984.

Friedman, Lawrence S., *William Golding,* Continuum (New York City), 1993.

Gindin, James, *Postwar British Fiction: New Accents and Attitudes,* University of California Press, 1962.

Gindin, J., *Harvest of a Quiet Eve: The Novel of Compassion,* Indiana University Press, 1971.

Golding, William, *Lord of the Flies,* Faber, 1954, published with an introduction by E. M. Forster, Coward, 1955, reprinted, 1978.

Golding, W., *The Spire,* Harcourt, 1964.

Golding, W., *The Hot Gates, and Other Occasional Pieces,* Harcourt, 1965.

Golding, W., *Darkness Visible,* Farrar, Straus, 1979.

Golding, W., *Rites of Passage,* Farrar, Straus, 1980.

Golding, W., *A Moving Target,* Farrar, Straus, 1982.

Green, Peter, *A Review of English Literature,* Longmans, Green, 1960.

Hynes, Samuel, *William Golding,* Columbia University Press, 1964.

Johnson, Arnold, *Of Earth and Darkness: The Novels of William Golding,* University of Missouri Press, 1980.

Kennard, Jean E., *Number and Nightmare: Forms of Fantasy in Contemporary Fiction,* Archon Books, 1975.

Kinkead-Weekes, Mark, and Ian Gregor, *William Golding: A Critical Study,* Faber, 1967.

Medcalf, Stephen, *William Golding,* Longman, 1975.

Oldsey, Bernard S., and Stanley Weintraub, *The Art of William Golding,* Harcourt, 1965.

Reilly, Patrick, *Lord of the Flies: Fathers and Sons,* Twayne, 1992.

Ries, Lawrence R., *Wolf Masks: Violence in Contemporary Fiction,* Kennikat Press, 1975.

Tiger, Virginia, *William Golding: The Dark Fields of Discovery,* Calder & Boyars, 1974.

*PERIODICALS*

*Atlantic,* May, 1965; April, 1984.

*Chicago Tribune,* October 7, 1983.

*Chicago Tribune Book World,* December 30, 1979; October 26, 1980; April 8, 1984.

*Commentary,* January, 1968.

*Commonweal,* October 25, 1968; September 26, 1980.

*Critical Quarterly,* summer, 1960; autumn, 1962; spring, 1967.

*Critique: Studies in Modern Fiction,* Volume 14, number 2, 1972.

*Detroit News,* December 16, 1979; January 4, 1981; April 29, 1984.

*Kenyon Review,* autumn, 1957.

*Life,* November 17, 1967.

*Listener,* October 4, 1979; October 23, 1980; January 5, 1984.

*London Magazine,* February-March, 1981.

*London Review of Books,* June 17, 1982.

*Los Angeles Times Book Review,* November 9, 1980; June 20, 1982; June 3, 1984; June 7, 1987, pp. 3, 6.

*New Republic,* December 8, 1979; September 13, 1982.

*New Statesman,* August 2, 1958; April 10, 1964; November 5, 1965; October 12, 1979; October 17, 1980; June 11, 1982.

*New Statesman & Society,* April 14, 1989, p. 34.

*Newsweek,* November 5, 1979; October 27, 1980; April 30, 1984.

*New Yorker,* September 21, 1957.

*New York Post,* December 17, 1963.

*New York Review of Books,* April 30, 1964; December 7, 1967; February 24, 1972; December 6, 1979; December 18, 1980.

*New York Times,* September 1, 1957; November 9, 1979; October 15, 1980; October 7, 1983; March 26, 1984; June 22, 1987.

*New York Times Book Review,* October 23, 1955; April 19, 1964; November 18, 1979; November 2, 1980; July 11, 1982; May 31, 1987, p. 44.

*Publishers Weekly,* May 15, 1987, p. 267.

*Quill and Quire,* July, 1989, p. 47.

*Saturday Review,* March 19, 1960.

*South Atlantic Quarterly,* autumn, 1970.

*Southern Review,* March, 1976.

*Spectator,* October 13, 1979.

*Time,* September 9, 1957; October 13, 1967; October 17, 1983; April 9, 1984; June 8, 1987.

*Times* (London), February 9, 1984; June 11, 1987.

*Times Literary Supplement,* October 21, 1955; October 23, 1959; June 1, 1967; November 5, 1971;

November 23, 1979; October 17, 1980; July 23, 1982; March 2, 1984; June 19, 1987, p. 653.
*Twentieth Century Literature,* summer, 1982.
*Village Voice,* November 5, 1979.
*Washington Post,* July 12, 1982; October 7, 1983; January 12, 1986.
*Washington Post Book World,* November 4, 1979; November 2, 1980; April 15, 1984.
*World Literature Today,* spring, 1988, p. 81; autumn, 1989, p. 681.
*Yale Review,* spring, 1960.

*OBITUARIES:*

PERIODICALS

*America,* July 31, 1993, pp. 6-7.
*Los Angeles Times,* June 20, 1993, p. A22.
*New York Times,* June 20, 1993, p. 38.
*Times* (London), June 21, 1993, p. 17.
*Washington Post,* June 20, 1993, p. B6.*

\* \* \*

**GONZALEZ, Justo L(uis) 1937-**

*PERSONAL:* Born August 9, 1937, in Havana, Cuba; son of Justo Bernardino (a professor, minister, and author) and Luisa (a teacher and author; maiden name, Garcia) Gonzalez; married second wife, Catherine Gunsalus (a theologian), December 18, 1973; children: (first marriage) Juana Luisa. *Education:* Attended University of Havana, 1954-57; Union Theological Seminary, Matanzas, Cuba, S.T.B., 1957; Yale University, S.T.M., 1958, M.A., 1960, Ph.D., 1961; University of Strasbourg, graduate study, 1958-59. *Religion:* Methodist.

*ADDRESSES: Office—*336 Columbia Dr., Decatur, GA 30021.

*CAREER:* Evangelical Seminary of Puerto Rico, professor of historical theology, 1961-69, dean, 1967-69; Emory University, Candler School of Theology, Atlanta, GA, assistant professor, 1969-71, associate professor of world Christianity, 1971-77; visiting professor of theology, Interdenominational Theological Center, 1977-88; adjunct professor of theology, Columbia Theological Seminary, 1988—. Consultant to the Ninth Province of the Episcopal Church and to the Church of the Province of the West Indies, 1969-74; consultant for the Fund for Theological Educa-

tion, 1987-88; consultant for Grants Program of Trinity Parish. Lecturer at seminaries and preacher for ecclesiastical gatherings.

*AWARDS, HONORS:* Yale University research fellowship, 1968.

*WRITINGS:*

*Revolucion y encarnacion,* La Reforma, 1965, second edition, 1966.
*Historia del pensamiento cristiano,* Methopress, Volume 1: *Desde los origenes hasta el Concilio de Calcedonia,* 1965, Volume 2: *Desde San Agustin hasta las visperas de la Reforma,* 1972.
(Editor) *Por la renovacion del entendimiento,* La Reforma, 1965.
*The Development of Christianity in the Latin Caribbean,* Eerdmans (Grand Rapids, MI), 1969.
*A History of Christian Thought,* Abingdon (Nashville, TN), Volume 1: *From the Beginnings to the Council of Chalcedon,* 1970, second edition, 1987, Volume 2: *From Augustine to the Eve of the Reformation,* 1971, second edition, 1987, Volume 3: *From the Protestant Reformation to the Present,* 1975, second edition, 1987.
*Historia de las misiones,* Methopress, 1970.
*Ambrosio de Milan,* Centro de Publicaciones Cristianas, 1970.
*Jesucristo es el Senor,* Caribe (Miami, FL), 1975.
*Itinerario de la teologia cristiana,* Caribe, 1975.
*Luces bajo el almud,* Caribe, 1977.
(With wife, Catherine Gunsalus Gonzalez) *Their Souls Did Magnify the Lord: Studies on Biblical Women,* John Knox (Atlanta, GA), 1977.
(With Gunsalus Gonzalez) *Sus almas engrandecieron el Senor,* Caribe, 1977.
(With Gunsalus Gonzalez) *Vision at Patmos: Studies in the Book of Revelation,* Friendship (New York City), 1978, reprinted, Abingdon, 1990.
*Y hasta lo ultimo de la tierra,* Caribe, Volume 1: *La era de los martires,* 1978, Volume 2: *La era de los gigantes,* 1978, Volume 3: *La era de las Tinieblas,* 1978, Volume 4: *La era de los altos ideales,* 1979, Volume 5: *La era de los suenos frustrados,* 1979, Volume 6: *La era de los reformadores,* 1980, Volume 7: *La era de los conquistadores,* 1980, Volume 8: *La era de los dogmas y las dudas,* 1983, Volume 9: *La era de los nuevos horizontes,* 1987, Volume 10: *La era inconclusa,* 1988.
(With Gunsalus Gonzalez) *Rejoice in Your Savior: A Study for Lent-Easter,* Graded Press, 1979.

(With Gunsalus Gonzalez) *Liberation Preaching: The Pulpit and the Oppressed,* Abingdon, 1980.

(With Gunsalus Gonzalez) *In Accord: Let Us Worship,* Friendship, 1981.

(Editor) *Proclaiming the Acceptable Year: Sermons from a Perspective of Liberation,* Judson (Valley Forge, PA), 1982.

*The Story of Christianity,* Harper (New York City), Volume 1: *Early and Medieval Christianity,* 1984, Volume 2: *From the Reformation to the Present,* 1985.

*Juntamente con Cristo,* Discipleship Resources (Nashville, TN), 1985.

*Juntamente con Cristo: Un comentario sobre los textos de Cuaresma y Semana Santa,* Ediciones Discipulado, 1985.

*Probad los espiritus: Un comentario sobre los textos de Adviento y Navidad,* Ediciones Discipulado, 1987.

(With Gunsalus Gonzalez) *Paul: His Impact on Christianity,* Graded Press, 1987.

*The Crusades: Piety Misguided,* Graded Press, 1988.

*Monasticism: Patterns of Piety,* Graded Press, 1988.

*The Theological Education of Hispanics,* Fund for Theological Education, 1988.

*Christian Thought Revisited: Three Types of Theology,* Abingdon, 1989.

(With Gunsalus Gonzalez) *A Faith More Precious than Gold: A Study of 1 Peter,* Horizons, 1989.

*Cristianismo: culto o profecia: el hecho religioso andino,* Ediciones Abya-Yala (Quito, Ecuador), 1989.

(With Francisco Rodriguez Cavero) *Entre la cruz y la espada: evangelizacion o adoctrinamiento en America Latina,* Fundacion Munoz Hermanos, 1989.

*La evangelizacion de la religosidad popular andina,* Ediciones Abya-Yala, 1990.

*Faith and Wealth: A History of Early Christian Ideas on the Origin, Significance, and Use of Money,* Harper, 1990.

*Manana: Christian Theology from a Hispanic Perspective,* Abingdon, 1990.

(Editor) *Each in Our Own Tongue: A History of Hispanic United Methodism,* Abingdon, 1991.

(Editor) *Voces: Voices from the Hispanic Church,* Abingdon, 1992.

*Out of Every Tribe and Nation: Christian Theology at the Ethnic Roundtable,* Abingdon, 1992.

(Editor with Anthony L. Dunnavants) *Poverty and Ecclesiology: Nineteenth-Century Evangelicals in the Light of Liberation Theology,* Liturgical Press (Collegeville, MN), 1992.

*Mentors as Instruments of God's Call: Biblical Reflections,* Division of Diaconal Ministry, United Methodist Church (Nashville, TN), 1992.

(With Gunsalus Gonzalez) *The Liberating Pulpit,* Abingdon, 1994.

*Santa Biblia: The Bible through Hispanic Eyes,* Abingdon, 1996.

(Editor) *Alabadle!: Hispanic Christian Worship,* Abingdon, 1996.

(Editor) *Church History: An Essential Guide,* Abingdon, 1996.

*Tres meses en la escuela de Mateo: Estudios sobre el Evangelio de Mateo,* Abingdon, 1996.

TRANSLATOR INTO SPANISH

H. R. Macintosh, *Types of Modern Theology,* Methopress, 1964.

Bernard Ramn, *Special Revelation and the Word of God,* Methopress, 1968.

Seward Hiltner, *Pastoral Counseling,* Methopress, 1971.

OTHER

Editor of *Apuntes,* a journal of Hispanic theology.

SIDELIGHTS: Justo L. Gonzalez told *CA:* "According to my wife, I was born with printer's ink for blood."*

\* \* \*

**GONZALEZ-CRUSSI, F(rank)  1936-**

PERSONAL: Born October 4, 1936, in Mexico City, Mexico; immigrated to United States, 1973; naturalized citizen, 1987; son of Pablo (a pharmacist) and Maria (a pharmacist; maiden name, Crussi) Gonzalez; married Ana Luz, December 22, 1961 (divorced, 1974); married Wei Hsueh (a research pathologist), October 7, 1978; children: (first marriage) Daniel, Francis Xavier, Juliana. *Education:* Universidad Nacional Autonoma de Mexico, B.A., 1954, M.D., 1961.

ADDRESSES: *Home*—2626 North Lakeview Ave., Chicago, IL 60614. *Office*—Department of Pathology, Childrens Memorial Hospital, 2300 Childrens Plaza, Chicago, IL 60614.

*CAREER:* Licensed to practice medicine in Indiana, Illinois, and Ontario; certified by American Board of Pathology, 1967, Canada Register, Ontario, 1970. Penrose Hospital, Colorado Springs, CO, intern, 1962; St. Lawrence Hospital, Lansing, MI, and Shands Teaching Hospital at the University of Florida, Gainesville, FL, resident in pathology, 1963-67; Queens University, Kingston, Ontario, assistant professor of pathology, 1967-73; Purdue University at Indianapolis, IN, associate professor of pathology, 1973-78; Northwestern University, Chicago, IL, professor of pathology, 1978—. Writer. Head of laboratories at Childrens Memorial Hospital, Chicago.

*MEMBER:* International Academy of Pathology, Society for Pediatric Pathology, American Society of Clinical Pathologists, Authors Guild, Authors League of America, Royal College of Physicians and Surgeons of Canada, Chicago Pathology Society, Society of Midland Authors.

*AWARDS, HONORS:* Best Nonfiction Award from the Society of Midland Authors, 1985, for *Notes of an Anatomist.*

*WRITINGS:*

(Editor) *Wilms Tumor (Nephroblastoma) and Related Renal Neoplasms of Childhood,* CRC Press (Boca Raton, FL), 1983.
*Notes of an Anatomist* (essays), Harcourt (New York City), 1985.
*Three Forms of Sudden Death; and Other Reflections on the Grandeur and Misery of the Body* (essays; includes "Some Expressions of the Body [in Four Movements]"), Harper (New York City), 1986.
*On the Nature of Things Erotic* (essays), Harcourt, 1988.
*The Five Senses,* Harcourt, 1989.
*The Day of the Dead and Other Mortal Reflections,* Harcourt, 1993.
*Suspended Animation: Six Essays on the Preservation of Bodily Parts,* photographs by Rosamond Purcell, Harcourt, 1995.

Also author of a medical book entitled *Extragonadal Teratomas.* Contributor to numerous medical journals.

*ADAPTATIONS:* The works of Gonzalez-Crussi were adapted for the stage by the Live Bait Theatrical Co. of Chicago in January, 1995, in a play entitled *Me-* *mento Mori,* by Sharon Evans (director) and Valerie Olney.

*SIDELIGHTS:* Pathologist F. Gonzalez-Crussi established himself as a noteworthy author with the publication of three nontechnical essay collections. Described as "witty" and "well-read" by Brett Singer in the *Los Angeles Times Book Review,* Gonzalez-Crussi colors his informal writings with the insight he has gained from three decades of practicing medicine. Critics credit him with renewing the essay as a viable literary form in the twentieth century and liken his style to that of classic writers, such as Herman Melville, Michel Eyquem Montaigne, and Charles Lamb.

Gonzalez-Crussi's first collection of essays, entitled *Notes of an Anatomist,* deals with a vast array of subjects, including corpses, ancient embalming techniques, the phenomenon of multiple births, bodily appendages, and natural monstrosities from a pathologist's perspective. Many critics considered the volume to be a rich and thought-provoking first effort that artfully blends the author's personal experience and wry humor with mythic and literary references. Gonzalez-Crussi spices his essays with historical asides. His use of allusions, ranging from the mention of sixteenth-century French king Henry IV's venereal diseases and Spanish painter El Greco's astigmatism to the style of a Federico Fellini film, prompted critic Dennis Drabelle to call him a "skilled wielder of literary references" in a review for *Washington Post Book World.*

John Gross, writing for the *New York Times,* suggested that *Notes of an Anatomist* "could also have been entitled 'A Pathologist's Apology'," as it attempts to purge doctors who perform autopsies of their presumed callousness. Gonzalez-Crussi asserted the nobility of pathologists in "The Dead as a Living," an essay from the volume that was cited in part in *Washington Post Book World:* physicians who search for the cause of their patients deaths, explained the author, are unequaled in their "interest in the dead as dead persons, rather than abstractions." In the same excerpt, the doctor went on to argue that pathologists regard a corpse as a unique repository of clues capable of disclosing the cause of an individual human beings death. Ironically, however, the highly personal postmortem examination also reveals man's sameness in what Gonzalez-Crussi, quoted by Edward Schneidman for the *Los Angeles Times Book Review,* calls "a most brutal way." The author reminds us, wrote Bruce Hepburn in an article for *New*

*Statesman,* of the disturbing but undeniable fact that "decomposition of one sort or other is our universal fate and that it is salutary for us all to keep our latter end in mind."

Critics applauded Gonzalez-Crussi's literary debut for both its form and content. D. J. Enright wrote in the *New York Times Book Review* that the essays "mix fact with speculation and gravity with humor, are rich in apposite and astounding anecdote and are elegant in expression." Schneidman echoed Enright's praise and expressed the consensus of the critics when he called the essays the "marvelously original and provocative" products of a "gifted" writer. *Notes of an Anatomist* earned Gonzalez-Crussi the Best Nonfiction Award from the Society of Midland Authors in 1985.

The authors follow-up volume of essays, *Three Forms of Sudden Death; and Other Reflections on the Grandeur and Misery of the Body,* centers on issues of aging and death. Allan J. Tobin, commenting on the doctor's treatment of a seemingly somber topic, wrote in the *Los Angeles Times Book Review:* "Gonzalez-Crussi deals less with the gloom of death than with the joy of life, especially of a life devoted to inquiry." Tobin suggested that just as the doctor examines physiological abnormalities in an effort to better understand normal life processes, he writes his essays in an attempt to explore timeless human mysteries: "There are only two themes worth writing . . . about," Gonzalez-Crussi stated according to Tobin, "love and death, *eros* and *thanatos.*"

The title *Three Forms of Sudden Death* refers to death by lightning, asphyxiation, and unknown causes, topics Gonzalez-Crussi discusses in the book along with thoughts on cannibalism, the female breast, and human emotions in what several critics have referred to as "pithy" and "engaging" essays. Gonzalez-Crussi's third publication, *On the Nature of Things Erotic,* marks a departure from the scientifically inspired writings that dominate the author's earlier collections. The essays deal with love, desire, and seduction, achieving "something that it is not too much to call wisdom," stated John Gross in the *New York Times.* Some reviewers expressed a desire for the author to offer his own theories on the subjects he addresses, rather than compile the thoughts of others, but most enjoyed his accounts of ancient Greek love diagnoses, medieval Chinese seduction, and the classical view of homosexuality as a sign of high culture.

While Gonzalez-Crussi has gained both critical and popular success as a writer, he remains a practicing pathologist and a professor at Northwestern University in Chicago, Illinois. As an author, he is the practitioner of a long-ignored art, "a true essayist," wrote Gross in an article for the *New York Times.* By following the paths of his imagination, Gonzalez-Crussi has touched upon what critics consider to be universal themes in essays of universal appeal.

Gonzalez-Crussi told *CA:* "In my books, I have attempted to join science and the humanities. I would like to produce works of literature inspired on medical and biological subjects—not scientific divulgation. *Notes of an Anatomist* originated from a desire to reflect on the personal experience of a pathologist. *Three Forms of Sudden Death* attempts to be a personal statement of perplexity at the limitations and strengths of the human body."

## BIOGRAPHICAL/CRITICAL SOURCES:

*PERIODICALS*

*Los Angeles Times Book Review,* July 7, 1985; December 7, 1986; March 27, 1988.
*New Statesman,* April 11, 1986.
*New York Times,* May 14, 1985; April 15, 1988.
*New York Times Book Review,* July 7, 1985; April 9, 1989; November 12, 1995, p. 8.
*Observer* (London), April 13, 1986.
*Vista,* November 26, 1989.
*Washington Post,* July 5, 1985.
*Washington Post Book World,* April 9, 1989.

\*    \*    \*

## GORES, Joe
See GORES, Joseph N(icholas)

\*    \*    \*

## GORES, Joseph N(icholas) 1931-
(Joe Gores)

*PERSONAL:* Surname rhymes with "roars"; born December 25, 1931, in Rochester, MN; son of Joseph Mathias (an accountant) and Mildred Dorothy (Duncanson) Gores; married Dori Jane Corfitzen, May 16, 1976; children: Timothy, Gillian. *Educa-*

*tion:* University of Notre Dame, A.B., 1953; Stanford University, M.A., 1961. *Politics:* Republican. *Religion:* Roman Catholic. *Avocational interests:* Skin diving, handball, weightlifting, hiking, African prehistory, travel.

*ADDRESSES: Home*—401 Oak Crest Rd., San Anselmo, CA 94960. *Office*—DOJO, Inc., P.O. Box 446, Fairfax, CA 94978. *Agent*—(Books) Henry Morrison, P.O. Box 235, Bedford Hills, NY 10507; (scripts) Joel Gottler, Renaissance/H. N. Swanson, 8523 Sunset Blvd., Los Angeles, CA 90069.

*CAREER:* Novelist, short story writer, film and television script writer. Has worked as a hod carrier, laborer, logger, stock clerk, truck driver, carnival worker, and assistant motel manager; Floyd Page's Gymnasium, Palo Alto, CA, instructor, 1953-55; L. A. Walker Co., San Francisco, CA, private investigator, 1955-57, 1959; David Kikkert & Associates, San Francisco, private investigator, 1959-62, 1965-66; Kakamega Boys Secondary School, Kakamega, Kenya, East Africa, English teacher, 1963-64; Automobile Auction Co., San Francisco, manager and auctioneer, 1968-76; story editor, *B. L. Stryker* (monthly mystery movie), Universal/ABC, 1988-89; currently affiliated with DOJO, Inc., Fairfax, CA. *Military service:* U.S. Army, 1958-59.

*MEMBER:* Mystery Writers of America (secretary, 1966, 1968; vice-president, 1967, 1969-70; general awards chair, 1976-77, 1992-93; member of board of directors, 1967-70, 1975-76; president, 1986); Writers Guild of America West, Crime Writers Association.

*AWARDS, HONORS:* Edgar Allan Poe Awards, Mystery Writers of America, 1969, for best first mystery novel for *A Time of Predators,* 1969, for best mystery short story for "Goodbye, Pops," and 1975, for best episode in a television dramatic series for "No Immunity for Murder" from *Kojak;* Falcon Award for best hard-boiled mystery novel, Maltese Falcon Society of Japan, 1986, for *Hammett.*

*WRITINGS:*

*NOVELS; UNDER NAME JOE GORES*

*A Time of Predators,* Random House (New York City), 1969.
*Dead Skip,* Random House, 1972.
*Interface* (also see below), M. Evans (New York City), 1974.

*Hammett* (also see below), Putnam (New York City), 1975.
*Gone, No Forwarding,* Random House, 1978.
*Come Morning* (also see below), Mysterious Press (New York City), 1986.
*Wolf Time,* Putnam, 1989.
*32 Cadillacs* (also see below), Mysterious Press, 1992.
*Dead Man,* Mysterious Press, 1993.
*Menaced Assassin,* Mysterious Press, 1994.
*Contract Null and Void,* Mysterious Press, 1996.

*FILM SCRIPTS; UNDER NAME JOE GORES*

*Interface,* Cinema Entertainment, 1974.
*Deadfall,* Twentieth Century-Fox, 1976.
*Hammett,* Zoetrope Studios, 1977-78.
*Paper Crimes,* P.E.A./United Artists, 1978.
*Paradise Road,* Paramount, 1978.
*Golden Gate Memorial* (television film), Universal, 1978.
*A Wayward Angel,* Solofilm/United Artists, 1981.
(With Kevin Wade) *Cover Story,* Columbia, 1985.
*Gangbusters,* Botfilm Productions, 1989.
*32 Cadillacs,* Fox-2000, 1996.

Also author of films (with Arthur M. Kaye) *Force Twelve,* 1971, (with Kaye) *Game without Rules,* 1972, and *Come Morning,* 1980.

*OTHER; UNDER NAME JOE GORES*

*Marine Salvage* (nonfiction), Doubleday (New York City), 1971.
(Editor) *Honolulu: Port of Call* (anthology), Comstock (Ithaca, NY), 1974.
(Editor with Bill Pronzini) *Tricks and Treats* (anthology), Doubleday, 1975.
*Mostly Murder* (collection), Mystery Scene Press, 1992.

Contributor of scripts to television series *Kojak, Eischeid, Kate Loves a Mystery, The Gangster Chronicles, Strike Force, Magnum, P.I., Mike Hammer, Remington Steele, Scene of the Crime, Eye to Eye, Hell Town, B. L. Stryker,* and *T. J. Hooker.* Also contributor to anthologies, including *Mystery Writers of America Annual Anthology, Boucher's Choicest,* and *Best Detective Stories of the Year.* Contributor of stories and articles to *Ellery Queen's Mystery Magazine, Argosy, Adam, Negro Digest,* and other periodicals.

*ADAPTATIONS: Hammett* was adapted into a film by Ross Thomas and Dennis O'Flaherty, produced by Francis Ford Coppola and directed by Wim Wenders, and released by Warner Brothers in 1982.

*WORK IN PROGRESS:* A novel tentatively titled *The Field of Bullets;* a novel entitled *Cons, Scams, and Grifts.*

*SIDELIGHTS:* Joe Gores worked as a private detective in San Francisco for more than ten years, beginning in 1955. Winner of three Edgar Allan Poe Awards, Gores is probably best known for his novel *Hammett,* which sets the real-life detective and mystery writer Dashiell Hammett in a fictional murder case in 1928. Although *Newsweek* reviewer Peter S. Prescott finds fault with Gores's narrative technique and *New York Times* critic Richard R. Lingeman believes Gores's portrayal of Hammett is superficial, according to Max Byrd, *Hammett* is "a splendid story, a candy-apple to the connoisseur." Reviewing the novel in the *New Republic,* Byrd writes that Gore's protagonist "sets out to clean up a corrupt society, . . . but his civic aim is constantly deflected by a revenge *motif* worthy of Jacobean drama and by Gores' obvious delight in the conventions of his genre." Byrd adds that "perhaps, but not likely, Gores had even more fun writing this book than we do reading it."

In his *Washington Post Book World* assessment of Gores's *Come Morning,* Lawrence Block claims "Gores is one of the better-kept secrets in crime fiction. . . . *Come Morning* is a pure pleasure to read. Please understand that the basic ingredients are nothing new. One man has something—spy secrets, a black bird, a fortune in diamonds. Others want to take it from him. . . . [Yet,] the plot is a honey, intricate, logical, fair, and constantly surprising. . . . Within the mystery field, Gores has won awards and fans. He deserves a wider audience, and this book should get it for him." According to Brian Garfield for the *Chicago-Sun Times, Come Morning* is the work of a novelist who has matured—"[Gores] has absolute control of his material: the book inspires a chill on the back of the neck—the short hairs are raised by a thrill of confidence that we are in the hands of a master who *knows.* . . . Although metaphors do not flood his pages (he won't stoop to that sort of pretentiousness), nevertheless there are images, doled out at frugal intervals—striking, apt, stunningly effective. They do what good prose is supposed to do: they show us new ways of perceiving things." Even within the novel's rush of action,

Garfield senses a "convincing warmth," and concludes that the work is the major event Gores's publishers claimed it would be: "Like a handful of previous writers . . . Gores brings a vivid new voice to America's literatures of the criminal on the run."

Gores once told *CA:* "I entered college thinking I wanted to be a cartoonist in a Milton Caniff-Hal Foster mode. But I soon realized I was intrigued by storytelling, so I quit drawing and started writing short stories, averaging 300 rejection slips a year until my first sale (to *Manhunt* for $65) four years after graduation. It was only years later, when I added film and TV to the novel and the short story, that I realized I had come full circle: I was back to telling stories in words *and* pictures.

"In 1968, Lee Wright of Random House wrote that if I ever wanted to write a novel she'd probably want to publish it. I immediately wrote *A Time of Predators,* Wright published it, and it won an Edgar. In 1974, Jack Laird, supervising producer of *Kojak,* wrote that if I ever wanted to write a *Kojak* episode, he'd probably want to buy it. I immediately wrote 'No Immunity for Murder,' Laird bought it, and it won an Edgar. I seem to keep backing into my career moves.

"While living in Africa I read Robert Ardrey's *African Genesis,* and a few years later Joseph Campbell's *The Hero with a Thousand Faces.* From these I came to understand what my basic fictional theme was: A hero who has been stripped of society's defenses must overcome danger and death armed only with the genetic survival skills inherited from his prehuman ancestors." Gores more recently added, "My 1994 novel *Menaced Assassin* addresses these concerns directly; while it is about a hit man, the spine of the book is a speech about the nature of human violence being made by the man the killer plans to make his final victim. It is the only novel I have written to which I felt it appropriate to append a bibliography."

Gores continued, "Writing is all I do and all I want to do. I try to write every day but [I] don't always make it—travel, for instance, makes the work schedule disappear."

*BIOGRAPHICAL/CRITICAL SOURCES:*

*PERIODICALS*

*Chicago-Sun Times,* March 2, 1986.
*Listener,* November 25, 1976.

*Los Angeles Times,* March 13, 1981.

*New Republic,* May 22, 1979.

*Newsweek,* September 8, 1975.

*New York Times,* September 4, 1975; July 1, 1983; February 19, 1986.

*New York Times Book Review,* August 24, 1969; August 11, 1972; May 14, 1978.

*Times Literary Supplement,* October 10, 1975.

*Washington Post Book World,* August 23, 1970; December 17, 1972; May 19, 1974; March 2, 1986.

\*    \*    \*

## GORTON, Kaitlyn
### See EMERSON, Kathy Lynn

\*    \*    \*

## GRANT, Matthew G.
### See MAY, Julian

\*    \*    \*

## GRENNAN, Eamon 1941-

*PERSONAL:* Born November 13, 1941, in Dublin, Ireland; son of Thomas P. (an educational administrator) and Evelyn (Yourell) Grennan; married Joan Perkins, 1972 (divorced, 1986); married Rachel Kitzinger (a college teacher); children: Kate, Conor, Kira. *Education:* National University of Ireland, University College, Dublin, B.A., 1963, M.A., 1964; Harvard University, Ph.D., 1973.

*ADDRESSES: Home*—Box 352, Vassar College, Poughkeepsie, NY 12601.

*CAREER:* Vassar College, Poughkeepsie, NY, member of English faculty, 1974—.

*AWARDS, HONORS:* NEA Award, 1991; Guggenheim fellowship, 1995; James Boatwright Poetry Prize from *Shenandoah* magazine, 1995.

*WRITINGS:*

*Wildly for Days,* Gallery Press (Dublin), 1983.

*What Light There Is,* Gallery Press, 1987.

*Twelve Poems,* Occasional Works, 1988.

*What Light There Is and Other Poems,* North Point Press (Berkeley, CA), 1989.

*As If It Matters,* Gallery Press, 1991; Graywolf Press (St. Paul, MN), 1992.

*So It Goes,* Gallery Press and Graywolf Press, 1995.

(Translator) *Selected Poems of Giacomo Leopardi,* Dedalus (Dublin), 1995.

*SIDELIGHTS:* Eamon Grennan is one of a handful of Irish poets who, like Seamus Heaney, Derek Mahon, and Paul Muldoon, live and teach, full or part-time, at American universities. As a result, his poems are often present-tense American experiences, past-tense Irish reminiscences, or a blending of these elements. Alfred Corn, writing in *Poetry,* cites how Grennan's "authentic sources are Irish," and how he displays the "specific virtues the Irish bring with them—humanity, verbal fluency, and a convincing pastoralism." His work has also been called characteristically Irish by Richard Tillinghast in *The New England Review* by having "a sense that life approaches at times the significance of ritual," by showing "the centrality in Irish life of the hearth," and by incorporating "the weather eye that the poet keeps out for presences other than the physical and earthly," giving Grennan's poetry "a largeness, a generosity, an unforced openness to experience that affirms what we have in common rather than the barriers we erect to divide us." By Grennan's depicting "things of the ordinary morning world," writes Robert Schultz in the *Hudson Review,* Grennan "works toward moments of quiet epiphany." Yet, adds Ben Howard in *Poetry,* in addition to Grennan's "eye for the elusive detail" is "an ear for the most reclusive sound," for, "like many Irish poets, bardic and modern, he is keenly aware of aural phenomena," as was his countryman James Joyce "with whom he shares a love of the fabric of words." This emphasis on sound, as Bill Tremblay comments on in the *American Book Review,* is Grennan's "most powerful element," using "assonance, internal rhyme, alliteration, oxymoron—a host of poetic devices in the context of free verse poems—to create a textured music." As a result, when Grennan writes, according to Edward Hirsch in *The New Republic,* "His quiet, well-crafted poems are painterly, sensible, shapely; they are eager, unrhetorical, straightforward, melodic. They are never extreme."

Although Eamon Grennan published three books of poems in Ireland between 1983 and 1988, it was not until his first American publication in 1989 of *What Light There Is And Other Poems* that American readers and critics began to notice him, and gave him, what Laurel Blossom in *Small Press* calls "a rousing welcome." The book collects together much of his early work, and is divided into three sections. The first section, "Wildly for Days," which was Grennan's first book, shows the influence of "the nature lyrics of the medieval Irish monks," according to Maurice Riordan in *Times Literary Supplement,* as he "writes impressionistically of birds, beasts, flowers and the weather," yet, as Hirsch adds, the work is balanced by a "central emotional sadness" which reflects the death of the poet's father and his own divorce and separation from his children. In the middle section, "A Single Window," while Hirsch points out how "the thirteen intermediate poems" form "a kind of stylistic bridge" between the early poems in "Wildly for Days" and the later work in "What Light There Is." Dillon Johnston, in the *Irish Literary Supplement,* notes Grennan's use of a "window-view" which connects him with contemporary Irish women poets Eilean Ni Chuilleanain and Medbh McGuckian. The third and title section, "What Light There Is," has poems which are "more fully developed, reaching broader levels of thematic significance, yet remaining grounded in close observation and strong feeling," according to Schultz.

*As If It Matters,* 1992, has been praised by Rand Brandes in the *Irish Literary Supplement,* for extending Grennan's "experimenting with light—playing with (optical) illusions, magnifications, and distortions, which are often centered in the kitchen" and for including poems which "record the breakup of the family, which is paralleled by images of decomposition and destruction in nature," as well as "poems of celebration and discovery." The book is both balanced and framed by what Howard calls "a pair of tender narrative poems." Section one, "Compass Readings," opens with "Two Climbing," a poem in which the poet and his twelve-year-old son from his first marriage go hiking in North Connemara, "pleased with ourselves / at some dumb male thing for which / he finds the word: *adventure,*" and which introduces what Brandes calls the central themes of the book, "defining oneself, familial continuity and discontinuity, and the regenerating powers of nature." Section two, "Things in the Flesh," ends with "Two Gathering," a poem in which the poet and his teenage daughter from his first marriage go gathering mussels to be eaten together, the meal and the hearth a continuity, and the gathering experience makes the poet feel "this wonderful abundance / offering itself up to us as if we were masters / of the garden, parts of the plenary sphere / and circle, our bodies belong-

ing / to the earth, the air, the water." In between are, according to Howard, "some thirty meditative-descriptive poems of medium length, most of them cast in the first-person, present-tense mode and many of them commemorating privileged moments." On the whole, *As If It Matters* is, Brandes states, "a book of studied interiors and harsh exposures" in which Grennan "brilliantly affirms" for his readers "the value of home," and "the need to take care of what we have."

*So It Goes,* 1995, finds Grennan considering midlife: "There comes in middle life a moment / when everything is very solid / and seems to stand foursquare / in its own hard, uncompromising light." Louis McKee, writing in *Library Journal,* believes that Grennan is "pensive and expansive. His hard-won maturity and insight enable him to cast light on the shadows and reveal the everyday wonders hidden there." According to *Publishers Weekly,* Grennan "plumbs his personal heritage in these 40-plus poems," where the "forms are varied, stanza length ranging from three lines to 50," and the "tone is meditative and pliant." McKee remarks that Grennan's "appreciation of the small things makes these poems memorable."

## BIOGRAPHICAL/CRITICAL SOURCES:

### PERIODICALS

*American Book Review,* July, 1990, p. 30.
*Booklist,* June 15, 1989, p. 61; March 15, 1992, p. 1331; November 1, 1995, p. 450.
*Choice,* October, 1992, p. 298.
*Hudson Review,* spring, 1990, p. 143; fall, 1992, p. 518.
*Irish Literary Supplement,* spring, 1988, p. 10; fall, 1992, p. 19-20.
*Library Journal,* June 15, 1989, p. 61; March 15, 1992, p. 92; November 15, 1995, p. 79.
*New England Review,* spring, 1993, p. 189-95
*New Republic,* June 11, 1990, p. 39.
*New Yorker,* December 14, 1992, p. 134.
*Poetry,* January, 1990, p. 287-89; January, 1993, p. 233-34.
*Publishers Weekly,* May 5, 1989, p. 74; January 27, 1992, p. 93; October 31, 1994, p. 55. October 23, 1995, p. 65.
*Times Literary Supplement,* March 15, 1985, p. 294.
*Small Press,* summer, 1992, p. 52.

*—Sketch by Robert Miltner*

# H-I

**HADITHI, Mwenye**
**See HOBSON, Bruce**

\* \* \*

## HAGUE, Richard 1947-

*PERSONAL:* Born August 7, 1947, in Steubenville, OH; son of James R. (an engineer) and Ruth (a homemaker; maiden name, Heights) Hague; married Pamela Korte (a potter), June 24, 1980; children: Patrick, Brendan. *Ethnicity:* "White Appalachian." *Education:* Xavier University, B.S., 1969, M.A., 1971. *Religion:* Roman Catholic. *Avocational interests:* "Science, in particular local geology and archaeology, and the powers and functions of the brain and memory; gardening, which I practice compulsively and yet with great enjoyment."

*ADDRESSES: Home*—6203 Erie Ave., Cincinnati, OH 45227. *Office*—Purcell Marian High School, 2935 Hackberry, Cincinnati, OH 45206.

*CAREER:* Purcell Marian High School, Cincinnati, OH, teacher and chairman of English department, 1969—. Adjunct lecturer at Xavier University; co-coordinator of Southern Appalachian Writers Cooperative, 1982, 1996; literary artist at Kentucky Institute for Arts in Education, University of Louisville, 1984; member of literary panel of Ohio Arts Council, 1984-87; member of poetry staff of Appalachian Writers Workshop, 1988, 1994. Gives writing workshops and lectures on poetry. Site manager of Madisonville Community Garden, 1987—.

*AWARDS, HONORS:* President's Award in Poetry from *Ohio Journal,* 1979, for "An Unsent Letter of Darwin's," and 1981, for "Moose Ridge Apple Wine"; Post-Corbett Award in Literary Arts from *Cincinnati Post,* 1982, for a continuing contribution to the arts in Cincinnati; grant from Greater Cincinnati Foundation, 1984; first prize in professional prose category from Ohio Educational and Library Media Association, 1985, for story "Whistling Woman and the Man of Light"; named co-poet of the year in Ohio by Ohio Poetry Day Association, 1985, for *Ripening;* runner-up for Poetry Center Prize from Cleveland State University, 1987, for *Possible Debris;* finalist, Associated Writing Program Award in creative nonfiction, 1991, for *Hitepokes, Night Fish, and the Jumping Buckeyes;* National First Prize, English-Speaking Union, 1994, for writing program; Ohio Arts Council Fellow, 1994; Arts in Education grant, Council for Basic Education, 1995; Marianist Education Consortium Grant, 1996.

*WRITINGS:*

*Crossings* (poems), Cincinnati Area Poetry Press, 1979.
*A Week of Nights Down River* (poems), privately printed, 1981.
*Ripening* (poems), Ohio State University Press (Columbus, OH), 1984.
*Possible Debris* (poems), Poetry Center, Cleveland State University, 1988.
*Mill and Smoke Marrow* (poems), Bottom Dog Press, 1991.
*In a Red Shadow of Steel Mills,* Bottom Dog Press, 1991.

Work represented in anthologies, including *I Have a Place,* edited by Jim Wayne Miller, Alice Lloyd

College, 1981; *Footsteps on the Mountain,* Appalachian Consortium Press, 1987; *Oyo: An Ohio River Anthology,* Volume II, Oyo Press, 1988; *In Buckeye Country,* Bottom Dog Press, 1994; *Old Wounds, New Words,* Jesse Stuart Foundation, 1994; *Appalachia Inside Out,* University of Tennessee Press, 1995; *Coffeehouse Poetry Anthology,* Bottom Dog Press, 1996; and *Down Home, Down Town: Urban Appalachians Today,* Kendall-Hum, 1996. Contributor to periodicals, including *Appalachian Heritage, Country Journal, Creative Nonfiction, English Journal, Gambit, Kiosk, Laurel Review, Open Places, Poetry, The Prose Poem: An International Journal,* and *Wooster Review.* Poetry editor of *Pine Mountain Sand and Gravel.*

*WORK IN PROGRESS: The Time It Takes Light: Poems in the Vicinity of Physics; Mortality,* poems.

*SIDELIGHTS:* Richard Hague told *CA* that one of the most important events of his career "was the growing realization that I came from a specific and interesting place, that I was an Ohioan, a border Appalachian, and that these places had value and significance. Becoming aware of my own roots, I lived alone on Greenbrier Ridge in southeastern Ohio for several summers, and it was these stays, and their attendant lessons, that shaped me early in my career, and continue to do so now. Recently, I have centered even more: now I am a resident of Madisonville, an old neighborhood in Cincinnati, and I am a husband and father and gardener there. These, too, shape my work more and more. I try to celebrate the local; I try to find in the commonly overlooked or misapprehended detail some significance that may allow me to speak to people elsewhere, to reach them where they live.

"My major areas of vocational interest are the teaching of writing, both prose and poetry; studying and teaching the literature of place, so-called regional literature, discovering in it the universal."

*BIOGRAPHICAL/CRITICAL SOURCES:*

PERIODICALS

*Appalachian Journal,* summer, 1985.
*Journal of Kentucky Studies,* September, 1993, pp. 57-65.
*Ohioana Quarterly,* spring, 1986.
*Western Ohio Journal,* spring, 1988.

## HAMILTON, David    1939-

*PERSONAL:* Born June 30, 1939, in Rothesay Bute, England; son of James Hay and Olive Hamilton; married Jean Duncan, 1982; children: Duncan, Alistair, Hazel. *Ethnicity:* "Scottish." *Education:* University of Glasgow, B.Sc., 1960, M.B., Ch.B., 1963, Ph.D., 1963, F.R.C.S., 1966. *Politics:* Labour.

*ADDRESSES: Agent*—David Fletcher, 58 John St., Penicuik, Midlothian, Scotland.

*CAREER:* Western Infirmary, Glasgow, Scotland, surgeon, 1963-84; Inverclyden Royal Trust, surgeon, 1988—. Partick Press, owner, 1984—.

*AWARDS, HONORS:* Research fellow, Oxford University, 1983-84; Murdoch Medal, 1995, for contributions to the history of golf.

*WRITINGS:*

*The Healers: A History of Scottish Medicine,* Canongate, 1981, second edition, 1987.
*A Good Golf Guide to Scotland,* Canongate, 1985.
*Early Golf: Glasgow,* Partick Press, 1985.
*Early Golf: Aberdeen,* Partick Press, 1986.
*The Monkey Gland Affair,* Chatto & Windus (England), 1986.
*Early Golf: St. Andrews,* Partick Press, 1987.
*The Brithers,* Patrick Press, 1989.
*Golf—Scotland's Game,* Partick Press, 1996.

*SIDELIGHTS:* David Hamilton told *CA:* "I try to bring serious-minded scholarship to the history of Scotland, notably in the areas of medicine and golf. My Partick Press books contain new material on the history of golf printed by letterpress in limited editions."

*BIOGRAPHICAL/CRITICAL SOURCES:*

PERIODICALS

*Times* (London), December 11, 1986.
*Times Literary Supplement,* September 19, 1986.

*    *    *

**HARGRAVE, Leonie**
**See DISCH, Thomas M(ichael)**

## HASZARD, Patricia Moyes 1923-
### (Patricia Moyes)

*PERSONAL:* Born January 19, 1923, in Bray, Ireland; daughter of Ernst (a judge in the Indian Civil Service) and Marion (Boyd) Pakenham-Walsh; married John Moyes (a photographer), 1951 (divorced, 1959); married John S. Haszard (an official of the International Monetary Fund), October 13, 1962 (died 1994). *Politics:* Liberal (non-party). *Religion:* Church of England. *Avocational interests:* Skiing, sailing, good food and wine, travel.

*ADDRESSES: Home*—P.O. Box 1, Virgin Gorda, British Virgin Islands, West Indies. *Agent*—Curtis Brown, Ltd., Haymarket House, 28/29 Haymarket, London, SW1Y 4SP England.

*CAREER:* Writer. Peter Ustinov Productions, Ltd., London, England, secretary, 1947-53; *Vogue,* London, assistant editor, 1954-58. *Military service:* British Women's Auxiliary Air Force, Radar Section, 1940-45; became flight officer.

*AWARDS, HONORS:* Edgar Allan Poe Award from Mystery Writers of America, 1970, for *Many Deadly Returns.*

*WRITINGS:*

MYSTERIES; UNDER NAME PATRICIA MOYES

*Dead Men Don't Ski,* Collins (London), 1959, Rinehart (New York City), 1960.
*Down among the Dead Men,* Holt (New York City), 1961, published in England as *The Sunken Sailor,* Collins, 1961.
*Death on the Agenda,* Holt, 1962.
*Murder a la Mode,* Holt, 1963.
*Falling Star,* Holt, 1964.
*Johnny under Ground,* Collins, 1965, Holt, 1966.
*Murder by 3's* (omnibus volume of mystery novels), Holt, 1965.
*Murder Fantastical,* Holt, 1967.
*Death and the Dutch Uncle,* Holt, 1968.
*Many Deadly Returns,* Holt, 1970, published in England as *Who Saw Her Die?,* Collins, 1970.
*Seasons of Snows and Sins,* Holt, 1971.
*The Curious Affair of the Third Dog,* Holt, 1973.
*Black Widower,* Holt, 1975.
*The Coconut Killings,* Holt, 1977, published in England as *To Kill A Coconut,* Collins, 1977.

*Who Is Simon Warwick?,* Collins, 1978, Holt, 1979.
*Angel Death,* Holt, 1980.
*A Six-Letter Word for Death,* Holt, 1983.
*Night Ferry to Death,* Holt, 1985.
*Black Girl, White Girl,* Holt, 1989.
*Twice in a Blue Moon,* Holt, 1993.
*Who Killed Father Christmas and Other Seasonable Demises,* Crippen & Landrew, 1996.

OTHER

*Time Remembered* (play; first produced in London, 1954; produced in New York, 1957), Methuen, 1955.
(With Peter Ustinov and Hal E. Chester) *School for Scoundrels* (screenplay), Continental Pictures, 1960.
*Helter-Skelter* (juvenile), Holt, 1968.
*After All, They're Only Cats,* Curtis Books, 1973.
*How to Talk to Your Cat,* Holt, 1978.

Contributor of short stories and articles to *Women's Mirror, Evening News* (London), *Writer, Ellery Queen's Mystery Magazine,* and other publications.

Moyes's books have been translated into fifteen languages.

*ADAPTATIONS:* The short stories "A Sad Loss" and "Hit and Run" were made into episodes of the British television program *Tales of the Unexpected.*

*WORK IN PROGRESS:* A mystery novel.

*SIDELIGHTS:* "One of the brightest contemporary practitioners of the puzzle-and-plot whodunit," as a *New York Times Book Review* critic describes her, Patricia Moyes Haszard writes mystery novels about Inspector Henry Tibbett of Scotland Yard and his wife, Emmy. Jean M. White of the *Washington Post Book World* calls them a "thoroughly engaging couple" and praises Moyes's "talent for overlaying mystery with witty, sophisticated social comment." Writing in the *New York Times Book Review,* Newgate Callendar sees Moyes as "carrying on the traditions of the classical British mystery." Similarly, Anthony Boucher, writing for the same publication, states that "Moyes is so good with people and professions and milieus that her books . . . keep reminding one more and more of the best work of [Ngaio] Marsh and [Margery] Allingham and other exemplary products of the Golden Thirties."

*BIOGRAPHICAL/CRITICAL SOURCES:*

PERIODICALS

*Listener,* April 7, 1977; January 11, 1979.
*Los Angeles Times Book Review,* October 6, 1985.
*New York Times Book Review,* July 26, 1964; May 31, 1970; February 22, 1981; May 16, 1982.
*Observer* (London), July 5, 1970; February 6, 1977.
*Saturday Review,* December 25, 1971.
*Spectator,* August 18, 1973.
*Times Literary Supplement,* August 13, 1964; July 16, 1970; November 12 1971; October 3, 1980; June 20, 1986.
*Washington Post Book World,* November 18, 1973; July 20, 1975; January 21, 1979.

\* \* \*

## HENKES, Robert    1922-

*PERSONAL:* Born October 28, 1922, in Kalamazoo, MI; son of Peter John (a policeman) and Veronica (Itsenhuiser) Henkes; married Frances Malerney, April 21, 1956; children: Catherine, Anne, Susan, Jane. *Education:* Drake University, B.F.A., 1948; University of Wisconsin, M.A., 1950; attended summer painting workshops at University of Michigan, 1955, and Michigan State University, 1956. *Religion:* Roman Catholic. *Avocational interests:* Track (member of national collegiate cross-country championship team, 1944-45), collecting antique glass, collecting original etchings and lithographs by American artists of the Depression decade.

*ADDRESSES: Home*—1124 Bretton Dr., Kalamazoo, MI 49006.

*CAREER:* Kalamazoo Institute of Arts, Kalamazoo, MI, instructor in painting, 1954-84; Nazareth College, Kalamazoo, professor of art, 1966-72. Instructor in art, Barbour Hall Boys School, Kalamazoo, 1968-84; director of community art education workshops for children and painting instructor at Adult Community Center, Kalamazoo. Has had one-man shows in Des Moines, IA; Milwaukee, WI; Racine, WI; and at Nazareth College, Kalamazoo College, Western Michigan University, Luther College, and Kinascott Gallery & Arts Council of Greater Kalamazoo, MI.

*MEMBER:* National Art Education Association, Western Arts Association, Michigan Art Education Association, Kalamazoo Council of the Arts, Delta Phi Delta.

*AWARDS, HONORS:* Awards for painting from South Bend Art Association, Grand Rapids Art Association, Detroit Artists, and Kalamazoo Institute of Arts.

*WRITINGS:*

*Orientation to Drawing and Painting,* International Textbook, 1965.
*Notes on Art and Art Education,* MSS Educational Publishing, 1969.
*Eight American Women Painters,* Gordon Press (New York City), 1977.
(Contributor) *Great Men,* Dial (New York City), 1978.
*The Crucifixion in American Painting,* Gordon Press, 1979.
*Insights in Art and Education,* Gordon Press, 1979.
*300 Lessons in Art,* J. Weston Walch, 1980.
*American Art Activity Book,* J. Weston Walch, 1982.
*Sport in Art,* Prentice-Hall (Englewood Cliffs, NJ), 1986.
*New Vision in Art,* International Universities Press (New York City), 1989.
*Art Projects Around the Calendar,* J. Weston Walch, 1990.
*American Women Artists of the 1930's & 1940's,* McFarland (Jefferson, NC), 1991.
*Themes in American Painting,* McFarland, 1993.
*The Art of Black American Women,* McFarland, 1993.
*Native American Artists of the 20th Century,* McFarland, 1995.
*Famous American Women in Portraiture,* McFarland, in press.
*Latin American Women Artists of the United States,* McFarland, in press.

FILMSTRIPS

*Open Your Eyes to Art,* J. Weston Walch, 1981.
*Twentieth Century American Painting,* J. Weston Walch, 1983.
*Hispanic Art,* J. Weston Walch, 1984.

OTHER

Contributor of more than two hundred articles to art and education journals.

*WORK IN PROGRESS: Haitian Painters,* for McFarland, 1998; *Ten American Humanist Painters; Painting Styles; Drawing in the Junior High School;*

*The Clown in American Art; Ten American Religious Painters; The Art Experience; The Crucifixion; Christ in Art; Spirituality of Abraham Rattner; Reflections of the Crucifixion; The Roadrunner,* novel; *All That We Had,* novel; *The Scars of War.*

*SIDELIGHTS:* Robert Henkes told *CA:* "Writing is essential to teaching and painting as the latter are essential to my writing. Successful teaching only reaches a small segment of society while the printed word reaches thousands in a single moment. Aside from contribution, work manipulation arouses the aesthetic experience. It is quite similar to composing a painting. Words can change man's spiritual condition as much as the color images of a canvas. My interest in art and sports led to the publication of *Sport in Art.* Other works, centered upon my religious background, have been *The Spirituality of Abraham Rattner, Christ in Art,* and *Crucifixion.*

"Correspondence with contemporary artists has been a great research technique for my writing and has led to memorable friendships. My writing day includes the reading of art and religious books and periodicals. I have been influenced by such writers as Thomas Merton and Fulton Sheen, and have been name as a religious writer by American painters, Umberto Romano and Abraham Rattner. I continue to paint religious themes which affect the tone of some of my writing."

Henkes later told *CA:* "Since my retirement from teaching in 1984, my writing has focused on the paintings of American women artists of the Depression and on the painting of ethnic groups such as Latin Americans, Native Americans and African Americans. My life is divided between writing and painting. Both creative processes serve to benefit others. I write and paint because both give me a purpose. My painting fulfills a spiritual need while my writing hopefully helps to further the careers of other artists aside from granting the laity biographical information. I hope to continue to write about artists of the ethnic communities and to paint religiously in thanksgiving for the opportunity to do so."

\*     \*     \*

**HERRON, Don   1952-**

*PERSONAL:* Born January 22, 1952, in Detroit, MI; son of Huston and Jimmie Louise (Ray) Herron.

*Education:* Attended Middle Tennessee State University, 1970-73.

*ADDRESSES: Home*—P.O. Box 982, Glen Ellen, CA 95442-0982.

*CAREER:* Dashiell Hammett Tour and Literary Walks, San Francisco, CA, owner and operator, 1977—; Underwood/Miller Publishers, San Francisco, editor, 1988-89; mystery-horror reviewer, *San Francisco Bay Guardian,* 1995.

*WRITINGS:*

*Echoes from the Vaults of Yoh-Vombis* (biography), privately printed, 1976.
*Dashiell Hammett Tour,* privately printed, 1979, third edition, City Lights (San Francisco), 1991.
*The Literary World of San Francisco and Its Environs,* City Lights, 1985, revised edition, 1996.
(Compiler) *Feast of Fear: Conversations with Stephen King,* Underwood/Miller (San Francisco), 1989.

*EDITOR*

*The Dark Barbarian: The Writings of Robert E. Howard,* Greenwood Press (Westport, CT), 1984.
*Reign of Fear: Fiction and Film of Stephen King,* Underwood/Miller, 1988.
*The Devil's Notebook: Collected Epigrams and Pensees of Clark Ashton Smith,* Starmont (Mercer Island, WA), 1990.
*The Selected Letters of Philip K. Dick, 1975-76,* Underwood/Miller, 1992.
*The Selected Letters of Philip K. Dick, 1977-79,* Underwood/Miller, 1993.

*OTHER*

Contributor to a number of books, including *Fear Itself: The Horror Fiction of Stephen King,* edited by Tim Underwood and Chuck Miller, Underwood/Miller, 1982; *The Penguin Encyclopedia of Horror and the Supernatural,* edited by Jack Sullivan, Viking, 1986; *100 Vicious Little Vampire Stories,* edited by Stephen Dziemianowicz, Barnes and Noble, 1995; and *Modern Fantasy Writers,* edited by Harold Bloom, Chelsea House, 1995.

*WORK IN PROGRESS:* Editing *The Letters of Dashiell Hammett,* with Josephine Hammer Marshall; *Willeford,* study of and interviews with Charles Willeford; a history of the urban adventurers' society, The San Francisco Suicide Club.

*SIDELIGHTS:* Don Herron told *CA:* "I think of myself as following, within my limitations, in the tradition of the great Chicago bookman Vincent Starrett, writing appreciatively of authors I like, spreading the word. But my city is San Francisco, and over the years I have done several books strictly for commercial reasons—to paraphrase Dr. Sam Johnson: Nobody but a blockhead ever wrote anything about Stephen King except for money. My allegiance to the works of Dashiell Hammett is intensely documented, and I'm proud to have helped with the revival of Charles Willeford's reputation in the 1980s (as Starrett, in the 1920s, helped rediscover Arthur Machen). I don't think that literary appreciation ought to be a dull pursuit, and I'm happy that some people have noticed that my best essays and books are funny."

*BIOGRAPHICAL/CRITICAL SOURCES:*

BOOKS

Wiley, Peter Booth, *A Free Library in This City,* Weldon Owen, 1996.

PERIODICALS

*Choice,* January, 1985.
*Los Angeles Times,* July 30, 1995.
*Los Angeles Times Calendar,* September 26, 1982.
*New York Times,* October 23, 1981; October 15, 1995.
*Wall Street Journal,* December 1, 1982.
*Washington Post,* January 29, 1989.

\* \* \*

**HIPPOPOTAMUS, Eugene H.**
  **See KRAUS, (Herman) Robert**

\* \* \*

**H. M. S.**
  **See KIRK-GREENE, Anthony (Hamilton Millard)**

**HOBSON, Bruce   1950-**
    **(Mwenye Hadithi)**

*PERSONAL:* Born September 21, 1950, in Nairobi, Kenya; son of Brian Hugh (in business) and Joan (Knell) Hobson; married Marian Cole (a homemaker), March 24, 1979; children: Amelia. *Education:* Queen Mary College, London, B.A. (with honors), 1973.

*ADDRESSES: Home and office*—P.O. Box 34247, Nairobi, Kenya. *Agent*—Leslie Hadcroft, Laurence Pollinger, 18 Maddox St., London, W1R 0EV, England.

*CAREER:* Worked as a conference manager, 1973-78; Concrete Jungle (horticultural business), Nairobi, Kenya, proprietor, 1983—.

*WRITINGS:*

(Editor) *Gardening in East Africa,* Kenya Horticultural Society, 1995.

JUVENILE; UNDER PSEUDONYM MWENYE HADITHI

*Greedy Zebra,* illustrated by Adrienne Kennaway, Little, Brown (Boston, MA), 1984.
*Hot Hippo,* illustrated by Kennaway, Little, Brown, 1986.
*Crafty Chameleon,* illustrated by Kennaway, Little, Brown, 1987, published in England as *Crafty Chamaeleon,* Hodder & Stoughton (London), 1987.
*Tricky Tortoise,* illustrated by Kennaway, Hodder & Stoughton, 1988.
*Lady Lion,* illustrated by Kennaway, Little, Brown, 1990.
*Baby Baboon,* illustrated by Kennaway, Little, Brown, 1993.
*Hungry Hyena,* illustrated by Kennaway, Hodder & Stoughton, 1994.
*Trunk Tales* (poem script for wildlife video), Rhino Ark, 1996.

*WORK IN PROGRESS:* A suspense novel; a romance novel about surfing.

*ADAPTATIONS: Greedy Zebra* has been adapted for video.

*SIDELIGHTS:* Bruce Hobson told *CA:* "I suspect everyone who enjoys reading positively knows, with burning certainty, that they will become a great writer. This usually happens in the teenage years, when the real world is still thinly veiled. Then, as it happened to myself, the chaos of adulthood tumbles the dream. The key is perseverance, gripping the string of the dream at all costs, never letting go.

"At the moment, I collect African myths and stories, traditionally spoken, not written, a great many of which are already lost to the new generations who crave pop music, fashionable clothes, and Western comics. These I present in a fashion that will please children of the Western world; they are always instinctive and somewhat moralistic, but amusing as well. It would be true to say that the majority of children's books reflect the laziness of our age— mindless entertainment en masse, coupled with the worship of that which is ugly-made-cute. Children are no longer taught to see the perfect beauty of an untouched butterfly's wing. They are, rather, persuaded to love fantastically ugly adult creations, such as cute space monsters. I would like to see new authors fill this well of froth with work that is no less entertaining, but more nourishing to the spirit.

"My books have been translated into Danish, German, Dutch, Shona, Xhosa, Zulu, Afrikaans, Chinese, and Japanese."

*       *       *

## HOLDSWORTH, Christopher (John)    1931-

*PERSONAL:* Born January 29, 1931, in Bolton, Lancashire, England; son of James Oliver (a farmer) and Catherine (Theakston) Holdsworth; married Juliet Clutterbuck, August 19, 1957 (divorced, 1976); children: Robert Edmund. *Education:* Cambridge University, B.A., 1953, M.A., 1956, Ph.D., 1960. *Religion:* Society of Friends (Quakers). *Avocational interests:* Playing cello and piano, travel.

*ADDRESSES: Home*—5 Pennsylvania Park, Exeter EX4 6HB, England.

*CAREER:* University of London, University College, London, England, assistant lecturer, 1956, lecturer, 1959-67, senior lecturer, 1967-73, reader in medieval history, 1973-77; University of Exeter, Exeter, England, professor of medieval history, 1977-91, head of department of history and archaeology, 1984-89; retired. Joseph Rowntree Charitable Trust, trustee, 1957—, chair, 1980-89.

*MEMBER:* Royal Historical Society (member of council, 1982-85, 1992-95), Society of Antiquaries.

*WRITINGS:*

*Rufford Charters,* four volumes, Thoroton Society (Nottingham), 1972-81.
(Editor with Diana Greenway and Jane Sayers) *Tradition and Change: Essays in Honour of Marjorie Chibnall,* Cambridge University Press (Cambridge, England), 1985.
*Steps in a Large Room: A Quaker Explores the Monastic Tradition,* Quaker Home Service (London), 1985.
(Editor) *Domesday Essays,* University of Exeter (Exeter, England), 1986.
(Editor with T. P. Wiseman) *The Inheritance of Historiography,* University of Exeter, 1986.
(Editor with Christopher Harpo, Bill and Janet Nelson) *Studies in Medieval History Presented to R. Allen Brown,* Boydell Press (Suffolk), 1989.
*The Piper and the Tune: Medieval Patrons and Monks,* University of Reading (Reading, England), 1990.

Contributor to composite volumes and history journals.

*WORK IN PROGRESS: Saint Bernard,* completion expected in 1998.

*SIDELIGHTS:* Christopher Holdsworth told *CA:* "My interest in history was sparked by David Knowles and Marjorie Chibnall when I was a student at Cambridge, although I had gained a lot from being at a private school in York and from being brought up in a medieval farm house.

"I chose for my doctorate to work on the writings of English Cistercians in the late twelfth century, and in some ways I have never gotten away from them and their world. Editing a huge corpus of charters taught me more about social and economic history, and my present book on Saint Bernard will, I hope, bring together the insights that I have gained over thirty years. *Domesday Essays* contains lectures given in Exeter to mark the nine hundredth anniversary and have a mainly regional interest.

"Having spent much of my professional life around monasticism, it was almost inevitable that when I was invited to give a public lecture at the annual meeting of British Quakers that I chose to reflect on it from a very personal point of view. It is a tribute to what I have gained from other Christians over the years."

HUDSON, Jeffrey
See CRICHTON, (John) Michael

*    *    *

*    *    *

**HOLMAN-HUNT, Diana**
See CUTHBERT, Diana Daphne Holman-Hunt

**INCOGNITEAU, Jean-Louis**
See KEROUAC, Jean-Louis Lebris de

# J

## JAY, Elisabeth 1947-

*PERSONAL:* Born February 8, 1947, in London, England; daughter of Brian Cyril (a clerk in holy orders) and Grace Amelia (Hogg) Aldis; married Richard Jay (a university lecturer), September 5, 1970 (separated, 1984); children: Anna Kate, Hugo William Aldis. *Education:* St. Anne's College, Oxford, B.A., 1969, M.Phil., 1971, D.Phil., 1975. *Religion:* Church of England.

*ADDRESSES: Home*—31 Stratfield Road, Summertown, Oxford, Oxfordshire OX2 7BG, England. *Office*—Westminster College, North Hinksey, Oxford, England.

*CAREER:* Westminster College, Oxford, England, lecturer, 1975-80, senior lecturer in English, 1981—. Tutor at Queen's University, Belfast, Northern Ireland, 1977-78; visiting professor at Ball State University, spring, 1984 and 1987-88.

*AWARDS, HONORS:* Oxford University, M.A. 1975, membership of English faculty, 1988.

*WRITINGS:*

*The Religion of the Heart: Anglican Evangelicalism and the Nineteenth Century Novel,* Clarendon Press (Oxford, England), 1979.
*Faith and Doubt in Victorian Britain,* Macmillan (New York City), 1986.
*Mrs. Oliphant: A Fiction to Herself, A Literary Life,* Clarendon Press, 1995.

*EDITOR*

*The Evangelical and Oxford Movements,* Cambridge University Press (New York City), 1983.
(With husband, Richard Jay) *The Critics of Capitalism: Victorian Reactions to Political Economy,* Cambridge University Press, 1986.
(And author of introduction) *The Journal of John Wesley: A Selection,* Oxford University Press (Oxford, England), 1987.
*The Autobiography of Mrs. M. O. W. Oliphant; A New and Full Text,* Oxford University Press, 1990.
Elizabeth Gaskell, *Life of Charlotte Bronte,* Penguin (New York City), 1996.

*WORK IN PROGRESS:* Gendered appropriations of Old Testament myths.

*SIDELIGHTS:* In writing *The Religion of the Heart,* Elisabeth Jay has, according to *Times Literary Supplement* critic Owen Chadwick, undertaken a tedious, demanding subject, that of the Victorian religious novel. The result, he commented, is "a useful contribution to the study of an oddly elusive frame of mind." Chadwick particularly appreciated the author's historical account of American evangelicalism and the insight the book provides on the attitudes and spiritual beliefs of such authors as Mrs. Guyton, who wrote *Thornycroft Hall.* Jay's history also explains the decline of evangelicalism, which resulted ultimately in the demise of the nineteenth-century religious novel.

Brian Martin, another *Times Literary Supplement* reviewer, also praised Jay's work as a religious historian. He described *The Evangelical and Oxford*

*Movements* as a stimulating collection, which "provokes arguments and invites questions." Martin found the editor's selections "valuable for students. . . . They are well chosen and show the conflict in belief between the Evangelicals and the Tractorians." The collection presents, in one volume, a highly diverse and otherwise inaccessible group of essays.

Jay told *CA:* "My initial work on nineteenth-century Anglican Evangelicalism was generated by an interest in discovering the roots of a belief and a mode of life that had informed my own upbringing. The further work on nineteenth-century religion grew from a conviction that religious movements develop and change in tension with competing beliefs and ideologies. The eclectic concerns of nineteenth-century novels make them a particularly rich field in which to work as one's own critical interests shift.

"Mrs. Oliphant, my current preoccupation, presents both a fascinating range of literary achievement: autobiographer, biographer, essayist, and novelist; and a life whose constant juggling of the concerns of work and single parenting is of immediate relevance to many twentieth-century readers. For me writing provides a space where I can discover what it is that I really think and justifies and refuels my teaching."

*BIOGRAPHICAL/CRITICAL SOURCES:*

PERIODICALS

*Times Literary Supplement,* February 15, 1980, May 13, 1983.

\*     \*     \*

**JEAN-LOUIS**
   **See KEROUAC, Jean-Louis Lebris de**

\*     \*     \*

**JONES, Madison (Percy, Jr.)**    **1925-**

*PERSONAL:* Born March 21, 1925, in Nashville, TN; son of Madison Percy and Mary Temple (Webber) Jones; married Shailah McEvilley, February 5, 1951; children: Carroll (Mrs. John S. Lofty), Madison III, Ellen, Michael, Andrew. *Education:* Van-

derbilt University, A.B., 1949; University of Florida, A.M., 1951, graduate study, 1951-53. *Avocational interests:* Hunting, fishing, sailing, sculpturing.

*ADDRESSES: Home*—800 Kuderna Acres, Auburn, AL 36830. *Agent*—Harold Matson Company, Inc., 276 Fifth Avenue, New York, NY 10001.

*CAREER:* Farmer and horse trainer in Cheatham County, TN, during the 1940s; instructor in English at Miami University, Oxford, Ohio, 1953-54, and at University of Tennessee, Knoxville, 1955-56; Auburn University, Auburn, AL, assistant professor, 1956-68, professor of English, 1968-87, Alumni Writer in residence, 1966-87, Distinguished Faculty Lecturer, 1980, currently professor emeritus. *Military service:* U.S. Army, Corps of Military Police, 1944-45; served in Korea.

*MEMBER:* Fellowship of Southern Writers, Alabama Academy of Distinguished Authors.

*AWARDS, HONORS: Sewanee Review* fellow, 1954; Alabama Library Association Book Award, 1967; Rockefeller fellow, 1968; Guggenheim fellow, 1973-74; Lytle Prize, 1992, for short fiction.

*WRITINGS:*

NOVELS

*The Innocent,* Harcourt (New York City), 1957.
*Forest of the Night,* Harcourt, 1960.
*A Buried Land,* Viking (New York City), 1963.
*An Exile,* Viking, 1967, published as *I Walk the Line,* Popular Library (New York City), 1970.
*A Cry of Absence,* Crown (New York City), 1971.
*Passage through Gehenna,* Louisiana State University Press (Baton Rouge), 1978.
*Season of the Strangler,* Doubleday (New York City), 1982.
*Last Things,* Louisiana State University Press, 1989.

OTHER

(With Thomas Davidson Dow) *History of the Tennessee State Dental Association,* Tennessee State Dental Association, 1958.

Work is represented in the anthologies *Best American Short Stories, 1953,* edited by Martha Foley, and *Stories of the Modern South,* edited by Benjamin Forkner and Patrick Samway. Contributor of short stories to *Perspective, Sewanee Review, Arlington Quarterly,* and *Delta Review.* Jones's manuscripts are collected at Emory University and Auburn University.

*ADAPTATIONS: An Exile* was filmed in 1970 as *I Walk the Line.*

*SIDELIGHTS:* Although Madison Jones has a devoted and enthusiastic following in certain (mostly Southern) circles, widespread critical and popular acclaim have proved elusive through much of his career. In the eyes of his admirers, however, he has been favorably compared to the classic Greek tragedians, as well as to more "modern" writers. Ovid Pierce notes in the *New York Times Book Review* that "outside of Faulkner, few writers have been able to command such a range of country with so much atmospheric detail . . . nor have they been able to capture so well the air of defeat over forgotten little towns." As a stylist, praise has also come Jones's way. Called "clean, spare, and subtle" by David Payne in the *Washington Post Book World,* Jones "offers us those little epiphanies of altered perspective that constitute fresh seeing." For the most part, Jones has made use of traditional themes, what Jonathan Yardley calls in *Partisan Review* "good, solid, 'Southern' material": small towns, fundamentalism, moonshine, racial tension, and loyalty to the Confederacy. Guilt—or hubris—and retribution are common preoccupations, as is the conflict between past and present and the destruction that can result when people refuse to accept what cannot be changed. The typically Southern concerns of place, community, and history also figure prominently in Jones's fictional world.

*The Innocent,* published in 1957, introduces themes of innocence corrupted by experience and the insinuation of past evils upon the present, as well as a symbolic and allegorical quality that would mark Jones's later work as well. The protagonist of Jones's first novel, Duncan Welsh, seeks to break with his past transgressions committed on a seven-year residency in the North and start a new life after he inherits farmland near his boyhood home in rural Tennessee. An allegory of the Agrarian movement of the first half of the twentieth century in which a Southern economy based on farming rather than industry was championed, *The Innocent* portrays the battle of idealism over reality. Welsh, an agrarian, tries to create an idealized pastoral community, but ultimately his hubris causes his downfall. Symbolism abounds: Welsh's growing obsession is reflected by

his Godlike but futile attempts to stop the extinction of a breed of horse; meanwhile he must confront the more sinister side of his own nature in the person of a local moonshiner who ultimately involves him in murder.

Jones's second novel, *Forest of the Night,* is set in the American frontier during the early part of the nineteenth century. Jonathan Cannon, an innocent, albeit enlightened, product of the philosophy of Rousseau, Paine, and Jefferson, follows the Natchez Trail from Nashville to Natchez, Mississippi, in hopes of discovering men living untouched by civilization in a Rousseauian "state of nature." What he discovers instead are the outlaw Harpe brothers— brutal, psychotic killers whom Jonathan eventually comes to resemble in his effort to survive. Jones's protagonist "becomes the very thing he abhorred in theory. . .," notes Sandy Cohen in the *Dictionary of Literary Biography.* "Eventually, Cannon, like John Locke and Edmund Burke, comes to the conclusion that society is a civilizing force."

"The story is largely imagined," Jones explains to *CA,* describing the historic backdrop of *Forest of the Night.* "There is a little about the Harpe brothers on record, but very little. We know what kind of men they were and a few things they did, but we don't even know with certainty what their end was. But I hope this much is clear: the virgin forest has become a forest of the night for the enlightened hero and the confrontation issues in the near extinction of his real humanity. It's the fatality of badly misreading the nature of things."

*A Buried Land,* considered one of Jones's best novels, echoes the themes of *Forest of the Night,* but in a more modern setting. Taking place in the Tennessee River Valley as the historic Tennessee Valley Authority dam projects were reshaping the Southern landscape, the novel follows a young attorney as he returns to the land of his youth, intent upon changing those around him to accommodate his more sophisticated attitudes. "He attempts," notes M. E. Bradford in *Contemporary Novelists,* "to bury the old world (represented by a girl who dies aborting his child) under the waters of the TVA; but its truths (and their symbol) rise to haunt him back into abandoned modes of thought and feeling."

Jones's fifth novel, 1971's *A Cry of Absence,* tells the story of Hester Glenn, a well-to-do, middle-aged woman whose obsession with decorum and "tradition" cause her to reject the changes taking place in the South during the post-World War II years. After learning that her youngest son was instrumental in stoning a young black civil rights activist to death, Hester at first denies his involvement, then suppresses the evidence. Eventually, however, as her old-fashioned attitudes become less and less acceptable to her peers, Hester is forced to reassess both her own and her son's behavior. Joseph Catinella of the *Saturday Review* attributes the success of *A Cry of Absence* to Jones's mastery of the tragic style. In short, he writes, reading *A Cry of Absence* is particularly affecting "not only because racial conflicts still exist but because Mr. Jones dramatically places our national turmoil in a poignant framework. Seldom have I found a novel this formal in structure, one so perfectly plotted and harmoniously designed, such a moving experience." The result, declares Catinella, is "a novel that in many respects is an astonishing technical performance by an impressive artist, a writer whose Southern themes transcend their region and embody universal truths."

*Last Things,* published in 1989, takes the modern South as its setting. While living conditions may have improved with time, the ills of modern society—adultery, drug trafficking, murder, cynicism, and an increasing sense of alienation, to name a few—have more than cancelled out such improvements. Through the moral breakdown of a poor white southerner named Wendell Corbin, Jones illustrates contemporary society's efforts to discard the moral precepts that once cemented the country's social fabric. As with his other works, *Last Things* mirrors Jones's view that, as Cohen explains, "not only will innocence always be corrupted by experience but . . . the innocent deserve some blame for their ignorance of the reality of evil."

Jones consistently sets his fiction in a Southern locale; as he once told *CA:* "I feel a strong attachment for the country of my childhood. Most people do in the South, probably more than people from other parts of the nation. Our sense of history has a lot to do with that, and for me as a writer this attachment to place has been indispensable. The familiar place offers inspiration and images to embody my ideas. Some images I remember from my childhood, and they retain a certain mystery for me.

"I could, of course, have seen fields of briars and buckbushes stretching to the horizon in other places. But I saw them in Tennessee, and for me they will always be associated with the country of my childhood. I hope that the mystery I feel in connection with the remembered images has been retained in my fiction."

*BIOGRAPHICAL/CRITICAL SOURCES:*

*BOOKS*

Binding, Paul, *Separate Country,* Paddington Press (New York City), 1979.
*Contemporary Authors Autobiography Series,* Volume 11, Gale (Detroit), 1990.
*Contemporary Literary Criticism,* Volume 4, Gale, 1975.
*Contemporary Novelists,* fifth edition, St. James Press (Detroit), 1991.
*Dictionary of Literary Biography,* Volume 152: *American Novelists since World War II, Fourth Series,* Gale, 1995.
Rubin, Louis, Jr., editor, *History of Southern Literature,* Louisiana State University Press, 1985.

*PERIODICALS*

*American Book Review,* October, 1979.
*Chicago Sunday Tribune,* February 24, 1957.
*Commonweal,* March 22, 1957; August 9, 1963.
*Harper's,* October, 1967.
*New Republic,* June 26, 1971.
*New York Herald Tribune Book Review,* March 13, 1960.
*New York Herald Tribune Books,* May 19, 1963.
*New York Times,* March 10, 1957; June 24, 1971.
*New York Times Book Review,* September 3, 1967; July 4, 1971; September 24, 1989, p. 48.
*Saturday Review,* February 23, 1957; July 10, 1971.
*Southern Humanities Review,* spring, 1991, pp. 194-96.
*Time,* February 25, 1957; June 21, 1971.
*Times Literary Supplement,* October 4, 1957.
*Washington Post,* January 27, 1982.
*Washington Post Book World,* July 18, 1971; October 15, 1989, pp. 4, 11.

\*    \*    \*

## JORDAN, Neil (Patrick) 1950-

*PERSONAL:* Born February 25, 1950 (some sources say 1951), in County Sligo, Ireland; son of an educator and a painter; married wife, Vivienne; children: (with wife) two daughters; Ben; (with Brenda

Rawn) Daniel. *Education:* University College, Dublin, B.A., 1968.

*ADDRESSES: Home*—2 Martello Terrace, Bray, County Wicklow, Ireland; and London, England. *Office*—Jenne Casarotto/Casarotto Company Ltd., Nat House, 60/66 Wardour St., London WIV 3HP, England; Palace Productions, 16-17 Wardour Mews, London W1, England.

*CAREER:* Film director, screenwriter, novelist, and short story writer. Formerly associated with a theater company in Dublin; cofounder, administrator, and chair of the board of Irish Writers Cooperative, 1974; creative adviser for John Boorman's film *Excalibur,* 1981; worked variously as a laborer, teacher, and saxophonist.

*AWARDS, HONORS:* Art Council bursary, 1976; *Guardian* Fiction Prize, 1979, for *Night in Tunisia and Other Stories; Evening Standard*'s most promising newcomer award, 1982, and Best First Feature Film Award from the Durban International Film Festival, 1983, both for *Angel; Sunday Independent* Arts Award—Cinema, 1984; named best director by the film section of British Critics Circle, 1984, London Critics Circle Award, Fantasy Film Festival Award, and Critics Prize from the Fantasporto Fantasy Festival, all for *The Company of Wolves;* Golden Scroll from the Academy of Science Fiction Fantasy and Horror Films for Outstanding Achievement, 1985; Golden Globe, Los Angeles Critics Circle Award, New York Film Critics Award, London Critics Circle Award, and Balladolid Award, all 1986, for *Mona Lisa;* People of the Year award (Ireland), 1986; Academy Award for Best Original Screenplay, 1993, for *The Crying Game.*

*WRITINGS:*

### NOVELS

*The Past,* Braziller (New York City), 1980.
*The Dream of a Beast* (also see below), Chatto & Windus (London), 1983, Random House (New York City), 1989.
*Nightlines,* Random House, 1995, published in England as *Sunrise with Sea Monster,* Chatto & Windus, 1995.

### SHORT STORIES

*Night in Tunisia and Other Stories* (also see below), Co-op Books (Dublin), 1976, Braziller, 1980.

*A Neil Jordan Reader* (contains *Night in Tunisia and Other Stories, The Dream of a Beast,* and *The Crying Game* [also see below]), Vintage Books (New York City), 1993.

Author of the stories "A Bus, a Bridge, a Beach" and "The Old-Fashioned Lift," both published in *Paddy No More,* Longship Press, 1978; and "The Artist" and "The Photographer," both published in *New Writing and Writers 16,* Humanities (Atlantic Highlands, NJ), 1979.

### SCREENPLAYS; AND DIRECTOR

*Angel,* Motion Picture Co., 1982, released as *Danny Boy,* Triumph Films, 1984.
(With Angela Carter) *The Company of Wolves* (adapted from a story by Carter), Cannon Group, 1984, released in the United States, 1985.
(With David Leland) *Mona Lisa* (released by Island Pictures, 1986), Faber & Faber, 1986.
*The Miracle,* Palace Pictures, 1991.
*The Crying Game,* Miramax Films, 1992.
*Interview with the Vampire* (screenplay was un-credited; adapted from the novel by Anne Rice), Geffen Pictures, 1994.
*Michael Collins: Screenplay and Film Diary,* Plume (New York City), 1996.

### DIRECTOR

*High Spirits,* Palace Pictures/Tri-Star, 1987.
*We're No Angels,* Art Linson/PAR, 1989.

### OTHER

Also author of plays and television scripts. Contributor of poetry to periodicals.

*WORK IN PROGRESS:* A novel; a film adaptation of Henry Fielding's novel *Jonathan Wild.*

*SIDELIGHTS:* Neil Jordan is widely regarded as one of the most imaginative and talented of a new generation of Irish writers. Although he is best known for his screenwriting and directing talents—demonstrated in such highly acclaimed films as *Mona Lisa* and *The Crying Game*—Jordan has also attracted substantial praise as a fiction writer. After producing an award-winning story collection at the age of twenty-five, Jordan wrote novels before turning to filmmaking. Acknowledging that his books are influenced by the works of early twentieth-century Irish writers William Butler Yeats and James Joyce, Jordan cites filmmakers Luis Bunuel and Federico Fellini as inspirations for his movies. Combining these influences, he has developed a singular style that consistently prompts critics to hail his work as lyrical, surrealistic, sometimes baffling, and often disturbing.

Jordan first demonstrated his creative talents with his collection *Night in Tunisia and Other Stories,* winner of the 1979 *Guardian* Fiction Prize. Critics compared the work, which is set in Ireland and centers on characters who suffer from spiritual numbness, to Joyce's short story collection *Dubliners.* "The people in *Night in Tunisia* are often 'suspended,' suffering a kind of detachment from the world and, more significantly, from themselves," explained Terence Winch, reviewing Jordan's work in the *Washington Post Book World.* Filled with what Winch called "insistent sexuality" heightened by a backdrop of the ceaseless surge of the ocean, the collection depicts such situations as two boys discovering homosexual love; a bored housewife who, searching for spiritual awakening, wanders into the sea; a laborer who kills himself after first pondering his attraction to the emotionless quality of mud and stone; and, in the book's title story, a young man who works out his frustrations through playing the saxophone.

"[Jordan's] writing has a quiet authority which draws you on even into the bleakest," announced Emma Fisher, critiquing *Night in Tunisia* for the *Spectator.* Winch concurred and described Jordan as "a unique writer." Although the reviewer noted that the collection "has its limitations," faulting the author's "obsessive" use of symbols and the unvarying emotional and physical terrain explored in each story, Winch concluded: "[Jordan's] fiction is poetic in the best sense of the word, which is to say that he manipulates certain images skillfully without using more words than necessary. This is an exciting book by the kind of writer who makes you curious about what he'll do next."

Jordan again won the favor of critics with his subsequent offering, *The Past,* a "rich, deeply textured first novel by an extraordinary new writer," stated Roger Dionne in the *Los Angeles Times.* Also set in Ireland, *The Past* introduces a young, nameless narrator who, upon discovering some picture postcards dating from 1914, sets out to find the truth of his origins. Through talking with his mother's old friend Lili, among others, and traveling to pertinent locations in Ireland, the narrator discovers that his

mother Rene was born out of wedlock to a politically active Irish actress. Rene herself eventually became an actress and a model. It was in the latter capacity that she met James and Luke Vance, a father-and-son team of photographers. The narrator deduces that one of the Vances was his father, but, due to unreliable recollections from Lili and Father Beausang, an elderly priest who knew the Vances, he has difficulty discovering which. Depicting significant scenes from the past through flashbacks and scattered remembrances, Jordan's novel demonstrates how the past intricately entwines with the present.

"*The Past* is many things," declared Dionne. "It is a sensitive evocation of Irish people and places beyond Dublin, an elaborate literary jigsaw puzzle, a kind of love story and a kind of detective story, but above all, an exercise in imagination." Widely considered an artful undertaking, the novel greatly impressed critics. Calling Jordan "one of the most original talents to emerge in the last decade," Francis King, writing in the *Spectator,* found *The Past* "boldly imagined [and] beautifully written" with prose that "has a splendid elasticity and vigour." Paul Taylor of the *Times Literary Supplement* agreed, judging Jordan's novel "exquisite" and "masterly." While arguing that the author's writing "reverberates with [the] periods" of Yeats and Joyce, Dionne added that the novel nonetheless "charts new territory for itself." The reviewer concluded: "Jordan's own voice is strong and deep and beautifully original. The publication of *The Past* is an event."

Jordan's second novel, *The Dream of a Beast,* was published in 1983. Set in Dublin, the novel focuses on a surrealistic metaphor and depicts another unnamed narrator who, sickened by his environment and a dull, meaningless life, slowly transforms into a mysterious creature that he imagined for an advertising campaign. Melding into his suburban surroundings, which also become strangely disfigured in the smoldering heat of an unbearable summer, the metamorphosing narrator represents man's desire to return to a more humanized state of heightened awareness; he ventures back to a sort of childlike consciousness, wherein colors, textures, and sounds evoke intense feelings and thoughts. This reawakening caused by the narrator's transformation eventually brings him closer to his wife and child, from whom he had previously alienated himself.

"Ultimately, then," observed *Los Angeles Times Book Review* contributor Alex Raksin, "*The Dream of a Beast* is an eloquent testament to the value of listening to the poetry of everyday life." Calling the book an "inspired, surrealistic novel" that "reveals the emotional currents swirling beneath the calm surface of suburban life," the reviewer remarked that Jordan presents his ideas with "great energy and creativity." Similarly, Lewis Jones in the *Spectator* termed the book a "highly poetic fantasy. . . . It's certainly beautifully written." *The Dream of a Beast* is "brilliantly portrayed with vivid, thoughtful imagery," Raksin assessed, and he reaffirmed that Jordan is "one of Ireland's preeminent fiction writers."

Although his books were enjoying critical success, Jordan became increasingly interested in film. While supporting himself through writing and playing saxophone in a band, Jordan also worked as a creative consultant for screenwriter and director John Boorman's 1981 film *Excalibur*. Later, Jordan wrote a documentary film for television concerning his experience working with Boorman. Unsatisfied with simply writing scripts, Jordan decided to both write and direct his next screen effort. In an interview with *CA,* he stated: "I got into film the way most writers do, out of a sense of dissatisfaction about the way the work was being handled by others. I decided to make films myself because I found that form of storytelling exciting and found that, to realize it correctly, I would have to direct my own work. I think it's comparable for many writers: many playwrights, many novelists, many screenwriters who get seriously interested in film as a medium of expression end up directing."

Jordan's directoral debut was the 1982 film *Angel,* released two years later in the United States as *Danny Boy.* Set in contemporary Northern Ireland where civil unrest prevails, *Danny Boy* depicts localized violence in the manner of bleak and ominous film noir. The picture introduces Danny, a jazz saxophone player who, after spending time in a bar and making love to a mute girl, witnesses a double murder. Once he recovers from the shock, Danny tracks down the murderers in order to kill them. Eventually, Danny's obsession with revenge not only takes him away from his music but gradually destroys him, his violent pilgrimage creating psychological chaos.

Like most reviewers of Jordan's work, the *Los Angeles Times*'s Michael Wilmington commended the filmmaker for his singular style. "There's bloody magic afoot in . . . *Danny Boy,*" observed the critic, "alchemy that sets it apart from the opening frames. The colors are a bit more scintillating than usual; the angles skewed; the camera mobile; the atmosphere pungent and rare." Wilmington concluded, "[Jordan's] images haunt you, just as the keening tones of *Danny Boy* ravish the ear. Melodious and dirge-like, echoing with fidelity and death, they are fit emblem for this movie ballad of a land where murder threads through the fabric of life, where blood spills endlessly and tears are a ceaseless stream, where the poetry lies dark, thick and hazy like a coat of fog, rising."

With his next film, *The Company of Wolves,* Jordan "once again orchestrated a piece of utter originality," according to John Coleman in a critique for the *New Statesman*. Strewn with Jordan's typically dreamlike imagery and surrealistic tone, the film—based on a story by British writer Angela Carter—recreates the well-known fable of "Little Red Riding Hood." The action of the movie takes place inside the fevered and continuous dreams of an adolescent girl, Rosaleen, as she wanders through dense woods, repeatedly meeting up with men who transform into werewolves before her. Ample with Freudian themes of sexual fear, the film becomes what Wilmington termed "a grand cautionary tale, wryly subverted, of the dangers of rampant sexuality and the wolfish heart of man." Released in England in 1984 and soon after in the United States, *The Company of Wolves* fared well in both countries.

Creating what reviewers unanimously dubbed an artistic thriller, Jordan scored a critical success in 1986 with *Mona Lisa,* which he cowrote with David Leland. When it premiered at the Cannes Film Festival, *Mona Lisa* immediately generated a stir of universal approval. Set in what Anna Kythreotis of the London *Times* described as "a brilliantly evoked, almost surreal . . . London of plush hotels, strip joints and streetwalkers," the film features Bob Hoskins as a good-hearted, though sometimes ill-tempered, ex-convict named George. George becomes a chauffeur for Simone, an elegant high-priced prostitute who previously practiced her profession in the often brutal red-light districts of London. Their relationship starts out stormy, but the two slowly earn each other's trust. George begins to refer to her as a "lady" and naively falls deeply in love with her; she becomes his "Mona Lisa," an object of mysteriously intriguing though unattainable love. When Simone realizes that George truly intends to protect her, she enlists him to find a teen-aged heroin-addicted streetwalker named Cathy, who was a former colleague of Simone's. Risking his life in the seamier sides of London, George finally finds Cathy and rescues her from the hands of his own corrupted boss, only to discover that Simone and Cathy are lovers.

"With astonishing elegance and skill, director Neil Jordan . . . weaves a touching, terrifying tale that mates the setting of London's sleazy underworld with a story of unrequited romance," wrote Lawrence O'Toole, reviewing *Mona Lisa* in *Maclean's*. The film drew further praise on many accounts. John Simon in the *National Review,* for example, thought that "in the exploration of the worlds of sexual degradation . . . Jordan comes up with some memorable images without much explicit detail, the horror made ineffable by being merely suggested." Commenting on the film's overall achievement, the reviewer concluded that *Mona Lisa* "is one of the painfully few movies these days whose appeal is to an adult audience. . . . It . . . strives to be a work of art."

Intent on extending his film repertoire across various cinematic genres, Jordan tried his hand at directing comedy with his 1988 film *High Spirits*. Returning to an Irish setting, Jordan depicts the Castle Plunkett, a dilapidated mansion whose owner, in an effort to save his home from creditors, promotes the place as a "haunted hotel" to attract American tourists. The film was generally criticized for trying to cater—with special effects and exaggerated humor—to American audiences. Declaring that Jordan "was much more at home in the dark, colloquial world of *Mona Lisa* . . . than he is in this one," the *New York Times*'s Janet Maslin denounced *High Spirits* for being "directed as broad, noisy slapstick." Likewise, Wilmington lamented, "Couldn't Irish poetry and American movies have had a happier marriage?" He added: "The American big-movie sex comedy conventions overwhelm Jordan's liberating poetry, his wild lyricism." Critics were no more enthusiastic about Jordan's next directoral offering, *We're No Angels,* which featured Robert De Niro and Sean Penn as escaped convicts in disguise as priests. After these films, Jordan decided he would never again work as a director for hire.

Jordan redeemed his reputation in 1992 with *The Crying Game,* which he wrote and directed. A complex story involving an IRA terrorist who becomes romantically involved with the fiancee of a British soldier he once held prisoner, *The Crying Game* "demolishes sexual and racial stereotypes," according to Jay Carr of the *Boston Globe*. Vincent Canby, reviewing the film for the *New York Times,* credited Jordan with writing an "efficient and ingenious"

script and creating an "elegant" film. "When the film's subplots, all of which are germane, are stripped away," Canby summarized, "*The Crying Game* becomes a tale of a love that couldn't be but proudly is." "Suspenseful and emotionally complex, skillfully mixing politics with affairs of the heart, *The Crying Game* is something unexpected, a challenging new way to tell a very old story," Kenneth Turan wrote in the *Los Angeles Times*. Jordan's screenplay for *The Crying Game* earned him an Academy Award. His next Hollywood project was the highly successful film adaptation of Anne Rice's novel *Interview with the Vampire;* Jordan worked on the uncredited screenplay and directed the film. According to Gene Siskel of the *Chicago Tribune,* "the occasionally gory film is really quite good, taking vampires seriously and depicting their underground world with some stunning imagery."

After completing *Interview with the Vampire,* Jordan returned to writing and produced another novel. He discussed the differences between working in film and writing fiction with Sean Abbot, a contributor to *At Random*. Abbot quoted Jordan as saying: "With a film you write a script and someone says, 'This is good, I would like to do it,' and then an actor gets excited about it, and soon enough you get all the people you've worked with before around you, and there's all this impetus to get the thing made and to finish it, whereas with the novel, there's only yourself; you have nothing to deal with except your own emotions. You have to dredge parts of yourself to the surface." He described this process as "emotionally and mentally exhausting" and concluded: "I do think writing prose is one of the hardest things there is to do. Any writer who has written serious fiction and also written screenplays or written for the theatre will tell you that."

Book reviewers celebrated Jordan's return to the novel; *Nightlines* (published in England as *Sunrise with Sea Monster*) was greeted with enthusiastic reviews. The plot embraced many elements common to Jordan's work, including a tangled love story and a background of Irish politics. The narrative begins during the Spanish Civil War. The protagonist, a young Irishman named Donal Gore, has been captured during the fighting and is in prison, awaiting execution. In his cell, he recalls his childhood, his uncommunicative father, and his love affair with his teacher—a woman his widowed father eventually married. The 'nightlines' of the title refer to the fishing lines he and his father routinely set in the evenings, a ritual that provided the only time Donal felt at peace with his father.

As the novel progresses, Donal is released from prison and returns home to find his father speechless and paralyzed by a stroke. Donal resumes his love affair with his stepmother and "for a while they live, the three of them, in a strange idyll that Jordan's canted vision and touch of quicksilver manage to extract from its melodramatic possibilities," wrote Richard Eder in the *Los Angeles Times Book Review.* Eder compared *Nightlines* to *The Crying Game,* finding that both narratives range "between the large-scale gestures of politics and the compacted incandescence of the personal."

Jordan's style in *Nightlines* is "direct, sparse and cool, with none of the lushness of what is still surely Jordan's masterpiece, *The Dream of a Beast,*" commented John Banville in the *Observer.* "However, despite the low-key tone of the book, the intense, almost religious conclusion lifts everything on to a strangely transcendent level." "The sea is a constant presence here," observed Michael Kerrigan in the *Times Literary Supplement.* "Every page seems permeated by the drear, muddy chill of the Irish Sea by the family home at Bray. Described in the bleakest of terms, it is none the less a source of comfort." Despite the sea's promise of insularity, Kerrigan argued, Jordan's novel implies that "to turn away from the world is merely to confront more disturbing problems within." Writing for the *Spectator,* James Simmons noted Jordan's "hint at a theme of 'multiple betrayal'"—Donal commits adultery with his father's wife and also aids the Irish authorities in their pursuit of some IRA saboteurs. However, Simmons lamented, the novel "doesn't illuminate anything except Irish weather and landscape. . . . [*Nightlines*] has some vivid and surprising scenes. But isn't that the best you can say about *The Crying Game?*" Kerrigan, on the other hand, found *Nightlines* "a work of considerable imaginative richness, raising historical questions of the highest importance and carrying an enormous emotional charge. Jordan combines a flair for seeing the story in every picture with the skill and discipline required to make every image tell."

## BIOGRAPHICAL/CRITICAL SOURCES:

### PERIODICALS

*At Random,* fall, 1995, pp. 56-58.
*Boston Globe,* July 14, 1991, p. 81; July 19, 1991, p. 27; December 13, 1992, p. B31; December 18, 1992, p. 51; January 17, 1993, p. B33; November 11, 1994, pp. 43.
*Chicago Tribune,* April 22, 1985; November 21, 1988; July 19, 1991, section 7, p. B28; December 13, 1992, pp. 6-7; December 18, 1992, section 7, p. H34; November 6, 1994, section 13, p. 10; November 11, 1994, section 7, p. B.
*Christian Science Monitor,* June 19, 1990, p. 10; July 19, 1991, p. F15; August 16, 1991, p. 12; August 16, 1992, p. 12; March 4, 1993, p. 11; November 14, 1994, p. 13.
*Commonweal,* July 11, 1986.
*Constitution* (Atlanta), August 16, 1991, p. D1; August 20, 1991, p. E5.
*Harper's Bazaar,* November, 1994, pp. 182-83.
*Journal-Constitution* (Atlanta), December 25, 1992, pp. B1, D1; November 11, 1994, p. P23.
*Los Angeles Times,* November 19, 1980; April 19, 1985; June 20, 1985; November 18, 1988; July 19, 1991, p. F15; November 25, 1992, pp. F1, F8; January 28, 1993, p. F1; November 11, 1994, p. F1.
*Los Angeles Times Book Review,* February 5, 1989; September 17, 1995, pp. 3, 10.
*Maclean's,* July 21, 1986.
*National Review,* July 18, 1986.
*New Republic,* June 23, 1986.
*New Statesman,* November 5, 1982; September 21, 1984.
*Newsweek,* May 6, 1985; June 16, 1986.
*New Yorker,* June 16, 1986.
*New York Times,* May 18, 1984; April 19, 1985; June 13, 1986; November 18, 1988; October 14, 1990, section 2, p. 18; July 3, 1991, p. C12; August 2, 1991, p. C11; September 26, 1992, p. A12; December 4, 1992, p. C3; January 19, 1993, p. C13; January 31, 1993, p. H11; October 28, 1993, p. C15; November 11, 1994, p. C1; November 13, 1994, section 2, p. 1; November 27, 1994, section 2, p. 26; June 2, 1995, p. D17.
*New York Times Magazine,* January 9, 1994, p. 22-5.
*Observer* (London), January 8, 1995, p. 19.
*People Weekly,* June 16, 1986.
*Spectator,* April 21, 1979; November 8, 1980; January 7, 1984; December 31, 1994, p. 25.
*Times* (London), September 6, 1986.
*Times Literary Supplement,* November 14, 1980; November 11, 1983; January 13, 1995, p. 21.
*Village Voice,* May 29, 1984; April 30, 1985; June 17, 1986.
*Wall Street Journal,* August 1, 1991, p. A10; December 10, 1992, p. A16; November 17, 1994, p. A22.

*Washington Post,* November 19, 1988; June 28, 1990, p. D7; July 14, 1991, p. G1, G7; July 19, 1991, p. WW41; January 30, 1992, p. C7; December 18, 1992, pp. D1, WW50; November 11, 1994, pp. D1, WW48; June 9, 1995, p. B7. *Washington Post Book World,* April 20, 1980.*

\*   \*   \*

## JUSTICE, Donald (Rodney) 1925-

*PERSONAL:* Born August 12, 1925, in Miami, FL; son of Vascoe J. (a carpenter) and Mary Ethel (maiden name, Cook) Justice; married Jean Catherine Ross (a writer), August 22, 1947; children: Nathaniel Ross. *Education:* University of Miami, B.A., 1945; University of North Carolina, M.A., 1947; attended Stanford University, 1947-48; State University of Iowa (now University of Iowa), Ph.D., 1954. *Avocational interests:* Composition in music, drawing and painting.

*ADDRESSES: Home*—338 Rocky Shore Dr., Iowa City, IA 52246.

*CAREER:* University of Missouri, Columbia, visiting assistant professor of English, 1955-56; Hamline University, St. Paul, MN, assistant professor of English, 1956-57; State University of Iowa (now University of Iowa), Iowa City, visiting lecturer, 1957-59, assistant professor, 1959-63, associate professor of English, 1963-66; Syracuse University, Syracuse, NY, associate professor, 1966-67, professor of English, 1967-70; University of California, Irvine, visiting professor of English, 1970-71; University of Iowa, professor of English, 1971-82; University of Florida, Gainesville, professor of English, 1982-92. Bain-Swiggett Lecturer, Princeton University, 1976; visiting professor, University of Virginia, Charlotte, 1980.

*MEMBER:* American Academy and Institute of Arts and Letters.

*AWARDS, HONORS:* University of Iowa, Rockefeller Foundation fellow in poetry, 1954-55; Lamont Poetry Selection, Academy of American Poets, 1959, for *The Summer Anniversaries;* Inez Boulton Prize, *Poetry* Magazine, 1960; Ford Foundation fellowship in theater, 1964-65; National Endowment for the Arts grant, 1967, 1973, 1980, and 1989; National Book Award nomination, 1973, for *Departures;* Guggenheim fellowship in poetry, 1976-77; Pulitzer Prize in poetry, 1979, for *Selected Poems;* Harriet Monroe Award, University of Chicago, 1984; National Book Critics Circle Award nomination, 1988, for *The Sunset Maker: Poems/Stories/A Memoir;* American Academy of Poets fellow, 1988; Bollingen Prize for poetry, 1991; Lannan Literary Award for poetry, 1996.

*WRITINGS:*

*POEMS*

*The Summer Anniversaries,* Wesleyan University Press (Middletown, CT), 1960, revised edition, University Press of New England (Hanover, NH), 1981.

*A Local Storm,* Stone Wall Press (Washington, DC), 1963.

*Night Light,* Wesleyan University Press, 1967, revised edition, University Press of New England, 1981.

(With Tom McAfee, Donald Drummond, and R. P. Dickey) *Four Poets,* Central College of Pella (Iowa), 1968.

*Sixteen Poems,* Stone Wall Press, 1970.

*From a Notebook,* Seamark Press, 1971.

*Departures,* Atheneum (New York City), 1973.

*Selected Poems,* Atheneum, 1979.

*Tremayne,* Windhover Press, 1984.

*The Sunset Maker: Poems/Stories/A Memoir,* Atheneum, 1987.

*A Donald Justice Reader: Selected Poetry and Prose,* Middlebury College Press (Middlebury, VT), 1991.

*New and Selected Poems,* Knopf (New York City), 1995.

*EDITOR*

Weldon Kees, *The Collected Poems of Weldon Kees,* Stone Wall Press, 1960, revised edition, University of Nebraska Press (Lincoln), 1992.

(Assistant editor) *Midland,* Random House, (New York City), 1961.

(With Alexander Aspel) *Contemporary French Poetry,* University of Michigan Press (Ann Arbor), 1965.

*Syracuse Poems,* Syracuse University Department of English (Syracuse, NY), 1968.

(With Robert Mezey) Henri Coulette, *The Collected Poems of Henri Coulette,* University of Arkansas Press (Fayetteville), 1990.

(With Cooper R. Mackin and Richard D. Olson) Raeburn Miller, *The Comma after Love: Selected Poems of Raeburn Miller,* University of Akron Press (Akron, OH), 1994.

*OTHER*

(Contributor) Paul Engle, editor, *On Creative Writing,* Dutton (New York City), 1964.

(Translator) Guillevic, *L'Homme qui se ferme/The Man Closing Up,* Stone Wall Press, 1973.

*Platonic Scripts* (essays), University of Michigan Press, 1984.

*The Death of Lincoln* (libretto), A. Thomas Taylor, 1988.

(With Betty Adcock) Poems recorded on audio cassette, Archive of Recorded Poetry and Literature, Washington, DC, March 21, 1989.

(With Eavan Boland) Poems recorded on audio cassette, Archive of Recorded Poetry and Literature, Washington, DC, October 15, 1992.

Works represented in numerous anthologies, including *New Poets of England and America,* Conrad Aiken's *Twentieth Century American Poetry,* A. J. Poulin's *Contemporary American Poetry,* Robert Richman's *The Direction of Poetry,* Donald Hall's *Contemporary American Poetry* and *The Structure of Verse.* Contributor to literary journals such as *Poetry, Antaeus, New Yorker, New Criterion,* and other magazines.

A collection of Justice's manuscripts is housed at the University of Delaware Library in Dover, Delaware.

*SIDELIGHTS:* "Those in a position to appreciate craft" in poetry have long admired the works of Donald Justice, Cathrael Kazin says in the *Dictionary of Literary Biography Yearbook: 1983.* "His first book, *The Summer Anniversaries,* was the Lamont Poetry Selection for 1959; *Departures . . .* was nominated for the 1973 National Book Award"; furthermore, she reports, since his *Selected Poems* won the Pulitzer Prize in 1979, "Justice has come to be recognized not only as one of America's most elegant and distinctive contemporary poets but also as one of its most significant." His credentials are a relatively small number of poems that focus on the theme of loss and reflect a remarkable mastery of prosody, or poetic technique. Even so, technical prowess "never calls attention to itself in Justice's understated work," claims *Southern Review* contributor Dana Gioia. The poet's presence is implied by his control of form, say reviewers, but otherwise Justice uses the poems to efface the self rather than to vaunt it. Because one way of diminishing the self is to relax its control over form, Justice has sometimes used chance methods (such as shuffling word cards together) to compose poems. Thus, writes Gioia, "Justice has published very little, but he has also distilled a decade of writing and experimentation in each new volume."

*The Summer Anniversaries* established Justice's reputation for attention to craft. The book, relates Greg Simon in the *American Poetry Review,* "consists of flawless poems, moving as inexorably as glaciers toward beautiful comprehension and immersion in reality." Writing in the *Washington Post Book World,* Doug Lang suggests, "Justice's concern for form is really a concern with experience" that seeks to be conveyed in "an appropriate arrangement of words." In his essay on Justice in *Contemporary American Poetry,* A. J. Poulin calls Justice "a master of what might be called sparse elegance. . . . [His] poems are moving because of his consummate linguistic, tonal, and formal exactitude." But less attention to form may have improved the poems in this first book, some readers suggest; *New York Times Book Review* contributor Charles Molesworth explains, "What some might see as proper formality might strike others as unnecessary stiffness." Looking back on these poems himself in a poem from his next book, *Night Light,* Justice reflects, "How fashionably sad those early poems are! / On their clipped lawns and hedges the snows fall."

As one would expect after this self-criticism, *Night Light* presents poems that "are not so tame, not so manicured as those in *The Summer Anniversaries,*" notes Joel O. Conarroe in a *Shenandoah* review. But reviewers hear the same tone in both books, and conclude that understatement is another Justice hallmark. According to Molesworth, for instance, poems "of small scale dooms and dim light" in the first book are followed by verses that depict a "twilight perspective verging on total darkness" in the second. For Alan Hollinghurst of the *New Statesman,* the poems seem to suffer from a "lack of color and surprise," or seem haunted "by a weary passivity, a lack of vitality that is unsupported by fastidious formal elegance." Others see the poetry's muted tones in a more favorable light. Offers Molesworth, "If you are the sort of reader who occasionally suspects too much of poetry's grandeur is 'prerecorded,' then the whisper of Donald Justice may be music to your ears."

Conarroe relates Justice's tone to his subject matter: "Justice brings a controlled, urbane intensity to his Chekovian descriptions of loss and of the unlived life, of the solitary, empty 'sad' world of those who receive no mail, have no urgent hungers—who, in short, lead their lives but do not own them." As a *Times Literary Supplement* reviewer phrases it, "People who fascinate [Justice] are elegiacally evoked by a handful of quiet images, and made fascinating to us. The poet conveys these remarkably suggestive images through a select troupe of words varied and repeated in a sustained, low-keyed music." The same reviewer defends the tone of a later book, *Departures:* "Poems draw our attention to the minute effects of language. In them we discover connexions of syntax to meaning that invite a second and third review. Truth, wisdom, drama become deeper, stronger, more genuine than ordinary speech can make them. . . . [*Departures*] reflects a familiarity with such standards and an acceptance of them."

Many critics note that if Justice sustains his mastery of craft from book to book, in *Departures* he achieves a command of poetic technique that surpasses nearly all earlier works. Remaining unsurpassed, feels Simon, is "the core of the book[,] . . . the absolutely indispensable *Sixteen Poems* that Justice published in a limited edition in 1970." Of these and the others in *Departures,* Simon comments: "The new Justice poem is no longer a set piece or still life, forced into shape, but vigorous and rhythmical composition, prosody at the limit of its kinetic potential. This remarkable new intention in Justice's work accounts for the fact that the forms of the best poems in *Departures* are invisible architecture. . . . It is intoxicating to see Justice now unfettered by the forms that circumscribed and dictated the action in his early poems; and to see him working with sources that are not only naturally energetic and new, but demanding in conception and daring in stance."

In the later books, for example, Justice proves himself "equally as willing to give a new twist to an old form. . . as he is to find a new form to fit the materials at hand," Lang observes. For Justice, this involves experimenting with deliberate "mistranslations" of poems in other languages, or with methods of composition that combine words at random until they suggest a statement or a form. These methods help the poet to focus more on his materials than on his conscious control over them. Justice himself sees such "chance" methods as "in its way, a formal approach," one which allows him "to see images a

little differently." Paul Ramsey, writing in the *Sewanee Review,* comments that Justice's poems composed in this way are prone "to fragmentation, to deconstructive poetics, to wandered and incompleted narrative. Yet his poetic integrity . . . bears Justice safely by such swamps and murmured gleams. His fragments sound completed. . . . His gift for order is an irresistible gift."

Lang relates that "some of the forms [Justice] finds are very direct and simple," while others are more complex, coming from the poet's sensitivity to patterns of sound. "Justice gives each poem structure according to its own weight and he shows great versatility in the process." Thomas Swiss remarks in *Modern Poetry Studies* that, as a result, "the reader feels the poet performing with a great sense of confidence, clearing a path for himself between the radical and the conservative." These claims are supported by the poem "Counting the Mad," says Robert Peters in the *American Book Review.* It is, he relates, "an echoing of one of the most famous of all children's poems, 'This little pig went to market.' But there are startling differences. . . . These people never get out to go to market. What the mad retain is the power to cry NO NO NO NO (all the way home) against their keepers' brutalizations and the horrors rampant within their own psyches. This is a stunning use of a simple form for complex purposes."

Gioia suggests that no other American poet has perfected as many poetic styles. "At times," he says, "*Selected Poems* reads almost like an anthology of the possibilities of contemporary poetry. There are sestinas, villanelles and ballads rubbing shoulders with aleatory poems [composed using chance methods], surreal odes, and . . . free verse. . . . A new technique is often developed, mastered, and exhausted in one unprecedented and unrepeatable poem." During the selection process credited in the title, Justice rewrote some poems and gave them a new sequence to make this "nearly perfect volume," writes Gioia, who finds "almost no bad poems . . . and quite a few perfect ones" in the book. In a *Parnassus* review, Vernon Young concurs, "I doubt if there are six poems in [*Selected Poems*] which could be claimed for the public sensibility. But Justice has written a dozen lyrics I'd call virtually incomparable."

The little autobiography to be found in Justice's oeuvre must be gleaned despite the poet's refusal to let his personality dominate his writing. "The principles of composition . . . really occupy him, not his own life," concludes *Yale Review* contributor Richard Wertime after reading the essays in *Platonic Scripts.* Swiss makes a similar observation, maintaining that Justice brings images of mirrors into the poems not, as some reviewers have seen it, to indulge a narcissistic impulse, but rather to point out how language and art can render, at best, only distorted images of the self. Citing the series of unanswered questions in the poem "Fragment: To a Mirror," Simon comments, "We confront the reticence of Justice, the obvious scarcity of lies. . ., the fact that Justice has produced fewer lines and fewer poems in twenty years than others . . . are able to publish in two. But reticence is an attitude toward writing that Justice has assumed with malice of forethought."

Particularly in "Poem," Swiss relates, "Justice speaks about the effacement of self" with an "agnostic and stoic" attitude: "You have begun to vanish. And it does not matter. / The poem will go on without you." In other poems, the speaker reports himself to authorities as a missing person, or views his own corpse from a distance. Thus, observes Jerome McGann in *Poetry* magazine, "His interior poems are not confessions. . . . Justice is too busy attending to the needs of his audience and his subjects ever to get preoccupied with himself." He rarely wanders from an abstract perspective, "and the result is a series of splendid labyrinths" and still points, devoid of comforting self-deceptions, McGann continues. "Given the air of remoteness so often hovering around them," notes Anthony Ostroff in the *Western Humanities Review,* "these poems bring us into a peculiarly intimate relationship with themselves."

That Justice does continue to write is due to his belief that art is a hedge against death and loss. In his essay "Meters and Memory," reprinted in *Platonic Scripts,* he explains how writing about loss enables him to endure it: "To remember an event is almost to begin to control it, as well as to approach an understanding of it; incapable of recurring now, it is only to be contemplated rather than acted on or reacted to. . . . The terror or beauty or, for that matter, the plain ordinariness of the original event, being transformed, is fixed and thereby made more tolerable. That the event can recur only in its new context, the context of art, sheers it of some risks, the chief of which may anyhow have been its transitory character." Submitting his materials to metrical structures is part of this process: "The meters . . . may

be . . . some psychological compulsion, a sort of counting on the fingers or stepping on cracks, magic to keep an unpredictable world under control." Furthermore, as Peters notes, because "art endures while life is brief," Justice's elegies mitigate the total loss of death. Observes Kazin, "In the guise of lamenting a loss, [the poems] perform acts of preservation"; resurrected by memory and ensconced in art, the lost friends of childhood, suicides, and other casualties gain an extended life. Justice succeeds, says Edward Hirsch in the *New York Times Book Review,* because "he counters our inevitable human losses with an unforgettable and permanent music." Justice, who is "the resident genius of nostalgia in the ever-expanding house of American poetry," deserves to be called "an elegiac poet of the first order."

Piano lessons Justice enjoyed as a child provide the central motif of *The Sunset Maker: Poems/Stories/A Memoir,* which seems like a "complex piece of music" dedicated to the working out of a single theme, "the pain and beauty of memory and loss," as Frances Ruhlen McConnel of the *Los Angeles Times* sees it. "Justice shows you how closely related to the pleasures of music are the pleasures of poetry" in its elegies and memoirs, some written in verse, some in prose. These come together most powerfully, she feels, in the book's final poem, which calls up from the past the six notes Justice can recall of a musical piece for cello and piano. These notes—because they are here written down—constitute the immortality of the musician who had composed the piece, Justice suggests. "On the whole," Bruce Bawer comments in the *Washington Post Book World,* "*The Sunset Maker* is a deeply affecting volume—a beautiful, powerful meditation by a modern master upon the themes of aging, lost innocence, and the unalterable, terrifying pastness of the past."

Of Justice's works as a whole, Gioia reflects, "There are no long poems in his canon, no epics, no dramas, none of those ambitious single poems on which most contemporary reputations are founded." Instead, says Poulin, Justice has eloquently chronicled "the depth of loneliness, the isolation, and the spiritual desolation at the heart of the twentieth century experience." Due to his penchant for "Mordancies of the Armchair," as Justice calls them in a later poem, the Pulitzer Prize-winner has produced, says Howard, "some of the most assured, elegant and heartbreaking . . . verse in our literature so far." To a *Times Literary Supplement* reviewer, this achievement seems more remarkable because Justice works with themes that are timeless: "If the large themes of love, heroism and death are to be handled, only a profoundly gifted poet will discover images that are not second-hand. Mr. Justice has this power." Howard observes, "There is a deep committed reverence about the way Justice celebrates . . . madness, love, old age, death. . . . But given such a burden altogether, and such a resonance, . . . the wonder is not that Donald Justice has written [so few poems]. . ., but that we have an elegant monument of fifty such poems [at least] to testify to his doomed transactions with life."

More important, perhaps the key to Justice's distinction as poet and critic is his love for "the cooler technical brilliancies" and "mysterious precisions" of classical metrics, as he calls them in *Platonic Scripts.* Proposing "that the anticlassical movement in current poetry is dead," to cite Wertime's paraphrase, Justice ventures: "A tradition could be put back together starting with not much more than this. Not forgetting rhythm; not forgetting truth."

*A Donald Justice Reader: Selected Poetry and Prose* gathers into one volume seventy-three poems and six prose pieces: three essays, two stories, and a memoir of Justice's Miami childhood. Writing in *Poetry,* Robert Richman calls Justice "one of our most reticent poets" whose volume of work is slim. Felix Stefanile, writing in *Christian Science Monitor,* calls this collection "a real gift" since "it is a sign of Donald Justice's clear, retentive mind that so many of these works, assembled over decades—verse and prose—talk to each other." The essay "The Invention of Free Verse" proposes that a commemorative tablet to be erected in Crawfordsville, Indiana, at Wabash College, to acknowledge Ezra Pound's deconstruction of the iamb, and to celebrate the time (1907) and the place (Crawfordsville) of the invention of modern poetry. The collection also includes examples of Justice's poems about time: "Certain moments will never change, nor stop being— / My mother's face all smiles, all wrinkles soon; /. . . All fixed into place now, all rhyming with each other" ("Thinking about the Past"), and his poems about place: ". . . this / Is Kansas the / Mountains start here / Just behind / The closed yes / Of a farmer's / Sons asleep / In their workclothes" ("Crossing Kansas by Train:"). A reviewer in *Virginia Quarterly Review* comments that "Justice certainly deserves the wider audience this selection from his poems and prose . . . is designed to produce" since he is "revered by other poets as a virtuoso craftsman."

*New and Selected Poems,* published four years later in 1995, offers another collection of Justice's poems. Michael Hoffman, writing in *New York Times Book Review,* comments about Justice's writing, which he considers "skillful and musical." Justice "probably has few peers when it comes to the musical arrangement of words in a line," he notes. The reviewer is critical, however, of what he finds to be "generic 50's-ish writing" full of the "values of the period, a kind of cleverness, neatness, . . . an easy relationship with the poems' own futility," which he finds "exemplified by far too many of the poems" in this collection. Since the book is composed of "cyclical forms, pantoums, villanelles, sestinas," which are "expressions of a sensibility that is itself highly literary," what the reader gets is "more like an anthology of literary effects." A writer for *Publishers Weekly,* however, acknowledges the work as a timeless retrospective compilation by a poet who has received the Lamont Prize, Pulitzer Prize, and Bollinger Prize, commenting that, "Until we see a complete collected works, this is probably the definitive Justice."

## BIOGRAPHICAL/CRITICAL SOURCES:

### BOOKS

*Contemporary Literary Criticism,* Gale (Detroit), Volume 6, 1976, Volume 19, 1981.
*Dictionary of Literary Biography Yearbook: 1983,* Gale, 1984.
Fussell, Paul, *Poetic Meter and Poetic Form,* Random House (New York City), 1965, revised edition, 1979.
Howard, Richard, *Alone with America,* Atheneum, 1969, revised edition, 1980.
Poulin, A. J., editor, *Contemporary American Poetry,* fourth edition, Houghton (Boston, MA), 1985.
Rubin, Louis D., *The History of Southern Literature,* Louisiana State University Press (Baton Rouge, LA), 1985.
Walsh, William J., *Speak, So I Shall Know Thee: Interviews with Southern Writers,* Down Home Press, 1993.

### PERIODICALS

*American Book Review,* January, 1982; April-May, 1993, p. 26.
*American Poetry Review,* March/April, 1976; May, 1988, p. 9.
*Antaeus,* spring/summer, 1982.

*Antioch Review,* winter, 1988, p. 102.

*Booklist,* January 1, 1992, p. 805.

*Boston Review,* June, 1987, p. 27.

*Choice,* February, 1985, p. 815.

*Christian Science Monitor,* April 20, 1992, p. 13.

*Hudson Review,* spring, 1974.

*Iowa Review,* spring/summer, 1980, pp. 1-21.

*Library Journal,* February 1, 1967; May 1, 1987, p. 71; December, 1991, p. 144.

*Los Angeles Times,* August 12, 1987.

*Missouri Review,* fall, 1980, pp. 41-67.

*Modern Language Studies,* winter, 1978-79.

*Modern Poetry Studies,* spring, 1980, pp. 44-58.

*Nation,* December 26, 1987, p. 803.

*New England Review and Bread Loaf Quarterly,* winter, 1984.

*New Statesman,* August 22, 1980, pp. 17-18; August 23, 1987, p. 28.

*New York Herald Tribune Books,* September 4, 1960.

*New York Review of Books,* October 16, 1975.

*New York Times Book Review,* February 19, 1961; March 9, 1980, pp. 8, 16; August 23, 1987, p. 20; December 27, 1992, p. 2; December 10, 1995, pp. 13-14.

*North American Review,* spring, 1974; spring, 1984.

*Ohio Review,* spring, 1975, pp. 40-63.

*Paris Review,* March, 1988, p. 490.

*Parnassus,* fall/winter, 1979, pp. 227-237.

*Partisan Review,* Volume 47, number 4, 1980, pp. 639-644.

*Perspective,* spring, 1962.

*Poetry,* October, 1974; October, 1984; September, 1989, p. 342; June, 1993, pp. 160-166; June, 1994, pp. 167-171; June, 1996, p. 168.

*Prairie Schooner,* Volume 47, 1973.

*Publishers Weekly,* August 28, 1995, p. 108.

*Punch,* January 15, 1988, p. 44.

*Saturday Review,* October 14, 1967, pp. 31-33, 99.

*Sewanee Review,* spring, 1974; summer, 1980, pp. 474-478; fall, 1980.

*Shenandoah,* summer, 1967.

*Southern Review,* summer, 1981.

*Southwest Review,* spring, 1980, pp. 218-220.

*Times Literary Supplement,* May 18, 1967; March 29, 1974; April 16, 1976; May 30, 1980, p. 620; April 15-21, 1988, p. 420.

*Tribune Books* (Chicago), June 21, 1987, p. 3.

*Virginia Quarterly Review,* summer, 1992, p. 101.

*Washington Post Book World,* February 10, 1980, p. 11; January 3, 1988.

*Western Humanities Review,* summer, 1974.

*Yale Review,* June, 1960, pp. 589-598; summer, 1985, p. 602; autumn, 1987, p. 124; spring, 1988.*

# K

KANE, Francis
See ROBBINS, Harold

\* \* \*

KARK, Nina Mary (Mabey)
See BAWDEN, Nina (Mary Mabey)

\* \* \*

KAUFMAN, Martin 1940-

PERSONAL: Born December 6, 1940, in Boston, MA; son of Irving (a meatmarket proprietor) and Rose (Langbort) Kaufman; married Henrietta Flax, December 22, 1968 (deceased); children: Edward Brian, Richard Lee (deceased), Linda Gail. *Education:* Boston University, A.B., 1962; University of Pittsburgh, M.A., 1963; Tulane University, Ph.D., 1969.

ADDRESSES: Home—666 Western Ave., Westfield, MA 01085. *Office*—Department of History, Westfield State College, Westfield, MA 01085.

CAREER: High school history teacher in Winter Haven, FL, 1964-65; Worcester State College, Worcester, MA, instructor in history, 1968-69; Westfield State College, Westfield, MA, assistant professor, 1969-72, associate professor, 1973-76, professor of history, 1977—, director of Institute for Massachusetts Studies, 1981—. *Military service:* U.S. Army Reserve, 1964-70.

MEMBER: American Association for the History of Medicine, Organization of American Historians, National Education Association.

AWARDS, HONORS: Distinguished service award, Westfield State College, 1981; John F. Ayer award for 1994, Bay State Historical League.

WRITINGS:

*Homeopathy in America: The Rise and Fall of a Medical Heresy,* Johns Hopkins University Press (Baltimore, MD), 1971.
*American Medical Education: The Formative Years, 1765-1910,* Greenwood Press, 1976.
*University of Vermont College of Medicine,* University Press of New England (Hanover, NH), 1979.
(Editor in chief) *Dictionary of American Medical Biography,* Greenwood Press, 1984.
(Editor in chief) *Dictionary of American Nursing Biography,* Greenwood Press, 1988.
*A Guide to the History of Massachusetts,* Greenwood Press, 1988.
(Editor, with others) *Education in Massachusetts: Selected Essays,* Institute for Massachusetts Studies, 1989.
(Editor, with others) *Labor in Massachusetts: Selected Essays,* Institute for Massachusetts Studies, 1990.

Contributor of articles to periodicals.

WORK IN PROGRESS: "Coeditor of a forthcoming book, *Political History of Massachusetts: Selected Essays,* and I am always working on the next issue of the *Historical Journal of Massachusetts,* including typesetting of articles, book reviews, book notes, and notes of historical interest."

*SIDELIGHTS:* Martin Kaufman told *CA:* "I am a hard-working historian and writer, and I have always tried to write for the intelligent layman, rather than for scholars. I am most proud of the fact that I have had articles published in *Sports Illustrated, American History Illustrated,* and *Yankee Magazine.* Indeed, in one week, millions of people read my article in *Sports Illustrated,* as compared to the thousand who perhaps have read any of my books over a fifteen year period.

"It is commonly said that 'into every life some rain must fall,' and my life is certainly evidence of the truth of that adage. In 1974, problems began with the birth of Richard Lee Kaufman, my second son. Ricky was multiply-handicapped, being unable to either walk or talk, and the care he required, combined with his severe behavior problem, resulted in a great turmoil within the house, and conflict within the family. From 1976, when we realized that Ricky had a serious problem, to 1981, when he was admitted into the Berkshire Children's Community in Great Barrington, Massachusetts, it was difficult to work, knowing how difficult it was at home. With Ricky at a residential school, the home life improved, but I thought that I would never be able to return to anything resembling a normal scholarly life, as we visited Ricky at least once a week, and there were always problems related to his needs. Ricky contracted pneumonia and died in April of 1984, and in many ways it was a Godsend to be released from being involved with his many problems. It was also a Godsend for him, as he would never have been able to develop normally; he would never have been able to walk or talk.

"Shortly after Ricky's death, however, I began to have severe headaches, much more severe than I had had since I was a child. In 1990, my wife insisted that I get professional help with the headaches, which led to the discovery that I had a large benign brain tumor which undoubtedly was responsible for the headaches. My wife took me to the Massachusetts General Hospital, where the tumor was surgically removed by one of the leading neurosurgeons in the world, Dr. Nicholas Zervas. At the time, I did not know that the operation was to be the beginning of a new set of problems. Since the tumor was on my pituitary gland, which monitors the body's production of a variety of hormones, either the tumor or its surgical removal resulted in damage to the pituitary. As a result, when I was tested it was found that I had low levels of testosterone, thyroid extract, and cortisone, and my endocrinologist, Dr. Burritt Haag, of the Bay State Medical Center, in Springfield, immediately initiated a program intended to replace the hormones that my body was no longer able to produce. I began taking synthyroid and cortisone steroids by pill, and every two weeks I returned to Dr. Haag's office for a testosterone injection. The cortisone steroids led to a new problem; steroids result in severe thirst and hunger, which led to my weight increasing from 150 to 210 pounds.

"Through all of my medical and surgical problems, my wife Henrietta (known to all as 'Honey') was always there, as my chauffeur, guide, and companion. Then, on Valentine's Day of 1993, she woke up with severe chest pains, which almost immediately was diagnosed as lung cancer. She was hospitalized, and radiation treatments began. Within a week, however, she was dead, at the age of fifty, depriving me of a wonderful wife and companion, and depriving my son and daughter of a wonderful mother.

"Even during times of sorrow, however, there always seems to be some humor, and that certainly was the case with the death of my 'Honey.' When Honey died, our daughter Linda was sixteen years old. While I lost a wife and companion, Linda lost her best friend, her shopping partner, and her closest confidante. Linda was obviously shocked at the loss of her mother; she barely came out of her room for several days, and then only to grab some food, or to go to the bathroom, before returning to her bedroom, which obviously was her sanctuary. I realized that I had to do something to help my daughter get through the problem. So I went into her room, intending to instill in her some hope for the future. 'Linda,' I said, 'I know it was a terrible shock to lose your mother. I know that you lost your best friend, and your companion. But Linda,' I declared, 'from now on, I'll be a mother and a father to you. If you have any problems, come to me and I'll help you solve them. And if you have any questions, come to me and I'll answer them for you.' Linda immediately responded: 'I do have a question.' 'That's wonderful,' I exclaimed, 'give me the question, and I'll give you the answer. I'll show you that I can be a father and a mother to you.' Then Linda asked her question, one that very few men have any idea how to answer, one that demonstrated to both of us that I could never replace her mother. The question was 'Daddy, how do you use a tampon?' My response was not at all sufficient. It was 'Carefully.'

"Through all of these personal and family problems, I continued to be thankful that I had professional obligations that served to keep me busy, and to get me away from those problems, at least temporarily. I had my professional position at Westfield State College, requiring me to teach three courses each semester, and putting me into contact with a number of very fine students who were interested in American history. And I had my position as editorial director of the *Historical Journal of Massachusetts,* which kept me busy reading and evaluating manuscripts submitted for publication, editing those manuscripts which were accepted for publication by the editorial board, requesting books for review and corresponding with book reviewers, and writing book note of those books which clearly did not warrant full-scale reviews.

"In addition, I became much more involved in the experiences of my children, who now were young adults. Ed graduated from the University of Massachusetts at Amherst, with honors, as a double-major in Spanish and Economics. While a student, he spent a year in Spain, and a semester in Ecuador, and then he decided that his goal in life was to get a Ph.D. in Romance Languages, and to become a college professor, like his father. He is currently a graduate student at Columbia University, in New York City, having received a five-year graduate fellowship providing him with tuition and over ten thousand dollars a year to cover his expenses. Linda is in her second year at the University of Massachusetts at Amherst, majoring in Psychology, and spending much of her time terrorizing the roads of Massachusetts, demolishing her two cars in the process.

"And I began to do some of my own writing, what I hope will result in a very personal account of the Kaufman family's encounter with the modern American medical care system. Hopefully, that will be my next book-length publication."

*BIOGRAPHICAL/CRITICAL SOURCES:*

PERIODICALS

*American Historical Review,* autumn, 1973; June, 1977; April, 1980.

\*    \*    \*

**KAVANAGH, Dan**
    **See BARNES, Julian (Patrick)**

**KEMERER, Frank R(obert) 1940-**

*PERSONAL:* Born October 22, 1940, in Minneapolis, MN; son of Robert W. (a business executive) and Marion (Nordin) Kemerer; married Barbara Kellner, May 7, 1971; children: Ann Elizabeth, Jennifer Lynn. *Education:* Stanford University, A.B. (history) and A.B. (political science), both 1963, M.A., 1968, Ph.D., 1975; University of Minnesota Law School, graduate study, 1963-64. *Politics:* Democrat.

*ADDRESSES: Home*—27 Timbergreen, Denton, TX 76205. *Office*—College of Education, University of North Texas, Denton, TX 76203.

*CAREER:* Blake School, Minneapolis, MN, teacher of history, speech, and journalism, and counselor, 1964-67, 1968-69; Stanford University, Stanford, CA, admissions officer, 1967-68; Latin School of Chicago, Chicago, IL, instructor and assistant headmaster, director of studies and counseling, 1969-72; Lick-Wilmerding School, San Francisco, CA, instructor and director, 1973-75; Stanford University, senior research associate, 1973-75; State University of New York College at Geneseo, College of Arts and Science, lecturer in political science, assistant to president, and director of college enrollment management, 1975-78; University of North Texas, Denton, professor of education law and administration, 1978-90, Regents Professor of law and administration, 1990—. Guest lecturer at colleges and universities, including State University of New York College at Brockport, Indiana University of Pennsylvania, Harvard University, and Stanford University; speaker at numerous national and regional conferences; chairman of various committees at University of North Texas, 1980—. Member of State University of New York negotiations advisory committee, 1975-78; consultant on education and management at universities.

*MEMBER:* American Association of University Administrators (member of board of directors, 1981-82), National Organization on Legal Problems of Education, Phi Kappa Delta, Kappa Delta Pi.

*AWARDS, HONORS:* Excellence in Governmental/Legislative Relations Award, State University of New York College and University Relations Council, 1976; University of North Texas, designated Regents Professor by board of regents, 1990, recipient of Toulouse Scholars Award in recognition of research and teaching excellence, 1993, awarded President's Council University Teaching Award, 1994; awarded

T. R. Fehrenbach Prize by Texas Historical Commission, 1990; Certificate of Distinction, from American Society of Writers on Legal Subjects, 1991, for *William Wayne Justice: A Judicial Biography.*

*WRITINGS:*

(With J. Victor Baldridge) *Unions on Campus: A National Study of the Consequences of Faculty Bargaining,* Jossey-Bass (San Francisco, CA), 1975.

*Understanding Faculty Unions and Collective Bargaining* (monograph), National Association of Independent Schools (Boston, MA), 1976.

(Contributor) Baldridge and Gary Lee Riley, *Governing Academic Organizations: New Issues, New Perspectives,* McCutchan (Berkeley, CA), 1977.

(With Ronald P. Satryb) *Facing Financial Exigency: Strategies for Educational Administrators,* Lexington Books (Lexington, MA), 1978.

(With Kenneth L. Deutsch) *Constitutional Rights and Student Life,* with textbook supplement and instructor's manual, West Publishing (Minneapolis, MN), 1979.

(With Baldridge) *Assessing the Impact of Faculty Collective Bargaining,* American Association for Higher Education (Washington, DC), 1981.

*Texas Teachers' Guide to School Law,* University of Texas Press (Austin), 1982.

(With Baldridge and Kenneth C. Green) *The Enrollment Crisis: Factors, Actors, and Impact,* American Association for Higher Education, 1982.

(With Baldridge and Green) *Strategies for Effective Enrollment Management,* American Association of State Colleges and Universities (Washington, DC), 1982.

*The Educator's Guide to Texas School Law,* University of Texas Press, 1986, 2nd edition (with Joe B. Hairston), 1990, 4th edition (with Jim Walsh), 1996.

*William Wayne Justice: A Judicial Biography,* University of Texas Press, 1990.

Also author of research reports and discussion papers. Contributor to journals, including *Educational Forum, Independent School, Journal of Higher Education,* and *Journal of Law and Education.*

*WORK IN PROGRESS:* With Kenneth Godwin and Valerie Martinez, *Vouchers for the Poor: Policy Issues in School Choice.*

*SIDELIGHTS:* Frank R. Kemerer told *CA:* "I didn't begin writing for publication until I had received a master's degree at Stanford University in 1968. My first publication was an article on nondirective counseling for college-bound students. It was included in an issue of the National Association of Independent School's magazine, *The Independent School Bulletin,* in 1971. Thereafter, I began contributing regularly to professional periodicals. When I returned to Stanford to complete a doctorate, I made an effort to turn every research paper into a published article. I also began to focus my writing on law-related subjects.

"After completing my doctorate at Stanford, I worked as an administrator and taught constitutional and civil liberties at a college in the State University of New York (SUNY) system. For some time I had been interested in writing a legal textbook that used student rights cases as a catalyst to encourage students to explore deeper issues in American society. The SUNY experience gave me the opportunity, and the result was a law book entitled *Constitutional Rights and Student Life.*

"My most satisfactory writing accomplishment is my biography of Judge William Wayne Justice published in 1991 by the University of Texas Press. Judge Justice is one of the most controversial and influential reform judges on the federal bench. The book received several awards and was extensively reviewed by journals and legal periodicals. I found the reviewer comments particularly gratifying.

"I now find myself writing about subjects as diverse as school vouchers and Texas school law. I still enjoy most of all writing about legal subjects. I hope that one of these days I will be able to write a book on the role of the First Amendment in education."

\*          \*          \*

**KERNAGHAN, Eileen    1939-**

*PERSONAL:* Born January 6, 1939, in Enderby, British Columbia, Canada; daughter of William Alfred (a dairy farmer) and Belinda Maude (Pritchard) Monk; married Patrick Walter Kernaghan, 1959; children: Michael, Susan, Gavin. *Education:* Attended University of British Columbia, 1956-59.

*ADDRESSES: Home*—New Westminster, British Columbia, Canada. *Office*—225 Townsend Pl., New Westminster, British Columbia, Canada V3L 1L4.

*CAREER:* Elementary school teacher in British Columbia, 1959-62; Burnaby Arts Council, Burnaby, British Columbia, secretary, office worker, and coordinator, 1979-84; freelance writer, 1984—. Operates Neville Books, a secondhand bookstore, with her husband in Burnaby.

*MEMBER:* SF Canada, Science Fiction Writers of America, Federation of British Columbia Writers, Burnaby Writers Society, The Lonely Cry.

*AWARDS, HONORS:* Silver Medal Award for original fantasy from *West Coast Review of Books,* 1980, for *Journey to Aprilioth;* Canadian Science Fiction and Fantasy (CASPAR) Award, 1984, for *Songs from the Drowned Lands: A Novel of High Fantasy,* and 1990, for short story, "Carpe Diem."

*WRITINGS:*

(Coauthor) *The Upper Left-Hand Corner: A Writer's Guide for the Northwest,* J. D. Douglas, 1975, 3rd edition, International Self-Counsel Press, 1986.
(Coauthor) J. Michael Yates, editor, *Light Like a Summons* (poetry), Cacanadadada Press, 1989.
(With Jonathan Kay) *Walking after Midnight* (nonfiction), Berkley Books (New York City), 1990.
*Dance of the Snow Dragon* (young adult fantasy novel), Thistledown Press (Saskatoon, Canada), 1995.

*"GREY ISLES" FANTASY TRILOGY; ACE BOOKS (NEW YORK CITY)*

*Journey to Aprilioth,* 1983.
*Songs from the Drowned Lands: A Novel of High Fantasy,* 1983.
*The Sarsen Witch,* 1989.

OTHER

Contributor to numerous anthologies, including *Tesseracts,* edited by Judith Merril, Porcepic Books, 1985; *The Blue Jean Collection,* edited by Pete Carver, Thistledown Press, 1992; and *The Year's Best Fantasy & Horror,* Ninth Annual Collection, edited by Ellen Datlow and Terri Windling, St. Martin's Press, 1996. Also contributor of poems, short stories and articles to various periodicals, including *Canadian Review, Dreams & Nightmares, Galaxy, Magazine of Speculative Poetry, Northern Journey, On Spec: The Canadian Magazine of Speculative Writing, PRISM International, Room of One's Own, Space and Time, TransVersions,* and *Woman-space.*

*WORK IN PROGRESS:* Recently completed *Winter on the Plain of Ghosts,* a prehistoric fantasy set in the bronze-age Indus Valley; untitled young adult fantasy novel.

*SIDELIGHTS:* In an interview with Frank Garcia for *Cross-Canada Writers,* Eileen Kernaghan indicates that she began writing for publication when she was approximately twelve years old. She started in science fiction but switched to fantasy when she realized her background in "the rules of the real world"—like biology, chemistry, and physics—were lacking. When asked why the fantasy genre appeals to her, she told Garcia: "I suppose, because in mainstream fiction, you know that the bad guys are probably going to win; whereas Fantasy good is still able to conquer evil. When your life, the country, and the whole world are in a mess, it's nice to read a book in which Order wins over Chaos. From a writer's point of view, what other genre allows you to create, populate and make up all the rules for an entire universe? It's the ultimate act of self-indulgence."

*Journey to Aprilioth,* the first novel in Kernaghan's fantasy trilogy, is set in 1970 B.C. It is the story of Nhiall, a religious novice forced to flee his land after accidentally killing a man. While traveling across the terrain of ancient Europe, Nhiall attempts to discover the last survivors of an even older civilization. This journey, however, is disrupted by numerous encounters with bandits and barbarians. According to *Vancouver Sun* contributor Leslie Peterson, the novel is "plausible" and "well balanced."

Kernaghan's second trilogy novel entitled *Songs from the Drowned Lands: A Novel of High Fantasy* won a Canadian Science Fiction and Fantasy Award in 1984. Events in this novel are set in an even earlier time than that of *Journey to Aprilioth,* with some people calling it a "prequel." As Melanie Conn explains in *Kinesis,* "*Songs from the Drowned Lands* is a pre-historic disaster novel which explores the mystery of Stonehenge and the disappearance of the Grey Isles beneath the sea. Each of the four 'Songs'—or novelettes—focuses on one character's response to foreknowledge of the coming disaster: What do people do when they know that the world is about to end?" When Conn heard Kernaghan read parts of *Songs from the Drowned Lands* aloud, she was "struck by the imagery and emotion of [Kernaghan's] writing."

Eileen Kernaghan told *CA:* "My major theme in the 'Grey Isles' trilogy is a traditional one in fantasy: the eternal struggle between order and chaos; the message, one of guarded, and long-term, optimism: civilizations rise as well as fall. Essentially, I just enjoy telling a good story. But people whose opinions I respect tell me that my books are about making choices, accepting responsibility, seeking values in something larger than oneself. Perhaps that's because I'm looking at the world of 2000 B.C. through twentieth-century A.D. eyes: a time when we must continue to make choices, with fewer and fewer real choices remaining to us."

Kernaghan described *Dance of the Snow Dragon* as "a young adult fantasy with a Tibetan Buddhist background, set in eighteenth- century Bhutan. Fantasy author Sean Stewart reviewed the novel thus[ly]: 'Battles and visions and sorcerer's magic dance like driven snow through this beautifully written tale about a yak-herder's son who sets out on a magical journey through the eternal Himalayas. This book delivers in spades that sense of wonder fantasy was always supposed to be about.'"

Karnaghan added: "I suppose [you] could say that all of my books arise out of my own quest for answers—my search for a set of beliefs that I find meaningful. The Shambhala legend is an archetypal spiritual quest—a physical journey which is also a metaphor for the inward psychological, emotional and spiritual journey towards enlightenment."

*BIOGRAPHICAL/CRITICAL SOURCES:*

*BOOKS*

Twigg, Alan, *Vancouver and Its Writers,* Harbour Publishing, 1986.

*PERIODICALS*

*Cross-Canada Writers,* Number 2, 1988.
*Edmonton Journal,* November 26, 1995, p. F7.
*Kinesis,* July-August, 1988.
*Quill and Quire,* June, 1995.
*Vancouver Sun,* June 26, 1981.

\*    \*    \*

**KEROUAC, Jack**
  **See KEROUAC, Jean-Louis Lebris de**

**KEROUAC, Jean-Louis Lebris de**    **1922-1969**
  **(Jean-Louis Incogniteau, Jean-Louis, Jack Kerouac, John Kerouac)**

*PERSONAL:* Born March 12, 1922, in Lowell, MA; died October 21, 1969, of a stomach hemorrhage in St. Petersburg, FL; buried in Lowell, MA; son of Leo Alcide (a job printer) and Gabrielle-Ange (a shoe-factory worker; maiden name, Levesque) Ker-ouac; married Frankie Edith Parker, August 22, 1944 (marriage annulled, 1945); married Joan Ha-verty, November 17, 1950 (divorced); married Stella Sampas, November 18, 1966; children: (second marriage) Jan Michele Hackett. *Education:* Attended Horace Mann School for Boys, New York, NY; attended Columbia College, 1940-42; attended New School for Social Research, 1948-49. *Religion:* Roman Catholic. *Avocational interests:* Reading, walking, late TV movies, and tape-recording FM musical programs.

*CAREER:* Writer. Worked at odd jobs in garages and as a sports reporter for the Lowell (MA) *Sun,* 1942; was a railroad brakeman with the Southern Pacific Railroad, San Francisco, CA, 1952-53; traveled around the United States and Mexico; was a fire lookout for the U.S. Agriculture Service in northwest Washington, 1956. *Military service:* U.S. Merchant Marine, 1942-43; U.S. Navy, 1943.

*MEMBER:* Authors Guild, Authors League of America.

*AWARDS, HONORS:* American Academy of Arts and Sciences grant, 1955; Allen Ginsberg and other poets created the Jack Kerouac School of Disembodied Poetics at the Naropa Institute in Boulder, Colorado; *Moody Street Irregulars: A Jack Kerouac Newsletter,* edited by Joy Walsh and Michael Basinski, was established in 1978.

*WRITINGS:*

(Under name John Kerouac) *The Town and the City,* Harcourt (New York City), 1950, reprinted under name Jack Kerouac, Grosset (New York City), 1960, reprinted, Harcourt, 1978.
(Under name John Kerouac) *Visions of Gerard* (also see below), Farrar, Straus (New York City), 1963, reprinted under name Jack Kerouac, McGraw (New York City), 1976.

Contributor to *Columbia Review* (under pseudonym Jean-Louis Incogniteau) and to *New World Writing* (under pseudonym Jean-Louis).

*NOVELS; UNDER NAME JACK KEROUAC*

*On the Road,* Viking (New York City), 1957, reprinted, Penguin (New York City), 1987, critical edition with notes by Scott Donaldson published as *On the Road: Text and Criticism,* Penguin, 1979.

*The Dharma Bums,* Viking, 1958, reprinted, Buccaneer Books (Cutchogue, NY), 1976.

*The Subterraneans* (also see below), Grove (New York City), 1958, 2nd edition, 1981.

*Doctor Sax: Faust Part Three,* Grove, 1959, reprinted, 1988.

*Maggie Cassidy: A Love Story,* Avon (New York City), 1959, reprinted, McGraw, 1978.

*Excerpts from Visions of Cody,* New Directions (New York City), 1959, enlarged edition published as *Visions of Cody,* McGraw, 1972 (published with *The Visions of the Great Rememberer,* by Allen Ginsberg, Penguin, 1993).

*Tristessa,* Avon, 1960 (published in England with *Visions of Gerard,* Deutsch, 1964), reprinted, McGraw, 1978.

*Big Sur,* Farrar, Straus, 1962, reprinted, McGraw, 1981, new edition with foreword by Aram Saroyan, Penguin, 1992.

*Desolation Angels,* Coward (New York City), 1965.

*Satori in Paris* (also see below), Grove, 1966, reprinted, 1988.

*Vanity of Duluoz: An Adventurous Education, 1935-46,* Coward, 1968.

*Pic,* Grove, 1971 (published in England with *The Subterraneans* as *Two Novels,* Deutsch (London), 1973; published with *Satori in Paris,* Grove, 1986).

Also author, with William S. Burroughs, of unpublished novel "And the Hippos Were Boiled in Their Tanks," and of unpublished novels "The Sea Is My Brother," "Buddha Tells Us," and "Secret Mullings about Bill."

*POETRY; UNDER NAME JACK KEROUAC*

*Mexico City Blues: Two Hundred Forty-Two Choruses,* Grove, 1959, reprinted, 1987.

*Hugo Weber,* Portents, 1967.

*Someday You'll Be Lying,* privately printed, 1968.

*A Lost Haiku,* privately printed, 1969.

*Scattered Poems,* City Lights (San Francisco, CA), 1971.

(With Albert Saijo and Lew Welch) *Trip Trap: Haiku along the Road from San Francisco to New York, 1959,* Grey Fox (San Francisco, CA), 1973.

*Heaven and Other Poems,* Grey Fox, 1977.

*San Francisco Blues,* Beat Books, 1983.

*Hymn: God Pray for Me,* Caliban (Dover, NH), 1985.

*American Haikus,* Caliban, 1986.

*Pomes All Sizes,* with introduction by Allen Ginsberg, City Lights, 1992.

*Old Angel Midnight,* Grey Fox, 1993, new edition edited by Donald Allen, with prefaces by Ann Charters and Michael McClure, Grey Fox, 1993.

*Book of Blues,* with introduction by Robert Creeley, Penguin, 1995.

*SOUND RECORDINGS; UNDER NAME JACK KEROUAC*

*Jack Kerouac Steve Allen Poetry for the Beat Generation,* Hanover, 1959.

*Jack Kerouac Blues and Haikus,* Hanover, 1959.

*Readings by Jack Kerouac on the Beat Generation,* Verve, 1959.

*The Jack Kerouac Collection,* Rhino (Santa Monica, CA), 1990.

*OTHER; UNDER NAME JACK KEROUAC*

(Contributor) *January 1st 1959: Fidel Castro,* Totem, 1959.

*Rimbaud,* City Lights, 1959.

*The Scripture of the Golden Eternity* (philosophy and religion), Corinth Books (Chevy Chase, MD), 1960, new edition, 1970, new edition with introduction by Eric Mottram, City Lights, 1994.

(Author of introduction) *The Americans,* photographs by Robert Frank, Grove, 1960, revised and enlarged edition, 1978.

*Lonesome Traveler* (autobiography), McGraw, 1960, reprinted, Grove, 1989.

(Ad lib narrator) *Pull My Daisy* (screenplay), Grove, 1961.

*Book of Dreams,* City Lights, 1961.

*A Pun for Al Gelpi* (broadside), [Cambridge], 1966.

*A Memoir in Which Is Revealed Secret Lives and West Coast Whispers,* Giligia (Aurora, OR), 1970.

*Two Early Stories,* Aloe Editions, 1973.

*Home at Christmas,* Oliphant, 1973.

(With Allen Ginsberg) *Take Care of My Ghost, Ghost* (letters), limited edition, Ghost Press, 1977.

*Une veille de Noel,* Knight, 1980.

(With Carolyn Cassady) *Dear Carolyn: Letters to Carolyn Cassady,* Unspeakable Visions (California, PA), 1983.

*Good Blonde & Others,* edited by Donald Allen, Grey Fox, 1993.

*Jack Kerouac: Selected Letters, 1940-1956,* edited with introduction and commentary by Ann Charters, Viking, 1995.

*The Portable Jack Kerouac* (omnibus volume), edited by Charters, Viking, 1995.

*A Jack Kerouac ROMnibus* (CD-ROM), Largely Literary Designs (Morrisville, NC), 1995.

Also author of *Before the Road: Young Cody and the Birth of Hippie,* and of *Not Long Ago Joy Abounded at Christmas,* 1972. Author of pamphlet, *Nosferatu* (Dracula), New York Film Society, 1960. Contributor to periodicals, including *Ark-Moby, Paris Review, Evergreen Review, Big Table, Black Mountain Review,* and *Chicago Review.* Contributor of regular column, "The Last Word," to *Escapade,* 1959-61.

One of Kerouac's notebooks is at the University of Texas, Austin; five notebooks and a typescript are in the Berg Collection of the New York Public Library; some of the author's correspondence with Allen Ginsberg is housed at the Butler Library of Columbia University; other letters are in the Gary Snyder Archives at the library of the University of California, Davis.

*ADAPTATIONS:* The Subterraneans* was adapted as a film of the same title by Metro-Goldwyn-Mayer in 1960, starring George Peppard and Leslie Caron; a play based on Kerouac's life and works was produced in New York in 1976; a film based on *On the Road* is scheduled for release in 1997.

*SIDELIGHTS:* Jean-Louis Lebris de Kerouac became famous as Jack Kerouac, author of *On the Road,* the novel that is considered the quintessential statement of the 1950s literary movement known as the Beat Generation. *On the Road* described the growing friendship of two men, Sal Paradise and Dean Moriarty, and their criss-crossing journeys over the American continent. On a deeper level, it was the story of the narrator's search for religious truth and for values more profound than those embraced by most of mid-twentieth-century America. In both form and subject *On the Road* was completely unlike the formal fiction that dominated the era, and was ridiculed accordingly by Kerouac's contemporaries in the literary establishment, who viewed it as "an insane parody of the mobility of automotive America," according to Dennis McNally in *Desolate Angel: Jack Kerouac, the Beat Generation, and America. On the Road* spoke to many readers, however, expressing their own unarticulated dissatisfaction with the repressive climate of the United States after World War II.

"It is difficult, separated as we are by time and temper from that period, to convey the liberating effect that *On the Road* had on young people all over America," wrote Bruce Cook in *The Beat Generation.* "There was a sort of instantaneous flash of recognition that seemed to send thousands of them out into the streets, proclaiming that Kerouac had written their story, that *On the Road* was their book." More and more people took their cue from Kerouac's novel and adopted a lifestyle that emphasized personal freedom over social conformity and expanded consciousness over material wealth. The mass media jokingly referred to these modern Bohemians as "beatniks" and portrayed Kerouac as their leader. In this position he achieved a celebrity status uncommon for a novelist—an uncomfortable role for Kerouac, a shy, insecure man ill-equipped to deal with fame. As the scattered beat scene evolved into the hippie counterculture of the 1960s, Kerouac continued to be named the progenitor of it all, but by that time he had withdrawn from public life, frustrated by critics' continuing attacks on his work. It was not until several years after his death that Kerouac began to be recognized as an important artist, one who, according to *Midwest Quarterly* contributor Carole Gottlieb Vopat, had "provided an enduring portrait of the national psyche; like Fitzgerald, he has defined America and delineated American life for his generation."

Kerouac was born to French-Canadian parents in the working-class "Little Canada" neighborhood of Lowell, Massachusetts, a mill town some thirty miles northwest of Boston. He spoke only French until the age of seven, and his French-Canadian heritage, along with the Roman Catholic faith in which he was raised, was a strong influence throughout his life. He was a highly imaginative child who created a private world of racing stables and sports teams, then wrote his own newspapers to report their performances. Diaries, radio plays, and a novel entitled "Jack Kerouac Explores the Merrimack" were some of his other childhood writing projects. He was an excellent student, and by the time he entered Lowell High School, he was also developing into a gifted athlete. It was his performance on the high school football team that provided his ticket out of Lowell: he was offered a football scholarship to Columbia University. New York City was a world away from Lowell. Forty percent of Kerouac's home town received some form of public assistance, but at the Horace Mann School (where he spent a year preparing for Columbia's Ivy League standards) his classmates were the heirs to Manhattan's fortunes. Kerouac seemed amusingly rustic to them, but he was well-liked, and his new friends guided his explorations of the city. He found its vibrancy and diversity inspirational.

Kerouac had a checkered career at Columbia. A broken leg kept him from playing much football in 1940, and his 1941 season was marked by disagreements with his coach. Furthermore, Kerouac was beginning to feel deeply troubled by the great shift in morals brought about by the Second World War. A whole way of life seemed to be vanishing, and as McNally observed, "Studying and practicing seemed trivial exercises in an apocalyptic world." Late in 1941 Kerouac left the university for a hitch in the Merchant Marine. In his off-duty hours he read the works of Thomas Wolfe and worked on a novel he called "The Sea Is My Brother." He returned briefly to Columbia in 1942, left to join the Navy, then found himself unable to submit to the military discipline of that service. This earned him some time in the psychiatric ward of Bethesda Naval Hospital, but he eventually received an honorable discharge for "indifferent character." Kerouac reentered the less-regimented Merchant Marine for some time before returning to New York City, although not to Columbia. It was at this time that he began to meet the people who would profoundly influence the rest of his life and his work—the people who would in fact be the core of the Beat Generation.

"Cutting away the amateurs, the opportunists, and the figures whose generational identification was fleeting or less than wholehearted on their own part, the Beat Generation—as a literary school—pretty much amounts to Kerouac and his friends William Burroughs and Allen Ginsberg," suggested Barry Gifford and Lawrence Lee in *Jack's Book: An Oral Biography of Jack Kerouac*. Allen Ginsberg was a seventeen-year-old Columbia freshman when he and Kerouac first met. The two became like brothers, excitedly discussing their literary and philosophical ideas. Several years older than Kerouac, William Burroughs was a shadowy figure who had worked as an adman, a detective, an exterminator, and a bartender. He served as Kerouac's tutor and mentor, introducing him to the works of Spengler, Nietzsche, and Celine. He also provided an intimate introduction to the underground society of Times Square, to morphine, and to amphetamines.

In 1945 his intense friendships, the mood of nihilistic despair, and Kerouac's heavy use of benzedrine took their toll. Thrombophlebitis made his legs swell painfully, and he was confined to a hospital bed. His father and mother had come to New York in search of factory work two years earlier; now Leo Kerouac began to die a painful death of stomach cancer. Released from the hospital, Jack returned not to his intellectual friends in the city, but to his parents' shabby home in Ozone Park. For many months he cared for his father, who berated his son for his aimless life, his worthless friends and his foolish artistic aspirations. On his deathbed Leo repeatedly made Jack swear to support his mother, and Jack promised that he would.

It was in the hope of fulfilling that promise that he returned to his mother's home after Leo's burial and began working on a new novel, an idealized autobiography that would be published in 1950 as *The Town and the City*. The book "reflected his return to family, replacing the New Vision aura of symbolic decadence with the style of his first love, Thomas Wolfe," remarked McNally. "The work was underlaid not only with his new insight into death but with the idealism of Goethe's autobiography *Dichtung und Wahrheit* (*Poetry and Truth*), Kerouac's main reading matter that summer and fall. . . . Goethe calmly rejected satire and preached an affirmative love of life, and more, told Jack that all of his work was merely 'fragments of a great confession'. . . . Jack worked at his own confession . . . for two years, grimly struggling from morning until late at night to recite the history of the Kerouacs and America."

Stretches of work on *The Town and the City* were broken by occasional visits to friends in New York. It was on one such trip that Kerouac met the man who would inspire some of his best work. Neal Cassady was the motherless son of a derelict from Denver, Colorado. He had been born in an automobile and was fourteen years old when he stole his first car. Cassady quickly became addicted to the feeling of freedom he experienced behind the wheel. By the time he was twenty-one, he'd stolen five hundred cars, been arrested ten times, convicted six times, and spent fifteen months in jail. McNally commented: "Twenty-year-old Neal swept into [Kerouac's] life like a Wild West siren singing freedom, kicks, a 'wild yea-saying overburst of American joy,' as Jack characterized him, enthusiastically flying after food and sex like a holy primitive, a 'natural man'; he was the embodiment of Jack's American dream."

The two men quickly developed an intense friendship, but when Cassady's plan to enter Columbia collapsed, he returned to Denver. Four months later,

Kerouac took a break from his work on *The Town and the City* to hitchhike west and join his friend. Once there, he found Cassady preoccupied by his love affairs with his mistress, his estranged fifteen-year-old wife, and Allen Ginsberg, so Kerouac continued on to San Francisco alone, then returned to New York by bus. This first of many restless journeys around the United States provided Kerouac with the ending he needed for *The Town and the City*. The finished book opened with a lyrical re-creation of a New England childhood, featuring a large, happy family with strong foundations. War scatters the family, however, and eventually even its anchor, the father, must tear up his roots and move to the city. His death there symbolized the final destruction of the idyllic way of life evoked in the novel's first half. In a final scene which prefigured the *On the Road* story, the most promising son turned his back on conventional success and took to the open road in search of a new way of life. *The Town and the City* was cordially reviewed upon its publication in 1950. Although there were objections to the message implied in the novel's closing scene, most critics noted the book's vitality and praised its style as powerful and evocative.

Kerouac was elated to be a published novelist, but by the time *The Town and the City* appeared he was struggling with his next book. Its subject was Neal Cassady. Kerouac wanted this new novel to reflect the fevered pace of modern life; the gracious prose he'd used in *The Town and the City* was inappropriate for that purpose. After several false starts, Kerouac found the inspiration for a new style in the letters he received from Cassady. Kerouac remembered them in a *Paris Review* interview with Ted Berrigan as "all first person, fast, mad, confessional, completely serious, all detailed." In one 40,000-word letter, Cassady described his seduction of a woman he met on a bus. It read "with spew and rush, without halt, all unified and molten flow; no boring moments, everything significant and interesting, sometimes breathtaking in speed and brilliance," as McNally quoted Ginsberg. Kerouac decided to model his book about Cassady on the style of these letters. Instead of revising, he would let the story assume its own shape, allowing details and impressions to accumulate as they do in life. Threading a long roll of paper through his typewriter so he would not have to pause at the end of each page, Kerouac sat down in April, 1951, to pour out the story of his friendship with Cassady. In twenty days he had completed a 175,000-word, single-spaced paragraph that was the first version of *On the Road*. McNally as-

sessed the author's output: "The sentences were short and tight, clickety-pop word bursts that caught the rhythm of the high-speed road life as no author before him ever had. . . . [The book was] bursting with energy, with a feeling of life struggling inside a deathly society, energy burning bright before the laws of entropy and the nation caught up."

"Spontaneous prose" was Kerouac's name for the high-speed writing method he was developing. *Dictionary of Literary Biography* contributor George Dardess explained what this style symbolized to the author: "'Spontaneous prose' was the way by which the inner mind, trapped as Kerouac finally felt it to be by social, psychological, and grammatical restrictions, could free itself from its muteness and take verbal shape in the outside world. The result of this liberation would not be chaotic, however, since the inner mind was innately shapely and would cause the words with which it expressed itself to be shapely. . . . Spontaneous prose became a metaphor for the paradoxes of the human condition as Kerouac, the Roman Catholic, conceived it: hopelessly corrupted and compromised, yet somehow, in ways only indirectly glimpsed and never fully understood, redeemable, even in the midst of its sin." Spontaneous prose had contemporary parallels in music and the visual arts, noted McNally: "At roughly the same time and place and in response to the same stimuli—a world at once accelerating and constricting—the painter Jackson Pollock and the musician Charlie Parker had accomplished similar revolutions in their own art forms. . . . All three men were working-class sons of matrifocal families who refused to 'adjust' to the conformist society of mid-century or the accepted styles of their disciplines, and for their efforts were labeled psychopaths and falsely associated with violence. Each ignored the critical authorities in their field and stood emotionally naked before their audiences, spewing words, notes, or paintdrops that were like the fiery rain of a volcano: The rain captured the passing moment in a luminous veil of particulars that depicted the universal as an expression of the artist's own self. . . . [Parker] played with the raw energy of a high-power line, and it was that stabbing electricity that Jack had attempted to put into *On the Road,* that mortal sense that the candle must burn furiously, else the times will surely snuff it out."

After retyping his giant roll of manuscript, Kerouac confidently submitted it to Robert Giroux, the editor who had handled *The Town and the City*. Giroux rejected it, becoming the first of many editors to do so. Part of the problem was the experimental prose, but even after Kerouac had reluctantly revised the manuscript to read in a more conventional style, he was unable to sell *On the Road*. The greatest barrier to its acceptance was the author's empathy with social outcasts. Kerouac wrote of the dignity and spirituality of blacks, Mexicans, hobos, and even drug addicts. His attitudes denied "complacency and middle-class notions of propriety and status"; they "seemed incomprehensible in 1957," wrote John Tytell in *Naked Angels: The Lives and Literature of the Beat Generation*. "One of the readers for Viking Press, for example, while appreciating Kerouac's lavish power, was dismayed by the raw sociology of the book, finding in it the quintessence of 'everything that is bad and horrible about this otherwise wonderful age we live in.' The characters were irredeemable psychopaths and hopeless neurotics who lived exclusively for sensation. This judgment, delivered prior to publication, can stand as a sign of how those born before the war would see the book."

*On the Road* was apparently unpublishable, but Kerouac remained passionately committed to his confessional style. In fact, the six years between *On the Road's* completion and its publication were the most productive of the author's life. He began a series of novels which he thought of as one vast story, in the tradition of Proust's *Remembrance of Things Past*. As he moved between New York, San Francisco, and Mexico City, Kerouac paused for intense writing sessions that yielded more than eight books, including *Tristessa, Doctor Sax: Faust Part Three,* and *Visions of Cody*. In them he told the stories of his family and friends, striving to do so with complete emotional honesty. His approach could be exhausting.

Kerouac wrote *The Subterraneans* in response to his breakup with a woman he called "Mardou Fox" in the book. On the day Kerouac realized their affair was over, he swallowed some benzedrine, inserted a roll of teletype paper in his typewriter, and in three days produced what is considered one of his best novels. Kerouac characterized that effort to Berrigan as "really a fantastic athletic feat as well as mental. . . . After I was done . . . I was pale as a sheet and had lost fifteen pounds and looked strange in the mirror." Kerouac was able to maintain unswerving faith in the value of his own writing, but he was tormented by the fact that no publisher would accept his work during those years. In 1954 he found a measure of relief from his frustration in his study of Buddhist texts. "It does not seem difficult to explain Kerouac's attraction to Buddhism," mused Dardess.

"Torn as he often was by the paradox of God's seemingly simultaneous presence and absence in the world he saw, Kerouac could seize with relief on Buddhism's annihilation of the paradox." Through his later novels, the author was one of the first people to introduce the concepts of Buddhism to the American public.

While Kerouac remained largely anonymous, some of his friends were becoming well known. In 1952 John Clellon Holmes published an article entitled "This Is the Beat Generation," using a term Kerouac had offhandedly coined to compare modern feelings of disillusionment with those of the Lost Generation writers. In 1955 Allen Ginsberg and other poets gave an influential reading at the Six Gallery in San Francisco, and were subsequently featured in a widely-read issue of *Evergreen Review*. Ginsberg's *Howl* was the subject of a highly-publicized obscenity trial in 1956. By that year there was sufficient public awareness of the emerging Beat writers for Viking Press to risk purchasing *On the Road,* after Kerouac agreed to extensive cuts, revisions, and name changes (Kerouac is "Sal Paradise" in the novel and Neal Cassady is "Dean Moriarty"). Its 1957 publication was hailed as "a historic occasion" in the *New York Times* by Gilbert Millstein, the editor who had earlier commissioned Holmes's "This Is the Beat Generation" article. He wrote: "*On the Road* is the most beautifully executed, the clearest and most important utterance yet made by the generation Kerouac himself named years ago as 'beat,' and whose principal avatar he is. Just as, more than any other novel of the Twenties, 'The Sun Also Rises' came to be regarded as the testament of the 'Lost Generation,' so it seems certain that 'On the Road' will come to be known as that of the 'Beat Generation'. . . . There are sections . . . in which the writing is of a beauty almost breathtaking. There is a description of a cross-country automobile ride fully the equal, for example, of the train ride told by Thomas Wolfe in 'Of Time and the River.' There are details of a trip to Mexico . . . that are, by turns, awesome, tender and funny. . . . 'On the Road' is a major novel."

Most critics perceived the book in a different light, however. McNally summarized: "The *Times Book Review* waffled, first praising the book as 'enormously readable and entertaining,' then dismissing it as 'a sideshow—the freaks are fascinating although they are hardly part of our lives'. . . . It was 'verbal goofballs' to *Saturday Review,* 'infantile, perversely negative' to the *Herald Tribune,* 'lack[ed] . . . seriousness' to *Commonweal,* 'like a slob running a temperature' to the *Hudson Review,* and a 'series of Neanderthal grunts' to *Encounter.* The *New Yorker* labeled Dean Moriarty 'a wild and incomprehensible ex-convict'; the *Atlantic* thought him 'more convincing as an eccentric than as a representative of any segment of humanity,' and *Time* diagnosed him as a victim of the Ganser Syndrome, whereby people weren't really mad—they only seemed to be." Mc-Nally concluded: "To understand *On the Road* one somehow needed an affinity for the intuitive and the sensual, for the romantic quest as opposed to the generally analytic realm of the critics. Since most critics had never experienced anything like the *Road,* they denied its existence as art and proclaimed it a 'Beat Generation' tract of rebellion, then pilloried it as immoral." "According to the critics who wrote these reviews, ecstasy, when it occurred in a non-institutional setting like the backseat of a car, was indistinguishable from mental and physical illness, filth, incoherence, deceit, criminal violence, degeneracy, and mindless folly," concurred Dardess. "This assumption said much, for those who had ears to hear it, about the depth of those critics' fears of their emotions and of their pride in the narrow limits of their intellects. But it did not say much of anything about *On the Road.*"

Readers ignored the critics' negative appraisal of Kerouac and made *On the Road* a best seller for many weeks. The book became a symbol for a rapidly evolving social movement. Kerouac was suddenly a celebrity, faced with many offers to explain the Beat phenomenon in lecture halls, on radio, and on television. Public speaking was a nerve-wracking ordeal for him, but he did his best to publicize his novel. Unfortunately, these engagements often ended with Kerouac "uselessly trying to explain mystical poetry to pragmatic reporters who wanted nothing from him but hot copy," suggested McNally. The adulation of his fans proved even harder for him to cope with than the hostility of his critics. More than once, the writer was mobbed by crowds who came to hear him read. "Abuse he could comprehend, but not the blankness of an image blinded fan," observed McNally. Kerouac began drinking heavily, and "the private person inside him began to crumble. . . . Even immersed in his booze, 'my liquid suit of armor, my shield which not even Flash Gordon's super ray gun could penetrate,' it was difficult for him to talk with people. Hungover and trembling, he groaned to John Holmes, 'I can't stand to meet anybody anymore. They talk to me like I wasn't me.' The fans wanted Jack to be Dean Moriarty, the free American cowboy, the limitless man who lived on life's mental

frontiers. What no one beyond friends knew was that *On the Road* was six years old and superseded by a body of work Jack considered superior."

Kerouac's stack of unpublished manuscripts ranged from the tender memories of a brother who died in childhood, simply expressed in *Visions of Gerard,* to the baroque surrealism of *Doctor Sax: Faust Part Three,* a novel of guilt and shadows. All of it was deemed unpublishable by *On the Road*'s editor. "Viking was not interested in bringing out a quirky legend, merely books," observed Gifford and Lee. Kerouac responded to the demand for a saleable manuscript with ten days of writing that produced *The Dharma Bums.* According to Gifford and Lee, *The Dharma Bums* was written "with an air of patient explanation, as though addressed to a book editor." Just as *On the Road* focused on Neal Cassady, *The Dharma Bums* provided a portrait of Gary Snyder, a poet and student of Oriental religions who had become Kerouac's friend in 1955. Viking again insisted that names be changed to avoid possible lawsuits, so Kerouac appeared as "Ray Smith," Snyder as "Japhy Ryder." *The Dharma Bums* characterized Ray and Japhy as modern religious wanderers in search of dharma, or truth. It is especially notable for Japhy Ryder's speech describing his vision of "a great rucksack revolution" of millions of young Americans, all becoming "Dharma Bums refusing to subscribe to the general demand that they consume . . . all that crap they didn't really want anyway such as refrigerators, TV sets, . . . certain hair oils and deodorants and general junk you finally always see a week later in the garbage anyway." It was an accurate prophecy of the hippies of the next decade.

The rest of Kerouac's work was published piecemeal, and never appeared as the interconnected series of novels he envisioned. *The Subterraneans, Doctor Sax: Faust Part Three, Maggie Cassidy: A Love Story, Mexico City Blues, Tristessa,* and *Lonesome Traveler* all came out within two years, most of them as inexpensive paperbacks. "Despite the fact that these titles included some of his strongest and most original spontaneous extended narrative, especially *Doctor Sax,* . . . the critics paid less and less attention to [Kerouac] as a serious writer in the furor over the emergence of the beat generation [as a social phenomenon]," wrote Ann Charters in *Dictionary of Literary Biography.* Alfred Kazin's comments on *The Dharma Bums* typify most critics' dismissal of Kerouac as an artist. Kazin wrote in *Harper's:* "It is ridiculous that novels can now be sent off as quickly as they are written and published immediately afterwards in order to satisfy the hopped-up taste of people who, when they open a novel, want to feel that they are not missing a thing. The sluttishness of a society whose mass ideal seems to be unlimited consumption of all possible goods and services is the reason for the 'success' of writers [like Kerouac]."

Kerouac was unable to finish any writing projects for almost four years after completing *The Dharma Bums* late in 1958. He made several false starts, but even in his mother's house, his privacy was invaded by reporters and teenaged admirers who slipped through his bedroom window to steal his journals. Finally Kerouac retreated to the tranquillity of a friend's cabin in California's remote Big Sur region, but once there he suffered a serious alcoholic breakdown, including a series of terrifying hallucinations of himself as a prize in a war between angels and devils. It took him a year to recuperate from the experience, but it provided him with the material for what Gifford and Lee referred to as "his capstone novel," *Big Sur,* "his single book dealing with the effects of the fame which had destroyed him." Ironically, when *Big Sur* was published in 1962 "it received excellent reviews, perhaps because it portrayed the 'King of the Beats' brought low, perhaps because of its frightening honesty."

But the joy had gone out of writing for Kerouac, as he told Ted Berrigan in a *Paris Review* interview: "I had a ritual once of lighting a candle and writing by its light and blowing it out when I was done for the night . . . also kneeling and praying before starting . . . but now I simply hate to write. . . . Frankly I do feel my mind is going. So another 'ritual' as you call it, is to pray to Jesus to preserve my sanity and my energy so I can help my family: That being my paralyzed mother, and my wife, and the ever-present kitties. . . . What I do now is write something like an average of 8,000 words a sitting, in the middle of the night, and another about a week later, resting and sighing in between. I really hate to write." Kerouac became increasingly reclusive throughout the 1960s, and in 1969 he died of a stomach hemorrhage caused by chronic alcoholism.

Several years after Kerouac's death, his book *Visions of Cody* was published. Like *On the Road, Visions of Cody* was a prolonged meditation on Neal Cassady. In fact, the opening section was one of the false starts Kerouac made on the story that eventually became *On the Road. Visions of Cody* covered the same events as Kerouac's most famous book, but it was written in a style so unusual that he'd only been

able to publish excerpts of it during his lifetime. When printed in its entirety in 1973, the book prompted *New York Times* reviewer Anatole Broyard to "propose, once and for all, a pox on 'spontaneity' in fiction. Spontaneity is a psychological, not a literary, quality. . . . The notion that what comes naturally is naturally welcome is one of the great idiocies of our age. What is *Visions of Cody* about? Well, I've read it and I'm damned if I know." But while reviews like Broyard's echoed the hostility of Kerouac's original critics, more of them reflected a growing respect for the author's work. Aaron Latham's *New York Times Book Review* assessment of *Visions of Cody* began by stating that "*On the Road* was the *Huckleberry Finn* of the mid-20th century," and went on to compare Kerouac to Thomas Wolfe, Louis-Ferdinand Celine, Mark Twain, and Jean Genet. "You will find some of Kerouac's very best writing in this book," summarized Latham. "It is funny. It is serious. It is eloquent. To read *On the Road* but not *Visions of Cody* is to take a nice sightseeing tour but to forgo the spectacular rapids of Jack Kerouac's wildest writing."

After Kerouac's death, his third wife sealed most of his papers and unpublished manuscripts. Only after her death were such items as Kerouac's voluminous correspondence and manuscript poems made available for publication by the heirs of his widow's estate. This accounts for the small publishing boom of Kerouac material beginning in 1992. Small presses such as City Lights Books and Grey Fox released new volumes of Kerouac's poetry, including *Old Angel Midnight* and *Pomes All Sizes.* Lawrence Ferlinghetti, who supervised the publication of *Pomes All Sizes,* told the *Los Angeles Times* that the work sheds light on a crucial period of Kerouac's life between 1954 and 1965. "It spans the last years of [Kerouac's] life," Ferlinghetti explained. "He became more and more alcoholic, and there's evidence of that in some of the poems." City Lights editor Nancy Peters likewise noted that the poems "show a side of [Kerouac] people don't think about. His sensitivity to the sadness of life is really apparent in this book."

Even more excitement was generated by the publication of some of Kerouac's correspondence, including *Jack Kerouac: Selected Letters 1940-1956,* edited by Ann Charters. The letters in the volume include those Kerouac wrote to Cassady and Ginsberg during the early years of their friendships, as well as correspondence with various book editors and with his first wife. In *Review of Contemporary Fiction,* Steven Moore called *Selected Letters* "the greatest addition to the Kerouac canon in recent years."

Chicago *Tribune Books* correspondent Thomas Mc-Gonigle likewise observed that with the publication of the volume, "the background to the writing of *On the Road* can be authoritatively filled in. No less important, these letters deepen our appreciation of how carefully crafted *On the Road* is and further confirm what is evident each time one re-reads the book—that it is a work of high literary ambition and a layered depth of meaning." The letters, McGonigle concluded, reveal Kerouac "to be overwhelmed by his passion for the printed word, by his hunger for experience and by his ability to describe both his passion and hunger in language that sings."

The mid-1990s also saw publication of an important omnibus volume, *The Portable Jack Kerouac,* also edited by Charters, and a CD-ROM devoted to the author entitled *A Jack Kerouac ROMnibus.* While the computer disk offers information on Kerouac and his friends—including video and audio presentations—the omnibus volume presents selections from a wide variety of Kerouac's writings, arranged in an order that suggests autobiography. Moore declared that *The Portable Jack Kerouac* is "just what is needed to elevate Kerouac from his lingering status as a Beatnik chronicler to his deserved status as one of the greatest American novelists of our century." In the *New Yorker,* Joyce Carol Oates contends that *The Portable Jack Kerouac* "may well be seminal in a reevaluation of Kerouac's position in the literature of mid-twentieth-century America—a richly varied affluence of 'high' and 'low' art that permanently changed the course of our fiction."

In the *Dictionary of Literary Biography,* Charters has called Kerouac's body of work "one of the most ambitious projects conceived by any modern writer in its scope, depth, and variety." Tytell commented similarly: "In so many ways there is something essentially American about Kerouac's writing; his restless energies could never settle for a final form, and each of his novels demonstrates an eager variety in their differences from each other, and from conventional expectations of what novels should be like." Seymour Krim told the *National Observer,* "The only way you can understand Kerouac is as an American phenomenon. He is in the great American tradition of fiction from Thomas Wolfe right back through Mark Twain to Herman Melville. He did a lot to bring our fiction back home. His wild enthusiasm for all that is right and wrong with the country is really unique." Latham also emphasized Kerouac's role in revitalizing twentieth-century American prose: "When an effete literary language . . . threatened to silence all other voices, Kerouac . . . discovered the vernacular."

Kerouac's freedom with language is generally acknowledged as a liberating influence on many writers who came after him, including Ken Kesey, Charles Bukowski, Tom Robbins, and Richard Brautigan, as well as songwriter Bob Dylan. His nakedly confessional style led to the subjective reportage or "New Journalism" of Hunter S. Thompson and Tom Wolfe. Latham related that "when *On the Road* made Jack Kerouac famous, [Truman] Capote delivered his famous one-liner: 'That's not writing, it's just type-writing.' But would he have written *In Cold Blood* as a non-fiction novel if Jack Kerouac had not helped to make the form respectable?"

Although Kerouac came to bitterly resent being cast as a social figurehead, his novels did make a significant impact on the lives of many who read them. According to Tytell, "*On the Road* still has a large and growing audience. For many, it was the book that most motivated dissatisfaction with the atmosphere of unquestioning acceptance that stifled the fifties; remarkably, despite the passage of time and its relative unpopularity among older university instructors, its audience grows, and young people especially gravitate to a force in it." Charters concluded: "What has been increasingly clear in the last twenty years is that the fabric of American culture has never been the same since 'Sal Paradise' and 'Dean Moriarty' went on the road. As Burroughs said, 'Kerouac opened a million coffee bars and sold a trillion Levis to both sexes. . . . Woodstock rises from his pages.'"

*BIOGRAPHICAL/CRITICAL SOURCES:*

*BOOKS*

Anstee, Rod, editor, *Jack Kerouac: The Bootleg Era: A Bibliography of Pirated Editions,* Water Row Press, 1994.
*Authors in the News,* Volume 1, Gale (Detroit, MI), 1976.
Balakian, Nona, and Charles Simmons, *The Creative Present: Notes on Contemporary American Fiction,* Doubleday (New York City), 1963.
Bartlett, Lee, *The Beats: Essays of Criticism,* McFarland (Jefferson, NC), 1981, pp. 115-26.
Cassady, Carolyn, *Heart Beat: My Life with Jack and Neal,* Creative Arts Book Co. (Berkley, CA), 1977.
Cassady, Carolyn, *Off the Road: My Years with Cassady, Kerouac, and Ginsberg,* Morrow (New York City), 1990.
Challis, Chris, *Quest for Kerouac,* Faber (Winchester, MA), 1984.

Charters, Ann, *Kerouac: A Biography,* Straight Arrow (San Francisco), 1973, reprinted, St. Martin's (New York City), 1994.

Charters, Ann, *A Bibliography of Works by Jack Kerouac, 1939-1975,* Phoenix Book Shop (New York City), 1975.

Clark, Tom, *Jack Kerouac,* Harcourt (San Diego, CA), 1984, reprinted, Paragon House (New York City), 1990.

*Concise Dictionary of American Literary Biography: The New Consciousness, 1941-1968,* Gale, 1987.

*Contemporary Literary Criticism,* Gale, Volume 1, 1973, Volume 2, 1974, Volume 3, 1975, Volume 5, 1976, Volume 14, 1980, Volume 29, 1984, Volume 61, 1990.

Cook, Bruce, *The Beat Generation,* Scribner (New York City), 1971.

*Dictionary of Literary Biography,* Gale, Volume 2: *American Novelists since World War II,* 1978, Volume 16: *The Beats: Literary Bohemians in Postwar America,* Gale, 1983.

*Dictionary of Literary Biography Documentary Series,* Volume 3, Gale, 1983.

Donaldson, Scott, editor, *On the Road: Text and Criticism,* Viking, 1979.

Feied, Frederick, *No Pie in the Sky: The Hobo as American Culture Hero in the Works of Jack London, John Dos Passos, and Jack Kerouac,* Citadel (Secaucus, NJ), 1964.

Fiedler, Leslie, *Waiting for the End,* Stein & Day (Briarcliff Manor, NY), 1964.

French, Warren, editor, *The Fifties: Fiction, Poetry, Drama,* Everett/Edwards (DeLand, FL), 1970.

French, *Jack Kerouac,* Twayne (Boston, MA), 1986.

Fuller, Edmund, *Man in Modern Fiction: Some Minority Opinions on Contemporary American Writings,* Random House (New York City), 1958.

Gaffie, Luc, *Jack Kerouac: The New Picaroon,* Postillion Press (Southfield, MI), 1977.

Gifford, Barry, *Kerouac's Town,* Capra (Santa Barbara, CA), 1973, revised edition, Creative Arts Book Co., 1977.

Gifford, and Lawrence Lee, *Jack's Book: An Oral Biography of Jack Kerouac,* St. Martin's (New York City), 1978, reprinted, 1994.

Ginsberg, Allen, *Allen Verbatim: Lectures on Poetry, Politics, Consciousness,* McGraw, 1974.

Hipkiss, Robert A., *Jack Kerouac: Prophet of the New Romanticism,* University of Kansas Press (Lawrence, KS), 1977.

Holmes, John Clellon, *Nothing More to Declare,* Dutton (New York City), 1967.

Huebel, Harry Russell, *Jack Kerouac,* Boise State University (Boise, ID), 1979.

Hunt, Tim, *Kerouac's Crooked Road: Development of a Fiction,* Archon Books (Hamden, CT), 1981.

Jarvis, Charles E., *Visions of Kerouac,* Ithaca Press (Lowell, MA), 1973, third edition, 1994.

Johnson, Joyce, *Minor Characters: A Young Woman's Coming-of-Age in the Beat Orbit of Jack Kerouac,* Anchor Books (New York City), 1994.

Jones, Granville H., *Lectures on Modern Novelists,* Carnegie Institute (Pittsburgh, PA), 1963.

Jones, James T., *A Map of Mexico City Blues: Jack Kerouac as Poet,* Southern Illinois University Press (Carbondale, IL), 1992.

Kerouac, Jack, *Lonesome Traveler,* McGraw, 1960.

Kerouac, and Allen Ginsberg, *Take Care of My Ghost, Ghost,* limited edition, Ghost Press, 1977.

Kerouac, and Carolyn Cassady, *Dear Carolyn: Letters to Carolyn Cassady,* Unspeakable Visions, 1983.

Lindberg, Gary, *The Confidence Man in American Literature,* Oxford University Press (Oxford, England), 1982.

McClure, Michael, *Scratching the Beat Surface: Essays on New Vision from Blake to Kerouac,* Penguin, 1994.

McDarragh, Fred W., *Kerouac and His Friends: A Beat Generation Album,* William Morrow (New York City), 1985.

McDarragh, Fred W. and Gloria S. McDarragh, *Beat Generation: Glory Days in Greenwich Village,* Schirmer (New York City), 1996.

McNally, Dennis, *Desolate Angel: Jack Kerouac, the Beat Generation, and America,* McGraw, 1979.

Milewski, Robert J., *Jack Kerouac: An Annotated Bibliography of Secondary Sources, 1944-1979,* Scarecrow (Metuchen, NJ), 1981.

Montgomery, John, *The Kerouac We Knew: Unposed Portraits: Action Shots,* Fels & Firn (Kentfield, CA), 1982.

Moore, Harry T., editor, *Contemporary American Novelists,* Southern Illinois University Press (Carbondale, IL), 1964.

Motier, Donald, *Gerard: The Influence of Jack Kerouac's Brother on His Life and Writing,* Beaulier Press (Harrisburg, PA), 1991.

Nicosia, Gerald, *Memory Babe: A Critical Biography of Jack Kerouac,* Grove, 1983, reprinted, University of California Press (Berkeley, CA), 1994.

Nisonger, T. E., *Jack Kerouac: A Bibliography of Biographical and Critical Material, 1950-1979,* Bull Bibliography, 1980.

Parker, Brad, *Jack Kerouac: An Introduction,* Lowell Corporation for the Humanities (Lowell, MA), 1989.

Parkinson, Thomas, editor, *A Casebook on the Beat,* Crowell (New York City), 1961.

Podhoretz, Norman, *Doings and Undoings,* Farrar, Straus, 1964.

Tanner, Tony, *City of Words,* Harper (New York City), 1971.

Tytell, John, *Naked Angels: The Lives and Literature of the Beat Generation,* McGraw, 1976.

Waldmeir, Joseph J., editor, *Recent American Fiction,* Houghton (Boston, MA), 1963.

Weinreich, Regina, *The Spontaneous Poetics of Jack Kerouac: A Study of Fiction,* Southern Illinois University Press, 1987.


*PERIODICALS*


*American Literature,* May, 1974.

*Atlantic,* July, 1965.

*Best Sellers,* February 15, 1968.

*Books,* December, 1966.

*Books Abroad,* summer, 1967.

*Books and Bookmen,* May, 1969.

*Chicago Review,* winter-spring, 1959.

*Chicago Tribune,* August 22, 1986; March 16, 1994, p. 8.

*Commonweal,* February 2, 1959.

*Contemporary Literature,* summer, 1974.

*Critique: Studies in Modern Fiction,* Volume 14, number 3, 1973.

*Detroit Free Press,* November 13, 1986.

*Detroit News,* November 23, 1995, p. 3F.

*Esquire,* June, 1983, pp. 158-60, 162-64, 166-67.

*Evergreen Review,* summer, 1958; spring, 1959.

*Harper's,* October, 1959.

*Hudson Review,* winter, 1959-60; spring, 1967.

*Illinois Quarterly,* April 1973, pp. 52-61.

*Listener,* June 27, 1968.

*Los Angeles Times,* September 19, 1986; September 20, 1986; June 4, 1992, p. 1E.

*Midwest Quarterly,* summer, 1973.

*National Observer,* February 5, 1968; December 9, 1968.

*New Republic,* April 24, 1995, p. 43.

*New Statesman,* November 23, 1973.

*Newsweek,* December 19, 1960.

*New Yorker,* March 27, 1995, pp. 96-100.

*New York Post,* March 10, 1959.

*New York Review of Books,* May 20, 1965; April 11, 1968.

*New York Times,* September 5, 1957; May 4, 1965; June 8, 1965; January 9, 1973; April 16, 1986; June 11, 1995, p. 8.

*New York Times Book Review,* May 2, 1965; February 26, 1967; February 18, 1968; January 28, 1973; April 9, 1995, p. 2.

*Observer* (London), November 19, 1967.

*Observer Review,* November 19, 1967.

*Paris Review,* summer, 1968.

*Partisan Review,* Volume 40, number 2, 1973.

*Playboy,* June, 1959.

*Prairie Schooner,* spring, 1974.

*Reporter,* April 3, 1958.

*Review of Contemporary Fiction,* Volume 3, number 2, 1983; spring, 1995, pp. 161-62.

*Saturday Review,* January 11, 1958; May 2, 1959; June 12, 1965; December 2, 1972.

*Small Press Review,* March, 1983.

*South Atlantic Quarterly,* autumn, 1974.

*Spectator,* November 24, 1967; March 28, 1969; August 10, 1974; August 24, 1974.

*Stand,* Volume 16, number 2, 1975.

*Tamarack Review,* spring, 1959.

*Time,* February 23, 1968.

*Times Literary Supplement,* May 26, 1966; February 1, 1968; March 27, 1969; April 6, 1973; November 2, 1973; September 13, 1974; April 22, 1977; September 1, 1995, p. 22.

*Tribune Books* (Chicago), March 26, 1995, pp. 1, 9.

*Village Voice,* September 18, 1957; November 12, 1958.

*Virginia Quarterly Review,* spring, 1973.

*Washington Post,* October 22, 1969; August 2, 1982.

*Washington Post Book World,* April 8, 1973; March 12, 1995, pp. 1, 14.


*OTHER*


*What Happened to Kerouac?* (documentary film), produced by Richard Lerner, 1986.

*A Jack Kerouac ROMnibus* (CD-ROM), Largely Literary Designs, 1995.


*OBITUARIES:*


*PERIODICALS*


*Detroit Free Press,* October 22, 1969.

*L'Express,* October 27-November 2, 1969.

*Newsweek,* November 3, 1969.

*New York Times,* October 22, 1969.

*Publishers Weekly,* November 3, 1969.

*Rolling Stone,* November 29, 1969.

*Time,* October 31, 1969.

*Variety,* October 29, 1969.

*Village Voice,* October 30, 1969; November 28, 1969.

*Washington Post,* October 22, 1969.*

**KEROUAC, John**
See KEROUAC, Jean-Louis Lebris de

\*    \*    \*

**KESSLER, Lauren J.   1950-**

*PERSONAL:* Born April 4, 1950, in New York, NY; daughter of Sidney (an auditor for the Internal Revenue Service) and Margarita (Falk) Kessler; married Thomas Hager (a magazine editor), July 7, 1984; children: Jackson, Zane, Elizabeth. *Ethnicity:* "Caucasian." *Education:* Northwestern University, B.S.J. (with honors), 1971; University of Oregon, M.S. (with honors), 1975; University of Washington, Seattle, Ph.D., 1980.

*ADDRESSES: Home*—Eugene, OR. *Office*—School of Journalism and Communication, University of Oregon, Eugene, OR 97403. *E-mail*—ljk@oregon.uoregon.edu.

*CAREER:* CNA Financial Corp., Chicago, IL, advertising copywriter, 1971-72; *Burlingame Villager,* Burlingame, CA, city hall reporter, 1972-73; Southern Illinois University, Carbondale, instructor in journalism, 1974-75; Linfield College, McMinnville, OR, assistant professor of communication, 1975-80; University of Oregon, Eugene, assistant professor, 1980-84, associate professor, 1984-91, professor of journalism, 1991—, director of graduate studies and research, 1986-88, 1994—.

*AWARDS, HONORS:* Annenberg scholar at University of Southern California, 1986; Sigma Delta Chi award, 1987, for social issues reporting; Council for the Advancement of Secondary Education (CASE) award, 1987, for excellence in magazine writing; Freedom Forum Professors Publishing grant, Gannett Foundation, 1992, and Frances Fuller Victor Literary Arts Award, 1994, both for *Stubborn Twig: Three Generations in the Life of a Japanese-American Family.*

*WRITINGS:*

*The Dissident Press: Alternative Journalism in American History,* Sage Publications (Beverly Hills, CA), 1984.
(With Duncan McDonald) *When Words Collide: A Journalist's Guide to Grammar and Style,* Wadsworth (Belmont, CA), 1984, new edition, 1996.

(With husband, Thomas Hager) *Staying Young: The Whole Truth about Aging and What You Can Do to Slow Its Progress,* Facts on File (New York City), 1987, published as *Aging Well,* Simon & Schuster (New York City), 1990.
(With McDonald) *Mastering the Message: Writing with Substance and Style,* Wadsworth, 1989.
*After All These Years: Sixties Idealism in a Different World,* Thunder's Mouth Press (New York City), 1990.
(With McDonald) *The Search: Information Gathering in the Information Age,* Wadsworth, 1991.
*Stubborn Twig: Three Generations in the Life of a Japanese-American Family,* Random House (New York City), 1993.
*Full Court Press: A Season of Women's Basketball,* Dutton (New York City), 1997.

Regional correspondent for *Salem Statesman-Journal,* 1976-78; Oregon correspondent for *Newsweek* magazine, 1987-90. Contributor to *Encyclopedia of the American West, American National Biography,* and *Dictionary of Literary Biography.* Contributor to periodicals, including *Self, Us, Modern Maturity, Working Mother, American Journalism,* and *Oregon Historical Quarterly.*

*SIDELIGHTS:* Lauren J. Kessler told *CA:* "I write in the genre of literary nonfiction, which melds the power of truth to the drama of fiction. I am motivated both by the story—its narrative thread, its subtexts and contexts, its enduring themes—and by the act of writing itself. Writing is how I learn, not just about my subjects but about myself. It is how I make connections, how I make sense of the world and my place in it. Writing for me is no longer an act of choice but one of necessity. When I am not writing, I do not feel quite human.

"I choose my nonfiction subjects because they are relatively small tales that open windows onto very big ideas. *After All These Years* examined the lives of 1960s radicals almost thirty years later. These small personal stories opened the window to larger issues of the formation and persistence of values in our fast-paced culture, the meaning of integrity, the nature of social responsibility. *Stubborn Twig* was an intimate chronicle of three generations in the life of one Japanese-American family, but it was not just a family biography. It was also a book about what it means to be an American, about being a stranger in a strange land, about the deep and persistent current of racism in our country. *Full Court* is ostensibly about one season in the life of a women's basketball team. But it is really about gender politics in sports, self-esteem, self-respect and the women who are in it to win it.

"My writing process has changed dramatically since I became a mother—now thrice over. Before children, when I hit a rough spot in a chapter, I whiled away the rest of the afternoon arranging pictures in photo albums and defrosting the refrigerator. Now I stay put and ride it out. I have to. I may have only two non-kid hours to write that day, and I'm not going to waste them."

\* \* \*

## KEYES, Daniel 1927-

*PERSONAL:* Born August 9, 1927, in Brooklyn, NY; son of William and Betty (Alicke) Keyes; married Aurea Vazquez (a fashion stylist, photographer, and artist), October 14, 1952; children: Hillary Ann, Leslie Joan. *Education:* Brooklyn College (now Brooklyn College of the City University of New York), A.B., 1950, A.M., 1961.

*ADDRESSES: Office*—Department of English, Ohio University, Athens, OH 45701. *Agent*—Marcy Posner, William Morris Agency, 1325 Avenue of the Americas, New York, NY 10019.

*CAREER:* Stadium Publishing Co., New York City, associate fiction editor, 1951-52; Fenko & Keyes Photography, Inc., New York City, co-owner, 1953; high school teacher of English, Brooklyn, NY, 1954-55, 1957-62; Wayne State University, Detroit, MI, instructor in English, 1962-66; Ohio University, Athens, lecturer, 1966-72, professor of English, 1972—, director of creative writing center, 1973-74, 1977-78. Supervising producer of television movie *The Mad Housers,* 1990. *Military service:* U.S. Maritime Service, senior assistant purser, 1945-47.

*MEMBER:* PEN, Societe des Auteurs et Compos-iteurs Dramatiques, Authors Guild, Authors League of America, Dramatists Guild (full voting member), Mystery Writers of America, MacDowell Colony Fellows.

*AWARDS, HONORS:* Hugo Award, World Science Fiction Convention, 1959, for "Flowers for Algernon" (short story); Nebula Award, Science Fiction Writers of America, 1966, for *Flowers for Algernon* (novel); fellow, Yaddo artist colony, 1967; fellow,

MacDowell artist colony, 1967; special award, Mystery Writers of America, 1981, for *The Minds of Billy Milligan;* Kurd Lasswitz Award for best book by a foreign author, 1986, for *Die Leben des Billy Milligan,* the German translation of *The Minds of Billy Milligan;* Edgar Allan Poe Award nomination, Mystery Writers of America, 1986, for *Unveiling Claudia: A True Story of a Serial Murder;* individual artists fellowship, Ohio Arts Council, 1986-87; Baker Fund Award, Ohio University, 1986; Award of Honor, Distinguished Alumnus Brooklyn College, 1988.

*WRITINGS:*

FICTION

*Flowers for Algernon* (novel), Harcourt (New York City), 1966, Modern Classics Edition, 1995.
*The Touch* (novel), Harcourt, 1968, published in England as *The Contaminated Man,* Mayflower (London), 1973.
*The Fifth Sally* (novel), Houghton (Boston), 1980.
*Daniel Keyes Collected Stories,* Hayakawa (Tokyo), 1993.
*Daniel Keyes Reader,* Hayakawa, 1994.

NONFICTION

*The Minds of Billy Milligan* (Book-of-the-Month Club selection), Random House, 1981, revised edition, with afterword, Bantam (New York City), 1982.
*Unveiling Claudia: A True Story of a Serial Murder,* Bantam, 1986.
*The Milligan Wars* (sequel to *The Minds of Billy Milligan*), Hayakawa, 1993, Bantam, 1996.

OTHER

Also contributor to numerous anthologies, including *Ten Top Stories,* edited by David A. Sohn, Bantam, 1964. Contributor of fiction to periodicals. Associate editor, *Marvel Science Fiction,* 1951.

Keyes's works have been translated into numerous foreign languages, including Danish, Dutch, French, German, Italian, Swedish, and Spanish.

"The Daniel Keyes Collection," a repository of papers and manuscripts, is housed at the Alden Library, Ohio University, Athens, OH.

*ADAPTATIONS:* Television play "The Two Worlds of Charlie Gordon," based on the short story "Flowers for Algernon," CBS Playhouse, February 22, 1961; feature film *Charly,* based on the novel *Flowers for Algernon,* starring Cliff Robertson, winner of an Academy Award for this role, Cinerama, 1968; two-act play *Flowers for Algernon,* adapted by David Rogers, Dramatic Publishing, 1969; dramatic musical *Charlie and Algernon,* first produced at Citadel Theater, Alberta, Canada, December 21, 1978, produced at Queens Theater, London, England, June 14, 1979, first produced in the United States at Terrace Theater, Kennedy Center, Washington, D.C., March 8, 1980, produced on Broadway at Helen Hayes Theater, September 4, 1980; other adaptations of *Flowers for Algernon* include: French stage play, first produced at Theater Espace Massalia, Marseille, France, October 11, 1982; Irish radio monodrama, first broadcast by Radio Telefis Eireann, Dublin, Ireland, October 25, 1983; Australian stage-play, produced by Jigsaw Theater Company, March, 1984; Polish stage play, adapted by Jerzy Gudejka, first produced at W. Horzyca Memorial Theater of Torun, Torun, Poland, March 3, 1985; Japanese stage play, first produced at Kinokuniya Theater, Tokyo, Japan, January 20, 1987; and a radio play, Czechoslovak Radio Prague, 1988.

*WORK IN PROGRESS:* A novel.

*SIDELIGHTS:* The author of several works focusing on psychological themes, Daniel Keyes told *CA* that he is "fascinated by the complexities of the human mind." Keyes is perhaps best known for his novel *Flowers for Algernon,* the story of Charlie, a mentally retarded man who is transformed into a genius by psychosurgery, only to eventually regress. *Flowers for Algernon,* which originally appeared as a short story in the *Magazine of Fantasy and Science Fiction,* is viewed by a *Times Literary Supplement* contributor as "a good example of that kind of science fiction which uses a persuasive hypothesis to explore emotional and moral issues. . . ." The reviewer continues that Keyes's ideas and speculations on the relationship between maturity and intelligence make *Flowers for Algernon* "a far more intelligent book than the vast majority of 'straight' novels. . . . Charlie's hopeless knowledge that he is destined to end in a home for the feeble-minded, a moron who knows that he is a moron, is painful, and Mr. Keyes has the technical equipment to prevent us from shrugging off the pain."

Two of Keyes's works, *The Fifth Sally* and *The Minds of Billy Milligan,* deal with the subject of multiple personalities and are dramatic recreations of

factual cases. The title character of *The Fifth Sally* is Sally Porter, a woman who harbors four personalities that embody her emotional states: Nola, an intellectual artist; Derry, a free-spirited tomboy; Bella, a promiscuous woman; and Jinx, a murderous personality. The novel examines the efforts of Sally and her doctor to fuse the four beings into one complete person. "This is an intriguing story," writes Mel Gilden in the *Los Angeles Times,* "but the reader is able to remain an observer rather than becoming emotionally involved. . . . Despite the intellectual distance maintained between Sally and reader, the book will reward almost anyone who reads it."

*The Minds of Billy Milligan* is based on the case of Billy Milligan, who was arrested on rape charges in Ohio in 1977 and who later became the first person in U.S. history to be acquitted of a major felony by reason of a multiple personality disorder. At the time of his arrest, Billy Milligan was found to possess no fewer than twenty-four personalities—three of them female—with ages ranging from three to twenty-four years old. Among Milligan's dominant personalities were Arthur, an Englishman in charge of all the others; Ragen, a violent Yugoslav who acted as physical protector; and Adalana, a nineteen-year-old lesbian who confessed to instituting the three rapes with which Milligan was charged. According to Keyes, these personalities, along with all the rest, would share "the spot"—control of Milligan's consciousness—whenever their distinctive qualities were needed.

The circumstances under which Keyes was contracted to write Milligan's story proved unusual: It was only after several of Milligan's selves read *Flowers for Algernon* that they agreed among themselves to work with the author. In *The Minds of Billy Milligan,* Keyes writes of a personality known as "The Teacher." The Teacher kept the memory of all the other beings in Milligan and provided much of the book's background information. Through the different personas, the author describes the life of a young man who had suffered years of mental and physical abuse at the hands of his stepfather, and how Milligan had sought solace and protection from the various people existing in him. After Milligan was arrested and sent to a correctional institution for observation, debate surfaced as to how to best classify his mental state. According to Robert Coles in the *New York Times Book Review,* "Keyes makes quite evident in *The Minds of Billy Milligan,* [that] historical tensions within the [medical] profession have yet to be resolved, and have, in fact, been given new expression in this instance. . . ." While the prosecuting attorneys insisted that Milligan be jailed, doctors and psychologists in Ohio debated the location and terms of such a patient's incarceration. "When he was found 'insane,'" Coles continues, "the arguments did not by any means abate. Was he a 'sociopath'—a liar, an impostor?. . . Was he a severely disturbed and dangerous 'psychotic' who required careful watching, lots of medication, maybe a course or two of electric shock treatment?"

Coles ultimately commends Keyes for telling "this complicated story well. It reads like a play: Billy's 'personalities' come onstage, leave to be replaced by others and then reappear." Peter Gorner finds this distracting; in a *Chicago Tribune* review of the book, he states that the author "interviews everybody, reconstructs, flashes back, and confuses the story in a chatty, conversational style. The alter egos seem to dance before our eyes like a stroboscope." However, in the opinion of David Johnston in the *Los Angeles Times*, "telling the stories of twenty-four different personalities would be a difficult task for any writer. To tell of two dozen personalities in one human body is an extremely complex task. Keyes, on balance, carries it off quite well. While it shortchanges the reader by limiting explanation of motives almost exclusively to Milligan's personalities, [*The Minds of Billy Milligan*] is nonetheless a fascinating work." Finally, *Washington Post Book World*, reviewer Joseph McLellan points out that "complexity is . . . the keynote of the Billy phenomenon and equally of its treatment by Daniel Keyes. The challenge of first unearthing this story . . . and then telling it intelligibly was a daunting one. He has carried it off brilliantly, bringing to the assignment not only a fine clarity but a special warmth, and empathy for the victim of circumstances and mental failings that made *Flowers for Algernon* one of the most memorable novels of the 1960s."

As in his two previous works, Keyes unravels the bizarre incidents in a mentally ill person's life in *Unveiling Claudia: A True Story of a Serial Murder.* Claudia Elaine Yasko, having known both the victims and the murderers in three Ohio killings in the late 1970s, fantasized herself as the murderer. She confessed to the homicides in 1978 but the charges were dropped once the real killers were accidentally discovered. Keyes's book records the incidents and attempts to explain why Yasko knew so much about the killings. Writes Gregor A. Preston in the *Library Journal,* "while not as intriguing as Billy Milligan, this is a masterfully told, absorbing story."

*BIOGRAPHICAL/CRITICAL SOURCES:*

*BOOKS*

Scholes, Robert, *Structural Fabulation,* University of Notre Dame Press (Notre Dame, IN), 1975.

*PERIODICALS*

*Chicago Tribune,* November 11, 1981.
*Library Journal,* July, 1986.
*Los Angeles Times,* December 12, 1980.
*Los Angeles Times Book Review,* January 3, 1982.
*New York Times Book Review,* November 15, 1981; August 24, 1986.
*Saturday Review,* March 26, 1966.
*Times Literary Supplement,* July 21, 1966.
*Village Voice Literary Supplement,* October, 1981.
*Washington Post Book World,* November 29, 1981.

\*    \*    \*

**KIRK-GREENE, Anthony (Hamilton Millard) 1925-**
**(Anthony H. M. Kirk-Greene; pseudonyms: Nicholas Caverhill, H. M. S., P. L. K., Yerima Yola)**

*PERSONAL:* Born May 16, 1925, in Tunbridge Wells, England; son of Leslie (a civil engineer) and Helen (Millard) Kirk-Greene; married Helen Margaret Sellar (a personal secretary), April 22, 1967. *Education:* Clare College, Cambridge, B.A. (with first class honors), 1949, M.A., 1954; Oxford University, M.A., 1967; graduate study at Cambridge University, 1955-56, Northwestern University and University of California, Los Angeles, 1958-59, and Edinburgh University, 1965-66.

*ADDRESSES: Home*—34 Davenant Rd., Oxford, England. *Office*—St. Antony's College, Oxford University, Oxford OX2 6JF, England.

*CAREER:* British Colonial Administrative Service, Northern Nigeria, district officer, 1950-57; Institute of Administration, Zaria, Nigeria, senior lecturer in government, 1957-60; Ahmadu Bello University, Zaria, associate professor of government and head of department, 1961-66; Oxford University, St. Antony's College, Oxford, England, senior research fellow in African studies, 1967-81, director of Oxford Colonial Records and Research Project, 1980-84,

University Lecturer in the Modern History of Africa, 1982-92, emeritus fellow, 1992—, director of foreign service program, 1986-90, Stanford University Center, Oxford, adjunct professor, 1992—.

Visiting professor, Syracuse University, 1961, University of California, Los Angeles, 1962, 1963, 1967, and 1968, University of Paris, 1971, 1973, and 1975, Scandinavian Institute of African Studies, 1974, and University of Calgary, 1977, and 1985; Hans Wolff Memorial Lecturer, University of Indiana, 1973; visiting fellow, Hoover Institution on War, Revolution, and Peace, 1975—; scholar in residence, Trent University, 1975. Consultant to Kenya Government, 1961, East African Staff College, 1969 and 1970, East African Community, 1972, and African Association for Public Administration and Management, 1975; British government elections supervisor, Zimbabwe, 1980. *Military service:* Royal War-wickshire Regiment, 1943-44; Indian Army, 8th Punjab Regiment, 1944-47; became captain.

*MEMBER:* International African Institute, African Studies Association (vice president, 1986-88; president, 1988-90), Royal African Society (vice president, 1995—), Royal Commonwealth Society (member of council, 1984-85), Royal Historical Society (fellow), Corona Club, Hawks Club.

*AWARDS, HONORS:* Harkness fellowship, 1958-59; member, Order of the British Empire, 1963; Canada Council fellowship, 1975; Leverholme emeritus fellowship, 1993-95.

*WRITINGS:*

*This Is Northern Nigeria: Background to an Invitation,* Government Printer of Northern Nigeria (Kaduna), 1956.

*Maiduguri and the Capitals of Bornu,* bilingual edition, Northern Regional Literature Agency (Zaria, Nigeria), 1958.

*Adamawa, Past and Present: An Historical Approach to the Development of a Northern Cameroons Province,* Oxford University Press for the International African Institute, 1958, new edition, Humanities, 1969.

(With Caroline Sassoon) *The Cattle People of Nigeria,* Oxford University Press, 1959.

(With Sassoon) *The Niger,* Oxford University Press, 1961.

*Barth's Travels in Nigeria,* Oxford University Press, 1962.

*The Principles of Native Administration in Nigeria: Selected Documents, 1900-1947,* Oxford University Press, 1965.

(With Sidney J. Hogben) *The Emirates of Northern Nigeria,* Oxford University Press, 1966.

(Compiler and translator) *Hausa ba dabo ba ne: A Collection of 500 Proverbs,* Oxford University Press, 1966.

(With Yahaya Aliyu) *A Modern Hausa Reader,* McKay, 1967.

*Crisis and Conflict in Nigeria: A Documentary Sourcebook,* two volumes, Oxford University Press, 1971, 2nd edition, 1993.

(Translator with Paul Newman) *West African Travels and Adventures: Two Autobiographical Narratives from Northern Nigeria,* Yale University Press, 1972.

(With Charles Kraft) *Teach Yourself Hausa,* University of London Press, 1973, 9th edition, 1990.

*Mutumin Kirkii: The Concept of the Good Man in Hausa* (monograph), University of Indiana, 1976.

*The Genesis of the Nigerian Civil War* (monograph), University of Uppsala, 1976.

(With Pauline Ryan) *Faces North: Some Peoples of Nigeria,* Pitkin Publications, 1975.

*A Biographical Dictionary of the British Colonial Governor,* Volume I: *Africa,* Hoover Institution, 1980.

*"Stay by Your Radios": Documentation for a Study of Military Government in Tropical Africa,* University of Leiden Press, 1981.

(With Douglas Rimmer) *Nigeria Since 1970: A Political and Economic Outline,* Holmes & Meier, 1981.

*The Sudan Political Service: A Profile in the Sociology of Empire,* Oxford University Press, 1982.

*The Literature on Francophone Africa in English,* Bordeaux, 1989.

*A Short History of the Corona Club,* London, 1990.

*A Biographical Dictionary of the British Colonial Service,* Zell, 1991.

*Nationalism and Arcadianism in the Sudan,* Oxford, 1993.

*Diplomatic Initiative: A Jubilee History of the Foreign Service Programme,* Oxford, 1994.

(With D. Bach) *Francophone Africa Since Independence,* Macmillan, 1994.

(With Vaughan) *Hamman Yaji: Diary of a Nigerian Chief,* Indiana, 1994.

*EDITOR*

*Lugard and the Amalgamation of Nigeria: A Documentary Record,* Cass, 1968.

(And author of introduction and preface) *Gazetteers of the Northern Provinces of Nigeria,* revised edition, Volume I: *The Hausa Emirates,* Volume II: *The Eastern Kingdoms,* Volume III: *The Central Kingdoms,* Volume IV: *The Highland Chieftaincies,* Cass, 1972.

*The Transfer of Power: The African Administrator in the Age of Decolonization,* Oxford University Press, 1979.

(And author of introduction) Margery Perham, *West African Passage: A Journey through Nigeria, Chad, and the Cameroons, 1931-1932,* P. Owen, 1983.

(With J. Stone) *Ethnicity, Empire and Race Relations,* RKP, 1986.

(With J. Stone) *Ethnicity, Empire, and Race Relations,* RKP, 1986.

(With Mahdi Adamu) *Pastoralists of the West African Savanna,* Manchester University Press, 1986.

(And author of introduction) Perham, *Pacific Prelude,* P. Owen, 1988.

*The Evolution of African History at British Universities,* World View Press, 1994.

### AUTHOR OF INTRODUCTION

C. J. Orr, *The Making of Northern Nigeria,* 2nd edition, Cass, 1965.

Heinrich Barth, *Travels and Discoveries in North and Central Africa,* centenary edition, Barnes & Noble, 1965.

Sonia Graham, *Government and Mission Education in Northern Nigeria,* Ibadan University Press, 1966.

P. A. Benton, *The Languages and People of Bornu,* Cass, 1968.

Barth, *The Vocabularies of Central African Languages,* Cass, 1970.

Frederick Lugard, *Political Memoranda,* Cass, 1971.

J. A. Burdon, *History of the Emirates of Northern Nigeria,* Gregg, 1973.

Lord Hailey, *Native Administration and Political Development in British Tropical Africa,* Kraus, 1979.

Charles Allen, *Tales from the Dark Continent,* Deutsch, 1979.

D. Ray and others, *African Studies: Into the 80s,* Vancouver, 1981.

M. S. Kisch, *Letters and Sketches from N. Nigeria (1910),* Gregg, 1992.

### OTHER

Author of *The Deans and Directors of Diplomatic Academies Conference: A Jubilee History,* [Washington, DC], 1994; with L. Diamond, *Nigeria's Transition Programme,* 1995; and *Britain's Overseas Civil Service,* in press. Also author of pamphlets and research papers on African history, governmental institutions, politics, and languages.

Contributor to numerous books, including *The Politics and Administration of Nigeria,* edited by L. Franklin Blitz, Praeger, 1966; *The English Language in West Africa,* edited by John Spencer, Longmans, Green, 1968; *African Studies since 1945,* edited by C. Fyfe, Longman, 1976; *The Transfer of Power in Africa: Decolonization 1940-1960,* edited by Prosser Gifford and W. Roger Louis, Yale University Press, 1982; *The Berlin West Africa Conference in 1885,* edited by W. Mommsen and R. E. Robinson, Oxford University Press, 1988; and *Sport in Africa: Essays in Social History,* edited by J. A. Mangan, Cass, 1992. Also contributor to *Dictionary of National Biography, Encyclopaedia Britannica, Encyclopaedia of Sub-Saharan Africa,* and of several hundred articles and reviews to African and historical journals; contributor of obituaries to *Daily Telegraph/Times.*

General editor, "Studies in African History" series, Methuen, 1971—, "Africana Publishing" series, Holmes and Meier, "Modern Africana Revivals" series, Gregg, and "Colonial Memoirs" series, Radcliffe; academic consultant, "Memoirs from Overseas," Radcliffe Press, 1990—; editorial advisor, *Journal of African Administration,* 1957-67, *African Affairs,* 1975—, *Culture et Developpement,* 1976—, and *International History of Sport,* 1986—.

**WORK IN PROGRESS:** A history of the British Colonial Administrative Service (project); the political history of modern Nigeria; colonial rule and decolon-ization; the District Officer in Africa and India.

### BIOGRAPHICAL/CRITICAL SOURCES:

*BOOKS*

Ranger, Terance, and Vaughan, Oluferni, editors, *Legitimacy and State in Twentieth-Century Africa; Essays in Honour of A. H. M. Kirk-Greene,* Macmillan, 1993.

*PERIODICALS*

*Times* (London), June 11, 1981.

*Times Literary Supplement,* September 25, 1981; January 20, 1984.

**KIRK-GREENE, Anthony H. M.**
    See **KIRK-GREENE, Anthony (Hamilton Millard)**


\*   \*   \*


**KLUGER, Richard   1934-**

*PERSONAL:* Born September 18, 1934, in Paterson, NJ; son of David (a business executive) and Ida (Abramson) Kluger; married Phyllis Schlain, March 23, 1957; children: Matthew Harold, Leonard Theodore. *Education:* Princeton University, B.A. (cum laude), 1956.

*ADDRESSES: Home*—Skillman, NJ. *Agent*—Georges Borchardt, Inc., 136 East 57th St., New York, NY 10022.

*CAREER:* Author, editor, critic. *Wall Street Journal,* New York City, city editor, 1956-57; *County Citizen,* New City, NY, editor and publisher, 1958-60; *New York Post,* New York City, staff writer, 1960-61; *Forbes* magazine, New York City, associate editor, 1962; *New York Herald Tribune,* New York City, general book editor, 1962-63, book editor, 1963-66; *Book Week,* New York City, editor, 1963-66; Simon & Schuster, New York City, managing editor, 1966-68, executive editor, 1968-70; Atheneum Publishers, New York City, editor in chief, 1970-71; Charterhouse Books, New York City, president and publisher, 1972-73.

*MEMBER:* Princeton Club of New York.

*AWARDS, HONORS:* National Book Award nomination and Sidney Hillman Prize, both 1976, both for *Simple Justice: A History of Brown v. Board of Education;* American Book Award nomination, 1986, and George Polk Prize, 1987, both for *The Paper: The Life and Death of the New York Herald Tribune.*

*WRITINGS:*

NOVELS

*When the Bough Breaks,* Doubleday (New York City), 1964.
*National Anthem,* Harper (New York City), 1969.
*Members of the Tribe* (Book-of-the-Month Club alternate selection), Doubleday, 1977.
*Star Witness,* Doubleday, 1979.

*Un-American Activities,* Doubleday, 1982.
*The Sheriff of Nottingham,* Viking (New York City), 1992.

NONFICTION

*Simple Justice: A History of Brown v. Board of Education,* Knopf (New York City), 1976.
(With wife, Phyllis Kluger) *Good Goods,* Macmillan (New York City), 1982.
*The Paper: The Life and Death of the New York Herald Tribune,* Knopf, 1986.
(With P. Kluger) *Royal Poinciana,* Donald I. Fine, 1987.
*Ashes to Ashes: America's Hundred-Year Cigarette War, The Public Health, and the Unabashed Triumph of Philip Morris,* Knopf, 1996.

OTHER

Contributor to *Harper's, Nation, New Republic, New York Times Book Review, Partisan Review,* and other periodicals.

*SIDELIGHTS:* In keeping with his claim that the quest for social justice in America is a unifying theme to his writing, Richard Kluger's acclaimed nonfiction work known as *Simple Justice: A History of Brown v. Board of Education,* relates a crucial event in the black population's struggle for equal rights in America. *Simple Justice* is Kluger's detailed analysis of the landmark U.S. Supreme Court case of 1954 which decided against segregation in the public school system. In the *New York Times Book Review,* Robert Conot finds Kluger's account "intriguing, encyclopedic and deeply researched. . . . Kluger tells the story in terms of the people involved, and so turns what might have been a dry text into an exceedingly human drama." Although Conot feels the book is too long and too detailed, he says, "In the final third of the book, when the focus is on the Supreme Court, the story is gripping." Additionally, *Time* reviewer Melvin Maddocks concludes that Kluger's "collage of facts and events, institutions and people eventually documents nothing less than a national change of heart."

After directing attention to the struggle of blacks for equal opportunity education in *Simple Justice,* "a similar impetus on behalf of American Jews led to [Kluger's] writing *Members of the Tribe,*" notes Lincoln Caplan in the *Saturday Review.* In this novel, set in the South in the late nineteenth and early twentieth centuries, Kluger draws on incidents of the Leo M. Frank trial which took place in Atlanta, Georgia, from 1913 to 1915. Accordingly, in *Members of the Tribe,* Seth Adler, a young Jewish lawyer originally from New York, defends a Jewish man accused of killing a fourteen-year-old Christian girl. As Caplan maintains, "Though mainly a work of imagination, the narrative draws on historical events and personalities to describe the growing pains of the post-bellum South and its awkwardness in accommodating not just blacks and Northerners but also Jews, who had special anxieties about assimilation." Likewise, *New York Times Book Review* critic Eli N. Evans expresses that Kluger "has written the best novel yet about the Jews who settled in the South. . . . Over the past [several decades] there has been just a handful of novels written about Jews of the South, and the Frank case is one of the reasons why: Southern Jews learned to keep a low profile; they were conditioned by an instinctive wariness against passing for white in that mysterious underland of America. . . . [Perhaps] Kluger's provocative fictionalization of the Frank trial and lynching is an appropriate first step toward dispelling the phantoms that have held back novels about this fascinating aspect of Jews in America as one example of the varieties of the white experience in the South."

Kluger worked as a book editor for the *New York Herald Tribune* during its final four years from 1962 to 1966. His 1986 account, or obituary as it has been called, of the *Tribune* is said by *Chicago Tribune* reviewer W. A. Swanberg to be a "Grade-A journalistic cliffhanger." According to Don Cook in the *Los Angeles Times Book Review,* Kluger, in *The Paper: The Life and Death of the New York Herald Tribune,* "has performed a vast labor of love and research on 131 years of Herald Tribune history, written with verve, style and skill." As has been viewed the case with *Simple Justice, The Paper*'s success is in part derived from its attention to individuals. Notes David Shaw in the *New York Times Book Review:* "*The Paper* was always far more a collection of individuals—and a reflection of their special sensibilities—than it was an institution, and Mr. Kluger does a remarkable job of bringing these people to life on the printed page." Included among those Kluger brings to life are the original founder and editor of the *New York Herald,* James Gordon Bennett, the original founder and editor of the *New York Tribune,* Horace Greeley, and James Bellows, the last editor of the merged *New York Herald Tribune. New York Times* reviewer Christopher Lehmann-Haupt believes Kluger's enthusiasm for his subject, "which is apparent everywhere," has made *The Paper* a success.

Kluger told *CA* that his quest for social justice in his writing is a "preoccupation which affects my fiction at least as much as my books of social history; novels of exquisite sensibility are not my metier. I believe that my country has thrived not because of its brash arrogance alone but because many of its people naively hold to the precepts with which the United States was endowed. The most patriotic of our citizens are not those who say, 'My country, right or wrong,' but those who call upon it to meet the high promise of its rhetoric and are willing, indeed compelled, to criticize it for its shortcomings and to act with compassion and strength toward that end. The true subversives, I think, are those who mindlessly cheer our every action and fear those—even hate those—who dissent or demur."

*BIOGRAPHICAL/CRITICAL SOURCES:*

*PERIODICALS*

*Best Sellers,* May 1, 1969.
*Chicago Tribune,* March 4, 1979; November 30, 1986.
*Detroit News,* August 15, 1982.
*Los Angeles Times Book Review,* November 23, 1986.
*Nation,* May 12, 1979.
*Newsweek,* July 13, 1964; January 26, 1976.
*New York Times,* February 22, 1977; September 23, 1977; February 28, 1979; July 22, 1982; October 30, 1986.
*New York Times Book Review,* January 18, 1976; September 25, 1977; February 25, 1979; July 25, 1982; October 26, 1986.
*Observer Review,* October 26, 1969.
*Saturday Review,* October 15, 1977.
*Time,* February 9, 1976; October 10, 1977; October 27, 1986.
*Virginia Quarterly Review,* autumn, 1969.
*Washington Post,* March 1, 1979.
*Washington Post Book World,* June 16, 1982; October 26, 1986.

\*      \*      \*

**KNYE, Cassandra**
**See DISCH, Thomas M(ichael)**

\*      \*      \*

**KORNBLUM, Allan      1949-**

*PERSONAL:* Born February 16, 1949, in New York, NY; son of Seymour (a social worker) and Anne (an elementary school teacher; maiden name, Epstein) Kornblum; married Cinda Wormley (a poet and administrator), August 19, 1972. *Education:* Attended New York University, 1967-68, and University of Iowa, 1970-72.

*CAREER:* Toothpaste Press, West Branch, IA, publisher and printer, 1970—. Instructor at Scattergood School, 1974-75.

*MEMBER:* West Branch Library Board Center for Book Arts.

*AWARDS, HONORS:* Small press grants from National Education Association, 1975-76, 1976-77, 1978-79, 1979-80; book design awards from Chicago Book Clinic, Midwestern Books Competition, and Windflower Press.

*WRITINGS:*

POETRY

*Famous Americans,* privately printed, 1970.
*Tight Pants,* privately printed, 1971.
(With Darrell Gray) *Good Morning: Fourteen Sonnets,* "J" Stone Press Weekly Special, 1975.
*The Salad Bushes,* Seamark Press, 1975.
*Threshold,* Toothpaste Press (West Branch, IA), 1976.
*Awkward Song,* Toothpaste Press, 1980.

Editor of *Toothpaste,* 1970-72, and *Dental Floss.*

*WORK IN PROGRESS:* Poems.

*SIDELIGHTS:* Allan Kornblum wrote to *CA:* "The essence of life is the same everywhere for everyone. Therefore it is the surface which interests me. My poems are full of coffee, the refrigerator, the towns where I have lived. Although my private studies of history would teach me otherwise, I refuse to view the world through eyes of despair. My poetry and life are open to both quiet and wild joys, open to my mother's cancer and death, open to a beer at The Peppermint Stable in West Branch. Sometimes I can't read enough, sometimes grade B movies are all I crave. If you're on Interstate 80 and pass through Iowa, give me a call."

*BIOGRAPHICAL/CRITICAL SOURCES:*

BOOKS

Tarachow, Michael, editor, *Toward a Further Definition,* Pentagram Press (Markesan, WI), 1977.*

KRAUS, (Herman) Robert 1925-
    (Eugene H. Hippopotamus, E. S. Silly, I. M. Tubby)

*PERSONAL:* Born June 21, 1925, in Milwaukee, WI; son of Jack (in real estate business) and Esther (Rosen) Kraus; married Pamela Wong, December 11, 1946; children: Bruce, William. *Education:* Attended Layton Art School, Milwaukee, 1942, and Art Students' League of New York, 1945.

*ADDRESSES: Home*—Ridgefield, CT.

*CAREER:* Cartoonist for national magazines, and author and illustrator of children's books; president of Windmill Books, Inc., New York City, beginning 1965; president of Springfellow Books, Inc., beginning 1972.

*AWARDS, HONORS: Whose Mouse Are You?* was named a notable children's book of 1970 by the American Library Association; *Herman the Helper* appeared on the *Horn Book* honor list and received the Children's Trade Book Award; *Milton the Early Riser* and *Owliver* were named notable children's books by the American Library Association; *Leo the Late Bloomer* was read on national television by First Lady Barbara Bush as part of her literacy campaign.

*WRITINGS:*

*Harriet and the Promised Land,* Windmill Books (New York City), 1968.
*Unidentified Flying Elephant,* Windmill Books, 1968.
*The Children Who Got Married,* Windmill Books, 1969.
*Animal Etiquette,* Windmill Books, 1969.
*Don't Talk to Strange Bears,* Windmill Books, 1969.
*Rumple-Nose Dimple and the Three Horrible Snaps,* Windmill Books, 1969.
*The Christmas Cookie Sprinkle Snitcher,* Windmill Books, 1969.
*The Rabbit Brothers,* Anti-Defamation League of B'nai B'rith (New York City), 1969.
*I'm Glad I'm a Boy, I'm Glad I'm a Girl,* Windmill Books, 1970.
*Whose Mouse Are You?,* Macmillan (New York City), 1970.
*Vip's Mistake Book,* Windmill Books, 1970.
*Bunya the Witch,* Windmill Books, 1971.
*Shaggy Fur Face,* Windmill Books, 1971.
*Ludwig, the Dog Who Snored Symphonies,* Windmill Books, 1971.

*Pipsqueak, Mouse in Shining Armor,* Windmill Books, 1971.

*Lillian Morgan and Teddy Morgan,* Windmill Books, 1971.

*The Tree That Stayed Up Until Next Christmas,* Windmill Books, 1971.

*Leo the Late Bloomer,* Windmill Books, 1971.

*Milton the Early Riser* (Junior Literary Guild selection), Windmill Books, 1972.

*How Spider Saved Halloween,* Parents Magazine Press (New York City), 1973.

*Big Brother,* Parents Magazine Press, 1973.

*Pip Squeaks Through,* Springfellow Press (New York City), 1973.

*Poor Mister Splinterfitz!,* Dutton (New York City), 1973.

*Rebecca Hatpin,* Windmill Books, 1974.

*Pinchpenny Mouse* (Junior Literary Guild selection), Windmill Books, 1974.

*Owliver* (Junior Literary Guild selection), Windmill Books, 1974.

*Herman the Helper* (Junior Literary Guild selection), Windmill Books, 1974.

*Three Friends* (Junior Literary Guild selection), Windmill Books, 1975.

*I'm a Monkey,* Windmill Books, 1975.

*The Night-Light Story Book,* Windmill Books, 1975.

*The Gondolier of Venice* (Junior Literary Guild selection), Windmill Books, 1976.

*Boris Bad Enough,* Windmill Books, 1976.

*Dinosaur Do's and Don'ts,* Windmill Books, 1976.

*Kittens for Nothing,* Windmill Books, 1976.

*The Good Mousekeeper,* Windmill Books, 1977.

(With son, Bruce Kraus) *The Detective of London* (Junior Literary Guild selection), Windmill Books, 1977.

*Noel the Coward,* Windmill Books, 1977.

*Another Mouse to Feed,* Windmill Books, 1980.

*Mouse Work,'* Windmill Books, 1980.

*Mert the Blurt,* Windmill Books, 1980.

*Puppet Pal Books* (contains *Herman the Helper Lends a Hand, Leo the Late Bloomer Bakes a Cake, Milton the Early Riser Takes a Trip,* and *Owliver the Actor Takes a Bow*), four volumes, Windmill Books, 1981.

*The King's Trousers,* Windmill Books, 1981.

*Leo the Late Bloomer Takes a Bath,* Windmill Books, 1981.

*Herman the Helper Cleans Up,* Windmill Books, 1981.

*See the Christmas Lights,* Windmill Books, 1981.

(With wife, Pam Kraus) *Box of Brownies,* four volumes, Windmill Books, 1981.

*Where Are You Going, Little Mouse?,* Greenwillow Books (New York City), 1986.

*Screamy Mimi,* Simon & Schuster (New York City), 1987.

*How Spider Saved Thanksgiving,* Scholastic Inc. (New York City), 1991.

*All My Chickens,* Western Publishing (Racine, WI), 1993.

*Dance, Spider, Dance!,* Western Publishing, 1993.

*Jack O'Lantern's Scary Halloween,* Western Publishing, 1993.

*Fables Aesop Never Wrote but Robert Kraus Did,* Viking (New York City), 1994.

*Near Myths: Dug Up and Dusted Off,* Viking, 1996.

*Big Squeak, Little Squeak,* illustrated by Kevin O'Malley, Orchard Books (New York City), 1996.

*Little Louie the Baby Bloomer,* HarperCollins (New York City), 1998.

A collection of Kraus's manuscripts is housed at Syracuse University.

*AUTHOR AND ILLUSTRATOR*

*Junior, the Spoiled Cat,* Oxford University Press (New York City), 1955.

*All the Mice Came,* Harper (New York City), 1955.

*Ladybug, Ladybug,* Harper, 1956.

*The Littlest Rabbit,* Harper, 1957.

*I, Mouse,* Harper, 1958.

*The Trouble with Spider,* Harper, 1962.

*Miranda's Beautiful Dream,* Harper, 1964.

*Penguin's Pal,* Harper, 1964.

*Mouse at Sea,* Harper, 1964.

*Amanda Remembers,* Harper, 1965.

*My Son, the Mouse,* Harper, 1967.

*Little Giant,* Harper, 1967.

(Under pseudonym Eugene H. Hippopotamus) *Hello, Hippopotamus,* Windmill Books, 1969.

*Daddy Long Ears,* Windmill Books, 1970.

*How Spider Saved Christmas,* Windmill Books, 1970.

*The Tale Who Wagged the Dog,* Windmill Books, 1971.

*Animal Families,* Windmill Books, 1980.

*See the Moon,* Windmill Books, 1980.

*How Spider Saved Turkey,* Windmill Books, 1981.

*The Old-Fashioned Raggedy Ann and Andy ABC Book,* edited by Pam Kraus, Windmill Books, 1981.

*Squeaky,* Simon & Schuster, 1982.

*Bumpy the Car,* Putnam (New York City), 1985.

*Ferddy the Fire Engine,* Putnam, 1985.

*How Spider Saved Valentine's Day,* Scholastic Inc., 1986.

*Spider's First Day at School,* Scholastic Inc., 1987.
*Happy City,* Simon & Schuster, 1987.
*Happy Farm,* Simon & Schuster, 1987.
*Spider's Home Town: A Story to Color,* Scholastic Inc., 1988.
*Here Comes Tardy Toad,* Silver Press (Englewood Cliffs, NJ), 1989.
*Ella the Bad Speller,* Silver Press, 1989.
*Good Morning, Miss Gator,* Silver Press, 1989.
*Miss Gator's School House,* Messner (New York City), 1989.
*Buggy Bear Cleans Up,* Silver Press, 1989.
*How Spider Saved the Baseball Game,* Scholastic Inc., 1989.
*Phil, the Ventriloquist,* Greenwillow, 1989.
*Daddy Long Ears Christmas Surprise,* Simon & Schuster, 1989.
*Daddy Long Ears Halloween,* Simon & Schuster, 1990.
*Private Eyes Don't Blink,* Warner Books (New York City), 1990.
*Spider's Baby-Sitting Job,* Scholastic Inc., 1990.
*Spider's Draw-a-Long Book,* Scholastic Inc., 1990.
*Creepy Hollow Ghostly Glowing Haunted House,* Warner Books, 1990.
*Boogie Woogie Bears Go Back to Nature,* Warner Books, 1990.
*Boogie Woogie Bears' Picnic,* Warner Books, 1990.
*Jack Galaxy, Space Cop,* Bantam (New York City), 1990.
*Klunky Monkey, New Kid in Class,* Bantam, 1990.
*Mixed-Up Mice Clean House,* Warner Books, 1990.
*Mixed-Up Mice in the Big Birthday Mix-Up,* Warner Books, 1990.
*Mummy Knows Best,* Warner Books, 1990.
*Mummy Vanishes,* Warner Books, 1990.
*Musical Max,* Simon & Schuster, 1990.
*The Phantom of Creepy Hollow,* Warner Books, 1990.
(With Bonnie Brook) *Squirmy's Big Secret,* Silver Press, 1990.
(With P. Kraus) *Wise Old Owl's Halloween Adventure,* Troll (Mahwah, NJ), 1993.
(With P. Kraus) *Wise Old Owl's Christmas Adventure,* Troll, 1994.
*Strudwick: A Sheep in Wolf's Clothing,* Viking, 1995.

*"THE BUNNY'S NUTSHELL LIBRARY" SERIES*

*The Silver Dandelion,* Harper, 1965.
*Juniper,* Harper, 1965.
*The First Robin,* Harper, 1965.
*Springfellow's Parade,* Harper, 1965.

*"THE NIGHT LIGHT LIBRARY" SERIES*

*Good Night, Little One,* Springfellow Books, 1972.
*Good Night, Little ABC,* Springfellow Books, 1972.
*Good Night, Little Richard Rabbit,* Springfellow Books, 1972.

*UNDER PSEUDONYM E. S. SILLY*

*Squeaky,* Windmill Books, 1982.
*Squeaky's One Man Band,* Windmill Books, 1982.

*UNDER PSEUDONYM I. M. TUBBY*

*I'm a Little Airplane,* Tubby Books, 1982.
*I'm a Little Fish,* Tubby Books, 1982.
*I'm a Little House,* Tubby Books, 1982.
*I'm a Little Tugboat,* Tubby Books, 1982.

*EDITOR*

Robert J. Flaherty, *Nanook of the North,* Windmill Books, 1971.
*Reggie Jackson's Scrapbook,* Windmill Books, 1978.

*ILLUSTRATOR*

Paul Anderson, *Red Fox and the Hungry Tiger,* Addison-Wesley (Reading, MA), 1962.
Carla Stevens, *Rabbit and Skunk and the Spooks,* Scholastic Book Services (New York City), 1968.
Stevens, *Rabbit and Skunk and the Scary Rock,* Scholastic Book Services, 1970.
Cleveland Amory, *Cleveland Amory's Animail,* Dutton, 1976.
Stevens, *Rabbit and Skunk and the Big Fight,* Scholastic Book Services, 1976.

*SIDELIGHTS:* A noted children's writer and illustrator, former president of Windmill Books, and a magazine cartoonist, Robert Kraus has enjoyed a long and varied career. Kraus began as a cartoonist, selling his first cartoon at the age of 10 to a local newspaper in his native Milwaukee. By the age of 16, he was selling cartoons to such magazines as the *Saturday Evening Post* and *Esquire.* His big break came with a sale to the *New Yorker,* the premiere cartoon market in the country. Soon Kraus was a regular cartoonist for the magazine, contracted to draw 50 cartoons a year.

After 15 years with the *New Yorker,* Kraus decided to try something new, turning his talents to writing and drawing children's books full time. This led him in 1965 to begin a new publishing company, Windmill Books, which specialized in children's picture books. At first, Kraus wrote the stories and his artist friends from the *New Yorker,* like Charles Addams and William Steig, drew the pictures. Soon Windmill Books was publishing a wide variety of children's books by many authors; some of the books were award winners. Jean F. Mercier, writing in *Publishers Weekly,* says that Windmill Books has "an enviable reputation." Among Kraus's publishing innovations was Tubby Books, small waterproof books for children to read in the bathtub. (The slogan: "They Float! The Unsinkable Book!") Unfortunately, in the early 1980s Windmill Books experienced legal difficulties with its distributor. Because of these troubles, Kraus was obliged to sign over the company and all its books to Simon and Schuster.

Since that time, he has focused his attention on writing and illustrating books for a number of different publishers. Kraus often writes of animal characters. Among the most popular are Owliver, an owl who likes to act, Herman, a well-meaning octopus, and Spider, a problem-solving insect.

*BIOGRAPHICAL/CRITICAL SOURCES:*

*PERIODICALS*

*Booklist,* March 15, 1990, p. 1471; July, 1990, p. 2092.
*Growing Point,* April, 1977.
*Horn Book Guide,* fall, 1993, p. 281; spring, 1994, p. 41.
*Kirkus Reviews,* July 15, 1990, p. 1004.
*New Yorker,* December 7, 1981.
*Publishers Weekly,* February 27, 1978; July 13, 1990, p. 52; March 7, 1994, p. 73.
*School Library Journal,* December, 1989, p. 84; February, 1990, p. 76; March, 1990, p. 195.

# L

## LANE, Patrick 1939-

*PERSONAL:* Born March 26, 1939, in Nelson, British Columbia, Canada; son of A. S. Red (in business) and E. M. (Titsworth) Lane; married Mary Hayden, 1958 (divorced, 1967); married Carol Beale, 1972 (divorced, 1978); companion of Lorna Crozier (poet); children: Mark Hayden, Christopher Patrick, Kathryn Mary, Michael John, Richard Patrick. *Education:* Graduated from high school in Vernon, British Columbia. *Politics:* Social democrat. *Religion:* Christian.

*ADDRESSES: Home*—Saskatchewan, Canada. *Office*—c/o Oxford University Press, 70 Wynford Dr., Don Mills, Ontario, Canada.

*CAREER:* Poet. Worker in Canada in logging camps, sawmills, and mines, 1957-62; office manager and purchasing agent in Vancouver, British Columbia, 1962-67; Very Stone House In Transit (formerly Very Stone House; publisher), Vancouver, editor, 1966-80. Writer in residence or instructor in creative writing at Notre Dame University, 1975, University of Manitoba, 1979, Saskatchewan summer school, 1979 and 1980, University of Ottawa, 1980, Manitoba Writer's School, 1980, University of Alberta, 1982, Library of Saskatoon, 1983, Globe Theatre Company of Regina, 1985, Concordia University (Montreal), 1987, University of Saskatoon, 1988-89, and University of Toronto, 1989.

*MEMBER:* League of Canadian Poets (vice-president), Writer's Union of Canada.

*AWARDS, HONORS:* Poet's award from York University, 1971; grants from Canada Council, 1973-74, 1976-78, and 1983-84, Ontario Arts Council, 1974, 1975, and 1978, Manitoba Arts Council, 1979, and Saskatchewan Arts Council, 1983; Governor General's Award for poetry, 1978, for *Poems: New and Selected;* National Magazine Award, 1985, for "Rabbits," a short story; CAA award for poetry, 1988; Dorothy Livesay Poetry Prize, 1996.

*WRITINGS:*

POETRY

*Letters from the Savage Mind,* Very Stone House (Vancouver, British Columbia), 1966.
*For Rita—in Asylum,* Very Stone House, 1969.
*Calgary City Jail,* Very Stone House, 1969.
*Separations,* New Books (Trumansburg, NY), 1969.
*Sunflower Seeds,* Western Press, 1969.
*On the Street,* Very Stone House, 1970.
*Hiway 401 Rhapsody,* Very Stone House, 1971.
*Mountain Oysters,* Very Stone House, 1971, 2nd revised edition, 1971.
*The Sun Has Begun to Eat the Mountain,* Ingluvin Publications (Montreal), 1972.
*Passing into Storm,* Traumerei Communications (Vernon, British Columbia), 1973.
*Beware the Months of Fire,* Anansi (Toronto), 1974.
*Certs,* College of New Caledonia, 1974.
*Unborn Things: South American Poems,* Harbour Publishing (Madeira Park, British Columbia), 1975.
*For Riel in That Gawdam Prison,* Blackfish Press, 1975.
*Albino Pheasants,* Harbour Publishing, 1977.
*If,* Dreadnaught Press, 1977.
*Poems: New and Selected,* Oxford University Press (Toronto), 1978.
(With Lorna Uher) *No Longer Two People,* Turnstone Press (Winnipeg, Manitoba), 1979.

*There Are Still the Mountains,* Very Stone House, 1979.

*The Measure,* Black Moss Press (Windsor, Ontario), 1980.

*The Garden,* League of Canadian Poets, 1980.

*Old Mother,* Oxford University Press, 1982.

*Woman in the Dust,* Mosaic Press (Oakville, Ontario), 1983.

*A Linen Crow, A Caftan Magpie,* Thistledown Press (Saskatoon, Saskatchewan), 1984.

*Selected Poems,* Oxford University Press, 1987.

*Winter,* Coteau Books (Regina, Saskatchewan), 1990.

*Mortal Remains,* Exile Editions (Toronto), 1991.

OTHER

*(Drawings),* Tundra Graphics, 1981.

*The Liberal Vision and the Death of Culture* (lecture), Saskatchewan Library Association, 1983.

(Editor) Catherine M. Buckaway, *Blue Windows,* Coteau, 1988.

*Milford and Me* (for children), illustrations by Bonnie McLean, Coteau Books, 1989.

*"How Do You Spell Beautiful?": And Other Stories,* Fifth House (Saskatoon, Saskatchewan), 1992.

(Editor with Lorna Crozier) *Breathing Fire: Canada's New Poets,* Harbour Publishing, 1995.

Work represented in anthologies, including *Storm Warning,* edited by Al Purdy, McClelland, 1971; *Skookum Wawa: An Anthology of the Canadian Northwest,* by Gary Geddes, Oxford University Press, 1975; *Fifteen Canadian Poets Plus Five,* by Geddes and Phyllis Bruce, Oxford University Press, 1978; *The Penguin Book of Canadian Verse,* edited by Ralph Gustafson, Penguin, 1975; and *Literature In Canada,* by Douglas Daymond and Leslie Monkman, two volumes, Gage, 1978.

Collections of Lane's manuscripts are housed at McMaster University, Hamilton, Ontario, and University of British Columbia, Vancouver, British Columbia.

SIDELIGHTS: Patrick Lane is the poet of the Canadian West, of the logging camps, mills, and the company towns of its interior, and of the desperate lives of the people who live and work there. Lane knows the land and people that he describes in his poetry. He was born and raised in British Columbia, far from Vancouver to the west and the larger Canadian metropolises to the east; he lived in the company towns and worked in the often wretched conditions there and in other western provinces. He found similar isolation and desperation in travels that took him to the backcountry and cities of North and South America. In a literary career that has continued to develop since the mid-1960s, Lane has captured images of these people and places in poetry that is considered among contemporary Canada's best. His poetry is a testament to all his experience and a reaction to it. Lane once told *CA,* "I think my reaction to all I saw—the inhumanity of man against man, the world I saw in the bush, the backcountry of years ago, my travels in South America—was a violent and absolute hatred. I saw horrifying things on the streets of Canada. . . . I lived with that kind of thing. And I reacted against it." As a result, writes Len Gasparini in *Canadian Literature,* Lane's "poems are mirrors with the spidery cracks of truth in them. He doesn't flinch from the ugliness and cruelty of life, but observes it with ironic compassion."

Lane's subject matter and his approach to poetry have earned him such titles as "maverick poet" and "red-neck poet." As Gasparini explains, "Lane's poems tell us about things we would like to forget. They are the acerbic documents of an imagination turned inside out. Lane records his impressions of reality with guts." Doug Fetherling comments in *Saturday Night,* "Lane's poems are more visceral than cerebral and are not abstract at all. At their most representative they focus on a specific person or place in his life, such as a whore or a lumberjack, a jail cell or a highway." Fetherling adds, "They are characterized by a general surefootedness and realism through which he sprinkles the occasional brilliant image, the odd burst of poetry so pure it makes you squirm."

Lane was inspired to take up poetry by his older brother, Red Lane, who had begun a promising career as poet himself before his death in 1964. The younger Lane published his first collection in 1966, *Letters from the Savage Mind.* Marilyn Bowering observes in the *Malahat Review* that a poem such as "The Myth Makers" (included in this collection), "parallels the development of any young poet, but the difference with Lane was his refusal to imitate anything he didn't know firsthand (family, job, no-job), an anti-intellectual/anti-ivory tower stand risking a literature of surfaces, but allowing him to develop slowly, a poetry that is justifiably self-confident." *Canadian Forum* contributor Peter Stevens also notes Lane's tight focus on his own experience. He finds that this personal experience contains a world: "The encroachments of age, the madness of political situations, childlessness, loneliness and anonymity in the big city, outbursts of violence are all fixed within the circle of himself and the environments he lives in, visits or remembers." Stevens recognizes that "sometimes these ordinary things reduce the poems to ordinariness." However, the reviewer finds, "The cumulative effect of these poems is to make the reader feel that this poet is an individual keenly observant about himself and the world around him, sensitive without being over-emotional, realistic without milking the realism too often. This is a very good collection."

Lane's 1978 collection, *Poems: New and Selected,* brings together the best from previous works such as *Beware the Months of Fire, Unborn Things: South American Poems,* and *Albino Pheasants.* This book won Canada's prestigious Governor General's Award. As the poems collected here illustrate, Lane "writes a tough-minded, anecdotal poetry full of narratives of the hard lives of ordinary people," observes Rosemary Sullivan in the *Canadian Forum.* "The voice he chooses is often raw and violent, and his best quality is a remarkable and moving empathy for all of life that is vulnerable and pained." Sullivan continues: "Lane has a fine gift for image, and writes of the tragic not histrionically but in understatement, deflecting attention to some small detail that is made to carry the full horror of the situation." This is one of the reasons Lane is considered one of Canada's best. In fact, according to *Queen's Quarterly* contributor Christopher Levenson, "Purely in terms of linguistic control, mastery of cadence and verse movement, and command of imagery, Patrick Lane . . . has to be classed along with John Newlove and Margaret Atwood as among Canada's most accomplished contemporary poets."

Yet, Levenson, like some other critics, finds Lane's portrayal of the violence around him troubling. "In Lane's case, what we are given is no dispassionate reportage: the poet frequently seems intoxicated by the violence and cruelty that he evokes. And when cruelty not only informs the subject matter but also, via imagery, permeates the manner of the poetry," maintains Levenson, "we are entitled to regret the absence of any controlling moral stance, just as we are entitled to ask whether a talent, no matter how remarkable, that indulges in gratuitous descriptions of cruelty can ever attain to greatness." Sullivan, on the other hand, believes that Lane's "poetic energy comes from a real understanding of violence" and that this "challenges our complacency." She is convinced that Lane "is a poet with staying power. There is a fine sensual energy in his work, as well

as humour, and at moments a depth of vision that make him the best of his generation of poets."

A decade (and a half dozen other collections) after *Poems: New and Selected,* Lane offered another selection of his best. *Selected Poems* contains poems published in the 1960s, 1970s, 1980s, and new works. Reviewers of this collection recognize the harsh nature of Lane's world and his unwavering commitment to show its brutality; yet, several suggest that the poet has not exploited the violence for its sensational effect. Lawrence W. Norfolk writes in the *Times Literary Supplement,* "His style is exact and he neither pities nor exalts the hard lives he describes. There is no recourse to myth." Barbara Carey notes in *Books in Canada,* "The raw material of Lane's work may truly be raw, but its sensibility is not." And Lawrence Sail of *Stand Magazine* sees the positive value of Lane's depiction of violence. "Unmediated, this might seem little better than a macho frontiersman's view of his native Canada," Sail admits, "but violence is both seen to be appalling and comprehended as a dark inheritance which is also the context for what may yet be defined as hope or love."

Carey observes in *Selected Poems* evidence that Lane has developed into a poet who "combines flesh-and-blood immediacy with a reflective quality that deepens the work." She adds, "Call it maturity, mellowing, the perspective of age, whatever—it makes for wonderful poems. The poet emerges from a detour into more abstract, philosophical work to deliver . . . remarkable poems."

*BIOGRAPHICAL/CRITICAL SOURCES:*

*BOOKS*

*Contemporary Literary Criticism,* Volume 25, Gale (Detroit), 1983.
*Contemporary Poets,* fifth edition, St. James Press (Detroit), 1991.
*Dictionary of Literary Biography,* Volume 53: *Canadian Writers since 1960, First Series,* Gale, 1986.
Musgrave, Susan, editor, *Because You Loved Being a Stranger: Fifty-five Poets Celebrate Patrick Lane,* Harbour Publishing (Madeira Park, British Columbia), 1994.
Woodcock, George, *Patrick Lane and His Works,* ECW Press (Toronto), 1984.

*PERIODICALS*

*Books in Canada,* February, 1979, p. 24; August, 1981, p. 18; December, 1987, p. 29; June, 1990, p. 42; May, 1992, p. 47; summer, 1992, p. 60.

*Brick,* fall, 1979, p. 5.

*Canadian Forum,* March, 1968, p. 282; May, 1974, p. 20; June, 1975, p. 40; March, 1979, p. 34; March, 1980, p. 38; March, 1983, p. 34; February-March, 1989.

*Canadian Literature,* winter, 1975, p. 92; autumn, 1976, p. 84; winter, 1981, p. 102; autumn, 1989, p. 220; summer, 1991, p. 158; fall, 1993, pp. 143, 184.

*Fiddlehead,* spring, 1967.

*Malahat Review,* January, 1978, p. 24.

*Queen's Quarterly,* summer, 1980, p. 279.

*Quill and Quire,* February, 1981, p. 48; December, 1991, p. 18; June, 1992, p. 25.

*Saturday Night,* August, 1972, p. 35.

*Small Press,* October, 1990, p. 91.

*Stand Magazine,* summer, 1990, p. 46.

*Times Literary Supplement,* August 18, 1989, p. 903.

\* \* \*

**LANGE, John**
See CRICHTON, (John) Michael

\* \* \*

**LANGE, John Frederick, Jr. 1931-**
**(John Norman)**

*PERSONAL:* Born June 3, 1931, in Chicago, IL; son of John Frederick and Almyra D. (Taylor) Lange; married Bernice L. Green, January 14, 1956; children: John, David, Jennifer. *Education:* University of Nebraska, B.A., 1953; University of Southern California, M.A., 1957; Princeton University, Ph.D., 1963.

*ADDRESSES: Office*—Department of Philosophy, Queens College of the City University of New York, Flushing, NY 11367.

*CAREER:* Hamilton College, Clinton, NY, instructor in philosophy, 1962-64; Queens College of the City University of New York, Flushing, NY, 1964—, began as assistant professor, professor of philosophy,

1976—. Former story analyst for Warner Bros., staff writer and technical editor for Rocketdyne Division of North American Aviation, and radio continuity writer. *Military service:* U.S. Army, personnel management specialist; became sergeant.

*MEMBER:* American Philosophical Association, Science Fiction Writers of America.

*WRITINGS:*

(Editor) Clarence I. Lewis, *Values and Imperatives: Studies in Ethics,* Stanford University Press (Stanford, CA), 1969.

*Cognitivity Paradox: An Inquiry Concerning the Claims of Philosophy,* Princeton University Press (Princeton, NJ), 1970.

UNDER PSEUDONYM JOHN NORMAN

*Imaginative Sex,* DAW Books (New York City), 1974.

*Time Slave,* DAW Books, 1975.

*Ghost Dance,* DAW Books, 1979.

UNDER PSEUDONYM JOHN NORMAN; "THE CHRONICLES OF COUNTER-EARTH" SERIES

*Tarnsman of Gor,* Ballantine (New York City), 1966.

*Outlaw of Gor,* Ballantine, 1967.

*Priest-Kings of Gor,* Ballantine, 1968.

*Nomads of Gor,* Ballentine, 1969.

*Assassin of Gor,* Ballantine, 1970.

*Raiders of Gor,* Ballantine, 1971.

*Captive of Gor,* Ballantine, 1972.

*Gor Omnibus: The Chronicles of Counter-Earth,* Sidgwick & Jackson, 1972.

*Hunters of Gor,* DAW Books, 1974.

*Marauders of Gor,* DAW Books, 1975.

*Tribesmen of Gor,* DAW Books, 1976.

*Slave Girl of Gor,* DAW Books, 1977.

*Beasts of Gor,* DAW Books, 1977.

*Explorers of Gor,* DAW Books, 1979.

*Fighting Slave of Gor,* DAW Books, 1981.

*Guardsman of Gor,* DAW Books, 1981.

*Rogue of Gor,* DAW Books, 1981.

*Savages of Gor,* DAW Books, 1982.

*Blood Brothers of Gor,* DAW Books, 1982.

*Kajira of Gor,* DAW Books, 1983.

*Players of Gor,* DAW Books, 1984.

*Mercenaries of Gor,* DAW Books, 1985.

*Dancer of Gor,* DAW Books, 1985.

*Renegades of Gor,* DAW Books, 1986.

*Vagabonds of Gor,* DAW Books, 1987.

*Magicians of Gor,* DAW Books, 1988.

*UNDER PSEUDONYM JOHN NORMAN; "TELNARIAN HISTO-
RIES" SERIES*

*The Chieftain,* Warner Books (New York City),
1991.
*The Captain,* Warner Books, 1992.
*The Kind,* Warner Books, 1993.

OTHER

Also author of radio scripts. Contributor of articles
to philosophy journals.

*SIDELIGHTS:* John Frederick Lange, Jr. is better
known by his pseudonym, John Norman, under
which he created the best-selling science fiction series "The Chronicles of Counter-Earth." The series
is set on Gor, a primitive planet on the other side of
the sun from Earth. Tarl Cabot is a former Earthling
who has chosen to live on Gor, and his many adventures make up the exciting series. In a letter to *CA,*
Norman describes the Gor books as "intellectual and
philosophical novels, as well as adventure novels."

Many critics fail to see the intellectual or philosophical aspects of Norman's books, however. They instead criticize the series for what they see as its
sexism and obsession with bondage and slavery. Richard E. Geis of *Science Fiction Review,* for example, writes that Norman "betrays an obsession, a
compulsion, to dwell repeatedly, endlessly, minutely,
on the subject of women slaves; how to use them,
handle them, discipline them, dominate them, create
them." Similarly, Theodore Sturgeon writes in the
*New York Times Book Review* that *Hunters of Gor*
"exhibits more of its author's total obsession with
stripping, tying, whipping, and submission." He
judges the book "good fare for kinks who find *The
Story of O* too intellectual." Speaking of *Explorers of
Gor,* a *Publishers Weekly* critic states that it is "an
unsavory and oddball collection of sexist, misogynis-
tic, and sadistic notions and fantasies."

In an article for *Extrapolation,* Mary Kenny Badami
examines Norman's Gor series from a feminist perspective and finds that the books "blatantly pander to
an audience which thrills at the imagined degradation
of a woman by a man, a perversion of sexuality
which is based on power and cruelty." She cites a
chapter in *Priest-Kings of Gor* in which the male
protagonist has captured the slave-girl Vika and "has
ordered her head shaved and imprisoned her in a
cage. . . . Vika acknowledges . . . that such humiliation is really what she has wanted all along." "Nov-

els like this," Badami concludes, "play right into
bondage fantasies and sadomasochism. Ultimately I
believe they are dangerous because they foster a rape
mentality."

Reviewers also criticize Norman's writing style. Reviewing *Fighting Slave of Gor,* Geis states: "Gor is
only a device, a stage setting, on which to act out [the
author's] power fantasy in exquisite, endlessly repetitive detail. As writing, this is simply terrible. As a
novel, this is simply terrible." A *Publishers Weekly*
critic calls *Explorers of Gor* "a story of a quest. . . .
However, any similarity to Wagner or Tolkien ceases
right there. . . . There's a fair adventure story buried
in here somewhere; the question is whether one wants
to look for it." Another *Publishers Weekly* critic finds
*Time Slave* to be "a real treat for bondage fanciers who
can work their way through the author's murky and
repetitious prose; others are apt to find it disgusting."

"I have been personally belittled and slandered,"
Norman asserts in *Fantasy Voices 1,* "by individuals
I do not even know, and who do not know me.
Sometimes, I wonder seriously about the sanity and
moral character of some of these individuals."
Norman points out that his books have been bestsellers. His publisher, Donald A. Wollheim, states in
an interview with *Science Fiction Review* that readers
"who dislike [the Gor books] are outnumbered more
than ten to one by readers who find in John Norman's novels exactly what pleases their imaginations
and makes daily life more bearable."

"I am well aware," Norman once told *CA,* "that my
views, which are based on history, tradition, and
biology, may not concur with those of certain current
political orthodoxies." Norman sees his work being
unfairly judged partly because of the views he presents. As he states in *Fantasy Voices 1,* "The Gorean
books have introduced new subject matter and new
ideas to science fiction. They have plowed new conceptual furrows; they have altered, in the thinking of
thousands, the conceptions and horizons of science
fiction. The borders of science fiction have been
extended by my work; new possibilities have been
delineated and explored. It is natural that these
changes would be felt as threatening to a vain, stale,
insecure establishment."

Addressing the complaint that the Gor stories glam-
orize rape, Norman told *CA:* "Rape is one of those
buzz words which often serves as a substitute for
putting reasons, and intelligence, and facts, on the
table. The Gorean books do celebrate male virility.

They also celebrate feminine response to strong, dominant males. What one of our critics calls the 'rape mentality' is nothing more than our old friend, male virility."

Speaking of the sex scenes presented in the Gor books, and the critical reaction to them, Norman explained to *CA:* "Strong sexual fantasy has been long recognized as clinically therapeutic. It is safe, sound, healthy, moral, and desirable. Check in with your local psychiatrist. Sex dramas, for example, can considerably enliven, and enhance, the sex lives of human beings. There is nothing immoral about applying the wonders and delights of the imagination to sexual experience. Too, it might be noted that some people desire strong sexual experiences, and thrill to have them. . . . Imaginative sex is wonderful. The critic activists' implicit insistence on *unimaginative sex* is their business. If they are content with an essentially subhuman sex life, a reduced sex life, one, in my view, beneath and unfit for a rational animal, one which dares not exceed the sexual outlook and practices of the cocker spaniel, squirrel, and turtledove, that is their business. Who am I to complain about what they choose to miss? One must, however, regret the tragic harm that the views of such individuals, with their uncritical, mindless espousal of the secular residue of pathological Puritanism, might inflict on the ignorant, on those who might otherwise be capable of a better life, and greater joys."

## BIOGRAPHICAL/CRITICAL SOURCES:

### BOOKS

Elliott, Jeffrey M., *Fantasy Voices 1,* Borgo Press (San Bernardino, CA), 1982.

### PERIODICALS

*Amazing Stories,* June, 1967.
*Extrapolation,* December, 1976.
*Fantastic Stories,* November, 1973.
*Galaxy,* July, 1976.
*New Worlds,* April, 1970.
*New York Times Book Review,* September 8, 1974.
*Paunch,* Number 48, 1977.
*Publishers Weekly,* November 11, 1974; October 13, 1975; February 6, 1978; January 29, 1979.
*Science Fiction Review,* November, 1979; May, 1980.
*Times Literary Supplement,* October 16, 1969; April 9, 1970.
*Worlds of If,* January/February, 1971; July/August, 1974.

## LAPINE, James (Elliot) 1949-

*PERSONAL:* Born January 10, 1949, in Mansfield, OH; son of David Sanford and Lillian (Feld) Lapine; married Sarah Marshall Kernochan (a screenwriter), February 24, 1985; children: Phoebe. *Education:* Franklin and Marshall College, B.A., 1971; California Institute of Arts, M.F.A., 1973.

*ADDRESSES: Home*—New York, NY. *Agent*—George Lane, William Morris Agency, 1350 Avenue of the Americas, New York, NY 10019.

*CAREER:* Worked as graphic designer and photographer; stage director and writer. Architectural League of New York, New York City, architectural preservationist, 1973-75; Yale University, New Haven, CT, resident graphic designer and later teacher at the drama school, beginning c. 1976; teacher at the Fashion Institute of Technology; director of stage productions, including *March of the Falsettos,* 1981, *A Midsummer Night's Dream,* 1982, *Merrily We Roll Along* (revised version), 1985, *Sunday in the Park with George,* 1986, *Into the Woods,* 1988, *The Winter's Tale,* 1989, *Falsettos,* 1992, and *Passion,* 1994; and director of films, including *Into the Woods* for PBS American Playhouse, 1988, *Impromptu,* 1989, and *Life with Mikey,* 1993.

*AWARDS, HONORS:* Obie Award from *Village Voice,* for *Photograph;* George Oppenheimer/Newsday Award, for *Table Settings;* award for best musical book from New York Drama Critics Circle, 1984, Pulitzer Prize for drama, 1985, and Olivier Award, all for *Sunday in the Park with George;* Antoinette Perry ("Tony") Award for best musical book from American Theatre Wing and League of American Theatres, award for best book of a musical from New York Drama Critics Circle, and Drama Desk Award, all 1988, and Evening Standard Award and London Critics Award, 1991, all for *Into the Woods;* Outer Critics Circle Award (with William Finn) for best musical, 1990, for *Falsettoland;* Tony Award for best musical book, 1992, for *Falsettos;* Tony Awards for best musical (with Stephen Sondheim) and best book of a musical, and Drama Desk Award for best book of a musical, 1994, for *Passion.* Received honorary degree from Franklin and Marshall College, 1994.

*WRITINGS:*

(And director) *Photograph* (play adapted from Gertrude Stein's poem), produced in New Haven at Yale Repertory Theatre in the 1970s, produced in New York City at Open Space Theatre, 1977.

(And director) *Table Settings* (play; produced Off-Broadway at Playwrights Horizons, March, 1980), Performing Arts Journal Publications, 1980.

(With William Finn; and director) *March of the Falsettos* (also see below; one-act musical; first produced Off-Broadway at Playwrights Horizons, 1981, produced at Lincoln Center, New York City, 1995), Plume (New York City), 1993.

(And director) *Twelve Dreams* (play; produced Off-Broadway at Public Theatre/Martinson Hall, December, 1981), Doubleday (New York City), 1982, revised edition, Dramatists Play Service (New York City), 1996.

(With Stephen Sondheim; and director) *Sunday in the Park with George* (two-act musical; lyrics and music by Sondheim, book by Lapine; first produced on Broadway at the Booth Theatre, May 2, 1984), Dodd, Mead (New York City), 1986.

(With Sondheim; and director) *Into the Woods* (two-act musical; lyrics and music by Sondheim, book by Lapine; first produced in San Diego at the Old Globe Theatre, November, 1986; produced on Broadway at the Martin Beck Theatre, November 5, 1987), Crown (New York City), 1988.

(With William Finn; and director) *Falsettoland* (also see below; one-act musical; first produced Off-Broadway at Playwrights Horizons, June 28, 1990), Plume, 1993.

(With William Finn; and director) *Falsettos* (two-act musical comprised of *March of the Falsettos* and *Falsettoland;* first produced on Broadway at the John Golden Theatre, April 29, 1992), Plume, 1993.

(And director) *Luck, Pluck, and Virtue* (play), produced at La Jolla Playhouse, 1993, and at Atlantic Theatre Co., 1995.

(With Stephen Sondheim; and director) *Passion* (one-act musical; produced on Broadway at the Plymouth Theater, 1994), Theatre Communications Group, 1995.

Work anthologized in *Wordplay V: New American Drama,* Performing Arts Journal Publications, 1986.

*ADAPTATIONS: Into the Woods* was adapted for television and broadcast on *American Playhouse,* PBS, 1988; *Passion* was filmed and broadcast by PBS, 1994.

*SIDELIGHTS:* James Lapine is an important Broadway writer and director. Though best known for his award-winning musicals written with songwriter Stephen Sondheim, Lapine has also written dramas.

He produced his first work, *Photograph,* in response to a challenge from students at Yale University's Repertory Theatre, where he had been teaching graphic arts. *Photograph,* which Lapine derived from Gertrude Stein's five-part poem, proved immensely popular at Yale, and upon playing at New York City's Open Space Theatre in 1977 it received an Obie Award from *Village Voice.*

Following the success of *Photograph,* which he had also directed, Lapine devoted himself more fully to a career in theater. In 1980 he directed the Off-Broadway production of his second play, *Table Settings.* This work concerns the interactions of various members of a middle-class Jewish family during several meals. Many of the characters are deliberate Jewish stereotypes—the tirelessly devoted mother, the nervous oldest son (a lawyer) married to a perky gentile—and Lapine continually exploits them for comic absurdity. "The characters and their well-nourished plights are as instantly recognizable as billboards," wrote Richard Eder in his *New York Times* review. "What Mr. Lapine has done is to work his particular kind of humor into them." Eder added that "quite a few of the sketches are amusing and many seem fresher than they are, thanks to the author's talent and the unexpected leaks he has let into his stereotypes." Walter Kerr, another *New York Times* critic, also considered Lapine an enterprising comic writer, remarking, "He just bends the universe a little and it works." In addition, Kerr praised the technical aspects of the Off-Broadway production, noting that the play was "sleekly staged and crisply, confidently acted by all present."

Lapine returned to Off-Broadway in 1981 with *Twelve Dreams,* an explicitly psychoanalytical drama—set in New England in the late 1930s—about a woman who dreams of ominous insects and animals. The heroine's father is a Freudian psychoanalyst who proves unable to fathom his daughter's nightmares. He plays host, however, to an elderly Jungian professor who interprets the dreams as timeless exemplifications of death and rebirth. Meanwhile, Europe becomes the scene of increasing political and social upheaval. As the situation there degenerates, so too does the heroine's health. Eventually, her dreams seem somehow related to the impending catastrophes of World War II and the Holocaust. Writing in the *New York Times,* Frank Rich praised *Twelve Dreams* as "an imaginative—and well produced—effort." He conceded that the play required some "enriching, filling in," but nonetheless commended "the brilliance of [Lapine's] overall conception."

In 1984 Lapine completed *Sunday in the Park with George,* his first collaboration with renowned Broadway songwriter Stephen Sondheim. This unusual musical explores the nature of creativity by focusing on the struggles of two artists. The first act concerns painter Georges Seurat as he created his mid-1880s pointillist masterpiece, *Sunday Afternoon on the Island of La Grand Jatte.* While at work on the vast canvas, Seurat contemplates his art and tunefully exchanges observations with his pregnant mistress, Dot. The second act, set one hundred years later, concerns Dot's great-grandson, also named George, who is devising an electronic light show. Much of this act details George's struggle to determine his own artistry in a world of increasing compromise and commercialism. Eventually, he finds self-confidence and strength as an artist. This breakthrough is celebrated in two of the musical's finest songs, "Children and Art" and "Move On."

*Sunday in the Park with George* was a great success when it began playing on Broadway in 1984. Among the musical's most enthusiastic supporters was *Newsweek*'s Jack Kroll, who hailed it as a work "of more daring and surprise than the American musical stage has seen in a long time." For Kroll, *Sunday in the Park with George* proved "not only a musical about an artist but a musical about art, about its triumphs, pains and its inescapable necessity." In addition, he lauded the musical for its innovation and thematic daring, and he concluded by commending it as a work of "beauty, wit, nobility and ardor."

Other reviewers concurred with Kroll's assessment of *Sunday in the Park with George.* *Time* reviewer Richard Corliss found it a demanding but ultimately rewarding work—"a shapely object of art." *Los Angeles Times* reviewer Sylvie Drake deemed it a considerable triumph for its creators. "Not only do Sondheim and Lapine break new ground," she declared, "but they fill in the details without compromising the non-plot's non-linear development." Equally impressed was the *Chicago Tribune*'s Richard Christiansen, who acclaimed *Sunday in the Park with George* as Broadway's "class act" of 1984. He described the musical as "a show of deep feelings on life and art" and acknowledged its "moments of breathtaking beauty."

Lapine and Sondheim continued their collaboration with the musical *Into the Woods.* This work, which has been described as a children's story for adults, features such prominent fairy-tale figures as Little Red Riding Hood, Cinderella, and Jack, the giant killer. In the first act, these and other characters share adventures and, as is usual in fairy tales, revel in

what is apparently a happy ending. The second act, however, explores what happens to these characters as their lives continue after the happy ending. Here loved ones die, marriages degenerate into resentment and mistrust, and moral issues grow distressingly complex. By work's end several characters are dead, and the survivors, confused and frightened, are only somewhat reassured of their continued well-being.

*Into the Woods* played Broadway beginning in 1987 and earned mixed reviews. Frank Rich, in his *New York Times* review, complained that Lapine's book "is as wildly overgrown as the forest," but he also acknowledged the musical's conception as "brilliant." Dan Sullivan, who reviewed *Into the Woods* in the *Los Angeles Times,* also expressed both dissatisfaction and delight. He described the first act as "dazzling" but dismissed the second one as "a letdown." In assessing the show's first half, Sullivan lauded inventive handling of the fairy-tale narratives. He wrote: "The fun . . . is to see how wittily Lapine and Sondheim work out the intersections of their stories. . . . The matching of story, character, words and music is elegant here." Sullivan claimed that the show lapsed into platitudes in the second half, though he suggested that more modifications might prove corrective.

Although reviewers were reserved in their overall praise for *Into the Woods,* the musical became a popular success and earned Tony Awards for best musical book and best score. A short time later, in a 1988 *CA* interview, Lapine discussed his future plans. "I would like to take a little break from doing big musicals," he admitted, "And though I would like to work with Steve [Sondheim] again, I think maybe we're going to take a little break from one another on the next go-round."

Though he would rejoin Sondheim in a few years, Lapine's next "go-round" was indeed with another collaborator. In 1981, Lapine had teamed up with William Finn to create *March of the Falsettos,* a one-act musical about a gay man's search for love and happiness inside and outside the traditional American family. Nine years later, in 1990, they reunited to produce a sequel, using the same characters, that would take into account the AIDS crisis that had so heavily affected the gay community. The result was a second one-act, *Falsettoland.* In 1992 Finn and Lapine combined the two Off-Broadway pieces into a single bill, *Falsettos,* for which the artists received Tony Awards for best score and best book.

The first act of *Falsettos,* which was conceived in the pre-dawn of the AIDS epidemic, before the disease was widely known and understood, concerns Marvin, a Jewish businessman in his early forties who, in his middle age, emerges from the closet, leaves his wife, Trina, and son, Jason, and runs away with Whizzer, a younger man. Marvin tries desperately to keep all the parts of his suddenly scattered life together—his love affair with Whizzer, his continuing affectionate relationship with his wife and the respect of his son. Amazingly, he is successful for awhile.

Eventually, though, the threads begin to unravel: Trina finds romance with Mendel, the family psychiatrist; Jason approaches puberty and notices girls; and Whiz-zer's fickleness dooms his relationship with Marvin. The act ends with a father-son reconciliation that nevertheless suggests a rocky road ahead. Two years pass between acts. During that time, Marvin explains in the opening number, a truce has been called in the family, Trina and Mendel remain happily married, Jason is being prepared for his bar mitzvah, and Marvin, still unattached, has become close friends with a lesbian couple next door. Whizzer rejoins the clan at one of Jason's little league baseball games and soon he and Marvin are together again. Complications arise when Whizzer is hospitalized with an unnamed malady (obviously meant to be AIDS) and Jason can't decide on whether to go through with his bar mitzvah. The sad yet funny solution, of course, and the climax to the show, is to hold the event in the hospital room where Whizzer lays dying.

Several critics commented on the unique style of *Falsettos*—its ability to be alternately tragic and hilarious and its inventive, soul-stirring songs masked by irreverent titles like "Four Jews in a Room Bitching" and "My Father's a Homo." In the *New York Times* Frank Rich suggested, "The songs are so fresh that the show is only a few bars old before one feels the unmistakable, revivifying charge of pure talent." Ken Mandel-baum of *Theatre Week* magazine wrote, "Though the second half of *Falsettoland* is profoundly moving, the first half is hilarious. Together, the two halves add up to a wonderful evening." A few reviewers placed the separate acts of "Falsettos" in their historical context. Gerald Weales noted in *Commonweal,* "Surprisingly, since it dates from the innocent gay days before AIDS was clearly perceived as the horror it has become, the first act is darker, tougher, funnier, more inventive than the later work." For Weales the "chirpiness" of the second act detracts from its serious themes. Thomas Disch, on the other hand, writing for the *Nation,* felt that

"Act I offers little that Act II doesn't provide in a more emotionally intense and/or musically effective form."

A relatively small cadre of critics disliked *Falsettos.* In the *New Leader,* for instance, Stefan Kanfer wrote, "Confused and insupportable rage puts the false in *Falsettos,* a show that advertises itself as breakthrough Broadway fare. In an unintended sense it is: the first major example of special pleading in four-fourths time." However, it received more praise than damnation. Frank Rich even contributed an afterword to the Plume published edition of the text in which he describes the experience of bringing his two young sons to see the show. Rich wrote, "I was . . . grateful to take my children to a show that depicts homosexuals neither as abject victims of prejudice or disease nor as campy figures of fun but as sometimes likable, sometimes smarmy, sometimes witty, sometimes fallible, sometimes juvenile, sometimes noble people no more or less extraordinary than the rest of us. In other words, gay people are just part of the family in *Falsettos,* and the values of Marvin's family are those of any other."

For his next creative effort, Lapine joined ranks with Sondheim again to produce *Passion,* an opera-style musical based on *Passione d'Amore,* a 1981 Italian film by Ettore Scola, which was in turn based on *Fosca,* an 1869 novel by Igino Ugo Tarchetti. The plot is a variation of sorts on *Beauty and the Beast,* told largely through a series of letters the principle characters exchange with one another. The setting is Italy in 1863. Giorgio, a handsome captain in the Italian army, has been transferred to a provincial outpost and must leave behind Clara, his beautiful, married mistress. When he arrives at his post he meets the regiment's commanding officer, Colonel Ricci, and his sickly cousin, the homely, disturbed Fosca.

When Giorgio shows Fosca some mild kindness, she is immediately enamored of him. Her love leads to obsession, though Giorgio makes it clear he has no feelings for her other than friendship. She eventually falls ill, pining for her captain, and Giorgio rushes to her bedside to console her. His sympathy for the pathetic Fosca leads him to agree to write a letter to her—an expression of love that she herself dictates.

Soon after, Giorgio also becomes sick and is sent home to recuperate. While there he asks Clara to leave her husband and run away with him, but she refuses, for the sake of her son. Giorgio returns to his camp where

Colonel Ricci challenges him to a duel over the honor of Fosca. On the evening before the duel Giorgio visits Fosca and surrenders to the passion she has awakened in his heart. While he loved Clara, he tells her, no one has ever loved him the way Fosca has.

In the duel the next morning Giorgio wounds the Colonel, then falls to the ground with an hysterical scream. The musical ends with the captain in a sanitorium, recovering from a mental breakdown. The Colonel has recovered from his wound and Fosca has died, leaving Giorgio to ruminate on the depth of passion they have shared.

Like their earlier collaborations, *Passion* garnered Sondheim and Lapine several awards, including Tony Awards for best musical, best original score (Sondheim) and best book (Lapine). Critical reaction, however, was less enthusiastic. In a *New Yorker* review titled "Love in Gloom," John Lahr complained, "What we get in this listless epistolary musical, where the main characters spend much of their time singing love letters to and from each other, is the results of Sondheim's recent experiments with the play's director and librettist, James Lapine: not the big heart but the dead heart; not the joy of the pleasure dome but the hush of the lecture hall; not dancing but reading."

John Simon, in *New York*, took Lapine and Sondheim to task for not providing greater variety within the book and music. "There have been musicals about which the complaint was that all the songs sounded similar," noted Simon, "this one goes a step further: All the songs sound the same. The score is a glutinous mass; although there are ample passages of dialogue, it comes across as through-composed."

Robert Brustein, however, revealed in the *New Republic*, "I know it is not seemly for a drama critic to admit to experiencing excessive feeling, especially over a work that, despite its (grudgingly given) Tony awards, is drawing a lot of scorn in sophisticated theater circles. But I am compelled to tell you that . . . *Passion* held me in its grip from the opening chords and had me sobbing uncontrollably at the end." Brustein's explanation for the abuse *Passion* had been taking in the press was that it "has been misidentified as a musical and mislocated in a Broadway house. The work is clearly an opera, and were it sitting where it belongs, on the stage of the Houston Grand Opera or the Chicago Lyric, I'm convinced it would have elicited the kind of respect it truly deserves."

Lapine continues to write and direct for both the theater and cinema, and usually works on several projects simultaneously. More directing opportunities are coming his way, and he has committed to a film version of *Falsettos* for Disney. "I like to keep busy," the writer/director told the *Los Angeles Times*. "I seem to function better when I'm doing a few things at once." The variety of subjects he has tackled in the past makes future projects difficult to predict, even for Lapine himself. "I like to work intuitively," he claimed. "Part of the fun is the mystery of where one simple idea can take you."

*BIOGRAPHICAL/CRITICAL SOURCES:*

*BOOKS*

*Contemporary Literary Criticism,* Volume 39, Gale (Detroit), 1986.
*Falsettos,* by William Finn and James Lapine, Plume, 1993.

*PERIODICALS*

*America,* September 24, 1994, p. 25.
*Chicago Tribune,* May 3, 1984; December 7, 1986.
*Commonweal,* October 9, 1992, pp. 22-23.
*Globe and Mail* (Toronto), November 7, 1987.
*Los Angeles Times,* May 20, 1984; November 26, 1984; November 6, 1987; August 1, 1993, p. 3.
*Nation,* June 8, 1992, pp. 797-799; June 13, 1994, p. 843.
*New Leader,* June 1, 1992, pp. 30-31; July 4, 1994, pp. 22-23.
*New Republic,* August 1, 1994, pp. 29-30.
*New York,* May 23, 1994, pp. 70-71; April 17, 1995, pp. 111-112.
*New Yorker,* May 23, 1994, p. 89.
*New York Times,* March 24, 1979; January 15, 1980; February 1, 1980; December 22, 1981; April 29, 1984; May 3, 1984; May 13, 1984; March 6, 1987; October 9, 1987; November 1, 1987; November 6, 1987; January 7, 1990; June 24, 1990; June 29, 1990, p. C3; June 13, 1994, p. C11.
*Newsweek,* May 14, 1984, pp. 83-4.
*Playbill,* January, 1988.
*Theatre Week,* July 16, 1990, pp. 42-43.
*Time,* May 14, 1984; May 23, 1994, p. 68.
*Times* (London), May 5, 1984.
*Washington Post,* November 6, 1987.

—*Sketch by Lane A. Glenn*

## LESSING, Doris (May) 1919-
### (Jane Somers)

*PERSONAL:* Born October 22, 1919, in Kermanshah, Persia (now Iran); daughter of Alfred Cook Taylor (a farmer) and Emily Maude McVeagh; married Frank Charles Wisdom, 1939 (marriage dissolved, 1943); married Gottfried Anton Nicholas Lessing, 1945 (marriage dissolved, 1949); children: (first marriage) John (deceased), Jean; (second marriage) Peter. *Education:* Attended Roman Catholic Convent, then Girls' High School, both in Salisbury, Southern Rhodesia (now Harare, Zimbabwe); left school at age 14.

*ADDRESSES: Agent*—c/o Jonathan Clowes Ltd., 10 Iron Bridge House, Bridge Approach, London NW1 8BD, England.

*CAREER:* Writer. Worked as a nursemaid, a lawyer's secretary, a Hansard typist, and a Parliamentary Com-missioner's typist while living in Southern Rhodesia, 1924-49.

*MEMBER:* National Institute of Arts and Letters, American Academy of Arts and Letters, Modern Language Association (honorary fellow), Institute of Cultural Research.

*AWARDS, HONORS:* Somerset Maugham Award, Society of Authors, 1954, for *Five: Short Novels;* short-listed for the Booker McConnell Prize, 1971, for *Briefing for a Descent into Hell,* 1981, for *The Sirian Experiments: The Report of Ambien II, of the Five,* and 1985, for *The Good Terrorist;* Prix Medicis Award for work translated into French, 1976, for *The Golden Notebook;* Austrian State Prize for European Literature, 1981; German Federal Republic Shakespeare Prize, 1982; Australian Science Fiction Achievement Award (Ditmars) nomination, 1982, for *The Sirian Experiments: The Report of Ambien II, of the Five;* W. H. Smith Literary Award, 1986, Palermo Prize, 1987, and Premio Internazionale Mondello, 1987, all for *The Good Terrorist;* Grinzane Cavour award (Italy), 1989, for *The Fifth Child;* honorary degree, Princeton University, 1989, and Harvard University, 1995; distinguished fellow, University of East Anglia, 1991; James Tait Black Memorial Book Prize, University of Edinburgh, and *Los Angeles Times* Book Prize, both 1995, both for *Under My Skin.*

*WRITINGS:*

*FICTION*

*The Grass Is Singing,* Crowell (New York City), 1950, reprinted, Penguin Books (New York City), 1991.
*This Was the Old Chief's Country* (stories), M. Joseph (London), 1952.
*Five: Short Novels,* M. Joseph, 1955.
*Retreat to Innocence,* M. Joseph, 1956.
*Habit of Loving* (stories), Crowell, 1958.
*The Golden Notebook,* Simon & Schuster (New York City), 1962, published with an introduction by the author, Harper Perennial (New York City), 1994.
*A Man and Two Women* (stories), Simon & Schuster, 1963.
*African Stories,* M. Joseph, 1964, Simon & Schuster, 1965.
*Briefing for a Descent into Hell,* Knopf (New York City), 1971.
*The Temptation of Jack Orkney and Other Stories,* Knopf, 1972, published in England as *The Story of a Non-Marrying Man and Other Stories,* J. Cape (London), 1972.
*The Summer before the Dark,* Knopf, 1973.
*The Memoirs of a Survivor,* Random House (New York City), 1975.
*Stories,* Knopf, 1978, originally published in England as *Collected Stories I: To Room Nineteen* and *Collected Stories II: The Temptation of Jack Orkney and Other Stories,* J. Cape, 1978.
(Under pseudonym Jane Somers) *The Diary of a Good Neighbor* (also see below) Knopf, 1983.
(Under pseudonym Jane Somers) *If the Old Could . . . ,* Knopf, 1984 (also see below).
*The Diaries of Jane Somers* (contains *The Diary of a Good Neighbor* and *If the Old Could . . .*), Random House, 1984.
*The Good Terrorist,* Knopf, 1985.
*The Fifth Child,* Knopf, 1988.
*The Doris Lessing Reader,* Knopf, 1989.
*The Real Thing: Stories and Sketches,* Harper-Collins (New York City), 1992, published in England as *London Observed: Stories and Sketches,* Harper-Collins (London), 1992.
*Playing the Game Graphic Novel,* HarperCollins, 1993.
*Winter in July,* Flamingo (London), 1993.
*Love, Again,* HarperCollins, 1996.

*"CHILDREN OF VIOLENCE" SERIES*

*Martha Quest,* M. Joseph, 1952.
*A Proper Marriage,* M. Joseph, 1954, reprinted, Plume (New York City), 1991.

*A Ripple from the Storm,* M. Joseph, 1958, reprinted, Plume, 1991.

*Landlocked,* Simon & Schuster, 1966, reprinted, Plume, 1991.

*The Four-Gated City,* Knopf, 1969, reprinted, Plume, 1991.

*"CANOPUS IN ARGOS: ARCHIVES" SERIES*

*Re: Colonized Planet V, Shikasta,* Knopf, 1979.

*The Marriage between Zones Three, Four, and Five,* Knopf, 1980.

*The Sirian Experiments: The Report of Ambien II, of the Five,* Knopf, 1981.

*The Making of the Representative for Planet 8,* Knopf, 1982.

*Documents Relating to the Sentimental Agents in the Volyen Empire,* Knopf, 1983.

*Canopus in Argos: Archives* (contains *Re: Colonized Planet V, Shikasta, The Marriage between Zones Three, Four, and Five, The Sirian Experiments: The Report of Ambien II, of the Five, The Making of the Representative for Planet 8,* and *Documents Relating to the Sentimental Agents in the Volyen Empire*), Vintage Books (New York City), 1992.

*NONFICTION*

*Going Home,* M. Joseph, 1957.

*In Pursuit of the English,* Simon & Schuster, 1961.

*Particularly Cats,* Simon & Schuster, 1967, revised edition published as *Particularly Cats—And Rufus,* Knopf, 1991.

*A Small Personal Voice: Essays, Reviews, Interviews,* Random House, 1975.

*Prisons We Choose to Live Inside,* Harper (New York City), 1987.

*The Wind Blows away Our Words,* Random House, 1987.

*African Laughter: Four Visits to Zimbabwe,* HarperCollins, 1992.

*Under My Skin* (autobiography), HarperCollins, 1994.

*PLAYS*

*Mr. Dollinger,* first produced in Oxford, England, at Oxford Playhouse, 1958.

*Each in His Own Wilderness,* first produced in London, England at Royal Court, March 23, 1958.

*The Truth about Billy Newton,* first produced in Salisbury, England, 1961.

*Play with a Tiger* (first produced in London at Comedy Theatre, March 22, 1962; produced in New York City at Renata Theatre, December 30, 1964), M. Joseph, 1962.

Also author of a libretto based on *The Making of the Representative for Planet 8,* for an opera by Philip Glass.

*OTHER*

*Fourteen Poems,* Scorpion Press, 1959.

*ADAPTATIONS: The Memoirs of a Survivor* was adapted into a film and released in 1983; *The Grass Is Singing* was adapted into a film by Michael Raeburn and released as *Killing Heat* in 1984.

*WORK IN PROGRESS:* Two volumes of autobiography.

*SIDELIGHTS:* Doris Lessing, whose long career as a novelist, short story writer, and essayist began in 1949, is considered among the most important writers of the postwar era. Since her birth in 1919 in Britain's sphere of influence in Persia (now Iran), Lessing has traveled widely, in geographical, social, political, psychological, and literary terms. These travels, as expressed in her writing, offer insights into life at distant outposts of the British Empire and at its core. They encounter people buffeted by personal, historical, and political forces, and they explore the major issues of the twentieth century: racism, communism, feminism, terrorism, and the destruction of the environment. "Lessing has written prolifically on everything from British colonialism . . . to the failure of ideology," comments Gail Caldwell in the *Boston Globe.* Adds the reviewer, "In more than 30 books, she's taken on the apocalyptic potential of a futuristic, Blade Runner London, the perils of the color bar in Africa, the life of a young girl growing up on the veld." This wide-ranging literary appetite is one of the defining characteristics of her work. "Critics have found it extremely hard to categorize Lessing," observes Fiona R. Barnes in the *Dictionary of Literary Biography,* "for she has at various stages of her life espoused different causes and been labeled over again." Barnes continues, "While she displays a powerful commitment to causes she views as vital to the survival of humankind, her greatest strength lies in her flexibility. She is always prepared to change her views to accommodate new insights and contradictions."

In 1924, Lessing's father took the family to Southern Rhodesia (now Zimbabwe) in search of a fortune growing corn and tobacco and panning for gold. The family found little fortune on its farm in a remote corner of the Rhodesian bush not far from the border with Mozambique. However, in her years growing up in the African wild, her stays in convent and government schools, and her brief career as a secretary and homemaker, Lessing found a wealth of literary inspiration. As Mark Mathabane notes in the *Washington Post Book World,* "The formidable problems of racial, social and economic injustice besieging the region of her formative years, its wondrous beauty and unfulfilled promise, left a permanent imprint on her. They molded her artistic temperament, politics and loyalties and made of her a highly original and activist writer." In 1949, Lessing left Africa behind for the heart of the empire, London. She also left behind most of her family—her brother, her two failed marriages, and her two children from her first marriage. With her son from her second marriage, she embarked on a new life in London as a writer. Her first novel, *The Grass Is Singing,* was published the following year.

Like many of the novels and short stories that would follow its debut, *The Grass Is Singing* deals with settings, characters, and issues very close to its author's experience—Rhodesian society and its apartheid. The central character of the novel is Mary Turner, the wife of a farmer in the African bush. Her affair with one of the African servants ends in her murder. "Mary Turner is a strange, sad woman, suffering under the burden of obligations imposed upon her as a white woman by the sad, strange conventions of a colonial settler society," writes K. Anthony Appiah in the *New Republic.* "The novel is intensely humane in its attentiveness to the minutest details of the mental life of this central character." In the opinion of *New York Review of Books* contributor J. M. Coetzee , this book represents "an astonishingly accomplished debut, though perhaps too wedded to romantic stereotypes of the African for present-day tastes." At the time of Lessing's debut in 1950, however, Appiah observes, "reviewers pronounced her the finest new novelist since the war."

Two years after her initial success, Lessing embarked on what would become a series of five autobiographical novels published over a period of seventeen years. This "Children of Violence" series has enjoyed wide critical acclaim. Marjorie M. Bitker writes: "There seems no doubt that this work will rank with the foremost fictional commentaries on events of our century up to and perhaps beyond the present." "The series' importance," says Florence Howe, is based on the fact that Lessing "is writing *bildungsroman* and at the same time . . . she is producing good political fiction. Her themes are major: the politics of race and war; . . . the West's changing attitude toward the Soviet Union; the shift from the Second World War to the cold war; worldwide revolutionary struggle against the West and capitalism; the problem of violence." To quote Lessing, "Martha [Quest, the protagonist] did not believe in violence. [Yet] Martha was the essence of violence, she has been conceived, bred, fed, and reared on violence . . . because she had been born at the end of one world war, and had spent all her adolescence in the atmosphere of preparations for another which had lasted five years and had inflicted such wounds on the human race that no one had any idea of what the results would be."

In "Children of Violence," according to Walter Allen, "Doris Lessing does for a young woman something very similar to what Arnold Bennett did in *Clayhanger* and D. H. Lawrence did in *Sons and Lovers* for a young man, but the closer parallel is probably with George Eliot. . . . Doris Lessing shows her kinship to George Eliot both in her technique here and in her sober, unsentimental scrutiny of behavior, motives and morals." Lessing's intent, writes Howe, is "extremely ambitious" and her success, of course, has been debated. "But the canvas large enough to contain world events and small enough to measure the growth of a human being is one that only the very greatest novelists have tried." He adds, "Martha's half-conscious identification of her own lot with the Africans', as she struggles against the tyranny of paternalistic personal relations, is a motif that lights the novel. Her personal wars are refractions of that other, greater war. And if she is slow to learn how to manage her wars, who is quick?" Bitker concludes that "the bare bones of the plot are the least of the riches of this work; its nuances, complexities and implications for our own time and country are unforgettable. For we, like Martha, are children of violence."

Lessing's major and most controversial novel is *The Golden Notebook,* published in 1962, wherein she brilliantly explores, as a *New Statesman* reviewer noted, what it is like to be "free and responsible, a woman in relation to men and other women, and to struggle to come to terms with one's self about these things and about writing and politics." Lessing considers the book to be "a novel about certain political and sexual attitudes that have force now; it is an attempt to explain them, to objectivize them, to set them in relation with each other. So in a way it is a social novel, written by someone whose training—or at least whose habit of mind—is to see these things socially, not personally." In its structure, the novel is really two novels, divided in four sections, and "the Golden Notebook." Lessing split it into four parts, she says, in order to "express a split person. I felt that if the artist's sensibility is to be equated with the sensibility of the educated person, then it is logical to use different styles to express different kinds of people." She feels that the "personality is very much what is remembered; [the form I used] enabled me to say to the reader: Look, these apparently so different people have got so-and-so in common, or these things have got this in common. If I had used a conventional style, the old-fashioned novel, which I do not think is dead by any means, . . . I would not have been able to do this kind of playing with time, memory and the balancing of people. . . . I like *The Golden Notebook* even though I believe it to be a failure, because it at least hints at complexity."

Robert Taubman expresses similar sentiments, although he is a bit confused concerning the book's structure. He calls the book "a very full novel: it not only burst the bounds of the short formal novel, as it set out to do, but overflowed its own bounds as well. It's pretty well inexhaustible on the way women think and behave, notably in the area where their personal feelings and social and political attitudes meet." But, he adds, "its unusual structure is less a matter of subtle organization than of simple, rather haphazard naturalism, . . . [or perhaps] an advance in naturalism." Neither Lessing nor the book's reviewers could foresee the impact it would have on women and feminism. But, as Gail Caldwell writes in a 1994 feature on the author, "Lessing's 1962 novel changed the face of modern English fiction and influenced a generation of women writers as well as readers. . . . Capturing the life of the mind from a female point of view, then displaying it in an arc of fractured brilliance, [it] emerged as a classic treatise by nature of the gap it filled."

Lessing explores the same concerns found in her novels in short stories and novellas. J. M. Edelstein believes that, on the basis of *African Stories* alone, "Doris Lessing must be counted as one of the most important fiction writers of our times." As political and social commentaries these stories "confirm in precise and painful detail, like stitches in a wound,

the abuse of the native population of Southern Rhodesia by the white settlers of British descent," writes Mary Ellmann. "Doris Lessing's work is an uninterrupted study of loneliness, but here it is particularly the isolation of a few white exiles, claiming vast strange land. . . . For her first thirty years . . . Doris Lessing seems to have listened to Southern Rhodesia as no other writer has been able to do. It remained, even after she had left it, all nature to her. As one associates her English work with flats and offices, one associates the African stories with swollen suns and moons, head-tail grass, and the secret constant stirring of animal life. . . . Africa is for her not only a society in which the white people use their exile like a weapon against the black; but also a place, supporting both white and black, which endlessly enacts the conflict of forms, the effort of every living thing, at the cost of other living things, to achieve what is right for itself, its sustenance and continuation. Africa, not England, impressed the knowledge of necessary cruelty."

After her initial flourishing as a writer during which time she explored the Africa of her youth from her new home in London, Lessing turned away from the mythic land of her past toward new settings: inner space and outer space. *Briefing for a Descent into Hell* is a novel of ideas based on Lessing's interest in the views of British psychiatrist R. D. Laing. In subsequent novels, Lessing continued to produce work that critiqued modern society. In contrast to the realism that marked her earlier novels, though, Lessing's work in this middle period—particularly her science fiction series titled *"Canopus in Argos: Archives"*—took startling new forms. In the five volumes of the *"Canopus"* series, Lessing explores the destruction of life brought about by catastrophe and tyranny. Paul Schlueter in the *Dictionary of Literary Biography* notes that in this series Lessing's "high seriousness in describing earth's own decline and ultimate demise is as profoundly apocalyptic as ever."

Following her foray into science fiction, Lessing again surprised readers and critics by publishing two novels under a pseudonym, Jane Somers. *The Diary of a Good Neighbor* and *If the Old Could* . . . contain typical Lessing themes: relations between women, the question of identity, and psychological conflict. Though Lessing was able to get the books published in both England and the United States, the books were generally ignored by critics and did not sell well. Lessing finally admitted that the works were her creation, saying that she had used the pseudonym to prove a point about the difficulties facing young writers. Without adequate marketing and publicity, noted Lessing, books by unknown writers are generally doomed to oblivion.

Since her pseudonymous period, Lessing has written *The Good Terrorist,* a satirical novel about romantic politics, and *The Fifth Child,* about a violent, antisocial child who wreaks havoc on his family and society. She has also produced nonfiction tomes, including *The Wind Blows away Our Words,* about war in Afghanistan during the 1980s.

In the most recent period of her life and literary career, Lessing seems to have come full circle. A nonfiction work and an autobiography mark her return to her homeland in Africa and to the preoccupations of her youth. After leaving Southern Rhodesia in 1949, Lessing had returned only once, in 1956. This era is recounted in her 1957 book *Going Home.* After this first homecoming, the white minority government blocked any future returns because of Lessing's criticism of apartheid. It was not until the 1980s, after years of civil war and thousands of deaths brought the black majority to power in the newly christened Zimbabwe, that Lessing could return. In *African Laughter: Four Visits to Zimbabwe,* she chronicles her trips to southern Africa in 1982, 1988, 1989, and 1992. On one level, this book offers the keen observations of a new nation's growing pains through the eyes of someone not an insider but not an outsider. She sees first a country trying to come to terms with the outcome of a long and bloody civil war based on race. In subsequent trips, she finds exuberance, corruption, and finally decline. "One is oneself fixed in the beam of Lessing's penetrating gaze from the first moments of the book," writes Appiah.

"Within [this book]," Mathabane believes, "Lessing gives us one of the most penetrating and evenhanded critiques of Zimbabwe as a new nation." He explains, "Lessing's portrait is without stereotype or sentimentality, and free of the overbearing shadow of South Africa and its larger-than-life problems of apartheid." For Appiah, however, Lessing's insights into the changes taking place in Zimbabwe are not complete because, as a white woman, she is unable to get inside the hearts and minds of the blacks. "Lessing shows us only the exterior of the black Zimbabweans," he points out, "but still we are in her debt for what that view teaches us about what is happening in Zimbabwe." In Appiah's final analysis, "What we learn from this book, then, is not so much

the political history of Zimbabwe in its first dozen years, but the psychic history of Southern Rhodesia, the inner history of the white settlers and what has become of them: the best of this book is the white man's story."

On another level, *African Laughter* represents a personal and literary odyssey for Lessing. As Vincent Crapanzano explains in the *New York Times Book Review,* "Mrs. Lessing's return to Africa was more than a return to an objectively describable land. It was also a return to memory, to the source of memory, to a mythic place that is constantly intercepted by an insistent reality that both confirms and subverts those memories, that place." Richard Stengel offers a similar view in the *Los Angeles Times Book Review.* He says, "In this elegant and elegiac memoir, Lessing not only returns to her native land but to her earliest themes as a writer. . . . While the book recounts her travels during four trips to Zimbabwe, it is really a Proustian journey to the past, a search for the fountainhead of her own artistic sensibility." Concludes Robert Oakeshott in the *Spectator,* "This [is a] marvelous book. It is delightful and profoundly moving by turns, and frequently both at the same time. Moreover, it is not too much to claim that it offers such a variety of subject matter as sometimes to defy classification."

*Under My Skin,* the first of a proposed three-volume autobiography, follows Lessing from her birth in 1919 to 1949, the year she left Southern Rhodesia for London and her life as a single mother and aspiring writer. She recounts her very early years in Persia, the railway journey across a Soviet Russia in disorder, the promising voyage to Africa, and the years in the bush and convent school. She also describes the lives of the Tayler family, their fellow whites, and the African majority around them. "*Under My Skin* . . . is not so much a recollection of her early life in Southern Rhodesia as a dissection of it," comments Martha Duffy in *Time.* She adds, "The chapters on childhood are marvelously, sometimes frighteningly, detailed." Roberta Rubenstein finds in *Tribune Books* that "*Under My Skin* makes for compelling reading because of Lessing's vivid reconstructions of decisive experiences and significant people of her childhood. Throughout, she juxtaposes descriptions of events that occurred in her youth— before she was capable of fathoming them—with her current unsentimental judgments of them." Although this is autobiography, it is Lessing, true to her strengths as an observer and writer. Duffy concludes: "Set down in blunt, fluent prose, it is the same mix of the practical and the speculative that marks all her writing. And, alas, the same lack of humor. But if that is a flaw, it also ensures the author's total engagement with any subject she tackles. That is what one reads Doris Lessing for: unsparing clarity and frankness."

As Michele Field points out in *Publishers Weekly,* a Lessing autobiography is not as much of an expose as one might think. "Because so much of Lessing's fiction has the ring of real experience, *Under My Skin* is more like her other books than most novelists' autobiographies would be." Carol Brightman finds this characteristic to be a negative. "Finding [the attributes of Lessing's fictional characters] writ large in Lessing's autobiography, however, somehow diminishes the effect, as if the fictional characters are not created at all but are justifications of the author's will." Janet Burroway comes to a different evaluation. She writes in the *New York Times Book Review,* "What is different is not that one is 'true' and the other fiction, but that the themes of a life remembered at this distance are more profound." She adds, "Finally, it may be Mrs. Lessing's most significant contribution is that she has lived and written not with an eye to transcendence or posterity but to experiencing her own time most fully."

*Under My Skin* combines with her earlier fiction and nonfiction to prove, in Mathabane's opinion, that "whatever her subject, Lessing is a surefooted and convincing storyteller. Her work possesses a universality, range and depth matched by that of few other writers in our time." And, as Schlueter remarks, "[Her] work has changed radically in format and genre over the years, . . . and she has been more and more willing to take chances fictionally by tackling unusual or taboo subjects. . . . And while it is commonplace to note that Lessing is not a stylist, that she is repetitive, and that her fiction too easily reflects her own enthusiasms at particular moments, . . . the fact remains that she is among the most powerful and compelling novelists of our century."

## BIOGRAPHICAL/CRITICAL SOURCES:

### BOOKS

Arora, Neena, *Nayantara Sahgal and Doris Lessing: A Feminist Study in Comparison,* Prestige Books/Indian Society for Commonwealth Studies (New Delhi, India), 1991.

Bigsby, C. W. E., *The Radical Imagination and the Liberal Tradition,* Junction Books, 1981, pp. 190-208.

Brewster, Dorothy, *Doris Lessing,* Twayne (Boston), 1965.

Burkom, Selma, and Margaret Williams, *Doris Lessing: A Checklist of Primary and Secondary Sources,* Whitston (Troy, NY), 1973.

Christ, Carol P., *Diving Deep and Surfacing: Women Writers on Spiritual Quest,* Beacon, 1980, pp. 55-73.

*Contemporary Literary Criticism,* Gale (Detroit), Volume 1, 1973, Volume 2, 1974, Volume 3, 1975, Volume 6, 1975, Volume 10, 1979, Volume 15, 1980, Volume 22, 1982, Volume 40, 1986.

Dandson, Cathy N., and E. M. Brown, editors, *The Lost Tradition: Mothers and Daughters in Literature,* Ungar (New York City), 1980, pp. 207-16.

*Dictionary of Literary Biography,* Volume 15: *British Novelists, 1930-1959,* Gale, 1983, Volume 139: *British Short Fiction Writers, 1945-1980,* 1994.

*Dictionary of Literary Biography Yearbook: 1985,* Gale, 1986.

Fahim, Shadia S., *Doris Lessing: Sufi Equilibrium and the Form of the Novel,* St. Martin's (New York City), 1994.

Gindin, James, *Postwar British Fiction,* University of California Press (Berkeley), 1962.

Greene, Gayle, *Doris Lessing: The Poetics of Change,* University of Michigan Press (Ann Arbor), 1994.

Holmquist, Ingrid, *From Society to Nature: A Study of Doris Lessing's "Children of Violence",* Gothenburg Studies in English, 1980.

Ingersoll, Earl G. (editor), *Doris Lessing: Conversations,* Ontario Review Press (Princeton, NJ), 1994.

Ipp, Catherina, *Doris Lessing: A Bibliography,* University of Witwatersrand Press, 1967.

Kaplan, Sydney J., *Feminine Consciousness in the Modern Novel,* University of Illinois Press (Champaign), 1975, pp. 136-72.

Kostelanetz, Richard, editor, *On Contemporary Literature,* Avon (New York City), 1964.

Laurenson, Diana, editor, *The Sociology of Literature: Applied Studies,* University of Keele Press (Newcastle, England), 1978, pp. 38-54.

Lessing, Doris, *Under My Skin,* HarperCollins, 1994.

Maschler, Tom, editor, *Declaration,* MacGibbon & Kee (London), 1959.

Morris, Robert K., *Continuance and Change: The Contemporary British Novel Sequence,* Southern Illinois University Press (Carbondale), 1972, pp. 1-27.

Morris, editor, *Old Lines, New Forces: Essays on the Contemporary British Novel, 1960-1970,* Fairleigh Dickinson University Press, 1976, pp. 12-37, 181-99.

Myers, Carol Fairbanks, *Women in Literature: Criticism of the Seventies,* Scarecrow Press (Metuchen, NJ), 1976, pp. 117-21.

Myles, Anita, *Doris Lessing: A Novelist with Organic Sensibility,* Associated Publishing House (New Delhi, India), 1991.

Narasimhaiah, C. D., editor, *Awakened Conscience: Studies in Commonwealth Literature,* 1978, pp. 307-14.

Newquist, Roy, editor, *Counterpoint,* Rand McNally (Chicago), 1964.

Pratt, Annis, and L. S. Dembo, editors, *Doris Lessing: Critical Studies,* University of Wisconsin Press (Madison), 1974.

Rigney, Barbara H., *Madness and Sexual politics in the Feminist Novel: Studies in Bronte, Woolf, Lessing, and Atwood,* University of Wisconsin Press, 1978, pp. 65-89.

Robinson, Sally, *Engendering the Subject: Gender and Self-Representation in Contemporary Women's Fiction,* State University of New York Press (Albany), 1991.

Rose, Ellen Cronan, *The Tree Outside the Window: Doris Lessing's Children of Violence,* University Press of New England (Hanover, NH), 1976.

Rowe, Margaret Moan, *Doris Lessing,* St. Martin's (New York City), 1994.

Rubenstein, Roberta, *Novelistic Vision of Doris Lessing,* University of Illinois Press, 1979.

Saxton, Ruth, and Jean Tobin, editors, *Woolf and Lessing: Breaking the Mold,* St. Martin's, 1994.

Schlueter, Paul, *The Novels of Doris Lessing,* Southern Illinois University Press, 1973.

Seligman, Dee, *Doris Lessing: An Annotated Bibliography of Criticism,* Greenwood (Westport, CT), 1981.

Shapiro, Charles, editor, *Contemporary British Novelists,* Southern Illinois University Press, 1964, pp. 48-61.

*Short Story Criticism,* Volume 6, Gale, 1990.

Showalter, Elaine, *A Literature of Their Own: British Women Novelists from Bronte to Lessing,* Princeton University Press (Princeton, NJ), 1977, pp. 298-319.

Steele, M. C., *Children of Violence and Rhodesia: A Study of Doris Lessing as Historical Observer,* Central Africa Historical Association, 1974.

Thorpe, Michael, *Doris Lessing's Africa,* Evans, 1978.

Tucker, Martin, *Africa in Modern Literature: A Survey of Contemporary Writing in English,* Ungar, 1967, pp. 175-83.

Wellwarth, George, *Theatre of Protest and Paradox,* New York University Press, 1964.

PERIODICALS

*American Imago,* spring, 1975.

*Arizona Quarterly,* winter, 1965.

*Belles Lettres,* summer, 1993, p. 30.

*Boston Globe,* July 29, 1992, p. 62; October 16, 1994, p. B18; November 13, 1994, p. B1.

*Chicago Daily News,* June 14, 1969.

*Chicago Tribune Book World,* October 30, 1979; April 27, 1980; January 24, 1982; September 29, 1985.

*Christian Science Monitor,* December 9, 1992, p. 13; November 17, 1994, p. 14.

*College English,* February, 1977.

*Columbia Forum,* spring, 1974.

*Commentary,* May, 1988.

*Commonweal,* January 28, 1966; May 7, 1971.

*Contemporary Literature,* winter, 1972; autumn, 1973; spring, 1975.

*Critique,* Volume 11, 1969; Volume 15, 1973; Volume 16, 1974; Volume 17, 1975.

*Globe and Mail* (Toronto), November 24, 1984; April 6, 1985; December 21, 1985; August 6, 1988.

*Iowa Review,* summer, 1973; fall, 1974.

*Journal of Narrative Technique,* September, 1974.

*Kenyon Review,* March, 1966.

*London Review of Books,* April 22, 1993, p. 22.

*Los Angeles Times,* March 1, 1983; July 6, 1983; May 10, 1984; January 14, 1988; June 25, 1992, p. E12; October 20, 1994, p. E8; December 8, 1994, p. E1.

*Los Angeles Times Book Review,* March 1, 1981; March 21, 1982; February 10, 1985; October 13, 1985; October 20, 1985; March 27, 1988; April 6, 1988; November 1, 1992, p. 2; September 5, 1993, p. 6.

*Macleans,* January 9, 1995, p. 66.

*Milwaukee Journal,* May 29, 1966.

*Modern British Literature,* fall, 1977.

*Modern Fiction Studies,* summer, 1975; spring, 1980.

*Modern Language Quarterly,* March, 1974.

*Mosaic,* spring/summer, 1980.

*Nation,* January 11, 1965; January 17, 1966; June 13, 1966; March 6, 1967; November 7, 1994, p. 528.

*New American Review,* Volume 8, 1972.

*New Leader,* April 19, 1971.

*New Republic,* June 28, 1993, p. 30.

*New Review,* November, 1974.

*New Statesman,* April 20, 1962; November 8, 1963.

*Newsweek,* October 14, 1985.

*New York,* October 26, 1992, p. 96.

*New York Review of Books,* December 22, 1994, p. 51; April 18, 1996, pp. 13-15.

*New York Times,* October 21, 1972; October 23, 1979; March 27, 1980; January 19, 1981; January 29, 1982; March 14, 1983; April 22, 1984; October 5, 1984; October 23, 1984; July 14, 1985; September 17, 1985; March 30, 1988; June 14, 1988; June 16, 1992, p. C16; November 2, 1994, p. C1.

*New York Times Book Review,* March 14, 1971; May 13, 1973; June 4, 1978; November 4, 1979; March 30, 1980; January 11, 1981; February 2, 1982; April 3, 1983; September 22, 1985; January 24, 1988; April 3, 1988; April 12, 1992, p. 13; October 18, 1992, p. 13; November 6, 1994, p. 1; April 21, 1996, p. 13.

*Partisan Review,* spring, 1966.

*Psychoanalytic Review,* spring, 1976.

*Publishers Weekly,* September 19, 1994, p. 47.

*Queen,* August 21, 1962.

*Ramparts,* February, 1972.

*Regionalism and the Female Imagination,* fall, 1978.

*San Francisco Review of Books,* Number 3, 1992, p. 25.

*Saturday Review,* April 2, 1966; March 13, 1971.

*Southern Review,* October, 1973.

*Spectator,* October 31, 1992, p. 38; October 22, 1994, p. 48.

*Studies in the Novel,* summer, 1972; summer, 1975; spring, 1979.

*Time,* October 1, 1984; October 7, 1985; November 21, 1994.

*Times* (London), March 19, 1981; June 2, 1983; August 12, 1985; October 7, 1985.

*Times Literary Supplement,* November 23, 1979; May 9, 1980; April 17, 1981; April 2, 1982; June 3, 1983; September 13, 1985; May 8, 1987; October 17, 1987; April 22, 1988; December 18, 1992, p. 8; December, 2, 1994, p. 11; April 5, 1996, p. 27.

*Tribune Books* (Chicago), January 31, 1988; March 20, 1988; July 26, 1992, p. 3; January 3, 1993, p. 3; October 23, 1994, p. 1.

*Twentieth Century Literature,* October, 1977.

*USA Today,* December 1, 1994, p. D9.

*Village Voice,* January 4, 1973; October 2, 1978.

*Washington Post,* September 24, 1984; October 1, 1984; October 24, 1984; June 11, 1992, p. B2; December 29, 1994, p. C1.

*Washington Post Book World,* October 21, 1979; November 4, 1979; April 6, 1980; January 25, 1981; March 21, 1982; April 24, 1983; September 22, 1985; March 20, 1988; April 19, 1992, p. 15; January, 10, 1993, p. 5; October 16, 1994, p. 14; March 31, 1996, p. 7.

*Wilson Library Bulletin,* May, 1965.

*Women's Review of Books,* March, 1995, p. 11.

*World Literature Written in English,* November, 1973; April, 1976.

\*    \*    \*

**LESTER, Andrew D(ouglas)  1939-**

*PERSONAL:* Born August 8, 1939, in Coral Ga-bles, FL; son of Andrew R. and Dorothy V. (Atkinson) Lester; married Judith A. Laesser (a marriage and family therapist), September 8, 1960; children: Scott, Denise. *Education:* Mississippi College, B.A., 1961; Southern Baptist Theological Seminary, B.D., 1964, Ph.D., 1968. *Religion:* Baptist.

*ADDRESSES: Office*—Brite Divinity School, Texas Christian University, Fort Worth, TX 76129.

*CAREER:* Youth minister at Baptist churches in Memphis, TN, 1960, Washington, MS, 1960-61, Jackson, MS, 1961-62, and Louisville, KY, 1966-67; ordained as Southern Baptist minister in 1962; pastor of Baptist church in Bryantsville, KY, 1962-66; Southern Baptist Theological Seminary, Louisville, KY, special instructor in psychology and religion, 1967-69; North Carolina Baptist Hospital, Winston-Salem, NC, assistant director of department of pastoral care, 1969-70, director of counseling services, 1970-71, director of School of Pastoral Care, 1971-77; Southern Baptist Theological Seminary, associate professor, 1977-82, professor of psychology of religion, 1982-91; Texas Christian University, Fort Worth, TX, professor of pastoral theology and pastoral counseling, 1991—. Pastoral counselor at Personal Counseling Service, Clarksville, IN, 1968-69 and 1977-85, and at Kilgore Samaritan Counseling Center, Louisville, KY, 1989-91. Visiting professor at Southeastern Baptist Theological Seminary and visiting lecturer at Wake Forest University, both 1972-77.

*MEMBER:* American Association for Marriage and Family Therapy (clinical member), American Association of Pastoral Counselors (diplomate), Association of Clinical Pastoral Education (chaplain supervisor), American Protestant Hospital Association (fellow of College of Chaplains), Society for Pastoral Theology, Theta Pi.

## WRITINGS:

*Sex Is More Than a Word,* Broadman (Nashville, TN), 1973.

*It Hurts So Bad, Lord!: The Christian Encounters Crisis,* Broadman, 1976.

(With wife, Judith L. Lester) *Understanding Aging Parents,* Westminster (Philadelphia), 1980.

*Coping with Your Anger: A Christian Guide,* Westminster, 1983.

*Pastoral Care with Children in Crisis,* Westminster, 1985.

*Hope in Pastoral Care and Counseling,* Westminster John Knox Press (Louisville, KY), 1995.

### EDITOR

(With Wayne E. Oates) *Pastoral Care in Crucial Human Situations,* Judson (Valley Forge, PA), 1969.

(With Gerald L. Borchert) *Spiritual Dimensions of Pastoral Care: Witness to the Ministry of Wayne E. Oates,* Westminster, 1985.

*When Children Suffer: A Sourcebook for Ministry with Children in Crisis,* Westminster, 1987.

### OTHER

Contributor to *Encyclopedia of Southern Baptists,* 1982, and to church magazines, including *Review and Expositor;* general editor for the "Resources for Living" series, 1989-90, and for a series of books on pastoral care and counseling, 1992—, both from Westminster John Knox Press; member of editorial boards of *Journal of Pastoral Care,* 1987—, and *Journal of Family Ministry,* 1994—.

SIDELIGHTS: Andrew D. Lester told *CA:* "I have always been interested in what psychology and theology can teach each other. My basic purpose for writing is to introduce lay-persons to some of the insights of psychology of religion and pastoral theology. Popular ideas about the Christian faith are often destructive to personhood. *Coping With Your Anger,* for instance, is an attempt to help Christians understand that the capacity for anger is part of the creation and not the result of sin. *Sex Is More Than a Word* has the same goal, to help Christians recognize that sex is one of God's gifts rather than some demonic aspect of selfhood. Both anger and sex can help fulfill life and add to love and intimacy if handled ethically."

## LEVINTHAL, Charles F(rederick) 1945-

PERSONAL: Born July 6, 1945, in Cincinnati, OH; son of Sam and Mildred (Greenburg) Levinthal; married Beth Kuby (a teacher), December 16, 1973; children: David, Brian. *Education:* University of Cincinnati, A.B., 1967; University of Michigan, M.A., 1968, Ph.D., 1971. *Religion:* Jewish.

ADDRESSES: Home—9 Royal Oak Dr., Huntington, NY 11743. *Office*—Department of Psychology, Hofstra University, Hempstead, NY 11550. *E-mail*—psycfl@vaxc.hofstra.edu.

CAREER: Hofstra University, Hempstead, NY, staff member, beginning 1971, professor of psychology, 1987—. *Military service:* U.S. Army Reserve, 1968-74.

MEMBER: Society for Neuroscience, American Psychological Association, Society for Psychophysiological Research.

## WRITINGS:

*The Physiological Approach in Psychology,* Prentice-Hall (Englewood Cliffs, NJ), 1979, 3rd edition published as *Introduction to Physiological Psychology,* 1990.

*Messengers of Paradise: Opiates and the Brain,* Anchor Press/Doubleday (New York City), 1988.

*Drugs, Behavior, and Modern Society,* Allyn & Bacon (Newton, MA), 1996.

Contributor to scientific journals.

SIDELIGHTS: Charles F. Levinthal told *CA:* "As an author, I have been interested in communicating to people the complex and intriguing relationship between our behavior and the workings of the human brain. All of my books have evolved from that basic motivating factor. *The Physiological Approach to Psychology* was written to introduce college students to the world of neuroscience research in simple and direct language, offering them ways of seeing the full range of their everyday experiences in terms of neurological processes.

"The message of *Messengers of Paradise* was, in a sense, more specific as well as more general. Its specific focus was on the discovery of brain-produced opiate-like substances called endorphins, one group among dozens of chemicals that enable the brain to function. I wanted to offer a chronicle of the important events surrounding the initial surge of discoveries between 1971 and 1975, the personal competitiveness and professional ambition among a small community of extraordinary scientists who made the major breakthroughs in this area of neuroscience research. I considered this story to be an example of the ways in which modern science operates as well as a look at an intimate side of science that most people never see or even imagine existing. At the same time, I set out to put in an evolutionary context the more general quesiton of why we have these amazing chemicals in the first place. An argument was made that endorphins have been central participants in the major changes in brain functioning over the course of evolution. The role of endorphins as powerful pain-killers can be linked to a continuing biological struggle for survival; endorphins-mediated feelings can be considered as key reinforcers for behaviors that emphasize interdependency and socialization. Finally, endorphins continue to guide the course of human cultural history, as biochemical reinforcers for the appreciation of beauty and accomplishment. In effect, endorphins have given us the means to be not only reactors to a biological world but also potential creators of new worlds.

"Most recently, in the textbook *Drugs, Behavior, and Modern Society,* I turned to the important issues of licit and illicit psychoactive drugs and their impact upon our contemporary society. This book integrated the practical concerns of young people today with an understanding of how drugs work in the body and on the mind, addressing in frank terms the controversies surrounding social policy with regard to drug abuse and misuse. In the United States today, as well as in most of the world, drugs affect our daily lives. They present a social paradox, combining the potential for good and for bad. As a society and as individuals, we can be the beneficiaries of drugs or their victims. Communicating the facts and the fictions regarding drug abuse is a necessary first step toward dealing with that paradox."

\*　　\*　　\*

## LOWBURY, Edward (Joseph Lister) 1913-

*PERSONAL:* Born December 6, 1913, in London, England; son of Benjamin William (a physician) and Alice (Halle) Lowbury; married Alison Young (a musician), June 12, 1954; children: Ruth, Pauline, Miriam. *Ethnicity:* White. *Education:* University

College, Oxford, B.A., 1936, B.M. and B.Ch., 1939; London Hospital Medical College, London, M.A., 1940; Oxford University, D.M., 1957.

*ADDRESSES: Home*—79 Vernon Rd., Birmingham B16 9SQ, England.

*CAREER:* Member of scientific staff, Medical Research Council of Great Britain, 1947-79; Birmingham Accident Hospital, Birmingham, England, bacteriologist in Medical Research Council Burns Research Unit, 1949-79; University of Aston, Birmingham, honorary professor of medical microbiology, 1979-89. Honorary research fellow, University of Birmingham, 1950-79. Consultant in bacteriology, Birmingham Regional Hospital Board, 1960-79; founder and honorary director, Hospital Infectional Research Laboratory, Birmingham, 1966-79. Consultant to United States on hospital-acquired infection, World Health Organization, 1965. *Military service:* Royal Army Medical Corps, 1943-47; became major (specialist in pathology).

*MEMBER:* Royal College of Pathologists (fellow), Royal College of Physicians (honorary fellow), Royal College of Surgeons (honorary fellow), Royal Society of Literature (fellow), Pathological Society of Great Britain and Ireland, British Medical Association, Hospital Infection Society (president, 1980-82).

*AWARDS, HONORS:* Newdigate Prize, 1934, for *Fire;* Matthew Arnold Memorial Prize, 1937; John Keats Memorial Lecturer, 1973; Everett Evans Memorial Lecturer and medal, 1977; D.Sc., University of Aston, 1977; A. B. Wallace Memorial Lecturer and Medal, 1978; LL.D., University of Birmingham, 1980; Officer, Order of the British Empire, 1979.

*WRITINGS:*

*POETRY*

*Fire,* Blackwell (London), 1934.
*Crossing the Line,* Hutchinson (London), 1947.
(With Terence Heywood) *Facing North,* Mitre Press, 1957.
*Metamorphoses,* Keepsake Press, 1960.
*Time for Sale,* Chatto & Windus (London), 1961.
*New Poems,* Keepsake Press, 1965.
*Daylight Astronomy,* Wesleyan University Press, Chatto & Windus, 1968.
*Figures of Eight,* Keepsake Press, 1969.
*Green Magic* (juvenile), Chatto & Windus, 1972.

*Two Confessions,* Keepsake Press, 1973.

*The Night Watchman,* Chatto & Windus, 1974.

*Poetry and Paradox: Poems and an Essay,* Keepsake Press, 1976.

(With John Press and Michael Rinere) *Troika: A Selection of Poems,* Daedalus Press, 1977.

*Selected Poems,* Celtion Press, 1978.

*A Letter from Masada,* Keepsake Press, 1982.

*Goldrush,* Celandine Press, 1983.

*Apocryphal Letters,* Sceptre Press, 1985.

*Birmingham! Birmingham!,* Keepsake Press, 1985, 2nd enlarged edition, 1989.

*Flowering Cypress,* Pointing Finger Press, 1986.

*A Letter from Hampstead,* Keepsake Press, 1987.

*Variations on Aldeburgh,* Mandeville Press, 1987, 2nd edition, 1989.

*Selected and New Poems,* Hippopotamus Press, 1990.

*Collected Poems of Edward Lowbury,* with introduction by John Press, University of Salzburg Press (Salzburg, Austria), 1993.

*First Light,* Keepsake Press, 1991.

*Mystic Bridge,* Hippopotamus Press, 1996.

(Editor and author of introduction) *Apollo: An Anthology of Poems by Doctor Poets,* Keynes Press, 1990.

### NONFICTION

(With wife, Alison Young, and Timothy Salter) *Thomas Campion: Poet, Composer, Physician* (biography and critical study), Barnes & Noble (New York City), 1970.

(With G. A. Ayliffe) *Drug Resistance in Antimicrobial Therapy,* C. C. Thomas (Springfield, IL), 1974.

(Editor with others) *Control of Hospital Infection: A Practical Handbook,* Chapman & Hall, 1975, 3rd edition, 1992.

(Editor with Alison Young) Andrew Young, *The Poetical Works of Andrew Young,* Secker & Warburg, 1985.

*Hallmarks of Poetry: Reflections on a Theme* (essays and addresses), University of Salzburg Press, 1995.

### OTHER

Contributor of chapters and articles to numerous books, including *The Scientific Basis of Medicine, Textbook of British Surgery, Recent Advances in Surgery, Recent Advances in Clinical Pathology, Chambers Encyclopedia,* and *Encyclopedia of Poets.* Editor of and contributor to *Widening Circles,* 1976, *Night Ride and Sunrise,* 1978, *Golden Treasury, A*

*Map of Modern Verse,* 1964, *The Poet Speaks* (recordings), and other collections. Contributor of poetry and medical and scientific articles to many periodicals, including *British Medical Journal, Encounter, Lancet, London Magazine, Nature, New York Times, Times Literary Supplement,* and *Southern Review.* Editor, *Equator* (Nairobi), 1945-46.

*WORK IN PROGRESS:* With Alison Young, *To Shirk No Idleness: A Critical Biography of Andre Young; One Might Live Twice,* an autobiography.

*SIDELIGHTS:* The two sides of the double life Edward Lowbury leads as a medical man and as a poet are "excitingly contrasted," he notes to *CA,* adding: "I write at weekends and on holiday, but store up memories and experiences for use at these times. The collaborative study on Thomas Campion reflects an interest of many years in Elizabethan music and poetry, and incidentally gave me an insight into the divided life of a seventeenth-century doctor-poet who was also a fine composer."

Lowbury told *CA:* "I write poems because I enjoy expressing thoughts, experiences, feelings and stories in verbal structures that seem to me alive, new and individual, to excite surprise and, at the same time, the seemingly opposite sense of inevitability. My verse is usually metrical and rhymed and I aim for clarity of meaning, though in poetry some ambiguities are inevitably and even desirable; by contrast, in my essays and scientific papers I strive to avoid ambiguity.

"I have written many essays in recent years on various aspects of poetry, art and science, including trying to assess the artistic merits of a poem.

"My poems usually arise from some experience that has moved me—in life, in art, sometime through the sound and sense of words, sometimes from medical experiences, occasionally through a humorous episode. Poems may erupt at any time, but I usually have short spells of writing separated by longer fallow periods."

*BIOGRAPHICAL/CRITICAL SOURCES:*

### BOOKS

Lovelock, Yann, *Physic Meet and Metaphysic: A Celebration for Edward Lowbury,* University of Salzburg Press, 1993.

*My Medical School,* Robson Books, 1978.

*PERIODICALS*

*Agenda,* Volume 21, number 4, 1989.
*Southern Review,* Volume 6, 1970.
*Times Literary Supplement,* June 13, 1986.

\* \* \*

## LUMLEY, Brian   1937-

*PERSONAL:* Born December 2, 1937, in Horden, England; married; wife's name, Barbara Ann.

*ADDRESSES: Home*—Torquay, England. *Office*—c/o Tor Books, 175 5th Ave., New York, NY 10010.

*CAREER:* Writer. Worked previously as a sawyer. *Military service:* British Army, 22 years.

*AWARDS, HONORS:* British Fantasy Award; *Fear* Magazine Fiction Award.

*WRITINGS:*

*The Caller of the Black* (stories), Arkham (Sauk City, WI), 1971.
*Beneath the Moors* (novel), Arkham, 1974.
*The Horror at Oakdene, and Others* (stories), Arkham, 1977.
*Khai of Ancient Khem,* Berkley Publishing (New York City), 1980.
*Ghoul Warning, and Other Omens* (poetry), Spectre Press, 1982.
*Psychomech,* Granada (London), 1984.
*Demogorgon,* Grafton (London), 1987.
*Synchronicity, or Something,* Dagon Press, 1988.
*Elysia: The Coming of Cthulhu,* Ganley Publishing (Buffalo, NY), 1989.
*The House of Doors,* Tor Books (New York City), 1990.
*Psychosphere,* Tor Books, 1992.
*Psychamok,* Tor Books, 1993.
*Fruiting Bodies and Other Fungi* (stories), Tor Books, 1993.
*Return of the Deep Ones,* Roc, 1994.

Also author of *The Second Wish and Other Exhalations,* 1995, *De Marigny's Dream-Quest, Dagon's Bell and Other Discords,* and *The Last Rite.* Contributor of stories to magazines.

*"TITUS CROW" SERIES*

*The Burrowers Beneath,* DAW Books (New York City), 1974.
*The Transition of Titus Crow,* DAW Books, 1975, revised edition, Ganley, 1992.
*Clock of Dreams,* Jove (New York City), 1978.
*Spawn of the Winds,* Jove, 1978.
*In the Moons of Borea,* Jove, 1979.
*The Compleat Crow,* Ganley Publishing, 1987.

*"TALES OF THE PRIMAL LAND" SERIES*

*The House of Cthulhu, and Other Tales of the Primal Land,* Weirdbook (Buffalo, NY), 1984, revised edition, 1991.
*The Compleat Khash, Volume I: Never a Backward Glance,* Ganley Publishing, 1991.
*Sorcery in Shad,* Headline (London), 1991.
*Tarra Khash: Hrossak!,* Headline, 1991.
*The Compleat Khash, Volume II: Sorcery in Shad,* Ganley Publishing, 1994.

*"NECROSCOPE" SERIES*

*Necroscope,* Grafton, Volume 1, 1986, Volume 2, 1988, Volume 3, 1989.
*Vamphyri!,* Tor Books, 1989.
*The Source: Necroscope III,* Tor Books, 1989.
*Deadspeak: Necroscope IV,* Tor Books, 1990.
*Deadspawn,* Tor Books, 1991.
*Necroscope: The Lost Years* (also see below), Tor Books, 1995.
*Resurgence* (second volume of *Necroscope: The Lost Years*), Tor Books, 1996.

*"DREAMLANDS" SERIES*

*Hero of Dreams,* Ganley Publishing, 1986.
*Ship of Dreams,* Ganley Publishing, 1986.
*Mad Moon of Dreams,* Ganley Publishing, 1987.
*Iced on Aran, and Other Dream Quests,* Ganley Publishing, 1992.

*"VAMPIRE WORLD" SERIES*

*Blood Brothers,* Tor Books, 1993.
*The Last Aerie,* Tor Books, 1993.
*Bloodwars,* Tor Books, 1994.

*SIDELIGHTS:* Brian Lumley is a prolific novelist and short story writer whose works include fantasy, horror, and science fiction. He has penned several series, including "Titus Crow," "Dreamlands," "Vampire World," "Necroscope," and "Tales of the Primal Land." Lumley has also won high praise for his innovative use of themes first created by noted 1930s horror writer H. P. Lovecraft in his "Cthulhu Mythos," a story series about an imaginary pantheon of malignant deities. Writing in *Voice of Youth Advocates*, Christy Tyson likened Lumley's work to a cross between that of Anne Rice and John Grisham, or Meredith Pierce and Stephen King. She observed that "Lumley deserves a wide audience . . . because his books don't compare to anything else being done by any single writer."

Lumley's series and novels are frequently interrelated. For example, the "Vampire World" trilogy stands on its own, yet has many ties to the "Necroscope" cycle. The Necroscope books are probably the author's best-known work, with the initial novel in the series having sold over 350,000 copies in paperback alone. Containing *Necroscope, Vamphyri!, The Source: Necroscope III, Deadspeak: Necroscope IV, Deadspawn,* and *Necroscope: The Lost Years,* this series relates the adventures of vampire hunter Harry Keogh. Keogh is a British intelligence agent and a "necroscope"—one who can communicate with the dead. He also has special abilities to travel easily through time and space. Through the course of the series, he conquers numerous members of the evil Vampire empire and dispatches them into exile. A *Publishers Weekly* reviewer described *Necroscope: The Lost Years* as a "ripping yarn of espionage and occult intrigue." The reviewer further commented, "Lumley's Necroscope novels are refreshing reminders that sometimes a vampire is just a bloody entertaining monster."

Lumley's "Vampire World" series—*Blood Brothers, The Last Aerie,* and *Bloodwars*—concerns Harry's twin sons, Nestor and Nathan Kiklu. Separated during a vampire raid, the brothers eventu-ally mature into opposites. Nestor becomes a vampire lord, bent on conquering the earth, while Nathan struggles to assume his father's mantle as master vampire hunter. Tyson called *The Last Aerie* a "complex, fast-paced, and challenging novel. . . . Lumley's writing is solid, his characters compelling, and his dual worlds equally credible. . . . His creatures are so horrifyingly real they make the Transylvanian version seem little more than a shadow of the real thing." A *Publishers Weekly* reviewer concurred that Lumley's vampire universe is "so vivid, with characters so real, that even the undead seem alive."

## BIOGRAPHICAL/CRITICAL SOURCES:

*PERIODICALS*

*Booklist,* November 15, 1995, p. 536.
*Fantasy Review,* August, 1984, p. 15; July-August, 1987, p. 51.
*Kirkus Reviews,* May 15, 1992, p. 630; November 15, 1992, p. 1400; June, 1993, pp. 744-45.
*Kliatt,* May, 1994, p. 18.
*Locus,* January, 1994, p. 44; April, 1994, p. 49; May, 1994, p. 50; November, 1994, p. 54; December, 1994, p. 59.
*Magazine of Fantasy and Science Fiction,* December, 1973, p. 39; April, 1976, pp. 62-66.
*Publishers Weekly,* March 6, 1978, p. 100; October 3, 1994, p. 55; November 20, 1995, p. 70.
*Rapport,* Volume 18, Number 6, 1995, p. 24.
*Science Fiction Chronicle,* October, 1994, p. 45.
*Small Press,* April, 1990, p. 41.
*Voice of Youth Advocates,* August, 1990, pp. 167-68; February, 1994, p. 383.
*Wilson Library Bulletin,* October, 1993, p. 102.

# M-N

## MACKEY, Sandra 1937-

*PERSONAL:* Born September 13, 1937, in Oklahoma City, OK; daughter of Velt (a funeral director) and Verna (a funeral director; maiden name, Richie) Sherman; married Dan Michael Mackey (a physician), December 22, 1961; children: Michael Colin. *Ethnicity:* "Anglo." *Education:* Central State College (now University), Edmond, OK, B.A., 1958; University of Virginia, M.A., 1966. *Politics:* "In limbo." *Religion:* Presbyterian.

*ADDRESSES: Home*—3590 Cloudland Dr. N.W., Atlanta, GA 30327; fax: 404-262-7176. *Agent*—Helen Rees, 308 Commonwealth Ave., Boston, MA 02116.

*CAREER:* Writer and lecturer, 1978—. Commentator on the Middle East for various media organizations. Member of Atlanta Symphony Associates.

*WRITINGS:*

*The Saudis: Inside the Desert Kingdom,* Houghton (Boston), 1987.
*Lebanon: Death of a Nation,* Congdon & Weed (New York City), 1989.
*Passion and Politics: The Turbulent World of the Arabs,* Dutton (New York City), 1992.
*The Iranians: Persia, Islam, and the Soul of a Nation,* Dutton, 1996.

Contributor of articles and reviews to newspapers.

*SIDELIGHTS:* Sandra Mackey told *CA:* "With its great petroleum resources and its emotions and complexities, the Middle East is central to Western inter-

ests. Because of its volatility, however, the area seems unintelligible to most westerners. What I attempt to do in my writing is to create a pattern for understanding people and events in the Middle East. The key to unraveling the enigmatic Saudis or the baffling Iranians is to engage the reader in the psychology and the society and, only then, begin to explore the political ramifications for the Middle East and for the West."

*BIOGRAPHICAL/CRITICAL SOURCES:*

*PERIODICALS*

*Chicago Tribune,* June 4, 1987.
*Christian Science Monitor,* May 7, 1987.
*Commonweal,* November 3, 1989, p. 602.
*New York Times Book Review,* July 12, 1987.
*School Library Journal,* January, 1990, p. 129.

*     *     *

## MANTEL, Hilary (Mary) 1952-

*PERSONAL:* Born July 6, 1952, in Derbyshire, England; married Gerald McEwen (a geologist), September 23, 1972. *Education:* Attended London School of Economics and Political Science, 1970; University of Sheffield, Jur.B., 1973.

*ADDRESSES: Agent*—A. M. Heath & Co., Ltd., 79 St. Martin's Ln., London WC1, England.

*CAREER:* Writer. Worked in a variety of jobs, including salesperson, social worker in a geriatric hospital, and secondary school English teacher, until 1986; lived and worked in Botswana, southern Africa, 1977-82, and Jeddah, Saudi Arabia, 1983-86. Fulltime writer in United Kingdom, 1986—.

*MEMBER:* Society of Authors.

*AWARDS, HONORS:* Shiva Naipaul Memorial prize for travel writing, 1987; fellow of the Royal Society of Literature, 1990; Cheltenham Festival Prize, Southern Arts Literary Prize, and Winifred Holtby Award, 1990, all for *Fludd;* Sunday Express "Book of the Year" Award, 1992, for *A Place of Greater Safety.*

*WRITINGS:*

NOVELS

*Every Day Is Mother's Day,* Chatto & Windus (London), 1985.
*Vacant Possession,* Chatto & Windus, 1986.
*Eight Months on Ghazzah Street,* Viking (London), 1988.
*Fludd,* Viking, 1990.
*A Place of Greater Safety,* Atheneum (New York City), 1992.
*A Change of Climate,* Atheneum, 1994.
*An Experiment in Love,* Holt (New York City), 1995.

SHORT STORIES

*New Writing,* Minerva, 1991.
*The Time Out Book of London Short Stories,* Penguin (Harmondsworth, Middlesex), 1993.
*New Writing 3,* Minerva, 1994.

Editor of *The Best of Best Short Stories 1986-95,* Minerva, 1995, and *The Daily Telegraph Book of Contemporary Short Stories,* 1995. Also contributor to *Best Short Stories of 1987,* Heinemann (London), 1987.

OTHER

Film critic for *Spectator,* 1987-91. Contributor of short stories and reviews to periodicals, including *London Magazine, London Review of Books, Literary Review,* and *Encounter.*

*SIDELIGHTS:* In her first book, *Every Day Is Mother's Day,* which *London Magazine* reviewer

John Mellors called "an accomplished novel of striking originality," Hilary Mantel "extracts comedy from the lives of misfits and the mentally disordered." Mantel depicts Colin Sidney, a history teacher who, while taking night classes in order to get away from his wife and children, meets and carries on an affair with Isabel Field, a young and unsatisfied social worker. Isabel meanwhile has been assigned the case of Muriel Axon—a mentally retarded woman living with her insane mother, Evelyn—who happens to live next door to Colin's sister. In portraying its characters' miserable, mad, and eccentric lives, the novel "starts as simple black comedy," explained *Daily Mail* columnist Auberon Waugh, "and then slips into a savage satire on the social services." Waugh proclaimed *Mother's Day* "one of the bleakest commentaries on contemporary English life I have ever read." And heralding Mantel as a "major new talent," Waugh commended the author for her "beautifully constructed" plot, her "vivid imagination," and "the pert, surreal precision of her characters' dialogue."

The same characters, setting, and style appear in Mantel's second book, *Vacant Possession,* a sequel to *Mother's Day.* This "exceptional novel," asserted *New Statesman* reviewer Bill Greenwell, is "filled with fiendish glee, all of it held in hysterical check by the writer's wry style. . . . It has a wittily nasty plot, but never gloats over its victims." The welfare services are again the object of Mantel's derision, but Greenwell noted that the author's satire "is finely tempered by the rampant ironies of the narrative." Mantel adds continuing crisis and excessive coincidence to her novel of "interlocking complexity and crafty irony," commented Greenwell. In *Vacant Possession* Muriel Axon had been institutionalized and, having just been released, proceeds to wreak revenge, for various reasons, upon a number of targets: Colin Sidney's family, including his wife, mother, and sister; Isabel Field, who had institutionalized her; and Isabel's father, who had sexually abused Muriel in the past.

Although the story is complicated, *Times Literary Supplement* reviewer Christopher Hawtree applauded Mantel's handling of plot in *Vacant Possession,* as her "succession of neatly juxtaposed scenes leaves one torn between horror and delight at the unfolding, malevolent design." Greenwell further praised Mantel's style, noting that the author's "violently observant" passages play "both . . . dangerously and brilliantly with the reader's sensibility." Enthusiastic about Mantel's first two works, the reviewer concluded: "If you read only one book—I mean two, of course—this year, make sure that Hilary Mantel wrote it (them)."

Mantel told *CA:* "In *Every Day Is Mother's Day* and its sequel, *Vacant Possession,* I wrote about the nature of time, prisons, ghosts, family life, marital discord, and social policy. Both novels were set in the north of England, but I wrote them while I was living abroad, and I think that factor made my perception of home sharper than it would have been otherwise. Distance makes things funny as well—when you move around a lot you are not obliged to take any society seriously. With those two books, I wanted to make people laugh; to make some points about social work theory and practice; and to give a picture of the state of England as I saw it.

"When I wrote *Every Day Is Mother's Day,* I was interested in Bruno Bettleheim's work on autism and his accounts of the victims of concentration camps; I had my social worker tell a story from one of his books. All my characters had created prisons for themselves, and the more they tried to break out, the more securely they found themselves confined. The ultimate prison is lack of imagination; the characters are so tightly sealed into their own worlds that they are oblivious to the dire events laying waste to everything around them.

"*Vacant Possession* is a much more exuberant book—with, however, a higher mortality rate among the characters. The starting point was the policy decision to close long-term hospitals for the mentally ill and mentally retarded, and release their former inmates into 'the community'—a community which on the whole did not want them and had done nothing to prepare for them. This policy frees Muriel Axon to take revenge on the people whom she believes have injured her. Though it is hard to imagine how the events of *Vacant Possession* could take place in real life, I hope that in the book they have a threatening logic of their own. Some people read it as a rather left-wing book, but one magazine called it 'Thatcherite.' I am quite happy for this uncertainty to continue.

"I have drawn material from periods spent living abroad—five years in Africa and three-and-one-half years in Saudi Arabia. *Eight Months on Ghazzah Street* is based on my experiences in Jeddah, Saudi Arabia, but it is certainly not a disguised autobiography. It is about Frances Shore, a young English-woman living in that city; her circle of British and American friends; and her involvement—which turns out to be a rather dangerous involvement—in the affairs of her Muslim neighbors.

"*Fludd* is a magic-realist novel set in Derbyshire, northwest England in 1956. The main character, Fludd, is a reincarnation of the sixteenth-century scholar and alchemist of the same name. One dark and stormy night, he arrives in an obscure moorland village, knocking at the door of the priest's house. He is assumed to be a new curate. He makes the parish revise its idea of itself, and absconds to a Manchester hotel with a young nun, his female spiritual counterpart. This is a Jungian fiction, and not a satire on the Catholic Church. Its events derive from my childhood.

"*A Place of Greater Safety* is a fictionalised study of the French Revolution. It is closely bound to historical fact, as far as that is established, and concentrates on the career of three prominent revolutionaries. I attempt to show why, to each of these three men, a personal revolution was necessary, and through them I tentatively explore the connections between the personal and the political. It is my biggest book, and I think it is my best.

"*A Change of Climate* is an attempt to explore how individuals cope with disaster, with tragic events: how do they find or manufacture the resources to carry on with day-to-day life, and how might they arrive at some form of reconciliation? The main characters are Ralph and Anna Eldred, an idealistic and naive young couple who are sent by an evangelical missionary society to South Africa, in the late 1950s, at a time when apartheid legislation is taking a grip. They spend eighteen months in a volatile Transvaal township, and are then jailed and threatened with deportation. To escape a return to England—which would make them feel like failures—they take a post as administrators of a small mission in Bechuanaland (now Botswana) on the fringe of the Kalahari desert. There, an unspeakable incident occurs—something that, quite literally, they are unable to speak about—and after their return to England, they do not talk about it to their children. Twenty years on, their secret begins to make its way from darkness to light.

"*An Experiment in Love* is set in the north of England during the 1950s/60s and in London between October 1970 and March 1971. In part it is a joke-variant of Muriel Spark's novel *The Girls of Slender Means.* It explores the question of how a girl invents herself into a woman, and considers what role models she will embrace as she moves into adulthood. Mrs Thatcher, who appears in the story but is not named, is one version of womanhood on offer. The book's concerns are: appetite (in its many meanings), hunger, nurturing, fertility, and envy. As in *A Place of Greater Safety* I want to hover at the point of interconnection between the personal and the political, but this book puts a feminist spin on the question."

*BIOGRAPHICAL/CRITICAL SOURCES:*

PERIODICALS

*Daily Mail,* March 28, 1985.
*London Magazine,* March, 1985.
*New Statesman,* May 30, 1986.
*Times Literary Supplement,* June 20, 1986.

\*     \*     \*

**MARCHAK, M(aureen) Patricia    1936-**
**(Maureen Marchak)**

*PERSONAL:* Born June 22, 1936, in Lethbridge, Alberta, Canada; daughter of Adrian Ebenezer and Wilhelmina Rankin (Hamilton) Russell; married William Marchak, 1956 children: Geordon Eric, Lauren Craig. *Education:* University of British Columbia B.A., 1958, Ph.D., 1970.

*ADDRESSES: Office*—Department of Anthropology and Sociology, University of British Columbia, 6303 Northwest Marine Dr., Vancouver, British Columbia, Canada V6T 2B2; fax: 604-822-6096. *E-mail*—marchak@arts.ubc.ca.

*CAREER:* Freelance writer, 1963-65; University of British Columbia, Vancouver, instructor, 1965-67, sessional lecturer, 1968-72, assistant professor, 1973-75, associate professor, 1975-80, professor of sociology, 1980—, head of department 1987-90, dean of faculty of arts, 1990-96. Sorokin Lecturer, University of Saskatchewan, 1982; guest lecturer, Queen's University, 1985; visiting professor, Carleton University, summer, 1986; Shastri-Indo-Canadian Institute Visiting Professor to India, 1987; David Alexander Memorial Lecturer, Memorial University, Newfoundland, 1995. Lecturer at conferences and association meetings. Director of research

on housing in North Vancouver, 1972. Member of Pacific Group of Canadian Centre for Policy Alternatives, 1983-85; member of committee on Yukon water resources, Westwater Research Institute, 1979-82. Canadian Registrar of Research and Researchers in the Social Sciences, 1981-86. Member of board of Ecotrust and the British Columbia Forestry Appeals Commission.

*AWARDS, HONORS:* Research grant from Institute of Industrial Relations, University of British Columbia, 1969-70; Social Science and Humanities Council of Canada, grants, 1977-78 and 1981-84, fellowships, 1984-85 and 1984-85; *Green Gold: The Forest Industry in British Columbia* was selected as one of the outstanding academic books of the year by the American Library Association, 1985; John Porter Memorial Book Prize from Canadian Association of Sociology and Anthropology, 1986, for *Green Gold: The Forest Industry in British Columbia;* named outstanding contributor by Canadian Association of Sociology and Anthropology, 1990; Commemorative Medal, Governor General of Canada, for "significant contributions to Canada," 1993.

*MEMBER:* Canadian Political Science Association, Canadian Sociology and Anthropology Association (president, 1979-80), Association for Canadian Studies (member of executive board, 1978-80), Royal Society of Canada (fellow), Forest History Association.

*WRITINGS:*

*Ideological Perspectives on Canada,* McGraw (Toronto), 1975, 3rd revised edition, 1987.
(Editor) *The Working Sexes,* Institute of Industrial Relations, University of British Columbia (Vancouver), 1977.
*In Whose Interests: An Essay on Multinational Corporations in a Canadian Context,* McClelland & Stewart (Toronto), 1979.
*Green Gold: The Forest Industry in British Columbia,* University of British Columbia Press (Vancouver), 1983.
(Editor with Neil Guppy and John McMullan) *Uncommon Property: The Fishing and Fish Processing Industries in British Columbia,* Methuen (Toronto), 1987.
*The Integrated Circus: The "New Right" and the Restructuring of Global Markets,* McGill-Queen's University (Montreal), 1991.
*Logging the Globe,* McGill-Queen's University, 1995.

*Racism, Sexism and the University: The Political Science Affair at UBC,* McGill-Queen's University, 1996.

OTHER

Contributor to many books. Contributor of articles and reviews to *London Journal of Canadian Studies, Canadian Public Policy, Journal of Business Administration, Queen's Quarterly,* and other publications. Book review editor of *Canadian Review of Sociology and Anthropology,* 1971-74; member of editorial board of *Studies in Political Economy,* 1980—, *Current Sociology,* 1982—, *Canadian Journal of Sociology,* 1986—, and *B. C. Studies,* 1988—.

SIDELIGHTS: M. Patricia Marchak told *CA* that her primary motivation for writing is "curiosity about the subjects and pleasure in the act of organizing ideas and writing. The biggest task for a new book is to organize the material so that it can be read and understood by someone who did not do the research or may not have started out with the same curiosity about the subject. I revise the text often, trying out various organizations and then, when the structure is okay, trying out various ways of saying things. I write on weekends and evenings, whenever I can find time.

"I am truly puzzled by the way human beings relate to one another, organize their societies, develop their cultures and by the relationship between humans and the rest of nature. My concern for the forests of my coastal home region has expanded to the forest regions of the world, and my last book was about the processes of deforestation across the globe."

\*        \*        \*

**MARCHAK, Maureen**
  **See MARCHAK, M(aureen) Patricia**

\*        \*        \*

**MARGOSHES, Dave    1941-**

PERSONAL: Born July 8, 1941, in New Brunswick, NJ; son of Harry (a journalist) and Berte (Shalley) Margoshes; married Ilya Silbar (a potter and librar-ian), 1963. *Education:* Attended Middlebury College, 1959-61; University of Iowa, B.A., 1963, M.F.A., 1969.

ADDRESSES: *Home*—2922 19th Ave., Regina, Saskatchewan, Canada S4T 1X5. *E-mail*—dmargos@ unibase.unibase.com.

CAREER: Writer. Worked as newspaper reporter and editor, 1963-75; Mount Royal College, Calgary, instructor in journalism, 1975-76 and 1981-84; Southern Alberta Institute of Technology, Calgary, instructor in journalism, 1976-77; *Calgary Herald,* Calgary, reporter, 1977-81; *Vancouver Sun,* Vancouver, British Columbia, reporter, 1984-86; University of Winnipeg, Winnipeg, Manitoba, writer in residence, 1995-96.

MEMBER: Writers Union of Canada, League of Canadian Poets, Saskatchewan Writers Guild (former board member).

AWARDS, HONORS: Poem of the year award, *Canadian Author and Bookman,* 1982, for "Season of Lilac"; League of Canadian Poets award, 1991; Saskatchewan Writers Guild Literacy award, 1990; Stephen Leacock Award for Poetry, 1996.

WRITINGS:

*Third Impressions* (stories), edited by John Metcalf, Oberon (Ottawa), 1982.
*Small Regrets* (stories), Thistledown Press (Saskatoon, Saskatchewan), 1986.
*Walking at Brighton* (poetry), Thistledown Press, 1988.
*Northwest Passage* (poetry), Oberon, 1990.
*Nine Lives* (stories), Thistledown Press, 1991.
*Saskatchewan: Discover Canada* (nonfiction), Grolier (Toronto), 1992.
*Long Distance Calls* (stories), Coteau Books (Regina, Saskatchewan), 1996.

Stories and poems represented in numerous anthologies, including *Metavisions,* Quadrant Press, 1983; *Open Windows,* Quarry Press, 1988; *Out of Place,* Coteau Books, 1991; *Lodestone,* Fifth House, 1993; and *Due West,* Coteau Books, 1996. Contributor of stories and poems to various periodicals, including *Canadian Forum, Canadian Literature, Dalhousie Review, Descant, Fiddlehead, Malahat Review, Poetry Canada Review, Prairie Fire, Prism International, Quarry, Queen's Quarterly,* and *Wascana Review.*

**MARLOWE, Katherine**
  See ALLEN, Charlotte Vale

\*     \*     \*

**MARSACK, Robyn (Louise)    1953-**

*PERSONAL:* Born January 30, 1953, in Wellington, New Zealand; married Stuart Airlie (a historian), July 21, 1984; children: one daughter. *Education:* Victoria University of Wellington, B.A., 1973; Oxford University, B.Phil., 1976, D.Phil., 1979.

*ADDRESSES: Home*—Glasgow, Scotland. *Office*—c/o Carcanet Press, 402-406 Corn Exchange, Manchester M4 3BY, England.

*CAREER:* Oxford University, Oxford, England, junior research fellow, 1979-82; Carcanet Press, Manchester, England, editor, 1982-87; freelance editor, 1987—.

*AWARDS, HONORS:* Scott-Moncrieff Prize, Translators Association, 1988, for translating *The Scorpion-Fish.*

*WRITINGS:*

*The Cave of Making: The Poetry of Louis MacNeice,* Oxford University Press (New York City), 1982.
*Sylvia Plath,* Open University Press (London), 1992.

*EDITOR*

(And author of introduction) *The Selected Poems of Edmund Blunden,* Carcanet (Oxford), 1982.
(And author of introduction) Thomas Bewick, *Selected Works,* Carcanet, 1989.
(And author of introduction) Mary Russell Mitford, *My Garden,* Houghton (Boston), 1990.

*TRANSLATOR*

Bruno Monsaingeon, *Mademoiselle: Conversations with Nadia Boulanger,* Carcanet, 1985, Northeastern University Press (Boston), 1988.
Nicolas Bouvier, *The Scorpion-Fish,* Carcanet, 1987.
Bouvier, *The Way of the World,* Marlboro (Marlboro, VT), 1992.
Nina Berberova, *Aleksandr Blok: A Life,* Braziller (New York City), 1996.

(With Stuart Airlie) *The Cambridge Illustrated History of the Middle Ages,* Volume II, Cambridge University Press (New York City), 1997.

Also translator of Robertson McCarta's *Walks in Provence,* 1989, and *Walking Through Brittany,* 1989. Contributor to books, including *About Edwin Morgan,* Edinburgh University Press (Edinburgh), 1990, and *La Liberte en Traduction,* Didier Erudition (Paris), 1991. Contributor to *Dictionary of Literary Biography.* Contributor of reviews and articles to *Notes and Queries, Verse, PN Review, Review of English Studies, Modern Language Review, Scotland on Sunday,* and *Professional Translator and Interpreter.*

\*     \*     \*

**MARTENS, E. A.**
  See MARTENS, Elmer A(rthur)

\*     \*     \*

**MARTENS, Elmer A(rthur)    1930-**
  (E. A. Martens)

*PERSONAL:* Born August 12, 1930, in Main Centre, Saskatchewan, Canada; immigrated to the United States, 1955; son of Jacob Henry (a farmer) and Susie (a housewife; maiden name, Nickel) Martens; married Phyllis J. Hiebert (a writer), August 24, 1956; children: Lauren, Frances (Mrs. Ken Friesen), Vernon, Karen (Mrs. Rick Bartlett). *Ethnicity:* "European." *Education:* University of Saskatchewan, B.A., 1954; University of Manitoba, B.Ed., 1956; Mennonite Brethren Biblical Seminary, B.D., 1958; Claremont Graduate School, Ph.D., 1972. *Avocational interests:* Photography.

*ADDRESSES: Home*—4850 East Rialto, Fresno, CA 93726; fax: 209-251-7212. *Office*—4824 East Butler, Fresno, CA 93727. *E-mail*—76331.1567@compuserve.com.

*CAREER:* Schoolteacher in Stewart Valley, Saskatchewan, 1954-55; pastor of Mennonite Brethren congregation in Fresno, CA, 1958-66; ordained minister of the Mennonite Brethren, 1959; Mennonite Brethren Biblical Seminary, Fresno, assistant professor, 1970-71, associate professor, 1972-74, professor of Old Testament, 1975-95, professor emeritus, 1995—, registrar, 1973-77, president, 1977-86. Director of Christian education at Mennonite Brethren church in Upland, CA, 1967; member of Mennonite World Conference in Brazil, 1972; teacher at seminaries abroad, including work at Pune, India; Nairobi, Kenya, 1986-88; Seoul, South Korea, 1991; and St. Petersburg, Russia, 1994.

*MEMBER:* Society for Biblical Literature, Institute of Biblical Research, Society for Antiquity and Christianity, Near East Archaeological Society.

*AWARDS, HONORS:* Sermon Award, National Association of Evangelicals, 1962, for "The Bible and Spiritual Awakening."

*WRITINGS:*

(Under name E. A. Martens) *Plot and Purpose in the Old Testament,* Inter-Varsity Press, 1981, revised edition published as *God's Design: A Focus on Old Testament Theology,* Baker Books (Grand Rapids, MI), 1994.

(Under name E. A. Martens) *Jeremiah: The Believer's Church Bible Commentary Series,* Herald Press (Scottsdale, PA), 1986.

(Editor with Ben C. Ollenburger and Gerhard Hasel) *The Flowering of Old Testament Theology: A Reader in Twentieth-Century Theology, 1930-1990,* Eisenbrauns (Winona Lake, IN), 1992.

Contributor to books, including *Early Jewish and Christian Exegesis,* edited by Craig Evans and William F. Stinespring, Scholars Press (Atlanta), 1987; *Retrospect and Prospect: Missiology at the Threshold of 2001,* edited by Hans Kasdorf and Klaus W. Mueller, Liebenzeller Mission, 1988; *Your Daughters Shall Prophesy: Women in Ministry in the Church,* edited by John E. Toews, Valerie Rempel, and Katie Funk Wiebe, Kindred Press (Hillsboro, KS), 1992; *Faith, Tradition, and History: Old Testament Historiography in Its Near Eastern Context,* edited by A. R. Millard, James Hoffmeier, and David W. Baker, Eisenbrauns, 1994; *Evangelical Dictionary of Biblical Theology,* edited by Walter A. Elwell, Baker Books, 1996. Member of translation team for *New American Standard Bible,* 1969-70, *New King James Version, International Children's Version* and *New Living Bible.* Old Testament editor of "Believer's Church Bible Commentary Series," Herald Press. Contributor to periodicals, including *Bulletin for Biblical Research.* Editor of *Direction,* 1976-81.

*WORK IN PROGRESS:* An annotated bibliography of Old Testament theology.

*SIDELIGHTS:* Elmer A. Martens told *CA:* "My motivation for writing has been that I had something to say and I had an inner compulsion to say it. The message needed to get out from my 'inners' to the world. I think of my writing as having something of a 'driveness' about it. Two teachers, both towering persons in their respective fields, supply something of motivation as well as a goal for my writing. My wife Phyllis, herself a writer, is influential in 'quality control.'"

Commenting on his writing process, Martens said that "through reading and writing, especially through tackling a problem in biblical interpretation, a concept, or even a thesis statement emerges. Through conversation with others and through reflection, the written project takes shape. I gather materials, enough to refine an initial idea. Then, while materials are yet far from fully gathered or researched, I push myself to get through a first draft—quite unpolished, often with large lacunae where investigation or writing or both needs yet to happen. Then begins the laborious part of rewriting, critiquing, modifying, not once but several times until clarity and dynamism characterize the piece.

"The subjects are religious, specifically biblical. My Christian faith, my experience as a pastor, my appreciation for good resources, and my goal to add to the reservoir of exposition and argument, are major reasons for working in the field of biblical theology. An ultimate passion is to assist the church, especially the pastors, with current and more in-depth resource material."

\*    \*    \*

**MARTINSEN, Martin**
  **See FOLLETT, Ken(neth Martin)**

\*    \*    \*

**MAXWELL, William (Keepers, Jr.) 1908-**

*PERSONAL:* Born August 16, 1908, in Lincoln, IL; son of William Keepers (an insurance executive) and Eva Blossom (Blinn) Maxwell; married Emily

Gilman Noyes, May 17, 1945; children: Katharine Farrington, Emily Brooke. *Education:* University of Illinois, B.A., 1930; Harvard University, M.A., 1931.

*ADDRESSES: Home*—544 East 86th St., New York, NY 10028; (summer) 1255 Baptist Church Road, Yorktown Heights, NY 10598.

*CAREER:* Novelist and short story writer. University of Illinois, Urbana, member of English faculty, 1931-33; *New Yorker,* New York, NY, member of editorial staff, 1936-76.

*MEMBER:* National Institute of Arts and Letters (president, 1969-72), American Academy of Arts and Letters.

*AWARDS, HONORS:* Friends of American Writers Award, 1938; National Institute of Arts and Letters grant, 1958; Howells Medal, American Academy of Arts and Letters, 1980; American Book Award, 1982 for *So Long, See You Tomorrow*; Brandeis University Creative Arts Award Medal for Fiction, 1984; Chicago Public Library Harold Washington Award, 1990; Chicago Tribune Heartland Award, 1995; PEN/Malamud Award for the short story, 1995; Mark Twain Award, 1995; Gold Medal for Fiction, American Academy of Arts and Letters, 1995; Ivan Sandrof Award for Lifetime Achievement in Publishing, National Book Critics Circle, 1995.

*WRITINGS:*

NOVELS

*Bright Center of Heaven,* Harper & Bros. (New York City), 1934.
*They Came Like Swallows,* Harper & Bros., 1937, revised edition, Vintage Books (New York City), 1960.
*The Folded Leaf,* Harper (New York City), 1945.
*Time Will Darken It,* Harper, 1948.
*The Chateau,* Knopf (New York City), 1961.
*So Long, See You Tomorrow,* Knopf, 1980.

OTHER

*The Heavenly Tenants* (fantasy for children), Harper, 1946.
*Stories,* Farrar, Straus (New York City), 1956.
*The Old Man at the Railroad Crossing and Other Tales* (stories), Knopf, 1966.
*Ancestors: A Family History,* Knopf, 1971.

*Over by the River, and Other Stories* (stories), Knopf, 1977.
(Editor) Charles Pratt, *The Garden and the Wilderness* (photographs), Horizon Press (New York City), 1980.
(Editor) Sylvia Townsend Warner, *Letters,* Chatto & Windus (London), 1982.
*Five Tales* (limited edition), Cummington Press (Omaha), 1988.
*The Outermost Dream: Essays and Reviews,* Knopf, 1989.
*Billie Dyer and Other Stories,* Knopf, 1992.
*Richard Bausch and William Maxwell Reading Their Short Stories* (sound recording), Archive of Recorded Poetry and Literature, Library of Congress (Washington, DC), 1992.
*All the Days and Nights: The Collected Stories of William Maxwell,* Knopf, 1995.
*Mrs. Donald's Dog Bun and His Home Away from Home,* illustrated by James Stevenson, Knopf, 1995.

Contributor of stories and book reviews to periodicals, including the *New Yorker, Paris Review, Harper's Bazaar, New England Review,* and *WigWag.*

*SIDELIGHTS:* Known for his work on the *New Yorker,* William Maxwell is also the author of nearly twenty books, including a family history which traces his ancestry back to American pioneers. Both his novels and stories alike have drawn praise from critics, and he has, on occasion, been compared to Sinclair Lewis, Henry Fuller, and Sherwood Anderson. With a "gentle wit" and an appreciation of rural America, Maxwell paints a picture of small-town life in the Midwest, untouched by the worldliness and loneliness of the big city. Maxwell once said that he does not consider his books to be nostalgic "in the strict sense." "I write about the past," he stated, "not because I think it is better than the present but because of things that happened that I do not want to be forgotten."

Many of Maxwell's books and stories are set in his home town of Lincoln, Illinois, or a fictional counterpart. *Chicago Tribune* contributor John Blades quoted Maxwell as explaining his preoccupation with Lincoln in this way: "To begin with, it was a very pretty town with elm trees meeting over the brick pavements, and a great deal of individuality in the houses, and the people as well. And because I left it when I was still a boy, my early memories are not overlaid by others, so the Lincoln of the first decades of this century is very vivid to me."

In fact, however, Maxwell has lived most of his life in New York City, where he settled in 1936. He already had one book published when he arrived in the city, and his publisher had given him letters of reference to three major magazines. Maxwell remembered in a *CA* interview that one was "to the *New Republic,* one to *Time,* and one to the *New Yorker.* I was unsuited for the *New Republic* because I was politically uninformed. I don't know if I was unsuited to *Time* as well; I got to the *New Yorker* before I got to *Time,* and they hired me, and that was that. There was a vacancy in the art department, and I found myself sitting in at the weekly art meeting, and on the following day I would tell the artists whether or not their work had been bought, and any changes in their drawings that the meeting wanted."

Maxwell eventually became one of the prestigious magazine's fiction editors, working with highly respected authors such as John O'Hara, J. D. Salinger, John Updike, and John Cheever. Asked in his *CA* interview about the *New Yorker*'s fiction style, he voiced the opinion that there was never a conscious attempt to create one; however, he allowed that "*New Yorker* editors tend to cut out unnecessary words and to punctuate according to the house rules, and most often the prose advances sentence by sentence in its effects, rather than by paragraphs in which any given sentence may not carry that much weight. The result is a certain density that may appear to be a 'style.' But when you consider the fiction writers who have appeared frequently in the magazine, for example, John Updike, John Cheever, John O'Hara, Vladimir Nabokov, Mary McCarthy, Mavis Gallant, Sylvia Townsend Warner, Shirley Hazzard, Eudora Welty, J. D. Salinger, Frank O'Connor, Maeve Brennan, and Larry Woiwode—it is immediately apparent that there is no style common to all of them."

Maxwell's trademark style has been described as "thoughtful, quiet, painfully compassionate but also painfully shy" by *Yale Review* contributor Wendy Lesser. Out of his six novels, *The Folded Leaf* has been singled out by a number of critics as a good example of Maxwell's "genuine artistry." A sensitive portrayal of the friendship between two adolescent boys of different temperament, the novel is, according to Diana Trilling, an "important social document." Edmund Wilson wrote that Maxwell "approaches such matters as fraternity initiations and gratuitous schoolboy fights, the traditional customs of childhood, from an anthropological point of view: . . . with careful, unobtrusive art, [he] has

made us feel all the coldness and hardness and darkness of Chicago, the prosaic surface of existence which seems to stretch about one like asphalt or ice. But there are moments when the author breaks away into a kind of poetic reverie that shows he is able to find a way out." Colby Walworth emphasized the difficulty of the theme, and praised Maxwell's "affectionate insight into the frailties of immaturity" in the characterizations of Lymie Peters and Spud Latham. Richard Sullivan concluded: "[The novel] does precisely, beautifully and completely what it sets out to do. . . . It is a satisfaction to read prose always so admirably controlled, so governed with distinction."

*They Came Like Swallows,* an account of the effects of a Spanish influenza epidemic on a close-knit family, has also drawn praise from critics. David Tilden called it an "unpretentious book, simple and straightforward and natural, unspoiled by sentimentality." Fanny Butcher concurred, "The children are as real as any children in literature. There is neither oversentimentalizing nor that sometimes too obvious . . . lack of sentiment in these simple and memorable pages." V. S. Pritchett mentioned the "lack of unity" in the novel, but noted that "otherwise the book is a sensitive, wistful reminiscence of family life."

Maxwell turned to a different theme in *The Chateau:* the American experience in Europe. According to Richard Gilman, he exercised "a trained, cool-tempered sensibility" in portraying the predicament of an American couple in postwar France. David Boraff called the work "a beguilingly old fashioned novel, almost Jamesian in its restraint and in its delineation of subtle shifts in consciousness." For Naomi Bliven, "*The Chateau* . . . is a large-scale work whose smallest details are beautifully made. The author has labored for the reader's case. His style is a joy— exact, moderate, from time to time amused or amusing, always compassionate, sometimes as startling as lightning. . . . This novel is fiction with the authenticity of a verified document, a history of what some citizens of the splintered Western World might say or mean to each other in our period." Elizabeth Bowen declared, "I can think of few novels, of my day certainly, that have such romantic authority as *The Chateau,* fewer still so adult in vitality, so alight with humor."

In her review of *Over by the River, and Other Stories,* Joyce Carol Oates praised "Maxwell's gifts as a writer" which "allow him to impose upon his material a gentle, rather Chekhovian sense of order:

whatever happens is not Fate but the inevitable working-out of character, never melodramatic, never pointedly 'symbolic.' " This collection of stories includes work written from as early as 1941 to 1977. Oates pointed out a few stories that she especially liked, and spoke of Maxwell's "vision." "He is not unaware of what might be called evil," she commented, "and he is willing to explore the possibility that, yes, civilization is in decline."

*So Long, See You Tomorrow* is according to Robert Wilson, "a summing up by Maxwell at the age of 71 of many of the most powerful experiences and concerns from his past work." In this novel, Maxwell recalls the death of his mother in the 1918 flu epidemic, and the family's subsequent move to Chicago. He also describes the tragedy which struck another Lincoln household: tenant farmer Clarence Smith finds out about his wife's love affair, kills her lover, and then commits suicide. Years later in Chicago, Maxwell comes face to face with Cletus Smith, Clarence's son, and the meeting stirs up painful memories for both boys.

A *New York Post* critic noted that the book "is filled with the sense of desolation and bewilderment which adults inflict upon their young, wounds like those of war, never fully healing, aching with each twinge of recollection. There is compressed into this small work the scope of Greek tragedy, a sense of time and place and the accumulated perception of a thoughtful and moving writer. William Maxwell makes one believe that the best traditions of American fiction continue to survive." White agreed: "His accomplishment is to present a fascinating tragedy enacted by sincere, gentle, reluctant participants—and to give his account the same integrity that marks their deeds." Likewise, Wilson praised Maxwell for "a marvelously evocative prose style, which suggests in its grace and simplicity a gentle wind brushing autumn leaves across the yards of those stately old houses that seemingly exist outside time compared to the lives of the families who pass through them."

Maxwell's nonfiction collection *The Outermost Dream: Essays and Reviews,* which covers a wide diversity of subjects, also won enthusiastic praise from book reviewers after it was published in 1989. Most of the items included in the book were previously published in the *New Yorker* magazine; many of the reviews focus on the diaries, biographies, and memoirs of nineteenth- and twentieth-century figures, including writers Virginia Woolf and E. B. White.

*New York Times Book Review* contributor Judith Baumel concluded that "in this one wonderful volume we get Mr. Maxwell's clear prose, his magical narrative and the attractions of his quirky mind."

Many of Maxwell's most widely acclaimed short stories appeared in *Billie Dyer and Other Stories* and *All the Days and Nights: The Collected Stories of William Maxwell.* Of the former, Carin Pratt remarked in the *Christian Science Monitor,* "His writing is simple and direct, poignant without being sentimental. . . . Reading these stories about when life was supposedly more simple than it is now makes you come away with the clear understanding that life has always been complicated and hard. . . . What's perhaps most appealing about this collection is that after finishing a story, you don't have to wonder what it's about. . . . [The author] . . . doesn't make you feel stupid by obscuring the meaning."

Mary Flanagan included some rare criticism of the author's writing in her generally favorable *New York Times Book Review* assessment of *All the Days and Nights.* "Mr. Maxwell's work is throughout balanced, gentle and humane. . . . [His] realism is permeated by a tender lyricism. Mellow and unhurried, his warm, amiable voice mixes the cultivated with the colloquial. His powers of description are remarkable. . . . But he can also ramble, sacrificing structure to discursiveness and flirting with the literary equivalent of easy listening. . . . The last few stories are so similar that I kept wondering whether I was rereading the same one." But Penelope Mesic was unqualified in her praise for *All the Days and Nights.* She declared in the *Chicago Tribune:* "Maxwell, dealing in very ordinary days and nights, makes them luminous by the skillful use of contrasts, as the impressionists made a dull rain-washed street shine—not by using colors of garish brightness but by using one tone to bring another into prominence. We feel this is not only an esthetic but a moral choice. Maxwell's constant effort is to give to whatever he observes its true colors and just value."

*BIOGRAPHICAL/CRITICAL SOURCES:*

BOOKS

*Dictionary of Literary Biography Yearbook,* Gale (Detroit), 1980.
*Contemporary Literary Criticism,* Volume 19, Gale, 1981.
Maxwell, William, *Ancestors: A Family History,* Knopf, 1971.

Maxwell, *Billie Dyer and Other Stories,* Knopf, 1992.

Steinman, Michael, editor, *The Happiness of Getting It Down Right: The Letters of Frank O'Connor and William Maxwell* Knopf, 1996.

*PERIODICALS*

*Booklist,* April 1, 1989, p. 1341.

*Boston Globe,* January 7, 1986, p. 25; January 7, 1986, p. 25; June 8, 1989, p. 86; February 25, 1992, p. 56; January 15, 1995, p. 62.

*Chicago Daily Tribune,* May 1, 1937; May 2, 1937.

*Chicago Tribune,* May 14, 1989, section 14, p. 7; February 9, 1992, section 14, p. 3; March 5, 1992, section 5, pp. 1-2; January 8, 1995, section 14, p. 3.

*Chicago Tribune Book World,* December 12, 1979.

*Christian Science Monitor,* May 26, 1937; December 17, 1946; September 9, 1948; March 27, 1992, p. 17.

*Commonweal,* April 7, 1961, p. 50; December 10, 1971; May 22, 1992, pp. 2021.

*Los Angeles Times Book Review,* January 22, 1995, p. 6; March 5, 1995, p. 9.

*Nation,* April 21, 1945; September 25, 1948, p. 353.

*New Republic,* September 10, 1977; January 26, 1980, pp. 39-40.

*New Statesman and Nation,* August 8, 1937, pp. 312-13; August 28, 1937.

*New Yorker,* March 31, 1945, pp. 81-82; September 4, 1948; March 25, 1961.

*New York Post,* January 12, 1980.

*New York Review of Books,* April 28, 1966, pp. 23-24; October 8, 1992, pp. 49-50.

*New York Times,* April 8, 1945; September 5, 1948; April 29, 1989, p. A15; May 14, 1989, section 7, p. 23; February 14, 1992, section C, p. 27; December 30, 1994, p. C31.

*New York Times Book Review,* September 9, 1934, p. 17; April 8, 1945, p. 3; September 5, 1948, p. 4; March 26, 1961; March 13, 1966, p. 5; August 8, 1971; May 14, 1989, p. 23; February 16, 1992, section 7, p. 7; February 28, 1993, p. 32; June 6, 1993, p. 54; January 22, 1995, pp. 3, 20.

*Publishers Weekly,* December 10, 1979, pp. 8-9; November 28, 1994, p. 43.

*Rapport,* vol. 18, no. 6, p. 21.

*Reporter,* May 25, 1961.

*Saturday Review of Literature,* September 15, 1934, pp. 109-10; May 1, 1937, p. 4; November 9, 1946; September 4, 1948.

*Time,* September 20, 1948.

*Times Literary Supplement,* August 21, 1937.

*Tribune Books,* December 6, 1992, p. 13.

*Washington Post,* January 18, 1995, section B, p. 2.

*Washington Post Book World,* January 13, 1980, pp. 1-2; April 30, 1989, p. 5; January 26, 1992, p. 1.

*Weekly Book Review,* April 8, 1945.

*Yale Review,* July, 1992, pp. 202-03.

\*    \*    \*

**MAY, J. C.**
  **See MAY, Julian**

\*    \*    \*

**MAY, Julian 1931-**
  **(Julian May Dikty; pseudonyms: Bob Cunningham, Lee N. Falconer, John Feilen, Matthew G. Grant, J. C. May, Ian Thorne, Jean Wright Thorne, George Zanderbergen)**

*PERSONAL:* Born July 10, 1931, in Chicago, IL; daughter of Matthew M. and Julia (Feilen) May; married Thaddeus "Ted" E. Dikty (a writer and publisher), 1953; children: Alan Samuel, David Bernard, Barbara Ellen. *Education:* Attended Rosary College, 1949-52. *Avocational interests:* Backpacking, canoeing, electronic music, gardening, jewelry making.

*ADDRESSES: Home and office*—P.O. Box 851, Mercer Island, WA 98040.

*CAREER:* Freelance writer. Booz Allen & Hamilton, Chicago, IL, editor, 1953; Consolidated Book Publishers, Chicago, editor, 1954-57; Publication Associates, editor and co-owner, Chicago, 1957-68, Naperville, IL, 1968-74, West Linn, OR, 1974-80, and Mercer Island, WA, 1980—. Has also worked in art design, art direction, commercial art, and photography.

*AWARDS, HONORS: Locus* Award for Best Science Fiction Novel, 1982, and Hugo and Nebula Award nominations, all for *The Many-Colored Land.*

*WRITINGS:*

*"THE SAGA OF PLIOCENE EXILE" SERIES*

*The Many-Colored Land,* Houghton (Boston), 1981.
*The Golden Torc,* Houghton, 1981.

*Brede's Tale* (short story), Starmont House (Mercer Island, WA), 1982.

*The Nonborn King,* Houghton, 1983.

*The Adversary,* Houghton, 1984.

*A Pliocene Companion: A Reader's Guide to The Many-Colored Land, The Golden Torc, The Nonborn King, The Adversary,* Houghton, 1984.

*"GALACTIC MILIEU" SERIES*

*Intervention: A Root Tale to the Galactic Milieu and a Vinculum between It and the Saga of Pliocene Exile,* Houghton, 1987, published in two volumes as *The Surveillance* and *The Metaconcert,* Ballantine (New York City), 1989.

*Jack the Bodiless,* Knopf (New York City), 1992.

*Diamond Mask,* Knopf, 1994.

*Magnificat,* Knopf, 1996.

*FANTASY FICTION*

(With Marion Zimmer Bradley and Andre Norton) *Black Trillium,* Doubleday (New York City), 1990.

*Blood Trillium,* Bantam Spectra (New York City), 1992.

*Sky Trillium,* Ballantine, 1997.

*JUVENILE NONFICTION*

*There's Adventure in Atomic Energy,* Popular Mechanics Press, 1957.

*There's Adventure in Chemistry,* Popular Mechanics Press, 1957.

*There's Adventure in Electronics,* Popular Mechanics Press, 1957.

*There's Adventure in Geology,* Popular Mechanics Press, 1958.

*There's Adventure in Rockets,* Popular Mechanics Press, 1958.

*You and the Earth beneath Us,* Children's Press (Chicago), 1958.

*There's Adventure in Jet Aircraft,* Popular Mechanics Press, 1959.

*There's Adventure in Marine Science,* Popular Mechanics Press, 1959.

*Show Me the World of Astronomy,* Pennington Press, 1959.

*Show Me the World of Electronics,* Pennington Press, 1959.

*Show Me the World of Modern Airplanes,* Pennington Press, 1959.

*Show Me the World of Space Travel,* Pennington Press, 1959.

*The Real Book about Robots and Thinking Machines,* Doubleday, 1961.

*There's Adventure in Astronautics,* Hawthorn, 1961.

*There's Adventure in Automobiles,* Hawthorn, 1961.

*Motion,* Accelerated Instruction Methods, 1962.

(With husband, T. E. Dikty) *Every Boy's Book of American Heroes,* Fell (New York City), 1963.

*They Turned to Stone,* Holiday House (New York City), 1965.

*Weather,* Follett (New York City), 1966.

*Rockets,* Follett, 1967.

*They Lived in the Ice Age,* Holiday House, 1968.

*Astronautics,* Follett, 1968.

*The Big Island,* Follett, 1968.

*The First Men,* Holiday House, 1968.

*Horses: How They Came to Be,* Holiday House, 1968.

*Alligator Hole,* Follett, 1969.

*Before the Indians,* Holiday House, 1969.

*Climate,* Follett, 1969.

*How We Are Born,* Follett, 1969.

*Living Things and Their Young,* Follett, 1969.

*Man and Woman,* Follett, 1969.

*Moving Hills of Sand,* Follett, 1969.

*Why the Earth Quakes,* Holiday House, 1969.

*Do You Have Your Father's Nose?,* Creative Educational Society, 1970.

*Dodos and Dinosaurs are Extinct,* Creative Educational Society, 1970.

(With others) *The Ecology of North America,* Creative Educational Society, 1970.

*The First Living Things,* Holiday House, 1970.

*How to Build a Body,* Creative Educational Society, 1970.

*Millions of Years of Eggs,* Creative Educational Society, 1970.

*A New Baby Comes,* Creative Educational Society, 1970.

*Tiger Stripes and Zebra Stripes,* Creative Educational Society, 1970.

*Why Birds Migrate,* Holiday House, 1970.

*Why Plants Are Green Instead of Pink,* Creative Educational Society, 1970.

*Wildlife in the City,* Creative Educational Society, 1970.

*Blue River: The Land beneath the Sea,* Holiday House, 1971.

*Cactus Fox,* Creative Educational Society, 1971.

*These Islands Are Alive,* Hawthorn, 1971.

*Why People Are Different Colors,* Holiday House, 1971.

*The Antarctic: Bottom of the World,* Creative Educational Society, 1972.

*The Arctic: Top of the World,* Creative Educational Society, 1972.

*Cascade Cougar,* Creative Educational Society, 1972.

*The Cloud Book,* Creative Educational Society, 1972.

*Deserts: Hot and Cold,* Creative Educational Society, 1972.

*Eagles of the Valley,* Creative Educational Society, 1972.

*Forests That Change Color,* Creative Educational Society, 1972.

*Giant Condor of California,* Creative Educational Society, 1972.

*Glacier Grizzly,* Creative Educational Society, 1972.

*Islands of the Tiny Deer,* Young Scott Books, 1972.

*The Land Is Disappearing,* Creative Educational Society, 1972.

*Living Blanket on the Land,* Creative Educational Society, 1972.

*The Mysterious Evergreen Forest,* Creative Educational Society, 1972.

*Plankton: Drifting Life of the Waters,* Holiday House, 1972.

*The Prairie Has an Endless Sky,* Creative Educational Society, 1972.

*Prairie Pronghorn,* Creative Educational Society, 1972.

*Rainbows, Clouds, and Foggy Dew,* Creative Educational Society, 1972.

*Sea Lion Island,* Creative Educational Society, 1972.

*Sea Otter,* Creative Educational Society, 1972.

*Snowfall!,* Creative Educational Society, 1972.

*What Will the Weather Be?,* Creative Educational Society, 1972.

*Birds We Know,* Creative Educational Society, 1973.

*Fishes We Know,* Creative Educational Society, 1973.

*Insects We Know,* Creative Educational Society, 1973.

*The Life Cycle of a Bullfrog,* Creative Educational Society, 1973.

*The Life Cycle of a Cottontail Rabbit,* Creative Educational Society, 1973.

*The Life Cycle of a Monarch Butterfly,* Creative Educational Society, 1973.

*The Life Cycle of an Opossum,* Creative Educational Society, 1973.

*The Life Cycle of a Polyphemus Moth,* Creative Educational Society, 1973.

*The Life Cycle of a Raccoon,* Creative Educational Society, 1973.

*The Life Cycle of a Red Fox,* Creative Educational Society, 1973.

*The Life Cycle of a Snapping Turtle,* Creative Educational Society, 1973.

*Mammals We Know,* Creative Educational Society, 1973.

*Reptiles We Know,* Creative Educational Society, 1973.

*Wild Turkeys,* Holiday House, 1973.

*How the Animals Came to North America,* Holiday House, 1974.

*Cars and Cycles,* Bowmar-Noble, 1978.

*The Warm-Blooded Dinosaurs,* Holiday House, 1978.

*JUVENILE BIOGRAPHIES*

*Captain Cousteau: Undersea Explorer,* Creative Educational Society, 1972.

*Hank Aaron Clinches the Pennant,* Crestwood, 1972.

*Jim Brown Runs with the Ball,* Crestwood, 1972.

*Johnny Unitas and the Long Pass,* Crestwood, 1972.

*Matthew Henson: Co-Discoverer of the North Pole,* Creative Educational Society, 1972.

*Mickey Mantle Slugs It Out,* Crestwood (Mankato, MN), 1972.

*Sitting Bull: Chief of the Sioux,* Creative Educational Society, 1972.

*Sojourner Truth: Freedom Fighter,* Creative Educational Society, 1972.

*Willie Mays: Most Valuable Player,* Crestwood, 1972.

*Amelia Earhart: Pioneer of Aviation,* Creative Educational Society, 1973.

*Bobby Orr: Star on Ice,* Crestwood, 1973.

*Ernie Banks: Home Run Slugger,* Crestwood, 1973.

*Fran Tarkenton: Scrambling Quarterback,* Crestwood, 1973.

*Gale Sayers: Star Running Back,* Crestwood, 1973.

*Hillary and Tenzing: Conquerors of Mount Everest,* Creative Educational Society, 1973.

*Kareem Abdul Jabbar: Cage Superstar,* Crestwood, 1973.

*Quanah: Leader of the Comanche,* Creative Educational Society, 1973.

*Thor Heyerdahl: Modern Viking Adventurer,* Creative Educational Society, 1973.

*Roberto Clemente and the World Series Upset,* Crestwood, 1973.

*Billie Jean King: Tennis Champion,* Crestwood, 1974.

*Bobby Hull: Hockey's Golden Jet,* Crestwood, 1974.

*Lee Trevino: The Golf Explosion,* Crestwood, 1974.

*O. J. Simpson: Juice on the Gridiron,* Crestwood, 1974.

*Roy Campanella: Brave Man of Baseball,* Crestwood, 1974.

*A. J. Foyt: Championship Auto Racer,* Crestwood, 1975.

*Arthur Ashe: Dark Star of Tennis,* Crestwood, 1975.

*Bobby Clarke: Hockey with a Grin,* Crestwood, 1975.

*Chris Evert: Princess of Tennis,* Crestwood, 1975.

*Evel Knievel: Daredevil Stuntman,* Crestwood, 1975.

*Evonne Goolalgong: Smasher from Australia,* Crestwood, 1975.

*Frank Robinson: Slugging toward Glory,* Crestwood, 1975.

*Janet Lynn: Figure Skating Star,* Crestwood, 1975.

*Pele: World Soccer Star,* Crestwood, 1975.

*Joe Namath: High Flying Quarterback,* Crestwood, 1975.

*Muhammad Ali: Boxing Superstar,* Crestwood, 1975.

*Vince Lombardi: The Immortal Coach,* Crestwood, 1975.

*Phil Esposito: The Big Bruin,* Crestwood, 1975.

*SPORTS NONFICTION*

*The Baltimore Colts,* Creative Educational Society, 1974.

*The Dallas Cowboys,* Creative Educational Society, 1974.

*The Green Bay Packers,* Creative Educational Society, 1974.

*The Kansas City Chiefs,* Creative Educational Society, 1974.

*The Miami Dolphins,* Creative Educational Society, 1974.

*The New York Jets,* Creative Educational Society, 1974.

*The Stanley Cup,* Creative Educational Society, 1975.

*The Super Bowl,* Creative Educational Society, 1975.

*The Indianapolis 500,* Creative Educational Society, 1975.

*The Kentucky Derby,* Creative Educational Society, 1975.

*The Masters Tournament of Golf,* Creative Educational Society, 1975.

*The U. S. Open Golf Championship,* Creative Educational Society, 1975.

*Wimbledon: World Tennis Focus,* Creative Educational Society, 1975.

*The World Series,* Creative Educational Society, 1975.

*The NBA Playoffs: Basketball's Classic,* Creative Educational Society, 1975.

*The Olympic Games,* Creative Educational Society, 1975.

*The PGA Championship,* Creative Educational Society, 1976.

*The Pittsburgh Steelers,* Creative Educational Society, 1976.

*The Winter Olympics,* Creative Educational Society, 1976.

*America's Cup Yacht Race,* Creative Educational Society, 1976.

*Boxing's Heavyweight Championship Fight,* Creative Educational Society, 1976.

*Daytona 500,* Creative Educational Society, 1976.

*Forest Hills and the American Tennis Championship,* Creative Educational Society, 1976.

*The Grand Prix,* Creative Educational Society, 1976.

*The Triple Crown,* Creative Educational Society, 1976.

*The Rose Bowl,* Creative Educational Society, 1976.

*The Washington Redskins,* Creative Educational Society, 1977.

*The Los Angeles Rams,* Creative Educational Society, 1977.

*The Minnesota Vikings,* Creative Educational Society, 1977.

*The New York Giants,* Creative Educational Society, 1977.

*The Oakland Raiders,* Creative Educational Society, 1977.

*The San Francisco 49ers,* Creative Educational Society, 1977.

*The Oakland Raiders: Superbowl Champions,* Creative Educational Society, 1978.

*The Baltimore Colts* (different from previous publication of same title), Creative Educational Society, 1980.

*The Cincinnati Bengals,* Creative Educational Society, 1980.

*The Dallas Cowboys* (different from previous publication of same title), Creative Educational Society, 1980.

*The Denver Broncos,* Creative Educational Society, 1980.

*The Green Bay Packers* (different from previous publication of same title), Creative Educational Society, 1980.

*The Kansas City Chiefs* (different from previous publication of same title), Creative Educational Society), 1980.

*The Miami Dolphins* (different from previous publication of same title), Creative Educational Society, 1980.

*The New York Jets* (different from previous publication of same title), Creative Educational Society, 1980.

*The Pittsburgh Steelers* (different from previous publication of same title), Creative Educational Society, 1980.

*The San Diego Chargers,* Creative Educational Society, 1980.

*NONFICTION; UNDER PSEUDONYM JOHN FEILEN*

*Air,* Follett, 1965.

*Deer,* Follett, 1967.

*Squirrels,* Follett, 1967.
*Dirt Track Speedsters,* Crestwood, 1976.
*Racing on the Water,* Crestwood, 1976.
*Winter Sports,* Crestwood, 1976.
*Four-Wheel Racing,* Crestwood, 1978.
*Motocross Racing,* Crestwood, 1978.

*NONFICTION; UNDER PSEUDONYM MATTHEW G. GRANT*

*A Walk in the Mountains,* Reilly and Lee, 1971.
*Buffalo Bill of the Wild West,* Creative Educational Society, 1974.
*Champlain: Explorer of New France,* Creative Educational Society, 1974.
*Chief Joseph of the Nez Perce,* Creative Educational Society, 1974.
*Clara Barton: Red Cross Pioneer,* Creative Educational Society, 1974.
*Columbus: Discoverer of the New World,* Creative Educational Society, 1974.
*Coronado: Explorer of the Southwest,* Creative Educational Society, 1974.
*Crazy Horse: War Chief of the Oglala,* Creative Educational Society, 1974.
*Daniel Boone in the Wilderness,* Creative Educational Society, 1974.
*Davy Crockett: Frontier Adventurer,* Creative Educational Society, 1974.
*DeSoto: Explorer of the Southeast,* Creative Educational Society, 1974.
*Dolly Madison: First Lady of the Land,* Creative Educational Society, 1974.
*Elizabeth Blackwell: Pioneer Doctor,* Creative Educational Society, 1974.
*Francis Marion: Swamp Fox,* Creative Educational Society, 1974.
*Geronimo: Apache Warrior,* Creative Educational Society, 1974.
*Harriet Tubman: Black Liberator,* Creative Educational Society, 1974.
*Jane Addams: Helper of the Poor,* Creative Educational Society, 1974.
*Jim Bridger: The Mountain Man,* Creative Educational Society, 1974.
*John Paul Jones: Naval Hero,* Creative Educational Society, 1974.
*Leif Ericson: Explorer of Vinland,* Creative Educational Society, 1974.
*Lewis and Clark: Western Trailblazers,* Creative Educational Society, 1974.
*Kit Carson: Trailblazer of the West,* Creative Educational Society, 1974.
*Lafayette: Freedom's General,* Creative Educational Society, 1974.

*Osceola and the Seminole War,* Creative Educational Society, 1974.
*Paul Revere: Patriot and Craftsman,* Creative Educational Society, 1974.
*Pontiac: Indian General and Statesman,* Creative Educational Society, 1974.
*Robert E. Lee: The South's Great General,* Creative Educational Society, 1974.
*Squanto: The Indian Who Saved the Pilgrims,* Creative Educational Society, 1974.
*Sam Houston of Texas,* Creative Educational Society, 1974.
*Susan B. Anthony: Crusader for Women's Rights,* Creative Educational Society, 1974.
*Ulysses S Grant: General and President,* Creative Educational Society, 1974.

*NONFICTION; UNDER PSEUDONYM IAN THORNE*

*Meet the Coaches,* Creative Educational Society, 1975.
*Meet the Defensive Linemen,* Creative Educational Society, 1975.
*Meet the Linebackers,* Creative Educational Society, 1975.
*Meet the Quarterbacks,* Creative Educational Society, 1975.
*Meet the Receivers,* Creative Educational Society, 1975.
*Meet the Running Backs,* Creative Educational Society, 1975.
*The Great Centers,* Creative Educational Society, 1976.
*The Great Defenseman,* Creative Educational Society, 1976.
*The Great Goalies,* Creative Educational Society, 1976.
*The Great Wingmen,* Creative Educational Society, 1976.
*King Kong,* Creative Educational Society, 1976.
*Mad Scientists,* Crestwood, 1977.
*Godzilla,* Crestwood, 1977.
*Ancient Astronauts,* Crestwood, 1977.
*Dracula,* Crestwood, 1977.
*Frankenstein,* Crestwood, 1977.
*Monster Tales of Native Americans,* Crestwood, 1978.
*The Bermuda Triangle,* Crestwood, 1978.
*Bigfoot,* Crestwood, 1978.
*The Loch Ness Monster,* Crestwood, 1978.
*UFOs,* edited by Howard Schroeder, Crestwood, 1978.

*NONFICTION; UNDER PSEUDONYM GEORGE ZANDERBERGEN*

*The Beatles,* Crestwood, 1976.
*Made for Music: Elton John, Stevie Wonder, John Denver,* Crestwood, 1976.

*Laugh It Up: Carol Burnett, Bill Cosby, Mary Tyler Moore,* Crestwood, 1976.
*Nashville Music: Loretta Lynn, Mac Davis, Charley Pride,* Crestwood, 1976.
*Stay Tuned: Henry Winkler, Lee Majors, Valerie Harper,* Crestwood, 1976.
*Sweetly Singing: Cher, Roberta Flack, Olivia Newton John,* Crestwood, 1976.

NONFICTION; UNDER PSEUDONYM BOB CUNNINGHAM

*Ten-Five: Alaska Skip,* Crestwood, 1977.
*Ten-Seven for Good Sam,* Crestwood, 1977.
*Ten-Seventy: Range Fire,* Crestwood, 1977.
*Ten-Thirty-Three: Emergency,* Crestwood, 1977.
*Ten-Two Hundred: Come on Smokey!,* Crestwood, 1977.

FILM NOVELIZATIONS; UNDER PSEUDONYM IAN THORNE

*The Wolf Man,* Crestwood House, 1977.
*The Creature from the Black Lagoon,* Crestwood House, 1981.
*Frankenstein Meets the Wolfman,* Crestwood House, 1981.
*The Blob,* Crestwood House, 1982.
*The Deadly Mantis,* Crestwood House, 1982.
*It Came from Outer Space,* Crestwood House, 1982.

OTHER

(Under pseudonym Jean Wright Thorne) *Horse and Rider,* Creative Educational Society, 1976.
(Under pseudonym Jean Wright Thorne) *Rodeo,* Creative Educational Society, 1976.
(Under pseudonym Lee N. Falconer) *A Gazetteer of the Hyborian World of Conan.* Starmont House, 1977.

Editor, "Life in God's Love" series, *Franciscan Herald,* 1963.

*ADAPTATIONS:* The 1951 novelette *Dune Roller* has been adapted for television and radio.

*WORK IN PROGRESS: Sky Trillium,* another novel in the "Trillium" fantasy series; the "Rampart Worlds" trilogy.

*SIDELIGHTS:* "I love action-filled science fiction. I am a fan. I have been accused of being a fan and I admit to it," Julian May tells Darrell Schweitzer in *Science Fiction Review.* After twenty-five years of earning her living by writing juvenile nonfiction

works to order, May's love for science fiction led her to return to the field in the 1980s with the four-volume "Saga of the Pliocene Exile." This epic series involving time travel, psychic powers, alien conquerors, and human determination has proven popular with readers who enjoy tales of adventure. As the author tells Schweitzer: "To me, SF should not be didactic, but rather a literature of entertainment. . . . I [have always] wanted to give the reader books that would be fun."

As a teenager, May was first introduced to the science fiction genre. She briefly became involved in what is known as science fiction "fandom," corresponding with other enthusiasts, editing a science fiction newsletter, and even organizing a convention in her hometown of Chicago. In 1951, her novelette "Dune Roller" was published in *Astounding,* the magazine edited by the legendary John W. Campbell, who had fostered the careers of writers like Isaac Asimov and Robert A. Heinlein. This story brought her to the attention of other editors—leading to the publication of her second story—as well as a young publisher named Ted Dikty, whom she married in 1953.

While "Dune Roller" achieved a wide readership, May left science fiction fandom and writing soon after her marriage. As she explained to Schweitzer, "In the 1950s you couldn't make a living writing science fiction unless you wrote a great volume of work, mostly short pieces for magazines. I am not that sort of writer." Instead, May took a job with a publishing company, where she wrote some 7,000 encyclopedia articles about science and natural history. She discovered a talent for producing nonfiction quickly, and in 1957 she turned freelance, forming an editorial services company with her husband that handled every aspect of book production, from research and writing to printing and binding.

May wrote almost 250 nonfiction books between 1957 and 1982, most of which dealt with science, sports, or biography. While these books gave her the chance to learn about new subjects and hone her writing skills, they provided little room for creativity—even the subjects were assigned by the publishers. As a result, May has explained, she had "little emotional involvement in my juvenile books. . . . I did not write my long list of books because of a creative itch, but because I was good at it and it paid the bills." The "itch" to write science fiction always remained, however, and as her children grew up and the royalties from her nonfiction works accumulated, she began considering a return to science fiction.

A homemade "diamond"-studded space suit May created for a science fiction convention provided the inspiration that led to her first novel. "At first I had no notion of writing a novel," the author tells Schweitzer, "but then as I was writing my other stuff, the damn costume would come creeping back into my subconscious mind and I would wonder what kind of character would wear something like that." May began jotting down notes and collecting research and by 1978 had the outline for a series of novels set in what she called the Galactic Milieu, a future in which humans with extraordinary mental powers such as telepathy and telekinesis have led Earth into a galaxy-wide civilization with several alien races. The author recognized that she might have difficulty marketing a story with such complex concepts, however, and decided to write a more conventional science fiction story first. This story became the "Saga of the Pliocene Exile," which is comprised of four volumes: *The Many-Colored Land, The Golden Torc, The Nonborn King,* and *The Adversary.*

Set in the early twenty-second century, *The Many-Colored Land* opens upon a near-utopian Earth where the social problems of previous years have been solved with the cooperation of the alien races that form the Galactic Milieu. For those unsatisfied with the new structure of society, however, there exists an intriguing option: a one-way trip to the past, six million years ago, through an invention called the Guderian field. Travellers have been passing through the timegate in Lyon, France, for over seventy years when a unique group of eight individuals makes the same trip. Once in the past, they discover that two related but warring races of aliens, the Tanu and the Firvulag, are already inhabiting this area of Europe, which they call the "Many-Colored Land"; the Tanu's advanced metapsychic powers have allowed them to enslave most of the 100,000 humans who have arrived there. The eight members of "Group Green" are witness to the unique relationships between the races that have developed, with some assimilating into the society and others rebelling. *The Many-Colored Land* is "an enjoyable book," Algis Budrys writes in the *Magazine of Fantasy Science Fiction,* adding that this "page-turner on an intelligent level" is "a book which signally rewards" science fiction readers of all stripes. A *Publishers Weekly* critic likewise calls the novel "a most enjoyable entertainment that will have readers eagerly turning pages and awaiting the promised sequel."

The Green Group's increasing involvement in and influence of Pliocene society makes up the action of

the series' second volume, *The Golden Torc.* Those humans with latent metapsychic abilities or skills otherwise useful to the Tanu have been fitted with collars, called torcs, that can enhance mental skills and stimulate pain or pleasure centers to ensure compliance. They discover some of the secrets of the Tanu, and one human, Aiken Drum, begins insinuating himself into the Tanu royal family, helping them prepare for ritual combat against the Firvulag. The other members of Green Group, originally consigned to labor camps, have managed to escape, kill a Tanu, and secure the cooperation of the Firvulag in searching for their ancient spaceship. Like the first volume, *The Golden Torc* is entertaining "as superhero adventure raised to its highest level," a *Publishers Weekly* critic states, adding that "May develops her premises seriously and gives her large cast of characters a surprising amount of life." "May seems to be trying to do everything at once," *Booklist* reviewer Roland Green similarly observes of *The Golden Torc*'s many characters, subplots, and themes. "She also seems to succeed most of the time—the book is as powerful and gripping as it is complex."

The third volume of the Pliocene Exile, *The Nonborn King,* relates the sweeping changes that occurred in the wake of a great flood. The human Aiken Drum has assumed kingship of the Tanu and has forged an uneasy peace with the Firvulag. He is beset by enemies from within and without, however, including a previously unknown threat: a band of metapsychics led by Marc Remillard, the leader of an unsuccessful rebellion against the Galactic Milieu who escaped through the timegate almost thirty years before. *The Nonborn King* "maintains the high standard of entertainment established" in previous volumes, a *Publishers Weekly* reviewer asserts, comparing May's skills in creating "richly plotted, extravagant adventures spun from a blend of myth and science" to those of Roger Zelazny. Elton T. Elliott concurs that this third volume "marks May's continued growth and maturity as a novelist," as he writes in *Science Fiction Review.* "There is a surety about her handling of the characters and narrative," he explains, and her writing "is as rich as ever, but more under control."

The saga concludes in *The Adversary,* in which the conflicts are consummated in a spectacular mental battle that could destroy the entire civilization of the Many-Colored Land. "In a rousing climax," Pat Royal comments in *School Library Journal,* the author "brings to a glorious and grand conclusion" her "extraordinarily complex and rich science fantasy." While *Fantasy Review* contributor Susan L.

Nickerson finds the conclusion somewhat disappointing, noting that "one of the dangers of using time travel as a plot device [is that] sometimes the reader already knows the result," she adds that the series is "still a cracking good story."

While the length and "dizzying scope" of this four-volume series makes for "a tough, complex mix of characters, groups and events to manage," Elliott asserts in *Science Fiction Review,* May "handles it admirably." The critic reserves special praise for the author's characterizations, adding that "Marc Remillard is one of the most memorable personalities to ever appear in science fiction. He's complex, utterly ruthless, . . . yet I found him sympathetic." Sue Martin remarks in the *Los Angeles Times Book Review:* "May has a delightful sense of the stately and the wickedly rude that works so well with a cast of decidedly pungent personalities. Her handling of dialogue and smooth and spicy." Assessing the author's "rousing, carousing carnival of a saga," Martin concludes: "Good job, May. The Pliocene will never be the same."

While May's epic has won praise and popularity as an exciting read, several reviewers have found more to the Pliocene Saga than just an adventure story. Todd H. Sammons remarks in *Twentieth-Century Science-Fiction Writers* that the series "is Wagnerian in scope: the principals number in the dozens, the chorus in the hundreds, and . . . May uses Freudian concepts or Jungian archetypes (sometimes both) as musical leitmotifs to characterize her human principals, as well as some of the important aliens." The use of these psychological theories was deliberate, May reveals in an interview with Robert A. Collins for *Fantasy Newsletter.* "In my novels, the archetypes, the undercurrents, the different levels of meaning are there. If you're not looking for them, I promise they won't get in the way of the blood and guts and sex and fun. But if you *are* looking, you can find something like six different levels, all deliberately put there. . . . I'm here to entertain us all: the guys looking for a good read as well as the academics who like to find strange things hidden away." Because "The Saga of the Pliocene Exile" contains so much information, May wrote *A Pliocene Companion* in 1984 to help readers enhance their enjoyment of the series. Complete with glossary, characters, maps, chronologies, and genealogies, this work is "a much needed guide," Martin writes in the *Los Angeles Times Book Review:* "I wish I'd had this when I was sailing through the series."

Since writing the four Pliocene books, May has investigated the origins of the Remillard family's powers and the Galactic Milieu in *Intervention,* which was republished as two books, *The Surveillance* and *The Metaconcert.* Beginning with the explosion of the first atomic bomb in 1945, *Intervention* presents an alternate Earth history which culminates in the telepathic call sent by Denis Remillard and his associates that leads to humanity's first contact with an alien culture. The novel "has the feel of historical fiction," Sammons writes, "and May uses an array of literary techniques to tell the story—memoirs, straight narration, dramatic dialogue, excerpts from actual speeches or reports, a television script," among other "sources." The development of the new intergalactic society is revealed further in the "Galactic Milieu" trilogy, consisting of *Jack the Bodiless, Diamond Mask* and *Magnificat.* These three works concern events that happen before the Pliocene Era books, explaining the events leading to the rebellion led by Marc Remillard.

*Jack the Bodiless* begins in the twenty-first century, as humanity's fate as a member of the Galactic Milieu is being decided by five alien races. The birth of Jack Remillard, whose extraordinary metapsychic potential indicates an evolutionary leap for humankind, also poses a problem, for his physical genetic defects are unacceptable under Milieu law. At the same time, a malevolent creature known only as Fury also comes into being, killing off many of the Remillards and jeopardizing Earth's entry into the Milieu. "May combines a compelling vision of humanity's future with the drama and political intrigue" of the Remillards' political involvements, Jackie Cassada says in *Library Journal.* While a *Publishers Weekly* reviewer believes May's narrow focus on the Remillard "elites" mars the novel, the critic nonetheless allows that *Jack the Bodiless* "is engaging and May's prose adequate to it."

In *Diamond Mask,* the story of Earth's fate within the Galactic Milieu continues. As Dorothea, or Dee, Macdonald begins to acknowledge her growing metapsychic powers, she assumes the identity of Diamond Mask and confronts the power of Fury and several renegade Remillards. Working in concert with Jack and Marc Remillard, Dee saves an entire planet from a catastrophic earthquake. A *Kirkus Reviews* critic labels *Diamond Mask* as "patchy and irritatingly inconclusive," but finds that May "handles both the psychic complication and the family interactions with pleasing skill." In *Library Journal,* however, Cassada praises May's book and the development of the trilogy, calling them "rich in intrigue and vibrating with creative energy." In *Metaconcert,* the concluding volume of the trilogy, May details the rebellion of Marc Remillard and reveals the secrets behind the evil entity known as Fury.

May has also ventured into fantasy writing with a series of novels that began with *Black Trillium,* a volume she coauthored with noted writers Marion Zimmer Bradley and Andre Norton, and continued with the solo effort *Blood Trillium.* The series is set on the World of Three Moons, which has been threatened by various sorcerers who can only be defeated by a certain powerful talisman. In *Blood Trillium,* as in the first book, three sisters must fulfill separate quests; unlike *Black Trillium,* May makes the book more positive by changing "its focus from the absolute destruction of evil to the possibility of its ultimate transformation," according to *Library Journal* reviewer Cassada. A *Publishers Weekly* critic notes that May's *Blood Trillium* is "a superior tale, giving life, character, and emotion to the Three Petals of the Living Trillium."

Late in her career, May has finally been able to devote her efforts to her first love, science fiction. She has a positive view of humanity's future, which she hopes to communicate in her works. "I am an optimist," she tells Collins. "I don't think we are going to die in a mushroom cloud. I think something great will happen. I don't know if there are flying saucers—if there *are* galactic civilizations they're quite sensible in leaving us alone until we have attained suitable enlightenment. But I *am* an optimist and it shows in my novels. I've been accused of being upbeat. I triumph in being upbeat! I don't know how successful I've been, but it's been a lot of fun."

May told *CA:* "Voluminous reading, especially in the field of science, eventually led me to science fiction—which remains my first love. My first published novelette," 'Dune Roller,' "became a minor classic in the field; but in the early 1950's it was not possible to earn a living writing sf, and so I turned to nonfiction. . . . My avalanche of books for young people includes many science titles, as well as biographies and sports books. I do the book design and art direction for many of my books, as well as write them. Because I am an experienced researcher and a fast writer, I am able to do nonfiction books very quickly.

"Because my juvenile writing has been a job rather than a sideline, I have never been anxious to talk about my work. I have little emotional involvement in my juvenile books, and this tends to disappoint young readers and librarians who have romantic ideas of authorhood. . . . The professional writer is at an economic disadvantage in this country unless he or she produces a Best Seller. Since juvenile books rarely attain such heights, the ambitious writer has no other recourse but to keep on truckin'—which, for better or worse, I have done. The result is manifest."

*BIOGRAPHICAL/CRITICAL SOURCES:*

*BOOKS*

Dikty, T. E. and R. Reginald, *The Work of Julian May: An Annotated Bibliography and Guide,* Borgo Press (San Bernardino, CA), 1985.
May, Julian, *A Pliocene Companion,* Del Rey Books (New York City), 1984.
*Twentieth-Century Science Fiction Writers,* 3rd edition, St. James Press (Detroit), 1991, pp. 534-35.

*PERIODICALS*

*Analog,* August, 1983, pp. 129-30.
*Booklist,* March 1, 1982, p. 848; November 1, 1991, p. 475.
*Book World,* November 10, 1968; November 9, 1969.
*Fantasy Newsletter,* March, 1983.
*Fantasy Review,* August, 1984, pp. 16-17.
*Kirkus Reviews,* February 15, 1994, p. 181.
*Kliatt,* winter, 1984.
*Library Journal,* December 1991, p. 202; June 15, 1992, p. 105; March 15, 1994, pp. 103-04.
*Los Angeles Times Book Review,* June 3, 1984, p. 6; December 9, 1984, p. 14.
*Magazine of Fantasy and Science Fiction,* October, 1981, pp. 29-37.
*Publishers Weekly,* March 6, 1981, p. 91; December 11, 1981, p. 53; December 24, 1982, p. 51; March 9, 1984, p. 101; December 20, 1991, p. 68; May 25, 1992, pp. 42-43; February 14, 1994, p. 83.
*School Library Journal,* November, 1984, p. 146.
*Science Fiction Review,* spring, 1983, p. 25; spring, 1984, p. 36; fall, 1984, pp. 33-36.
*Times Literary Supplement,* October 16, 1969.
*Voice of Youth Advocates,* February, 1985, p. 339.
*Washington Post Book World,* March 28, 1982, p. 22.
*Young Reader's Review,* May, 1968.

## McCARTHY, Kyle 1954-

*PERSONAL:* Born July 11, 1954, in Havana, Cuba; immigrated to United States, 1960; daughter of Francis Lewis (a journalist) McCarthy and Ruth (a designer licensing agent; maiden name, Constad) McCarthy Manton; married Ron Bozman (a filmmaker and photographer), August 8, 1988; children: Regan. *Ethnicity:* "Caucasian." *Education:* Hampshire College, B.A., 1975.

*ADDRESSES: Home*—300 Central Park West #12J-1, New York, NY 10024. *E-mail*—ftforum@aol.com.

*CAREER:* Assistant director of feature films and television films; film researcher, 1976—. Free-lance travel writer, 1983—. Founder and editor of *The Family Travel Forum,* 1996—.

*MEMBER:* Directors Guild of America, New York Women in Film, Asia Society, Friends of the New York Public Library.

*WRITINGS:*

(With John Levy) *Greece and the Turkish Aegean Coast on Twenty-Five Dollars a Day,* Simon & Schuster (New York City), 1983, sixth edition published as *Frommer's Greece on Forty-Five Dollars a Day,* MacMillan (New York City), 1994, seventh edition, 1996.
(With Levy) *Dollarwise Guide to Southeast Asia,* Prentice-Hall (Englewood Cliffs, NJ), 1989.
(With Levy) *Frommer's Comprehensive Travel Guide: Thailand,* Frommer (New York City), 1991, second edition, 1994.
*Frommer's Comprehensive Travel Guide: Bangkok,* second edition, Frommer, 1994, published as *Bangkok Cityguide,* MacMillan, 1994.

Contributor to periodicals and newsletters, including *The China Daily, Conde Nast Traveler, Departures, Backpacker, Great Expeditions, The Dollarwise Traveler,* and *Pan Am Clipper.*

*WORK IN PROGRESS:* A teleplay for a travel series for children.

*SIDELIGHTS:* Kyle McCarthy told *CA:* "My free-lance career in still photography and location scouting for motion pictures was frequently punctuated by long periods of travel. A 1981 trip to China made obvious the need for an in-depth, practical travel guide for independent young professionals. A literary agent steered me to Arthur Frommer, and that is how my travel-writing career began. I know that honest, forthright guidebooks are invaluable to the adventurous traveler.

"Since becoming a parent, I've learned that honest, forthright information is also critical to the success of family journeys. That's why I'm excited about a new multimedia venture that will utilize my research and writing toward a databank for the next millennium."

\*   \*   \*

## McKINNEY, Jack
### See DALEY, Brian

\*   \*   \*

## MEEKS, Wayne A. 1932-

*PERSONAL:* Born January 8, 1932, in Aliceville, AL; son of Benjamin LaFayette (a stationmaster) and Winnie (Gavin) Meeks; married Martha Fowler (a freelance artist), June 10, 1954; Suzanne, Edith, Ellen. *Education:* University of Alabama, B.S., 1953; Austin Presbyterian Theological Seminary, B.D., 1956; University of Tuebingen, graduate study, 1956-57; Yale University, M.A., 1963, Ph.D., 1965.

*ADDRESSES: Office*—Department of Religious Studies, Yale University, P.O. Box 208287, New Haven, CT 06520.

*CAREER:* Ordained Presbyterian minister, 1956; Presbyterian Campus Christian Life, Memphis, TN, university pastor, 1957-61; Dartmouth College, Hanover, NH, instructor in religion, 1964-65; United Ministry to Yale, New Haven, CT, university pastor, 1965-66; Indiana University at Bloomington, assistant professor, 1966-68, associate professor, 1968-69; Yale University, New Haven, CT, associate professor, 1969-73, professor of religious studies, 1973—, Woolsey Professor of Biblical Studies, 1985—, chair of department, 1972-75, director, division of the humanities, 1988-91.

*MEMBER:* American Academy of Religion, Society of Biblical Literature (president, 1985), Studorium Novi Testamenti Societas, Phi Beta Kappa.

*AWARDS, HONORS:* Fulbright fellow to University of Tuebingen, 1956-57; Kent fellow, 1962-65; National Endowment for the Humanities senior fellow, 1975-76; Guggenheim fellow, 1979-80; honorary doctorate, University of Uppsala (Sweden), 1990; elected corresponding fellow of the British Academy, 1992.

*WRITINGS:*

*Go from Your Father's House,* John Knox (Atlanta), 1964.

*The Prophet-King,* E. J. Brill (Long Island City, NY), 1967.

(With R. L. Wilken) *Jews and Christians in Antioch in the First Four Centuries of the Common Era,* Scholars Press (Missoula, MT), 1978.

*The First Urban Christians: The Social World of the Apostle Paul,* Yale University Press (New Haven, CT) , 1983.

*The Moral World of the First Christians,* Westminster John Knox, 1986.

*The Origins of Christian Morality: The First Two Centuries,* Yale University Press, 1993.

EDITOR

*The Writings of St. Paul,* Norton (New York City), 1972.

(With F. O. Francis) *Conflict at Colossae: A Problem in the Interpretation of Early Christianity,* Society of Biblical Literature (Missoula, MT), 1973.

(With J. Jervell) *God's Christ and His People,* Universitetsforlaget (Oslo, Norway), 1977.

*Zur Soziologie des Urchristentums,* Kaiser (Munich, Germany), 1979.

Grant, Robert M., *Gods and the One God,* Westminster John Knox, 1986.

Stambaugh, John E. and Balch, David L., *The New Testament in Its Social Environment,* Westminster John Knox, 1988.

(With David L. Balch and Everett Ferguson) *Greeks, Romans, and Christians: Essays in Honor of Abraham J. Malherbe,* Fortress Press (Philadelphia), 1990.

(With Abraham J. Malherbe) *The Future of Christology: Essays in Honor of Leander E. Keck,* Fortress Press, 1993.

OTHER

Contributor to various symposia and festschrifts. Contributor of articles to the *History of Religions,*

*Journal of Biblical Literature,* and *Journal for Study of the New Testament.* Also general editor, *Library of Early Christianity,* Westminster Press, 1982-87, and *Harper's Study Bible,* HarperCollins, 1993; associate editor, *Harper's Bible Commentary,* HarperCollins, 1988.

*WORK IN PROGRESS:* A book of historical case studies analyzing the use of the Bible to support moral abominations—such as slavery and anti-Semitism—and seeking to discover what lessons might be learned about the use and abuse of scripture in religious communities.

*SIDELIGHTS:* Wayne A. Meeks told *CA:* "*The First Urban Christians* established me as a pioneer in the social history of ancient Christianity. The book has now appeared in Italian, Spanish, Portuguese, Japanese, Korean, and German editions; in an afterword to the German edition, Professor Gerd Theissen called it 'a "classic" of sociohistorical research on the New Testament.'

"In the eighties, I turned back from general problems of social history to a long-standing interest in the basis of ethical judgments in the traditions and practices of religious communities. Still confining myself narrowly to the early years of the Christian movement, I produced first *The Moral World of the First Christians,* included in a series I was editing for Westminster Press, intended as textbooks for college and seminary use. Several graduate seminars at Yale, in which students of ethics, ancient Christian history, and the New testament took part, helped me to shape my research agenda. Conversations with colleagues in these fields and several series of lectures, at Colgate-Rochester Divinity School, Austin Presbyterian Theological Seminary, and, finally, the Speaker's Lectures at Oxford University in 1990 and 1991, helped me approach *The Origins of Christian Morality* as a sequence of case studies. I compared my approach with that of an ethnographer, arguing that the formation of a community and the formation of moral dispositions are part of our dialectical process."

*BIOGRAPHICAL/CRITICAL SOURCES:*

BOOKS

White, L. Michael and O. Larry Yarbrough, editors, *The Social World of the First Christians: Essays in Honor of Wayne A. Meeks,* Fortress Press, 1995.

*PERIODICALS*

*Anvil,* Volume 12/2, 1995.
*Christian Century,* October 16, 1994.
*Commonweal,* March 24, 1995.
*New York Times Book Review,* April 3, 1983.
*Sociology of Religion,* Volume 56/1, Spring, 1995.
*Theology Today,* July, 1995.
*Times Literary Supplement,* October 7, 1983.
*Washington Post Book World,* April 10, 1983.

\* \* \*

**MERINGOFF, Laurene Krasny**
   **See BROWN, Laurene Krasny**

\* \* \*

**MEYERS, Jeffrey**    **1939-**

*PERSONAL:* Born April 1, 1939, in New York, NY; son of Rubin and Judith Meyers; married Valerie Froggatt (a teacher), October 12, 1965; children: Rachel. *Education:* University of Michigan, B.A., 1959; University of California, Berkeley, M.A., 1961, Ph.D., 1967. *Politics:* Socialist. *Religion:* None. *Avocational interests:* Travel (Asia, Africa, the Near East, Europe), tennis.

*ADDRESSES: Home*—Kensington, CA. *Agent*—Sandra Dijkstra Literary Agency, 1155 Camino Del Mar, Suite 515, Del Mar, CA 92014.

*CAREER:* University of California, Los Angeles, assistant professor of English, 1963-65; University of Maryland, Far East Division, Tokyo, Japan, lecturer in English, 1965-66; Tufts University, Boston, MA, assistant professor of English, 1967-71; writer in London, England, 1971-74; Christie's, London, in rare books department, 1974; University of Colorado, Boulder, associate professor of English, 1975—; University of Kent, Canterbury, 1979-80; University of Massachusetts, Amherst, 1982-83.

*MEMBER:* Royal Society of Literature (fellow).

*AWARDS, HONORS:* Fellowships from American Council of Learned Societies, 1970, and Huntington Library, 1971; Fulbright fellowship, 1977-78; Guggenheim fellowship, 1978.

*WRITINGS:*

*Fiction and the Colonial Experience,* Rowman & Littlefield (Totowa, NJ), 1973.
*The Wounded Spirit: A Study of 'Seven Pillars of Wisdom',* Martin, Brian & O'Keeffe (London), 1973; revised edition, *The Wounded Spirit: T. E. Lawrence's Seven Pillars of Wisdom,* St. Martin's (New York City), 1989.
*T. E. Lawrence: A Bibliography,* Garland Publishing (New York City), 1974.
*A Reader's Guide to George Orwell,* Thames & Hudson (London), 1975, Littlefield (Totowa, NJ), 1977.
(Editor and author of introduction and notes) *George Orwell: The Critical Heritage,* Routledge & Kegan Paul (Boston), 1975.
*Painting and the Novel,* Barnes & Noble (New York City), 1975.
*Catalogue of the Library of the Late Siegfried Sassoon,* Christie's (London), 1975.
*A Fever at the Core: The Idealist in Politics,* Barnes & Noble, 1976.
*George Orwell: An Annotated Bibliography of Criticism,* Garland Publishing, 1977.
*Homosexuality and Literature, 1890-1930,* Athlone Press, 1977.
*Married to Genius,* Barnes & Noble, 1977.
*Katherine Mansfield: A Biography,* Hamish Hamilton, 1978, New Directions Publishing (New York City), 1980.
(Editor and author of introduction) *Four Poems,* by Katherine Mansfield, Stevens, 1980.
*The Enemy: A Biography of Wyndham Lewis,* Routledge & Kegan Paul, 1980, Routledge & Kegan Paul, (Boston), 1982.
(Editor) *Wyndham Lewis: A Revaluation: New Essays,* McGill-Queen's University Press (Montreal), 1980.
*D. H. Lawrence and the Experience of Italy,* University of Pennsylvania Press (Philadelphia), 1982.
(Editor and author of introduction and notes) *Hemingway: The Critical Heritage,* Routledge & Kegan Paul, 1982.
(Editor and author of introduction and chapter) *The Craft of Literary Biography,* Schocken (New York City), 1985.
(Editor and author of introduction) *D. H. Lawrence and Tradition,* University of Massachusetts Press (Amherst), 1985.
*Disease and the Novel, 1880-1960,* St. Martin's, 1985.
*Hemingway: A Biography,* Harper (New York City), 1985.

(Editor and author of introduction) *Wyndham Lewis,* by Roy Campbell, University of Natal Press (Pietermaritzburg, South Africa), 1985.

(Editor and author of introduction and chapter) *The Legacy of D. H. Lawrence: New Essays,* St. Martin's, 1987.

*Manic Power: Robert Lowell and His Circle,* Arbor House (New York City), 1987.

(Editor and author of introduction and notes) *Robert Lowell: Interviews and Memoirs,* University of Michigan Press (Ann Arbor), 1988.

(Editor and author of introduction and chapter) *The Biographer's Art: New Essays,* New Amsterdam Books (New York City), 1989.

*The Spirit of Biography* (selected essays), UMI Research Press (Ann Arbor), 1989.

(Editor) *T. E. Lawrence: Soldier, Writer, Legend: New Essays,* St. Martin's, 1989.

*D. H. Lawrence: A Biography,* Knopf (New York City), 1990.

(Editor) *Graham Greene: A Revaluation: New Essays,* St. Martin's, 1990.

*Joseph Conrad: A Biography,* Scribner (New York City), 1991.

*Edgar Allan Poe: His Life and Legacy,* Scribner, 1992.

*Scott Fitzgerald: A Biography,* HarperCollins (New York City), 1994.

*Edmund Wilson: A Biography,* Houghton (Boston), 1995.

*Robert Frost: A Biography,* Houghton, 1996.

(Editor) *Early Frost: The First Three Books,* Ecco Press (New York City), 1996.

*Bogart: A Life in Hollywood,* Houghton, 1997.

Contributor to books, including *Essays by Divers Hands,* volume 44, edited by Angus Wilson, Boydell & Brewer, 1986; and periodicals, including *London, Sewanee Review,* and *Virginia Quarterly Review.*

*SIDELIGHTS:* Jeffrey Meyers is a prominent and prolific biographer of literary figures. The frequency with which his books appear leads critic James Atlas, in the *New York Times Book Review,* to call him "indefatigable" and his output "prodigious," although Atlas finds the quality of Meyers's books inconsistent. Meyers, who has likened his work to that of an investigative journalist, turned to literary biography after a significant career in literary criticism. "Meyers began writing primarily as a literary critic who used biography to explicate texts," writes Mark Allister in *Dictionary of Literary Biography,* "and he has since become primarily a biographer who occasionally interprets literature." Allister sees

Meyers's use of information on writers' lives in his critical works as foreshadowing his emergence as an author of full-fledged biographies. For instance, *The Wounded Spirit: A Study of 'Seven Pillars of Wisdom'* analyzes British soldier-adventurer T. E. Lawrence's memoir as a work of literature, but explores aspects of Lawrence's life as well.

Meyers's penchant for telling life stories became further apparent in two group biographies. *A Fever at the Core: The Idealist in Politics* deals with people involved in both the arts and political activism, while *Married to Genius* looks at the marriages of several authors. One of these authors was the influential British short-story writer and poet Katherine Mansfield, who subsequently became the subject of Meyers's first full-length biographical work. *Katherine Mansfield: A Biography* provides details on areas of Mansfield's life that had been covered either superficially or not at all by her previous biographers, including her husband, John Middleton Murry. While Murry had depicted Mansfield and their relationship in only the most flattering manner, Meyers discusses Mansfield's numerous love affairs with both men and women, as well as her husband's infidelities and coldness. Some reviewers find the book cruel to Mansfield, while others contend Murry was not as evil as he was portrayed by Meyers. Still others praise Meyers's extensive research—he interviewed every person acquainted with Mansfield—and find that his work casts new light on this literary life.

In the Mansfield book, Meyers did not write extensively about the times in which she lived or provide much opinion on her work. However, *The Enemy: A Biography of Wyndham Lewis,* "is rich in such details," according to Allister. Lewis produced many works of poetry, fiction, and nonfiction (in addition to numerous paintings and drawings), but is not as well known as his early-twentieth-century contemporaries, such as T. S. Eliot, D. H. Lawrence, and Ezra Pound, and is frequently confused with another writer, D. B. Wyndham Lewis. Lewis's reputation also has suffered because of his early support of Adolf Hitler, although he later turned against Hitler. Meyers's biography, several reviewers say, contributes to a greater understanding of Lewis. The book is "richly informative, fair, lively, and in every good sense disinterested," writes Denis Donoghue in *New York Review of Books.* Bernard Bergonzi in *Times Literary Supplement* notes that Meyers is by no means a Lewis partisan, but has written a biography that is "solid and well documented, without being pointlessly massive or tediously long." However, while Bergonzi finds Meyers's evaluation of Lewis's writings "cautious and sensible," he also considers it "quietly dismissive of a good part of the oeuvre."

For his next biographical work, Meyers chose as his subject a writer far more famous than Mansfield or Lewis—one of the giants of twentieth-century American literature, Ernest Hemingway. *Hemingway: A Biography* was the first full-fledged biography of the writer to appear since Carlos Baker's *Ernest Hemingway: A Life Story* in 1969. Meyers made an effort to gather material that had not been included in Baker's book; among his finds was a Federal Bureau of Investigation dossier on Hemingway, indicating the agency's head, J. Edgar Hoover, wished to destroy Hemingway's standing as a writer (Hoover thought Hemingway was a communist). Christopher Lehmann-Haupt, a reviewer for the *New York Times,* finds Meyers's book well organized, "a relief . . . after Professor Baker's shapeless gathering of a million facts." Meyers, according to Lehmann-Haupt, "is able to illuminate what he considers the major turning points of Hemingway's life" and produce "an absorbing tragic portrait." In *Voice Literary Supplement,* Mario Vargas Llosa says the book "adds to as well as corrects" the Baker work and "is the most complete biography" of Hemingway.

Raymond Carver, writing in the *New York Times Book Review,* has a different view: "There's little in this book that Carlos Baker . . . didn't say better. Mr. Baker, despite his blind spots, was far more sympathetic to the work and, finally, more understanding of the man." Carver also asserts, "Adulation is not a requirement for biographers, but Mr. Meyers's book fairly bristles with disapproval of his subject." Carver notes that Meyers devotes much space to Hemingway's large ego (which Meyers claims affected his work adversely), excessive drinking, and ill treatment of his loved ones. *Los Angeles Times Book Review* contributor Irving Marder does not object to Meyers's discussion of Hemingway's personal failings, but sees other flaws in the book: "One is a style so graceless and so imprecise that, at crucial points, there is only ambiguity." Vargas Llosa, while admiring the book's thoroughness, argues that Meyers does not really explain how Hemingway was able to distill the events of his life and various aspects of his personality into literature—including works that Vargas Llosa considers Hemingway's best, the novels *The Sun Also Rises* and *A Farewell*

*to Arms,* "and a handful of outstanding stories." Lehmann-Haupt is bothered by Meyers's dismissal of the possibility that Hemingway's ultramasculine persona was a reaction to insecurity about his sexual identity. "This peculiar bias . . . leaves a gaping hole at the very heart of his otherwise impressive treatment," Lehmann-Haupt says.

Meyers returned to group biography with *Manic Power: Robert Lowell and His Circle.* He deals with Lowell and three other poets who were his contemporaries: John Berryman, Randall Jarrell, and Theodore Roethke, adding an epilogue on Sylvia Plath. All had significant personal problems that informed their poetry. Mark Allister considers the book successful as biography, less so as a study of the poets' art. *Times Literary Supplement* critic Michael Hofmann, however, lambasts Meyers's work as "witless, censorious, treacherous and sloppy."

British writer D. H. Lawrence, whose art and life had figured in some of Meyers's previous works, was the author's next biographical subject. In *Times Literary Supplement,* Julian Symons calls *D. H. Lawrence: A Biography* a "robust, energetic book" and "probably the best biography" of the controversial Lawrence, once vilified for the sexual explicitness of his novels, later condemned as displaying a supremacist attitude toward women. *New York Review of Books* critic Noel Annan praises Meyers's work in sorting out the various versions of events in Lawrence's life and refers to the book as "dispassionate . . . a cool, not cold, analysis." Paul Delany, writing for *London Review of Books,* finds Meyers's assertion that Lawrence's problems in life were due to his relationship with his mother far too facile, but terms the book as a whole "readable, judicious and authoritative." Christopher Hawtree's *Spectator* review, however, criticizes the book as having "a perfunctory air" and "lacking all rhythm and underplaying much of the subject's existence." Nancy Mairs of *Los Angeles Times Book Review* lauds Meyers for illuminating the relationship between Lawrence's life and his work, while finding Lawrence's work too plentiful to allow the biographer to do so in all cases. The book, though, is an "admirable introduction" to Lawrence, she says.

*Joseph Conrad: A Biography,* featuring the Polish-descended seaman who became a highly regarded British novelist, fulfills the need for a book "that makes overall sense of the myriad, often contradictory, facts of Conrad's life," according to Jay Parini in *Los Angeles Times Book Review.* Parini finds the book's second half "beautifully focused on the author's life of writing," providing insight into the creative process that produced such works as *Heart of Darkness* and *Lord Jim,* and also praises the account of Conrad's little-known love affair with Jane Anderson, an American newspaper reporter. To Peter Kemp of *Times Literary Supplement,* however, the story of the relationship is "wonky erotic conjecture"; he finds Meyers's evidence that the affair was consummated quite unconvincing. Kemp also sees little that sheds new light on any other aspect of Conrad's life or work: "Meyers is happiest with the obvious," he asserts. J. A. Bryant, Jr., while calling the book "neatly crafted" in *Sewanee Review,* terms it "most interesting when [Meyers] is presenting the details of Conrad's life, least interesting when he is reviewing or analyzing the novels." Joyce Carol Oates, writing for *New York Times Book Review,* pronounces *Joseph Conrad* "never less than a workmanlike amalgam of known and new material; at its best, it is sensitively written, and clearly inspired by a great admiration for its subject."

*Edgar Allan Poe: His Life and Legacy* brought a reaction from some critics that was similar to a reaction to the Conrad book: that it fills a void. This book and Kenneth Silverman's *Edgar Allan Poe: Mournful and Never-Ending Remembrance,* published shortly before Meyers's work, are entries in the "relatively new field" of mature, balanced, Poe biographies, writes Lloyd Rose in *Washington Post Book World.* Previously, Rose says, biographers tended either to damn or to idealize Poe, known both for his self-destructive way of life and his still-popular stories and poems of the supernatural. According to Rose, "Meyers is sympathetic but dispassionate towards his subject, which strikes me as exactly the right approach towards such a difficult man." Chicago *Tribune Books* reviewer Colin Harrison terms Meyers's chronicle a "solid, thoughtful biography" and *New Statesman and Society* contributor Robert Carver finds it "elegantly written, important and endlessly fascinating." Carver praises Meyers's insights into Poe's work and his influence as well as his life. In *Times Literary Supplement,* Arthur Krystal considers both Meyers's and Silverman's books "admirably executed" but writes that "it is Meyers who, untempted by psychoanalytic theories, better conveys Poe's . . . literary travails." But Erik Rieselbach, in *American Spectator,* compares Meyers's work unfavorably to Silverman's. Meyers "includes almost nothing that can't be found more fully discussed in Silverman," Rieselbach contends.

Meyers chronicled the life of another self-destructive writer in *Scott Fitzgerald: A Biography.* Merle Rubin, reviewing the book for *Christian Science Monitor,* says it "focuses on the aspects of [Fitzgerald's] personality that made it hard for him to achieve his full potential as an artist"; these aspects include his alcoholism and his troubled marriage to Zelda Sayre. While Meyers, according to Rubin, does not fully reconcile Fitzgerald's flaws with his virtues, the biographer manages to "allow the pathos and curious heroism of his subject to merge for themselves." Some other reviewers find Meyers's portrayal of Fitzgerald less tolerant, even unkind. The book has an "all but sneering tone," writes John Updike in *New Yorker.* Updike asserts that "Mr. Meyers, like the practitioners of celebrity-centered tabloid journalism, shows his subjects no respect." Similarly, Michiko Kakutani of *New York Times* faults Meyers for taking "a snide, patronizing tone" and pronounces the biography "an ugly and superfluous book about a major American artist who deserves a better biographical fate." Kakutani sees value in Meyers's discussion of how Fitzgerald was influenced by numerous writers (including two of Meyers's previous subjects, Poe and Conrad) but on the whole finds the book gives short shrift to Fitzgerald's writing, especially to his "masterpiece, *The Great Gatsby.*"

Brad Leithauser, though, in *New York Review of Books,* expects that Meyers will "take some knocks for focusing so insistently on Fitzgerald's dissipations" but deems such a focus justified: "Fitzgerald's ruinous life-style . . . was not something tangential or supplemental to his work." Fitzgerald's novels and short stories are based to a great degree on his own experiences, Leithauser notes, and Fitzgerald's nemesis, liquor, figures largely in the makeup of his two most famous characters—the bootlegger Gatsby and the alcoholic psychiatrist Dick Diver of *Tender Is the Night.* Leithauser finds that Meyers has drawn "an appealingly pitiful portrait" and, while offering little in the way of new interpretations of Fitzgerald's life or work, has provided "an encyclopedic enumeration of the real-life counterparts that stood behind Fitzgerald's creations."

Meyers's next subject was a contemporary and friend of Fitzgerald's, Edmund Wilson, who was a literary critic, essayist, historian, poet, fiction writer, and general man of letters. *Edmund Wilson: A Biography* was the first full-scale biography of Wilson, a fact that is not surprising, according to Elizabeth

Hardwick in *New Yorker,* because Wilson wrote so extensively about himself; his voluminous diaries and journals, she asserts, are daunting competition for any biographer, and she does not find Meyers's work wholly satisfactory. "Meyers has brought together the grand flow of Wilson's work and life, including all the flirtations, the drinking, and the marital discord," Hardwick writes. "But he has not been able to recreate in his own pages the subject's brilliant mind and spirit." In *New York Times Book Review,* James Atlas also notes the challenge that Wilson's autobiographical writings pose, but concludes that "somehow Mr. Meyers has produced a highly engaging book. Lively, well proportioned, insightful about the life and work, his brisk narrative puts it all together." *New York Times* reviewer Christopher Lehmann-Haupt considers the book "fascinating" and worthwhile in its assessment of Wilson's literary significance, but is "leery of a tendency on Mr. Meyers's part to emphasize the negative" in his subject's personal life. "Perhaps because [Meyers] wrote this intensely detailed book in a single year . . . he was unable to bring to his story a perspective that might have prevented some of his material from coming across as nasty gossip," Lehmann-Haupt comments.

In 1996, Meyers came out with *Robert Frost: A Biography,* which some reviewers see as a necessary corrective to Lawrance Thompson's highly unflattering biography of this major American poet. Michiko Kakutani of *New York Times* calls Meyers's work "a judicious book that serves as a welcome antidote to Thompson's angry screed and to [Meyers's] own earlier exercises in literary destruction." In *New York Times Book Review,* however, Miranda Seymour contends that Meyers "is not at his thorough and disciplined best in this book . . . [He] seems to have been unable to get under his subject's skin. The Frost he offers is no less an egotistical monster than the man described by Thompson." She also questions the value of Meyers's detailed recounting of Frost's extramarital affair with Kathleen Morrison. Joseph Parisi, a critic for Chicago *Tribune Books,* deems the biography balanced: Meyers, he says, does not hesitate to point out Frost's personal flaws, but also gives "sympathetic explanations" for them. Parisi judges the book's discussion of Frost's poems to be somewhat superficial, but Kakutani praises many of the insights Meyers offers—such as his discussion of the life experiences Frost reflected in one of his best-known poems, "The Road Not Taken." *Robert Frost,* Kakutani adds, "is by far Mr. Meyers's most persuasive and thoughtful biography yet."

*BIOGRAPHICAL/CRITICAL SOURCES:*

*BOOKS*

*Contemporary Literary Criticism,* Volume 39, Gale (Detroit), 1986.
*Dictionary of Literary Biography,* Volume 111: *American Literary Biographers, Second Series,* Gale, 1991.

*PERIODICALS*

*American Spectator,* March, 1993, pp. 58-59.
*Bloomsbury Review,* November-December, 1995.
*Christian Science Monitor,* August 7, 1990, p. 13; April 22, 1991, p. 13; May 10, 1994, p. 15.
*Journal and Constitution* (Atlanta), May 8, 1994, p. N10.
*London Review of Books,* January 24, 1991, pp. 22-23; November 10, 1994.
*Los Angeles Times Book Review,* May 23, 1982, p. 16; December 8, 1985, p. 2, 6; July 22, 1990, pp. 1, 13; June 23, 1991, p. 10.
*Nation,* June 12, 1995, pp. 840-44.
*New Statesman and Society,* October 16, 1992, pp. 39-40.
*New Yorker,* May 3, 1989, pp. 166-67; June 27, 1994, pp. 186-94; May 8, 1995, pp. 85-89.
*New York Review of Books,* April 29, 1982, pp. 28-30; January 17, 1991, pp. 10-14; August 11, 1994, pp. 14-16.
*New York Times,* April 15, 1994, p. C29; May 1, 1995, p. C15; May 17, 1995, p. C18; October 21, 1995, p. C22; April 23, 1996, p. C16.
*New York Times Book Review,* November 17, 1985, pp. 3, 51-52; April 14, 1991, pp. 15-16; April 30, 1995, pp. 6-7; May 19, 1996, p. 8.
*Observer,* June 9, 1985, p. 25.
*Publishers Weekly,* September 27, 1985, p. 90; September 18, 1987, p. 166, May 22, 1995, p. 38.
*Sewanee Review,* summer, 1992, pp. 461-66.
*Spectator,* September 1, 1990, p. 30; June 4, 1994, p. 37.
*Times Literary Supplement,* October 31, 1980, pp. 1215-16; July 19, 1985, p. 795; October 18, 1985, pp. 1171-72; December 13, 1985, pp. 1415-16; August 1, 1986, pp. 837-38; May 26-June 1, 1989, p. 578; September 7-13, 1990, p. 940; November 15, 1991, pp. 3-4; October 16, 1992, p. 28.
*Tribune Books* (Chicago), October 18, 1992, pp. 1, 7; May 29, 1994, pp. 3, 10; May 26, 1996, pp. 1, 11.
*Voice Literary Supplement,* March, 1986, pp. 6-7.

*Washington Post Book World,* September 6, 1992, pp. 3, 7.*

—*Sketch by Trudy Ring*

* * *

## MIDDLETON, Christopher 1926-

*PERSONAL:* Born June 10, 1926, in Truro, Cornwall, England; son of Hubert Stanley (a professor of music) and Dorothy (Miller) Middleton; married Mary Freer, April 11, 1953 (divorced, 1970); children: Sarah, Miranda, Benjamin. *Education:* Merton College, Oxford, B. A., 1951, D.Phil., 1954.

*ADDRESSES: Home*—Austin, TX. *Office*—Department of German, University of Texas, Austin, TX 78712.

*CAREER:* Zurich University, Zurich, Switzerland, lecturer in English, 1952-55; University of Texas, Austin, visiting professor, 1961-62, professor of German literature, 1966—; King's College, University of London, London, England, lecturer, 1955-65, senior lecturer, 1965-66. Exhibition of forty collages with texts, "The Troubled Sleep of America", at the Laguna Gloria Art Museum, Austin, TX, 1982. *Military service:* Royal Air Force, 1944-48; became sergeant.

*AWARDS, HONORS:* Sir Geoffrey Faber Memorial Prize, 1964, for *Torse 3: Poems, 1949-1961;* Guggenheim fellow, 1974-75; National Endowment for the Humanities fellow, 1980; Schlegel-Tieck Translation Prize, 1986; Max-Geilinger-Stiftung Prize, 1987-88, for translations; Neustadt Prize nomination, 1992.

*WRITINGS:*

*The Metropolitans* (libretto), Alkor, 1964.
*Der Taschenelefant* (title means "The Pocket Elephant"), Verlag Neue Rabenpresse, 1969.
*Wie wir Grossmutter zum Markt bringen* (title means "As We Bring Grandmother to Market"), Eremiten-presse, 1970.
*Bolshevism in Art, and Other Expository Writings,* Carcanet Press (Manchester, England), 1978, Humanities Press (Atlantic Highlands, NJ), 1980.

*The Pursuit of the Kingfisher* (essays), Carcanet Press, 1983.

*POETRY*

*Poems,* Fortune Press (London, England), 1944.
*Nocturne in Eden,* Fortune Press, 1945.
*Torse 3: Poems, 1949-1961,* Harcourt (New York City), 1962.
(With David Holbrook and David Wevill) *Penguin Modern Poets 4,* Penguin (New York City), 1963.
*Nonsequences: Selfpoems,* Longmans, 1965, Norton (New York City), 1966.
*Our Flowers and Nice Bones,* Fulcrum Press, 1969.
*The Fossil Fish: 15 Micropoems,* Burning Deck (Providence, RI), 1970.
*Briefcase History: 9 Poems,* Burning Deck, 1972.
*Fractions from Another Telemachus,* Sceptre Press, 1974.
*Wild Horse,* Sceptre Press, 1975.
*The Lonely Suppers of W. V. Balloon,* David Godine, 1975.
*Razzmatazz,* W. Thomas Taylor (Austin, TX), 1976.
*Eight Elementary Inventions,* Sceptre Press, 1977.
*Carminalenia,* Carcanet Press, 1980.
*Woden Dog,* Burning Deck, 1982.
*111 Poems,* Carcanet Press, 1983.
*Two Horse Wagon Going By,* Carcanet Press, 1987.
*Selected Writings,* Carcanet Press, 1989.
*The Balcony Tree,* Carcanet Press, 1992, Sheep Meadow, 1993.
*Some Dogs,* Enitharmon Press (London, England), 1993.
*Intimate Chronicles,* Sheep Meadow, 1996.

*PROSE*

*Pataxanadu and Other Prose,* Carcanet Press, 1977.
*Serpentine,* Oasis Books (London, England), 1985.

*EDITOR*

(With others) *Ohne Hass und Fahne* (title means "Without Hate and Flag"), Rowolt Verlag, 1959.
(And translator with Michael Hamburger) *Modern German Poetry, 1910-1960: An Anthology with Verse Translations,* Grove (London and New York City), 1962.
(And translator with William Burford) *The Poet's Vocation: Selections from the Letters of Hoelderlin, Rimbaud and Hart Crane,* University of Texas Press, 1962.

(And selector of texts and editor) *German Writing Today,* Penguin (Harmondsworth, England), 1967.

*Selected Poems by Georg Trakl,* J. Cape, 1968.

(And author of introduction, and translator with others) *Selected Poems of Goethe,* Suhrkamp Insel (Boston, MA), 1983.

(And translator with others) Lars Gustafsson, *The Stillness of the World before Bach,* New Directions (Newton, NJ), 1988.

*TRANSLATOR*

Robert Walser, *The Walk and Other Stories,* Calder, 1957.

(With others) Gottfried Benn, *Primal Vision,* New Directions, 1960.

(With others) Hugo von Hofmannsthal, *Poems and Verse Plays,* Pantheon (New York City), 1961.

(With Hamburger) Guenter Grass, *Selected Poems,* Harcourt, 1966.

Walser, *Jakob von Gunten,* University of Texas Press (Austin, TX), 1969.

Friedrich Nietzsche, *Selected Letters,* University of Chicago Press (Chicago, IL), 1969.

(With Hamburger) Grass, *Poems,* Penguin, 1969, published as *Selected Poems,* 1980.

Christa Wolf, *The Quest for Christa T.,* Farrar, Straus (New York City), 1970.

(With Hamburger) Paul Celan, *Selected Poems,* Penguin, 1972.

Friedrich Hoelderlin and Eduard Moerike, *Selected Poems,* University of Chicago Press, 1972.

Grass, *Inmarypraise,* Harcourt, 1974.

Elias Canetti, *Kafka's Other Trial: The Letters to Felice,* Schocken (New York City), 1974.

(With Hamburger) Grass, *In the Egg, and Other Poems,* Harcourt, 1977.

Walser, *Selected Stories,* Farrar, Straus, 1982, Vintage, 1983.

Gert Hofmann, *The Spectacle at the Tower,* Fromm (New York City), 1985.

Hofmann, *Our Conquest,* Fromm, 1985.

Hofmann, *The Parable of the Blind,* Fromm, 1987.

Hofmann, *Balzac's Horse and Other Stories,* Fromm, 1988.

(With Leticia Garza-Falcon) *Andalusian Poems* (from Spanish versions of the Arabic), David Godine (Boston, MA), 1993.

*OTHER*

Also author of *Anasphere,* Burning Deck.

*SIDELIGHTS:* Christopher Middleton is "one of the most scrupulous of British poets involved in following the innovations of modernism," according to Douglas Dunn of *Encounter.* Writing in the *Times Literary Supplement,* George Steiner praises Middleton's "characteristic tautness, his sinewy elegance and reach of invocation". Middleton has earned a considerable reputation for his translations as well. As Alfred Corn remarks in the *New York Times Book Review,* Middleton "is a distinguished translator of Goethe, Rilke and Trakl, among others." Steiner believes that Middleton "is at his best when he writes as a translator, when he places his own gifts at the exigent service of a master."

"Although its roots are in surrealism . . . and German Expressionism," Brian Swann comments in the *Library Journal,* "Middleton's poetry is unlike any other. He specializes in lively juxtapositions, incongruities of collage, the play of forms. . . . Vistas recede in a number of poems into the prehistoric so we are aware of mysterious correlations." One of Middleton's continuing concerns has been the shaping of each individual poem to suit its particular subject. "His concern to produce an individual structure of perception for every place, thought and experience he writes about," notes Alan Brownjohn in the *New Statesman,* "results in a ceaseless and challenging originality." Alan Young of the *Dictionary of Literary Biography* describes Middleton as a writer who sees "the art and craft of writing as a hazardous, disruptive, and visionary enterprise, one in which the poet as maker undertakes to shape a language into original ways of saying and, therefore, of knowing for a shaken and uncertain world."

Because of his beliefs about what poetry should be, Middleton is often at odds with the British poetry mainstream. In his collection of essays entitled *The Pursuit of the Kingfisher,* Middleton calls for an "exigent poetry, hard-bitten poetry, which goes to the limits of the conceivable and thus relocates the centre." He also decries the "suave poetry" which he sees as dominating the British literary scene. Steiner argues that Middleton's "linguistic range, the severe seriousness of his conception of the role of the poet and of the poet's reader in these 'terrible times', his unembarrassed celebration of the visionary, 'transcendent' potentialities in art and the imagination, are correctives to the retrenched provincialism of the current English manner."

Middleton's approach has not always been popular with the critics, who sometimes misunderstand his intentions or do not appreciate his innovations. Even some critics who understand his intentions believe that Middleton does not always succeed in fulfilling them in his poems. Corn, for one, states that Middleton's "effort is to escape the artifice of received literacy, and he has at least succeeded in doing that; his poems don't sound like anyone in particular, not even his models. The gain brings with it definite losses." Reviewing *Pataxanadu and Other Prose* for the *Times Literary Supplement,* Alan Young claims that Middleton "likes to make up new rules and does not really seem to care which way he is playing. . . . *Pataxanadu and Other Prose* . . . exhibits more than ever before those cultivated eccentricities of Middleton's art which by turns fascinate, mystify and exasperate his readers."

Among Middleton's most successful poetry collections is *The Lonely Suppers of W. V. Balloon,* a book that "ranges through many countries, times, and moods, but [exhibits] throughout a consistently high level of performance," according to Young in his *Dictionary of Literary Biography* article. Writing in the *Chicago Review,* Jay Parini finds *The Lonely Suppers of W. V. Balloon* to be "a daring and, largely, successful book." The collection moved Brownjohn to call Middleton "easily the most intelligent and serious of our innovators, a poet with a disconcerting knack of making it new in a different way in almost every poem." Dunn, in his review of the book, called Middleton "a poet of considerable importance—an avant-garde poet we can actually *read.*"

The collection *111 Poems,* a selection from several of Middleton's books, has also been well received by the critics. Writing in the *London Review of Books,* Denis Donoghue states that "metrically inventive and various, these poems are remarkably alive to 'the unknown thing beside us'; they listen for 'the due sound', and, as if watching birds, register 'the timed flight of words.'" Although acknowledging Middleton's reputation as "a poet of re-markable oddity," John Mole of *Encounter* finds in his review of the book that "Middleton can write fine poems." And Mole explains that Middleton's work is often concerned with "definitions of poetry—its possibilities and limits." In similar terms, Robert Nye remarks in the London *Times* that Middleton "has a reputation for being eccentric to the point of obscurity. The present volume shows that reputation to be more apparent than real." Nye compares Middleton to Wordsworth: "Middleton demonstrates that the essence of his talent is for a kind of passionate description not all that far away from Wordsworth. . . . I very much like both the tone and the substance."

Although Middleton has lived in Texas for over thirty years—and is, as Steiner explains, "at odds with what he takes to be the English literary, spiritual climate"—he is still a vital part of the contemporary English poetry scene. As Young notes in the *Dictionary of Literary Biography,* "Middleton has been an increasingly important influence on writing in English since the mid-1950s. His poems, stories, translations, and essays have demonstrated consistent refusal to disregard the more unsettling discoveries of both romanticism and high modernism."

## BIOGRAPHICAL/CRITICAL SOURCES:

*BOOKS*

*Contemporary Literary Criticism,* Volume 13, Gale (Detroit), 1980.
*Dictionary of Literary Biography,* Volume 40: *Poets of Great Britain and Ireland since 1960,* Gale, 1985.
Middleton, Christopher, *The Pursuit of the Kingfisher,* Carcanet Press, 1983.
Young, Alan, *Dada and After: Extremist Modernism and English Literature,* Humanities Press, 1981.

*PERIODICALS*

*Chicago Review,* Volume 29, number 1, 1977.
*Encounter,* September, 1975; October, 1979; December, 1983.
*Hudson Review,* autumn, 1962.
*Library Journal,* November 15, 1975.
*London Magazine,* February, 1966.
*London Review of Books,* October 4, 1984.
*New Statesman,* December 24, 1965; September 5, 1975; June 3, 1983.
*New York Times Book Review,* October 24, 1982; May 20, 1984; November 15, 1987.
*Ninth Decade,* Number 2, 1983.
*Observer* (London), January 2, 1966.
*PN Review,* Number 18, 1980.
*Stand,* spring, 1981.
*Times* (London), June 9, 1983.
*Times Literary Supplement,* February 17, 1966; January 13, 1978; May, 16, 1980; March 9, 1984.
*Voice Literary Supplement,* March, 1982.
*Yale Review,* autumn, 1963.

## MILLER, Arthur 1915-

*PERSONAL:* Born October 17, 1915, in New York, NY; son of Isidore (a manufacturer) and Augusta (Barnett) Miller; married Mary Grace Slattery, 1940 (divorced, 1956); married Marilyn Monroe (an actress), June, 1956 (divorced, 1961); married Ingeborg Morath (a photojournalist), 1962; children: (first marriage) Jane Ellen, Robert Arthur; (third marriage) Rebecca Augusta, Daniel. *Education:* University of Michigan, A.B., 1938. *Avocational interests:* Carpentry, farming.

*ADDRESSES: Home*—Roxbury, CT. *Agent*—International Creative Management, 40 West 57th St., New York, NY 10019.

*CAREER:* Writer, 1938—. Associate of Federal Theater Project, 1938; author of radio plays, 1939-44; dramatist and essayist, 1944—. Also worked in an automobile parts warehouse, the Brooklyn Navy Yard, and a box factory. Resident lecturer, University of Michigan, 1973-74.

*MEMBER:* Dramatists Guild, Authors League of America, National Institute of Arts and Letters, PEN (international president, 1965-69).

*AWARDS, HONORS:* Avery Hopwood Award from the University of Michigan, 1936, for *Honors at Dawn,* and 1937, for *No Villain: They Too Arise;* Bureau of New Plays Prize from Theatre Guild of New York, 1938; Theatre Guild National Prize, 1944, for *The Man Who Had All the Luck;* Drama Critics Circle Award, 1947, for *All My Sons,* and 1949, for *Death of a Salesman;* Antoinette Perry Award, 1947, for *All My Sons,* 1949, for *Death of a Salesman,* and 1953, for *The Crucible;* Donaldson Award, 1947, for *All My Sons,* 1949, for *Death of a Salesman,* and 1953, for *The Crucible;* Pulitzer Prize for drama, 1949, for *Death of a Salesman;* National Association of Independent Schools Award, 1954; L.H.D. from University of Michigan, 1956, and Carnegie-Mellon University, 1970; Obie Award from *Village Voice,* 1958, for *The Crucible;* American Academy of Arts and Letters gold medal, 1959; Anglo-American Award, 1966; Emmy Award, National Academy of Television Arts and Sciences, 1967, for *Death of a Salesman;* Brandeis University creative arts award, 1969; George Foster Peabody Award, 1981, for *Playing for Time;* John F. Kennedy Award for Lifetime Achievement, 1984; National Medal of the Arts, 1993; Antoinette Perry Award

nomination, 1994, and Olivier Award (London), 1995, both for *Broken Glass.*

*WRITINGS:*

*PLAYS*

*Honors at Dawn,* produced in Ann Arbor, MI, 1936.
*No Villain: They Too Arise,* produced in Ann Arbor, MI, 1937.
*The Man Who Had All the Luck,* produced on Broadway at Forest Theatre, November 23, 1944.
*All My Sons* (three-act; produced on Broadway at Coronet Theatre, January 29, 1947; also see below), Reynal (New York City), 1947, reprinted, Chelsea House (New York City), 1987.
*Death of a Salesman* (two-act; produced on Broadway at Morosco Theatre, February 10, 1949; also see below), Viking (New York City), 1949, reprinted, Chelsea House, 1987, published as *Death of a Salesman: Text and Criticism,* edited by Gerald Weales, Penguin (New York City), 1977.
(Adaptor) Henrik Ibsen, *An Enemy of the People* (produced on Broadway at Broadhurst Theatre, December 28, 1950), Viking, 1951.
*The Crucible* (four-act; produced on Broadway at Martin Beck Theatre, January 22, 1953), Viking, 1953, published as *The Crucible: Text and Criticism,* edited by Weales, Viking, 1977.
*A View from the Bridge,* [and] *A Memory of Two Mondays* (produced together on Broadway at Coronet Theatre, September 29, 1955; also see below), Viking 1955, published separately, Dramatists Play Service (New York City), 1956, revised version of *A View from the Bridge* (produced Off-Broadway at Sheridan Square Playhouse, January 28, 1965; also see below), Cresset (Philadelphia, PA), 1956, reprinted, Penguin, 1977.
*After the Fall* (produced on Broadway at American National Theatre and Academy, January 23, 1964), Viking, 1964, reprinted, Penguin, 1980.
*Incident at Vichy* (produced on Broadway at American National Theatre and Academy, December 3, 1964), Viking, 1965.
*The Price* (produced on Broadway at Morosco Theatre, February 7, 1968; also see below), Viking, 1968, reprinted, Penguin, 1985.
*The Creation of the World and Other Business* (produced on Broadway at Shubert Theatre, November 30, 1972), Viking, 1972.
*Up from Paradise,* with music by Stanley Silverman (musical version of *The Creation of the World*

*and Other Business;* first produced in Ann Arbor, MI at Trueblood Theatre, directed and narrated by Miller, April, 1974; produced Off-Broadway at Jewish Repertory Theater, October 25, 1983), Viking, 1978.

*The Archbishop's Ceiling* (produced in Washington, DC, at Eisenhower Theatre, Kennedy Center for the Performing Arts, April 30, 1977), Dramatists Play Service, 1976.

*The American Clock* (first produced in Charleston, SC, at Dock Street Theatre, 1980; produced on Broadway at Harold Clurman Theatre, 1980), Viking, 1980.

*Elegy for a Lady* [and] *Some Kind of Love Story* (one-acts; produced together under title *Two-Way Mirror* in New Haven, CT, at Long Wharf Theatre, 1983), published separately by Dramatists Play Service, 1984.

*Playing for Time* (stage adaptation of screenplay; produced in England at Netherbow Art Centre, August, 1986; also see below), Dramatic Publishing, 1985.

*Danger: Memory! Two Plays: "I Can't Remember Anything" and "Clara"* (one-acts; produced on Broadway at Mitzi E. Newhouse Theatre, Lincoln Center for the Performing Arts, February 8, 1987), Grove (New York City), 1987.

*The Golden Years,* Dramatists Play Service, 1990.

*The Last Yankee,* Dramatists Play Service, 1991, reprinted as *The Last Yankee: With a New Essay about Theatre Language,* Penguin, 1994.

*The Ride Down Mt. Morgan* ( first produced in London at Wyndham's Theatre, October, 1991), Viking Penguin, 1992.

*Broken Glass* (first produced on Broadway at the Booth Theater, April, 1994), Viking Penguin, 1994.

### SCREENPLAYS

(With others) *The Story of G.I. Joe,* United Artists, 1945.

*The Witches of Salem,* Kingsley-International, 1958.

*The Misfits* (United Artists, 1961; also see below), published as *The Misfits: An Original Screenplay Directed by John Huston,* edited by George P. Garrett, Irvington, 1982.

*The Price* (based on play of same title), United Artists, 1969.

*The Hook,* MCA, 1975.

*Fame* (also see below), National Broadcasting Company (NBC-TV), 1978.

*Playing for Time,* Columbia Broadcasting System (CBS-TV), 1980.

*Everybody Wins,* Orion Pictures, 1990, Grove Weidenfeld (New York City), 1990.

### FICTION

*Focus* (novel), Reynal, 1945, reprinted with introduction by the author, Arbor House (New York City), 1984.

*The Misfits* (novella; also see below), Viking, 1961.

*Jane's Blanket* (juvenile), Collier (New York City), 1963.

*I Don't Need You Anymore* (stories), Viking, 1967.

*"The Misfits" and Other Stories,* Scribner (New York City), 1987.

*Homely Girl: A Life,* Peter Blum (New York City), 1992, Viking, 1995.

### NONFICTION

*Situation Normal* (reportage on the army), Reynal, 1944.

*In Russia,* with photographs by wife, Inge Morath, Viking, 1969.

*In the Country,* with photographs by Morath, Viking, 1977.

Robert A. Martin, editor, *The Theatre Essays of Arthur Miller,* Viking, 1978, revised and expanded edition with introduction by Robert A. Martin and Steven R. Centola and foreword by Arthur Miller, published by Da Capo Press, 1996.

*Chinese Encounters,* with photographs by Morath, Farrar, Straus (New York City), 1979.

*Salesman in Beijing,* with photographs by Morath, Viking, 1984.

*Timebends: A Life* (autobiography), Grove, 1987.

*Arthur Miller and Company: Arthur Miller Talks about His Work in the Company of Actors, Designers, Directors, Reviewers, and Writers,* edited by Christopher Bigsby, Methuen (London), 1990.

*Arthur Miller in Conversation,* Northouse & Northouse (Dallas, TX), 1993.

### OMNIBUS VOLUMES

(Also author of introduction) *Arthur Miller's Collected Plays* (contains *All My Sons, Death of a Salesman, The Crucible, A Memory of Two Mondays,* and *A View from the Bridge*), Viking, 1957.

Harold Clurman, editor, *The Portable Arthur Miller* (includes *Death of a Salesman, The Crucible, Incident at Vichy, The Price, The Misfits, Fame,* and *In Russia*), Viking, 1971, reprinted with new material, Penguin, 1995.

(Also author of introduction) *Collected Plays, Volume II*, Viking, 1980.

CONTRIBUTOR

William Kozlendko, compiler, *One-hundred Non-Royalty Radio Plays*, Greenberg, 1941.

Edwin Seaver, editor, *Cross-Section 1944*, Fischer, 1944.

Erik Barnous, editor, *Radio Drama in Action*, Farrar & Rinehart (New York City), 1945.

Margaret Mayorga, editor, *The Best One-Act Plays of 1944*, Dodd (New York City), 1945.

Joseph Liss, editor, *Radio's Best Plays*, Greenberg, 1947.

H. William Fitelson, editor, *Theatre Guild on the Air*, Rinehart, 1947.

*One-Act: Eleven Short Plays of the Modern Theatre*, Grove, 1961.

*Six Great Modern Plays*, Dell (New York City), 1964.

*Poetry and Film: Two Symposiums*, Gotham (New York City), 1973.

OTHER

Contributor of essays, commentary, and short stories to periodicals, including *Collier's, New York Times, Theatre Arts, Holiday, Nation, Esquire,* and *Atlantic.* The University of Michigan at Ann Arbor, the University of Texas at Austin, and the New York Public Library have collections of Miller's papers.

ADAPTATIONS: *All My Sons* was filmed by Universal in 1948 and adapted for television by the Corporation for Public Broadcasting in 1987; *Death of a Salesman* was filmed by Columbia in 1951 and adapted for television by CBS-TV in 1985; *The Crucible* was filmed in France by Kingsley-International in 1958 and was made into an American feature film, 1996; *A View from the Bridge* was filmed by Continental in 1962; *After the Fall* was filmed for television by NBC-TV in 1969.

SIDELIGHTS: Arthur Miller is widely recognized as a preeminent playwright of the modern American theatre. Miller's realistic dramas explore the complex psychological and social issues that plague humankind in the wake of the Second World War: the dangers of rampant materialism, the struggle for dignity in a dehumanizing world, the erosion of the family structure, and the perils besetting human rights. Several of Miller's best-known plays—*All My*

*Sons, Death of a Salesman,* and *The Crucible*—have been performed for well over forty years, and according to Benjamin Nelson in *Arthur Miller: Portrait of a Playwright,* they "continue to endure, . . . in fact gaining in strength and impact." Nelson sees the many plays in the Miller canon as "stunning dramatic achievements." Viewers, he notes, "are jolted by the immediate emotional impact of something real, something vibrantly alive exploding at them with a burst of meaning and a ring of truth. The impact is hardly accidental. Miller's plays are products of a meticulous craftsman with an unerring sense of the theater and the ability to create meaningful people in striking situations." In an era marked by theatrical experimentation, much of it at the expense of theme and message, Miller has concentrated on portraying life as it is lived and on proving, in his own words, that "we are made and yet are more than what made us." Walter Kerr observes in *Twentieth Century Interpretations of "The Crucible"* that Miller has "not only the professional crusader's zeal for humanity, but the imaginative writer's feel for it—how it really behaves, how it moves about a room, how it looks in its foolish as well as its noble attitudes."

An earnest sense of social responsibility is one earmark of an Arthur Miller play. For the playwright, writes Neil Carson in *Arthur Miller,* "man is inescapably social, . . . and it is impossible to understand an individual without understanding his society. . . . Miller focuses on the point of intersection between the inner and outer worlds." Whether Miller's plays are set in America or abroad, he reveals characters who are the products of their environments, as well as societies that may support individuals or imprison them, or both. Conflicts arise sometimes from a character's assault on the prevailing order and sometimes from his too willing acceptance of shallow values. *New York Times* contributor Mel Gussow contends that in play after play, Miller "holds man responsible for his—and for his neighbor's—actions. Each work is a drama of accountability." This is not to suggest that Miller serves as a political reformer who seeks to overthrow established mores; rather, he explores the inescapable bonds between human beings and the terrible tolls exacted when people deny those bonds. In *Arthur Miller: A Collection of Critical Essays,* Tom F. Driver writes: "The foremost asset Arthur Miller possesses as a playwright is his knowledge that the theatre must dedicate itself to public matters. He has an acute sense of his audience as persons to be addressed, never merely spectators to be tolerated."

If the plays begin at the point where a character's personal, social, and economic selves meet, they ultimately explore the character's dawning recognition of his moral imperatives. *Los Angeles Times* correspondent Judith Szarka claims that the author's most famous works confront issues raised "when a character is forced to consider the morality of his actions or the validity of his motivating ideals. Whether the protagonist accepts guilt or denies it, transcends the dissolution of cherished ideals or is destroyed along with them, reveals that person's priorities and instincts." Carson observes that Miller "seems almost medieval in his concern with such topics as conscience, presumption, despair and faith. Miller is quintessentially an explorer of the shadowy region between pride and guilt. His characters are a peculiar combination of insight and blindness, doubt and assertiveness, which makes them alternately confront and avoid their innermost selves." Some Miller characters are victorious in their struggles for selfhood; others cannot make the leap of recognition and are consigned to despair. The playwright champions those who achieve essential dignity through an awareness of the dignity of others. Nelson suggests that in most Miller dramas "the possibility of responsibility and action is restored. . . . And because this possibility permeates his work, Arthur Miller is one of the most rebellious writers in modern drama. His continuing exploration of the ramifications of determinism and free will, guilt and responsibility, drift and action, represents his revolt against a theater singing dirges of woe."

The nuclear family offers a favorite context for Miller's dramas. According to Allan Lewis in *American Plays and Playwrights of the Contemporary Theater,* much of Miller's work consists of family plays "in which the social issue is revealed through the personal dilemma. The family is a microcosm of a world beyond, and the behavior of an individual in love, sex, or parental relations is evidence of the choices imposed by social necessity." Carson also declares that one of Miller's strengths "is his penetrating insight into familial relationships." Many of Miller's fictitious families revolve around a dominant though not necessarily admirable father, a devoted but beleaguered mother, and two sons who quietly compete for parental approval. In *Arthur Miller: A Collection of Critical Essays,* Harold Clurman writes: "The shock which shatters Miller's dramatic cosmos always begins with the father's inability to enact the role of moral authority the son assigns to him and which the father willy-nilly assumes. The son never altogether absolves the father for his de-

fection nor is the father ever able to forgive himself for it. Each bears a heavy burden of responsibility to the other." The parents need not even be alive and active in the drama to exert an influence, because Miller's characters are deeply rooted in the past. *Encounter* essayist Ronald Hayman notes that the plays "cannot move forwards without moving backwards" to crucial prior moments that are then "made to exist as if they have been preserved in amber."

Although none of Miller's theatre work is specifically autobiographical, it has been strongly influenced by his particular life experiences. An early influential event was the Great Depression of the 1930s. Miller was born in New York City in 1915, and until 1929 he lived the comfortable life of an upper middle class businessman's son. Then the stock market collapsed, and his father, a coat manufacturer, was forced out of work. First his parents sold their luxury items, one by one, to pay the bills. Later the family had to move from the spacious Harlem apartment of Miller's youth to a tiny house in Brooklyn. Miller told the *New York Times* that the Depression "occurred during a particularly sensitive moment" for him. "I was turning 14 or 15 and I was without leaders," he said. "This was symptomatic not just of me but of that whole generation. It made you want to search for ultimate values, for things that would not fall apart under pressure." Like many others at the time, Miller was attracted to the tenets of socialism; Clurman suggests that the young man realized "it was not financial stress alone that shook the foundations of American life at that time but a false ideal which the preceding era, the Twenties, had raised to the level of a religious creed: the ideal of Success."

Lacking funds for college tuition, and not having earned the grades to merit a scholarship, Miller determined to work until he could afford to enter a university. His job at a Manhattan auto parts warehouse exposed him to yet another troubling social conundrum: anti-Semitism. Being Jewish, he was hired only reluctantly, and occasional comments by his fellow employees let him know that his faith was held against him. Eventually he overcame the prejudice and made friends at the warehouse, but the experience enhanced his desire to change some of society's damaging attitudes. While he was saving portions of his salary for college, Miller read voraciously on his own and spent the routine hours at his job thinking about what he had read. Nelson contends that Miller's reading before college brought him "the first sense that writing could be a way of communicating, of defining experience, shaping chaos, making some kind of sense out of apparent senselessness."

In the midst of the Depression Miller entered the University of Michigan where, to quote Nelson, "the atmosphere was one of challenge rather than despairing finality." An undistinguished high school student, Miller had to prove himself capable of college work in his first year. That accomplished, he matured into a good scholar who spent his spare hours writing for the college newspaper and working as a custodian in a research laboratory that housed several hundred mice. During a mid-semester break in his sophomore year, he turned his hand to playwriting in hopes of winning a prestigious (and lucrative) Avery Hopwood Award from the university. His first play, *Honors at Dawn,* won the award in 1936. The next year he won again with *No Villain: They Too Arise.* Both dramas tackled themes that would later fuel his major works: the sins committed in the name of "free enterprise," sibling rivalry, and moral responsibility to family and community. *Modern American Playwrights* author Jean Gould writes: "In his plays Arthur Miller was to question and to sit in judgment against the false values of the past and present, as yet a distant outcome of his college years, but already clearly outlined in his early manuscript plays."

The Hopwood Awards and a Bureau of New Plays Prize from the Theatre Guild of New York enabled Miller to find writing jobs right out of college. In 1938 he worked briefly for the Federal Theater Project, then he began to turn out radio dramas. Although radio work paid well, Miller yearned to do plays for the stage. He got his chance in 1944, when his work *The Man Who Had All the Luck* had its Broadway premiere. An investigation of man's ability to determine his own fate, the play serves as "a kind of simple alphabet of ideas that will be developed later," according to Sheila Huftel in *Arthur Miller: The Burning Glass. The Man Who Had All the Luck* folded shortly after its opening, and Miller went on to other non-theatrical projects. One of these, a nonfiction book entitled *Situation Normal,* examined the lives and attitudes of ordinary soldiers going to battle in World War II. The other, a novel called *Focus,* explored the irrationality of anti-Semitism. *Focus* was a modest success on the book market; Huftel observes that the work "is a dramatist's novel: tense in construction and dynamic in climax. The reader is driven by it as tragedy commands an audience, partly by technique but mainly by intensity." Despite the lackluster showing

of his first Broadway play and the success of his novel, Miller felt drawn back to the theatre. By 1947 he had crafted a major play from the bare bones of a true wartime incident.

*All My Sons* is Miller's first successful "drama of accountability." In the play, an aging businessman comes to the anguished recognition that his responsibility extends beyond his immediate family to the wider world of humankind. Having sold defective merchandise to the army, and having lied to protect his business when the merchandise caused war planes to crash in battle, the businessman learns that he has in fact caused the death of one of his own sons. His other son, also a war veteran, savagely rebukes him for his warped sense of morality. In *Arthur Miller: A Collection of Critical Essays,* Gerald Weales notes that the businessman, Joe Keller, is "an image of American success, who is des troyed when he is forced to see that image in another context—through the eyes of his idealist son." The son, Chris, has learned from his war experiences that relatedness is not particular but universal; he is shocked by his father's unscrupulous renunciation of that knowledge. Huftel writes that in *All My Sons,* "Miller is concerned with consciousness, not crime, and with bringing a man face to face with the consequences he has caused, forcing him to share in the results of his creation." In his introduction to *Arthur Miller's Collected Plays,* the author himself suggests that the play lays siege to "the fortress of unrelatedness. It is an assertion not so much of a morality in terms of right and wrong, but of a moral world's being such because men cannot walk away from certain of their deeds."

*All My Sons* won numerous awards and established Miller as a young playwright of promise. Nelson writes: "More than any of Miller's subsequent plays, *All My Sons* is a drama in the service of a message. Fortunately the message is dramatic and substantial, and the play is rooted in enough human conflict and complexity so that it never deteriorates into an illustrated editorial." Gould likewise styles the work "a sincere, moving, at times gripping drama of ideas." The play has been revived many times and has been filmed as a movie and as a teleplay. Directing his remarks to the continuing pertinence of the story, *Washington Post* contributor Joseph McLellan concludes that *All My Sons* is "rather a period piece" now, but even so, "the passions with which it deals— family loyalty, greed, self-deception, cowardice and remorse—are timeless, and it builds them into a structure like that of a classic tragedy."

With the box office proceeds from *All My Sons* Miller bought a farm in rural Connecticut. There he built himself a studio and began to work on another drama. It was produced in 1949 under the title *Death of a Salesman,* and it received overwhelming critical and public acclaim. The play centers on the emotional deterioration of Willy Loman, an aging and not too successful salesman who can hardly distinguish between his memories of a brighter past and his setbacks in the dismal present. In the course of the play Willy grapples with the loss of his job and the failure of his two grown sons to achieve wealth, and with it, presumably, happiness. Nelson writes of Willy: "Shot through with weaknesses and faults, he is almost a personification of self-delusion and waste, the apotheosis of the modern man in an age too vast, demanding and complex for him. . . . He personifies the human being's desire, for all his flaws, to force apart the steel pincers of necessity and partake of magnificence." Willy does aspire to greatness for himself and his sons, but he champions a success ethic that is both shallow and contradictory—the cult of popularity, good looks, and a winning personality. "From the conflicting success images that wander through his troubled brain comes Willy's double ambition—to be rich and to be loved," notes Weales. Facing ruin, Willy still cannot relinquish his skewed values, and he becomes a martyr to them. His sons must come to terms with their father's splintered legacy and determine the essence of his ultimate worth. *New York Times* contributor Frank Rich observes that *Death of a Salesman* "is most of all about fathers and sons. . . . The drama's tidal pull comes from the sons' tortured attempts to reconcile themselves to their father's dreams."

Because Willy struggles valiantly for money and recognition, and then fails on both accounts, some critics see *Death of a Salesman* as an indictment of the American system. In *Newsweek,* Jack Kroll suggests that the drama is "a great public ritualizing of some of our deepest and deadliest contradictions. It is a play about the misplaced energy of the basic human material in American society." The message Miller sends in the work is not so simple, however. Nelson writes: "One of the strengths of *Death of a Salesman* is its refusal to pin blame exclusively on a person, an institution, or even on an entire society. Although Willy Loman's destruction is partly the fault of his family and the failure of certain values propounded by society, it is no less his own doing." Indeed, while Willy adheres to an adolescent code of values, his son Biff and his neighbor Charley represent alternative reactions to family and society. According to

R. H. Gardner in *The Splintered Stage: The Decline of the American Theater,* the play is "an affirmation of the proposition that persistent application of one's talents, small though they may be, pays off. And this, after all, is the substance of the American dream."

On one point most critics agree: *Death of a Salesman* is one of the significant accomplishments of modern American letters. In *The Forties: Fiction, Poetry, Drama,* Lois Gordon calls it "the major American drama of the 1940s" and adds that it "remains unequalled in its brilliant and original fusion of realistic and poetic techniques, its richness of visual and verbal texture, and its wide range of emotional impact." *New York Times* columnist Frank Rich concludes that *Death of a Salesman* "is one of a handful of American plays that appear destined to outlast the 20th century. In Willy Loman, that insignificant salesman who has lost the magic touch along with the shine on his shoes after a lifetime on the road, Miller created an enduring image of our unslaked thirst for popularity and success." According to John Gassner in the *Quarterly Journal of Speech,* Miller "has accomplished the feat of writing a drama critical of wrong values that virtually every member of our middle-class can accept as valid. It stabs itself into a playgoer's consciousness to a degree that may well lead him to review his own life and the lives of those who are closest to him. The conviction of the writing is, besides, strengthened by a quality of compassion rarely experienced in our theatre."

Miller rose to prominence during a particularly tense time in American politics. In the early 1950s many national leaders perceived a threat of communist domination even within the borders of the United States, and public figures from all walks of life fell under suspicion of conspiring to overthrow the government. Miller and several of his theatre associates became targets for persecution, and in that climate the playwright conceived *The Crucible.* First produced in 1953, *The Crucible* chronicles the hysterical witch-hunt in seventeenth-century Salem, Massachusetts, through the deeds of one courageous dissenter, John Proctor. As John Gassner notes in *Twentieth Century Interpretations of "The Crucible,"* Miller's motivation "plainly included taking a public stand against authoritarian inquisitions and mass hysteria. . . . It is one of Miller's distinctions that he was one of the very few writers of the period to speak out unequivocally for reason and justice." If Miller began his researches into the Salem witch trials with the communist-hunting trials in mind, he soon uncovered a deeper level for his prospective drama. In his autobiography, *Timebends: A Life,* Miller writes: "The political question . . . of whether witches and Communists could be equated was no longer to the point. What was manifestly parallel was the guilt, two centuries apart, of holding illicit, suppressed feelings of alienation and hostility toward standard, daylight society as defined by its most orthodox proponents." What Miller reveals in *The Crucible,* to quote *University College Quarterly* essayist John H. Ferres, is the tenet that "life is not worth living when lies must be told to one's self and one's friends to preserve it."

Early reviewers of *The Crucible* saw the play—and often denounced it—as an allegory for the McCarthy hearings on communism. That view has been revised significantly in the wake of the work's continuing popularity. "For a play that was often dismissed as a political tract for the times, *The Crucible* has survived uncommonly well," states Ferres. Robert A. Martin offers a similar opinion in *Modern Drama.* The play, writes Martin, "has endured beyond the immediate events of its own time. . . . As one of the most frequently produced plays in the American theater, *The Crucible* has attained a life of its own; one that both interprets and defines the cultural and historical background of American society. Given the general lack of plays in the American theater that have seriously undertaken to explore the meaning and significance of the American past in relation to the present, *The Crucible* stands virtually alone as a dramatically coherent rendition of one of the most terrifying chapters in American history." In *Twentieth Century Interpretations of "The Crucible,"* Phillip G. Hill speaks to the play's pertinence. To quote Hill, the work remains "a powerful indictment of bigotry, narrow-mindedness, hypocrisy, and violation of due process of law, from whatever source these evils spring." Edward Murray concludes in *Arthur Miller, Dramatist* that *The Crucible* "remains one of Miller's best plays and one of the most impressive achievements of the American theater."

The eight-year period following the first production of *The Crucible* was extremely hectic and ultimately dispiriting for Miller. In 1955 he divorced his first wife, and the following year he married actress Marilyn Monroe. At the same time, his supposed communist sympathies caused his expulsion from a script-writing project based on New York City's Youth Board, and he was denied a passport renewal by the State Department. Shortly after his celebrated second marriage, Miller was subpoenaed to appear before the House Un-American Activities Committee, where he was queried about his political beliefs. Miller admitted to the Committee that he had attended a few informal Communist Party meetings many years earlier, but he refused to name others who had attended the meetings even when the Committee insisted he do so. *Dictionary of Literary Biography* essayist Jeffrey Helterman writes: "In a classic case of life imitating art, Miller took the precise position Proctor took before his Puritan judges. Just as Proctor is willing to implicate himself but refuses to name other dabblers with witchcraft, so Miller named himself, but refused to identify any others involved in communist-front activities." Miller was charged with contempt of Congress and was tried and convicted in 1957. His conviction was overturned on appeal the next year. Nelson concludes: "In a time when men and women were being enticed and coerced into giving up their cores and identities, the author of *The Crucible* remained himself. It was a knowledge and a victory that reached far beyond any court decision."

Just before Miller's political problems began in earnest, he brought another production to Broadway. It consisted of two one-act plays, *A Memory of Two Mondays* and *A View from the Bridge.* Both are set in working-class Manhattan; *A Memory of Two Mondays* dramatizes a young man's escape from the crushing boredom of work in a warehouse, and *A View from the Bridge* chronicles the death of a misguided Italian longshoreman. Of the two, *A View from the Bridge* has had a longer and more varied theatrical life. After critics found the one-act version lacking in motive and detail, Miller expanded the work to two acts. The longer production had a successful run in London and has been revived several times in New York. In *A View from the Bridge,* writes Helterman, Miller "creates his contemporary classical tragedy." Eddie Carbone, the hero, accepts two illegal immigrants into the home he shares with his wife and his young niece. When one of the immigrants falls in love with the niece, Eddie reacts with irrational anger. Eventually Eddie breaks the most important unwritten law of his ethnic community—he turns the immigrants over to the authorities for deportation. *Washington Post* contributor David Richard concludes that the expanded version of *A View from the Bridge* "gives the chase to some elemental emotions and it is willing to tell a raw, compelling story about human beings in deep conflict. That willingness makes all the difference.

There's matter here for actors to sink their teeth into; reason for them to square off, eyes blazing, on the sidewalk."

Marriage to one of Hollywood's biggest stars brought Miller numerous unforeseen problems. The couple found themselves hounded by reporters at every turn, and Monroe relied on Miller to help her make business and artistic decisions. Helterman observes: "Despite her deference to his work habits, Miller soon fell into Monroe's orbit rather than vice versa." This difficulty was compounded by Monroe's deep-seated emotional problems and her barbiturate dependency, both of which predated her marriage to Miller. Still Miller found many admirable and poignant qualities in his famous wife, and he wrote a movie script, *The Misfits,* that reflected some of those qualities. Filmed in 1961, *The Misfits* gave Monroe a chance to perform a role with depth. Although the movie was not a box-office success, it has been praised in retrospect for its script and for John Huston's directing. The story explores the last breaths of the wild West cowboy myth through three luckless drifters and an anguished divorcee who search for permanence in a world of purposeless flux. "Threatened with isolation, personal and social, these people and this way to life define instability," notes Huftel. "This film script is like a city built on shifting sand; through it a search is going on for something stable in the face of change, for a way to live, and for a way out of chaos." Shortly after *The Misfits* finished shooting, Monroe filed for divorce, and Miller was plunged back into the relative obscurity he needed in order to write plays.

*The Misfits* and subsequent works such as *After the Fall* and *Incident at Vichy* introduced a new theme in Miller's work—man's hopeless alienation from himself and others. *Critical Quarterly* contributor Kerry McSweeney maintains that the horrors of World War II as well as his more personal problems caused Miller to reject his vision of possible social harmony among humankind. "His characters now grope alone for values to sustain their dissipating lives and each value, once discovered, slips again into ambiguity," writes McSweeney. "Most frightening of all is the realization that human corruption, once attributed to conscious deviation from recognizable moral norms, is now seen as an irresistible impulse in the heart of man. The theme of universal guilt becomes increasingly and despairingly affirmed." Also affirmed, however, is the possibility of redemption through an understanding of self and an abrogation of destructive impulses—a realization achieved with great difficulty. According to Clurman, the proposition that people can still relate one to another "takes on a new meaning; a new light is shed on the injunction of human responsibility. Each of us is separate and in our separateness we must assume responsibility even in full awareness of that separateness." Quentin, the protagonist of *After the Fall,* is the first Miller character to tackle these issues.

*After the Fall* is "the testimony of a life—a mind made visual," observes Huftel. The drama consists of a series of recollections from the mind of Quentin, an attorney facing the consequences of his actions for the first time. To quote Helterman, the play's action "is expressionistic throughout, using an open space in which various people and events come and go, always confronting Quentin's judging mind. In this episodic structure the recurrent matter to be resolved is the nature of guilt, the limits of personal responsibility for the lives of others, and the means of expiation for crimes real or imagined. Three crises in Quentin's life are vividly presented: Nazi death camps, the suicide of Quentin's beautiful but neurotic wife, Maggie, and Quentin's confrontation with the anti-Communist House Committee on Un-American Activities." Confessional in nature, *After the Fall* "resolved many of the problems which had vexed Miller throughout his writing career," according to C. W. E. Bigsby in *Twentieth Century Literature.* "It served to exorcise his personal sense of guilt but, more significantly, provided evidence that he had finally evolved a consistent concept of the relation between human freedom and human limitations."

When *After the Fall* was first produced in 1964, it met with a round condemnation from the critics. Many of them felt that the play unfairly exploited Miller's relationship with Marilyn Monroe, and her subsequent suicide, for the purpose of high drama. Nelson calls the attacks on the play "blatantly unfair" and adds that by concentrating on the work's parallels to Miller's actual life "many critics and viewers wholly missed the genuine stature of the finest play Miller had written since *The Crucible.*" Robert Hogan likewise contends in *Arthur Miller* that *After the Fall* "was so obviously based on Miller's life that its true merits were at first difficult to see. . . . At any rate, *After the Fall* is Miller's most intellectually probing play." Huftel's description of the work sums up its impact. "It is as if someone took his life and tore it up in front of you, the while explaining why he was doing it. It seems incredible that any hope at all can be pulled out of such darkness. For this reason, people may see the pain, but not the point—see that every hope is blasted with insight, and yet that insight is all that will save you."

Nazi atrocities continued to dominate Miller's thematics in his next play, *Incident at Vichy*. Returning to stark realism, the work explores human reactions to irrational and unavoidable sadism. Nelson suggests that the drama exposes "not the villainy of the Nazis—which is scarcely worth reiterating—but the involvement of human beings with justice and injustice, self-preservation and commitment to others, which make for some of the conditions responsible for Nazism's growth and, by strong implication, for its possible resurrection." *Incident at Vichy* highlights one man's sacrificial gesture to save the life of a Jewish doctor otherwise destined for the extermination camps. In Nelson's words, one movement of the play "is toward despair, toward the loss of hopes, illusions, and rationalizations, toward the inadequacy of reason and logic as well as faith, toward the erosion of any value that might possibly endow the word humanity with some positive meaning." In the core of the work, Nelson continues, Miller "is grappling with *complicity,* not *equality,* in evil. . . . He is not claiming that we are all equally guilty of injustice in the world, but rather that very few of us, for all our avowed decency, are wholly innocent." *Incident at Vichy* is another of Miller's plays that has been revived and restaged many times in New York and elsewhere. In a *New York Times* review, Richard F. Shepard concludes: "This is Arthur Miller at his most searching and provocative, peeling the leaves of motivation as though they were coming off of an artichoke, always more remaining to shroud the core. It is a play that makes you think."

In 1969 Miller wrote *The Price,* one of his most successful Broadway plays. The work reprises his family dramas, this time with two middle-aged brothers who meet in an attic to dispose of their deceased parents' furniture. Old jealousies and self-righteous alibis flare as the brothers compare lives and bemoan lost opportunities. Helterman finds *The Price* "a most traditional piece of theater, harking back to *All My Sons,* not only in its theme of defining the price one pays for the choices in life, but also in its technique of the characters uncovering the past by retelling events to reveal one incompletely understood motive after another in their present lives." Speaking to the play's power to move viewers, *Modern Drama* correspondent Orm Oeverland writes: "Two hours in an attic with old furniture and four people—and the experience in the theater is of something organic,

something that comes alive and evolves before us on the stage." Nelson likewise calls *The Price* a "powerful and provocative" work and concludes that it is "a play of the heart and for the heart, and although it advocates very few truths, it unmistakably and hauntingly has caught many."

Miller's more recent stage works have enjoyed longer runs in England than in the United States. This is due in great part to the costs of mounting a Broadway production; plays must be fantastic successes immediately or they are forced to fold. In his autobiography Miller addresses this difficulty: "The problem is not that the American theatre has no place for great plays but rather that it doesn't support good ones, the ground from which the extraordinary spring." *The American Clock,* Miller's 1980 portrait of the Great Depression, is one production that fared better in London than it did in New York. During the show's pre-Broadway run Miller tinkered with it endlessly, endeavoring to satisfy the demands of directors and producers. Still the show failed. The London production returned faithfully to Miller's original concept, and the play was a hit. Watching it in London, Miller writes in *Timebends,* he "felt the happy sadness of knowing that my original impulse had been correct in this work; but as had happened more than once before, in the American production I had not had the luck to fall in with people sufficiently at ease with psychopolitical themes. . . . I had hopelessly given way and reshaped a play for what I had come to think of as the Frightened Theatre."

Several other Miller plays, including *Danger, Memory!, The Archbishop's Ceiling,* and *The Ride Down Mt. Morgan* have met with similar fates, proving far more popular with English, French, and German audiences than with Americans. Even *Broken Glass,* Miller's first Broadway play in more than a decade, ran only ten weeks in New York and much longer in London. In a 1994 profile for the *Los Angeles Times,* Miller praised the British system of subsidized theatre for its support of plays with artistic as well as commercial merit. In Britain, he said, "they can still play something twice a week to a half-empty house because somebody believes it's valuable. It makes the difference between feeling that you're in a world of art or a world of business." Miller also characterized the Broadway of the 1990s as "post-crisis, in catastrophe. . . . This is theater as a form of banking."

*Broken Glass* offers a disturbing portrait of a middle-aged Jewish couple living in New York City in 1938.

After hearing about the Nazi atrocities of *Kristallnacht* on her radio, Sylvia Gellburg develops hysterical paralysis in her legs. Her husband, himself in deep conflict about his heritage, seeks professional help for her, only to be challenged on his own views by the attending physician. "This play, as a play, is precisely what I wanted it to be and is beautifully performed," Miller told the *Los Angeles Times* of the Broadway version. "Its audiences, I dare say, have been spellbound." *Broken Glass* ran for ten weeks on Broadway, garnering mostly positive reviews and an Antoinette Perry (Tony) Award nomination for best drama of 1994. According to *Chicago Tribune Books* contributor Penelope Mesic, the work "confronts us with both the horror of seeing a peaceful, supposedly civilized Germany lose its human face, and the shame of the casual, almost lazy anti-Semitism that was standard practice in America."

Ever active and energetic, Miller has become an international traveller and spokesman for human rights and artistic freedom. As the first international president of PEN he opened the Soviet Bloc nations to that organization and offered its support to imprisoned and persecuted writers. *New York Times Book Review* contributor Roger Shattuck observes that Miller "was the only American famous enough and courageous enough in 1966 to inject new vitality into PEN International." Indeed, Miller resuscitated the dwindling organization and has seen it grow in prominence and power. He has also seen his best-known plays produced in such unlikely locales as Moscow and Bejing, where *Death of a Salesman* was one of the first American dramas to be performed. Miller directed the Bejing production of *Salesman* himself, with the help of translators. In *Concise Dictionary of American Literary Biography: The New Consciousness, 1941-1968,* Helterman writes: "That [Miller] was able to motivate [Chinese] actors who had survived the cultural revolution and that a play so embedded in American capitalism was able to reach the audience in the capital of communism is testimony that the play's true message is more personal and human than sociological." Miller claims in *Timebends* that the Chinese reaction to *Death of a Salesman* confirmed "what had become more and more obvious over the decades in the play's hundreds of productions throughout the world: Willy was representative everywhere, in every kind of system, of ourselves in this time . . . not simply as a type but because of what he wanted. Which was to excel, to win out over anonymity and meaninglessness, to love and be loved, and above all, perhaps, to *count.*"

Willy Loman may not have won out over anonymity, but his creator certainly has. Respect for Miller's artistic accomplishment has come from all quarters and is renewed each time a Miller work is revived. Tom F. Driver lists the playwright's special strengths: an "acute awareness of the 'public' nature of theatre, the desire to see and report life realistically, an unwillingness to settle for a merely positivist version of reality, and a desire to see a theatre of 'heightened consciousness.'" Driver adds: "By putting these concerns before the public, Arthur Miller has shown that his sights are higher than those of any of his competitors at the Broadway box office. The fact that such concerns exist in a playwright of his prominence is proof that our theatre is still alive." Robert W. Corrigan addresses the same idea in his contribution to *Arthur Miller: A Collection of Critical Essays.* As Corrigan sees it, Miller's "passionate concern that attention be paid to the aspirations, worries, and failures of all men—and, more especially, of the little man who is representative of the best and worst of an industrialized democratic society—has resulted in plays of great range and emotional impact. . . . Miller's own sense of involvement with modern man's struggle to be himself is revealed in his own growth as an artist and has made him one of the modern theatre's most compelling and important spokesmen." *American Drama and Theater in the 20th Century* essayist William Heyen concludes that Miller's characters "will be asking us for a long time how we must live in the world. Their presence, their humanity as they strain to realize themselves, is staggering."

Arthur Miller turned eighty years old in 1995 and celebrated that milestone by continuing to write new works at his 400-acre Connecticut farm. His ongoing career marks him not only as "America's greatest living playwright," to quote Jan Breslauer in the *Los Angeles Times,* but also "the most senior of the country's actively working serious dramatists." Breslauer further comments that, with so many young artists opting to write for the medium of film, Miller may well be "the last of a breed."

Miller has had much to say about the art of playwrighting over the years, both from a personal and a judgmental standpoint. Reflecting on his own career, he told the *New York Times:* "There's an intensification of feeling when you create a play that doesn't exist anywhere else. It's a way of spiritually living. There's a pleasure there that doesn't exist in real life. You get swept up in a free emotional life—

and you can be all those other people. . . . That's when you're most alive."

*BIOGRAPHICAL/CRITICAL SOURCES:*

*BOOKS*

*Authors in the News,* Volume 1, Gale (Detroit, MI), 1976.

Bhatia, S. K., *Arthur Miller,* Heinemann (New York City), 1985.

Bigsby, C. W. E., *Confrontation and Commitment: A Study of Contemporary American Drama, 1959-66,* University of Missouri Press (Columbia, MO), 1968.

Bigsby, C. W. E., *A Critical Introduction to Twentieth-Century American Drama,* Cambridge University Press (Cambridge, England), 1984.

Bloom, Harold, *Arthur Miller's "Death of a Salesman,"* Chelsea House, 1996.

Bloom, *Arthur Miller's "The Crucible,"* Chelsea House, 1996.

Bogard, Travis, and William I. Oliver, editors, *Modern Drama,* Oxford University Press (Oxford, England), 1965.

Brown, John Russell and Bernard Harris, editors, *American Theatre,* Edward Arnold (Baltimore, MD), 1967.

Brustein, Robert, *The Third Theatre,* Knopf (New York City), 1969.

Carson, Neil, *Arthur Miller,* Grove, 1982.

Centola, Steven R., editor, *The Achievement of Arthur Miller: New Essays,* Contemporary Research Press, 1995.

Cohn, Ruby, *Dialogue in American Drama,* Indiana University Press (Bloomington, IN), 1971.

Cole, Toby, editor, *Playwrights on Playwrighting,* Hill & Wang (New York City), 1961.

*Concise Dictionary of American Literary Biography: The New Consciousness, 1941-1968,* Gale, 1987.

*Contemporary Literary Criticism,* Gale, Volume 1, 1973; Volume 2, 1974; Volume 6, 1976; Volume 10, 1979; Volume 15, 1980; Volume 26, 1983; Volume 78, 1993.

Corrigan, Robert W., editor, *Arthur Miller: A Collection of Critical Essays,* Prentice-Hall (New York City), 1969.

Dekle, Bernard, *Profiles of Modern American Authors,* Charles E. Tuttle (Rutland, VT), 1969.

*Dictionary of Literary Biography,* Volume 7: *Twentieth-Century American Dramatists,* Gale, 1981.

Downer, Alan S., editor, *The American Theatre Today,* Basic Books (New York City), 1967.

Duprey, Richard A., *Just off the Aisle: The Ramblings of a Catholic Critic,* Newman Press, 1962.

Evans, Richard, *Psychology and Arthur Miller,* Dutton (New York City), 1969.

Ferres, John H., editor, *Twentieth Century Interpretations of "The Crucible,"* Prentice-Hall (Englewood Cliffs, NJ), 1972.

French, Warren, editor, *The Forties: Fiction, Poetry, Drama,* Everett/Edwards (Deland, FL), 1969.

Gardner, R. H., *The Splintered Stage: The Decline of the American Theater,* Macmillan (New York City), 1965.

Gassner, John, *Dramatic Soundings: Evaluations and Retractions Culled from 30 Years of Dramatic Criticism,* Crown (New York City), 1968.

Gilman, Richard, *Common and Uncommon Masks: Writings on Theatre, 1961-1970,* Random House (New York City), 1971.

Glassman, Bruce, *Arthur Miller,* Silver Burdett Press (Englewood Cliffs, NJ), 1990.

Gould, Jean, *Modern American Playwrights,* Dodd, 1966.

Griffin, Alice, *Understanding Arthur Miller,* University of South Carolina Press, 1996.

Hayashi, T., *Arthur Miller and Tennessee Williams,* McFarland (Jefferson, NC), 1983.

Hogan, Robert, *Arthur Miller,* University of Minnesota Press (Minneapolis, MN), 1964.

Huftel, Sheila, *Arthur Miller: The Burning Glass,* Citadel (Secaucus, NJ), 1965.

Hurrell, John D., editor, *Two Modern American Tragedies: Reviews and Criticism of "Death of a Salesman" and "A Streetcar Named Desire,"* Scribner, 1961.

Lewis, Allan, *American Plays and Playwrights of the Contemporary Theatre,* Crown Publishers, 1970.

Madden, David, editor, *American Dreams, American Nightmares,* Southern Illinois University Press (Carbondale, IL), 1970.

Martin, Robert and Steven Centola, editors, *The Theater Essays of Arthur Miller,* Da Capo Press (New York City), 1978, revised and expanded, 1996.

Martin, Robert, editor, *Arthur Miller: New Perspectives,* Prentice-Hall, 1982.

Martine, James J., editor, *Critical Essays on Arthur Miller,* G. K. Hall (Boston, MA), 1979.

Miller, Arthur, *Arthur Miller's Collected Plays,* Viking, 1957.

Miller, Arthur, *Collected Plays, Volume II,* Viking, 1980.

Miller, Arthur, *Timebends: A Life,* Grove, 1987.

Moss, Leonard, *Arthur Miller,* Twayne (Boston, MA), 1967.

Murphy, Brenda, *Miller: Death of a Salesman,* Cambridge University Press, 1995.

Murray, Edward, *Arthur Miller, Dramatist,* Ungar (New York City), 1967.

Murray, Edward, *The Cinematic Imagination: Writers and the Motion Pictures,* Ungar, 1972.

Nelson, Benjamin, *Arthur Miller: Portrait of a Playwright,* McKay, 1970.

Porter, Thomas, *Myth and Modern American Drama,* Wayne State University Press (Detroit, MI), 1969.

Rahv, Philip, *The Myth and the Powerhouse,* Farrar, Straus (New York City), 1965.

Roudane, Matthew C., editor, *Approaches to Teaching Miller's "Death of a Salesman,"* Modern Language Association (New York City), 1995.

Sheed, Wilfrid, *The Morning After,* Farrar, Straus, 1971.

Siebold, Thomas, editor, *Readings on Arthur Miller,* Greenhaven Press, 1997.

*Twentieth Century Interpretations of "Death of a Salesman,"* Prentice-Hall, 1983.

Tynan, Kenneth, *Curtains,* Atheneum (New York City), 1961.

Vogel, Dan, *The Three Masks of American Tragedy,* Louisiana State University Press (Baton Rouge, LA), 1974.

Wager, Walter, editor, *The Playwrights Speak,* Delacorte (New York City), 1967.

Warshow, Robert, *The Immediate Experience: Movies, Comics, Theatre and Other Aspects of Popular Culture,* Doubleday (New York City), 1962.

Weales, Gerald, *American Drama since World War II,* Harcourt (New York City), 1962.

Weber, Alfred and Siegfried Neuweiler, editors, *Amerikanisches Drama und Theater im 20. Jahrhundert: American Drama and Theater in the 20th Century,* Vandenhoeck & Ruprecht, 1975.

Welland, Dennis, *Arthur Miller,* Grove, 1961, revised edition published as *Miller: The Playwright,* Methuen (New York City), 1979, reprinted, 1983.

White, Sidney, *Guide to Arthur Miller,* Merrill, 1970.

*PERIODICALS*

*American Theatre,* May, 1986.
*Atlantic,* April, 1956.
*Book Week,* March 8, 1964.
*Catholic World,* May, 1950.
*Chicago Tribune,* September 30, 1980; April 20, 1983; February 17, 1984; April 30, 1985; November 27, 1987; September 16, 1990, pp. 22-23; August 20, 1995, p. 2.

*Chicago Tribune Books,* November 15, 1987; May 29, 1994, p. 6.
*Christian Science Monitor,* April 26, 1994, p. 12; April 27, 1994, p. 17.
*College English,* November, 1964.
*Commentary,* February, 1973.
*Commonweal,* February 19, 1965.
*Critical Quarterly,* summer, 1959.
*Criticism,* fall, 1967.
*Dalhousie Review,* Volume XL, 1960.
*Detroit Free Press,* March 5, 1967.
*Detroit News,* November 25, 1973.
*Educational Theatre Journal,* October, 1958; October, 1969.
*Emory University Quarterly,* Volume XVI, 1960.
*Encounter,* May, 1957; July, 1959; November, 1971.
*Esquire,* October, 1959; March, 1961.
*Globe and Mail* (Toronto), May 19, 1984.
*Harper's,* November, 1960.
*Horizon,* December, 1984.
*Hudson Review,* September, 1965; summer, 1968.
*Life,* December 22, 1958.
*Listener,* September 27, 1979.
*Literary Criterion,* summer, 1974.
*Los Angeles Times,* April 10, 1981; November 27, 1982; March 26, 1983; June 10, 1984; June 15, 1984; May 26, 1986; February 14, 1987; November 15, 1987; June 19, 1994, p. 8.
*Los Angeles Times Book Review,* November 8, 1987.
*Maclean's,* September 16, 1985.
*Michigan Quarterly Review,* summer, 1967; fall, 1974; spring, 1977; summer, 1985.
*Modern Drama,* March, 1975; December, 1976; September, 1977; September, 1984.
*Nation,* July 19, 1975.
*New Leader,* November 3, 1980.
*New Republic,* May 27, 1972; July 19, 1975; May 6, 1978.
*New Statesman,* February 4, 1966.
*Newsweek,* February 3, 1964; December 11, 1972; July 7, 1975; November 16, 1987.
*New York,* May 15, 1972; July 7, 1975.
*New Yorker,* July 7, 1975.
*New York Herald Tribune,* September 27, 1965.
*New York Review of Books,* March 5, 1964; January 14, 1965.
*New York Times,* February 27, 1949; October 9, 1955; July 6, 1965; June 17, 1979; May 27, 1980; September 30, 1980; November 16, 1980; June 12, 1981; January 30, 1983; February 4, 1983; February 10, 1983; February 13, 1983; October 23, 1983; October 26, 1983; March 30, 1984; May 9,

1984; October 5, 1984; September 15, 1985; February 9, 1986; February 16, 1986; February 1, 1987; February 9, 1987; November 2, 1987; June 11, 1989, p. 19.

*New York Times Book Review,* October 14, 1979; June 24, 1984; November 8, 1987; December 24, 1995, p. 10.

*New York Times Magazine,* February 13, 1972.

*Observer,* March 2, 1969.

*Paris Review,* summer, 1966; summer, 1968.

*Plays and Players,* July, 1986.

*Publishers Weekly,* November 6, 1987; August 28, 1995, pp. 101-02.

*Quarterly Journal of Speech,* October, 1949.

*Renascence,* fall, 1978.

*Saturday Review,* January 31, 1953; June 4, 1966; July 25, 1970.

*Sewanee Review,* winter, 1960.

*Studies in Short Fiction,* fall, 1976.

*Theatre Arts,* June, 1947; April, 1953; October, 1953.

*Theatre Journal,* May, 1980.

*Time,* December 6, 1976; October 15, 1984; August 18, 1986; May 4, 1987; November 23, 1987.

*Times* (London), April 21, 1983; April 3, 1984; July 4, 1984; July 5, 1984; September 5, 1984; April 19, 1985; August 8, 1986; August 28, 1986; October 31, 1986; December 20, 1986; February 14, 1987; February 19, 1987; March 5, 1987.

*Times Literary Supplement,* December 25-31, 1987.

*Tulane Drama Review,* May, 1958; Volume IV, number 4, 1960.

*Twentieth Century Literature,* January, 1970.

*University College Quarterly,* May, 1972.

*Variety,* August 30, 1993, p. 26.

*Virginia Quarterly Review,* summer, 1964.

*Washington Post,* October 26, 1969; October 1, 1979; October 16, 1980; October 26, 1980; December 15, 1980; February 13, 1983; February 19, 1984; February 27, 1984; March 2, 1984; February 22, 1987; November 23, 1987.

*Wilson Library Bulletin,* May, 1965.

*World Literature Today,* Volume 67, number 2, 1992, p. 383.*

—*Sketch by Anne Janette Johnson*

\*    \*    \*

**MOYES, Patricia**
    See HASZARD, Patricia Moyes

**MYLES, Symon**
    See FOLLETT, Ken(neth Martin)

\*    \*    \*

**NISKANEN, William Arthur, Jr.**    1933-

*PERSONAL:* Born March 13, 1933, in Bend, OR; son of William Arthur (a businessperson) and Nina (McCord) Niskanen; married Helen Barr, August 3, 1957 (divorced, 1978); children: Lia Anne, Pamela Cay. *Education:* Harvard University, B.A., 1954, University of Chicago, M.A., 1955, Ph.D., 1962.

*ADDRESSES:* c/o Publicity Director, Edward Elgar Publishing Co., Old Post Rd., Brookfield, VT 05036.

*CAREER:* Rand Corp., Santa Monica, CA, economist, 1957-62; Office of Secretary of Defense, Arlington, VA, director of special studies, 1962-64; Institute for Defense Analyses, Arlington, division director, 1964-70; Office of Management and Budget, Washington, DC, assistant director, 1970-72; University of California, Berkeley, professor of economics, 1972-75; Ford Motor Co., Dearborn, MI, director of economics, 1975-80; Council of Economic Advisors, Washington, DC, member, 1981-85; Cato Institute, Washington, DC, chairperson, 1985—.

*MEMBER:* American Economic Association, Public Choice Society.

*WRITINGS:*

*Bureaucracy and Representative Government,* Aldine-Atherton (Hawthorne, NY), 1971.

*Structural Reform of the Federal Budget Process,* American Enterprise Institute (Washington, DC), 1973.

*Bureaucracy—Servant or Master?: Lessons from America,* Institute of Economic Affairs (London), 1973.

(With others) *Tax and Expenditure Limitation by Constitutional Amendment: Four Perspectives on the California Initiative,* Institute of Governmental Studies (Berkeley), 1973.

*Reagonomics: An Insider's Account of the Policies and the People,* Oxford University Press (New York City), 1988.

(Editor with James A Dorn) *Dollars, Deficits and Trade,* Kluwer Academic (Boston), 1989.

*Bureaucracy and Public Economics,* Elgar (Brookfield, VT), 1994.

Coeditor of *Benefit-Cost Annual,* 1971-72.

*WORK IN PROGRESS:* Research on behavior of government organizations.

\*     \*     \*

**NORMAN, John**
    **See LANGE, John Frederick, Jr.**

# O

## OAKLEY, Graham 1929-

*PERSONAL:* Born August 27, 1929, in Shrewsbury, England; son of Thomas (a shop manager) and Flora (Madeley) Oakley. *Education:* Attended Warrington Art School, 1950. *Avocational interests:* Music.

*ADDRESSES: Home and office*—Kellaways Mill, North Chippenham, Wiltshire, England.

*CAREER:* Freelance artist and book illustrator. Scenic artist for English repertory companies, 1950-55; Royal Opera House, designer's assistant, 1955-57; worked at Crawford's Advertising Agency, 1960-62; British Broadcasting Corporation, television set designer for motion pictures and series, including *How Green Was My Valley, Nicholas Nickleby, Treasure Island,* and *Softly, Softly,* 1962-67. *Military service:* Served in the British Army, 1947-49.

*AWARDS, HONORS:* Kate Greenaway Medal nomination, 1976, and *New York Times* best illustrated children's book of the year citation, 1977, both for *The Church Mice Adrift; Boston Globe-Horn Book* Award illustration special citation, and American Library Association notable book citation, both 1980, both for *Graham Oakley's Magical Changes;* Kate Greenaway Medal nomination, and Kurt Maschler Award runner-up, both 1982, both for *The Church Mice in Action.*

*WRITINGS:*

### SELF-ILLUSTRATED CHILDREN'S BOOKS

*Graham Oakley's Magical Changes,* Macmillan (London), 1979, Atheneum (New York City), 1980.

*Hetty and Harriet,* Macmillan, 1981, Atheneum, 1982.
*Henry's Quest,* Macmillan, 1985, Atheneum, 1986.
*Once upon a Time: A Prince's Fantastic Journey,* Macmillan, 1990.
*The Foxbury Force,* Macmillan, 1994.

### SELF-ILLUSTRATED; "CHURCH MICE" SERIES

*The Church Mouse* (also see below), Atheneum, 1972.
*The Church Cat Abroad* (also see below), Atheneum, 1973.
*The Church Mice and the Moon* (also see below), Atheneum, 1974.
*The Church Mice Spread Their Wings,* Macmillan, 1975, Atheneum, 1976.
*The Church Mice Adrift,* Macmillan, 1976, Atheneum, 1977.
*The Church Mice at Bay,* Macmillan, 1978, Atheneum, 1979.
*The Church Mice at Christmas,* Atheneum, 1980.
*The Church Mice in Action,* Macmillan, 1982, Atheneum, 1983.
*The Church Mice Chronicles* (contains *The Church Mouse, The Church Cat Abroad,* and *The Church Mice and the Moon*), Macmillan, 1986.
*The Diary of a Church Mouse,* Macmillan, 1986, Atheneum, 1987.
*The Church Mice and the Ring,* Atheneum, 1992.

### ILLUSTRATOR

John Ruskin, *The King of the Golden River,* Hutchinson (London), 1958.
Hugh Popham, *Monsters and Marlinspikes,* Hart-Davis (London), 1958.

Popham, *The Fabulous Voyage of the Pegasus,* Criterion (London), 1959.

Robert Louis Stevenson, *Kidnapped,* Dent (London), 1960, with N. C. Wyeth, Crown (New York City), 1989.

David Scott Daniell, *Discovering the Bible,* University of London Press (London), 1961.

Charles Kervern, *White Horizons,* University of London Press, 1962.

Mollie Clarke, adapter, *The Three Feathers: A German Folk Tale Retold,* Hart-Davis, 1963, Follett (New York City), 1968.

Richard Garnett, *The White Dragon,* Hart-Davis, 1963, Vanguard (New York City), 1964.

Garnett, *Jack of Dover,* Vanguard, 1966.

Patricia Ledward, *Grandmother's Footsteps,* Macmillan, 1966.

Taya Zinkin, *Stories Told Round the World,* Oxford University Press (New York City), 1968.

Brian Read, *The Water Wheel,* World's Work, 1970.

Tanith Lee, *Dragon Hoard,* Farrar, Straus (New York City), 1971.

Elizabeth MacDonald, *The Two Sisters,* World's Work, 1975.

Also illustrator of Mollie CLarke's *Skillywidden,* 1965, and *The Bird-Catcher and the Crow-Peri,* 1968, and of Robert Ogilvie's *The Ancient World,* 1969. Oakley's books have been translated and published in Germany and Japan.

*ADAPTATIONS: The Church Mouse* was adapted for videocassette by Live Oak Media, 1988.

*SIDELIGHTS:* British author and illustrator Graham Oakley is recognized for his strong storytelling abilities and his satirical presentation of modern society. The text and elaborate illustrations in his books work together to convey witty and often hilariously comic stories. In his popular "Church Mice" series, for example, Oakley uses the adventures of a group of lively mice and their protector, Sampson the cat, to ridicule such contemporary figures as scientists, the media, and hippies. And in his other works, Oakley uses a similar combination of understated writing and vastly populated pictures—the pictures supplying the story with more meaning than that found in the words alone. "Oakley's witty stories are books to be *enjoyed*—and how often is this vital ingredient missing from children's picture books," points out Edward Hudson in *Children's Book Review.* Elaine Edelman, writing in the *New York Times Book Review,* maintains: "Oakley is one of the craftiest picture-book people working today." As Jane Langton

comments in a *New York Times Book Review* article on *The Church Mice Adrift,* the "brilliant author-artist . . . draws like an angel."

Born in Shrewsbury, England, Oakley attended the Warrington Art School before beginning his career as a scenic artist for repertory companies in London. He then moved on to the Royal Opera House in Covent Garden where he worked as a design assistant, later joining the British Broadcasting Corporation (BBC-TV) as a television set designer before choosing to become a free-lance author and illustrator. It was while he was working as an illustrator for Macmillan that Oakley first envisioned the fictitious English country town of Wortlethorpe as the setting for a series of children's books. "I was going to open with a high view on top of the town and a series of stories about each building, starting with the church and moving on to the library and the town hall, but the first book, *The Church Mouse* was so successful I never got to the library," explains Oakley in an interview with Barbara A. Bannon for *Publishers Weekly.*

*The Church Mouse,* the first book in the "Church Mice" series, introduces the mice who populate the church in Wortlethorpe along with their guardian Sampson the cat. This strange alliance between cat and mice is explained by the setting of the story—Sampson has heard so many sermons on brotherly love and meekness that he thinks of mice as his brothers. Originally, there is only one mouse, Arthur, occupying the church, but he goes to the parson and asks if his town friends can live in the church for free if they perform chores and do odd jobs. All is well until Sampson dreams he is back in his mouse hunting days and wakes up to find himself chasing mice around the church. Before the situation can be dealt with, though, a burglar comes to the church that same night and Sampson and the mice save the day. "The story goes with a swing and the slapstick and circumstantial detail are livened with a measure of wit," observes Margery Fisher in *Growing Point. The Church Mouse* is filled with "fascinating activities" asserts a *Times Literary Supplement* contributor, adding: "Oakley shows in this book how effectively words and pictures can be grafted together so that our understanding of the story depends on the combination of the two."

Later books in the "Church Mice" series have the occupants of the Wortlethorpe church taking part in a number of equally amusing adventures. In *The*

*Church Cat Abroad,* Oakley has Sampson travelling to an exotic South Sea island to shoot a commercial for cat food in order to earn some money to fix the church's roof. Hudson comments in his review of *The Church Cat* Abroad that it is "a story full of humorous incidents and superb illustrations. Oakley is a true artist of the highest calibre with an ability to create and exploit humorous situations to the full." *The Church Mice in Action,* published in 1982, also has Sampson doing something he would rather not in order to earn money to fix up the church. This time he has entered a cat show, but events take an unexpected turn when he is kidnapped by horrible men on a tandem bicycle. The mice, who have been arguing over whether or not it is fair to lure the other cats into fights to give Sampson a better chance, are able to rescue him and all is well in the end. "In *The Church Mice in Action,*" assert Donnarae MacCann and Olga Richard in the *Wilson Library Bulletin,* "Oakley creates a book for all ages by combining satiric cartoons, a tongue-in-cheek literary style, and a cleverly improbable story line."

Oakley departs from the town of Wortlethorpe with his 1979 *Graham Oakley's Magical Changes,* in which he "embarks on a technical experiment in picture-book making that is likely to become a landmark in the history of the genre," describes Elaine Moss in *Signal.* The pages of the book contain no words and are split in half horizontally so that they can be mixed and matched in over five hundred different combinations. The images created revolve around six slender cylinders on the left side pages and four thicker ones on the right, creating such surreal combinations as six city gentlemen holding umbrella handles attached to a full clothesline above their heads, and a four poster bed supporting a railway arch with a thundering train racing over it. "By creating such juxtapositions between the ordinary and the fabulous Oakley emphasizes the strangeness of life," relates Jon C. Stott in *World of Children's Books.* "Most books with half pages for flipping are gimmicks; *Magical Changes* is not—it offers an often humorous, often ironic commentary on life." With *Graham Oakley's Magical Changes,* Leigh Dean concludes in *Children's Book Review Service,* "Oakley has touched the eye, the imagination, and the emotions at a depth where words seem inadequate to describe the genius of this book."

Oakley creates a humorous fictional world—populated by foxes—in *The Foxbury Force,* where police and crooks have created a comfortable relationship in which the robbers will steal their booty but then al-

low themselves to be caught each time. Trouble comes when the crooks decide to have a real robbery, and the Foxbury Force must rely on their long-unused resourcefulness to catch them after they burglarize a castle. *The Foxbury Force,* in the words of a critic for *Junior Bookshelf,* is "relentlessly funny."

Deviating from the "Church Mice" series again, Oakley presents two hens in *Hetty and Harriet* who are in search of the perfect place to live. The trip is Harriet's idea, and Hetty goes along partly because she is bullied into it, but also because she really has nothing better to do. During the course of their search, the two hens encounter a number of dangers in both the country and the city. Worst of all is the egg production plant, but they manage to escape such threats and end up finding the ideal home—the farmyard from which they began. Writing in the *School Library Journal,* Kenneth Marantz comments that "details of nature, or tongue-in-cheek signs in town, abound. Both text and illustration exude the joy of fine storytelling." Finding the book a "delight," Linda Yeatman concludes in the *British Book News:* "Oakley has developed his own special blend of lifelike representation and fantasy in children's books and Hetty and Harriet is a superb example of his skill."

Another quest story, *Henry's Quest,* is set in the future and centers around a young boy's search for a mythical substance—gasoline. The world that Oakley presents is one in which civilization has returned to an age similar to that of medieval times. The country in which Henry lives is surrounded by a large forest, and because the king once read an old copy of *King Arthur and the Knights of the Round Table,* it is alive with the same kinds of things found in the book, such as knights and chivalry. When the king wants to marry off his daughter, he decides to send the suitors on a quest for the substance known as gasoline. Although Henry is only a shepherd-boy and not a knight, he is allowed to participate. He begins his journey through the forest, passing technological gadgets, such as televisions, that have been thrown aside as junk. On the other side of the forest is an evil civilization in which he finds not only gasoline, but also industrialism and corruption. He brings all of these things home, but none, not even the gas, seems to catch on. "The text is very subtle, as funny as it is serious, and the pictures are the stuff of dreams and nightmares, rich with literary and historical illusion," relates Elizabeth Ward in *Washington Post Book World.* "*Henry's Quest* is definitely not a book to be taken too lightly."

While many of his books have been praised for their illustrations, Oakley stretched his artistic skills to their experimental limits in the award-winning *Graham Oakley's Magical Changes.* Unlike his other books, *Magical Changes* has no text. In this "brilliant and bizarre" book, as Leigh Dean describes it in *Children's Book Review Service,* Oakley presents a painting containing vertical bars on each of thirty-two horizontally-split pages. By turning either the top or bottom of the pages, the reader may discover over 4,000 new illustrations linked by continuous bars. For example, as Elaine Moss, writing in *Signal,* explains, a picture of six men carrying six umbrellas (their handles are the bars) becomes a picture of men holding six lollipops (the bars are the lollipop sticks), or six spaghetti strands. The result, as a reviewer for *Publishers Weekly* observes, is either "comic or fearful surrealism." After noting that the "basic," unflipped pictures are "in themselves, satiric," *World of Children's Books* reviewer Jon C. Stott concludes that *Magical Changes* "offers an often humorous, often ironic commentary on life."

## BIOGRAPHICAL/CRITICAL SOURCES:

### BOOKS

Chevalier, Tracy, editor, *Twentieth-Century Children's Writers,* 3rd edition, St. James Press, 1989, pp. 732-33.

*Children's Literature Review,* Volume 7, Gale (Detroit), 1984, pp. 212-223.

Cullinan, Bernice E., Mary K. Karrer, and Arlene M. Pillar, *Literature and the Child,* Harcourt, 1981, pp. 115-160.

Moss, Elaine, *Children's Books of the Year: 1974,* Hamish Hamilton, 1975, p. 54.

### PERIODICALS

*Babbling Bookworm Newsletter,* November, 1979, p. 3.

*Booklist,* November 15, 1992, p. 610.

*Bulletin of the Center for Children's Books,* June, 1982; May, 1983; March, 1987, p. 133.

*British Book News,* spring, 1982, p. 3.

*Children's Book Review,* spring, 1974, p. 12; spring, 1975, p. 14.

*Children's Book Review Service,* June, 1980, p. 103.

*Growing Point,* November, 1972, pp. 2027-2028; October, 1973, p. 2245; December, 1974, p. 2541; January, 1979, p. 3450.

*Horn Book,* June, 1979, p. 294; August, 1983, p. 434.

*Junior Bookshelf,* April, 1979, pp. 99-100; February, 1982, p. 19; August, 1990, p. 165; June, 1994, p. 97.

*New York Times Book Review,* December 10, 1972, p. 8; May 4, 1975, p. 42; May 2, 1976, p. 46; May 8, 1977, p. 41; May 30, 1982, p. 14.

*Publishers Weekly,* February 26, 1979, pp. 74-75; February 15, 1980, p. 110; January 9, 1981, p. 76; February 11, 1983, p. 71; February 13, 1987, p. 91.

*Punch,* January 16, 1980.

*School Librarian,* November, 1990, pp. 143-144.

*School Library Journal,* May, 1973, pp. 65, 67; December, 1973, p. 44; April, 1975, p. 46; April, 1976, pp. 62-63; April, 1977, p. 56; March, 1979, p. 143; May, 1980, p. 62; October, 1980, p. 162; April, 1982, p. 61; December, 1986, p. 107.

*Signal,* January, 1980, pp. 3-7.

*Spectator,* November 11, 1972, pp. 759-760.

*Times Educational Supplement,* November 21, 1980, pp. 29-30; November 19, 1982, p. 32; March 6, 1987, p. 37.

*Times Literary Supplement,* November 3, 1972, p. 1327; November 23, 1973, p. 1440; December 5, 1975, pp. 1452-53; December 10, 1976, p. 1551; November 28, 1986, p. 1345.

*Washington Post Book World,* September 14, 1986, p. 11.

*Wilson Library Bulletin,* October, 1983, p. 131.

*World of Children's Books,* Volume 6, 1981, p. 26.

\* \* \*

**OCKHAM, Joan Price**
**See PRICE, Joan**

\* \* \*

**O'DRISCOLL, Dennis 1954-**

*PERSONAL:* Born January 1, 1954, in Thurles, County Tipperary, Ireland; son of James F. (a salesman and horticulturist) and Catherine (a homemaker; maiden name, Lahart) O'Driscoll; married Julie O'Callaghan (a writer), September, 1985. *Ethnicity:* "Irish." *Education:* Institute of Public Administration, Certificate of Public Administration, 1972; attended National University of Ireland, University College, Dublin, 1972-75.

*ADDRESSES: Home*—Blackrock, Ireland. *Office*—c/o International Customs Branch, Castle House, South Great George's St., Dublin 2, Ireland.

*CAREER:* Revenue Commissioners, Dublin, Ireland, executive officer, 1970-76, higher executive officer, 1976-83, assistant principal officer, 1983—. Writer in residence at National University of Ireland, University College, Dublin, 1987-88; literary organizer of Dublin Arts Festival, 1977-79.

*MEMBER:* Irish United Nations Association (member of council, c. 1975-80).

*AWARDS, HONORS:* Grants from Irish Arts Council, 1985 and 1996.

*WRITINGS:*

(Editor with Peter Fallon) *The First Ten Years: Dublin Arts Festival Poetry,* Dublin Arts Festival, 1979.
*Kist* (poems), Dolmen Press (Mountrath, Ireland), 1982.
*Hidden Extras* (poems), Anvil Press/Dedalus Press, 1987.
(With others) *Five Irish Poets,* White Pine Press (Buffalo, NY), 1990.
*Long Story Short* (poems), Anvil Press/Dedalus Press, 1993.
*The Bottom Line* (poem), Dedalus Press, 1994.
*Quality Time* (poems), Anvil Press/Dedalus Press, in press.

Contributor of about two hundred articles and reviews to periodicals, including *Poetry, London Magazine, Harvard Review, Southern Review,* and *Poetry Review.* Editor of *Poetry Ireland Review,* 1986-87.

*WORK IN PROGRESS:* A book of critical and autobiographical essays.

*SIDELIGHTS:* Dennis O'Driscoll told *CA:* "I have a demanding (and not very interesting!) full-time job. As a result, much of my literary activity is concentrated on weekends. I therefore write only the poems that absolutely insist on being written, that will not go away however much I may initially resist them. Although I dislike my job, I am suspicious in certain respects of poetry as a career, if it leads to a lot of unnecessary (and unconvincing) poems being written. I prefer to write *criticism* in my 'uninspired' periods.

"Many of my poems are about the physical frailty of people and the tenuous hold we have on life. Other themes include the small frustrations of everyday life and the drabness and monotony of routines involving unfulfilling jobs and suburban neighborhoods. Although my themes are often serious, even grim, the poetry tends to undercut solemnity through irony."

*BIOGRAPHICAL/CRITICAL SOURCES:*

PERIODICALS

*Cobweb* (Maynootu), Number 10, 1994.
*Irish Literary Supplement,* Volume 2, number 2, 1983.
*Sunday Tribune* (Dublin), September 19, 1982; August 2, 1987; March 13, 1994.
*Times Literary Supplement,* October 1, 1993.

\*　　\*　　\*

**OINAS, Felix J(ohannes)　1911-**

*PERSONAL:* Born March 6, 1911, in Tartu, Estonia; came to the United States in 1949, naturalized in 1955; son of Ernst (a businessperson) and Marie (Saarik) Oinas; married Lisbet Kove (a librarian), July 10, 1937; children: Helina (Mrs. Charles Anthony Piano), Valdar. *Ethnicity:* "Estonian." *Education:* Attended Budapest University, 1935-36; Tartu University, M.A., 1938; additional study at University of Heidelberg 1946-48; Indiana University, Ph.D., 1952. *Religion:* Evangelical Lutheran.

*ADDRESSES: Home*—2513 East Eighth St., Bloomington, IN 47401. *Office*—Department of Slavic Languages and Literatures, Ballantine Hall 502, Indiana University, Bloomington, IN 47405. *E-mail*—mwducket@indiana.edu

*CAREER:* Budapest University, Budapest, Hungary, lecturer in Finno-Ugric languages, 1938-40; Baltic University, Hamburg, Germany, lecturer in Estonian language, 1946-48; Indiana University at Bloomington, lecturer, 1951-52, instructor, 1952-55, assistant professor, 1955-61, associate professor, 1961-65, professor of Slavic and Finno-Ugric languages and fellow of the Folklore Institute, 1965-71, professor emeritus, 1971—.

*MEMBER:* American Association of Teachers of Slavic and East European Languages Linguistic Society of America, American Folklore Society, Finno-Ugrian Society (fellow), Finnish Academy of Sciences, Finnish Literary Society (fellow), Baltisches Forschungsinstitut (fellow), Finnish Folklore Society (fellow).

*AWARDS, HONORS:* Fulbright grant, 1961-62; Guggenheim grants, 1961-62 and 1966-67; Ford International Studies grants, 1962 and 1967; Fulbright-Hays grant, 1964-65; American Philosophical Society grant, 1965; American Council of Learned Societies travel grant, 1973; National Endowment for the Humanities research grant, 1974; Arthur Puksow Foundation first prize award, 1980.

*WRITINGS:*

*Petoefi,* Estonian Literary Society, 1939.
*The Karelians,* Human Relations Area Files Press (New Haven, CT), 1955.
*The Development of Postpositional Cases in Balto-Finnic Languages,* Finno-Ugric Society, 1961.
*Estonian General Reader,* Indiana University Publications (Bloomington, IN), 1963, 2nd edition, 1972.
*Basic Course in Estonian,* Indiana University Publications, 1966, 4th edition, 1975.
*Studies in Finnic-Slavic Folklore Relations,* Finnish Academy, 1969, 2nd edition, 1992.
*Kalevipoeg kuetkeis ja muid esseid,* Mana (Alexandria, VA), 1979.
*Vargamae tode ja oigus,* Valis-Eesti, 1984.
*Studies in Finnic Folklore,* Finnish Literature Society, 1985.
*Essays on Russian Folklore and Mythology,* Slavica Publishers (Columbus, OH), 1985.
*Surematu Kalevipoeg* (title means "Immortal Kalevipoeg"), Keel ja Kirjandus (Tallinn), 1994.

*EDITOR*

(With Karl Inno) *Eesti,* Eesti Rahvusfond, 1949.
*Language Teaching Today,* Research Center, Indiana University (Bloomington, IN), 1960.
(With Stephen Soudakoff) *The Study of Russian Folklore,* Department of Slavic Languages and Literatures, Indiana University (Bloomington), 1971, Mouton (The Hague, Netherlands), 1975.
(Coeditor) *Tractata Altaica: Denis Sinor sexagenario optime de rebus altaicis merito dedicata,* Otto Harrassowitz, 1976.
(Coeditor) *Folklore Today: Festschrift in Honor of Richard M. Dorson,* Research Center, Indiana University, 1976.

*Heroic Epic and Saga: An Introduction to the World's Great Folk Epics,* Indiana University Press, 1978.
*Folklore, Nationalism and Politics,* Slavica Publishers, 1978.
(And author of introduction) *European Folklore: Readings from the Journal of the Folklore Institute,* Trickster Press (Bloomington, IN), 1981.
*Kuidas kirjanikud kirjutavad* (title means "How Writers Write"), Eesti Kirjanike Kooperatiiv, 1992.

*OTHER*

Contributor of numerous articles to *Word, Journal of American Folklore, Slavic Review, General Linguistics, Studia Fennica,* and other publications. Review editor, *Slavic and East European Journal,* 1957-64.

*WORK IN PROGRESS:* Working on problems of mythology and ancient history.

*SIDELIGHTS:* Felix J. Oinas told *CA:* "My field of research is rather broad, and includes Slavic, Finno-Ugric, and Siberian folklore, mythology, literature, and languages. This variety of interests provides me with an abundance of fascinating research problems, frequently cross-cultural, which can then be viewed from a unifying vantage point. I am currently applying myself to intensive research in an effort to make up for the ten years lost during World War II."

Oinas later told *CA:* "I usually work concurrently on 3 or 4 problems or themes, on which I have new ideas or points of view. I collect material for them from all possible sources. At the same time I work on them in my thought, structuring the material and solving the questions that arise. When the material for one of them has been collected, threshed out in my thoughts and partially worded in my mind, I put it down. As a matter of fact, because of this preparation, my pen runs almost by itself. I have been following the same procedure in almost all my writings."

*BIOGRAPHICAL/CRITICAL SOURCES:*

*BOOKS*

eZygas, Egle Victoria and Peter Voorheis, editors, *Folklorica: Essays for Felix J. Oinas,* Research Institute for Inner Asian Studies (Bloomington, IN), 1982.
Feldstein, Ronald F., compiler, *Feliz Johannes Oinas Bibliography,* Brill (Keoln), 1981.

**ORENSTEIN, Frank (Everett) 1919-**

*PERSONAL:* Born June 22, 1919, in New York, NY; son of Charles and Cecile (Kobliner) Orenstein. *Education:* Dartmouth College, B.A., 1940; University of Chicago, M.A., 1942.

*ADDRESSES: Home*—P.O. Box 244, Gardiner, NY 12525.

*CAREER:* U.S. Department of State, Washington, DC, senior project director for Voice of America evaluation staff, 1950-52, chief of evaluation staff for International Educational Exchange program, 1952-56; McCann Erickson, New York City, manager of television and print research and project director of market and motivation research, 1956-60; Newspaper Advertising Bureau, New York City, vice president and director of research, 1960-77; writer, 1977—. *Military service:* U.S. Army, 1942-46.

*MEMBER:* Mystery Writers of America, American Association for Public Opinion Research, American Sociological Association, Market Research Council, Newspaper Research Council.

*AWARDS, HONORS:* Sidney Goldish Award, International Newspaper Promotion Association, 1975, for "a significant, continuing contribution to newspaper research."

*WRITINGS:*

*Murder on Madison Avenue,* St. Martin's (New York City), 1983.
*The Man in the Gray Flannel Shroud,* St. Martin's, 1984.
*A Candidate for Murder,* St. Martin's, 1987.
*Paradise of Death,* St. Martin's, 1988.
*A Killing in Real Estate,* St. Martin's, 1989.
*Off with the Old,* St. Martin's, 1991.
*A Vintage Year for Dying,* St. Martin's, 1994.

# P

## PADOA-SCHIOPPA ROSTORIS, Fiorella 1945-

*PERSONAL:* Born May 5, 1945, in Rome, Italy; daughter of Leopoldo and Doris Nacmias; married Tommaso Padoa-Schioppa; children: Camillo, Caterina, Costanza. *Education:* University of Bocconi, Ph.D. (magna cum laude), 1968; Massachusetts Institute of Technology, M.S., 1970.

*ADDRESSES: Home*—Via Bradano 34, 00199 Rome, Italy. *Office*—ISPE Co. Vittorio Emanuele II 282, 00186 Rome, Italy. *Agent*—Eulama S. R. L., Via guido de Ruggiero 28, 00142 Rome, Italy.

*CAREER:* University of Rome, Rome, Italy, associate professor, 1977-80, professor, 1989—; University of Trieste, Trieste, Italy, professor, 1980-83; Postgraduate School of Public Administration, Rome, professor, 1984-89. Oxford University, Jemolo fellow at Nuffield College, 1992. Chief of various projects for the Italian National Research Council, 1985-87, 1992—; European Community, member of jury for young scientists contest, 1990-94, member of academic advisory group on state AIDS policy, 1992—; Institute of Studies for Economic Planning, president, 1993—; Aspen Institute Italia, member of general council, 1994—; helped prepare Italian national report for the Fourth World Conference on Women, organized by the United Nations in Beijing, China, 1994; consultant to International Monetary Fund and Organization for Economic Cooperation and Development.

*WRITINGS:*

*IN ENGLISH*

(Editor) *Mismatch and Labour Mobility,* Cambridge University Press, 1991.

*Italy, The Sheltered Economy: Structural Problems of the Italian Economy,* Oxford University Press, 1993.

*Excesses and Limits of the Public Sector in the Italian Economy: The Ongoing Reform,* Routledge (London), 1996.

*IN ITALIAN*

*Scuola e classi sociali,* Il Mulino (Bologna, Italy), 1974.

*La forza lavoro femminile,* Il Mulino, 1977.

(With husband, Tommaso Padoa-Schioppa) *Agenda e non-agenda. Limiti e crisi della politica economica,* Edizioni Comunita (Milan, Italy), 1984.

(Editor with Tommaso Padoa-Schioppa) *Reddito, interesse, inflazione,* Einadi (Torino, Italy), 1987.

*L'Economia sotto tutela. Problema strutturali dell'intervento pubblico in Italia,* Il Mulino, 1990.

(Editor) *Squilibri e rigidita' nel mercato del lavoro italiano: rilevanza quantitativa e proposte correttive,* Franco Angeli (Milan, Italy), 1992.

(Editor) *Struttua di mercato e regolamentazione nel trasporto aereo,* Il Mulino, 1995.

(With G. De Arcangelis) *Esercizi di micro e macroeconomia,* Hoepli (Milan, Italy), 1995.

*OTHER*

Contributor to economic texts, including *Europe's Unemployment Problem,* edited by J. H. Dreze and Ch. R. Bean, MIT Press, 1990; and *Empirical Approaches to Fiscal Policy Modelling,* edited by A. Heimler and D. Meulders, Chapman and Hall, 1993.

Director of economic book series for the publisher Hoeply (Milan, Italy). Contributor of articles to economic journals, including *Metroeconomica, European Economic Review, Public Finance,* and *Politica Economica.*

*WORK IN PROGRESS:* Editing *Pensioni e risanamento della finanza pubblica,* for Il Mulino. Research on macro economics, labor economics, the welfare state, and women's studies.

\* \* \*

### PAGTER, Carl R(ichard) 1934-

*PERSONAL:* Born February 13, 1934, in Baltimore, MD; son of Charles Ralph and Wilhemina (Amelung) Pagter; married Linda Wolfard, August 6, 1962 (divorced, February, 1978); married Judith Elaine Rorabaugh (a musician), May 6, 1978; children: (first marriage) Cameron Roger (deceased), Corbin Christopher. *Ethnicity:* "Caucasian." *Education:* Diablo Valley College, A.A., 1953; San Jose State College (now University), B.A. (with great distinction), 1956; University of California, Berkeley, J.D., 1964. *Politics:* Republican. *Religion:* Protestant.

*ADDRESSES: Home*—17 Julianne Ct., Walnut Creek, CA 94595; fax: 510-328-1820; and Route 1, Box 280, Barboursville, VA 22923. *Office*—Kaiser Cement Corp., 2680 Bisitop Dr., Suite 225, San Ramon, CA 94583.

*CAREER:* Kaiser Industries Corp., Oakland, CA, law clerk, 1963-64, counsel, 1964-70, associate counsel at office in Washington, DC, 1970-73, counsel, 1973-75, director of government affairs for Eastern Region in Washington, DC, 1975-76; Kaiser Cement Corp., San Ramon, CA, vice-president, secretary, and general counsel, 1976-88, consultant and general counsel, 1988—. Professional banjoist and vocalist, 1960—; leader of the string band Country Ham, 1975—. Past president and director of Kaiser Oakland Federal Credit Union; director of League to Save Lake Tahoe, 1965-73; member of Industrial Sector Advisory Committee for Construction, 1984-88, chairman of committee, 1986-88; consultant to Mitsubishi Cement Corp., Rohrer and Associates, and Northern California Asphalt Producers Association. *Military service:* U.S. Navy, air intelligence, 1957-61. U.S. Naval Reserve, 1961-77; became commander.

*MEMBER:* American Bar Association, American Folklore Society, American Society of Corporate Secretaries, California Folklore Society, California Bluegrass Association (founder, 1974; life member; director, 1979—; chairman of board of directors, 1984—), Contra Costa County Bar Association, Phi Kappa Phi, Phi Alpha Theta, Oakland Athletic Club, University Club (Washington, DC).

*WRITINGS:*

(With Alan Dundes) *Urban Folklore from the Paperwork Empire,* University of Texas Press (Austin), 1975, reprinted as *Work Hard and You Shall Be Rewarded,* Indiana University Press (Urbana), 1978.
(With Dundes) *When You're Up to Your Ass in Alligators: More Urban Folklore from the Paperwork Empire,* Wayne State University Press (Detroit), 1987.
(With Dundes) *Never Try to Teach a Pig to Sing,* Wayne State University Press, 1991.
(With Dundes) *Sometimes the Dragon Wins: Yet More Urban Folklore from the Paperwork Empire,* Syracuse University Press (Syracuse, NY), 1996.

Contributor to *Western Folklore* and *Papers of the Kroeber Anthropological Society.* Associate editor of *California Law Review,* 1962-64.

*WORK IN PROGRESS:* A new book on urban office folklore.

*SIDELIGHTS:* Carl R. Pagter told *CA:* "I am fascinated with and extremely interested in folklore, particularly urban office folklore, urban legends, and traditional music. I am a life member of the California Bluegrass Association, which I founded in 1974. The association hosts an annual music festival in Grass Valley, California, and sponsors concerts throughout the year.

"I actively perform and promote old-time and bluegrass music. My wife and I formed the band Country Ham in 1975. We play at music festivals and other events throughout the United States, and we have eleven recordings on the Vetco label. A large part of our repertoire is American traditional music: gospel songs, fiddle tunes, and instrumentals, ballads, and songs of long ago.

"It was my appreciation for traditional music and bawdy songs that sparked my interest in broader forms of folklore. This led eventually to the lifelong collaboration with professor Alan Dundes and the publication of our books."

*BIOGRAPHICAL/CRITICAL SOURCES:*

*PERIODICALS*

*Chicago Tribune,* February 5, 1988.

\*   \*   \*

**PAULSEN, Gary   1939-**

*PERSONAL:* Born May 17, 1939, in Minneapolis, MN; son of Oscar and Eunice Paulsen; married third wife, Ruth Ellen Wright (an artist), May 5, 1971; children: James Wright. *Education:* Attended Bemidji College, 1957-58; and University of Colorado, 1976. *Politics:* "As Solzhenitsyn has said, 'If we limit ourselves to political structures we are not artists.'" *Religion:* "I believe in spiritual progress."

*ADDRESSES: Home*—Leonard, MI. *Agent*—Jonathan Lazear, 430 First Ave., N., Suite 516, Minneapolis, MN 55401.

*CAREER:* Has worked variously as a teacher, electronics field engineer, soldier, actor, director, farmer, rancher, truck driver, trapper, professional archer, migrant farm worker, singer, and sailor; currently a full-time writer. *Military service:* U.S. Army, 1959-62; became sergeant.

*AWARDS, HONORS:* Central Missouri Award for Children's Literature, 1976; *The Green Recruit* was chosen one of New York Public Library's Books for the Teen Age, 1980, 1981, and 1982, and *Sailing: From Jibs to Jibing* was chosen in 1982; *Dancing Carl* was selected one of American Library Association's Best Young Adult Books, 1983, and *Tracker* was selected in 1984; Society of Midland Authors Award, 1985, for *Tracker; Dogsong* was chosen one of Child Study Association of America's Children's Books of the Year, and was a Newbery Honor Book, 1986; *Hatchet* was named a Newbery Honor Book, 1988; *The Winter Room* was named a Newbery Honor Book, 1990; Parents' Choice award, 1991, for *The Boy Who Owned the School: A Comedy of Love;* ALAN Award, 1991; Western Writers of America Spur award, 1991, for *Woodsong.*

*WRITINGS:*

*NOVELS*

*The Implosion Effect,* Major Books (Canoga Park, CA), 1976.
*The Death Specialists,* Major Books, 1976.
*The Foxman,* Thomas Nelson (Nashville, TN), 1977.
*Winterkill,* Thomas Nelson, 1977.
*Tiltawhirl John,* Thomas Nelson, 1977.
*C. B. Jockey,* Major Books, 1977.
*The Night the White Deer Died,* Thomas Nelson, 1978.
*Hope and a Hatchet,* Thomas Nelson, 1978.
(With Ray Peekner) *The Green Recruit,* Independence Press (Independence, MO), 1978.
*The Spitball Gang,* Elsevier/Nelson, 1980.
*The Sweeper,* Harlequin (Tarrytown, NY), 1981.
*Campkill,* Pinnacle Books (New York City), 1981.
*Clutterkill,* Harlequin, 1982.
*Popcorn Days and Buttermilk Nights,* Lodestar Books (New York City), 1983.
*Dancing Carl,* Bradbury (Scarsdale, NY), 1983.
*Tracker,* Bradbury, 1984.
*Dogsong,* Bradbury, 1985.
*Sentries,* Bradbury, 1986.
*The Crossing,* Paperback Library, 1987.
*Hatchet,* Orchard Books, 1987.
*Murphy* (western), Walker & Co. (New York City), 1987.
*The Island,* Orchard Books, 1988.
*Murphy's Gold* (western), Walker & Co., 1988.
*Murphy's Herd* (western), Walker & Co., 1989.
*Night Rituals,* Donald I. Fine, Inc., 1989.
*The Boy Who Owned the School: A Comedy of Love,* Orchard Books, 1990.
*Canyons,* Delacorte (New York City), 1990.
*Kill Fee,* Donald I. Fine, Inc., 1990.
*Woodsong,* illustrated by Ruth Wright Paulsen, Bradbury, 1990.
*The Cookcamp,* Orchard Books, 1991.
*Monument,* Delacorte, 1991.
*The River,* Delacorte, 1991.
*The Winter Room,* Dell (New York City), 1991.
*A Christmas Sonata,* Delacorte, 1992.
*Clabbered Dirt, Sweet Grass,* paintings by R. Paulsen, Harcourt (New York City), 1992.
*The Haymeadow,* Doubleday (New York City), 1992.
*Dogteam,* Delacorte, 1993.
*Murphy's Stand* (western), Walker & Co., 1993.
*Nightjohn,* Delacorte, 1993.
*Sisters/Hermanas,* Harcourt, 1993.
*The Car,* Harcourt, 1994.
*Legend of Red Horse Cavern,* Dell, 1994.

*Rodomonte's Revenge,* Dell, 1994.
*Winterdance: The Fine Madness of Running the Iditarod,* Harcourt, 1994.
*Call Me Francis Tucket,* Delacorte, 1995.
*The Tent: A Tale in One Sitting,* Harcourt, 1995.

SHORT STORIES

*The Madonna Stories,* Van Vliet & Co., 1989.

NONFICTION

(With Raymond Friday Locke) *The Special War,* Sirkay, 1966.
*Some Birds Don't Fly,* Rand McNally (Chicago), 1969.
*The Building a New, Buying an Old, Remodeling a Used, Comprehensive Home and Shelter Book,* Prentice-Hall (New York City), 1976.
*Farm: A History and Celebration of the American Farmer,* Prentice-Hall, 1977.
(With John Morris) *Hiking and Backpacking,* illustrated by R. Paulsen, Simon & Schuster (New York City), 1978.
*Successful Home Repair: When Not to Call the Contractor,* Structures, 1978.
(With Morris) *Canoeing, Kayaking, and Rafting,* illustrated by John Peterson and Jack Storholm, Simon & Schuster, 1979.
*Money-Saving Home Repair Guide,* Ideals (State College, PA), 1981.
*Beat the System: A Survival Guide,* Pinnacle Books, 1983.
*Eastern Sun, Winter Moon: An Autobiographical Odyssey,* Harcourt, 1993.
*Father Water, Mother Woods: Essays on Fishing and Hunting in the North Woods,* Delacorte, 1994.

JUVENILE

*Mr. Tucket,* Funk & Wagnall (New York City), 1968.
(With Dan Theis) *Martin Luther King: The Man Who Climbed the Mountain,* Raintree (Milwaukee, WI), 1976.
*The Small Ones,* illustrated by K. Goff and with photographs by W. Miller, Raintree, 1976.
*The Grass Eaters: Real Animals,* illustrated by Goff and with photographs by Miller, Raintree, 1976.
*Dribbling, Shooting, and Scoring Sometimes,* Raintree, 1976.
*Hitting, Pitching, and Running Maybe,* Raintree, 1976.
*Tackling, Running, and Kicking—Now and Again,* Raintree, 1977.

*Riding, Roping, and Bulldogging—Almost,* Raintree, 1977.
*The Golden Stick,* Raintree, 1977.
*Careers in an Airport,* photographs by Roger Nye, Raintree, 1977.
*The CB Radio Caper,* illustrated by John Asquith, Raintree, 1977.
*The Curse of the Cobra,* illustrated by Asquith, Raintree, 1977.
*Running, Jumping and Throwing—If You Can,* photographs by Heinz Kluetmeier, Raintree, 1978.
*Forehanding and Backhanding—If You're Lucky,* photographs by Kluetmeier, Raintree, 1978.
*Downhill, Hotdogging, and Cross-Country—If the Snow Isn't Sticky,* photographs by Willis Wood and Kluetmeier, Raintree, 1979.
*Facing Off, Checking, and Goaltending—Perhaps,* photographs by Melchior DeGiacomo and Kluetmeier, Raintree, 1979.
*Going Very Fast in a Circle—If You Don't Run out of Gas,* photographs by Kluetmeier and Bob D'Olivo, Raintree, 1979.
*Launching, Floating High, and Landing—If Your Pilot Light Doesn't Go Out,* photographs by Kluetmeier, Raintree, 1979.
*Pummeling, Falling, and Getting Up—Sometimes,* photographs by Kluetmeier and Joe DiMaggio, Raintree, 1979.
*Track, Enduro, and Motocross—Unless You Fall Over,* photographs by Kluetmeier and others, Raintree, 1979.
(With Art Browne, Jr.) *TV and Movie Animals,* Messner (New York City), 1980.
*Sailing: From Jibs to Jibing,* illustrated by R. Paulsen, Messner, 1981.
*Voyage of the Frog,* Orchard Books, 1989.
*Harris and Me: A Summer Remembered,* Harcourt, 1993.

"CULPEPPER ADVENTURES" SERIES

*The Case of the Dirty Bird,* Dell, 1992.
*Dunc's Doll,* Dell, 1992.
*Culpepper's Cannon,* Dell, 1992.
*Dunc Gets Tweaked,* Dell, 1992.
*Dunc's Halloween,* Dell, 1992.
*Dunc Breaks the Record,* Dell, 1992.
*Dunc and the Flaming Ghost,* Dell, 1992.
*Amos Gets Famous,* Dell, 1993.
*Dunc and Amos Hit the Big Top,* Dell, 1993.
*Dunc's Dump,* Dell, 1993.
*Amos's Last Stand,* Dell, 1993.
*The Wild Culpepper Cruise,* Dell, 1993.
*Dunc's Undercover,* Dell, 1993.

*Dunc and Amos and the Red Tattoos,* Dell, 1993.
*Dunc and the Haunted House,* Dell, 1993.
*Cowpokes and Desperadoes,* Dell, 1994.
*Prince Amos,* Dell, 1994.
*Coach Amos,* Dell, 1994.
*Amos and the Alien,* Dell, 1994.
*Dunc and Amos Meet the Slasher,* Dell, 1994.
*Dunc and the Greased Sticks of Doom,* Dell, 1994.
*Amos's Killer Concert Caper,* Dell, 1995.
*Amos Gets Married,* Dell, 1995.
*Amos Goes Bananas,* Dell, 1995.
*Dunc and Amos Go to the Dogs,* Dell, 1995.

*"GARY PAULSEN WORLD OF ADVENTURE" SERIES*

*Escape from Fire Mountain,* Dell, 1995.
*Rock Jockeys,* Dell, 1995.

*PLAYS*

*Communications* (one-act play), produced in New Mexico, 1974.
*Together-Apart* (one-act play), produced at Changing Scene Theater, 1976.

*OTHER*

Also author, with Roger Barrett, of *Athletics, Ice Hockey, Motor-Cycling, Motor Racing, Skiing,* and *Tennis,* all 1980. Also author of *Meteor.* Contributor of more than two hundred short stories and articles to periodicals.

*ADAPTATIONS: Dogsong* (filmstrip with cassette), Random House/Miller-Brody, 1986; *Dancing Carl* was first a narrative ballet for two dancers with original music by John Collins and choreography by Nancy Keller—a seven-minute version of it was aired on Minnesota Public Television.

*SIDELIGHTS:* "I was an 'army brat,' and it was a miserable life," Gary Paulsen once explained. "School was a nightmare because I was unbelievably shy, and terrible at sports. I had no friends, and teachers ridiculed me. . . . One day as I was walking past the public library in twenty-below temperatures . . . I went in to get warm and to my absolute astonishment the librarian . . . asked me if I wanted a library card. . . . When she handed me the card, she handed me the world."

Now a prolific author of coming-of-age stories, novels, and how-to books aimed at a younger audience, Paulsen has also written nonfiction works on such topics as hunting, trapping, farming, animals, medi-

cine, sports, and outdoor life. Paulsen trapped and hunted as a youth and ran the Iditarod (a 1200-mile Alaska dogsled race) in 1983, and the subjects of most of his books reflect this experience with the wilderness. *Tracker,* for instance, tells the story of a thirteen-year-old boy who must hunt alone for the first time to put meat on the table. Paulsen describes the spiritual relationship that develops between the hunter and his prey and how the deer's acceptance of death helps the boy come to terms with his grandfather's imminent death. *Dogsong* is a story of a boy's coming of age on the northern tundra. Eugene J. Lineham in *Best Sellers* praises Paulsen's writing style, noting: "There is poetic majesty in the descriptions without a touch of condescension to the young."

In Paulsen's novel *Hatchet,* the pilot of a single-engined plane has a heart attack and dies, crashing his plane in the Canadian wilderness. Brian Robeson, the sole passenger, must put aside his troubled thoughts about his parents' divorce and try to survive with just the hatchet that his mother had given him as a parting gift. Brian uses his hatchet in numerous ways, such as striking it against a rock to make sparks for a fire and using it to sharpen sticks for tools. The tension surrounding Brian's struggle to survive is enhanced by Paulsen's "staccato, repetitive style," according to a *Kirkus Reviews* contributor, who notes *Hatchet* is a "plausible, taut, . . . [and] spellbinding account." Comparing Paulsen to best-selling authors Robert Cormier and Paula Fox, *Christian Science Monitor*'s Stephen Fraser claims that *Hatchet* "deserves special attention. Written in terse, poetic prose, it is an adventure story in the best tradition."

*Dancing Carl* deviates from Paulsen's adventure stories and focuses on interpersonal relationships. When two twelve-year-old boys first meet Carl, the enigmatic man in the flight jacket, they think he is an alcoholic and a bum. They quickly learn that Carl is much more than that; he takes over the skating rink with the power of his presence, and over the course of the winter, he becomes the topic of the whole town's conversations. With his dance-like movements he expresses his emotions, and the people who watch are made to feel things too, such as repentance for a violent act, happy memories of someone who just died, Carl's pain and terror of his war experience, and Carl's love for a woman. "Readers will come away with a sense of having met an intriguing person," according to Jane E. Gardner in the *School Library Journal.* "Filled with poetry and with life," praises Dorcas Hand in *Horn Book,* "[*Dancing Carl*] is not only an insightful, beautifully written story for children but for readers of any age."

Another book that touches on the subject of war and its effect on lives is *Sentries,* a collection of stories about four young people who are given the opportunity to make their lives a success during peacetime and three young men whose lives are destroyed by choices made during war. The peacetime tales relate the stories of a girl who chooses between her Indian heritage and the white world, a migrant worker who commits to working with beet harvesters, a daughter who proves that she is as capable as any son, and a gifted rock musician who creates a new music. These stories are juxtaposed with tales expressed through four battle hymns set during World War II and the Vietnam War. The purpose of these veterans' tales of mental and physical suffering and the looming threat of nuclear war are to ensure that readers do not take their choices and opportunities for granted and to encourage them to be sentries to protect their rights and freedoms. The juxtaposition of the war and peacetime chapters "conveys, better than philosophizing, the interconnections of life," according to *New York Times Book Review*'s Doris Orgel. Noting that *Sentries* "is strange [and] hard to pigeonhole," Orgel finds that although the protaganists do not interact and the combined tales do not create a novel, the "stories produce a unified effect." And, *Voice of Youth Advocates*'s Evie Wilson hails Paulsen for his "literary excellence" in his selection of stories that serve to remind us of the potential of "the formidable human waste nuclear war promises."

Paulsen's novels continue to reflect the author's interest in nature and the people who derive their sustenance from the outdoors. In *The Cookcamp,* a young boy learns some valuable lessons about life and love from his grandmother, who works as a cook for a deep-woods road crew. "This short novel has almost unbelievable poignancy," comments Patty Campbell in the *New York Times Book Review.* Susan M. Harding, writing in *School Library Journal,* concurs by noting that *The Cookcamp* offers a "depth of imagery and emotion" which makes the book "superb for readers just old enough to look back."

In books like *Nightjohn* and *Mr. Tucket,* Paulsen draws on history for literary inspiration. The twelve-year-old heroine of *Nightjohn* is a slave who awaits the day when she will be designated a "breeder" by her master. As Sarny tries to deal with this unpleasant eventuality, she surreptitiously takes reading lessons from an older slave named John. John pays a high price for being Sarny's teacher—two of his toes are cut off—but he is eventually able to escape and establish an underground school. In *Mr. Tucket,* fourteen-year-old Francis Tucket has a number of hair-raising adventures when he is captured by the Pawnee after drifting away from his family's Oregon-bound wagon train. After Francis escapes from the tribe, a one-armed fur trader named Jason Grimes continues the young teen's frontier education.

The traumas that go hand-in-hand with coming of age are also present in *The Car,* Paulsen's 1994 novel about a teen who deals with emotional upheaval by working on a car kit. Terry pours the frustration and anger he feels about his parents' separation into long hours with his tools, building the convertible his father never finished. In his review of *The Car* for *School Library Journal,* Tim Rausch calls the author's characters "interesting to [young adults] . . . the action is brisk."

Rosa and Traci of *Sisters/Hermanas* have little in common—at least on the surface. Rosa is an illegal immigrant who turns to prostitution in order to survive; Traci is a well-liked junior high schooler whose biggest concerns revolve around cheerleading tryouts and new clothes. Both teens, however, are deeply obsessed with beauty and its impact on their future happiness. The two young women's lives ultimately intersect at a mall, where both girls are forced to face some unpleasant realities. This tale of culture clash and youthful dreams is especially unique in that the entire text appears in both English and Spanish. Summing up the novel for the *Los Angeles Times Book Review,* Yvonne Sapia terms the work "brief, ambitious, and told quite poetically."

Paulsen's own colorful life was the basis for the author's 1993 autobiographical book entitled *Eastern Sun, Winter Moon: An Autobiographical Odyssey.* Among the events chronicled are Paulsen's journey by car across the country to meet his long-absent father, his family's unsettling life in the Philippines, and the dissolution of his parents' marriage. While noting that the memoir lacked a certain depth of introspection, Tim Winton in the *Los Angeles Times Book Review* nevertheless finds the book to be "no less powerful and dignified for its painful silences."

"I write because it's all I can do," Paulsen once commented. "Every time I've tried to do something else, I cannot." The author continues to write—even though the task is often daunting to him—because he wants his "years on this ball of earth to mean something. Writing furnishes a way for that to happen. . . . It pleases me to write—in a very literal sense of the word."

*BIOGRAPHICAL/CRITICAL SOURCES:*

*BOOKS*

*Children's Literature Review,* Volume 19, Gale (Detroit), 1990.

*PERIODICALS*

*Best Sellers,* July, 1985.
*Christian Science Monitor,* November 6, 1987, p. B5.
*Horn Book,* August, 1983, pp. 446-47.
*Kirkus Reviews,* August 1, 1987, pp. 1161-62.
*Library Journal,* February 15, 1993.
*Los Angeles Times,* December 12, 1987.
*Los Angeles Times Book Review,* March 21, 1993, pp. 1, 11; February 27, 1994, pp. 2, 13.
*New York Times Book Review,* June 29, 1986, p. 30; May 22, 1988; May 5, 1991, pp. 22-23.
*School Library Journal,* May, 1983, p. 84; May, 1994, pp. 131-32.
*Voice of Youth Advocates,* October, 1986, p. 148; June, 1994.
*Writer's Digest,* January, 1980.*

\* \* \*

**PINTO, John A.    1948-**

*PERSONAL:* Born February 28, 1948, in Cincinnati, OH; son of Daniel J. (a teacher) and Mary (a teacher; maiden name, Abel) Pinto; married Margaret Hopkin, June 12, 1971; children: Nicholas, James. *Education:* Harvard University, B.A., 1970, Ph.D., 1976.

*ADDRESSES: Office*—Department of Art and Archeology, Princeton University, Princeton, NJ 08544.

*CAREER:* Smith College, Northampton, MA, professor of art history, 1976-88; affiliated with Princeton University, Princeton, NJ, 1988—.

*MEMBER:* College Art Association of America, Society of Architectural Historians.

*AWARDS, HONORS:* Alice Davis Hitchcock Award, Society of Architectural Historians, and George Wittenborn Memorial Award, Art Libraries Society of North America, both 1996, both for *Hadrian's Villa and Its Legacy.*

*WRITINGS:*

*The Trevi Fountain,* Yale University Press (New Haven, CT), 1986.
(With William L. McDonald) *Hadrian's Villa and Its Legacy,* Yale University Press, 1995.

*WORK IN PROGRESS:* A book on eighteenth-century Roman architecture.

*BIOGRAPHICAL/CRITICAL SOURCES:*

*PERIODICALS*

*Times Literary Supplement,* August 15, 1986.

\* \* \*

**P. L. K.**
  **See KIRK-GREENE, Anthony (Hamilton Millard)**

\* \* \*

**POPENOE, David    1932-**

*PERSONAL:* Surname is pronounced *Pop*-en-oe; born October 1, 1932, in Los Angeles, CA; son of Paul (a family life specialist) and Betty (Stankovitch) Popenoe; married Katharine Sasse, July 18, 1959; children: Rebecca, Julia. *Education:* Antioch College, A.B., 1954; University of Pennsylvania, M.C.P., 1958, Ph.D., 1963. *Politics:* Democrat. *Religion:* Religious Society of Friends (Quaker).

*ADDRESSES: Home*—92 Moore St., Princeton, NJ 08540. *Office*—Office of the Dean, Faculty of Arts and Sciences, 77 Hamilton St., Rutgers University, New Brunswick, NJ 08903.

*CAREER:* Brandywine Valley Association, West Chester, PA, staff associate, 1953-54; Philadelphia Redevelopment Authority, Philadelphia, PA, program planner II, 1956-58; Newark Central Planning Board, Newark, NJ, senior planner, 1958-59; Rutgers University, New Brunswick, NJ, assistant director of research and education, Urban Studies Center, 1961-64, director of research and education, Urban Studies Center, 1965-69, associate professor of urban planning at Livingston College, 1967-69, associate professor, 1969-77, professor of sociology at Douglass College, 1978—, chair and graduate director of department of sociology, 1979-85, associate dean for social sciences, 1988—, professor II, 1989—. Adjunct professor of public administration, New York University, 1964-65, 1967-68; lecturer in sociology, University of Pennsylvania, 1965-66; visiting professor, department of sociology, University of Stockholm, 1972-73, 1974, 1977, and National Swedish Building Research Institute, 1975; visiting scholar, Centre for Environmental Studies, London, 1978.

Member of the community mental heath planning committee for the state of New Jersey, 1964; member of the sub-committee on housing and community affairs for the state of New Jersey, 1966; member of the task force on housing for the Board of National Missions, United Presbyterian Church in the USA, 1967; member of the national board of directors, Planners for Equal Opportunity, 1965-68; United States-Sweden Fulbright Commission, Stockholm, Sweden, 1972-73; member of the national research council evaluation panel, National Science Foundation Graduate Fellowships in the Behavioral and Social Sciences, 1975-76; member of the national screening committee in sociology for the Fulbright Program, 1977-81; member of the scholarly advisory panel; 1989—, and board of directors, 1991— for the Institute for American Values, New York City; member of the experts advisory board for the National Parenting Association, New York City, 1993—. Invited participant for Project Knowledge 2000, Bicentennial Conference on the National Sciences Foundation, Leesburg, VA, 1976; chair, board of trustees, 1976-79, and honorary member of board, 1979—, American Institute of Family Relations, Los Angeles, CA; chair, Research Board, 1990—, and cochair, 1991—; Council on Families in America, New York City; head, National Family Project, The Communitarian Network, Washington, DC, 1994—. *Military service:* U.S. Army, 1954-56.

*MEMBER:* International Sociological Association, International Society of Family Law, American Association of University Professors, American Institute of Certified Planners, American Planning Associa-

tion, American Sociological Association, Society for the Advancement of Scandinavian Studies, Human Behavior and Evolution Society.

*AWARDS, HONORS:* Research grants from National Institute of Mental Health, 1965, Rutgers Research Council, 1971, 1973-75, 1986, and National Swedish Building Research Institute, 1977; Rutgers Research Council faculty fellowship, 1972-73; Fulbright visiting lectureship, Israel, Greece, and Spain, 1973; Swedish Kennedy fellowship, 1975; Thord-Gray Memorial Fund grant from American Scandinavian Foundation, 1985-86 (declined); Senior Fulbright research scholarship, 1972-73, 1985-86; American Council of Learned Societies/Ford fellowship, 1985-86.

*WRITINGS:*

*Sociology* (introductory text), Prentice-Hall (Englewood Cliffs, NJ), 1971, 10th edition, in press.

*The Suburban Environment: Sweden and the United States,* University of Chicago Press (Chicago), 1977.

*Private Pleasure, Public Plight: American Metropolitan Community Life in Comparative Perspective,* Transaction Books (New Brunswick, NJ), 1985.

*Disturbing the Nest: Family Change and Decline in Modern Societies,* Aldine de Gruyter (New York City), 1988.

*Life without Father: Compelling New Evidence that Fatherhood & Marriage are Indispensable for the Good of Children and Society,* The Free Press, 1996.

Also principal author of *Marriage in America: A Report to the Nation,* Council on Families in America.

*EDITOR*

*The Urban-Industrial Frontier: Essays on Social Trends and Institutional Goals in Modern Communities,* Rutgers University Press (New Brunswick, NJ), 1969.

(With Robert Gutman) *Neighborhood, City and Metropolis: An Integrated Reader in Urban Sociology,* Random House (New York City), 1970.

(With Willem van Vliet, Harvey Choldin, and William Michelson) *Housing and Neighborhoods: Theoretical and Empirical Contributions,* Greenwood Press (Westport, CT), 1987.

*OTHER*

Contributor to various publications, including *Housing and Neighborhoods,* edited by van Vliet and others, Greenwood Press, 1987; *Handbook of Housing and the Built Environment in the United States,* edited by E. Huttman and van Vliet, Greenwood, 1988; *Individualism Reconsidered: Readings Bearing on the Endangered Self in Modern Society,* Center for Religion, Self, and Society (Princeton, NJ), 1992; *Values and Public Policy,* edited by H. J. Aaron, T. E. Mann, and T. Taylor, Brookings Institution (Washington, DC), 1994; and *Handbook of Environmental Sociology,* edited by R. Dunlap and Michelson, forthcoming.

Also contributor of articles and reviews on sociology, urban studies, and social planning to professional journals, as well as popular periodicals, including *American Behavioral Scientist, Greek Review of Social Research, Journal of Marriage and the Family, The Public Interest, The Public Perspective, The Responsive Community, Television and Families,* and *USA Today.*

Editor with Gutman of a special issue of *American Behavioral Scientist* devoted to urban studies, February, 1963; editor of special issue of *Urban Education,* April, 1971; editorial advisor, *Research in Community Sociology,* 1988—.

*SIDELIGHTS:* David Popenoe told *CA:* "My recent writings have focused on the decline of marriage and the family in modern societies and its personal and social consequences. As cochair of the Council on Families in America, I was principal author of its *Marriage in America: A Report to the Nation.* My thinking is increasingly influenced by the new field of evolutionary psychology with its neo-Darwinian paradigm."

\*   \*   \*

**POSNER, Barry Z(ane)   1949-**

*PERSONAL:* Born March 11, 1949, in Hollywood, CA; son of Henry and Delores Ginsberg (Gearhart) Posner (small business owners); married Jacqueline Schmidt (a college administrator), July 23, 1972; children: Amanda Delores. *Education:* University of California, Santa Barbara, B.A. (with honors), 1970; Ohio State University, M.A., 1972; University of Massachusetts, Ph.D., 1976. *Avocational interests:* Tennis, golf, travel.

*ADDRESSES: Office*—Leavey School of Business Administration, University of Santa Clara, Santa Clara, CA 95053. *E-mail*—bposner@scuacc.scu.edu.

*CAREER:* University of Santa Clara, Santa Clara, CA, assistant professor, 1976-82, associate professor and professor of management, 1982—; associate dean, 1986-90. Executive Development Center, managing partner, 1993—; member of board of directors of Big Brothers/Big Sisters and Center for Excellence in Nonprofits.

*MEMBER:* Academy of Management, American Psychological Association.

*AWARDS, HONORS:* President's Award for faculty distinction, University of Santa Clara, 1984; Book of the Year award, American Society of Health Care Executives, 1989.

*WRITINGS:*

(With Warner H. Schmidt) *Managerial Values and Expectations,* American Management Association (Saranac Lake, NY), 1982.
(With Schmidt) *Managerial Values in Perspective,* American Management Association, 1983.
(With J. M. Kouzes) *The Leadership Challenge: How to Get Extraordinary Things Done in Organizations,* Jossey-Bass (San Francisco, CA), 1987, 2nd edition, 1995.
(With W. A. Randolph) *Effective Project Planning and Management,* Prentice-Hall (Englewood Cliffs, NJ), 1988.
(With Randolph) *Getting the Job Done,* Prentice-Hall, 1992.
(With Kouzes) *Credibility,* Jossey-Bass, 1993.
(With Kouzes) *Leadership Practices Inventory: Trainer's Manual,* Pfeiffer (San Diego), 1993.

Contributor of more than one hundred articles to business and management journals. Associate editor of *Journal of Management Inquiry;* former member of editorial review board of *Exchange: The Organizational Behavior Teaching Journal.*

*SIDELIGHTS:* Barry Z. Posner told *CA:* "As a management consultant and scholar I write for several audiences. With my academic colleagues I write for other academics in the hope of contributing to the 'science' of management. For practitioners I both translate the management science into its 'artistic' components and contribute to the humanization of the work place."

**POWER, Margaret 1950-**

*PERSONAL:* Born October 7, 1950, in London, England; daughter of Christopher and Margaret Mary (Gallagher) Lonergan; married Thomas Power (a heating engineer), February 28, 1976; children: Eliza. *Ethnicity:* "Irish." *Education:* Portsmouth Polytechnic, B.A. (with honors), 1973; Garnett College, post-graduate certificate in education, 1974; University of London, post-graduate diploma in communications, 1988. *Religion:* Roman Catholic.

*ADDRESSES: Home*—2 Norwich Rd., Northwood, Middlesex HA6 1NA, England. *Office*—Department of Adult and Continuing Education, Kilburn Polytechnic, Barrett's Green Rd., London N.W.10, England.

*CAREER:* Kilburn Polytechnic, London, England, lecturer in English and communications, 1978-93.

*WRITINGS:*

*Goblin Fruit* (novel), Journeyman Press, 1987.
*Lily* (novel), Simon & Schuster (New York City), 1994.
*Porphyria's Lover* (novel), Simon & Schuster, 1995.

*SIDELIGHTS:* Margaret Power told *CA:* "My writing draws upon the Gothic tradition in nineteenth-century poetry and fiction in order to explore the emotional distortions exerted by gendered subjectivity. As well as being influenced by those stunning nineteenth-century familial groups of writers and artists, the Brontes, Brownings, and Rossettis, I greatly admire the work of Angela Carter, Joyce Carol Oates and, above all, Jean Rhys."

\*    \*    \*

**PRAWER, S(iegbert) S(alomon) 1925-**

*PERSONAL:* Surname is pronounced "Prah-ver"; born February 15, 1925, in Cologne, Germany; came to England, 1939; naturalized British citizen, 1945; son of Marcus (owner of a clothing business) and Eleonora (Cohn) Prawer; married Helga Alice Schaefer, December 25, 1949; children: David Marcus (died, 1968), Daniela Sylvia, Deborah Joy, Jonathan Roy. *Education:* Attended Jesus College, Cambridge; Christ's College, Cambridge, B.A.,

1947, M.A., 1950; University of Birmingham, Ph.D., 1953; Cambridge University, Litt.D., 1962; Oxford University, M.A. and D.Litt., 1969. *Avocational interests:* Portrait drawing.

*ADDRESSES: Home*—Queen's College, Oxford OX1 4AW, England.

*CAREER:* University of Birmingham, Birmingham, England, assistant lecturer, 1948-51, lecturer, 1951-58, senior lecturer in German, 1958-63; University of London, Westfield College, London, England, professor of German, 1964-69; University of Oxford, Taylor Professor of German Language and Literature, 1969-86, professor emeritus, 1986—. Visiting professor at numerous colleges and universities, including Harvard University, 1968, Hamburg University, 1969, and Australian National University, 1980. Queen's College, Oxford, fellow, 1969—, Dean of Degrees, 1978-93. Visiting fellow of Knox College, Dunedin, New Zealand, 1976, Humanities Research Centre, Australian National University, 1980, Tauber Institute, Brandeis University, 1981-82, and Russell Sage Foundation, 1988. Honorary director of London University Institute of Germanic Studies, 1966-68, honorary fellow, 1987—. Freelance graphic artist, 1986—.

*MEMBER:* British Comparative Literature Association (president, 1984-87, honorary fellow), English Goethe Society (vice president; member of council, 1964-84; former president), British Academy of Language and Literature (fellow), British Academy of Language and Literature (fellow), Conference of University Teachers of German in Great Britain and Northern Island, Modern Language Association of America (honorary member).

*AWARDS, HONORS:* Goethe Medal, 1973; Isaac Deutscher Memorial Prize, 1977, for *Karl Marx and World Literature;* D.Phil., Cologne University, 1984; Friedrich Gundolf Prize, German Academy, 1986; D.Litt., University of Birmingham, 1988; Gold Medal of the German Goethe Society, 1995.

*WRITINGS:*

*German Lyric Poetry,* Routledge & Kegan Paul (London), 1952.
*Moerike und seine Leser* (title means "Moerike and His Readership"), E. Klett (Stuttgart, Germany), 1960.
*Heine's "Buch der Lieder": A Critical Study,* Edward Arnold (London), 1960.

*Heine: The Tragic Satirist,* Cambridge University Press (Cambridge, England), 1961.

(Editor and translator) *The Penguin Book of Lieder,* Penguin (London), 1964.

(Editor with V. J. Riley) *Theses in Germanic Studies: 1962-67,* Institute of Germanic Studies, University of London, 1969.

(Editor with R. H. Thomas and Leonard W. Forster) *Essays in German Language, Culture, and Society,* Institute of Germanic Studies, University of London, 1969.

(Editor) *The Romantic Period in Germany,* Schocken, 1970.

(Editor) *Seventeen Modern German Poets,* Oxford University Press (Oxford, England), 1971.

*Comparative Literary Studies: An Introduction,* Duckworth (London), 1973.

*Karl Marx and World Literature,* Oxford University Press, 1976.

*Caligari's Children: The Film as Tale of Terror,* Oxford University Press, 1978.

*Heine's Jewish Comedy: A Study of His Portraits of Jews and Judaism,* Oxford University Press, 1983.

*A. N. Stencl: Poet of Whitechapel,* Oxford Centre for Postgraduate Hebrew Studies (Oxford, England), 1984.

*Frankenstein's Island: England and the English in the Writings of Heinrich Heine,* Cambridge University Press, 1986.

*Israel at Vanity Fair: Jews and Judaism in the Writings of W. M. Thackery,* E. J. Brill (Long Island City, NY), 1992.

Also editor of a version of the screenplay for the film *Das Kabinett des Dr. Caligari.* Contributor of numerous articles on German, English, and comparative literature to scholarly journals, including *Cambridge Journal, German Review, Modern Language Review,* and *Modern Philology.* Coeditor, *Oxford German Studies,* 1971-75, and *Anglica Germanica,* 1973-79.

*WORK IN PROGRESS:* Graphic artwork; a book on Germany and the Germans in the writing of W. M. Thackery.

*BIOGRAPHICAL/CRITICAL SOURCES:*

*PERIODICALS*

*New York Review of Books,* February 16, 1984.
*Observer* (London), August 14, 1983.
*Review of English Studies,* November, 1994, p. 587.

*Times Literary Supplement,* February 1, 1974; February 4, 1977; December 2, 1983; August 21, 1987.
*Victorian Studies,* autumn, 1993, p. 162.

\*    \*    \*

**PRICE, Joan    1931-**
  **(Joan Price Ockham)**

*PERSONAL:* Born May 20, 1931, in Phoenix, AZ; daughter of Fred V. (in business construction) and Loreen (Ackley) Price; married; children: Joan, Judy. *Education:* Attended Colorado Agricultural and Mechanical College (now Colorado State University), 1949-53; University of Arizona, B.S., 1955; Springfield College, M.S., 1956; Arizona State University, M.A., 1968, Ph.D., 1973. *Avocational interests:* Nature, animals.

*ADDRESSES: Office*—Department of Philosophy, Mesa Community College, 1833 West Southern, Mesa, AZ 85201.

*CAREER:* Mesa Community College, Mesa, AZ, professor of philosophy, 1968-95, chair of department, 1978-88, professor emeritus, 1995—; creator of Religious Studies Department, chair of Articulation Committee. Lecturer on religion and philosophy.

*MEMBER:* Arizona State Philosophy Instructional Council, Phoenix Friends of Jung (secretary), Teilhard de Chardin Society (member of board of directors), East-West Philosophical Society (member of board of directors).

*WRITINGS:*

*A Very Special Burro* (children's book), Naylor, 1966.

(Under name Joan Price Ockham) *Introduction to Sri Aurobindo's Philosophy,* University of Pondicherry Press (India), 1975.

*Truth Is a Bright Star,* Celestial Arts (Millbrae, CA), 1982.

*New Age Philosophy,* Ginn Press (Needham, MA), 1988.

*Medicine Man* (children's book), Royal Fireworks Publishing, 1997.

*Hawk in the Wind* (children's book), Royal Fireworks Publishing, 1997.

Also author of *Horse, Dog and Little Stray Cow* (children's book), 1989. Contributor of articles to periodicals, including *Vision 90, Quest Journal,* and *World Humanities Journal.*

*WORK IN PROGRESS:* A philosophy textbook for Wadsworth Publishing.

*SIDELIGHTS:* Joan Price told *CA:* "I write because I must. It fills an inner need for expression. I am especially interested in religious studies and the mystical views in psychology, philosophy, and comparative religion. Knowing one's inner self is especially vital today in the world of computers and technology. The human elements—human values, search for truth, and sharing world views—are necessary for balance in the world and for an understanding of people as whole beings."

\* \* \*

**PYGGE, Edward**
    See BARNES, Julian (Patrick)

\* \* \*

**PYNE, Stephen J(oseph) 1949-**

*PERSONAL:* Born March 6, 1949, in San Francisco, CA; son of Joseph R. (a special agent of the Federal Bureau of Investigation) and Barbara (Boles) Pyne; married Sonja Sandberg, May 14, 1977; children: Lydia Virginia. *Education:* Stanford University, B.A., 1971; University of Texas, M.A., 1974, Ph.D., 1976.

*ADDRESSES: Home*—Glendale, AZ. *Office*—Department of American Studies, Arizona State University West, Phoenix, AZ.

*CAREER:* Grand Canyon National Park, Grand Canyon, AZ, fire control aid at North Rim, summers, 1967-69, foreman of fire crew at North Rim, summers, 1970-81, park ranger at Desert View, winter, 1976-77; University of Iowa, Iowa City, assistant professor of history, beginning 1981; Arizona State University West, Phoenix, currently professor of American studies. Research coordinator at U.S. Forest Service's History Office, winters, 1977-81.

*MEMBER:* History of Science Society, American Association for the Advancement of Science, American Historical Association, Forest History Society.

*AWARDS, HONORS:* Smithsonian Institution fellow, 1974; National Humanities Center fellow, 1979-80; National Endowment for the Humanities fellow (in Antarctica), 1981-82; MacArthur fellow, 1988-93; *Los Angeles Times* Book Prize, 1995, for *World Fire: The Culture of Fire on Earth.*

*WRITINGS:*

*Grove Karl Gilbert: A Great Engine of Research,* University of Texas Press (Austin), 1980.
*Fire in America: A Cultural History of Wildland and Rural Fire,* Princeton University Press (Princeton, NJ), 1982.
*Dutton's Point: An Intellectual History of the Grand Canyon* (monograph), Grand Canyon Natural History Association (Grand Canyon, AZ), 1982.
*Introduction to Wildland Fire: Fire Management in the United States,* Wiley (New York City), 1984, second edition (with Patricia L. Andrews and Richard D. Laven), 1996.
*The Ice: A Journey to Antarctica,* University of Iowa Press, 1986.
*Fire on the Rim: A Firefighter's Season at the Grand Canyon,* Weidenfeld & Nicolson (New York City), 1989.
*Burning Bush: A Fire History of Australia,* Holt (New York City), 1991.
*World Fire: The Culture of Fire on Earth,* Holt, 1995.

Contributor of articles and reviews to *New Republic, New York Times Book Review, BioScience, Journal of American History, Natural History,* and other periodicals.

*WORK IN PROGRESS: Vestal Fire,* a history of fire in Europe.

*SIDELIGHTS:* Stephen J. Pyne "is recognized as the world's leading authority on wildfire," according to Mike Davis in the *Nation.* In four books covering the role of fire in human history, he has examined how fire has helped to shape human culture throughout the world. As Pyne writes in his book *World Fire: The Culture of Fire on Earth:* "Fire and humans have co-evolved, like the bonded strands of a DNA molecule. . . . Ignore fire history and you dismiss one of the truly defining attributes of *Homo sapiens.*"

David Darlington, writing in *Audubon,* argues that "to label Pyne a historian is almost to do him an intellectual disservice. . . . Pyne boasts a consciousness composed of equal parts historian, ecologist, philosopher, critic, poet, and sociologist." Pyne himself tells Joseph A. Cincotti of the *New York Times Book Review:* "I've called myself a scholar on fire and a pyromantic. . . . I've had to create those names to explain what I do." Pyne once told *CA:* "I am basically interested in nature, and in the ways in which people do things with the natural world and how they understand that world."

Pyne's interest in fire began the summer after he graduated from high school. While working for the park service at the Grand Canyon, Pyne was called upon to assist the fire crew in putting out a wildfire at the Canyon's North Rim. He tells Roger Adelson in the *Historian:* "That's where I think my life really began because practically all the things I've written about in one way or another trace back to that experience."

Pyne spent the next fifteen summers working at the Grand Canyon, a period he records in *Fire on the Rim: A Firefighter's Season at the Grand Canyon.* In this book Pyne focuses on the firefighters' work during a composite season of the ones he spent at the Grand Canyon. The fires at the Grand Canyon are often started by lightning. Fire crews are sent to the site, and they prevent the fire from spreading to tourist areas. Some 35 fires occur every season. Fires are necessary, since they rejuvenate the forest by promoting fresh growth. But they are also dangerous to those who visit the Grand Canyon. Pyne details this conflict between opposing needs while telling his story of how the fire crews do their job. "Pyne," writes Rachel Russell in *BioScience,* "shows his fire crew fighting not just fire, but also boredom and bureaucracy." Andrew H. Malcolm observes in the *New York Times Book Review* that "thankfully, there is no strident advocacy here" and concludes that *Fire on the Rim* is "an enlightening and entertaining journey through the woods."

Pyne's studies of the history of fire began with *Fire in America: A Cultural History of Wildland and Rural Fire.* In this book Pyne provides an overview of the history of fire management in the nation's wilderness areas. "Carefully researched, clearly written, and authoritative, this pioneering work brings together a vast amount of useful information," according to P. J. Coleman in the *Library Journal.*

Dennis Smith in the *New York Times Book Review* calls *Fire in America* "the biggest, most ambitious and fact-filled book yet about woodland, brush and prairie fires in the United States."

In *Burning Bush: A Fire History of Australia,* Pyne explores the history of fire management in Australia, a continent where fire is a constant threat because of the dry conditions and where it is also a necessity for some plant life to survive at all. The seeds of the eucalyptus, for example, the most common tree in Australia, need fire to crack open and germinate. But Australia also suffers from fires that consume hundreds of square miles, destroying homes and businesses and killing people and animals alike. This relationship to fire has shaped Australian culture in numerous ways, Pyne argues. W. H. New, writing in *Canadian Literature,* explains that "Pyne tells not only how fire came to Australia but also how it transformed the landscape and in so doing changed the way people comprehend the world." Writing in the *Quarterly Review of Biology,* Allen Keast refers to "Pyne's massive essay" as "a stimulating and thought-provoking piece of work." Jill Ker Conway, in a review of *Burning Bush* for the *New York Times Book Review,* concludes that Pyne "has produced a provocative work that is a major contribution to the literature of environmental studies."

Upon winning a MacArthur fellowship in 1988, which provides the recipient with $250,000 over a five-year period, Pyne decided to take the opportunity to write a fire history of the world. Combined with the books he published earlier, and with the upcoming *Vestal Fire,* which covers fire history in Europe, Pyne's *World Fire: The Culture of Fire on Earth* completes the epic history. "*World Fire* and its companion volumes," writes Davis, "constitute a vast, Diego Rivera-like mural of singular fire histories." "Pyne's talent and achievement," Darlington believes, "is that he has not only assembled an exhaustive and eloquent account of the relationship [between humans and fire] but also demonstrated, again and again, the particular ways in which it disrobes us in all our desperate humanity and mortality."

*BIOGRAPHICAL/CRITICAL SOURCES:*

*PERIODICALS*

*Audubon,* September, 1995, p. 90.
*BioScience,* November, 1989, p. 733.

*Booklist,* January 15, 1991, p. 986; March 15, 1995, p. 1291.

*Boston Globe,* June 18, 1995, p. B48.

*Canadian Literature,* autumn, 1992, p. 198.

*Esquire,* December, 1984, p. 112.

*Historian,* autumn, 1994, pp. 1-16.

*Library Journal,* April 1, 1995, p. 121.

*Los Angeles Times Book Review,* November 21, 1982, p. 3; January 18, 1987, p. 4.

*Nation,* October 2, 1995, p. 362.

*Natural History,* April, 1991, p. 82.

*Nature,* November 19, 1987, p. 287; April 11, 1991, p. 539.

*Newsweek,* May 1, 1989, p. 74.

*New York Times Book Review,* August 15, 1982, p. 3; January 11, 1987, p. 11; December 18, 1988, p. 34; May 14, 1989, p. 7; March 10, 1991, p. 8.

*Quarterly Review of Biology,* September, 1993, pp. 451-452.

*Science,* February 18, 1983, p. 838.

*Times Literary Supplement,* November 5, 1982, p. 1215.

*Virginia Quarterly Review,* winter, 1983, p. 8.

*Wall Street Journal,* June 7, 1989, p. A30.

*Washington Post Book World,* July 2, 1995, p. 13.

*Western American Literature,* winter, 1989, p. 379.

*Whole Earth Review,* fall, 1991, p. 92.

*Wilson Quarterly,* winter, 1983, p. 137.

# R

## RAKEL, Robert E(dwin) 1932-

*PERSONAL:* Born July 13, 1932, in Cincinnati, OH; son of Edwin J. (a laundry driver) and Elsie (a secretary; maiden name, Machino) Rakel; married Peggy A. Klare; children: Barbara, Cindy Zajicek, Linda, David. *Education:* University of Cincinnati, B.S., 1954, M.D., 1958. *Politics:* Independent. *Religion:* Roman Catholic.

*ADDRESSES: Home—*2420 Underwood, Houston, TX 77030. *Office—*Family Practice Center, 5510 Greenbriar, Houston, TX 77005.

*CAREER:* St. Mary's Hospital, Cincinnati, OH, intern, 1958-59; U.S. Public Health Service Hospital, Seattle, WA, resident in internal medicine, 1959-61; Monterey County Hospital, Salinas, CA, resident in general practice, 1961-62; private practice of medicine in Newport Beach, CA, 1962-69; University of California, Irvine, assistant professor, 1969-71, associate professor of family practice, 1971, chair of family practice program, 1969-71; University of Iowa, Iowa City, professor of family practice and head of department, 1971-85; Baylor College of Medicine, Houston, TX, associate dean for academic and clinical affairs, Richard M. Kleberg, Sr., professor, and chair of department of family medicine, 1985—.

Chair of department of general practice at Orange County Medical Center, 1968-71; member of executive committee at Hoag Memorial Hospital, 1967-70, director of family practice residency program, 1969-71; member of medical staff of Mercy Hospital, Iowa City, 1971-85; First Angus Memorial Lecturer, University of Toronto, 1984; chief of family practice service, St. Luke's Episcopal Hospital, Houston, TX, 1985—. Member of organizing board of directors of Costa Mesa Memorial Hospital, 1968-69; member of advisory council of Patient Care Systems, 1970-76; member of board of trustees, New Age Hospice of Houston, Inc., 1986—; member of board of trustees, Institute of Religion, Texas Medical Center, Houston, 1986—. People to People Family Practice Delegation leader, China, 1983. Consultant to Bureau of Health Manpower, Department of Health and Human Services, National Heart, Lung and Blood Institute, and Health Learning Systems, Inc.

*MEMBER:* World Organization of National Colleges, Academies, and Academic Associations of General Practice, American Academy of Family Physicians (fellow; president of Orange County California Chapter, 1969; member of board of directors of California Academy of Family Physicians, 1970-72), Council of Academic Societies, National Board of Medical Examiners (member of board of directors, 1975-79), American Board of Family Practice (charter diplomate; member of board of directors, 1973-79; vice president, 1977-79; chair of research and development committee, 1971-79, and examination committee, 1974-79), American Board of Medical Specialties (member of specialty evaluation committee, 1978-81), American Medical Association (member of governing council of section on medical schools, 1986—), Association of American Medical Colleges, Society of Teachers of Family Medicine (member of board of directors, 1971-79), History of Medicine Society (founder and chair at University of Iowa, 1978-85, and at Baylor College of Medicine, 1986—), Texas Medical Association, American Osler Society (president, 1994), Cosmos Club.

*AWARDS, HONORS:* Mead-Johnson scholarship from American Academy of Family Physicians, 1971; Thomas W. Johnson Award from American Academy of Family Physicians, 1973, for outstanding contribution to family practice and education; Wade and Harold Mack Chair in Family Medicine from Ogden Surgical Society, 1983; F. Marian Bishop Leadership Award, Society of Teachers of Family Medicine Foundation (STFM), 1992.

*WRITINGS:*

(Author of foreword) R. J. Cadoret and L. J. King, *Psychiatry in Primary Care,* Mosby, 1974.
*Principles of Family Medicine,* Saunders, 1977.
(Author of foreword) Adrian E. Flatt, *The Care of Minor Hand Injuries,* 4th edition (Rakel was not associated with earlier editions), Mosby, 1979.
(Author of foreword) L. R. Mercier and F. J. Pettid, *Practical Orthopedics,* Year Book Medical Publishers, 1980.
(Author of foreword) R. G. Feldman, *Neurology for the Everyday Practice of Medicine,* Thieme-Stratton, 1984.
(Author of foreword) *The Fifteen Minute Hour,* second edition, Praeger (Westport, CT), 1993.
*Essentials of Family Practice,* Saunders, 1993.

*EDITOR*

*Selected References in Family Medicine,* Society of Teachers of Family Medicine, 1973.
(With H. F. Conn and T. W. Johnson) *Family Practice* (textbook), Saunders, 1973, 5th edition (sole editor; published as *Textbook of Family Practice),* Saunders, 1995.
*Year Book of Family Practice,* Year Book Medical Publishers, 1977-87.
*Conn's Current Therapy,* Saunders, 1984.
*Saunders Manual of Medical Practice,* Saunders, 1996.

*FILMS*

*The Office Record: Making It Work for Your Practice,* released by Network for Continuing Medical Education and Sleep Center at Pennsylvania State University, 1979.
*Disturbed Sleep: Five Case Problems,* released by Network for Continuing Medical Education, 1980.

*OTHER*

Also editor and coordinator of Volume 18 of series "Procedures for Your Practice Patient Care"; contributor to various publications, including the *Encyclopaedia Britannica,* and *The Persisting Osler II,* edited by J. A. Barondess and C. G. Roland, Krieger (Malabar, FL), 1994; also contributor of articles and reviews to journals.

*Female Patient,* associate editor, 1978—, associate editor-in-chief, 1981-86; associate editor of *Emergency Department News,* 1979-81. Also member of editorial board of *Update International,* 1973-74, *Continuing Education for the Family Physician,* 1974—, *Infectious Disease,* 1978-88, *Primary Cardiology,* 1978-89, *Archives of Internal Medicine,* 1979-90, *Journal of Clinical Psychopharmacology,* 1980-90, *Consultant,* 1981—, and *Journal of the American Medical Association,* 1982-93.

*SIDELIGHTS:* Robert E. Rakel told *CA:* "As a bibliophile since youth, I welcomed the opportunity to become involved in editing medical texts after ten years in practice, followed by three years in teaching. As of January 1, 1996, I have written or edited over 30 books. Although publishing gives me a great deal of satisfaction, I still enjoy writing because it is a stimulus to learn."

\*　　\*　　\*

## REYNOLDS, Barbara    1914-

*PERSONAL:* Born June 13, 1914, in Bristol, Gloucestershire, England; daughter of Alfred Charles (a composer) and Barbara (a singer; maiden name, Florac), Reynolds; married Lewis Thorpe (a professor of French at the University of Nottingham), September 5, 1939; children: Adrian Charles, Kerstin. *Ethnicity:* "White." *Education:* Attended schools in Detroit, MI, 1922-26, Chicago, IL, 1926-27, and St. Paul's Girls School, London, England, 1927-32; University College, University of London, B.A. (honors in French), 1935, B.A. (honors in Italian), 1936, Ph.D., 1948; Cambridge University, M.A., 1940. *Religion:* Church of England.

*ADDRESSES: Home*—220 Milton Rd., Cambridge CB4 1LQ, England; fax: 01223-424894.

*CAREER:* London School of Economics, University of London, London, England, assistant lecturer in Italian, 1937-40; Cambridge University, Cambridge, England lecturer in Italian, 1940-62; University of

Nottingham, Nottingham, England, lecturer in Italian and warden of a hall of residence, 1963-69, reader in Italian studies, 1969-78. Member of council of senate, Cambridge University, 1960-62.

*MEMBER:* Society for Italian Studies (honorary secretary, 1948-52; member of executive committee, 1946-62), University Women's Club (chair, 1988—), Dorothy L. Sayers Society (chair; president, 1994—).

*AWARDS, HONORS:* Silver Cultural medal, 1964, for services to Italian culture; Edmund Gardner Prize, 1964, for original Italian scholarship; Monselice International Prize, 1976, for translation of Lodovico Ariosto's *Orlando Furioso: The Frenzy of Orlando, a Romantic Epic;* Cavaliere Ufficiale al Merito della Repubblica Italiana, 1978.

*WRITINGS:*

(Editor and author of introduction and notes, with K. T. Butler) *Tredici novelle moderne,* Macmillan (New York City), 1947, 2nd edition, Cambridge University Press (New York City), 1959.
*The Linguistic Writings of Alessandro Manzoni: A Textual and a Chronological Reconstruction,* Heffer, 1950.
(Editor) M. A. Orr, *Dante and the Early Astronomers,* 2nd edition, Wingate, 1956.
(General editor and chief contributor) *The Cambridge Italian Dictionary,* Cambridge University Press, Volume 1, 1962, Volume 2, 1980.
(Translator with Dorothy L. Sayers) Dante Alighieri, *The Comedy of Dante Alighieri, the Florentine: Paradise,* Penguin (New York City), 1962.
(With husband, Lewis Thorpe) *Guido Farina,* Valdonega (Verona), 1967.
(Translator) Dante, *La vita nuova: Poems of Youth,* Penguin, 1969.
*Concise Cambridge Italian Dictionary,* Cambridge University Press, 1975.
(Translator) Lodovico Ariosto, *Orlando Furioso: The Frenzy of Orlando, a Romantic Epic,* Penguin, Volume 1, 1975, Volume 2, 1977.
(Editor) *Cambridge-Signorelli Italian-English, English-Italian Dictionary,* Cambridge University Press, 1986.
(Editor with William Radice) *The Translator's Art: Essays in Honor of Betty Radice,* Penguin, 1987.
*The Passionate Intellect: Dorothy L. Sayers' Encounter with Dante,* Kent State University Press (Kent, OH), 1989.
*Dorothy L. Sayers: Her Life and Soul,* St. Martin's (New York City), 1993.

*The Letters of Dorothy L. Sayers, 1899-1936: The Making of a Detective Novelist,* Hodder & Stoughton (London), 1995, St. Martin's, 1996.

Contributor of stories and poetry to the *Detroit News.* Managing editor and co-founder of *Seven: An Anglo-American Literary Review.*

*WORK IN PROGRESS: The Letters of Dorothy L. Sayers, 1937-1943: The Making of a Playwright.*

*BIOGRAPHICAL/CRITICAL SOURCES:*

PERIODICALS

*Times* (London), September 19, 1987.
*Times Literary Supplement,* May 9, 1986.

\*    \*    \*

**RIKKI**
**See DUCORNET, Erica**

\*    \*    \*

**ROBBINS, Harold   1916-**
**(Francis Kane, Harold Rubin)**

*PERSONAL:* Original name, Francis Kane; took name Harold Rubin (some sources list as Rubins) when adopted in 1927; name legally changed to Harold Robbins; born May 21, 1916, in New York, New York; married Lillian Machnivitz, 1937 (divorced, 1962); married Grace Palermo (divorced, 1992); married Jann Stapp, February 14, 1992; children (second marriage): Caryn, Adreana. *Education:* Attended public high school in New York City.

*ADDRESSES: Home*—Palm Springs, CA. *Office*—c/o Simon & Schuster, 1230 Avenue of the Americas, New York, NY 10020.

*CAREER:* Novelist. Worked as a grocery clerk, cook, cashier, errand boy, and bookies' runner, 1927-31; in food factoring business during 1930s; Universal Pictures, New York City, shipping clerk in warehouse, 1940-41, executive director of budget and planning, 1942-57.

*WRITINGS:*

NOVELS

*Never Love a Stranger,* Knopf (New York City), 1948, reprinted, Pocket Books (New York City), 1985.

*The Dream Merchants,* Knopf, 1949, reprinted, Pocket Books, 1987.

*A Stone for Danny Fisher* (also see below), Knopf, 1952, reprinted, Pocket Books, 1985.

*Never Leave Me,* Knopf, 1953, reprinted, Pocket Books, 1978.

*79 Park Avenue* (also see below), Knopf, 1953, reprinted, Pocket Books, 1982.

*Stiletto,* Dell (New York City), 1960, reprinted, 1982.

*The Carpetbaggers* (also see below), Trident Press, 1961, reprinted, Pocket Books, 1987.

*Where Love Has Gone,* Trident Press, 1962, reprinted, Pocket Books, 1987.

*The Adventurers,* Simon & Schuster (New York City), 1966, reprinted, Pocket Books, 1987.

*The Inheritors,* Trident Press, 1969, reprinted, Pocket Books, 1985.

*The Betsy,* Trident Press, 1971, reprinted, Pocket Books, 1985.

*The Pirate,* Simon & Schuster, 1974.

*The Lonely Lady,* Simon & Schuster, 1976.

*Dreams Die First,* Simon & Schuster, 1977.

*Memories of Another Day,* Simon & Schuster, 1979.

*Goodbye, Janette,* Simon & Schuster, 1981.

*Spellbinder,* Simon & Schuster, 1982.

*Descent from Xanadu,* Simon & Schuster, 1984.

*The Storyteller,* Simon & Schuster, 1985.

*The Piranhas,* Simon & Schuster, 1986.

*Three Complete Novels* (contains *The Carpetbaggers, 79 Park Avenue,* and *A Stone for Danny Fisher*), Outlet Book Company (New York City), 1994.

*The Raiders,* Simon & Schuster, 1994.

*The Stallion,* Simon & Schuster, 1996.

*Tycoon,* Simon & Schuster, 1997.

Also author of *The Survivors,* a television series for American Broadcasting Co. (ABC), 1969-70.

*ADAPTATIONS: Never Love a Stranger* was filmed by Allied Artists in 1957; *A Stone for Danny Fisher* was filmed as *King Creole* by Paramount in 1958; *The Carpetbaggers* was filmed by Paramount in 1963; *Where Love Has Gone* was filmed by Paramount in 1964; *Nevada Smith,* based on a character in *The Carpetbaggers,* was filmed by Paramount in 1966; *The Adventurers* was filmed by Paramount in

1968; *Stiletto* was filmed by Avco-Embassy in 1970; *The Betsy* was filmed by Allied Artists in 1978; *Dreams Die First* was filmed by American International in 1979; *79 Park Avenue* was filmed as a television miniseries.

*WORK IN PROGRESS: Wishing Well,* a novel that follows the development of the bottled water industry; an autobiography.

*SIDELIGHTS:* Each day, some 40,000 people buy a Harold Robbins novel, while total sales of his books stand at nearly three-quarters of a billion copies worldwide. Sales figures for individual titles are also phenomenal. *The Carpetbaggers* has gone through more than seventy printings and sold over eight million copies; *79 Park Avenue* has sold more than five and a half million copies; *Never Love a Stranger* and *Dreams Die First* have each topped three million in sales. None of Robbins's novels has sold less than 600,000 copies. The books have also been translated into thirty-nine languages and are on sale in sixty-three countries around the world. Many have been made into popular films as well.

Because of these impressive statistics, Robbins calls himself the best novelist alive. "There's not another writer being published today," he tells Leslie Hanscom of the *Pittsburgh Press,* "whose every book—every book he's ever written—is always on sale everywhere, and that's gotta mean something. . . . You can find my books anywhere in the world in any language."

The typical Robbins novel is a long, intricately plotted story loaded with illicit sex, graphic violence, and powerful conflicts between members of the international jet set. Often they are also exposes of a sort, taking the reader behind the scenes of a glamorous and respected industry to reveal the secret corruption there. Often, too, the characters are thinly veiled versions of famous people in business and high society. The best of Robbins's novels are "fun to read, full of outrageous people and complicated plot lines, not to mention lots of supposedly sizzling sex," as Joy Fielding writes in the Toronto *Globe and Mail.*

Robbins divides his books into two categories. The first are the adventure novels like *The Carpetbaggers* which focus on the Machiavellian power plays of unscrupulous captains of industry. The second type is what Robbins calls his Depression novels. These are, Dick Lochte explains in the *Los Angeles Times Book Review,* "close in style and substance to the hardboiled novels of the '30s in which tough street kids fight their way out of the proletarian jungle to achieve wealth and power." These latter books are largely based on Robbins's own life story, which in many ways sounds fantastic enough to be fiction.

Robbins began life as Francis Kane, an abandoned infant whose parents were unknown. Raised in a Roman Catholic orphanage in New York's tough Hell's Kitchen area, Robbins was placed in a series of foster homes as a youth. When the last of his foster parents, a Manhattan pharmacist, adopted him in 1927, he was given the name of Harold Rubin. He used the name of Harold Robbins when he turned to writing in the 1940s and has since made it his legal name.

At the age of fifteen, Robbins left home to begin a series of low-paying jobs in New York City. He worked as a bookies' runner, a cook, a clerk, and an errand boy, yet none of these jobs in the Depression years of the 1930s provided much opportunity for the ambitious Robbins. But while working as an inventory clerk in a grocery store, Robbins noted that fresh produce was difficult to find. The food distribution system of the time was so bad that some crops were rotting in the fields while store shelves were empty. Robbins got into the food factoring business, buying options on farmers' crops that were in demand in the city and selling the options to canning companies and wholesale grocers. By the time he was twenty, Robbins was a millionaire.

But in 1939, with war looming in the public mind, Robbins speculated in crop futures and lost. Reasoning that a major war would cut off or sharply reduce shipments of sugar, thus sending prices upward, Robbins invested his fortune in sugar at $4.85 per hundred pounds. Unfortunately, the Roosevelt administration chose to freeze food prices, and sugar was frozen at $4.65 per hundred pounds. Robbins went bankrupt. He took a job with the Universal Pictures warehouse in New York City as a shipping clerk. When he uncovered overcharges made to the company in excess of $30,000, Robbins was promoted, eventually becoming the executive director of budget and planning.

It was while working for Universal Pictures that Robbins first began to write. A vice president of the company overheard Robbins complain about a novel that the studio had bought for filming. He challenged Robbins to write a better book himself, and Robbins

took him up on the offer. The resulting six-hundred-page novel was sent to an agent and within three weeks the publishing house of Alfred Knopf accepted the book for publication.

*Never Love a Stranger,* still Robbins's personal favorite of his novels, appeared in 1948. Although the book's candid approach to sex caused the police in Philadelphia to confiscate copies, many reviewers found it a realistic portrayal of a tough New York City orphan coming of age. Drawing heavily on Robbins's own experiences on the streets of Manhattan, the story revolves around the hustlers and racketeers of that city and recounts the protagonist's efforts to find his place in the world. N. L. Rothman of the *Saturday Review of Literature* notes that "Robbins' writing is strong, his pace varied, and his invention admirable."

Robbins followed his initial success with *The Dream Merchants,* a novel set in the Hollywood film world and telling of the rise of Johnny Edge, a movie entrepreneur. The novel also traces the rise of Hollywood itself. Budd Schulberg of the *Saturday Review of Literature* finds that "the upward climb of immigrant shopkeepers to positions of power in the industry of mass entertainment makes colorful history and entertaining reading, [but] Mr. Robbins never quite succeeds in re-creating them as vital fictional characters." Citing Robbins's daring sex scenes, the reviewer for the *Christian Science Monitor,* M. W. Stoer, complains that "it is regrettable that a book with so much in it that is otherwise entertaining and tempered with warm humanity should have been allowed to lapse into such tastelessness." But the *New York Post*'s Lewis Gannett judges the novel more favorably. "Robbins," Gannett writes, "knows the great Hollywood art: he keeps his story moving, shifting expertly from tears to laughter and from desperation to triumph."

Perhaps the most critically praised of Robbins's novels is *A Stone for Danny Fisher,* the story of a poor Jewish boy's struggle to succeed in the New York of the 1930s and 1940s. James B. Lane, writing in the *Journal of Popular Culture,* claims that the book "recorded the epic battle of ethnic groups against inconsequentialness, and the disintegration of their rigid moral, ethical, and cultural standards under the stress and strain of survival." James Kelly of the *New York Times,* despite some reservations about the novel's believability, praises Robbins's "vivid characterization" and "feeling for individual scenes." Thomas Thompson of *Life* speculates that had

Robbins ended his career with *A Stone for Danny Fisher,* the novel "would have reserved him a small place in literature."

However, Robbins went on to write many more best-selling novels, few of which have received a sympathetic hearing from the critics. Evan Hunter of the *New York Times Book Review,* for instance, argues that "in true pulp style Mr. Robbins never tries to evoke anything except through cliche. . . . His people never simply say anything. They say it "shortly' or "darkly,' or they "growl' or "grunt' it." Reviewing *Spellbinder* for the *Chicago Tribune Book World,* Frederick Busch states that "the book is the paginated equivalent of television: shallow, semiliterate, made of cliches and stereotypes, full of violence and heavy breathing. People who love TV love such books." Reviewing *The Betsy* for *Books and Bookmen,* Roger Baker calls it "about as realistic and pungent as Batman. . . . The superficiality of the characters is beyond belief; the mechanical setting-up of the sexual bouts is crude; and the fact that everyone in the saga seems either vicious or bats or both doesn't help at all." Fielding even claims that Robbins's work has worsened over time: "Robbins keeps churning them out, seemingly oblivious to the fact that his already cardboard characters have turned to paper, that his plots have virtually disappeared, and that . . . his sex scenes [are] not only silly but downright pathetic."

But not all critics have been so harsh with Robbins. In his review of *The Storyteller,* for instance, Lochte admits that "in describing the art of economic survival in the 1940s—how deals were cut with Brooklyn crime bosses, Manhattan publishers and Hollywood studio heads—Robbins shows how good a writer he is. His prose is lean and straightforward, with a keen, cynical edge." Robert Graecen of *Books and Bookmen* points out that "nobody can accuse Harold Robbins of not telling a story. He knows how to handle narrative and keep the novel on the move." Lane argues that "Robbins, the bestselling American novelist, has been spurned and overlooked by literary critics because of the alleged mediocrity of his work. Nevertheless, he has won public affection by portraying identifiable life-situations in a realistic and titillating manner. His characters resemble the common man even as their bizarre exploits, fascinating sex lives and heroic struggles exude an air of Walter Mitty."

Despite the usual scorn his work receives from the critics, Robbins has fared quite well with the reading public. His books have set phenomenal sales records, while his *The Carpetbaggers* is estimated to be the fourth most-read book in history. The profits from such overwhelming popularity assuaged some of the critical barbs. For a time Robbins lived in a style as lavish as any he could create in his fiction, with mansions in several glamourous locations, private planes, Rolls-Royces and other luxury automobiles, and an 85-foot yacht moored in the Mediterranean, equipped with "with two beautiful French whores I hired as decorations," as the author recalls to Bettijane Levine of the *Los Angeles Times.*

Robbins lost most of his fortune in the late 1980s, however, "due to illness, financial naivete, divorce or indulgence," according to Levine. Sales of his books began to sag slightly at that time. *The Pirhanas* was widely criticized as a dull, muddled potboiler, and numerous reviewers claimed that Robbins had been eclipsed by younger writers "who can outsex, outviolence and outgross him," in the words of *New York Times Book Review* contributor Ed Weiner. In 1985, the writer took a serious fall while stepping out of his shower. He crushed one hip and fractured the other. Surgery meant to correct the injuries caused severe nerve damage. An implant intended to block the pain was ineffective, and he became progressively more debilitated and confined to a wheelchair. For nearly a decade, he was unable to write.

Robbins began a determined effort to restart his career in the mid-1990s, assisted by his third wife, Jann. Always wise to the ways of marketing, he began his comeback with a sequel to his most popular book, *The Carpetbaggers. The Raiders* continues the saga of Jonas Cord, the ruthless tycoon loosely based on Howard Hughes. This time around, Jonas incurs the wrath of the Mafia, dodges Senate hearings on his business practices, and discovers an illegitimate son who is now of an age to compete with his father. Joyce Slater, a reviewer for the *Atlanta Journal-Constitution,* admits that she approached the novel with some trepidation, but she lauds Robbins's effort: "This old guy's still got the right stuff." A *Publishers Weekly* reviewer also gives an approving nod to *The Raiders,* noting that while the author "hasn't matched the potboiling heat of *The Carpetbaggers* here, this is still his most entertaining novel in years. . . . Robbins can still make readers turn the pages through cliff-hanging chapters and a gallery of eccentric characters." The reviewer concludes that *The Raiders* is a "lively follow-up to a commercial fiction classic."

Robbins followed the success of *The Raiders* with another sequel. *The Stallion* picks up where *The Betsy,* his expose of the automobile industry, left off. As usual, the plot is a fast-paced blend of money, sex, and revenge. "The international art world, the Japanese impact on the auto industry and a blood feud provide a fascinating global web of subplots in bedchambers and boardrooms as Robbins spins his lascivious, melodramatic tale," a *Publishers Weekly* reviewer reports. "While this novel may not be the powerhouse *The Betsy* was, it has wheels and is a worthy successor."

Discussing the vicissitudes of his life with Levine, Robbins declared that although he now owns only one house, is largely immobilized, and lives with almost constant pain, he is "very happy. . . . I may have lost a lot, in terms of money, but I don't miss it. In fact, I have more now than I ever had. Without Jann, I'd be nothing. . . . [She] gives me such unbelievable support that it makes me realize how much I have now that I never had before. Our home, our relationship, the things we share and look forward to together. It's more meaningful than anything. . . . Maybe I'm finally growing up. . . . Maybe we all get old enough that we don't think about [sex] anymore. We think about the good things we have in our lives. The warmth and the affection."

*BIOGRAPHICAL/CRITICAL SOURCES:*

*BOOKS*

*Biography News,* Gale (Detroit), 1975.
*Contemporary Literary Criticism,* Volume 5, Gale, 1976.

*PERIODICALS*

*Advocate,* August 22, 1995, pp. 38-42.
*Atlanta Journal-Constitution,* June 23, 1991, p. N8; January 8, 1995, p. N10.
*Booklist,* October 15, 1994, p. 372; November 1, 1995, p. 435.
*Books and Bookmen,* April, 1971.
*Chicago Tribune,* August 18, 1991, section 14, p. 7; January 22, 1995, section 14, p. 6.
*Chicago Tribune Book World,* February 3, 1980; January 2, 1983.
*Christian Science Monitor,* October 28, 1949.
*Coronet,* February, 1970.
*Globe and Mail* (Toronto), January 25, 1986.
*Journal of Popular Culture,* fall, 1974.

*Life,* December 8, 1967.
*Los Angeles Times,* May 31, 1991, p. E1; March 15, 1995, pp. E1, E4.
*Los Angeles Times Book Review,* September 12, 1982; February 16, 1986; July 7, 1991, p. 6.
*Newsday,* April 16, 1966.
*Newsweek,* June 6, 1966.
*New Yorker,* March 15, 1952; June 17, 1961; November 29, 1969; April 1, 1996, p. 72.
*New York Post,* March 31, 1966; February 4, 1967; September 6, 1969; June 24, 1972.
*New York Times,* March 7, 1948; March 9, 1952; June 25, 1961; February 28, 1965.
*New York Times Book Review,* June 25, 1961; November 18, 1979; June 7, 1981; September 5, 1982; April 29, 1984; January 26, 1986; July 7, 1991, p. 7.
*People Weekly,* July 19, 1976; July 22, 1991, p. 21.
*Pittsburgh Press,* March 16, 1975.
*Publishers Weekly,* October 31, 1994, pp. 42-43; November 6, 1995, p. 81.
*Punch,* June 12, 1974.
*Saturday Review of Literature,* May 22, 1948; October 29, 1949.
*Time,* December 13, 1971, p. E7; November 11, 1974.
*Tribune Books* (Chicago), August 18, 1991.
*TV Guide,* April 11, 1970.
*Variety,* November 5, 1969.
*Virginia Quarterly Review,* autumn, 1984, p. 130.
*Washington Post,* November 29, 1979; October 5, 1983; July 25, 1991, p. D1.
*Washington Post Book World,* July 5, 1981.

*OTHER*

*I'm the World's Best Writer—There's Nothing More to Say* (television documentary), ITV Network, 1971.

\* \* \*

**ROEBUCK, Derek   1935-**

*PERSONAL:* Born January 22, 1935, in Stalybridge, England; son of John (a postal worker) and Jessie (a bookbinder) Roebuck; married Susanna Hoe (a writer), August 18, 1981; children: two sons, one daughter. *Education:* Hertford College, Oxford, M.A., 1960; University of New Zealand, M.Com. *Avocational interests:* Cricket, music.

*ADDRESSES: Home*—Flat 5B/1 Cavendish Heights, Jardine's Lookout, Hong Kong. *Office*—Law Department, City University of Hong Kong, Kowloon, Hong Kong.

*CAREER:* Solicitor in England, 1957-62; Victoria University of Wellington, Wellington, New Zealand, lecturer in law, 1962-67; University of Tasmania, Hobart, Australia, senior lecturer, 1967-69, professor of law, 1969-78; Amnesty International, London, head of research at International Secretariat, 1979-82; University of Papua New Guinea, Port Moresby, professor of law, 1982-87; City University of Hong Kong, Kowloon, professor of comparative law, head of department of law, and dean, 1987—.

*MEMBER:* Chartered Institute of Arbitrators, Law Society (England and Hong Kong), Selden Society.

*WRITINGS:*

*Law in the Study of Business,* Pergamon (Elmsford, NY), 1967.
(With Peter C. Duncan and Alexander Szakats) *Law of Commerce,* Wellington, Sweet & Maxwell, 1968.
(Editor with David E. Allan and Mary E. Hiscock) *Asian Contract Law: A Survey of Current Problems,* Melbourne University Press (Melbourne), 1969.
(With Allan, Hiscock, and others) *Credit and Security: The Legal Problem of Development Financing,* ten volumes, Queensland University Press, 1974.
*Law of Contract: Text and Materials,* Law Book Co., 1974.
(With Wilfred Burchett) *The Whores of War,* Penguin (New York City), 1977.
(With D. K. Srivastava and J. Nonggorr) *Context of Contract,* University of Papua New Guinea Press, 1984.
(With Srivastava and Nonggorr) *Pacific Contract Law,* University of Papua New Guinea Press, 1987.
*The Background of the Common Law,* Oxford University Press (New York City), 1988, 2nd edition, 1990.
*Cheques,* Hong Kong University Press (Hong Kong), 1989, 2nd edition, 1991.
(With Carole Chui) *Hong Kong Contracts,* Hong Kong University Press, 1989, 2nd edition, 1991.
(Editor) *Law Relating to Banking in Hong Kong,* Hong Kong University Press, 1993, 2nd edition, 1994.

(With Srivastava and Zafrullah) *Banking Law in Hong Kong,* Buttersworth (London), 1995.
(With Dobinson) *Introduction to the Law of the Hong Kong SAR,* Sweet & Maxwell, 1996.

*GENERAL EDITOR*

*Digest of Hong Kong Contract Law,* Peking University Press (Peking), 1995.
*Criminal Law of Hong Kong: A Descriptive Text,* Peking University Press, 1995.
*Criminal Procedure of Hong Kong: A Descriptive Text,* Peking University Press, 1996.
*Digest of Hong Kong Criminal Law,* Peking University Press, 1996.

\*    \*    \*

## ROSOWSKI, Susan J(ean) 1942-

*PERSONAL:* Born January 2, 1942, in Topeka, KS; daughter of William H. and Alice E. (Winegar) Campbell; married James R. Rosowski (a professor of botany), June 22, 1963; children: Scott Merritt, David William. *Education:* Whittier College, B.A., 1964; University of Arizona, M.A., 1967, Ph.D., 1974.

*ADDRESSES: Home*—3405 South 28th St., Lincoln, NE 68502. *Office*—Department of English, University of Nebraska, Lincoln, NE 68588-0333.

*CAREER:* University of Nebraska—Lincoln, instructor, 1971-76; University of Nebraska—Omaha, assistant professor, 1976-78, associate professor of English, 1978-82; University of Nebraska—Lincoln, associate professor, 1982-86, professor of English, 1986-91, Adele Hall Professor, 1991—. Berdahl-Rolvaag Lecturer, Augustana College, 1986; lecturer, University of California, Davis, 1989; visiting scholar, Williamette University, 1989; visiting scholar, St. Lawrence University, 1990. Co-director of National Seminar on Willa Cather, 1983; executive council member, Center for Great Plains Studies, University of Nebraska, 1984-87; member of board of governors of Willa Cather Pioneer Memorial and Educational Foundation, 1982—; member of Nebraska Center for the Book.

*MEMBER:* Council of Editors of Learned Journals, Modern Language Association, American Literature

Association, Western Literature Association (member of executive council, 1980-83; vice president, 1984-85; president-elect, 1985-86; president, 1986-87), American Association of University Professors, Society for Textual Editing, Margaret Fuller Society, Ellen Glasgow Society.

*AWARDS, HONORS:* Danforth associate, Danforth Foundation, 1980; Great Teacher Award, University of Nebraska—Omaha, 1981; Annis Chaikin Sorensen Award for distinguished teaching in the humanities, University of Nebraska—Lincoln, 1986; Fletcher Pratt fellow, Bread Loaf Writers Conference, 1989; recognition award for contributions to students, University of Nebraska—Lincoln, 1990 and 1994; received university honors program proclamation for "support and dedicated service to the honors program," University of Nebraska—Lincoln, 1991; Mildred R. Bennett Nebraska Literature Award, Nebraska Center for the Book, 1994; named honorary Nebraska author, Nebraska Literary Heritage Association, 1995.

*WRITINGS:*

(With Billie Jo Inman and Ruth Gardner) *Reading and Exercises for English I* (textbook and manual), University of Arizona (Tucson), 1967, 2nd edition, 1968.

(Editor with Helen Stauffer) *Women and Western American Literature,* Whitston Publishing (Troy, NY), 1982.

*The Voyage Perilous: Willa Cather's Romanticism,* University of Nebraska Press (Lincoln), 1986.

(Editor and contributor) *Approaches to Teaching Cather's "My Antonia,"* Modern Language Association of America (New York City), 1989.

(Editor) *Cather Studies,* University of Nebraska Press, Volume 1, 1990, Volume 2, 1993, Volume 3, in press.

(With Karl A. Ronnig) *A Lost Lady,* University of Nebraska Press, 1997.

Contributor to numerous books, including *Dictionary of Literary Biography* and *Twentieth-Century Western Writers.* General editor, with James Woodress, of "Cather Edition" series, University of Nebraska Press, 1992—. Contributor of articles on Willa Cather and other writers to journals, including *Studies in the Novel, Studies in the Literary Imagination, Novel, Western American Literature, Journal of Narrative Technique, Modern Fiction Studies, Great Plains Quarterly, Women's Studies, English Journal,*

*Prairie Schooner,* and *Literature and Belief.* Guest editor, "Cather in the Classroom" special issue, *Nebraska English Journal,* fall, 1991. Member of editorial board, *Willa Cather Pioneer Memorial Newsletter,* 1989—, and *American Literary Realism;* member of advisory board, *Prairie Schooner,* 1990—.

*WORK IN PROGRESS:* Editing further volumes in the "Cather Edition" series with James Woodress; *The Birth of a Nation: Gender, Creativity, and the Significance of the Frontier in American Literature.*

*SIDELIGHTS:* Susan J. Rosowski once told *CA:* "Work on Willa Cather has enabled me to combine my personal and professional interests in an extremely satisfying way. Cather contributed heroic women to a western American literature dominated by a masculine ethos, and she provided revelations of spiritual value in a modern tradition dominated by themes of alienation and loneliness. Cather once wrote, 'Miracles . . . rest not so much upon faces or voices or healing power coming suddenly near to us from afar off, but upon our perceptions being made finer, so that for a moment our eyes can see and our ears can hear what is there about us always.' Her writing offers the 'miracle' of such moments."

\*   \*   \*

**ROSS, Bernard L.**
**See FOLLETT, Ken(neth Martin)**

\*   \*   \*

**ROSTKOWSKI, Margaret I.   1945-**

*PERSONAL:* Surname is pronounced "Ros-*kow*-ski"; born January 12, 1945, in Little Rock, AR; daughter of Ralph Carlisle (a pathologist) and Charlotte (a registered nurse; maiden name, Leuenberger) Ellis; children: David Lee, Diovannie. *Education:* Middlebury College, B.A., 1967; University of Kansas, M.A.T., 1971. *Politics:* Democrat. *Religion:* Society of Friends (Quakers).

*ADDRESSES: Home*—2830 Marilyn Dr., Ogden, UT 84403. *Office*—Ogden High School, 2828 Harrison Blvd., Ogden, UT 94403. *Agent*—Ruth Cohen, P.O. Box 7626, Menlo Park, CA 94025.

*CAREER:* Teacher of English, French, and reading at middle schools in Ogden, Utah, 1974-84; Ogden High School, Ogden, teacher of English and writing, 1984—.

*MEMBER:* National Education Association, Society of Children's Book Writers, National Council of Teachers of English, League of Women Voters, Utah Education Association, Ogden Education Association, Ogden City Arts, Friends of Weber County Library, Delta Kappa Gamma, Phi Delta Kappa.

*AWARDS, HONORS:* Golden Kite Award from the Society of Children's Book Writers, 1986, the Children's Book Award from the International Reading Association, 1987, and the Jefferson Cup from the Virginia Library Association, 1987, all for *After the Dancing Days;* the novel was also listed among the Best Books for Young Adults and Notable Children's Books by the American Library Association, 1986.

*WRITINGS:*

*After the Dancing Days* (young adult novel), Harper (New York City), 1986.
*The Best of Friends* (young adult novel), Harper, 1989.
*Moon Dancer* (young adult novel), Harcourt (San Diego), 1995.

Member of advisory board for *Rough Draft.*

*SIDELIGHTS:* Margaret I. Rostkowski told *CA:* "My writing is a direct outgrowth of my twenty-six years of teaching. I am sustained and nourished by daily contact with my teenage writing students, who challenge me with their honesty, their questions, and their innocence. My first two books have been written from my own questions and my desire to speak to some of the concerns I see troubling my students. I feel fortunate to be able to combine the worlds of teaching and writing (hard as it often is), as my research material walks through the door every day.

"In the years before I began my first novel, I was preparing to write, gathering material, accumulating moments worth reconstructing on paper. All that came before is now material to think and write about: the summer games my brother and sister and I played behind our house in Utah; the parachute jump I did at age nineteen; the visits to the Catholic hospital where my father was a doctor; the smell of sagebrush and wet ground in southern Utah. Not high drama, but all material than can be used as impetus or embroidery for a story.

"In using memory, I never repeat an exact story but I extract the feelings. Since living with other people in families is one of the greatest challenges of life, I am drawn to write about families and the tangled thread of love, memory and hate that bind families. I am also drawn to the complexities of friendship in the teenage years, when who a young person is or may become hangs in the balance and is so vulnerable to the influence of others.

"In high school, a wonderful teacher, George Taylor, taught me all the important things I needed to know about writing and teaching writing. In the years between high school and that January day when I began *After the Dancing Days,* I attended Middlebury College and the University of Kansas, married, had two sons, taught school, traveled, loved the animals and friends that entered my life. In short, I prepared to write. And now I write as often as the rest of my life allows me to do.

"Teaching enriches my life and writing. I have the best teaching assignment possible: working with high school seniors who are about to leave for college as well as with a wide mix of students who want to write. My students give me ideas, models, language for characters, as well as an idea about which questions and issues are important at their age.

"My books begin with questions, with things I want to explore and learn about. *After the Dancing Days* began when I wondered what life would be like for someone so badly mutilated that people turned away from him in horror. *The Best of Friends* began when my students asked me to write about the period of the Vietnam War, a time they are curious about but find few adults willing to discuss. *Moon Dancer* began when I first visited the Anasazi villages in southern Utah and felt the presence of people who had been gone for six hundred years.

"I enjoy all of writing: the first excitement of falling in love with characters, the thrashings out of plot, the revision, the hard work of finding the feeling buried beneath the surface of the moment. In trying to write as well and as honestly as I can, I follow a few practices: I read widely and constantly, talk to other writers, explore the land where I live, play the piano, walk with my dogs every day. And always, in my head, I write."

**RUBEL, Marc (Reid) 1949-**

*PERSONAL:* Born June 19, 1949, in Los Angeles, CA; son of Harry and Sadie (Derfner) Rubel; married Maria Beistegui; children: two. *Education:* San Francisco State University, B.A., 1971.

*ADDRESSES: Agent*—Ronda Gomez, c/o Broder, Kurland, Webb, Uffner, 9242 Beverly Blvd., Beverly Hills, CA 91302.

*CAREER:* Writer.

*AWARDS, HONORS:* James D. Phelan Award in literature, 1972.

*WRITINGS:*

*Almost Summer* (screenplay), Universal, 1977.
*Xanadu* (screenplay), Universal, 1980.
*Windy Story* (screenplay), Towa Productions, 1982.
*Flex* (novel), St. Martin's (New York City), 1983.

(With Dori Pierson) *Obsessed With a Married Woman* (teleplay), American Broadcasting Companies (ABC-TV), 1983.
(With Pierson) *The Impostor* (teleplay), ABC-TV, 1984.
(And coproducer) *Prince of Bel Air,* ABC-TV, 1984.
*Big Business* (screenplay), Touchstone, 1988.

Contributing editor of *Surfing.*

*BIOGRAPHICAL/CRITICAL SOURCES:*

*PERIODICALS*

*Los Angeles Times Book Review,* October 16, 1983.

*       *       *

**RUBIN, Harold**
    **See ROBBINS, Harold**

# S

## SAFIRE, William 1929-

*PERSONAL:* Born William Safir, December 17, 1929; name legally changed to Safire; son of Oliver C. and Ida (Panish) Safir; married Helene Belmar Julius (a jewelry-maker), December 16, 1962; children: Mark Lindsey, Annabel Victoria. *Education:* Attended Syracuse University, 1947-49. *Politics:* Libertarian conservative.

*ADDRESSES: Office—New York Times,* 1627 Eye St. NW, Washington, DC 20006. *Agent—*Morton Janklow, 598 Madison Ave., New York, NY 10036.

*CAREER:* New York Herald-Tribune Syndicate, reporter, 1949-51; WNBC-WNBT, correspondent in Europe and Middle East, 1951; WNBC, New York City, radio-TV producer, 1954-55; Tex McCrary, Inc., vice president, 1955-60; Safire Public Relations, Inc., New York City, president, 1961-68; The White House, Washington, DC, special assistant to the President and speechwriter, 1968-73; *New York Times,* Washington, DC, columnist, 1973—. Member of Pulitzer Prize Board, 1995—. *Military service:* U.S. Army, 1952-54.

*AWARDS, HONORS:* Pulitzer Prize for distinguished commentary, 1978, for articles on Bert Lance.

*WRITINGS:*

*The Relations Explosion,* Macmillan (New York City), 1963.
(With M. Loeb) *Plunging into Politics,* McKay (New York City), 1964.

*The New Language of Politics,* Random House (New York City), 1968, 3rd edition published as *Safire's Political Dictionary: The New Language of Politics,* 1978, revised and enlarged edition published as *Safire's New Political Dictionary: The Definitive Guide to the New Language of Politics,* 1993.
*Before the Fall,* Doubleday (New York City), 1975, published as *Before the Fall: An Inside View of the Pre-Watergate White House,* Da Capo Press (New York City), 1988.
*Full Disclosure* (novel; Literary Guild selection), Doubleday, 1977, limited edition with illustrations by George Jones, Franklin Library, 1977.
*On Language* (collection of weekly columns), Times Books (New York City), 1980.
*Safire's Washington,* Times Books, 1980.
*What's the Good Word?,* Times Books, 1982.
(Compiler with brother, Leonard Safir) *Good Advice,* Times Books, 1982.
*I Stand Corrected: More on Language* (collection of weekly columns), Times Books, 1984.
*Take My Word for It: More on Language* (collection of weekly columns), Times Books, 1986.
*Freedom* (novel; Book-of-the-Month Club main selection), Doubleday, 1987.
*You Could Look It Up: More on Language,* Times Books, 1988.
*Words of Wisdom,* Fireside Books (St. Louis), 1990.
*Language Maven Strikes Again* (collection of weekly columns), Holt (New York City), 1990.
*Coming to Terms* (collection of weekly columns), Doubleday, 1991.
*The First Dissident: The Book of Job in Today's Politics,* Random House, 1992.
(Compiler and author of introduction) *Lend Me Your Ears: Great Speeches in History,* Norton (New York City), 1992.

(Compiler with L. Safir) *Good Advice on Writing: Writers Past and Present on How to Write Well,* Simon & Schuster (New York City), 1992.

*Quoth the Maven* (collection of weekly columns), Random House, 1993.

*In Love with Norma Loquendi* (collection of weekly columns), Random House, 1994.

*Sleeper Spy* (novel), Random House, 1995.

*Watching My Language* (collection of weekly columns), Random House, 1996.

Also author of *Fumblerules: A Light-Hearted Guide to Grammar and Good Usage,* 1990, and, with L. Safir, *Leadership,* 1990. Author of political column "Essay," in *New York Times,* and "On Language" column in *New York Times Magazine.* Contributor to *Harvard Business Review, Cosmopolitan, Playboy, Esquire, Reader's Digest, Redbook,* and *Collier's.*

*SIDELIGHTS:* William Safire has worn several hats in his varied career: speechwriter for President Richard Nixon, language commentator for the Sunday *New York Times Magazine,* political commentator for the *New York Times,* novelist, and historian. Safire does not pull his punches, and has made both friends and enemies on all sides of political and linguistic issues. According to J. A. Barnes in the *National Review,* "whether you love [Safire] or you hate him, you cannot afford to skip over him." *Time* contributor Paul Gray appreciates Safire's lack of rigidity: "William Safire has largely made his reputation through epigrammatic feistiness and hit-and-run repartee. . . . His twice-a-week columns continue to display reportorial zeal and refreshing unpredictability." Safire is also quick to alert his readers to governmental figures who run amuck. *Washington Post* contributor Eleanor Randolph notes: "The years in public relations and the White House seem to have given [Safire] an ear for sour notes on both sides—among those in power in the government and those in power in the press." And when speaking of his commentaries on English-language usage, some critics view Safire as an institution. David Thomas in the *Christian Science Monitor* observes that "Safire may be the closest we have to a clearinghouse for hearing, seeing, and testing how we're doing with the language."

Safire began his career as a public relations writer, took a job as speechwriter for Spiro Agnew in the 1968 presidential campaign, and eventually became a senior speechwriter for President Nixon. He left his position, however, before the bugging of Watergate and was finishing his memoir of the Nixon White House when the president resigned. Because of the timing of its completion, *Before the Fall* almost missed publication entirely. The book painted a fairly positive view of the administration and was rejected by William Morrow, who also demanded back their advance. But eventually the book was published by Doubleday.

*Newsweek's* Walter Clemons calls *Before the Fall* "a puffy, lightweight concoction, served up for the faithful." Clemons complains that "Safire is protective of Nixon, reserving his harshest judgment for the deviousness and drive for power he attributes to Henry Kissinger." But *Atlantic* contributor Richard Todd gives the book credit for being "full of interesting data on the theme that Safire identifies as crucial to the Nixon Administration: its sense of the world as "us' against "them.'" And Daniel Schorr, in the *New York Times Book Review,* recounts Safire's description of Nixon's desire for "understanding and perspective," and notes: "If Nixon gets the kind of understanding he wants, this book will surely have helped a lot. In any event [*Before the Fall*] . . . will still be an enormous contribution to understanding the phenomenon called Nixon."

Safire's first novel, *Full Disclosure,* also deals with a president in danger of losing his office. His fictional leader, Sven Ericson, has been blinded from a bump on the head received while closeted in a Pullman berth with a female member of the White House press corps. The plot concerns whether the Twenty-fifth Amendment, regarding disabled presidents, will be used to oust Ericson. *New Republic* contributor Stephen Hess says *Full Disclosure's* strength comes from the fact that it "is about presidential politics by a man who intimately knows presidential politics." But a *Saturday Review* contributor questions the work's literary value, claiming that the story's political puzzle is "the book's one redeeming feature." The critic adds, however, that by exploring Ericson's uncertain position, "Safire not only cooks up a fiery stewpot of political ambitions, but produces a dramatic warning of the [Twenty-fifth Amendment's] possible abuse."

Safire's columns on language for the *New York Times* are widely read and enjoyed. In several books, he has reprinted column selections and his readers' replies. *On Language* gives examples of correct and incorrect usage, and explores word origins as well. In the *Saturday Review,* John Ciardi explains Safire's position toward communication in *On Language* as "neither an [etymologist] nor an expert on usage. He is a keen reporter at his splendid best in such reports as the one here labeled 'Kissingerese,' a star coverage of the idiom of Henry the Pompous." Ciardi continues: "I am engaged and rewarded by this maculate Safire, and even more so when he is attended by his letterwriters." Other reviewers also enjoy Safire's interaction with his readers. "Although what Safire has discovered about word origins and their current usage made good reading, the inclusion of what his readers have to add makes them even more so," states *Christian Science Monitor* contributor Maria Lenhart. And, according to D. J. Enright in the *Encounter,* "Safire's relations with his Irregulars are highly interesting, and help to generate much of the comedy in this almost continuously entertaining book."

*Freedom,* a heavily detailed historical novel, is the author's longest work. When Safire submitted the manuscript to his publisher after working on it for seven years, the triple-spaced copy ran 3,300 pages. When Doubleday found the book too large to bind, Safire had to cut at least one section; still, the final product was 1,152 pages. In *Freedom,* Safire again uses his Washington experience to describe the capital between June of 1861, and January 1, 1863. The story opens with Lincoln's issue of the Emancipation Proclamation and focuses on the president's role during the early Civil War years. *New York Review of Books* contributor C. Vann Woodward describes Safire's Lincoln as "a Lincoln racked by debilitating depression (which he called melancholia), agonizing over the daily choice of evils, and seeking relief in one of his that-reminds-me stories. He is by turns Saint Sebastian, Machiavelli, Pericles, and an oversize, countrified Puck."

Safire explains his attitude toward Lincoln to Alvin P. Sanoff for *U.S. News & World Report:* "It's impossible to approach Lincoln honestly with a spirit of reverence and awe. He is a secular and not a religious figure. He wasn't martyred; he was assassinated. Approaching Lincoln as a political figure, which is what he was, you can appreciate him." Still, Safire concludes that "I've come to the conclusion that he was, indeed, the greatest President, with the possible exception of Washington, because he was so complex and so purposeful. When you see him with all the warts, when you see his drawbacks and his failures and his shortcomings, then you see his greatness." The author explains to *Publishers Weekly* contributor Trish Todd that one of the greatest issues facing the U.S. government at that time is the contemporary problem of "how much freedom must be

taken away from individuals in order to protect the freedom of the nation." And while Safire feels that Lincoln occasionally went too far in suspending individual liberties, he told Eleanor Randolph for the *Washington Post:* "If [Lincoln] were running today, I'd vote for him. I think he had his priorities straight." Randolph continues, "straight priorities mean having a core of beliefs that are worth all the harassment and trouble that come with leadership."

While *Freedom* has received much popular and critical acclaim, some reviewers dislike the book's focus. Woodward feels Safire has almost neglected the presence of blacks in the Civil War: "One book of the nine into which the novel is divided is indeed entitled 'The Negro,' but it is largely concerned with other matters, with only four or five pages on blacks, and most of that is what whites said or did about them, not what they said and did themselves." Woodward adds, "as a whole [blacks] are granted fewer than twenty-five lines of their own to speak. None of their prominent leaders are introduced, and Frederick Douglass is not mentioned. . . . Nowhere does this huge book face up squarely to the impact of slavery and the complexities of race." Other critics have found the book too lengthy and detailed. But while *Los Angeles Times Book Review* contributor Winston Groom finds the book "often ponderous, tedious and maddening to plow through," he feels that reading *Freedom* is worth the effort: "It's a story that ought to be read by every American, and for that matter everyone else in the world, because it so graphically presents how our grand experiment in democracy has actually worked in a time of extreme stress. . . . [*Freedom*] enlivens and elucidates a period of American history that remains crucial for anyone with the faintest interest in what we, the American people, are all about." And Chicago *Tribune Books* contributor John Calvin Batchelor calls *Freedom* "a mountain to dazzle and assault," states that it is "loving, cogent, bottomlessly researched, [and] passionately argued," and claims the book "is guaranteed to exhaust the reader like no other intellectual endeavor, yet in the end it delivers a miracle."

Safire ventured further into new writing territory with *The First Dissident: The Book of Job in Today's Politics.* Safire had long been fascinated by Job, the Biblical figure whose faith was tested by his many troubles and who sought an explanation from God. Published in an American presidential election year, 1992, the book led Kenneth L. Woodward to report in *Newsweek:* "In this campaign season's most improbable political meditation, Safire has published . . .

a sometimes wise and frequently witty demonstration of how Job's confrontation with Ultimate Authority can illuminate the power struggles in Washington and vice versa." Safire's interpretation of Job is a far cry from the most widely held view of him. He is usually held up as a model of long-suffering patience, but Safire views him as a righteous, rebellious, "even blasphemous" figure "who demands that God explain himself or stand guilty of abusing his own authority," explains Woodward. "He is in short, the original political contrarian, a fellow who, in another era, might just find work as a brave, truth-telling columnist."

*Christian Science Monitor* contributor Marshall Ingwerson notes that extensive study informs the book, and he remarks that "Safire's own concept of God is of a powerful—but not all-powerful—creator who leaves it to man to carve out justice in the world." But while Ingwerson and Woodward both credit the author with serious theological intent, another reviewer, Jonathan Dorfman, finds *The First Dissident* a disappointing, superficial book. Writing in the *Washington Post Book World,* he finds promise in Safire's stated premise, "to discern political lessons in Job and the book's relevance to modern politics," but goes on to say: "You begin the book with high expectations. Five minutes later, you realize that the author reduces the gravity of Job to a trifle with all the moral freight of 'Larry King Live.'" Dorfman further castigates Safire for trivializing Job's suffering by comparing him to politicians such as Gary Hart and Bert Lance. The reviewer deems Safire's discussion of Job and Lincoln more appropriate, though: "In his meditation on Lincoln and Job, Safire drops his street-smart style; the tone is somber, fit for the gravity of the subject. . . . [The essay is] an elegiac lament that atones for much of his frivolity on the angry howl of Job."

Safire tried another new genre in 1995 with *Sleeper Spy,* a novel of espionage. *New Yorker* reviewer David Remnick characterizes it as "an old-fashioned Washington-Moscow thriller. It features a hundred billion dollars, a sexy network newsie, a K.G.B. mole, lots of secret agents, and a hero who is . . . 'the world's greatest reporter.'" In the story, a Russian spy who has been working in finance in the United States is given a small fortune to invest and increases it many times over. With the breakup of the Soviet Union and the deaths of his spymasters, however, the agent is left on his own, pursued by various factions. Reviewers are mixed in their assessment of Safire's skill in handling this type of thriller.

"Interesting as all this is conceptually, it makes for a highly cerebral and talky novel—a mind game," finds Morton Kondracke, contributor to the *New York Times Book Review,* adding, "Toward the end the reader is made to feel that the writer is having most of the fun, some of it at the expense of the reader, who's suddenly told without warning that things presumed to be facts simply aren't." Yet Kondracke allows that *Sleeper Spy* "certainly does engage the mind and, on a few occasions, stir the pulse." *New York Times* reviewer George Stade is critical of Safire's handling of plot and dialogue, saying the author "has the skills of a reporter but not those of a storyteller."

Remnick is more generous, calling *Sleeper Spy* "a great big ice-cream cone of a book: predictable, sweet fun." Jonathan Kirsch also finds much to praise. In the *Los Angeles Times* he dubs *Sleeper Spy* "a smartly done spy story with enough surprises to set it apart from the ordinary run of espionage fiction." The book, he says, "crackles with wit and savvy." Kirsch concludes: "The author enjoys himself most when he gives us the world according to William Safire, a world beset with plots and conspiracies, a world in which brains count and the good guys (and gals) win."

## BIOGRAPHICAL/CRITICAL SOURCES:

### BOOKS

*Contemporary Literary Criticism,* Volume 10, Gale (Detroit), 1979.

### PERIODICALS

*Atlantic,* July, 1975; March, 1979.
*Boston Globe,* May 17, 1995, p. 5; July 25, 1995, p. 6.
*Chicago Tribune,* August 4, 1988; November 10, 1993, section 7, p. 4.
*Christian Science Monitor,* January 12, 1981; December 31, 1984; January 11, 1993, p. 15.
*Commentary,* April, 1993, p. 56.
*Economist,* November 21, 1992, p. 107.
*Encounter,* April, 1981.
*Entertainment Weekly,* November 10, 1995, p. 55.
*Esquire,* April, 1994, p. 84.
*Forbes,* October 26, 1992, p. 26.
*Los Angeles Times,* November 14, 1992, p. B4; September 10, 1993, p. E10; September 20, 1995, p. E4.

*Los Angeles Times Book Review,* August 30, 1987; December 20, 1992, p. 2.

*National Catholic Reporter,* February 5, 1993, p. 25.

*National Review,* November 28, 1980; March 29, 1993, p. 66.

*New Republic,* July 9-16, 1977; February 16, 1987.

*Newsweek,* March 3, 1975; August 31, 1987; November 9, 1992, p. 81; January 31, 1994, p. 41.

*New York,* December 21, 1992, p. 107.

*New Yorker,* August 21, 1995, pp. 116, 118.

*New York Review of Books,* September 24, 1987.

*New York Times,* November 5, 1992, p. C20; September 4, 1995, p. A15.

*New York Times Book Review,* February 23, 1975; July 21, 1991, p. 18; November 8, 1992, p. 14; October 31, 1993, p. 9; September 18, 1994, p. 20; September 17, 1995, p. 15.

*People,* December 4, 1995, p. 36.

*Playboy,* November, 1992, p. 63.

*Publishers Weekly,* April 30, 1982; March 29, 1987; April 12, 1991, p. 51; August 10, 1992, p. 61; June 7, 1993, p. 58; July 11, 1994, p. 70; July 31, 1995, p. 67.

*Saturday Review,* July 9, 1977; November, 1980.

*Time,* August 31, 1987; December 11, 1995, p. 95.

*Tribune Books* (Chicago), August 9, 1987; October 17, 1993, p. 8; September 17, 1995, p. 6.

*U.S. News & World Report,* August 24, 1987.

*Vanity Fair,* November, 1992, p. 148.

*Washingtonian,* August, 1991, p. 66.

*Washington Post,* August 24, 1987; November 23, 1992, p. B2; December 1, 1995, p. F1.

*Washington Post Book World,* August 27, 1995, p. 5.

*Wilson Library Bulletin,* March, 1994, p. 95.

 

\*    \*    \*

 

## SEYMOUR-SMITH, Martin    1928-

*PERSONAL:* Born April 24, 1928, in London, England; son of Frank and Marjorie (Harris) Seymour-Smith; married Janet de Glanville, September 10, 1952; children: Miranda Catherine, Charlotte Consuelo. *Education:* St. Edmund Hall, Oxford University, B.A., (with honors), 1951. *Politics:* Independent. *Religion:* Independent.

*ADDRESSES: Home*—36 Holliers Hill, Bexhill-on-Sea, Sussex, England. *Agent*—John Johnson Esq., 10 Suffield House, 79 Davies St., London W.1, England.

*CAREER:* Tutor to Robert Graves's son in Deya, Mallorca, 1951-54; schoolmaster in various schools, 1954-59; freelance writer, 1959—; poetry editor, *Isis,* 1950-51; editorial assistant, *The London Magazine,* 1955-56; poetry editor, *Truth,* 1955-57; poetry editor and critic, *Scotsman,* 1964-66; literary adviser, Hodder & Stoughton, 1963-65; general editor, Gollancz Classics, 1967-69. *Military service:* British Army, served in Middle East, 1946-48; became sergeant.

*WRITINGS:*

POEMS

(With Rex Taylor and Terence Hards) *Poems,* Longmans, Green (London), 1952.

*Martin Seymour-Smith,* Fantasy Press (London), 1953.

*All Devils Fading* (poems), Divers Press (Mallorca), 1953.

*Tea with Miss Stockport* (poems), Abelard Schuman (London), 1963.

*Reminiscences of Norma: Poems, 1963-1970,* Barnes & Noble (New York City), 1970.

*Wilderness: 36 Poems, 1972-93,* Greenwich Exchange (London), 1994.

NONFICTION

*Robert Graves* (critical monograph), Longmans, Green, for British Council, 1956, revised edition, 1970.

*Bluff Your Way in Literature,* Wolfe (London), 1966, Cowles (New York City), 1968.

*Poets Through Their Letters,* Holt (New York City), 1969.

*Fallen Women: A Sceptical Enquiry into the Treatment of Prostitutes, Their Clients and Their Pimps, in Literature,* Nelson (London), 1969.

*Guide to Modern World Literature,* Wolfe, 1973, published as *Funk and Wagnalls Guide to Modern World Literature,* Funk & Wagnalls (New York City), 1973, revised edition published as *The New Guide to Modern World Literature,* Bedrick (New York City), 1985.

*The Dent Dictionary of Fictional Characters,* Dent (London), 1974, revised edition published as *Dictionary of Fictional Characters,* The Writer (Boston), 1992.

*Sex and Society,* Hodder & Stoughton (London), 1975.

*Who's Who in Twentieth-Century Literature,* Holt, 1976.

*An Introduction to Fifty European Novels,* Pan Books (London), 1979, published as *A Reader's Guide to Fifty European Novels,* Barnes & Noble, 1980.

*The New Astrologer,* Sidgwick & Jackson (London), 1981, Macmillan (New York City), 1982.

*Robert Graves: His Life and Work,* Hutchinson (London), 1982, Holt, 1983.

*How to Succeed in Poetry without Really Reading or Writing,* Anvil Press (London), 1986.

*Rudyard Kipling,* St. Martin's (New York City), 1989.

*Hardy,* St. Martin's, 1994.

*Gnosticism: The Path of Inner Knowledge,* Harper (San Francisco), 1996.

*EDITOR*

*Shakespeare's Sonnets* (critical edition), Heinemann, 1963, revised edition, 1964.

(Compiler) *A Cupful of Tears: Sixteen Victorian Novelettes,* Wolfe, 1964.

Ben Jonson, *Every Man in His Humour* (critical edition), Benn, 1966, Methuen (London), 1986.

(With James Reeves) *A New Canon of English Poetry,* Barnes & Noble, 1967.

(With Reeves) Andrew Marvell, *The Poems of Andrew Marvell,* Barnes & Noble, 1969.

*Cumulative Index to the Shakespeare Quarterly, Volume 1-15, 1950-1964,* AMS Press, 1969.

(With Reeves) *Inside Poetry,* Barnes & Noble, 1970.

*Longer Elizabethan Poems,* Barnes & Noble, 1972.

Robert Graves, *Collected Poems,* Cassell (London), 1975, revised edition, 1986.

(With Reeves) Walt Whitman, *Selected Poems of Walt Whitman,* Heinemann (London), 1976.

*The English Sermon, Volume 1: 1550-1650,* Carcanet (Cheadle, England), 1976.

Thomas Hardy, *The Mayor of Casterbridge,* Penguin (London), 1978.

*Novels and Novelists: A Guide to the World of Fiction,* St. Martin's, 1980.

Joseph Conrad, *Nostromo,* Penguin, 1984.

Conrad, *The Secret Agent: A Simple Tale,* Penguin, 1985.

*From Bed to Verse,* Souvenir (London), 1991.

(With Andrew Kimmens) *World Authors, 1900-1950,* H. W. Wilson, 1996.

Contributor to *New Statesman, Truth, Encounter, Times Literary Supplement, Spectator, Financial Times, London Magazine, Sunday Telegraph, Listener,* and other periodicals, and to British Broadcasting Corp. European service.

Seymour-Smith's papers are housed at the Harry Ransom Humanities Research Center, University of Texas at Austin.

*SIDELIGHTS:* Martin Seymour-Smith writes successful books in a wide variety of genres: poems, guides, critical editions, anthologies, collections of letters, sociological texts, and literary dictionaries. He wrote the first monograph on poet and novelist Robert Graves. He has edited works by such prominent English writers as William Shakespeare, Joseph Conrad, Thomas Hardy, and Ben Jonson. Most notable, however, are Seymour-Smith's biographies of such prominent literary figures as Robert Graves, Rudyard Kipling, and Thomas Hardy. Writing in the *Dictionary of Literary Biography,* Angus Somerville calls Seymour-Smith "an uncompromisingly honest and independent writer [who] has never been less than interesting and usually succeeds in challenging his readers' assumptions."

As the author of many literary guides, Seymour-Smith has provided succinct overviews to much of the world's literature. Christopher Lehmann-Haupt, writing in the *New York Times,* calls *The New Guide to Modern World Literature* a book which shows Seymour-Smith's "omnivorous knowledge and his sharp and outspoken opinions." Tom D'Evelyn, writing in the *Christian Science Monitor,* praises the book for how well it "guides the general reader through the labyrinth of modern national languages and literature," and for putting "a vast number of texts in context, both cultural and literary; yet, for all its size (nearly fourteen hundred pages), the effect of the book is intimate." Critic Claire Tomalin, speaking of the book *Poets Through Their Letters* in the *New Statesman,* praises it as "much more than an anthology; it is a grand magpie's nest stuffed with anecdotes, discoveries, quotations, textual analysis, lively arguments with other critics and biographers; a few raucous cries of abuse issue from it too." She notes positively that the work is further enhanced by the fact that "as a practicing poet himself, the author advances some of his own ideas about the nature of poetic activity."

Speaking to *CA,* Seymour-Smith has explained this relationship between the poet, critic, and poet-as-critic by stating that his "chief interest is in poetry and in writing poetry, an activity I associate directly with the way I live. As a critic I am partly preoccupied with presentation of original and unmodernized texts. As an annotator my approach is psychological, although I try to argue, initially, from the text rather than from the facts of the author's life. I distrust abstractions, and am opposed to (although sympathetic with) the views of such 'scientific' critics as Wimsatt. My general approach is eclectic."

The first of Seymour-Smith's three major literary biographies, upon which a large portion of his scholarly reputation rests, is *Robert Graves: His Life and Work.* The seed for this work was planted in the years 1951 to 1954 when Seymour-Smith, just graduated from Oxford and developing his poetic skills, was employed by Robert Graves as his son's tutor on the Spanish island of Mallorca. Graves, a prolific writer of nearly 140 books, is best known for *I, Claudius,* an historical novel set in ancient Rome and adapted into a popular television series and *Goodbye to All That,* a book Donald Hall in the *New York Times Book Review* calls "arguably the finest English account of the Great War." Despite his many books in a variety of genres, Graves always considered himself to be primarily a poet, and it is this argument that Seymour-Smith presents in his biography of the author.

Readers learn much from Seymour-Smith's biography of Graves. He tells of the marriage triangle between Graves, his first wife Nancy Nicholson, militant feminist and mother of their four children, and American poet Laura Riding. He further reveals how the arrival of Irish journalist Geoffrey Phibbs into the circle led not only to Riding's scandalous suicide attempt, but also to the eventual breakup of the marriage of Graves and Nicholson. The scandal aside, Seymour-Smith shows how collaboration between Riding and Graves led to such successful literary endeavors as publication of *A Survey of Modernist Poetry* in 1927. Seymour-Smith suggests that Graves was first and foremost a writer of love poems to a white goddess, and argues that the role of the white goddess was played by Graves' wife Nancy, lover Laura Riding, second wife Beryl Graves, and a variety of young female "muses" on Mallorca between 1950 and 1975.

Kieran Quinlan in *World Literature Today* writes that "this volume should provoke sympathetic examination of Seymour-Smith's contention that Graves is 'the foremost English-language love poet of this century.'" Novelist and critic Anthony Burgess, writing in the *Times Literary Supplement,* concludes that "Seymour-Smith has produced an admirable biography and a shrewd commentary on Graves's work."

In his introduction to *Rudyard Kipling: A Biography,* the second of his major works on literary figures, Seymour-Smith states that in writing the book he "speculated boldly" concerning the life of Kipling. This bold speculation produced a book that caused controversy when it was first released in England. David Trotter in the *Times Literary Supplement* explains that Seymour-Smith's "thesis is that Kipling was a closet homosexual," and that "his method is to review the major events of Kipling's life and the major writings in the light of his bold speculations. Homosexuality becomes the key to all mythologies." Such events as Kipling's relationship with Harry Holloway, a young man with whom he shared a room as a boy while his parents were in India, his friendship first with American publisher Wolcott Balestier and then his marriage to Wolcott's sister, Caroline, are seen by Seymour-Smith as evidence for a latent homosexuality overlooked by previous biographers of Kipling. Craig Raine, reviewing the biography for *Punch,* notes further that Seymour-Smith's "boldest speculation" is that Kipling's book *Stalky & Co.* "makes it clear that Kipling found flogging a turn-on, while [the story] "Danny Deever" shows that, William Burroughs-like, Kipling was unhealthily interested in hanging." As Charles DeFanti asserts in *Children's Literature,* Seymour-Smith is "a thoroughly psychoanalytic (though not Freudian) biographer, who places much weight on trauma and psychic lesions in the formation of human character" and whose "case is convincing, since he is the first biographer to have had full access to the surviving Kipling archives since the death of Elsie Kipling." Nonetheless, as Kate Chisholm states in the *Times Educational Supplement,* "when Martin Seymour-Smith tried to breathe life into his biography of Rudyard Kipling, he aroused the wrath of the British Establishment." Still, DeFanti reminds readers that "no one biography is capable of presenting the basic 'truth,'" so readers "must insist upon interpretation, preferably using competing versions of the life."

Seymour-Smith's third major literary biography is *Hardy,* a life of English novelist Thomas Hardy, which James Buchan in the *Spectator* calls "a typical old-fashioned literary biography, full of learning and sometimes flashing with insight." Hardy is considered by many writers a difficult subject for a biography. Hardy himself burned his personal papers after the death of his first wife, then wrote an autobiography which he left to his second wife, Florence, to publish under her own name as a biography. But Florence revised sections of the book to put Hardy's first wife, Emma, in a bad light. Hardy was also a man who tended to reinvent himself, enjoying careers as an architect, then a novelist, and finally a poet. Samuel Hynes in the *Times Literary Supplement* believes that Seymour-Smith is "right to insist on Hardy's intellectual capacities and range of knowledge," that he "does another good turn by insisting that Hardy was a religious man," that he is "sensible and sympathetic" to Hardy's sexuality, and that he treats Hardy's social personality in a generous way. Poet and critic Brad Leithauser, reviewing the book in *Time,* finds that Seymour-Smith does "an admirable job of promoting Hardy's poetry above all else" since his "life makes clear that his poetry is paramount."

Seymour-Smith's biography of Hardy is over 800 pages long and, as Adam Thorpe notes in the *Los Angeles Times Book Review,* the book "is not scholarly, or at least eschews the usual trappings of that ilk such as footnotes, appendices and exhaustive bibliographies." But James Kincaid in the *New York Times Book Review* nonetheless finds the biography to be "massively enjoyable. As it sets about savagely refuting all other lives of Hardy, it slips in a very intelligent, oddly delicate story of its own," producing a Hardy who "lives a life that seems far more canny, flexible, good-natured and certainly engaging than any we had been presented with before."

## BIOGRAPHICAL/CRITICAL SOURCES:

### BOOKS

*Dictionary of Literary Biography,* Volume 155: *Twentieth-Century British Literary Biographers,* Gale (Detroit), 1995.

### PERIODICALS

*AB Bookman's Weekly,* February 6, 1967, p. 511.
*American Literature,* December, 1985, p. 707.
*American Reference Book Annual,* 1977, p. 572; 1982, p. 623; 1986, p. 424; 1993, p. 488.
*Atlanta Journal and Atlanta Constitution,* February 4, 1990, p. L8.
*Atlantic,* January, 1995, p. 108.
*Best Sellers,* May, 1983, p. 56.
*Biography,* fall, 1984, p. 363.
*Booklist,* December 1, 1969, p. 433; September 15, 1973, p. 78, 114; September 15, 1976, p. 205; July 15, 1980, p. 1650; March 15, 1983, p. 942; April 15, 1986, p. 1196; August, 1992, p. 2035; December 15, 1994, p. 730.

*Books,* August, 1987, p. 19; March, 1989, p. 24.
*Books and Bookmen,* June, 1971, p. 59; July, 1971, p. 61; September, 1971, p. 18; August, 1973, p. 16; June, 1976, p. 7; August, 1982, p. 23; September, 1983, p. 37.
*Book World,* April 6, 1969, p. 6.
*Boston Globe,* December 18, 1994, p. B16.
*British Book News,* April, 1980, p. 243; September, 1982, p. 569; April, 1987, p. 214.
*Chicago Tribune,* January 15, 1995, p. 5.
*Children's Literature,* 1992, p. 180.
*Choice,* May, 1970, p. 387; January, 1974, p. 1703; October, 1976, p. 962; December, 1976, p. 1298; July, 1981, p. 1530; May, 1983, p. 1292; November, 1985, p. 430.
*Christian Century,* March 23, 1993, p. 288.
*Christian Science Monitor,* July 5, 1985, p. B2.
*Contemporary Review,* September, 1973, p. 163.
*Critic,* January, 1981, p. 8.
*Economist,* May 29, 1982, p. 97; August 24, 1985, p. 84.
*Encounter,* August, 1971, p. 73; July, 1973, p. 55.
*Esquire,* September, 1985, p. 20.
*Guardian Weekly,* February 27, 1971, p. 18; May 30, 1976, p. 22; May 23, 1982, p. 22; February 27, 1983, p. 18.
*Hudson Review,* winter, 1983, p. 735; summer, 1991, p. 189.
*Illustrated London News,* winter, 1990, p. 94.
*Kliaat Young Adult Paperback Book Guide,* winter, 1978, p. 21.
*Library Journal,* April 15, 1969, p. 1635; August, 1973, p. 2264; April 15, 1977, p. 874; August, 1980, p. 1637; October 15, 1982, p. 1993; January 15, 1983, p. 126; February 1, 1985, p. 86; June 1, 1985, p. 117; January, 1995, p. 103.
*Listener,* February 26, 1970, p. 266; March 25, 1971, p. 381; January 22, 1976, p. 91; May 20, 1982, p. 23.
*London Review of Books,* February 3, 1983, p. 8; March 16, 1989, p. 13; September 8, 1994, p. 18.
*Los Angeles Times Book Review,* March 6, 1983, p. 1; October 13, 1985, p. 10; January 15, 1995, p. 1.
*National Review,* January 21, 1983, p. 58; March 18, 1983, p. 334.
*New Republic,* February 28, 1983, p. 32; March 6, 1995, p. 42.
*New Statesman,* January 31, 1969, p. 159; January 2, 1970, p. 20; March 19, 1971, p. 393; December 5, 1975, p. 727; April 22, 1977, p. 538; December 20, 1985, p. 62.
*New York Review of Books,* August 18, 1983, p. 38.

*New York Times,* January 25, 1983, p. 25; November 25, 1985, p. 19.

*New York Times Book Review,* March 20, 1983, p. 14; December 18, 1994, p. 3.

*Observer* (London), April 4, 1971, p 36; June 10, 1973, p. 37; November 30, 1975, p 27; June 6, 1976, p. 29; December 7, 1980, p. 29; May 16, 1982, p. 30; September 25, 1983, p. 31; December 1, 1985, p. 17; May 24, 1987, p. 24; July 19, 1987, p. 23; February 19, 1989, p. 44; October 21, 1990, p. 59; January 30, 1994, p. 21.

*Publishers Weekly,* February 17, 1969, p. 154; June 6, 1980, p. 78; May 26, 1982, p. 859; December 3, 1982, p. 54; October 24, 1989, p. 47; November 17, 1989, p. 39.

*Punch,* July 4, 1973, p. 25; February 10, 1989, p. 39.

*Reference and Research Book News,* May, 1993, p. 39.

*Reference Services Review,* July, 1973, p. 21.

*Scotsman,* November 9, 1963.

*Southern Humanities Review,* summer, 1984, p. 277.

*Spectator,* September 8, 1967, p. 275; March 7, 1969, p. 306; November 29, 1969, p. 757; June 23, 1973, p. 788; June 5, 1982, p. 22; January 29, 1994, p. 39.

*Time,* February 7, 1983, p. 80; January 16, 1995, p. 74.

*Times Educational Supplement,* December 26, 1986, p. 23; January 11, 1991, p. 30; February 4, 1994, p. 12.

*Times Literary Supplement,* October 14, 1965, p. 912; February 13, 1969, p. 154; March 12, 1970, p. 278; April 14, 1972, p. 429; October 26, 1976, p. 1359; January 28, 1977, p. 111; July 25, 1980, p. 832; May 21, 1982, p. 547; July 9, 1982, p. 731; February 3, 1989, p. 99; March 18, 1994, p. 3; August 2, 1995, p. 840.

*USA Today,* December 13, 1985, p. 4D.

*Virginia Quarterly Review,* winter, 1981, p. 18; autumn, 1983, p. 124; summer, 1990, p. 91.

*Wall Street Journal,* December 27, 1994, p. A14.

*Washington Post,* March 4, 1990, p. 5; January 5, 1995, p. 3.

*Washington Post Book World,* September 28, 1980, p. 8; January 30, 1983, p. 1; March 4, 1990, p. 5; January 15, 1995, p. 3.

*West Coast Review of Books,* March, 1990, p. 35.

*Wilson Library Bulletin,* November, 1973, p. 259; October, 1985, p. 68.

*World Literature Today,* spring, 1977, p. 341; autumn, 1983, p. 641.

—*Sketch by Robert Miltner*

## SILLY, E. S.
### See KRAUS, (Herman) Robert

\*   \*   \*

## SIMON, (Marvin) Neil 1927-

*PERSONAL:* Born July 4, 1927, in the Bronx, New York; son of Irving (a garment salesman) and Mamie Simon; married Joan Baim (a dancer), September 30, 1953 (died, 1973); married Marsha Mason (an actress), 1973 (separated, 1983); married Diana Lander, 1987 (divorced, 1989; remarried, 1990); children: (first marriage) Ellen, Nancy. *Education:* Attended New York University, 1946, and University of Denver.

*ADDRESSES: Office*—c/o Albert Da Silva, 502 Park Ave. #10-G, New York, NY 10022.

*CAREER:* Playwright. Warner Brothers, Inc., New York City, mail room clerk, 1946; Columbia Broadcasting System (CBS), New York City, comedy writer for Goodman Ace, late 1940s; comedy writer for Robert W. Lewis' *The Little Show,* radio, late 1940s; comedy writer for *The Phil Silvers Arrow Show,* National Broadcasting Co., Inc. (NBC-TV), 1948, *The Tallulah Bankhead Show,* NBC-TV, 1951, Sid Caesar's *Your Show of Shows,* NBC-TV, 1956-57, *The Phil Silvers Show,* CBS-TV, 1958-59, *The Garry Moore Show,* CBS-TV, 1959-60, for *The Jackie Gleason Show* and *The Red Buttons Show,* both CBS-TV, and for television specials. Producer of motion pictures, including *Only When I Laugh,* Columbia, 1981, *I Ought to Be in Pictures,* Twentieth-Century Fox, 1982, and *Max Dugan Returns,* Twentieth-Century Fox, 1983. *Military service:* U.S. Army Air Force Reserve; sports editor of *Rev-Meter,* the Lowry Field, CO, base newspaper, 1946.

*MEMBER:* Dramatists Guild, Writers Guild of America.

*AWARDS, HONORS:* Academy of Television Arts and Sciences Award (Emmy), 1957, for Sid Caesar's *Your Show of Shows,* and 1959, for *The Phil Silvers Show;* Antoinette Perry Award (Tony) nomination, 1963, for *Little Me* and *Barefoot in the Park,* 1968, for *Plaza Suite,* 1969, for *Promises, Promises,* 1970, for *Last of the Red Hot Lovers,* 1972, for *The Prisoner of Second Avenue,* and 1987, for *Broadway Bound;* Tony Award for best playwright, 1965, for *The Odd Couple,* for best drama, 1985, for *Biloxi*

*Blues,* and 1991, for *Lost in Yonkers;* Writers Guild Award nomination, 1967, for *Barefoot in the Park; Evening Standard* Drama Award, 1967, for *Sweet Charity;* Sam S. Shubert Foundation Award, 1968; Academy of Motion Picture Arts and Sciences Award (Oscar) nomination, 1968, for *The Odd Couple,* and 1978, for *California Suite;* Writers Guild Award, 1969, for *The Odd Couple,* 1970, for *Last of the Red Hot Lovers,* 1971, for *The Out-of-Towners,* and 1972, for *The Trouble with People;* named Entertainer of the Year, *Cue* magazine, 1972; Academy of Motion Picture Arts and Sciences Award (Oscar) nomination and Golden Globe Award nomination, 1975, for *The Sunshine Boys,* and 1977, for *The Goodbye Girl;* L.H.D., Hofstra University, 1981; New York Drama Critics Circle Award, 1983, for *Brighton Beach Memoirs;* elected to the Theater Hall of Fame, Uris Theater, 1983; a Neil Simon tribute show was held at the Shubert Theater, March 1, 1987; Pulitzer Prize for Drama, and Drama Desk Award, both 1991, both for *Lost in Yonkers;* the Neil Simon Endowment for the Dramatic Arts has been established at Duke University.

*WRITINGS:*

*PLAYS*

(With William Friedberg) *Adventures of Marco Polo: A Musical Fantasy* (music by Clay Warnick and Mel Pahl), Samuel French (New York City), 1959.

(Adaptor with Friedberg) *Heidi* (based on the novel by Johanna Spyri; music by Warnick), Samuel French, 1959.

(With Danny Simon) *Come Blow Your Horn* (also see below; first produced in New Hope, PA, at the Bucks County Playhouse, August, 1960; produced on Broadway at the Brooks Atkinson Theatre, February 22, 1961; produced on the West End at the Prince of Wales Theatre, February 17, 1962), Doubleday (New York City), 1963.

*Barefoot in the Park* (also see below; first produced, under title *Nobody Loves Me,* in New Hope, PA, at the Bucks County Playhouse, 1962; produced on Broadway at the Biltmore Theatre, October 23, 1963; produced on the West End, 1965), Random House (New York City), 1964.

*The Odd Couple* (also see below; first produced on Broadway at the Plymouth Theatre, March 10, 1965; produced on the West End at the Queen's Theatre, October 12, 1966; revised version first produced in Los Angeles at the Ahmanson Theatre, April 6, 1985; produced on Broadway at the Broadhurst Theatre, June, 1985), Random House, 1966.

*Sweet Charity* (also see below; musical; based on the screenplay *The Nights of Cabiria* by Federico Fellini; music and lyrics by Cy Coleman and Dorothy Fields; first produced on Broadway at the Palace Theatre, January 29, 1966; produced on the West End at the Prince of Wales Theatre, October 11, 1967), Random House, 1966.

*The Star-Spangled Girl* (also see below; first produced on Broadway at the Plymouth Theatre, December 21, 1966), Random House, 1967.

*Plaza Suite* (also see below; three one-acts entitled *Visitor from Hollywood, Visitor from Mamaroneck,* and *Visitor from Forest Hills;* first produced on Broadway at the Plymouth Theatre, February 14, 1968; produced on the West End at the Lyric Theatre, February 18, 1969), Random House, 1969.

*Promises, Promises* (also see below; musical; based on the screenplay *The Apartment* by Billy Wilder and I. A. L. Diamond; music by Burt Bacharach; lyrics by Hal David; first produced on Broadway at the Shubert Theatre, December 1, 1968; produced on the West End at the Prince of Wales Theatre, October 2, 1969), Random House, 1969.

*Last of the Red Hot Lovers* (also see below; three acts; first produced in New Haven at the Shubert Theatre, November 26, 1969; produced on Broadway at the Eugene O'Neill Theatre, December 28, 1969; produced in London, 1979), Random House, 1970.

*The Gingerbread Lady* (also see below; first produced in New Haven at the Shubert Theatre, November 4, 1970; produced on Broadway at the Plymouth Theatre, December 13, 1970; produced in London, 1974), Random House, 1971.

*The Prisoner of Second Avenue* (also see below; first produced in New Haven at the Shubert Theatre, October 12, 1971; produced on Broadway at the Eugene O'Neill Theatre, November 11, 1971), Random House, 1972.

*The Sunshine Boys* (also see below; first produced in New Haven at the Shubert Theatre, November 21, 1972; produced on Broadway at the Broadhurst Theatre, December 20, 1972; produced in London, 1975), Random House, 1973.

*The Good Doctor* (also see below; musical; adapted from stories by Anton Chekhov; music by Peter Link; lyrics by Simon; first produced on Broadway at the Eugene O'Neill Theatre, November 27, 1973), Random House, 1974.

*God's Favorite* (also see below; first produced on Broadway at the Eugene O'Neill Theatre, December 11, 1974), Random House, 1975.

*California Suite* (also see below; first produced in Los Angeles, April, 1976; produced on Broadway at the Eugene O'Neill Theatre, June 30, 1976; produced in London, 1976), Random House, 1977.

*Chapter Two* (also see below; first produced in Los Angeles, 1977; produced on Broadway at the Imperial Theatre, December 4, 1977; produced in London, 1981), Random House, 1979.

*They're Playing Our Song* (also see below; musical; music by Marvin Hamlisch; lyrics by Carol Bayer Sager; first produced in Los Angeles, 1978; produced on Broadway at the Imperial Theatre, February 11, 1979; produced in London, 1980), Random House, 1980.

*I Ought to Be in Pictures* (also see below; first produced in Los Angeles, 1980; produced on Broadway at the Eugene O'Neill Theatre, April 3, 1980; produced in London at the Offstage Downstairs, December, 1986), Random House, 1981.

*Fools* (also see below; first produced on Broadway at the Eugene O'Neill Theatre, April, 1981), Random House, 1982.

*Brighton Beach Memoirs* (also see below; first produced in Los Angeles at the Ahmanson Theatre, December, 1982; produced on Broadway at the Alvin Theatre, March 27, 1983), Random House, 1984.

*Biloxi Blues* (also see below; first produced in Los Angeles at the Ahmanson Theatre, December, 1984; produced on Broadway at the Neil Simon Theatre, March, 1985), Random House, 1986.

*Broadway Bound* (also see below; first produced at Duke University, October, 1986; produced on Broadway at the Broadhurst Theatre, December, 1986), Random House, 1987.

*Rumors* (first produced in San Diego in the Old Globe Theater in 1988; produced on Broadway at the Broadhurst Theatre, November 17, 1988), Random House, 1990.

*Lost in Yonkers* (first produced in New York City at the Richard Rodgers Theatre, 1991), Plume, 1991.

*Jake's Women* (produced on Broadway at the Neil Simon Theatre, March 24, 1992), Samuel French, 1993, Random House, 1994.

*Laughter on the 23rd Floor* (produced on Broadway at the Richard Rodgers Theatre, November 22, 1993; produced on the West End, 1996), Random House, 1995.

*London Suite* (produced Off-Broadway at the Union Square Theatre, April 9, 1995), Samuel French, 1996.

OMNIBUS COLLECTIONS

*The Comedy of Neil Simon* (contains *Come Blow Your Horn, Barefoot in the Park, The Odd Couple, The Star-Spangled Girl, Promises, Promises, Plaza Suite,* and *Last of the Red Hot Lovers*), Random House, 1971, published as *The Collected Plays of Neil Simon,* Volume 1, New American Library (New York City), 1986.

*The Collected Plays of Neil Simon,* Volume 2 (contains *The Sunshine Boys, Little Me* [also see below], *The Gingerbread Lady, The Prisoner of Second Avenue, The Good Doctor, God's Favorite, California Suite,* and *Chapter Two*), Random House, 1979.

*The Collected Plays of Neil Simon,* Volume 3 (contains *Sweet Charity, They're Playing Our Song, I Ought to Be in Pictures, Fools, The Odd Couple—Female Version, Brighton Beach Memoirs, Biloxi Blues,* and *Broadway Bound*), Random House, 1992.

UNPUBLISHED PLAYS

(Contributor of sketches) *Tamiment Revue,* first produced in Tamiment, PA, 1952-53.

(Contributor of sketches, with D. Simon) *Catch a Star!* (musical revue), first produced on Broadway at the Plymouth Theatre, November 6, 1955.

(Contributor of sketches, with D. Simon) *New Faces of 1956,* first produced on Broadway at the Ethel Barrymore Theatre, June 14, 1956.

(Adaptor) *Little Me* (musical; based on the novel by Patrick Dennis), music by Coleman, first produced on Broadway at the Lunt-Fontanne Theatre, November 17, 1962, produced on the West End at the Cambridge Theatre, November 18, 1964, revised version produced in New York, 1981.

(Contributor of sketch) *Broadway Revue* (satirical musical revue), first produced in New York City at the Karmit Bloomgarden Theatre, November, 1968.

(Editor of book for musical) *Seesaw* (based on *Two for the Seesaw* by William Gibson), first produced on Broadway, March 18, 1973.

*The Goodbye Girl* (musical; based on Simon's screenplay), lyrics by David Zippel, music by Marvin Hamlisch, first produced on Broadway at the Marquis Theatre, March 4, 1993.

SCREENPLAYS

*Come Blow Your Horn* (based on Simon's play of the same title), Paramount, 1963.

(With Cesare Zavattini) *After the Fox* (also known as *Caccia alla volpe*), United Artists, 1966.

*Barefoot in the Park* (based on Simon's play of the same title), Paramount, 1967.

*The Odd Couple* (based on Simon's play of the same title), Paramount, 1968.

*The Out-of-Towners,* Paramount, 1970.

*Plaza Suite* (based on Simon's play of the same title), Paramount, 1971.

(With Arnold Margolin and Jim Parker) *Star Spangled Girl,* Paramount, 1971.

*Last of the Red Hot Lovers* (based on Simon's play of the same title), Paramount, 1972.

*The Heartbreak Kid* (based on short story by Bruce Jay Friedman), Twentieth Century-Fox, 1972.

*The Prisoner of Second Avenue* (based on Simon's play of the same title), Warner Bros., 1975.

*The Sunshine Boys* (based on Simon's play of the same title), Metro-Goldwyn-Mayer, 1975.

*Murder by Death,* Columbia, 1976.

*The Goodbye Girl,* Warner Bros., 1977.

*The Cheap Detective,* Columbia, 1978.

*California Suite* (based on Simon's play of the same title), Columbia, 1978.

*Chapter Two* (based on Simon's play of the same title), Columbia, 1979.

*Seems Like Old Times,* Columbia, 1980.

*Only When I Laugh* (based on Simon's play *The Gingerbread Lady*), Columbia, 1981.

*I Ought to Be in Pictures* (based on Simon's play of the same title), Twentieth Century-Fox, 1982.

*Max Dugan Returns,* Twentieth Century-Fox, 1983.

(With Edward Weinberger and Stan Daniels) *The Lonely Guy* (based on the novel *The Lonely Guy's Book of Life,* by Bruce Jay Friedman), Universal, 1984.

*The Slugger's Wife,* Columbia, 1985.

*Brighton Beach Memoirs* (based on Simon's play of the same title), Universal, 1986.

*Biloxi Blues* (based on Simon's play of the same title), Universal, 1988.

*The Marrying Man,* Hollywood Pictures, 1991.

*Lost in Yonkers* (based on Simon's play of the same title), Columbia, 1993, published as *Neil Simon's Lost in Yonkers: The Illustrated Screenplay of the Film,* Newmarket Press (New York City), 1993.

*OTHER*

*The Trouble with People* (teleplay), NBC-TV, 1972.

*Plaza Suite* (teleplay; based on Simon's play of the same title), ABC-TV, 1987.

*Broadway Bound* (teleplay; based on Simon's play of the same title), ABC-TV, 1992.

*Jake's Women* (teleplay; based on Simon's play of the same title), CBS-TV, 1996.

*Rewrites: A Memoir* (autobiography), Simon & Schuster, 1996.

*Neil Simon Monologues: Speeches from the Works of America's Foremost Playwright,* edited by Roger Karshner, Dramaline (Rancho Mirage, CA), 1996.

*London Suite* (teleplay; based on Simon's play of the same title), NBC-TV, 1996.

(Contributor) *Hold Fast Your Dreams,* edited by Carrie Boyko and Kimberly Colen, Scholastic (New York City), 1996.

Also coauthor of teleplay *Happy Endings,* 1975.

*ADAPTATIONS:* In addition to the films for which Simon also wrote the screenplay, *Sweet Charity,* written by Peter Stone, directed by Bob Fosse, and starring Shirley MacLaine, was filmed by Universal in 1969.

*SIDELIGHTS:* "When I was a kid," playwright Neil Simon tells Tom Prideaux of *Life,* "I climbed up on a stone ledge to watch an outdoor movie of Charlie Chaplin. I laughed so hard I fell off, cut my head open and was taken to the doctor, bleeding and laughing. . . . My idea of the ultimate achievement in a comedy is to make a whole audience fall onto the floor, writhing and laughing so hard that some of them pass out." For some thirty years Simon's comedies have dominated the Broadway stage and have been adapted as popular Hollywood films as well. As David Richards explains in the *Washington Post,* Simon's comedies have run "forever on Broadway and made him pots of money, after which they were turned into movies that made him pots more." Such plays as *Barefoot in the Park, The Odd Couple, Plaza Suite, The Prisoner of Second Avenue, The Sunshine Boys,* and the autobiographical trilogy of *Brighton Beach Memoirs, Biloxi Blues,* and *Broadway Bound,* have ensured Simon a position as "one of America's most popular and prolific playwrights" and "the most formidable comedy writer in American theatre," as Sheila Ennis Geitner reports in *Dictionary of Literary Biography.*

Even though Simon's plays are often "detonatingly funny," as a critic for *Time* claims, in recent years they have grown more serious, confronting issues of importance, the humor developing naturally from the characters and their interactions. With these plays, Simon has gained a new respect for his work. "Simon's mature theatre work," Robert K. Johnson writes in *Neil Simon,* "combines comedy with moments of poignance and insight." Speaking of the Tony Award-winning *Biloxi Blues,* Frank Rich of the *New York Times* argues that Simon "at last begins to examine himself honestly, without compromises, and the result is his most persuasively serious effort to date." In his review of the same play, Clive Barnes of the *New York Post* calls it "a realistic comedy of the heart" and allows that it "is funny, often heartrendingly funny, but nowadays Simon will not compromise character for a laugh."

Simon began his career as a radio writer in the 1940s. He and his brother Danny Simon worked as a team, writing comedy sketches for radio personality Goodman Ace. In the 1950s the pair graduated to television, working with such popular entertainers as Sid Caesar, Phil Silvers, and Jackie Gleason, and with such other writers as Mel Brooks and Woody Allen. But after some ten years in the business, Simon wanted out. "I hated the idea of working in television and having conferences with network executives and advertising executives who told you what audiences wanted and in what region they wanted it," Simon tells the *New York Times Magazine.* With the success of his play *Come Blow Your Horn,* written with Danny, Simon was finally able to leave television and devote his efforts to the stage. He has never regretted the move. As he tells Richards, "I would rather spend my nights writing for an audience of 1,000, than an audience of 14 million."

Since the initial success of *Come Blow Your Horn,* which ran for eighty-four weeks on Broadway, Simon has seldom had a disappointing reception to his work. His second play, *Barefoot in the Park,* ran for over 1,500 performances on Broadway; *The Odd Couple* for over 900 performances; *Plaza Suite* for over 1,000 performances; and *Last of the Red Hot Lovers* and *The Prisoner of Second Avenue* ran for over 700 performances each. Richards notes that "all but a handful of Simon's plays" have made a profit, while Simon is reputedly "the richest playwright alive and arguably the richest ever in the history of the theater." "Most of Simon's plays . . .," Richard Christiansen remarks in the *Chicago Tribune,* "have been good box office. [And] he still holds the record for having the most plays running simultaneously on Broadway (four)." Speaking of Simon's phenomenal career, Christine Arnold of the *Chicago Tribune* calls him "America's most successful playwright, more prolific and far less troubled than Tennessee Williams, more popular than Eugene O'Neill or Lanford

Wilson or Sam Shepard. Critics may dismiss or embrace his work, but they cannot dispute his genius for creating plays that resonate for vast audiences."

Although Simon's plays have dealt with a wide range of situations and characters, certain elements recur in all of them. The setting is usually Simon's hometown of New York, the characters are often native New Yorkers, and their problems are similar to those experienced by Simon himself. *Come Blow Your Horn,* for instance, is a thinly-disguised version of Simon and brother Danny coming of age and leaving home, *The Odd Couple* stems from Danny's experience of sharing an apartment with a divorced friend, and *Chapter Two* concerns Simon's recovery following the death of his first wife in 1973. Simon tells Leslie Bennetts of the *New York Times* about how he has incorporated events from his own life into his plays: "The theme is me, my outlook on life. If you spread [my career] out like a map, you can chart my emotional life: some of the growth, some of the changes, some of the side trips."

Critics often point out that Simon has an admirable ability to accurately depict American domestic life. "Simon has a gift for sketching America in small-scale situations," states Joe Brown of the *Washington Post.* Writing in the *Humanist,* Julius Novick claims that Simon immerses "himself in the minutiae of modern American upper-middle-class existence, which no one conveys with more authority—or, anyhow, more assiduity—than he."

Simon's plays usually focus on the members of one family or on a small group of friends, and often concern the more disruptive problems of modern life: divorce, urban crime and congestion, conflicts between children and parents, infidelity. These conflicts occur in a closed environment: an apartment or the family home. "Many of my plays [deal] with people being dumped together in a confined space, physically and emotionally," Bennetts quotes Simon as explaining. He uses this confined space with expert skill. David Kehr of the *Chicago Tribune* claims that Simon has "a kind of genius—a genius for stagecraft, the art of getting characters on and off a stage as unobtrusively as possible and of finding plausible, natural excuses for restricting a whole range of dramatic action to the confines of a single set. As a master of logistics, Simon is without peer."

Although Simon's plays are often concerned with domestic troubles, they nonetheless find humor in these painful situations. In his critique of *The Odd*

*Couple* for the *Saturday Review,* Henry Hewes explains that Simon "makes comic cadenzas out of our bleats of agony." Simon's characters, Hewes maintains, "are blissfully unhappy but the pain of what they do to each other and to themselves is exploded into fierce humor." In his analysis of what makes Simon's plays funny, T. E. Kalem of *Time* finds that "the central aspect of his plays is that the central characters are not funny at all. They never laugh, and they are frequently utterly miserable. . . . Why does the audience laugh? Two reasons suggest themselves. The first is the catharsis of relief—thank God, this hasn't happened to me. The second is to ward off and suppress anxiety—by God, this might happen to me." Speaking to Paul D. Zimmerman of *Newsweek,* Simon explains: "My view is 'how sad and funny life is.' I can't think of a humorous situation that does not involve some pain. I used to ask, 'What is a funny situation?' Now I ask, 'What is a sad situation and how can I tell it humorously?'"

This fusion of the sad and funny in Simon's work is noted by several critics who see it as a central reason for his theatrical success. Marilyn Stasio writes in her review of *Last of the Red Hot Lovers:* "There is nothing at all funny about the painfully neurotic and really quite profoundly unhappy characters in this play, which is actually about the disintegration of our moral codes and the chaos which such a breakdown has made of our emotional lives. What makes the play so wildly funny is not its author's vision, for Simon's is close to tragedy, but his conceptualization of that vision as high comedy-of-manners. It is neither the personae of the characters nor the situations of their drama which Simon treats humorously, but only the superficial foibles which they have erected as elaborate defenses against their own anxieties." Prideaux argues that Simon's comic characters—who, like his audience, are usually from the middle class—offer something more than simple entertainment. "By making a modern audience feel that its foibles and vices are not too serious because he makes them seem so funny," Prideaux writes, "Simon is also selling a sort of forgiveness: absolution by laughter."

In her *Neil Simon: A Critical Study,* Edythe M. McGovern argues that in his early plays Simon also advocates compromise and moderation. In *Barefoot in the Park,* for instance, a newly married couple are opposites: she is spontaneous; he is overly careful. Their different outlooks on life threaten to pull them apart. But by play's end, they have moderated their behavior so that they can live comfortably together. "Simon," McGovern writes, "has made a point here

regarding the desirability of following a middle course in order to live pleasurably without boredom, but with a sensible regard for responsibility."

The same theme is returned to in *The Odd Couple,* in which two divorced male friends share an apartment, only to find that the disagreeable personality traits which led them to get divorces also make their living together impossible. They are "two rather nice human beings who will never be able to communicate with one another simply because each man has a completely different way of viewing the world and is committed to what amounts to an extreme position with no intention of compromise," as McGovern explains. Their unyielding attitudes lead to an angry confrontation and eventual break. In showing the consequences of their inability to compromise, Simon again argues for "a middle course rather than an extremely polarized position," McGovern writes. Speaking of Simon's handling of such important themes in his comedies, McGovern claims that "to Neil Simon, . . . the comic form provides a means to present serious subjects so that audiences may laugh to avoid weeping."

But not all critics have been kind to Simon. Some believe his long string of hit comedies to be filled with funny one-liners and little else. Jack Kroll of *Newsweek* refers to Simon's image as "Gagman Laureate." Writing in his *Uneasy Stages: A Chronicle of the New York Theater, 1963-73,* John Simon claims that "the basic unit of [Simon's] playmaking is the joke. Not the word, the idea, the character, or even the situation, but the gag. It kills him if here and there a monosyllable resists funnying up, if now and then someone has to make a move that won't fracture the audience." According to Gerald M. Berkowitz, writing in *Players,* "Simon is a critical embarrassment. . . . A Neil Simon comedy makes the audience laugh. . . . [But] the secret of his special comic talent is a matter of pure technique; . . . it is not the content of his plays, but the manner in which the content is presented that generates most of the laughter."

For many years, Simon was taken less than seriously even by critics who enjoyed his work. A *Time* reviewer, for example, once claimed that "Santa Claus is just an alias for Neil Simon. Every year just before Christmas, he loads up packets of goodies and tosses two unbridled hours of laughter to Broadway audiences." Johnson notes that many people saw Simon as "a sausage grinder turning out the same pleasing 'product' over and over again. The 'product' is a play or movie realistic in style and featuring New Yorkers who spout a lot of funny lines." Geitner remarks that Simon's reputation as "the most formidable comedy writer in American theatre . . . prevented his being considered a serious dramatist by many critics."

With the autobiographical trilogy *Brighton Beach Memoirs, Biloxi Blues,* and *Broadway Bound* in the 1980s, however, critical opinion about Simon's work has improved enormously. Speaking of the critical reception of *Brighton Beach Memoirs,* Richards explains that "the critics, who have sometimes begrudged the playwright his ability to coin more funny lines per minute than seems humanly possible, have now decided that he has a very warm heart." And *Biloxi Blues,* his twenty-first Broadway play, won Simon in 1985 his first Tony Award for best drama. (He had twenty years earlier won the Tony for best playwright.)

The trilogy is based on Simon's own childhood and youth in the 1930s and 1940s, although he tells Charles Champlin of the *Los Angeles Times:* "I hate to call it autobiographical, because things didn't necessarily happen, or happen to me. It's an Impressionist painting of that era and that place. But there are bits and pieces of me in several of the characters." *Broadway Bound* is close enough to the truth, however, for William A. Henry III of *Time* to report that both Simon "and his brother Danny have wept openly while watching it in performance."

*Brighton Beach Memoirs* is set in the Brooklyn of 1937 and tells of a Jewish family, the Jeromes, and their financial troubles during the Depression. When an aunt loses her job, she and her son move in with the Jeromes, and the family, now seven people in a cramped house, must survive their financial crisis and the aggravatingly close proximity to each other. Rich explains that "Simon uses the family's miseries to raise such enduring issues as sibling resentments, guilt-ridden parent-child relationships and the hunger for dignity in a poverty-stricken world." Simon's alter ego is the family's teenage son, Eugene, who comments on his family's problems in asides to the audience. Eugene, Richards explains, "serves as the play's narrator and [his] cockeyed slant on the family's tribulations keeps the play in comic perspective."

The play earned Simon some of the best reviews of his career. Brown writes that *Brighton Beach Memoirs* has "plenty of laughs," but "Simon avoids

the glib, tenderly probing the often-awkward moments where confused emotions cause unconscious hurts. . . . Simon's at his best, finding the natural wit, wisecracking and hyperbole in the words and wisdom of everyday people." Barnes finds *Brighton Beach Memoirs* to be "a very lovely play." He continues: "I am certain—if the kids of our academic establishment can get off their pinnacles and start taking Simon as seriously as he deserves—*Brighton Beach Memoirs* will become a standard part of American dramatic literature."

Eugene Jerome joins the Army in *Biloxi Blues,* the second play of the trilogy. The story follows Eugene through his ten weeks of basic training in Biloxi, Mississippi. During this training, one recruit is jailed for his homosexuality; one comes into constant conflict with his superior officers; and Eugene faces anti-Semitic insults from another soldier. Eugene, an aspiring writer, records these events faithfully in his diary, learning to examine his life and the lives of his friends honestly, and developing personal values in the process. Eugene's dream of becoming a writer is greatly furthered when he is assigned to work on an Army newspaper instead of being sent to the front, a fortunate turn of events that nonetheless makes him feel guilty.

Eugene's Army career is virtually identical to Simon's own stint in the military. Simon explains to Michiko Kakutani of the *New York Times* that writing the play was an act of self-discovery: "I wanted to know how this extremely shy, not enormously well-educated boy came to do what I consider a very hard thing to do—write plays. I wanted to see how I became the person I am. I seem to be, in my own mind, a very unlikely candidate for success."

This self-examination has been well received by the critics, who find that Simon realistically presents life in the Army. "For all the familiarity of its set pieces," Dan Sullivan of the *Los Angeles Times* says of *Biloxi Blues,* "it feels like life, not 'Gomer Pyle.'" Critics have also been impressed with how Simon subordinates the play's humor to its more serious concerns. As Howard Kissel writes in *Women's Wear Daily, Biloxi Blues* "is certainly Simon's best play, to my mind the first in which he has had the courage to suggest there are things that matter more to him than the reassuring sound of the audience's laughter. My admiration for the play is deep and unqualified." Richards claims that *Biloxi Blues* "may be the most touching play ever written about the rigors of basic training."

The story of Eugene Jerome continues in *Broadway Bound,* in which Eugene and his older brother, Stan, become comedy writers, leave home, and take jobs with a major network radio show. The breakup of their parents' marriage, the family's resistance to their new profession, and Eugene's realization that life does not contain the happy endings found in art form the basis of the plot. Danny Simon tells Nina Darnton of the *New York Times* that *Broadway Bound* "is the closest in accuracy" of the three autobiographical plays.

Eugene's mother is the primary character in *Broadway Bound.* "Through much of the comedy," Christiansen notes, "she has been the needling, nagging Jewish mother who gets the old, familiar laughs. But by the end of the play, with her personal life a shambles, she has turned into a creature of great sorrow and weariness, as well." After recounting to Eugene the story of how she once danced with actor George Raft—an exhilarating and romantic moment she still recalls fondly—Eugene asks his mother to dance with him. "In this," Kroll observes, "perhaps the most delicate and highly charged moment in any Simon play, we feel the waste of a woman's unlived life and the shock of a young man who feels in his arms the repressed rhythm of that life." Eugene "sees that behind his mother's depressed exterior," Mel Gussow comments in the *New York Times,* "is the heart of a once vibrant and hopeful young woman; she is someone who has been defeated by the limits she has imposed on her life."

According to Sylvie Drake of the *Los Angeles Times,* *Broadway Bound* is "the third and best and final segment of Simon's semiautobiographical trilogy. . . . There is plenty of comedy left, but of a different order. The one-liners are gone, replaced by a well-timed visceral humor that is coated in melancholy." Drake concludes that *Broadway Bound* is Simon "not only at his finest, but at his most personal and complex." Similarly, although he sees some flaws in *Broadway Bound,* Rich admits that it "contains some of its author's most accomplished writing to date—passages that dramatize the timeless, unresolvable bloodlettings of familial existence as well as the humorous conflicts one expects." And Holly Hill, writing for the London *Times,* believes that Eugene's mother "is the most masterful portrait Neil Simon has ever drawn."

Simon finally received critical recognition of his status as one of America's major playwrights in 1991, when his play *Lost in Yonkers* won both a Pulitzer Prize for Drama and a Tony Award for best drama. The play, which tells the story of a dysfunctional Jewish-American family during World War II, is "closer to pure surrealism than anything Mr. Simon has hitherto produced," writes David Richards in the *New York Times,* "and take[s] him several bold steps beyond the autobiographical traumas he recorded in *Brighton Beach Memoirs* and *Broadway Bound.*" "No longer content to dramatize divisive arguments around the family table," the critic continues, "he has pulled the family itself out of shape and turned it into a grotesque version of itself. These characters are not oddballs, they're deeply disturbed creatures. Were it not for his ready wit and his appreciation for life's incongruities, *Lost in Yonkers* could pass for a nightmare."

*Lost in Yonkers* is the story of how Eddie Kurnitz is forced by his economic circumstances to leave his two young sons, Arty and Jay, in the care of his severe, overbearing German-born Jewish mother. Grandma Kurnitz has tried to encourage self-reliance among her children by exercising strict discipline in her home, but she has only succeeded in scarring them emotionally. She continues to exert her authority over her gangster son Louie and her mentally-impaired daughter Bella. "The two children," David Richards declares in his *New York Times* review of the show, "are our sole connection to a world of conventional relationships and values." "During the eight months Jay and Arty spend with their relatives," Richards continues, "Bella takes it into her addled head that she's going to leave home, marry the usher at the local movie house, open a restaurant and have babies—more or less in that order." Grandma opposes Bella's show of individuality, and, with Arty's and Jay's help, Bella stages her own defiance of the family matriarch. "We are relieved, at the end, when the father reappears," writes James S. Torrens in *America.* "And the youngsters, who have made it through the same ordeals as their parents . . . can be seen as having survived. *Lost in Yonkers* touches all the chords."

Critics have remarked on how Simon's recent plays—including *Lost in Yonkers* and his autobiographical trilogy—turn from straight comedy toward the depiction of suffering. "Over the last decade," David Richard writes in the *New York Times,* "pain has slowly crept into the comic world of Neil Simon. Although his popularity remains undiminished, his increasing willingness to recognize that the uproariously funny can also be ineffably sad may be freeing him from the taint of craven commercialism." "He was already a past master at depicting the sundry ways people get on one another's nerves," the critic writes in a *Washington Post* article on Simon's career. "What have surfaced increasingly in his mature works are the hurt, the sadness and the longings that possess his characters. In *Lost in Yonkers, . . .* the ache and the absurdity of living are inextricably interwoven."

Simon returned to straight comedy in two farces: *Rumors* (1988) and *Jake's Women* (1992). In both cases critics remarked that the plays seemed almost too lightweight after the successes of his autobiographical plays and *Lost in Yonkers*. *Rumors* is "a self-described farce," reports Frank Rich in the *New York Times*, "that has nothing on its mind except making the audience laugh. And not exactly in the Moliere manner. Maybe I've led a charmed life, but I can't recall hearing this many toilet jokes since the ninth grade." "*Rumors* is about as silly a play as can be imagined," declares Leah D. Frank in the *New York Times*. *Jake's Women* received "scathing" reviews in the *Los Angeles Times*, states *New York Times* reporter Mervyn Rothstein, and "the San Diego critics said it needed a lot of work but had promise."

*Jake's Women* and Simon's next play, *Laughter on the 23rd Floor* (1993) both failed to make a profit, in part because of the expense of Broadway productions. When *Laughter on the 23rd Floor*—based on stories from Simon's life working of Sid Caesar's *Your Show of Shows*—met with good reviews and had a decent run but was less than a financial success, Simon declared his intention to open his next play Off-Broadway. "When we closed *Laughter on the 23rd Floor* after nine months on Broadway," Simon tells *New York Times* contributor Richard Rosen, "we had lost six, seven, eight hundred thousand dollars. I had a meeting with my producer, and he figured out that if we had the same number of people coming to the theater here, we would've made our money back and a very decent profit." *London Suite,* a series of four one-act plays, opened off-Broadway in 1995 and later travelled successfully to Chicago.

Although primarily known for his plays, Simon also has written a score of popular films. These include the screen adaptations of many of his own hit plays—including *Barefoot in the Park, The Odd Couple,* and *The Sunshine Boys*—as well as such original screenplays as *The Cheap Detective, Murder by Death,* and *The Goodbye Girl*. Simon's best screen work is found in films where he creates a desperate situation,

Vincent Canby argues in the *New York Times*. Simon's "wisecracks define a world of mighty desperation," Canby writes, "in which every confrontation, be it with a lover, a child, a husband, a friend or a taxi driver, becomes a last chance for survival. When he writes a work in which the desperation is built into the situations, Mr. Simon can be both immensely funny and surprisingly moving."

But not all critics appreciate Simon's film work. Gene Siskel of the *Chicago Tribune,* for one, declares: "I dread going to see a movie of Neil Simon's. In fact, I would see anything but a Disney live-action film rather than a Neil Simon movie. Anything. Even a mad-slasher movie." Simon's adaptations of his own plays, while often good box office, have sometimes been criticized for being too stagey, like "photographed plays," as Johnson puts it. Yet, most of Simon's films, especially *The Heartbreak Kid* and *Only When I Laugh,* have been extremely popular with audiences and critics alike.

*The Heartbreak Kid* concerns a young couple who get divorced during their honeymoon in Florida after the husband meets another woman. Simon creates humor in this film, as Johnson allows, "out of situations which are not basically surefire comedy material." It is this blend of the humorous and the essentially tragic—with the humor emerging naturally from the actions and speech of the characters—which makes *The Heartbreak Kid* "the best film created thus far from a Neil Simon script," Johnson believes.

*Only When I Laugh* was also a critical success for Simon. It tells the story of Georgia Hines, an alcoholic Broadway actress who, despite rehabilitation, cannot beat her dependence. Georgia "is one of the most interesting, complicated characters that Mr. Simon, the master of the sometimes self-defeating one-liner, has ever written," according to Canby. Johnson finds *Only When I Laugh* "one of the most absorbing pieces of work that Simon has written."

"Writing is an escape from a world that crowds me," Simon tells John Corry of the *New York Times*. "I like being alone in a room. It's almost a form of meditation—an investigation of my own life." He explains to Henry how he begins a play: "There's no blueprint per se. You just go through the tunnels of your mind, and you come out someplace." Simon admits to Zimmerman that the writing process still frightens him. "Every time I start a play," he explains, "I panic because I feel I don't know how to do it. . . . I keep wishing I had a grownup in the room who would tell me how to begin." Accepting his success as a writer has also been difficult. "I was depressed for a number of years," Simon tells Corry. The opening of a new play filled him with guilt. It took psychoanalysis, and a consultation with his second wife's swami, before Simon learned to enjoy his accomplishments.

Simon writes on a daily basis, although much of his work is never completed. Richards reports that "Simon's desk overflows with the plays he's begun over the years. On an average, for every one he finishes, there are 10 he abandons after 15 or 20 pages." Generally, if Simon gets past page thirty-five he will finish the play, a process that takes four months for a first draft, longer for the final draft. *Come Blow Your Horn,* for example, was rewritten twenty times before Simon was satisfied with it. In *Broadway Bound,* Simon has his alter ego, Eugene, say: "I love *being* a writer. It's the writing that's hard."

Despite the difficulty involved in writing, Simon has managed to produce an impressive body of work. A new Simon comedy every theatrical season has been a Broadway staple for three decades. Henry calls him "America's foremost stage comedist" and places Simon "in the top rank of American playwrights." Rich calls him "not just a show business success but an institution." After surveying Simon's many achievements during his long career as a writer for the stage and screen, Johnson concludes by calling him "one of the finest writers of comedy in American literary history."

## BIOGRAPHICAL/CRITICAL SOURCES:

### BOOKS

*Authors in the News,* Volume 1, Gale (Detroit), 1976.
*Contemporary Literary Criticism,* Gale, Volume 6, 1976; Volume 9, 1979; Volume 31, 1985; Volume 39, 1986; Volume 70, 1991.
*Dictionary of Literary Biography,* Volume 7: *Twentieth-Century American Dramatists,* Gale, 1981.
Johnson, Robert K., *Neil Simon,* Twayne (New York City), 1983.
Kerr, Walter, *Thirty Plays Hath November,* Simon & Schuster (New York City), 1969.
McGovern, Edythe M., *Neil Simon: A Critical Study,* Ungar (New York City), 1979.
Monaco, James, *American Film Now,* Oxford University Press (New York City), 1979.

Simon, John, *Uneasy Stages: A Chronicle of the New York Theater, 1963-73,* Random House, 1975.

### PERIODICALS

*America,* May 20, 1961; May 29, 1965; April 1, 1989; May 4, 1991, pp. 496-97.
*American Film,* March, 1978.
*Chicago Tribune,* March 26, 1982; April 7, 1986; November 2, 1986; December 31, 1986; August 23, 1989; December 13, 1992, section 13, pp. 4-5; November 23, 1993, section 4, p. 20; October 8, 1995, section 7, p. 8.
*Christian Science Monitor,* January 17, 1970; November 11, 1970; March 31, 1992, p. 11; May 18, 1993, p. 13; December 7, 1993, p. 15; April 17, 1995, p. 14.
*Commonweal,* November 15, 1963; April 2, 1965; October 9, 1992.
*Critic's Choice,* December, 1969.
*Cue,* January 3, 1970; January 15, 1972.
*Daily News* (New York City), April 4, 1980; April 7, 1981; March 29, 1985.
*Entertainment Weekly,* July 16, 1993; November 19, 1993.
*Horizon,* January, 1978.
*Hudson Review,* spring, 1978.
*Humanist,* September/October, 1976.
*Life,* April 9, 1965; March 6, 1970; May 7, 1971.
*Los Angeles Times,* December 5, 1982; December 11, 1982; August 24, 1984; December 15, 1984; April 6, 1985; April 8, 1985; December 6, 1986; December 25, 1986; March 25, 1988; November 19, 1988; November 23, 1988; August 19, 1989; September 8, 1989; March 10, 1990; April 7, 1990; April 30, 1995, section C, pp. 7, 86-87.
*Macleans,* May 18, 1992.
*Nation,* March 4, 1968; July 3, 1976; May 11, 1992, pp. 642-43.
*National Observer,* November 20, 1971.
*New Republic,* January 16, 1971.
*New Statesman,* November 1, 1974.
*Newsweek,* January 9, 1967; February 26, 1968; February 2, 1970; November 23, 1970; December 10, 1973; April 26, 1976; February 26, 1979; April 14, 1980; April 20, 1981; December 15, 1986; March 4, 1991; March 15, 1993; December 6, 1993.
*New York,* January 13, 1975; April 11, 1983; March 29, 1985.
*New Yorker,* January 10, 1970; December 23, 1974; March 11, 1991; March 15, 1993; December 20, 1993; December 20, 1993, pp. 135-38.

*New York Post,* December 22, 1966; November 12, 1971; April 7, 1981; March 28, 1983; March 29, 1985.

*New York Times,* August 4, 1968; December 2, 1968; December 31, 1969; November 17, 1971; December 9, 1973; December 12, 1974; December 22, 1974; December 1, 1977; June 23, 1978; December 22, 1978; December 19, 1980; March 23, 1981; April 5, 1981; April 7, 1981; April 12, 1981; September 23, 1981; March 25, 1983; March 27, 1983; March 28, 1983; April 3, 1983; March 29, 1985; April 1, 1985; April 7, 1985; April 16, 1985; June 9, 1985; August 29, 1986; November 30, 1986; December 5, 1986; December 14, 1986; December 25, 1986; December 26, 1986; January 8, 1987; January 25, 1987; August 17, 1987; December 9, 1987; March 25, 1988; April 15, 1988; November 13, 1988, pp. 13, 41; November 18, 1988, p. C3; December 25, 1988, p. 5; April 8, 1990, p. C3; March 3, 1991, pp. 1, 7; April 10, 1991, p. A21; May 13, 1991, p. C12; June 3, 1991, pp. C11, C16; December 8, 1991, p. 23; April 5, 1992, pp. 5, 37; October 20, 1994, pp. C15, C20; March 26, 1995, pp. 7, 13; April 10, 1995, pp. C9, C11.

*New York Times Magazine,* March 7, 1965; March 22, 1970; May 26, 1985; February 17, 1991, pp. 30-32, 36, 57, 64.

*Philadelphia Inquirer,* March 27, 1988.

*Playbill,* January, 1969.

*Playboy,* February, 1979; July, 1991.

*Players,* February/March, 1972; September, 1977.

*Plays and Players,* February, 1975; July, 1975; September, 1977.

*Saturday Review,* March 27, 1965.

*Seventeen,* November, 1979.

*Show Business,* January 10, 1970.

*Spectator,* November 2, 1974.

*Time,* November 1, 1963; January 12, 1970; January 15, 1973; December 23, 1974; April 8, 1985; December 15, 1986; November 28, 1988; April 8, 1991; May 24, 1993; December 6, 1993.

*Times* (London), April 20, 1983; April 10, 1985; December 4, 1986; January 3, 1987; June 4, 1987.

*TV Guide,* November 4, 1972.

*Variety,* December 24, 1969; February 25, 1970; November 4, 1970; September 8, 1971; December 27, 1972; December 5, 1973; March 2, 1992; January 4, 1993; November 22, 1993.

*Village Voice,* January 8, 1970.

*Vogue,* April 1, 1968; October 1, 1968; January 1, 1970.

*Washington Post,* January 13, 1970; February 9, 1971; April 10, 1983; December 14, 1984; April 6, 1985; July 16, 1985; June 12, 1986; September 12, 1986; October 19, 1986; December 25, 1986; December 26, 1986; March 25, 1988; September 9, 1993, section MD, p. 5; April 1, 1995, section C, pp. 1-2; December 3, 1995, section G, p. 6.

*Women's Wear Daily,* November 15, 1971; April 4, 1980; March 29, 1985.

*World Journal Tribune,* December 22, 1966.

\*    \*    \*

## SNOW, Philip (Albert) 1915-

*PERSONAL:* Born August 7, 1915, in Leicester, England; son of William Edward (an organist and shoe factory clerk) and Ada Sophia (Robinson) Snow; married Mary Anne Harris, May 2, 1940; children: Stefanie Dale Vivien Vuikamba (Mrs. Peter Edward Waine). *Education:* Christ's College, Cambridge, B.A., 1937, M.A. (with honors), 1940. *Avocational interests:* South Sea islands.

*ADDRESSES: Home*—Gables, Station Rd., Angmering, Sussex BN16 4HY, England.

*CAREER:* Government of Fiji and Western Pacific, Provincial Commissioner, Magistrate, and Assistant Colonial Secretary, 1938-52; Justice of the Peace, Warwickshire, England, 1952-75, West Sussex, 1976—. Bursar, Rugby School, 1952-76; examiner on Pacific Subjects, Oxford and Cambridge Universities, 1955—. Founder, Fiji Cricket Association, 1946, vice-patron, 1952—; captain, Fiji Cricket Team, New Zealand First-Class Tour, 1948; permanent representative, Fiji on International Cricket Conference, 1965-95. Member, First World Cup Committee, 1971-75; chairman, Associate Member Countries, 1982—. Leader of expedition to Vanua Levu, Fiji, to investigate rock carvings, 1949. Literary executor and executor of Lord C.P. Snow. *Wartime service:* Aide de camp to Governor and Commander in Chief, Fiji, 1939; Air Raids Precautions Officer, Lautoka, Fiji, 1942-44; Fiji Government liaison officer to U.S. and New Zealand forces, 1942-44.

*MEMBER:* National Independent Schools Bursars Association of Great Britain, Northern Ireland, and Commonwealth (vice-chair, 1959-61; chair, 1961-

64), Royal Anthropological Institute (fellow), Royal Society of Arts (fellow), Marylebone Cricket Club (London), Hawks Club (Cambridge), Mastermind Club (London), Scragglers of Asia Cricket Club (London), De Flamingo's (Holland).

*AWARDS, HONORS:* Foreign Specialist award, U.S. Government, 1964, for *Visits to Schools and Universities in U.S.A. and Canada;* Member, Order of the British Empire, 1979, on recommendation of Government of Fiji; National Award (with Stefanie Snow Waine) for second best history/biography, Arts Council of Great Britain, 1979, for *The People from the Horizon: An Illustrated History of the Europeans among the South Sea Islanders;* Officer, Order of the British Empire, 1985; special honorary life membership, Marylebone Cricket Club, for services to international cricket; Fiji Independence Silver Jubilee Medal, 1995.

*WRITINGS:*

*Civil Defense Services,* Fiji Government Printer, 1942.
(Editor) *Fiji Civil Service Journal,* Fiji Government Printer, 1945.
*Cricket in the Fiji Islands,* Whitcombe & Tombs (New Zealand), 1949.
*Rock Carvings in Fiji,* Fiji Society, 1953.
*The Nature of Fiji and Tonga,* Discovery, 1956.
(With D. M. Sherwood and F. J. Walesby) *Visits to Schools and Universities in U.S.A. and Canada,* Public Schools' Bursars' Association of U.K. and Commonwealth, 1964.
(Editor, author of introduction, and contributor) *Best Stories of the South Seas,* Faber & Faber (London), 1967.
*Bibliography of Fiji, Tonga, and Rotuma,* Volume 1, University of Miami Press (Baltimore, MD), 1969.
(With daughter, Stefanie Snow Waine) *The People from the Horizon: An Illustrated History of the Europeans among the South Sea Islanders,* Phaidon (England), 1979.
*Stranger and Brother: A Portrait of C. P. Snow,* Macmillan (New York City), 1982, Scribner (New York City), 1983.
*The Rarest Printed Work on the Pacific? A Bibliographer's Proposition,* Volumes 1-4, Fiji Museum Journal, 1988.
*Years of Hope,* St. Martin's (New York City), 1996.
*Time of Renewal,* St. Martin's, 1996.
*The Star Raft: China's Encounter with Africa,* Cornell University Press (Ithaca, NY), 1988.

Also author of *Bula,* 1959, and, with J. S. Woodhouse, of *Visit of Her Majesty the Queen and H.R.H. Prince Philip to Rugby School on the Occasion of the Quatercentenary Year,* 1967; also editor, with G. K. Roth, of *Fijian Customs,* 1944. Contributor to reference works, including *The Far East and Australasia, Wisden Cricketers Almanack, The World of Cricket,* and *Dictionary of National Biography.* Author of introduction for books, including *Kidnapping in the South Seas* by George Palmer, Dawsons of Pall Mall, 1972; and *Viti* Berthold Seeman, Dawsons of Pall Mall, 1972. Contributor of articles on the Pacific to the *Times* (London), *Daily Telegraph, American Anthropologist, Journal of Polynesian Society, Discovery, Journal de la Societe des Oceanistes, Sunday Times, Times Literary Supplement, Fiji Museum Journal, Journal of Pacific History, Journal of the Royal Anthropological Institute,* and *Journal of the Royal Geographical Society.* Author of foreword/preface of a number of volumes on cricket or Fiji, including *Tales of the Fiji Islands* by Anne Gittins, Acorn Press, 1991.

*WORK IN PROGRESS:* A history of the Pacific.

*SIDELIGHTS:* Philip Snow, younger brother of the late Right Honorable Lord C. P. Snow of Leicester, was for fourteen years a Colonial Administrator in Fiji. One result of this was his *Bibliography of Fiji, Tonga, and Rotuma,* a "compilation which [is] not merely valuable but essential to any workers in the Pacific area or students of its history," according to a *Times Literary Supplement* reviewer. Others were his biography *Stranger and Brother: A Portrait of C. P. Snow,* and later, *Years of Hope.* For both books, he used a series of letters from C. P. Snow written during the second World War and in the period immediately following it.

"The definitive biography [of C. P. Snow] has yet to be written; it will be a monumental task for somebody, and must be some way off," Philip Snow states in the foreword to his biography. "In the meantime, without attempting any sort of analysis of his work—though I have identified many of the characters in the *Stranger and Brother* series—" he continues, "I have set out to paint an informal picture of a man who has been the main influence in my life." Reviewers echo the author's assessment; for instance, Victoria Glendinning, a reviewer for the *Listener,* asserts that the book "is neither a formal or a critical biography, and the personality of the painter is not excluded from the work." Edward M. White, writing in the *Los Angeles Times Book Review,* states,

"This is not a critical work or one which will add much to one's appreciation of the novels," but declares, "this loving and pleasant tribute offers the guilty pleasures of personality to those who would enjoy the man as well as the books." *Washington Post Book World* contributor Edward M. Yoder Jr. appraises *Stranger and Brother* as "a useful guide to a major accomplishment in old-fashioned storytelling, and to the remarkable man who achieved it." In 1996, Snow issued *Years of Hope,* and he told *CA* that a "main theme" of this work was his "reflections and observations on life in the pacific." "A further account of [my] relationship with C. P. Snow is paramount" in *A Time of Renewal,* also written in 1996. Snow considers both these books "companion volumes."

Philip Snow is proficient in the Hindi and Fijian languages. He possesses what is probably the best private collection on Pacific literature in the United Kingdom, and the best collection in the world of the works of Lord Snow and his wife, Pamela Hansford Johnson.

*BIOGRAPHICAL/CRITICAL SOURCES:*

*BOOKS*

Gorman, G. E. and J. J. Mills, *Fiji* (World Bibliographical Series), Clio Press (Oxford, England), 1996.

Johnson, Pamela Hansford, *Important to Me: Personalia,* Macmillan, 1974, Scribner, 1975.

Knox-Mawer, June, *Tales from Paradise,* B.B.C. Ariel, 1986.

Martin-Jenkins, Christopher, *World Cricketers. A Biographical Dictionary,* Oxford University Press, 1996.

Snow, Philip, *Stranger and Brother: A Portrait of C. P. Snow,* Macmillan, 1982, Scribner, 1983.

Swanton, E. W., *Follow On,* Collins, 1977.

*PERIODICALS*

*Atlantic,* April, 1983.
*Best Sellers,* May, 1983.
*British Book News,* May, 1980; March, 1983.
*Choice,* May, 1970.
*Daily Mail* (London), October 7, 1982.
*Daily Telegraph* (London), January 28, 1952; December 12, 1953; June 23, 1958; February 10, 1966; March 5, 1970; March 2, 1973; March 9, 1973; December 2, 1976; November 27, 1979; November 18, 1982; October 27, 1983; January 5, 1984; March 26, 1984.

*Fiji Times,* April 13, 1996.
*History Today,* April, 1980.
*Listener,* October 28, 1982.
*London Review of Books,* November 18, 1982.
*Los Angeles Times Book Review,* April 17, 1983.
*National Review,* March 18, 1983.
*New Statesman,* November 5, 1982.
*Spectator,* October 16, 1982; December 18, 1982.
*Times* (London), June 10, 1954; July 6, 1960; February 18, 1967; July 11, 1968; July 21, 1971; July 11, 1973; July 27, 1977; March 9, 1981; October 27, 1983; April 12, 1984; August 17, 1987; August 19, 1987.
*Times Literary Supplement,* August 26, 1950; June 23, 1957; August 15, 1968; June 18, 1970; January 7, 1983.
*Washington Post Book World,* May 7, 1983.

\*    \*    \*

**SOMERS, Jane**
  **See LESSING, Doris (May)**

\*    \*    \*

**SPENCE, Jonathan D(ermot)   1936-**

*PERSONAL:* Born August 11, 1936, in England; son of Dermot Gordon Chesson (poet) and Muriel (Crailsham) Spence; married Helen Alexander, September 15, 1962; children: Colin Chesson, Ian Alexander. *Education:* Cambridge University, B.A., 1959; Yale University, Ph.D., 1965.

*ADDRESSES: Office*—Department of History, Yale University, New Haven, CT 06520.

*CAREER:* Yale University, New Haven, CT, assistant professor, 1965-71, professor of Chinese history, beginning 1971, currently George Burton Adams Professor of History and chair of department. *Military service:* British Army, 1954-56; became first lieutenant.

*MEMBER:* Council on East Asian Studies (chair)

*AWARDS, HONORS:* Christopher Book Award, 1975, for *Emperor of China: Self-Portrait of K'ang-Hsi; Los Angeles Times* Book Award, 1982, and Harold D. Vursell Memorial Award, American

Academy-Institute of Arts and Letters, 1983, both for *The Gate of Heavenly Peace: The Chinese and Their Revolution, 1895-1980;* Gelber Prize, 1990, for *Chinese Roundabout: Essays in History and Culture.*

*WRITINGS:*

*Ts'ao Yin and the K'ang-Hsi Emperor, Bondservant and Master,* Yale University Press (New Haven, CT), 1966.

*To Change China: Western Advisers to China, 1620-1960,* Little, Brown (Boston), 1969, published in England as *The China Helpers: Western Advisers to China, 1620-1960,* Bodley Head, 1969.

*Emperor of China: Self-Portrait of K'ang-Hsi,* Knopf (New York City), 1974.

*The Death of Woman Wang* (novel), Viking (New York City), 1978.

(With John E. Wills, Jr.) *From Ming to Ch'ing: Conquest, Region and Continuity in Seventeenth-Century China,* Yale University Press, 1979.

(With Paul Cohen and Steven Levine) *The Historical Precedents for Our New Regulations with China,* East Asia Program (Washington, DC), 1980.

*The Gate of Heavenly Peace: The Chinese and Their Revolution, 1895-1980,* Viking, 1981.

*The Memory Palace of Matteo Ricci,* Viking, 1984.

*The Question of Hu* (biography), Knopf, 1988.

*The Search for Modern China,* Norton, (New York City), 1990.

*Chinese Roundabout: Essays in History and Culture,* Norton, 1992.

*God's Chinese Son: The Taiping Heavenly Kingdom of Hong Xiuquan,* Norton, 1996.

(With Annping Chin) *The Chinese Century: The Photographic History of the Last Hundred Years,* Random House, 1996.

*SIDELIGHTS:* Jonathan D. Spence writes books of Chinese history which employ various of organization and approach. "No one writes history—Chinese or any other kind—exactly as Spence does," Harrison E. Salisbury claims in the *Chicago Tribune Book World.* In his *Emperor of China: Self-Portrait of K'ang-Hsi,* Spence splices together contemporary accounts of a seventeenth-century Chinese ruler to fashion a kind of autobiography. In *The Death of Woman Wang,* he fuses the official history of a seventeenth-century Chinese province, the memoirs of a local magistrate, and a collection of contemporary short stories into a historical novel. *The Gate of Heavenly Peace: The Chinese and Their Revolution, 1895-1980* presents recent Chinese history as seen

and lived by China's writers and artists. And *The Memory Palace of Matteo Ricci* is a biography of a sixteenth-century Jesuit missionary to China organized around the mental images used in a Medieval memory system. Because he "brings imagination and literary flair to his material," these books have won Spence "a high reputation," as John Gross reports in the *New York Times.*

One of Spence's most successful books is *The Gate of Heavenly Peace,* winner of two major awards in the field of historical writing. Tracing the turbulent history of modern China, *The Gate of Heavenly Peace* does not tell of the political leaders of the time nor of the common people. It focuses instead on China's intelligentsia and records how they both inspired and served the forces of political change and were often the first victims of those changes. As Kenneth J. Atchity explains in the *Los Angeles Times Book Review,* "Spence shows us history through the perceptions of individuals who—in a more or less minor key, relative to Sun Yat-sen and Mao—were affected by these movements and whose souls helped shape these dreams." In particular, the book follows the careers of three people: the Confucian scholar Kang Youwei, the writer Lu Xun, and the novelist Ding Ling.

"No one has quite done Chinese history like this before," Jay Mathews writes in the *Washington Post Book World.* Mathews believes that Spence "brings alive the men and women who made the revolution, uncovering their bedtime fantasies, personality conflicts, sexual weaknesses and irrational rages." Similarly, Richard Harris of the London *Times* calls *The Gate of Heavenly Peace* "a book that brings China to life better than almost any other written about China since [the revolution]."

Spence's book also provides a valuable insight into the nature of the Chinese revolution. As Stuart Schram writes in the *Times Literary Supplement,* "Spence illuminates in a way no one else has done before, important aspects of the revolution, and in the process brings us closer to a full understanding of its meaning." "Spence has woven a magical symphony," Salisbury writes, "that tells us as no conventional history could of the agony of a nation in awesome labor, giving birth, as it were, to its own future."

In *The Memory Palace of Matteo Ricci,* Spence recreates the China of the sixteenth century and the work of the Jesuit missionaries of the time. In doing so, he also sketches a panoramic overview of the relationship between Europe and the East. The book's title comes from Ricci's memory system, which he used to remember vast amounts of information. His memory feats astounded his Chinese friends. At one gathering, Ricci was given a list of 500 Chinese characters to memorize. He read them back correctly and then, to the astonishment of the Chinese, recited them correctly in backward order as well. The system he used was based on a mental "memory palace"—a series of vividly-imagined rooms. In each room was stored visual representations of the items to be remembered. As the user of the system imagines a walk through these rooms, the visual images trigger the proper memories in the proper order.

*The Memory Palace of Matteo Ricci* is organized around eight pictures—four used in Ricci's memory system and four religious wood-cuts he chose to illustrate one of his books. Spence uses these pictures as starting-points to discuss such topics as sixteenth-century warfare, commerce, and religious thought. "Spence cuts across the fabric of history from many different angles and directions," H. J. Kirchhoff writes in the Toronto *Globe and Mail,* "allowing Ricci's choices of illustration and explication to direct our gaze toward the Chinese of the sixteenth century, and toward the Jesuits who so determinedly and imaginatively proselytized them." As Marvin R. O'Connell observes in the *Washington Post Book World,* "Spence has employed Ricci's preoccupation with mnemonics to fashion an ingenious structure in which to bring together a history of China and Europe during Ricci's lifetime. . . . [It is] a genuine tour de force."

Spence employed a more conventional structure in *The Search for Modern China.* The author begins this study in 1600, during the era when the Ming dynasty was crumbling. Progressing chronologically through the centuries, he demonstrates that since that time, China has continually struggled to hold together a vast nation which seems always to be on the verge of falling apart. Fear of such fragmentation is one of the major sources of China's traditional closed-door policy. Spence examines the many ways in which China has attempted to protect itself from outsiders and their influence, and analyzes the ways that these attitudes come into play in modern China.

"To understand the burdens and opportunities embedded in China's past there is no better place to start than Jonathan D. Spence's excellent new book," asserts Vera Schwarcz in the *New York Times Book*

*Review.* Nicholas R. Clifford concurs in *Commonweal* that Spence's book offers unusually clear insights into "*China's* history, rather than a China seen through Western eyes, or a China that simply responds to the actions of others." Writing in *Publishers Weekly,* Chris Goodrich names *The Search for Modern China* "a significant contribution to the history of our time." Originally conceived as a textbook, Spence's book proved to have wide appeal; it was on the *New York Times* bestseller list for three weeks.

Spence followed *The Search for Modern China* with *Chinese Roundabout: Essays in History and Culture.* "A new book by Jonathan Spence is always a cause for celebration," enthuses Kate Lowe in *History Today,* "and this volume containing a collection of twenty-five of what he considers some of his best articles and review essays will allow new generations to catch up easily on missed treats The range [of the book] is breathtaking, from Confucianism to sea slugs, and from Tianamen under the Ming and Qing, to an appreciation of Arthur Waley." Lowe points out that although his books are popular, Spence has sacrificed none of his academic integrity. J. D. Brown makes a similar point in a Chicago *Tribune Books* review, describing Spence as "a clear and lively writer who is also inventive and witty, [and] at the same time a painstaking scholar." Allowing that Spence's style is occasionally "a bit dry," Brown goes on to add: "It is also various and possesses an element of unpredictability, which can produce results that are, at once, surprising, entertaining and inspired As these essays show, Spence at his best employs an adventurous imagination to blow away the layers of dust that have obscured China's past and made the present so bewildering."

In his next offering, *God's Chinese Son: The Taiping Heavenly Kingdom of Hong Xiuquan,* Spence chose to focus on one bizarre, violent episode in nineteenth-century China—the Taiping Rebellion, instigated by Hong Xiuquan. The son of a farming couple, Hong aspired to become a mandarin, and so traveled as a young man to Canton to take the Confucian examinations. After failing several times, he fell ill and experienced a baffling, vision-filled delirium. Beginning to read a Bible given to him by a missionary, Hong came to believe that he was the Second Son of God. He became an itinerant preacher and attracted legions of followers. Eventually, he called for the destruction of the government, and nearly achieved it; however, his own cult was eventually wiped out by religious excesses and self-destructive paranoia.

A *Publishers Weekly* reviewer calls it a "strange, compelling tale" and credits Spence with being "a first-rate storyteller [who] recounts this extraordinary event with verve, offering sharp insights into the political dangers of religious fanaticism." Marie Arana-Ward also commends the author on his achievement. She writes in the *Washington Post Book World,* "Weaving what is already well known about the Taiping Rebellion with information from newly discovered documents inscribed by Hong, Spence gives us a magnificent tapestry of those apocalyptic days. It is a story that reaches beyond China into our world and time: a story of faith, hope, passion, and a fatal grandiosity."

Spence's unique presentations of history, Michael Feingold maintains in the *Voice Literary Supplement,* "may be on the thin edge of ethical procedure. For the lay reader, however, they're infinitely more entertaining than the ponderous sobriety, overlaid with econometric tables and French theorizing, that history as a field has become. . . . If Spence's tactics are maddening, they're also revelatory, making us think about the life behind history as a drier recitation of facts never could." David Lattimore of the *New York Times Book Review* cites *Emperor of China, The Death of Woman Wang,* and *The Gate of Heavenly Peace* as works in which Spence "employs a similar method of delicate interweaving and transition. These are works of carefully thought out, accurately annotated history, which, with their well-observed detail and extensive quotations, propel us among the very sights and sounds and emotions of the time. They exemplify a high historical art, worthy tributes to Clio, muse of history." Salisbury describes Spence as "a poet-historian of China, whose images bring to us the true fragrance of the East, the limitless breadth of China, the deep wells of its culture, the harshness of its cruelties, the continuity of the Chinese ethos."

*BIOGRAPHICAL/CRITICAL SOURCES:*

*BOOKS*

*Bestsellers 90,* issue 4, Gale (Detroit), 1991.

*PERIODICALS*

*America,* September 29, 1990, p. 190.
*American Spectator,* December, 1990, p. 52.
*Boston Globe,* November 16, 1988, p. 85; May 6, 1990, p. B51; July 2, 1992, p. 67.

*Chicago Tribune,* May 13, 1990, section 14, p. 1; July 12, 1992, section 14, p. 3.
*Chicago Tribune Book World,* October 11, 1981.
*Commonweal,* August 10, 1990, pp. 462-63.
*Economist,* June 2, 1990, pp. 95-96.
*Globe and Mail* (Toronto), June 29, 1985.
*Historian,* spring, 1995, pp. 626-27.
*History and Theory: Studies in the Philosophy of History,* May, 1992, pp. 143-52.
*History Today,* February, 1993, p. 57; December, 1993, pp. 55, 57.
*Library Journal,* May 15, 1992, p. 103.
*Los Angeles Times,* November 20, 1988, p. B1.
*Los Angeles Times Book Review,* December 27, 1981; November 25, 1984; May 27, 1990, p. 1.
*Nation,* September 2, 1978.
*New Leader,* July 9, 1990, p. 17.
*New Statesman & Society,* September 29, 1989, p. 38; June 8, 1990, p. 34.
*Newsweek,* May 22, 1978; November 9, 1981.
*New Yorker,* April 3, 1989, pp. 109-115.
*New York Review of Books,* May 18, 1978; May 31, 1990, p. 16; November 5, 1992, pp. 51-53; February 29, 1996, pp. 39-42.
*New York Times,* October 12, 1981; November 21, 1984; May 10, 1990, p. C19.
*New York Times Book Review,* July 16, 1969; June 11, 1978; October 18, 1981; December 2, 1984; December 18, 1988, p. 7; May 13, 1990, pp. 1, 32; December 2, 1990, p. 81; February 4, 1996, p. 6.
*Publishers Weekly,* March 16, 1990, p. 56; May 4, 1990, pp. 48-49; April 20, 1992, p. 42; November 27, 1995, p. 62.
*Times* (London), February 18, 1982.
*Times Literary Supplement,* August 19, 1983; September 27, 1985; February 12, 1993, p. 26.
*Tribune Books* (Chicago), July 12, 1992, pp. 3, 9.
*U.S. News and World Report,* May 28, 1990, p. 62.
*Voice Literary Supplement,* December, 1984.
*Washington Post Book World,* November 22, 1981; December 23, 1984; April 22, 1990, p. 1; January 21, 1996, pp. 1, 14.
*Yale Review,* autumn, 1969.*

\*          \*          \*

**SPENDER, Stephen (Harold) 1909-1995**

*PERSONAL:* Born February 28, 1909, in London, England; died July 16, 1995, in London; son of Edward Harold (a journalist and lecturer) and Violet

Hilda (Schuster) Spender; married Agnes Marie Pearn, 1936 (divorced); married Natasha Litvin (a pianist), 1941; children: (second marriage) Matthew Francis, Elizabeth. *Education:* Attended University College, Oxford, 1928-30.

*CAREER:* Writer. Elliston Chair of Poetry, University of Cincinnati, 1953; Beckman Professor, University of California, 1959; visiting lecturer, Northwestern University, 1963; Clark lecturer, Cambridge University, 1966; Mellon lecturer, Washington, DC, 1968; Northcliffe lecturer, University of London, 1969; visiting professor at University of Connecticut, 1968-70, University of Florida, 1976, Vanderbilt University, 1979, and University of South Carolina, 1981; University of London, University College, London, England, professor of English, 1970-77, professor emeritus, 1977-95.

Counselor in Section of Letters, UNESCO, 1947. Fellow of Institute of Advanced Studies, Wesleyan University, 1967. Consultant on poetry in English, Library of Congress, Washington, DC, 1965. *Wartime service:* National Fire Service, fireman, 1941-44.

*MEMBER:* PEN International (president, English Centre, beginning in 1975); American Academy of Arts and Letters and National Institute for Arts and Letters (honorary), Phi Beta Kappa, Beefsteak Club.

*AWARDS, HONORS:* Commander of the British Empire, 1962; Queen's Gold Medal for Poetry, 1971; named Companion of Literature, 1977; knighted by Queen Elizabeth II, 1983; *Los Angeles Times* Book Award in poetry nomination for *Collected Poems, 1928-1985,* 1986; honorary fellow, University College, Oxford; D.Litt. from University of Montpelier, Cornell University, and Loyola University.

*WRITINGS:*

POETRY

*Nine Experiments: Being Poems Written at the Age of Eighteen,* privately printed, 1928.
*Twenty Poems,* Basil Blackwell (Oxford, England), 1930.
*Poems,* Faber (London), 1933, Random House (New York City), 1934.
*Perhaps* (limited edition), privately printed, 1933.
*Poem* (limited edition), privately printed, 1934.
*Vienna,* Faber, 1934.
*At Night,* privately printed, 1935.
*The Still Centre,* Faber, 1939.

*Selected Poems,* Random House, 1940.
*I Sit by the Window,* Linden Press (New York City), c. 1940.
*Ruins and Visions: Poems, 1934-1942,* Random House, 1942.
*Poems of Dedication,* Random House, 1947.
*Returning to Vienna, 1947: Nine Sketches,* Banyan Press (Chicago), 1947.
*The Edge of Being,* Random House, 1949.
*Sirmione Peninsula,* Faber, 1954.
*Collected Poems, 1928-1953,* Random House, 1955, revised edition published as *Collected Poems, 1928-1985,* Faber, 1985.
*Inscriptions,* Poetry Book Society (London), 1958.
*Selected Poems,* Random House, 1964.
*The Generous Days: Ten Poems,* David Godine (Boston), 1969, enlarged edition published as *The Generous Days,* Faber, 1971.
*Descartes,* Steam Press (London), 1970.
*Art Student,* Poem-of-the-Month Club (London), 1970.
*Recent Poems,* Anvil Press Poetry (London), 1978.
*Dolphins,* St. Martin's (New York City), 1994.

PLAYS

*Trial of a Judge: A Tragedy in Five Acts* (first produced in London at Rupert Doone's Group Theatre on March 18, 1938), Random House, 1938.
(Translator and adapter with Goronwy Rees) *Danton's Death* (first produced in London, 1939; adaptation of a play by Georg Buechner), Faber, 1939.
*To the Island,* first produced at Oxford University, 1951.
(Adapter) *Lulu* (adaptation from plays by Frank Wedekind; also see below), produced in New York, 1958.
(Translator and adapter) *Mary Stuart* (adaptation of a play by Johann Christoph Friedrich von Schiller; produced on the West End at Old Vic, 1961; produced on Broadway at Vivian Beaumont Theatre, November 11, 1971), Faber, 1959, reprinted, Ticknor & Fields, 1980.
(Translator and adapter) *The Oedipus Trilogy—King Oedipus, Oedipus at Colonos, Antigone: A Version by Stephen Spender* (three-act play; revision of play produced at Oxford Playhouse, 1983), Faber, 1985.

ESSAYS

*The Destructive Element: A Study of Modern Writers and Beliefs,* J. Cape (London), 1935, Houghton (Boston), 1936, reprinted, Folcroft (Folcroft, PA), 1970.

*Forward from Liberalism,* Random House, 1937.

*The New Realism: A Discussion,* Hogarth (London), 1939, Folcroft, 1977.

*Life and the Poet,* Secker & Warburg (London), 1942, Folcroft, 1974.

*European Witness,* Reynal, 1946.

(Contributor) Richard H. Crossman, editor, *The God That Failed: Six Studies in Communism,* Harper, 1950.

*Learning Laughter,* Weidenfeld & Nicolson (London), 1952, Harcourt, 1953.

*The Creative Element: A Study of Vision, Despair, and Orthodoxy among Some Modern Writers,* Hamish Hamilton (London), 1953, Folcroft, 1973.

*The Making of a Poem,* Hamish Hamilton, 1955, Norton, 1962.

*The Imagination in the Modern World: Three Lectures,* Library of Congress (Washington, DC), 1962.

*The Struggle of the Modern,* University of California Press (Berkeley, CA), 1963.

*Chaos and Control in Poetry,* Library of Congress, 1966.

*The Year of the Young Rebels,* Random House, 1969.

*Love-Hate Relations: A Study of Anglo-American Sensibilities,* Random House, 1974.

*Eliot,* Fontana, 1975, published as *T. S. Eliot,* Viking, 1976.

*Henry Moore: Sculptures in Landscape,* Studio Vista (London), 1978, C. N. Potter, 1979.

*The Thirties and After: Poetry, Politics, People, 1933-1970,* Random House, 1978.

(Contributor) *America Observed,* C. N. Potter, 1979.

(With David Hockney) *China Diary* (travel guide), with illustrations by Hockney, Thames & Hudson, 1982.

*In Irina's Garden with Henry Moore's Sculpture,* Thames & Hudson, 1986.

*EDITOR*

W. H. Auden, *Poems,* privately printed, 1928.

(With Louis MacNeice) *Oxford Poetry 1929,* Basil Blackwell, 1929.

(With Bernard Spencer) *Oxford Poetry 1930,* Basil Blackwell, 1930.

(With John Lehmann and Christopher Isherwood) *New Writing, New Series I,* Hogarth, 1938.

(With Lehmann and Isherwood) *New Writing, New Series II,* Hogarth, 1939.

(With Lehmann and author of introduction) *Poems for Spain,* Hogarth, 1939.

*Spiritual Exercises: To Cecil Day Lewis* (poems), privately printed, 1943.

(And author of introduction) *A Choice of English Romantic Poetry,* Dial, 1947.

(And author of introduction) Walt Whitman, *Selected Poems,* Grey Walls Press (London), 1950.

Martin Huerlimann, *Europe in Photographs,* Thames & Hudson, 1951.

(With Elizabeth Jennings and Dannie Abse) *New Poems 1956: An Anthology,* M. Joseph (London), 1956.

(And author of introduction) *Great Writings of Goethe,* New American Library, 1958.

(And author of introduction) *Great German Short Stories,* Dell, 1960.

(And author of introduction) *The Writer's Dilemma,* Oxford University Press, 1961.

(With Irving Kristol and Melvin J. Lasky) *Encounters: An Anthology from the First Ten Years of "Encounter" Magazine,* Basic Books, 1963.

(With Donald Hall) *The Concise Encyclopedia of English and American Poets and Poetry,* Hawthorn, 1963, revised edition, Hutchinson, 1970.

(And author of introduction) *A Choice of Shelley's Verse,* Faber, 1971.

(And author of introduction) *Selected Poems of Abba Kovne* [and] *Selected Poems of Nelly Sachs,* Penguin, 1971.

*The Poems of Percy Bysshe Shelley,* Limited Editions Club (Cambridge), 1971.

*D. H. Lawrence: Novelist, Poet, Prophet,* Harper, 1973.

*W. H. Auden: A Tribute,* Macmillan, 1975.

*Herbert List: Junge Maenner,* Twin Palms, 1988.

*Hockney's Alphabet,* Random House/American Friends of AIDS Crisis Trust, 1991.

*TRANSLATOR*

(And author of introduction and, with J. B. Leishman, commentary) Rainer Maria Rilke, *Duino Elegies* (bilingual edition), Norton, 1939, 4th edition, revised, Hogarth, 1963.

(With Hugh Hunt) Ernst Toller, *Pastor Hall* (three-act play), John Lane, 1939; also bound with *Blind Man's Buff* by Toller and Denis Johnson, Random House, 1939.

(With J. L. Gili) Federico Garcia Lorca, *Poems,* Oxford University Press, 1939.

(With Gili) *Selected Poems of Federico Garcia Lorca,* Hogarth, 1943.

(With Frances Cornford) Paul Eluard, *Le Dur desir de Durer,* Grey Falcon Press, 1950.

(And author of introduction) Rilke, *The Life of the Virgin Mary (Das Marien-Leben)* (bilingual edition), Philosophical Library, 1951.

(With Frances Fawcett) Wedekind, *Five Tragedies of Sex,* Theatre Arts, 1952.

(With Nikos Stangos) C. P. Cavafy, *Fourteen Poems,* Editions Electo, 1977.

Wedekind, *Lulu Plays and Other Sex Tragedies,* Riverrun, 1979.

*OTHER*

*The Burning Cactus* (short stories), Random House, 1936, reprinted, Books for Libraries Press, 1971.

*The Backward Son* (novel), Hogarth, 1940.

(With William Sansom and James Gordon) *Jim Braidy: The Story of Britain's Firemen,* Lindsay Drummond, 1943.

(Author of introduction and notes) *Botticelli,* Faber, 1945, Pitman (London), 1948.

(Author of introduction) Patrice de la Tour du Pin, *The Dedicated Life in Poetry* [and] *The Correspondence of Laurent de Cayeux,* Harvill Press, 1948.

*World within World: The Autobiography of Stephen Spender,* Harcourt, 1951, reprinted with an introduction by the author, St. Martin's, 1994.

*Engaged in Writing, and The Fool and the Princess* (short stories), Farrar, Straus (New York City), 1958.

(With Nicholas Nabokov) *Rasputin's End* (opera), Ricordi (Milan), 1963.

(Contributor with Patrick Leigh Fermor) *Ghika: Paintings, Drawings, Sculpture,* Lund, Humphries, 1964, Boston Book and Art Shop, 1965.

(Reteller) *The Magic Flute: Retold* (juvenile; based on the opera by Mozart), Putnam, 1966.

(Author of introduction) *Venice,* Vendome, 1979.

*Letters to Christopher: Stephen Spender's Letters to Christopher Isherwood, 1929-1939, with "The Line of the Branch"—Two Thirties Journals,* Black Sparrow (Santa Barbara, CA), 1980.

(Author of introduction) *Herbert List: Photographs, 1930-1970,* Thames & Hudson, 1981.

(Contributor) Martin Friedman, *Hockney Paints the Stage,* Abbeville Press, 1983.

*The Journals of Stephen Spender, 1939-1983,* Random House, 1986.

*The Temple* (novel), Grove, 1988.

(Author of preface) David Finn, *Evocations of "Four Quartets",* Black Swan, 1991.

Editor, with Cyril Connolly, of *Horizon,* 1939-41; coeditor, with Melvin J. Lasky, 1953-66, and corresponding editor, 1966-67, *Encounter;* co-founder of *Index on Censorship* (bimonthly magazine). Contributor to numerous anthologies.

*SIDELIGHTS:* Stephen Spender was a member of the generation of British poets who came to prominence in the 1930s, a group—sometimes referred to as the Oxford Poets—that included W. H. Auden, Christopher Isherwood, C. Day Lewis, and Louis MacNeice. In *World within World: The Autobiography of Stephen Spender* the author speculated that the names of the members of the group became irreversibly linked in the minds of critics for no other reason other than having their poems included in the same important poetic anthologies of the early thirties. However, in *The Angry Young Men of the Thirties* Elton Edward Smith found that the poets had much more in common and stated that they shared a "similarity of theme, image, and diction." According to Smith, the poets also all rejected the writing of the immediately preceding generation. Gerald Nicosia reached the same conclusion in his *Chicago Tribune Book World* essay on Spender's work. "While preserving a reverence for traditional values and a high standard of craftsmanship," Nicosia wrote, "they turned away from the esotericism of T. S. Eliot, insisting that the writer stay in touch with the urgent political issues of the day and that he speak in a voice whose clarity can be understood by all." Comparing the older and younger generations of writers, Smith noted that while the poets of the 1920s focused on themes removed from reality, "the poets of the 1930s represented a return to the objective world outside and the recognition of the importance of the things men do together in groups: political action, social structure, cultural development."

Spender's name was most frequently associated with that of W. H. Auden, perhaps the most famous poet of the thirties; yet some critics, including Alfred Kazin and Helen Vendler, found the two poets dissimilar in many ways. In the *New Yorker,* for example, Vendler observed that "at first [Spender] imitated Auden's self-possessed ironies, his determined use of technological objects. . . . But no two poets can have been more different. Auden's rigid, brilliant, peremptory, categorizing, allegorical mind demanded forms altogether different from Spender's dreamy, liquid, guilty, hovering sensibility. Auden is a poet of firmly historical time, Spender of timeless nostalgic space." In the *New York Times Book Review* Kazin similarly concluded that Spender "was mistakenly identified with Auden. Although they were virtual opposites in personality and in the direction of their talents, they became famous at the same time as 'pylon poets'—among the first to put England's gritty industrial landscape of the 1930's into poetry."

The term "pylon poets" refers to "The Pylons," a poem by Spender which many critics described as typical of the Auden generation. The much-anthologized work, included in one of Spender's earliest collections, *Poems,* as well as in his compilation of a lifetime's accomplishments, *Collected Poems, 1928-1985,* is characteristic of the group's imagery and also reflects the political and social concerns of its members. Smith recognized that in such a poem "the poet, instead of closing his eyes to the hideous steel towers of a rural electrification system and concentrating on the soft green fields, glorifies the pylons and grants to them the future. And the non-human structure proves to be of the very highest social value, for rural electrification programs help create a new world of human equality."

The decade of the thirties was marked by turbulent events that would shape the course of history: the world-wide economic depression, the Spanish Civil War, and the beginnings of the Second World War. Seeing the established world crumbling around them, the writers of the period sought to create a new reality to replace the old, which in their minds had become obsolete. According to D. E. S. Maxwell, commenting in his *Poets of the Thirties,* "the imaginative writing of the thirties created an unusual *milieu* of urban squalor and political intrigue. This kind of statement—a suggestion of decay producing violence and leading to change—as much as any absolute and unanimous political partisanship gave this poetry its marxist reputation. Communism and 'the communist' (a poster-type stock figure) were frequently invoked." For a time Spender, like many young intellectuals of the era, was a member of the Communist party. "Spender believed," Smith noted, "that communism offered the only workable analysis and solution of complex world problems, that it was sure eventually to win, and that for significance and relevance the artist must somehow link his art to the Communist diagnosis." Smith described Spender's poem, "The Funeral" (included in *Collected Poems: 1928-1953* but omitted from the 1985 revision of the same work), as "a Communist elegy" and observes that much of Spender's other works from the same early period as "The Funeral," including his play, *Trial of a Judge: A Tragedy in Five Acts,* his poems from *Vienna,* and his essays in *The Destructive Element: A Study of Modern Writers and Beliefs* and *Forward from Liberalism* deal with the Communist question.

*Washington Post Book World* contributor Monroe K. Spears considered "The Funeral" one of Spender's least successful poems, but nevertheless acknowl-edged that it reveals some of the same characteristics of the poet as his better work: "an ardent idealism, an earnest dedication that leaves him vulnerable in his sympathy for the deprived and exploited, his hopes for a better world, [and] his reverence for greatness and heroism, especially in art." Critics noted that Spender's attitudes, developed in the thirties, continued to influence the poet throughout his life. As Peter Stansky pointed out in the *New Republic:* "The 1930s were a shaping time for Spender, casting a long shadow over all that came after. . . . It would seem that the rest of his life, even more than he may realize, has been a matter of coming to terms with the 1930s, and the conflicting claims of literature and politics as he knew them in that decade of achievement, fame, and disillusion."

Spender continued to write poetry throughout his life, but it came to consume less of his literary output in later years than it did in the 1930s and 1940s. The last collection of poems published before his death was *Dolphins.* "To find him still reaching out at 85— the same age as [English novelist and poet Thomas] Hardy was when he published his last poems—is confirmation of the old truism that feeling is not an optional extra of humans but bred in the bone," commented William Scammell in the *Spectator.* In the title piece, Spender turns his attention to those creatures of the sea which have captivated poets for centuries. "For him, their movements constitute a kind of scripture, communicating at an ontological level beyond merely human speech," observed Peter Firchow in *World Literature Today.* "Their message is utterly simple, the simplest and most basic of all: 'I AM.'" For several critics, these two words spoke volumes about Spender's poetry. In a *Times Literary Supplement* review, Julian Symons explained, "If Stephen Spender ever intended to create a poetry of 'direct social function,' the idea was long ago abandoned in favour of a concern to express in verse his own true beliefs and attitudes, about which he remains permanently uncertain."

Firchow found that most of the poems in *Dolphins* did not live up to the high standards that Spender had set in his previous work, but the reviewer did admit that "two long autobiographical poems, 'A First War Childhood' and 'Wordsworth,' come close." Symons praised Spender's long poem about the life of Arthur Rimbaud. "The sequence is successful in part because Spender can have found no difficulty in imagining himself both Rimbaud and [Paul] Verlaine, in part because of his strong dramatic sense," wrote the reviewer. "Yet the most striking poem here records not the insight of the witness, but the anguish of the absentee," observed Boyd Tonkin in the *New States-man and Society.* "'History and Reality' pays hom-age to the Jewish, Catholic and quasi-Marxist thinker Simone Weil, who starved herself in solidarity with Hitler's victims."

Despite Spender's status as one of the leading poets of the twentieth century, a number of critics have noted his value beyond his poetry. Symons main-tained, "As one looks back, Spender's principal achievement seems to have been less his poems or any particular piece of prose than the candor of the ceaseless critical self-examination he has conducted for more than half a century in autobiography, jour-nals, criticism, poems." Peter Stansky also observed that Spender was at his best when he was writing autobiography. The poet himself seemed to have pointed out this fact when he wrote in the postscript to *Thirties and After: Poetry, Politics, People, 1933-1970:* "I myself am, it is only too clear, an autobi-ographer. Autobiography provides the line of conti-nuity in my work. I am not someone who can shed or disclaim his past."

The past often became the subject of Spender's writ-ing in the eighties. Particularly *The Journals of Stephen Spender, 1939-1983, Collected Poems, 1928-1985,* and *Letters to Christopher: Stephen Spender's Letters to Christopher Isherwood, 1929-1939, with "The Line of the Branch"—Two Thirties Journals* placed a special emphasis on autobiographi-cal material that reviewers found revealed Spender as both an admirable personality and a notable writer. In a *New York Times Book Review* commentary by Samuel Hynes on the collection of Spender's letters, for instance, the critic expressed his belief that "the person who emerges from these letters is neither a madman nor a fool, but an honest, intelligent, troubled young man, groping toward maturity in a troubled time. And the author of the journals is something more; he is a writer of sensitivity and power." Discussing the same volume in the *Times Literary Supplement* Philip Gardener noted, "If, since the war, Spender's creative engine has run at less than full power, one remains grateful for his best work, the context of which is fascinatingly provided by these letters and journals."

One of Spender's earliest published works of autobi-ography, *World within World,* came to be emblematic of the author's candor, commitment to honesty, and longevity. First published in 1951, the book created a stir for Spender's frank disclosure of a homosexual relationship he had had at around the time of the Spanish Civil War. The relationship ended when Spender married. Spender's ex-lover then ran off to fight in Spain; Spender ended up going after him to try to get him out of the country. The book earned a second life when it became the subject of another controversy in the 1990s. In 1993, American writer David Leavitt published his novel *While England Sleeps,* in which a writer has a homosexual affair that follows many of the events of Spender's life but adds more explicit sexual detail. Feeling his integrity and his literary license threatened, Spender accused Leavitt of plagiarism. He also filed a lawsuit in Brit-ish courts to stop the British publication of the book, charging the American novelist with copyright in-fringement and violation of a British law that assures authors the right to control adaptations of their work. In 1994, Leavitt and his publisher, Viking Penguin, agreed to a settlement that would withdraw the book from publication; Leavitt made changes to *While England Sleeps* for a revised edition.

During this period of intense attention focused on *World within World,* St. Martin's reprinted the auto-biography with a new introduction by Spender. As a result, many readers were afforded the opportunity to discover or rediscover Spender's work. "With the passage of time," commented Eric Pace in a *New York Times* obituary, "'World within World' has proved to be in many ways Sir Stephen's most endur-ing prose work because it gives the reader revealing glimpses of its author, Auden and Mr. Isherwood and of what it was like to be a British poet in the 1930's."

In the final analysis, "Some of Spender's poems, criticism, memoirs, translations have contributed to the formation of a period, which to some extent, they now represent . . . ," Robert Craft observed in his *New York Review of Books* critique of *The Journals of Stephen Spender, 1939-1983.* "Yet Spender him-self stands taller than his work. The least insular writer of his generation and the most generous, he is a kinder man—*hypocrite lecteur!*—than most of us deserve."

*BIOGRAPHICAL/CRITICAL SOURCES:*

*BOOKS*

Connors, J. J., *Poets & Politics: A Study of the Careers of C. Day Lewis, Stephen Spender and W. H. Auden in the 1930s,* Yale University Press (New Haven, CT), 1967.

*Contemporary Literary Criticism,* Gale (Detroit), Volume 1, 1973, Volume 2, 1974, Volume 5, 1976, Volume 10, 1979, Volume 41, 1987.

David, Hugh, *Stephen Spender: A Portrait with Background,* Heinemann (London), 1992.

*Dictionary of Literary Biography,* Volume 20: *British Poets, 1914-1945,* Gale, 1983.

Kulkarni, H. B., *Stephen Spender: Poet in Crisis,* Blackie, 1970.

Kulkarni, H. B., *Stephen Spender: Works and Criticism: An Annotated Bibliography,* Garland, 1976.

Maxwell, D. E. S., *Poets of the Thirties,* Barnes & Noble, 1969.

O'Neill, Michael, and Gareth Reeves, *Auden, MacNeice, Spender: The Thirties Poetry,* St. Martin's, 1992.

Pandey, Surya Nath, *Stephen Spender: A Study in Poetic Growth,* Humanities Press (Atlantic Highlands, NJ), 1982.

Reilly, Catherine W., *English Poetry of the Second World War: A Biobibliography,* G. K. Hall (Boston), 1986.

Sasidharan, K. P., *Poets in a Changing World: A Study of the Progressive Movement in Poetry,* Konark Publishers (Delhi, India), 1991.

Smith, Elton Edmund, *The Angry Young Men of the Thirties,* Southern Illinois University Press (Carbondale, IL), 1975.

Stanford, Derek, *Stephen Spender, Louis MacNeice, Cecil Day Lewis: A Critical Essay,* Eerdmans (Grand Rapids, MI), 1969.

Sternlicht, Sanford V., *Stephen Spender,* Twayne, 1992.

Weatherhead, A. Kingsley, *Stephen Spender and the Thirties,* Bucknell University Press (Cranbury, NJ), 1975.

Whitehead, John, *A Commentary on the Poetry of W. H. Auden, C. Day Lewis, Louis MacNeice, and Stephen Spender,* E. Mellen Press (Lewiston, NY), 1992.

*PERIODICALS*

*American Scholar,* Winter, 1988, p. 148.
*Boston Globe,* November 12, 1993, p. 45.
*Chicago Tribune Book World,* January 12, 1986.
*New Republic,* September 23, 1978; August 1, 1988, p. 52.
*New Statesman and Society,* February 26, 1988, p. 22; February 25, 1994, p. 41.
*New Yorker,* November 10, 1986; February 28, 1994, p. 72; January 8, 1996, p. 58.
*New York Review of Books,* January 25, 1979; April 24, 1986.

*New York Times,* February 17, 1994, p. C24; February 20, 1994, sec. 4, p. 14.
*New York Times Book Review,* February 1, 1981; January 26, 1986; September 11, 1988, p. 20; September 4, 1994, p. 10.
*New York Times Magazine,* April 3, 1994, p. 36.
*People,* December 25, 1995, p. 166.
*Publishers Weekly,* February 21, 1994, p. 10; March 20, 1995, p. 16.
*Spectator,* February 26, 1994, p. 37.
*Times Literary Supplement,* April 17, 1981; February 18, 1994, p. 10.
*Washington Post,* February 17, 1994, p. A1; October 26, 1993, p. F1.
*Washington Post Book World,* January 12, 1986.
*World Literature Today,* spring, 1995, p. 367.

*OBITUARIES:*

*PERIODICALS*

*Boston Globe,* July 18, 1995, p. 33.
*Current Biography,* September, 1995, p. 59.
*Economist,* July 22, 1995, p. 97.
*Entertainment Weekly,* July 28, 1995, p. 15.
*New Statesman,* July 28, 1995, p. 41.
*Newsweek,* July 31, 1995, p. 51.
*New York Times,* July 18, 1995, p. B11.
*Time,* July 31, 1995, p. 23.
*Washington Post,* July 18, 1995, p. C1.*

\*        \*        \*

**STONE, Zachary**
**See FOLLETT, Ken(neth Martin)**

\*        \*        \*

**SULLIVAN, Rosemary        1947-**

*PERSONAL:* Born August 29, 1947, in Montreal, Quebec, Canada; daughter of Michael Patrick and Leanore M. (Guthrie) Sullivan. *Education:* McGill University, B.A., 1968; University of Connecticut, M.A., 1969; University of Sussex, Ph.D., 1972.

*ADDRESSES: Home*—45 Benlamond Ave., No. 4, Toronto, Ontario, Canada M4E 1Y8. *Office*—Department of English, Erindale College, University of Toronto, 296 North Building, Mississauga, Ontario, Canada.

*CAREER:* University of Dijon, Dijon, France, research assistant, 1974; University of Bordeaux, Bordeaux, France, research associate, 1975; University of Victoria, Victoria, British Columbia, assistant professor of English, 1976-78; University of Toronto, Erindale College, Mississauga, Ontario, assistant professor, beginning 1978, currently associate professor of English. Lecturer at universities and academic gatherings. Reviewer for Canadian Broadcasting Corp. (CBC-Radio).

*MEMBER:* Writers' Union of Canada.

*AWARDS, HONORS:* Canada Council fellowship, 1978-79; Gerald Lampert Memorial Award for best first poetry collection, 1986, for *The Space a Name Makes;* Governor General's Award for nonfiction, 1995, for *Shadowmaker: The Life of Gwendolyn MacEwen;* has also received the Brascan Silver Medal and grants from Canada Council, Ontario Arts Council and Toronto Arts Council.

*WRITINGS:*

*Theodore Roethke: The Garden Master,* University of Washington Press (Seattle), 1975.
(Editor) *Stories by Canadian Women,* Oxford University Press (Toronto), 1984.
*The Space a Name Makes* (poems), Black Moss Press (Windsor, ON), 1986.
(Editor) *More Stories by Canadian Women,* Oxford University Press, 1987.
(Editor) *Poetry by Canadian Women,* Oxford University Press, 1989.
*By Heart: Elizabeth Smart, a Life,* Viking (Toronto), 1991.
*Blue Panic* (poems), Black Moss Press, 1992.
*Shadowmaker: The Life of Gwendolyn MacEwen,* HarperCollins (New York City), 1995.

Also author of a monograph, *Robertson Davies.* Contributor to *Crossing Frontiers, New Poetry, Descant, Malahat Review, Queen's Quarterly,* and *Canadian Forum.*

*SIDELIGHTS:* Rosemary Sullivan has established a reputation as a biographer of literary figures, an anthologist of Canadian women's literature, and a poet. As a literary biographer, Sullivan "has two great virtues," writes Joan Givner in *Quill & Quire.*

"The first is the ability to shape a compelling story and tell it with incomparable grace. . . . Her other virtue . . . is a deeply felt understanding of and respect for the creative process and for the intensity of the life that feeds it." Sullivan's anthologies of Canadian women's poetry and fiction have been critical successes, while her own poetry has earned her the Gerald Lampert Memorial Award.

In *Theodore Roethke: The Garden Master* Sullivan traces the development of American poet Roethke's work, focusing on "the metaphysical aspects," as Helen McNeil writes in the *Times Literary Supplement.* Writing in *World Literature Today,* J. M. Morrison believes that "Sullivan is principally concerned with psychological patterns in Roethke's life and work. . . . [Sullivan] supplements her psychological expertise with a thorough knowledge of the relevant poetic and mystical traditions." McNeil finds that Sullivan "gives wise and sensitive readings of many of [Roethke's] poems." Walter Waring in *Library Journal* finds that although Sullivan's "style and method are scholarly, she writes with sensitivity and perception."

Sullivan turned her attention to Canadian expatriate novelist Elizabeth Smart in her study *By Heart: Elizabeth Smart, a Life.* Smart, who had four children with the married English poet George Barker, is best known for the autobiographical novel *By Grand Central Station I Sat Down and Wept.* After the novel's appearance in 1945, Smart published no new work for some thirty years, working instead as an advertising copywriter and magazine editor during this time. Sullivan explains in her study that she wanted to write "a feminist biography," but Elspeth Cameron in *Canadian Forum* believes that "Smart's life is not well suited to what Sullivan wants to demonstrate." Cameron argues that Smart "was infantile and self-centred all her life, hardly the free and independent spirit Sullivan wants us to admire." Although Sherrill Grace in *Canadian Literature* admits that Sullivan's biography "does not encourage me to re-read Smart's published work. . . . Nevertheless, it is an interesting biography written with sensitivity and care." Writing in *Contemporary Review,* Geoffrey Heptonstall concludes that *By Heart* is a "sympathetic and compelling book" and a "true story of what a woman's patience can endure, and of what her resolution can achieve."

In *Shadowmaker: The Life of Gwendolyn MacEwen,* Sullivan wrote of another Canadian literary woman.

Gwendolyn MacEwen, a poet whose work earned her a Governor General's Award, died at the age of 46 from alcoholism. Sullivan's biography uncovers the secret side of a woman who, although a lifelong writer, left behind no personal letters or diaries. Reviewing the biography for *Maclean's,* John Bemrose notes that it possesses "an incisive, empathetic immediacy that raises it above the cumbersome, overly detailed work of so many biographers. And while it reveals a great deal about MacEwen, it never presumes to explain everything."

*Stories by Canadian Women* and *More Stories by Canadian Women,* Sullivan's anthologies of Canadian women's literature, gather together examples of the best short fiction written by Canadian women from the country's earliest settlement to the present-day. As Cathy Matyas, reviewing the first anthology, notes in *Essays on Canadian Writing:* "The main criterion for Sullivan really *did* seem to be quality, and the result is an admirably cohesive anthology of short fiction." Speaking of the second anthology, which focuses on the work of contemporary writers, W. H. New in *Books in Canada* praises its inclusion of "alternative traditions in Canadian writing" and finds that, "as with Sullivan's earlier volume, this is a book to absorb rather than to rush through."

With the success of her collections of Canadian women's fiction, Sullivan edited *Poetry by Canadian Women,* a representative collection of the best Canadian women's poetry. Joe Rosenblatt, writing in *Books in Canada,* explains that, "having culled a century and a half from the corpus of Canadian women's poetry, Sullivan places these gems under a variant roof with a historical and evolutionary nexus to hold the poetical works together." "Flipping through the pages, through the centuries, is an entertaining, enlightening, and (inevitably for many women) *affirming* experience," Louise McKinney claims in *Quill & Quire.*

Sullivan's own poetry has appeared in two collections, *The Space a Name Makes* and *Blue Panic.* Sullivan's poems are often concerned with how larger social processes shape our lives. The poems in *Blue Panic,* as Sue Schenk writes in *Canadian Literature,* tell of the "human desire to locate a narrative thread that would allow us to make sense of our lives." Sullivan's poems are "lean and vigorous, with the colloquial directness of a documentary film," according to Barbara Carey in *Books in Canada. The Space a Name Makes* won Sullivan a Gerald Lampert Memorial Award for best first poetry collection.

Sullivan told *CA:* "I lived four years in England, two in France, and have traveled widely. My Canadian background—the complexity of living in two cultures, French and English, both of which are in a process of profound cultural change—is at the root of my particular view of the world."

## BIOGRAPHICAL/CRITICAL SOURCES:

### PERIODICALS

*Books in Canada,* March, 1985, p. 24; April, 1985, p. 42; November, 1986, p. 26; October, 1987, pp. 31-32; May, 1989, p. 36; May, 1991, p. 45.
*Canadian Forum,* March, 1985, pp. 38-39; August, 1991, pp. 26-28; January/February, 1996, pp. 42-43.
*Canadian Literature,* summer, 1992, pp. 146-149; autumn, 1992, pp. 169-170.
*Canadian Materials,* July, 1989, pp. 194-195.
*Contemporary Review,* April, 1993, pp. 217-218.
*Essays on Canadian Writing,* fall, 1986, pp. 140-143.
*Library Journal,* May 1, 1976, p. 1123.
*London Review of Books,* November 21, 1991, pp. 13-14.
*Maclean's,* April 8, 1991, p. 50; October 2, 1995, p. 62.
*New Statesman & Society,* November 1, 1991, p. 46.
*Observer* (London), November 3, 1991, p. 68.
*Quill and Quire,* January, 1988, p. 22; June, 1989, p. 40; February, 1991, p. 29; September, 1995, p. 61; February, 1996, p. 38.
*Saturday Night,* May, 1991, p. 52.
*Spectator,* November 2, 1991, p. 43.
*Times Literary Supplement,* January 27, 1978, p. 79.
*World Literature Today,* spring, 1977, p. 285.*

# T-V

## TAN, Amy (Ruth) 1952-

*PERSONAL:* Born February 19, 1952, in Oakland, CA; daughter of John Yuehhan (a minister and electrical engineer) and Daisy (a vocational nurse and member of a Joy Luck Club; maiden name, Tu Ching) Tan; married Louis M. DeMattei (a tax attorney), April 6, 1974. *Education:* San Jose State University, B.A., 1973, M.A., 1974; postgraduate study at University of California, Berkeley, 1974-76. *Avocational interests:* Billiards, skiing, drawing, piano playing.

*ADDRESSES: Home*—San Francisco, CA. *Office*—Random House, 201 E. 50th St., 22nd floor, New York, NY 10022. *Agent*—Sandra Dijkstra, 1155 Camino del Mar, Del Mar, CA 92014.

*CAREER:* Writer. Alameda County Association for Mentally Retarded, Oakland, CA, language consultant to programs for disabled children, 1976-81; MORE Project, San Francisco, CA, project director, 1980-81; worked as reporter, managing editor, and associate publisher for *Emergency Room Reports* (now *Emergency Medicine Reports*), 1981-83; freelance technical writer, 1983-87.

*AWARDS, HONORS:* Commonwealth Club gold award for fiction, Bay Area Book Reviewers award for best fiction, American Library Association's best book for young adults award, nomination for National Book Critics Circle award for best novel, and nomination for *Los Angeles Times* book award, all 1989, all for *The Joy Luck Club; The Kitchen God's Wife* was a 1991 *Booklist* editor's choice and nominated for Bay Area Book Reviewers award; Best American Essays award, 1991; honorary LHD, Dominican College, 1991.

*WRITINGS:*

NOVELS

*The Joy Luck Club,* Putnam (New York City), 1989.
*The Kitchen God's Wife,* Putnam, 1991.
*The Hundred Secret Senses,* Putnam, 1995.
*The Year of No Flood,* Putnam, 1995.

JUVENILE; ILLUSTRATED BY GRETCHEN SCHIELDS

*The Moon Lady,* Macmillan (New York City), 1992.
*The Chinese Siamese Cat,* Macmillan, 1994.

SCREENPLAY

(With Ronald Bass) *The Joy Luck Club*, Hollywood Pictures, 1993.

OTHER

Also author of short stories, including "The Rules of the Game." Work represented in *State of the Language,* edited by Christopher Ricks and Leonard Michaels, second edition, University of California Press (Berkeley), 1989, and *Best American Essays, 1991* edited by Joyce Carol Oates, Ticknor & Fields (New York City), 1991. Contributor to periodicals, including *Atlantic Monthly, McCall's, Threepenny Review, Grand Street,* and *Seventeen.*

*ADAPTATIONS: The Joy Luck Club* was released on audiocassette by Dove, as was *The Kitchen God's Wife,* 1991. *The Joy Luck Club* was adapted for the stage by Susan Kim and produced in China in 1993.

*SIDELIGHTS:* Amy Tan's novels, *The Joy Luck Club, The Kitchen God's Wife,* and *The Hundred Secret Senses,* have been enthusiastically received by critics as well as the book-buying public. Focusing on the lives of Chinese-American women, Tan's books introduce characters who are ambivalent, as she once was, about their Chinese background. Tan remarked in a *Bestsellers* interview that though she once tried to distance herself from her ethnicity, writing *The Joy Luck Club* helped her discover "how very Chinese I was. And how much had stayed with me that I had tried to deny." Upon *The Joy Luck Club*'s release, Tan quickly became known as a gifted storyteller, a reputation she upheld with the publication of *The Kitchen God's Wife* and *The Hundred Secret Senses.* Impressed with *The Joy Luck Club, Detroit News* contributor Michael Dorris proclaimed Tan "a writer of dazzling talent."

Despite her achievements, Tan's literary career was not planned; in fact, she first began writing fiction as a form of therapy. Considered a workaholic by her friends, Tan had been working ninety hours per week as a freelance technical writer. She became dissatisfied with her work life, however, and hoped to eradicate her workaholic tendencies through psychological counseling. But when her therapist fell asleep several times during her counseling sessions, Tan quit and decided to curb her working hours by delving into jazz piano lessons and writing fiction instead. Tan's first literary efforts were short stories, one of which secured her a position in the Squaw Valley Community of Writers, a fiction writers' workshop. Tan's hobby soon developed into a new career when her first novel, *The Joy Luck Club,* was published in 1989.

Set in the late 1980s, *The Joy Luck Club* details the generational and cultural differences between a young woman, June, and her late Chinese mother's three Chinese friends. June's mother and the three older women had formed the Joy Luck Club, a social group, in San Francisco in 1949. Nearly forty years later, June's mother has died. The surviving members, the "aunties," recruit June to replace her mother, then send her to China to meet her stepsisters and to inform them of the mother's death. When June expresses reservations about her ability to execute this assignment, the older women respond with disappointment. June then realizes that the women rightly suspect that she, and their own daughters, know little of the women's lives and the strength and hope they wished to give the next gen-

eration. Throughout the novel, the various mothers and daughters attempt to articulate their own concerns about the past and the present and about themselves and their relations.

*The Joy Luck Club* was praised as a thought-provoking, engaging novel. In *Quill and Quire,* Denise Chong assessed: "These moving and powerful stories share the irony, pain, and sorrow of the imperfect ways in which mothers and daughters love each other. Tan's vision is courageous and insightful." In her review for the Toronto *Globe and Mail,* Nancy Wigston declared that Tan's literary debut "is that rare find, a first novel that you keep thinking about, keep telling your friends about long after you've finished reading it." *Time* reviewer John Skow found the work "bright, sharp-flavored," adding that it "rings clearly, like a fine porcelain bowl." Some critics were particularly impressed with Tan's ear for authentic dialogue. Carolyn See, for instance, wrote in the *Los Angeles Times Book Review* that Tan ranks among the "magicians of language." Dorris placed the book within the realm of true literature, which "is writing that makes a difference, that alters the way we understand the world and ourselves, that transcends topicality, and by those criteria, *The Joy Luck Club* is the real thing."

Tan followed *The Joy Luck Club* with *The Kitchen God's Wife,* in which a young woman in California realizes a greater understanding of her mother's Chinese background. A generation gap exists between the two heroines: Mother Winnie has only awkwardly adapted to the relatively free-wheeling ways of American, particularly Californian, life; daughter Pearl, on the other hand, is more comfortable in a world of sports and fast food than she is when listening, at least initially, to her mother's recollections of her own arduous life in China. As Winnie recounts the secrets of her past, including her mother's mysterious disappearance, her marriage to a psychotic and brutal man, the deaths of her first three children, and her journey to America in 1949, Pearl is able to view her mother in a new light and gathers the courage to reveal a secret of her own.

Critics hailed *The Kitchen God's Wife,* admiring its poignancy and bittersweet humor. Sabine Durrant, writing in the London *Times,* called the book "gripping" and "enchanting," and Charles Foran, in his review for the Toronto *Globe and Mail,* proclaimed Tan's work "a fine novel" of "exuberant storytelling and rich drama." In a *Washington Post Book World* review, Wendy Law-Yone asserted that Tan exceeded the expectations raised by her first book, declaring that *"The Kitchen God's Wife* is bigger, bolder and, I have to say, better" than *The Joy Luck Club.* Referring to *The Kitchen God's Wife* in a *Time* review, Pico Iyer affirmed, "Tan has transcended herself again."

In her third novel, Tan shifted her focus from the mother-daughter bond to the relationship between sisters. The main characters in *The Hundred Secret Senses* are half-sisters Olivia and Kwan. Olivia is the daughter of an American mother and a Chinese father who died before her fourth birthday. In adulthood, she is a pragmatic, somewhat priggish yuppie. Kwan, her Chinese half-sister, arrives in her life when she is six. Twelve years older than Olivia, clumsy, and barely able to speak English, Kwan is an immediate source of resentment and embarrassment to Olivia. Kwan's belief that she can speak with spirits is anther source of humiliation, one that leads her stepfather to commit her for electroshock therapy. Through the years, Olivia treats Kwan rudely and dismissively, yet her older sister remains devoted to her and is determined to awaken Olivia to the reality of the spirit world. To this end, the two travel to China, where Kwan believes they lived another life together in an earlier century.

For some reviewers, Tan's use of the supernatural posed a problem. Claire Messud, for example, wrote in the *New York Times Book Review* that Tan's evocation of the spirit world was unconvincing, and that "to accept the novel as anything more than a mildly entertaining and slightly ridiculous ghost story, the reader must also make [a] demanding leap of faith, turning a blind eye to rash improbabilities and a host of loose ends. For this reader, at least, that leap was not possible." She noted, however, that Kwan was "a memorable creation. . . . Kwan gently forces Olivia to face the worst in herself and, in so doing, to find her strengths. We could all do with such a sister."

*New York Times* reviewer Michiko Kakutani also expressed a mixed opinion of Tan's third novel. She praised it as "a contemporary tale of familial love and resentment, nimbly evoked in Ms. Tan's guileless prose," but qualified that it was "unfortunately overlaid by another, more sensational tale of reincarnation that undermines the reader's trust." She went on: "Of course, there's nothing inherently implausible about ghosts. Maxine Hong Kingston handled similar material with consummate ardor and grace in 'The Woman Warrior,' but Ms. Tan doesn't seem to know how to make Kwan's beliefs in the spirit world palpable or engaging." She affirmed, however, that "Ms. Tan is able to create enormously sympathetic people who inhabit some middle ground between real life and the more primary-colored world of fable. In doing so, she draws the reader into these characters' lives, and into the minutiae of their daily concerns."

Some other commentators were unreserved in their enthusiasm for *The Hundred Secret Senses.* Chicago *Tribune Books* contributor Penelope Mesic stated that the book contained "three qualities almost never found together: popularity, authenticity and excellence." Mesic concluded the work is an "effortless mix of invention and reliance on reality that makes Tan's fiction so engrossing—a kind of consistency of action that suggests one could ask anything about a character and Tan could answer. She provides what is most irresistible in popular fiction: a feeling of abundance, an account so circumstantial, powerful and ingenious that it seems the story could go on forever." Gail Caldwell of the *Boston Globe* declared that *The Hundred Secret Senses* is simply "the wisest and most captivating novel Tan has written."

## BIOGRAPHICAL/CRITICAL SOURCES:

### BOOKS

*Bestsellers 89,* issue 3, Gale (Detroit), 1989, pp. 69-71.

*Contemporary Literary Criticism,* Gale, Volume 59, 1990.

Kramer, Barbara, *Amy Tan, Author of* The Joy Luck Club, Enslow Publishers (Springfield, NJ), 1996.

*Notable Asian Americans,* Gale, 1995.

### PERIODICALS

*America,* May 4, 1996, p. 27.

*Boston Globe,* November 10, 1992, p. 69; May 21, 1993, p. 23; September 19, 1993, p. 77; October 22, 1995, p. B37.

*Canadian Literature,* summer, 1992, p. 196.

*Chicago Tribune,* August 6, 1989; March 17, 1991; September 26, 1993, section 13, p. 20; November 9, 1995, section 2C, p. 16.

*Christian Science Monitor,* September 16, 1993, p. 11.

*Critique,* spring, 1993, p. 193.

*Detroit News,* March 26, 1989, p. 2D.

*Economist,* December 12, 1992, p. 101.

*Fortune,* August 26, 1991, p. 116; December 28, 1992, p. 105.

*Globe and Mail* (Toronto), April 29, 1989; June 29, 1991, p. C8.

*Journal and Constitution* (Atlanta), November 26, 1995, p. K11.

*Kirkus,* September 1, 1992, p. 1135.

*Life,* April, 1994, p. 108.

*London Review of Books,* July 11, 1991, p. 19.

*Los Angeles Times,* March 12, 1989; May 28, 1992, p. E7; September 5, 1993, "California" section, p. 8; September 8, 1993, p. F1; October 30, 1995, p. E4.

*Los Angeles Times Book Review,* March 12, 1989, p. 1; July 5, 1992, p. 10; December 6, 1992, p. 10.

*Ms.,* November, 1991; November-December, 1995, p. 88.

*New Statesman and Society,* July 12, 1991, pp. 37-38; February 16, 1996, p. 38.

*Newsweek,* April 17, 1989, pp. 68-69; June 24, 1991, p. 63; November 6, 1995, p. 91.

*New York,* March 20, 1989, p. 82; June 17, 1991, p. 83.

*New York Times,* July 5, 1989; September 8, 1993, p. C15; November 17, 1995, p. C29.

*New York Times Book Review,* March 19, 1989, pp. 3, 28; June 16, 1991, p. 9; November 8, 1992, p. 31; October 29, 1995, p. 11.

*People,* April 10, 1989, pp. 149-50.

*Publishers Weekly,* July 7, 1989, pp. 24-26; April 5, 1991, pp. 4-7; July 20, 1992, pp. 249-50; August 9, 1993, pp. 32-34; July 11, 1994, p. 78; September 11, 1995, p. 73.

*School Library Journal,* September, 1992, p. 255.

*Time,* March 27, 1989, p. 98; June 3, 1991, p. 67.

*Times* (London), July 11, 1991, p. 16.

*Times Educational Supplement* (London), August 4, 1989, p. 19; August 2, 1991, p. 18; February 5, 1993, p. 10; January 16, 1995, p. 16.

*Times Literary Supplement* (London), December 29, 1989, p. 1447; July 5, 1991, p. 20.

*Tribune Books* (Chicago), March 12, 1989, pp. 1, 11; November 5, 1995, pp. 1, 11.

*USA Today,* October 5, 1993, p. D12.

*Wall Street Journal,* September 1, 1992, p. A12; August 19, 1993, p. A8; September 9, 1993, p. A18; December 6, 1994, p. B1.

*Washington Post,* October 8, 1989; May 21, 1993, p. WW16; May 27, 1993, p. D9; September 21, 1993, pp. D1, D10; September 24, 1993, p. WW47; October 23, 1995, p. D1.

*Washington Post Book World,* March 5, 1989, p. 7; June 16, 1991, pp. 1-2.

## TARR, Herbert  1929-1993

*PERSONAL:* Surname originally Targovik; born September 10, 1929, in Brooklyn, NY; died of liver cancer, November 18, 1993, in Roslyn Heights, NY; son of Isidore and Anna (Rubinfeld) Targovik. *Education:* Brooklyn College (now of the City University of New York), B.A. (magna cum laude), 1949; Columbia University, M.A., 1951; Hebrew Union College-Jewish Institute of Religion, New York, NY, B.H.L., 1953, M.H.L. and Rabbi, 1955.

*CAREER:* Teacher at Temple Rodeph Sholom, New York, NY, 1953, and Temple Beth Sholom, Roslyn, NY, 1954-56; Temple Beth Zion, Buffalo, NY, rabbi, 1958-60; Westbury Temple, Westbury, NY, rabbi, 1960-63; freelance writer, 1963-93. *Military service:* U.S. Air Force, chaplain, 1956-58.

*MEMBER:* Central Conference of American Rabbis, New York Board of Rabbis, Nassau-Suffolk Board of Rabbis.

*WRITINGS:*

*The Conversion of Chaplain Cohen* (novel), Geis, 1963.

*Heaven Help Us!,* Random House (New York City), 1968.

*A Time for Loving,* Random House, 1973.

*So Help Me God!,* Times Books (New York City), 1979.

*A Woman of Spirit,* D. I. Fine (New York City), 1989.

*MUSICALS*

*Heaven Help Us!* (adaptation from novel), produced on Broadway, 1969.

*SIDELIGHTS:* Former rabbi Herbert Tarr, stated *Publishers Weekly* interviewer Beth Levine, was a person who felt it was "important to write about admirable people and important issues." A native Brooklynite, Tarr was educated at a yeshiva school and later attended rabbinical school while studying comparative literature and drama at Columbia University. Tarr became a best-selling author in 1963 with his novel *The Conversion of Chaplain Cohen.* "'Kvetch-22,' it could have been called," wrote Marvin Kitman in the *New York Times Book Review*—the story of the struggles of a Air Force rabbi trying to come to terms with military life. The book was rejected by thirty-two publishers and seventeen agents, Levine explained, before it was finally accepted by Bernard Geis. "Geis loved the book . . . and gave Tarr a $750 advance. On the strength of that sum, Tarr resigned from his congregation." The story sold about 700,000 copies in its first few years of publication.

*The Conversion of Chaplain Cohen* launched Tarr on a writing career that lasted for thirty years. In his second novel *Heaven Help Us!* Tarr continued his examination of contemporary Judaism with the story of suburban rabbi Gideon Abel, whose religious emphasis conflicts with the worldly preferences of his parishioners. "Rabbi Abel's congregation sees the Temple as a social centre and a business," explained a *Times Literary Supplement* reviewer. "Faced with his committed brand of Judaism, they complain that 'that man is too much of a Jew, and runs too tight a Temple'; whereas Rabbi Abel has received from his old teacher the view that 'on the outside Jews are making believe they're Jews, but inside they're all of them Rotarians.'" "Mr. Tarr writes of all this," declared *New York Times* contributor Richard F. Shepard, "with a conviction and fervor, masked in humor, that is in the best prophetic tradition."

After *A Time for Loving,* a third novel set in ancient Israel and depicting the love of an aging King Solomon for Shulamith, a peasant girl, Tarr returned to the subject of secularism and contemporary Judaism in *So Help Me God!* This is the story of a young man, Andrew Baron, who tries to dodge the draft for the Vietnam War by enrolling in rabbinical school. The catch is that Baron is not Jewish, and he has to undergo a crash course in Jewish traditions, customs, and practices. Eventually Baron ends up in Soviet Russia, assisting Jewish activists. His commitment to Judaism grows along with his self-respect, and, stated a *Publishers Weekly* contributor, "the novel, too, attains depth and poignancy, while never losing its by-now bittersweet humor." "Like his other novels," wrote Andrea Caron Kempf in *Library Journal,* "this one is a gentle sermon, laced with humor, on the art of being Jewish."

*A Woman of Spirit* takes a quite different look at modern Jewish life. Its protagonist is a Polish Jewish woman named Hannah Brody who discovers after her husband's death that she is very well-off. She treats herself to a cruise and "falls in love, travels, moves to an upscale neighborhood and discovers that her mindless doodlings were actually the work of a latent, talented artist," according to a *Publishers Weekly* reviewer. "Everyone should enjoy this trib-

ute," stated a contributor to *Kirkus Reviews,* "to a *bubbe* with the mostest." Levine declared that Tarr wrote the book in part as a tribute to his mother—who, like Hannah, was born in Polish Galicia—and in part as a way to improve the image of the Jewish mother as presented in Philip Roth's *Portnoy's Complaint.* "Tarr is nothing so much as a professional *tummler,*" Levine explained—"Yiddish for someone who likes to stir things up. . . . His forum may change but his intent remains the same: to make people reassess their lives and their involvement in the world that surrounds them."

## BIOGRAPHICAL/CRITICAL SOURCES:

*PERIODICALS*

*Booklist,* March 1, 1973, p. 620; December 1, 1979, p. 543; September 1, 1989, p. 38.
*Kirkus Reviews,* September 1, 1996, p. 1279.
*Library Journal,* August, 1979, p. 1592.
*New York Times,* June 12, 1969, p. 45.
*New York Times Book Review,* January/June, 1968, pp. 6-7; January/June, 1973, p. 24.
*Publishers Weekly,* May/June, 1969, p. 59; September/October, 1972, p. 49; July 2, 1979, p. 96; September 29, 1989, p. 60; December 1, 1989, pp. 40-41.
*Spectator,* January 31, 1969, p. 142.
*Times Literary Supplement,* February 20, 1969, p. 175.
*Washington Post Book World,* June 22, 1969, p. 13.

## OBITUARIES:

*PERIODICALS*

*Chicago Tribune,* November 21, 1993, p. 10.
*New York Times,* November 19, 1993, p. B6.
*Washington Post,* November 20, 1993, p. C5.*

\* \* \*

**TATE, Joan 1922-**

*PERSONAL:* Born September 23, 1922, in Tonbridge, Kent, England; married, 1945; children: two daughters, one son.

*ADDRESSES: Home*—7 College Hill, Shrewsbury SY1 1LZ, England.

*CAREER:* Freelance writer, translator, and publisher's reader.

*MEMBER:* PEN International, Amnesty International, Swedish English Literary Translators' Association (SELTA).

*WRITINGS:*

CHILDREN'S FICTION

*Coal Hoppy,* illustrated by J. Yunge-Bateman, Heinemann (London), 1964.

*The Crane,* illustrated by Richard Wilson, Heinemann, 1964.

*Jenny,* illustrated by Charles Keeping, Heinemann, 1964.

*Lucy,* illustrated by Wilson, Heinemann, 1964.

*The Next-Doors,* illustrated by Keeping, Heinemann, 1964, Scholastic (New York City), 1976.

*Picture Charlie,* illustrated by Laszlo Acs, Heinemann, 1964.

*The Rabbit Boy,* illustrated by Hugh Marshall, Heinemann, 1964.

*The Silver Grill,* illustrated by Marshall, Heinemann, 1964, Scholastic, 1976.

*Bill,* illustrated by George Tuckwell, Heinemann, 1966.

*The Holiday,* illustrated by Leo Walmsley, Heinemann, 1966.

*Mrs. Jenny,* illustrated by Keeping, Heinemann, 1966.

*Tad,* illustrated by Walmsley, Heinemann, 1966.

*The Tree,* illustrated by George Tuckwell, Heinemann, 1966, published as *Tina and David,* Nelson (Nashville), 1973.

*Bits and Pieces,* illustrated by Quentin Blake, Heinemann, 1967.

*The Circus and Other Stories,* illustrated by Timothy Jacques, Heinemann, 1967.

*The Great Birds,* Almqvist & Wiksell (Stockholm), 1967, Blackie (London), 1976.

*Letters to Chris,* illustrated by Mary Russon, Heinemann, 1967.

*Luke's Garden,* illustrated by Quentin Blake, Heinemann, 1967, Hodder & Stoughton (London), 1976, published as *Luke's Garden and Gramp: Two Short Novels,* Harper (New York City), 1981.

*The New House,* Almqvist & Wiksell, 1967, Pelham, 1976.

*The Old Car,* Almqvist & Wiksell, 1967.

*Polly,* Almqvist & Wiksell, 1967, Cassell (London), 1976.

*The Soap Box,* Almqvist & Wiksell, 1967.

*The Train,* Almqvist & Wiksell, 1967.

*Wild Martin and the Crow,* illustrated by Richard Kennedy, Heinemann, 1967.

*Sam and Me,* Macmillan (New York City), 1968.

*The Ball,* illustrated by Mary Dinsdale, John Dyke, and Prudence Seward, Macmillan, 1969.

*The Caravan,* Almqvist & Wiksell, 1969.

*The Cheapjack Man,* illustrated by Richard Rose, Jenny Williams, and Mary Dinsdale, Macmillan, 1969.

*Clipper,* Macmillan, 1969, published as *Ring on My Finger,* 1971, Scholastic, 1976.

*Edward and the Uncles,* Almqvist & Wiksell, 1969.

*The Gobblydock,* illustrated by Rose, Williams, and Dinsdale, Macmillan, 1969.

*The Letter,* Almqvist & Wiksell, 1969.

*The Lollipop Man,* illustrated by Dinsdale, John Dyke, and Prudence Seward, Macmillan, 1969.

*The Nest,* illustrated by Seward, Macmillan, 1969.

*Out of the Sun,* Heinemann, 1969.

*Puddle's Tiger,* Almqvist & Wiksell, 1969.

*The Secret,* Almqvist & Wiksell, 1969.

*The Treehouse,* illustrated by Dinsdale, Macmillan, 1969.

*Whizz Kid,* Macmillan, 1969, published as *Not the Usual Kind of Girl,* Scholastic, 1974, published as *Clee and Nibs,* Penguin (New York City), 1990.

*Gramp,* illustrated by Robert Geary, Chatto Boyd and Oliver, 1971, revised edition, Pelham, 1979, published as *Luke's Garden and Gramp: Two Short Novels,* Harper, 1981.

*The Long Road Home,* Heinemann, 1971.

*Wild Boy,* illustrated by Trevor Stubley, Chatto Boyd and Oliver, 1972, Harper, 1973.

*Wump Day,* illustrated by John Storey, Heinemann, 1972.

*Ben and Annie,* illustrated by Dinsdale, Brockhampton Press, 1973, Doubleday (New York City), 1974.

*Dad's Camel,* illustrated by Margaret Power, Heinemann, 1973, new edition, Red Fox/Anderson Press, 1991.

*Dinah,* Almqvist & Wiksell, 1973.

*Grandpa and My Sister Bee,* illustrated by Leslie Wood, Brockhampton Press, 1973.

*Jock and the Rock Cakes,* illustrated by Carolyn Dinan, Brockhampton Press, 1973.

*Journal for One,* Almqvist & Wiksell, 1973.

*The Man Who Rang the Bell,* Almqvist & Wiksell, 1973.

*The Match,* Almqvist & Wiksell, 1973.

*Night Out,* Almqvist & Wiksell, 1973.

*Taxi!,* Schoeningh, 1973.

*Dirty Dan,* Almqvist & Wiksell, 1974.

*Ginger Mick,* Heinemann, 1974, revised edition, Longman (London), 1975.

*The Runners,* illustrated by Douglas Phillips, David & Charles (London), 1974, revised edition, Longman, 1977.

*Sunday's Trumpet,* Almqvist & Wiksell, 1974.

*The Thinking Box,* Almqvist and Wiksell, 1974.

*Zena,* Almqvist & Wiksell, 1974.

*Your Dog,* Pelham, 1975.

*Billoggs,* illustrated by Stubley, Pelham, 1976.

*Crow and the Brown Boy,* illustrated by Gay Galsworthy, Cassell (London), 1976.

*The House That Jack Built,* Pelham, 1976.

*Polly and the Barrow Boy,* illustrated by Galsworthy, Cassell, 1976.

*Turn Again, Whittington,* Pelham, 1976.

*You Can't Explain Everything,* Longman, 1976.

*See You and Other Stories,* Longman, 1977.

*See How They Run,* Pelham, 1978.

*Cat Country,* Ram, 1979.

*Jumping Jo the Joker,* illustrated by Maggie Dawson, Macmillan, 1984.

NONFICTION AND FABLES FOR CHILDREN

*Going Up,* three volumes, Almqvist & Wiksell, 1969-74.

*Your Town,* illustrated by Virginia Smith, David & Charles, 1972.

*How Do You Do?,* three volumes, Schoeningh, 1973-76.

*The Living River,* illustrated by David Harris, Dent (London), 1974.

*Disco Books* (contains *Big Fish, Tom's Trip, The Day I Got the Sack, Girl in the Window, Supermarket, Gren, Day Off,* and *Moped*), eight volumes, illustrated by Galsworthy, Jill Cox, and George Craig, Cassell, 1975.

*Your Dog,* illustrated by Babette Cole, Pelham, 1975.

*On Your Own,* two volumes, Wheaton (Exeter), 1977-78.

*Frankie Flies,* Macmillan, 1980.

*Club Books* (contains *The Jimjob, The Totter Man, Trip to Liverpool,* and *New Shoes*), four volumes, illustrated by Craig and Cox, Cassell, 1981.

(With M. Wiese) *How to Go Shopping,* Hirschgraben, 1982.

(With M. Wiese) *How to Get Help,* Hirschgraben, 1983.

(With M. Wiese) *How to Eat Out,* Hirschgraben, 1983.

*The Fox and the Stork and Other Fables* (fables from Aesop), illustrated by Svend Otto S., Pelham, 1985.

*Avalanche!,* illustrated by Otto S., Pelham, 1987.

*The Donkey and the Dog* (fable from Aesop), illustrated by Otto S., Pelham, 1987.

*Twenty Tales of Aesop,* illustrated by Otto S., Pelham, 1987.

OTHER

Also translator of more than 140 books from Swedish, Danish and Norwegian into English. Contributor of poems and short stories to anthologies.

Tate's work has been translated into several languages. A collection of her manuscripts is housed in the Kerlan Collection, University of Minnesota, Minneapolis.

*ADAPTATIONS: Gramp* was adapted for British Broadcasting Corp. (BBC) radio in 1971.

*WORK IN PROGRESS:* A series of nonfiction books on the theater arts, including *Shadow Theater of Thailand, Shadow Theater of China, Shadow Theater of Indonesia, Shadow Theater of the Middle East, Shadow Theater of India,* and *Shadow Theater of Malaysia.* Two children's fiction titles, *Catspoon and Fiddle* and *Jimmy.*

*SIDELIGHTS:* Joan Tate is best known for her short novels written for adolescents. A typical Tate book is "topical, full of snappy dialogue, and [has] a plot that is relevant and interesting to teenagers," according to Jean Russell in *Twentieth-Century Children's Writers.* Tate, who is fluent in Swedish, has also written young adult titles in simple English for second-language readers in Sweden, Norway, Denmark, Finland, and Germany, and she is a translator of books for both children and adults.

Writing in *Something about the Author Autobiography Series (SAAS),* Tate describes her early books as stories "for young people who were no longer children, who hadn't started reading when they were four, who had never read a whole book, who had no books at home and whose parents never or rarely went into a library or a bookshop." These books Tate continues, were meant for readers who "wanted books about the real life they actually lived themselves, not stories about bunny rabbits or squirrels going shopping or improbable 'adventure' stories." Because of this focus, Tate wrote about young people who "went dancing, drove cars, got into trouble, got out of trouble, wept or laughed or hurt themselves, stories with a beginning, middle, but very rarely a conclusive end."

The 1966 work *Tina and David,* published in England as *The Tree,* is indicative of how Tate presented a sensitive interaction between teenage protagonists. In this novel eighteen-year-old David is painfully shy of girls, so shy that he cannot talk to them. But when he runs into a former classmate, Tina, with whom he used to exchange notes in school, he finds a new strategy to communicate. One day Tina discovers a note left by David in a tree by her usual bus stop. From this fragile beginning, the two form a real friendship that soon blossoms into love, and when the tree is cut down Tina is saddened, but David realizes they no longer need this form of communication. A reviewer in the *Bulletin of the Center for Children's Books* concludes that Tate's sensitivity in handling the relationship was "affective and realistic."

Tate's early books were so successful in reaching their audience that she was asked by a Swedish publisher to write the same sort of books for second-language readers in Sweden as well. *The Great Birds,* published first in Stockholm and then a decade later in England, tells the story of the loner Mark who has a phobia about airplanes until meeting—through a shared hobby of bird watching—a pilot from a nearby air base and taking an unexpected flight. The theme of this book, notes Margery Fisher in *Growing Point,* "is developed with the shrewd sympathy typical of Joan Tate's writing."

Another favorite of Tate's realistic young-adult novels is *Whizz Kid,* published in the United States as *Not the Usual Kind of Girl,* a "kind of love story," as Tate describes it in *SAAS.* "Actually, the story is about what happens when the girl's boyfriend gets out of the car for a moment to relieve himself on the way back from a football match and completely disappears. The story is told in two halves, first her view of what happened, and then, secondly, his." It was a story popular enough with readers to be published in Danish, Norwegian, and French, with a main character, Clee, who is "wonderfully crisp and unique," according to a *Times Literary Supplement* reviewer.

Another story about a boy and girl, *Ben and Annie,* is about two young people who live in the same apartment house. Annie is confined to a wheelchair and Ben communicates with her via a second-hand intercom rigged up by his father. Ben takes Annie for outings to the park and shopping, but when Ben and a friend playfully push Annie down a hill, this is misunderstood by an onlooker. Thinking that the boys are somehow torturing the girl, this adult reports the incident to Annie's parents, who end the friendship. Written in the present tense and with large blocks of dialogue, the story has "a strong feeling of immediacy," Paul Heins notes in *Horn Book,* concluding that the book was "skillful for its condensation and powerful for its presentation of the emotions of childhood." A contributor to *Bulletin of the Center for Children's Books* concurs, calling *Ben and Annie* a "short and poignant story." A *Publishers Weekly* reviewer praises Tate for the fact that she didn't "prettify the ending. . . . The reader's sense of loss . . . is acute."

Tate's career has spanned four decades and over a hundred original publications. But to the author, her career seems quite ordinary. "In reality," Tate writes in *SAAS,* "I am quite an ordinary person who spends almost every day in working hours banging away on a machine in a small room in a small house in a small market town in an agricultural area of England near Wales, and the post office does quite well out of me." Of her more recent work, Tate has said: "Nowadays I am largely occupied with translations of Scandinavian literature, of which there is a great deal, and today it is beginning to be noticed everywhere outside Scandinavia. It's a good life."

*BIOGRAPHICAL/CRITICAL SOURCES:*

*BOOKS*

*Something about the Author Autobiography Series,* Volume 20, Gale (Detroit), 1995.
*Twentieth-Century Children's Writers,* 4th edition, St. James Press (Detroit), 1995.

*PERIODICALS*

*Bulletin of the Center for Children's Books,* April, 1970, p. 135; February, 1974, p. 102; May, 1974, p. 151; November, 1974, p. 55; October, 1981, p. 38.
*Growing Point,* March, 1975, p. 2579; July, 1976, p. 2919; November, 1976, p. 2988; March, 1977, p. 3060; January, 1979, p. 3443; January, 1986, p. 4549; September, 1987, p. 4872.
*Horn Book,* December, 1973, p. 596; December, 1974, p. 694; October, 1981, p. 545.

*Junior Bookshelf,* April, 1975, p. 137; April, 1976, p. 109.

*Kirkus Reviews,* February 1, 1969, p. 108; September 1, 1973, p. 973; September 15, 1973, p. 1045; July 15, 1974, p. 744; February 1, 1982, p. 137.

*Library Journal,* October 15, 1969, p. 3836; January 15, 1974, p. 219; May 15, 1974, p. 1478.

*Publishers Weekly,* August 5, 1974, p. 58.

*School Library Journal,* September, 1976, p. 97; September, 1981, p. 142.

*Times Literary Supplement,* March 14, 1968, p. 258; April 2, 1971, p. 385; July 2, 1971, p. 775; December 3, 1971, p. 1512; April 28, 1972, p. 481; November 3, 1972, p. 1335; December 8, 1972, p. 1497; April 6, 1973, p. 387; September 28, 1973, pp. 1123, 1127; December 6, 1974, p. 1373; November 21, 1980, p. 1324.

*Voice of Youth Advocates,* October, 1981, p. 38.

\*   \*   \*

**THOMPSON, Kenneth W(infred)    1921-**

*PERSONAL:* Born August 29, 1921, in Des Moines, IA; son of Thor Carlyle and Agnes (Rorbeck) Thompson; married Lucille Elizabeth Bergquist (deceased), February 4, 1948; married Beverly Cornelia Bourret; children: (first marriage) Kenneth Carlyle, Paul Andrew, James David; (second marriage) Carolyn Annette. *Education:* Augustana College, Sioux Falls, SD, A.B., 1943; University of Chicago, M.A., 1948, Ph.D., 1950. *Avocational interests:* Travel, gardening, exercise, watching football and basketball.

*ADDRESSES: Home*—369 Normandy Dr., Charlottesville, VA 22903. *Office*—Miller Center of Public Affairs, University of Virginia, P.O. Box 5106, Charlottesville, VA 22905.

*CAREER:* University of Chicago, Chicago, IL, lecturer in social sciences, 1948, assistant professor of political science, 1951-53; Northwestern University Evanston, IL, assistant professor of political science and chair of international relations committee, 1951-55; Rockefeller Foundation, New York City, consultant in international relations, 1953-55, assistant director, 1955-57, associate director, 1957-60, director for social sciences, 1960-61, vice president, 1961-74; University of Virginia, Charlottesville, Common-

wealth Professor of Government and Foreign Affairs, 1975-78, White Burkett Miller Professor of Government and Foreign Affairs, 1979-86, J. Wilson Newman Professor of Government and Foreign Affairs, 1986—, director of Miller Center of Public Affairs, 1978—. Seminar associate, Columbia University, 1957—. Featured lecturer at numerous colleges and universities; trustee, member of board of directors, or director of numerous institutes, educational organizations, and colleges. *Military service:* U.S. Army, Infantry and Intelligence, 1943-45, Counter-Intelligence, 1944-46.

*MEMBER:* International Studies Association, American Political Science Association, Council of Foreign Relations, United Nations Association of the United States of America, American Committee on East West Accord (committee member), American Universities Field Staff (member of governing board), Society for Religion in Higher Education (fellow), American Academy of Arts and Sciences (fellow), Council on Religion and International Affairs (director of ethics and foreign policy project), Phi Beta Kappa, Sigma Nu, Raven Society, Century Club.

*AWARDS, HONORS:* LL.D., University of Notre Dame, 1964, Bowdoin College, 1972, St. Michael's College, 1973, and St. Olaf College, 1974; L.H.D., West Virginia Wesleyan University, 1970, Nebraska Wesleyan College, 1971, University of Denver 1984, and Augustana College, 1986; Annual Medal, University of Chicago, 1974.

*WRITINGS:*

(With Karl de Schweinitz) *Man and Modern Society: Conflict and Choice in the Industrial Era,* Holt (New York City), 1953.

*Ethics and National Purpose* (pamphlet), Church Peace Union, 1957.

*Christian Ethics and the Dilemmas of Foreign Policy,* Duke University Press (Durham, NC), 1959.

*Political Realism and the Crisis of World Politics: An American Approach to Foreign Policy,* Princeton University Press (Princeton, NJ), 1960, reprinted, University Press of America (Lanham, MD), 1982.

(With Ivo D. Duchacek) *Conflict and Cooperation among Nations,* Holt, 1960.

*America Diplomacy and Emergent Patterns,* New York University Press (New York City), 1962.

*The Moral Issue in Statecraft: Twentieth-Century Approaches and Problems,* Louisiana State University Press (Baton Rouge, LA), 1966.

(With Hans J. Morgenthau and Jerald C. Brauer) *U.S. Policy in the Far East: Ideology, Religion, and Superstition,* Council on Religion and International Affairs (New York City), 1968.

*Foreign Assistance: A View from the Private Sector,* University of Notre Dame Press (Notre Dame, IN), 1972.

*Higher Education for National Development,* Interbook, 1972.

*Reconstituting the Human Community,* Hazen Foundation, 1972.

*Understanding World Politics,* University of Notre Dame Press, 1975.

(With James Rosenau and Gavin Boyd) *World Politics,* Free Press (New York City), 1976.

*Interpreters and Critics of the Cold War,* University Press of America, 1978.

*Ethics, Functionalism and Power in International Politics: Crisis in Values,* Louisiana State University Press, 1979.

*Masters of International Thought,* Louisiana State University Press, 1980.

*The Moral Imperatives of Human Rights: A World Survey,* University Press of America, 1980.

*Morality and Foreign Policy,* Louisiana State University Press, 1980.

*Cold War Theories, Volume 1: World Polarization, 1943-53,* Louisiana State University Press, 1981.

*The President and the Public Philosophy,* Louisiana State University Press, 1981.

*American Diplomacy and Emergent Patterns,* University Press of America, 1983.

*Winston Churchill's World-View,* Louisiana State University Press 1983.

(With Morgenthau) *Politics among Nations,* 6th revised edition, Knopf (New York City), 1984.

*Toynbee's Philosophy of History and Politics,* Louisiana State University Press, 1985.

*Moralism and Morality in Politics and Diplomacy,* University Press of America, 1985.

*Theory and Practice in International Relations,* University Press of America, 1987.

*Traditions and Values in Politics and Diplomacy,* Louisiana State University Press, 1989.

*Schools of Thought in International Relations,* Louisiana State University Press, 1996.

*EDITOR*

(With Morgenthau) *Principles and Problems of International Politics: Selected Readings,* Knopf, 1950, reprinted, University Press of America, 1982.

(And contributor and author of introduction with Joseph E. Black) *Foreign Policies in a World of Change,* Harper (New York City), 1963.

(With Barbara R. Fogel) *Higher Education and Social Change: Promising Experiments in Developing Countries,* Volumes 1-2, Praeger (New York City), 1976.

(With Robert J. Myers) *Truth and Tragedy: A Tribute to Hans J. Morgenthau,* New Republic Press (Washington, DC), 1977.

(With Louis J. Halle) *Foreign Policy and the Democratic Process: The Geneva Papers,* University Press of America, 1978.

(With Herbert Butterfield) *The Ethics of History and Politics,* University Press of America, 1979.

*Papers on Presidential Disability and the Twenty-Fifth Amendment by Six Medical, Legal and Political Authorities,* University Press of America, 1988

*SERIES EDITOR*

*The Virginia Papers on the Presidency: The White Burkett Miller Center Forums,* Volumes 1-27, University Press of America, 1979-96.

*American Values Projected Abroad,* Volumes 1-20, University Press of America, 1980-83.

*The American Presidency: Principles and Problems,* Volumes 1-3, University Press of America, 1982-84.

*The Credibility of Institutions, Policies and Leadership,* Volumes 1-20, University Press of America, 1983-86.

*The Presidential Nominating Process,* Volumes 1-4, University Press of America, 1983-86.

*The Presidency and the Press,* Volumes 1-6, University Press of America, 1983-86.

*Portraits of American Presidents,* Volumes 1-11, University Press of America, 1983-92.

*Ethics and Foreign Policy,* Volumes 1-2, Transaction Books, 1984-85.

*The American Presidency: Perspectives from Abroad,* Volumes 1-2, University Press of America, 1986.

*Presidential Transitions and Foreign Policy,* Volumes 1-9, University Press of America, 1986-95.

*The Presidency and Science Advising,* Volumes 1-7, University Press of America, 1986-88.

*Rhetoric and Political Discourse,* Volumes 1-20, University Press of America, 1987-88.

*Arms Control,* Volumes 1-13, University Press of America, 1987-88.

*The Presidency and Arms Control,* Volumes 1-3, University Press of America, 1990-96.

*OTHER*

Also author of monograph series on international affairs, 1974—. Contributor to numerous anthologies on politics, foreign policy, cultural affairs, theology, education, and history; contributor of articles to periodicals, including *Reporter, World Politics, Interpretation, Worldview,* and *International Organization.* Contributing editor, *Christianity and Crisis,* 1956-62, and *Worldview,* 1969—; member of editorial board, *International Organization,* 1956-76, *Virginia Quarterly Review, Society,* and *Atlantic Quarterly;* associate editor, *Review of Politics,* 1974—.

*WORK IN PROGRESS: History of the Cold War; The Post Cold War and After.*

*SIDELIGHTS:* Kenneth W. Thompson told *CA:* "My motivation is to search for enduring principles of foreighn policy and international relations. I seek to make a contribution in both theory and practice, through my edited work in particular. I aim to serve the beleaguered decision-maker.

"Two major figures in political theory and international politics have been formative influences on me: Reinhold Neibuhr and Hans J. Morgenthau.

"I write early mornings and evenings and weekends. The condition and future of the world inspired me ot write on international relations."

*BIOGRAPHICAL/CRITICAL SOURCES:*

*PERIODICALS*

*American Political Science Review,* March, 1994, p. 257.
*Christian Century,* December 13, 1967.
*Journal of the History of Ideas,* October, 1993, p. 704.
*Political Science Quarterly,* December, 1963.
*Reference and Research Book News,* September, 1994, p. 28.
*Review of Politics,* fall, 1993, p. 738.
*Times Literary Supplement,* March 5, 1982.
*Virginia Quarterly Review,* summer, 1967; autumn, 1994, p. 132.

\* \* \*

**THORNE, Ian**
   **See MAY, Julian**

**THORNE, Jean Wright**
   **See MAY, Julian**

\* \* \*

**TRUMAN, (Mary) Margaret    1924-**

*PERSONAL:* Born February 17, 1924, in Independence, MO; daughter of Harry S. (the U. S. president) and Elizabeth Virginia (Wallace) Truman; married E. Clifton Daniel, Jr. (a newspaper editor), April 21, 1956; children: Clifton, William, Harrison, Thomas. *Education:* George Washington University, A. B., 1946. *Politics:* Democrat. *Religion:* Episcopalian.

*ADDRESSES: Agent*—Scott Meredith, Scott Meredith Literary Agency, Inc., 845 Third Ave., New York, NY 10022.

*CAREER:* Writer. Opera coloratura, touring nationwide and appearing on radio and television, 1947-54; host of radio program "Authors in the News," 1954-61; co-host, with Mike Wallace, of radio program "Weekday," 1955-56; host of television program "CBS International Hour," 1965; summer stock actress. Director of Riggs National Bank, Washington, DC; trustee of Harry S. Truman Institute at Georgetown University; secretary of Harry S. Truman Scholarship Fund.

*AWARDS, HONORS:* L.H.D., Wake Forest University, 1972; Litt.D., George Washington University, 1975; H.H.D., Rockhurst College, 1976.

*WRITINGS:*

(With Margaret Cousins) *Souvenir: Margaret Truman's Own Story,* McGraw (New York City), 1956.
*White House Pets,* McKay (New York City), 1969.
*Harry S. Truman* (Book-of-the-Month Club selection), Morrow (New York City), 1972.
*Women of Courage,* Morrow, 1976.
*Bess W. Truman,* Macmillan (New York City), 1986.
*First Ladies,* Random House (New York City), 1995.

*MYSTERY NOVELS*

*Murder in the White House* (Book-of-the-Month Club alternate selection), Arbor House (New York City), 1980.

*Murder on Capitol Hill,* Arbor House, 1981.

*Murder in the Supreme Court* (Book-of-the-Month Club alternate selection), Arbor House, 1982.

*Murder in the Smithsonian,* Arbor House, 1983.

*Murder on Embassy Row,* Arbor House, 1984.

*Murder at the FBI,* Arbor House, 1985.

*Murder in Georgetown,* Arbor House, 1986.

*Murder in the CIA* (also see below), Random House, 1987.

*Murder at the Kennedy Center* (also see below), Random House, 1989.

*Murder at the National Cathedral* (also see below), Random House, 1990.

*Murder at the Pentagon,* Random House, 1992.

*Murder on the Potomac,* Random House, 1994.

*Margaret Truman: Three Complete Mysteries* (contains *Murder in the CIA, Murder at the Kennedy Center,* and *Murder at the National Cathedral*), Wings Books (New York City), 1994.

*Murder at the National Gallery,* Random House, 1996.

OTHER

Also editor of *Letters from Father: The Truman Family's Personal Correspondence,* Arbor House, 1981, and *Where the Buck Stops: Personal and Private Writings of Harry S. Truman,* Warner Books (New York City), 1989.

*ADAPTATIONS:* Film rights to *Murder in the White House* have been sold to Dick Clark Cinema Productions; *Murder at the Kennedy Center* was released on cassette by Recorded Books (Prince Frederick, MD), 1990.

*SIDELIGHTS:* When Margaret Truman published her first mystery novel in 1980, *Murder in the White House,* some observers were skeptical. As the daughter of U.S. President Harry S. Truman, she had long been a familiar figure to the nation's news media and had garnered a reputation as a concert singer, radio and television personality, and nonfiction writer. But her move to fiction writing was unexpected, even by her. Although she had long been a reader of mystery novels, trying her hand at writing one was accidental. Speaking to Carol Lawson of the *New York Times Book Review,* Truman explained: "I had been working on a nonfiction book—a history of White House children—but lost interest in it. I was with my agent one day . . . , and I told him I had an idea for a mystery: *Murder in the White House.* I don't know where those words came from." Because she had unique credentials to write a mystery set in the White

House, having lived there for seven years during her father's administration, her agent encouraged her to do the book. "It's a combination of the setting and my name," Lawson quotes Truman as saying about the book's appeal. "Seeing my name with this setting startles people, don't you think?"

*Murder in the White House* centers on the murder of Lansard Blaine, the corrupt Secretary of State, who is found strangled to death in the family quarters of the White House. Because Blaine had been a shady businessman, a powerful politician, and a womanizer, there are numerous suspects in the case. "Blaine may have been put out of business by one of these females," Chris Chase of the *Chicago Tribune* explains, "or he may have been killed by the agent of a foreign power . . . , or he may have been killed by 'someone fairly highly placed in the White House.'" The ensuing investigation of the murder exposes personal and political scandals among the First Family and their staff.

Critics were divided as to the merits of *Murder in the White House,* pointing out that Truman handled some elements of the novel better than others. William French of the Toronto *Globe and Mail* notes that "Miss Truman seems to have studied Agatha Christie on how to introduce false leads, point to the wrong suspect and generally confuse the issue. She does this with a certain amount of technical dexterity, but it's too mechanical and juiceless." Edwin J. Miller of *Best Sellers* maintains that the idea for the novel "could have made a first-rate book," but that Truman's story was only an "excellent outline." Peter Andrews of the *New York Times Book Review* claims that "a bit more thought and some rudimentary editing might have turned the book into a really interesting story. . . . All the evidence indicates that Margaret Truman is capable of doing much more interesting work than this." Reactions from the reading public were far more positive. *Murder in the White House* made the best-seller lists, was optioned for a television movie, and earned Truman over $200,000 for the paperback rights alone.

After her initial success as a mystery writer, Truman settled into a one-novel-a-year writing schedule. In each one, she has continued to draw on her intimate knowledge of Washington and its environs, setting her mysteries in such famous locations as the CIA headquarters, the Supreme Court, the Smithsonian Institution, the U.S. Congress, and the offices of the FBI. Her characters are bureaucrats, diplomats, and other influential men and women in Washington society; she views them with a cynical eye. Her plots are complicated and fast-moving, while the Washington milieu is painted with precision.

Each subsequent entry in Truman's Washington mystery series has proven to be popular with readers, even though some critics voice continuing reservations about the books' quality. Discussing *Murder at the National Cathedral* in the *New York Times Book Review,* Marilyn Stasio refers to Truman as "a stodgy writer," yet she gives the author credit for being "a stickler for authenticity" and for doing a good job summoning up her "imposing setting." A *Publishers Weekly* contributor agrees that *Murder at the National Cathedral* is "well served by the rich ecclesiastical accoutrements of its solemn setting," but complains that "Truman's mystery unravels disappointingly in a melodramatic, arbitrary resolution." In this reviewer's opinion, "gentlemanly Mac and lively Annabel [Truman's sleuthing protagonists] deserve a more convincing vehicle." *Murder on the Potomac* is "polished and capably written," states a writer for *Rapport,* but "the characters never achieve any depth and the story is void of intensity. The result is a cozy, but ultimately uninvolving mystery. . . . The story also lacks the sense of danger or immediacy which would make it thrilling, instead of merely interesting. *Murder on the Potomac* succeeds as an entertaining diversion, but as a mystery it is only passable."

Other reviewers are more generous in their praise for Truman's writing ability, however. Charles Champlin remarks in the *Los Angeles Times Book Review* that in *Murder at the Pentagon* "the plotting indeed is satisfyingly convoluted and the large-scale resolution worthy of [Robert] Ludlum." Writing about the same mystery, Burke Wilkinson declares in the *Christian Science Monitor:* "Margaret Truman 'knows the forks' in the nation's capital and how to pitchfork her readers into a web of murder and detection." Jean M. White of the *Washington Post Book World* concludes that Truman "writes a lively Washington scene with the sure hand of one who knows her way around the streets, institutions, restaurants, watering holes, people and politics."

Despite the success of her mystery novels, Truman has admitted on several occasions that she does not find writing to be a pleasant activity. "Writing," she told *CA,* "is the hardest and most exacting career I've ever had." And Truman has had several careers. For many years before she began to write, Truman was a concert singer. She debuted in 1947 on a national radio program with the Detroit Symphony Orchestra and was soon touring the nation, performing a program of operatic arias and light classics. Live concerts soon led to regular appearances on radio and television, and in 1949 she signed a recording contract with RCA-Victor Records. In 1956, Truman married Clifton Daniel, an editor at the *New York Times.* Except for acting in summer stock, Truman quit her performing work at this time.

She was prompted to write her first book, *Souvenir: Margaret Truman's Own Story,* only because an unauthorized biography was in the planning stages and she wanted to head it off. *Souvenir* recounts incidents from her childhood in Missouri, her years living in the White House as the president's only child, and her successful career as a concert singer. N. L. Browning of the *Chicago Sunday Tribune* calls the book "a fascinating chronicle. . . . It projects the simple dignity, warmth, and genuine modesty of a plain, unaffected midwest girl." Ishbel Ross of the *New York Herald Tribune Book Review* finds *Souvenir* to be "a gracefully written tale of an average American girl drawn by chance into the White House."

After the success of *Souvenir* in 1956, Truman did not write another book until 1969, when her *White House Pets,* a far less ambitious work, enjoyed some popularity with readers. But in 1972 Truman completed a project she had long wanted to do, a biography of her father. Her biography, published as *Harry S. Truman,* provides a behind-the-scenes look at Harry Truman as president and family man, revealing his personal side in a way no other biography could. In her review for the *Christian Science Monitor,* Pamela Marsh explains that in this book, the former president is "shown through the eyes of a deeply loving, loyal daughter" who "can give what no one else can, a closeup of an undramatic man dramatically thrust into awesome power—and coping with it." Vera Glaser of the *Akron Beacon Journal* calls the book "a warm memoir based on her father's personal papers and [Margaret Truman's] own recollections." While disagreeing with some of the book's partisan judgments about Truman and his administration, Wilson C. McWilliams of the *New York Times Book Review* sees value in the portrait it gives of Truman. He finds that "it is the personal, familial side of [Truman's] biography that makes it valuable. . . . Every anecdote adds human dimension to the Trumans as a family and to Harry as a man." The book has sold well over one million copies and was a selection of a major book club.

In 1986 Truman followed up her success by publishing a biography of her mother, entitled *Bess W. Truman,* a book considered by several critics to be of special interest for its intimate portrait of the president's wife. Because her mother preferred to burn her correspondence rather than let historians read it, little is known of Bess Truman's private thoughts and emotions. Her daughter's biography is one of the few personal accounts available. It is, according to Helen Thomas of the *New York Times Book Review,* "a refreshing, real and touching biography." Similarly, a critic for *Time* calls the book "a gentle, warmhearted biography." A. L. Yarnell of *Choice* lauds *Bess W. Truman* as "the most revealing view of the personal side of the Truman relationship now available."

Although White maintains that Truman "has proved herself to be a competent professional writer of mysteries" and both her mystery novels and biographies have been best-sellers, Truman is nonetheless still uneasy about the writing life. "I am always glad," she told *CA,* "when a book or a magazine article is finished. I promise myself never to write another one, but I shall probably do one."

*BIOGRAPHICAL/CRITICAL SOURCES:*

BOOKS

Truman, Margaret, *Souvenir: Margaret Truman's Own Story,* McGraw, 1956.

PERIODICALS

*Akron Beacon Journal,* March 3, 1974.
*Armchair Detective,* spring, 1986.
*Best Sellers,* July, 1980.
*Biography News,* April, 1974.
*Booklist,* May 1, 1996, p. 1470.
*Chicago Sunday Tribune,* May 27, 1956.
*Chicago Tribune,* July 6, 1980.
*Chicago Tribune Book World,* June 21, 1981.
*Choice,* September, 1986.
*Christian Science Monitor,* January 3, 1973; July 3, 1992, p. 13.
*Globe and Mail* (Toronto), June 26, 1980.
*Kirkus Reviews,* August 15, 1990, p. 1134; February 15, 1992, p. 229; April, 1994, p. 441.
*Los Angeles Times Book Review,* November 1, 1987; May 10, 1992, p. 12.
*New York Herald Tribune Book Review,* May 20, 1956.
*New York Times,* April 24, 1980; June 24, 1983.
*New York Times Book Review,* December 24, 1972; July 20, 1980; August 17, 1980; April 13, 1986; October 28, 1990, p. 41.
*People,* June 16, 1980.
*Publishers Weekly,* August 3, 1990, pp. 65-66; April 25, 1994, p. 60.
*Rapport,* January, 1992, p. 28; September-October, 1994, p. 26.
*School Library Journal,* March, 1996, p. 234.
*Time,* May 19, 1986.
*Washington Post,* June 27, 1983.
*Washington Post Book World,* July 19, 1981; August 18, 1985; November 15, 1987; June 19, 1994, p. 6.

\*   \*   \*

**TUBBY, I. M.**
 **See KRAUS, (Herman) Robert**

\*   \*   \*

**UNSWORTH, Barry (Forster)   1930-**

*PERSONAL:* Born August 10, 1930, in Durham, England; son of Michael (an insurance salesman) and Elsie (Forster) Unsworth; married Valerie Moor, May 15, 1959; children: Madeleine, Tania, Thomasina. *Education:* University of Manchester, B.A. (with honors in English), 1951.

*ADDRESSES: Office*—Hamish Hamilton, 22 Wrights Lane, London W8 5TZ, England. *Agent*—Giles Gordon, Anthony Sheil Associates, Lauranpolku 1 a 35, 01360 Vantaa 36, Finland.

*CAREER:* Norwood Technical College, London, England, lecturer in English, 1960; University of Athens, Athens, Greece, lecturer in English for British Council, 1960-63; Norwood Technical College, lecturer in English, 1963-65; University of Istanbul, Istanbul, Turkey, lecturer in English for British Council, 1965—; Writer in residence, Liverpool University, 1984-85, and Lund University, Sweden, 1988. *Military service:* British Army, Royal Corps of Signals, 1951-53, became second lieutenant.

*AWARDS, HONORS:* Heinemann Award for Literature, Royal Society of Literature, 1974, for *Mooncrankers Gift;* Arts Council Creative Writing fellowship, Charlotte Mason College, Ambleside, Cumbria, 1978-79; Literary fellow, Universities of Durham and Newcastle, 1983-84; Booker Prize (joint winner), 1992, for *Sacred Hunger.*

*WRITINGS:*

NOVELS

*The Partnership,* Hutchinson (London), 1966.
*The Greeks Have a Word for It,* Hutchinson, 1967.
*The Hide,* Gollancz (London), 1970.
*Mooncrankers Gift,* Allen Lane, 1973, Houghton (Boston), 1974.
*The Big Day,* M. Joseph (London), 1976, Mason/Charter, 1977.
*Pascalis Island,* M. Joseph, 1980, published in America as *The Idol Hunter,* Simon & Schuster (New York City), 1980.
*The Rage of the Vulture,* Granada (London), 1982, Houghton, 1983.
*Stone Virgin,* Hamish Hamilton (London), 1985, Houghton, 1986.
*Sugar and Rum,* Hamish Hamilton, 1988.
*Sacred Hunger,* Hamish Hamilton, 1992, Doubleday/Nan A. Talese, (New York City), 1992.
*Morality Play,* Doubleday/Nan A. Talese, 1995.
*The Hide,* Norton, 1996.
*After Hannibal,* Hamish Hamilton, 1996, published as *Umbrian Mosaic* Nan Talese, 1997.

OTHER

(With John Lennox Cook and Amorey Gethin) *The Students Book of English: A Complete Coursebook and Grammar to Advanced Intermediate Level,* Blackwell (London), 1981.

Also author of television play, *The Stick Insect,* 1975.

*ADAPTATIONS:* A film adaptation of *Pascalis Island* is being produced by Avenue Entertainment.

*SIDELIGHTS:* Barry Unsworth's novels have garnered him wide critical acclaim and recognition as one of the finest historical novelists writing in English. Winner of Britain's prestigious Booker Prize in 1992, Unsworth has time-traveled in his fiction to such places as turn-of-the-century Constantinople in *The Rage of the Vulture,* to Renaissance Venice in *Stone Virgin,* to an 18th-century slave ship in *Sacred Hunger,* and to 14th-century Yorkshire in *Morality Play.* Amy Gamerman, interviewing Unsworth for

the *Wall Street Journal,* writes "few contemporary writers have been as bold in mining history's provocative recesses for their fiction." Though Unsworth has been well regarded in England since the 1970s, it is only with his more recent novels that he has won international acclaim.

*Sugar and Rum,* published in 1988, is the story of a writer blocked in his attempts to write an historical novel on the slave trade. Unsworth's research for this novel led to his next work, as he explained in a *Wall Street Journal* interview: "I thought—well, couldn't I maybe do the novel that he was blocked about." The result was *Sacred Hunger. Sacred Hunger*'s central character is one Matthew Paris, a doctor who signs on as ship's surgeon on the maiden voyage of his uncle's slave-trading ship. The ship is captained by a man Paris describes as "an incarnation, really, of the profit motive," a man who throws a group of sick passengers—bound for sale into slavery—overboard because while there is no market for sick slaves, there is insurance compensation for lost cargo. The slaves and crew, partly at Paris's instigation, mutiny, killing the captain and setting up a would-be utopia in Florida where blacks and whites live, ostensibly, as equals. This paradise is itself eventually brought to ruin by the "sacred hunger" for money and power.

Critics have widely praised *Sacred Hunger*'s moral and philosophic aims and import. In the *Times Literary Supplement,* Mark Sanderson writes that the author is, in this and other of his novels, "concerned with nothing less than the fall of man." He goes on to write that "the concepts of justice, liberty and duty are debated through the medium of a genuinely exciting historical adventure." Several critics, such as Adam Bradbury, writing in the *London Review of Books,* read Unsworth's themes as commentary upon contemporary times: "It is hard to escape the impression that Unsworth is talking about the economic miracle with which we are supposed to have been blessed in the Eighties. But he is going further, chipping away at the fundamentals of capital trade with the question gradually emerging: would man, free and happy in a state of nature, still seek to accumulate wealth by enslaving others? Don't know, is the resounding reply."

Unsworth's next novel, *Morality Play,* concerns a young monk-errant in 14th century England who joins up with a traveling troupe of actors. When the troupe's stock morality play, the "Play of Adam," fails to draw paying crowds, they decide to make current events—the murder of a local boy—the focus of the onstage drama. "It has been in my mind for years now that we can make plays from stories that happen in our lives," says the troupe's leader. "I believe this is the way that plays will be made in the times to come." Their choice thus prefigures the evolution of modern western drama.

At least one critic, Marc Romano writing for the *Boston Review,* finds his credulity stretched too far by this novelistic strategy. "The historical shift from morality plays based on stock figures," Romano writes, "to modern drama based on psychological realism was a qualitative leap. . . . Psychological realism . . . asks its audience to draw its own conclusions. . . . That, in the end, *Morality Play* never manages to do—it is determined to tell modern readers about the history of drama, . . . even at the expense of its own credibility as a historical novel." Yet the *Los Angeles Times Book Review*'s critic, Charles Nicholl, yields a more sanguine take on Unsworth's narrative intent. He contrasts the inn-yard stage with the jousts taking place on the feudal manor, where "knights and ladies play their parts in a performance that reinforces the hierarchies and assumptions of feudal society." "The play," Nicholl writes, "does something different: it questions and explores, and . . . creates an area of comment and debate." Nicholl argues that Unsworth's intent in recapitulating the evolution of theatrical modernism is to tell a story "about the capacity of art . . . to create new meanings, and thereby new possibilities, in the lives of its audience."

Critics have taken particular note of Unsworth's historical evocation of the earthy, impoverished atmosphere in which much of *Morality Play* is staged, his "wintry scenes, hard-bitten lives etched against a background of frost and snow . . . the presence of hunger and plague; the daily oppression of feudal society," to quote Nicholl. And though Romano writes that the author "has the misfortune . . . of using history as a device rather than recreating it," Janet Burroway, in the *New York Times Book Review,* praises his subtlety in this regard: "Mr. Unsworth has the art to enter the sensibility of a period—its attitudes, assumptions and turns of phrase—so convincingly that he is able to suggest subtle yet essential parallels between an earlier era and our own."

In spite of his evident success as a novelist, Unsworth himself, in the *Wall Street Journal* inter-

view, expresses a writer's dissatisfaction with his finished product: "The idea is so radiant and the conception so exciting, and somewhere the shadow falls between the idea and the execution. . . . I always feel that I did the best I could, I just didn't do proper justice to it." Unsworth's critics have tended to be less harsh. The London *Observer*'s Jonathan Keates, writing specifically of *Stone Virgin,* sums up the tenor of general critical response to Unsworth's recent novels: "the cumulative effect of such consistently sound storytelling is to remind us of an almost vanished art, to which Unsworth holds the enviable key."

*BIOGRAPHICAL/CRITICAL SOURCES:*

*BOOKS*

*Contemporary Literary Criticism,* Gale (Detroit), Volume 76, 1993.

*PERIODICALS*

*Atlanta Journal and Atlanta Constitution,* October 11, 1992, p. K13.
*Books,* March, 1990, p. 21; March, 1992, p. 5; November, 1992, p. 18; January, 1993, p. 15, p. 21.
*Books and Bookmen,* October, 1986, p. 37.
*Book World,* September 13, 1992, p. 2; November 1, 1992, p. 15; November 28, 1993, p. 12.
*Boston Globe,* August 9, 1992, p. B38.
*Boston Review,* February/March, 1996, p. 34.
*British Book News,* October 1985, p. 624.
*Chicago Tribune,* August 9, 1992, p. 1.
*Contemporary Review,* October, 1985, p. 213; July, 1992, p. 43.
*Kirkus Reviews,* January 15, 1986, p. 88; May 15, 1992, p. 636.
*Library Journal,* March 1, 1986, p. 110; July, 1992, p. 130.
*Listener,* September 19, 1985, p. 28; December 1, 1988, p. 33.
*London Review of Books,* June 11, 1992, p. 27.
*Los Angeles Times Book Review,* August 2, 1992, p. 3; November 12, 1995, p. 2.
*New Statesman,* August 15, 1985, p. 28; August 8, 1986, p. 29.
*New Statesman & Society,* February 28, 1992, p. 45; October 16, 1992, p. 41.
*Newsweek,* January 28, 1983.
*New Yorker,* May 26, 1986, p. 106.
*New York Times,* November 20, 1980; February 7, 1983; December 23, 1992, p. C15.

*New York Times Book Review,* January 11, 1981;
March 13, 1983; April 6, 1986, p. 27; August
28, 1988, p. 32; July 19, 1992, p. 3, p. 23;
December 12, 1993, p. 36; June 5, 1994, p. 60;
November 12, 1995, p. 11.

*Observer* (London), July 21, 1985, p. 22; July 27,
1986, p. 23; September 18, 1988, p. 43; September 13, 1992, p. 55; October 18, 1992, p.
59; November 22, 1992, p. 64; March 31, 1993,
p. 62; May 30, 1993, p. 62.

*Publishers Weekly,* January 31, 1986, p. 363; May
11, 1992, p. 52; May 22, 1995, p. 55; August
21, 1995, p. 43; November 6, 1995, p. 60.

*Punch,* August 13, 1986, p. 45.

*Spectator,* August 24, 1985, p. 25; November 21,
1992, p. 42, p. 43.

*Stand,* spring, 1990, p. 75.

*Times* (London), June 19, 1980; July 25, 1985; June
11, 1992, p. 4.

*Times Educational Supplement,* October 7, 1988, p.
34; April 3, 1992, p. 32.

*Times Literary Supplement,* August 30, 1985, p. 946;
September 16, 1988, p. 1014; February 28,
1992, p. 23.

*Tribune Books* (Chicago), August 9, 1992, p. 1;
December 6, 1992, p. 13; November 14, 1993,
p. 8.

*USA Today,* December 7, 1992, p. D6.

*Wall Street Journal,* December 5, 1995, p. A16.

*Washington Post,* January 24, 1981; September 13,
1992; October 14, 1992, p. C2.

*Washington Post Book World,* April 3, 1983.*

—*Sketch by Frank DeSanto*

\*   \*   \*

## VERNANT, Jean-Pierre 1914-

*PERSONAL:* Born January 4, 1914, in Provins,
France; son of Jean (a journalist) and Anna
(Heilbron) Vernant; married Lida Nahimovitch (a
professor), November 30, 1939; children: Claude.
*Education:* Sorbonne, University of Paris, agrege de
philosophie, 1937.

*ADDRESSES: Home*—112 Grande Rue, 92310 Sevres,
France. *Office*—Department of Ancient Religions,
College de France, 11 Place Marcelin, Berthelot,
75005 Paris, France.

*CAREER:* In charge of research at Centre National de
la Recherche Scientifique, 1948-57; director of studies at Ecole Pratique des Hautes-Etudes, 1957-75;
College de France, Paris, professor of the comparative study of ancient religions, 1975-84, honorary
professor, 1984—. *Military service:* French Army,
1937-45, served in infantry; became lieutenant colonel; received Croix de Guerre and Croix de la Liberation, was made commander of French Legion of
Honor.

*MEMBER:* Academie Royale de Belgique (associe),
American Academy of Arts and Sciences (foreign
honorary member), British Academy (corresponding
fellow).

*AWARDS, HONORS:* Honorary doctorate from University of Chicago, 1979, and University of Bristol,
1987; Medaille d'r, Recherche Scientifique francaise,
1984; Premio di Storia San Marino, 1991; Award for
Humanistic Studies, American Academy of Arts and
Sciences, 1992.

*WRITINGS:*

*Les Origines de la pensee greque,* Presses
Universitaires de France, 1962, translation pub-
lished as *The Origins of Greek Thought,* Cornell
University Press (Ithaca, NY), 1982.

*Mythe et pensee chez les grecs: Etudes de
psychologie historique,* Maspero (Paris), 1965,
translation by Janet Lloyd published as *Myth and
Thought among the Greeks,* Routledge & Kegan
Paul (Boston), 1983.

(Editor) *Problemes de la guerre en Grece ancienne*
(title means "Problems of War in Ancient
Greece"), La Haye, Mouton & Co., 1968, 2nd
edition, 1985.

(Author of introduction) Marcel Detienne, *Les
Jardins d'Adonis,* Gallimard, 1972, translation
published as *The Garden of Adonis,* Bollingen,
1993.

(With Pierre Vidal-Naquet) *Mythe et tragedie en
Grece ancienne,* Maspero, 1972, translation by
Lloyd published as *Myth and Tragedy in Ancient
Greece,* Harvester Press (Brighton, England),
1981.

*Mythe et societe en Grece ancienne,* Maspero, 1974,
translation by Lloyd published as *Myth and Society in Ancient Greece,* Harvester Press, 1980.

(With Detienne) *Les Ruses de l'intelligence: La Metis
des grecs,* Flammarion, 1974, translation by
Lloyd published as *Cunning Intelligence in Greek
Culture and Society,* Humanities (Atlantic Highlands, NJ), 1978.

(Contributor) *Divination et rationalite* (title means "Divination and Rationality"), Seuil, 1974.

*La Cuisine du sacrifice en pays grec,* Gallimard, 1979, 2nd edition, 1983, translation by Paula Wissing published as *The Cuisine of Sacrifice among the Greeks,* University of Chicago Press, 1989.

*Religions, histoires, raisons* (title means "Religion, History, Reason"), Maspero, 1979.

(With Gherardo Gnoli) *La Mort, les morts dans les societes anciennes,* Cambridge University Press (New York City), 1982.

*La Mort dans les yeux: Figures de l'autre en Grece ancienne,* Hachette, 1985, 2nd edition, 1986.

(With Vidal-Naquet) *Mythe et tragedie deux,* Decouverte, 1986.

(With Charles Malamoud) *Corps des dieux,* Gallimard, 1986.

(With Vidal-Naquet) *Oedipe et ses mythes,* Complexe, 1988.

(With Vidal-Naquet) *Travail et esclavage en Grece ancienne,* Complexe, 1988.

*L'individu, la mort, l'amour,* Gallimard, 1989.

*Mythe et religion en Grece ancienne,* Seuil, 1990.

*Figures, idoles, masques* (lectures and essays) Julliard, 1990.

*Mortals and Immortals* (essays), edited by Froma Zeitlin, Princeton University Press (Princeton, NJ), 1991.

*Passe et Present Contributiones a une Psychologie historique,* two volumes, Edizioni di Storia e Letteratura (Rome), 1995.

*The Greeks,* translated by Charles Lambert and Teresa Lavender Fagan, University of Chicago Press, 1995.

*SIDELIGHTS:* Jean-Pierre Vernant told *CA:* "My work tries to be a contribution to the foundation of a historical anthropology of ancient Greece." About the body of Vernant's work, Charles Segal notes in *Arethusa* that "one is struck by the coherence and the logical progression of his thought, his feeling for the integral relation between literature and society, language and social institutions." Segal admires the writer's depth of study and concludes, "Vernant's work is of seminal importance."

*Myth and Society in Ancient Greece,* a collection of Vernant's essays, illustrates the relationship between myth and societal institutions in ancient Greek culture. According to John Gould in a *Times Literary Supplement* review, the essays analyze myth comparatively, "refer[ring] the logic of the myth to a network of related concepts which makes up the 'deep structure' of ancient Greek thinking about the social nature of man." Gould judges Vernant's book to be "an important work, of rare intelligence, stimulating and discerning."

*BIOGRAPHICAL/CRITICAL SOURCES:*

PERIODICALS

*Arethusa,* spring, 1982; fall, 1982.
*Times Literary Supplement,* August 22, 1980; October 29, 1982; November 12, 1982; September 26, 1986.

\*    \*    \*

**VINCENT, Claire**
**See ALLEN, Charlotte Vale**

# W-Z

## WAIN, John (Barrington) 1925-1994

*PERSONAL:* Born March 14, 1925, in Stoke-on-Trent, Staffordshire, England; died of a stroke, May 24, 1994, in Oxford, England; son of Arnold A. (a dentist) and Anne Wain; married Marianne Urmston, 1947 (divorced, 1956); married Eirian James, 1960 (died, 1988); married Patricia Dunn, 1989; children: (second marriage) William, Ianto, Tobias. *Education:* St. John's College, Oxford, B.A., 1946, M.A., 1950. *Avocational interests:* Walking, canoeing.

*CAREER:* St. John's College, Oxford University, Oxford, England, Fereday Fellow, 1946-47; University of Reading, Reading, England, lecturer in English literature, 1947-55; writer and critic, 1955-94. Churchill Visiting Professor at University of Bristol, 1967; visiting professor at Centre Experimental de Vincennes, University of Paris, 1969; George Elliston Lecturer on Poetry at University of Cincinnati; Professor of Poetry at Oxford University, 1973-78. Director of Poetry Book Society's festival, London, 1961.

*MEMBER:* Oxford Union Society.

*AWARDS, HONORS:* Somerset Maugham Award, 1958, for *Preliminary Essays;* Royal Society of Literature fellow, 1960; Brasenose College creative arts fellowship from Oxford University, 1971-72; James Tait Black Memorial Prize and Heinemann Award from Royal Society of Literature, both 1975, both for *Samuel Johnson;* Whitbread Literary Award, 1985, for *The Free Zone Starts Here;* honorary degrees from the University of Keele and the University of Loughborough, both 1985; honorary fellow, St. John's College, Oxford, 1985-94.

*WRITINGS:*

FICTION

*Hurry on Down* (novel), Secker & Warburg (London), 1953, published as *Born in Captivity,* Knopf (New York City), 1954, published as *Hurry on Down,* Viking (New York City), 1965, reprinted with a new introduction by the author, Secker & Warburg, 1978.

*Living in the Present* (novel), Secker & Warburg, 1955, Putnam (New York City), 1960.

*The Contenders* (novel), St. Martin's (New York City), 1958.

*A Travelling Woman* (novel), St. Martin's, 1959.

*Nuncle and Other Stories* (short stories), Macmillan (London), 1960, St. Martin's, 1961.

*Strike the Father Dead* (novel), St. Martin's, 1962.

*The Young Visitors* (novel), Viking, 1965.

*Death of the Hind Legs and Other Stories* (short stories), Viking, 1966.

*The Smaller Sky* (novel), Macmillan, 1967.

*A Winter in the Hills* (novel; also see below), Viking, 1970.

*The Life Guard* (short stories), Macmillan, 1971, Viking, 1972.

*King Caliban and Other Stories* (short stories), Macmillan, 1978.

*The Pardoner's Tale* (novel), Macmillan, 1978, Viking, 1979.

*Lizzie's Floating Shop* (juvenile), Bodley Head (London), 1981.

*Young Shoulders* (juvenile), Macmillan, 1982, published as *The Free Zone Starts Here,* Delacorte (New York City), 1982.

*Where the Rivers Meet* (novel), Hutchinson (London), 1988.

*Comedies* (novel; sequel to *Where the Rivers Meet*), Hutchinson, 1990.

*Hungry Generations* (novel; sequel to *Comedies*), Hutchinson, 1994.

*POETRY*

*Mixed Feelings,* University of Reading (Berkshire), 1951.

(Contributor) D. J. Enright, editor, *Poets of the Fifties,* [London], 1955.

*A Word Carved on a Sill,* St. Martin's, 1956.

(Contributor) Robert Conquest, editor, *New Lines,* [London], 1956.

*Weep before God,* St. Martin's, 1961.

*A Song about Major Eatherly,* Qara Press (Iowa City), 1961.

(Contributor) Chad Walsh, editor, *Today's Poets,* Scribner (New York City), 1964.

*Wildtrack,* Macmillan, 1965, Viking, 1966.

*Letters to Five Artists,* Macmillan, 1969, Viking, 1970.

*The Shape of Feng,* Covent Garden Press (London), 1972.

*Feng,* Viking, 1975.

*Poems for the Zodiac* (limited edition), Pisces (London), 1980.

*Thinking about Mr. Person,* Chimaera Press (Kent), 1980.

*Poems, 1949-1979,* Macmillan, 1981.

*The Twofold,* Hunting Raven Press (Somerset), 1981.

*Mid-week Period Return: Home Thoughts of a Native,* Celandine Press (Stratford-upon-Avon), 1982.

*PLAYS*

*Harry in the Night,* first produced in Stoke-on-Trent, England, 1975.

*You Wouldn't Remember* (radio play), first produced by British Broadcasting Corporation (BBC), 1978.

*A Winter in the Hills* (radio play; adapted from the author's novel), 1981.

*Frank* (radio play; first produced by BBC), Amber Lane Press (Oxford), 1984.

*Good Morning Blues* (radio play), first produced by BBC, 1986.

*Johnson Is Leaving: A Monodrama,* Pisces, 1994.

*NONFICTION*

*Preliminary Essays,* St. Martin's, 1957.

*Gerard Manley Hopkins: An Idiom of Desperation,* Oxford University Press (London), 1959, reprinted, Folcroft Editions (Folcroft, PA), 1974.

(Contributor) Tom Maschler, editor, *Declaration,* MacGibbon & Kee, 1959.

*Sprightly Running: Part of an Autobiography,* Macmillan, 1962, St. Martin's, 1963.

*Essays on Literature and Ideas,* St. Martin's, 1963.

*The Living World of Shakespeare: A Playgoer's Guide,* St. Martin's, 1964.

*Arnold Bennett,* Columbia University Press (New York City), 1967.

*A House for the Truth: Critical Essays,* Macmillan, 1972, Viking, 1973.

*Samuel Johnson* (biography; Book-of-the-Month Club selection), Macmillan, 1974, Viking, 1975.

*Professing Poetry,* Macmillan, 1977, Viking, 1978.

*Dear Shadows: Portraits from Memory,* J. Murray (London), 1986.

*EDITOR*

*Contemporary Reviews of Romantic Poetry,* Barnes & Noble (New York City), 1953.

*Interpretations: Essays on Twelve English Poems,* Routledge & Kegan Paul (London), 1955, Hillary (New York City), 1957, 2nd edition, Routledge & Kegan Paul, 1972.

*International Literary Annual,* two volumes, J. Calder, 1958, 1959, Criterion, 1959, 1960.

Frances Burney d'Arblay, *Fanny Burney's Diary,* Folio Society (London), 1961.

*Anthology of Modern Poetry,* Hutchinson, 1963.

(Author of introduction and notes) *Pope,* Dell (New York City), 1963.

(Author of introduction) Thomas Hardy, *The Dynasts,* St. Martin's, 1966.

*Selected Shorter Poems of Thomas Hardy,* Macmillan, 1966.

*Selected Stories of Thomas Hardy,* St. Martin's, 1966.

*Shakespeare: Macbeth; a Casebook,* Macmillan, 1968, Aurora Publications (Nashville, TN), 1970.

*Shakespeare: Othello; a Casebook,* Macmillan, 1971.

*Johnson as Critic,* Routledge & Kegan Paul, 1973.

Samuel Johnson, *Lives of the English Poets,* Dent (London), 1975, Dutton, 1976.

*Johnson on Johnson: A Selection of the Personal and Autobiographical Writings of Samuel Johnson,* Dutton, 1976.

*Edmund Wilson: The Man and His Work,* New York University Press (New York City), 1978 (published in England as *An Edmund Wilson Celebration,* Phaidon Press [Oxford], 1978).

*Personal Choice: A Poetry Anthology,* David & Charles (North Pomfret, VT), 1978.

(With wife, Eirian Wain) *The New Wessex Selection of Thomas Hardy's Poetry,* Macmillan, 1978.

*Anthology of Contemporary Poetry: Post-War to the Present,* Hutchinson, 1979.

*Everyman's Book of English Verse,* Dent, 1981.

Arnold Bennett, *The Old Wives' Tale,* Penguin, 1983.

James Hogg, *The Private Memoirs and Confessions of a Justified Sinner,* Penguin, 1983.

*Oxford Anthology of English Poetry,* Oxford University Press, 1990.

(And author of introduction) *The Journals of James Boswell, 1762-1795,* Yale University Press (New Haven, CT), 1991.

*OTHER*

(With Ted Walker) *Modern Poetry* (sound recording), BFA Educational Media, 1972.

*The Poetry of John Wain* (sound recording), Jeffrey Norton, 1976.

Geoffrey Halson, editor, *A John Wain Selection,* Longman, 1977.

(Translator from Anglo-Saxon) *The Seafarer,* Grenville Press, 1982.

*Open Country,* Hutchinson, 1987.

Contributor to numerous periodicals, including *New Republic, Observer, New Yorker, Times Literary Supplement, Saturday Evening Post, Harper's Bazaar,* and *Ladies' Home Journal.* Founding editor of *Mandrake,* 1944.

*SIDELIGHTS:* For more than forty years, John Wain, a British man of letters, devoted his energies primarily to writing. The diversity of his output demonstrated his commitment to his craft—from 1951 until his death in 1994, he penned novels, short stories, poetry, critical essays, and a highly acclaimed biography, *Samuel Johnson.* According to *Dictionary of Literary Biography* contributor A. T. Tolley, Wain's novels and stories "make up one of the more substantial bodies of contemporary fiction in English," while his poetry "stands as an important contribution to his total achievement and displays that concern with the life of literature in our day that has permeated his work." Wain was likewise commended for his critical judgments that proved him "adamantly committed to the mystery of literary truths that can advance the universal human experience," in the words of *Dictionary of Literary Biography* essayist Augustus M. Kolich. Kolich called Wain "an iconoclast who is uncompromising in his

dedication to the belief that in a world where 'destruction and disintegration' are the norm, only the artist's creative language can clear the ruins and establish a foundation for heroic individualism." Wain's writings pursued this high ideal in an unpretentious and readable style; Susan Wood noted in the *Washington Post Book World* that the author, while an Oxford graduate, "is no dour Oxford don. . . . Instead, he typifies the very best of what one might call 'Englishness'—good sense, moderation, a feeling for language, erudition without pretension, and wit."

Addressing Wain's fiction specifically, *Esquire* critic Geoffrey Wolff commented: "From his first novel, *Hurry on Down* (1953), Wain has concerned himself with contemporary English manners, with the small choices that comprise a program of values. . . . Wain writes about boredom, the killing regularity of diminished, stunted lives; because he is so skilled a writer, he creates an accurate evocation of the awful coziness and regularity of English conventions." Wain was also preoccupied, in much of his work, with the survival of individual dignity and purpose in a world where bullying and domination often prevail. Kolich stated: "In Wain's criticism of contemporary English society, his target is clearly the totalitarian consciousness which has as its object the manipulation and domination of the small child in all of us— that part of our self-concept that naturally sees through folly and pretense and always expects to be left uncontrolled and free. Hence, Wain's fiction is above all morally pledged to a set of values that aim at offending the status quo, when it seems either silly, absurd, or oppressive, and championing commonsense individualism, whenever it can be championed in a world of antiheroes."

This theme of individual rebellion is particularly prevalent in *Hurry on Down,* the novel that established Wain among the clan of writers known as "angry young men" in postwar Great Britain. Set in a provincial town similar to the one in which Wain himself was raised, *Hurry on Down* describes the picaresque adventures of Charles Lumley, a cynical youth who contrives to avoid the respectable middle-class lifestyle expected of him because of his education and upbringing. *Times Literary Supplement* reviewer Blake Morrison suggested that Lumley could be seen "as representative of a 'less deceived' postwar generation hostile to old values and intent upon radical political change. He and other new heroes in fiction were the subject of much journalistic discussion—discussion which ensured *Hurry on Down*'s success." According to Kolich, Wain came to be identified with his alienated protagonist, even though the author was never comfortable with the way many critics associated him with the "angry decade" movement. Morrison even suggested that the true political significance of the Lumley character "lies in his concern to avoid commitments and his willingness to adapt himself—both features of an era when not anger and rebellion but 'Butskellism' and 'the End of Ideology' were dominant ideals." In any case, *Hurry on Down* was a commercial and critical success for Wain. *South Atlantic Quarterly* contributor Elgin W. Mellown claimed that the work "holds the reader by its verisimilitude and artfully contrived though seemingly unposed candid-camera shots of English life in the late forties and early fifties." In his book *Tradition and Dream: The English and American Novel from the Twenties to Our Time,* Walter Allen concluded that *Hurry on Down* made Wain "the satirist of this period of social change."

Disillusioned Englishmen figure in many of Wain's subsequent novels, including *Strike the Father Dead, The Contenders,* and *The Smaller Sky.* Kolich wrote: "In the process of breaking away from the confines of economic and social success and the seductive powers of competitive capitalism, Wain's heroes still must face the unsettling business of reordering their lives outside the conventional set plans that either religion or business might offer. . . . Very often, . . . they seem lost and unable to cope with the shifting emotional currents generated by those toward whom they feel drawn." In general, critics found Wain's novels of the late 1950s and 1960s less successful than his debut fiction work. As Mellown described it, Wain "commands an almost flawless technique and can write in a truthful, accurate, and revealing way about human beings interacting on the personal level; but when he looks beyond these individuals and attempts to put them into a larger focus or to give them a wider significance, their thoughts and beliefs condemn them as second-rate." In his book entitled *Postwar British Fiction: New Accents and Attitudes,* James Gindin contended: "For the kind of point Wain is making about the contemporary world that he depicts with such specificity, force, and intelligence, he does require some tangible expression of the value of the personal and the humane. But the form of expression often lacks a comic richness that would avoid both the brittle gimmick and the heavy sediment of emotion." Undaunted by the sometimes harsh criticism, Wain continued to produce fiction. His later works found favor with reviewers, and, in retrospect, his seriousness of purpose and sheer pro-

ductivity led Mellown to suggest that "these [early] novels are the most impressive output of any of the postwar British writers."

Kolich described *A Winter in the Hills,* Wain's 1970 novel, as "perhaps the most typical . . . in terms of themes and characters." The story concerns a philologist who moves to North Wales and becomes involved in a local bus driver's efforts to thwart a business takeover. *Newsweek* contributor Raymond A. Sokolov found the work "an unashamedly romantic, heroic, plot-heavy, character-ridden, warm piece of narration with a beginning, a middle and an end. . . . Wain proves there is still much life in the old tricks." A *Times Literary Supplement* reviewer asserted that *A Winter in the Hills* "goes farther, perhaps, in defining and developing Mr. Wain's basic concerns as a writer than most of his earlier works; and does it with a growing maturity and conviction." The reviewer noted Wain's continuing interest in the quality of individual living, and added, "Observing social situations, catching hints of character and motive in conversational habits, contriving elaborate and efficient plots—these continue to be [Wain's] strengths."

*The Pardoner's Tale,* published in 1978, proved even more popular than *A Winter in the Hills.* In *Time,* R. Z. Sheppard called the work a "thoughtful treatment of two middle-aged men joyfully making fools of themselves over younger women." The book is a novel-within-a-novel; an author, Giles Hermitage, seeks to resolve his own romantic misadventures by writing about a fictitious businessman and *his* encounter with a woman. The resulting pastiche of stories evokes "a steady sensuous glow that warms the brain," according to Sheppard. *Saturday Review* correspondent Carole Cook contended that it is Wain himself who "shines as the hero" in *The Pardoner's Tale.* "He has beaten the clock," Cook wrote, "enticed us into the game, and held us so captivated by his voice of a man desperate for a second chance at life that it becomes, word by word, our own." Amy Wilentz argued a different viewpoint in the *Nation.* She found *The Pardoner's Tale* a "well-intentioned book," but subsequently declared that there is "so little true atmosphere in Wain's book that his characters, who are sporadically well drawn, also seem shadowy and displaced." Conversely, D. A. N. Jones praised the novel in the *Times Literary Supplement.* "The lineaments of gratified desire are persuasively drawn," Jones asserted. "Precise details of plot and character dissolve into an amorous haze, spreading delight. . . . John Wain's novel is written in a warmly forgiving spirit; and this, together with its engaging riggishness, contributes to the reader's delight."

In an essay for the *Contemporary Authors Autobiography Series,* Wain claimed that his book about Samuel Johnson was "the most successful work of my middle life." *Samuel Johnson* provided a comprehensive biography of one of England's leading literary figures, written expressly for the general reader. Many critics praised the account not only for its accessibility to the non-academic public, but also for its subtle reflections on the literary life in any age. *Harper's* reviewer Jack Richardson wrote: "To John Wain, Johnson is not only a great figure in literature, he is also a magnificent companion, someone who brings with him a feeling of good company when met for the first time or recalled for the hundredth; and it is this feeling which Wain wishes to celebrate, and which makes *Samuel Johnson* more than anything else a narrative of friendship." In the *Nation,* Robert L. Chapman stated: "John Wain's own stature as a literary-academic person assures us a voice both authoritative and eloquent" in *Samuel Johnson,* but the author is still "less interested in the precise delineation of a dead man than in the appraisal of an immortal colleague. . . . I cherish the lively, novelistic quality of [Wain's] book, where I can see an idea being born, growing, and at last enforcing itself as the prime focus of meaning."

Anatole Broyard offered further commendations for *Samuel Johnson* in the *New York Times:* "A good biography of a great man is one of the best ways to define the society he concentrated in himself. Mr. Wain's *Samuel Johnson* is a brilliant picture of 18th-century England, too." *New York Times Book Review* contributor Christopher Ricks called the work "vividly humane" and suggests that it "does justice to the range and depth of this just and merciful man. . . . It is a noble story nobly told." Ricks added: "Johnson's was essentially a commemorative spirit, and Mr. Wain's biography is a dignified achievement because it too is undertaken in a commemorative spirit. Not 'let me tell you about this man,' but 'let us remember together this man.'" As George Gale concluded in the *Spectator,* Wain's biography "is at the end seen to be a very substantial work of synthesis, intuitive understanding and intellectual grasp. . . . We are left with . . . a work which, by persuading us of the stature of its subject, establishes at the same time a very considerable stature of its own."

Wain's poetry is also seen as a significant contribution to the body of English letters since 1945. Tolley explained that, in his early poems, Wain is "affronting the whole modernist poetic, where the emphasis had been on the image, on the maximization of sensory impact, and where generalizations had been seen as the enemies of the poetic. Wain . . . is comfortable with a poetry of statement. However, these [early] poems are far from being doctrinaire literary stunts. Many stand out as simple and passionate statements on what have proved to be some of Wain's abiding themes: love, isolation, honesty, and sympathy for the deprived. . . . Poems . . . seemingly artificial . . . survive as expressions of tenderness." Wain is perhaps better known for his long poems such as *Wildtrack, Feng,* and *Letters to Five Artists.* "Wain's devotion to the long poem," wrote Tolley, "is at once courageous and surprising in view of his steady adherence to the realistic tradition in his novels. Whatever may be said about his attainment in his longer poems, he has not been content with the diminished ambitions that have often led to diminished poetry in Britain the last quarter of a century." According to Philip Gardner in the *Times Literary Supplement,* Wain, "concerned with the communication both of humane values and of an imaginative response to experience, . . . sometimes errs on the side of too much clarity: over-insistent, he button-holes the reader or goes on too long." Derek Stanford expressed a different opinion in *Books:* "Wain's unitary theme is the relationship between art and life—particularly that between the individual work and the individual producer. . . . All in all, *Letters to Five Artists* is full of vigorous poetry, written in sinewy masculine language but without any of that paraded toughness sometimes indulged in by the New Movement." A *Times Literary Supplement* reviewer concluded that there is "no deliberate order or consistency in Mr. Wain's reflections, except for the unity given by an underlying compassion."

In 1973 Wain was elected to the prestigious Professor of Poetry chair at Oxford. He held the chair for five years, giving lectures on subjects that reflected his critical concerns. These lectures are collected in *Professing Poetry.* Kolich contends that, as a literary critic, Wain projects an iconoclasm "derived from a privately felt moral sense of self-determination, a concept that he hopes can be shared by a community of equals, scholars and artists, working toward 'the establishment of a hierarchy of quality.'" According to Herbert Leibowitz in the *New York Times Book Review,* Wain "detests the art chatter and sensationalism of the modern age, with its denial of complexity and the rich diapason of language. For Wain, the imagination is under siege by an 'insistence on explicitness,' 'intellectual slapstick' replaces thought, and our art 'abandons the search for standards' by stupidly rejecting the past." As might be expected of one educated at and honored by Oxford, Wain's critical judgments reside "in his devotion to the idea that the study of the best literature that has been written can provide the criteria for the best judgments," Kolich concluded.

For many years before his death, Wain experienced deteriorating health and increasing blindness due to diabetes. Despite his disabilities, he worked diligently to complete his last major literary achievement—a trilogy of novels based on his life at Oxford. *Where the Rivers Meet* was the first in the trio, followed by *Comedies* and *Hungry Generations*. Their protagonist was Peter Leonard, a lower-middle-class youth who attends Oxford on a scholarship. The widening gap between Peter and his family and the young man's struggle to adapt to his new environment are convincingly portrayed. *Spectator* reviewer Raymond Carr singled out a wedding episode as "a superb set piece," and called Peter's relationship with his family "subtly and movingly done." Carr and other commentators pointed out, however, that Peter's insatiable sexual appetite dominated the book inappropriately. "At times Wain appears to have a bet on with himself to see how many different ways he can find of describing erectile tissue," complained Hugh Barnes in the *Observer*. John Melmoth concluded in *Times Literary Supplement* that *Where the Rivers Meet* is "sprawling, randy, over-long, self-indulgent and disingenuously plain-blokeish. True to a certain type of English fiction, it is too relaxed about its own limitations, and the narrator is content to describe himself as 'a philistine.'"

David Buckley also commented negatively about the character of Peter, stating in his *Observer* review of *Hungry Generations* that "it is difficult to like the narrator." John-Paul Flintoff was more generous, finding Peter merely "determinedly unsensational," but he voiced the opinion that Wain's material had grown thin: "Yet another sketch of Oxford is not enough to fuel a trilogy. Certainly, in terms of raw experience, this volume offers good value: not only divorce, but remarriage, birth and death too. But the human interest, until late in the story, is dreary." More favorably received was Wain's nonfiction memoir, *Dear Shadows: Portraits from Memory*. The author's character sketch of Marshall McLuhan was singled out by many reviewers for special praise.

"As a writer I have regarded my basic material as the word rather than as this or that literary form," Wain stated in the *Contemporary Authors Autobiography Series*. Wain refused to be classified as "primarily" one specific sort of writer—novelist, poet, or essayist. "I am always primarily what I am doing at the moment," he explained. The author also claimed that he knew from an early age that he intended to write, the career being "not a profession but a condition." He offered these thoughts on literature: "The books I most admire are those that take human life as I know it and live it from day to day and describe it honestly and lovingly, and illuminate it fearlessly. As a novelist I have always seen myself as contributing to the central tradition of the novel, the tradition that grew up in the eighteenth century, which means recognisable human beings in familiar settings, doing the kind of things that you and I do, with all the usual consequences. . . . Everything important, everything lyrical and tragic and horrifying and uplifting and miraculous, is there in our ordinary lives if we can open our eyes and see it."

Mellown observed that Wain, who labored "within a tradition sustained by the living presence of earlier literature," was a writer who consciously developed his skills over three decades. Of all the so-called former "angry young men," according to Mellown, Wain "represents perhaps better than any other the traditional British novelist. His output (in both quantity and versatility) and its quality cause him to be reckoned an outstanding figure of his generation." In the *Atlantic*, Benjamin DeMott concluded that in his sober manner, Wain avoided gags, touched on hard subjects, celebrated classic authors, and produced, on occasion, "an elevated, unironic, unself-protective case for Art-in-the-large."

*BIOGRAPHICAL/CRITICAL SOURCES:*

*BOOKS*

Allen, Walter, *Tradition and Dream: The English and American Novel from the Twenties to Our Time*, Phoenix House, 1964.
Allen, *The Modern Novel*, Dutton, 1965.
Allsop, Kenneth, *The Angry Decade*, P. Owen, 1958.
Burgess, Anthony, *The Novel Now: A Guide to Contemporary Fiction*, Norton (New York City), 1967.

_Contemporary Authors Autobiography Series,_ Volume 4, Gale (Detroit), 1986.

_Contemporary Fiction in America and England, 1950-1970,_ Gale, 1976.

_Contemporary Literary Criticism,_ Gale, Volume 2, 1974, Volume 11, 1979, Volume 15, 1980, Volume 46, 1988.

_Dictionary of Literary Biography,_ Gale, Volume 15: _British Novelists, 1930-1959,_ 1983, Volume 27: _Poets of Great Britain and Ireland, 1945-1960,_ 1984, Volume 139: _British Short-Fiction Writers, 1945-1980,_ 1994, Volume 155: _Twentieth-Century British Literary Biographers,_ 1995.

Enright, D. J., _Conspirators and Poets,_ Dufour (Chester Springs, PA), 1966.

Fraser, G. S., _The Modern Writer and His World,_ Penguin, 1964.

Gerard, David, _My Work as a Novelist: John Wain,_ Drake Educational Associates (Cardiff, Wales), 1978.

Gerard, _John Wain: A Bibliography,_ Meckler (New York City), 1987.

Gindin, James J., _Postwar British Fiction: New Accents and Attitudes,_ University of California Press (Berkeley), 1962.

Karl, Frederick R., _The Contemporary English Novel,_ Farrar, Straus (New York City), 1962.

Maschler, Tom, editor, _Declaration,_ MacGibbon & Kee, 1959.

O'Connor, William Van, _The New University Wits and the End of Modernism,_ Southern Illinois University Press (Carbondale, IL), 1963.

Ries, Lawrence R., _Wolf Masks: Violence in Contemporary Poetry,_ Kennikat (Port Washington, NY), 1977.

Salwak, Dale, _John Braine and John Wain: A Reference Guide,_ G. K. Hall (Boston), 1980.

Salwak, _John Wain,_ G. K. Hall, 1981.

Salwak, _Interviews with . . . Britain's Angry Young Men,_ Borgo (San Bernardino, CA), 1984.

Wain, John, _Sprightly Running: Part of an Autobiography,_ Macmillan, 1962, St. Martin's, 1963.

Wain, _Dear Shadows: Portraits from Memory,_ John Murray, 1986.

PERIODICALS

_Atlantic,_ May, 1979.

_Best Sellers,_ October 15, 1971.

_Books,_ February, 1970; June, 1970.

_Books Abroad,_ summer, 1967.

_Books and Bookmen,_ October, 1967.

_Commonweal,_ February 10, 1967.

_Contemporary Review,_ October, 1978; January, 1979.

_Esquire,_ April 10, 1979.

_Globe and Mail_ (Toronto), June 16, 1984.

_Harper's,_ July, 1975; July, 1979.

_Listener,_ October 12, 1967; October 26, 1978.

_London Magazine,_ November, 1956; October, 1967.

_London Review of Books,_ September 1, 1988, pp. 24-25; June 5, 1986, p. 10.

_Los Angeles Times,_ May 17, 1970.

_Los Angeles Times Book Review,_ August 6, 1978.

_Nation,_ October 5, 1970; April 19, 1975; April 7, 1979.

_New Leader,_ July 3, 1978.

_New Republic,_ March 15, 1975.

_New Statesman,_ October 6, 1967; May 19, 1978.

_Newsweek,_ September 14, 1970; February 17, 1975.

_New Yorker,_ April 28, 1975; May 7, 1979.

_New York Review of Books,_ April 14, 1966; March 23, 1967; February 20, 1975.

_New York Times,_ February 13, 1975; December 26, 1978; April 6, 1979.

_New York Times Book Review,_ January 25, 1959; October 24, 1965; December 18, 1966; September 13, 1970; March 19, 1972; July 29, 1973; March 16, 1975; March 25, 1979.

_Observer,_ October 8, 1967; May 3, 1970; December 20, 1970; May 4, 1986, p. 23; June 26, 1988, p. 42; July 3, 1994, p. 20; November 13, 1994, p. 22.

_Poetry,_ February, 1978.

_Punch,_ October 11, 1967; May 21, 1986, p. 51; July 1, 1988, p. 52.

_Saturday Review,_ May 7, 1955; July 27, 1957; October 16, 1965; December 3, 1966; February 8, 1975; April 28, 1979.

_South Atlantic Quarterly,_ summer, 1969; autumn, 1979.

_Spectator,_ May 16, 1970; November 30, 1974; May 3, 1986, p. 26; July 30, 1988, pp. 26-27; October 8, 1988, p. 38.

_Stand,_ Volume XVII, number 1, 1975-76.

_Time,_ April 2, 1979.

_Times_ (London), January 7, 1984; April 24, 1986.

_Times Educational Supplement,_ July 20, 1956; June 20, 1986, p. 25.

_Times Literary Supplement,_ July 26, 1963; July 29, 1965; September 30, 1965; October 3, 1966; October 5, 1967; July 3, 1969; February 12, 1970; April 30, 1971; November 19, 1971; March 8, 1974; November 22, 1974; September 26, 1975; February 24, 1978; May 19, 1978; October 13, 1978; November 17, 1978; February 27, 1981; July 10, 1981; October 15, 1982; April 25, 1986, p. 445; July 8, 1988, p. 758; August 12, 1994, p. 23.

*Wall Street Journal,* December 21, 1992, p. A7.
*Washington Post Book World,* February 23, 1975; October 8, 1978; April 22, 1979; May 13, 1984.
*Wilson Library Bulletin,* May, 1963.
*World Literature Today,* spring, 1979.
*Yale Review,* winter, 1967.

*OBITUARIES:*

*PERIODICALS*

*Los Angeles Times,* May 27, 1994, p. A28.
*New York Times,* May 26, 1994, p. D22.
*Washington Post,* May 31, 1994, p. D7.*

\* \* \*

## WALKER, Margaret (Abigail) 1915-

*PERSONAL:* Born July 7, 1915, in Birmingham, AL; daughter of Sigismund C. (a Methodist minister) and Marion (a music teacher; maiden name Dozier) Walker; married Firnist James Alexander, June 13, 1943 (deceased); children: Marion Elizabeth, Firnist James, Sigismund, Margaret Elvira. *Education:* Northwestern University, B.A., 1935; University of Iowa, M.A., 1940, Ph.D., 1965. *Religion:* Methodist.

*ADDRESSES: Home*—2205 Guynes Street, Jackson, MS 39213. *Office*—Department of English, Jackson State College, Jackson, MS 39217.

*CAREER:* Worked as a social worker, newspaper reporter, and magazine editor. Livingstone College, Salisbury, NC, member of faculty, 1941-42, professor of English, 1945-46; West Virginia State College, Institute, West Virginia, instructor in English, 1942-43; Jackson State College, Jackson, Mississippi, professor of English, 1949-79, director of Institute for the Study of the History, Life, and Culture of Black Peoples, 1968-79. Lecturer, National Concert and Artists Corp. Lecture Bureau, 1943-48. Visiting professor in creative writing, Northwestern University, spring, 1969. Staff member, Cape Cod Writers Conference, Craigville, Massachusetts, 1967 and 1969. Participant, Library of Congress Conference on the Teaching of Creative Writing, 1973.

*MEMBER:* National Council of Teachers of English, Modern Language Association, Poetry Society of America, American Association of University Professors, National Education Association, Alpha Kappa Alpha.

*AWARDS, HONORS:* Yale Series of Younger Poets Award, 1942, for *For My People;* named to Honor Roll of Race Relations (national poll conducted by the New York Public Library), 1942; Rosenthal fellowship, 1944; Ford fellowship for study at Yale University, 1954; Houghton Mifflin Literary fellowship, 1966; Fulbright fellowship, 1971; National Endowment for the Humanities fellowship, 1972; D.Lit., Northwestern University, 1974; D.Let., Rust College, 1974; D.F.A., Dennison University, 1974; D.H.L., Morgan State University, 1976; Feminist Press Literary Award, 1989, for lifetime achievement.

*WRITINGS:*

*POETRY*

*For My People,* Yale University Press (New Haven, CT), 1942.
*Ballad of the Free,* Broadside Press (Detroit), 1966.
*Prophets for a New Day,* Broadside Press, 1970.
*October Journey,* Broadside Press, 1973.
*This Is My Century: New and Collected Poems,* University of Georgia Press (Athens), 1989.

*OTHER*

*Jubilee* (novel), Houghton (Boston), 1965.
*How I Wrote "Jubilee,"* Third World Press (Chicago), 1972, expanded edition published as *How I Wrote "Jubilee" and Other Essays on Life and Literature,* edited by Maryemma Graham, Feminist Press at the City University of New York (New York City), 1990.
(With Nikki Giovanni) *A Poetic Equation: Conversations between Nikki Giovanni and Margaret Walker,* Howard University Press (Washington, DC), 1974, published with new postscript, 1983.
*Richard Wright, Daemonic Genius: A Portrait of the Man, A Critical Look at His Work,* Warner Books (New York City), 1988.
*Margaret Walker Interview with Kay Bonetti* (audio recording), American Audio Prose Library (Columbia, MO), 1991.

Contributor to anthologies, including *Black Expression,* edited by Addison Gayle, Weybright & Tally (New York City), 1969; *Many Shades of Black,* edited by Stanton L. Wormley and Lewis H.

Fenderson, Morrow (New York City), 1969; and *Understanding the New Black Poetry: Black Speech and Black Music as Poetic References,* edited by Stephen Henderson, Morrow, 1973. Also contributor to periodicals, including *The Crisis, Negro Digest, Opportunity, Phylon, Poetry, Saturday Review, Virginia Quarterly,* and *Yale Review.*

*ADAPTATIONS: Jubilee* was adapted as an operetta by Donald Dorr and produced in Jackson, Mississippi, in 1977, and excerpts read by the author have been recorded on audio tape, American Audio Prose Library, 1991.

*SIDELIGHTS:* When twenty-seven-year-old Margaret Walker's *For My People* won the Yale Younger Poets Series Award in 1942, she became one of the youngest African-American writers to have published a book of poetry in the twentieth century. Walker also became the first woman of color in the United States to be honored in a prestigious literary competition. Since that time, her novel, *Jubilee,* has been acclaimed by scholars and critics as the first truly historical black American novel; it was also the first work by a black writer to speak out for the liberation of the black woman. Two cornerstones of a literature that affirms the African folk roots of black American life, *For My People* and *Jubilee* have also been called visionary in their look forward, toward a new cultural unity for black Americans.

The title of Walker's *For My People* denotes the subject matter of "poems in which the body and spirit of a great group of people are revealed with vigor and undeviating integrity," according to Louis Untermeyer in the *Yale Review.* Here, in long ballads, Walker draws sympathetic portraits of characters such as the New Orleans sorceress Molly Means; Kissie Lee, a tough young woman who dies "with her boots on switching blades"; and Poppa Chicken, an urban drug dealer and pimp. Other ballads give a new dignity to John Henry, killed by a ten-pound hammer, and Stagolee, who kills a white officer but eludes a lynch mob. In an essay in *Black Women Writers (1950-1980): A Critical Evaluation,* Eugenia Collier notes that "Using . . . the language of the grass-roots people, Walker spins yarns of folk heroes and heroines: those who, faced with the terrible obstacles which haunt Black people's very existence, not only survive but prevail—with style." Soon after it appeared, *For My People* found a large readership; three printings were needed to satisfy popular demand.

Some critics find fault with the sonnets in *For My People,* but others deem it generally impressive. In *Black American Literature: A Critical History,* Roger Whitlow elaborates on the title poem: "The poem, written in free verse, rhythmically catalogues the progress of black American experience, from the rural folkways, religious practices, and exhausting labor of the South, through the cramped and confusing conditions of the northern urban centers, to what she hopes will be a racial awakening, blacks militantly rising up to take control of their own destinies." "The final stanza is a reverberating cry for redress," Collier adds. "It demands a new beginning. Our music then will be martial music; our peace will be hard-won, but it will be 'written in the sky.' And after the agony, the people whose misery spawned strength will control our world. This poem is the hallmark of Margaret Walker's works. It echoes in her subsequent poetry and even in her monumental novel *Jubilee.* It speaks to us, in our words and rhythms, of our history, and it radiates the promise of our future. It is the quintessential example of myth and ritual shaped by artistic genius."

Reviewers praise Walker's control of poetic technique in "For My People." As Dudley Randall writes in *The Black Aesthetic,* "The poem gains its force . . . by the sheer overpowering accumulation of a mass of details delivered in rhythmical parallel phrases." To cite Richard K. Barksdale in *Black American Poets between Worlds, 1940-1960,* "it is magnificently wrought oral poetry. . . . In reading it aloud, one must be able to breathe and pause, pause and breathe preacher-style. One must be able to sense the ebb and flow of the intonations. . . . This is the kind of verbal music found in a well-delivered down-home folk sermon." By giving the poem a musical rhythm, Walker underscores the poem's message, observes Barksdale: "The poet here is writing about the source of the Black peoples' blues, for out of their troubled past and turbulent present came the Black peoples' song." Walker steps forward to remind her people of the strength to be found in their cultural tradition as she calls for a new, hopeful literature that can inspire social action.

"If the test of a great poem is the universality of statement, then 'For My People' is a great poem," states Barksdale. The critic explains in Donald B. Gibson's *Modern Black Poets: A Collection of Critical Essays* that the poem was written when "worldwide pain, sorrow, and affliction were tangibly evident, and few could isolate the Black man's dilemma from humanity's dilemma during the depression years or during the war years." Thus, the power of resilience presented in the poem is a hope Walker holds out not only to black people, but to all people—to "all the adams and eves." As she once remarked, "Writers should not write exclusively for black or white audiences, but most inclusively. After all, it is the business of all writers to write about the human condition, and all humanity must be involved in both the writing and in the reading."

*Jubilee,* an historical novel, is the second book on which Walker's literary reputation rests. First published in 1965, it is the story of a slave family during and after the civil war. The novel took Walker thirty years to write, during which she married a disabled veteran, raised four children, taught full time at Jackson State College in Mississippi, and earned a Ph.D. from the University of Iowa. The lengthy gestation, she believes, partly accounts for the book's quality. As she told Claudia Tate in *Black Women Writers at Work,* "Living with the book over a long period of time was agonizing. Despite all of that, *Jubilee* is the product of a mature person," one whose own difficult pregnancies and economic struggles could lend authenticity to the lives of her characters. "There's a difference between writing about something and living through it," Walker added. "I did both. I think I was meant to write *Jubilee.*"

The story behind *Jubilee*'s main characters, Vyry and Randall Ware, was an important part of Walker's life even before she began to write it down. As she explains in the essay *How I Wrote "Jubilee,"* she first heard about the "slavery time" in bedtime stories told by her maternal grandmother. When old enough to recognize the value of her family history, Walker took initiative, "prodding" her grandmother for more details, and promising to set down on paper the story that had taken shape in her mind. Later on, she completed extensive research on every aspect of the black experience touching the Civil War, from obscure birth records to information on the history of tin cans. "Most of my life I have been involved with writing this story about my great grandmother, and even if *Jubilee* were never considered an artistic or commercial success I would still be happy just to have finished it."

Soon after *Jubilee* was published, Walker was awarded a fellowship from Houghton-Mifflin, and a mixed reception from critics. Granting that the novel is "ambitious," *New York Times Book Review* contributor Wilma Dykeman nevertheless deems it "un-

even." Arthur P. Davis, writing in *From the Dark Tower: Afro-American Writers, 1900-1960,* suggests that the author "has crowded too much into her novel." Even so, say reviewers, the novel merits praise. Abraham Chapman of the *Saturday Review* appreciates the author's "fidelity to fact and detail" as she "presents the little-known everyday life of the slaves," their music, and their folkways. In the *Christian Science Monitor,* Henrietta Buckmaster comments: "In Vyry, Miss Walker has found a remarkable woman who suffered one outrage after the other and yet emerged with a humility and a mortal fortitude that reflected a spiritual wholeness." Dykeman concurs, "In its best episodes, and in Vyry, 'Jubilee' chronicles the triumph of a free spirit over many kinds of bondages." Later critical studies of the book emphasize the importance of its themes and its position as the prototype for novels that present black history from a black perspective. Claims Whitlow, "It serves especially well as a response to white 'nostalgia' fiction about the antebellum and Reconstruction South."

Walker's *Prophets for a New Day,* a slim volume of poems, was completed in 1970. Unlike the verses in *For My People,* which, in a Marxist fashion, names religion an enemy of revolution, *Prophets for a New Day* "reflects a profound religious faith," according to Collier. "The heroes of the sixties are named for the prophets of the Bible: Martin Luther King is Amos, Medgar Evars is Micah, and so on. The people and events of the sixties are paralleled with Biblical characters and occurrences. . . . The religious references are important. Whether one espouses the Christianity in which they are couched is not the issue. For the fact is that Black people from ancient Africa to now have always been a spiritual people, believing in an existence beyond the flesh." One poem in *Prophets* that harks back to African spiritualism is the "Ballad of Hoppy Toad," with its hexes that turn a murderous conjurer into a toad. Though Collier feels that Walker's "vision of the African past is fairly dim and romantic," the critic goes on to say that this poetry "emanates from a deeper area of the psyche, one which touches the mythic area of a collective being and reenacts the rituals which define a Black collective self." Perhaps more importantly, in *Prophets,* says Collier, Walker depicts "a people striking back at oppression and emerging triumphant."

Walker published a compilation of her poetry, *This Is My Century,* in 1989. Containing one-hundred poems that extend back to her early work published in *The*

*Crisis* magazine and including the classic "For My People," *This Is My Century* also features thirty-seven new poems, including "Farish Street" and "The Labyrinth of Life." As a retrospective, the volume clearly illustrates the consistency of Walker's humanitarian voice, her social and political concerns, and her position as a pivotal figure among Southern writers. Calling Walker a "poet of vision, of the flow of past not only into present, but of a reach into the future," Florence Howe praises many of Walker's poems included in the anthology. "For those of us who have lived through three (or more) decades of change know that we are only at the beginning (or at best in the middle) of much more to come," writes Howe in her review of *This Is My Century* for the *Women's Review of Books*. "This 1942 poem ["The Struggle Staggers Us]" speaks with immediacy not only to the contemporary women's movement, . . . but to a world that needs to solve the problems of poverty if it is ever to have racial and ethnic harmony inside nations and among them."

Throughout her career as a poet and teacher, Walker has written numerous essays, many of which are anthologized in 1990's *How I Wrote Jubilee and Other Essays on Life and Literature*. A half-century of African-American intellectual thought is illuminated through Walker's commentary on culture, literature, and social issues that include the importance of the family, racism, religion, academia, and the place of women—especially Black women—in society. Among the fourteen essays and speeches in the collection is "Black Women in Academia," which recounts an experience wherein Walker was turned down for financial assistance by the dean of the school where she had taught English for twenty years. And her feminist consciousness can be seen in one of her later essays, entitled "Rediscovering Black Women Writers in the Mecca of the New Negro," in which Walker lauds the work of several almost-forgotten African-American women writers.

*Richard Wright, Daemonic Genius: A Portrait of the Man, A Critical Look at His Work,* published in 1988, is based on Walker's personal relationship with the noted author of *Native Son* during the 1930s, when the two worked together on the W. P. A.'s Federal Writers Project in New York City. Concentrating on Wright's intellectual development—his pan-Africanism, Marxist-humanism, and existentialism—Walker places him securely in the forefront of twentieth-century American culture. She argues that the development of Wright's worldview was grounded in the South and attempts to provide an

honest assessment of the psychological perspective that would shape his work as a writer. "Wright is too important to be lost in the confusion of race and politics and racist literary history and criticism so evident in the twentieth century," Walker writes. Of particular interest is Walker's description of her personal relationship with her subject. As Waldo E. Martin Jr. notes in the *Washington Post Book World*, Walker "takes great pains to describe as a platonic and intellectual relationship clearly affected her deeply then and, judging from the intensity of the description, the impact lingers. Walker convincingly suggests that Wright's attitude toward her reflected his hatred of women in general and black women in particular. . . . Played off against the psychosexual tension of their friendship, Walker's repeated and incisive critiques of Wright's misogyny assume at once a personal and political quality."

Barksdale relates that Walker's books owe little to her relatively privileged academic life and much to a rich cultural sensibility gained in her youth: "There was . . . New Orleans with its . . . folk mythology, its music, . . . and its assortment of racial experiences to be remembered and recalled." There was also the shaping influence of Walker's parents. Born in Jamaica but educated at Atlanta's Gammon Theological Institute, her father Sigismund was a Methodist preacher, her mother, Marion, was a musician. "So [the poet] grew up in a household ruled by the power of the word, for undoubtedly few have a greater gift for articulate word power than an educated Jamaican trained to preach the doctrine of salvation in the Black South," Barksdale remarks. In such a home, survival "without mastery of words and language was impossible," he adds. Because of such a background, Walker felt destined for an academic career.

Walker's career was characterized by opposition and difficulty. Walker reflects in her interview with Tate: "I'm a third-generation college graduate. Society doesn't want to recognize that there's this kind of black writer. I'm the Ph.D. black woman. That's horrible. That is to be despised. I didn't know how bad it was until I went back to school [to teaching] and found out." With her older children nearing college age, Walker had taken leave from her position at Jackson State University to earn an advanced degree in hopes that it would lead to a greater salary. She returned, only to be slighted by the administration. Eventually, she developed the school's Black studies program, attaining personal fulfillment only during the last years of her career as an educator.

Such discouragements have not kept Walker from producing works that have encouraged others. *For My People, Jubilee,* and *Prophets for a New Day* are valued for their relation to social movements of twentieth-century America; translated into seven languages, *Jubilee* has inspired readers worldwide. In 1937 the poem "For My People" called for a new generation to gather strength from a militant literature. The black literature of the 1960s—including the autobiographies of Malcolm X, Eldridge Cleaver, Huey Newton, and Angela Davis—would answer that challenge, according to C. W. E. Bigsby in *The Second Black Renaissance: Essays in Black Literature.* Her example over the years has also proved to be instructive. "She has revealed the creative ways in which methods and materials of the social science scholar may be joined with the craft and viewpoint of the poet/novelist to create authentic black literature," reads the epilogue of *How I Wrote "Jubilee."* "She has reaffirmed for us the critical importance of oral tradition in the creation of our history. . . . Finally, she has made awesomely clear to us the tremendous costs which must be paid in stubborn, persistent work and commitment if we are indeed to write our own history and create our own literature."

## BIOGRAPHICAL/CRITICAL SOURCES:

### BOOKS

Bankier, Joanna, and Dierdre Lashgari, editors, *Women Poets of the World,* Macmillan (New York City), 1983.

Baraka, Amiri, *The Black Nation,* Getting Together Publications, 1982.

Bigsby, C. W. E., editor, *The Second Black Renaissance: Essays in Black Literature,* Greenwood Press (Westport, CT), 1980.

Braxton, Joanne M., and Andraee Nicola McLaughlin, editors, *Wild Women in the Whirlwind: Afra-American Culture and the Contemporary Literary Renaissance,* Rutgers University Press (New Brunswick, NJ), 1990.

*Contemporary Literary Criticism,* Gale (Detroit), Volume 1, 1973, Volume 2, 1976.

Davis, Arthur P., *From the Dark Tower: Afro-American Writers, 1900 to 1960,* Howard University Press, 1974.

*Dictionary of Literary Biography,* Gale, Volume 76: *Afro-American Writers, 1940-1955,* 1988, Volume 152: *American Novelists since World War II, Fourth Series,* 1995.

Emanuel, James A., and Theodore L. Gross, editors, *Dark Symphony: Negro Literature in America,* Free Press, 1968.

Evans, Mari, editor, *Black Women Writers (1950-1980): A Critical Evaluation,* Anchor/Doubleday (New York City), 1982.

Gayle, Addison, editor, *The Black Aesthetic,* Doubleday, 1971.

Gibson, Donald B., editor, *Modern Black Poets: A Collection of Critical Essays,* Prentice-Hall (New York City), 1983.

Jackson, Blyden, and Louis D. Rubin, Jr., *Black Poetry in America: Two Essays in Historical Interpretation,* Louisiana State University Press (Baton Rouge), 1974.

Jones, John Griffith, in *Mississippi Writers Talking,* Volume 2, University of Mississippi Press, 1983.

Kent, George E., *Blackness and the Adventure of Western Culture,* Third World Press, 1972.

Lee, Don L., *Dynamite Voices I: Black Poets of the 1960s,* Broadside Press, 1971.

*Margaret Walker's "For My People": A Tribute,* photographs by Roland L. Freeman, University Press of Mississippi, 1992.

Miller, R. Baxter, editor, *Black American Poets between Worlds, 1940-1960,* University of Tennessee Press (Knoxville), 1986.

Pryse, Marjorie, and Hortense J. Spillers, editors, *Conjuring: Black Women, Fiction, and Literary Tradition,* Indiana University Press (Bloomington), 1985.

Redmond, Eugene B., *Drumvoices: The Mission of Afro-American Poetry—A Critical Evaluation,* Doubleday, 1976.

Tate, Claudia, editor, *Black Women Writers at Work,* Continuum (New York City), 1983.

Walker, Margaret, *How I Wrote "Jubilee" and Other Essays on Life and Literature,* edited by Maryemma Graham, Feminist Press at the City University of New York, 1990.

Whitlow, Roger, *Black American Literature: A Critical History,* Nelson Hall, 1973.

### PERIODICALS

*Atlantic,* December, 1942.

*Belles Lettres,* summer, 1990, p. 32; spring, 1991, p. 2.

*Best Sellers,* October 1, 1966.

*Black World,* December, 1971; December, 1975.

*Books,* January 3, 1973.

*Book Week,* October 2, 1966.

*Callaloo,* May, 1979; fall, 1987.

*Christian Science Monitor,* November 14, 1942; September 29, 1966; June 19, 1974.

*CLA Journal,* December, 1977.

*Common Ground,* autumn, 1943.
*Ebony,* February, 1949.
*English Journal,* November, 1993, p. 31.
*Freedomways,* summer, 1967.
*Mississippi Quarterly,* fall, 1988; fall, 1989.
*National Review,* October 4, 1966.
*Negro Digest,* February, 1967; January, 1968.
*New Republic,* November 23, 1942.
*New York Times,* November 4, 1942.
*New York Times Book Review,* August 2, 1942; September 25, 1966.
*Opportunity,* December, 1942.
*Publishers Weekly,* April 15, 1944; March 24, 1945.
*Saturday Review,* September 24, 1966.
*Times Literary Supplement,* June 29, 1967.
*Washington Post,* February 9, 1983.
*Washington Post Book World,* February 16, 1989.
*Women's Review of Books,* July, 1990, p. 41; December, 1990, p. 29.
*Yale Review,* winter, 1943.*

\* \* \*

## WATSON, Ian 1943-

*PERSONAL:* Born April 20, 1943, in St. Albans, England; son of John William (a postmaster) and Ellen (Rowley) Watson; married Judith Jackson, September 1, 1962; children: Jessica Scott. *Education:* Balliol College, Oxford, B.A. (first class honors), 1963, B.Litt., 1965, M.A., 1966.

*ADDRESSES: Home*—Daisy Cottage, Banbury Rd., Moreton Pinkney, Near Daventry, Northants, NN11 35Q, England. *Agent*—c/o Victor Gollancz Ltd., Wellington House, 125 Strand, London WC2N 0BB, England.

*CAREER:* University of Dar es Salaam, Dar es Salaam, Tanzania, lecturer in literature, 1965-67; Tokyo University of Education and Keio University, Tokyo, Japan, lecturer in English, 1967-70; Birmingham Polytechnic, Birmingham, England, lecturer, 1970-75, senior lecturer in complementary studies (science fiction and futures studies) for School of the History of Art in Art and Design Center, 1975-76; writer, 1976—. Temporary lecturer, English department, Japan Women's University, Tokyo, 1968-69. Writer in residence, Nene College, Northamptonshire, England, 1984.

*MEMBER:* Science Fiction Writers of America, Science Fiction Foundation (London; member of governing council, 1974-90).

*AWARDS, HONORS:* John W. Campbell Memorial Award runner-up, World Science Fiction Convention, 1974, for *The Embedding;* Prix Apollo, 1975, for French translation of *The Embedding;* Premios Zikkurath, 1978, for Spanish translation of *The Embedding;* Orbit Award, 1976, and British Science Fiction Association Award for best paperback book published in Britain, both 1978, both for *The Jonah Kit;* Southern Arts Association literary bursary, 1978; Hugo Award nomination for best short story, World Science Fiction Convention, 1979, for "The Very Slow Time Machine"; British Science Fiction Award runner-up for best short story, 1981, for "The World SF Convention of 2080"; Hugo Award nominee, World Science Fiction Convention, and Nebula Award nominee, Science Fiction Writers of America, both 1984, both for *Slow Birds and Other Stories;* Prix Europeen de Science Fiction, 1985, for work as a novelist; British Science Fiction Association Award runner-up for best short story, 1987, for "Jingling Geordie's Hole"; Arthur C. Clarke Award finalist, 1989, for *Whores of Babylon;* British Fantasy Award finalist, 1989, for "Lost Bodies"; Eastercon Award finalist, 1990, for "Eye of the Ayatollah"; Eastercon Award finalist and British Science Fiction Association Award runner-up, both 1993, both for "The Coming of Vertumnus"; guest of honor at numerous science fiction conventions.

*WRITINGS:*

NOVELS

*The Embedding,* Gollancz (London), 1973, Scribner (New York City), 1975.
*The Jonah Kit,* Gollancz, 1975, Scribner, 1976.
(With wife, Judith Jackson Watson) *Orgasmachine* (French translation of original English manuscript), Editions Champ-Libre, 1976.
*The Martian Inca,* Scribner, 1977.
*Alien Embassy,* Gollancz, 1977, Ace (New York City), 1978.
*Miracle Visitors,* Gollancz, 1978.
*God's World,* Gollancz, 1979, Carrol and Graf (New York City), 1990.
*The Gardens of Delight,* Gollancz, 1980, Pocket Books (New York City), 1982.
(With Michael Bishop) *Under Heaven's Bridge,* Gollancz, 1981, Ace, 1982.

*Deathhunter,* Gollancz, 1981, St. Martin's (New York City), 1986.

*Chekhov's Journey,* Gollancz, 1983, Carrol and Graf, 1989.

*Converts,* Granada (London), 1984, St. Martin's, 1985.

*Queenmagic, Kingmagic,* Gollancz, 1986, St. Martin's, 1986.

*The Power* (horror), Headline (London), 1987.

*Meat,* (horror) Headline, 1988.

*The Fire Worm* (horror) Gollancz, 1988.

*Whores of Babylon,* Paladin (London), 1989.

*The Flies of Memory,* Gollancz, 1990.

*Nanoware Time* (bound with *The Persistence of Vision,* by John Varley), Tor (New York City), 1991.

*Lucky's Harvest (The First Book of Mana),* Gollancz, 1993.

*The Fallen Moon (The Second Book of Mana),* Gollancz, 1994.

*Hard Questions,* Gollancz, 1996.

### *"BLACK RIVER/YALEEN" TRILOGY; NOVELS*

*The Book of the River,* Gollancz, 1984, DAW (New York City), 1986.

*The Book of the Stars,* Gollancz, 1985, DAW, 1986.

*The Book of Being,* Gollancz, 1985, DAW, 1986.

### *"WARHAMMER 40,000 SERIES"; NOVELS*

*Inquisitor,* Games Workshop (Brighton, West Sussex), 1990.

*Space Marine,* Boxtree, 1993.

*Harlequin,* Boxtree, 1994.

*Chaos Child,* Boxtree, 1995.

### *SHORT STORY COLLECTIONS*

*The Very Slow Time Machine,* Ace, 1979.

*Sunstroke and Other Stories,* Gollancz, 1982.

*Slow Birds and Other Stories,* Gollancz, 1985.

*The Book of Ian Watson* (includes nonfiction), Ziesing (Willimantic, CT), 1985.

*Evil Water and Other Stories,* Gollancz, 1987.

*Salvage Rites and Other Stories,* Gollancz, 1989.

*Stalin's Teardrops,* Gollancz, 1991.

*The Coming of Vertumnus,* Gollancz, 1994.

### *OTHER*

*Japan: A Cat's Eye View* (juvenile), Bunken (Osaka, Japan), 1969.

*Japan Tomorrow* (juvenile), Bunken, 1977.

(Editor) *Pictures at an Exhibition: A Science Fiction Anthology,* Greystoke Mobray (Cardiff, Wales), 1981, Borgo (San Bernardino, CA), 1987.

(Editor with Bishop) *Changes: Stories of Metamorphosis: An Anthology of Speculative Fiction about Startling Metamorphoses, both Psychological and Physical,* Ace, 1982.

(Editor with Pamela Sargent) *Afterlives: An Anthology of Stories about Life after Death,* Vintage (New York City), 1986.

Also contributor of stories to science fiction anthologies. Contributor of stories and articles to science fiction magazines and literary journals, including *Chicago Review, London Magazine, Ambit, Interzone, Transition,* and *Transatlantic Review. Foundation: The Review of Science Fiction,* features editor, 1975-90, consultant editor, 1990—. European editor of *Science Fiction Writers of America Bulletin.*

Ian Watson's manuscripts are housed at the Science Fiction Foundation, North-East London Polytechnic.

*SIDELIGHTS:* According to a reviewer for the *Washington Post Book World,* Ian Watson is "probably the best thinker" in British science fiction. "I'm attempting to alter the states of mind of my readers, to make them more conscious of the operating programs that are running their brains—the sort of thing that John Lilly refers to as 'metaprogramming,'" Watson tells Charles Platt in *Dream Makers: The Uncommon People Who Write Science Fiction.* "I'm interested in ways of examining the structure of your thinking, and trying to present narratives that make people think a bit about the pattern and style of their thoughts, and what alternative thought-structures they could enter into. That is what I say science fiction ought to be about, presenting you with an alternative-reality paradigm, a different way of conceptualizing reality and the universe." Watson's novels and stories present an ongoing fictional exploration of the nature of being and reality, language and memory, morality and religion—in other words, of humankind's metaphysical, epistemological, and spiritual relationship to the universe. Both Spider Robinson in *Analog Science Fiction/Science Fact* and Alex de Jonge in the *Spectator* admit that Watson's books are not easy to read, but recommend them strongly. Robinson in particular views Watson's multiplicity of ideas as one of his strengths: "Daring, heady stuff . . . not to be missed by the thoughtful, and not in a million years to be taken for light entertainment."

Watson's first novel, *The Embedding,* involves the search for a primary language which, if discovered, may provide clues to understanding the nature of reality. Charles Platt in *Dream Makers* says, "The book suggests that an isolated group of children, educated to think differently, would inhabit a different reality from ours, with different natural laws." Similar themes are explored in *The Jonah Kit,* in which the universe is discovered to have existed for only a few microseconds after its creation and a whale is imprinted with a human soul, and in *The Martian Inca,* in which an extraterrestrial microorganism accidentally infects both a group of Andean natives and a pair of American astronauts. In each case, a character's perception of the universe which surrounds him changes, and, for that character at least, the universe itself changes correspondingly.

Baird Searles and his co-editors in *A Reader's Guide to Science Fiction* call Watson's *The Embedding* "a serious, difficult and fascinating book, one that assumes its reader's intelligence." Gerald Jonas, writing for the *New York Times Book Review,* praises Watson's first two novels as "distinguished by an irresistible blend of narrative energy and intellectual interest"; but he says of *The Martian Inca,* "the book fails to cohere. The ideas, while fascinating in themselves, are not really dramatized. . . . However, with all its faults, it is still superior to most contemporary sf." Eric Korn, in the *Times Literary Supplement,* finds the *The Jonah Kit* "flawed in realization." He continues, "Most of the characters exist only to break the exposition up into easy chunks of dialogue." However, Korn says of *Miracle Visitors,* Watson's novel about the origin of UFOs, "There is, as usual, a richness of character and description."

*God's World* and *The Gardens of Delight* are less about the perception of reality and the evolution of consciousness than about the nature of God. *God's World* concerns a trip to heaven. Angels appear at sacred places all over the globe, inviting humanity to join God, who lives in a star system some distance away. A spaceship with neo-crusaders aboard sets out, using technology provided by the angels, but, on their arrival, the humans' expectations are shattered. They find themselves in a world with its own heaven, which can be reached by dreaming or death, but they discover that the struggle between good and evil is not nearly as simple as it seems. *The Gardens of Delight* is based on the triptych painting "The Garden of Delights" by Hieronymus Bosch; its center panel, filled with outsized animals, bizarrely shaped vegetables, and nude men and women, is interpreted by some as a surrealistic vision of life after death, while the left and right panels are generally believed to represent the Garden of Eden and Hell, respectively. Watson's novel tells the story of a spaceship crew's search for God against the backdrop of Bosch's allegorical work. Mysterious immortal beings, in an attempt to bring purpose to their existences, have been molding worlds to fit what they have learned about other forms of life. A chance encounter with colonists from Earth causes the aliens to transform one world into a living replica of Bosch's painting. When another spacecraft arrives some years later, its crew begins a search for the aliens, who fancy themselves "God."

"I am less enthusiastic about *God's World* than any of the previous novels," Korn remarks. "It seems, if not perfunctory, at least hurried in relation to its theme." Alex de Jonge, writing in the *Spectator,* holds a different view, stating that *God's World* "is quite as good as [Watson's] earlier works . . . never for a moment do we feel the author has overreached himself," and calls it "a work of great distinction." Similar differences of opinion surround *The Gardens of Delight;* Gay Firth comments in the London *Times* that Watson is attempting in *Gardens* to retell a story which has been "better described by Dante and Bunyan." On the other hand, Tom Easton, writing for *Analog Science Fiction/Science Fact,* says, "*Gardens* is a strange book, as strange as Bosch's original painting. But Watson has handled the imagery well, emerging with a story that could stand discussion in terms of Bunyan and Dante. It's an allegory that denies itself even as it says perfection of the soul is possible." In Watson's own opinion, these two studies of the search for God, although alike, represent views from opposite angles. He told David Langford in *Science Fiction Review:* "*GW* and *Gardens* are mirror images in the sense that, in the former, the journey to an objective alien world is presented as a journey through imaginative space, the physical starship journey being also a journey through the imagination—whereas, in the latter, the creators (who are also the inhabitants) of the alien Bosch-world have to imagine (and create) a human starship arriving there, in order to understand their own reality."

The *Black River/Yaleen* trilogy is probably Watson's most popularly successful work. Comprised of *The Book of the River, The Book of the Stars,* and *The Book of Being,* the trilogy takes place in a fantasy world divided by a sentient river. On one side of the river lies a female-dominated society; on the other, a male-dominated society. If men try to cross the river, it drives them insane. The action of the trilogy centers on the travails of its female protagonist, Yaleen, as she unravels and confronts the origins and meaning of this world. Although more adventure-oriented than much of Watson's other work, the *Black River/ Yaleen* trilogy still contains a good deal of speculation on the nature of reality and the universe.

Critical reaction to the *Black River/Yaleen* trilogy was mixed. Arguing that a male novelist can indeed create a feminist utopia, Jonas in the *New York Times Book Review* says that Watson "outdoes himself" with *The Book of the River.* Easton in *Analog Science Fiction/Science Fact* comments that he did not review *The Book of the River* because he "felt you didn't need my comments to know how good it was." Easton finds *The Book of the Stars* "a little farfetched," but concludes that Watson "tells the tale vigorously and convincingly." A *Booklist* reviewer argues that *The Book of the Stars* is "too discursive, too philosophical, and too slow in pace," but concludes that those with a "taste for [Watson's] work will enjoy this tale." A *Kirkus Reviews* critic has similar objections to *The Book of Being* but also concludes that fans of Watson will find "a suitable and worthy conclusion, with . . . cosmic complications aplenty."

*Queenmagic, Kingmagic* is a fantasy that mirrors the game of chess. Two kingdoms, white Bellogard and black Chorny, engage in a recurring battle, with individual characters representing various chess pieces. The plot of the book revolves around a pawn and his companions who travel through several alternate worlds in an attempt to break this endless cycle. Writing in *Voice of Youth Advocates,* Judy Kowalski states that "the worlds Watson creates are thought provoking about the games we play and the rules we follow." Kelvin Johnston in the *Observer* finds *Queenmagic, Kingmagic* "much more robust than the general run of fantasy novels." Chris Morgan in *Fantasy Review* describes it as "a less cerebral novel than one is used to from Watson, and none the worse for that."

Watson's first book of the 1990s, *The Flies of Memory,* is a continuation of a previously published story. According to Mary Gentle in the *Washington Post Book World, The Flies of Memory* "has all the bravura that space opera should have, without being any such thing." Alien invaders, the flies of the title, land on Earth. Their goal is not to conquer the planet, but rather to memorize and recreate its most

famous architectural accomplishments. When, despite their apparently peaceful intentions, the aliens' rights to do so are challenged, parts of famous Earth cities vanish and reappear on Mars. An expedition is then sent to Mars to rescue the human survivors that have been transported along with the cites. Gerald Jonas in the *New York Times Book Review* finds the novel "engaging," but is critical of its "paragraphs of pseudoscientific explanation." Gentle concludes: "Deep-structure reality, Nazis on Mars, and a memory-construct voodoo mama are only a few of the sparks the book throws off as it whirls—all purely science fiction, all grounded in respectable speculation, all wonderfully gonzo."

Watson's two-volume *Book of Mana* epic, based in part on Finnish folk legends, is the story of Lucky Sariola, an interstellar Earth colonist in Kaleva who discovers an asteroid lifeform that responds to storytelling. A *Books* reviewer calls *Lucky's Harvest,* the first book in the set, "vibrant, challenging and multi-layered," concluding that *Lucky's Harvest* is Watson's "finest work to date." Farren Miller, writing in *Locus,* states that "Watson isn't content with any mere tomfoolery of enchanted swords, pale maidens, and ravening monsters, linked to sf with a little rubber science; there's a sharp, rational mind at work (and play) in *Lucky's Harvest.*"

Watson once told *CA:* "The Science Fiction I am interested in should be scientific—in that it deals with the impact of scientific ideas and discoveries; and however farfetched these ideas or discoveries may be, they should be dealt with from a standpoint of realism, not fantasy or magic. But at the same time, SF should be metaphorical—in that it functions as a tool for thinking about the world and its future, Man and the Universe, flexibly and boldly. . . . SF should be contradictory, in that it envisages a multiplicity of possible futures. SF should be rooted in a sense of Man (adequate characterization, not puppets; sense of real social milieu). Yet it should be this without being 'earthbound' (by refusing to consider the nature of Alien experience or the Universe at large). Indeed, it must try to tackle ultimate questions: about the nature of reality, about the origin and significance of the Universe, and of life within this Universe."

*BIOGRAPHICAL/CRITICAL SOURCES:*

*BOOKS*

Clute, John, and Peter Nicholls, *The Encyclopedia of Science Fiction,* St. Martin's, 1993, p. 1302.

Mackey, Douglas A., *The Work of Ian Watson: An Annotated Bibliography and Guide,* Borgo, 1989.

Platt, Charles, *Dream Makers: The Uncommon People Who Write Science Fiction,* Berkeley Publishing (New York City), 1980.

Pringle, David, *Science Fiction: The 100 Best Novels,* Xanadu (Goochland, VA), 1985.

Searles, Baird, Martin Last, Beth Meacham, and Michael Franklin, editors, *A Reader's Guide to Science Fiction,* Avon (New York City), 1979.

Staicar, Ted, editor, *Critical Encounters II: Writers & Themes in Science Fiction,* Ungar (New York City), 1982.

*PERIODICALS*

*Analog Science Fiction/Science Fact,* March, 1979; June, 1979; September, 1982; October, 1986.

*Booklist,* May 1, 1986; October 15, 1986.

*Books,* September/October, 1993.

*Economist,* August 20, 1983.

*Fantasy Review,* August, 1984; April, 1985; July, 1985; November, 1985; May, 1986; November, 1986.

*Kirkus Reviews,* April 1, 1986; September 1, 1986.

*Locus,* February, 1991, p. 60; January, 1994, p. 15.

*New Statesman,* April 24, 1987.

*New York Times Book Review,* July 20, 1975; September 12, 1976; November 27, 1977; March 9, 1986; September 21, 1986; July 8, 1990, p. 22; February 9, 1992, p. 20.

*Observer* (London), February 20, 1983; August 5, 1984; December 26, 1986; December 28, 1986, p. 20; April 26, 1987.

*Publishers Weekly,* April 11, 1986; October 10, 1986; November 14, 1994, p. 56.

*Punch,* June 13, 1984; December 12, 1984; November 6, 1985; June 4, 1986.

*Science Fiction Chronicle,* November, 1987, p. 53.

*Science Fiction and Fantasy Book Review,* January, 1982; July, 1983.

*Science Fiction Review,* spring, 1982; winter, 1982; summer, 1985; spring, 1986.

*Scream Factory,* spring, 1996.

*Spectator,* August 26, 1978; January 12, 1980; September 13, 1980.

*Times* (London), February 3, 1980; March 3, 1983; October 31, 1985.

*Times Literary Supplement,* September 11, 1973; May 23, 1975; July 8, 1977; January 27, 1978; May 30, 1980; July 18, 1980; September 10, 1982.

*Voice Literary Supplement,* October, 1984; July, 1985.

*Voice of Youth Advocates,* June, 1988, p. 98.

*Washington Post Book World,* July 26, 1981; March 28, 1982; April 28, 1985; January 26, 1992, p. 6.

*West Coast Review of Books,* July, 1979.

\* \* \*

## WILSON, August 1945-

*PERSONAL:* Born Frederick August Kittel in 1945, in Pittsburgh, PA; son of Frederick August (a baker) and Daisy (a cleaning woman; maiden name, Wilson) Kittel, and stepfather, David Bedford; married second wife, Judy Oliver (a social worker), 1981 (marriage ended); married Constanza Romero (a costume designer); children: (first marriage) Sakina Ansari.

*ADDRESSES: Home—*Seattle, WA. *Office—*c/o John Breglio, Paul Weiss Rifkind Wharton & Garrison, 1285 Avenue of the Americas, New York, NY 10019.

*CAREER:* Writer. Cofounder (with Rob Penny), scriptwriter, and director of Black Horizons on the Hill (theatre company) Pittsburgh, PA, 1968-78; scriptwriter for Science Museum of Minnesota, St. Paul, 1979.

*AWARDS, HONORS:* Award for best play of 1984-85 from New York Drama Critics Circle, 1985, Antoinette Perry ("Tony") Award nomination from League of New York Theatres and Producers, 1985, and Whiting Writers' Award from the Whiting Foundation, 1986, all for *Ma Rainey's Black Bottom;* Outstanding Play Award from American Theatre Critics, 1986, Drama Desk Outstanding New Play Award, 1986, New York Drama Critics Circle Best Play Award, 1986, Pulitzer Prize for drama, Antoinette Perry Award for best play, and award for best Broadway play from Outer Critics Circle, all 1987, all for *Fences;* John Gassner Award for best American playwright from Outer Critics Circle, 1987; named Artist of the Year by *Chicago Tribune,* 1987; Literary Lion Award from New York Public Library, 1988; New York Drama Critics Circle Best Play award, and Antoinette Perry Award nomination for best play, both 1988, both for *Joe Turner's Come and Gone;* Drama Desk Outstanding New Play Award, New York Drama Critics Circle Best Play Award, Antoinette Perry Award for Best Play, American Theatre Critics Outstanding Play Award, and Pulitzer Prize for drama, all 1990, all for *The Piano Lesson;* Black Filmmakers Hall of Fame Award, 1991; Antoinette Perry Award nomination for best play, and American Theatre Critics' Association Award, both 1992, both for *Two Trains Running;* Clarence Muse Award, 1992; recipient of Bush and Guggenheim Foundation fellowships.

*WRITINGS:*

*Jitney* (two-act play), first produced in Pittsburgh, PA, at the Allegheny Repertory Theatre, 1982.

*Ma Rainey's Black Bottom* (play; first produced in New Haven, CT, at the Yale Repertory Theatre, 1984; produced on Broadway at the Cort Theatre, October, 1984; also see below), New American Library (New York City), 1985.

*Fences* (play; first produced at Yale Repertory Theatre, 1985; produced on Broadway at 46th Street Theatre, March, 1987; also see below), New American Library, 1986.

*Joe Turner's Come and Gone* (play; first produced at Yale Repertory Theatre, 1986; produced on Broadway at Barrymore Theatre, March, 1988; also see below), New American Library, 1988.

*The Piano Lesson* (play; first produced in New Haven at the Yale Repertory Theatre, 1987; produced on Broadway at Walter Kerr Theatre, 1990; also see below), New American Library, 1990.

(And author of preface) *August Wilson: Three Plays* (contains *Ma Rainey's Black Bottom, Fences,* and *Joe Turner's Come and Gone*), afterword by Paul C. Harrison, University of Pittsburgh Press (Pittsburgh), 1991.

*Two Trains Running* (first produced at Yale Repertory Theatre, 1990, produced at Walter Kerr Theatre, 1992), New American Library/Dutton, 1993.

*Seven Guitars* (first produced in Chicago at Goodman Theatre, 1995), Dutton, 1996.

*The Piano Lesson* (teleplay; adapted from his play), "Hallmark Hall of Fame," CBS-TV, 1995.

Also author of the plays *The Homecoming,* 1979, *The Coldest Day of the Year,* 1979, *Fullerton Street,* 1980, *Black Bart and the Sacred Hills,* 1981, and *The Mill Hand's Lunch Bucket,* 1983. Author of the book for a stage musical about jazz musician Jelly Roll Morton. Work represented in *A Game of Passion: The NFL Literary Companion,* Turner, 1994, *Selected from Contemporary American Plays,* 1990, and *The Poetry of Blackamerica,* Adoff. Contributor to periodicals, including *Black Lines* and *Connection.*

*WORK IN PROGRESS:* A screenplay adaptation of *Fences.*

*SIDELIGHTS:* August Wilson has been hailed since the mid-1980s as an important talent in the American theatre. He spent his childhood in poverty in Pittsburgh, Pennsylvania, where he lived with his parents and five siblings. Though he grew up in a poor family, Wilson felt that his parents withheld knowledge of even greater hardships they had endured. "My generation of blacks knew very little about the past of our parents," he told the *New York Times* in 1984. "They shielded us from the indignities they suffered." Wilson's goal is to illuminate that shadowy past with a series of plays, each set in a different decade, that focus on black issues. *Ma Rainey's Black Bottom, Fences, Joe Turner's Come and Gone, The Piano Lesson, Two Trains Running,* and *Seven Guitars* are part of this ambitious project.

Wilson has noted that his real education began when he was sixteen years old. Disgusted by the racist treatment he endured in the various schools he had attended until that time, he dropped out and began educating himself in the local library. Working at menial jobs, he also pursued a literary career and successfully submitted poems to black publications at the University of Pittsburgh. In 1968 he became active in the theatre by founding—despite lacking prior experience—Black Horizons on the Hill, a theatre company in Pittsburgh. Recalling his early theatre involvement, Wilson described himself to the *New York Times* as "a cultural nationalist . . . trying to raise consciousness through theater."

According to several observers, however, Wilson found his artistic voice—and began to appreciate the black voices of Pittsburgh—after he moved to St. Paul, Minnesota, in 1978. In St. Paul Wilson wrote his first play, *Jitney,* a realistic drama set in a Pittsburgh taxi station. *Jitney,* noted for the fidelity with which it portrayed black urban speech and life, had a successful engagement at a small theater in Pittsburgh. Wilson followed *Jitney* with another play, *Fullerton Street,* but this work failed to strengthen his reputation.

Wilson then resumed work on an earlier unfinished project, *Ma Rainey's Black Bottom,* a play about a black blues singer's exploitation of her fellow musicians. This work, whose title role is named after an actual blues singer from the 1920s, is set in a recording studio in 1927. In the studio, temperamental Ma Rainey verbally abuses the other musicians and presents herself—without justification—as an important musical figure. But much of the play is also set in a rehearsal room, where Ma Rainey's musicians discuss their abusive employer and the hardships of life in racist America.

Eventually, the musicians are all revealed to have experienced, in varying degrees, racist treatment. The most resigned member is the group's leader, a trombonist who has learned to accept racial discrimination and merely negotiates around it. The bassist's response is to wallow in hedonism and ignore his nation's treatment of blacks, while the pianist takes an intellectual approach to solving racial problems. The group's trumpeter, however, is bitter and cynical. He is haunted by the memory of his mother's rape by four white men. Tensions mount in the play when the sullen trumpeter clashes with Ma Rainey and is fired. The manager of the recording studio then swindles him in a recording rights agreement, and a subsequent and seemingly insignificant incident precipitates a violent act from the trumpeter, who has simply endured too much abuse. The London *Times*'s Holly Hill called the play's climactic moment "a melodramatically violent act."

*Ma Rainey's Black Bottom* earned Wilson a trip to the O'Neill Theatre Center's National Playwrights Conference. There Wilson's play impressed director Lloyd Richards from the Yale Repertory Theatre. Richards worked with Wilson to refine the play, and when it was presented at Yale in 1984 it was hailed as the work of an important new playwright. Frank Rich, who reviewed the Yale production in the *New York Times,* acclaimed Wilson as "a major find for the American theater" and cited Wilson's ability to write "with compassion, raucous humor and penetrating wisdom."

Wilson enjoyed further success with *Ma Rainey's Black Bottom* after the play came to Broadway later in 1984. The *Chicago Tribune*'s Richard Christiansen reviewed the Broadway production as "a work of intermittent but immense power" and commended the "striking beauty" of the play's "literary and theatrical poetry." Christiansen added that "Wilson's power of language is sensational" and that *Ma Rainey's Black Bottom* was "the work of an impressive writer." The London *Times*'s Hill agreed, calling Wilson "a promising new playwright" and hailing his work as "a remarkable first play."

Wilson's subsequent plays include the Pulitzer Prize-winning *Fences,* which is about a former athlete who forbids his son to accept an athletic scholarship, and *Joe Turner's Come and Gone,* which concerns an ex-convict's efforts to find his wife. Like *Ma Rainey's Black Bottom,* these plays underwent extensive rewriting. Guiding Wilson in this process was Lloyd Richards, dean of Yale's drama school and director of the school's productions of Wilson's plays. "August is a wonderful poet," Richards told the *New York Times* in 1986. "A wonderful poet turning into a playwright." Richards added that his work with Wilson involved "clarifying" each work's main theme and "arranging the material in a dynamic way."

Both *Fences* and *Joe Turner's Come and Gone* were praised when they played on American stages. The *New York Times*'s Frank Rich, in his review of *Fences,* wrote that the play "leaves no doubt that Mr. Wilson is a major writer, combining a poet's ear for vernacular with a robust sense of humor (political and sexual), a sure instinct for cracking dramatic incident and passionate commitment to a great subject." And in his critique of *Joe Turner's Come and Gone,* Rich speculated that the play "will give a lasting voice to a generation of uprooted black Americans." Rich contended that the work was "potentially its author's finest achievement yet" and described it as "a teeming canvas of black America . . . and a spiritual allegory."

In 1990, Wilson claimed his second Pulitzer Prize, this time for *The Piano Lesson.* Set during the Great Depression of the 1930s, this drama pits brother against sister in a contest to decide the future of a treasured heirloom—a piano, carved with African-style portraits by their grandfather, an enslaved plantation carpenter. The brother wants to sell it to buy land, while the sister adamantly insists that the instrument carries too much family history to part with. Acclaim for the play was widespread, although some commentators were put off by the supernatural elements that came to play in the climax of this otherwise realistic piece. "When ghosts begin resolving realistic plays, you can be sure the playwright has failed to master his material," wrote Robert Brustein in the *New Republic.* Brustein also found the play overlong and repetitious, and asserted that Wilson's focus on the effects of racism was limiting him artistically. Others praised the work unreservedly, however, including Clive Barnes of the *New York Post.* He declared: "This is a play in which to lose yourself—to give yourself up . . . to August Wilson's thoughts, humors and thrills, all caught in a microcosm largely remote for many of us from our own little worlds, yet always talking the same language of humanity." Frank Rich of the *New York Times* wrote that Wilson has given "miraculous voice" to the black experience, and William A. Henry III of *Time* dubbed the play's piano "the most potent symbol in American drama since Laura Wingfield's glass menagerie" in the Tennessee Williams classic. Barnes concluded: "This is a wonderful play that lights up man. See it, wonder at it, and recognize it." Wilson later adapted *The Piano Lesson* for a "Hallmark Hall of Fame" television production. It was judged a success by John J. O'Connor, who wrote in the *New York Times:* "If anything, *The Piano Lesson* is even more effective in this shortened version."

*Two Trains Running* continued Wilson's projected ten-play cycle about black American history. The play, which came to Broadway in 1992, is set in a run-down diner on the verge of being sold. Reactions by the diner's regular patrons to the pending sale make up the body of the drama. Some critics, such as the *New Yorker*'s Mimi Kramer, found the play less subtle and dramatic than its predecessors, but *Newsweek*'s David Ansen praised the "musical eloquence" of Wilson's language, which he felt enhanced a "thematically rich" work. And Henry wrote in *Time* that *Two Trains Running* is a "delicate and mature" play that shows Wilson "at his lyrical best."

*Two Trains Running* was followed in 1995 by *Seven Guitars*. Set in the 1940s, it recounts the tragic story of blues guitarist Floyd Barton, whose funeral opens the play. Action then flashes back to recreate the events of Floyd's last week of life. *Seven Guitars* was the first major production of a Wilson play without the direction of Richards, who was forced to abandon the project due to illness. The task of directing fell to Walter Dallas, whose staging at the Goodman Theatre in Chicago William Tynan characterized as "skillful" in a *Time* review. Yet the critic's overall assessment was mixed. "Part bawdy comedy, part dark elegy, part mystery," he wrote, "August Wilson's rich new play, *Seven Guitars,* nicely eludes categorization. . . . But though full and strong in its buildup, the play loses its potency as it reaches its climax. . . . Though Floyd is as charming and sympathetic a protagonist as we could want, the surprising truth is that his death has little effect on us. We leave the theater entertained and admiring but not truly moved." Vincent Canby differed markedly in his judgment, writing in the *New York Times:* "Though the frame of 'Seven Guitars' is limited and employs only seven characters, Mr. Wilson writes so vividly that the play seems to have the narrative scope and depth of a novel. When the curtain comes down, it's

difficult to remember which characters you've actually seen and which you have come to know only through stories recollected on stage. . . . 'Seven Guitars' plays with such speed that you begin the journey one minute, and the next thing you know, you're leaving the theater on a high."

Further praise came from *Newsweek* reviewer Jack Kroll, who called *Seven Guitars* "a kind of jazz cantata for actors," with "a gritty, lyrical polyphony of voices that evokes the character and destiny of these men and women who can't help singing the blues even when they're just talking." The play, he continued, "bristles with symbolism" and with "anguished eloquence." Kroll found the protagonist's death "shocking, unexpected, yet inevitable" and the characters overall "not victims, wallowing in voluptuous resentment," but "tragic figures, bursting with the balked music of life."

Discussing Wilson's body of work, Lawrence Bommer stated in the *Chicago Tribune,* "August Wilson has created the most complete cultural chronicle since Balzac wrote his vast 'Human Comedy,' an artistic whole that has grown even greater than its prize-winning parts." As for the playwright, he has repeatedly stressed that his first objective is simply getting his work produced. "All I want is for the most people to get to see this play," he told the *New York Times* while discussing *Joe Turner's Come and Gone.* Wilson added, however, that he was not opposed to having his works performed on Broadway. He told the *New York Times* that Broadway "still has the connotation of Mecca" and asked, "Who doesn't want to go to Mecca?"

*BIOGRAPHICAL/CRITICAL SOURCES:*

*BOOKS*

*Black Literature Criticism,* Gale (Detroit), Volume 3, 1992.
*Contemporary Literary Criticism,* Gale, Volume 39, 1986, Volume 50, 1988, Volume 63, 1991.
*Drama Criticism,* Gale, Volume 2, 1992.
Elkins, Marilyn, editor, *August Wilson: A Casebook,* Garland (New York City), 1994.
Hartigan, Karelisa V., *Within the Dramatic Spectrum,* University Press of America (Lanham, MD), 1986, pp. 177-86.
Kolin, Philip C., *American Playwrights since 1945: A Guide to Scholarship, Criticism, and Performance,* Greenwood Press (Westport, CT), 1989, pp. 518-27.

Nadel, Alan, editor, *May All Your Fences Have Gates: Essays on the Drama of August Wilson,* University of Iowa Press (Iowa City), 1994.

Pereira, Kim, *August Wilson and the African-American Odyssey,* University of Illinois Press (Urbana), 1995.

Shannon, Sandra Garrett, *The Dramatic Vision of August Wilson,* Howard University Press (Washington, DC), 1995.

*PERIODICALS*

*African American Review,* spring, 1996, p. 99.

*Boston Globe,* February 3, 1995, section 3, p. 47.

*Chicago Tribune,* October 15, 1984; June 8, 1987; December 17, 1987; December 27, 1987, pp. 4-5; January 20, 1993, p. section 1, p. 20; January 24, 1993, section 13, pp. 8-9; January 26, 1993, section 1, p. 16; January 15, 1995, section 13, pp. 16-17, 21.

*Chicago Tribune Book World,* February 9, 1986, pp. 12-13.

*Christian Science Monitor,* October 16, 1984, pp. 29-30; March 27, 1987, pp. 1, 8; March 30, 1988, p. 21.

*Ebony,* January, 1985; November, 1987, pp. 68, 70, 72, 74.

*Esquire,* April, 1989, pp. 116, 118, 120, 122-27.

*Essence,* August, 1987, pp. 51, 111, 113.

*Journal and Constitution* (Atlanta), October 17, 1993, p. N1; October 13, 1994, p. D11; January 9, 1995, p. D5.

*Los Angeles Times,* November 24, 1984; November 7, 1986; April 17, 1987; June 7, 1987; June 8, 1987; June 9, 1987; February 6, 1988.

*Maclean's,* May 28, 1990, p. 62; May 18, 1992, pp. 56-57.

*Massachusetts Review,* spring, 1988, pp. 87-97.

*Nation,* April 18, 1987, p. 518; June 1, 1990, pp. 832-33; June 8, 1992, pp. 799-800.

*New Republic,* May 21, 1990, pp. 28-30.

*Newsweek,* April 6, 1987; April 11, 1988, p. 82; April 27, 1992, p. 70; February 6, 1995, p. 60.

*New York,* April 6, 1987, pp. 92-94; May 7, 1990, pp. 82-83.

*New Yorker,* April 6, 1987, p. 81; April 11, 1988, p. 107; April 30, 1990, p. 85; April 27, 1992, p. 85.

*New York Newsday,* April 20, 1987, p. 47.

*New York Post,* March 28, 1988; April 17, 1990.

*New York Times,* April 11, 1984; April 13, 1984; October 12, 1984; October 22, 1984, p. C15; May 5, 1985, p. 80; May 6, 1986; May 14, 1986; May 19, 1986, p. C11; June 20, 1986; March 27, 1987, p. C3; April 5, 1987, II, pp. 1, 39; April 9, 1987; April 17, 1987; May 7, 1987; December 10, 1987; December 11, 1987; March 27, 1988, pp. 1, 34; March 28, 1988, p. C15; January 30, 1989, p. 69; April 17, 1990, p. C13; March 10, 1991, section 2, pp. 5, 17; January 25, 1995, pp. C13-C14; February 3, 1995, p. D26; February 5, 1995, section 2, pp. 1, 5.

*New York Times Book Review,* March 3, 1996, p. 22.

*New York Times Magazine,* June 10, 1987, pp. 36, 40, 49, 70.

*People,* May 13, 1996, p. 63.

*Saturday Review,* January-February, 1985, pp. 83, 90.

*Theater,* fall-winter, 1984, pp. 50-55; summer-fall, 1986, pp. 64; summer-fall, 1988, pp. 69-71.

*Theatre Journal,* December, 1994, pp. 468-76.

*Time,* April 6, 1987, p. 81; April 27, 1987; April 11, 1988, pp. 77-78; January 30, 1989, p. 69; April 27, 1992, pp. 65-66; February 6, 1995, p. 71.

*Times* (London), November 6, 1984; April 18, 1987; April 24, 1987.

*Variety,* February 26, 1996, p. 175.

*Vogue,* August, 1988, pp. 200, 204.

*Washington Post,* May 20, 1986; April 15, 1987; June 9, 1987; October 4, 1987; October 9, 1987.*

\*      \*      \*

**WING, J(ohn) K(enneth)    1923-**

*PERSONAL:* Born October 22, 1923. *Education:* Received M.D. and Ph..D. from University of London.

*ADDRESSES: Office*—College Research Unit, Royal College of Psychiatrists, 11 Grosvenor Crescent, London SW1X 7EE.

*CAREER:* Medical Research Council, Social Psychiatry Unit, London, England, director, 1965-89; Institute of Psychiatry, Denmark Hill, England, and London School of Hygiene, London, England, professor of social psychiatry, 1970-89, professor emeritus, 1989—; Royal College of Psychiatrists Research Unit, director, 1989-94, consultant, 1994—. *Military service:* Royal Naval Volunteer Reserve, 1941-45; became lieutenant.

*WRITINGS:*

(With G. W. Brown, M. Bone, and B. Dalison) *Schizophrenia and Social Care,* Oxford University Press (Oxford), 1966.

(Editor) *Early Childhood Autism,* Pergamon (Oxford), 1966.

(Editor with E. H. Hare) *Psychiatric Epidemiology,* Oxford University Press, 1970.

(Editor with R. Bransby) *Psychiatric Case Registers,* H.M.S.O., 1970.

(With Brown) *Institutionalism and Schizophrenia,* Cambridge University Press (Cambridge), 1970.

(With A. M. Hailey) *Evaluating a Community Psychiatric Service,* Oxford University Press, 1972.

(With J. E. Cooper and N. Sartorius) *Measurement and Classification of Psychiatric Symptoms: An Instructional Manual for the PSE and Catego Program,* Cambridge University Press, 1974.

*Reasoning about Madness,* Oxford University Press, 1978.

(Editor) *Schizophrenia: Toward a New Synthesis,* Academic Press (London), 1978.

(With J. Leach) *Helping Destitute Men,* Tavistock, 1979.

(Editor with R. Olsen) *Community Care for the Mentally Disabled,* Oxford University Press, 1979.

(Editor with P. Kielholz and W. M. Zinn) *Rehabilitation of Patients with Schizophrenia and with Depression,* Hans Huber (Bern), 1981.

(Editor with Paul Bebbington and Lee N. Robins) *What Is a Case?: The Problem of Definition in Psychiatric Community Surveys,* McIntyre (London), 1981.

(Editor with Brenda Morris) *Handbook of Psychiatric Rehabilitation Practice,* Oxford University Press, 1981.

(Editor) *Long-term Community Care: Experience in a London Borough,* Cambridge University Press, 1982.

(Editor with wife, Lorna Wing) *Psychoses of Uncertain Aetiology,* Cambridge University Press, 1982.

(Editor) *Contributions to Health Services Planning and Research,* Gaskell (London), 1989.

(Editor with G. Thornicroft and C. R. Brewin) *Measuring Mental Health Needs,* Gaskell, 1992.

(Editor) *Measurement for Mental Health: Contributions from the College Research Unit,* College Research Unit (London), 1995.

(Editor with Sartorius and T. B. Ustun) *Diagnosis and Clinical Measurement in Psychiatry: An Instruction Manual for the SCAN System,* Cambridge University Press, 1996.

*WORK IN PROGRESS:* Investigation of social factors in causation and treatment of psychiatric disorders; protocol for measuring quality of mental health services; brief scale for routine measurement of mental health problems; guidelines for the management of violence in mental health settings.

\*   \*   \*

## WITTLIFF, William D. 1940-

*PERSONAL:* Born in 1940 in Taft, TX; married; wife's name Sally; children: Reid, Allison. *Education:* University of Texas, graduated 1963.

*ADDRESSES: Home*—Austin, TX. *Office*—Encino Press, 510 Baylor St., Austin, TX 78703.

*CAREER:* Encino Press, Austin, TX, founder and publisher, 1963—; screenwriter, director, and producer of motion pictures, 1978—; photographer. Former member of executive board of trustees, Sundance Institute. Photographs exhibited in numerous galleries, including the National Cowboy Hall of Fame, the Palacio de Bellas Artes in Mexico City, and the Texas Capitol.

*MEMBER:* Academy of Motion Picture Arts and Sciences, Texas Philosophical Society, Texas Institute of Letters (president, 1974-78; member of executive council, 1979-90; fellow, 1993).

*AWARDS, HONORS:* Christopher Award, 1985, for *Country;* seven Emmy Awards, National Association of Television Critics Award for Best Mini-series and Best Television Program, D.W. Griffith Award for best television mini-series, National Board of Review, International Monitor Award for best achievement in entertainment programming, Golden Globe Award, George Foster Peabody Award for best television mini-series, Wrangler Award for best western television feature, National Cowboy Hall of Fame, and Writers Guild of America Award for best teleplay, all 1989, all for *Lonesome Dove;* Western Heritage Award for outstanding fictional television drama, National Cowboy Hall of Fame, 1993, for *Ned Blessing: The Story of My Life and Times;* Western Heritage Award for outstanding motion picture, National Cowboy Hall of Fame, three Golden Globe Award nominations, including best motion picture, and three Academy Award nominations,

Academy of Motion Picture Arts and Sciences, all 1994, all for *Legends of the Fall.*

*WRITINGS:*

*SCREENPLAYS*

*Thaddeus Rose and Eddie,* Columbia Broadcasting System (CBS), 1977.

(With Melissa Mathison and Jeanne Rosenberg) *The Black Stallion,* United Artists, 1979.

(With Carol Sobieski and John Binder) *Honeysuckle Rose,* Warner Brothers, 1980.

(And producer) *Raggedy Man* (also see below), Universal, 1981.

(And co-producer) *Barbarosa,* Universal, 1982.

(And co-producer) *Country,* Touchstone, 1984.

(And director and co-producer) *Redheaded Stranger,* R.H.S. Productions and Pangaea Films, 1986.

(And executive producer with Suzanne de Passe) *Lonesome Dove* (based on the novel by Larry McMurtry), CBS, 1989.

(And executive producer) *Ned Blessing: The Story of My Life and Times,* CBS, 1993.

(And executive producer) *The Cowboy Way,* Universal, 1994.

(And producer with Ed Zwick and Marshall Herskowitz) *Legends of the Fall,* Bedford Falls/ Pangaea, 1994.

*OTHER*

(Editor with Sheila Ohlendorf) *The Horsemen of the Americas: An Exhibition From the Hall of the Horsemen of the Americas,* University of Texas Humanities Research Center (Austin, TX), 1968.

(With Sara Clark) *Raggedy Man* (novel), Pinnacle (New York City), 1979.

*SIDELIGHTS:* Screenwriter William D. Wittliff, who has won critical praise as an authentic and sensitive portraitist of rural and western America, often explores through his work the conflict between regional myths of rugged individualism and the actual human vulnerability of his characters. "The ultimate theme of all my films is people need people," he explains in an interview with *American Film's* Mike Greco. "I am interested in looking for what is at the base of the human heart."

Wittliff began developing his interest in western literature and folklore into a career in 1964, when he founded Encino Press, an Austin-based publisher of limited edition books by Texas authors. His real

aspiration, however, was to write himself, and although he tried his skill at short stories, essays, and poems, his efforts were frustrated. "I cried bitter tears about not being able to write," he tells Greco. "My hand was trying to make a pretty sentence, but my head was full of images." Finally, in 1973, Wittliff tried to write a film script based on a story his grandfather had told him about a boy who, in the 1890s, had had his ears cut off for stealing cattle. The script eventually became the screenplay for the movie *Barbarosa,* and Wittliff at last found the writing form best suited to his highly visual imagination.

His first produced screenplay, *Thaddeus Rose and Eddie,* appeared in 1978 as a television movie broadcast by the Columbia Broadcasting System (CBS). The story, which focuses on a pair of aging Texas bachelors who come to the realization that their freewheeling ways have kept them from building meaningful relationships, attracted the attention of director-producer Francis Ford Coppola, who signed Wittliff on as a co-writer for his 1979 adventure film, *The Black Stallion.* Based on a children's novel of the same title, *The Black Stallion* proved a successful collaboration, winning critical commendations for its skillful evocation of the imaginative and emotional world of childhood.

In 1980 Wittliff entered a creative partnership with country music star Willy Nelson, who asked him to write a script for Nelson's first feature film, *Honeysuckle Rose.* In the movie Nelson plays a middle-aged country singer on the Texas honky-tonk circuit, Buck Bonham, who becomes romantically involved with one of his backup singers, his best friend's young daughter, played by Amy Irving. Buck ultimately has to choose between his infatuation with Irving and his responsibilities to his wife and family. Though Wittliff found the film's theme compelling, he took issue with what he felt was director Jerry Schatzberg's unrealistic depiction of life on the road, and he was critical of *Honeysuckle Rose* after it was released.

A more successful film, in Wittliff's estimation and in the view of many critics, was *Barbarosa,* which also cast Nelson in a leading role. The movie's title character is a rugged outlaw who had been provoked into killing several members of his wife's family on his wedding night, and who now must roam the bleak Texas countryside pursued by the rest of the clan. In his wanderings Barbarosa encounters and befriends a young man wanted for murder, and the two join forces to elude their enemies. Defying bullets and ambushes, Barbarosa becomes an outlaw legend who earns even the grudging admiration of his pursuers. Reviewing *Barbarosa* for the *New York Times,* Janet Maslin calls it "the best western in a long while," and deems it "an entertaining movie, not a self-important one" in its treatment of the classic genre themes of vengeance and personal valor.

Wittliff drew upon his own boyhood experiences to write a screenplay for the 1981 film *Raggedy Man,* which concerns a woman's struggle for dignity. Set in Texas in the 1940s, the story centers on Nita Longley, a lonely mother of two small boys who is abandoned by her husband and trapped in a deadend job as a small-town telephone operator. When a sailor on leave from duty enters Nita's life and becomes her lover, the Longley family is happily reformed. Their joy is short lived, however, because intolerant townspeople brand Nita a "loose" woman, and when the sailor returns to his ship she suffers an attempted rape. In the film's pivotal scene, Nita is rescued from her attackers by a crippled, enigmatic village handyman known as the Raggedy Man. The movie ends on a hopeful note as Nita discovers her own hidden potential and finally demands the respect that is due her. *New York Times*'s Vincent Canby praises the performance of Sissy Spacek as Nita and calls *Raggedy Man* "a movie of sweet, low-keyed charm." With his co-author Sara Clark, Wittliff adapted the screenplay as a novel, which was published under the same title.

Another strong and resourceful woman is the central character of Wittliff's 1984 motion picture *Country,* which he scripted and, with actress Jessica Lange, produced. Set in contemporary Iowa, the film is about a farm family facing bankruptcy because of excessive debts and low farm commodity prices. Lange starred in the film as Jewell Ivy, a mother who leads her family fight against the Farmers Home Administration, the government agency that is calling in loans and threatening foreclosure on land that Jewell's family has worked for generations. When Jewell's husband breaks down under the pressure, Jewell continues the battle alone. The film climaxes in an emotional scene in which Jewell disrupts a forced auction of the Ivy family possessions. As Canby remarks in the *New York Times, Country* displays "the sharp edge of informed journalism." He adds that "more than any other recent commercial film, [it] is genuinely interested in very specific social and economic conditions. It takes farmers seriously."

In the *American Film* interview with Greco, Wittliff offers his reflections on why and how he writes. He explains that writing, for him, is "making conscious what has been unconscious. Things hit the paper from out of nowhere. They're not thought out; they're felt through images in the mind. It doesn't happen all the time, but it's the thing I pray for. I want to disappear and have those moments when the thing I'm putting on paper becomes so real that I'm no longer leading but following." Wittliff further remarks that he is interested in directing and producing films primarily to exercise control over how his writing is interpreted: "I don't think my stuff is in the lines. It's in between the lines. It's not what the dialogue says but it's the spaces." He concludes, "I know the spaces better than anyone else."

In 1985, Wittliff and his wife, Sally, founded the Southwestern Writers Collection of original books and manuscripts at Texas State University.

*BIOGRAPHICAL/CRITICAL SOURCES:*

PERIODICALS

*American Film,* June, 1981.
*Chicago Tribune,* April 4, 1980; October 5, 1984.
*Los Angeles Times,* October 5, 1984.
*New York Times,* September 18, 1981; July 25, 1982; September 28, 1984.
*Southern Living,* March, 1982.
*Washington Post,* October 5, 1984.

\*    \*    \*

**WOLFF, Tobias (Jonathan Ansell)   1945-**

*PERSONAL:* Born June 19, 1945, in Birmingham, AL; son of Arthur Saunders (an aeronautical engineer) and Rosemary (Loftus) Wolff; married Catherine Dolores Spohn (a clinical social worker), 1975; children: Michael, Patrick, Mary Elizabeth. *Education:* Oxford University, B.A. (with first class honors), 1972, M.A., 1975; Stanford University, M.A., 1978.

*ADDRESSES: Office*—Department of English, Syracuse University, Syracuse, NY 13244-1170. *Agent*—Amanda Urban, International Creative Management, 40 West 57th St., New York, NY 10019.

*CAREER:* Stanford University, Stanford, CA, Jones Lecturer in Creative Writing, 1975-78; Syracuse University, Syracuse, NY, Peck Professor of English, 1980—. Member of faculty at Goddard College, Plainfield, VT, and Arizona State University, Tempe. Former reporter for *Washington Post. Military service:* U.S. Army, 1964-68 (Special Forces, 1964-67); served in Vietnam; became first lieutenant.

*MEMBER:* PEN, Associated Writing Programs.

*AWARDS, HONORS:* Wallace Stegner fellowship in creative writing, 1975-76; National Endowment for the Arts fellowship in creative writing, 1978 and 1985; Mary Roberts Rinehart grant, 1979; Arizona Council on the Arts and Humanities fellowship in creative writing, 1980; Guggenheim fellowship, 1982; St. Lawrence Award for Fiction, 1982, for *In the Garden of the North American Martyrs;* PEN/ Faulkner Award for Fiction, 1985, for *The Barracks Thief;* Rea Award for short story, 1989; *Los Angeles Times* Book Prize for biography, and National Book Critics Circle Award finalist, both 1989, and Ambassador Book Award of the English Speaking Union, all for *This Boy's Life: A Memoir;* Whiting Foundation Award, 1990; Lila Wallace-*Reader's Digest* Award, 1993; Lyndhurst Foundation Award, 1994; National Book Award finalist, and Esquire-Volvo-Waterstone's Prize for Nonfiction (England), both 1994, and *Los Angeles Times* Book Award for biography finalist, 1995, all for *In Pharaoh's Army: Memories of the Lost War.*

*WRITINGS:*

*Ugly Rumours,* Allen & Unwin (London), 1975.
*In the Garden of the North American Martyrs* (short stories), Ecco Press (New York City), 1981, published in England as *Hunters in the Snow* (also see below), J. Cape (London), 1982.
(Editor) *Matters of Life and Death: New American Stories,* Wampeter (Green Harbor, ME), 1982, hardcover edition, 1983.
*The Barracks Thief* (novella; also see below), Ecco Press, 1984, published as *The Barracks Thief and Other Stories,* Bantam (New York City), 1984.
*Back in the World* (short stories; also see below), Houghton (Boston, MA), 1985.
(Editor) *A Doctor's Visit: The Short Stories of Anton Chekhov,* Bantam, 1987.
*The Stories of Tobias Wolff* (contains *Hunters in the Snow, Back in the World,* and *The Barracks Thief*), Picador (London), 1988.

*This Boy's Life: A Memoir,* Atlantic Monthly Press (New York City), 1989.
(Editor) *The Picador Book of Contemporary American Stories,* Picador, 1993.
(Editor and author of introduction) *The Vintage Book of Contemporary American Short Stories,* Random House (New York City), 1994.
*In Pharaoh's Army: Memories of the Lost War* (memoir), Knopf (New York City), 1994.
(Editor) *Best American Short Stories,* Houghton, 1994.
*The Night in Question: Stories,* Knopf, 1996.

Work is represented in over fifty anthologies. Contributor of short stories and book reviews to periodicals, including *Atlantic Monthly, New Yorker, Esquire, Vanity Fair, Harper's, TriQuarterly,* and *Antaeus.*

*ADAPTATIONS: This Boy's Life: A Memoir* was made into the movie *This Boy's Life,* 1993, produced by Art Linson, directed by Michael Caton-Jones, starring Robert De Niro as Wolff's stepfather, Ellen Barkin as Wolff's mother, and Leonardo DiCaprio playing Wolff as a teenager. *This Boy's Life* has also been released on audiocassette.

*WORK IN PROGRESS:* A short story collection.

*SIDELIGHTS:* Tobias Wolff, short story writer, novelist, memoirist, editor and journalist, has received critical acclaim since the publication of his first collection of short stories in 1981. Both *Los Angeles Times* book reviewer James Kaufman and *New Statesman* contributor Bill Greenwell label the stories of *In the Garden of the North American Martyrs* "impressive," and the *Chicago Tribune*'s Bruce Allen deems it "one of the most acclaimed short-story collections within memory." In the twelve tales which comprise *In the Garden of the North American Martyrs,* according to *Nation* reviewer Brina Caplan, Wolff "scrutinizes the disorders of daily living to find significant order; in the best of [these] stories . . . he informs us not only of what happened but of why it had to happen as it did. . . . Distant in age, class and geography, [his characters] have in common lives crowded with the results of previous choices." *Best Sellers* reviewer James C. Dolan advises: "relax and enter into the sometimes comic, always compassionate world of ordinary people who suffer twentieth-century martyrdoms of growing up, growing old, loving and lacking love, living with parents and lovers and wives and their own weaknesses."

Among the characters of *In the Garden of the North American Martyrs*—all of whom, claims Alane Rollings of the *Chicago Tribune,* readers can "care for"—are a teenage boy who tells morbid lies about his home life, a timid professor who, in the first genuine outburst of her life, pours out her opinions in spite of a protesting audience, a prudish loner who gives an obnoxious hitchhiker a ride, and an elderly couple on a golden anniversary cruise who endure the offensive conviviality of the ship's social director. Rollings concludes that "Wolff's ironic dialog, misfit heroes, and haphazard events play beautifully off the undercurrent drift of the searching inner mood which wins over in the end." *New York Times Book Review* critic Le Ann Schreiber admires Wolff's avoidance of "the emotional and stylistic monotone that constricts so many collections of contemporary short stories," pointing out that "his range, sometimes within the same story, extends from fastidious realism to the grotesque and the lyrical. . . . He allows [his] characters scenes of flamboyant madness as well as quiet desperation, moments of slap-happiness as well as muted contentment." In addition, observing that the time covered by the collection's stories varies from a few hours to two decades, Schreiber declares Wolff's vision "so acute" and his talent "so refined" that "none of them seems sketchy" and that in fact, they evoke our "amazed appreciation."

Wolff's novella *The Barracks Thief* won the prestigious PEN/Faulkner Award as the best work of fiction of 1984. Linda Taylor writes in the *Times Literary Supplement* that "*The Barracks Thief* is a book to be taken in all at once: the ingenuousness of the narration and the vulnerability of the characters are disarmingly seductive." Narrated retrospectively by one of three paratroopers stationed at Fort Bragg, North Carolina, during the Vietnam years, the story focuses on an event that leaves a lasting impression on the trio. Assigned to guard a nearby ammunition dump on a steamy Fourth of July evening in 1967, they face the threat of an approaching forest fire. The temptation to allow the dump to ignite and explode proves exhilarating and unites them in a bond of friendship. "The world of *The Barracks Thief* contains no answers," observes *New York Times* reviewer Walter Kendricks. "We are left to make up our own minds whether it is better to die spectacularly or to dribble on for decades in safe conventionality." Kendricks also hails Wolff's "boundless tolerance for the stupid sorrow of ordinary human entanglements" and his "command of eloquent detail." *America* critic Andre Dubus concludes, "If words on

paper could make sounds, you would hear me shouting now, urging you to read this book."

Wolff's 1985 short story collection, *Back in the World,* derives its title from the expression used by servicemen during the Vietnam War to refer to postwar life at home in the United States. The experience of returning home, however, proves more disillusioning than hopeful to the veterans in Wolff's stories. Feeling alienated from society and powerless to change their circumstances, his characters capitulate to whatever life deals them, only briefly—if at all—challenging fate. They seek relief from their cheerless, detached existence in drugs, casual sex, and, as the *Chicago Tribune*'s Allen observes, "contriving falsely romantic or interesting versions of themselves and their experiences." Yet, *New York Times* reviewer Michiko Kakutani notes that Wolff suggests for these people "the power of some kind of redemption in their fumbling efforts to connect with one another, and even in their sad attempts to shore up their dignity with their pipe dreams and clumsy fictions." This "power of . . . redemption," according to Kakutani, "enables these characters to go on, and it is also what invests these stories with the burnished glow of compassion."

While admitting a preference for *In the Garden of the North American Martyrs* and *The Barracks Thief,* Russell Banks of the *New York Times Book Review* nevertheless calls two of the stories in *Back in the World* "as fine as anything . . . Wolff has written." *Washington Post Book World* reviewer Jonathan Penner objects to Wolff's choice of a third-person narrator for all the stories, arguing that the use of such a voice blocks revelation of a character's "inner world" of thoughts and feelings. Kakutani of the *New York Times* also finds weakness in the "narrative machinery" of some of the stories, yet commends the "gleaming moments that display . . . Wolff's quick eye, his gift for meticulous observation." Penner agrees that "Wolff does so much well that his gifts are continually evident. His ear is sharp for every kind of speech. He can be very funny. He can be lyrical. His people display consistency and irrelevance—that odd blend of the mechanical and the random that we embrace as free will. His decorative surfaces turn out to be weight-bearing. His details, innocently planted, germinate." Kakutani, who describes Wolff as a "masterful storyteller" and "natural raconteur," further reflects that "in the end, though, what really makes the finest of these stories so compelling is the author's sympathy for his characters, his clear-eyed but generous sense of their weaknesses, their frustrations and disappointments."

Wolff's next work, *This Boy's Life: A Memoir,* "is about growing up, as inevitably any such memoir must be," comments Jonathan Yardley in the *Washington Post Book World.* The book addresses Wolff's teenage years, when he and his mother moved from Florida to Utah to Washington State to escape her abusive boyfriend. Wolff had lost contact with his father and brother (writer Geoffrey Wolff, author of *The Duke of Deception: Memories of My Father,* an autobiography about his youth spent with their father) following his parents' divorce. In Washington his mother remarried, and Wolff experienced difficulties with his new stepfather. Yardley remarks that, in part, *This Boy's Life* "is the story of what happens to a child when the peculiarities of a mother's romance place him at the mercy of a man who is neither his father nor his protector, but it is not a self-pitying lament and it is not really a tale of abuse and neglect."

*New York Times Book Review*'s Joel Conarroe notes the literary quality of the book: "*This Boy's Life* is apparently straight autobiography—the facts, attired in their exotic garments. The book, however, reads very much like a collection of short stories, each with its own beginning, middle and end. Lifted from their context, the individual chapters would be at home in the fiction pages of any good magazine." Francine Prose makes a similar observation in the *New York Times Magazine:* "*This Boy's Life* reads like the work of a writer who has long understood himself to be 'surrounded by stories.' Its strategy is novelistic; details have been altered, events ordered and edited, to give Wolff's memoir the shape of fiction." Prose adds that "Tobias Wolff admits to having omitted things from *This Boy's Life*—real events he chose to leave out lest the true account of his life seem too markedly patterned and shaped. 'It would have seemed too contrived,' he says. 'Too much like a novel.'"

Richard Eder of the *Los Angeles Times Book Review* is drawn to the more somber side of the work: "The art in this memoir is its nakedness. It is stripped of pose; it has the courage to be a record, not of survival but of destruction." Eder adds that the book "is a desperate story. The desperation is conveyed in a narration that is chilly and dispassionate on the whole, vivid in its detail, and enlivened by disconcerting comedy." Yardley also recognizes the an-

guish visible in parts of the book, writing in the *Washington Post Book World* that "Wolff's is a story of guile and accommodation and pain and apprehension, and he tells it as such; no false triumphs or epiphanies are to be found here."

The *New York Times Book Review*'s Conarroe questions the veracity of Wolff's memoir, arguing that there "may or may not be convincing reasons to believe everything Mr. Wolff tells us. He is, by his own admission, a fabricator who learned at his father's knee that is it pointless to stick with facts when fantasy is so much more rewarding." Overall, Conarroe concludes that the book is "literate and consistently entertaining—and richer, darker, and funnier than anything else Tobias Wolff has written." *New York Times* critic Christopher Lehmann-Haupt argues that Wolff "is clearly searching for a writer's persona in *This Boy's Life.* He is learning the arts of disguise and illusion." Lehmann-Haupt concludes that Wolff's mastery "lies in the superb storytelling that is in evidence here, and in the creation of the boy Jack, who teaches us something new about the alienated world of childhood."

Some critics consider Wolff's acclaimed memoir *In Pharaoh's Army: Memories of the Lost War,* to be a logical continuation of *This Boy's Life.* Yet, the author tells Nicholas A. Basbanes in a *Publishers Weekly* interview that the book is not a sequel: "I'm a really different person in the new book. I see it as a story about a young man going off to war, and the kind of moral transformations that take place." The book, which was nominated for the National Book Award in 1994 and received England's Esquire-Volvo-Waterstone's Prize for Nonfiction, recounts the author's one-year Vietnam tour of duty in the Mekong Delta village of My Tho in thirteen chapters, or "episodes." Paul Gray comments in *Time,* that each "of Wolff's thirteen chapters reads like a rigorously boiled-down short story, but the effects never seem artificial or contrived," and calls the book a "terse, mesmerizing memoir."

*In Pharaoh's Army* focuses on events which took place during the Vietnam War. But as Basbanes notes in *Publishers Weekly,* readers who are "in search of riveting battle scenes will have to look elsewhere; of far greater moment is the maturation of Tobias Wolff. The immature lieutenant who arrives in the war zone returns home as a man ready to spend four years at Oxford University (1968-72) and to begin his life as a writer." Judith Coburn observes in *Washington Post Book World* that "Mostly [Wolff] tells stories, awful, hilarious stories, often at his own expense, of what it was like day-to-day, trying to get by." Similarly, an *American Heritage* reviewer describes the writing as "relaxed, utterly lucid prose" and characterized the book as "melancholy and hilarious by turns." A reviewer for *Publishers Weekly* calls the book an "intense, precisely observed memoir," while the *New York Times Book Review*'s Bruce Bawer finds that the book "in style and tone has much in common with the low-key domestic minimalism of Raymond Carver and Ann Beattie."

The memoir treats aspects of the Vietnam War through the use of spare, uncomplicated prose. Although Wolff does not write specifically of atrocity and carnage, critics infer abominations from the very simplicity of his stories. Richard Eder suggests in the *Los Angeles Times Book Review,* that "because there was no actual horror, we see more clearly what underlay the horror." Coburn comments in the *Washington Post Book World* that "Wolff's strategy is to tell his story in an elegantly simple style and with a deceptively casual voice. The tension between this form and the horror of the war's content made this reader, anyway, feel by the book's end as if somehow I had gone out of my mind without noticing." While Bawer, in the *New York Times Book Review,* questions the "limitations" of Wolff's literary style applied to the horrors and intensity of war, he nonetheless declares: "There is a great deal of precise, evocative writing here." Gray comments in *Time* that the war taught Wolff "how to portray life as both desperately serious and perfectly absurd."

## BIOGRAPHICAL/CRITICAL SOURCES:

### BOOKS

*Contemporary Literary Criticism,* Volume 39, Gale (Detroit), 1985, Volume 64, 1990.
*Dictionary of Literary Biography,* Volume 130: *American Short-Story Writers Since World War II,* Gale, 1993.
Hannah, James, *Tobias Wolff: A Study of the Short Fiction,* Twayne (New York City), 1996.
Wolff, Tobias, *This Boy's Life: A Memoir,* Atlantic Monthly Press, 1989.
Wolff, *In Pharaoh's Army: Memories of the Lost War,* Knopf, 1994.

### PERIODICALS

*America,* September 8, 1984.
*American Heritage,* November, 1994, p. 120.
*Best Sellers,* November, 1981.
*Bloomsbury Review,* March/April, 1995, p. 13.
*Booklist,* September 1, 1994, p. 2.
*Boston Review,* December, 1985.
*Chicago Tribune Books,* January 22, 1989.
*Chicago Tribune Book World,* October 18, 1981; December 8, 1985.
*Esquire,* October, 1994, p. 133.
*Globe and Mail* (Toronto), February 8, 1986.
*Hudson Review,* summer, 1982; autumn, 1986.
*Life,* September, 1990, p. 95.
*Los Angeles Times Book Review,* January 3, 1982; November 17, 1985; January 8, 1989, p. 3; November 5, 1989, p. 12; June 6, 1993, p. 15; October 16, 1994, pp. 3, 10.
*Nation,* February 6, 1982, p. 152.
*New England Review and Bread Loaf Quarterly,* autumn, 1986.
*New Statesman,* July 23, 1982, p. 22; August 12, 1983, p. 27.
*Newsweek,* January 23, 1989, p. 64; October 24, 1994, p. 78.
*New York,* April 12, 1993, p. 58.
*New York Times,* November 25, 1981; October 2, 1985, p. 27; October 28, 1985; October 30, 1985; January 12, 1989.
*New York Times Book Review,* November 15, 1981, p. 11; June 2, 1982; October 17, 1982, p. 45; October 20, 1985, p. 9; October 5, 1986, p. 58; January 15, 1989, p. 1; November 27, 1994, p. 10.
*New York Times Magazine,* February 5, 1989, p. 22.
*North American Review,* June, 1982.
*People Weekly,* October 7, 1985.
*Publishers Weekly,* August 29, 1994, p. 55; October 24, 1994, pp. 45-46; August 5, 1996.
*San Francisco Review of Books,* March/April, 1995.
*Time,* December 2, 1985, p. 99; February 6, 1989, p. 70; October 31, 1994, p. 81.
*Times* (London), May 4, 1989; May 11, 1989.
*Times Literary Supplement,* March 14, 1975, p. 269; July 30, 1982, p. 815; January 24, 1986; November 6, 1987, p. 1227; May 13, 1988, p. 532; May 12, 1989.
*Village Voice,* January 31, 1989.
*Virginia Quarterly Review,* spring, 1982.
*Wall Street Journal,* January 3, 1989.
*Washington Post Book World,* December 26, 1982, p. 12; November 3, 1985, p. 5; January 22, 1989, p. 3; November 6, 1994, pp. 3, 12.
*Writer's Digest,* August, 1989, p. 52.

**YEVTUSHENKO, Yevgeny (Alexandrovich)   1933-**

*PERSONAL:* Name is transliterated in some sources as Evgenii Evtushenko, Yevgeniy Yevtushenko, or Evgeny Evtushenko; born July 18, 1933, in Stanzia Zima, Siberia, U.S.S.R. (now known as Russia); son of Alksandr Gangnus (a geologist) and Zinaida Yermolayevna (a geologist and singer) Yevtushenko; married Bella Akhmadulina (a poet), 1954 (divorced); married Galina Semyonovna Sokol (a literary translator), 1962 (divorced); married Jan Butler, 1978 (divorced); married Masha Novikova (a physician), 1986; children: (with Sokol) one; (with Butler) two; (with Novikova) two. *Education:* Attended Gorky Literary Institute, 1951-54. *Politics:* Communist. *Religion:* "Revolution."

*CAREER:* Poet, filmmaker, actor, and author. Worked on geological expeditions in Kazakhstan, U.S.S.R. (now known as Russia), 1948, and the Altai, 1950. Elected to the Soviet Congress of People's Deputies, 1989. Appearances in films include *Take-Off,* 1979, and *The Kindergarten,* 1983.

*MEMBER:* International PEN (vice-president of Russian center), Gorky Literary Institute, Writer's Union.

*AWARDS, HONORS:* U.S.S.R. Commission for the Defense of Peace award, 1965; U.S.S.R. state prize, 1984; Order of Red Banner of Labor; finalist for Ritz Paris Hemingway award for best 1984 novel published in English, 1985, for *Wild Berries.*

*WRITINGS:*

POETRY IN ENGLISH

(With others) *Red Cats,* City Lights (San Francisco), 1961.
*Selected Poems,* translated from the Russian by Robin Milner-Gulland and Peter Levi, Dutton (New York City), 1962.
*Yevtushenko* (young adult), edited by Milner-Gulland, Penguin Books, 1962.
*Selected Poetry,* Pergamon (Elmsford, NY), 1963.
*Winter Station,* translated from the Russian by Oliver J. Frederiksen, C. Gerber, 1964.
*The Poetry of Yevgeny Yevtushenko, 1953-1965,* translated from the Russian and edited by George Reavey, October House (Stonington, CT), 1964.
*Bratskaya GES,* Russian Language Specialties, 1965, translation by Tina Tupikina-Glaessner, Igor Mezhakoff-Koriakin, and Geoffrey Dutton published as *New Works: The Bratsk Station,* Praeger

(New York City), 1966, published as *The Bratsk Station and Other New Poems,* Praeger, 1967.
*The City of Yes and the City of No and Other Poems,* translated from the Russian by Tupikina-Glaessner, Mezhakoff-Koriakin, and Dutton, Sun Books (Albuquerque, NY), 1966.
*Yevtushenko's Reader: The Spirit of Elbe, A Precocious Autobiography, Poems,* Dutton, 1966.
*Poems,* translated from the Russian by Herbert Marshall, Dutton, 1966.
*Poems Chosen by the Author,* translated from the Russian by Milner-Gulland and Levi, Collins, 1966, Hill & Wang (New York City), 1967.
*New Poems,* Sun Books, 1968.
*Bratsk Station, The City of Yes and the City of No, and Other New Poems,* translated from the Russian by Tupikina-Glaessner, Dutton, and Mezhakoff-Koriakin, Sun Books, 1970.
*Flowers and Bullets & Freedom to Kill,* City Lights, 1970.
*Stolen Apples,* Doubleday (New York City), 1971.
*Kazan University and Other New Poems,* translated from the Russian by Dutton and Eleanor Jacka, Sun Books, 1973.
*From Desire to Desire,* Doubleday, 1976.
*The Poetry of Yevgeny Yevtushenko* (bilingual edition), Marion Boyars, 1981.
*Invisible Threads,* Macmillan (New York City), 1982.
*Almost at the End,* translated by Antonina W. Bouis, Albert C. Todd, and Yevtushenko, Henry Holt, 1987.
*The Face behind the Face,* translated by Arthur Boyars and Simon Franklin, Marion Boyars (New York City), 1987.
*Early Poems,* translated by George Reavey, Marion Boyars, 1989.
*Early Poems,* Marion Boyars, 1989.
*The Collected Poems, 1952-1990,* edited by Albert C. Todd and James Ragan, Henry Holt, 1991.
(Compiler and author of introduction) *Twentieth Century Russian Poetry: Silver and Steel, an Anthology,* edited by Albert C. Todd, Max Hayward, and Daniel Weissbort, Doubleday, 1993.

Also author of *Love Poems,* 1977, and *Ivan the Terrible and Ivan the Fool,* 1979.

POETRY IN RUSSIAN

*Razvedchiki Gryadushchego* (title means "The Prospectors of the Future"), Sovietsky Pisatel, 1952.
*Tretii Sneg* (title means "Third Snow"), Sovietsky Pisatel, 1955.

*Shosse Entusiastov* (title means "Highway of the Enthusiasts"), Moskovskii Rabochii, 1956.

*Obeschanie* (title means "Promise"), Sovietsky Pisatel, 1957.

*Luk i lira* (title means "The Bow and the Lyre"), Zara Vostoka, 1959.

*Stikhi Raznykh Let* (title means "Poems of Several Years"), Molodaya Gvardia, 1959.

*Yabloko* (title means "The Apple"), Sovietsky Pisatel, 1960.

*Vzmakh Ruki* (title means "A Wave of the Hand"), Molodaya Gvardia, 1962.

*Nezhnost: Novyii Stikhi* (title means "Tenderness: New Poems"), Sovietsky Pisatel, 1962.

*Posie Stalina* (title means "After Stalin"), Russian Language Specialties, 1962.

*Kater Sviazi* (title means "Torpedo Boat Signalling"), Molodaya Gvardia, 1966.

*Kazanskii universitet* (title means "Kazan University"), Tatarskoe knizhnoe izd-vo, 1971.

*Net let,* Khudozh (St. Petersburg), 1993.

*PLAYS*

*Bratsk Power Station,* produced in Moscow, 1968.

*Under the Skin of the Statue of Liberty,* produced in 1972.

*SOUND RECORDINGS*

Dmitri Shostakovich, *Symphony No. 13: Babi Yar* (lyrics by Yevtushenko), Russian Disc, 1993.

*OTHER*

*A Precocious Autobiography,* translated from the Russian by Andrew R. MacAndrew, Dutton, 1963.

*Wild Berries* (novel; originally published c. 1981 in U.S.S.R.), translated by Antonina W. Bouis, Morrow, 1984.

*Roubles in Words, Kopeks in Figures and Other Stories,* translated by Natasha Ward and David Iliffe, Marion Boyars, 1985.

*Ardabiola,* St. Martin's (New York City), 1985.

*Divided Twins: Alaska and Siberia,* Viking, 1988.

*Fatal Half Measures: The Culture of Democracy in the Soviet Union,* edited and translated by Antonina W. Bouis, Little, Brown (Boston), 1991.

(Author of foreword) *The Russian Century: A Photographic History of Russia's 100 Years* (text by Brian Moynahan; photographs researched by Annabel Merullo and Sarah Jackson), Random House, 1994.

(Author of introduction) *St. Petersburg* (principal photographer, Fritz Dressler; project editor, Wilhelm Klein), Houghton Mifflin, 1994.

(Author of introduction) Erez Yakin, *The Silent City,* Kitchen Sink Press, 1995.

*Ne umira prezhde smerti: Russka, skazka* (autobiographical novel), Liberty Publishing, 1993, translation by Antonina W. Bouis published as *Don't Die before You're Dead,* Random House, 1995.

Writer and director of films, including *The Kindergarten,* released in the U.S.S.R. in 1983, and *The End of the Musketeers.*

*SIDELIGHTS:* As with few other living poets, Yevgeny Yevtushenko's career sharply illustrates the relationship between poetry and politics. While there exists a long Western tradition of politically engaged poetry, poets in the West have generally remained, as poet Percey Bysshe Shelly said, "the unacknowledged legislators of the world." But in the Soviet Union, the political nature and power of poetry, and literature in general, have been more often recognized. This is evident in the persecution of various writers, including Alexander Solzhenitsyn, who have been considered subversive or as political threats.

Yevtushenko has always frankly embraced his political role as a poet by incorporating both public and personal themes in his work and speaking out on current events. Consequently, his stature among the Soviet literati has fluctuated despite his insistence that he is a loyal, revolutionary Soviet citizen. Following the death of Stalin, the morally outraged tone and revolutionary idealism of Yevtushenko's early poetry were enthusiastically received by young Russians and generally tolerated by the post-Stalin authorities. During the 1950s, Yevtushenko's books were published regularly and in 1960, he was permitted to travel outside the Soviet Union to give poetry readings in Europe and the United States.

Occasionally, however, Yevtushenko overstepped his privileged bounds and found himself caught up in political controversy. One such situation developed in 1960 with the publication of *Babi Yar.* The title of the poem refers to a ravine near Kiev where 96,000 Jews were killed by Nazis during the German occupation; because the poem attributes anti-Semitism to Russians as well as Germans, Yevtushenko was criticized. He was also reprimanded in 1963 for allowing, without official permission from the state, the publication of *Notes for an Autobiography* in the French newspaper, *L'Express.* On still other occasions, Yevtushenko has been censored because of his political "indiscretions." In 1968, he wrote a letter condemning the Soviet Union's occupation of Czechoslovakia. The negative response the letter provoked resulted in a cancellation of a performance of *The Bratsk Station.* In 1974, he sent a telegram to Soviet official Leonid Breshnev expressing concern for the safety of Solzhenitsyn after his arrest. Shortly after Yevtushenko's letter was received, a major recital of his work was canceled.

In the West, Yevtushenko's reputation has also been unstable, though often in inverse relation to his reputation at home. In 1968, when he was nominated for an Oxford professorship, Kingsley Amis denounced him as a pawn of the Communist Party; his defenders, including Arthur Miller and William Styron, affirmed his integrity with evidence of his protests against the Czechoslovakian invasion. Yet, in 1972, he headlined an enormously successful recital in New York City which also featured James Dickey and Stanley Kunitz.

Despite a flair for publicity and occasional successes at recitals, Yevtushenko's popularity has declined in the United States as his poetry becomes more available. When *Bratsk Station* appeared in 1967, Rosemary Neiswender praised his "technical virtuosity" and Andrew Field dubbed him "the best of the political activists writing editorials in verse form." But two of Yevtushenko's most recent collections of poetry have caused some critics to question his writing ability. J. F. Cotter, in a review of *Stolen Apples,* wrote that "Yevtushenko is simply not that great a poet." Gerard Grealish was even less kind in his dismissal of *From Desire to Desire.* "Yevtushenko is the Rod McKuen of Russia," Grealish wrote. "Both men have captured the popular mind and neither man can write poetry. It is sad."

Nevertheless, Yevtushenko remains a major literary figure in the post-Stalinist Soviet Union. Comparisons to past Russian poets, including Voznesensky and early Mayakovsky continue to be made, and Yevtushenko persists in speaking out for his art and his political ideals. "It goes without saying that the dogmatists used, still use, and will go on using every opportunity they can find to arrest the process of democratization in our society," wrote Yevtushenko in *A Precocious Autobiography.* "I have no rosy illusions about that."

During the 1980s, Yevtushenko began to experiment with literary forms outside of poetry. His first novel,

*Wild Berries,* was a finalist for the Ritz Paris Hemingway prize in 1985. Featuring numerous plot shifts, the novel ostensibly celebrates Russian philosophy and existence but is similar to an American thriller in its emphasis on action, sex, and exotic locales. While Soviet critics faulted Yevtushenko's emphasis on the miseries of war rather than Soviet military triumphs, Western commentators praised Yevtushenko. Susan Jacoby, for instance, writing in the *New York Times Book Review,* characterized him as a "hybrid of Walt Whitman and Norman Mailer— with all the extravagant enthusiasms, risk-taking, self-promotion, blundering and talent that might be expected from such a creature."

Yevtushenko continued his experimentation with prose in such works as the 1984 novel *Ardabiola,* which combines elements from several genres and features chapters written in diverse styles. The plot turns on a scientist's discovery of a cure for cancer and what happens after he is mugged, develops amnesia, and forgets about his discovery. Yevtushenko's narrative satirizes Russian life—to good effect, according to numerous reviewers. Writing in the *Listener,* John Mellors declared that *Ardabiola* is "good entertainment, with flashes of humour and a fascinating poet's-eye view of life in the USSR. The denouement is unashamed fantasy wrapped round a hard truth: new creations, in art or science, will not go away all that easily—even if their inventors neglect them."

Work from Yevtushenko's most productive years as a poet was presented in *The Collected Poems, 1952-1990.* The collection demonstrates the poet's changing styles over the years, yet for all its variety, *Collected Poems* is "a consistent narrative, dominated by the haunted figure of a Russian poet," stated Carol Rumens in *New Statesman & Society.* Yevtushenko, she continued, is "as deeply rooted as any of his breed, sent by success and the mid-20th-century publicity machine into dizzy orbit between the two arch-enemies of the cold war, beaming messages first to one, then the other, and emotionally involved in both. A complex character, living in highly complex times, Yevtushenko often likes to picture himself as a skinny, wily Siberian street urchin, living off his wits." The reviewer took note of the "breezy energy and the sometimes *macho* swagger" that marked the early works, and contrasted it to the mood of his later poems, which she referred to as "somewhat darker; the swagger has gone and, whether contemplating himself or his society, the poet sees doom and exhaustion: rust, ghosts, chasms, things smashed." Commenting on the collection in *World Literature Today,* Patricia Pollock Brodsky affirmed that *Collected Poems* "reflects Yevgeny Yevtushenko's poetic career in microcosm: vast and uneven, sometimes irritating, often appealing, and ever astonishing in its variety. . . . [It] provides the reader with numerous opportunities to become acquainted with this engaged and engaging poet, one of the important, questioning voices of our age." Yevtushenko's commitment to poetry was also demonstrated in his work on the collection entitled *Twentieth-Century Russian Poetry: Silver and Steel, an Anthology.* For this volume, he selected writings from 23 poets, ranging from Boris Slutsky, who was born in 1919, to Aleksei Parshchikov, born in 1954.

Yevtushenko was elected to the Soviet Congress of People's Deputies in 1989 and thereafter became one of the leaders of the democratic movement. During the attempted coup in August 1991, he remained in the Parliament Building while it was surrounded by tanks. There, he composed a poem to voice his opposition of a return to totalitarianism and his support of Boris Yeltsin's leadership. When the coup attempt crumbled, he read an English translation of his poem to Western television reporters.

Many of Yevtushenko's speeches and essays on Soviet democratic reform were collected in the book *Fatal Half Measures: The Culture of Democracy in the Soviet Union,* published in 1992. The book was highly praised by numerous reviewers for its insights into Soviet culture. "Yevtushenko has been almost everywhere. He knows almost everybody. He remembers it all and he writes wonderfully. This is what makes *Fatal Half Measures* such a feast. For anyone interested in Soviet society and especially those of a literary bent, it is truly a delight," enthused Lee B. Croft in *World Literature Today.* Sally Laird was slightly less wholehearted in her endorsement of the book, noting in her review for the *Observer* that Yevtushenko at times lapsed into cliche and recitation of the official Soviet canon. She concluded, however, that "he speaks a language people understand: bold, simple, witty, *punchy,* even when some punches are pulled, it inspires the *desire* for courage, and that is important. These are the writings not of a brilliant mind but of a sympathetic heart, and therein lies their immense appeal." Laird went on to praise Yevtushenko for illuminating the suffering and humiliation of ordinary Soviet citizens and concluded that *Fatal Half Measures* should be required reading for those critical of Russia's "new 'materialism'."

Yevtushenko offered another take on the historic events of 1991 in *Don't Die before You're Dead,* an autobiographical novel. Although the coup and the events surrounding it provide the primary action in the book, the real drama lies in the ways in which ordinary people cope with this extraordinary situation. "People may like this book, or they may not," the author asserted in an interview, quoted by Anthony Wilson-Smith in *Maclean's.* "Either way, they should accept that it represents Russia the way it is." Wilson-Smith went on to describe *Don't Die before You're Dead* as "sprawling, bombastic, occasionally overwrought, and filled with black humor." Yevtushenko's emotions and characters, Wilson-Smith continued, are all "instantly recognizable to anyone familiar with the alternately challenging and deadening qualities of everyday existence in Russia. . . . The real charm . . . lies in the skill with which he reflects the contradictory elements that vie for control of the Russian soul."

## BIOGRAPHICAL/CRITICAL SOURCES:

### BOOKS

Alexandrova, Vera, *History of Soviet Literature,* Doubleday, 1963.
Blair, Katherine Hunter, *A Review of Soviet Literature,* Ampersand, 1966.
Brown, Edward James, *Russian Literature since the Revolution,* Collier, 1963.
Carlisle, Olga, *Voices in the Snow,* Random House, 1962.
*Contemporary Literary Criticism,* Gale (Detroit, MI), Volume 1, 1973, Volume 3, 1975, Volume 13, 1980, Volume 26, 1983, Volume 51, 1989.
Hayward, Max and Leopold Labedz, editors, *Literature and Revolution in Soviet Russia,* Oxford University Press, 1963.
Yevtushenko, Yevgeny, *A Precocious Autobiography,* Dutton, 1963.

### PERIODICALS

*America,* November 13, 1971.
*Book Week,* February 26, 1967.
*Boston Globe,* February 26, 1992, p. 13.
*Chicago Tribune,* October 22, 1993, section 1, p. 24.
*Chicago Tribune Book World,* August 19, 1984.
*Christian Science Monitor,* March 8, 1991, pp. 10-11; December 3, 1993, p. 12.
*Library Journal,* January 15, 1967.

*Life,* February 17, 1967.

*Listener,* August 23, 1984, p. 27.

*London Review of Books,* December 6, 1984, pp. 20-21.

*Los Angeles Times,* January 27, 1982; October 9, 1984; April 1, 1987; November 12, 1988; January 18, 1993, pp. F1, F5; October 1, 1993, pp. A1, A6-A7.

*Los Angeles Times Book Review,* July 22, 1984; December 7, 1986.

*Maclean's,* June 12, 1995, pp. 60, 62.

*National Review,* July 17, 1987; December 14, 1984, pp. 47-48.

*New Republic,* June 22, 1987.

*New Statesman,* August 3, 1984, p. 27.

*New Statesman & Society,* March 15, 1991, p. 37; July 5, 1991, p. 39.

*Newsweek,* August 27, 1984.

*New Yorker,* April 15, 1985, pp. 110-26.

*New York Review of Books,* November 2, 1984, pp. 28-31.

*New York Times,* June 22, 1984, p. C25; June 9, 1985; June 18, 1985; February 2, 1986; April 16, 1986; June 20, 1987; January 2, 1988; January 19, 1988; January 23, 1991, p. C16; September 14, 1991, p. 4; January 16, 1993, p. 15; July 24, 1993, p. 4.

*New York Times Book Review,* July 15, 1984, p. 11; June 23, 1985, p. 13; June 28, 1987, p.12; December 25, 1988.

*Observer,* August 16, 1987, p. 22; June 16, 1991.

*Paris Review,* spring-summer, 1965.

*Progressive,* April, 1987.

*Publishers Weekly,* October 2, 1995, p. 54-55.

*Time,* May 25, 1987, p. 65.

*Times* (London), July 13, 1983; November 2, 1984; September 27, 1984; January 18, 1986.

*Times Literary Supplement,* November 6, 1981; August 26, 1988; June 14, 1991, pp. 3-4; January 7, 1994, p. 8.

*Washington Post,* February 21, 1987; January 2, 1988; May 17, 1988; July 8, 1989.

*Washington Post Book World,* July 22, 1984, p. 9; June 14, 1987, pp. 3-4.

*World Literature Today,* winter, 1992, p. 159; winter, 1992, pp. 156-57.*

\*    \*    \*

**YOLA, Yerima**
  **See KIRK-GREENE, Anthony (Hamilton Millard)**

**YOUNGBLOOD, Ronald F. 1931-**

*PERSONAL:* Born August 10, 1931, in Chicago, IL; son of William C. (a banker) and Ethel (Arenz) Youngblood; married Carolyn Johnson, August 16, 1952; children: Glenn, Wendy. *Education:* Valparaiso University, B.A., 1952; Fuller Theological Seminary, B.D., 1955; Dropsie College for Hebrew and Cognate Learning, Ph.D., 1961. *Religion:* Baptist.

*ADDRESSES: Office*—Bethel Theological Seminary West, 6116 Arosa St., San Diego, CA 92115.

*CAREER:* Bethel Theological Seminary, St. Paul, MN, assistant professor, 1961-65, associate professor, 1965-70, professor of Old Testament, 1970-78; Wheaton Graduate School, Wheaton, IL, professor, 1978-81, associate dean, 1978-80, dean, 1980-81; Trinity Evangelical Divinity School, Deerfield, IL, professor, 1981-82; Bethel Theological Seminary West, San Diego, CA, professor, 1982—. Has spent four summers in Europe as translator-editor of the New International Version of the Old Testament, sponsored by International Bible Society.

*MEMBER:* International Bible Society (vice chair and member of board), Evangelical Theological Society, Near East Archaeological Society (secretary and member of board).

*AWARDS, HONORS:* Gold Medallion Award for best reference book, 1996, for *Nelson's New Illustrated Bible Dictionary.*

*WRITINGS:*

*Great Themes of the Old Testament,* Harvest Publications (Chicago), 1968, revised edition published as *The Heart of the Old Testament,* Baker Book House (Grand Rapids, MI), 1971.

*Special Day Sermons,* Baker Book House, 1973, revised edition, 1989.

*Faith of Our Fathers,* Regal Books (Ventura, CA), 1976.

*How It All Began,* Regal Books, 1980.

*Exodus,* Moody (Chicago), 1983.

(Editor with Morris Inch) *The Living and Active Word of God,* Eisenbrauns (Winona Lake, IN), 1983.

*Themes from Isaiah,* Regal Books, 1983.

(Coeditor with Merrill C. Tenney) *What the Bible Is All About,* revised edition (Youngblood not associated with first edition), Regal Books, 1983.

(Editor) *Evangelicals and Inerrancy,* Thomas Nelson (Nashville, TN), 1984.

(Coeditor with Walter C. Kaiser, Jr.) *A Tribute to Gleason Archer,* Moody, 1986.

(Editor) *The Genesis Debate: Persistent Questions about Creation and the Flood,* Thomas Nelson, 1986.

*The Book of Genesis: An Introductory Commentary,* Baker Book House, 1991.

*New Compact Key Reference Concordance,* Thomas Nelson, 1992.

*The Book of Isaiah: An Introductory Commentary,* Baker Book House, 1993.

*Bible Concordance,* Thomas Nelson, 1993.

Author of introduction to William Henry Green, *The Unity of the Book of Genesis,* Baker Book House, 1979, and John D. Davis, *Genesis and Semitic Tradition,* Baker Book House, 1980. Assistant editor, *Baker Encyclopedia of the Bible* (two volumes), 1988; associate editor, *New International Version Study Bible,* Zondervan, 1985; consulting editor, *Nelson's Illustrated Bible Dictionary,* 1986, and Volumes 3 and 4 of *The New International Version Interlinear Hebrew-English Old Testament,* Zondervan, 1982 and 1985; Old Testament editor, *Wycliffe Exegetical Commentary,* Moody; general editor, *Nelson's New Illustrated Bible Dictionary,* Thomas Nelson, 1995; executive editor, *New International Reader's Version of Bible,* Zondervan, 1996. Contributor of numerous articles and book reviews to books and journals, including *Journal of Biblical Literature, Bulletin of American Schools of Oriental Research, Journal of the Evangelical Theological Society, Journal of the Ancient Near East Society of Columbia University, Bible Review, Moody Magazine,* and *Jewish Quarterly Review.* Editor, *Journal of the Evangelical Theological Society.*

*WORK IN PROGRESS:* Commentary on *Judges,* for Eerdmans.

*SIDELIGHTS:* Ronald F. Youngblood is fluent in Hebrew and has made eleven trips to the Middle East.

\*          \*          \*

**ZANDERBERGEN, George**
**See MAY, Julian**